ENCYCLOPAEDIA OF TRACK AND FIELD
(In 3 Vol.)

YOGRAJ THANI, RACHNA
& DEEPAK JAIN

Vol. 1

SPORTS PUBLICATION

Delhi-110 052

Published by:

Lokesh Thani

SPORTS PUBLICATIONS

H.O. 4264/3, Ansari Road, Darya Ganj, New Delhi-110002
B.O. WP-474, Ist Floor, Shiv Market, Ashok Vihar, Delhi-52
Phones: 3246532, 7241050, 7562163
Website: *www.sportsbookshouse.com*

I.S.B.N. – 81-7879-56-4

PRINTED IN INDIA 2003

Laser Typeset by:

JAIN MEDIA GRAPHICS

B-4/40-A, Lawrence Road, (Keshav Puram),
(Near Chandni Restaurant),
New Delhi-110035

Printed by:

CHAWLA OFFSET PRINTERS

Delhi-110052

Price: Rs. 3000/- (3 Vol.)

VOL. I

PART 1

SPRINTING

CONTENTS

PART 2

RUNNING

CONTENTS

PART 1
SPRINTING

CHAPTER 1

INTRODUCTION TO SPRINTING

Sprints are defined as including all races in which the contestant runs at full speed over the entire distance on the flat. Although the running distances vary, the upper limit is usually considered 300 yards. Outdoor meets ordinarily include but two sprint races, namely, the 100-yard and the 220-yard dashes. One finds distance of 40 yards, 50 yards, 60 yards, 70 yards, and 80 yards on the indoor program. The determining factor in the indoor distances is usually the amount of space available.

There are two sprint races on the program of the Olympic games. They are the 100-meter race, comparable to the 100-yard dash, and the 200-meter race, paralleling the 220-yard dash.

The universality of running and the apparent simplicity of sprinting requirements are no doubt responsible for the fact that there is usually no dearth of candidates for the sprint events. Although it is true that almost anyone can run, it is another matter to run fast. It is indeed a surprise to many when they learn that running sprint races involves techniques which are equally as difficult as those required for many of the other events on the track and field program.

A study of the records of champions during the past half century reveals the fact that more than one second has been cut from the time required to run the 100-yard dash. The records show also that the 220-yard dash is now run more than three seconds faster than in early contests.

It is the purpose of this discussion to point out the methods which are believed to be responsible for improvement in sprinting time.

Sprinting as a race category includes all distances up to 400 meters, with the 400 meters classified as a long sprint. Races beyond 400 meters usually fall into the category of middle distance, though elite athletes may sprint much of the distance.

The act of sprinting occurs in every race, including the marathon. As the competitive distance increases from the very short sprints (50-and 60-meter dashes) to longer distances, so the demands on the athlete change. In short sprints, the athlete races on stored energy supplies (anaerobic capacity). As the race distance increases, so does the demand on the athlete's anaerobic capacity, and the aerobic capacity begins to be taxed as well. Long distance races require tremendous aerobic capacity and place less demand on the athlete's stored (anaerobic) energy supplies. Thus, the balance of anaerobic-aerobic training must change according to the competitive distance raced.

Good sprinting requires fast reactions, good acceleration, and an efficient style of running. The sprinter must also develop an excellent sprint and maintain top speed for as long as possible. A season's training usually begins with drills to develop power, technique, and sprint endurance. As the competitive season approaches, reduce power and sprint endurance training and emphasize "quality" high-speed sprinting: The athlete attempts to sprint at top speed with as much relaxation and lack of tension as possible. Most technique training will be completed in the preseason and never fully forgotten during the competitive period. For a beginner faced with a short season and little time to prepare, training should concentrate on improving basic sprinting technique and the ability to relax while sprinting at top speed.

CHAPTER 2

HISTORY OF SPRINTING

Racing short distances has been a part of the competitive play of every civilization and has been described in the literature of almost every people. Certainly it was an important part of the ancient Greek Olympics. In fact, until the fourteenth officially recorded Olympiad, the *stade* race covering one length of the stadium, which varied in distance from 192 to 210 meters, was the only running event on the program. E. Norman Gardiner has made an exhaustive and interesting study of these ancient games, of the conditions under which the competitions were held, and of the equipment used. He states that no time comparisons are possible, for the Greeks kept no such records, had no watches by which to measure time, and in the erection of their stadia had no set distance for their length. The signal to start was given by a herald calling go or perhaps by a blast of the trumpet as in the chariot race. And woe to him who sought a flying start, for long forked rods were handily present, and "Those who start too soon are beaten says Andeimantus to Themistocles in the historic council before Salamis."

Incidentally, the threat of physical punishment is not entirely unknown in modern times. For instance, Webster tells a story of how Arthur Duffey, the Georgtown champion, while touring England had an even more threatening experience.

The style of the ancient sprinters are portrayed on Greek vases to an amazingly accurate degree, considering their lack of photographs. The runners are well upon their toes, their knees well raised, their bodies erect, and their arm action vigorous. Clearly, style in sprinting is a natural, ancient, and little-changed art.

Modern organised sprint races had their origin in professional racing, which was very prevalent in England during the entire 19th century and in much less organised fashion in this country until about 1910. The story of methods, stratagems, and gambling in professional racing forms one of the most fascinating pages in all sports history, one that needs organisation and a printed record before those who participated are entirely gone. From the standpoint of form development, one of the best of the scattered writings is that by William Curtis, written in 1899 and reproduced in How to Sprint.

During the early years of American amateur athletic sport, all the methods of management were naturally copied from the professionals. Running was limited almost entirely to matches, as there were no open competitions in which athletes could enter, and the distances were in nine cases out of ten one of the two extremes—one hundred yards or ten miles. As there were but two starters in these match races, the method of getting away were more primitive than at present and had been cunningly devised by veteran professionals to give the expert an advantage over the novice.

Several styles were in common use, the oldest being what was called the "break start". The judge stood on the starting line, the men went back fifteen or twenty paces, stood side by side, joined fingers lightly and trotted up to the judge. As they passed on either side of him, his body broke the touch of their fingers and they dashed away at full speed. If the judge thought the start fair, he said nothing, but if he thought either man had an unfair advantage they were recalled....

However, the cunning of professional runners had devised methods of outwitting inexperienced opponents. A few steps from the judge the expert would slacken his trot and the other almost invariably would do the same. Just as he reached the judge the expert would suddenly quicken. As it required some fraction of a second for the other to follow this example, the men would pass the judge almost exactly abreast, the expert more than likely a few inches in the rear, but he would be running, while the other was only trotting. The advantage thus gained would amount to two or three yards in the first twenty-five yards of the race.

A more complicated style was the "mutual consent" start. A line was drawn across the track, fifteen or twenty feet starting scratch. The men were placed between these lines and told to start by mutual consent, and whenever both men touched the ground in front of the starting scratch at the same time with any part of their persons it was considered as start.

A race of this kind between two experts was amusing. The men stood between the lines facing each other, pranced up to the starting mark sideways, and the one who was ahead would put his foot down over the mark, hoping that the other would follow. If he did, it would be a start, with the first man a foot or two in front; but if the second man did not like the start, he held back, did not put his foot over the mark, and the first man was ordered back for a fresh trial.

Starts of this style frequently lasted over an hour, especially if one of the runners was not extremely anxious for a race, and eventually this system was modified by inserting in the articles of agreement, a clause substantially as follows: "Start by mutual consent; if not off inside an hour [or some other specified time], then to start by pistol". Resort to the pistol was necessary in so many cases that it gradually supplanted the mutual consent system, and became the customary way of starting sprints.

These professional wolves usually travelled and prowled in pairs, one going first to a town , securing some employment, exhibiting his proficiency as a runner to a select few, and finally making a match with and beating the local champion. Then the winner would explain that he knew a man in a neighbouring town who thought he could run, and whose friends would back him heavily, but who really was several yards slower than championship speed and could be easily beaten. Negotiations would be opened with the stranger and a match arranged. All the men who had won on the first race wished to double their gains, while those who lost won, of course; the town was pretty thoroughly cleaned of money, and the partners changed their names and moved to fresh harvest fields.

If, after beating the local champions in races on even terms and under ordinary conditions, any money still remained in sight, the professionals tried to secure it by offering contests on lovel terms, and with such conditions as seemed to the uninitiated, foolhardy and sure to lose. One of these was called the "lying down start." The novice stood in his usual position, while the professional would lie flat on his back, with his head at the scratch and his feet pointing away from the finish, and the race started by pisto shot. To men unacquainted with this trick, it seemed as if the novice must win, and elderly know-it-alls, standing about, shifted their quids and wisely drawled out: "Why, Jimmy will be down to the other end before that fellow gets started."

But it did not work that way. When the pistol sounded, the professional turned on his face, rose to his hands and feet, and found himself in the attitude now universally adopted by present day sprinters (the crouch start), and which is much better than the old fashioned erect position. This preliminary movement cost the professional about half a second, or five yards, and as this was about half the handicap, he could beat the novice in 100 yards. He usually caught his man near the seventy-fifth yard mark.

It seems rather evident how such experiments in starting would naturally lead to the trial of a crouch start. However, it appears to be generally accepted that this method of starting did not begin of starting did not begin until 1887. Mike Murphy, the remarkable University of Pennsylvania, Yale, and Olympic track coach, took credit in his book for inventing it:

The crouching start was introduced by me. This was in 1887, at Yale, and Charles H. Sherrill was the athlete who first demonstrated its superiority. When the used it in his first race, he was laughed at, and the starter. Thinking that Sherill did not know how to start, held up the race to give him instructions..

The Hahn book, How to Sprint, carried a picture of the "first public appearance of the crouch start in America," taken at the Rockaway Hunt Club games, May 12, 1888, which shows Sherrill, alone out of four sprinters, down on his marks in a crouched position. However, in another picture of the start of the race in which John Owen set a new 100 yards world's record of:09.8 on October 11, 1890, all the starters, including Owen, are in a standing start position. The caption states that "Owen was trained for thisrace by the late Michael C. Murphy." Apparently the crouch start had its difficulties in selling itself even to those athletes trained by its inventor.

Most of the earliest stand-up starters used what was called the "dab." The body weight was well balanced on the forward foot with the same arm forward, that is, left foot and left arm were forward, in contrast to the normal opposite-arm-forward position. A very short and fast "dab" was taken with the forward foot at the same time the opposite arm was swung sharply forward. Apparently it was thought that the quicker movement of the front foot achieved greater acceleration than the slower, more forceful action of the back leg. In later years. however, this assumption has been found to be false, and the initial push in stand-up starting now comes from the back leg, and a normal arm swing is used.

The development of correct body, leg, and arm position in making the crouch start occurred very early in modern track history. Pictures of Arthr Duffey, champion from 1900 to 1903, show him in a crouched starting position that, in general, is identical with what champion sprinters use today. Further, his ideas then are still sound. He emphasizes that "often the arms are not used to full advantage," that the primary push comes from the front leg although "both legs must be called into action at one moment," that "at the report of the pistol, the left arm is swung directly ahead, flexed at the elbow, the right arm swinging directly backwards," and, lastly, "the necessity for forward action, by lifting the knees in a straight line and jabbing directly downward, without any of the side deviation which is such a common fault with the novice sprinter."

Although written a half century ago, each of these points is almost unchanged today in the written and spoken instruction of our best coaches. However, through the years, there has been a great deal of experimentation about the correct position of the hands and feet and the right placement of body weight when in the set position. Duffey writes of his method as being the "Kangaroo start," without explaining the name's origin. Around 1925, this same general position was called the "orthodox" start position, although by that time accepted practice placed the front foot from 8 to 10 inches back of the starting line.

At the time Larry Snyder was coaching Jesse Owens (1936) and other fine sprinters, he believed a position which "crowded" the starting line was best. When starting from holes, "if the boys's foot is within 8 inches to a foot away from the starting line, never more than afoot, I feel that boy is ahead of the one whose front foot is 18 inches back." When starting from blocks, "he will probably have the front foot 2 of 3 inches from the starting line," Snyder has not consistently followed these instructions through the years, but they illustrate the trends of thinking and of trial-and-errir efforts that coaches were attempting throughout the country.

Early in the 1920's, a so-called Australian start (mow commonly called the "bunch start because the feet are close together) placed the front foot 17 to 19 inches back of the starting lineand the back foot 10 to 12 inches behind the front. This elongated position did not gain rapid favour for it seemed to put the sprinter that much farther from the starting line. However, the research studies of Bresnahan and Tuttle proved that this position was fastest of all in producing clearance of the starting blocks. This conclusion influenced increased use of the "bunch" start until by the 1950's it had become probably the most common of all.

However, in 1952, two pieces of research pointed out that reaction time to a gun is not the same as printing time during the first score or so or yards. A man might clear his blocks in a short time and yet not have either the momentum or the good balance that would et him into fast action toward the finish line. Both studies concluded that the "bunch" start was actually the; east efficient. Henry states:

It is clear that the 16 and 21 inch toe-to-toe distance is the best... The 11 inch "bunch" start is definitely the poorest of the four. While it is true that this position gets the runner off the blocks quickest, he is going slower as he leaves them and never recovers from this disadvantage.

These conclusions argue that the old "orthodox" start with the back knee at some point between the toe and the arch of the opposite foot is best, and we are likely to see a more widespread use of this style by future sprinters.

A similar history cannot be traced for the development of form in sprinting proper, for sprinting is such a natural, universal, and relatively simple activity that style is present without specialized coaching. Undoubtedly, Mel Patton in action appeared very much like Lon Myers in 1880, or even like wing-footed Ulyssses in ancient Greece. Without question, the precise emphasis of modern coaching upon higher knee action or increased foot and ankle bounce has produced increased speeds, but such changes are either too minute or too transitory to furnish an excuse for a history.

Similarly, the development of form during the finish has followed an uncertain path. As far back as 1904, J.W. Morton attempted a "throw"at the finish, which is still advocated by some good coaches today:

At about twenty yards from the tape I take a long breath, quickly pulling myself together for a final effort. At this point a thrill seems to pass through my muscles; I travel much faster and, should it be a close finish, at about 8 feet from the tape I throw myself from collapsing by the left leg.

Charley Paddock, "world's fastest human" during the 1920's, made occasional and successful use (according to his coach, Dean Cromwell) of a full jump at the finish. Paddock frankly admitted that this leap"has been referred to as 'grand-stand play' and the 'freak finish of a freak performer,'" yet he firmly believed that "the jump has won so many more races for me than it lost that I an do no less than suggest it to the sprinter who runs high and has the patience to learn it, and the courage to use it."

Other methods of making the finish apparently also had an early origin. The lunge finish, which consisted of throwing the body well forward with the chest out and the arms far down and back, originated with Arthur Duffey.

Arthur Duffey was one of the first to scientifically use it. The Boston boy employed the lunge in a race against Bernie Wefers of the New York Athletic Club, who was American champion in 1895-96-97, and he won by the width of a hand. Wefers saw the advantage of the lunge, and at once set out to improve upon this method of finishing if possible. And his studies resulted in the introduction of a still better style.

This new finish was soon known as the "shrug", and it was accomplished by throwing the side of the body into the string with one hand held high, and the other held back behind the body. The forward lean of the "lunge" was maintained in the "shrug" but the tape could be broken 6 inches sooner, since the side of the body can be brought that much nearer the string than the chest. . . .

This "shrug" finish first perfected by Bernie Wefers has grown in popularity during the past thirty years until today it is in general use by a majority of the best sprinters throughout the world.

A SHORT HISTORY OF PERFORMANCE

It is interesting to note that, unlike other events in track and field, the history of performance in the sprints does not parallel a history of form development and that therefore the former story cannot rightly be told under the latter heading. However, a brief summary of performance seems both necessary and of interest.

The story can well begin with John Owen, the first man to run 100 yards under 10 seconds officially. For years Owen's performances aroused intense argument, particularly because Owen competed for the Detroit Athletic Club. That such a "backwoods' organization should sire an upstart sprinter who could challenge the supremacy of the East was, well, somewhat unthinkable. But his :09.8 at Analostan Island, Washington, D.C., in 1890, could not seriously be questioned. To this day, however, the habit of using 10 second as the standard for judgement has persisted. The not infrequent expression, "He ran 2 feet inside, or outside, evens" (that is, inside or outside an exact 10 seconds) is but one such carry-over.

Although tied seven ties in the next twelve years, Owen's record was not broken until 1902, when Arthur Duffey, 5'7" tall and 138 pounds in weight, after three years of great sprinting as a prep school and Georgetown University runner, beat an excellent field in :09.6 in the ICAAAA championships. It should be remembered, of course, that only fifth-second watches were being used at this time and that therefore improvements in records could only come about in units of 2 yards or more. It is small wonder, therefore, that it was not until 28 years later, on May 10, 1930, that a new time of :09.4 was officially posted.

No record of sprinting would be complete without a special comment on Charley Paddock, the most dramatic and widely publicized sprinter of all time. Perhaps because of their professional background, the sprints up to about 1930, were the piece de resistance at every track meet, much as the mile is today. Paddick, coming near the end of this predominance in the minds of spectators, raised it to fever pitch, aided of course by a sprinkle of California "foofaraw" amd 'Hollywooditis." Not only did be tie the 100 yard record on six different occasions; he also broad-jumped through the finish tape to set records at 90 yards (.08.8), 110 yards (:10.2),125 yards (:12.0), 130 yards (:12.4), 150 yards (14.2), 200 yards (19.0), 300 yards (:30.2), and 300 meters (:33.2). They were all unofficial, of course, as international records, but they attracted the headlines and the spectator as nothing had since Paul Revere's sprint through old Boston Town.

The writer will never forget the occasion at the Penn relays in 1926 when Charley, beautifully arrayed in baby-blue striped shorts and white track shoes, really rough down the house,. In their efforts to see the world's fastest human, the spectators broke through the retaining wall of the stadium and came spilling out on the track, but fortunately they were too late to stop cheerful Charley from continuing on to a new record at well, the exact distance is forgotten, but it was probably around 147.3 yards. A showman? Most certainly, but a great sprinter and a fine sportsman as well. With official timers, Charley ran :09.5 on several occasions, but of course was not able to receive credit for tenth-second timing.

One of the most underrated and hard-luck sprinters was George Simpson of Ohio State University. Dogged by leg injuries throughout his career, he pulled up short again in the 1928 final Olympic trials. However, in 1929, he returned to his best form and ran the first official :09.4 for 100 yards in history. Unfortunately for him, he was also the first record breaker to use the new starting blocks, and, since they had not yet been adopted by the IAAF, this discredited his time.

It took a college sophomore to turn the trick at last. Frank Wykoff, of the University of Southern California, had won the national 100 meter championship in 1928, just after graduation from high school, had been a close second to Simpson in the National Collegiates in 1929, and broke through to run:09.4 officially not only in May, 1930, but again in the National Collegiates in June of that year.

There the record remained for 18years, being tied only by Jesse Owens, of Ohio State University, on the greatest of all his days, May 25, 1935. It is of interest to record that on this occasion large dialed tenth-second watches were used with hands that move in tiny segments and therefore stop between as well as on the tenth-second markers. The hands of all three official watches were actually closer to :09.4, but of course the slower time had to be recorded officially. Further, the starter for the race was W.J Monilaw, who was very insistent in his starting that the "set" should be held at least 2 second so that the chances of a "flyer" would be minimized. He used to argue that it was not enough to prevent a man from "beating the gun":; he should not even start "with the gun." A certain time should elapse between the sound of the gun and the first body movement. It may well be that Owens performance that day was even greater than we now officially recognize.

However, it was Mel Patton, also of Southern California, who first ran :09.3 officially on May 15, 1948, at the Fresno relays. D.H. Potts, an astute and reliable observer, wrote of the race as follows:

In a special 100 yard event Mel faced his conqueror of 1947, LIoyd LaBeach [a great sprinter but not ordinarily a fast starter.- J.K.D.]. After several false starts, which added to the already high tension, the field was away. Mel was off flying, while LaBeach was left at the post. At 20 yards Mel had a 3 foot lead. Nor could LaBeach close on him until the final 20 yards. But he couldn't make it as Mel hit the tape a foot ion front and became the first man to run an official :09.3.

Conjecture is warranted over just how great these two sprinters were. If LaBeach could make up 2 feet in 80 yards on a man who is running :09.3, LaBeach was potentially the greatness were dissipated by his :20.2 for the 220 in 1949.

The history of performance in the 100-meter dash follows a similar pattern, although the names, interestingly enough, are not identical. Paddock, in 1921, and Eddie Tolan (the University of Michigan's 1932 Olympic games winner), in 1929, established a mark of :10.4. This was lowered to :10.3 by Percy Williams in 1929.

Then came Jesse Owens with another world's record of :10.2 in winning the National Collegiates in the Olympic year 1936. There it remained for 14 years. Tied by Hal Davis, of the University of California, in 1941, and by Lloyd LaBeach, UCLA, and Barney Ewell, Penn State, in 1948, it was finally broken by LaBeach on October 7, 1950, at Guayquil, Ecuador. Meet officials seemed certain that all was in good order in this race: yet as late as Aprill 1952 this record has not been officially accepted by the IAAF.

A world's record in the 220-yard dash was first made by Bernie Wefers in 1896 when he ran :21.2. An amazing double performance by Charley Paddock in 1921, in which he twice took .4 second off the old record, placed it at :20.8. Roland Locke, of the University of Nebraska, lowered it a full fifth of a second to :20.6. After tenth-second timing was accepted, Jesse Owens, for the third time in a single day, on May 25, 1935, created a new world's record of :20.3. There the record remained for 14 years, untied and unbroken, until Mel Patton ran :20.2 in a dual meet against U.C.L.A. on May 7, 1949.

CHAPTER 3

LEARNING TIPS IN SPRINTING

The preparation for a sprint race does not start the night before, but on the first day of training; and a lot depends on the life-style the athlete leads thereafter. There is a saying 'you cannot burn a candle at both ends' — well, an athlete cannot afford to burn a candle at all ! Sleep is probably one of the most important factors governing an athlete's performance. If you go to bed late after a hard day's work and training, not only does your work suffer the next day, but your training suffers too as you are both mentally and physically tired. The problems do not stop there. Training goes on because it has to, and therefore there is an ongoing downhill situation with the body's resources being constantly drained. The amount of sleep you need varies from individual to individual, and each athlete will know how much he or she needs to be able to cope with living and training.

FOOD

Food is another important factor. The usual requirement is plenty of the right kind. The food balance is crucial because if too much of the wrong kind of food is eaten then the wrong kind of weight is gained (i.e., fat rather than muscle), upsetting the strength/weight ratio. Similarly, if not enough is eaten then weight and power are lost. So the right amount of food is essential to be able to train and build muscles which, in turn, will help you to run faster. It is natural to gain weight when training, as muscle develops, but do not go berserk — remember it gets a bit hard going propelling 100kg (224lb) along a 100-metre straight !

So what is the right kind of food? A cooked or good breakfast is essential, especially if you train twice a day. Fruit juice, cereal, eggs, toast and honey — or any combination of these — should suffice. Lunch should be a cooked meal if possible but, even if this is not practicable, the food should be substantial and not just a pie and a pint at the local. Another cooked meal after training, to replace lost calories, should round off one's eating for the day. Meals should be balanced, using meat, fish, chicken, potatoes, fresh fruit and vegetables, bread and cheese. Meals should be varied and appetising. Added vitamins have always been controversial, but by taking them at least you know you have covered all possibilities and will not lack anything. Other dietary ingredients which should not be neglected are electrolyte replenishment (e.g. salt) and minerals essential to the body's metabolism.

When to eat is almost as important as what to eat. It is an impossible to run on a full stomach as on an empty stomach. If you have nothing in your stomach then your body has nothing with which to replace used energy. It is up to the individual to work out for himself the ideal time to eat before a race, but the normal time it takes for a full meal to be digested is around three to four hours.

CLOTHING

Once the inside of the body has been taken care of, then we must take a look at the outside. An athlete's kit is an important in training as it is in competition. Training kit must always be fresh and clean — not only will it make the athlete feel better, but training companions will appreciate the gesture! One must wear enough clothes to be warm but not so many that free movement is hindered. Remember, it is easier to take items of clothing off if one is too warm than it is to add clothing if one is not warm enough. The basic essentials are a tracksuit or loose-fitting trousers and jumper, with waterproof covering if possible — even an old mackintosh is better than nothing.

If you can only afford to buy certain items then the first priority is your footwear. You can wear any kind of clothing to train in, but you must have the correct footwear, otherwise you will cause injuries to your feet which can stop you competing. Training shoes should be firm and fairly solid with good supporting areas within the shoe. Ideally two pairs of spikes should be purchased — one pair for competition and one pair for training. The competition spikes should feel special and light when put on, compared with the training spikes which should be comfortable, supportive and fairly long-lasting. The same goes for running kit; if you have a special vest and shorts (may be in your club colours) try not to wear them for training. This all adds to your well-being before a race. You feel different and look good. Although it will not necessarily turn you into a world-class sprinter, if you feel clean, healthy and a bit special, it certainly will help. When Allan won the Golden Sprints in 1981 it was a very cold, wet evening, but because he had three complete changes of clothing with him he always lined up wearing dry, warm clothes. This plays a large part in the feeling of well-being, especially if one's opponents are wearing wet clothes and shoes!

WARM-UP

Once the athlete has prepared himself to run, what can he do to make himself ready immediately prior to a race? The warm-up is probably more important than the race itself because if the warm-up is not performed properly then the athlete cannot do himself justice when the race begins.

Allan never jogs during a warm-up! That may seem strange as 90 per cent of athletes jog two or three laps during a warm-up. So if not, why not? We feel that by doing strides, starting off slowly and gradually increasing in speed, he can still concentrate on his running technique by the same means as he would while sprinting, whereas if he jogged he would be unable to run in the same way. After striding, a lot of stretching and mobility work should then take place to prepare the body for the task ahead. The purpose of stretching is to take the muscles through a greater range than they have to achieve during a race; in this way the muscles are not being asked to do anything they have not done before. Stretching is also important because as the muscles become stronger they become tighter, and this tightness would restrict the length of stride if a strict mobility programme were not adhered to.

The general rule for stretching is to start at the top and work your way down:

1. Rolling the head — Rotate the head, passing through as large a circumference as possible in both directions.

2. Arm rotation — Keeping the arm straight and close to the ears, rotate the arm in both directions.

3. Hip circles — Using only the pelvic area, circle the hips in both directions, again passing through as large a circumference as possible. This exercise can be extended by circling the upper body as well and then further by using the arms as well so that the whole body moves in a circle.

4. Side bends — Keeping the legs straight and the body in alignment, slide the hand down the leg as far as possible. Repeat on the other side.

5. Calf stretches — Leaning against a wall, walk, walk the feet out until it is difficult to keep the heels flat on the ground, and then alternately lift and lower the heels.

6. Lunges —

(a) With both feet facing forward, place one leg in front of the other, wide apart, and try to force the thigh of the back leg onto the ground while keeping the trunk upright. The front knee should be over the front foot, which should have the heel on the ground. Again this exercise should be done equally to both sides, each leg in turn in front of the other.

(b) The same exercises as (a) but with the back foot on its side.

7. Hamstring stretches —

(a) Lying on your back with both hands supporting the hips off the ground, alternately stretch out each leg with the other one in a relaxed position.

(b) Lying on your back, grasp one leg behind the knee with both hands and pull the knee into the chest. Slowly straighten the leg and then pull the toes downwards thus creating a good stretch up the back of the leg. Relax the leg afterwards by allowing the lower leg to flop.

8. Hip circles — Bend the leg and draw it across the body, then, keeping the leg bent, open it up, before straightening and returning to the opposite leg, which remains straight throughout. This should look like a type of breast-stroke leg kick with one leg.

These are only a few of the hundreds of exercises available, and everyone has their own favourites. The most important factor to remember is never to jerk stretching movements. The sequence of stretching is:

stretch - hold - relax - stretch - hold - relax.

The important areas to stretch as far as sprinters are concerned are: (a) hips (b) abductors (c) hamstrings (d) shoulders. (a) and (b) are important because these are the restricting muscles in terms of stride length, (c) because these are sprinter' 'achilles heels' and seem to cause most problems, and (d) if the shoulders are tight then they limit the amount of drive from the arms.

This whole programme should take approximately thirty minutes and should then be followed by more strides, still in training shoes. The spikes should then be put on just before starting to do the practice starts. It is important that the spikes are not put on until this moment, nor should any articles of clothing be removed except in extremely hot conditions. Only too often do we see juniors warming up in spikes, wearing only a tee-shirt and shorts? The aim of a warm-up is to prepare the body, both physically and mentally, for the task ahead; this means not only raising the body temperature but warming up the muscles inside as well. It is not good warming up and then stripping off ten minutes before a race begins, as the body will soon cool down and become stiff even before you start.

The entire warming-up procedure should take approximately forty to fifty minutes and this should immediately precede the start of the race. Sometimes, however, a race meeting will be running behind schedule, and it is therefore important continually to check the times of the races beforehand and to adjust your warm-up time accordingly. In major Games such as the Olympics, European, Commonwealth etc., the athletes must report in some cases as much as forty minutes before the start of the race, so that too has to be taken into consideration. The warm-up timing should be well-rehearsed beforehand; it is just as important not to warm up too early as it is not to be rushed.

On completion of the race the athlete must put on his track gear and remove the spikes immediately; failure to do so could result in a chill, stiffness or, even worse, an injury. Avoid the temptation to discuss the race with anyone before putting on warm clothing and doing a warm-down.

A warm-down is not quite so important to a sprinter as it is to a middle/long-distance runner, but even so it has a place in the finishing off of a race. Again, while most athletes jog, we go back to striding, but this time we decrease the speed of each stride as opposed to increasing. It is important to return the pulse rate and body temperature to normal in order to prevent stiffness and a build-up of impurities in the muscles.

CHAPTER 4

TYPES OF COMPETITORS IN SPRINTING

Sprinters do not readily conform to a classification by types since athletes having a wide range of characteristics are listed as champions. Top flight sprinters are seldom found who weigh less than 130 pounds or more than 170 pounds. They range in height from 5 feet 7 inches to 6 feet 3 inches. Sprinting has been termed a young man's event, a statement borne out by the fact that rarely has an American sprinter maintained championship form after the age of twenty-five years.

The tall sprinter is characterised by long lower extremities, equipped with long powerful muscles. The short sprinter compensates for muscle length found in his taller opponent by possessing strong thick muscles. Since driving power is the chief prerequisite for fast sprinting, it matters little whether it is derived from a long slender muscle or a short thick one.

PHYSICAL QUALIFICATION

If an athlete is to become a fast sprinter, there are a number of inherent qualities which he must possess. Among these are (1) short reaction time, (2) short reflex time, (3) pure dominance, (4) motor mindedness, and

(5) strong power of inhibition.

1. Reaction Time —Since many of the adjustment required of a sprinter are voluntary in nature, the athlete who can make them quickly and efficiently is at a distinct advantage. It has been proved that there is a high correlation between sprinting ability and reaction time.

2. Reflex Time — In view of the fact that it is generally agreed that a fast start is conducive to a fast race, the sprinter possessing a short reflex time is obviously at an advantage. This means that the athlete profits by having a short reflex time and is well on his way before his slower opponent is off his marks. Actual measurements have shown that champion sprinters have a short reflex time than those requiring a longer interval to cover an equal distance.

3. Dominance — When manual acts, such as starting the sprints, are performed, lead preference is usually given to one side of the body. There is good evidence that dominance is an inherited characteristic. Individuals who give lead performance to the right side of the body are said to be right dominant. Those who show preference to the left side are designated as left dominant, while those who show no preference, lack dominance (ambidextrous).

In starting the sprint, the right dominant athlete places this right foot back and when he leaves the marks a definite sequence of movements is executed. The left dominant individual places the left foot back and likewise performs a definite sequence of movements.

It has been demonstrated that an individual who shows no preference in body lead is likely to execute a mixed movement pattern in leaving the marks, regardless of the foot placed back. Such a situation interferes with coordination in getting into the first stride.

Advising hurdlers to reverse the feet at the start of a race, for the purpose of approach adjustment, no doubt causes an interference in coordination in getting into the first strides. However, it is believed that in some instances the loss in time in getting into stride is overbalanced by the benefit derived by the change in number of strides.

4. Motor Mindedness — Through practice, the athlete must be able to reduce all of the acts of skill in any event to a reflex pattern, that is, he must be able to do them without thinking. Whenever an athlete is able to execute his event automatically, he can rest assured that he has the technique truly mastered. The sprinter is not to be criticized for driving off his marks at the click of a gun, the cough of an official, or at any other clear-cut stimulus. Such a response by a sprinter is evidence that his attention is fixed on the act of starting (motor mindedness) rather than on the report of the gun (sensory mindedness).

5. Inhibition — When an athlete is participating in any event, his attention must be focused on the task at hand. This means that when a sprinter is running a race he is literally deaf to everything around him. A well-trained competitor is able to inhibit response to any distraction, whether it is the cheering of the spectators, the derogatory remarks of a bystander, or the advice of a teammate.

EQUIPMENT

During the first few weeks of the preliminary season the athlete may find it advantageous to use moderately short spikes in order to avoid shin-splints. On hard tracks sharper spikes, shorter in length, are desirable, while on a loose or wet course, longer spikes serve best.

CHAPTER 5

THE TECHNIQUES OF SPRINTING

In attempting to master the techniques of sprinting, the beginner must recognise the fact that this event involves something more than being able to run rapidly. There are physical, physiologic, and psychologic adjustments which must be made and with which he must be familiar. For the sake of clarity in presentation, the sprints are broken up into the following components: (1) the start, (2) the running strides, (3) the coast, (4) the finish.

1. THE START—It is generally recognized that a good start is a prerequisite to a winning performance. Ways for reducing the starting time of the sprinter have been considered for many years. One of the most outstanding changes in the start which reduced the time in getting under way was the adoption of the crouch, some fifty years ago. In the discussion which follows, items of technique which the sprinter must consider, if he is to become efficient, are presented.

A. FOOT SUPPORT

There are two opinions on the matter of support for the feet at the start of the sprints. One is that holes in the track can be used as a means of foot support, while the other is that starting blocks on top of the track be used.

If holes in the track are used, they should be dug so as to present a solid back surface. The depth and the size of the hole depend on the size of the foot. A hole to be most effective and safe should be dug deep enough so that the back spikes, when the foot is in position, firmly engage the back of the hole. The rear surface of the front hole should be slanted at an angle of approximately 45 degrees. The rear surface of the hole for the back foot should be at an angle of approximately 90 degrees with the surface of the track.

The essential requirement of any supports on top of the track are that they may be quickly placed, adjusted to suit the angles of the feet, firmly fastened to the track, and speedily removed from the course.

The adjustment of the foot-supporting surfaces of the starting blocks is the same as that for holes, namely, 90 degrees for the back and 45 degrees for the front block, but this may be shifted to suit the competitor.

Those who recommend starting blocks as a substitute for holes in the track do so because they believe that blocks present a firmer and more reliable support, are more quickly and accurately arranged for the start, are removed from the track rapidly, and do not mar the running surface of the track.

B. TYPES OF STARTS

A study of the starting positions assumed by trained sprinters reveals the fact that there is a rather wide variation in the distances at which they space their feet. The more commonly used positions are as follows:

1. The Bunch Start — This position is defined as one in which the toe of the back foot is placed opposite the heel of the front foot while in a standing position. This start represents the one extreme in foot spacing since sprinters seldom place the feet closer together than

described in the bunch start. Experimental evidence shows that this type of foot spacing permits the fastest getaway.

2. The Medium Start — In this start the knee of the back leg is placed opposite the front of the arch of the front foot, in a kneeling position.

C. THE POSITION OF THE HANDS AND ARMS

The hands are placed so that the weight rests on the thumbs and fingers. Some sprinters prefer to place the weight on the thumb and second joint of the fingers, while others throw their weight on the thumb and knuckles. The guiding factor is the comfort of the sprinter. Care should always be taken so that the hands are not in front of the scratch line.

In the position "on the marks" the arms should be fully extended and not flexed at the elbow. They should be far enough apart to insure free knee action in getting "set". The sprinter should remember that the arms and hands are so placed that there is no feeling of discomfort. He should be in a state of sharply defined balance.

D. THE POSITION OF THE HIPS

The height to which a sprinter elevates the hips in relation to the shoulders in the "set" position depends on the type of foot spacing employed. As a rule, the shorter the longitudinal spacing, the higher are the hips elevated. In the bunch start the hips are usually about 25 degrees higher than the shoulders. This angle becomes less for the medium start and still less for the elongated position. Many good competitors favour a hip position which is as high as possible and yet consistent with the type of foot spacing employed.

E. POSITION OF THE HEAD AND EYES

In the "set" position the sprinter looks down the track

as far as consistent with his body position. If a sprinter starts from a position in which the trunk is parallel with the track, he can see some distance without cramping his neck. However, when the high hip position is employed, the distance of vision is reduced. In any event a sprinter should raise his head high enough so that he can see far enough ahead to guide the direction of his body.

After the start the eyes are focused in the direction of the run. Imbalance and loss of stride may result if a runner turns his head to see what is going on around him. The sprinter should give whatever information he desires through peripheral vision and sound, just as in hurdling.

F. POSITION OF THE TRUNK

When the sprinter is on his marks, waiting for the command, "Get set" the position of the body may vary from one in which the centre of weight is well behind the knee on the ground, to one in which the centre of weight is well in front of it. This depends on the type of foot spacing employed and the forward tilt of the trunk. The points to bear in mind are the comfort of the contestant and the efficiency with which the hips are raised to the "set" position. If the trunk is tilted to its backward limit, there is but little weight on the arms, and, when the command, "Get set" is given, the sprinter must move his trunk forward and upward. If the body position is too far forward, the athlete is conscious of undue strain on the arms and hands. A short foot spacing (bunch start) is more conducive to extreme forward trunk tilt than the longer foot spacing (elongated start). For any given spacing, the determining factor in the degree of trunk tilt is the amount of leg bend and hip elevation. If the forward lean is too extreme, the back leg is likely to be too straight and thus detract from its drive. An "on the marks" position which permits the sprinter to get "set" merely by raising the hips in the most desirable.

G. BREATHING

There is a lack of uniformity among authorities as to the most effective breathing habits which should be established in sprint racing. The point which a sprinter must consider in any type of breathing habit is that sufficient air must be provided for his race.

A common procedure followed by many sprinters is to breath forcefully for two or three minutes before getting on the marks. This seems to be a logical procedure since by so doing the carbon dioxide in the blood is reduced and an increased oxygen supply is furnished.

The breathing habits of the sprinter in the "set" position are reflex, that is, involuntary. It has been demonstrated that when the sprinter is in the "on the marks" position, breathing is normal. As soon as the command, "Get set", is given, the sprinter takes a deed breath, exhales slightly, and then holds the breath in the inspiratory phase until the gun is fired. The breathing habits of the sprinter in the "set" position are paralleled by the golfer concentrating on a putt or the marksman aiming at the target.

No set rule is laid down to govern the breathing of a sprinter after he leaves his marks. Some coaches recommend that he hold his breath for a full 100 yards. Others make no recommendation to the athlete. Here again it is a question of supplying the body with sufficient oxygen and eliminating sufficient carbon dioxide to ward off fatigue as long as possible. There are not sufficient scientific data at hand to support any set practice in the matter of breathing during the actual running of sprint races.

The sprinter should always bear in mind that the better the physical condition and the more efficient the warm-up, the less will be the air requirements during the course of a sprint.

H. ATTENTION

When the sprinter is notified by the official that his race is about to start, he must give his undivided attention voluntarily to the preliminary preparations which are necessary so that he will be ready to "take his marks" when the command is given. As soon as the sprinter takes his marks, the attention is then turned to the finer bodily adjustments in preparation for the command, "Get set". Competent starters allow an interval of 10 to 12 seconds between these commands.

When the command, "Get set", is given, the sprinter assumes the "set" position, in which the driving muscles become tense, breathing ceases, and extraneous stimuli are shut out. Attention is focused involuntarily on the act of starting. In fact, the athlete becomes an automatic responding mechanism.

The sprinter must remember that attention is a fluctuating phenomenon, reaching its peak, then subsiding, coming back to its peak again. If the sprinter is to get the best start, the peak of attention and the firing of gun must coincide.

Since attention fluctuation is involuntary, the coincidence of attention and the sound of the gun lies largely in the hands of the official. If the gun is fired too soon, the peak of attention may not yet be reached, and, if the sprinter is held too long in the "set position, attention may have reached its peak and may be in the subsiding phase when the gun is fired. It has been demonstrated that the peak of attention and the report of the gun are closest together when the holding time is 1.5 seconds. This is about 2 seconds after the command, "Get set", is given.

I. FORCE EXERTED BY THE LEGS

When the sprinter leaves his marks, he should execute a vicious drive with both legs. The amount of force exerted and the distribution of this force depend on the spacing of the feet. When the feet are close together as in the bunch start, the greatest drive is executed by the front foot. As the foot spacing is increased the tendency is towards an equilization of the force exerted by the legs. In what has been defined as the medium start, the force exerted by the legs is approximately equal. As the foot spacing is increased still further, the force exerted by the back leg exceeds that applied by the front, as is the case in which the elongated foot spacing is assumed at the start of the race.

It is of interest to note that the force applied by the front leg is independent of foot spacing, remaining constant in all the starts described. However, as the space between the feet is increased, so also is the force exerted by the back leg increased. Since this is true, then as the foot spacing is increased, the total force exerted by the legs is increased. As a matter of general information, it might be stated that the average sprinter exerts a force represented as 195, pouns with the front foot. When the feet are close together, as in the bunch start, the average sprinter exerts a pressure of 150 pounds with the back foot. As the foot spacing is increased, the pressure exerted by the back foot increases, reaching 195 pounds in the medium position and 210 pounds in the elongated start.

J. THE SEQUENCE OF MOVEMENTS IN LEAVING THE MARKS

The sequence of the movement which a sprinter follows when he leaves his marks depends on his dominance (footedness or handedness). The right dominant individual places his right foot back. The movement pattern employed in leaving the marks is reflex, similar to the hand-foot relationship when walking. The order of movements of the right dominant individual is left hand, right foot, and left foot. For the left dominant sprinter the movement sequence is: right hand, left hand, left foot, and right foot.

It is of interest to note that a well-trained sprinter requires from 0.3 to 0.4 second to leave his marks after the gun is fired.

K. THE RESPONSE TO THE GUN

Through practice the sprinter should learn to respond to the firing of the gun automatically, that is, without giving it any thought. An individual who is able to start in such a manner is said to be motor minded. The sprinter who finds it necessary first to think about the report of the gun before he starts is described as sensory minded and loses valuable time at the start of a race.

L. THE COMMANDS

When the stage is all set, the official notifies the contestants that the race is about to begin. After preliminary instruction, each sprinter assumes a position in such proximity to his foot supports the little time is lost in getting placed when the command to do so is given. As soon as the sprinters are ready, the official gives the commands as follows:

1. "Get on Your Marks" — Sufficient time is allowed for the contestant to get settled on the marks. During this interval of 10 to 12 seconds, he concludes his body adjustment, making sure that he is ready to quickly assume a position from which he can drive viciously.

2. "Get Set" — The position "on the marks" is such that most of the body weight is on the right knee. When the command, "Get Set" is given, the hips are raised into

starting position by contracting the extensor muscles of both legs and thighs. This throw the body weight on the feet and arms. The sprinter must remember that because a vicious drive is to be executed by both legs, the back leg must carry its share of the body weight if the drive is to be most effective. In the "set" position the arms are used for balance and support.

The degree of inclination of the trunk, the elevation of the hips, the direction of the head and eyes, and the placement of the hands and arms have been previously determined by the athlete himself. Through practice he must learn to assume quickly the desired body position when the command, "Get Set" is given. When the contestant has assumed this position and becomes steady, he is said to be "set". All musculature involved in driving off the marks is tense, ready to execute quick, powerful movements.

To get the most out of a start the contestant must become an automatic (reflex) organism.

3. The Gun — The sprinter must be ready to go any instant after he is "set". Of course, it must be realized that the interval which the contestant is held in the "set" position is entirely in the hands of the official. The sprinter who is physically and mentally poised may be likened to the powder in the shell that is about to be fired. When the spark contacts the powder, it explodes with great force and likewise when the gun is fired the sprinter's energy is automatically exploded and he springs forward with a vicious drive.

2. THE RUNNING STRIDES

During the running strides the body is propelled forward chiefly by the pushing action of the driving leg. The function of the recovery leg is to get into position for the next stride as expeditiously as possible, with a minimum waste of energy.

The arms constitute the balancing mechanism for keeping the body aligned, and they also act as a part of the reflex movement pattern developed naturally through walking and running.

The way in which power is applied to the body by the legs, and the adjustments of the arms for balance depends on the striding action. A study of sprinting justifies the breaking of it into the component part of (a) the starting strides, (b) the transitional strides, and (c) the top-speed strides. The movement described are based on the assumption that the sprinter places his right foot back in the starting position.

A. The Starting Strides

The two starting strides are defined as beginning when the right foot first applies force against the back block and ending the instant before it leaves the ground the second time.

Forward propulsion at the beginning of the first stride is initiated by the back leg. The beginning of the back leg drive is followed very quickly (approximately 0.01 second) by the driving action of the front leg. For a time, both legs are applying force to the body simultaneously. The application of front leg power to the forward propulsion of the body lasts considerably longer (more than twice as long for the average sprinter) than the application of back leg force.

As the force is applied by the legs, the shoulders are raised somewhat higher than the hips. Simultaneously, the hands leave the ground in their natural sequence. The hip-shoulder change is the beginning of the straightening of the trunk lean. This straightening process continues until the sprinter reaches top speed.

At the conclusion of the push-off, the back leg starts forward. A combination of the pushing force of the left leg, and the backward reaction to the forward swing of the right leg tends to swing the right hip backward. This disalignment is overcome by the compensating reaction force of the swinging of the arms. The right arm is swung back slightly bent, with the bent left arm is swung forward somewhat toward the midline of the body. Although the height of arm swing varies, the hands usually come up to about the shoulder level. The force of arm swing is proportional to the force of the leg drive. Since the drive off the blocks is vicious, the arm swing is powerful.

The right foot is brought forward and placed on the ground, the knee forming almost a right angle. The length of the first stride depends on both the length of legs and the type of start used. This is the shortest stride of the sprint (18 inches to 28 inches in front of the starting line) since the necessarily low body position limits its length.

Almost instantaneously after the right foot hits the ground, the left foot leaves its support. It is brought forward in the same manner as described for the right except this stride is slightly longer than the first and the trunk is slightly more erect. With the moving of the left foot forward, the arms execute a forceful action, opposite in direction to their movement when the right foot moved forward. Here again, the forceful arm action to align the body with the direction of the run.

The paramount point to be remembered is that during the first two strides, terrific force must be applied by both legs accompanied by a forceful swing of both arms. It is power in the leg drive that brings about the achievement of maximum acceleration. This completes the first, two-stride section of the sprint.

B. The Transitional Strides

The average sprinter continues to accelerate for a distance of 10 to 15 yards from the starting line and requires from six to nine strides. During this time there is a gradual transition from what we have called the starting strides to the strides characteristic of full speed.

Throughout the transitional period there is a progressive lengthening of the strides and a gradual straightening of the trunk angle. As the trunk becomes more erect, the recovery knee becomes straighter as the foot contacts the ground.

The principle involved in this section of the sprint is that since the trunk lean is greater, the centre of weight is closer to the ground, and of necessity the strides are shorter than the full-speed strides. During this phase of the sprint, the knee bend of the recovery leg, when the foot contacts the track, varies among different athletes (the bend is greater in the first stride and becomes less and less until it becomes constant at full speed). From the beginning of the sprint through the period of accleration, the driving leg executes a terrific backward thrust by extending both the knee and ankle. To this force is added a powerful backward extension of the hip. As full speed is approached and the knee becomes straighter when the foot hits the ground, the backward knee thrust becomes less, almost vanishing as an effective forward propelling force.

During the transitional strides, when the foot touches the ground, it must be moving backward with an adequate amount of speed.

C. The Full-Speed Stride

The sprinter is said to be at full speed when he ceases to accelerate to further increase his speed. As full speed is attained, there is no further change (decrease) in trunk angle, and the strides become uniform in length. Full-speed strides differ in character from the transitional strides.

A single stride is defined as the distance between the toe of the right foot and the toe of the left. In other words, it is but one step. However, for the purpose of this discussion a complete cycle (two steps) is described. This cycle is defined as beginning when the right foot leaves and the ground and ending when it leaves the ground a second time. A full-speed cycle is divided into the recovery phase and the driving phase.

1. The Recovery Phase — The problem involved in the recovery phase is twofold, that is, first, to move the leg forward as expeditiously as possible with the minimum waste of energy and, second, to place it in the optimum position for the execution of the drive following the recovery.

In order to achieve recovery in the most economical fashion the knee is flexed so that when the leg is brought forward, the heel is carried high under the buttock. As the thigh swings out forward to a position almost horizontal with the ground the foot is moved forward, then downward and backward in a pawing motion. The foot contacts the ground almost directly under the centre of weight with the right knee bent only slightly.

The background rate of movement of the foot when it contacts the ground must be adequate. It should be moving backward, relative to the centre of weight of the body, at a rate of speed which is as great or slightly greater than the forward speed of the body relative to the track.

2. The Driving Phase — As the recovery leg comes forward, its toe contacts the track with the knee very slightly bent and with the heel sinking until it almost touches the ground. The driving forces of the leg are at once applied. Since the knee is fairly straight, but little power is derived from straightening it further. At this stage there occurs a strong thrust of the right foot accompanied by a powerful backward sweep of the whole

right leg. These movements are chiefly responsible for the forward propulsion of the body. Power continues to be applied, and the body is propelled forward as long as the right toe contacts the track.

Although there is a slight vertical bounding of the body in sprinting, the movement is chiefly forward. The downward phase of the bound is partially compensated by the straightening of the driving leg, which raises the body as it moves forward.

Here, as in all strides, when the right leg is thrust backward and the left leg swung forward, there is a tendency toward a trunk twist to the right. This action is counter-balanced by swinging the left arm backward and the right arm forward, thus keeping the trunk aligned in the direction of the run.

As soon as the power of the drive has been expended and the right toe leaves the ground, the driving leg becomes the recovery leg.

3. THE COAST

The so-called rest period practiced by some runners in fast races of 220 yards or more is known as coasting. This rest period is sometimes designated as "freewheeling". Although it has no place in the 100-yard dash or shorter races, it is used to advantage in the longer events, up to and including 880 yards.

As a sprinter goes charging down the track, the driving musculature is tense, and contractions are perhaps more powerful than the optimum requirements for maximum speed. The trained sprinter can learn through experience to run in a more relaxed manner for a few strides at about the midpoint of a race. The sprinter may profit by taking a deep breath during this period. The well-trained sprinter is able to coast without loss of form and with no apparent loss of speed.

In learning to coast, the novice usually experiences a loss of speed. However, he soon learns how to relax or let up a little without suffering loss of momentum. Many feel that it is better for a runner to obtain an instant of relaxation midway in the race at the risk of speed loss if such a practice saves him from "tying-up" at the finish.

4. THE FINISH

Assuming that top speed has been reached at the end of the 15-yard section and can be maintained throughout the race, the finish consists of a continuation of top-speed striding to a point several yards beyond the finish yarn. This added objective insures breasting the yarn at top speed.

If a sprinter is striding the cinders at top speed, there are no body position changes (gathering for a jump, or turn) which he can make which will increase his momentum. In fact, it seems to us that any change in good running form, as the sprinter approaches the yarn, is very likely to detract from forward propulsion. However, many fast sprinters claim that they gain an advantage by either jumping, lunging, or turning into the finish yarn.

It is believed that any alteration of striding action which interferes with the synchronization of the leg and body movement, or which detracts from the power of the driving leg, reduces speed at the finish, as well as in any other section of the sprint. Furthermore, a sprinter who is able to put additional power into a lunge or jump at the yarn has not been running at full effort.

CHAPTER 6

ESSENTIALS OF CORRECT FORM IN SPRINTING

Although sprinting is usually considered as including only the 100-and 220-yard dashes, the various points of good form they require are so much like those needed in the quarter mile that the essentials of correct form in the three events will be considered here as a unit. Special comment will be made, of courses, where differences occur. Such a discussion of correct form can best be divided into four parts:the starting position, the starting action, the sprinting action, and the finish action.

The starting position. Certain characteristics of correct starting position are the same for all sprinters and have found general agreement among coaches. Among these are position of the arms and hands, angles of the head and eyes, distribution of body weight when set" position and the line of the back when in the "set" position .Each will be considered in turn.

1. Better coaches agree that the arms should be a trifle wider than vertical from the shoulders when viewed from in front and that the hands should be supported as high on the fingers as possible, in an inverted "V"

position. Where finger strength does not permit such placement, special exercises should be taken to strengthen them. However, the fingers can be bent at the second joint temporarily and support be provided there. This position is more comfortable and some prefer it for that reason alone. However, increased height of the shoulders, which comes from finger-tip support, gives better balance and greater drive.

2. Similarly, there is general agreement that the eyes should be focused on a spot from 5 to 20 feet in front of the starting line. This placement avoids the upward leap that tends to result form watching the finish line, as well as the partially blind stumble that often accompanies a completely downward focus on the starting line itself. The head position is consistent with that of the back and of the eyes, thus permitting a relaxed neck and a forward drive of the upper forehead rather than the disastrous upward and forward lift of the face.

3. The weight of the body when in the "set" position should be so distributed that good balance can be achieved during the initial starting action. Most of the weight will necessarily be felt on the hands, but enough should rest upon the front foot to permit a full application of power by the front leg. This statement requires exact interpretation by each sprinter in terms of his own balance and drive, but the principle is certain.

4. The line of the back when in the "set" position should, in most cases, be slightly downward toward the shoulders. The first action after the gun immediately lifts the shoulders several inches to a point where their centre of weight is directly in line with that of the hips and the initial drive of the rear leg. If their weight is too low relative to that of the hips, good balance will be lost and the free striding action of the legs diminished. The runner will feel as though he were falling. If the hips are relatively low, either the back foot will be placed too far

behind the line or a closer placement will force the back leg into a cramped and weak position. Men for whom a horizontal line of the back is most helpful are usually short-legged or, more rarely, long-armed.

5. It should be realized that various positions of the feet, the eyes, the forward balance, and so forth, combined with later movements of the arms, legs, and head, all tend to balance one another. A poor foot position can be partially balanced by a proper placement of weight or a proper focus of the eyes. An ill-balanced"set" position can be partially compensated for by proper use of the arms and head during the first action out of the blocks.

Throughout this discussion, the use of starting blocks has been assumed, for they are now required at almost all big meets at all levels of competition. The controversy over their acceptance was long and sometimes heated but their advantages in economy of time, in safety, and in convenience are so great as to have now established their permanent use.

Proper placement of these blocks has been a matter of disagreement among coaches and athletes since their inception, but in recent years a series of research studies, culminating in the work of Henry of the University of California, seems to have fixed their location within rather definite limits. Henry's statistical analysis of his data led to the following conclusions:

1. The highest proportion of best runs and the smallest proportion of poorest runs result from starting with a 16-inch stance. [A separation of 16 inches between the two blocks.- J.K.D.]. A 21-inch stance is nearly as good.

2. An elongated stance of 26 inches results win greated velocity leaving the blocks, but the advantage is lost within the first 10 yards. [This loss might have been caused by improper use of other factors: poor

balance when set, incorrect angle of the head and eyes when set and of the body during the first few yards, failure to pick up the knees and thus secure full strides, and so forth.-J.K.D.].

3. Use of the 11-inch bunch start results in clearing the blocks sooner but with less velocity than securred from medium stances, resulting in significantly slower time at 10 and 50 yards.

4. Reaction time is uninfluenced by block spacing and uncorrelated with speed in the sprints.

5. Leg length is not important in determining the best block spacing and is unrelated to 50 yard sprinting ability.

6. With block spacing held constant, speed in the sprint is significantly related to how closely the individual approaches the ideal start (defined as the early development and maintenance of full maximal thrust with each leg until the respective blocks are cleared as a necessary result of forward motion).

7. Although the rear leg develops considerably more force than the front, the latter contributes twice as much to the block velocity because its impulse has a longer duration.

Special emphasis should be placed upon conclusions (4) and (6), and (7), which clearly distinguish between time spent in clearing the blocks (the primary basis for the conclusions of Bresnahan and Tuttle previously cited) and body velocity out of the blocks. The latter is much the more important.

The second method places the weight further forward so that the shoulders are already advanced an inch beyond the starting ling. In this case, getting "set" merely involves lifting the hips with no forward action at all. Thus the "set" position is more simply and consistently taken. The sprinter must make his own choice. If his fingers are weak and barely able to withstand the strain of being "set" for 2 seconds, the former method will be preferred. If they are strong, the latter has advantages.

GET SET

At the command "Get Set," the hips are pushed upward (and forward if the "on your marks" position requires it) to a point where the back leg is in its most instantaneously powerful position. There should be no weight on the back foot, but there should be definite pressure of the foot against its block. The gun does not initiate this push against the block; rather, it releases the inhibitory flexor muscles, which have held the extensor muscles in check. In the sprinter of average build, this position will raise the hips so that they will be slightly higher than the shoulders; but the back leg is the more essential guide. Charles Werner, who coached Barney Ewell and has had good success at Penn State College with sprinters generally, has for many years emphasized the drive from the back foot. He argues that since the back leg is in a more immediately powerful position, concentration of attention should be placed there. In contrast, Larry Snyder, of Ohio State University, emphasizes the front-leg drive.

The primary weight of the body will be on the hands, although an effort should be made to shift this weight to the front foot. Like the back leg, the forward leg should push vigorously against the block , waiting for release by the gun. The eyes remain focused on the same spot from 5 to 20 feet down the track as in the "on your marks" position.

At the word "set," a full breath will normally be taken and then further breathing stopped. This lifting and fixing of the chest is a normal and involuntary aspect of all positions involving concentration and explosive power. It permits both a fixing of attention and a muscular readiness.

In summary, the "set" position should be firmly and steadily fixed. The counter forces of the muscles of the legs and the weight of the body should be balanced so that the position can be held a full 2 seconds with reasonable comfort and steadiness. Yet the body should be sufficiently forward so that release of the hands would produce a forward fall on the face, did not the quick action of the rear leg prevent it. Attention should be on the explosive action of release and forward drive. The gun is merely the agent of release. If attention is upon the gun, a slower reaction will result, for attention then need to shift from sound to movement. Hoyt of Michigan felt he had aided many sprinters by insisting that they concentrate in practice upon the quickest possible forward action of the back leg. Their reaction time to the gun became shorter after constant drill on this point.

"Go," the starting action. The over-all effect of the gun should be to drive the centre of gravity of the body in a straight line to the finish tape or, more practically, to a point at least 10 yards down the track. It certainly should not produce an upward and then forward action, which comes from too much weight back on the feet. It this straight-line action is kept clearly in mind, the essential factor in the start lies in "falling with balance-that is, in keeping the weight just so far forward that the updriving knees and legs can partially but not quite catch balance. It should be understood, of course, that this rhythmic and recurring loss and catching of balance is a major factor in running. It is simply accentuated in the start.

The eyes are the key to this forward action and the primary safeguard against jumping up before driving forward. If the angle of focus of the eyes is correct, the body angle will usually be correct also. They should move slowly and steadily from their initial downward focus to the sprinting angle.

Leg action should of course be as rapid as possible and yet should provide a natural full stride. Neither a chopping of strides nor any undue effort to increase stride lengths during the first 15 yards will produce best results.

It is important to emphasize that the "set" position and the first movements of the start should be directed toward producing the greatest possible body momentum at 20 yards out. To concentrate on immediate reaction to the gun or gaining momentum only during the first 5 yards may defeat the main purpose. Sprinters who ask, "Why is it that I'm ahead at 5 yards but seem to lose my lead after that point?" Will find the probable solution here. For this reason, starting drills should always be for no less than 20 yards.

Arm action is of tremendous importance throughout the start. The studies of Bresnahan and Tuttle establish first movement as coming from the arms. The left arm, assuming a starting position in which the right leg is back, is thrown straight ahead with only a slight bend at the elbow; the right arm, straight back. The most important aspect of this movement is that it should place the arms in proper position for an effective arm drive during the next few strides. If the arm is chopped upward, it will straighten the body and shorten arm action. If it is too forcefully thrown, the shoulders may be drawn out of line. Quickness is essential, but quickness is not the same as power of force.

During the start and the entire sprint, the arms will be swung quickly, even vigorously, back and forth, but most certainly not in such a way as to lessen balance or to increase muscular tension. The forward hand should not rise above the level of the shoulders, nor should the rear hand drive more than 8 inches back of the hip.

Each stride will be longer than the one preceding it. However, the stride of most sprinters is not naturally as long as it should be to give greatest acceleration. Daily and careful drill must emphasize the need for lengthening these strides without decreasing leg speed. Higher knee action and certainly increased bounce and spring from the feet and ankles will be very helpful. The rear foot should be brought forward as close to the ground as possible and placed quickly, of course, usually not more than 18 to 24 inches from the starting line. Mel Patton, however, placed his first step as much as 30 inches beyond the starting line. He was tall, of course, and added a swing of the hip to the action of his naturally long legs. The section on practice methods will consider this entire action further.

The head during the start and the entire sprint should be exactly in line with the trunk of the body and the rear leg just before the foot leaves the ground. It should be possible to draw a single straight line at this stage of the action running the length of the leg, the spinal column, the neck, and the back of the head. As long as the head is in this relaxed, balanced position, upper body tension, the greatest single fault of sprinters, will be at a minimum.

Breathing should be as normal as possible in the 100-and 220-yard dashes, when starting and when sprinting. Under highly competitive conditions, very few sprinters are ale to maintain normal breathing; yet it should be emphasized that holding the breath increases body tension generally. Actually, the amount of oxygen taken in is not directly a factor in performance in these short events, but relaxation is, and all possible means, such as breathing should be used to achieve it. In many cases, where sprinters are tense, concentration upon one or two points in the race at which breaths are taken deliberately will often prove of value.

The sprinting action. There are four main aspects of sprinting action: (1) the maintenance of relaxation and forward body lean, (2) the action of the arms, (3) length of stride, and (4) bounce from the feet and ankles. Relaxation, it needs to be said again and again, means the full contraction of muscles when needed in the action and the full relaxation of muscles when not needed Champions often state that their best performances feel "easy" and not at all like maximum performances. For example, when Jesse Owens made his four world's records in a single day, on May 25, 1935, seemingly all but one of the viewers were convinced that this was only the beginning. He was only a college sophomore and everything he had done had looked so easy, almost careless. The one exception was Charles Hoyt, then coach of the University of Michigan team. Hoyt argued on the basis of this absence of tension that this was the greatest day Owens would ever experience. His point was substantiated three weeks later when Owens, showing marked tension in his entire upper body, was defeated in the 100-yard dash Eulace Peacock in :09.5. The commonly used phrase, "The real champion makes 'em look easy," could well be put, "Make 'em look easy and increase your chances to be a real champion."

One of the better means of keeping relaxed is by maintaining a proper forward angle of the head and trunk. The eyes are the primary means for this and should be focused at less than the horizontal. To lift the eyes is to lift the head and arms, to straighten the trunk, and to create tension in the entire action. Sprinters vary in body angle. A few carry the trunk as far forward as 30 degrees beyond the vertical. This gives them an excellent forward drive and smoothness, but they have difficulty in bringing their knees and feet forward for a full stride as well as in avoiding a wasteful kick-up behind. Far too many run with a vertical trunk, which increases tension and greatly decreases the forward drive. This is especially disastrous during the finish, where loss of forward lean is the greatest single cause of poor sprinting.

A further key to relaxation lies in the second aspect of sprinting action, arm carriage. Vigorous action of the arms, which emphasizes the forward motion, can increase body momentum, but if it is obtained at the expense of general relaxation, it would be far better to consider the arms as balancing agents only. Charles Hoyt, coach of Eddie Tolan, Sam Stoller, and many other fine sprinters, rarely stressed arm action in his coaching except as a means to balance and poise. Old-time sprinters used to carry corks in their hands when sprinting and grasped them tightly as a means of concentrating on forceful arm action. However, they were found to be a detriment to ease of action and were abandoned before 1925. In contrast, Jesse Owens sometimes sprinted with his fingers outstretched but this also is not a natural, relaxed action and did not occur in his best running. Insofar as possible, regardless of the vigour of the arm action, the hands should be held in the same easy position they naturally fall into at the sides when entirely forgotten. To do this is extremely difficult for most men as they try for greater power, but it is a necessary part of every best performance.

To find a proper arm position, the hands should first he lifted to a point even with the hipbone. The angle that the forearm now makes with the upper arm should remain unchanged. There should be no straightening of the arm as it swings forward, nor when it swings backward. Certainly there should be no upward drive of the hand and decrease of the elbow angle as the hand comes forward. This latter action has somehow gained acceptance in certain parts of the country and has detracted from relaxation and performance. The writer has often compared correct action to that of a doll with a fixed elbow angle of about 90 degrees; the shoulders are able to swing on only a very short are of 10 degrees, and therefore the arms are forced to swing freely from a pin driven through the shoulders. Their action is much more that of a freely swinging pendulum than that of a forward-driving power unit.

The third aspect, length of stride, will vary, of course, with the physical characteristics of the sprinter. Eddie Tolan, 5'7" tall, had a 12 stride (from right foot to right foot or left to left); Owens, 5' 10½ tall, a 14½ stride;Metcaklfe, 6'1" a 17' stride. Yet stride is also an acquired trait. Eddie Tolan, for example, started college with an 11' stride. Constant attention to higher knee action and to increased reach and reaction with the forward foot made the difference. Apparently, Eddie acquired this additional length of stride with very little loss of leg speed. If so, he acquired at least 5 yards in 100 yards by this method alone.

Dean Cromwell constantly emphasized the importance of bounce in working with his sprinters. For him this word summarized all the resilient reaction of the feet from the ground, much as a rubber ball bounces from the ground. Certainly the development of such bounce would greatly aid an increase in stride length.

To have bounce in one's stride does not mean that one's entire body bounce while sprinting. On the contrary, time spent in the air is time lost. A line showing the rise and fall of the head or the hips should approximate a horizontal straight line with only minor cress and troughs. To have bounce is to have the muscles and tendons of the legs, ankles, and feet in such excellent condition in terms of quickness and resilience that they react instantly at the very touch of the ground.

Bounce is a matter of natural inheritance, but it can be greatly increased by proper training and exercise. As the toe first strikes the ground, the ankles must be completely relaxed, thus cushioning landing and permitting the foot to drop down for a full forward and upward spring at the end of its stride. This requires great explosive force in the relevant muscles and great elasticity in foot and ankle tendons. Only months of precise conditioning can produce them.

The finish action. Action at the finish includes two phases, that of the last 15 yards and that of the upper body at the finish line. Without question, the most important problem during the last 15 yards is to maintain relaxation. On the surface, it would seem foolish to emphasize increased arm or leg action at this point, when the almost universal tendency is to be trying too hard already. In general, wise coaching will place relaxation above increased drive until the sprinter has permanently mastered the art. On the other hand, by a strange paradox, specific emphasis upon increased effort at this point forces the sprinter to relax just prior to the finish and to carry such ease of action through the tape.

The writer first learned this lesson in watching the development of Eddie Tolan (Michigan '31). Eddie's two coaches had rich personal experiences in coaching. Steve Farrell, then head coach at Michigan, had been a great professional sprinter and was the only American ever to win the lucrative English Sheffield Handicap twice (one of these times he did it under the name of McDonald, a not unusual circumstance but a most interesting story). Assistant coach at Michigan during Eddie's first two years and head coach from 1930 to 1939 was Charles Hoyt, who, as a Grinnell College man, held the world's record for the 220-yard dash around the turn. These two coaches worked assiduously with Eddie Tolan, even during the indoor season when the distance was only 60 yards, trying to teach him to finish. They insisted that he run his fastest throughout the entire race and yet that he "pick it up even faster" during the last 15 yards. For example, Jack Campbell, a fine sprinter, was placed 2 or 3 feet ahead of Tolan at the start. Tolan was instructed to stay with him for 45 yards, in itself a close to top performance; but then Eddie was to "go get him" in that last burst at the finish. In order to go even faster, Tolan learned to be more relaxed, not to run slower but to run more easily during the middle part of his race. Somehow his ease of action carried through to the finish. Tolan in high school strained every muscle of his body from the start to the finish of his race; Tolan at the 1932 Olympics was a picture of smoothness and ease of action. His natural ability was great, of course, but it was the years of persistent and specific drilling on pickup, on increased length of stride, on relaxation, and on finish that really brought the finest of all gold medals.

The second aspect of the finish, action of the upper body at the tape, must also e carefully supervised lest more be lost than gained. Above all, such action should in no way interfere with rhythm and balance of the forward drive of the legs. This is extremely difficult to accomplish and therefore many excellent coaches are content to teach a simple sprint on through the tape. The athlete concentrates on straight-ahead action 5 yards beyond the finish line with no special arm movements to catch the judges' eyes.

Whatever special action, if any, is taken should occur at the last possible moment on the last stride. Even the champions occasionally fail in this respect. For example, movies of the finish of the 1939 National Collegiate 100 yard dash show the winner with his left shoulder far forward in an excellent "shrug" position. Unfortunately, the "shrug" began three full strides before the finish so that much more was lost in balance and drive than was gained through the shrug. It is the old story of a good action poorly timed. This effort cannot in any way increase body speed. Rather, it attempts to pick up a few inches at the tape and to attract the attention of the finish judges by an accentuated body lean or sideward throw of the shoulders. A grandstand jump at the finish, such as used by Charles Paddock, can only lose speed, despite the contrary opinion of Charley and his coach. On the other hand, great victories are often won in the sprints by inches and the margin of victory can well be that acquired through either a lunge or a shrug at the tape.

The lunge consists of throwing the chest well forward and the arms down and back, thus producing a pronounced forward lean that can gain inches, although not the full foot often claimed for it.

The shrug combines the forward lean of the lunge with a throw of one arm, shoulder, and side of the body upward and forward while throwing the opposite arm down and back. Thus the width of the body is presented to the tape rather than its thickness, and more inches are gained. Certainly it is an attractive finish in the true sense of the word and may pull the winning nod.

In the writer's opinion, the greatest value of a special action at the tape lies in its tendency to relax the sprinter .The necessity for using judgement as to proper timing of this action and, even more, the necessity for doing something different is an excellent deterrent to desperate, all-out body tension.

Where any doubt exists of the sprinter's ability to master either of these finish forms, the best plan is to sprint right on through and beyond the tape.

CHAPTER 7

CONSTRUCTION AND CARE OF FACILITIES AND EQUIPMENTS IN SPRINTING

Wherever one finds strong track and field teams, one will also discover, almost invariably soundly constructed facilities, well-maintained for both practice and meets; adequate and well-organised equipment; and, basic to it all, groundkeepers and equipment men who are well-paid and interested in their jobs. Many are the record achievements that might properly have been credited to the construction engineer, or to the groundsman who gave the track "just one more brush and roll", then raked and brushed and rolled it once again.

The most important essential in constructing track and field facilities is a sound plan and upon the wide experience of many other persons and institutions as well as upon a careful analysis of local conditions and local needs. The latter condition is just as important as the former. One might feel safe in adopting the recommendations of a recent survey based upon the opinions of 177 track coaches. Yet actually such a recommendation is merely an average opinion that might be entirely out of place considering local conditions and needs. Ralph Young, Director of Athletics at Michigan State College, mentioned in a talk before the National Track Coaches Association that he had spent two years in planning their outdoor track, had personally visited most of the best tracks in the country, and had secured detailed plans from 60 different coaches and colleges, including four foreign countries and the International Olympic Committee. In addition, he used the college's Agricultural Department in making soil analyses and selections, its climatologists for information about prevailing winds and their effect on direction of runways, and so forth, and of course its engineers for all aspects of actual construction.

How many, many times in discussing track facilities the writer has heard the complaint, "If only they had planned a little better and built the thing right in the first place". They needs of both spectators and participants, local soil beds and available soils, rainfall during the months of competition, prevailing winds, presence of other athletic facilities or parking areas, the extent and kind of use to which the facility will be put during its many years of service—each of these and many other details demand and most careful consideration. For example, in order to meet the increasing needs of its great Relay Carnival, the University of Pennsylvania rebuilt its track in 1951 to provide 12 lanes of 38 inches each all the way round. On its Friday program, in which there are innumerable 440-yard relay heats, this meant a saving of 45 minutes and a great increase in spectator appeal. Few track programs would require so many lanes or such width of track.

TRACK CONSTRUCTION

Track dimensions—All outstanding tracks in the Far West, the Middle West, and the East are 440 yards in length but vary in the radius of their curves from 97'6" at Ohio State to 127 feet at Stanford. There is a growing tendency in track presentation to start and finish all races as much as possible in front of the spectators. This leads to more frequent running around the curves and to a greater need for increased radi and widths of track on the curves. The best hurdle lane is 50 inches wide, and thus a total track width of 25 feet is required for 6 lanes of hurdles. This point of view explains the request, in the Athletic Journal's 1952 survey, for a track 5 feet wider than that requested in Henry Schulte's 1930 survey. Coaches agree that best conditions for participants occur in the 220-, 440-, and 220-yard low hurdles when a 250-yard straightway is provided. Consequently, they are loath to eliminate this feature even though increasingly concerned about better vision for spectators.

DRAINAGE

The nature and extent of the problem of drainage is dependent almost entirely upon local conditions of soil and weather during the track season. At the University of Nebraska, for example, the track bed is almost pure sand and therefore required a minimum of excavation and rough fill. On such a track, the more it rains, the faster the track is likely to be. Other tracks, in contrast, have been laid on low marshy ground where there is much rainfall in the spring. Full tiling and use of storm sewers would therefore be necessary. Normally, however, full excavation of from 21 to 24 inches with rough and medium filling, as indicated later, will take care of all requirements.

Where drainage tile is required, only an engineer can decide just how much and where to put it. At Drake University, 48 lines of 4-inch tile were laid laterally to the track in coarse cinder ditches so that they passed beneath the track curbing and emptied into the track infield. Since the track is built 4 feet above the infield, both the subsoil and surface layers are pitched to the inside. At Michigan State, catch basins were located every 35 feet both inside and outside the track. On the infield side of the curb, a path 2 feet wide and 13½ inches deep was excavated all around the track. After 6-inch tiles were loosely laid, they were covered by 10½ inches of coarse gravel and cinders, with 3 inches of fine gravel on the surface. Later, this path was found to be usable for practice purpose even during the rainy season. Each locale has its own problems, which require specific planning.

ROUGH FILL

There is general agreement throughout the country on the use of either heavy clinkers or 3-to-4-inch stone, either crushed or in the form of gravel, for the initial coarse layer. Local conditions will determine its depth, although about 20 inches is usually considered adequate. To hurry settling and provide an early even top surface, this layer is usually rolled thoroughly. However, such rolling is dangerous to tile and sometimes crushes coarse cinders.

MIDDLE LAYER

On top of the rough fill, it is common practice to place about 6 inches of coarse cinders such as would be retained on a ¾"-mesh screen.

TOP DRESSING

Tradition in the United States suggests a mixture of 1 part clay or clay loam to 2 parts "front" or "head-end" cinders. These latter were the hard little cinder pellets that were caught by the locomotive stack screen and dropped back into the head-end of the fire box to be shovelled out at the roundhouse. Unfortunately, the use of softer coals and the expense of saving such material has made good head-end cinders almost unavailable. Ordinary boiler cinders crush easily and either turn to dust and blow away or, worse, remain in the track to form an impervious hardpan when dry and mud when wet. Much care should therefore be taken in selecting cinders, for they can easily negate much of the expense and care of building the track.

Without doubt, American coaches should be turning to science and research for the discovery of better materials for top dressing on their running tracks. Actually, our knowledge of what is best for fast running as well as best for maintenance is quite uncertain and based almost entirely upon opinion. On the one hand, for example, we hear respected coaches speaking of tracks that have "life" or "bounce" or "resilency". Yet they also praise the fast clay tracks of the West Coast or of the University of Chicago fieldhouse, which have no "give" or "bounce" whatsoever. In writing of Stanford's new track, the engineer, J.H.McDonald, stated that "every track in order to have a 'jarless', yet firm surface must be cushioned". The builders therefore very carefully placed 1½ inches of redwood bark 12 inches below the surface, under cinders, clay, and crushed rock, to provide a "cushion" against too solid a foundation. How really effective was this procedure? One of the virtues claimed for cinder tracks generally is that they are easier on the legs in both practice and meets than harder and less buoyant surfaces. Yet teams working on indoor wooden tracks or on the surfaces at the Chicago, Michigan State, or Purdue fieldhouses certainly have no more "shin splints" or sore muscles, and possibly fewer, than where tracks are softer and tend to give with each sprinting stride. It seems clear that we actually know very little on this and related subjects and that careful research in the future is needed to establish the facts of the case and the best materials to use for both track and field facilities.

Greater differences of opinion concerning the right materials and right proportions for top dressing were found by the 1952 Athletic Journal survey than on any other subject. The average opinion was given as 3 parts of cinders to 1 of clay, but at least a dozen alternatives were suggested, several of which had many adherents. Proportions of 4:1, 3:1, 2:1, 1:1, 1:2, and 1:3 of cinders and clay all had their advocates. Brick dust and clay was suggested by five coaches. The addition of peat moss and sawdust was mentioned as helping to hold moisture in the track. In the West, where oil-burning makes cinders almost nonexistent, experiments with "decomposed" granite and clay, sifted carbon with clay, decomposed lava ash, or crushed limestone have been tried and have their supporters.

THE CURB

Opinion is almost unanimous that concrete curbing provides the best and most permanent material. Present rules suggest a curb that rise 4 inches above the track, and common practice makes it 4 inches wide. Its depth in the ground is determined by the frost line and should be established so that no heaving during the winter months can possibly occur. Wood that has been well creosoted has often been used, but at best it provides only a dozen years of use. Old railroad rails have also been used, but one would have difficulty in finding such material available today. Undoubtedly the most unique and spectacular of all curbing was a hollow plastic tube, with fluorescent lighting, which was used at the indoor Purdue relays.

TRACK GRADING

Accepted practice in the construction of tracks is to make the top surface exactly level. Excess surface water will run to the surface drains on either or both the inside and outside of the track while the porous track materials absorb the remainder. However, constant use of the inside lane tends to lower this part of the track, and groundsmen all too frequently fail to maintain its height. On nine-tenths of the tracks of the country, inspection following a heavy rain will discover water standing around the inside 2 or 3 lanes of the track, just where it is least wanted in either practice or meet competition. All plans for both construction and maintenance should keep this serious problem in mind.

FIELD LAY-OUTS

An ideal plan for track and field facilities requires careful consideration of many factors. Foremost among these are (1) the requirements of best athletic competition, (2) the needs of spectators, (3) the costs of construction, and (4) the cost and ease of maintenance. Michigan State's outdoor track probably accomplishes the first two of these considerations more completely than any other track in the world. On the other hand, both its original cost and the tremendous daily care required for such extensive facilities make their adoption at other schools very difficult. Note that the pole vault and broad jump use the same runway. Since wind directions determine the direction of run in both instances, no interference can result. In such case, groundsmen will maintain both runways equally well. Where there are separate places for these two events, with two runways for each, there is an almost universal tendency to neglect the runway opposed to the prevailing winds. Then, when an emergency forces their use, poorer competitive conditions almost always result. In the writer's judgement, it is easier and even cheaper to maintain a single runway with two pits than a single pit with two runways. Furthermore, the runways are likely to be more consistently maintained.

However, each of these plans assumes a field that is used exclusively for track and field athletics, an all-too-infrequent occurrence. The requirements of football and other sports using the field force the placement of field events outside the gridiron. As a matter of interest, such requirements undoubtedly influenced the decision early in the history of track and field as to the length of a running track. From a spectator's standpoint, a smaller track—220 yards, for example—with wide curves would have provided a much more interesting prospect. Undoubtedly this is one of the great reason for the popularity of indoor track in the East and Middle West. Everything occurs directly in front of everyone and the athletes become clearly viewed personalities rather than distant blurs with arms and legs. The fertile brain of the man who was probably track's greatest innovator, Ben Ogden, of Temple University, has proposed an outdoor horseshoe stadium around a 220-yard track. The 100 and high hurdles would be down the centre of the field, the 220 and low hurdles around one curve. This would be a little rough on these latter contestants but wonderful for the spectator. A fair crowd would seem large and encourage pre-game ticket buying, whereas even a good track crowd in a football stadium seems lost and disappointing.

Regardless of the merits of such a field, the fact remains that in the great majority of cases, the lay-out of track facilities must allow for an inner field that cannot be invaded. In such instances, a plan will prove adequate.

CONSTRUCTION OF FIELD EVENT FACILITIES

In general, the plan for excavation, drainage, and choice of materials will be consistent with that followed in constructing the track itself. However, because runways and circles can be raised as well as covered by waterproof materials, there is a lesser tendency to provide special and costly drainage systems. These two reasons, added to the need for a running surface that is more firm and resistant to concentrated use, also produce a tendency to use a higher proportion of clay or clay loam in the top dressing mixture.

The runway in the pole vault should be from 120 to 140 feet in length. Where a single runway is used with two pits or where the pole vault and broad jump are combined, a length of 150 feet is best. The runway width should, in general, be 4 feet but should be determined by maintenance considerations—the width of the brushes and rollers that will be used, for example. In most cases, it will be found best to raise the level of the runway at least 3 inches above that of the surrounding ground, and thus prepare for unusually heavy rainfall. On innumerable occasions, the success or failure of an entire year's preparation for the big championship meet has been determined by facilities rather than by the ability or the perfection of preparation of the athletes. Simply to laugh off a soggy runway with "That's the breaks of the game" is infuriating to one who knows that it was actually laziness or lack of interest that created the "break", rather than the untouchable gods of chance.

The pole vault pit is now misnamed. The term is undoubtedly derived from the outmoded custom of digging into the ground to form a softer surface for landing. Today, such a practice is, or should be, unthinkable and should call down the wrath of other coaches, contestants, and spectators alike. If a coach wishes to discourage vaulting, he could think of no more certain method. The more modern term should be a "pole vault mound", for the landing area should always be a mound of thin shavings and sawdust at least 2 and preferably 3 feet high. One of the greatest deterrents to best performances in the pole vault is the fear of injury in making a landing. Such a mound, if at least 16 feet wide by 12 feet deep as demanded by National Collegiate rules, is the best means of removing such fear. Its expense is not great, although rain, wind, and the neighbourhood kids do require that it be covered by canvas at all times when not in actual use. Excavation is a single shovel's depth and that the permanent fill below ground level can be of almost any soil mixed with sawdust to prevent the jar of a rare thrust-down through the mound itself. Once the track season is over, the shavings can be bagged up again and put under cover for the next year.

Extra bags of shavings should be placed completely around the mound to hold the loose shavings in place, and also against any protruding boards or pole vault standards that might prove injurious to the vaulter. Such assurance of freedom from injury is almost guaranteed to add 6 inches or even a foot to the average vaulter's performance.

Materials other than shavings have been and are being tried, of course. Sawdust, shavings and sand, tanbark, a foam rubber mattress on top of bed springs and cottonseed hulls all have their advocates. Ben Ogden, of Temple University, has invented a kind of circus net held up to a 6- or 8-foot height by weights and pulleys, which wafts the vaulter as gently as a feather to the ground. Out of such concern for increased safety and comfort will eventually come ever greater world's records.

Indoors, it is occasionally or even regular necessary to move the pole vault pit to make room for bleachers or other sports events In the Chicago fieldhouse, shavings and sawdust used to dumped wherever the event was to be held, sometimes along the wall, other times in the centre. By erecting the pit 3 feet high and taking special precautions to stamp down the shavings a little before anyone vaulted, no injuries occurred from the hard clay surface undereath. A different device was erected in Yost Field House at the University of Michigan. A strong wooden box 16' × 12' in size and 24 inches deep was raised from the hard ground on 5 steel dollies. Shavings were heaped in the box to a height of 3½ to 4 feet from the ground. The runway side of the box was low, with bags of shavings holding the pit material in place. All wooden edges were covered with mats and shavings bags. Vaulters could run into the box and even through if necessary. Visting vaulters cleared heights that were consitent with their efforts elsewhere. The great advantage of this device was that it could be run into an out-of-the-way corner in just a few minutes and back again when needed.

The lay-out for the take-off area should follow a half-circle. This permits an equal number of steps on the prepared surface, regardless of the angle from which the run is made. The all-too-common practice of cutting in directly to the high jump standard, forming an area resembling a truncated triangle, is unfair to the jumpers who approach from the extreme left or right.

The entire area should be built up at least an inch above the surrounding ground and sloped so that water will run off toward either natural or artificial drainage systems. Constant rolling, which is so important to good high jumping, will gradually lower this, so that each year new materials must be added.

The pit must, according to National Collegiate and High School rules, be at least 16 feet long and 12 feet wide. Height is not essential, but accepted practice calls for a mound of sawdust or thin shavings and sand that is about 12 inches above the ground. All boards used to hold the dirt walls of the pit in place should be covered with bags of sawdust.

In rainy areas, especially before meets, canvas covers for both the pit and the take-off areas will prove invaluable.

Best practice in those institutions that take pride in maintaining excellent field facilities is to set aside an area about 10′ × 24′ in size for each weight event. This permits iron circles to be moved in practice as use may suggest. National College and High School rules state that the circumference of weight circles shall be marked by an iron or wooden bank, sunk flush with the ground; but for practice purposes they can be moved from place to place on the ground surface. Having areas of this size also makes possible easier maintenance, for the entire area can be brushed and rolled with the same machines as in the other field events. As usual, the type of surface varies with climatic conditions. When these are ideal, clay is considered best; when poor, a cinder-loam mixture will be most satisfactory. It is always best to raise the surface above the surrounding ground level and to provide both drainage and run-off means.

In the Northeastern states, where spring is late and often wet, concrete circles for shot, discus, and hammer throwing are rapidly gaining favour. They provide consistently level and nonslippery surfaces that are identical at all institutions. They are somewhat more costly to construct but require almost no care. Further, they can be used throughout the entire year whenever temperatures or snowfall conditions permit.

One of the greatest deterrents to excellent javelin throwing in the United States is the grass runways that are still considered adequate in both high schools and colleges. Their use is excused on the grounds that lack of space does not permit a special and permanent runway for the javelin. And this can actually be the case. But if record distances are expected, a firm footing not ordinarily provided by turf must be assured.

National rules have recently been changed to conform with international standards. At the present time, the run-up for the javelin shall be marked by 2 parallel lines 13′ 1½″ apart and the throw shall be from behind an arc of a circle drawn with a radius of 26′ 3″. Such are shall consist of a band made of wood or metal 2¾ inches in width sunk flush with the ground.

In Europe, this run-up is constructed like that of the pole vault and broad jump, with a curb enclosing a raised runway made of clay or a clay-cinder mixture. This permits the firm footing that is so necessary to the fast momentum and great distances achieved in European styles of throw.

TRACK MAINTENANCE

First concern during the pre-season period is to gain every possible assurance that both drainage and seepage are adequate. Early spring rains will bring into clear evidence the low areas in the track, and additional top dressing should be applied to produce the grading level desired.

However, seepage is equally important and needs special consideration. In cold climates, where the frost line goes well under the surface, the upper inches of cinders and clay are well loosened and seepage occurs naturally. Where winter freezing is not so deep, and certainly with indoor cinder tracks, annual discing or harrowing to a depth of from 2 to 4 inches will prove beneficial. The hardpan produced by waterning and rolling will be thus broken up and the top layer renewed. The depth of this discing must be governed by the depth of the track's top dressing, so that larger cinders are not brought to the surface.

Some groundsmen resort to deep manual raking to produce this result, but this is not likely to be deep enough to break through the hardpan. In any case, no heavy machinery should be used on the track until it has been thoroughly brushed and dragged to a level and consistent surface. Each groundskeeper usually has his favourite device for this smoothing process. Most use push or pull brushes that are from 4 to 6 feet wide. Some like first to drag the track with a heavy steel bar or I-beam. Others use a large steel door mat with added bags of sand to weight it down. Brushing after the use of such drags is always worth while.

If needed, watering should always follow this levelling work, never proceed it. Using the exact amount of water is an important and tedious task. Hand sprinkling is time consuming and almost never consistent in its application similar to but smaller than ordinary street-sprinkling wagons have been used and provide a consistent amount of water, but they are expensive and are generally considered a nuisance to fill and use. At Stanford and other Western and Southern schools, where the climate during the track season is generally dry, permanent sprinkling pipes and sprayers have been installed around the track so that a single turn of a valve will water a large section exactly as needed.

The question of rolling can be answered only in terms of the type of construction and local conditions. In many cases, the top surface of the track is hard enough. In others, rolling merely produces a surface firmness, which quickly gives way under the flying spikes of track men. In many instances, where drainage and seepage are adequate, the best means of securing surface firmness is to give the track a thorough soaking. Many a great record has been made on tracks where rain with its myriad hammers has just tapped out a durable and spike-gripping surface.

With few exceptions, heavy rolling is not recommended, for it hardens the upper layers and destroys the value of the early discing. If the binding qualities in the track are not effective with light rolling, heavier rolling will probably also be of little use.

In summary, a running track is a mirror of the personal interest and energy of its groundskeeper. His pride in the perfection of all details of construction and maintenance should equal that of the coach in all aspects of the track team and its program.

CARE OF EQUIPMENT

As with the problem of maintenance, proper care of equipment depends upon possession adequate space, a proper place for everything, and an equipment man who knows and takes a personal pride in his job. He must be a handy man who can do anything and everything. He should be a carpenter, a seamstress, a shoe repairman, a gunsmith, a record clerk, and, perhaps above all, a patient and likeable personality who gets his fun out of life by helping others.

Such a man will ask and plead and demand until finally he has enough shelves and drawers for every item of equipment in all sports. He will smilingly accept one or twenty pairs of track shoes at night and somehow have them cleaned or repaired and ready for use the next day. He will take a coach's idea for a new piece of practice equipment and delightedly produce the finished product with his own improvements. He can take a sheet of aluminum and make a protective device for a hurdler's ankle or knee bone. He can construct a method of hanging javelins so they will not warp and will store them where they will not dry out. He's usually one of the least honoured men on the departmental staff, but he's certainly one of the most valuable. At least the team members know his worth, even though the salary dispenser usually does not.

The equipment room—The first essential of the equipment room is adequate space; the second, maximum use of space. There never can be shelves enough or bins enough or drawers enough. Reserving an area for working space at least 10′ × 10′ in size, one can begin by installing as many shelves as possible. Their width and height is very important if space is to be best utilized. A complete list of all equipment should furnish a guide in this matter. In general, an adequate equipment room for track and field athletics will include:

1. Shelves for practice sweat clothes, divided into small, medium, and large sizes.
2. Shelves for practice shorts and shirts, divided by sizes.
3. Shelves for new shoes: indoor, outdoor, and rubber-soled.
4. Shelves divided into 24 compartments 12 inches wide by 10 inches high, for keeping meet clothes and shoes separate and ready for each man.
5. Shelves two sets divided into either 6 or 12 compartments, for old shoes by sizes.
6. Closet, cedar-lined, for hanging and storing wool meet suits and sweal shirts. A large cedar-lined box may suffice.
7. Locked drawer for guns, shells, and stop watches.
8. Floor bin for shots, weights, discuss, and so forth.
9. Storage space for scales and various measuring devices for javelin, discuss, and so forth.
10. Device for hanging a dozen javelins for everyday use.
11. Work bench and full set of carpenter's tools.

12. Shoe repair equipment, including stretching devices.
13. Sewing machine for cloth and heavier fabrics.
14. Steel filing cabinet for records of equipment issued, inventories, equipment catalogues, and so forth.
15. Small steel cabinet with many small drawers and compartments for various sizes of track spikes, nails, screws, bolts and so forth.
16. Horizontal pipes for the hanging and drying sweat clothes, meet suits, and so on.

CHAPTER 8

IMPORTANCE OF SPRINTING TRAINING IN TRACK AND FIELD

In the last few decades sports have gained tremendous popularity all over the globe. The popularity of sports is still increasing at a fast pace and this happy trend is likely to continue in the future also. When one looks at the history of the modern Olympic games one sees the number of sports for which competitions are held at Olympic games has increased steadily. The total number of participating countries and sportsmen has also increased steadily. In addition to Olympic sports, indigenous sports have also become popular in each country. Several new sports like sky-diving, skating, motor-racing have also come into existence and are quite popular with the masses. The television and press are giving much more coverage to sports and have become effective medium to carry sports to millions and millions of people around the world. Sports have become an important social and cultural activity of the modern world which is being given the rightful place it deserves by the nations and societies of the world.

Sports serve vital social and cultural functions the importance of which can hardly be exaggerated. The contribution of sports towards the overall welfare of the human society may be capsuled in the following points:—

Sports help in the all round development of human personality.

Provide ample and healthy means for recreation and relaxation of human mind and body.

Are effective for rehabilitation and social adjustment of the injured, sick and handicapped.

Provide opportunities for social interaction thereby fostering peace and understanding among different people, nations, races, religions etc.

Perform prevention and curative functions for several disease and ailments inflicting human body and mind.

Provide healthy and socially acceptable opportunity for the people and nations to compete against each other thereby touching heights of excellence of human endeavour and attainment.

Keeping in mind the aims, organisation and means of sports activities the sports are classified into several areas, e.g., performance sports, physical education, rehabilitation sports, fitness and leisure sports, adventure sports etc. Each area of sports caters to the requirements and demands of a particular section of the society. The area of performance sports has gained much more publicity and importance than the other areas. It has it's own structure and organisation, cadre of functionaries and a science which exclusively deals with this area. The principle aim of performance sports is to prepare sports persons for giving high sports performances.

The area of performance sports is not merely a glamourous area of sports, it also fulfils certain valuable social functions due to which it has been accorded high importance all over the world. It contributes towards the all round development of personality and enhances the horizons of awareness among the competing sportsmen with regard to the fact that they are representing particular states or countries of their origin. It inculcates in the youth a fervent desire to excell. For this they have to discipline themselves for carrying out rigorous training over a number of years. International champions become model to be emulated by their people especially by the youth. They are considered national heroes and the nation feels proud of them. Television has added new social dimension to performance sports as millions of people watch their chosen representatives taking part in international competitions. People rejoice at their victories and feel sad when they lose. Victory or defeat of their sportsmen/team is perceived as the victory or defeat of the nation.

Performance sports aim at high sports performances and for the physical and psychic capacities of sportsmen are developed to extreme limits. This normally does not happen in other areas of human activity. As a result, performance sports yield valuable knowledge about the limits to which human performance and various performance factors can be developed. It also leads to discovery of means and methods for improving various physical and psychic capacities (performance factors) to exceptionally high levels. This knowledge can be fruitfully applied to other areas of sports and human activity.

Sprinter's performance is indeed an aspect of complex human performance which has several aspects or dimensions. Hence several disciplines of sports science are required to work in a co-ordinated manner to explore the nature of sprinter's performance and the process of improving sprinter's performance. In the last few decades several disciplines of sports science have been established e.g., sports medicine, sports physiology, sports training, sports bio-mechanics, sports psychology, sports pedagogy, sports nutrition and so on. The sports science is still in its state of infancy and in the near future more sports science disciplines are likely to emerge. Some of these disciplines have already emerged, e.g., sports statistics, sports biochemistry, sports neuro-physiology, sports cybernetics etc.

All the disciplines of sports science have their own areas of study which in all cases is a certain aspect of sports performance and sports training. Each discipline has its own qualified cadre of workers as well as means and methods of investigation. Except the training science, all other disciplines have the cadre/workers who are taken from their respective mother sciences and they then specialise in the concerned sports discipline. This is not the case in science of training in which the cadre is recruited from the sports itself. This is for obvious reasons. Science of training, unlike other disciplines, studies sports performance and sports training in totality and not just one aspect of the whole. This discipline carries the most important responsibility of creating knowledge and assimilating and collecting knowledge from all sports disciplines and on its basis to formulate theories, principles etc., to determine how the sports training should be planned, organised, implemented and regulated.

Training science is further divided into two separate but highly interrelated and interdependent areas. One is the General Theory and Methods of Sports Training (GTMT). It is also called Science of Training (ST) or Training Methods (TM). Second area comprises of Theories and Methods of Training of different sports (TMT). The main task of ST is to study the principles and fundamentals of sports training for all sports. The subject matter of TMT is also the same but it is limited to only one sport. It operates at the specific level whereas ST operates at a general level.

Science of sprinting training is a recent entrant to the field of sports science. Earlier only the theories and methods of individual sports existed. The reasons for the emergence of ST as a separate sports science discipline are several. TMT by it's very nature is limited to a single sport. It cannot study the problems or areas of training common to a number of sports. Hence it is not in a position to investigate and formulate theories and principles of training applicable to all sports. Moreover, TMT is preoccupied with the specific technical aspects of a sport. It's cadre i.e., coaches/trainers have no time to study important fundamental aspects of training e.g., training and competition load, talent, motor development etc. To formulate valid theories and principles one has to study the training process in all sports i.e., from a general aspect.

The sports science disciplines have improved at a very fast pace in the past few decades. The knowledge gained by these disciplines has to be understood by the coaches do not have sufficient scientific background and training to make full and effective use of the knowledge acquired by the sports science disciplines. This creates a gap between scientists and coaches. The science of training, with its workers having sufficient background of science and sports, are able to fill this gap and can become mediator between the scientists and the coaches.

Science of training also fulfils an important didactical task for the professional preparation of coaches. The students after studying sprinting's training are in a better position to comprehend the theory and methods of training of their sport. With this objective in mind in many countries the curriculum for the study courses for coaches contain this subject and due weighted is given to it. The subject of sprinting's training has proved to be of high utility to the students and is also very popular among them.

Science of training is relevant not only in performance sports, it is equally important for other areas of sports also, e.g., physical education, rehabilitation, fitness and leisure sports, physical training of military etc. In these areas the training is mainly, directed towards the development of fitness and health. Science of training contributes tremendously towards the achievement of such aims of these areas of sports. The recent trends in the further development of sports science indicates that in the near future the subject matter of sprinting training will be expanded to include the problems and tasks of training in all the areas of sports.

HISTORY OF SCIENCE OF SPRINTING TRAINING

Theories and methods of training have existed since time immemorial. One finds mention of these in the history of mankind. The Egyption, Greek, Roman, Chinese, Indian and other ancient civilisations used special method of physical preparation for training soldiers and sportsmen. Some basic principles of training like continuity, progression of load, specificity were recognised and widely practised in ancient times. But these theories and methods were generally for the physical preparation only. A distinct science of sports training however, did not come into existence till the latter half of the twentieth century.

The modern Olympic movement brought recognition to the cultural and social functions of sports. Sports once again became a respectable activity and several popular sports acquired organisational infrastructure at national and international levels. The physical education also gained strength from the modern Olympic movement and it acquired the status of an important science in the beginning of the present century. As sports are the principal means of physical education therefore, in the initial stages of its development, the discipline of sports training was developed as a part of physical education. With the rapid increase in the popularity of modern Olympics and alongwith it of performance sports the discipline of sports training also assumed more important leading to its further development.

Science of sprinting training as an independent sports science discipline is hardly 30 years old. Before this we find theories and methods of training scattered in different sports and sports science. Physical education and theory and method of some popular sports like track and field, football, boxing, swimming etc., are principal source out of which the science of sprinting developed as a scientific discipline. Sports medicine is another science which contributed significantly toward the development of sprinting training.

A very powerful impetus for the development of sprinting training came from the performance sports. The process of preparing ahletes for winning world level competitions led to the emergence of a new profession in sports, i.e., the profession of coaching. In several countries, especially Europe, it was realised that coaching is a highly complex and scientific job and, therefore, coaches must undergo special course for this purpose as is the case in respect of physical education teachers. As the principal objective of coaches is to train sportsmen for high level performance, therefore, all available knowledge about theory and methods of training must be brought together in a systematic and integrated manner in order to impart it to the coaches. This task was accomplished in many East European countries by establishing a separate sports science discipline of sprinting training as a research and teaching subject in the sports colleges and universities. It is interesting to note that sprinting training got established as a separate subject only in those countries in which we find professional courses begin run by sports collages and universities for coaches. In countries like England, U.S.A., Canada etc., the subject of sprinting training has still not clearly emerged as a separate entity as there we still do not have proper professional courses for coaches. But in the near future, there are indications that such courses will be started in these countries also and sprinting training will emerge as a separate science discipline.

Till the first half of 20th century the subject matter of sprinting training scattered in different sports, physical education and sports medicine. In the late forties and early fifties there were some attempts to formulate systematic and complete theories of different components of training e.g., strength, endurance, techniques etc. But still no attempt was made to put forward a body of knowledge systematically covering all the aspects and components of sprinting training. The year 1957 is important in the history of sprinting training and sports science as in this year a book on sprinting training titled "Trainingslehre" (Training Science) written by Dietrich Harre was published in GDR. This was the first book to present all aspects of training in a systematic and scientific manner. This book, since then, has undergone several revisions and is considered a classic in the field of sprinting training.

In the sixties the pace of development of sprinting training picked up momentum. The contributions came mainly from GDR and USSR. In GDR another important book titled "Bewegunqslehre" (movement science) written by Kurt Meinel was published in 1960. This book did not cover all the aspects of training but confined itself to the problems of co-ordination, technique training, movement assessment and motor development. This book has also been revised several time. The Soviet sports scientists also made significant contributions towards the development of sprinting training. They limited their efforts to specific areas or elements of sprinting training. In the early sixties in USSR the book "Periodisierung des Sportlichen Trainings" (Periodisation of sprinting training) written by L.P.Matweyew was published. This book revolutionised the concepts of planning and periodisation of sprinting training. Like Harre's book on sprinting training the book of Matweyew is also considered as a landmark in the development of sprinting training.

In the early seventies more books on different aspects of sprinting training were published in USSR. Verchosankij wrote a book on special strength, Zaciorkij on motor abilities, Farfel on movement control and Kusnezov on strength. It was only in late seventies that a book dealing with all the aspects of sprinting training was published in USSR. This book titled, "Grundlagen des Sportlichen Trainings" (basics of sprinter training) written by L.P.Matweyew was published in 1977. In the same year in F.R.G. a book "Grundlugen der Trainingslehre" (basics of training science) written by D. Martin was published. The second part of this book, however, was published in 1980 and deals with the problems of periodisation, planning, regulation of training etc. Another book on GTMT written by M.Letzelter of FRG was published in 1978.

The contributions to the developments of sprinting training in the late seventies and eighties are still coming from mainly two countries, i.e., GDR and USSR. In addition to revising the earlier books, the sports scientists from these two countries have written several books on the subject matter of sprinting training and have thereby further developed the subject. In addition to the publication of books on GTMT the sports scientists of GDR and USSR have also been publishing numerous articles and papers on different topics of sprinting training. The total amount of literature produced by GDR and USSR on sprinting training is several times more than the one produced in all the countries of the world put together.

The development of sprinting training in U.K. North America, South America, Africa, Asia and Australia is lagging far behind. GDR and USSR have become the leaders and other countries are trying to follow them. But unfortunately, still majority of the countries have not realised the importance of this subject and, therefore, this subject till now not been established as a separate sports science discipline. In English language there is hardly any book dealing with all the aspects of training. The English translation of German or Russian books are the exceptions in this regard. Most of the books in English on sprinting training only deal with the motor abilities. Important among these are given below:—

1. Scientific Basis of Athletic Conditioning. By Jenson and Fischer, 1979.
2. Athletic Training and Physical Fitness. By J.H.Wilmore, 1977.
3. Sports Training Principles. By F.W.Dick, 1979.
4. The Scientific Aspects of Sports Training. Bt A.W. Taylor. 1975.
5. Towards Better Coaching. By F.S.Pyke. 1980.

In India sprinting training was first introduced as a teaching subject by the Netaji Subhas National Institute of Sports, Patiala in the early seventies. In the various colleges of physical education and university departments of physical education the subject of sprinting training has still not been introduced as a separate subject. It is mostly taught as a part of science of coaching for a particular sport. A significant contribution towards establishing sprinting training as a separate science discipline was made by Hardayal Singh by writing a book on this subject. The book titled "Sports Training: General Theory and Methods" was published by NSNIS in 1984. NSNIS contributed tremendously towards the establishment and developments of sprinting training in India by creating separate departments of sprinting training at its various teaching centres.

From the above discussion it becomes amply clear that sprinting training is a new science and is developing at a very rapid pace. In view of the ever increasing popularity of sports, especially performance sports, the sprinting training will continue to develop further at a fast pace. Sprinting training in the past had mainly devoted itself to performance sports. But at present with the sports fast becoming a part and parcel of daily life activity of humans of different ages, professionals and by serving different aims and objectives of different sections of human society the sprinting training has to widen its field of study. There are new challenges and tasks for sprinting training to face and in future sprinting training is bound to gain in stature and significance.

SUBJECT MATTER OF THE SCIENCE OF SPRINTING TRAINING

Every science has to very clearly define and delimit the subject matter which it purports to study. This is essential in order to justify its existence as a science. Physics studies energy, chemistry studies the matter as a physical entity and biology studies the vital functions of life of plants and animals. It is difficult to pin point what is the real object of study of sprinting training. This problem is there because sprinting training focuses on sports which is a complex biological, social and psychological process. Sprinting training which is a distinct type of human activity and like all human activities it is multidimensional and this problem is further aggravated by the fact that its object of study is also a direct concern of theory and methods of various sports. As a result the borders of the subject matter of sprinting training as a practical necessity overlap the borders of the subject matter of several sciences and practically all sports.

The sprinting training studies the theory and ingredients required for a sprinter generally. It studies all the components or parts of athletic training as well as the sprinting training in its entirely as a complex process of preparation of sportsmen and human beings for better sports performance or physical performance. In doing so it does not limit its study to sprinting training for one sport only but for all the sports. The sprinting training also does not limits its study of theory and methods of training to any one aspect of training e.g., psychological, physiological etc., but attempts to integrate all such aspects into the actual and practical phenomenon of sprinting training. Other sports sciences do not go beyond a certain aspect of training i.e., they tend to study only one aspect of the complex multidimensional human activity of sprinting training.

The sprinting training distinguishes itself from other sports science disciplines by its characteristic of studying theory and methods of training from a practical point of view. It studies the actual planning, implementation, disciplines focus their attention on studying their own aspects of the components of the training but these disciplines do not study or describe in which way the knowledge discovered by them should be used effectively in the planning, implementation, assessment and regulation of sprinting training. This task is the subject matter of sprinting training.

Sprinting training is a conscious human activity. Also, it is a goal oriented activity. Therefore, it is obligatory for ST to include in its subject matter the study of sports performance and performance capacity. Without an understanding of sports performance and performance capacity no effective and meaningful theories and methods of training are possible. As a consequence sprinting training gives high weightage to studying the nature and genesis of sports performance in training and competition. Similarly, a large portion of sprinting training is devoted to the study of performance capacity which further comprises of physical condition (physical fitness), technique and coordinative abilities, tactics, physique and psychic factors.

Sports performance are to be achieved in sports competition. It is, therefore logic to include competition as a subject matter of sprinting training. The relationship between competition and performance is well known. Hence here the sprinting training tries to study the effect of competitions on sports performance and to use it for better training and for better preparation of sportsmen for competitions.. The competition theory in sprinting training has a very high relevance for performance sports. But for the other areas of the sports it is not of much relevance.

The study of sports performance, performance capacity, sprinting training and competitions from the actual subject matter of sprinting training. The other topics which are also to be studied by sprinting training are there because without studying these the above mentioned objects of study can not be properly studied. These topics are: Motor development, training load, talent identification and its development, education through sports, regulation of sprinting training and so on.

Relationship of Sprinting Training With Sports and Sports Science Disciplines

Science of sports training has emerged as a discipline of central important in physical education as well as sports science. It is an integrative science which attempts to collect relevant information and knowledge about the various aspects and components of sports training from the actual process of training in different sports and also from various other sports disciplines. Its function is not limited to collecting of information and knowledge but goes much beyond it. It analyses and synthesises this information in the light of actual practise and applicability of these into the training process. It formulates theories and methods for the planning, implementation, assessment and regulation of sports training. These theories and methods as such or in the form of principles, fundamentals, rules guidelines etc., are given over to the various sports for application in their specific fields.

Its relationship with the sports and sports science disciplines is a two way traffic. On the one hand it is collecting information and knowledge about sports training from sports and sports science disciplines and on the other hand it is also giving back information and knowledge back to these sports and sports science disciplines after analysing and synthesising these in the form of theories and methods etc.

WHAT IS SPRINTING TRAINING?

Sports of training is fast emerging as an independent research and teaching discipline in the field of sports science. It has multifarious functions to perform which are presented below in brief:—

It studies sports performance, sports training, sports competition from a general view point. For this purpose it has its own methods of investigation. It works in close combination which individual sports and other sports science disciplines to achieve its objective. The knowledge gained by sprinting training is given back to the sports and sports disciplines for their use. It also acts as a medium of conveyance of information from sports to sports science disciplines and vice versa. It acts as a filter and interpreter for the exchange of knowledge between sports and sports science disciplines.

Sprinting training an important role in the development of theories and methods of sports. It provides technical assistance and guidance to the sports coaches and sports teachers to study and develop their sports. To the sports science disciplines it contributes by helping them to understand the vital aspects and details of various aspects of theories and methods of training thereby enabling them to focus on problems of real practical importance.

The knowledge about theory and methods of training, gained by sprinting training in the area of performance sports; forms the basis of training in other areas of sports and physical education. In the recent past this function of sprinting training has gained immense importance because of increasing popularity of sports and physical activities for health, recreation, rehabilitation, prevention and cure of disease and so on. The physical education is fast being applied as an obligatory subject in schools and colleges all over the world. For achieving its aims and objectives physical education is now increasingly taking the help of sprinting training.

The terminology of sports and physical education was facing the problem of being not clear, precise, uniform and universally accepted terminology is a serious draw back and limitation for the science of sports. Sprinting training because of its close proximity with sports and sports science disciplines is attempting to evolve a uniform and standard terminology for use in sports training, competition and other aspects of sports.

As a teaching discipline sprinting training helps the students of sports, physical education and sports science disciplines to get a better and clear view of the theories and methods of training. This has proved to be very helpful to the students in order to understand their own fields of study with greater depth.

The word "training" has been a part of human language since ancient times. It denotes the process of preparation for some task. This process invariably extends to a number of days and even months and years. The term 'training' is widely used in sports. There is, however, some disagreement among sports coaches and also among sports scientists regarding the exact meaning of this word. Some experts, especially belonging to sports medicine, understand sports training as basically doing physical exercises. Several terms used in training e.g., strength training, interval training, technical and tactical training reflect this line of thinking.

The regular and systematic use of physical exercises, however, does not guarantee maximum improvement in performance. The effect of these exercises is increased or decreased by a multitude of factors. Some of these factors, if ignored, lead to a drastic reduction in the efficacy of physical exercise. Most important among these are sports equipment and implements, verbal instructions, means of recovery, means of assessment of performance capacity, nutrition, psychological means and so on. In order to achieve best results, all these factors or means are to be used in addition to or along with physical exercises. The physical exercises and the other means or factors are to be judiciously applied in a systematic manner. The process of preparation of a person for improving his performance, therefore, should not be confined only to physical exercises.

The complex nature of sports training involving physical exercises alongwith other means becomes obvious when one looks at the training of advanced sports means and measures from several sports science disciplines e.g., sports medicine, sports physiology, nutrition, physio-therapy, sports psychology, sports biomechanics and so on. It can be stated as a principle that higher the level of sports performance, more is the involvement of sports science disciplines. It, however, does not mean that the role of a coach become less but the held taken by the coach from the sports scientists increases. The planning, implementation and control of training is still the sole responsibility of the coach.

Sprinting training is done for improving sports performance. The sports performance, as any other type of human performance, is not the product of one single system or aspect of human responsibility. On the contrary, it is the product of the total personality of the sports person. The personality of a person has several dimensions e.g., physical, physiological, social and psychic. In order to improve sports performance the social and psychic capacities of the sports person also have to be improved in addition to the physical and physiological ones. In other words, the total personality of a sportsman has to be improved in order to improve his performance. Sports training, therefore, directly and indirectly aims at improving the personality of the sportsman. No wonder, therefore sprinting training is an educational (i.e., pedagogical) process.

Sprinting training is a systematic process extending over a long period. For best results the system of training has to be based and conducted on scientific facts and lines. Where it is not possible to do that, the training has to be based on the results of successful practice which has withstood the test of time. Sport science has still not been able to provide a scientific base for all the aspects and elements of training. Many things are still based on the results of successful practice which on deeper analysis is also a method of science to prove or disprove a theory. Moreover, the principal characteristic of a science is the existence of a systematised body of knowledge. The science of sports training has its own systematised body of knowledge and hence is a science in itself.

A definition of sports training has to be worked out in the light of above discussed nature of training. A few definitions, however, as given by some experts may well be presented as below :—

"Sports training is a planned and controlled process in which, for achieving a goal, changes in complex sports motor performance, ability to act and behaviour are made through measures of content, methods and organisation". (Martin 1979).

"Sports training of sportsman represents a multisided process of purposeful utilisation of the total complex of factors (means, methods and conditions) which help in the development of the sportsman and ensure a necessary level of his sports performance ability". (Matwejew 1981).

"Sports training, based on scientific knowledge, is a pedagogical process of sports perfection which through systematic effect on psycho-physical performance ability and performance readiness aims at leading the sportsman to high and the highest performance. Through active and conscious interaction with the given demand in sports training, the sportsman's personality develops according to the norms and standards of socialist society". (Harre 1986).

"Sports training is a scientifically based and pedagogically organised process which through planned and systematic, effect on performance ability and performance readiness aims at sports perfection and performance improvement as well as at the contest in sports competition" (Thiess and Schnabel 1986).

Now, it is quite obvious that various endeavours have been made at different levels to advance acceptable definition of the vital process of sports training. After considering the nature of sports training as viewed by some eminent authorities on this subject, the following definition of sports training is proposed :—

Sports training is a pedagogical process, based on scientific principles, aiming at preparing sportsmen for higher performance in sports competitions.

BASIC PRINCIPLES OF SPRINTING TRAINING

Sprinting training aim at improving the performance of sprint persons. The sprinter's performance depends on several factors. The performance of a sprint person primarily depends on his performance capacity which is a complex of five groups of factors. All these factors, therefore, are the principal aims of sprinting training. The constitution or physique is almost completely genetically determined and hence cannot be improved by training. But the other four groups of factors are trainable to a greater or lesser extent. These four, therefore, are generally considered to be the aims of sprinting training.

1. Physical Fitness or Condition

The physical fitness or condition is the sum total of five motor abilities namely strength, speed, endurance, flexibility and co-ordinative abilities. These five motor abilities and their complex (e.g., strength endurance, explosive strength etc.) are the basic prerequisites for human motor actions. Therefore, the spriter's performance in sprinting depends to a great extent on these abilities. The improvement and maintenance of physical fitness or condition is perhaps the most important aim of sprinting training. Each sports require a different type of fitness training or conditioning is required for different sports. Some sports like distance running require a high level of endurance but a low level of other motor abilities. Sports like shooting and archery do not require a high level physical condition.

2. Technical Skill

Sprints performance are possible only through sports motor actions or movements. The performance of a sprint persons is significantly affected by the skill with which these actions or movements are executed by a sprint's person. The acquisition of sports technical skills, therefore, is an important aim of sprinting training. In all sports one or more skills have to be acquired by doing technique training. The role of technical skills in different sports, however, is different. In sports in which only one or two simple movements have to be learnt the role of technical skills is less. But in sports in which several difficult movements difficult and their variations are to be mastered the roie of technical skills increases manifold e.g., gymnastics, football etc. In team games, combat sports etc., the technical skills serve as basic element of tactical actions which are indispensable for good performance in these sports. Even in sports depending largely on fitness or condition the technical skills are important for economy and efficiency of simple movements like running, swimming, jumping, lifting and throwing.

TACTICAL EFFICIENCY

Tactical efficiency consists of three elements: knowledge of competition rules and possibilities of exploiting various internal and external factors for achieving best possible results; tactical abilities and tactical skills. Tactical efficiency is important in all sports but its role is different in different sports. Tactical efficiency is of paramount importance in team games, combat sports and racket sports. These sports, therefore, are also called tactical sports. The role of tactics in individual sports is limited e.g., throws, gymnastics, weight lifting etc. The contribution of tactics toward sprints performance increases with the improvement in performance. The total volume of tactical training, also increases with the increase in the level of performance.

4. Education

Sprints performance is the product of the total personality of the sprint person. It is highly erroneous to think that sprints performance is determined exclusively by the physique and physical qualities. Sprints performance is a psycho motor performance and for its improvement through training as well as for achieving it in a competition. The sprint person depends heavily on his qualities of head and heart. These qualities or abilities can be classified into five groups given below :—

(a) Beliefs, values, motives, interests, attitudes etc.

(b) Cognitive abilities e.g., perception, thinking, memory etc.

(c) Emotional abilities, e.g., control of emotions.

(d) Personality traits e.g., regularity, sincerity, hardwork.

(e) Habits, e.g., habits of eating, sleeping, hygiene, spending of leisure time etc.

The above mentioned five groups of qualities and abilities enable the sprintpersons to compete successfully in a competition. It is also of equal importance to realise that these qualities also enable a sprintperson to do training effectively and systematically for a number of years.

The sprinting training aims at improving these qualities through proper selection and implementation of various means and methods of training. In other words, sprints training is an educational or pedagogical process. Without understanding this aspect of sprint training a sprintperson has a very low chance of achieving high sprint performance.

CHARACTERISTICS OF SPRINTING TRAINING

Sprinting training is not mere physical activity involving physical movement or actions. Such type of physical activity is common to several types of human activities e.g., play, dance, physical or manual work like house hold work, work in industries and factories. In addition to physical activity the sprint training possesses more characteristics which are explained below in brief:—

1. Performance in a Sprints Competition

Sprint training aims at achieving high performance in sprints competition. It is a process which is spread over a long period of time. It is a competition and performance oriented process. It is not just play or recreational activity, but a serious activity.

2. Planned and Systematic

Modern age is the age of science. Different sciences

are exploring different dimensions of human nature and human performance. In order to achieve best results the knowledge from these sciences has to be incorporated in the process of sprints training. In other words sprints training is based on scientific facts and principles. Where science is silent it is based on results of successful training/practice which has repeatedly withstood the test of time. Theories and methods of training are, therefore, either supported or by time tested practice.

4. Coach as a Leader

Sprints training is always assessed, planned, organised and implemented by a coach or a sprints teacher or some other person. A coach controls everything. He bears the overall responsibility for the effectiveness and success of training. As the performance level of a sprintsman improves the coach has to take the help of sprints scientists more and more. But at no time does his responsibility as a coach decreases. The dominant position of the coach is not an indication of total dependence of sprintperson on the coach. Sprintperson, with the passage of time, should become more and more independent. He should assume more responsibilities and should be involved in planning, implementation and assessment of training. But the responsibility of the coach to guide and help him in achieving high performance remains intact.

5. Development and Exploitation and Reserves

A person, in spite of his best intentions and efforts, cannot fully use his phychic and biological capacities to the maximum. Some reserves are always left untapped. This is particularly evident in sprinting. Many times the sprint person is not even aware of the limits of his performance. The sprints training aims at finding these hidden reserves and makes the sprintperson aware of it. Sprints training also aims at further development of these reserves. This characteristic of sprints training is unique as in other areas of human activity is rarely pushed to the ultimate limits of his performance i.e., super human efforts.

6. Controlled Daily Routine

Sprints training is not play or recreation. It is hard and exacting. Besides, in order to do training regularly with best effects, the sprintpersons has to adjust his other activities, i.e., training should take precedence over other activities. As a result the sprintspersons control their day to day routine in such a manner that they are able to do training once or twice a day with high effect. When we look at this important and vital characteristic of training, we realise that spintpersons must possess a high sense of self discipline, a quality shared by all champions.

Educational Process

Sprinting training is basically an educational or pedagogical process. It strives to develop all the aspects of personality. Without developing the personality sprint training and high performance are not possible. Therefore, personality development and performance development are two interrelated and interdependent aspects of sports training.

7. Educational Process

Sprinting training is a planned, systematic and scientific process of preparation of sprintpersons for high performance. To achieve this aim different means and methods are used. These means and methods are not static in nature. These are being constantly improved, modified and new ones being discovered by the sports science disciplines. Valuable contributions are made by implementing these means and methods in different forms and under different conditions. The process of scientific observation, experimentation, analysis and synthesis is an important characteristic of sprints training in modern age. Sprints training, therefore is a continuous process of perfection, improvement and creation of means and methods of improving sports performance and factors of performance.

TRAINING STRUCTURE

Sprinting training is a complex process of preparation of sprintspersons. It consists of various parts, phases, cycles, proportions of training elements, load dynamic etc. Thiess and Schnabel (1987) define training structure as follows :—

"Structure of internal interdependence of important aspects, parts and phases of training process, their lawful relationship and interaction as well as their general sequence". The training structure is based on the laws and principles of sports training and aims at systematic development of sports performance.

Training structure is primarily characterised by the following :—

Parts of training based on the performance structure and demand profiles.

Purposeful order of training parts.

The proportions and interrelationships of training parts, e.g., proportion of general and special preparation, conditioning and technical training.

Temporal sequence and change in the training parts with respect to training state, age, periodisation etc.

Load dynamic, e.g., volume, intensity.

The structure of sprints training can be studied and analysed either from its cross-sectional or longitudinal aspect. The training plan for a training session is an example of training structure depicting the cross-sectional view of training on a particular day. The longitudinal view of training structure is exemplified by a training plan for a longer period e.g., Annual plan or Olympic cycle plan.

The structure of training basically comprises of training elements/parts and their interrelations. But it is important to note that structure of training is in fact structure of long term process covering several years. With the passage of time the training structure also undergoes change. For the purpose of planning and analysis of training the cross-sectional and longitudinal aspects of training structure both are important.

It is also important for the students of sprint training to understand that the principal aim is always to study the process of training in its entirety. Hence, the study of strength and strength training is incomplete till we learn how to integrate strength training effectively with the actual process of training over short and long periods. This applies to all elements, parts, aspects, phases of the complex training process. This is one of the reasons for understanding cross-sectional and longitudinal aspects of sprints training.

MODEL OF SPRINTS TRAINING

The implementation of training process is a difficult take.

The starting point of sprints training is the determination of aim of sprints training. This is primarily done by the coach after a thorough analysis of various factors. The sports scientists and the sprintsman are also involved in the fixation of the aim. It is not sufficient to determine the general aim only. It is also essential to set time for different factors on which performance depends. It is preferable to split the aim into sub-aims to be achieved after definite periods of training. While determining the aims the coach must set aims for personality as well as for performance.

On the basis of set aims and objectives for personality and performance development the coach makes shorter and bigger training plants to achieve these aims and objectives. On the basis of these plans he organises the actual training process. Under his direct guidance, supervision and help the sprinter does the training. In the planning and implementation of training the sports scientists, physician and sprinters are also involved. The quality and extent of their involvement depends on the judgment, experience, and knowledge of the coach.

During the process of training and also during competitions the coach, through observation, tests, controls, competition results, gets the feed-back about the effect of training on the sprinters and on his performance. The sprinter and the sports scientists also get feed-back about training and competition performance. On the basis of this feed-back the coach periodically makes an analysis and assessment of training and performance. In this process the sports scientists are also involved as they can give valuable information about the various factors of performance capacity. The sprinter is also involved in order to take him into confidence and also to teach him how to analyse and assess training and performance.

Society plays an important role in the implementation of the training process. Its contribution is direct as well as indirect. The coach, sportsman, sports scientists and other persons involved in training are part and parcel of society. They are all subject to social influences through family members, friends, colleagues, associations, press, T.V. etc. Besides the infrastructure required for the sprint training and sprints competitions, is directly or indirectly provided by the society. Social recognition, praise, criticism, apathy have all pervasive effect on the training process. Society provides the basic prerequisites for successful implementation of training and competition system. It is not an exaggeration to say that training and competitions satisfy social needs and hence society provides for the implementation and success of this system.

Different nations or societies of the world, in the process of their development, have evolved different sports systems. The sports systems of socialist countries are vastly different from the sports systems of European and American systems. Each country has a system which suits its social, political, and economic conditions. System of one country may not prove to be good for another country. These systems have to be gradually evolved and cannot be changed in a sport span of two or three years.

In the end it must be pointed out that the success of sports training process depends on several factors particularly social, political and economical conditions. A coach or sports teacher alone cannot guarantee its success. Society has to consciously take up the responsibility of making it a success. This does not mean that the coach can be absolved of his responsibility. He has a very crucial and pivotal role to play. He should be a scientist and an artist both to train the sprinter. His job is to coach, and coaching is the art of successfully training the sprinter for higher performance and better results.

CHAPTER 9

IMPORTANT COMPETITIVE TIPS IN THE 100-YARD DASH

WARMING UP

The 100-yard dash is a controlled explosion of energy. It is an all-out effort, but it must be channelled into the fight muscles and only the right muscles at the right time. The process of warming up, therefore, has the dual function of preparing the body for greatest possible effort while at the same time concentrating and controlling energy output so as to produce best results. Its most obvious aspect is activity-the jogging, repeated wind sprints, exercises, and preliminary starting that are the habit of every trained sprinter. After these, the engine is at a temperature that makes fastest action possible.

The viscosity or resistance within the muscle is lessened. The power of the muscles to contract is greater and the time they require for relaxation is decreased. Reaction time to a stimulus is lowered. This internal warm-up cannot be judged from surface perspiration, which might come from high atmospheric temperatures regardless of activity.

Rather, it is a problem of blood circulation, of nerve reaction, and of muscle fluidity, all of which arise only through vigorous action.

A second aspect is emotional excitement and its control. The release of adrenaline into the blood stream, which normally accompanies warming up as well as highly competitive situations, is an emergency mechanism that places the body in the best possible condition for maximum effort. Without its exciting presence, the sprinter would be greatly handicapped-in fact, entirely incapable of doing his best.

Yet, unless this explosive stimulant is controlled, the sprinter will struggle futilely for his best speed. Control comes through months and even years of drill on the mechanics of form. To some it seems to come naturally and easily. By others it must be acquired. However, in all cases, an established routine of warm-up, of massage just before the race, of knowing the starter and his methods, and of setting one's starting blocks will all prove of great aid.

REPORTING AT THE STARTING LINE

The wise sprinter will report at the start with plenty of time to prepare himself but not so early as to make waiting a nervous strain. He should bring his own blocks, for he knows their make-up and best use. Whenever possible, he should watch the starter in his handling of the earlier races and prepare his own plans accordingly. Sweat clothes should be kept on until the starter asks for their removal. Shoe laces should have been checked earlier to see that they are new and properly tied.

The matter of being friendly with one's opponents at the start is an individual problem. For some, to do so will aid in maintaining poise and relaxation at the start. For others, concentration upon the matter at hand will advise against it. It is such considerations that should determine one's actions and not social propriety. Good sportsmanship is better shown by being prepared on time so that the others are not kept waiting or by getting a best possible start with not thought of "beating the gun."

In many cases, the last few minutes may well be spent in concentrating one's faculties and reviewing the forthcoming race. Mental alertness at the start is essential. It implies a focusing of attention upon the job at hand and permits no wandering to lesser details.

TAKING MARKS

Having been one of the first to take a position of readiness, the sprinter should get into his blocks unhurriedly. Fidgeting at this point hurts everyone, but most of all the one who does it, for the mind needs this time in which to prepare itself, to clear the channels for action. Reaction time is directly related to the degree and direction of attention.

GET SET

The speed with which the sprinter gets "get" is dependent upon his confidence in and the consistency of the starter. One of the most irritating and inexcusable aspects of present-day track athletics is the use of poorly trained starters. This is particularly the case where indoor racing has over emphasized the spectator and the importance of record breakings. However, until starters become more dependable, sprinters must be ready for anything.

With good starting, a man should move into "set" position smoothly and unhurriedly. Being "set" means to be physically poised and well balanced for hair-trigger action, but equally to be mentally alert and pin-pointed toward the initial drive off the blocks.

GO

There should be no guessing at the gun. The shameful performances of experienced sprinters in big-time indoor meets in which as many as a dozen false starts are taken in their efforts to "beat the gun" are a disgrace to the sprinters, to their coaches, and to the honour codes of track athletics itself.

No man can legitimately go "with the gun," even though he did not move a single muscle before it sounded. Physiologists report that at least 0.1 second is required between stimulus and response in activities such as sprinting. Therefore, no shorter time can legitimately elapse between the gun and first movement. Unfortunately, starters have ignored this fact and major record applications are signed for races in which reaction time to the gun was zero.

Good sportsmen in sprinting will concentrate on getting out as soon after the gun as possible. This is not exclusively a matter of quick reaction to the gun, but rather of total action out of the blocks. Ralph Metcalfe is generally admitted to have had one of the fastest finishes of all time, and Coach Snyder credited him with having greater "sheer speed" in 1936 than even the great Owens. Furthermore, Snyder closely examined movies of the 1936 Olympic 100-meter race and noted that Metcalfe's reaction to the gun was the quickest of any of the sprinters. How then could he lose the race? The answer apparently lies in his manner sued his belief that, for him, quick starting lay in placing the feet down as rapidly as possible. Consequently, his first foot was within 8 inches of the starting line and his next six strides very short and chopping down rather than reaching out. It seems clear that he lost yards in the first 10 yards of the race and never quite made them up at the finish. One can only conjecture what longer strides at the start might have accomplished for him.

SPRINTING ACTION

According to the excellent studies by A.V. Hill, full momentum is reached at between 30 and 50 yards. Once it is attained, the sprinter consciously relaxes. He does not slow down, In fact, if he has been trying too hard, he may even speed up at this point. But the muscles unrelated directly to sprinting are relaxed and a so-called "float" occurs. It is necessary to repeat that this "float" is not a lessening of speed; rather, it is simply a lessening of tension. It would be foolhardy to run less than one's fastest at any time in a distance as short as 100 yards. Yet, paradoxical as it may sound, all good coaches advocate a pickup or lift in the last 15 to 25 yards. The story already told of Eddie Tolan in the 60-yard dash is very much in point here. How many times the writer has listened wonderingly to himself saying, "No, you do not slow down at all in the middle of your race, but you should pick up speed in your finish." The words are somehow meaningless; but the effect of them has seemed to be worth while.

During this "float," a man's arms and hands do not "drop a little," nor do his shoulders swing a trifle more freely, nor does "his body angle lean forward a degree or two," as is so often stated in coaching literature. There are no changes the human eye can normally detect, but the sprinter can feel the difference in body tension and is aided by it.

THE FINISH

Even though the sprinter is already running his fastest, even though the coach urges him to run even faster, the top sprinter will somehow manage to keep relaxed throughout the finish. It takes remarkable poise to feel the wolf's hot breath at one's back and yet "take it easy." But constant drill over many months, even years, can accomplish much.

One of the most inexcusable errors in sprinting is to try to sneak a look at one's opponents. Nothing else can destroy concentration, poise and form quite so quickly.

COMPETITIVE HINTS IN THE 220-YARD DASH

The most commonly accepted practice today in running the 220 is to consider it as having three parts: the pickup, the "float," and the finish. The average 220 man will gain top speed during the first 60 yards of his race, relax into a "float" for about 100 yards, and then "pick it up" in a finish of about 60 yards.

This method is well illustrated by Mel Patton's description of his win in the 1948 Olympic 220 over Barney Ewell: "He had been studying Barney's methods of running the 220 and he discovered just where he turned it on in most of his races. So he just turned it on a little sooner and got an early enough jump on him to carry through to the finish."

However, an increasingly large number of progressive coaches regard the race as a single unit in which the man sprints as fast as he can but with minimum tension all the way. If maximum velocity is gained six seconds out from the start, the problem is then one of maintaining this type speed as long as possible and yet have minimum deceleration at the finish. The curve of velocity should not fall away during the middle 100 yards and then pick up again at the finish. Rather, it should very gradually but consistently fall away after the 60-yard mark through to the finish. This is implied in Snyder's description of Owens and Draper, in the talk just cited, as sprinters who could "relax and yet maintain top speed all the way through."

Inexperienced or immature sprinters will be wise to follow the "float" method until they have learned to relax at full speed. They may lose some races by misjudging the distance of their kick at the finish, but the experience gained will be worth it. Many coaches and fine sprinters follow such tactics as those suggested by Mel Patton. Although not looking over at their opponent, they "feel" his exact location and the effort he is making and adjust their own race accordingly. This is particularly effective when a man has definite confidence in his own finish and can run just behind his opponent's shoulder throughout the middle of the race. As Cromwell says, however, "I do not advise runners to base their hopes for 220 victories on the superiority of their own intellects. If they will learn how to run their best 220 in advance, knowing when to ease off from the opening burst of speed to the coast and when to go from that to the final gather, they are more likely to win than if they depend on out marting the opposition.

But the man who is specializing in the 220 and has made a careful study of it competitively, who knows how to sprint without tension, and who is well conditioned and physically mature will follow the "maximum speed, minimum deceleration" plan. Someday such an athlete will run under 20 seconds for the 220.

There will be no time in which to relax into a "float." Spectators will say he just sprinted all-out all the way, but as in the case of the best performances of Jesse Owens, they will be excited about how easy and loose he looked. They'll be certain he could have done much better had he really tried, but, like Owens and Patton, his easiest one will be his best.

IMPORTANT QUESTIONS AND ANSWERS

What about types of sprinters and sprinting styles? The very prevalent practice of attempting to type sprinters and sprinting styles leads in most instances to misunderstanding and poor training methods. There are, of course, sprinters who are tall, light of weight, and long-striding, just as there are others who are short, stocky, and explosive. There are sprinters who are "drivers" and others who light-footedly "float" over the ground. But to classify sprinters as being of two types of whatever category tends to blur understanding, and not clarify it. Effective coaching occurs only through careful study of the individual and of his particular characteristics.

How can the length of the first ten strides be increased withoutn slowing leg action? Only be constant and attentive drill over months, even years. Such drill can take many forms: sprinting the length of a football field, touching each 5-yard line with the left or the right foot; sprinting over low hurdles placed far enough apart to force slight overstriding; deliberately exaggerating stride length and action in warm-up work and thus stretching and strengthening leg muscles and tendons; constantly exercising foot and ankle muscles to produce maximum bounce or resilience of stride. Each coach and athlete will have his own favourite exercise for this purpose; but the only real answer lies in persistent drill.

When working on a dirt or cinder track, the writer has found the following procedure very worth while. Brush a wide lane 30 yards long from the starting blocks. After the sprinter is well warmed up, have him go all-out for a tape at 20 yards tow or even three times. Scratch a line on the trach at each of his footprints. Now have him move his blocks 2 feet over and run through again and again, deliberately trying to increase the lengths of his strides while still sprinting for the tape. It will be fond in most cases that he can pickpup as much as 3 feet in 20 yards with very little difficulty but that his form feels unnatural and tense.

Now drill day after day, week after week, month after month, until this same length of stride is produced with perfect freedom from tension and with equal leg speed.

When first attempting this exercise, get out the steel tape and write down the measurements of each stride, so that months later improvement can be measured accurately. When running competitive starts for 20 yards, remind the sprinter of the importance of maintaining the new stride action, for it is here that the real test of learning occurs. If he can't do it in competition, nothing has been gained.

How are age and performance related in sprinting? Best performances in sprinting come at anearlier age than do those in any other event in track and field athletics. The factors affecting speed of movement apparently develop very early in life, and constant practice from childhood on in the mechanics of last running apparently develop a mastery of its skills that coaching and precise training can do comparatively little to improve. In contrast to the record in distance and skill events, the writer is aware of only two great champion sprinters who ran their best after the age of 25: E. Mac Donald Bailey, British West Indies, 100 meters-:10.4, age 30, and Barney Ewell, Penn State, 100 meters-:10.2, age 30.

To the contrary, almost every one of the world's greatest sprinters made sensational records while still in high or prep school and while under 19 years of age. To list all such men would be both tedious and unnecessary. But certainly the names of Arthur Duffey, Howard Drew, Charley Paddock, Frank Wykoff, Jesse Owens, Clyde Jeffrey, and Charlie Borah are sufficiently impressive to prove the point. Almost all these men ran within 1/5 second of their all-time best while still in high school, and none of them improved more than 2/5 second.

Of course, 1/5 second means over 2 yards in distance, a very significant improvement that must be made if the athlete hopes to maintain in college and amateur ranks the supremacy he possessed at the secondary level. A gain of 2 yards more than justifies all the practice and training necessary to produce it. On the other hand, 2 yards is not to be compared with tens of seconds in distance running, feet in the shot, or yards in the javelin and discus.

Actually, sprinters are no more born rather than made than are athletes in any other event; yet their early development does provide a certain justification for the saying.

What characterizes a good starting block? All starting blocks must fulfill two basic requirements: firmness of base from which the drive from each foot can be made, and complete and rapid adjustability. A block that cannot be set firmly in the ground or that gives way even once in a hundred times simply cannot be used. Nor can one that takes too much time or ingenuity to adjust, or that does not provide sufficient variety of adjustment to permit every sprinter to use it. Some blocks carry numbered guide lines by which the sprinter can permanently and exactly fix the position of each foot.

In general, the single-unit block is stedier and more durable that those having a separate unit for each other. On the other hand, some of the latter are more convenient when travelling, for they can be carried in the sprinter's equipment bag. This is a definite advantage, for use of one's own blocks aids both confidence and consistency of performance.

In certain sections of the country, a single type of block is almost universally adopted in college meets, thus making personal blocks unnecessary, but high schools and small colleges are still far from this ideal situation.

What about a sprinter's shoes? Question a coach who has had great success with his sprinters and you will discover a man who is vitally interested in sprint footwear. Sprinter's should fit perfectly, and they require great care in their selection and their maintenance. Comfort is of course important, but a close fit is more so. Every good sprinter should have special shoes for meets only, which he has broken in over a period of weeks, even months. He will probably have used over-all stretches as well as spot stretchers in his efforts to get them exactly right. Such perfectly fitted shoes will greatly increase both the bounce and the confidence that are so essential to success. That they should be well and light made is taken for granted. One must take care that such shoes do not lift and thereby cause the loss of the nail of the big toe. The answer lies in proper trimming of the nail, not in longer shoes.

ORGANIZATION OF PRACTICE FOR THE 100-AND 220-YARD DASHES

For no other event on the track and field program is it as difficult to recommend an average or typical training schedule as for the sprints. Coaches differ greatly in their training programs, and every good coach varies his own program to fit the needs of the individual sprinter. Here again it should be recalled that typical sprinters never exist. There are only individual men with individual needs. For this reason, no single "recommended" or "typical" training schedule will be given here. Rather, an attempt will be made to give an understanding of the principles and methods involved.

Of the scores of so-called "typical" training schedules that have accumulated in the writer's files, four have been selected: first, because they present somewhat contrasting schedules, and second, because each of the selected coaches has worked with successful sprinters.

The schedules are all for midseason, after one or two meets have been held.

These four schedules have been presented in the approximate order of amount of work required. Many detailed comparisons of the amount of work be each man for each day could be made, but they would be both unfair and misleading. It is certain that if each of these four coaches were asked to write a training schedule for the sprints without referring to the schedules presented here, he would submit one quite different in its details.

On the basis of these schedules of numerous write-ups in articles and books, and of the athlete's own observations and experiences, what are the essential consideration in building a schedule?

1. The importance of adequate early-season conditioning. There should be at least six weeks of informal exercise away from the coach and the starting gun, progressively strenuous to strengthen all body muscles. The chances of muscle injury are in inverse proportion to the number of weeks of such work. Sprinting requires explosive power, and power comes only through many weeks of repeated, short, and increasingly fast effort.

2. The importance of drill. The numerous details and skills of starting and sprinting can be learned only through correct practice, repeated time after time. A study of any great sprinter will reveal that a vast amount of developmental work and drill upon details occurred somehow and sometime, regardless of the light training schedules recommended by their coaches.

3. The importance of underwork during the competitive season. Two days of nonstrenuous work is now sufficient, usually on Tuesday and

Wednesday. Often one day is enough. Thursday ordinarily is light and Friday brings complete rest.

4. The necessity of a proper warm-up for all fast work. The energy output of the warm-up will usually exceed that of the workout itself.

5. All-out fast work should always be taken early in the workout before fatigue is present; endurance work should come at the end. Fatigue increases the chances of muscle injury.

6. In the final analysis, the problem of training for the sprints is at least as much as a mental as a physical one. A sprinter without confidence is beaten before he starts, and confidence can be coached and acquired just as deliberately as sprinting skill. A hundred times as many sprinters have been beaten through lack of confidence as through overconfidence.

CHAPTER 10

THE 440-YARD DASH IN SPRINTING

Very early in the game, before 1870, it was recognized that a man could not sprint all-out for much more than 100 yards and that therefore the 440 should be considered as endurance race. Best tactics were considered similar to those of the 880 or mile, in which one ran easily, with a good deal of speed held in reserve, for the first three-fourths of the race and then finished with what was left. In general, quarter-milers were not specialists. For instance, in 1868, E.J.Colbeck won the English championships in :50.4, after having first taken a second place in the 100-yard dash and a first in the 880 in 2:02, for a new English record. A much more startling example was Lawrence "Lon Myers, one of the all-time greats of track athletics.

Myers held every American record, from the 50-yard dash to the mile. In 1880, he competed in seven races in a single afternoon and won four American championships in the 100, 220, 440 and 880. In 1881, he won the English championships in a best time of :48.6. Unquestionably, Myers was capable of better time than this. He had been timed at :05.5 for 50 yards, :10 for 100 yards, and 20.0 for 200 yards, as well as 1:55.5 for the half mile. No times are available for the first 220 of his :48.6 race, a fact which in itself indicates that coaches and athletes were not then conscious of the importance of this knowledge. But we can assume that it was relatively slow by modern standards, and that Myers was much more "win conscious" than "time conscious".

However, we do know that Wendell Baker, of Harvard, ran :23.2 for his first 220 in establishing a record of :47.6 in 1886. This was1.2 seconds slower than his best time of :22.0 for the 220 gave him split times of :23.2 and :24.2, reasonably close to even pace. In passing, the circumstances and handicaps under which this race and many other similar races of this time were held should prove of interest. Tracks then were not the permanent and precisely "dressed" affairs of today, nor were running shoes so dependable. As a tune-up for the 440 record trial, baker had just equalled the world's record of :10 for the 100-yard dash, but had burst his left shoes in the effort.

With no spare shoes, and facilities for repairs missing, it was decided to continue. Under the watchful eyes of George Goldie of the New York A.C., G.A. Avery of the Manhattan A.C., and other competent officials, a quarter mile straightaway was measured off. The loose upper surface of the track was scraped, the temperature was recorded as 81 degrees, a scarcely perceptible wind was noted, the timers took their places, and the trial was on.

Baker was off at the crack of the pistol, running the first 220 yards in :23.2 . . . . At the furlong post, G.P.Cogswell of Harvard joined his teammate. His was the task of drawing Baker out to the utmost. With expert judgment and burning speed, Baker passed 350 yards in 37s; at 400 yards the time was a shade under 43s. At the finish line the officials looked on in amazement, as Baker, running with one shoe, flashed another burst of speed to snap the tape in :47.6. . . .

His left foot bleeding slightly after the race. Baker explained what had happened. At 250 yards he had attempted to kick off the torn shoe; at 285 yards he let it loosen and fly off. With his bare foot digging into the dirt track and the tape 155 yard away. Baker simply get and spurted on to a new record.

Several items are of importance. First, it is of interest that so-called the world's records of this period were not official, for the International Amateur Athletic Federation was not organized until 1913. A race with no other competitors running the full distance would not be recognized today. Second, that the track had just been scraped certainly embarrasses our modern demands for surface perfection. But, more to our present purpose, according to this observers, Baker "flashed another burst of speed... and spurted on to a new record". This remark would indicate that Baker had been "saving something for the end" and had certainly not been running all-out. His best times of :10 and :22 for the 100 and 220 support this view.

Although no times for the 220 are available, Maxie did carry a faster pace when he ran :47 for a 440 straightway in 1900. At the 350 mark he was :36.4: at the :42.2, both of which compare favourably with Myers :37 and :42.9. Long also had been timed in :10 flat for the 100, so it would appear that his potential speed was not greater than that of Baker. On the basis of these times, one might hazard the guess that Long was about :22.8 at the 220 post.

The first official world's record for the 440 was made by Ted Meredith of the University of Pennsylvania :47.4 in 1916, at 24 years of age. Meredith's record remained for 15 years, unbeaten and untied, and the close association between the 440 and the 880 that he fixed in the minds of coaches and athletes continued to influence their thinking and their methods. All coaching books printed during this period and up to 1932 either include the 440 in their chapter on middle-distance events or, if they give it separate consideration, do so in middle-distance terms. For example, Douglas Lowe, an excellent example of the 440-880 combination runner, writing in 1929, argued the case as follows :

It is, strictly speaking, a mistake to describe the average method of running the quarter, no matter how rapidly and brillinatly, as sprinting, which implies top-gear the whole way and even time, or faster, unless one is prepared to call half-miling sprinting also, on the ground that one attempts to go his fastest all the way, capping a 53-54 first quarter with whatever burst of energy one may!

Therefore it is probably more logical to confine the term sprinting to races up to and including 300 yards, grouping the quarter with middle distance events, and in particular because most quarter-milers, unless they are pure sprinters attempting an unusually lengthy event, methods of running and tactics similar to those in the half-mile.

This point of view was supported by at least two influences. The extensive publicity given to Paavo Nurmi's use of the stop watch and his insistence upon the value of even pace undoubtedly had its effect, even upon quarter-milers. Further, the work of such physiologists as A.V.Hill, who, in working in 1925 with eight Cornell runners, concluded that men could not go top speed for much more than 50 yards, certainly questioned the wisdom of trying to sprint too fast and too far in the 440. Coaches therefore emphasized a slower first 220 and a more even pace.

On the opposing side, however, came the evidence gained from actual experience. American tracks, unlike those in Europe and England, adopted the use of the chute, a straightaway of about 220 yards, in running the quarter. In such a race there are no lanes and it is a distinct advantage to have the pole position around the curve. Consequently, there was intense competition in a field of six to eight runners to be first at the 220 mark. The first half of the race became more and more rapid—to the point, in fact, where the ordinary 880 man simply could not stay within striking distance of his sprinting rival. Quite naturally, the slow quarter-miler moved up to the 880, where first-lap times were also getting faster, and coaches in desperation were shifting their sprinters to the 440.

Cromwell emphasizes the lesson that should have been learned from the great victory of Eric Liddell, of Scotland, in the 1924 Olympic 400-meter championships. Liddell was best known as a 100 and 220 sprinter, having best times of :09.7 and :21.74, but when religious scruples led him to refuse to run the 100 trials on Sunday, he shifted his efforts to the 400. With almost no experience in the event, he sprinted all-out to a clear lead at the 200 post in :22.2, and with both form and judgment gone, as it was thought, ripped through the tape in :47.6 for a new Olympic record. Cromwell speaks of Liddell's performance as a revelation, but apparently few coaches had eyes to see. The faster that men ran the first 220, the more coaches and physiologists cried that they were wasting energy and working against best time. Most of the answers to these critics agreed that :22 was much too fast, but that keen competition made it necessary. To win they had to stay up, and staying up meant a fast sprint for the pole.

Resigned to their fate, coaches and runners adopted a "float" in the middle of the race. Meredith's book entitled Middle Distance Running, in 1925, strongly recommended this method, as did F.A.M. Webster in his excellent chapter on the 440:

The sprinter type of quarter-miler uses a different method. He goes all out for 75 to 100 yards in the hope of winning the inside berth at the bend of the track. As soon as he has got position, or covered his maximum sprint distance, he relaxes, by dropping his arms a little, and so adjusts his action that he runs lower on the ball of the foot than he would in the sprint action, and his stride lengthens out. He also begins to breathe regularly. On this action he floats through until 140 yards from the finish. Then he gets up on his toes again, sets arms and legs going to a livelier pitches his body forward to the true finishing angle and lets himself go for the tape.

Then, in the Olympic year of 1932, came the tremendous duals between Ben Eastman of Stanford and Bill Carr of Pennsylvania. Eastman had tied the 440 record at :47.4 in 1931 in a great dual with Vic Williams of Souther California and had just broken the world's 880 record with a 1:50.9. Then, in late May, in a special record attempt at Palo Alto, he cut the 440 time down to :46.4. But on July 4, the relatively unknown Carr, whose quarter-miling had been almost exclusively on relay teams, won the ICAAAA over Eastman at Berkeley, California, in :47 flat and then in the Olympics made a world's record by running 400 meters in :46.2. Quite apart from the great competitive thrills these races provided, which, incidentally, were stimulated by old rivalries between the East and West, they also proved a testing ground for the old argument over whether a fast 880 man could defeat a sprinter with endurance and just how each would go about doing it. American coaches, including Richard Templeton of Stanford, have consistently assumed that the half-miler would be forced to set a very fast pace and thus run the "kick" out of the legs of the sprinters. Certainly Eastman attempted just this, for, although he seldom ran the 220 and had a best unofficial time of :21.6, he covered the first 220 of the

Olympic quarter in :21.4—unheard-of time and "crazy" pace judgment. Yet Carr stayed on his heels and was able to run faster than Eastman at the finish and thus go on to win. Where was the traditional "float" in such a race? Eastman certainly didn't let down at any point, for he was trying to build up a lead, nor could Carr do any such special relaxing as Webster's instructions suggest, for he stayed at Eastman's shoulder all the way and must have run within a few tenths of a second of his best previous time.

The experts shrugged their shoulders, explained that competitive conditions sometimes force one to ignore economy of effort, and somehow brushed aside the fact that the world's record had been broken by 1.4 seconds. Physiologically, a pace of :21.4—:24.8 simply did not make sense.

Yet seven years later, in 1939, when Rudolph Harbig of Germany, ran his surprising :46 for 400 meters, he also sprinted the first 200 meters in :21.8, just :3 seconds that his best time for the 200 meters of :21.5. This gave him a split of :21.8—:24.2. Actually, Harbig's abilities as a sprinter may have been very high, for although seldom sprinting, he had officially made :10.6 for the 100-meter dash.

Dean Cromwell was fully aware of these times and methods, and his own quarter-milers—Vic Williams, Harold Smallwood, Erwin Miller, Hubert Kerns, et al.—Were certainly trained as sprinters and contributed to the tendency to an ever-faster first 220. Yet, writing in 1940, this unquestionably great coach stated:

Experienced runners always cover the first 220 yards faster than the second furlong. If you will time a 50 second quarter-miler of the sprinter type, you will find that he usually runs the first half of his race in close to :24.5 seconds and the second half in :25.5. If the runner is the half-miler type, his first furlong will usually be 2 seconds faster than the second 220, and his furlong times will be approximately 24 and 26 seconds.

A good general rule is to train the half-miler type to run the opening 220 yards 2 seconds faster than the second furlong and to coach the sprinter type to cover his first 220 only 1 second faster than his last one.

Statements such as this are an inherent part of coaches thinking even today, and they occur constantly in coaching clinics. That there should be a basic difference between the 440-yard dash and all the longer endurance runs seems unexplainable physiologically. Economy of energy output in the latter races demands close to even pace. How can it be that quarter-miling should be so different?

Yet the fast initial pace continued, almost without exception. No times for the first 220 are available for the marvellous National AAU 400-meter race in 1940 in which Grover Klemmer of the University of California ran :46 flat, Hubert Kerns and Cliff Bourland of Southern California :46.1, and the sixth man; :46.9. However, Al Diebolt, of Colgate, fourth in :46.4, was a very fine sprinter and pulled out the field at a very fast pace for the first 300 yards.

And then came the greatest trio of all time, Herb McKenley, Arthur Wint, and George Rhoden, all natives of the little island of Jamaica with a population of only 1 1/3 million people. McKenley first attracted world attention by running :46.2 for the 440 in May, 1946, a new world's record. The race started on the 220 straightway and the writer, clocking the 220 time very carefully, was amazed to see :20.9 on his watch dial. Two weeks earlier, McKenley had made his best personal record for the 220 of :20.6, so that, like Harbig, he had run within :3 second of his potential speed. Just a year later, on June 5, 1948, at Berkeley, California, McKenley again ran :20.9 for the 220 in establishing a new world's record of :46. Apparently, even McKenley thought a slower 220 would bring better results, for he confided to a newspaperman just before the National AAU meet in July that he planned to take it easier this time. Certainly his 220 time of :21.1 was slower, but so was his total time of :46.3.

At the London Olympics, McKenley was faced by Arthur Wint and by Mal Whitfield, who had already won the 800-meter title in 1:49.2. Herb confronted the dual problem of beating Wint, against whom he had run many times but whom he had never beaten, and establishing a new Olympic and world's record, to which his previous over-all performances certainly entitled him. He felt his only hope of doing either was to burn up the first 220 and, if possible, establish an 8-yard lead over. Wint at the 300 mark. Somehow, perhaps because of the soft London track, perhaps because of the tension engendered by Wint, he did neither. His time of :21.4 did give him 8 yards over Wint's :22.2 at the 220, but his deceleration from this point on was very marked and Wint pulled up within 5 yards at 300 and to a 3-yard win in :46.2. Note that in this race, McKenley ran :21.4—:25.1; and Wint :22.2—:24.0. Perhaps the most potent factor of all was McKenley's fear of Wint's strong finish and Wint's supreme confidence. Spectators and movies were strongly impressed by the difference in relaxation between the two men. Was it Wint's more evenly paced race that won for him, or was it these psychological factors that made the difference?

During the next two years, McKenley broke the :47 flat mark on 53 different occasions, an almost unbelievable record. And in almost every case he piled up a lead by the 220 mark, not merely through superior ability over his competitors but as a matter of running policy. His earlier mark of :20.6 remained his best for the 220.

If McKenley found that such an "insane" pace produced results, perhaps others might do likewise. At least George Rhoden thought it was worth a trial. After winning the 1949 National AAu 400-meter race in surprising :46.4, Rhoden competed in a series of races in Europe, sometimes with and sometimes without McKenley as a competitor. On August 15, 1950, Rhoden met McKenley at Stockholm running 400 meters around two turns. Quercetani tells the story of this attempt by Rhoden :

At Halsingborg on August 13 McKenley won a solo race in :46.0. Two days later at Stockholm he met Rhoden. Herb drew the fifth lane, George the sixth. Rhoden got off the marks faster than his rival and had 2 meters on Herb down the backstretch. McKenley was marvelous around the last turn and Rhoden's lead had been reduced to 1 meter as they entered the homestretch. A furious battle saw McKenley close the gap slowly but steadily to finally come within ½ meter of the leader. But the latter held on to the end and won by that margin. The timers caught Rhoden in :46.0 and McKenley in :46.1.

At Eskilstuna on August 22 Rhoden decided to have a record attempt. He competed in the 400 meters against Sherman Miller, best American quartermiler in the high school department, and Sven-Erik Nolinge of Sweden. Eskilstuna's Tunavallen stadium has a 426 meters track which has been often described as Sweden's fastest. Under ideal weather conditions Rhoden ran the best race of his carrer. He breezed the first 200 meters in :20.9 and he went on to negotiate the second half of the distance as smoothly as ever. At the tape 3 watches caught him in :45.8—one-tenth better than McKenley's official 400 meters record.

No time is given in this write-up for the 200 meters in the first race, but if Rhoden had two meters on McKenley, we may be sure the time was not slower than :21 flat.

Up to this point, the incidence related have constituted a rather clear and certain argument in support of our thesis. Now, however, comes the story of the 1952 Olympic final between Rhoden, McKenley, Wint, Whitfield, Matson of San Francisco, and Hass of Germany. Following the general background as here related, one would have expected a blistering pace during the early stages of the race. However, Rhoden (:22.2) McKenley (:22.7), and Whitfield (:22.9) were content to let 31-year-old Wint set the pace at :21.7. A glance at the quarter-mile record chart will show that this is the slowest pace (that is, for Rhoden or McKenley) ever set for a race under 47 seconds. Yet Rhoden, by pouring it on during the third 110 yards, and McKenley, by a tremendous spurt in the final straightaway, were able to come within 1/10 second of the best ever recorded, with a shared time of :45.9. Apparentaly, Wint's pace was 2/10 second faster than he had ever recorded for 200 meters (his best distance was probably over rather than under 400 meters), and he remarked after the race that he had made a great mistake in judgment in going out so fast.

What is the significance of these figures? First, that human ultimates in quarter-miling have not yet been reached. Second, that final answers concerning the highest efficiency in human endurance and the nature of human fatigue have not yet been given. And third, that probably the best practice in terms of pace will lie somewhere between the "insane" (pre-1952) McKenley pace and the even pace unanimously advocated by the physiologists.

One other factor needs to be specially noted here, that of age. These men who run under :47 for the 440 are unquestionably running very close to their true physiological capacity in terms of speed-endurance. A.V.Hill's eight subjects, six of whom were track men but only two quarter-milers or less, began to lose maximum speed after only 70 yards amd by 190 yards had lost as much as 12 per cent. Men trained specifically for speed endurance can be assumed to run much more efficiently than this and yet somewhere within the limits implied by Hill's work. To run the first 200 meters of a 400-meter race within .3 seconds of one's best is surely reaching close to the maximum in human ability to withstand fatigue. It therefore demands maturity as well as excellent conditioning.

To the coach's best knowledge, the youngest man ever to run under :47 was Godfrey Brown of England, who was just 21 when he placed second in :46.7 to Archie Williams in the 1936 Olympics, Carr and Eastman were both 22 in their best year; Archie Williams and Klemmer, 23 when at their best; Ted Meredith, 24 in 1916; Harbig, 26 in 1939; Wint, 26 in 1948; McKenley, 28 in 1950, and Rhoden, 25 when he won the 1952 Olympic championship in :45.9. The best age for men who are strictly sprinters has been between 19 and 23; that for speed-endurance men, as in the 440, is definitely several years older. The human machine needs added years for full development and highest efficiency.

ESSENTIALS OF CORRECT FORM

Correct running form in the 440 is identical to that previously described in discussing the 100 and 220. The only difference between the 220 and the 440 is one of degree, and this is so slight that even the most sharp-eyed observer can hardly detect a change. Coaches may argue that the 440 requires even greater relaxation than the 220, but here again the noticeable difference in form will be nil. No additional discussion of form is therefore needed here.

METHODS OF MAKING BEST TIME

The gist of the history of quarter-mile running as previously outlined can be summarized as (1) a change from thinking of the 440 as a middle-distance run to assuming that it is an endurance sprint and (2) a change from a sprint—float—sprint method to running the entire distance as fast as one can and still finish the race with minimum deceleration and with poise and control.

The results of an interesting and valuable piece of research, based on records by 54 individuals have been published by Henry. He concludes :

1. That men generally reached their top speed about 6 seconds after leaving the starting blocks.

2. That "it is physiologically impossible for the runner, after he has reached his peak velocity, to maintain it for more than about 15 or 20 yards".

3. That an earlier study by Sargent showed "that the energy cost of running increases as the 3.8th mathematical power of the speed".

4. That "it can be said with confidence that in so far as the physiological limit is involved in setting records, a steady pace will result in faster time for the 220 and 440 as well as the half, the mile, and the 2 mile".

Two comments are in order:

First, the difference between the theory advanced in this section and that of even-pace running, as Henry and others recommend, may not be so great as it seems to be at first. Second, human fatigue and performances involving fatigue are not merely physical phenomena;

to attempt to estimate capacity in a psychophysical action by exclusively physical measures has serious limitations.

Without a single exception, every piece of writing on coaching that is in the writer's possession, and the list is quite complete, is uncertain in its approach and torn between the facts of what has been happening on the track ever since 1900, when Maxie Long ran :22.8 for the first 220 of a :47 flat quarter, and the physiological theory of efficient even-pace running. For example, we have already noted Cromwell's keen interest in Liddell's sprinting methods as contrasted with his belief that the half-miler type should run the first 220 a full second faster than the sprinter type of quarter miler. This is inconsistent, for it advises a man of lesser speed to run faster early in the race than one of greater speed. No wonder the former is completely run out at 350 yards and is so often beaten. The sprinter does not win so much from his own superior sprinting ability as from his opponent's senseless waste of energy and slow-down finish. This problem will receive further discussion later.

At another point, Cromwell states :

The ideal manner to run the race in championship time is to cover the first furlong as very close to top speed, then stride through the next 100 to 120 yards at a slower pace, and finally to pull up to top speed over the last 100. The slowing down process at the end of the first 220 is necessary to give the runner a chance to recuperate from the fatigue of the first burst of speed.

Godfrey Brown, England's record holder for the quarter mile, first called attention to the fallacy in this statement. Many runners have refuted its assumptions in their competitive efforts, but, to the coach's knowledge, Brown is impressed with what he calls "the McKenley method" of fast-half running, but cites several possible weaknesses:

A third weakness may well lie in the fact that this method usually implies a marked decrease in effort and speed over the third quarter of the race, with a full-out effort to fight off further deceleration in its last quarter. Such a fluctuation seems to constitute an unnecessary qualification of the even-pace law. He admit that there should be an over-all deceleration over the body of the race, but he maintain that the deceleration should be gradual and smooth—like clockwork running down.... Obviously deceleration is going to be setting in [during the closing stage of the race—J.K.D.], and the man who finishes strongly will be the man who can fight off this tendency most successfully.

This point cannot be stressed too strongly—that in a correctly run 400 meters the strong finisher is the man who slows down least. In a mile race the strong finisher hits up a speed above the average speed at which he runs his race, but the runner who is able to do this at the end of a quarter-mile has run his race badly, because he has distributed his effort badly.

This statement is consistent with the facts of quarter-miling and should be carefully considered by every coach and 440 man. It is an essentially different point of view from the one shown by coaches in their writing, although not by runners in their actions. In considering what pace a particular 440 man should run, the first question has traditionally been in terms of the total time the athlete is striving for. If this is to be :52 he is then advised to run his first 220 about 2 seconds faster than his second, i.e., :25—:27.

The approach to the "maximum speed, minimum deceleration" method is quite different. The first question now is, "What is the maximum speed at which this boy can run 220 or 300 yards?" And the second is, "How little does he need to slow down and relax during the first two-thirds of his race to permit him to finish with a minimum of deceleration during the last 100 yards or so?" This method does not think of the race as having three parts: an initial sprint to the 220, a "float" around the curve, and a finish. Rather, the race is a smoothly co-ordinated unit. Ideally, there is no point at which any change in style or effort occurs. A man simply runs as smoothly and as fast as possible all the way.

Certainly, none of these sentences would be any surprise to Mr. Cromwell or, for that matter, to many other fine coaches, for most of their thinking and coaching have been along similar lines. In 1941, at the meetings of the National College Track Coaches in California, the coaches had been questioning Cliff Bourland, a :46.2 quarter-miler, about the mechanics of his "float". Cliff had implied that there were a few minor from differences between this "float" and his finish. When asked his opinion, Cromwell answered positively that no changes in form occurred, that there was no settling of the body or dropping of the arms. "In fact, Mr. Champion, merely drop his tension and everything else remains the same".

A champion should be able to go all the way, without recourse to a letdown or a time-consuming "float". This is a realistic recognition of the necessity for sprinting all the way with only enough deceleration to maintain relaxation through the finish line. In all his answers, Bourland maintained that there was no particular distance to which he sprinted wide open. "It depends on how he feel. Sometime he just keep going as fast as he can, and then he let down. Sometimes it takes him a little longer. He can't tell." This is sound, for it implies no definite point before and after which the form, and probably the pace, is different.

In summary, the quarter mile is an endurance sprint in which maximum acceleration is first achieved and momentum maintained to the finish line with the least possible deceleration. As Brown has stated, the strongest man at the finish is not the one who increases his pace most but rather the one who slows down the least. The problem lies, then, in knowing in each competition just what pace will produce this result. For world's champion runners, it is only from .3 to .5 second slower at the 220 than their best effort for the 220 alone. This is not to say that they run an exact distance, say 220 yards, at a certain pace and then do something different. Rather, they attempt a smooth pace all the way.

Such a method of running the 440 has its merits regardless of age or ability level. It will work equally well whether the final time is 46 or 56 seconds. If a runner is in poor condition, his pace will be slower throughout; but deceleration will occur on the same general basis as when he is in excellent condition. The race will in all cases be run as a single unit and not on a three-part plan of start—float—finish.

COMPETITIVE TACTICS IN THE 440

Indoors. In indoor racing, a quarter-miler must almost invariably be in either first or second place throughout the race if he hopes to win. Occasionally, the field will open up and permit a lesser-placed runner to slide through to the tape, but no one should plan on it. In most cases, an experienced runner of lesser ability can beat a superior opponent if he has the lead throughout. By picking up the pace on the straighaways and relaxing around the curves, the following runner is kept constantly off balance.

The latter's best chance is to concentrate on a single all-out effort that will surprise the leader. If this fails, the only other chance will come during the final straightaway.

A man hoping to place only third or fourth in a field of six men may often do better by relaxing in last position until the final straightaway. The others will have been constantly off balance and under constant tension in their efforts to improve their positions and will have little with which to meet his challenges at the end.

Generally speaking, the race is so short and fast that a man has but one opportunity to accomplish his goal. The trick lies in determining just when and how to make the effort. When the extent spot is determined, kick with surprising quickness and determination. Go all-out with certainty, with nothing being held back. A man of confidence and control will sometimes ease up and drop back a foot or two going into a curve but will then begin to move all-out in the middle of the curve. By the time he reaches the leader, his momentum is up and his chances thereby improved.

In nine cases out of ten, one should plan to complete a pass during the first third of a straightaway. If one miscalculates, there is still time to sprint the final two-thirds. However, just because this is the rule and men expect such tactics, the experienced man will occasionally upset the situation by turning it on when least expected, during the last one-third of the straightaway or even when going into a curve.

Outdoors. So many differences occur in individuals and in competitive conditions that no single statement on tactics can be accepted completely. However, the following points merit consideration:

1. Every curve that is run in the second lane adds about three yards to the length of the race.
2. Third position or less around the last curve holds the danger of letting the leader or leaders get away. One must either let them go or attempt to pass on the curve, a wasteful procedure.
3. For most men, second spot around the last turn is a more relaxing position psychologically than

being in front. Actually, however, the front runner dominates the situation and has the advantage if he possesses the poise and racing judgment to make use of it.

4. The strong slow runner will do best to concentrate upon his time at the 330-yard mark and will run steadily all the way, striving for minimum deceleration during the last 100 yards.
5. The sprinter who is in poor condition has two choices, either (a) to stay well back, to cover the first 300 yards as easily as possible and still stay in the running, and then to kick with whatever is left, or (b) to use his superior speed in running a good 200 yards or so, to relax quite markedly around the curve and thus hold back fatigue, and again to sprint at the finish. The latter is most likely to pay off.
6. The sprinter in good condition has no worries. If time is important, he can go all the way, running the 220 within less than 1 second of his best and the 330 within 2 seconds of his best. If running merely to win, he should simply stay out of boxes, and never underestimate his opponent.
7. Under highly competitive conditions, the race will most often be to the man who has best maintained poise, relaxation, and control of both mental alertness and physical co-ordination. Carr over Eastman, Rhoden over McKenley in his :46 flat effort, and Wint over McKenley are all excellent examples. Note that Rhoden was a front runner all the way and yet maintained control throughout.
8. When running in lanes all the way, or if the situation permits one to ignore the dangers of lost yardage around the last curve, the athlete should run at his own pace for the first 220, but

concentrate his best efforts in terms of both momentum and relaxation upon the third 110 yards of the race. It is here that the real test lies. Those of faint heart will let down too much in their overconcern for relaxation; those who strive desperately and fearfully to maintain their lead will soon lose both poise and momentum. The Carrs, the Wints, and the Rhodens continue unruffled in both nerve and muscle to the finish tape.

9. In qualifying races, always complete the last 20 yards with a strong finish. Carelessness at this point—letting down too soon and being unable to recover in time—has often produced a mere spectator at the final. If saving energy is important, do it during the third quarter of the race.

10. The quarter mile, when not turn in lanes, inevitably produces a battle for the first turn, whether from the chute or the middle of the oval. When the field is fewer than five or six, position at this point is not quite so vital; but in a large field, a man hoping to place first, second, or third must secure a good spot around the curve. The energy saved by dropping back and thus avoiding the jostling will be more than lost in attempting to improve one's position later. Probably the besy one can do in this case is to wait until the others have lost their fight, and then go all-out at the finish. Incidentally, if a man lacks the speed to secure a good position, he is probably misplaced and should make plans to run the 880 next year.

If in doubt as to whether to try for a front or back position around the first curve, always gamble in the quarter mile on the front position. In longer races just the opposite is true, but in the quarter mile, the extra energy expended will almost invariably pay dividends.

11. If in the lead and thinking only of winning, the man with superior speed will maintain his lead but should husband his strength by easing up around the curves and just holding his lead on the straightaway. He can then outsprint the field on the final stretch. If, as so often happens, he relinquishes the lead to a stronger opponent somewhere on the back stretch, he loses control of the pace. The latter can now pour it on all the way, hoping to build up a lead or kill off his opponent's speed. If he can maintain poise and control while doing this, the advantage is his. Of course, if he is relatively inexperienced or is "afraid" of his sprinting rival, he is in a pressure position and quite likely to tie up when the sprinter lets go at the finish. Here, as always, the twin admonitions of "Know thyself" and "Know thy opponent" are vitally important.
12. When planning to jump an opponent, do so with determination and quickness making every effort to surprise him and thereby pick up a 2- to 5-yard lead before he is aware of it. Usually this can happen only by starting the final sprint earlier than usual and therefore is a matter of confidence in one's own ability to carry the pace through on the finish.

IMPORTANT QUESTIONS AND ANSWERS

How can the half-miler type of 440 man beat the sprinter?

This question implies one runner of lesser sprinting ability but either greater natural endurance or better physical condition and a contrasting runner with speed but comparatively little strength. American coaches, traditionally, have advised the half-miler to go all-out, all the way, to lead at the 220 at all costs and thereby either run the "sprint" right out of the sprinter or build up such a lead that he cannot be caught at the finish. There is an element of truth in such advice; but it is sufficiently false to make the difference between winning and losing in many cases.

More exactly, the half-miler should run his own race, not the one into which his opponent tries to force him. He should not necessarily lead at the 220. His real question should be, "What is the momentum curve for the entire race that will bring me home in a time that is better than that which my opponent can run?" Such a question will not focus attention upon any single point, such as 200 or 250 yards, at which he should have a 4-yard or 6-yard lead on his opponent. Rather, it implies a knowledge of the runner's own best possible time for the 220 of, say, :22.6, and therefore of his own ability to carry a pace of :23.6, and of :36.1 for 330 yards. He should know that he will then suffer a minimum deceleration of :13.9 for the final 110 yards and make a total time of :50 for the race. His attitude can then be, "if my opponent can make better time than that, he will win, and good luck to him. At least I shall have done my best".

The hopes of the half-miler in such a race will primarily in approximately the third quarter of the race, between 220 and 330 yards. He knows that the first 220 has been harder on himself than on his opponent, for the latter's greater natural speed has made the pace easier. But if his pace is maintained beyond the 220 with very little deceleration, the advantage begins to shift to the stronger of the two. In general, the faster the pace of this third 110 yards, the better it is for the half-miler and the more difficult is the lot of the sprinter or of the man in poor conditions. If a man is mature and well conditioned, he should win most of his races here.

Should Eastman, the half-miler, have beaten the sprinter Carr in the 1932 Olympics? From the way the two men looked during the finish, the answer is a definite "No". Yet it seems to the writer that Eastman ran Carr's race. He hit :21.4 for the 220, which was probably too fast even for Carr, who had never beaten :21.2 officially. Certainly it was too fast for Eastman with a best 220 time of :21.6! Had Eastman run about :21.9 or :22 instead, his pace for the next 150 yards could have been proportionally faster and his chances of either getting away from Carr or of wearing away Carr's finish would have been improved. This is pure speculation, of course, but it serves to illustrate the basic point of this argument.

What is proper timing for each fourth (each 110 yards) of the quarter mile?

Obviously the answer to this question must be in terms of the individual. However, certain criteria are of value:

1. The faster the man, the easier a fast pace is for him.
2. The more mature or the better-conditioned the man, the nearer the pace for the 220 and 330 can approach his speed capacity and still permit him to finish with minimum deceleration.
3. The primary question in all cases is, "How fast and steadily can the first three-fourths of the race be run without necessitating excessive deceleration during the final one-fourth?"

Does the 440 make greater demands physically than other distances?

The best answer is both "Yes" and "No". Yes, because the distance is short and runners are more willing to go all-out all the way. There are no mental reservations, no time for awareness of feeling tired; therefore, the chances of reaching one's true physiological limit are increased

On the other hand, the answer is also "No", for even when such all-out running has occurred, less actual energy has been consumed. Recovery is rapid, so that within 40 minutes the runner can repeat with an even better performance. When Rhoden ran :45.8 in 1950, he doubled back in 20 minutes for a :10.6 100-meter win and then tripled 40 minutes later for a :45.4 leg on a 1600-metre relay.

What About Relaxation in the Quarter Mile?

The problem of relaxation in the 440 seems to have special significance. The demand for great speed over a distance well beyond man's sprinting abilities places major emphasis upon both mental and physical control. In such a race, the feelings of fatigue, with their numbing and disco-ordinating effects, do not creep into consciousness. Rather, they burst through the threshold of awareness with a disconcerting rout of form and poise that demands the utmost of aggressive control. In no other race is there so much or such a prevalent loss of form at the finish as in the quarter mile. This loss is as much a mental as a physical phenomenon and should be considered as such in all coaching efforts. In a very real and practical sense, relaxation is primarily a state of mind.

Organization of Practice

Quarter-miling should be fun, both in practice and in the meets. True, it calls for long and careful conditioning and puts a severe immediate strain upon the athlete's neuro-muscular and circulatory systems. Yet the conditioning can be entirely in terms of speed work and should involve a great deal of group running "for fun". The danger of overwork in either practical or meets is not great so long as the boy's enthusiasm and interest are maintained.

Over-all training plans should attempt to get the men in top condition at least three weeks before the major competition. The task is then comparatively easy. Race tactics, pace work, and speed work, with plenty of rest thrown in, will then produce that mental-emotional edge that identifies the champion. Work should be assigned primarily in accordance with the runner's attitude and emotional control. As usual, confidence here is half the battle.

1. The quarter-mile is both a sprint and a maximum-endurance event. These two facts must be kept constantly in mind in all planning of practice. The faster a man can run, either the easier it is for him to sprint at a lesser pace or the faster he can carry the first two-thirds of his race. The more endurance he has, the less will be his tendency to slow down during the last one-third of his race.
2. Practice five days a week is desirable, although less can be taken after good basic condition is attained.
3. Starting practice at 20 yards and sprinting 60 yards or more should be a part of almost every day's practice.
4. The best endurance workout for quarter-milers lies in sprinting repeatedly distances up to 300 yards. For example, three 220's within one second of best time and with less than 5 minutes rest between is an excellent speed-endurance workout.
5. Sprint work should strive for greater speed, of course, but never at the cost of greater tension or loss of form.
6. Knowledge of exact pace is as important for the quarter-miler as for the miler and must be acquired in practice with equal care and drill.

7. To run the full distance in practice "for time" is never advisable. Selection of the team provides the only exception to this rule.

8. Over-all body exercises are desirable; special exercises of the abdominal and back muscles are essential. Development of the ankle and foot muscles and tendons is even more important for quarter-milers than for sprinters.

9. The best single workout for a group of quarter-milers is an endless relay. This event involves speed, endurance, baton practice, group competition, and pace judgment. Each man on the relay team runs a series of three or more 220's. It begins as does any relay, but the last man on each team passes the baton back to the first man and the whole process if repeated one or more times. There should be an odd number of men on each team; two teams of five or even seven men are best. Having seven men gives longer rest periods, and thus faster 220's can be run.

SUGGESTED PRACTICE SCHEDULE

This schedule is merely indicative of possibilities and will fit no man's actual workout program. It is suggestive of early-season practice, when physical condition is good and emphasis upon speed work has begun. Top-speed running that is completely relaxed is basic to everything that is done. This cannot be stressed too much.

Monday: 6-8 starts and sprints at 80-150 yards, no finish tape or time taken. Emphasize group work and fun—baton passing, wind sprints over 3 or 4 laps in groups of 3-5 men, endless relays.

Tuesday: 6-8 starts, 2 or 3 sprints with tape and watch at 80-150 yards. Two 350's at 440 racing speed with 20 minutes rest between. If possible, get times at 110, 220, and 330 yards. These are primarily for pace judgment for the coming Saturday's race. A 50-second quarter-miler should run them in about 38.5 seconds.

Wednesday: Starts, 4-6 sprints at 60-80 yards, 3-5 220's. If trying primarily for endurance, shorten the rest period between; if primarily for speed, lengthen it. Even better, organize an endless relay in which each man is timed at the exact pace the coach assigns to him.

Thursday: Starts 4-6 sprints, perhaps a little pace or form work. Group wind sprints "for fun".

Friday: Rest for Saturday's competition.

CHAPTER 11

TEACHING TIPS IN SPRINTING

POINT 1 : LEAD-UPS

Lead-up activities for sprinting emphasize quick reactions, the development of coordination, and acceleration. You must teach participants to react to visual, auditory, and tactile signals. Chase, tag games, and relays are excellent for this purpose and also emphasize the competitive aspect.

Shadow Run

Pairs run freely. Runner 1 tries to shake off 2, who shadows1. 2 tries to remain in tagging the distance of runner 1 throughout. On the signal, the runners change roles. Be sure to use sufficient space in this lead-up activity to avoid collisions!

Reaction and Acceleration Drill

Teams (3 to 4 per team) line up behind a starting line. On the signal, the first member of each team sprints around his or her team's cone, set 20 to 25 meters away. The runner then turns and sprints back to tag the next runner in the team. (Be sure to allow sufficient space between teams for the turnaround).

Variation

Athletes use different starting positions (e.g., sitting, lying, kneeling, or the set position in sprint starts).

Shuttle Relay

Split teams into 2 groups (*i* and *ii*) with 3 to 4 students in each group. On the signal, the 1st member of group *i* sprints to cross a ling 20 meters away. That runner then tags the 1st member of group *ii*, who sprints back. The sequence is repeated with the 2nd runner of group *i*, and so forth.

Variation

Team members exchange a baton or use a hand tag. Students can use different starting positions as listed for the reaction and acceleration drill.

Chase and Tag

Pair off members of Team 1 with opponents in team 2. All members of team 1 run slowly to a line 15 meters ahead. The runners touch the line and then accelerate back to the starting line. Members of team 2, in a ready position 4 to 5 meters behind the line, attempt to tag their opponents in team 1 after the line has been touched and before members of team 1 can get back to the safety of their starting line.

COACHING DRILLS

Run slowly to the line; there is no need to sprint.

When the athlete get near the line, he should straighten his body for the turn around—he do not want to be leaning forward.

Pivot quickly and accelerate as fast as he can to safety.

Variation

Cones can be placed on the 15 meter line. Members of team 1 run to touch (or circle) the cone and sprint back to the safety of the starting line. Vary the starting positions of team 2 (e.g., kneeling, lying, sitting, or the sprint-start set position).

Pendular Relay

Divide athletes into 2 groups with 3 to 4 in each group. The groups face each other 20 to 25 meters apart. Sprinter A sprints the 20- to 25- meter distance, circles around the back of the team, and tags sprinter B from the rear. Sprinter B sprints, and sprinter C shifts into sprinter A's position to receive the tag from sprinter C.

COACHING DRILLS

The athlete should crouch down and look back over his shoulder for the tag. He should be ready to accelerate.

Variation

Runners use a baton, and they should determine the type of exchange.

Circle Relay

On the signal, runner *i* of each team (from 4 to 8 per team) sprints around the outside of the circle and tags the *ii* member of the team who has moved out to the circumference of the circle. Runner *ii* repeats and tags runner *iii*. (Be sure to make the circumference of the circle large enough so that runners are able to get sufficient traction when running on the curve!)

Variation

Vary starting positions (e.g., sitting, lying, kneeling, or the sprint-start set position). Runners use a baton, and they determine the type of exchange.

POINT 2 : SPRINTING TECHNIQUE

The following drills all play a large part in the improvement of sprinting technique. They have been set in groups—drills to improve coordination and sprinting techniques, drills to improve leg power and acceleration, and drills to improve sprint endurance—according to the desired effect. Select examples from each group when planning an instructional period.

IMPORTANT DRILLS TO IMPROVE COORDINATION AND SPRINTING TECHNIQUE

An acceptable method for developing sprinting technique is to practice the correct elements slowly in a "clockwork", formalized manner. Once beginners learn the correct actions and grasp the necessary rhythm, their speeds of movement are increased. Novices will find these drills quite strenuous. Recommended distances are from 10 to 15 meters with 2 to 3 repetitions. Students can use a loose easy walk as a recovery.

High-Knee Marching

Each participant marches forward slowly, forcefully driving the thigh of the leading leg up to horizontal. The arms are bent at 90 degrees at the elbow. The supporting leg extends fully up onto the toes as the participant lifts the opposing knee.

COACHING DRILLS

Lift each thigh to horizontal.

The sprinter should work his arms forward and backward, not across his body.

The sprinter should push up vigorously onto his toes with each step.

High-Knee Marching With Extention of the Lower Leg

This differs from the previous practice in that the lower leg is extended after the thigh has been raised to horizontal. The drill is performed in the following sequence.

The performer extends up onto the toes of the left leg, raises the right thigh to horizontal, and extends the lower right leg. The right foot is placed down on the ground, and the left foot steps forward normally to repeat the sequence.

The performer extends up onto the toes of the right leg, raises the left thigh to horizontal, and extends the lower left leg. The left foot is placed down on the ground, and the right foot steps forward normally to repeat the sequence.

These steps are repeated in sequence; the lower leg is extended with each elevation of the thigh.

COACHING DRILLS

The sprinter should keep his vision directly forward, and relax his shoulders.

He should keep his arms held at 90 degrees at the elbows.

He should lift his thigh as close to horizontal as he can. When his thigh is in the air, he should kick his lower leg forward and step down to repeat.

High-Knee Skipping With Lower Leg Extension

This drill is quite strenuous; 3 to 4 short individual efforts, each followed by a rest, are sufficient to begin with for novices. The skipping action is similar to that done with a rope. Instead of walking, as with the previous drill, the performer pretends to be skipping a rope. The thighs are raised to horizontal, and the lower leg is kicked out to an extended position. The performer looks straight ahead, holds the arms at 90 degrees at the elbows, and swings them forward and backward vigorously.

COACHING DRILLS

The sprinter should concentrate on his legs.

He should forget about the arm action to begin with.

He should get the action started by skipping in place. Then move forward very slowly and try to keep the skipping action going.

Think of a rhythm of "up-extend, up-extend".

Add the arm action once you have the legs working.

High-Knee Running With Lower Leg Extension

This stimulates the prancing action of a horse. Movement forward is still slow, but the speed of the legs resembles running in place. The performer can begin with simple high-knee running and then include the lower leg extension once the rhythm of the high-knee lift is established.

COACHING DRILLS

The sprinter should set up the rhythm while running in place, and then try to move forward at a slow jog. Slowly increase the speed of his legs.

The performer shuold look forward and keep his arms working hard forward and backward throughout.

Seat Kicks

Each athlete moves slowly forward, kicking up the heels to the rear and attempting to hit the buttocks. This practice helps to establish the pattern of leg movement to the rear of the body and also stretches and loosens the quadriceps.

COACHING DRILLS

The sprinter should start by running in place and kicking his heels up easily to his rear.

Begin moving slowly forward, kicking his heels up higher as he go.

He should concentrate only on getting his heels up to your rear (there is no need to lift the thighs upward).

He should not do worry if he can not hit his seat with your heels to begin with.

Work on raising the heels as high as possible.

Sprint Arm Action

In this practice, the athlete concentrates on maintaining the angle of the arms at the elbow (90 degrees) together with a forward and backward swing that must be parallel to the direction of run. This is initially practiced standing still, then walking and therefore jogging and sprinting.

COACHING DRILLS

The performer should pull his elbows back and upward.

He should relax his hands and the muscles of his face; let his jaw hang.

He should look directly ahead the lean forward slightly.

He should let the legs work on their own; concentrate on the arms.

High-Knee Running Followed by Acceleration Sprints

Each runner moves forward slowly 5 meters, emphasizing high-knee lift without lower leg extension. On the signal, runners sprint forward for approximately

10 meters, accelerating as vigorously as possible.

COACHING DRILLS

The sprinter should keep the upper body upright during the high knee lift. On the signal, lean forward and drive powerfully with his legs to accelerate.

He should work his arms forward and backward as vigorously as he can, not across his body.

He should look straight ahead; do not lean back.

Counting Strides Over a Selected Distance

The athlete sprints at medium to high speed over 20 to 25 meters, while you count the number of strides the athlete takes to run the distance. The athlete must try to maintain the same tempo throughout and maintain good technique without overstriding.

COACHING DRILLS

Concentrate on drive (supporting leg), lift (leading thigh), and reach (lower leg).

The athlete should look forward; relax and work his arms as powerfully as possible.

He should concentrate on good form.

He should not turn his sprint into a series of bounding long jumps!

Testing Leg Speed

Athletes run in place while counting how many leg beats (i.e., foot contacts with the ground) they can make in 10 seconds, 15 seconds, and 20 seconds. He call out the time. (A partner can help count the number of beats).

COACHING DRILLS

Lift each foot just clear of the ground each time.

Concentrate throughout on sheer speed of leg action. Use short, fast arm movements.

1/2 and 3/4 Speed Sprints

The emphasis in this practice is on maintaining the sprinting form established in earlier practices while maintaining the required speed without strain or tightening up. The participant uses a sprint start or flying start, and the distance run depends on maturity and fitness. Beginners run 25 to 30 meters, more mature athletes 45 to 50 meters.

COACHING DRILLS

The sprinter should think of good drive, knee lift, and arm action.

He should relax as he run;

He should let the muscles of his face and hands relax.

He should not drop his backward or swing his arms across his body.

He should keep the arms and knees swinging directly back and forth.

He should force his elbows back and up with each arm swing.

Flat-Out Sprinting

Using a flying start, the athlete runs a selected distance that is marked by 2 lines. The starter start the watch when the athlete crosses the first line, and an assistant signals by lowering an arm when the athlete crosses the second line (the finish). For beginners, an acceptable distance is 35 to 40 meters, but mature athletes will sprint farther. The number of repetitions and rest periods will depend upon fitness and maturity (2 to 3 for beginners).

COACHING DRILLS

The athlete should work on maintaining good sprinting form throughout; do not tighten up in an attempt to sprint faster.

He should look forward; relax his face and hands and run on the balls of his feet.

DRILLS TO IMPROVE LEG POWER AND ACCELERATION

These activities are very demanding. Use them sparingly with beginners, and increase intensity and repetitions slowly. Students should practice on a cushioned surface, such as mats or grass. The recommended number of repetitions for beginners is 2 to 3, with walking rests between each effort.

Distance Hopping

Each participant hops 2 to 3 paces with the left leg, then repeats the same action with the right leg. With each hop, athletes swing their arms forward and upward and drive with their legs as powerfully as possible. The thigh of the free leg is lifted to horizontal on each hop.

COACHING DRILLS

The athlete should swing his arms forward and upward vigorously as possible to help gain distance.

He should drive powerfully with each jumping leg.

Make each hop the same size.

He should not hop for height; drive for distance.

He should try the hopping sequence from standing and then from a 2- to 3-step run-up.

Bounding (Striding) for Distance

This is a favourite drill of triple jumpers. Each

bounding stride is long and reaching, and 2 to 3 are performed in sequence.

COACHING DRILLS

Lean forward slightly and jump long and low, not upward; keep the momentum going.

Make each bounding stride about the same size.

The performer should drive forward and upward with his arms on each stride.

Try the bounding strides from a standing start and then from a 2- to 3-step run-up.

Rabbit Hops

These are two-legged jumps, 2 to 3 performed in sequence. Students see who can cover the greatest distance after 3 jumps.

COACHING DRILLS

Drive forward as powerfully as possible with each jump.

The sprinter should be sure to synchronize the actions of his arms; swing them up and forward as he drive with his legs.

COMBINATIONS OF HOPPING AND BOUNDING OVER LOW OBSTACLES

Bamboo canes set across cones (or low elastic highjump "bars") are combined with mats to form a series of low obstacles. These are set in a sequence that forces the performer to strive for distance on each of 3 to 4 successive jumps. Mats cusion the landings. The performer make the sequence of required hops and bounds.

COACHING DRILLS

Do not high jump the obstacles.

The sprinter should use the drive of his legs and his arm lift to "float" as long as he can with each jump.

He should imagine himself as a ball that has been thrown forward and down at the ground.

He should endeavour to simulate the series of long, low bounces that the ball would make.

High-Knee Running, Moving Backward, Then Forward

The ground begins by running in place, emphasizing high-knee lift. On the first signal they shift to slow backward running (with high-knee lift). On the second signal they revert to slow forward running with high-knee lift. Recommended distance for beginners is 5 meters, backward, then 5 meters forward.

COACHING DRILLS

The performer should keep his knees working high and as fast as possible. Listen to the rhythm of his footballs and try to keep this rhythm both fast and regular.

He should lean his upper body slightly backward when he move backward.

He should tilt his body forward to shift forward.

He should keep his knee lift going as fast as possible.

Sprinting With Partner Resistance

Using a strap or belt, one athlete pulls another along like a horse and cart. The sprinter (horse) wears the strap or belt around the abdomen, with the partner (cart) holding the lines and providing a mobile but gentle resistance. The resistance should be sufficient to make the horse work as vigorously as possible, as though sprinting flat-out. Both horse and cart move forward 10 meters at a speed equivalent to a fast jog. A surface that provides sufficient traction will be necessary. Partners change roles after 2 to 3 repetitions.

COACHING DRILLS

Cart

Do not stop the horse from moving forward. Give just enough resistance so that the horse can really lean into the action and work the legs and arms as vigorously as possible.

Lean backward to provide the right amount of resistance.

Horse

Lean forward and work your legs and arms as hard as you can! See if you can overcome the resistance the cart is giving you.

Drills to Improve the Leg Power and Acceleration of the Mature Athlete

These drills are intended for the mature athlete who has worked beyond elementary sprinting drills and who has developed additional leg power during the off-season through weight training and other complementary activities.

A novice attempting the following drills is likely to experience extreme muscle soreness. Do not allow beginners to be hasty. They should progress slowly, working at drills appropriate to their levels of maturity.

Running, Bounding, and Jumping Up Stairs

Running, bounding, hopping and jumping are performed up stairs; as the athlete's leg power increases, steeper stairs are used. This is a familiar activity for football players who run and bound up stadium steps as part of their training. Introduce this activity on steps that are low (shallow) and wide enough to allow plenty of room for each landing and takeoff. Initially, have students practice one type of jump at a time in order not to disrupt rhythm. Later, use combinations of all types of jumps. Experienced athletes may also bound down shallow stairs using a controlled double leg take off and double-leg landing. Note. This practice demands excellent control and is particularly stressful on the legs. It is not a drill for beginners.

COACHING DRILLS

The athlete should keep his eyes on the steps throughout.

Drive as powerfully as he can and lift his thighs with each jump.

Remember to swing his arms forward and upward.

Rest and breath deeply once he has reached the top of the steps.

Depth or Rebound Jumping—"Plyometrics"

Depth or rebound jumping develops explosiveness and elastic rebound in the leg muscles. The performer steps (or jumps) down from the top of a vaulting box onto the floor and immediately rebounds up onto another box. Sprinters and jumpers, particularly the triple jumper, frequently use this activity.

These drills are very strenuous and extremely demanding. They demand a specific technique for landing at the end of the jump and are recommended only for physically mature athletes who have already developed power in the legs with considerable bounding, jumping, and strength training (squats). These drills are not intended for novices.

Drills to Improve Sprint Endurance

Rolling Sprints

Teams of four (or more) jog or run slowly around the track. At the signal, runner *iv* to the front of the team. On the next signal, runner *iii* sprints to the front and so on. Reducing the time between signals and increasing the size of teams will increases the intensity. One full lap of a 400-meter track is adequate for beginners.

Running Inclines

Athletes run up moderate inclines of 250 to 400 meters at 1/2, 3/4, and full speed. Increase repetitions as athletes stamina and fitness improve. Athletes can use the walk to the base of the incline as the recovery.

Continuous Relays

Form a team of 9 members. Each team member runs 50 meters on a 400-meter track; number 1 runs 50 meters then passes the baton to or tage number 2, and waits at number 2's position for the next round of exchanges. Number 9 moves into number 1's position to receive the tag (or baton) from number 8.

Fartlek

This is a varied cross-country course of 2 to 3 miles. Students alternate short bursts of sprinting with jogging.

Interval Sprints

Participants sprint the curve and jog or walk the straightaway on a 400-meter track; or they sprint 50 meters and jog or walk 200 to 300 meters. They repeat the interval 3 to 4 times.

The length and type of rest depends on the fitness and performance ability of the athlete. The pulse rate provides a good measure; if the pulse falls below 120 beats per minute at the end of the rest, the next repetition can begin. If the pulse stays above 120, the intensity of training is too high and should be reduced.

INTENSE SPRINT TRAINING FOR THE MORE MATURE ATHLETE REPETITION SPRINT STARTS WITH MAXIMUM EFFORT OVER 40 TO 60 METERS

Each athlete works through a complete sprint start sequence of commands; at the sound of the gun, the athlete sprints flat-out over 40 to 60 meters. The selected distance and the number of repetitions will depend on individual fitness and ability. An example is 4 to 6 repetitions with a 2- to 3-minute pause between each. This improves the sprinter's anaerobic endurance and will also improve coordination and sprinting power.

Repetition Sprints From a Flying Start

The athlete accelerates over 30 meters and then sprints with maximum effort for 20 to 30 meters. The distance and the number of repetitions will depend on individual fitness and ability. For example, the athlete can perform 2 to 3 repetitions with rest pauses of 2 to 3 minutes. This helps to improve anaerobic endurance and coordination while the athlete runs at high speed.

Ins and Outs

"Ins and Outs" is a common name given to periods of high-speed sprinting followed by equal distances of loose, relaxed, fast running. For example, the athlete can run 100 to 150 meters in the following manner: out—20 meters of relaxed, fast running; in—20 meters at high speed; out—20 meters of relaxed, fast running. The objective is to imprcve sprint endurance and coordination.

Repetitive Relays

Sprinter 1 accelerates over 40 meters and passes a baton to or tags sprinter 2. Sprinter 1 takes the position of sprinter 2, who repeats the sprinter 3. Sprinter 3 jogs back to the start and tags. Sprinter 4, who is waiting at the start and who repeats the process. The objective is to improve anaerobic endurance.

100-Meter Repeats

These repeats are run at 80 to 90 percent of the individual's 100-meter best performance. The number of repetitions will vary depending on fitness, and the rest period should be long enough to allow for full recovery. (This type of training is often used by 400-meter runners).

POINT 3: SPRINT STARTS

After the "on your marks" command has been issued, the athlete is positioned in the blocks with the body weight resting equally on the rear knee and the hands. The arms are shoulder-width apart, and the hands are to the rear of the line. The fingers and thumb form a *V*. The shoulders are rotated forward, slightly ahead of the hands (7 to 8 centimetres or 3 to 4 inches).

The stronger leg normally drives from the front block, because contact with this block is longer. The forward foot on the blocks is commonly 1-3/4 to 2 foot lengths from the starting line. The rear foot on the blocks is usually 1-1/2 foot lengths behind the front foot. Breathing is steady and regular.

In the "set" position, the athlete is like a coiled spring. The athlete's seat is raised up and forward so that the angle of the leading leg is approximately 80 to 90 degrees at the knee, the rear leg 110 to 130 degrees at the knee. The body weight is equally supported by arms and legs and both feet are well in contact with the blocks.

The back and the head from a straight line, and the athlete looks directly forward at the ground. The athlete holds the shoulders in their position slightly ahead of the vertical plane of the hands. On the set command, the athlete holds his or her breath.

At the sound of the gun, the forward leg extends vigorously and the knee of the rear leg is driven forward. The arms work vigorously to counterbalance the powerful action of the legs. The athlete inclines the body forward for the first 5 to 6 meters of the race. Beyond this distance the sprinter assumes a more upright sprinting position for the rest of the race. By 40 meters, the sprinter is fully upright.

Sprinters use three basic block positions, which vary in the distance between the front and rear block and also in the distance that the blocks are set from the line. These distances will be determined by the body position required following the set command.

The best position for each athlete depends upon the individual sprinter's body length, leg length, leg power, and coordination. Leg length is the most important single characteristic determining block position.

Starting Practice

Each participant walks forward, stops, and places both feet together on a line. On a single each individual leans forward slowly. Once the body weight is tilted sufficiently to require a step forward, the participants sprint forward 15 to 20 meters.

COACHING DRILLS

Who can tilt forward the farthest and begin sprinting without stumbling?

The athlete should keep his knees swinging directly forward when he accelerate;

He should endeavour to avoid turning the knees and feet outward.

He should drive with his legs as powerfully as possible as he accelerate.

He should lift his thighs to horizontal.

He should lift his elbows as high as possible to the rear with each arm swing.

Touch the Ground Drill

The group jogs slowly, abreast, and in a line. On a signal each individual touches the ground with both hands, momentarily simulating a set position, and immediately sprints for 10 to 15 meters. Participants then resume the jog, and on the signal they repeat the set position and sprint. Repeat 3 to 4 times.

COACHING DRILLS

The sprinter should not worry about his body position when he touch the ground.

He should be sure the fingers and thumb of both hands touch the ground simultaneously on each signal.

He should accelerate as fast as he can.

Developing Explosive Drive From the Set Position

The group jogs slowly, abreast, and in a line. On a signal each participant rotates 180 degrees with a small jump, dropping immediately into a momentary set position and sprinting in the opposite direction for 10 to 15 meters. On the next signal, athletes repeat the sequence. Dropping from a small jump into a set position and driving out of the set position helps students develop a feel for the explosive response needed in a sprint start.

COACHING DRILLS

The sprinter should not jump high in the air as he turn around; otherwise he will collapse into the set position and find it even more difficult to get out of it.

Only the feet and hands should touch the ground in the set position;

The sprinter should not sink all the way down onto his knees.

He should lean forward and work his arms and legs as vigorously as possible as he accelerate.

Variation

Abreast in a line; the group moves slowly backward with high-knee lift until you give a whistle blast. Participants immediately drop into the set position and sprint forward to cross a line that is 10 meters ahead. They re-form the line and repeat the sequence.

Running Lines and Practising the Set Position

Draw chalk lines on the ground 5 meters apart. From a standing start position, participants run to the farthest line (25 meters), jump turn, drop momentarily into a set position, run back to the start, jump turn, drop into a set position, run to the next nearest line (20 meters), and repeat.

COACHING DRILLS

This is not a race; run at medium speed, and use a low jump for the turnaround.

Drive with your legs as vigorously as possible out of the set position.

"On Your Marks, Get Set, Go"

Using a standing start, participants lean forward and relax down into the "on your marks" position. On the command, each raises his or her seat into the set position. You move from one runner to the next and correct individual positions. On a signal, the group sprints for 10 to 15 meters.

COACHING DRILLS

The sprinter should make sure that his arms are shoulder-width apart.

The sprinter's thumb and fingers should form a *V* to the rear of the starting line.

The athlete should set his shoulders slightly ahead of his hands on the "on your marks" command. Then simply raise your seat with the "get set" command.

Concentrate on achieving the correct angle at the knees with the "set" position.

Partners as Starting Blocks

Using a partner as blocks, each athlete can work through a complete sprint start sequence, experimenting with various foot positions and distances between the front and rear blocks. You should assist each individual in finding the correct block positions. Students with longer legs will find the correct starting position by setting the blocks further apart and further from the starting line.

COACHING DRILLS

If the athletes are acting as blocks for his partner, he should use the flat of his feet as blocks and be ready to resist the leg drive that will occur when the whistle blows.

He should lean backward, straighten his arm, and be sure to turn his fingers to the rear. This makes him more stable and helps him to resist the backward drive of the performer practising the start.

Sprint Start and Acceleration Practice

At your signal, runners practice starting and accelerating using starting blocks, and other participants act as judges at the finish line, 20 to 30 meters away. A second line is set 2 to 3 meters beyond the finish line. Initially require novices to run through the tape and continue sprinting to the second line. Once the athletes understand that they must sprint through the finish, they can try pushing their chests forward at the tape. With practice they can attempt a partial lean. Avoid having novices attempt excessive lean at the finish, because this will cause stumnling. First practice this drill on 25 to 30 meters of straightaway, then the same distance on a curved segment of track.

COACHING DRILLS

The athlete should line up his starting blocks so that you sprint on a tangent towards the inside edge of the lane.

He should lean inward as he sprint around the curve and swing his right arm more powerfully than the left.

He should keep his feet parallel to the curve;

He should not turn his feet or knees outward.

He should look forward and swing his arms forward and backward, not across your body.

Sprint through the tape as though the finish is really at the second line.

When practicing the lean, the sprinter should drive his chest ahead of his arms and lean toward the tape when he is approximately one full stride away. The performer should not jump at the tape or lean too early, or he will stumble.

CHAPTER 12

CHARACTERISTICS OF THE SPRINTING

BODY BUILD

Sprinters appear to be the least distinguishable of track and field participants. There are tall, short, heavy, light and medium-sized sprinters. Extremely short-legged sprinters often have difficulty holding their own with taller sprinters in 220-yard and longer sprints.

Probably the ideal body build for a sprinter would be a height of about 6 feet with light bones, good musculature, especially around the thigh region, light musculature in the calf of the leg (at least not thick ankles and heavy calf muscles placed low on the leg), and long, slender feet. Nevertheless, a boy with physical characteristics that would seem detrimental to his performance may become a fast runner, because he: (a) has very fast muscular movement of the legs, called leg speed; (b) uses good body mechanics; (c) has a long stride; (d) has confidence in his ability; and (e) has determination of train and to win.

TEMPERAMENT AND AGE

The sprinter is often nervous and high strung. Whether this results from experience in an explosive, competitive situation or is a natural condition is debatable. Certainly such qualities alone will not create a potential sprinter, but having favourable physical characteristics to go along with such a temperament may be an advantage. Evidence in relation to age seems to indicate that speed belongs to youth, buy some great sprinters have been able to keep their speed until the age of 30 or longer. However, this is only possible when they train regularly every year.

SPRINTER'S ATTRIBUTES

Fenn has found that the faster runners have the following movement characteristics: (1) longer length of stride; (2) faster number of steps (strides) per second; (3) greater height in front leg lift; (4) ground contact with a larger angle with the horizontal, therefore less wasted energy in forward pressure on the ground; and (5) less up-and-down movement of the body's centre of weight.

After a 6 year experimental program conducted on sprinting during the years 1950-1954 at the University of Southern California, the following still applicable conclusions were drawn:

1. When starting, the stronger leg should be placed on the front block. Fifteen untrained sprinter achieved better time in a 5-yard sprint by using the stronger leg against the front block.

2. Response time to the starting signal does not appear to be an important factor in the time required to run a given dash distance. There is a great difference between quickness of movement and speed of movement when starting and in sprinting. It is important to use proper running form off the blocks and throughout the race.

3. Removal of the rear block so that the sprinter starts with use of only the front block adversely affects

starting speed. This research was done to test the importance of the rear block in starting.

4. The optimum time for holding a sprinter at the "set" position is slightly beyond 1½ seconds. The response time to the starting gun is slower when the holding time is longer than 2 seconds.

5. The medium elongated starting stance was found at the time of the program to be best. Now the bunch starting position (mean distance 10.9 inches or slightly longer between the blocks) appears to be the most effective.

6. There appears to be no relationship between the amount of pressure exerted against the blocks and the time recorded in running a specified distance (5 yards in this case). The greatest force exerted against the blocks did not yield the fastest time for the performer.

7. When starting, the average good sprinter's rear leg exerts considerably more force than the front leg on the blocks, but the force from the front leg is applied for a longer time. It would seem from the findings in this study that the runner should attempt to get the rear foot into action against the ground as soon as possible.

Starting Position

Modern types of starting positions vary considerably. The most common are described below :—

Bunch Starting Position

This position is determined by having the runner place the top of the back foot opposite the rear edge of the heel of the front foot. Use of this position usually means the blocks are placed from 10 to 13 inches apart. Many top sprinters are using the bunch start today. It usually enables the sprinter to leave the blocks faster than in the other starts. In the bunch start, the sprinter's hips are high and he tends to leave the blocks very fast. However, it is a very difficult position to maintain if the starter holds the runner in the "set" position beyond 2 seconds.

Medium Starting Position

This position is not determined by a fixed distance between feet, but by a varying one, and experimentally has been shown in the past to have been the most effective, but is not considered so today. To determine this position the runner places the knee of his rear leg opposite the foot of the front leg at any place beyond the line opposite the toe of the front foot and up to, but not including, a position opposite the heel of the front foot. The average position would involve the knee of the rear leg being opposite the middle arch of the front foot. The sprinter determines the best position for his own use through experience or by going to an experimental running track, where devices test his speed for a given distance using various starting position.

Elongated Starting Position

This position is the extreme opposite of the bunch start. The method used to determine the distance between blocks is to have the runner place the knee of his rear leg opposite the back of the heel of the front foot, or at any location beyond this distance. Very few sprinters use this starting stance, since the feet are placed at too great a distance apart for almost all sprinters. The runner is unable to cause his body to fall forward fast enough to give him a fast start.

Starting and Sprinting Procedures

Based upon coaching experience and experimental evidence, the following starting procedures are suggested :—

1. The blocks should be set at the sprinter's preferred distance. It is recommended that the bunch or medium position be used by most sprinters, with the blocks 11 to 15 inches apart.

2. If the distance of the front foot from the starting line has not been determined through experience, a beginning reference point may be found by placing the front block the distance of two full hand "spans" from the front line. Modification of this distance should be made as experience and study dictate. This would mean that the rear block would be about 25 to 30 inches from the starting line. The front leg in a starting "set" position in the past formed an angle of about 80°. It was thought that this leg angle enabled the front leg to support the rear leg effectively as it swungs through for the first step. However, many good sprinters have recently tended to extend completely or nearly the rear leg when they are in the "set" position. This position tends to make the sprinter go forward more easily during his first step.

3. A standing position immediately behind the block is assumed.

4. One or two moderately deep breaths are taken when the starter says, "Go to your marks".

5. A position directly in front of the blocks is taken, the hands placed on the ground, and the feet backed into the starting blocks, placing first the front and then the rear foot against the blocks. (If sufficient training has not been experienced, it is suggested that the stronger leg be placed in front. If leg and foot strength devices, such as dynamometers, are not available, a crude method may be used to determine the stronger foot. The

sprinter stands erect with both feet together. Someone gently pushes him from the rear in the small of the back. Usually he will support his weight with his stronger leg, thus stepping forward with the weaker leg in the first step).

6. The hands are then dusted off and the rear knee is kept on the ground.
7. The hands are now placed on the ground and the wrists rotated outward so that the thumb and index finger are just behind the starting line, spread and parallel. The body weight is borne on the fingers; only the finger tips and thumb tips of each hand should be in contact with the ground. (Where finger strength is too weak to permit the sprinter to be up on his finger tips, special types of finger tip push-up exercises should be used to stengthen them. The fingertip position increases the forward lean and enables the runner to get off faster).
8. The arm should hang in a perpendicular line from the shoulders to the ground, with the two thumbs about 8 inches apart. (Some sprinters may prefer to have the hands slightly wider than shoulder width. Some few even use a very wide hand spread of as much as 20 or more inches).
9. The head should be loose, relaxed, and allowed to hang down.
10. At the command "set", one quick breath may be taken before the body weight moves upward and forward over the hands, so that all that is necessary is to pull and the hands out to the side to start to fall forward. The legs then move fast enough to keep the body from falling. (Enough weight should be felt on the front foot to permit a firm application of force against the block. There is no felt weight kept on the rear foot).

The sprinter should be less balanced in the "set" position if the starter holds him for less than 2 seconds. (When he is held for 2 seconds or longer, he will have assumed a more stable position—that is, with feet placed farther apart in the blocks). He must have such an unstable position in order to fall forward when he releases his hands as support. His attention should be focused on sound, and any little noise would cause him to start immediately. He should concentrate, after hearing the sound, on moving off the blocks as soon as possible.

11. The hips at "Set" are raised to a point slightly above the shoulders, so that as the runner leaves the blocks he lifts his shoulders just above the hips. The force from the legs is then directed forward and only slightly upward. The idea of having the force from the legs go through the centre of the body and continue in a straight line to the finish tape points out to the sprinter the importance of being in a forward-lean positions at "set", and of letting the legs continuously catch the body before it falls in its progress to the finish line, in a rhythmical, smooth motion. However, to set an initial goal of a short distance (such as 5 yards) only enables the runner to reach that particular point rapidly. Often the sprinter fails to maintain his pace from that point on because his body is too far forward. When practicing sprint starting, the goal selected should be a distance of more than 20 yards.

12. The eyes at "set" are focused on a point on the ground directly in front of the body, so that the head hangs down and is relaxed. Some coaches content that the sprinter should look at a point 3 to 20 yards, down the track preparatory to starting. However, it is suggested that the raised head in the "set" position is tense.

13. The runner should concentrate on taking the first step as rapidly as possible.

LEAVING THE BLOCKS

The following additional points are presented for the sprinter to follow as he leaves the block.

1. At the sound of the gun, the slightly bent arm, opposite the stepping leg (rear leg at start), is quickly, but gently, thrust forward at shoulder level, but not as far as possible. The other arm is moved vigorously toward the rear so that the arms will move in opposition to the legs. The first actual movement in starting is the cocking of the rear foot preparatory to taking a step. The front foot is then cocked (flexed) just before the arms start their movement. The arms are actually hanging in front of the body when the first step is taken. This position keeps the body weight in front of the feet.

2. The first step should be 18 to 30 inches from the starting line and slightly inward from a straight line down the track. The foot taking the first step should still be behind the weight centre line of the body, and should barely clear the ground in moving forward. Any lifting of the foot upward throws the body of the sprinter upward and prevents him from moving forward rapidly.

3. The foot is pointed almost straight ahead as it strikes the ground (exception: on the first step, the foot is turned slightly inward). Excessive toeing inward or outward decreases foot and leg action. However, knee position is the real key to the sprinter's ability to direct his body in as straight a line as possible. The knee must be pointed in the direction of the run in order for the sprinter to move linearly. Slight toeing-out may not be as

disadvantageous as once thought if the knee is pointed straight ahead. In fact, young Mike Goodrich of Indiana, as well as Charlie Greene of Nebraska, run with a definite toeing-out action.

4. The head should be raised gently as the runner leaves the block so that he focuses on a spot 20 to 30 feet down the track ahead of him as he moves forward.

5. The sprinter should slowly come to a completely upright position. Each succeeding step should be longer until he reaches this upright position. For most sprinters, this means that they have covered a distance of 10 to 15 yards before attaining their upright running position. If it were possible to have a higher effective starting position, full running stride could be achieved more rapidly. Short-legged sprinters reach this position sooner than long-legged ones.

6. The first few strides after leaving the blocks are fairly long, but not exaggerated in length. Short choppy steps should not be used.

   Reaction time off the blocks is not correlated with speed in the sprints. However, the better start each runner gets, the greater is his opportunity for running an ideal race. Probably the two most important factors are that the sprinter gets a firm, fast start and attempts to maintain top speed as long as possible.

7. Upon reaching full running position, the sprinter should pull his hips under him and attempt to roll his hips as he runs, thereby increasing the length of each stride. Since a sprinter reaches his maximum speed at approximately 65 yards from the start, or in approximately 6 seconds, the sprinter who is among the leaders at this point will

win the race if he can come closer than the others to maintaining this speed for the remainder of the race.

8. The use of proper arm and leg action is obviously extremely important. Going off the blocks, the sprinter should have strong arm action, with the movement to the front and rear made as fast as possible. As the sprinter reaches his full running position, the arm action should be rapid but executed somewhat more in front of the body. The movement of the bent arm to the front is rapid, but easy, so that the body will not react to the front arm movement with a backward motion. The arms should move slightly in toward the middle of the body, but not much higher than shoulder level. This slightly inward swinging motion is necessary for smooth, relaxed action because of the anatomical connection of the arm with the rest of the body, and the way in which the chest muscles pull the arms forward and inward. If the sprinter tends to tense his arms as he runs, it may be better to have him cut down the action of the arms, and swing them gently and easily in rhythm with the legs for balance purposes only.

9. During the sprint, the hand should be slightly cupped with the thumb pushing against the forefinger. Ability to relax the arm is an important factor in enabling the runner to secure entire body relaxation while running. Pushing the thumb against the forefinger helps prevent the arm from becoming tense.

10. The legs, from the first step until slightly beyond the upright running position, are moved vigorously with a high knee lift. The high knee lift should be continued throughout a 100-yard sprint, but the

foot action against the ground is not as vigorous when the sprinter uses longer strides.

Observation of the marks made on the ground by the feet of top sprinters (shoes covered with white chalk) has shown that there are deep holes in the ground after the first 5 or 6 strides, with the heel plainly visible. After that, the holes are much smaller, with the heel hitting very lightly and the marks barely visible. The movement of the leg to the rear is such that the foot goes somewhat higher than the knee. However, too much kick up in the rear appears to be unnecessary, does not add anything to the speed of movement, and results in loss of time.

The knee lift in front should be high, almost even with the top of the hip. The leg and foot are extended forward so that a long stride is taken, with the foot striking the ground in a pawing-like action. The sprinter should move his legs as fast as he can and still take as long a strides as possible. However, leg speed should not be unduly sacrificed for a longer stride.

11. The body lean forward as the start is extreme (almost as far as the sprinter can lean without falling). This angle of lean gradually decreases until the vertical position is assumed as the runner reaches his upright running position. While running, the leg of the rear foot, at the point of fullest extension, should be in a straight line with the back and the head. Some top runners have even been found to lean slightly backward during the latter portion of the race. However, it is impossible to run forward without having the rear leg and foot, the motive force, exerting effort from the rear of the centre of the body weight.

It is essential that the head be kept up during the run. Many beginning sprinters hold their heads down during the first few strides after leaving the blocks, especially those who have a tendency to stand up at the start. This gives them a false illusion of gradually coming up to an erect running position. Unfortunately, they are working at a mechanical disadvantage and may lose because of their poorer initial form.

12. The running form throughout should be smooth and seemingly effortless. Gallping, rolling of the head and body from side to side, excessive movement of the hands and arms, and clenching of the teeth, which makes the neck and face muscles bulge, will decrease running speed.

13. The feet and ankles move rapidly in a bounce-like action to increase the speed of leg and foot movement.

By way of summary to this point, after the sprinter has come to an upright running position, he should run with a long unexaggerated stride varying according to his leg length and general build—probably somewhere between 6 and 9 feet (from right foot to left foot). He should use a high lift, employ fast arm action, and keep a straight back.

SOME SPRINT ESSENTIALS

Several additional comments about sprinting should be made. The great sprinters of the past learned to relax when they ran. One step in accomplishing relaxation is to let the swinging leg move partially unchecked until just before the vigorous thrust of the foot against the ground. Using the arms in such a manner that the forward motion is extremely easy and not under control of the muscles except a necessary for fast backward movement also helps in relaxing the runner. The back and the rear and front of the neck are among the areas apt to show most strain.

To alleviate this strain, which often begins in the hands and arms, it is necessary for relaxation to begin in the hands and face. Rolling the lip outward, or letting the lower jaw sag by opening the mouth, aids in relaxing the front of the neck and the face. The head and neck may be relaxed by keeping the head in line with the back. Lifting the head high at the start tends to tense the neck and back muscles.

During the time the runner is accelerating, and especially while he is attempting to maintain his speed, it is important that he not overexert himself. This is not an easy skill to learn. Every runner has a maximum rhythm of leg movement beyond which he cannot go. Trying to exceed this rhythm of movement slows and "ties up" the runner.

Two breaths taken at the start of a sprint, and another as the runner gets "set", as previously mentioned, enable the runner to hold his breath during part of a 100-yard race, usually for the duration of a 60-yard sprint. Taking one or two breaths at the beginning of a race also tends to relax the runner before he leaves the blocks. As the 80-yard mark in the 100-yard sprint, one breath should be taken for a good supply of oxygen and to enable the runner to relax and run more easily at the finish. For distances, beyond 100-yards. breathing normally seems to be the best technique, but the runner should take one or more breaths at the start. Almost all runners hold their breath during an all-out effort, such as the last 25 yards of a long race.

The sprinter who attempts to leap, jump, shrug, or twist as he finishes a race is actually diminishing his speed with these extra motions. He should run through the tape and go beyond it about 10 yards before slowing up. An extra motion at the last moment may sometimes attract the judges eyes, but if the finish of the race is photographed, the runner who continues running through the tape shows to greatest advantage in a close finish. If any extra movement at the finish is necessary, it should be accomplished during the last stride.

SPECIAL COMMENTS ABOUT 220-YARD DASH

The records reveal not only that the time for the 220 has been gradually decreased during the last 60 years, but that more and more runners are able to equal previous "best" records. This is a race in which the contestant should attempt to run the entire distance at near maximum speed, and which calls for both top speed and more endurance than does the 100-yard dash. Certain special running techniques should be employed to enable the runner to maintain speed as long as possible.

The physical qualifications of the 220-yard sprinter are the same as those for the 100-yard sprinter, with only a few differences. Although there are exceptions, it is possible for an extremely short, heavy, quick runner to make a reasonably good 100-yard dash man, even a top one. Most of this physical type have difficulty in running a fast race beyond this distance because of weight and lack of length of stride. Occasionally, a fast runner who also competes in field events can run a good 100-yard race, but because of lack of training does not have the endurance to run an effective 220. Since the 220-yard dash is run on a curve, the runner must be able to sprint under control throughout the turn.

Age is often a factor to consider in selecting participants for the 220 in high school competition. An older boy frequently has the greater strength and endurance needed to run this distance more effectively. A good 440-yard runner can usually run a good, and sometimes a great, 220-yard sprint race when he has enough speed, because he already has sufficient endurance.

Most of the techniques of performance apply to both the 100 and 220. Not every good 100-yard sprinter can become good in the 220, but records indicate that, with proper training, more than 80 per cent of the 100-yard sprinters can become effective 220-yard runners.

HELPFUL HINTS

In addition to the previously mentioned factors, there are others that should be mastered for success in the 220-yard sprint.

1. The distance should be run with maximum speed and minimum tension. This means being able to relax sufficiently to maintain speed as long as possible after accelerating to the maximum. Maximum acceleration is reached in about 6 seconds after leaving the blocks. An inexperienced 220-yard runner will need a pattern to follow in running this distance. Such a pattern may be : (a) run the first 60 to 70 yards at top speed. (b) Relax and run as fast as possible without trying too hard for 90 to 100 yards. The running technique employed here is often called the "float". This is actually an erroneous idea, since there should be no conscious effort to slow up. (c) Attempt to run the last remaining 50 to 60 yards faster, with as little as possible Inexperienced 220-yard sprinters need to know how to judge the effort necessary in relation to the distance to be travelled. It is essential that the sprinter know how to pace himself so that he does not expend his effort before the finish of the race.

Many of today's top 220 sprinters accelerate up to about 65 yards, and relax, but run the remaining distance as fast as possible. Occasionally they "pour it on" in the last 20 yards.

2. In running the 220-yard race, the runner should be under control as he approaches the curve. He should run the inside edge of his lane, increase speed on the

curve, and maintain speed in a relaxed manner to the finish. A curve can be run most effectively if the stride is not broken and there is no slowing down.

When running indoors on cinder or board tracks, it is imperative that the sprinter accelerate on part of the straighaway, be under control when coming into the curve, and speed up on the curve, with the outside leg placed wide so that the legs are in a wide stance as the curve is taken. The runner then should push in toward the curve with this outside leg.

3. The 220-yard sprinter should develop enough endurance through repeated 220-yard runs and/or overdistance runs (300-yards) to run this race effectively.

4. He should develop speed by running repeated 50- and 75-yard sprints.

5. In preparation for, and competition in, the sprints in early season, the sprinters should drill on the fundamental skills of performance-starting, proper arm and leg action, relaxation, maximum speed with minimum effort, and gaining endurance. The midseason schedule should include work on skills considered to need most attention. This is the time to perfect form. The late season program should be characterized by reduction in the intensity of practice sessions and concentration on top winning performance in each meet.

CHAPTER 13

COMMON ERRORS AND THEIR CORRECTIONS IN SPRINTING

In sprinting, as in any other track or field event requiring the timing of interrelated movements, there exists the possibility of error in each and every action. Those imperfections quite frequently encountered by the beginner are discussed as follows :—

1. IN THE START

The axiom, "A good start is half the battle", may not be literally true in sprinting, but most authorities recognize that the athlete first underway has the best chance of winning the race. Therefore, any errors at the onset of the contest detract from fast time.

Should the holes or starting blocks be too far from the starting line, the thighs and legs are too straight to permit maximum driving effort. In case they are too close to the starting line, the athlete not only will suffer discomfort but also will lose leverage because the various parts of the body are folded up too much.

Extreme lateral spacing of either holes or blocks causes the competitor to leave the marks with a twisting motion. The distance recommended is approximately eight inches from centre of heel to centre of heel.

If the arms are spread too far apart in the "set" position or if placed in a bent manner, the chest will be too low, thus necessitating extra effort to bring it to running posture.

Should the hips be too high in the "set" position, both legs will be too straight and will not have the maximum drive. Efficiency is lost likewise if the hips are too low. It follows, then, that for a given athlete there is one most effective elevation of the hips which depends on his height and the type of foot spacing he employs.

Any extreme position of the head and neck constricts breathing and causes discomfort. If the focus of the eyes during a race is taken from the course and turned on the other contestant, attention is diverted and imperfections in full-effort striding may result.

If the trunk lean is too far forward, the athlete is out of balance. On the contrary, if the lean is insufficient, the movement of the body is less forward and more upward and forward than good form dictates.

Faults in breathing occur more frequently before the start than during either the start or the race. Excessive deep breathing should be avoided. The sprinter must find by experience how much of this he can profitably do. He is urged not to carry forced respiration to the point of dizziness. From the time of the command, "Get set", to the time of the gunshot, as was previously pointed out, breathing is automatic. During the race the sprinter should ventilate the lungs sufficiently to ward off air hunger. Fortunately, it is safe to place respiration, during the race, in the hands of nature.

The ramifications caused by inattention are very numerous and briefly stated any act which detracts from attention is an error.

Insufficient pressure on the legs, while in the set position, especially the back leg, detracts from the drive. The movement desired is not merely a lifting, but an extremely vigorous pushing action.

Some athletes needlessly delay making preparation for the start and are thrown into a state of confusion when the official calls, "Starters ready". In haste, many tasks requiring minute adjustments are improperly attended to.

Athletes have committed faults by becoming too tense when "on the marks". At the command, "Get set", they may err by wrongfully snapping the trunk forward. Both the speed and the force of this extra rapid movement are frequently so great as to destroy delicate balance. A less common error consists in overdelay of the same movement.

Once in the "set" position, the chief error occurs in failing to hold a finely poised position until the gunshot. Awaiting the gun is but a part of the technique, and the sprinter should not make the mistake of being caught "flat-footed" when the gun is fired. It is an unsportsman-like act and a strategical error to anticipate the gunshot, or in common parlance, "to try to beat the gun". The fact that one runner leaves the marks before the gun is fired does not justify the others leaving with him. The rules state that any athlete, not only the first offender, shall be panalized for committing a false start. The first official warning on account of a false start is considered a penalty because on the second offense the athlete is disqualified.

In case one or more of his rivals commits a false start, the athlete should remain on the marks until the official gives the recall command such as "up" or "break". He then should step back from the marks and limber up. Breaking from the marks when motivated by some extraneous sound such as a cough, the click of a camera, or the pounding of a hammer is not an error. This is evidence that the athlete is properly poised so that at the report of the gun, he automatically releases his force.

2. IN THE RUNNING STRIDES

Some athletes make the mistake of trying to lengthen the first stride in the start out of proportion to the body position. This interferes with getting into the correct running stride. Since the force of the swing of the arms depends on the force of the leg drive, it follows that either insufficient or too much arm power in the swing throws the body out of balance.

Running in other than a straight line is a fault in any stage of the race. Since body alignment is maintained chiefly through the arm swing, exaggerated cross-arm movement and low arm carriage are errors. If the trunk is brought to a nearly erect position too early during the transitional strides, forward driving power is lost.

Alteration in the length of the strides, reduction of the pushing force, variation in the angle of the trunk lean, or deviation from mechanically sound stride execution are the common pitfalls to be avoided during the top-speed stride section of the race. Although coasting is recommended in races from 220 yards to 880 yards, inclusive, it is not approved in the 100-yard dash.

3. IN THE COAST

The most common mistaken in the use of the coast is occasioned by the misinterpretation of its purpose. The beginner frequently "applies the brakes" or decreases his cadence. The objective is to provide a momentary period of relaxation about the middle of the race as an assurance against "tying-up" toward the finish. Athletes have made the mistake of executing the coast too early in the race, thus leaving a large portion of the contest to be run without a semirest. Others have overdelayed the coast until partial fatigue seriously hampered their ability to relax.

4. IN THE FINISH

The most flagrant error at the finish is an unconscious slowing up by the runner at the sight of the approaching yarn. We believe that it is an error to alter top-speed striding form in the closing yards of the contest. This conclusion is reached through mechanical, physiologic, and psycholgoic analyses of all through pertaining to the finish.

To summarize, the various phases of the art of running are highly individualized. Each runner must learn through analysis, practice, and racing experience the application of good form.

GENERAL ERRORS AND THEIR CORRECTIONS IN SPRINTING

1. Error

The athlete runs in a "sitting" position. The legs never fully extend, and there is no forward body lean.

Reasons

The driving leg is not extending, and the upper body is leaning backward.

Remedy

The athlete should practice leg strengthening activities, sequence hopping with right and left leg, running on inclines, and bounding strides mixed with sprinting.

2. Error

The arms are not swinging in the direction of the run.

Reasons

The shoulders and torso twist and rotate during the sprint, and the line of vision is incorrect. The head swings around, and the arms swing across the chest.

Remedy

The athlete should work to correct the arm action while running in place or sprinting at 1/2 and 3/4 speed. The line of vision should be directly ahead.

3. Error

The athlete runs with the head tilted back or with the upper body inclined backward.

Reasons

The torso and head position is incorrect, and vision is not directly ahead. The athlete may have weak abdominal muscles.

Remedy

The athlete should practice running in place, then change to running backward followed by running forward. Emphasize correct angle of head and torso. Have the athlete practice starts from a crouch and front-lying position, emphasizing correct position of head and torso. The athlete can also do abdominal exercises.

4. Error

The athlete has poor forward and upward thrust of the thigh of the leading leg.

Reasons

The athlete may have weak quadriceps, poor flexibility in the hip area, or poor coordination between arms and legs.

Remedy

The athlete should practice high-knee running, skipping and bounding exercises, and repetitive hopping and jumping.

5. Error

The athlete does not run in a straight line down the track.

Reasons

The athlete may be running with the head back, running with the eyes closed, or tightening up during the run.

Remedy

The athlete should practice running down a line, keeping vision directly ahead. Also helpful are repetitions sprints with increasing speed on each sprint; emphasize head and torso position.

6. Error

The athlete appears extremely tense. Fists are clenched, shoulders tight, and muscles of the face tense.

Reason

Tension is caused by inexperience and lack of training in relaxing while running at speed. The athlete wrongly feels that tension equals maximum effort and speed.

Remedy

Have the athlete practice running with the jaw relaxed and the fingers loose (as though carrying an egg in the fingers of each hand).

7. Error

In the set position, the athlete's shoulders are behind the hands, and the body weight is back over the legs.

Reasons

Weight is not equally distributed over arms and legs. The shoulders are not far enough forward, or blocks may be too far back from the starting line.

Remedy

Correct the positioning of the blocks. Have the athlete practice lifting his or her weight up and shifting the shoulders forward so that they are slightly ahead (i.e., in front) of the hands.

8. Error

In the set position, the angle of the leading leg is too small (much less than 90 degrees)

Reasons

The starting blocks are set too close to the line. The seat is not raised high enough in the set position.

Remedy

Correct the starting position. With the use of a partner, the athlete works at lifting into the correct starting position.

9. Error

In the set position, the angle of the leading leg is too large (much more than 90 degrees).

Reasons

The legs are almost fully extended, and the seat is lifted too high in the set position.

Remedy

Correct as for the previous error.

10. Error

In the set position, the athlete's back remains parallel to the ground.

Reasons

The athlete's vision is on the finish line, and the blocks are too far apart.

Remedy

Correct the line of vision, instructing the athlete to took at a point approximately 1 to 1-1/2 meters ahead of the hand position. Set blocks closer together.

11. Error

The athlete stands up or jumps up out of the blocks. The initial strides from the blocks are short and weak.

Reasons

Immediately after the gun is fired, the athlete elevates the upper body and raises the head and the line of vision. The athlete has poor drive from the blocks and during the strides that follow and may have poor leg power.

Remedy

Correct the angle of the body out of the blocks during the first 2 to 3 strides. Have the athlete practice working the arms and legs vigorously immediately after the gun is fired. Improve the athlete's leg power with jumping, bounding, hopping, and weight training.

12. Error

The athlete stumbles or staggers from the blocks.

Reasons

The athlete has poor or incorrect arm action or drive from the legs. The legs are driven out to the sides instead of in the direction of the run. The athlete may have poor leg power.

Remedy

At the gun, the athlete must drive vigorously from the blocks; arms must work as vigorously as legs. The athlete should also try leg-strengthening activities.

CHAPTER 14

TIMING AND STARTING TECHNIQUE IN SPRINTING

The jobs of timing and starting sprint races are extremely difficult and require the same careful training and study as do the events themselves. Certainly they cannot rightly be left to one of the extra men in the athletic department or to the fellow "who used to do a little sprinting himself once and ought to do all right". He can not possibly do all rights unless the job is a matter of real personal concern to him and unless he has found means of practicing his job as assiduously as do the sprinters themselves.

Timing. The essential factor in accurate timing is consistency of reaction. Quick reaction is not in itself of importance, although it is probable that a quicker reaction will be more consistent than a slower one. But consistency is all-important. In starting a watch, there must of course be a certain lag in time between the sight of the flash of the gun and the actual starting of the watch. Similarly, it is absolutely essential to proper timing that this identical lag in time should occur between the instant the winner's chest crosses the finish line and the stopping of the watch. Few timers make sufficient allowance for their own reaction time. They assume that, since the race ends and the finish is judged as the runner touches the tape, their watches should stop at this same instant. They forget they were not equally fast in starting their watches. Unquestionably many record certificates have been signed by timers who have ignored this fundamental requirement of proper timing.

In a study entitled the "Correlation Between Mechanical and Stop-Watch Timing", based on the timing of 320 races, Graflund concluded that "stop watch times were consistently shorter than the mechanical times, by an average amount of .092 second" and that "the gain in time seems to be at the tape", where anticipation of the finish was faster than at the start. Of course, such conclusions refer only to the particular timers he used in his experiment and to their method of timing, but the same situation is occasionally present elsewhere.

For these reasons, timers cannot be correctly placed in stands away from the finish post, for they will then inevitably stop their watches too soon. It has been seriously suggested that all timers should wear old-fashioned horse blinders that would force them to see straight ahead only. They then would be as unready for the finish as they are for the starting flash of the gun. They would watch the runners approach to within 15 yards of the tape (note that same time lag here as between "Get set" and "Go" at the start), then turn their eyes exclusively on the finish line. Only such timing should produce legitimate records.

In passing, it may be of value to cite the case of Professor Philip Diamond of the University of Michigan, who as head timer at Michigan track meets for over 20 years has insisted upon just such an approach to the job of timing. His timers have all been hand-picked and carefully trained at practice time trials as well as in meets. No, they do not wear blinders, but Diamond insists upon a procedure just as effective. "Watch for that back foot", he admonishes; "see it cross the finish line, then press the old forefinger. If a new record shows on the watch dial, you can be sure the former record holder was given a fair deal". It was Diamond and Diamond-trained men who timed Jesse Owens" fast :09.4.

Quite obvious, and yet often neglected, is the fact that any timer is only as accurate as the watch he is using. The stop watch is an even more delicate machine than an ordinary timepiece and requires the greatest of care if it is to maintain its accuracy. Synchronization of watches by an official watch repairman who understands stop watch will provide immediate correctness, but a little careless handling will soon remove it. A watch swinging heedlessly from a chain or being taped "just a little" to make it start is a source of actual pain to a man who takes pride in his timing. A good timer will know his own watch as a garage man knows his own car. He knows it also has to be warmed up a little before doing its best work. He knows that when wound very tightly, it gains just a little, or when allowed to run too long without winding, it loses. He knows that a vertical or horizontal position while it is running makes a slight variation in the time for a mile or two-mile run. And, above all, he knows that being able to sign that record certificate intelligently and with a clear conscience is more important than signing it at all.

STARTING

In similar although augmented fashion, reaction time and training are essential to good starting. In starting, however, quickness rather than consistency of reaction is primarily important. Unless the starter is "on edge", so to speak, and unless there is a little adrenalin circulating through his own system when he calls the men to their marks, he can hardly hope to get them away together and within the limits of their reaction times to the sound of the gun.

The job of a starter is not merely to see that no one moves before the gun fires. Actually, no one can move legitimately until more than 0.1 second after the gun sounds. Studies of reaction times in sprint starting are few but conclusive on this point. The time for human reaction to a hearing stimulus has been established as from 0.110 to 0.182 second. Actually, since sprinters are a highly select group in terms of muscular quickness, the range within a group of sprinters is very much less than this. It can therefore be assumed that any man who has a lead of more than a single foot on the field in the first yard of the race has actually anticipated the gun and has gained an illegal start. Starters constantly excuse a "flyer" on the grounds that he did not move a muscle before the gun; but that is not the only requirement.

Further, a good starter should rarely fire the gun when one or more men have broken from their "set" positions. Such men should rightly have one "break" against them; but, according to the rules, if the gun is fired as they go out, the entire start is cancelled. As soon as sprinters realize that the gun undoubtedly will be fired, even on a "break", they begin to gamble and to attempt to outguess the starter. For the starter to be able to withhold his fire despite the movement before him requires a careful study of right methods, complete relaxation, instantaneous reaction and constant practice. When consideration is given to the endless time and care and tremendous energy that sprinters and coaches put into perfecting their skills, it seems clear that the games committee has a special obligation to procure a starter who knows the job and does it at least as well as the sprinters do theirs.

The many aspects of the job of starting require more detailed discussion:

1. The Starter's Responsibility

It is the sole responsibility of the starter to get the runners out of their blocks together, within the range and the limits of their reaction times to the sound of the gun. He has complete jurisdiction over the situation and his decisions cannot be revoked by any other official. Further, it is his obligation to aid all starters in every way possible to do their best work. There is no rivalry between starter and athletes to see which can get the better of the other. On the contrary, he should make it clear before the competition ever begins that his job is to help them, that he will be firm in enforcing the rules of the game, and that his methods will be completely dependable and as fair as he can make them. Such an approach is a part of this entire discussion.

2. Preliminary Instructions

Without wasting a single moment of time, the starter should put the men as much at their ease as possible by a few quick explanations of his method. The men are of course in a state of high nervous tension. They wish to know exactly what is to be done but certainly are impatient with long-winded admonitions, even though these are entirely well intentioned. All starting blocks should be firmly and correctly placed and preliminary warm-up starts taken, without the aid of the starter's gun, of course.

Large meets may call for special instructions, and these should be given by the starter. Such information as the following may be desirable :—

"This is the first heat of the 100-yard dash. Two men in each heat qualify for the final". Or, "This is the final of the 100-yard dash; six men running, five men to place".

Or, "We are running in lanes all the way". Or, "There are no lanes in this race. If you cut across the pole lane, be sure you are not impeding the progress of anyone. There are inspectors at all points of the track".

Once these preliminaries are over and an "all-clear" response is secured from the finish judges and starters, the men should be instructed to remove their sweat clothes. The starter is responsible for seeing that this and other adjustment of personal equipment are done together and that no one delays the start by last-minute changes. A few men are certain to be slower than the others—slower to report, slower to get their blocks in pace, slower to make all necessary preparations. Such methods are sometimes characteristic of the athlete; sometimes they are part of a deliberate plan on his part to upset the poise of the other runners. In either case, the starter can give them little consideration. Spectators and other competitors demand conformity to a set procedure.

The starter will now take a position where he can view all aspects of the start clearly and where he can be seen by the official timers. Almost all starters move just to the left or right of the track and about 15 feet ahead of the starting line. A few men remain on the line, and Franz Miller, the excellent German starter at the 1932 and 1936 Olympic games, stood 12 to 15 feet behind the line. Being in front seems to have the advantage, however, of catching any movement before the gun as well as of identifying the offender afterwards.

The arm holding the gun is raised vertically. A bright-coloured hat, or even just a single sleeve or jacket, worn by the starter will aid the timers. The starter's eyes are now focused not at any one or more of the men but at a spot in the centre of the track about 6 feet in front of the line. His attention is upon the entire field of vision rather than on any one point in it. Thus he will be aware of all movement and yet will not be unduly affected, at least to the point of pulling the gun trigger, by any one action.

The hand holding the gun is completely relaxed with no pressure at all on the trigger finger. Such relaxation also aids the starter in maintaining control. Firing the gun is achieved by suddenly contracting all the muscles of the hand.

3. "Take Your Marks"

The researchers have found it worth while to use a preliminary phrase to alert everyone when all is ready. "All right, we're ready now", or "now, boys" will warn those who need extra time to get on their marks or hurry those who may be adjusting shirt tails. Almost immediately there follows the command. "Take your marks". There is no limit in the rule books for the time between this command and "Get set". Each man should be allowed sufficient time to adjust himself properly, physically and mentally, and yet not so much as to be unfair to other competitors. If one or more competitors are having difficulty with their blocks or other equipment, all the men should be brought to their feet by the command of "Stand up", or simply, "up, come up".

4. "Get Set"

When all seem ready, the starter calls out loudly but not sharply, "Get se-e-et" or "Se-e-et". His tone of voice will influence the manner in which the men proceed. A sharp, quick, and loud "Set" will almost scare them into popping up. However, since he intends to wait a full 2 seconds in accordance with the rules, he should suggest steadiness and poise by a clearly heard yet calm commands.

5. "Go"

The rules state that at least 2 seconds shall elapse between "Get set" and "Go". This is not an absolute time requirement, but rather is a guide by which the starter can judge his timing. Under no circumstances should this period be less than 1½ seconds. Yes, he can often "get away with" such a tactic in any given race, but immediately the word will travel rapidly around, "Better watch that starter from now on. He fired it fast that last time and you'd better be ready for anything". The entire atmosphere of calm and confidence has been destroyed and nothing the starter can now do will restore it.

Two seconds is a long time under such tense condition. It is a definite strain upon everyone concerned and some starters are inclined to argue that any time after .5 second is quite all right. However, the moment such fast starting is used, men will begin to "guess the gun" and gamble on getting away.

It is the practice that has produced the unfortunate situation that occurs almost annually in the big indoor meets, where over a dozen attempts to get the men away together have failed and where starters have resigned their positions because meet managers have refused their right to disqualify men from the race for false starting. Coaches with well-trained men should refuse to permit their sprinters to compete at all under such conditions.

If anyone moves or is off balance before the gun is fired, the starter should quickly call everyone to his feet and begin again. If any have touched the ground or the starting line, one "false start" shall be called against them. Men must hold their positions until the starter calls, "Come up", or they are liable to penalty.

Common practice, however, is to penalize only the man who broke first or those who broke instantly with him. The importance of calling "Come up" instantly is therefore apparent. If the gun is fired, no penalty can be called upon anyone.

After his second false start, a man is disqualified from the race. This is a heavy penalty, especially in important meets, and good starters do what they can to avoid it. Yet if the over-all approach has been as here suggested, and careful consideration has been given to being fair and consistent with everyone, the starter should face his decision with a clear conscience and meet the frequently hot-headed coach with calmness and assurance.

CHAPTER 15

IMPORTANCE OF RELAY RACING IN SPRINTING

Relay racing has been part of man's culture since the dawn of history. However, the distance to be run and the type of exchanges used have varied. Only recently have the distances been standardized and the baton become the usual exchange device.

In some sections of the country and at certain times of the year, relay events are the main attraction on the track schedule. Some of the various types of relays are sprint (440, 880, 1 mile), sprint and distance medleys, 2-mile, 4-mile, and shuttle hurdle. The 440 and 1-mile relays are the events scheduled in most dual meets, and are on the program at the national, international and Olympic Games levels of competition.

In the 1968 Olympics, the 400-meter relay world record of :38.6 was tied or broken four times prior to the finals. The final race was, without question, the greatest 400-meter relay race ever run, as the first five teams all tied or broke the world record. The United States led the contest with outstanding performances from Charlie Greene, Mel Pender, Ronnie Ray Smith, and Jim Hines in the unbelievable time of :38.2. They were followed by Cuba in :38.35, France in :38.4, Jamaica in :38.4, and

East Germany in :38.6. The 1968 Olympic team composed of Vince Matthews (:45.0), Ron Freeman (:43.2). Larry James (:43.8), and Lee Evans (:44.4) ran an astounding 2:56.1 in the 1600- meter relay.

This was a new Olympic and world record. Kenya's team tied the former Olympic and world record with most respectable 2:59.0. The United States team members were never pressed, and ran for the most part 10 to 20 yards in front of the nearest competition, with each team member averaging :44.025 per 40 meters.

Relay racing constitutes a phase of running and/or sprinting. (The sprints include up to the 440-yard dash being run by each runner. For example, the mile relay involves 4 quarter-mile sprinters). The sprint relays require real baton passing skills, while the distance relays are more dependent upon the running ability of the anchor man.

THE SPRINT RELAYS

The sprint relays are the fastest and the most dependent on good baton exchange of all types of relay racing. Fast sprint relay time is made possible by correct baton passing. A relay team composed of good, but not great, sprinters may win a sprint relay race almost solely because of superior ability in baton passing.

The baton must be passed from one sprinter to another within the specified 20-meter passing zone. (There are markers placed 10 meters to either side of the end of each 110 yards of a 440-yard relay; at the end of each 220 of the 880-yard relay; at the end of each 440 of a 1-mile relay; and so on). In the 440-and 880-yard relays, the outgoing runners may, in addition, start outside of the exchange zone or more than 10 meters (11 yards) as a leadup to the regular passing zone. This starting point must be marked outside of the track. However, the exchange of the baton must take place within the passing zone. In the other relays, the outgoing runner must always start inside the exchange zone, and also complete the pass within the prescribed 20-meter distance.

The sprinters in the 440 and 880 relay races should pass the baton to one another at top speed. This means that the baton is usually passed near the end of the 20-meter zone so that the receiving member may be running his fastest. He will often have been running about 25 to 28 meters when he receives the baton. However, some coaches wish the pass to be made at the end of 10 meters to reduce the possibility of fouling.

The first man to run for the sprint relay team is usually the best or second best sprinter on the team. This leadoff man must be fast enough to keep up with the other runners, and should probably be the fastest starter on the team. He starts from the blocks as a sprinter does and holds the baton in his hand in such a manner that he is able to support his weight on his fingers and still keep the baton between his thumb and the fleshy part of the hand supported by the little finger. Some runners prefer to grasp the baton with the two middle fingers and support their weight in the set position with the little finger, forefinger, and thumb.

Another method is to hold the baton with the last two fingers and held support the weight with the thumb and first two fingers. The baton should be grasped toward the rear so that over half of it extends beyond the front part of the hand.

The second runner is usually the slowest sprinter, but one who has enough speed for the relay team to remain in contention after he finishes his portion of the relay.

The third man is the third best sprinter on the team. He should make up any loss has occurred when the second man ran, or at least not lost any distance, so that the anchor man is not placed at too great a disadvantage.

The anchor man is either the best or second best sprinter on the team and the strongest competitor.

In the 440-yard relay, the men's abilities to run the curve may affect the order in which they run, since two or three of them will run on the curves. This is also true in the 880-yard relay. The lane assigned to the team may also become a factor in determining the order of running.

Runners in the 440-yard and 880-yard relays use what is commonly referred to as a blind or nonvisual pass (baton exchange). The responsibility for the success of this pass falls on both runners, but the major burden lies with the incoming runner. He must hit the target (hand) perfectly the first time.

Thus, the four runners must spend hours practicing exchange of the baton with one another. They must come to know each other so well that they become a smooth-running unit. The outgoing runner's responsibility is to present a perfect target, and also to start running at precisely the right moment.

Establishment of the proper takeoff spot for the receiving runner requires that the runners work with one another until an exchange is made with both runners running at top speed. The takeoff spot for the receiver is usually 6 to 10 yards away from the first restraining line. When the incoming runner hits this mark, the outgoing runner, who has assumed a crouched sprinter's start, starts his sprint. The outgoing runner's sole purpose is to accelerate as fast as possible before the incoming runner reaches him.

He must sprint, pumping with both arms, for a distance of 10 to 15 yards, then he extends his hand to the rear in order to receive the baton from the incoming runner. If the members of the team have worked together for a considerable time practicing the exchange, the rear hand of the outgoing runner should reach its position just as the baton is placed in it. This, of course, is an ideal situation, but the runners must work toward making a perfect pass.

In the mile relay the same general order of running is used. The 4 quarter-milers, however, finish slower and more tired than do men increases as the distance becomes longer.

Thus, a good anchor man is vital in the distance relays, in which some coaches place the slowest man at the start and move on up to the fastest as anchor man. This idea could be used even in the mile relay if the runners were temperamentally constituted to run their best when behind.

The order of the men running the medley relay is dictated by the distance each man runs. Each man is selected for his ability to run a specific distance. In the sprint medley relay the following distances are run: 220 yards (first to leadoff man), 220 yards (second man), 440 yards relay the distances are: 440 yards (first or leadoff man), 880 yards (second man), 1,320 yards (third man), and 1 mile (anchor man). In the 480 shuttle high hurdle race the men are usually selected to run in the same order as in the sprint relays.

With the advent of the additional 10-meters starting leadup area in the sprint relays, a number of changes came about in the methods used in the exchanging of the baton. Although the old left to right hand exchange is still used in the longer relays and by some coaches, it was not thought fast enough by some world authorities. The changing of the baton from the right hand of the incoming runner to the left hand of the outgoing runner had a tendency to cause other problems which resulted in loss of speed. Now the right to left and left to right method is most commonly used. The leadoff man starts with the baton in his right hand and keeps it there for his portion of the race. As he approaches the second runner, he utilizes his speed to advantage and runs on the inside portion of the curve. The second man starts on the outside of the land, where he has a less tight during his leg of the relay. The third man takes the baton in his right hand and keep it there during his running section.

The fourth man takes the baton in his left hand for the same reason as the number 2 runner. It is believed that adoption of the additional runway area caused the teams to develop this different method of exchanging the baton.

While there are many accepted methods of passing the baton, the one recommended for use (in accordance with the above passing method). The exchange is fast, and the baton is in the proper position for the next exchange to be made without moving it from one hand to the other after it is received.

In the 480-yard shuttle high hurdle race, no baton is exchanged. A restraining line is placed 1 yard in front of the starting line. When the individual who is hurdling crosses this line with any part of his body, his teammate may start running and hurdling his portion of the race.

DISTANCE RELAYS

In a relay race run a distance longer than 220 yards, the method used to exchange the baton is somewhat different from that presented for the sprint relays. The type of pass used in these races is referred to as an open or visual pass. The major responsibility in executing the visual pass rests with the outgoing runner. Here, as in the sprint relays, practice is essential, as the runners must know one another extremely well. The incoming runner concentrates on his running and on getting the baton to the outgoing runner. The outgoing runner, after taking the baton from the incoming runner, starts on his leg of the relay. The outgoing runner must gauge the speed as well as the physical condition of the incoming runner. He must be able to recognize any sign of fatigue displayed by the incoming runner in order not to leave too soon or too fast on his leg of the race.

Many distance relay teams are now utilizing a semivisual pass which is very similar to the sprint pass. In this method, the outgoing runner watches the incoming runner very closely. If the latter is running strongly, the receiver will turn and run with his hand back in anticipation of receiving the pass. He does not leave as quickly as he might in the sprint relay race, but he does accelerate at about ¾ speed. The incoming runner thus must "charge" into the passing zone. Many runners make the mistake of decelerating as they approach the exchange zone, thinking that their portion of the race is over. When using this later method of exchange, deceleration by the incoming runner would be disastrous.

SUMMARY AND FURTHER SUGGESTIONS

1. In sprint relays (including the mile), the speed of the baton exchange is very important.
2. The runners should hold the baton firmly, but not tightly.
3. The baton must be exchanged within a 20-meter zone. A midline is placed at 10 meters to enable the runners to judge their location in the zone.
4. In the 440-yard and 880-yard sprint relays, the second, third, and fourth runners may assume a

position to begin their portion of the race not more than 10 meters outside of the starting zone.

5. If the incoming runner runs past his receiver after the exchange, the receiver has failed to start running soon enough, and tenths of seconds have been lost. Conversely, the receiver must be careful not to start too soon and run away from his teammate. The incoming runner's speed at the time of the exchange should be equal to that of the outgoing runner.
6. In the sprint relays, excepting the mile, almost the full passing zone should be used, so that the receiver has time to gain speed. A great deal of practice will be necessary in order that the runners know one another's speed and movements well.
7. In the sprint relays, excepting the mile, it is the responsibility of the incoming runner to see that the baton is exchanged accurately and firmly. However, the receiver, after running 10 to 15 yards and then extending his arms to the rear, should not move his arm up and down, thereby making a poor target for the incoming runner.
8. The incoming runner should deliver the baton in the mile relay and longer distances with his left hand to the right hand of the receiver. (In the sprint relays, using the new method, it is right to left, left to right, and right to left)
9. Runners in the mile relay and long distances should, after receiving the baton with the right hand, shift it immediately to the left hand. This is done in the first two or three strides. However, the anchor man need not shift the baton from his right to left hand.
10. Before taking off, the receiver in the 440-yard sprint relay should let the incoming runner be farther

from the restraining line than would the receiver in the 880-yard relay. This spot is usually about 7½ yards for the 440 and 6½ yards for the 880-yard relay men; the distance generally diminishes as the distance of the relay increases. The speed of the incoming runner helps determine the exact distance, especially in the case of the longer relays.

11. The usual baton exchange method used in sprint relays, excluding the mile, is known as the nonvisual or blind type. Runners in the mile or longer relay usually use a visual type of exchange.
12. The extended hand to the rear (palm up) position appears to the fastest method of exchanging in short sprint relays.
13. In the short relays, the receiver watches the incoming man until he reaches a designated spot, and thereafter must not look back. Many runners have a signal that they use when the incoming man delivers the baton—the incoming runner yells "go" or some similar expression. Many coaches consider this a dangerous habit, especially when there may be many runners yelling commands which could confuse the outgoing runner. Practice on the fundamentals of passing and confidence in one another's abilities will help eliminate the need for the use of commands during the exchange.
14. Almost all sprint relays are run in lanes throughout the entire race. In such a case, the incoming man, after passing the baton, must be careful to jog along only in his lane. If he moves out of his lane before all runners have finished their portion of the relay race, he may cause slower runners to spill. As a result, his team would be disqualified.
15. In relay races in which the runner cuts to the pole

after a designated distance, a fast starter should almost always be used as leadoff man.

16. The usual order of running in the sprint relays is second fastest runner first, slowest runner second, third fastest third, and fastest runner last or anchor.

17. In the longer distance relays in which lanes are not used for all runners, the position of the receiving runner in the exchange zone is sometimes determined by the position of the passing runner as he comes off the turn into the straightaway. The team in first place gets lane 1, the second place team lane 2, and so on, until all team are placed.

18. In the sprint medley (220 yards, 440 yards, 880 yards), both nonvisual and visual types of exchanges are often used. To utilize the speed of the shorter distance runners, it is wise to start the 440 and 880 runners at the midpoint of the exchange zone; the runner who is running the longeı distance will then run 10 meters less than if he uses the total exchange zone.

19. The type of exchange indicated in 18 can also be utilized to great advantage in the distance medley—440 yards. 880 yards, 1,320 yards, 1 mile. The man running the shorter distance does not make his exchange to the outgoing runner until he is in the latter part of the exchange zone.

The training program prescribed for the various relay runners is dictated by the distance they will run in the relay. That is, sprint relay runners will practice sprinting and distance relay runners will practice distance running.

CHAPTER 16

IMPORTANT COMPONENTS OF SPRINTING

STRENGTH

Strength is a conditional ability, i.e., it depends largely on the energy liberation processes in the muscles. Strength is also perhaps the most important motor ability in sports as it is a direct product of muscle contractions. All movement in sports are caused by muscle contractions and, therefore, strength is a part and parcel of all motor abilities, technical skills and tactical actions. Strength and strength training, therefore, assume high importance for achieving good performance in all sports. The role of strength training for achieving good performance in all sports. The role of strength training for general health, good posture and for prevention of injuries is usually overlooked which in the long run can prove harmful. Zimmermann has very rightly pointed out the positive effects of strength training on muscles, bones, joints, heart, circulatory system, metabolism and nervous system.

Strength is the ability to overcome resistance or to act against resistance. Strength should not be considered a product of only muscular contractions. It is, in fact, a product of voluntary muscle contractions caused by the neuro-muscular system.

In sports movements, strength always appears in some combination with the duration and speed of movement i.e., in combination with endurance and speed abilities. In each sports movement strength appears in a different form. When we attempt to generalise the forms in which strength finds expression in movements, the strength ability can be divided into three types described below :—

a. Maximum Strength

It is the ability to overcome or to act against maximal resistance. It is measured by finding out the maximum resistance which can be overcome or the maximum force which can be applied by the muscles. The maximum strength is a motor ability and involves force application during a voluntary movement. The muscles normally are capable of generating higher magnitudes of force if stimulated electrically. The electrical stimulation causes maximal contraction of all motor units in a muscle which normally cannot be achieved voluntarily except under extreme emotional state of fear, anger etc. The force values achieved through electrical stimulation are indicators of biological capacity of the neuro-muscular system for strength application. It is called absolute strength. Maximum strength is not important in majority of the sports.

It is important only in those sports in which very heavy resistances have to be tackled e.g., weight lifting, throws, etc. In many sports, however, there are phases of movement when the muscles, must apply maximal or near maximal force e.g., cross position on roman rings, start and acceleration phase in sprints, take off in jumps. In such sports maximum strength is important. The importance of maximum strength lies in the fact that in majority of the sports as the basis for good explosive strength and strength endurance.

b. Explosive Strength

It is a combination of strength and speed abilities. It can be defined as the ability to overcome resistance with high speed. Depending on the nature of combination of strength and speed the explosive, strength can be further sub-divided into start strength, strength speed (power) and speed strength.

Start strength, is the ability to develop maximal muscle force during the starting phase of the movement e.g., sprint start, weight lifting etc. Strength speed is the ability to overcome heavy resistances with high speed e.g., throws, jumps, etc. Speed strength is the ability to overcome lower resistances with high speed e.g., team games, combat sports (lower weight categories). The explosive strength is of different nature in cyclic and acyclic movements (e.g., power).

Explosive strength always finds expression in motor movements, i.e., it is a form of dynamic strength. Explosive strength performances, are markedly influenced by the level of motor co-ordination required for a movement e.g., inter and intra muscular co-ordination.

As a result explosive strength is highly specific to the nature of a movement and for its development of specific movements (or part of these movements) have to be used as exercises. A high percentage of movements in sports is of explosive nature and involves overcoming of some external resistance or of one's own body weight. Explosive strength, therefore, is important in most of the sports. Even in endurance sports, explosive strength is important for start as well as for "spurt" phases.

c. Strength Edurance

Like explosive strength it is also a product of two motor abilities. It is the ability to overcome resistance or to act against resistance under conditions of fatigue. Strength endurance can be a form of static or dynamic strength depending on the fact whether the movement is static (iso-metric) or dynamic (iso-tonic). Depending on the nature of the combination of strength and endurance the strength endurance can be further classified into proper strength and endurance strength.

Strength endurance is the ability of overcome high resistance or to act against high resistance under conditions of fatigue e.g., in combat sports, long duration events requiring strength e.g., Pole Vault. Endurance strength is needed for activities in which low resistances are to be tackled e.g., swimming, road cycling etc. In all sports movements, whether fast or slow, movements have to be done under lesser or higher conditions of fatigue. Even for sprints some amount of strength endurance is required in the last phase or in heats.

Strength endurance, therefore, is important in most of the sports. In sports, depending on the nature of movements the above mentioned strength abilities can appear in complex form. In weight lifting and throws the strength required is a combination of maximum strength and explosive strength. This combination is also known as power. In Volleyball explosive strength appears in combination with strength edurance and is popularly referred to as power endurance. In sports where maximal resistances are to be tackled under fatigue conditions the strength required is a combination of maximum strength and strength endurance.

In sports in addition to the above mentioned terms of strength, there are some more terms which are used. These are briefly described below :—

Static Strength

It is the ability to act against resistance. It is also called iso-metric strength.

Dynamic Strength

It is the ability of overcome resistance. It is also known by the name of iostonic strength.

Relative Strength

It is not a strength ability. It is simply a ratio which we get by dividing maximum strength with body weight. In several sports the strength ability of a sportsman can be assessed better. If it is considered in relation to his body weight. This is relevant in sports in which during the competition the main resistance to be overcome is the body weight of the sportsman e.g., gymnastics, jumps, weight category sports like weight lifting and wrestling.

The aim of strength training in these sports is to improve the relative strength either by reducing body weight or by increasing the maximum strength without increasing the body weight. The relative strength has a distinct relationship with body weight:higher the body weight lower is the relative strength.

General Strength

It is also not a separate strength ability. It is understood to be a complex product of all strength abilities needed for satisfactory tackling of normal resistances in sports. It is impossible to define general strength. This term, however, in general usage means general ability to tackle resistances not specific to any sport. It is also understood to be overall body strength generally needed for training and sports competitions.

Special Strength

It is the ability to tackle resistance in a particular

sport. It is not a strength ability in itself. It can be any strength ability (maximum strength or explosive strength or strength endurance) required for a specific sport. The special strength in weight lifting is maximum strength. Similarly, special strength in long jump is explosive strength.

FACTORS DETERMINING STRENGTH

Strength is a highly trainable motor ability. Before taking up a discussion of the means and methods for improving strength, it is essential to know the factors on which strength depends. This will help us in understanding the nature of strength as well as the proper and effective formulation of strength training. The important factors which determine strength are given below :—

(A) Muscle Cross Section

The muscle cross section indicates the size of the muscle. It is an accepted fact that bigger and larger muscles can generate more force. The force which can be generated by one square centimetre of muscle ranges from about 6-10 kp. This is nearly the same in males and females. Men, however, are stronger because they have much larger muscle mass as compared to women. Strength can be increased by increasing the muscle cross section (hypertrophy) through appropriate means and methods of strength training. In women high muscle hypertrophy is not possible due to the lower level of male sex hormones. The misconception that women will get big muscles due to strength training, therefore, is not scientifically tenable.

(B) Muscle Fibre Spectrum

The muscles consist of muscle fibres which are basically of two type: fast twitch fibres (white fibres) and slow twitch fibres (red fibres). The fast twitch fibres can contract faster and can produce more force. On the contrary for a longer duration. The fast which have a high percentage of fast twitch muscle fibres, therefore, can produce more strength. The size of such muscles can also be considerably increased through strength training.

The proportion of these two types of muscle fibres is largely strength training. The proportion of these two types of muscle fibres is largely genetically determined and can not be changed through training or by some other means. The muscle fibre spectrum, however, has a wide range of variation from muscle to muscle and from individual to individual. The persons who have muscles with favourable muscle fibre spectrum, therefore, have better strength ability and trainability for strength.

(C) Co-ordination

The level of strength is markedly affected by co-ordination. The role of co-ordination in strength performance can be discussed from the three levels of co-ordination involved in tackling or overcoming a resistance.

(i) Skill:— The process of overcoming or acting against resistance involves some type of movement involving muscles of more than one body part. The best results are achieved if this movement is done skilfully. The skill can be acquired through motor learning and as a result the strength performance can be improved. The role of technical skill in strength performance is one of the main topics of interest of sports bio-mechanics.

(ii) Inter muscular co-ordination:—The inter muscular co-ordination refers to the proper temporal and dynamic co-ordination between different muscles and muscle groups (muscle synergy) which are contracting to overcome or tackle a resistance. Good co-ordination at this level makes is possible to achieve the summation of individual forces generated by different muscles thus resulting in a higher resultant force.

(iii) Intra-muscular co-ordination:—The intra muscular co-ordination refers to the co-ordination among different motor units within a muscle. A muscle can contract with greater force if all the contracting motor units (whether slow twitch or fast twitch motor units) contract in a manner which enables greater force production.

The improvement in co-ordination is the second most effective means of improving strength. The added advantage here is less increase in muscle size for achieving higher strength performance. Hence in sports where strength improvement without any appreciable increase in body weight is desirable the strength improvement should aim at the improvement of co-ordination. The inter and intra muscular co-ordination is beyond conscious control of humans but can be significantly improved by using appropriate methods of strength training.

(D) Energy Supply

The ultimate source for muscle contraction is the rate and amount of energy supply through chemical reactions taking place in the muscles.

The energy for muscle contraction is primarily obtained through the break down of phosphogens (ATP and CP). The amount of phosphogen stores is, therefore, important for strength performance or tackling resistances with high speed. However, the speed with which the energy can be supplied is of crucial importance. The rate and amount of energy supply can be improved through training.

(E) Body Weight

It is generally known that heavier persons are stronger than lighter persons. This is particularly true in case of trained sportsmen. The positive relationship between body weight and strength can be partly explained by the larger muscle mass of bigger and heavier persons. The other reasons for complete understanding of this relationship, however, are not clear. Perhaps greater mass of bones, connective tissues, and, possibly also, fat tissues is essential to support large muscles. All this results in more body weight.

(F) Psychic Factors

Certain psychic factors like motivation, arousal, emotions of anger, aggression etc., have a marked affect on strength performance. It has been proved that psychic factors limit the individual's capacity to fully utilise his strength capacity or potential. A fully aroused state of mind with the determination to apply maximum force results in a very strong nerve impulse leading to activation of larger number of motor units. The trained sportsmen are able to push their psychological limits to a significant extent.

Strength is also influenced to a lesser or greater extent by the following factors :—

Physique and Constitution

The length of the muscle at the time of contraction.

Strength and stability of the musculo-skeletal system.

Bio-mechanical factors like leverage and angle of pull.

IMPROVEMENT OF STRENGTH

The training for improvement of strength is an important part of training for all sports. This is discussed under the following four points :—

(a) Physical exercises.

(b) Types of muscle contraction.

(c) Methods of strength training.

(d) Organisation of strength training.

Physical Exercises

Different types of physical exercises are used with or without additional resistance to improve and maintain strength. These exercises can be broadly divided into two groups :—

1. Physical Exercises With Additional Resistance

These exercises form the principal means for the improvement and maintenance of strength. Most commonly used and most effective exercises with additional resistance are the weight training exercises. These exercises are done with additional weights e.g., barbel, dumbbell, iron shoes, cattleball and so on. These exercises are very effective for the improvement of maximum strength and explosive strength. The weight training exercises, however, are strenuous and require mastery of technique before these can be effectively used. Exercises with heavy weights are not advisable for children and beginners. These exercises with high resistance are also not of high importance in sports in which sportsman does not have to tackle high resistance.

In addition to weight training exercises there are other exercises with additional resistance which are quite effective for the development of explosive strength and strength endurance. These exercises, however, are not very effective for the development of maximum strength. These exercises can be divided into the following groups :—

Exercises with medicine balls, sand bags, bench etc.

Exercises with partner.

Exercises with elastic material e.g., chest expander, rubber tube etc.

Iso-metric exercises.

Exercises with environmental resistance e.g., sand, slope, wind, etc.

The above mentioned exercise can be done by sportsmen of all hues and ages. These do not require a high degree of skill and are more interesting as rich variation is possible. Exercises with partner or with medicine balls etc., are very effective for strength development of children and beginners. These are also very interesting and motivation for children especially combat type of partner exercises. The exercises with elastic material have their limitations as the nature of muscle contraction in such exercises is very different from the nature of muscle contraction during sports movement.

2. Physical Exercises With One's Own Body Weight As Resistance

There are innumerable exercises in which the body weight of the sportsman acts as resistance for improving the strength e.g., all types of jumps, wall bar exercises for strength, pull ups, rope climbing, sit ups etc. These exercises if properly done are very effective for improving explosive strength and strength endurance. In sports in which relative strength is important these exercises form the principal means of strength improvement. Most of these exercises can be done without any equipment. The load intensity in these exercises is automatically related to one's own body weight. In several sports and in cases where weight training equipment is not available the strength can be effectively developed through exercises with one's own body weight as resistance.

TYPES OF MUSCLE CONTRACTION

In sports movements the muscle contraction is of two types: static and dynamic. A third type is achieved by a combination of static as well as dynamic contraction.

Static Muscle Contraction

This is also called the iso-metric muscle contraction. In this type of muscle contraction there is no significant change in the length of the contracting muscle. As a result there is no external movement at the joint concerned. In sports there is movement of various limbs and body parts during a motor action, therefore, iso-metric or static contractions are not common types of muscle contraction in sports. But it must not be over looked that during a motor action certain body parts must be held statically to achieve proper body posture, balance etc. Hence certain muscle groups are always contracting iso-metrically while some other muscles are contracting dynamically to cause the movement with desired speed, force and amplitude.

Dynamic Muscle Contraction

This type of muscle contraction is also called iso-tonic or auxo-tonic muscle contraction. In this type of contraction the muscle lengthens or shortens. When during contraction the length of a muscle decreases it is called concentric contraction and when the length increases it is called eccentric contraction. Because of the shortening or lengthening of the muscle/muscles during dynamic contraction there is always a resultant movement at the concerned joint or joints.

In sports the dynamic muscle contractions are very common. But it is important to note that in majority of the cases the dynamic muscle contraction is a specific combination of concentric and eccentric contractions. The most common combination is eccentric-concetric contraction. This happens in all explosive movements like jumps, throws etc. In the initial phase of the movement (i.e., preparatory phase) the concerned muscles are stretched and then they contract explosively.

By abruptly stopping the stretching of a muscle initial force or tension is developed which is further increased by vigorous concentric contraction. The resultant force produced by a combination of eccentric and concentric contraction is considerably more than what can be produced by any other type of contraction. The concentric-eccentric type of muscle contraction is very rare in sports. It occurs when a resistance is moved to a certain point and is then slowly it is brought back as is the case in some movements in gymnastics.

COMBINATION OF DYNAMIC AND STATIC CONTRACTION

This type of muscle contraction is also not very common in sports. But in some sports like gymnastics we can see this type of contraction. For example, in assuming 'L' position on Romna rings or parallel bars the abdominal muscles first contract concentrically to bring the legs in the proper position. Then this position is maintained for the required duration by the static contraction of the abdominal muscles.

The gradual lowering of the legs from this position is made possible by the eccentric contraction of abdominal muscles. The combination of static contraction followed by dynamic (concentric or eccentric) is much more rare. From the above discussion about the type of muscle contraction it is clear that in sports as a rule the movements are caused by a specific combination of two or more types of muscle contraction. A pure static or dynamic contraction rarely occurs. While selecting exercises for the development of specific strength the type of muscle contraction should be used as a basic criterion.

It should also be kept in mind that during a sports movement, especially whole body movement, the various muscle groups of the body contract in one way or the other to make the movement execution correct and effective. In addition to the types of muscle contraction, the nature and magnitude of tension developed by the muscles during the movement is also important for correct selection of exercises for the development of specific strength.

METHODS OF STRENGTH IMPROVEMENT

(A) Maximum Strength

The methods used for the improvement of maximum strength are variations of repetition method. These methods can be classified according to the types of muscle contraction during the exercise.

I. Dynamic Concentric Method

In this method heavy resistances are overcome repeatedly. In order to overcome the resistance the muscles contract concentrically. Depending on the magnitude of load or resistance this method has two variations which are described below :—

(a) Maximal Resistance Method

In this method the resistance (intensity) is from 80-100% of the maximum. There are 1-10 repetitions in a set and total number of sets is 3-10. Complete recovery is given between the sets. The speed of movements is from smooth to explosive.

This method is very effective for improving the maximum strength. If the movements are done with speed then this method also leads to improvement in explosive strength. The maximal resistance method is very effective in improving the inter and intra-muscular co-ordination. It also results in significant hypertrophy of muscles.

(b) Sub-Maximal Resistance Method

This method is very effective for improving maximum strength and explosive strength at the same time. Due to sub-maximal resistances used this method does not lead to much hypertrophy of the muscles thereby not resulting in significant increase in body weight.

II. Dynamic Eccentric Method

In this method the muscles have to act against resistance by contracting eccentrically. It has the following variations :—

(a) Slow Eccentric Method

In this method the muscles are forced to contract eccentrically but with more than 100% of their force. The sportsman is required to gradually lower a resistance which is more than his maximum strength ability.

(b) Reactive Method

In this method the muscles are first made to stretch against resistance before contracting them maximally. This method is very effective for the development of maximum strength and explosive strength.

Jumpers and volleyball players have been using this method since long for the development of explosive strength. It is also called depth jumping. The sportsman stands on a bench or a box and then jumps down. Immediately after landing he jumps forward. At the time of landing due to the force of gravity the knee 'give in' a little causing the quadriceps muscles to stretch. But this 'give in' is only partial and is simply for absorbing the force of landing. This puts considerable tension on the quadriceps. From this bent position the sportsman now contracts the quadriceps maximally to jump up or forward.

For depth jumping the height of the box or bench should be from 40-120 cm. A higher height has not been found to be effective. The height, however, should be selected according to the strength ability of the sportsman. Stronger persons can use more height. Landing should be on toes trying not to let the heels touch the ground. Hartmann and Tunneman recommend that one must land with 120-140° knee angle and should 'give in' up to 90-100° as the optimum range of bending is 30-50°. They are also of the opinion that depth jumps with additional weights have not proved to be effective.

In depth jumping one should do 6-10 repetitions in each set with 5-8 minutes of rest in between. Total number of jumps in a training session should not be more than 50. For using reactive method for the muscles of trunk and upper extremities special equipment have to be designed which can enable stretching of muscles against resistance before maximal contraction. Verschosankij describes such a possibility with the concerned muscle to stretch.

The sportsman is supposed to react quickly by contracting his muscles explosively. The reactive method is a very strenuous method and hence can only be used with well conditioned sportsmen. For children and beginners, however, the mild form of reactive method can be used effectively e.g., continuous jumps on the ground.

III. Iso-Kinetic Method

This method was first introduced by J.J. Perrine in 1968. This method involves a special type of muscle contraction called iso-kinetic contraction. In iso-kinetic contraction the muscle applies maximal force throughout the range of movement. In iso-tonic contraction the muscle applies maximal force only at a particular angle of it's range of movement. The iso-kinetic contraction, however, is not a common type of muscle contraction in sports movements. This is a strong limitation of the iso-kinetic method. Specially designed machines are necessary for using iso-kinetic method for strength development. The speed of contraction can be adjusted according to the individual.

While doing the exercise the sportsman should consciously keep applying maximal force throughout the range of movement. By lowering or increasing the speed of contraction as well as by fixing the number of repetitions the iso-kinetic method can be effectively used for the development of maximum strength or explosive has been found to be effective for the improvement of maximum strength alongwith explosive strength.

The other load factors should be similar to the method of using maximal or sub-maximal resistance. The contribution of iso-kinetic method, because of non sport specific type of muscle contraction, to strength improvement and to performance improvement has yet to be scientifically investigated and proved. However, in water sports like swimming, rowing etc., this method has proved to be effective because in these sports the muscle contraction resembles iso-kinetic contraction.

IV. Static Method

In this method iso-metric exercises are used for the development of strength. Iso-metric contractions are mostly unspecific to sports movements. As a result the strength improved through iso-metric exercises is usually not of much value in sports. But inspite of this disadvantage iso-metric exercises have certain positive points and hence can be used for strength training. These exercises need less time and equipment and can be done practically anywhere. Moreover, iso-metric exercises can prove of great value for the maintenance of strength in case of injury or when other strength exercises cannot be performed.

The iso-metric exercises are very monotonous. These exercises, in the case of children and untrained persons, lead to the building up of 'compression effect' within the chest cavity during maximal exertion phase. This tends to stop or restrict the blood supply to and from the heart and lungs.

This can have harmful effect on children and untrained persons. Harre recommends limited use of iso-metric exercises for strength improvement. He suggests that these should be used as additional means of strength training and their volume should not exceed 10% of total strength training volume. To overcome the unwanted effect of iso-metric type of muscle contraction the iso-metric exercises should be combined with some movement or the muscle should be exercised iso-metrically at 3-4 angles of its range of movement. For better control of iso-metric exercises these should be done with known weights or equipments where the tension developed by the muscles can be easily known.

(B) Explosive Strength

Explosive strength, unlike maximum strength, is a highly specific motor ability. The explosive strength performance is always coupled with the specific load and movement structure of an exercise or motor action. As a result explosive strength is mainly developed through special and competition exercises.

The explosive strength performance depends largely on the muscle cross-section, contraction speed and intra-muscular co-ordination. As explosive strength is highly movement specific, therefore, the role of technique or skill should never be under estimated.

Depending on the magnitude of resistance and the specificity of movements the explosive strength has a different nature in different sports. In sports where high resistance are to be tackled the explosive strength depends markedly on maximum strength. In these sports, therefore, both these strength abilities have to be developed sequentially or parallely. An improvement in maximum strength automatically does not lead to an improvement in explosive strength. Special exercises are needed to ensure this conversion. It is, therefore, better if training for maximum and explosive strength is harmoniously combined.

Some methods, discussed for the improvement of maximum strength, are also very effective for the improvement of explosive strength. These methods are: method of sub-maximal loads, reaction method and iso-kinetic method. When using these methods for the improvement of explosive strength the following adjustments should be made :—

The magnitude of resistance should be selected according to the nature of sport.

Exercises resembling the competition activity should be used.

Stress during the exercise should be on speed of movement with proper movement execution.

In addition to the above mentioned methods for improving explosive strength the following two methods are also used :—

I. Using Special and Competition Exercises With Changed Resistance

Due to the specific nature of explosive strength this method is being used increasingly for improving explosive strength. This can take two directions (a) using resistance which is more than the resistance tackled during the competition. (b) Using resistance less than the resistance tackled in the competition. In the first variation the stress is on improving strength element and in the second variation the stress is on speed element.

The change in resistance, however, should be only so much that the load structure and movement structure of the competition movement does not change significantly. When using a special exercise the range of resistance which can be used is, however, larger. The application of this method is illustrated below with examples from some selected sports :—

(a) Various types of jumps with additional resistance e.g., weight jackets of 3-5% of body weight.

(b) Short sprints on slope with inclination of not more than 10%.

(c) Using heavier or lighter shot for putting the shot.

(d) Wrestling with a heavier or lighter partner or exercises with a dummy.

This method is also applied commonly in the form of a specific variation called contrast method. In this method an exercise is done alternately with higher and lower resistance. For shot put Kuznezov recommends the following variation : lighter shot (one throw): standard shot (two throws) the heavier shot (one throw).

II. Intensive Interval Method

This method can be effectively used for team and

combat sports. The exercises are special exercises which resemble partly with the structure of the competition activity. Scholish recommends the following load factors for this method when weight training exercises are to be used.

(C) Strength Endurance

Strength endurance can be classified as an endurance ability also. Like explosive strength it is also a complex motor ability and is the product of strength and endurance. Sports in which heavy resistances have to be tackled under conditions of fatigue the strength endurance depends considerably on maximum strength. But if the resistance to be tackled is less than 30% of the maximum strength then the strength endurance is not dependent on maximum strength.

Most of the methods for improvement of strength endurance are variations of interval method or continuous method. For better effect of strength endurance training either special or competition exercises are used with minor adjustments regarding resistance and duration/volume of training. As a rule the resistances used in training should approximately the resistance tackled in competition.

I. Extensive Interval Method

II. Intensive Interval Method

III. Use of Special Competition Exercise with Higher Resistance.

Strength endurance, like explosive strength, is a specific ability. Therefore, in the recent past there is an increase trend to use special and competition exercises with higher resistance for sufficiently longer periods for improving specific strength endurance. These exercises are done either according to the principles of interval method or continuous method. Some examples from selected sports are given below :—

(a) Sand running by long distance runner.

(b) Swimming against the current.

(c) Cycling against wind or with increased friction on the wheels.

(d) Playing on loose surface.

(e) Playing hockey with heavier sticks or with weight jackets.

(f) Wrestling or boxing with a heavier partner for a duration longer than that of a normal competition bout.

While using this method cares should be taken to ensure proper movement execution. The increased resistance should not result in significant change in the structure of the exercise. The total volume of training with these exercises should guarantee enough volume of training under high conditions of fatigue.

IV. Circuit Training

Circuit training has proved to be a very effective method for improving strength endurance. It offers rich variation of exercises and load structure.

STRENGTH TRAINING FOR MUSCLE HYPERTROPHY

In body building, and in some other sports also, strength training should result in high degree of muscle hypertrophy (i.e., increase in muscle size) or an increase in body weight.

It is a common and strong wish in boys and men to have large and well proportioned muscles. Some sportsmen, who are thin and lean, also require increase in body weight through increase in muscle mass. In sports, it is not advisable to achieve higher body weight by increasing boy fat. Moreover, due to genetic factors some individuals can never gain significant increases in body weight by increasing body fat. The only sensible and logical way of increasing body weight especially for sportspersons is by increasing muscle mass.

All types of strength training does not produce equal amount of muscle hypertrophy. The training methodology in this regard has been investigated and experimented by the body building experts. They have found that strength training with a certain type of load leads to best results. The actual mechanism of muscle hypertrophy is, however, still not clear. On the basis of a review of literature a theoretical concept regarding muscle hypertrophy is presented below :—

The stimulus for increasing in muscle size is given by an imbalance in break down and synthesis of ATP and other muscle proteins. This imbalance is caused when the muscles work at a particular speed for a sufficiently long duration. The muscles should contract against resistances which are 80-90% of the maximum.

The work phase should last for about 20-30 sec., in order to cause significant reduction in muscle ATP. Longer duration allows ATP re-synthesis through glycolyis or oxidation thus preventing acute shortage of ATP. The muscles, however, should contract or work at a speed which allows high rate of ATP splitting and should also lead to extreme exhaustion within the recommended duration of load phase. The acute low level of ATP is a stronger stimulus for muscle protein anabolism (i.e., build up) after the training activity, (i.e., during recovery).

The strength training for muscle hypertrophy has to be based on the theory explained above. As a result the strength training of body builders differs significantly from other sportsmen. Training for good and fast muscle hypertrophy is very strenuous and demanding.

It must be, however, stressed that the real effect is caused during the last few repetitions. Therefore, as a principle one should do as many repetitions as possible by forcing oneself. When he can no longer complete the movement himself then little external help is advisable to do another 2-3 repetitions.

This completely exhausts the concerned muscles and there are normally sensations of pain and discomfort. Such type of training, however, must be complemented with rich protein diet.

The training for muscle hypertrophy is also done for improving maximum and explosive strength hence it is advisable for all sports in which the performance depends significantly on these two abilities provided the increase in body weight is desirable.

ORGANISATION OF STRENGTH TRAINING

The organisation of strength training deals with actual process of doing strength training in a training session. It, basically, comprises of two things (a) Method of arrangement of strength exercises (b) loading procedure during a strength exercise.

A. Method of Arrangement of Exercises

This has three variations which are explained below:—

1. Station Training

This is the most common variation and is effective for the improvement of all strength abilities especially maximum strength and explosive strength. In station training the required number of repetitions and sets of an exercise are completed before starting the next exercise.

2. Set Training

This variation is suitable for developing strength

endurance. But it is also effective for improving maximum and explosive strength with an element of endurance. Two to three exercises are done in the form of a set. One set of each exercise is done in rotation before starting the next set.

In set training, if not otherwise required, the exercises for different muscle groups should be selected. This enables one to have shorter recovery periods thus reducing the total duration of exercise.

3. Circuit Training

It is a very popular and effective variation for the improvement of strength endurance. In circuit training several exercises are done one after the other. Completing of one set of each exercise in rotation is called one round. There are normally three or more rounds in circuit training. In circuit training there are generally 5-12 exercises. It can be done according to any of the three basic methods of conditioning. But, generally it is done according to continuous or interval method.

B. Loading Procedures

The loading procedures relate to the resistance and number of repetitions of a strength exercise. The important loading procedure are described below :—

1. Constant Resistance-Constant Repetitions

In this procedure an exercise is done with a fixed resistance and fixed number of repetitions in a set. It has two principal variations :—

(a) With low resistance

Here the resistance is generally from 40-60% of the maximum strength. The number of repetitions is large. It is good for parallel development of maximum strength and strength endurance, for example: 20×50%, 20×50%,

20×50%.

(b) With High Resistance

Here the resistance is high to maximal. The total number of repetitions is large but each set consists of only 2-4 repetitions. This procedure is good for the improvement of maximum strength without significant muscle hypertrophy. Example: 2×95%, 2×95%, 2×95%, 2×95%, 2×95%.

2. Increasing Resistance—Constant Repetitions

In this procedure the resistance is progressively increased from set to set but the number of repetitions is kept constant. This procedure is based on Delorme's principle. Delorme and Watkins suggested the following procedure:—

1st set of 10 repetitions with 50% of 10 RM.

2nd set of 10 repetitions with 75% of 10 RM.

3rd set of 10 repetitions with 100% of 10 RM.

10 RM is the maximum resistance with which 10 repetitions can be done. This procedure is very commonly used for rehabilitation purposes. It is also safe and effective when used for children and beginners. The variations of this procedure with more emphasis on higher number of repetitions with higher resistance are good for the development of maximum and explosive strength.

3. Changing Resistance—Changing Repetitions

In this procedure the resistance and number of repetitions change from set to set. It has two variations:—

(a) Progressive Procedure

The resistance increases from set to set while the number of repetitions decreases. When higher resistances are used this procedure is quite effective for the development of maximum strength. This procedure is also called pyramid training. Example: 5×80%, 4× 85%, 3×90%, 2×95%, 1×100%.

(b) Progressive-Regressive Procedure

Here in the first half the resistance is progressively increased while decreasing the repetitions. In the second half the resistance is gradually decreased while increasing the repetitions. This procedure when used with higher resistance is good for improving the maximum strength coupled with endurance.

For instance: 5×80%, 3×90%, 1×100%, 3×90%, 5×80%.

4. Decreasing Resistance-Constant Repetitions

This procedure is also called Oxford Method. Willmore has also described this procedure. In this procedure 100 repetitions of an exercise are done in sets of 10 repetitions. The first set is done with 10 RM and in the following sets the resistance is reduced proportitonately to enable the sportsman to do 10 repetitions. This method is good for parallel development of maximum strength and strength endurance. Due to the nature of load this procedure is also good for muscle hypertrophy.

5. Contrast Method

This procedure/method of strength training is described by Bachcevanow. In this procedure the sets are done alternately with high and low resistance e.g., 60%; 30%; 70%; 35%; 80%; 40%. The resistance is increased in steps over a period of weeks. According to Harre this method can be effectively used for parallel development of maximum strength and explosive strength.

The contrast method, however, can be done with another variation: 2-3 sets with higher resistance followed by 2-3 sets with 5-10% lower resistance.

RELATIONSHIP OF STRENGTH WITH OTHER PERFORMANCE FACTORS

Strength has important relationship with several performance factors. This knowledge is vital for proper and effective formulation of training of these performance factors. Relationship between strength and flexibility has always been a topic of interest. In the past it was wrongly understood that strength training will lead to decrease in flexibility.

But now it has been proved that strength training does not necessarily lead to deterioration of flexibility. Strength training causes higher muscle tone and leads to shortening of the muscle. But if strength training is properly supplemented with flexibility exercises then the flexibility can be effectively maintained. Hartmann and Tunnemann cite the example of champion weight lifters having excellent hip and ankle flexibility to prove this point. The flexibility exercises tend to lengthen the muscles, thereby causing some amount of loss of strength. It is, therefore, advisable to always go for some judicious combination of strength and flexibility exercises when improving either flexibility or strength.

Too much increase in muscle size, due to mechanical or physical obstruction (muscle boundness), can negatively affect the range of movement at certain joints e.g., shoulder, neck.

This effect can be countered by increasing the suppleness of the concerned muscles through stretching exercises. The relationship between strength (especially explosive strength) and speed is well-known. Speed performance can be improved rapidly by improving the explosive strength of the concerned muscle groups. A decrease in strength always has negative effect on speed performance.

Rapid increase in strength accompanied with increased muscle tone resulting in decreased flexibility can become problematic for good speed performance especially in cyclic sports. In addition to decrease in speed performance it can also lead to muscle injuries by disturbing the neuro-muscular co-ordination. This effect, however, can be effectively countered through flexibility exercises.

Speed training on the other hand can also lead to significant gains in strength especially of children and beginners e.g., short distance sprints with maximum intensity. The relationship of strength with endurance is usually not considered important; but it is necessary to know the strength training over long periods, without sufficient endurance training, can result in decrease in endurance performance. The reverse is also true. Endurance training for long periods, without sufficient strength training, leads to considerable loss of strength. This is due to the metabolic and structural changes which take place in the muscle fibres. Due to endurance training the muscles lose size.

The muscle fibres also adapt for endurance work. Both these factors lead to loss of strength. On the contrary by strength training the muscles gain in size and also adapt for work loads of short duration and high intensity, thereby, causing decrease in endurance. It is, therefore, necessary to take preventive steps to ensure maintenance of strength and endurance when training for either strength or endurance. Muscle contraction is the primary cause of movement.

Therefore, any change caused by strength training in the speed and force of muscle contraction tends to disturb the neuro-muscular co-ordination i.e., skill. This effect can be further aggravated by decreases in flexibility caused by strength training. The rapid increase in strength especially maximum or explosive strength always has negative effect on skill or co-ordination. This effect can be effectively tackled by first improving the strength to the desired level and then doing concentrated technique training for some days or weeks so that the higher level of strength is properly integrated into the skill by the co-ordinative process. Simultaneous development of strength and skill can solve the problem, but is not always possible due to limitations of time available as both these factors require high training volumes for their effective development.

EXERCISES FOR SPECIFIC STRENGTH

An exercise for strength training will result in the improvement of specific strength if the structure of the exercise is the same, or at least largely resembles, with that of the competition activity. The structure of an exercise has two aspects : load structure and movement structure. It would be ideal to use the competition activity itself with optimally higher resistance. But practical experience shows that the use of competition activity does not produce desirable results as the resistance in these exercises cannot be increased beyond a certain limit. Therefore, in training one has to use exercises which resemble competition movement.

It is important to know how an exercise should be selected for the improvement of specific strength. Verschosanski recommends that such an exercise must resemble the competition movement in at least five respect as given below :—

1. Amplitude and direction of movement.
2. Accentuated phase of movement amplitude.

3. Magnitude of strength application.

4. Speed with which the maximum force application is achieved.

5. Type and manner of muscle work.

For practical application the above mentioned five aspects are explained with examples as follows :—

1. Amplitude and Direction of Movement

The amplitude and direction of movement are part and parcel of the spatial or kinematic aspect of the movement (i.e., movement structure). The amplitude is the range through which a joint or body part moves. The direction of movement implies the direction, as well as the angle, in which the force is applied.

The bench press commonly used for strength development of shot putters is not a specific exercise for the improvement of specific strength. In Bench press the muscles apply force at a right angle to the trunk whereas in actual shot put the muscles apply force at approximately 42°.

From this aspect inclined bench press is more specific. Sprinters have been using knee lifts with iron shoes for the development of specific strength of hip flexors. But when this exercise is done from standing position the amplitude of movement is shorter as compared to that of the actual movement during sprint. It would be a specific strength exercise if the hip flexion can start from beyond the normal standing position. This can be done by lying supine on an inclined bench with the leg, to be exercised, hanging down. Such an exercise can also be done with the help of a partner who holds the leg from the ankle and stands behind the exercising sportsman. In this exercise the sportsman should start movement, against the resistance offered by the partner, from a semi extended hip position.

2. Accentuated Phase of Movement Amplitude

The magnitude of force application in different sports movements is different. But as a rule the maximum application of force takes place only in a certain phase of the total moment amplitude. This phase is called the accentuated phase of movement amplitude. In sports, majority of the movements are explosive in nature, i.e., are ballistic movements. In such movements the maximum application of force takes place in the initial phase of the movement.

Exercises with elastic materials e.g., rubber bands are not specific strength exercises for most of the sports because in these exercises the muscles have to apply force throughout the movement amplitude. The force application, in fact, increases with the movement. Similarly for swimmers exercises with weights are not specific strength exercises because in swimming the muscles apply force throughout the movement amplitude.

Magnitude of Strength Application

For the specific strength improvement the muscles must apply force which is slightly more than that during the competition activity or movement. The exercises with too much resistance leads to considerable changes in the structure of the exercise and as a result lose their effectiveness for specific strength improvement.

Strength exercises with too heavy implements are not effective for the improvement of specific strength, e.g., standing puts with 10Kg. shot, sprinting uphill with a slope of more than 10%, too heavy rackets etc. Similarly, efforts to improve specific strength by running or jumping with too heavy weight jackets is also not effective and purposeful. It is, however, important to note that the limit to how much resistance can be used in the exercise depends on the level of strength and skill of the sportsman. Strong and skillful persons can use comparatively higher resistances.

Speed of Achieving Maximum Force Application

Depending on the nature of movement the maximum force application is achieved after different time intervals in different movements. This can be effectively determined by electro-myography and bio-mechanical procedures. In ballistic or explosive movements the muscles develop tension very fast and achieve maximal values in the initial phase of the movement itself. Hence, for these sports, exercises of ballistic nature are suitable. But in sports in which the muscles develop tension gradually and rhythmically the exercises have to be specially designed to imitate this condition.

Type and Manner of Muscle Work

In sports the muscles contract in different ways to produce a variety of movements. It is rarely a pure iso-metric or pure iso-tonic muscle contractions. As a normal rule in sports the muscle contractions are combination of two or more types e.g., static-dynamic or eccentric-concentric muscle contractions. Moreover, in sports the movements are whole body movements which means that several muscle groups of the body are contracting simultaneously and one after the other to enable the proper execution of movement.

Therefore, while selecting an exercise for specific strength it is very important to ensure that the type and manner of muscle work during exercise must imitate or at least resemble with that of the competition movement.

In all jumping movements the muscles of hip, knee and ankle contract in eccentric-concentric manner. Therefore, for specific strength development jumps with resistance are more effective than simple squats. In some cyclic sports like swimming, cycling, rowing etc., the muscles contract rhythmically i.e., there are phases of high tension and low tension during muscle contraction.

For these sports exercises which make the muscles contract in a similar rhythm are, therefore, specific exercises for strength. It is important here to consider not only one or two major muscle groups involved in the movement but all the important muscle groups of the body which contribute to the successful execution of the movement.

SPEED

Speed, like strength and endurance, is a conditional ability. It has a complex nature as it depends to a considerable extent on the central nervous system. Due to this fact the exact nature of speed abilities is difficult to discover and understand. Moreover, because we can influence the functioning of central nervous system only to a very limited extent, therefore, speed performance can not be improved to considerable extent, therefore, speed performances can not be improved to considerable extent as is the case in strength and endurance.

Besides because of the high role of co-ordinative processes in a speed performance the improvement of speed has to be done with specific means and methods. Speed ability should not be equated with mechanical speed which is equal to the distance covered per unit of time. In several sports actions no distance is covered at all. Speed ability primarily signifies the ability to execute motor movements with high speed. These movements may be cyclic or acyclic in nature. Theiss and Schnabel give the following definition of speed :—

"It is the performance prerequisite to do motor actions under given conditions (movement task, external factors, individual prerequisites) in minimum of time". In spite of the complex and specific nature and low trainability speed ability is of high importance in all sports except sports.

Speed performances appear in different form in various sports. These have a different nature in cyclic sports as compared to acyclic sports. From general point of view we can have five type of speed abilities : reaction ability, movement speed, acceleration ability, locomotor ability and speed endurance. Reaction ability in reality, is not a speed ability as it depends entirely on co-ordinative processes. It is a co-ordinative ability.

But traditionally, it has been considered a speed ability and the training of reaction ability is, most of the time, inseparably linked with the training of movement speed. It is, therefore, being dealt with here along with the other speed abilities. Speed endurance is an endurance ability but training of speed endurance involves training of speed. Because of this reason it has also been included under speed abilities.

From the above discussion it becomes clear that there are only three speed abilities, i.e., movement speed, acceleration ability and locomotor ability. Some experts also name movement frequency as a separate speed ability. But movement frequency by it self can not be given the status of a speed ability. In several sports, especially cyclic sports, certain movement are repeatedly done at a high frequency but this frequency rarely reaches the maximum possible values.

Movement frequency, therefore, should be understood as an important prerequisite for acceleration ability and locomotor ability. A short explanation of the above mentioned five speed abilities is given below :—

Reaction Ability

It is the ability to react effectively and quickly to a

signal. In sports, signals can be of different type e.g., visual, tactile, acoustic. Depending on the degree of complexity of the reaction required the reaction ability can be further differentiated into simple and complex reaction ability.

Movement Speed

It is the ability to do a single movement in minimum of time. Movement speed is of high relevance in acyclic sports. In cyclic sports it is important in the initial phase (e.g., start movement) or in some phases during the hurdle event. In acyclic sports movement speed is very closely bound with technique and tactical action. Depending on the nature of the movement the ability of movement speed depends on a different complex of factors in different sports. But it generally depends heavily on explosive strength and technique.

Acceleration Ability

It is the ability to achieve high speed of locomotion from a stationary position or from a slow moving position. Acceleration ability depends to a great extent on explosive strength, technique and movement frequency. Performances in sprint events are determined to a great extent by acceleration ability. Acceleration ability is also of crucial importance in all team games and racket sports where high running speeds are to be achieved over short distances.

Locomotor Ability

It is the ability to maintain maximum speed of locomotion for maximum possible duration or distance. Locomotor ability is important in only a few sports or events, e.g., 100m and 200m in track and field, short sprints in track cycling and speed skating. In swimming, rowing etc., locomotor ability is not of much importance because all events last for more than 40 sec. On the other hand in these sports speed endurance is of high importance. Locomotor ability depends to a great extent on mobility of the nervous system which allows for high movement frequency. It further depends on technique, ability to relax and emplosive strength. The trainability of locomotor ability is very low:

Speed Endurance

It is the ability to do sports movements with high speed under conditions of fatigue. Speed endurance is a combination of speed and endurance abilities. it is of a different nature in cyclic and noncyclic sports. In cyclic sports the speed endurance is required to continue movements with high speed in spite of the rapid accumulation of fatigue during the activity. In noncyclic sports the speed endurance is required to fatigue e.g., repeated sprints in football. Speed endurance depends considerably on anaerobic capacity, technique and psychic factors.

Factors Determining Speed

Speed abilities are trainable to a very limited extent due to its marked dependence on the functioning of the central nervous system. In practice, therefore, speed performance are commonly improved not directly by improving the functioning of central nervous system but indirectly by improving the various factors on which the speed performance depends. It is, therefore, of great practical importance to know the factors which determine speed performance. These factors are explained below :—

(A) Mobility of the Nervous System

During all speed performances the muscles have to contract and relax at maximal possible speed e.g., in sprints. This rapid contraction and relaxation of muscles is possible only if the concerned motor centres in the

CNS can undergo rapid excitation and inhibition. This is called the mobility of the nervous system. When this rapid excitation and inhibition of motor centres takes place at maximal speed and for some seconds then the excitation process tends to spread to the neighbouring motor centres (irradiation) causing unnecessary tension in the body and thereby resulting in deterioration in speed performance.

The mobility of the nervous system is trainable to a limited extent. It seems to be determined to a great extent by genetic factors. When muscles contract and relax repeatedly in a definite sequence then the nervous system tends to adapt to this thereby resulting in "speed barrier".

(B) Explosive Strength

The speed performances depend to a great extent on explosive strength of the muscles concerned. This fact is especially vital for speed performances in which some resistance has to be tackled. Because of the importance of explosive strength and its high trainability most of the times speed performances are improved by improving explosive strength.

Explosive strength further depends on muscle composition, muscle size and muscle co-ordination (inter and intra-muscular co-ordination). It also depends on metabolic processes. Except muscle composition all other factors can be improved through training. The relative proportion of fast twitch and slow twitch fibres determines to a great extent the maximum possible speed with which a muscle can contract. But this is not trainable as it is genetically determined.

Good sprinters have a very high proportion of fast twitch fibres whereas endurance athletes have a very high proportion of slow twitch fibres. According to Hartmann and Tunnemann sprinters have fast twitch fibres up to 90% in soleus muscle whereas long distance men have slow twitch fibres up to 90% in the same muscle. The muscle composition, however, is characterized by high inter muscular and individual differences.

(C) Technique

Technique is an important factor determining speed performance. Unlearnt movements cannot be done at high speed. This is particularly applicable to complex and difficult movements. Moreover, good technique enables the sportsman to fully utilise his strength, flexibility etc., to achieve high speed. The movement speed in gymnastics, combat sports etc., is highly dependent on technique or skill. Like explosive strength technique is also very commonly an aim of training for improving speed performance.

(D) Bio-chemical Reserves and Metabolic Power

For maximal speed performance the muscles need high amount of energy at a very high rate of consumption. For this purpose the phosphogen stores in the muscles should be enough. Moreover, the metabolic process of energy production must take place at a very high pace. For this purpose, sufficient amount of non-oxydative enzymes is essential. Acceleration ability, locomotor ability and speed endurance are particularly dependent on the bio-chemical reserves and metabolic power.

(E) Flexibility

Flexibility includes the stretchability of the muscles and mobility of the joints. Good flexibility allows for optimum range of movement without much internal resistance, thereby positively affecting speed. Flexibility also enables full utilisation of explosive strength. Low flexibility leads to excessive internal resistance, muscle tension and less than optimum strength application.

(F) Psychic Factors

Speed depends considerably on certain psychic factors. Important among these are optimum arousal and motivation, attention and concentration, ability to relax and the ability to maximally mobilise one self for a short duration. In addition to these factors the anticipation ability is of high importance for quick reactions.

The ability to relax the non contracting body parts and muscles has been found to be of high importance for speed performances especially acceleration, locomotor and speed endurance abilities. But unfortunately this ability seems to depend much on the central nervous system and as a consequence it cannot be significantly improved.

All the speed abilities do not depend to the same extent on the various factors mentioned above. Each speed ability is relatively independent of other speed abilities. In other words each speed ability depends on a different complex of the factors described above.

IMPROVEMENT OF SPEED ABILITIES

I. Reaction Ability

In sports reaction ability is required to react quickly and effectively to various signals and changing situations. Reaction time is a component of reaction ability which also includes the time of reaction or response. Hence, in sports the speed of movement (i.e., response) is an important part of the total reaction.

Reaction time is most commonly taken as a measure of reaction ability. But it must be considered that reaction time does not include the reaction itself. It is the time interval between the signal and the start of the movement. In sports, except in a few events like 100 m sprint, reaction ability cannot be judged simply by considering the reaction time. The speed and correctness of the reaction also has to be considered. But if other things are constant then reaction time assumes high importance for the judgement of reaction ability. Reaction time can be further broken into the following six parts :—

(a) Time taken by the signal to reach the sense organs.

(b) Time taken by the sense organ to generate a nerve impulse.

(c) Time taken by the nerve impulse to reach the concerned centres in the CNS.

(d) Time taken by CNS to generate a motor nerve impulse.

(e) Time taken by the motor nerve impulse to reach the muscle.

(f) Time taken by the muscle to begin the contraction (laten time).

Reaction ability can be divided into various types according to the type of signal or according to the nature of the response. According to the type of signal we can classify reactions into three types: visual reactions, acoustic reactions and tactile reactions.

Tactile reactions are the fastest where as the visual reactions are the slowest. According to the nature of reaction the reaction ability can be divided into two types : simple reaction ability and complex reaction ability. Vilkner, however, mentions three types of reaction abilities : simple, complex, and selection reaction abilities.

According to Vilkner simple reaction ability is involved when only part body movements are to be done on a signal whereas complex reaction ability involves the movement of whole body e.g., sprint start.

Simple Reaction Ability

In simple reactions the signal and response are both known to the sportsman e.g., sprint start. Simple reaction ability is of importance in starts in swimming, cycling and track and field sprint events. In these sports the sportsman learns the reaction or movement as a skill and, therefore, reaction time is a reliable measure of simple reaction ability. Studies conducted on reactions to sound and light signals reveal some important facts:—

(a) Women have longer reaction time as composed to men.

(b) In track and field reaction time increases with the distance to be run.

(c) Elite sprinters have an average reaction time of about 0.12 sec.

(d) Reaction time of different body parts is different. Arms are faster than legs and hands are faster than the arms.

(e) Good sprinters are stable in reaction time performance.

(f) Reactions are slower if the movement to be executed is complex or unlearnt.

(g) Emotions specially anger, fear have an 'inverted U' relationship with reaction time.

The methods for improvement of simple reaction ability are given below :—

(A) General Method

Playing different types of games in which quick reactions are frequently required is a general but effective method for improving simple reaction ability of children and beginners. It improves the reaction ability to a certain extent after which further improvement is possible through specific reaction exercises.

(B) Reacting Repeatedly on a Signal

In this method specific reaction exercises are done. The sportsman react repeatedly and with maximal effort to a signal e.g., sprint starts. The reaction exercises are arranged in series and 3-4 with full rest is between. To increase variation the nature of signal and response can be varied e.g., the tone and intensity of sound or light signal.

(C) Part Method

This method aims at improving the movement time and reaction separately. For the improvement of movement time the factors on which it depends are improved e.g., technique, explosive strength. Reaction time is, however, improved through reaction exercises.

(D) Sensory Method

This method was first explained by Zaciorskij in 1971. Since then this method has been suggested by other experts also e.g., Martin, Matweyew and Singh. The sensory method is based on the assumption that reaction ability is very intimately linked with the ability to differentiate time intervals. The application of the method is done in stages described below :—

1. The sportsman reacts (e.g., 10m. sprint) with maximum speed on a signal. After each reaction he is told the time taken for the exercise.
2. The sportsman reacts repeatedly to a signal but with increasing speed. After the reaction he is asked to tell the time he has taken for the exercise. The time keeper or the coach then tells him the

actual time he has taken. In this way his subjective judgement of time differentiation is improved.

3. The sportsman reacts repeatedly to a signal but with different speeds. His subjective assessment of time is continuously compared with the time taken by a timing device.

The sensory method should be used after the other methods have been exhausted.

Complex Reaction Ability

Complex reaction ability is needed when there is uncertainty about the signal or response or both. This is the case in team games and combat sports. The sportsman does not know on which signal he should react and in what manner. The time of occurrence of signal also may not be certain. Complex reaction ability is partly dependent on the simple reaction ability. It also depends to a great extent on two factors which have to be improved to improve complex reaction ability. These factors are : anticipation of the signal and quick selection of correct response. Complex reaction ability, therefore, involves selection and decision making processes. The possibility of improvement of these two factors is discussed below :—

A. Anticipation

For quick and correct reaction the sportsman should be able to correctly anticipate the movement or action of the opponent. This should be timely in order to allow for a correct and quick response. Sportsman should be trained for good anticipation as in tactical sports the opponent tries to conceal his intention/movement in order to lead the sportsman to wrong anticipation. The ability to anticipate depends primarily on three things explained below :—

1. Movement Structure

Knowledge of movement structure can help the sportsman to anticipate the movement by correctly judging the preparatory phase movements of an action. The sportsman, however, should not be hasty in reaching a conclusion because preparatory movements can form part and parcel of a fake movement. Moreover, the sportsman should also always keep in mind the probability of occurrence of a movement e.g., in boxing and wrestling when a sportsman is in a certain position then only few limited number of movements are possible.

2. Tactical Pattern

All sportsmen, to a limited or greater extent, from the habit of doing only certain definite movements when they are in a definite situation. A knowledge of this helps the sportsman to anticipate the actions of an opponent. The observation and study of these patterns, as a principle, should form part and parcel of tactical preparation for obvious reasons.

3. Experience

For good anticipation there is no substitute for experience. Therefore, sportsmen must participate in many competitions and should face different opponents and situations.

B. Selection of Correct Response

This involves the process of selection. This depends on the ability of the sportsman to decide which will be the best response. In order to save time and to respond quickly it is better to link certain signals with certain responses. This can be done by devising appropriate drills and letting the sportsman practise these again and again. These drills, however, should not be highly automatised otherwise the sportsman is unable to change the response if the situation so demands. Quick selection of correct response depends to a great extent on the experience of the sportsman.

In addition, it is also determined by quick thinking, correct perception of the situation, emotional control and creativeness.

II. Acceleration Ability

Acceleration ability, like all other speed abilities, can be improved directly or indirectly. It is improved indirectly by improving explosive strength, technique, flexibility etc.

For the direct improvement of acceleration ability short sprints are the best means. The distance or duration of these sprints is based on practical experience as well as on some research findings. Henry found that sprinters achieve their maximum speed in about 6 seconds after the stationary start. Farfel, Zdanov, and Furnadziev and Petkova also found that irrespective of the performance level and age the maximum speed is achieved in 5-6 sec., after the start.

Harre however, states that the duration for achieving maximum speed is lesser in case of lower level sprinters. Teichgrabber also suggests shorter durations for children and lower level sprinters. Jung found that in 80 m sprint men achieved maximum speed at about 45 m whereas women achieved it at about 25 m.

III. Locomotor Ability

It is the ability to maintain maximum speed of locomotion for maximum duration possible. According to Gundlach the speed ranges from 99-100% of maximum during the phase of maximum locomotion speed. He found that in track and field sprints it can last from 20-45 m. but this phase of maintenance of maximum speed is different for different persons depending on their age and performance level. The locomotor ability depends heavily on the mobility of the CNS and on the ability of the sportsman to relax his non involved body parts and muscles during the phase of maximum speed. Hence sprints for locomotor ability must be done with conscious effort to achieve during the sprint. As it is mostly difficult to improve locomotor ability, therefore, much stress should be laid on the improvement of those factors which determine locomotor ability.

All these factors are not significantly trainable e.g., mobility of the CNS and relaxation ability. But technique, explosive strength etc., are trainable to a high degree.

IV. Movement Speed

Movement speed is of importance in acyclic events and sports e.g., throws, gymnastics, combat sports etc. In these sports the movement speed is very closely linked with technique and tactics of the sports. Depending upon the nature of speed it further depends heavily on explosive strength, flexibility, co-ordinative abilities, attention etc. Movement speed is most frequently improved indirectly by improving technique, explosive strength and other determining factors. The indirect method has proved to be very effective. But sometimes, especially during the competition period the movement speed has to be improved directly and for this purpose the specific movement is practised in the following three manners :—

A. Repeating the Movement with Maximum Speed

The concerned movement is executed again and again with maximum speed. It is important to take the time taken to complete the movement as feedback is very important for improving movement speed. In some sports the concerned movement can be done several times without pause e.g., in boxing. In such cases the time of total repetition should be taken.

B. Practising the Movement under easier Conditions

The movement is executed at maximum possible speed under condition which enable higher speed. For example this can be achieved in the following manners:—

(a) By reducing the resistance e.g., in shotput.

(b) By doing the movement on a faster surface.

(c) By using external help e.g., use of jump boards etc.

When making the conditions easier care should be taken to ensure proper movement structure. Too easy movement execution may prove harmful for the motor co-ordination required for the movement. It is also advisable to meaningfully combine the movement practice under easier and normal conditions in a training session.

C. Practising with a Faster Rhythm

Each movement has its own rhythm. If during the movement execution a slightly faster rhythm is given for outside the sportsman is able to do the movement faster. The rhythm to be given should correspond to the actual rhythm of the movement and should be properly given otherwise it will tend to slow the sportsman and will also have a negative effect on motor co-ordination.

The training for movement speed requires a high degree of concentration and attention. This should always be ensured for best results. The training should also ensure correct movement execution. In order to achieve high speed the sportsman tends to do the movement incorrectly. Hence a constant and effective check is required in this regard.

The training for movement speed should be done by using the specific movement. During practise the other normal requirements on the movement during competition should also be ensured for best results.

V. Speed Endurance

Speed endurance can be improved significantly through training. For its improvement both indirect and direct methods should be used as both are effective methods. In indirect method effort should be made to improve anaerobic capacity (especially lactacid tolerance), explosive strength and technique.

Harre stresses the importance of basic endurance training for speed endurance. He is of the opinion that the amount of basic endurance training in speed endurance sports should be quite high upto 90% of the total training volume in the preparatory period.

A. Repetition Method

This method when used with specific movement can be highly effective for improving speed endurance but for its success a good level of basic endurance is a necessary prerequisite. Harre suggests two variations of this method which can be effective for cyclic sports.

1. Repetitions with high speed over distances which are 2/3 to double of competition distance e.g., temp runs up to 300 m in track and field.

2. Repetitions with maximum speed over distances which are 10-20% longer than the competition distance.

In the above mentioned two variations required number of repetitions are done with complete recovery in between the repetitions. When the repetitions are done with maximal or near maximal speed then considerably long recovery periods are needed. But if the speed is low then shorter recovery periods are needed and the repetitions can be arranged in series of 2-4 repetitions.

B. Intensive Interval Method

This method is more suitable for the improvement of speed endurance in team games, combat sports and racket sports. In this method cyclic movements like running, cycling etc., can be used or specific movements of a sport can be used. The exercise is done at maximum or near maximum speed for a short distance or duration after which there is incomplete recovery of short duration.

The load and recovery phase can also be determined according to the typical competition load structure of a sport. In combat sports like wrestling, boxing and judo special circuits of 4-8 special exercises can be made and done according to intensive interval method for the improvement of speed endurance.

SPEED BARRIER

In sports which depend predominantly on speed the improvement of speed performance is hindered by speed barrier. When the improvement of speeds stops and it cannot be further improved inspite of continuing speed training we call it a speed barrier.

It is difficult to exactly pin point the reasons for the occurrence of speed barrier. According to Harre it occurs when the children's training is one sidedly directed at speed improvement through speed exercises and in high performance training the special exercises for explosive strength are ignored.

He, however, calls speed barrier as a 'motor stereotype'. The reasons for the occurrence of speed barrier perhaps relate to the functioning of CNS. When speed training is done with maximum speed using specific movement then the CNS has to function repeatedly in the same manner with same speed. If this is repeated too often then the CNS functioning becomes stabilised and can result in a sort of automatisation. This automatisation does not allow the CNS to function at a higher speed than to which it is habituated. Speed training, therefore, it self results in the occurrence of speed barrier.

On the one hand one has to use specific movements at maximum speed for improvement of speed. But on the other hand this is repeated too often the chances of speed barrier increases. The problem of speed barrier can be tackled in two ways. These are explained below :—

A. Delaying of Speed Barrier

In the initial stages of training the occurrence of speed barrier can be delayed by improving speed performance predominantly by using non specific means and methods. This means the speed performance should be improved primarily by improving strength, technique and other factors which determine speed. Zaciorskij has explained this method with the example of a 100 m sprinter. His performance can be improved up to about 10.0 or 10.2 by adopting general means. But if specific means are adopted then the speed barrier may occur at 11.0 sec thereby making further progress very difficult.

B. Overcoming Speed Barrier

In spite of whatever means, general or specific, are adopted for improving speed performance the speed barrier occurs sooner or later. The advantage of using general means is that it will occur at a much higher level of performance. The speed barrier can be possibly overcome or tackled in two ways mentioned below :—

1. The sportsman is enabled to do the movement faster by adopting certain means. In track and field sprinters can do this by running down hill with optimum slope or by running behind motor at optimum speed while

holding it from behind. Doing the movement accompanied by faster rhythm or under easier conditions also helps in overcoming speed barrier. The main purpose of using all these means is to somehow force the CNS to function at a higher speed that it is used to. Once this is accomplished a few times, the sportsman must try to accomplish the same under normal conditions.

2. Speed barrier is the result of some sort of automatisation of CNS functions controlling and regulating speed performance. If the sportsman does not do the concerned movements for a sufficiently long time then this automatisation becomes weak and can be overcome with less effort. This can be done to overcome speed barrier. The sportsman should not do the specific movements for several weeks. During this period he should concentrate on improving explosive strength of the concerned muscles, flexibility etc. After this 'break' of speed training the sportsman should again resume speed training, if needed under easier conditions. There are high chances that he will be able to overcome the speed barrier.

ENDURANCE

Endurance, like strength, is a conditional ability. It is primarily determined by energy liberation processes. The ability of the human body to maintain a certain level of energy production forms the physiological basis of endurance. Due to it high importance for health and training and competition and also due to its physiological determinants, which can be relatively easily studied, it is an ability which has been studied in great detail and depth by the physiologists. Endurance is directly or indirectly of high importance in all sports.

It is however not easy to define endurance. Nabatnikowa brings this into focus by presenting definitions given by several experts. Disagreement among experts is much more regarding the definition types of endurance e.g., special endurance, speed endurance, strength endurance etc. But there is agreement regarding the following aspects of endurance:—

It relates to doing work for a long time or period.

It relates to working under fatigue conditions.

It involves a large number of muscles.

It involves work efficiency.

Harre defines endurance as the ability to resist fatigue. Thiess and Schnabel also define endurance as the resistance ability to fatigue. Martin and Matweyew have also used the concept of 'ability to resist fatigue' for defining endurance. The author presents the following definitions of endurance :—

"Endurance is the ability to do sports movements, with the desired quality and speed, under conditions of fatigue".

Without an understanding of fatigue caused by training and competition load and the psycho-physiological systems involved in countering the effects of fatigue one cannot fully grasp the nature of endurance. Because of the overwhelming contributions made by sports physiology the psychic aspect of endurance is often overlooked. But it is important to realise that endurance is as much a product of physiological functions as of psychic functions. This act has been proved time and again by successful endurance athletes.

IMPORTANCE OF ENDURANCE

Endurance is a very important ability in sports. But

at the same time it is an ability that important of which is often overlooked in several sports. Endurance is the product of all psychic and physical organs and systems. No other motor ability depends so much on the working capacity of complete psycho-physical apparatus of humans as endurance.

All other performances factors depend on one or more parts of this psycho-physical apparatus and a result are directly or indirectly affected by endurance. The importance of endurance is discussed below under two headings sports and health:—

SPORTS

In sports endurance ensures optimum speed of motor actions. The ability to maintain pace or tempo of an exercise or during a competition is impossible without the requisite level of endurance. Good endurance also ensures high quality or skill of movement execution which finds expression in accuracy, precision, rhythm, consistency etc.

Under conditions of fitigue the sportsman tends to lose motor co-ordination, concentration, mental alertness etc. This clearly points out the importance of endurance for tactical efficiency.

Endurance training results in the improvement of functioning of various organs and systems of the human body. This in turn improves the ability to recover quickly from training and competition load. At the same time endurance activities enable the sportsman to better resist the fatigue i.e., to delay the fatigue. The ability to withstand fatigue and to recover faster from the fatigue enable the sportsmen to tackle higher training volumes with higher intensity in a training session, week, month or year. Higher training load leads to improvement in performance. From this point of view, therefore, endurance is of high importance.

The importance of endurance for recovery assumes much more relevance during competition i.e., in between heats, rounds, matches on successive days etc.

HEALTH

Endurance activities have been found to be of high volume for maintenance of good organic health, for increasing the general resistance against infection and for cure and treatment of various diseases and metabolic disorders.

Koinzer pointed out the stabilisation effect of endurance activities on health of adults and children. He further argued that endurance activities in childhood have a stabilising effect on health in later stages of life also. Cooper points out the positive effect of endurance activity on various physiological systems e.g., cardiorespiratory, digestion, metabolism etc. He also states that these activities have a preventive and curative effect on a number of health problems e.g., blood pressure, cardiac disorder, diabetes etc.

Israil found that children who do regular sports fall sick less frequently, they have better resistance to infections, can tolerate extreme temperatures better and their wounds heal faster. Neumann discovered that endurance loads with 70-80% of best performance intensity and over 60 min. duration have the best effect for the prevention and therapy of heart-circulatory and metabolic disorders.

The increasing awareness about the health stabilising, preventive and curative effect of sports especially endurance activities have resulted into mass movements for participation in such activities. Such movements are gaining momentum and popularity all over the world. The medical profession is actively encouraging and helping this movement.

TYPES OF ENDURANCE

Endurance performances are of different nature in different sports. These can be divided into various groups according to the dominant similarities in endurance performance. For different groups of sports and thereby classification of endurance can be done on the basis of two criteria: nature of activity and duration of activity. For team games, combat and racket sports the first classification is used. For cyclic sports lasting for more than 40-45 sec. both classification can be used through the second one is more frequently in use.

CLASSIFICATION ACCORDING TO NATURE OF ACTIVITY

This classification is based on the type of activity for which endurance is needed. From this aspect endurance is of the following three types :—

I. Basic Endurance

It is the ability to do movements involving large number of muscles, at a slow pace for prolonged periods e.g., jogging, swimming, walking at moderate speed for periods lasting more than 30 minutes. For sedentary and untrained persons the duration can be significantly less. As the activity is done at slow pace (below anaerobic threshold), therefore the energy is supplied predominantly by aerobic process of energy liberation. Due to this fact, it is also referred to as aerobic endurance.

However, the term basic endurance is better as it reflects the psycho-motor nature of this ability better. Basic endurance activities do not result in appreciable lactic acid concentrations in the blood. Basic endurance, as it depends on the aerobic process, forms the base for all types of endurance. Without a sufficient level of basic endurance other types of endurance are difficult to improve. It, however, should not be confused with local muscular endurance which is the ability to do part movements against resistance under conditions of fatigue. Local muscular endurance is a special form of strength endurance.

II. General Endurance

It is the ability to do sports movements of general nature under conditions of fatigue. General endurance is not specific to any sport and is developed through general exercises. It is very difficult to precisely say what is general endurance as it enables the sportsman to work under fatigue conditions caused by different types of movements done with different intensity and for different duration spans. But it must be differentiated from basic endurance which enables the sportsman to do movements at slow pace but for long durations.

General endurance, therefore, implies the ability to do various types of movements with higher or lower intensity for sufficiently long period. But this period is much shorter than required for basic endurance activity. In simple words general endurance enables a sportsman to do various types of exercises without getting unduly tired. As general endurance exercises can be done with high or low intensity; therefore, the energy liberation depends on a combination of aerobic and anaerobic metabolism.

III. Specific Endurance

It is the ability to do sports movements of a particular sport under conditions of fatigue. Depending on the nature of sport, the specific endurance may be largely determined by aerobic or anaerobic metabolism or by a certain combination of both. In a cyclic sports specific endurance is intricately combined with technical and tactical components of performance capacity. In endurance sports, in which movements are done at slower pace but for long duration (e.g., marathon), the specific endurance can be practically equated with basic endurance.

CLASSIFICATION ACCORDING TO DURATION OF ACTIVITY

This classification is applicable to cyclic sports only. The classification is based on physiological factors. It is not an established fact that energy production for activities lasting for different duration is dependent on a different type of combination of metabolic factors. For activities lasting up to 40-45 seconds the energy is produced mainly through phosphogen splitting and glycolysis.

But as the duration of the activity increases the contribution of glycolysis to energy production decreases while the contribution to oxydation increases. For very long duration activities the utilisation of fats for energy production is much more than for comparatively short duration activities. From the viewpoint of duration of activity, endurance can be divided into 4 types. This classification is based on the concept of Harre. The activities which last for less than 20-22 seconds are not endurance activities. These are speed activities.

I. Speed Endurance

This ability is required for cyclic activities lasting up to 45 seconds. The 400 m sprint in track and field is a classical example of speed endurance ability. This ability is highly dependent on the power and capacity of glycolytic mechanism of energy production. The phosphogens (alactacid metabolism) also contribute significantly towards energy production. Glycolysis results in very high amount of lactic acid concentration in the muscles and as a result is one of the dominant fatigue producing factors in such activities. Very high amount of oxygen debt is recorded in speed endurance activities.

A highly developed ability of the muscles, to continue contracting with required speed and force, under high lactic acid concentration is a primary prerequisite for good performance in speed endurance activities. In activities which last up to 20-22 seconds the energy production is almost completely achieved by alactacid metabolism (i.e., splitting of ATP and CP).

II. Short Time Endurance

This endurance ability is needed for cyclic activities lasting from about 45 seconds to two minutes. The 800 m run in track and field is a typical example of short time endurance activity. In short time endurance activities the energy is produced by a combination of glycolysis and oxydation. The contribution of alactacid mechanism is more than that of oxydation. As a result short time endurance activities result in high amount of lactic acid concentration in the muscles and blood. Because of comparatively longer duration of activity the lactate values can exceed those found in speed endurance activities. Short time endurance depends to a significant extent on speed endurance and strength endurance.

III. Medium Time Endurance

This ability is required for cyclic activities lasting from 2-11 minutes. Typical examples of cyclic activities requiring medium time endurance are 1500m and 3000m in track and field and 100m in rowing. The energy production for activities of this duration is achieved by a combination of glycolysis and oxydation. The activities lasting for about 3min. 40 sec. are the activities in which contribution of glycolysis and oxydation is nearly equal. But for longer duration activities the contribution of glycolysis steadily decreases. The contribution of alactacid metabolism is practically nil. For oxydation the source of energy is muscle glycogen which due to limited duration of activity cannot be depleted to a significant extent and as a result is not a limiting factor for performance. Due to involvement of glycolysis in medium time endurance activities, lasting up to eleven minutes, high concentrations of lactic acid are produced.

IV. Long Time Endurance

The long time endurance is needed for cyclic activities lasting more than eleven minutes. The energy production is achieved mainly from oxydation of glycogen. For activities lasting upto 30 minutes significant amount of energy production is achieved through glycolysis. But for longer duration activities the contribution of glycolysis is very less. For marathon run nearly the total amount of energy required is released by oxydation.

There is, however, one significant change in energy production. For activities lasting more than 30 minutes the energy production by oxidation of fatty acids (fat metabolism) increases steadily with the increase in the duration of activity. Depending on the nature of energy production as a result of duration of activity long time endurance can be divided into three types. For good performance in long time endurance activities, the glycogen stores in the muscles and liver assume great importance.

These often become limiting factors as low level of muscle glycogen and blood sugar can reflexibly accelerate the onset of fatigue. The performance here also depends to a great extent on basic endurance.

FACTORS DETERMINING ENDURANCE

Endurance is one motor ability which has been a subject of keen study by experts of sports physiology. As a result we have a much better insight into the factors and prerequisites which determine endurance ability. But the study of psychic factors of endurance is still lagging behind and we do not have clear picture of the role of various psychic factors having a decisive influence on endurance performance.

The study of psychic aspect of endurance is crucial for further improvement of endurance performances. The list of factors which determine endurance is very exhaustive and for details the reader is advised to refer to text books of sports physiology. For the sake of presenting these factors systematically all the factors can be grouped into four major factors i.e., aerobic capacity, anaerobic capacity, movement economy and psychic factors. These are explained below :—

I. Aerobic Capacity

The aerobic capacity is measured by the maximum amount of oxygen which can be consumed by the working muscles in one minute (VO_2 max.). When VO_2 max. is divided by the body weight of the sportsman then we get the relative VO_2 max. i.e., the amount of oxygen consumed per kilogram of body weight per minute.

For endurance activity a continuous flow of oxygen has to ensured to the muscle cells for the liberation of energy. In case of higher speeds the energy can be partly or completely released in the absence of oxygen; but after the cessation of activity the required oxygen (called oxygen debt) has to be supplied to the muscles. The human body gets oxygen from the atmosphere and is then transported to the muscles where it is consumed.

The ultimate amount of oxygen therefore depends primarily on three factors. But as energy liberation has to continue for long periods, therefore, the energy reserves are also important constituents of aerobic capacity.

(a) Oxygen Intake

The oxygen intake is the amount of oxygen which can be taken into the blood stream from the atmosphere. If oxygen intake is more, then there are favourable chances of achieving higher VO_2 max. The oxygen intake depends on the vital capacity which further depends on the lung size number of active unit lung alveoli, strength of respiratory muscles, size of the chest cavity etc. Once the oxygen is inside the lungs it has to be absorbed into the blood through diffusion.

The rate and amount of oxygen diffusion from the lungs to the blood depends on several factors e.g., temperature, partial pressure of oxygen in the lungs and blood, the amount of haemoglobin in the blood and so on.

It is generally agreed that oxygen intake is not a limiting factor for endurance performance in healthy and well trained sportsmen.

(b) Oxygen Transport

The amount of oxygen taken into the blood from the lungs has to be transported to the working muscles. More oxygen transport means more oxygen available to the muscles for consumption. The oxygen transport depends on two things. The amount of oxygen which the blood has absorbed from the lungs and the ability of the cardiocirculatory system to carry this quickly to the muscles for consumption.

The amount of oxygen absorbed into the blood mainly depends on the speed of blood flow through the lungs and also on the blood haemoglobin concentration. The concentration of blood haemoglobin is important as the oxygen can be transported only when it combines with the haemoglobin to form oxy-haemoglobin. The concentration of blood haemoglobin is healthy persons and sportsmen is about 14-15%. This is indifferent to training, i.e., it cannot be improved by training.

The carrying of oxygen, in the form of oxy-haemoglobin, to the muscles is dependent on the capacity of the heart. A bigger and stronger heart can pump out more blood in each stroke volume thus considerably increasing the amount of blood pumped out per minute (cardiac out put).

The size and strength of the heart can be considerably increased through training. A bigger and stronger heart, achieved through training is called 'Athlete's heart' well trained endurance athletes have much bigger and heavier hearts with greater stroke volume and cardiac out put.

(c) Oxygen Uptake

The oxygen from the blood has to be taken up by the muscle cells and then consumed. The oxygen uptake depends on the rate of diffusion which is further determined by the speed of blood flow, temperature and partial pressures of oxygen in the blood and of carbon-dioxide in the muscle cells. The oxygen uptake is facilitated if capillarisation is good. The speed and amount of oxygen consumption also depends on the number, size and metabolic capacity of the mitochondria.

It is now being increasingly realised that the metabolic capacity of the muscle cell is the ultimate limit of aerobic capacity and aerobic power. The systems of oxygen intake and transport are well developed in endurance sportsmen, and hence normally do not act as a limitation of aerobic capacity or aerobic power (rate of oxygen consumption). The metabolic capacity and power of muscle cell depends primarily on the number and size of mitochondria an the amount of oxydative enzymes helping in oxydation.

Fortunately, these are trainable to a significant extent. But the range to which these can be improved depends to a great extent on genetic factors.

(d) Energy Reserves

The amount of muscle glucogen has a decisive effect on activities lasting longer than 30 minutes. The muscles store glucose in the form of glycogen. When the activity is to be done at moderate speed than the energy is largely derived from the oxydation of muscle glycogen. The depletion of muscle glycogen beyond a certain level results in the onset of fatigue. The activities which last for very long periods (e.g., marathon) lead to extreme depletion of muscle glycogen. It also leads to consumption of liver glycogen and blood sugar which further adds to the degree of fatigue.

The discovery of the role of muscle glycogen in endurance performance has led to introduction of diet manipulation before and during long duration activities. For extremely long duration activities fatty acids are also used as energy fuel. But the total amount of stored fats in the human body is so much that it is practically inexhaustible during a single but extremely long duration activity. Hence, it is not a limiting factor for endurance performance.

During sports activities the muscles can use three substances as fuel for energy production. These substances are : phosphogens, carbohydrates and fats. These, however, are used differently for activities depending on the speed or pace of activity. For example slow activity like normal walking, sitting, standing etc., fat is used. When the activities are faster, oxydation of fat and carbohydrate takes place; and when the speed is still faster, it is oxydation of carbohydrate alone. In case of still faster activities glycolysis replaces oxydation. When the activity is done at maximum or near maximum speed, the energy is derived from the phosphogens.

AEROBIC CAPACITY AND ENDURANCE PERFORMANCE

It has been a common practise by physiologists to determine VO_2 max. (i.e., aerobic capacity) in order to judge the endurance of a sportsman. But latest findings in exercise physiology have altered this concept to a significant extent. The important conclusions having some relevance for endurance and endurance training are given below :—

(a) The aerobic capacity is determined to a great extent by genetic factors. Astrand and Rodahi and Hollman et al are of the view that aerobic capacity is genetically determined by up to 70-80%. This means that through training VO_2 max. values cannot be improved considerably, especially in case of well trained sportsmen.

(b) The VO_2 max. values are not reliable measures for judging the potential for performance in endurance events. The lower level of VO_2 max. can be effectively compensated by good technique, motivation and good training state. Astrand and Rodahl found that some marathon runners of world elite class have quite modest VO_2 max. values i.e., below 70ml/kg/min. Neumann also states that typical VO_2 max. value for elite athletes have changed very little during the last thirty years. This means that the improvement in endurance performances in the past 30 years cannot be a result of an increase in VO_2 max.

(c) Much more important than the VO_2 max. value is the ability of the sportsman to work for longer times at speeds of 100% VO_2 max. or close to it (i.e., percent utilisation of VO_2 max.). This ability is highly trainable and perhaps partly explains the improvement in endurance performance inspite of stable or unchanged values of VO_2 max. Astrand and Rodahl found that well trained athletes, including marathon runners, can exercise for hours with O_2 uptake around 70-80% of their maximum with little or no increase in blood lactate concentrations. All this signifies that for assessment of endurance improvement the changes taking place at sub maximal level should be given more weightage.

This is reflected by the findings that well-trained endurance sportmen have significantly higher threshold level in terms of VO_2 max. For example, Neumann reports that untrained persons start using glycolytic metabolism (i.e., Anaerobic metabolism) in exercises surpassing 60% of VO_2 max. whereas trained and well-trained at 80% and 90-95% of VO_2 max. respectively.

(d) The inadequate explanations and answers offered by sports physiology regarding the nature and extent of aerobic capacity's contribution towards endurance performance is slowly giving rise to the trend to look for answers in other factors of endurance namely technique, psychic factors and anaerobic capacity.

II. Anaerobic Capacity

It is the capacity of organism to work in the absence of oxygen. In the absence of oxygen the energy production for the muscle contractions can take place in two ways:— (a) through splitting of ATP and CP (i.e., phosphogens). This mechanism of energy production is called alactacid mechanism as it does not lead to formation of lactic acid; (b) by glycolysis of muscle glycogen (i.e., carbohydrate).

This is also called lacatcid mechanism as it results in the formation of lactic acid.In the muscles the total amount of stored phosphagens is only sufficient for activities with maximal intensity lasting up to 8-10 seconds. Hence, alactacid mechanism is of crucial importance for speed performance. But in activities of speed endurance nature the alactacid mechanism must function alongwith glycolysis to ensure high intensity of activity. The glycolysis process during anaerobic work primarily aims at rapid resynthesis of creative phosphate which is further required for rapid re-synthesis of ATP (adenosine triphosphate). The end product of glycolysis is lactic acid.

The glycolytic processes achieve its maximal values after 40-45 sec. of maximal effort. The lactic acid concentration in the muscles reach maximal value and inhibit muscle contractions. Therefore lactic acid is the limiting factor in speed endurance activities.

The anaerobic capacity is required to a lesser or greater extent for all sports performances depending on endurance. Even in long time endurance activities the anaerobic capacity for sudden bursts of short duration at the beginning or end or in between. The anaerobic capacity depends on the following factors :—

A. Phosphogen Stores

Stores of ATP and CP are crucial for anaerobic capacity. This is so because muscles derive energy only from ATP which is stored in very less amount in the muscles. Therefore ATP has to be rapidly resynthesised by CP the stores of which are also limited. CP is re-synthesised by glycolysis. But large stores of ATP and CP relieve pressure on the glycolysis thereby resulting in lesser amount of lactic acid production. The phosphagen stores can be increased significantly through training. Alongwith the phosphagens certain non-oxydative enzymes are also crucial for anaerobic energy production. The amount of these enzymes can also be increased by training.

B. Buffer Capacity

High concentrations of lactic acid are detrimental for endurance performance of short duration as it tends to inhibit muscle contraction. To avoid this lactic acid is quickly pushed into the blood where it lowers the blood pH value, i.e., makes blood more acidic. The maintenance of blood pH valued within a range of 7.1 to 7.5 is crucial for the normal functioning of the body. Therefore, the incoming lactic acid has to be neutralised or converted into something which is less acidic. This is done by some substances in the blood which are collectively referred to as alkali resers.

The total capacity of the alkali reserve to counter the effects of lactic acid in blood is called buffer capacity. A higher buffer capacity will ensure longer duration of glycolysis which is indispensable for endurance performances of short duration. The alkali reserve, however, cannot be improved significantly through training. Some amount of lactic acid can be removed from blood by oxydation but this process is very slow and can be effective for removal of lactic acid during recovery break.

C. Lactic Acid Tolerance

In endurance performances of short duration the ability to effectively tolerate higher concentration of lactic acid is of very high importance. Due to limited amount of alkali reserve the lactic acid concentration inevitably increases in the blood and the body is forced to work under highly acidic condition of blood.

High lactate values in blood also slow down the removal of lactic acid from the working muscles. As a result muscle lactate values also increase rapidly. Now only the ability to tolerate high lactate concentration can enable the sportsman to continue the activity with the same speed.

Fortunately through training the lactic acid tolerance can be significantly improved. The performance in 400, 800 m and 1500 m in track and field depends significantly on lactic acid tolerance.

D. Aerobic Capacity

The anaerobic capacity depends, to a significant extent, on aerobic capacity. During speed endurance and short time endurance performance the total energy required is produced by a certain combination of alactacid, lactacid and oxydative metabolic processes. A higher level of aerobic capacity has a sparing effect on glycolytic (i.e., lactacid) and alactacid mechanisms. This fact is demonstrated by higher anaerobic threshold levels in endurance trained sportsmen. In nontrained persons the lactic acid production begins at work rates of about 60-50% of VO_2 max. This happens in case of highly endurance trained sportsmen at about 85% VO_2 max. or even higher.

III. Movement Economy

The endurance performances depend to a great extent on movement economy. A sportsman who can run or swim at a given pace with less energy expenditure can continue with the same speed for longer duration or can run or swim a given distance with a higher speed. Technique in endurance sports, therefore, aims at movement economy. Saziorskij found that in long distance events the sportsmen with good running technique spend less energy than those having poor technique.

The good running raise their C.G. less higher, their unnecessary movements are less and they conserve and utilise kinetic energy for running. Fox and Costill found that marathon runners require 5-10% less energy than the middle distance runners when running at same speed. In some endurance sports like long distance swimming, rowing, cycling etc., the role of technique for energy, conservation assumes very high significance. In these sports poor technique leads to a lot of energy wastage, thereby markedly affecting the performance.

IV. Psychic Factors

The contribution of psychic factors towards endurance performance can hardly be over estimated. Endurance performances, because of high degree of fatigue involved, are always a result of a sportsman's fight and resistance against the uncomfortable and painful sensations and feelings which are an enevitable part of endurance activity. Endurance performance, therefore, depends to a high degree on motivation, will power, ability to resist and tolerate discomfort, pain and agony, ability to push oneself beyond one's capacity and so on.

These qualities of head and heart are important for endurance competition as well as for endurance training. Endurance athletes are characterised by qualities of hard work, preseverance, determination and by a distinct type of temperament and personality. Fortunately, many of the psychic factors important for good endurance performance can be significantly improved through training and other means.

IMPROVEMENT OF ENDURANCE

A vast amount of literature is available on means and methods of endurance improvement. But most of it is devoted to the development of aerobic and anaerobic capacity or their components. Very less literature is available on means and methods of improving endurance techniques and this is mostly covered under the aspect of technique. Literature on means and methods for improving the psychic factors of endurance performance and training is practically non-existing.

As training volumes in endurance training are reaching their saturation point, therefore in the future stress is shift to this aspect of endurance, which however has not been explored and studied so far. Before discussing the methods of endurance improvement the student must understand the cardinal principle of endurance improvement. Endurance performance represents the sportsman's fight or struggle with extreme degrees of fatigue. An endurance training becomes effective only when the sportsman gets tired to a significant extent. The longer and frequently a sportsman trains under extreme conditions of fatigue the more improvement of endurance takes place. Endurance training without pain and agony is not endurance training in the correct sense.

Every one cannot do this for a period stretching over a number of years. The ability to do this however is to be developed progressively and systematically over long period. The various methods for improving endurance are basically of four types. These are explained below along with their physiological and training effects :—

I. Continuous Method

In this method an exercise is done for long time without any break or pause. Because of the long duration of work the intensity is low. The continuous method has four variations which are explained below:—

(A) Slow Continuous Method

In this variation the sportsman exercises at a certain speed without any pause for very long durations. Long cross country runs are typical examples of slow continuous method. In this method the speed or pace of exercise is determined according to heart rate. For trained sportspersons the hear rate during the exercise should be from 140-160 beats per minute.

The volume, in terms of total duration should not be less than 30 minutes. The total duration, in case of endurance athletes can go up to 2 hours or even more. Cyclic activities like running, cycling, walking etc. are used for this method. Effects of slow continuous method, because of relatively low intensity and very high training volume, are mainly limited to the muscles. Far reaching changes or adaptations take place in the muscle. Some of the most important changes are : increase in muscle glycogen and liver glycogen, increase in capilliarisation, increase in the quantity of oxydative enzymes, increase in the number and size of mito-chondria, better thermo-regulation, improvement in movement economy. In addition it also positively effects fat metabolism for exercise, control and regulation of endurance activity, general resistance and so on. It also has positive effect on heart and lungs.

Slow continuous method, however, results in decrease in muscle size and strength. The changes, caused by this method, in the muscles on the whole aim at adapting the muscle for slow long duration efforts. The psychic effects of this method are also important. It improves will-power and ability to work under progressively increasing fatigue for long duration. It leads to self discipline and self conquest.

(B) Fast Continuous Method

In this variation the work is done at fast but unchanging pace for long durations without any break. Heart rate is normally between 160-180 beats/minute. The total volume or duration should be not less than 20 minutes for trained sports persons. Because of higher intensity the fast continuous method is more strenuous and exhaustive. For best results the exercise should be done with a heart rate of about 175-180 i.e., about 90-100% of VO_2 max. This speed is called critical speed as it approximates the speed at which lies the anaerobic threshold in trained sportsmen.

Training at such an intensity pushes the anerobic threshold level still up in terms of speed. In other words it improves the percent utilisation of VO_2 max. Fast pace method is very effective for improving the VO_2 max. It significantly improves the capacity of the muscles to consume maximal amount of oxygen for long duration. There is highly significant increase in number and size of mitochondria and quantity of oxydative enzymes. Fast method however has less effect on capilarisation, muscle glycogen, movement economy etc. But due to higher intensity and involvement of glycolytic mechanism to some extent (especially towards the end) this method has positive affect on anaerobic capacity. It also does not lead to much decrease in muscle size and strength. It is a strong stimulus for structural changes in the heart and lungs.

(C) Variable Pace Method

In this method the exercise of done continuous but with changing pace or speed. The heart rate normally ranges between 140-180 beats/minute. The total duration or volume ranges from about 15 minutes to 1 hour. Because of speed, which is pre-planned, this method is very strenuous and can be used by trained sportsmen only. Depending on the dynamics of speed this method can be used to improve aerobic or anaerobic capacity or both at the same time.

(D) Fartlek Method

Fartlek is Swedish word meaning 'speed play'. In

stricter sense it is a variation of variable pace method. In Fartlek the change of pace or speed is not pre-planned. The sportsman changes the speed on his own during the activity according to the terrain, surrounding and his feelings. Therefore, this method requires more self discipline in order to be effective. Like variable pace method in fartlek also the heart rate fluctuates between 140-180 beats/minute. The total volume and duration are also similar to variable pace method. The physiological and training effect are also, therefore, the same.

II. Interval Method

Interval method is perhaps the most versatile method for improving endurance of various types. In interval method, the exercise is done at relatively high intensity with intervals of incomplete recovery. Interval method is based on the following principle: Work should be done with sufficient speed and duration so that the heart rate goes up to 180 beats/min. After this there should be a recovery period and when the heart rate comes down to 120-130 beats/min. the work should be started again.

The training load in interval method, therefore, can be controlled by repeatedly checking the heart rate. The effect of interval method is determined by the variables of interval method which are the following :—

- Speed of work.
- Duration of work.
- Duration of recovery.
- Number of repetitions.
- Nature of recovery.

By proper manipulation of the above mentioned variables the interval method can be used in several ways each having a different physiological and training effect. However, from general point of view interval method is of two types : (A) Intensive interval method and (B) Extensive interval method. In intensive interval method the intensity is from 80-90%. Whereas in extensive interval method the intensity is from 60-80%. Interval method, by proper manipulation of the five variables, can be used for the improvement of any type of endurance or any prerequisite of endurance.

Some typical examples of interval method for different purposes are given below :—

(A) For Heart and Circulatory System

This variation of interval method is also called Freiburger interval training.

(B) For Aerobic Capacity

This variation is recommended by Zaciorskij.

(C) For Lactic Acid Tolerance

(D) For Improving VO_2 max.

The interval method has been used most frequently, and with good results, in cyclic sports like track events, swimming, rowing, cycling etc. In these sports, due to the nature of interval method, it cannot be very effective for the improvement of specific endurance which is of continuous nature. The continuous and repetition methods are more suitable for the improvement of specific endurance in these sports. The interval method, however, can be very effectively used for the improvement of specific endurance in team games, combat sports and racket sports. The activities in these sports are of interval nature.

Therefore, for specific endurance, the interval method should be used with special or competition exercises. It is not obligatory to use only an exercise of cyclic nature (e.g., running or swimming) for using interval method.

Any exercise can be done, general or specific, according to interval method. Some typical examples are given below:—

(a) Boxing

Sparring with partner at very high tempo for 15-20 seconds followed by a recovery of about 15-20 seconds.

(b) Hockey/Football

Dribbling with the ball at high speed for 10-15 seconds followed by a recovery of about 20 sec.

(c) Vollyball

Spiking repeatedly for 20-30 sec. followed by a recovery of 20-30 sec.

CONTROL OF INTERVAL METHOD BY HEART RATE

The interval method requires the art of checking heart rate during the training. Therefore, the coach and the sportsmen should learn to check heart rate at rest and immediately after or before starting the next repetition. At rest the heart rate can be checked easily from the radial artery at the wrist. But checking of heart rate correctly immediately after the exercise needs some practice. The heart rate can be checked from two places on the body after the exercise: from the carotid artery in the neck or from the chest. For checking the heart rate from the carotid artery the sportsman should place his finger tips lightly on the carotid artery on the side of the neck directly below the jaw.

Care should be taken not to apply much pressure otherwise the blood flow to brain may be hampered. Checking of heart rate from the chest is much simpler. One should place one's hand on the left side of the chest just over the heart. After the exercise the hand can very easily feel the beating of the heart. The heart rate after the exercise falls down very rapidly. Therefore, immediately after the exercise and without wasting any time, the heart rate should be checked.

As the heart rate is rapidly decreasing after exercise, therefore, the heart beats should be counted only for 6 to 10 seconds. This should then be multiplied by 10 or 6 to get the actual heart rate in a minute. Correct counting of heart beats is very essential as even a small error of one beat, when multiplied by 10 or 6, is also accordingly multiplied. It is not essential to check heart rate always or after and before each repetition.

The coach and sportsman should learn to subjectively associate the symptoms of fatigue with different heart rates. In this way the monotony of constant heart can be considerably reduced.

III. Repetition Method

The repetition method is characterised by high intensity (90-100%) of work with intervals of complete recovery. It is the best method for the improvement of speed abilities including speed endurance. In endurance training, the repetition method is used to improve components or factors of specific endurance or of anaerobic capacity. For the improvement of specific endurance the repetition method is used in the form of repetitions of the complete distance or part distance with the purpose of improving pace judgement of competition tactics. Certain components of anaerobic capacity like phosphogen stores, non oxydative enzymes and lactic acid tolerance can be effectively improved by repetition method.

For the improvement of phosphogen stores and alactacid metabolism short sprints lasting for about 6-8 seconds are effective. These sprints should be done in series of 3-4 repetitions with complete recovery in between the series.

The lactic acid tolerance can be improved by exercising at maximal or near maximal intensity for about 40-45 seconds or even little longer. This should be repeated 3-5 times with complete recovery in between the repetitions.

IV. Competition Method

Endurance training without participation in sufficient number of competitions is incomplete. Competitions are not only essential for the improvement of specific endurance but are also important for various psychic qualities essential for good endurance performance.

These are also effective for the development of endurance tactics. The competition method is used in endurance training in three forms : (a) endurance test and controls (b) competition in other events, sports or the specific event with minor changes in distance/ duration etc. (c) competitions in the specific event. The competition method in its three forms should be used quite frequently (also in preparatory period) for the improvement of endurance and its components. For example, cross country competitions in the preparatory period have proved to be very effective for endurance sports like middle and long distance running, long distance swimming, walking etc.

This helps in improving the basic endurance along with the required psychic qualities.

NUTRITION AND ENDURANCE PERFORMANCE

Recent studies have indicated the endurance performance can be significantly improved by dietary manipulation a few days or immediately before the competition. Glucose intake before and during long duration competitions is well known as it helps in maintaining the blood sugar level thereby delaying the onset of fatigue.

In sports dietary manipulation for endurance performance is of two types which are explained below:—

I. Carbohydrate Loading

This is based on the fact that initial level of muscle glycogen has a direct relationship with endurance performance especially in events which last longer than 30 minutes. Astrand and Rodahl state that "at work rates exceeding 75% of individual's VO_2 max., the initial glycogen content in the skeletal muscles is decisive for the individual's ability to sustain such exercise for more than an hour".

It has been found that if the muscle glycogen content is improved then the endurance performance also improves. The following three methods of carbohydrate loading can be used in sports training :—

HIGH CARBOHYDRATE DIET

Three to four days before the competition the sportsman is given high carbohydrate diet. By this method the muscle glycogen content can be significantly increased. According to Bergstrom et al the glycogen content can be improved by this method up to 25 gm/kg. of muscle weight. This is the simplest and the safest method of carbohydrate loading. The other two methods are more complicated and risky.

GLYCOGEN DEPLETION FOLLOWED BY HIGH CARBOHYDRATE DIET

Muscle glycogen is first depleted by doing hard training for 3-4 days and having carbohydrate low diet. Muscle glycogen depletion is best possible by adopting slow continuous method. After this the sportsman consume high carbohydrate diet for the next 3-4 days before the competition. During these days the sportsman does not do any hard training.

By this method the muscle glycogen content can be nearly doubled.

GLYCOGEN DEPLETION, CARBOHYDRATE LOW DIET, CARBOHYDRATE HIGH DIET

This method is much more complex and risky and should not be used without expert guidance. Glycogen is first depleted through hard training over 3-4 days. After this the muscle glycogen is further reduced by going on carbohydrate poor diet for about three days. This is followed by 3-4 days of high carbohydrate diet.

By this method maximal increase in muscle glycogen contents can be achieved. During high carbohydrate diet no hard training should be done. However hard training can continue during low carbohydrate diet. Carbohydrate loading, through proved to be effective for endurance performance, should be done carefully. It can have unfavourable side effects. Following suggestions are given in this regard :—

(A) Carbohydrate loading is effective for endurance performance which last for more than 30 minutes.

(B) High Carbohydrate intake in the 3-4 hour period before the competition is not advisable as it can lead to lowering of blood sugar due to reflexively increased secretion of insulin harmone.

(C) Increased muscle glycogen is always accompanied by increased storage of water in the muscles. One gram of muscle glycogen is stored alongwith 3-4 gm. of water. A total of 1-2 kg. extra water can be stored as a result of carbohydrate loading. This may generate uncomfortable feeling in a sportsman.

(D) The process of carbohydrate loading should be done at the correct time because increased muscle glycogen can be retained by the body for a maximum period of 2-4 days.

(E) Carbohydrate loading should be attempted in stages. If there are no complications then the whole process should be attempted.

(F) Carbohydrate loading should not be attempted too often. In a year it should be done at the maximum 2-4 times.

(G) Expert help from a nutritionist, dietition, physiologist, and a physician is essential to avoid possible harmful side effects of carbohydrate loading.

BI-CARBONATE INGESTION

In the past few years some studies have indicated that endurance performance in short duration events like 400m, 800m, 1500m, can be significantly increased by bicarbonate ingestion 1-2 hours before the competition. Astrand and Robahl also state that "biocarbonate ingestion can probably improve performance in anaerobic events such as 400-1500m races". Gledhill, while pointing out the positive effect of bicarbonate ingestion for events of not more than 4 min. duration, cautions that it can lead to side effects in many athletes about one hour after ingestion.

He suggests that the dosage should be about 300mg/ kg. of body weight i.e., 21gm for a 70kg. athlete. This should be ingested in the form of capsules (aprox. of 1.5gm) over a period of 2 hours alongwith a small amount of water. After the ingestion warm-up and competition should follow. Biocarbonate ingestion or soda loading does not come under banned drugs.

But more research and experimentation is needed to explore the nature, mechanism and possible side effects before it can be recommended for use for short duration endurance events.

ALTITUDE TRAINING FOR ENDURANCE

Since 1968 Mexico Olympics the topic of training at altitudes of about 2000-2400m has been of much interest. It is a common belief among coaches and athletes of endurance sports that a short period of endurance training at altitude will help them to improve their endurance performance at sea level. However, whether altitude training actually helps is still debatable.

High altitude exposes the human body to several effects of altitude. These are mainly lesser gravitation, lesser concentration of oxygen in the atmosphere, lesser wind or air resistance, lower temperature etc. These effects amount to greater stress on the oxygen transport system as a result of which some adaptations take place e.g., higher concentration of haemoglobin in the blood to tolerate hypoxic conditions. All these adaptation suggest better aerobic capacity. But research studies indicate no significant difference in endurance performance after return to sea level.

At altitude, however, the sportsman has to significantly reduce his training volume. Also, he is not able to maintain the same training intensity due to hypoxic conditions. The lower training volume and intensity, therefore, tend to nullify the positive physiological adaptations due to altitude. The net result of a training camp at altitude, therefore, is no significant change in endurance performance.

FLEXIBILITY

Flexibility is a motor ability which is not clearly a conditional or a co-ordinative ability. It depends partly on energy liberation process and partly on the coordinative processes of the CNS. In common usage flexibility is often equated with stretchbility, elasticity, suppleness, mobility etc. But as a scientific term flexbility means much more than what is conveyed by any of these terms. Flexibility can be defined as the ability to execute movements with greater amplitude or range.

Stretchability and elasticity are the special qualities of the muscles and ligament by which these can be stretched and can regain their normal length without any adverse effect on the concerned tissue. Suppleness denotes the ability of a muscle to remain in a state of low tension there by allowing for smooth and easy movements of the limbs. Mobility pertains to the degree of movement possible in different planes at a joint.

Stretchability, elasticity, mobility and suppleness, therefore, are a part and parcel of flexibility as these represents different capacities which enable the person to execute movements with greater amlitude. Flexibility is measured by determining the range of movement possible at a joint. This has given to the notion that flexibility is joint specific. But in actual sports movements the ranges of movement is the product of range of movements possible at more than one joint. For a greater amplitude, therefore, some degree of co-ordination of different joint movement is a necessary prerequisite.

In all sports movements, however, a maximum range of movement at all joints is not required. The normal amplitude required is less than the maximum possible. But a higher level of flexibility enables to achieve the required movement amplitude easily without much muscle tension etc.

IMPOTANCE OF FLEXIBILITY

Flexibility has important inter-relationship with other performance factors. It, therefore, determines the other factors to a lesser or greater extent. The importance of flexibility is explained briefly as follows :—

(1) Flexibility is a necessary prerequisite for maximal development of movement force and speed. Greater range of movement enables the muscles to develop more force and speed.

(2) Flexibility allows movements with minimum of muscle tension and internal resistance. It, therefore, has a energy saving effect. Good flexibility, therefore, helps in achieving higher movement economy.

(3) The motor learning requires adequate level of flexibility of the concerned joints. For example learning of back stroke in swimming is impossible without good shoulder flexibility. Inadequate flexibility always leads to errors in movement execution and in order to remove these errors the flexibility has to be improved. Because of its effect on the technique, flexibility also assumes importance for tactical skills.

(4) Flexibility is indispensable for prevention of injuries. Elasticity, stretchability and suppleness of muscles and ligaments helps in absorbing the shocks and external forces tending to cause an injury. But it must be pointed out here that flexibility helps to prevent injuries only if it is optimum. If the joints are overflexible then the chances of injury increase. In other words the stability of a joint is maximum when its flexibility is optimum.

TYPES OF FLEXIBILITY

Flexibility is of two types as described below :—

(a) Passive Flexibility

The ability to do movements with greater amplitude with external help is called passive flexibility e.g., stretching exercise with the help of a partner. The passive flexibility is always more than active flexibility and is largely determined by the joint structure and stretchability of the muscles and ligaments. Passive flexibility is the basis of active flexibility.

(b) Active Flexibility

The ability to do movement with greater amplitude without external help is called active flexibility e.g., stretching a joint by a sportsman himself without any external help. Active flexibility is always less than the passive flexibility and a large difference between the two indicates lack of muscle strength or co-ordination or both. Active flexibility is also of two types, static and dynamic. Static flexibility is required for movements done while the sportsman is standing, sitting or lying. Dynamic flexibility is required for executing movements with greater amplitude when the sportsman is moving. The dynamic flexibility is always less than static flexibility and is heavily dependent on the motor co-ordination.

CO-ORDINATIVE ABILITIES

In the past, five motor abilities were recognised as components of physical fitness. These were strength, endurance, speed, flexibility and agility. But since one and a half decade the term agility has been gradually replaced by the term co-ordiantive abilities.

It was increasingly felt that if the concept of agility can be discarded and replaced by the concept of co-ordinative abilities, it will be more scientific and practical and will help in clearing the confusion. Blume in his path breaking effort suggested that in place of agility there should be seven co-ordinative abilities which are important in sports. This will help in formulating the guidelines for improvement of each co-ordinative ability separately and will also help in better understanding of the role of co-ordinative factor in sports. The theory of co-ordinative abilities is still in a stage of infancy. Though there is rapidly increasing acceptance of the term co-ordiantive abilities yet there is no agreement regarding the number of co-ordinative abilities important for sports.

The methodology of improving different co-ordinative abilities is also yet not available in full detail. But in the near future it is expected that a clear cut system of mean and methods for improving each and every co-ordinative ability will be evolved.

NATURE AND DEFINITION OF CO-ORDINATIVE ABILITIES

Co-ordinative abilities are primarily depend on the motor control and regulation process of CNS. The theory of motor co-ordination, therefore, is the basis for understanding the nature of co-ordinative abilities. For each co-ordinative ability the motor control and regulation processes function in a definite manner. When a particular aspect of these functions is improved then the sportsman is in a better position to do a certain group of movements which for their execution depend on this type of CNS functioning pattern. This also explains the difference between a co-ordinative bility and motor skill. For a coordinative ability the control regulation processes are required to function in a particular manner whereas in case of a skill these processes are automatised to a great extent.

Co-ordinative abilities have also important and strong links with the motor skills as motor co-ordination forms the basis of both. Co-ordinative abilities become effective in movements only through the motor abilities and activity determined drives and cognitive processes.

In the end the important characteristics of co-ordinative abilities are summarised in the following points :—

A. The motor co-ordination processes form the basis of co-ordinative abilities. Hence co-ordinative abilities belong to the performance factor. Technique/co-ordination.

B. As the control and regulation processes of motor co-ordination can only be influenced through the process of afference and reafference (i.e., feed back) therefore, the various sense organs involved in motor co-ordination are the necessary biological prerequisites for the improvement and perfection of co-ordinative abilities. The functional capacity of these sense organs determines the level of co-ordinative abilities to a great extent.

C. Co-ordinative abilities find expression in the quality of movement as well as in the ability to learn movements. The movements on the other hand are essential for the improvement of co-ordinative abilities.

D. Co-ordinative abilities always appear in a complex combination with one another as well as with the conditional abilities, and processes of will, cognition and other psychic factors involved in the process of action or behaviour regulation.

E. Co-ordinative abilities have general and specific aspects both.

SIGNIFICANCE OF CO-ORDINATIVE ABILITIES

Co-ordinative abilities are an expression of motor co-ordination which is of crucial importance in sports movements. The importance of co-ordinative abilities is discussed below in four points :—

(i) The movement quality depends to a great extent on co-ordinative abilities. The rhythm, flow, accuracy, constancy, amplitude etc., of a movement are expressions of motor co-ordination and hence highly dependent on co-ordinative abilities. In technical sports beautiful and graceful movements are a product of well developed technical skills and co-ordinative abilities.

ii. The speed of learning of skill and its stability is directly dependent on the level of various co-ordinative abilities. Motor learning ability is a product of co-ordinative abilities. In sports lesser or greater number of motor skills have to be leant. Besides, the sportsmen are also required to learn the exercises needed for training and for recovery, relaxation etc. Well developed co-ordinative abilities, therefore, assume high importance in all sports. Their importance assumes very high significance in sports in which sportsmen are required to continuously keep learning more and more new movements with higher degree of difficulty e.g., gymnastics. The success of re-learning, frequently needed in many sports, depends on motor learning ability.

iii. Co-ordinative abilities are also needed for maximal utilisation of conditional abilities, technical skills and tactical skills. Without the adequately developed co-ordinative abilities, a sportsman can not make maximum use of his psycho-biological capacities and reserves.

iv. The co-ordinative abilities, to a great extent, determine the maximum limits to which sports performance can be improved in several sports especially the sports which depend largely on technical and tactica factors. Because of this reason assessement of co-ordinative abilities and the possibilities of their further development form an important part of the process of talent identification in sports.

BRIEF DESCRIPTION OF CO-ORDINATIVE ABILITIES

In sports seven co-ordinative abilities are important. In different sports the relative importance of these abilities is, however, different.

A. Differentiation Ability

It is the ability to achieve a high level of fine tuning or harmony of individual movement phases and body part movements. It finds expression in high degree of accuracy and movement economy. Differentiation ability depends on conscicus and precise perception of temporal, dynamic and spatial parameters of movement execution and their comparison with the similar parameters of movement concept at different levels of control and regulation. The high level of differentiation ability depends on movement experience (i.e., motor memory) and the degree of mastery over motor action. It enables the sportsman to perceive micro-differences regarding the temporal, dynamic and spatial aspects of movement execution.

B. Orientation Ability

It is the ability to determine the change the position and movements of the body in time and space in relation to a definite field of action (e.g., playing field, boxing ring, apparatus and/or a moving object (e.g., ball, opponent, partner). The perception of position and movement and the motor action to change the body position should be understood as a unity for the ability for space-time oriented movement regulation.

C. Coupling Ability

It is the ability to co-ordinate body part movement (e.g., movement of hand, feet, trunk etc.) with one another and in relation to a definite goal oriented whole body movement. Coupling ability is especially important in sports in which movements with a high degree of difficulty have to be done e.g., gymnastics, team games.

In a team game like football the foot movement for ball control or dribbling have to be coupled with the whole body movement of running, jumping etc. In gymnastics and also in wrestling the movements of hands, legs, trunk and head have to be successfully combined to achieve a certain goal. In sports, depending on the nature of activity, the movement coupling can be either successive or simultaneous.

D. Reaction Ability

It is the ability to react quickly and effectively to a signal.

E. Balance Ability

It is the ability to maintain balance during whole body movements and to regain balance quickly after the balance disturbing movements.

Balance ability is a necessary prerequisite for all types of movements. Static balance is required for the execution of all movements whether slow or fast, part body movement or whole body movement. Static balance ability develops to a significant extent through various activities in childhood. Dynamic balance ability is important in sports in which frequent and rapid change of body position is required e.g., gymnastics, ski jump etc. In these sports the performance has positive relationship with dynamic balance.

F. Rhythm Ability

It is the ability to perceive the externally given rhythm and to reproduce it in motor action. It also denotes the ability to reproduce a rhythm, existing in motor memory, in motor action.

In some technical sports like gymnastics, figure skating the sportsman has to perceive an external rhythm, given in the form of music, and to express it in his movements. In many sports rhythm is not given from outside. In these cases the sportsman has to make use of the rhythm stored in his motor memory. This is essential for effective motor learning as well as for high quality of movement execution.

G. Adaptation Ability

It is the ability to adjust or completely change the movement programme during the movement on the basis of changes or anticipated changes in the situation. The situational changes may be expected ones or may suddenly take place. The movement adjustment in cyclic sports takes place primarily by the adjustment of the spatial, dynamic and temporal parameters of movement e.g., in running, cycling etc.

RECENT TRENDS IN CO-ORDINATIVE ABILITIES

It is not possible here to discuss the improvement of all the seven co-ordinative abilities separately and in detail. In addition to the limitation of space, the unsatisfactory level of methodology for the improvement of these co-ordinative abilities is the principal reason for this.

(1) The principal method is varied practice and the principal means are learnt physical exercises

Inspite of the fact that co-ordinative abilities are determined by the control and regulation processes, the best method for effective development of these abilities is practising physical exercises. The control and regulation processes are the processes of motor co-ordination and hence are best affected by doing gross motor movements.

The movements, however, should be practised with enough variation. For best effects the movements to be used should have already been learnt to a sufficient degree by the sportsman. Unlearnt movements cannot be used for the training of co-ordinative abilities.

(2) General and Special exercises should be used

Each co-ordinative ability has a general and special aspect. In the initial stages general exercises for the development of general co-ordinative abilities should be dominantly used. But later on special exercises should be used more and more to ensure best effect for performance improvement in a sport.

(3) The movements should be done correctly and consciously

The execution of movement is made possible by control and regulation processes. Incorrect execution of movement will force the control and regulation processes to take place differently and hence to give a different sort of sensations and feelings to a sportsman. As a result he forms wrong associations between movement image and movement sensations and consequently is unable to correctly grasp and understand the verbal instructions of the coach or the teacher. It is, therefore, essential that movement is executed correctly.

(4) Additional means for improving motor sense organs should be used

These co-ordinative abilities depend heavily on the functional capacity of various sense organs e.g., optic, acoustic, tactile, kinesthetic and vestibular. The functional capacity of these organs can be improved by doing exercises during which the sportsman remains comparatively physically passive.

For instance, exercises to improve perepheral vision from sitting or standing position; exercises on the turn table to improve vestibular functional capacity; exercises to improve tactile or kinesthetic perception by use of various types and intensity of touch signals or through use of tensiometer or dynamometer respectively. These exercises, however, should be used as additional exercises only.

(5) Accentuated development of co-ordinative abilities

A physical exercise always has a complex effect. It will lead to improvement of several conditional and co-ordinative abilities. For example typical obstacle runs or agility run are good for improving a number of co-ordinative abilities alongwith speed and strength. But a faster and effective improvement of coordinative ability is possible if the exercise is modified to ensure the improvement of a single co-ordinative ability.

(6) There should be a rich variation of exercises

For the improvement of co-ordinative abilities a limited number of exercises do not give desired results. Each set of exercises have their effect for a certain period of time. Therefore, the exercises should be changed frequently. A rich and continuous variations of exercises used is of utmost importance to ensure continuous development.

(7) There should be a systematic increase in the difficulty of Co-ordination

To ensure continuous improvement in co-ordinative abilities the degree of difficulty of physical exercises should be systematically increased. There are unlimited possibilities of doing this. The important methods of increasing the degree of difficulty commonly used in sports are described in brief :—

(i) Variation in movement execution

The variation in movement execution can be achieved by bringing some change in the phases of movement or changing the complete movement to some extent. The temporal and spatial parameters of movement execution are changed more frequently e.g., doing the movement with slower or faster rhythm, increasing the movement amplitude; change in the starting position or end position.

(ii) Variation in external conditions

Here the possibilities are practically unlimited. The change in external conditions to increase degree of difficulty is frequently achieved by (a) changing the weight, size, shape or height of apparatus/implement/ball (b) changing the surface (c) changing the partner (d) changing the distance between the equipments, players etc. (e) changing the ground dimensions.

(iii) Combination of movements

Combination of two or more movements is very frequently used to increase the difficulty of co-ordination. Movement combinations can be successive or simultaneous combinations. Most common movement combinations are running and jumping, catching and throwing, running and throwing, running and dribbling and so on.

(iv) Change in Information uptake

The co-ordination performances depend on the information uptake and synthesis. The sportsman receives information about the movement from his different motor sense organs. If these pieces of information from the important sense organ/organs are reduced, changed or completely stopped then the degree of difficulty increases manifold.

(v) Practice against time

If the exercise is required to be done with high speed then the difficulty of coordination increases considerably. But, for effective use of this method the sportsman should use only those exercises the technique of which he has already mastered. For effective use of this method the exerciser should be done against time. The decrease in the duration to complete the exercise indicates an improvement in co-ordination.

(vi) Practice under fatigue

Fatigue, whether general or specific, has a deteriorating effect on motor co-ordination. Hence co-ordinative abilities training under conditions of fatigue can be effective. But, like in the earlier method, only thoroughly learnt exercises should be used. According to this method exercises should be done after some sort of strenuous training, e.g., endurance training.

CHAPTER 17

THE TECHNIQUES OF SPRINT RELAY

There are two types of sprint relay in the Olympic Games: the 4×100-meter relay and the 4×400-meter relay.

The objective in the 4×100-meter relay is for runners to pass the baton while the both sprint at top speed. A nonvisual (or blind) pass is used, which means that the outgoing runner has no need to look back or turn and reach for the baton. The 4×100-meter relay has three change-over zones, each 20 meters in legth, and prior to each change-over zone is a 10-meter acceleration zone. The outgoing runner is allowed to accelerate within the 10-meter acceleration zone provided that the baton is exchanged in the 20-meter change-over zone.

In the 4×400-meter relay, only the first lap and the bend of the second lap are run in lanes. There are no chance-over zones as in the 4×100-meter relay, and a visual exchange is used rather than a blind pass, due to the fatigue and slower speed of the incoming runner. The outgoing runner turns to face the incoming runner's hand rather than being given the baton.

In the 4×100-meter relay, elite athletes usually place a check mark 20 to 30 foot length from the start of the acceleration zone, and the outgoing runner begins accelerating when the incoming runner hits this check mark. A call from the incoming runner indicates when the outgoing runner must reach back for the baton. Usually the exchange occurs approximately 5 meters prior to the end of the change-over zone.

With practice, the outgoing runner learns exactly where the exchange will occur and so is prepared for the call of the incoming runner. As excellent 4×100-meter relay team sprints well and moves the baton at top speed. Good arm stretch must be used during the exchange so that each athlete runs the shortest possible distance during his or her leg of the relay.

There are various methods for passing the baton, each with advantages and disadvantages. Four methods are explained in this chapter: two are elementary and are recommended for beginners.

In both of the elementary exchanges, the receiving runner shifts the baton from one hand to the other. For more advanced performers, this chapter provides two alternate exchanges: the alternate upsweep exchange and the alternate downsweep exchange. With these methods the baton stays in the receiving hand, alternating from right hand to left one runner to the next. Of the two, the alternate downsweep is recommended.

COACHING TIPS

Relays involve large numbers of athletes, and it is important that change-over zones are well controlled by officials. After passing the baton, competitors must stay in their lanes rather than immediately move to the infield of the track, because slower teams may be coming up on the inside lanes. An athlete who hinders another team will have his team disqualified. Officials should control the movements of athletes to and from baton exchange areas; this will minimize the risk of fatigued athletes wandering into throwing sectors or disturbing those in other events. The safety precautions concerning sprints and sprint starts apply to relays.

There are two fundamental exchange techniques used for passing the baton; the upsweep technique and the downsweep technique.

THE UPSWEEP TECHNIQUE

The incoming runner passes the baton with an upward, pushing motion and pushes the baton as far as possible into the hand of the outgoing runner. The outgoing runner grips the baton between the *V* formed by the fingers and the thumb of the receiving hand.

The upsweep technique can be applied to three methods of baton exchange: the outside exchange, the inside exchange, and the alternative upsweep exchange. The outside and inside exchanges are considered elementary methods and are recommended for novices. The technique used in the alternative upsweep exchange is advanced and is recommended for more mature and experienced athletes.

THE DOWNSWEEP TECHNIQUE

The incoming runner passes the baton with a downward, forward, pushing motion onto a "platform" provided by the hand of the outgoing runner, who reaches back to grip the upper 1/3 of the baton.

The downsweep technique is most commonly used in the alternate (downsweep) exchange. Like the alternate upsweep exchange, the alternate downsweep exchange is an advanced method and is recommended for more mature and experienced athletes. Elite relay teams may use either technique because each exchange has advantages and disadvantages. However, the majority of elite teams use the downsweep exchange.

OUTSIDE AND INSIDE BATON EXCHANGES

The outside and inside exchanges are so named because the runner carrying the baton runs either to the outside or inside 1/2 of the lane for the exchange. In both exchanges, the incoming runner passes the baton with an upsweep motion into the *V* formed by the fingers and the thumb of the outgoing runner. The outgoing runner then shifts the baton as quickly as possible from the receiving hand to the other hand in preparation for the next change-over. This aspect of the outside and inside exchanges classifies them as elementary and less efficient than the alternate exchanges, in which the outgoing runner does not shift the baton.

CHARACTERISTICS OF THE OUTSIDE EXCHANGE

With this exchange, the incoming runner carries the baton in the left hand, passing it with an upsweep motion. The outgoing runner receives the baton in the *V* formed by the thumb and fingers of the right hand. During the exchange, the incoming runner runs to the outside of the lane, while the outgoing runner waits on the inside of the lane looking back over the right shoulder, keeping the left foot forward, and using a standing start or modified crouch start.

The outgoing runner receives the baton in the right hand and immediately shifts it to the left, running from the inside of the lane toward the outside for the next exchange. Subsequent runners repeat the exchange sequence in the same fashion.

ADVANTAGES OF THE OUTSIDE EXCHANGE

The upsweep action of this exchange complements the running arm action. Plus, the outgoing runner receives the baton in the right hand, which is most commonly the favoured hand. Because the method of baton exchange is the same for the whole team, substituting or shifting runners from one position to another is made easier. Finally, the outsider exchange is easy for youngsters to learn.

DISADVANTAGES OF THE OUTSIDE EXCHANGE

This exchange can hinder the sprinting actions of the second and third runners, who must shift the baton from one hand to the other. Also, the first and third runners run farther using the outside exchange than using the inside exchange.

CHARACTERISTICS OF THE INSIDE EXCHANGE

The incoming runner carries the baton in the right hand, passing the baton with an upsweep motion. The outgoing runner receives the baton in the *V* formed by. the them and fingers of the left hand. During the exchange, the incoming runner runs to the inside of the land, while the outgoing runner waits on the outside of the lane, looking back over the left shoulder, keeping the right foot forward, and using a standing start or modified crouch start. The outgoing runner receives the baton in the left hand and immediately shifts it to the right, running from the outside of the lane toward the inside for the next exchange. Subsequent runners repeat the exchange sequence in the same fashion.

ADVANTAGES OF THE INSIDE EXCHANGE

The upsweep exchange complements the running arm action, and because the method of exchange is the same for the whole team, substituting or shifting runners from one position to another is made easier. The first and third runners run shorter distances using the inside exchange as compared with the outside exchange. Looking back for the incoming runner is more comfortable when the outgoing runner is standing on the outside of the lane. Finally, the inside exchange is easy for youngsters to learn.

DISADVANTAGES OF THE INSIDE EXCHANGE

The second and the third runners must shift the baton from one hand to other, which hinders the sprinting action. Runners receive the baton in the left hand, which is commonly a less favoured hand.

ADVANCED EXCHANGES—THE ALTERNATE UPSWEEP EXCHANGE DOWNSWEEP EXCHANGE

Advanced relay runners use two advanced baton exchanges: the alternate upsweep exchange and the alternate downsweep exchange.

ALTERNATE UPSWEEP EXCHANGE

In the alternate upsweep exchange, the incoming runner lifts or swings the baton upward into the *V* formed by the palm and thumb of the outgoing runner's hand. This action is exactly the same as used for the outside and inside exchanges, but the outgoing runner does not shift the baton from one hand to the other. The incoming runner gives as much of the baton to the outgoing runner as possible, and to do this both runners try to make the giving and receiving hands contact during the exchange.

ADVANTAGES OF THE ALTERNATE UPSWEEP EXCHANGE

Runner 2 and 3 do not have to shift the baton from one hand to the other; sprinting action is not hindered. Runner 2 and 3 run the shortest possible distances, and the upward sweep of the baton complements the running arm action.

DISADVANTAGES OF THE ALTERNATE UPSWEEP EXCHANGE

Because each runner in the team has a specific task to perform, rearranging or substituting runners within a team is made more difficult. Also, each runner receiving the baton has less of the baton to grasp and is frequently forced to readjust the grip on the baton, often by hitting the base of the baton on the thigh, which greatly increases the risk of dropping the baton (particularly during the last exchange).

ALTERNATE DOWNSWEEP EXCHANGE

Using this exchange, the incoming runner grips the base of the baton and passes it with a pushing downsweep action into the palm of the outgoing runner, who grips the upper extremity of the baton. Once the outgoing runner's receiving arm is rotated down and forward, the upper extremity of the baton becomes the base, and the baton is ready for the next exchange.

ADVANTAGES OF ALTERNATE DOWNSWEEP EXCHANGE

This exchange allows for the greatest possible distance between the two runners during the exchange. The incoming runner grips the lower 1/3 of the baton, and the outgoing runner grips the upper 1/3; the distance between the two runners is two outstretched arms plus 1/3 of the baton. As with the alternate upsweep exchange, runners 2 and 3 have shorter distances to run, and runners do not shift the baton from 1 hand to the other.

DISADVANTAGES OF THE ALTERNATE DOWNSWEEP EXCHANGE

The pushing downsweep action of this exchange is contrary to the running arm action, and efforts to achieve arm stretch and baton distance between the two runners may cause a loss of rhythm and running speed. Because each runner in the team has a specific task to perform, rearranging or substituting runners within a team is made more difficult.

COMMON CHARACTERISTICS OF THE ALTERNATE UPSWEEP AND ALTERNATE DOWNSWEEP EXCHANGES

The alternative upsweep and alternate downsweep exchanges have several common characteristics. These involve positioning and duties of team members.

POSITIONING OF TEAM MEMBERS

The positioning of team members in the lane is the same for both techniques; both exchanges require the first team member to sprint on the inside edge of the lane, the second to sprint and pass the baton on the outside edge of the lane, and the third to sprint and pass on the inside edge of the lane.

FIRST EXCHANGE

Runner 1 runs along the inside of the lane, carrying the baton in the right hand. Runner 2 waits on the outside of the lane, looking back over the left shoulder. As runner 1 approaches, runner 2 accelerates along the outside of the lane and receives the baton in the left hand, where the baton remains. Runner 2 continues to run along the outside of the lane.

SECOND EXCHANGE

Runner 3 waits on the inside of the lane, looking back

or over the right shoulder. As runner 2 approaches (with the baton in the left hand), runner 3 accelerates along the inside of the lane and receives the baton in the right hand. With the baton remaining in the right hand, runner 3 continues to run along the inside of the lane.

THIRD EXCHANGE

Runner 4 waits on the outside of the lane, looking back over the left shoulder. As runner 3 approaches (with baton in right hand), runner 4 accelerates along the outside of the lane and receives the baton in the left hand. With the baton remaining in the left hand, runner 4 runs in a straight line to the finish.

DUTIES OF 4×100-METER RELAY TEAM MEMBERS

Each member of a 4×100-meter relay team performs specific duties, which apply regardless of whether the team uses an elementary or an advanced exchange.

Runner 1

This runner must be a reliable starter (no false starts), must run well on the curve, and must be skilled at handing off the baton. This runner runs approximately 105 meters from the start to the point where the baton is exchanged.

Runner 2

Runner 2 must be skilled at receiving and handing off the baton and must be able to sprint well over long distances. Runner 2 can be a tall athlete, because this runner has no curves to run. Runner 2 runs approximately 125 meters from the acceleration zone to the point where the baton is exchanged.

Runner 3

This runner must be good at receiving and handing

off the baton, must be an excellent curve runner, and must be able to sprint over long distances. Runner 3 runs approximately 125 meters from the acceleration zone to the point where the baton is exchanged.

Runner 4

Runner 4 must be skilled at receiving the baton and able to maintain good form while under pressure; this runner must have plenty of fighting spirit. Runner 4 runs approximately 120 meters from the acceleration zone to the finishing line.

TEACHING TACTICS

Drill 1: Lead-Ups

The following lead-up activities progress toward the outside and inside exchanges. These lead-up activities emphasize games of chase and tag, sprint starts, and modified baton exchanges.

Chase

Mark out an area 20 meters by 20 meters. Members of team 2 run freely within the area; members of team 1 stand on the perimeter. On the signal, one member from team 1 attempts to tag any player from team 2. If tagged, that player must leave the area. The first member of team 1 sprints back and tags the next member of his or her team, who tries to "capture" another player from team 2. How much time did team 1 take to tag all the members of team 2? Teams change roles when all members of team 2 have been captured.

Variations

Set a time limit. How many of the opposing team are captured within the time limit? Or, allow pairs of the chasing team to enter the area to tag their opponents. If you have a larger area, have one complete team chase the other: who is last to be tagged? How much time did it take?

Red Versus White

Pairs sit facing each other 1 to 2 meters (3 to 6 feet) apart; one member from each pair is "red", the other is "white". When you call "red", red students must react as fast as possible by leaping up, turning, and sprinting to the safety of a line 10 meters to their rear without being tagged by the whites. If the call is "white", the reverse occurs.

Coaching Points

Use this lead-up as a chance to practice your sprint start. When you turn to sprint away, roll sideways into the set position and work your arms and legs as powerfully as possible, as though from a sprint start!

Variation

Participants lie, kneel, or sit in their starting positions. This may require some adjustment in the 1- to 2-meter spacing so that the chase remains competitive

Touch and Go

Team A members assume standing start positions. Members of team B run to touch with their feet a line 4 to 5 meters from team A. Team B members turn and attempt to sprint to safety behind a line 15 to 20 meters to the rear. Team A cannot start pursuing until team B members have touched the 4- to 5-meter line. Team A members attempt to tag team B members before they reach the safety of the starting line.

Coaching Points

Run slowly to the line; be prepared to accelerate in the opposing direction.

After the sprinter have pivoted around, he should drive with his legs and work his arms vigorously as he accelerate.

Variation

Team A begins in a set position. On the signal, members of team B run to pick up tennis balls or relay batons placed on the 4- to 5-meter line. They then turn and sprint to the safety of the 15-to 20-meter line.

Tag

Teams of 3 to 4 athletes line up to the rear of a starting line. The first member of each team races to a ling 20 to 25 meters away and then back to the starting line to tag the next runner in the team, who repeats the sequence. Each runner goes to the rear of his or her team. Which team finishes first?

Variations

Students can use different starting positions (e.g., lying, kneeling, sitting, or the sprint-start position). Or, place cones 20 to 25 meters away from each team; team members run around the cones instead of to a line. For another variation, a baton can be handed from one team member to the next.

Shuttle Relay With Baton Exchange

Split teams into two groups (1 and 2), which face each other 20 to 25 meters apart. The first runner from group 1 sprints to pass a baton to the first member of group 2, who sprints back to pass the baton to the second member of group 1. The sequence of exchanges is complete and the race is over when all runners on a team have changed sides.

Pendular Relay

Set up posts 20 to 25 meters apart. Runners from each

team sprint around post 1 and tag the next runner to the rear of post 1.

Visual Baton Relay

Holding a baton, the first runner sprints around a post and hands the baton to the next member of the team. Both runners visually control the exchange of the baton. The first runner can use a sprint start.

Coaching Points

Outgoing runner

Begin running when the incoming runner is 3 to 4 strides away. In this exchange, the performer should look back and extend his arm backward to receive the baton. This type of exchange is similar to that used in the 4×400-meter relay.

Circular Relay

Runners stand in a line inside the circle. The first runner, standing at the circle's edge, sprints around the outside of the circle, and the next team member moves to the circumference and assumes a sprint-start set position. A tag on the shoulder from the incoming runner sets the next runner going. Be sure to make the circumference of the circle large enough to give sufficient traction; too tight a curve will cause runners to slip.

Variation

Place a check mark on the circumference of the circle 3 to 4 large strides back from the starting point for each team. When the whistle blows and the first runner has started sprinting around the circle, the second runner moves to the starting point and watches for the first runner to pass the check mark. When the first runner hits the check mark the second runner will turn and start accelerating. Both athletes attempt to pass the baton while sprinting. Do not emphasize a particular exchange at this stage in the teaching sequence. Any type of exchange is acceptable as long as both athletes pass the baton while sprinting.

Coaching Points

Look back for the incoming runner, and watch for the point when he or she hits the check mark. Start running at that instant.

Drill 2 : Tips for Elementary and Advanced Exchanges

Use the following drills for teaching all exchanges, whether elementary or advanced. The main elements of each drill will be the same, although the specifics of the baton pass will depend on the type of exchange you are teaching. The following drills use an elementary (outside) exchange as an example.

Static Baton Exchange Practice

Groups of 3 or 4 students stand 1-1/2 meters apart, one behind the other. This distance is sufficient to require good arm stretch during the baton exchange. The last athlete in each line holds a baton. Students pass the baton with the left hand to the right hand of the runner in front. The baton carrier calls "stick" or a similar verbal command, and on this call the receiving athlete places the right hand back to receive the baton, holding the right arm angled at approximately 45 degrees. The baton is swung up into the *V* formed by the thumb and fingers. The receiving athlete immediately shifts the baton from the right hand to the left. When the front group member receives the baton, all group members rotate 180° and the practice is repeated. Use differing calls for each team and separate the teams sufficiently so that there is no confusion among receiving runners answering the call from the baton carriers.

Coaching Points

Baton carrier

Hold the base of the baton and rotate your hand downward so the baton forms a straight line from the forearm.

Hit the baton into the *V* of the receiving hand, making sure you do not hit the receiver's finger tips!

Give the receiving runner the top 1/3 of the baton.

Baton receiver

Hold your receiving hand steady at 45 degrees; do not wave the hand around. Thumb and fingers must be well spread.

Grip the top 1/3 of the baton with the receiving hand. Immediately bring the hand across the front of your body and grip the base of the baton with the opposite hand, ready for the next pass.

Static Baton Exchange Using Sprint Arm Action

Groups of 2, 3 or 4 students stand 1-1/2 meters apart, one behind the other. Each athlete assumes a slight forward body lean and mimcs the arm action used when sprinting. At the call, the receiver's hand is placed back, and the last person in each line passes the baton to the receiver. The receiver immediately shifts the baton from the right to the left hand, repeats the arm action (but not the leg action) of running 2 or 3 times, and then calls for the next exchange.

Coaching Points

Flex your arms at the elbows and swing them back and forth slowly.

Lean your upper body forward as though sprinting.

Listen for the call.

When you receive the baton, mimic running for at least 2 to 3 arm actions, then make the call for the next exchange.

Baton Exchange Practice—Jogging Slowly

Use the same organization as the previous drill. Team members must maintain a distance of two arms stretch plus 1/3 of the baton between each pair of runners. On the call, the baton is passed forward from one runner to the next as they jog slowly. If runners are in pairs, the rear runner can pass the baton and then run ahead to receive the next pass.

When groups of 3 and 4 are running slowly, the following practices can be employed. The baton can be dropped to the side after the last exchange. The runners pass by, and the rear runner picks up the baton to repeat the sequence of passes. (This method only works well if all the athletes are sprinting slowly). Or, the rear runner can sprint to the front of the team immediately after passing the baton; this sequence is repeated continuously. In another variation, the last runner to receive the baton steps to the side and allows the 3 runners to the rear to pass by. Runners then repeat the sequence of passes fro the rear of the team.

Coaching Points

Run slowly to begin with, and concentrate on the baton passes.

Position yourself the correct distance from other athletes so that both arms are fully extended when the baton is passed.

Do not put your arm back until you hear the call.

Avoid running too close to the athlete in front of you prior to making the call.

Baton Exchange Practice

Students practice this drill at 41/2 to 3/4 speed, then at full speed. When students are running at speed, they must maintain the required distance between runners in order to make these passing practices effective. The front runner should set the pace, and those to the rear then establish the correct distances for passing the baton.

Coaching Points

Baton receiver

Hold your arm steady to receive the baton.

Spread your fingers and thumb wide to provide a good target.

Alternate Upsweep Baton Exchange Practice

Four runners begin sprinting easily in single file. After the front runner has established the pace, students set the passing distance of 2 arms 'stretch'. The rear runner carries the baton in the right hand, gripping the baton at the base. After the call, the rear runner makes the pass with an upsweep into the outstretched left hand of the receiving runner. Students continue to pass the baton (alternating left- and right-hand passes) to the front of the team.

Coaching Points

Baton Carrier

Be sure to make your hand contract the receiver's hand during the exchange; give as much of baton as possible.

Remember that each receiving runner gets less and less of the baton to hold; runners need to be able to grip as close to the base of the baton as possible.

Baton Receiver

Once the sprinter receive the baton, he should not shift it from one hand to the other. Grip as close to the base of the baton as possible so you have as much baton as possible above his hand.

Avoid having to hit the base of the baton on your thigh to reposition your grip.

Alternate Downsweep Baton Exchange Practice

Four runners in file begin sprinting easily. After the front runner has established the pace, runners set the passing distance of 2 arms stretch plus 1/3 of the baton. The rear runner holds the baton by the base in the right hand. On the call, this runner pushes the baton downward onto the platform formed by the left hand of the receiving runner. Gripping the upper 1/3 of the baton, the receiving runner rotates the arm down and forward and prepares to pass the baton with a downsweep push onto the right hand of the next runner in line. Runners alternate passing the baton in this fashion to the front of the team.

Coaching Points

Baton carrier

Push the baton down onto the hand of the receiving runner and give only the upper 1/3 of the baton. The upper 1/3 becomes the base of the baton when the receiving runner begins the arm forward for the next pass.

Baton receiver

Be sure to hold the receiving arm parallel to the ground. This gives a flat platform as a target for the runner passing the baton.

Introduction to the Acceleration Zone, Change-Over Zone, and Use of Check Marks

Pair runners of approximately equal sprinting ability. One runner stands ready on a midline with a check mark initially placed approximately 4 to 6 meters (5 to 6 long strides) to the rear. The other, as the incoming runner, sprints from a line 25 meters back. When the incoming runner hits the check mark, the outgoing runner turns and sprints as fast as possible toward a line 25 meters ahead. The incoming runner attempts to catch up with the outgoing runner by the time they reach the 25-meter line. Adjust check marks so that the tag occurs when both runners are sprinting flat-out (this will usually be close to the 25-meter line). Runners then use a baton in order to practice a selected exchange method. The check mark is shifted back one large stride to allow for the arm stretch and baton distance between the two runners.

The outgoing runner waits for the incoming runner to hit the check mark and then turns and accelerates. The baton exchange should occur near the 25-meter line.

Crouched Starting Position of the Outgoing Runner

Use the previous drill to teach the outgoing runner several skills, such as using a crouched position and looking back over the shoulder for the incoming runner. Other skills to teach at this time include the correct stance on the outside of the lane, looking back over the left shoulder, and reaching back with the receiving hand only on the call of the incoming runner.

Coaching Points

Outgoing runner

Accelerate as vigorously as possible as soon as you see the incoming runner hit the check mark; stay in your 1/2 of lane until you receive the baton.

The incoming runner must catch you and give you the baton, so do not slow down.

Listen for the call; only then do you put your arm back for the baton. Do not put your arm back until you hear the call.

The complete baton exchange should take no more than 2 to 3 strides.

Incoming runner

If you are supposed to run to the inside half of the lane, be sure you do so. Do not run directly behind the outgoing runner, otherwise you'll find yourself treading on his or her heels.

Call and extend your arm only when you are within distance to give the baton, not before.

Do not run with the baton arm continuously outstretched.

Reach forward with the baton only when in passing distance.

Baton Exchange on the Track Using Acceleration and Change-Over Zones

Again using the previous two drills, participants work in pairs and practice the required exchange. It is useful to have third member observe and help to establish the positioning of check marks. For another variation, the incoming and outgoing runners practice the exchange running from straightaway into curve and from curve into straightaway.

Repetitive Acceleration and Change-Over Zone Practice

When runner A, the incoming runner, passes the check mark, runner B, who is ready at the start of the 10-meter acceleration zone, sprints to receive the baton in the 20 meters of the change-over zone. Runner B sprints to pass the baton to runner C. The check mark is initially placed 4 to 6 meters back from the acceleration zone and is later readjusted. After passing the baton, runner A takes the starting position of runner B, and runner B takes the position of runner C.

You decide the distance run to the next change-over; the recommended distance is 25 meters. Additional runners can also be included in the practice so that each runner has a longer rest period between sprints.

Young athletes need not use the full 10 meters of the accleration zone. The line indicating the start of the acceleration zone can be used as the check mark for the incoming runner. The outgoing runner then stands well within the 20 meters of the change-over zone. This gives a young sprinter a line to use as a check mark and also ensures that the baton exchange occurs in the change-over zone and not in the acceleration zone (which is illegal). Adjust the starting position of the outgoing runner and his or her check mark so that the baton exchange occurs approximately 5 meters from the far end of the change-over zone.

Continuous Relay Practice Using 8 Runners

Use check marks, but do not use specific change-over zones. The 8 athletes run 50 meters each. After the exchange, runners jog back to their individual starting positions to receive the baton the second time around.

Continuous Relay Practice Using 9 Runners

Each runner sprints 50 meters; no specific acceleration or change-over zones are used. Runners i and ix are stationed at the start. Runner i carries the baton to runner ii and stays at that position to receive the baton the second time around. Runner ix steps into track to fill the position vacated by runner i.

If runners use an alternative exchange, the first runner carries the baton in the right hand. On the next circuit, this athlete must receive and pass the baton with the left hand. This variation also requires a shift from the outside to the inside of the lane for the reception.

Continuous Relay Practice Using 12 Runners

Each runner sprints the full 100 meters plus additional distances for acceleration and change-over. Runner i sprints around the curve, passes the baton to runner ii, and then goes to the end of the team stationed at the first change-over. Runner ii sprints the straightaway, passes the baton to runner iii, and goes to the end of the team stationed at the second change-over, and so on. Immediately after the first runner from each change-over group has sprinted away with the baton, the next member steps onto the track. An alternate exchange will demand an ability to receive and pass the baton with either hand.

PART 2
RUNNING

CHAPTER 1

INTRODUCTION TO RUNNING AND ITS IMPORTANCE IN TRACK AND FIELD

The recent revival of the Olympic Games has stimulated athletes throughout the world to perfect their bodies in size, strength, symmetry, and agility. The fact that fifty nations of the world are making advance preparations for the approaching Olympic indicates the universal desire to attain perfection in physique and body vigour, with the olive wreath, the symbol of the Olympic champion, as the objective.

The Greeks stressed competition in athletics for a twofold purpose : first, to supply physically fit soldiers and, second to fulfil as nearly as possible their love for artistic beauty in body activity.

Running and leaping exercises put the Greek soldier in readiness for offensive and defensive tactics. Throwing missiles or weights such as the discus and javelin developed strength and accuracy in casting implements of war. Self-defence was taught by participation in sports which involved body contact, such as wrestling and boxing.

Sculptor and poet alike glorified the virile, robust, and symmetrically developed physique as is evidenced by the statues and poems still available to us today. On the other hand, imperfect physical development was regarded as a disgrace, a sign of laxity in training and education, and the poorly formed individual was subject to ridicule. From thucydides we learn that athletic events among the Greeks were conducted with the athletes absolutely naked. Thus, with no garments to hide his bodily defects, the Greek youth set about developing himself, always keeping in mind the aim of attaining ideal physical beauty and proportion. But a fine specimen of manhood alone did not fulfil the warrior's ideals for it was also necessary that he demonstrate his speed, accuracy, endurance, and bravery on the field of competition.

Athletic competition and religion were associated in the life of the Greeks and this fact undoubtedly added to the unusual vitality of the games. Because the ideal of grace and beauty in all things was a part of the religion of the Greek athlete, he naturally entered into the spirit of the competition with genuine emotional fervour.

The rich material rewards bestowed upon Olympic winners led to professionalism and diminished enthusiasm for amateur sport. Music as well as athletics suffered from the professional spirit if we are to judge from the plutus of aristophanes hermes.

The rise and development of athletics in Greece is being paralleled in our day and age. We are remained by some writers today that the overemphasis on victory, the excess publicity, and the superabundant hero worship which caused the decadence of Greek sport is likely to cause the downfall of amateur sport in modern times. Professional tendencies crowded out amateur ideals in Grecian sport. Is it possible that history will repeat itself? Steps to avert this are being taken by local, national, and international sports-governing bodies throughout the world. They are uniting in efforts to uphold the ideals of amateur sports and to maintain athletics in proper balance with other human activities.

It is difficult to decide exactly how the interaction of all the factors caused the loss of amateur ideals and the granting of material rewards upon winners in place of the simple olive wreath, but one can conjecture that these changes were but evidences of the changing philosophy of the Greeks before the fall of the country.

Following the Greek era of high development in athletics, Latin literature records in the Aeneid of Virgil the funeral games of anchises which include athletic contests. Teutonic history sets forth in the Nibelungenlied the accomplishments of siegfried, a champion in sprinting, stone hurling, and spear throwing. Early Anglo-Saxon literature describes the deeds of Beowulf particularly in long distance swimming. Celtic contributions of historical significance in sports are recorded by John O'Reilly, who portrays Cuchullin as the all-round champion of that nation. In the events contested by this superman was the roth-cleas or wheel-feat which is apparently a forerunner of the modern hammer throw. Scottish Caledonian games are well remembered by track and field enthusiasts of a generation ago. In The Lady of the Lake, the Scot, Douglas, was acclaimed for his weight-throwing ability when he succeeded in outdistancing all other competitors in throwing the caber. This implement is a long heavy beam used for tossing in Gaelic games as a trial of strength.

The athletic events found on the present schedule of the track and field program in America are directly linked with the rise of modern English dating from about 1850. The first track and field meet between the two leading English Universities, Oxford and Cambridge, was held in 1864. In 1868 noncollegiate contests were sponsored by the newly formed London Athletic Club.

In America, track and field began to prosper shortly after the English revival of amateur participation. The Amateur Athletic Union of America (collegiate and noncollegiate participants) and the Intercollegiate Association of Amateur Athletes of America (collegiate only) each conducted their first championship contests in 1876.

The National Collegiate Athletic Association, organized in 1905, draws its membership from institutions comprising about eighty-five American college athletic conferences. Many of these conferences have conducted annual track and field championships since 1890. The National Collegiate Athletic Asscoation staged its first track and field championship in 1921.

A majority of the allied associations of the Amateur Athletic Union sponsor periodical competitive events in track and field. These contests are climaxed by the national championships in individual events, relay races, and team championships.

The various states of the United States have organized interscholastic athletic associations since the turn of the century. In 1920 the National Federation of State High School Athletic Associations was formed for the purpose of standardizing rules and regulations in contests for competition at secondary school level. This body is represented on the track and field rules committee of the National Collegiate Athletic Association.

Interstate high school competition was coordinated at the founding of the University of Chicago Interscholastic Meet in 1901 by Amos Alonzo Stagg, although the University of Pennsylvania previously conducted high school competition in the Penn Relays which originated in 1895. In 1993 scholastic competition on a national scale was disapproved in principle by the National Federation of State High School Athletic Associations.

For youth below the high school age, the Public Schools Athletic League of New York has pioneered in competition scaled to meet the physical abilities of young people. Besides these associations and schools, municipalities throughout the land have offered recreational and competitive programs in local systems of parks and playgrounds.

The almost universal interest in track and field events has stimulated participation and competition. At the present time the study of the techniques involved in these sports has become a science worthy of the thought and attention of a profession which is trying, through scientific investigation, to improve technique and skill for all, as well as to cut tenths of a second from running times and to increase jumping and throwing distances by fractions of an inch for the expert performer.

It is quite simple to lump into a single word the tasks for any distance runner aspiring to further excellence: train. However, that word embraces a multiplicity of assignments. We see the following requirements for distance runners as ideally giving them the best chance for achieving success:

1. Find a competent coach or advisor with whom to work, and try to learn as much as possible about the dynamics of training: what work loads best improve fitness, what kinds of changes occur with training, why adequate recovery following tissue breakdown from training is so crucial, and how to realize in advance when more breakdown will be counterproductive to improved fitness development.

2. Define and create a development plan based on achievable goals.

3. Do the physical and mental training necessary to improve performance.

4. Develop a support system for maintaining good health, preventing overtraining, and monitoring fitness/performance assets and liabilities composed of qualified people who can interact effectively with both athlete and coach.

5. Evaluate the results of development by a combination of carefully planned periodic time trials, laboratory physiological evaluation, and races.

6. Document the results of training, racing and physiological/health evaluation over time using charts, graphs, or notes and thus obtain a record that permits objective assessment.

7. Enter each major competitive period with confidence, and deliver good performances.

The purpose of this chapter is to help athletes achieve success in distance running and to help the coaches and scientists working with them. The chapter provide the scientific foundation, that apply this basic information in a practical way for optimal athletic performances. It discuss some of the essentials of physiology and biomechanics that relate to movement in general and running in particular; then outlines the function of skeletal muscles, which permit the movement to occur; explain relevant aspects of energy metabolism, since it is energy derived from the breakdown of foods that permits muscles to function. This chapter connect the information on movement, muscles, and metabolism that is the basis on which the science of training and competing relies; outlines the means by which the cardiopulmonary system ensures the distribution of fuels and oxygen (O_2)—so essential for high-level work—to the various organs that interact to permit athletic performance. Since performance fitness is essentially a measure of the operating capabilities of these organ systems, we introduce here the details of evaluating a runner's aerobic and anaerobic fitness appropriate physiological testing protocols.

Some parts of this chapter will seem challenging to understand, especially for those not well versed in biology and chemistry. Do not devote excessive time to details. The best approach at first is to see the forest, not the tree. Then, as the basic concepts become clear, re-read the examples to help develop a conversational knowledge that will permit exchange of ideas among friends. Carrying even a basic knowledge into the chapter will set the stage for understanding the logic of the practical concepts described and should provide a background of information that will clarify the more technical details.

Based on a fairly comprehensive scientific understanding of athlete performance, specifically discuss the design of training plans. It introduces the concept of periodization, or systematic design, of a training plan and emphasizes the running-related activities for that plan; then integrates all the other aspects of total-body fitness needed to convert a trained monitoring body composition for best performance.

Once athletes understand their bodies and how to train for fitness, it is time to race; an event-by-event analysis of racing strategies for the primary Olympic distance events, along with a special section on road racing. We hope that the presentation of strategies and ideas will serve as a catalyst for athletes to develop their own additional strategies as they enter the "School of Hard Knocks" that is the essence of hard-fought competition.

It examines the problem of managing the enormous

physiological and psychological stress load of athletes whose goal is top-level training and competition. This chapter offers strategies to effectively read the signs of overload and to deal objectively with appropriate behaviours to reduce the stressors that are causing the decline in performance. Some athletes train so arduously that overuse and overtraining result in exhaustion and injury, which can ruin their careers. Athletes willingness to overtrain must instead be refined into a more reasoned approach of identifying what is necessary and how to master it. Important in this process is interaction with a practical and knowledgeable coach or advisor, who can help athletes design a useful plan, and with a good sport scientists, who can help monitor progress using the consistent laboratory profiling technology. (It would be ideal, of course, for athletes to team up with a coach who is a sport scientist, or a sport scientist who also is a coach—but those are rare birds indeed!). Some perspective on the roles of assistive personnel is appropriate at this point.

Where there is life, there is movement. Walking and running are intricate motor skills that develop over time, with repeated practice, and are our most familiar forms of movement. Running is often considered humanity's oldest form of sport—a simple test of the ability of move quickly from the starting line to the finish. The Olympic motto Citius, Altius, Fortius literally means faster, higher, braver (or swifter, higher, stronger, the more common translation). From ancient Greece to modern times, running fast and far has been popular.

The desire to know how to run faster or farther is as old as our willingness to try harder. Talented athletes very often are highly motivated, even to the extent that their enthusiasm may need toning down rather than gearing up. Running is a neuromuscular skill, performed in accordance with the principles of biomechanics and dependent on metabolic energy. Practice, it is often said, makes perfect. When inefficient movement patterns are refined out of a runner's natural style through months of practice, which we call training, movement economy improves, permitting potentially greater speed or endurance. But it is not just practice that brings perfection. Knowing how to practice is essential; athletes must have an effective plan derived from the best information available about the kinds of work that will bring improvement. The results of that practice then can provide essential feedback for more refined activity.

As soon as runners begin to improve their abilities over time through training, they become desirous of any and all information that might enhance this development. Coaches also continually search for answers to questions that might provide them with additional knowledge to help their athletes acquire the winning edge over their competitors. How is running acquired as a skill? How do the nervous and musculoskeletal systems interact to permit running to occur? Can an individual's running style be improved, and would this likely improve competitive performance abilities? How can running injuries be prevented? What occurs during the training process that makes muscles more fatigue-resistant? Are these changes related solely to the neuromuscular system, or does the cardiovascular system contribute to these changes? Because energy is required for movement, how are the various available fuels converted into energy? However, lots of things to be achieved by the coaches as well as the athletes to capture the image of one nation's glory.

CHAPTER 2

THE SCIENCE OF RUNNING

Kinesiology is the science of human motion. It utilizes relevant principles from such disciplines as anatomy, physiology, and physics and applies them appropriately to the understanding of bodily movement. Our particular interest is to better understanding the movement patterns that permit running. Each structure contributing to such body movements acts in obedience to biomechanical and physiological principles. Understanding these principles puts us in a better position to identify the best plan for helping runners become more skilled in their sport. Because running is such a fundamental aspect of human movement, it is a skill learned quite early in life. Improved skill combined with the benefits of training contribute to performance enhancement. Thus, one runners are in their high school, college, and postcollegiate years, increases in performance ability are achieved primarily through greater fitness.

TERMINOLOGY AND CONCEPTS

We define movement as a positional change by any segment of the body. A more complex movement pattern is thus a sequence of movements in a particular time-space relationship. Running is a specifically structured movement pattern. Sometimes the phrases motor activity or motor pattern are substituted for movement pattern. A motor skill is defined as a group of simple, natural movements oriented toward achieving a predetermined goal. Three primary demands on muscular performance are imposed in acquiring any motor skill: strength, endurance, and speed. Coordination links these three together to permit smoothly executed movement patterns.

Fundamental motor skills set the stage for the development of more advanced and specialized motor activities. Fundamental motor patterns thus are the general sequence of movements required to perform a fundamental skill. A small child just beginning to run a few steps has acquired fundamental motor patterns for running. Over time and with practice, marked improvement will occur. This refinement has various features that constitute the developmental motor pattern. As this developing athlete becomes more accomplished over time, the steady improvement in competence beyond the fundamental running motor pattern will be obvious to all. Thus, motor skills are learned. Inborn, natural (unconditioned) responses are eventually modified to permit their triggering by other than natural (conditioned) stimuli in new combinations and sequences. This occurs because the plasticity of the nervous system permits reinterpretation (and, it is hoped, a refinement) of nervous input over time and with repetition.

When asked to run laps around a 400-m track at a specific pace, novice runners typically demonstrate considerable variation in lap times. If the runner is asked to maintain a 75-second(s) pace, for example, for six laps, with half a minute(min) rest between laps, variation of as much as 2 to 3 s and more for each lap can be common. Not so with the majority of experienced distance runners, who after years of good coaching can achieve a consistent sense of pace, despite weather or progressive fatigue, that over distances from 200 to 800m may not vary by more than a few tenths of a second.

A sport skill is a fundamental skill that has been refined and specialized to permit participation in a particular sport. Thus, whereas the simple act of running may be a fundamental skill, the art of running competitively is a sport skill. The concept of form or style refers to the visual effect produced by motor patterns. If the visual effect is smooth and efficient, then good form (style) ought to relate at least to some extent with increased skill. Finally, performance describes an assigned motor activity. A sport performance is thus an assigned, specialized sport activity with the intent of producing the best possible display of motor patterns.

ABILITY VERSUS CAPACITY

In all activities—athletic, artistic, literary—individuals who have subjected themselves to the same levels of intensive training typically demonstrate different levels of ability. The inference is that they must have started with unequal capacities to learn. There is thus a distinction between ability and capacity. Capacity is synonymous with readiness for use, whereas ability presupposes training. Each individual is thus endowed with a general motor capacity analogous to his or her general intellectual capacity. Whereas capacity is a condition, ability can be observed and measured. An ability is invariably the result of training, and the degree of ability is related to the quantity of such training. The common phrase inherent ability really refers to capacity.

The capacity of the brain to develop new motor patterns seems almost unlimited. Incorporation of incoming new sensory information leads to further perceptive and cognitive integration, which in turn permits progressively more effective motor responses. Not only can we create movements in the images of out thinking, but we also can improve their execution. This mental assimilation comes from training. There is no substitute for proper training if movement patterns are to develop optimally. The extent of performance improvement is greatest among athletes whose development programs have been not only very intense but also most specific to the sport skills being developed. Thus, the primary key to success is doing the correct amount of the type of training that best promotes the desired outcome: in the case of distance running, more endurance and more speed.

In essence, we are suggesting that the acquisition of human skills presupposes not only physical abilities but also the realization of distinct aims. The latter in turn are conceived in the image of historical, social, cultural, and scientific precedents. Thus, developing athletes become aware of the excellence of past athletes (such as Olympic Jesse Owens), identify with a particular event (such as the short sprints) and develop a yearing for excellence (such as a desire also to compete in the Olympic Games someday). This provides a base for their motivation and goal-setting toward achieving excellence (through collaboration with coaches who have demonstrated competence).

DEVELOPMENT OF SKILL IN MOVEMENT

Both training and technique are essential in improving sport skill levels. The human body is a self-optimizing machine in that it gradually adapts to a given movement challenge by improving the efficiency with which that movement is performed. This presumably permits the imposition of an even greater challenges, with eventual adaptation to that as well. Peak physical performance occurs when limits to further adaptation are reached. Peak performance is essentially the result of a balance between natural abilities (both physical and mental) and proper training. The results of training are seen in the biochemical and physiological adaptations occurring within cells. Skill is seen in improved movement pattern efficiency; outwardly we see an improved running style.

At least five characteristics are observable as a skilled performer optimizes energy expenditure to permit the highest quality of performance :

1. Balance and coordination improve, thereby reducing postural work.

2. Unnecessary and exuberant movements are eliminated.

3. Necessary movements are refined to ensure that these occur in the proper direction, with optimal quickness to minimize loss of kinetic energy.

4. The most important muscles for movement (the prime movers) are used more effectively, including the most efficient coordination of agonist muscles opposing motion and either are relaxed or stabilize the involved joints when the agonists are active), and synergistic muscles (those assisting the prime movers). The result is minimal energy devoted to initiating the movement, minimal opposing resistance, and minimal force required to terminate or reverse the direction of movement.

5. Continually controlled movements are gradually replaced by ballistic strokes.

This final characteristic needs further elaboration. For practical purposes, the limiting factor in the rapidity of a movement—be it tapping a finger or running down a street—is set by the natural movement frequency of the involved body part; this is its resonance. A reciprocal movements such as running is essentially a series of ballistic strokes. A ballistic stroke can be conceptualized here as a single oscillation of a moving pendulam formed by the arm or leg. Movement is initiated by sudden generation of tension in shortening muscles until acceleration has been completed, at which time the limb continues to move under its own momentum. As movement patterns are being learned, the stroke velocity is slow because of uncertainty, and tension application may occur throughout much of the range of motion. As skill is acquired, movement velocity increases. With it there is a gradual shift from prolonged muscle activity through the range of motion to short ballistic bursts that initiate limb acceleration in the precise direction and extent required to complete the movement.

Like acceleration, a decelerating action caused by tensions generation in the antagonistic muscles continues for sufficient time to revers the movement and initiate a ballistic stroke in the opposite direction. If the optimal resonant frequency of a limb is exceeded, movement becomes less efficient because more energy is required. Resonance thus limits the rate of running through limitation of stride frequency. Once the optimal frequency is attained, greater velocity occurs by lengthening the stride. This is achieved by strengthening, which comes with proper training over time. This explains why, for any aspiring great runner, the two fundamental determinants of running fast are stride length and stride frequency.

These concepts can help us understand the developmental process as runners progress from novice to elite levels. For example, if we compare two runners, each running at the same percentage of their maximal performance capacity and having the same height and leg length, the stronger and more powerful elite-level runner typically takes a stride that is several centimetres (cm) longer. This brings the thigh of the lead leg forward at closer to the maximal velocity permitted by resonance. In turn, this increased velocity requires more intense tension generation in the agonist muscles, and an equally greater relaxation of the antagonists to accommodate the increased range of motion.

If the quadriceps muscles, for example, are the agonist muscles providing forward thrust in running, then the hamstrings are the antagonists. Inflexible hamstrings can thus limit efficient stride maintenance at higher running intensities or can be prone to injury if the much stronger quadriceps group stretches them inappropriately. Thus, optimal relationships among muscle strength, muscle length, and joint range of motion are important not only for promoting faster-paced running, but also for promoting injury-free improvement in performance. As an accompaniment to a training plan that includes various patterns of running to provide specific development, we also recommend a plan to develop these other more general aspects of fitness commonly called total-body conditioning.

BRAIN INITIATION AND EXECUTION OF MOVEMENT

Many regions of the brain and spinal cord interact as a team to set the stage for and permit initiation of functionally useful and efficient movement. The cerebral cortex, as the seat of our volitional thoughts, is only one of the regions in the brain involved in directing movement. Many other brain and spinal cord regions are also involved with movement, and they interact with the cerebral cortex. Gaining a complete understanding of this topic would require some college courses in neuroanatomy and neurophysiology, but for our purposes, such advanced knowledge is not needed. We can briefly discuss some of the more important concepts, and these will be perfectly adequate for our understanding of how running occurs as a form of organized movement.

It is useful to view movement as a phenomenon in direct conflict with posture. Movement causes variable changes in the position of the body parts over time. In contrast, posture is exactly the reverse of movement. The body position is fixed. To resolve this paradox, the renowned neurologist Derek Denny-Brown suggested that we think of movement as simply a series of postures.

The reticular formation in the brain stem plays a fundamental role. This is the oldest part of the brain, responsible for the three primary requirements of postural maintenance :—

1. Support against gravity.
2. Orientation in space.
3. Balance.

Cues from several sensory systems help to satisfy this responsibility. The visual system provides visual orientation in space. The vestibular system in the inner ear provides cues about the position of the centre of mass as well as changes in acceleration or deceleration. Neuromuscular spindles distributed among all the skeletal muscle fibres detect static as well as dynamic muscle length. Golgi tendon organs detect changes in tension or force in skeletal muscles. These various receptors are often grouped together as proprioceptors.

The cerebellum is another primitive brain region, acting like a computer to process incoming information from several levels of sophistication—volitional, automatic, and reflexive. It interacts with both the reticular formation and the cerebral cortex to ensure that volitional commands for movement sequences produce the most efficient and coordinated result possible while still maintaining appropriate posture.

The signals to initiate movement originate in regions just below the cerebral cortex, notably the limbic system and hypothalamus. Here is where motivation and the urge to move (the drive to act) are developed. Stimuli from these areas then activate regions of the cerebral cortex known as association areas, which generate signals to permit synthesis of movement patterns. Signals going to the cerebellum result in movement patterns involving ballistic strokes and great precision. Signals sent to the basal ganglia just below the cerebral cortex create movement templates that provide postural compensation when the movement begins. Both the basal ganglia and cerebellum send their integrated movement pattern signals back to the cerebral cortex, specifically to its motor pyramidal region (so called because many of its large cell bodies resemble small pyramids),

Initiating signals are then sent from the cerebral cortex down through the spinal cord to the various muscles involved in both movement and postural maintenance. The beginning movement and postural alteration are monitored in exquisite detail via action of the proprioceptors. Such incoming information is used by the brain to help the determine how much volitional outpur is required to permit efficient and effective movement.

ACQUIRING SKILL THROUGH TRAINING

Achievement in sport is essentially the product of testing capabilities (how well one performs in either a competition, a time trial, or a practice session) and skill level. Motivation is required for both, but it is particularly influential in providing the persistence required for the training and practice necessary to improve skill levels. For achievement in any endeavour, one needs at least the following :—

1. Reasonable capabilities for that activity.
2. The capacity (motivation plus environment) to train

diligently.

3. Effective use of learned skills in a test situation.

Observing and thinking by themselves do not suffice for the acquisition of skills. In sports as well as the arts, a long period of conditioning and practice precedes mastery of a task. The personal history of every champion athlete reveals the determining role played by intensive and dedicated training. Sustained practice of precisely designed movement sequences establishes advanced levels of control, differentiation, and precision of motor patterns that are beyond the integrative control of untrained individual. Along with basic neuromotor skill, the cognitive qualities of awareness and judgment are also required for performance excellence.

The eventual goal of motor learning is to develop the ability to perform with minimal conscious concern for exactly how the performance is being achieved. Frequent practice of a complex skill helps make it automatic rather than voluntary, and the increasing smoothness thereby reduces error frequency. The execution of all rapid movements depends greatly on timing—generating and relaxing tension in individual muscles in a closely planned sequence. People vary in their abilities to store such movements sequences within the brain. Considerable time is spent practising to develop one's potential within the complex neurological framework that permits movement patterns in the context of postural balance. Once movement patterns have been learned, attention needs only to be shifted from the elements of the task to the initiating signal for skill competence. Thus, bowlers are taught to take their stance and then focus on the pins rather than on the ball or their body arms but rather at the oncoming ball being returned or served. Although running involves much more fitness than technique because it is not a complex, technique-oriented activity, there are useful skill-related hints that runners can focus on while running to perform more efficiently. These will be suggested shortly.

Runners in a race automatically select a stride length, stride frequency, and breathing rate that fit their level of exertion and running velocity. This permits other aspects to be dealt with more from a cognitive view point, such as assessing their own level of perceived exertion and how it seems to compare with the level of runners around them (listening to their breathing patterns, viewing their expressions, etc.) and determining the appropriateness of tactics for improving race position. Is this automatically selected combination of stride length and stride frequency in fact always the most energy efficient? To answer this question, we need to better understand some of the basic applications of biomechanics to running.

RUNNING-SPECIFIC MOVEMENT

Successful distance runners improve steadily with training and experience minimum setbacks from structural injury in any parts of the connecting limbs (bones, tendons, muscles, joints). More training can bring better fitness and thus better performance capabilities, but only within limits. The challenge is to identify those limits before they are reached. This is primarily because the large volumes of training required to improve fitness result in an enormous net impact stress on the feet and legs, which predisposes an athlete to injury.

Runners aspiring to excellence are in almost no-win situation. Running is required as training to improve running skills. As records become more difficult to break, more training (quantity, quality, or both) is required to achieve the performance level necessary for such a feat. This is true for individual records (personal best) as much as for world, Olympic, or school records. The greater the volume or intensity of distance run, the greater the stress and thus the risk of injury. Even one run provides enormous stresses to the lower limbs. Not to train very extensively makes one ill-prepared to compete successfully with those who have done so but have not (yet) been injured. At the top level, it is not unusual for an elite 10,000-m runner or marathoner to have several-week blocks of endurance-oriented training that can exceed 100 mi (161 km) each week (Kaggestad 1987). Using the arithmetic format, a calculation of the number of footstrikes or amount of landing force for such a week gives results that are almost unimaginable. Try the calculations first, before you try the endurance training!

It should be clear that the conflict between the need for training for improvement and the limit imposed by load-related stress that results in injury has stimulated considerable interest in understanding what occurs during a running cycle, how biomechanics can be improved, and how the weakest links, which might predispose a runner to injury as repetitive stress accumulates, can be identified. If improved running mechanics in fact can decrease the energy costs associated with the muscular forces of running, the resulting improved efficiency should decrease the O_2 cost of running at any given submaximal pace. Presumably, this ought to increase the maximal maintainable pace, thereby improving performance. Athletes and coaches ought to understand these basic concepts, including the proper terminology related to running biomechanics. They then can communicate more effectively with the various experts—biomechanists, podiatrists, orthopedists, and other coaches—who have the skills to assist them in identifying optimal training conditions for performance enhancement with freedom from injury.

SCIENTIFIC DOCTRINES

At least four important principles of biomechanics explain what occurs during a running cycle. Understanding these principles permits greater appreciation for the limb and postural adjustments that occur.

Force Must Be Applied to Change the Velocity of an Object in Motion

In humans, muscular tension generation serves as the producer of force. This force can start, accelerate, decelerate, stop, or change direction of movement. As an example, a runner experiences a slight loss of velocity during the airborne phase of each stride. Thus, to maintain continuity of motion, appropriate accelerative force must be applied by the support leg at takeoff.

Integration of Linear and Angular Motion Permits Optimal Performance of Movement Patterns

The lower limbs function by flexion and extension through the range of motion of their joints. The pelvis transmits the body weight to the alternating surface-striking limbs through the hip joints and the lumbothoracic spine. As the lower limbs alternate from support phase through swing phase, thigh extension and flexion are accompanied by rotary movements (to increase stride length), as well as abduction and adduction at the hips and lateral flexion and rotation of the spine. All these movements about various planes need to be complementary and not contradictory.

The Longer the Lever, the Greater the Potential Linear Velocity at its End

In running, this principle is utilized in reverse. Thus, the knee of the recovery leg and the arms as well are bent in order to shorten these limb levers and bring them forward with a smaller energy requirement.

For Every Action There is a Reaction Equal in Amount but Opposite in Direction

With every running footstrike, the landing surface pushes back with a force equal to the impact force, driving the runner upward and forward in a direction opposite that of impact.

There are, of course, additional biomechanical principles that describe the kinds of activities runners engage in during training.

UNDERSTANDING PODIATRIC PRINCIPLES

Podiatrists consider walking and running as an integrated series of anatomic rotations that propel the body through space. The so-called kinetic chain of bones that cope with the impact forces upon landing and the push-off forces upon takeoff extend from the spine to the foot. These bones include, in sequence, the lumbar spine, pelvis, proximal lower limb (femur), distal lower limb (tibia and fibula), rear foot (calcaneus and talus), midfoot (navicular and cuboid), and forefoot (cuneiforms, metatarsals, and phalanges). Joints connect each of these various bony links: the pelvis (hip to femur), the knee (femur to tibia), the ankle or talocrural joint (tibia and fibula to talus), the subtalar or talocalcaneal joints (talus to calcaneus), the two midtarsal joints—talonavicular and calcaneocuboid (talus to navicular), the two midtarsal joints—talonavicular and calcaneocuboid (talus to , and so on, through to the metatarsophalangeal joints (metatarsal bones to phalanges).

Muscles, tendons, ligaments, bones, and joint capsules work together to disipate and manage the rotatory, angular, and compressive forces that occur during a gait cycle. Muscles are particularly important because they initiate movement, stabilize bones, and decelerate or dampen movement forces resulting from sudden weight bearing. Muscle fatigue reduces this protective function, increasing the risk of injury to the other tissues in the kinetic chain.

The body has three axes of rotation: frontal, sagittal, and transverse. Relative to the foot, frontal plane rotation represents inversion and eversion, sagittal plane represents abduction (external rotation) and adduction (internal rotation). One confusing aspect of foot mechanics is that the ankle, subtalar, and midtarsal joints have axes of rotation that are oblique to these three body movement planes. Movements of these joints have components of all three motions. Thus, pronation consists of dorsiflexion, calcaneal eversion, and external rotation, whereas supination consists of plantar flexion, calcaneal inversion, and internal rotation. The talus bone lies just below the tibia and above the calcaneus and thus is a pivotal structure in linking the tibia and above the calcaneus and thus is a pivotal structure in linking the movements of the lower leg and foot. When it articulates with the tibia to form the ankle joint, it works as part of the foot to permit dorsiflexion and plantar flexion. When it articulates with the calcaneus at the subtalar joint, it works as part of the leg to permit pronation and supination.

The support phase of a running gait cycle consists of three distinct periods: footstrike, midsupport, and takeoff (sometimes called contact, midstance, and toeoff). During forward recovery there are also three periods: follow-through, forward swing, and foot descent. The follow-through and foot descent periods are sometimes also known as the periods of float.

THE SEQUENCE OF MOVEMENT IN A RUNNING CYCLE

It may be briefly described what occurs as a runner's limbs proceed through one running cycle. The relevant terminology and concepts are familiar to podiatrists, biomechanists, and orthopedists interested in gait, but this body of knowledge ought to be familiar to coaches and athletes as well. Several good reviews describe rather precisely what occurs during running (Adelaar 1986; James and Brubaker 1972; Mann, Moran, and Dougherty 1986; Slocum and Bowerman 1962; Slocum and James 1968). More than one set of descriptive terms exist for identifying the various aspects of gait cycle for running; we will use that of Slocum and James.

Running and walking are both fundamental skills, but they differ from many other such skills in that the movement patterns is designed to be continuous, without interruption. We move one foot in front of the other, with the arms on each side moving synchronously but in the direction opposite that of the legs. Thus, as the left leg and right arm are moving forward, the right leg and left arm are moving backward. (This information makes it easy to tell when the runners still to reduce problems with lens focusing—on the covers of running magazines). In both walking and running the trunk should lean forward minimally to reduce the load on postural muscles, which will be stressed least if they keep the large percentage of body weight made up by the trunk and head (60%) directly over the point of ground support.

The most important feature that distinguishes running from walking is that in running there is a period during which the runner is airborne, which does not occur during walking.

Although the period of free float is the most noticeable difference between walking and running, there are other differences as well. First, in walking the forward foot touches down heel first, before the toe of the other foot has pushed off. During running the push-off becomes so strong that the body is launched into the air; running is thus a kind of bounding. Second, in running the elbows flex more acutely. This shortens the arm level and thereby allows more rapid arm swing as stride rate increases. In contrast, during walking the arms are nearly extended. Third, greater vertical displacement of the trunk (the bounding aspect) occurs with running than with walking. Last, there is more hip, knee and ankle activity to accommodate the greater stresses with running than with walking. At landing a runner experiences a rapid knee and hip flexion and ankle dorsiflexion in response to the need for greater shock absorption. With walking there is ankle plantar flexion, not dorsiflexion.

Running velocity is the product of stride length and stride frequency. Stride length is best measured from the toe of the landing shoe rather than from the back of the heel. Although walking is almost universally a heel-to-toe action, some runners do not land on their heels. The majority of talented runners (60%) land on forefoot, a sizable number land on the midfoot (30%), and the remaining 10% are rearfoot strikes (Cavanagh, Pollock, and Landa 1977). The forefoot is better able to absorb stress than the rearfoot, an advantage for forefoot strikers.

The period of midsupport continues until the heel starts to rise upward into takeoff. During this time Julianne's foot must convert itself from a supple, mobile structure to a rigid lever to adequately support what at her pace can be two or three times her body weight. This changes does not depend so much on muscle action as on change in position of the subtalar and midtarsal joints of the foot, the anatomic shape of the bones establishes this rigid lever for forward propulsion. Thus, the knee joint extends, the lower extremity rotates externally, the calcaneus inverts, the midtarsal joint locks, and the foot becomes a rigid lever. The propulsive force is a thrust backward and downward, resulting from a combination of hip extension (gluteal and hamstring muscles), knee extension (quadriceps group), and ankle plantar flexion (soleus and gastrocnemius). The end result is a rise in the centre of mass as the body becomes airborne. The wider forefoot than rearfoot helps provide balance and also increases the weight-bearing surface area.

The reversal of limb directions requires time and energy. Hip flexion and forward rotation of the pelvis start moving the left thigh forward. Studied by Mann, Moran and Dougherty (1986) suggest that hip flexion, achieved through action of the iliacus and psoas muscles, is probably the single most important contributor to forward limb movement. Whereas the iliacus muscle has its origin at the base of the sacrum and the anterior surface of the ilium, the psoas muscle originates on the bodies and intervertebral cartilage of the last thoracic and all the lumbar vertebrae, as well as the transverse bony processes of the lumbar vertebrae. Both muscles then attach by the same tendon to that portion of the femur known as the lesser trochanter.

Knee flexion, which is mainly passive, assists this hip flexion by shortening the lever arm, thus permitting the thigh to move forward at a velocity considerably faster than the body's forward velocity. As soon as maximal hip flexion has been reached and the thigh farthest off the ground, the final float period, called foot descent, begins. Final preparations are made for the footstrike that will initiate the next cycle. Quadriceps muscle activity promote knee extension for maximal forward movement of the lower limb. The hamstrings then slow the forward movements of the foot and leg by generating tension, antagonizing any additional knee extension. In showing this limb movement, the hamstrings lenthen.

CHAPTER 3

THE DISTANCE RUNNING

The art of distance running lies in distributing one's energies as efficiently, completely, and rapidly as possible over any distance in which endurance is a primary factor. Basically the problem is the same, whether the length of run be 440 yards or the marathon distance of 26 miles 385 yards. In this discussion, however, direct attention will be given only to the regular school events : the 880, the mile, and, for colleges, the two-mile.

That great improvement in performance in these events has occurred at all competitive levels during the past 75 years is clearly evident. For example, more high school runners bettered 4:35 for the mile run in 1950 than did college runners in 1925. However, the reasons for such improvement are less clear and invite careful consideration. Among the more important are the following :

1. The natural human drive for recognition carries on without regard for the difficulty of achievement; the greater the challenge, the greater the response.
2. There is more intensive and widespread interest in track performances at all age levels.
3. The incentives and rewards for achievement have been increased at all age levels.
4. More men are competing and for a longer period of years.

5. Facilities and equipment are greatly improved and extensively available.
6. Attitudes toward time have changed. What was formerly thought impossible is now commonplace. This has occurred at all levels—high school, college and world.
7. Fear of heart or other organic injury through overwork has been removed.
8. The number of weeks of training each year has greatly increased at all age levels.
9. The number of competitions within each seasons has greatly increased.
10. Coaches have become more numerous and their training methods have improved.

TRAINING SYSTEMS IN DISTANCE RUNNING

Although there are no distinct and separate systems of training in distance running, there are certain broad points of view by which various systems can be distinguished. For example, the traditional American method of working entirely on the track under the close supervision of a professional coach is seemingly quite in contrast to the North European methods of running without direct or personal coaching and primarily along wood paths or through the fields. Further, within each of these systems there are those who believed in the primary efficacy of steady over-distance running and are opposed to others who are convinced that, under their particular training conditions, they under-distance and easy work will produce best results.

An adequate understanding of distance training is not possible without at least a basic knowledge of the similarities and differences of these systems as well as of the advantages and weaknesses of each.

THE ORTHODOX SYSTEM

The traditional orthodox system has two distinguishing characteristics: (1) a professional coach is always present and is expected to assign a specific workout to each man each day, and (2) all running is done on immediately next to a carefully prepared cinder track. It should be pointed out that only in America does each educational institution employ a trained and full-time coach whose activities are exclusive the promotion and teaching of athletics. In Europe and England there are a few national coaches who conduct clinics and travel into all sections of the country to advise athletes and certain part-time and often unpaid coaches. Older and more experienced athletes, perhaps graduate students who are still active in sports, provide most of the direct coaching. It is significant, for example, that the two most recent English books on track athletics were written, and excellently written too, by amateur members of athletic clubs who are still competing in their events. To Americans such lack of supervision can seem neither healthful nor productive of best efforts. We argue that a coach is a balancing and safety factor against extreme and unwise effort. Yet others counter by stating that the American system, with its primary emphasis upon winning regardless of inequalities of competition, has produced just the opposite result and that the coach is driving force toward greater specialization and greater effort. It is therefore important that an unbiased and realistic analysis of both the advantages and weaknesses of our system be made.

ADVANTAGES

1. It provides direct supervision of all practice work. Most American runners are still boys who lack the maturity and the knowledge to have proper judgment concerning the amount and kind of practice. On the one hand, there is the demand

from medical and education authorities to prevent overexertion and other harmful sports practices by providing adult leadership; on the other, there is the undoubted difficulty of the average boy in distinguishing between the feelings of fatigue and its actuality, which results in his crying "enough" long before the greatest practice benefits have been derived.

2. It provides a flat and smooth surface. This permits extreme speed work, which is so essential to American training and in part explains our success in Olympic competition at such shorter distances as the 800-meter. Of the first 12 Olympic games all titles have been won by either Americans (6 champions) or British Empire athletes (6 champions) who have placed a similar emphasis upon speed work.

3. It provides a better opportunity for pace work. The presence of a coach and a measured track seems essential to the development of good judgment of the right pace for an exact distance. Such judgment is learned only through repeated practice, day after day, and would be greatly delayed and dulled under any other system.

4. It is efficient as a teaching situation. It appears almost self-evident that the nose proximity of a wise and experienced teacher, as well as of other, more mature members of the team, should provide an ideal opportunity for learning the techniques and attitudes of running without wastefully repeating the mistakes of one's predecessors. Our record books teem with the names of those who had to be encouraged, challenged, pushed, and even coerced into doing better than they could do.

5. It permits a larger and in some ways better group

atmosphere. A large group leads to better team morale generally and to a more enthusiastic attitude toward practice. In many of our schools and colleges, students cannot report for practice at the same hour. Confinement of practice to a small outdoor or indoor area permits latecomers to join the group running.

6. It is undoubtedly the best system in developing a well-balanced and winning team. The careful observations made daily by the coach permit him to select the right men for the right events, with the allowance for the strengths and weaknesses of the opposing team. Further, it permits men in the same event to know each other's capabilities and to assist each other in practice and in meets for the sake of the team.

7. It hurries the learning and training process. The persistent drive toward excellence forces American coaches to attempt to bring a boy to a high level of performance during the youthful years of 16 to 22, when American boys are in school and therefore in competition. European runners begin serious athletic competition at a later age and continue on to the age of 30 or even 35, about 10 years longer than the average American.

8. It aids the runner to build a greater resistance to fatigue. Increased resistance to fatigue is one of the factor in endurance and results from running a little faster and farther each day—from digging deeper and deeper, so to speak. The stimulus of the coach's presence can be a help in achieving this. Such digging deeper need not be a tearing-down process, as is sometimes protested. On the contrary, if intelligently conducted, it is the only means of developing the heart and circulatory system as well as the other mechanism for

counteracting fatigue.

9. It requires a shorter period of time for each session. This is increasingly important in most of our schools, for the time now free for recreation and sports is becoming all too short.

DISADVANTAGES

1. The American system has a marked tendency to develop runners who are dependent upon the coach. It is usually he who decides what event shall be run, at what speed, and in what manner, not only in practice but in meets as well. Admiting the youthfulness of American school athletes, training methods should move a rapidly as possible not merely from inability to excellence in performance but also from dependence to independence, and from ignorance to knowledge by the athlete. It is the athlete who must run and who must know. The presence of a mature coach, whose ego is naturally flattered by their need for his help, is an all-too-enticing substitute for the athlete's own analysis of the situation, his own decision, and his own responsibility for results.

2. It has a tendency to ignore the truism that the essential object of sports is recreation. Although the professional coach, generally speaking, is a man of integrity and great value as an educator of American youth, the system of which he is an essential part often emphasizes winning, specialization, and the drive for perfection beyond their true value to the participants. The urge for more and more, and better and better, often reaches a point of no return, at which efforts the futile and even detrimental to everyone concerned. The coach, although but one phase of the system, must accept his share of the responsibility for its excesses.

3. It emphasizes a lip-after-lap, day-after-day, week-after-week monotony of practice, which deadens the fun and enthusiasm for running that are essential factors in continued good performance. Many devices can be used to minimize this weakness, yet the sameness of the surroundings and the running surface place unavoidable limitations.

4. It stresses a consciousness of the exact number of laps run each day. Consequently, there is an exaggeration of the feelings of being tired. To Americans, a mile to be walked or run is a relative long way, and our runners are likely to interpret number of miles covered from this point of view.

5. It places great stress upon the judgment of the coach concerning the amount of work needed. Although the athlete's feelings are deceptive, they are often a better basis for decision than are the "cold" opinions of even the expert. Further, the athlete alone knows his off-the-track training record—his late hours for whatever reasons, good or otherwise, his sense of a cold coming on, his worries concerning personal problems. Few boys like to bother the coach with these matters.

6. It leads to the development of "shin splints" and other muscular difficulties with the foot and lower leg. The constant running day after day on relatively hard tracks places great strain on the leg muscles, and quite occasionally leads to a lengthy lay-off from all work. Mr. Holmer, the Swedish Olympic coach, speaks of the irritating and deadened "hard muscle" developed by track running as contrasted to the soft and quick muscle produced by the pine-needled paths of Sweden.

7. It undoubtedly cuts down the number of miles

covered each day and possibly reduces the number of fast swings as well. The entire psychology of the American system is away from a play atmosphere, of running for the sake of running. The practice session is, as its name implies, a workout, running for the sake of some later reward or later satisfaction. At its worst, it becomes drudgery. In contrast, "Fartlek" or speed-play, is self-imposed and more likely to be fun.

8. It is seldom truly individualized. Even those coaches who protest most violently against training schedules and for consideration of individual differences have a tendency to run men in groups. The star may get individual attention; the other, lesser runners tage along and often take work that is entirely unsuited to their development.

"FARTLEK", OR SPEED-PLAY

The unparalleled success of Swedish distance runners during the last few decades has aroused tremendous interest among American coaches in their training methods. In response to their inquiries, Gosta Holmer, the Swedish Olympic coach, wrote with a frankness and an open-heartedness that are in refreshing contrast to the narrow nationalism shown in other areas of human endeavour.

It is not the races that make the runner but rather his training methods. In Sweden we saw ourselves conquered by the Finns; we gained a certain standard, until I, in the middle of 1930, decided to try to create something new, something that suited our mind and the nature of our country. I rejected the American opinion, that the runners

The running should be done on cross-country where the surface is soft and spingy, although in the large cities, where it is difficult to get to a forest, you should make a path on or around a sport field, and make the path soft by covering it with sawdust.

The athlete should train from one to two hours each day, according to the following schedule :—

1. Easy running from five or ten minutes (as a warm-up).
2. Steady, hard speed for one to two km. [5/8 mile to 1¼ mile].
3. Rapid walking for about five minutes.
4. Easy running, broken by wind-sprints of from fifty meters to sixty meters [55 yards to 65 yards] and repeated until you feel a little tired.
5. Easy running with three or four swift steps now and then. (In reality, these swift steps would be like the sudden speeding up of a runner during a race when he tries to fight off a challenger who is trying to pass him. The body suddenly lurches forward, and three or four quick, sudden steps are taken).
6. Full speed uphill 150 meters to 200 meters [165 yards to 220 yards].
7. Fast pace for one minute following this trial of strength described in (6).

The above described work can be repeated until the end of the period of the workout; but every athlete should well remember that he must not feel tired but rather stimulated after the training.

The extent to which this program is followed is of course dependent upon the individual, his time, his energies, and the phase of season. In Track and Field News, Cordner Nelson states :—

Mid-season training is different. As Fred Wilt pointed

out in the third article of this series, some runners use little or nothing except Fartlek. But for those who want to see a fairly typical program as recommended by Holmer, here are schedules for the mile ... :

Monday—1. Fartlek 45 minutes.

2. First 440 of race.

3. Repeat 2 or 3 times.

4. Walking and easy running to complete 2 hours.

Tuesday—1. Fartlek 20 minutes.

2. 880 on track.

3. Repeat within an hour.

Wednesday—Walk in woods 2 hours.

Thursday—Same as Monday, but run uphill 2 to 9 times for 150 yards each time during Fartlek.

Friday—Same as Tuesday, but run 4 440's instead of 2 880's, each lap one second slower than racing speed.

Saturday—Rest.

Sunday—Warm up and run a mile.

Remember :—these schedules are not blueprints. Each athlete must use his head.

The Swedes are extremely practical about fitting the schedule to the needs of the individual. For example, Holmer says: "It is wrong to give a student at yale the same work in training as a man who, in the struggle of life, has to walk ten miles".

A further interpretation and development of "Fartlek" is made by S.A. Tomlin in the British publication, The Athlete :

The runner practice "Fartlek" twice each week during early training and once each week during competitive periods, over the country or on grass sports field.

Speed is added by 220 yards bursts on the track two or three times each week. The runner does a series of such bursts at a speed faster than the average speed of his race. For instance, a 4 mins. 24 secs. miler runs each 220 yards at an average speed of 33 secs. His speed training would then be 220 yards in 28/29 secs. He runs 220 yards, walks back to the starting point and repeats, doing this until he begins to feel weary. The training is then finished off with about 30 minutes of easy running on the soft grass.

On other days the training consists of walking and easy running for 1-2 hours, the exercise being eased off to suit personal reactions, and stopped before fatigue occurs.

The schedule of training into four progressive periods of activity :—

(1) Conditioning period : January to mid-April. Walking, easy running and indoor gymnastic exercises.

(2) Pre-seasons : Mid-April to mid-May. Running work and "Fartlek" with some speed training.

(3) Early competitive season : Mid-May to early July. Training as above but one competition each week.

(4) Competitive season : Early July to September. Amount of training according to amount of racing.

ADVANTAGES

1. "Fartlek" provides a natural pattern of activity. Children or even young animals play hard for-a while, then rest until they are ready to play hard again. So with "Fartlek". After a short warm-up period, a group of runners will take a series of

sprints as challenges from within the group may stimulate them. A period of easy jogging or walking will ensue until gathering energies urge them to speed work again. If the members of the group have similar abilities and are in similar condition, they do not exhaust themselves, for there are no external pressures and they have done only what they themselves have decided to do and at the pace they wanted to do it.

2. It develops self-dependent and resourceful runners. The lack of a coach makes it necessary for the individual to think out his own program of running and his own solutions. He and his companion runners must decide where to run, how far, and at what pace. Their very lack of certainty leads to discussion and at least an attempt at intelligent understanding. Given years of time and maturity, as among European runners, this is a tremendous asset.

3. It encourages men to try different competitive distances on the track. Working half-milers, milers, and two-milers together make them realize that their races are fundamentally the same, the difference being only in the distance over which they have to spread their energies. Such men are more relaxed about coming competition and certainly more valuable in relay meets or other meets calling for unusual distances for certain men.

4. Its proponents claim it is physically and mentally invigorating and refreshing. Holmer writes "When you feel tired then relax by walking in a wood or park listening to the song of the birds. It is not only the body that gets tired but the mind as well. What you are able to do in one hour spread over two. You should not have a disagreeable feeling after a

training outing. A man who thinks he will attain his goal only by training hard from day to day will be richer only by bitter experience." In any case, it avoids the monotony of daily round-the-track running.

5. The daily training session is approached from a time basis rather than a mileage basis. "Fartlek" runners start out to run for one or two hours. Consequently, they are not nearly so conscious of actual distance covered nor of their own fatigue. They cover more miles, yet do not feel so tired. Much of fatigue is the result of an attitude of mind; we feel tired largely because we think we ought to be tired.
6. The softer running surfaces of woods and field paths lead to a softer and more relaxed muscle and to less soreness.
7. It probably leads to an earlier date for the first spring practice session. There is no waiting for the track to be brushed and rolled. Consequently, men are in better physical condition, or at least have attained condition at an easier and more healthful pace.
8. The soft but probably uncertain footing of woods paths leads to a shorter, more efficient, and more relaxed stride, which is advantageous for distances beyond the one-mile run. American long-distance men undoubtedly have a tendency to overstride.

DISADVANTAGES

1. It provides no direct supervision of practice. The youth of American runners and our over-all attitude toward sports make adult supervision advantageous from the standpoint of health as well as of successful and efficient organization.

2. It provides little opportunity for pace work or for teaching the numerous details of race tactics and team organization. The complex American track schedule of both indoor and outdoor running on tracks of different sizes, plus a variety of types of meets—dual meets, championship meets, and relay meets—makes such teaching essential.
3. It does not permit an emphasis upon extreme speeds as is common practice on smooth American cinder tracks. For this reason, "Fartlek" runners are not so likely to do well at the 880 or mile distances as at the longer runs.
4. It is a slower method of developing runners for competition and of their learning how to run. The point might be argued as being an advantage, for its very slowness implies a sounder physical and emotional development. However, from a high school competitive standpoint. It is a disadvantage.
5. It has a tendency to neglect the individual runner. This is particularly true where he indicates little promise for the future and soon becomes discouraged by his futile efforts to stay up with the groups. Runners are not so likely to help him as would a coach, whose responsibility is for the whole squad and for many future years. Such runners "of little promise" are often the backbone of future teams.
6. It requires more time each day.
7. It requires woods or grass paths, preferably with a varied topography.

These are seldom available to our city high schools and are often absent in our colleges.

THE MODERN SYSTEM

Modern training methods in distance running assume the no coach can teach a man as much about himself as he can discover through his own self-initiated study and practice; that the sport exists for the boy and no urge toward excellence and specialization should unduly influence the ideal of a well-rounded persons and of a sound mind in a sound body; and, finally, that great competitive success can be attained through determination, intelligence, and confidence even though training is at a minimum level. The true sportsman practices running because to run is enjoyable; and he competes because the association with other sportsmen, the thrill of meeting their greatest challenge, and the anticipation of victory are all worth while in themselves, quite apart from the acclaim and rewards of actual success.

This point of view is basic in the book athletics, written in 1929 by two great English track champions, Douglas Lowe and Arthur Porritt, and has clearly influenced the writers of the chapters on running in the recent book Athletics, published in 1951 by the Achilles club. Admitting the importance and even the necessity of athletic "giants", Lowe and Porritt considered such perfection in performance as being primarily valuable as an incentive and a guide to thousands of average boys throughout the nation, and they thought strenuous practice and specialized training were unwarranted and unwise for growing school boys.

In training of all kinds it is never wise to do too much. The object of training is not to break records or to exhaust oneself, but to improve style and technique and to store up energy for the race. For this reason, it is an excellent thing, once stamina is assured, to practice over distances which are shorter than the race. There is no question about being able to stay the course in races—excitement and fitness will always carry one home. Therefore, a quarter-miler will benefit if he goes 300 yards; a half-miler, 440 or 600; a miler, half or two-thirds of a mile. And one should avoid running oneself out in practice—that is not the aim of training. If possible one should seek final polish and have "all-out" runs in actual races; and if things can be arranged, it is a sound plan to scheme a series of graded races which will gradually bring one on week by week to faster times...

The length of time required for special training, once the runner is fit, as a minimum, about two or three weeks, provided the system of graded races advocated above practicable. Naturally, longer time is required to study technique. The frequency of training depends, largely upon the individual—how much he does at time, how much technique he has to acquire, and whether he plays other games which can supplement his training and, incidentally, help to keep him from staleness. But three times a week at the most should suffice; and when racing begins and one is fit, only one run a week besides the Saturday race is necessary or, indeed, wise, else there is a risk of staleness. Slight undertaking is better than too mush, which nauseates.

Should it happen that the athlete is anxious to attempt two or more middle distance events, the first advice is that of Punch—"Do not". Undoubtedly the ideal is one man one man one event; and this is quite sufficient exercise if there are heats on the same day.

Truly, for the modern, running has been a recreation. One might brush away the naïveté of these statements on the grounds that they were written over 20 years age and that our superior knowledge and running of today refute his beliefs. Yet the cruel fact is that Mr. Lowe defeated the world not only in 1924 but again in 1928 in the still good times of 1:52.4 and 1:51.8.

For further evidence, one can list such great names as A.N.S. Jackson, A.G.Hill, B.G.D. Rudd, G.H. Stallard, Thomas Hampson, John Cornes, Jack Lovelock, Sidney Wooderson, and Roger Bannister, all of whom, along with many others, inclined toward Lowe's beliefs and methods and yet were truly great performers in world competition.

In talking with Roger Banniste (mile—4:07.8, and 4th in the 1952 Olympic 1500-meter—3:46) in April, 1951, and watching his workouts, the writer gained the impression that the present point of view of modern runners and their amount of training is much more extreme than that expressed by Lowe and Porritt. Yet the influence of Lowe and those of similar mind is still clearly evident in both English writings and practice methods. After observing the 1952 Olympics, in which preliminaries, semifinals, and a final were run in the 1500-meter race and where runners had to break or approach the world's record in several instances merely to place in the competition, one cannot refrain from speculating whether modern respect for a gentleman's sports code or their pride in success in international competition will predominate.

Evaluation of the modern system. How can it be that a system of training that is so much in contrast to the almost never-ending and strenuous work of both the European and American systems is yet able to produce such excellent competitive results? Several considerations suggest themselves :—

1. The modern system has been most successful at the 800-meter distance, slightly less so at the 1500-meter, and, with certain recent exceptions, quite futile in the longer runs. In other words, modern athletes have demonstrated that their under-work method is effective at the shorter distances, where physiological factors are, conceivably, less vital.

2. The modern speak of competitive "peaks", of preparing for a particular race as the one goal of a season of running. They have not demonstrated an ability to run equally well on successive week ends of a long season.

3. They are proudly conscious of a national tradition of competitive spirit, of "muddling through" until the going gets really tough and crucial, but then coming through when the big chips are down. They believe in their ability to compete successfully against the world's best in sports, particularly in the 800- and 1500-meter runs. Apparently, the modern believe that genius in running is made up of about 40 parts of inspiration to 60 parts of perspiration, whereas the American an Swedish systems assume the more common definition of only 10 per cent inspiration and 90 per cent perspiration.

Three conclusions might be reached. First, as long as one is not running over the mile distance and does not intend to race seriously week after week through a long season, it is porsible to race exceedingly well on an underwork, under-distance program of training. Second, determined confidence actually is half the battle; when it is present, physiological factors function at maximum efficiency. Third, if the 40 parts of modern inspiration and quiet confidence could be added to 90 parts of perfect physiological training, the result would be more than 100, and that, fellow sports lovers, would mean new world's records.

FUNDAMENTALS OF TRAINING FOR DISTANCE RUNNING

In the light of this detailed discussion of the advantages and disadvantages of the various training systems of the world, what seem to be the basic essentials of training that every runner and every coach must utilize if their programs are to prove most efficient and most helpful?

Running, gradually increases over a period of months in distance, speed, and intensity, is an invigorating, mentally wholesome, and organically sound activity that will continue to build up the healthy boy and in no sense tear him down. The medical profession in the past has had a tendency to think of health as implying freedom from disease or impairment and to argue that exercise is not a primary health factor. Yet true health is a positive term, implying efficient and vigorous use of the organism. A healthy organ or muscle group is an efficient and powerful means to energetic action and not merely a motor capable of supporting a minimum sedentary existence. Certainly such an organ is not easily injured or strained.

If it now agreed that cardiac enlargements are the result of pre-existing disease and the normal heart cannot be dilated beyond its physiological limit, nor will a bout of strenuous exercise "strain" the healthy heart muscle or cause it to fail—the evidence taken in review indicates that athletic pursuits, especially of a strenuous nature, may cause a moderate but definite increase in cardiac bulk. This, however, is purely physiological and is proportioned to, or only slightly in excess of, a development of the skeletal muscles; the ratio of heart weight to body weight show no change or a very moderate one".

Present-day physiologists and psychologists generally agree that the healthy human being is naturally protected against major organic injuries that might occur from fatigue and that the discomforts and even pains of fatigue are themselves a defence against overexertion. An untrained individual will normally give up an endurance exercise soon after the discomforts of early fatigue appear, and even the incentives of the group or of the coach are not likely to push him far beyond this point. Such fatigue is primarily psychological and not at all an evidence of exhaustion. Even the all-too-frequent cases of men dropping "exhausted" at the finish line are very little related to physical fatigue but rather to the mental attitudes of giving up once the finish line is crossed.

Only when there takes place muscular or organic development that is beyond its present and later value to the runner can there be a question of worth-whileness, but in the all-too-short period of practice time now available to high school and college students this is an impossibility.

The most effective secret to success in running lies in running, running, running, any place and any time, primarily because running is fun but also because the possible outcomes of running are worth working for. This statement seems obvious and simple, and yet it is in large measure forgotten and ignored by a large percentage of runners. If one can assume varied running speeds, including a certain proportion of sprint work, it can be stated definitely that the amount of improvement in physical and mental condition for distance running is directly proportional to the amount of running done. All other contributing factors are secondary. Certainly the circulatory system or the muscle structures have neither knowledge nor interest in the time of day, or the type of running surface, or whether a coach with a stop watch is present. Though apparently, silly, this statement needs careful consideration, especially by the athletes themselves. Their almost universal concern that a coach should watch and time almost every lap they run; their belief that they have a correct attitude when they fulfil exactly whatever definite assignment their coach has given them; their habit of asking the coach, "What do we have to do today?"; their pride in their knowledge of jut how many laps they have covered in practice—all these matters point toward a basically unsound approach to training. The important thing is to run. Run on every surface that permits running. Run at every speed the footing allows. Run in the morning and at night, not because two more miles will add another fraction to physical condition, but because running has become a habit and, more than that, an enjoyable habit. The protest that most of our runners come from cities where the opportunities for this kind of running are very limited will hardly hold water. Sidewalks afford smooth and even, though hard, surfaces. Cushioned, rubber-soled, lightweight shoes are available, inexpensive, and entirely comfortable. The boy who really wants to be a runner will not hold back for lack of the soft pine-needled paths of the Scandinavian runners. He'll run under any and every condition, for only by running can he hope to become a champion runner.

Greg Rice, the great Notre Dame two-miler of the 1938-1945 era, states the case most capably :—

The paramount prerequisite for condition, the basis of success, is hard, diligent work. There is no escape. As soon as one no longer desires to make the self-sacrifice necessary for complete preparation he should then forget about winning any races or even competing...

Distance runners themselves prove that work, miles of competition, and training are required as they do not blossome into starts until they have matured. It is not an overnight sport. Years are an important factor in one's developing progress. So do not become too anxious for favourable results, look for a steady and slow betterment and then one day you will discover you are a start. The self-denial and hard work will have left many fond memories.

The darkness of this note seems necessary since with the proper attitude one can obtain a much higher objective. Knowledge of what is required makes it easier to overcome the ups and downs of the long period of development without unnecessary discouragement. Discouragement will often face that individual, but his interest will find bolstering from the knowledge of the hardships of others and it will aid him to re-initiate his desire for personal success and better American distance runners.

The day's training completed, bundle up and return to my room. A shower and if not too tired to eat, out on the streets for a belated dinner. When all was done it was time for sleep and another day.

However, highest achievement in competitive running comes only through right practice. Despite contrary opinions by a few older amateurs, it seems like common sense to assume that right practice for high school and college runners should occur primarily on the track under the guidance of a wise and experienced professional coach. Those who are oversold on the Swedish system of "Fartlek" feel that work on the track is not essential, but their arguments are not persuasive. Pace judgment is best learned by the beginning runner under competitive conditions and on tracks similar if not identical to those to be used in actual competition. Racing tactics are best learned with the advice of a coach rather than the long and hard way on the track through one's own mistakes in competition. Self-confidence, so essential to successful running, comes primarily through doing well what is to be done, but it can be increased through practice performances as well as in meets and especially when a wise teacher plans for its acquisition as deliberately and carefully as for more physical factors. All this is not to say that so-called right practice can be a full substitute for the background of running just suggested; rather, a sound running background is a prerequisite and a worth-while accompaniment to right practice.

Running, if properly organized and motivated, can and should be fun. It is essential to the maintenance of large numbers of boys out for track and for the continued enthusiasm of the individual athlete that running of some kind "for the fun of it" be both encouraged and planned. In our urge to complete the serious business of getting ready for next Saturday's meet, we coaches are prone to ignore this vital principle.

Wise coaching places great emphasis upon the individual runner's responsibility for all phases of the learning process. The job of a coach is primarily to help a boy do better what he is quite capable of doing very well alone and thus reach self-dependence, more quickly and more adequately. To learn to think while in action is far more desirable educationally and practically than to learn to follow orders. One of the greatest values of track and field athletics lies in the fact that the boy is on his own, once the competition starts. He must make his own decisions, and depend upon his own abilities and courage. Only that type of coaching which best develops these qualities will prove most effective.

A planned schedule of work is desirable but must be very flexible. A training schedule must always be adjusted to the immediate and long-time needs of the individual runner and to the particular conditions of practice. Furthermore, the success of a given workout is not determined merely by the degree to which it fulfils a plan's intended outcome but, equally important, by what the athlete thinks he accomplished. What progress does he think he is making? Has he gained in self-confidence and enthusiasm?

A succession of repeated speed runs of from 50 to 44 yards each, interspersed with restful jogs or walks, is the best endurance workout yet devised for distance running. This principle has been used by many different coaches using different systems, and it produces excellent results in every case. The old-timers called it "taking ins and outs". Some use the term "wind sprints"; others, "swings"; Swedish coaches, "Fartlek", or "speed-play". Basically they all mean about the same things, but each coach places a different emphasis upon the importance and value of such work, as well as upon the length and number of sprints and the over-all strenuousness of the work.

General developmental exercises as a part of each day's practice are certainly essential to a well-balanced physique and do contribute to better running. Pride in personal appearance will determine their extent, but at even a minimum level they should limber, stretch, and strengthen the muscles and tendons.

Running at an even pace in distance running is essential to best time. On its surface this principle appears to need little support, yet competitive practice finds it almost entirely ignored. At both the high school and college levels, runners continue to set a much faster than average pace for the first quarter of the race. Physiologically speaking, there can be few doubts that this practice is wrong. It is definitely established that the efficiency of increased running speed decreases not in arithmetic but in geometric proportion—Sargent placed it at the 3.8 power.

More directly, however, it is now generally accepted that physical condition is an extremely specific bodily state and that even a very minor change in the nature of the exercise or in its rhythm will produce a new fitness and a new efficiency of action. Cureton reports, for example, that "Zuntz found that a dog trained to walking on the level was not trained to walking uphill". Similarly, Steinhaus places great emphasis upon the perfection of specific movements as one of the major gains in efficiency from training.

It seems clear that an important part of each week's practice should be devoted to pace running and to the development of a perfect relaxation and rhythm while running at a particular pace.

The gold medals in distance running usually go to those who have learned to stay well up in the pack with a minimum of effort and who have learned that they can always sprint regardless of pace or fatigue. There are really two principles here, yet they are allied. The assurance that one can always sprint provides the incentive to stay up with the leaders. Only by staying up can a final sprint be effective. The important emphasis here, however, is upon establishing the certain knowledge that one can always sprint regardless of the feelings of fatigue. Such certainly is best developed by taking short sprints at the end of the workout when apparently tired.

Feeling tired is not necessarily being tired, and one of the essentials of correct training is the development of callousness toward the feelings of fatigue. Only true physical necessity should bring about a slowing of pace. This statement implies a basic change in our understanding of the nature of human fatigue. It considers the human being as a psychophysical organism in which body and mind cannot be separated. It thinks of fatigue not merely as the encumbering effects of the action of an inefficient machine, but also as a defence mechanism against increased fatigue and exhaustion. It assumes that the feelings of fatigue—breathlessness, fears, discomforts, even loss of clarity of consciousness—come very early in the fatigue process and that they are related to true exhaustion much as the discomforts of an empty stomach and related to starvation.

The reverse of this principle is that if one can avoid consciousness of the feelings of fatigue, one postpones, and, in a sense, actually avoids fatigue itself. One of the best stories illustrating the beneficial effects of keeping one's mind off one's own performance and feelings during a race is told by Armas Valste, the Finnish Olympic coach. In an important distance race between Sweden and Finland, the latter had entered two men, Salminen and Pekuri. Salminen was the winner of the 10,000-meter Olympic race in 1936, but was not at all in the best of condition. Pekuri, although a fine runner, was a relative newcomer, and Salminen was asked to do all that he could to be of assistance to him. Salminen stated afterward that throughout the race his mind was on his teammate and that at no time was he aware of his own feelings. With about 800 meters to go, he suddenly realized that he was not at all tired. Sprinting ahead, he went on to win, making one of the finest times of his entire career. Apparently even the most experienced runners need means by which they can forget their own troubles.

The more difficult problems in the process of getting in condition are more mental than physical. This is true not only in maintaining high morale throughout day-by-day practice during approximately ten months of the year, but equally so in building the athlete's confidence that he can meet successfully the steadily increasing demands of competition throughout this season and those that are approaching. The mentally conditioned runner knows what he can do and how he can do it best. He knows the strengths, the weaknesses, and the probable running tactics of his opponents, and has a calm belief in his own ability to meet their challenge. He has a sense of pace and knows that he can adjust that pace to changing conditions during the race. He has developed a mental toughness or even callousness to the discomforts of fatigue and feels a certainly that he can always sprint no matter how tired he may feel. He has learned to maintain a mental alterness throughout all stages of the race, particularly during the third quarter, when the feelings of fatigue are most noticeable. He has learned how to keep himself awake by picking up his pace, by changing his style, or by concentrating his mind outside his own feelings and thereby avoiding the dulling effects of fatigue.

Knowing and having confidence in all these matters will cause him to sleep better, digest his food better, and most certainly run better. More races are lost through the nervous and emotional fatigue brought on by worry during the days prior to the race than are brought on by physical overwork during the same period. The coach must make more careful plans for preventing and removing such worry than for the workouts themselves.

It is quite likely that the major improvements in the coaching of distance runners in the next few decades will come about through a clearer understanding of the significance of this principle. The problems of keeping men interested in running and in improvement, of maintaining and increasing their confidence in their running abilities despite the presence of men with better times on the squad or among their opponents, of co-operating in all group workouts and still maintaining individual initiative and assurance—these are the matters that cause greatest concern among good coaches.

Without question, the author's most noteworthy experience with this matter of co-operation between team members was in his work with the Hume twins, Ross and Bob, at the University of Michigan during the years 1943 to 1946. In high school, under the very fine coaching of Dick Mason at Canonsburg, Pennsylvania, Ross consistently ran the 880 and Bob the mile. During their freshman year at Michigan, it became apparent that their physical abilities were very similar and there was every reason to expect that Ross and Bob would be able to run together in the mile and then go back into either the 880 or the two-mile. Under this plan, however, it was found that one of the boys always failed to do his best work. Careful observation finally brought out the realization that the two boys simply could not do well running against each other. As a twin, neither could think that he should deliberately try to beat the other. During their first year of varsity competition, as sophomores, the boys were therefore separated in their events. Ross ran the mile and the 880, and Bob the two-mile. However, toward the close of the year, it became apparent that Bob was not likely to gain a liking for the longer event and that neither of the boys was running up to his potential.

During the fall of their junior year, a plan was mapped out for them by which they were to assume that they were not going to run against each other but rather with each other, and that even though it should result in the loss of the race, they were to come in together at all times. Immediately, a tremendous improvement in attitudes as well as in performance resulted. Not only were they much more relaxed in practice toward each other, but their more happy frame of mind permitted them to give great encouragement to a number of other runners who were competing on the team. Not only did Bob and Ross tie for the Indoor Conference mile championship, but Michigan found it possible to take all five places in the event. Later in the year, they tied for the first in the National Collegiate championships by finishing stride for stride and hand in hand in 4:14.6. Certain coaches criticized this procedure on the grounds that a single champion should always be selected. Had that been the Humes understanding a third man would probably have been the winner.

STYLE IN DISTANCE RUNNING

Style in distance running is an individual matter. True, there is an ideal form for each even, which coaches believe produces a perfect balance between maximum speed and maximum economy of effort. But it is always a particular individual's economy of effort that is important. Whatever produces this economy is, for him, good style, whether or not it conforms to traditional concepts of perfect style. In no other area of track athletics does daily practice for style begin at such an early age. After all, running begins at the age of three or four years, and style is likely to be definitely established by the time a boy reaches high school or college. Any setting or changing of style should therefore be very cautious and always within the range of individual's own natural and developed habits.

Necessary differences in pace produce natural differences in style at the various distances—the half-mile, the mile and the two-mile. However, the increased similarity of training that is how commonly practiced for these three events, is gradually eliminating these differences to a point where they require no special teaching emphasis.

The elements of proper style can be logically considered under six headings: the over-all action, body angle, arm swing, foot placement, rear-leg lift, and length of stride.

The over-all action. In general, the details of style are unimportant if the over-all action is efficient, smooth, and relaxed. The arms and legs should swing rhythmically and smoothly back and forth and should in no way be driven. In general, all actions should contribute toward movement along a straight line: feet will point straight ahead, shoulders and hips will not swing unduly off centre, and arms will move slightly across the body in such a way as to aid balance and the forward movement. A pronounced hip swing does permit a longer stride but detracts greatly from efficiency of action. Without question, overstriding is one of the more serious faults of distance runners.

The so-called picture runner or stylist is undoubtedly so referred to because the style that coaches feel is ideal happens to be natural to him. Not that he was necessarily "born that way". Rather, his natural physical proportions and muscular structure made it possible for coaching to produce a style that was, at one and the same time, his own and "ideal".

In contrast, one need only recall the awkward arms and haggard, strained face of the world's greatest distance runner, zatopek, as he won three Olympic distance titles in Helsinki, to realize that an "ideal" style is not necessary to great success.

Body angle. In most cases, proper body angle is a natural trait. As a matter of natural balance, the body will begin to lean forward as the pace increases. All human movement is a process of falling with balance, a constant and rhythmic loss and recovery of balance. On this basis, one can hardly prevent the increased angle of speed running. The problem, if one exists, usually lies in maintaining the body as a whole in a straight line, which should run from the point of balance on the ground, through the backbone, and to the top of the back of the head. The solution to such a problem usually lies in proper placement of the eyes and the head. In almost every case, when the eyes are focused at the proper place on the ground ahead, and the head is thus brought into proper position, the correct body angle will follow automatically. The point upon which the eyes should be focussed will vary with individual styles and also with the sped of the pace, moving from about 10 yards for the half-miler toward 100 yards for the long-distance man.

Arm swing. The action of the arms should be a relaxed and rhythmic swing from the shoulder girdle. Balance and rhythm are certainly the primary consideration, and to many good coaches they are the only one. The writer, at least, finds it difficult to agree with those who constantly call out to their protégés, "drive those arms, drive those arms!" In the first place, the forward propelling power of any such movement in "speeding up the leg action", as they put it, is highly questionable, and certainly, the possible gain is nullified by the loss of rhythm, relaxation and smoothness. Arm action will of course speed up and become more energetic as pace increases, particularly as the final sprint is unleashed. But such action is a part of the entire body action and should not be given special emphasis.

In giving instructions for proper arm carriage, the writer follows a rather set pattern :—

1. Drop your hands to your side and relax them completely. Note how the fingers are not extended but partially contracted.

2. Place the thumbs and forefingers lightly together.

3. Lift the hands to a level even with or below the hips, keeping them relaxed.

4. Let the arms swing from the shoulder girdle as the arms of a doll might swing on a pin through the shoulders. Do not drive them, let them go of their own weight and inertia. Relax, relax!

5. The angle of the forearm with the upper arm remains the same at all times and certainly does not permit the hands to swing high and close to the face. Rather, they should remain low and at ease.

Once a proper arm swing is developed, the runner should forget his arms and hands entirely, unless it might be to make certain they are relaxed. If they become heavy and tired while running, dropping them and even shaking them will help to bring recovery. Men having such difficulty should, first, try for a more relaxed and easy arm action and, second, take special exercises for the arms, especially one that is identical with the arm swing while running—standing in place and swinging, not driving, the arms very rapidly back and forth for some minutes.

Foot placement. The details of foot placement will, like other aspects of form, depend upon (1) the individual and his developed style of running, and (2) his speed and distance. As always, economy of effort is the primary consideration, but where speed is increasingly important, as in the half-mile, length and springiness of stride should be carefully coached and practiced. At all three distances—the 880, the mile, and the two-mile, the landing should be made first on the ball of the foot. In the 880, the weight will drop only lightly and buoyantly on to the heel; in the two-mile, a greater concern for economy will permit a somewhat greater process of settling and relaxing to occur before bouncing back to the ball and toes. Quite naturally, with a more forward lean of the body in the faster run, there will be a lighter and quicker riding forward of the body weight.

But such differences are a natural aspect of each event, and as modern training methods for the 880, the mile, and the two-mile become more and more alike, they will tend to grow less and less. In a fine talk before the National Collegiate Track Coaches Association in New York City on January 12, 1950, Fred Wilt, noted American distance runner, gave an extensive and sound discussion of this problem of foot placement.

Rear-leg lift. Generally speaking, writings on coaching in this country and abroad have suggested that the backward lift of the rear lower leg is wasteful of time and energy and have emphasized a full forward-reaching stride and knee lift. For example, according to an analysis of slow-motion pictures by Dean Cromwell, the great Finnish champion Paavo Nurmi "used a free stride of medium length with a considerable forward thrust and a good knee lift, the feet never rising higher behind than the knee. His ankles were remarkably relaxed, and he came down almost flat-footed, the heel touching the ground, but very lightly."

However, today, certain coaches, particularly those of Sweden, strongly advocate a free upward and backward swing of the rear foot as the leg starts forward. Such a rear lift swings the lower leg and heel close to the upper biceps. This shortens the weight arm of the leg lever and the length of the leg pendulum and thereby increases the efficiency of the action. As the upper leg swings forward, the lower leg falls easily and rhythmically downward and forward. The knee swings just far enough forward and upward to permit the foot to clear the ground. There is no attempt to lengthen the stride, no forward reaching or pointing of the toes, for such action promotes tension and waste of energy. This tends to produce a minimum of bounce in the stride, although no one could deny the natural bound of the foot and ankle that was such a beautiful aspect of Gunder Hagg's action.

This rear-leg lift is not at all a deliberate backward throw a kick. Rather, it is a natural and relaxed follow-through and follow-up of the push of the rear foot from the ground. Ordinarily, there is no need for specific coaching of this action. To the contrary, its greatest asset is its naturalness. On the other hand, where misunderstanding or coaching has emphasized a maximum length of stride, with no "waste action in the rear and a high knee lift", relaxation and economy of action have been lost and specific correction will be needed.

For other than such exceptional cases, attention to the complete relaxation, naturalness, and rhythm of the total action should suffice.

Length of stride. Modern training emphasizes sprinting and sprint action. It is inevitable therefore that many runners will employ the high-toed, bouncing, and long-striding action of the sprinter and the quarter-miler. Such a wasteful stride requires correction if distances over one-half mile are to be run successfully. Cross-country work and "Fartlek" will usually take care of the difficulty, but sometimes coaching is required.

In offering suggestions to American distance during the past few years, European coaches have placed great stress upon the importance of a short economical stride. Capozzoli, the great little Georgetown University two-miler who established an American undergraduate record of 8:55.3 (January 17, 1953), attributes much of his improvement since the 1952 Olympics to the shortening of his stride.

Certainly Emil Zatopek, greatest of all long distance runners, used an amazingly short stride and minimum knee lift. In watching him, one often wondered how he was able to run so fast with so little bounce and drive.

In summary, the matter of length of stride is important and demands careful judgment. Obviously, the longer the race, the more crucial economy of effort and shortness of stride become.

RACING TACTICS

General considerations. Perhaps the most intriguing but at the same time the most tragic aspect of track athletics is racing tactics. A slight hesitancy here, a single step to the inside there, a few seconds miscalculation of the right pace or in the timing of the final kick—any of these or other seemingly minor errors will throw away months and years of careful preparation and sacrifice. The race is not always to either the swift or the strong, but to the clever, the skilful, and the constantly wary.

1. In competitive running, Socrates instruction, "Know thyself", must always be supplemented by, "Know thy opponent". Racing tactics, if not based on such knowledge, are blind and often futile. One must be a student of one's self in each day's practice and each week's competition, but equally a student of one's opponents at every possible opportunity.

As witness, F.A.M.Webster writer of New Zealand's great miler, Dr. Jack Lovelock, the 1936 1500-meter Olympic champion.

Time for the first time 1200 meters of the Olympic race had been fast—3:06.9; yet, knowing the finishes of Cunningham and Beccali, the 1932 Olympic winner, Lovelock chose to sprint almost the entire last lap. His time for the last 300 meters was : 40.9, the equivalent of :54.5 for the last 400 meters!

A dozen similar, although less world-shaking, memories crowd in upon the writer, for such carefully planned victories are the sweetest of all and the best remembered. Suffice it here to say that carefully laid, although flexible, planning of a race based upon track conditions and upon each man's strengths and weaknesses is excellent assurance of an easy and rested mind before the race and victory at the end of it.

2. All planning must carefully consider the distance to be run, the size of the track, the number of competitors, their over-all abilities, and the specific

abilities of the best runners. Such planning is particularly important indoors, where straightaways are so short, position so essential, and opportunities for gaining it so few and so quickly lost. Even so experienced a runner as Don Gehrman suffered his first loss in the mile during the 1951 indoor season by drowsing momentarily in second position behind Stewart Ray while Fred Wilt jumped him from behind with 1¼ laps to go. The 3 yards gained thereby were enough to produce the winning medal.

3. Plans must always be flexible and include at least one alternative. Not only are track conditions uncertain, but it should be assumed that the opponent is at least equally cunning. Obviously, crowded indoor tracks make all plans most precarious.

4. Once plans are made, a quiet belief in them will put the mind and emotions at ease. Worry during the few days prior to a race is certainly useless and can be a serious factor in creating fatigue. Many a man has fussed and fumed for days over his coming race and so vitiated his nervous energy and will to win as to make effective performance impossible.

5. The man with the best sprint is more likely to get the pole lane at the start as well as the gold medal at the finish. The pole lane, or at least a good early position, is especially vital to indoor running and to such shorter runs as the half mile. Therefore, practice in starting with the sprinters is one of the best of all pre-meet tactics.

6. In any case, all tacticians must concede that the man who makes the best final time is always the winner. To get out in front and stay there all the way is the simplest and best of all tactics.

7. Most important of all, even the most cunning of tactics should confirm the faith that track men are good sportsmen. They are friendly and considerate before the

race, unwilling to use unfair means during the race, gracious in victory, and cheerfully generous in defeat.

TACTICS WHEN SETTING THE PACE

1. The primary problem as well as the primary opportunity in setting the pace lies in the third phase of the race, when fatigue dulls the will and muscles feel heavy and lethargic. This is the time when the ordinary runner allows the pace to fall or lags behind, whereas the real champion pace-setter pours it on. To point up the importance of this stage of every race, here is the story of the NCAA 1950 two-mile run as told by Cordner Nelson:

This was to be the greatest race in collegiate history. There was Jim Newcomb, USC's Indian who had never lost in any kind of school competition, and who had run a 4:07.7 mile the previous week. There was Warren Druetzler who ran the equivalent of a 9:01 2-mile last year in Europe. There was Don McEwen, a 21-year-old Michigan sophomore from Canada who had run 9:02. These were the big three, but men like Dick Hart, Bob Black, Bill McGuire, and Dick Church threatened to scare the NCAA record of 9:02.6.

Jim Brown of Arkanasas led for the first lap in 66, followed by McEwen. Whitney Overton led at the half in 2:14.5. McEwen was still second, followed by red-headed Herb Semper of Kanasas, and Hart. McEwen took the lead, passing the three quarters in 3:24, trailed by McGuire, Semper, Hart, Newcomb, Fox of Missouri, Overton, Druetzler, Black, and Fitzmorris of Colorado in that order. McEwen passed the mile in 4:32.5, followed by McGuire, Newcomb, Semper, Druetzler, Black and Hart. Then McEwen began to pour it on. His fifth lap, in 67½, opened up a ten yard lead on Newcomb, with Druetzler another 20 yards back and Semper and Black following. McEwen ran his sixth lap in 66.

Newcomb, completely bewildered but this amazing pace, was now four seconds behind, but still in the running. Semper was third, seven seconds behind Newcomb and leading Druetzler and Black. Another 66 second lap by MeEwen cracked Newcomb completely. The chief lost all his remaining energy and fell 12 seconds behind. Semper ran 8:07 for 1¾ miles, only three seconds behind Newcomb. Druetzler was trailing Semper, but Black dropped out. The last lap was anti-climatic. McEwen, completely run out, stagered around in 70 seconds. Newcomb, who had lost all his fight, matched that time, but summoned up some of his reserve to outsprint Semper to the tape. McGuire dropped out on the last lap.

1. McEwen; 2. Newcomb; 3. Semper; 4. Druetzler; 5. Hart.

2. An even pace makes for best time, for it implies maximum physical efficiency, rhythm, and relaxation. However, special conditions make such a pace difficult, unwise, and often impossible:

A crowded field on an indoor track may force a man to go out fast, to take an early lead, and therefore to adopt an altogether too rapidly early pace.

An opponent with a strong discourage the others. Such an effort is likely to prove successful only against an easily disheartened competitor.

Almost universal practice sets a pace for the 880 in which the first 440 is conditions determine this difference, not economy of physical energy.

In actual competition, an even pace seldom occurs, for excess nervous energy and the fight for position hurries the first phase of the race and the feelings of fatigue slow the third phase. However, third factors being equal, every effort should be made to avoid such inefficient running.

3. In a large field of runners, the man leading at the end of the first 440 of the mile or the two-mile is certain to be much too fast for an even pace and probably has paid too great a price for his leading position. This is particularly true outdoors, where longer straighaways make a later play for position a wiser plan. Indoors, careful consideration must be given to the relative values of the best position and a more even pace. To be well back in the field may bring a better pace, but this advantage is often lost in at attempt to gin position later in the race. However, experienced and mature runners follow this method almost invariably when running in a crowded field. They begin to move up after the first 880 and then pour it on after the mile, when men are tired and less combative. Such a practice is questionable in the mile indoors, but usually effective in the two-mile both indoors and out.

4. To discourage one's opponents, it is usually wise to pick up speed a little when a lead is challenged, but a marked change of pace can occur only once or twice without affecting endurance.

5. The use of pacemakers is a questionable practice at best, but is certainly unethical when it deliberately slows or blocks an opponent's progress and should bring disqualification.

6. To lead is more fatiguing (at least psychologically) to most athletes than to follow.

7. Once in the lead, the runner should realize he is now where he planned to be and should confidently search for rhythm, smoothness, and relaxation.

8. If passed when leading, the prospective winner should immediately move a half lane out to avoid being boxed.

9. The runner should think of others during the race—

their position, their condition, their probable timing of tactics. It will keep his mind off his own fatigue and alert for quick decisions.

10. Inexperienced runners should never look around. Many of the best European runners do look back at their opponents, but only their extensive experience and skill make it permissible.

11. A runner should always sprint at least two strides beyond the finish line, regardless of the length of his lead or the certainty of his place. Many races have been lost by relaxing just before the finish line.

12. Mental alertness, which is essential to pace when leading, can be maintained only by detailed planning and experimentation.

One example of such deliberate planning is to be found in the careers of Lash, Deckard, Trutt, and Smith of the University of Indiana, Billy Hayes finest quarter and probably the fines group of runners ever to compete together on a single American university team. For example, as far back as April 24, 1937, these four men combined their forces to establish a new world's record for the four-mile relay of 17:16.1. In practice and upon many occasions in one- and two-mile races, Billy Hayes had his men change the lead repeatedly at the end of each 220 yards of the entire race. This practice was accepted as being an inefficient one from a physical standpoint, but it had the deliberate purpose of maintaining mental alertness against the growing effects of fatigue; as such, it was certainly worth while and, at least in that respect, successful.

13. Correct pace is particularly important in the 880, for lap times come too late in the race to permit a satisfactory adjustment of mistakes.

When following pace.

1. The key question in racing is, "What is the minimum distance within which the athlete can outrun his opponents?" Perhaps it is the last 50 yards, the last 150, the last 440, the last 880, or even the full distance. Every plan to win must include the answer to this question. Whitfield, of Ohio State, picked up his winning lead in the 1948 Olympic 800-meter run between 400 and 600 meters. Had he waited for the last 220, he very probably would have lost to Wint and Barten. Later conversations with him make it seem likely that he made this decision some two months earlier and practiced accordingly.

2. Knowing pace is essential to every runner, even the one who considers himself a follower. Pace will determine the timing of his final kick, and occasionally may force him to take the lead himself through the greater part of the race.

3. A strong finishing kick means little unless one is close enough to the leaders to make it effective and in a sufficiently open position to permit one to maneuver when ready. The instances in which such effort occurs too late and from too far back are countless, for they occur in almost every track meet whether in the elementary grades or in world's championships.

4. When passing, never stop to ask permission or be polite. Do it quickly, unexpectedly, and with determination. "Jumping" an opponent is an art requiring study and practice, but it pays great dividends.

5. Where straighaways are short, as in indoor running, most passing should occur in the first third of the straightaway. The decision to pass must come earlier and with certainty. Come off the curve

somewhat wide, fast, and entirely unannounced.

6. Passing on the curve means increasing the dinstant to be run and should occur only when necessary or when there is a certainty of successful surprise. A single curve run in the second lane adds about 3 yards to the race. Such an attempt produced results for Herb Barten (university of michigan 49) over Don Gehrman (University of Wisconsin 50) in the indoor. Big Ten mile championships. With Gehrman in second spot, Barten in fourth, and 300 yards to go, Barten suddenly sprinted all out in the middle of the curve, just where least expected. In 30 yards he had a 5-yard lead, enough to insure the title.

7. When following, the inside lane is usually dangerous, and in the last stages of the race it may be fatal to success. Many an intended winner running in second place, inside, has watched almost the entire field pass him before he had a chance to move out and up.

8. When following and planning to win, the safest position is in second spot, a half lane wide, about 18 inches from the curb, on the leader's right shoulder. Such a position permits one to meet every challenge, to move out and up with those taking the lead, or to feint them back into place if they are halfhearted.

9. As soon as a runner has found his position, he should for rhythm and relaxation. This running position, whether first, second, third or tenth, is maintained throughout the middle half of the race at a minimum expenditure of energy in order best to assure the intended final place. The best position plus maximum economy of effort brings success.

10. In almost all instances, the advantage in

competitive racing lies with the man running in second position, for from this spot he can control much of the race and still maintain complete relaxation. If the pace is too slow, he can, by running a little closer on the leader's shoulder, stimulate him to increase it; if too fast, the realization that he is being closely followed will cause the leader to run with greater tension and thereby either unconsciously slow the pace or incur a disproportionate degree of fatigue.

TRAINING SCHEDULES

Common practice in articles or books on coaching is to protest against the presentation and rigid use of training schedules and to warn readers that all work should be individualized, but in the end to provide schedules which are all too often passed on to the athletes with little change or variation. The following material is organized with the intent to minimize this danger by presenting many alternative workouts and describing their values and uses, but leaving actual choice to the coach or athlete.

A major portion of this chapter has been devoted to an understanding of the many bases upon which such choice should be made. However, in summary, the coach should determine his plans for the coming week by considering the following :—

1. The exact distance each man will run in competition on the following Saturday.

2. Each individual's opponent, his ability, and his method of running in competition.

3. Each individual's strengths and weaknesses not only in terms of the competition this week but throughout the season.

4. The relative youth and experience of each

individual.

5. The time of season (pre-season, early season, late season) and the overall relative emphasis upon over-distance, under-distance, pace work, and speed work.

6. The over-all weekly organization—long, easy work on Monday, hard, under-distance work on Tuesday, and so on.

7. Over-all team consideration—improvement of squad morale, the need for aiding a teammate in pace or in gaining confidence, and so forth.

Only item 5 has not received adequate attention earlier. Ordinarily, there are three competitive seasons in a school year—fall cross-country, winter indoor track, and spring outdoor track. Similarly, there are three periods during the school year during which major emphasis is placed upon background or over-distance work. By far the most important of these is the fall cross-country season, without which it is impossible to secure a proper "bottom" or background of strength and endurance. This does not imply, of course, that during the fall exclusive concern is with over-distance work. On the contrary, each week and in fact each day will include within its practice a portion of speed work and pace judgment. But looking at the season as a whole its major emphasis is upon endurance and distance.

A similar emphasis is present during the pre-indoor and the pre-outdoor seasons. As the year progresses, this emphasis decreases, of course, yet there is need in March or early April to go back to the long work of the fall. Not only in such practice sound physically, but it affords the athlete a period of pleasurable change which often has the effect of a layoff or vacation.

Balancing these three periods of over-distance work, there should be three periods in which speed and under-distance work are primary. These will occur toward the end of the fall cross-country season, increasingly throughout the winter competitive season, and especially during the spring outdoor season. As over-distance work becomes less important, increased concentration upon faster under-distance work takes its place, to the point where during the late outdoor season almost exclusive attention may be given to speed. Yet throughout these "speed" periods, the continuous concern for variety and balance between the elements of good performance will lead coaches to include some distance work in each week's workout. Such over-distance practice does not necessarily mean an even-paced trial run at over the distance. Rather, it may come from the preliminary "play" period (erroneously called a "warm-up"), where distance is covered quite unconsciously.

Common elements in planning. Basically, the approach to weekly and daily schedule plans is the same for all distances events (half-mile, mile, two-mile). The traditional plan—Monday, over-distance; Tuesday, under-distance; Wednesday, trials or speed-work; Thursday, pace work; Friday, rest; and Saturday, race—applies equally well to each of these three events. Similarly, the organization within each day for each event follows a basic pattern—preliminary work, wokrout, and easy jogging—and is of equal value for each of the three events.

The weekly schedule. The almost universally accepted pattern for each week's workout seems to have been adopted very early in the history of American track training.

Monday : Usually a day of no time trials and few assignments of definite distances at stated times. The primary objective is a gain in endurance while relaxing mentally from the tensions of the preceding Saturday's competition. The adages, "There's no fun like work, if you enjoy the work" and, "if you wish to get real work out of a boy, see to it he thinks it's fun", are particularly applicable on this day. Group work in the nature of speed-play, preferably away from the track, accomplishes this purpose, as do such games as "circulators" or "follow-the-leader", as indicated later under "Practice Procedures". Some coaches assign to some men at certain times of the season the definite task of covering one the one-half to two times their distance at a specific pace. Most coaches utilize the opportunity for pace and rhythm work.

Tuesday : Either a day of all-out time trials, of under-distance work at specified times, or of repeated speed work. Time trials are often at three-fourths the distance—that is, 660 yards for half-milers, three-fourths of a mile for milers, and one and one-half miles for two milers.

Wednesday : Wednesday accomplishes whatever was not taken care of on Tuesday. If time trials are over, speed work is now in order, and vice versa. If by time trials is meant an all-out effort at a given distance, they might well occur on Tuesday, for then the men are rested and most likely to do their best. Sometimes such an effort is worth while and even necessary. Perhaps a man needs the confidence that a fine performance for a shorter distance will give him.

On the other hand, if by the time trials is meant a timed workout at three-fourths the distance at the exact pace that will be attempted on the forthcoming Saturday, followed by repeated sprints to bring speed and endurance, they might come best on Wednesday. The all-out speed work should occur on Tuesday. Such speed work sometimes produces tight and even sore muscles and therefore is placed as far away from the coming meet as possible.

Thursday : Because it follows two days of relatively hard work and is put two days from Saturday's competition, Thursday is traditionally a day of easy work and primarily pace work. Learning rhythm, relaxation, pace, and the particular method by which the coming opponents are to be beaten is all important. A freedom from tension during the practice is essential, as well as a deliberate effort to clear up all uncertainties and possible worries. The runner's mind will then be at ease during the next two days.

Friday : Friday means rest only physically but mentally and emotionally. Whatever can be done to remove the tensions of anxiety should be done. A careful review of possible problems that might arise on Saturday and their solution may help. Perhaps a light workout will aid proper sleep that night and thereby refresh the runner.

The daily practice period. Our terminology of "warm-up, workout, jog, and shower" is not basically sound, and a better description is needed that will be refreshing and intriguing.

The numerous academic and other activities of schools and colleges of the United States do not permit a practice period of more than about one and one-half hours on the track. Ordinarily, such a length of time is sufficient. A shorter period, however, tends to hurry practice and to remove the sense of freedom and fun that is necessary to best results.

1. Preliminary speed-play. This period will vary from 40 down to about 20 minutes of all types of group running. Much of it, perhaps all of it, could take place off the track. There is little consciousness of the exact amount of work done, but actually it is considerable. As a matter of fact, the purpose of this period is to get in as much as the time will permit. Certainly the traditional

warm-up is entirely inadequate. Some days, the emphasis will be upon pace work and the runners will organize their groups accordingly. Other days, it will be speed-play, off the track, and through the woods. In almost all cases it will include about 10 minutes of upper-body and arm exercises as an aid to running but also as a matter or pride in good posture and a well-proportioned body.

To maintain group morale, each member should know what kind of work the leader intends to do and should be able to make certain individual adjustments to it. Otherwise it becomes drudgery.

2. The special assignment. Specific distances and times will be agreed upon in terms of each individual's abilities and needs. Most coaches now believe in more than one continuous effort and expect the athlete to repeat and improve upon his first attempt, or at least to finish up with additional pace work or speed work. About 30 minutes, including resting and running again, is required to accomplish this.

3. The finishing jog. This period of 10 minutes of restful jogging and walking is an important phase of every day's practice. Such work is the best way of preventing and removing muscular soreness and general body fatigue. Further, it relaxes the boy from the tensions of the earlier practice and encourages better digestion of the evening meal and a better rest that night.

POSSIBLE PRACTICE PROCEDURES

1. Speed-play. Repeated sprints of varying length, interspersed with restful jogs, taken off the track and preferably along wood or field paths. Limits are set on a time basis rather than on the distance covered—20, 30, 40 minutes of running. The method is to sprint repeatedly until tired, rest by jogging or walking then sprint against until tired, and so forth.

2. "Circulators". A good warm-up procedure. Have from six to twelve men run in line around the track at a rather slow pace. The last man should always be coming up to take the lead. Warn the men against accelerating the pace.

3. "Follow-the-leader", endurance work. Put a dozen men under a leader who will determine when, where, and for what distance they will sprint. Assign two managers, one to handle the starts, the other to judge finishes. After a proper warm-up, the leader designates a start and a finish line at whatever distance he may wish. The manager at the finish picks only the last two or three men from each sprint and tells them to jog and keep jogging together on the grass. After four or five such sprints, the best men are excused to go ahead with their individual assignments. The others who have been jogging on the grass are brought back into the game and the whole process is repeated.

4. Competitive pace work. (a) Run a group of dozen or more men together, for relatively slow 220's or 440's at an assigned pace. All men will try to hit the assigned pace. Time the last man and the first man. If the last man is closer to the assigned time, cut the first two men out of the competition; if the first man is closer, cut the last two men off. Be sure to assign something to do those who have been cut off from the competition; otherwise, they'll be wasting time.

5. Competitive pace work. (b) Assing different paces to different individual runners or pairs of runners, all for the same distance. Establish a penalty for missing pace, e.g., all men missing the pace by more than two seconds must keep trying until they run two consecutive races within one second of the assigned time.

6. Competitive pace relays. Select men for relay teams

in which paired men run the same distance but not at the same speed. Assign a speed for each man on each team. The winning team is the one for which the total error from the assigned pace is the least. Obviously, it will be necessary to have two watches for each team so that each man will be individually timed.

7. Pace work. Run the full distance by running the first half of the race at definitely less than racing speed, but picking up the second half to the pace to be run the following week-end. Repeat.

8. Pace work. Run several times at three-fourths the distances. Run the first one-half at less than racing speed, but pick up on the last one-fourth. Finish up each race feeling that the full distance could have been covered. This workout is very valuable in placing emphasis upon the third quarter of a race and upon decreasing the speed of the first half of each race.

9. Time trial. Run for time at over the distance. Usually this is done at one and one-half times the distance; three-fourths of a mile for 880 men, one and one-half miles for milers, and three miles for two-milers. This method is occasionally used for time trails during the early season when confidence in being able to carry the full distance is lacking. It is sometimes used for pace work by having the final half of the distance run at racing speed.

10. Time trial. Run three-fourths of the distance for time, all-out.

11. Time trial. Run three-fourths of the distance at the pace at which the full distance will be run on the coming Saturday. Rest one minute, then run the final one-fourth all-out, or run a series of sprints.

12. Time trial. Run the full distance to be run on Saturday, but run the first three-fourths at a slower-than-

race speed, going all-out on the final one-fourth. This may help an inexperienced runner by giving him an idea of the distance. Under ordinary conditions, few coaches believe in running the actual distance all-out in practice.

13. Time trial. Run time trials in which, for example, 880 men and milers race against each other for three-fourths of a mile. Much friendly rivalry can be established at these in-between distances, with everyone benefiting.

14. Competitive relays. These are ordinary relays in which paired men run all-out at the distance assigned to them.

15. Repeated fast work on the track. The distance to be covered, the speed of running, and the time interval of jogging or walking will all be specified by the coach according to his intended outcomes for the day. If endurance is the primary factor, times will be slower and the rest interval shorter.

16. Endless relays. Time excellent workout has in it all the ingredients of a well-rounded practice. Two or three relay teams of four, five, six, or seven men each are organized by the coach. Men should be paired off in terms of ability and told to run varying distances, i.e., the first pair will run 220's at :26 each; the second pair 220's at :28 each; the third, 440's at :60 each, and so on. Each pair will run two or three or four times, as the coach may wish. If three times, the first two will be on a pace basis, and therefore the teams will keep close together during these early runs. As the No. 1 runners come up for their third run, competition begins and men go all-out.

For best results, two watches are needed for each team, or all runs should be timed to get the most benefit and the most fun. Each man runs more than once and the last man passes the baton back to the first man without any halt in proceedings.

It will be noted that such a session includes pace judgment, endurance work, speed work, racing tactics, and baton practice. In the early season, use fewer men on each team but assign a slower pace throughout. It is then more of an endurance session. In the later season, increase the number of men on each team, making the rest period longer, but speed up the pace assignments. It then becomes a real speed workout.

17. Sprint work. This consists of all-out sprinting from the starting blocks at short distances, from 30 to 150 yards.

18. Pace work. What is called for here is repeated work for pace at one-fourt or one-half the distance.

IMPORTANT QUESTIONS ABOUT DISTANCE RUN

What about body types in selecting men for different events? Many students of track and field spend much time in attempts to discover the ideal body types for each of the events on the program. The height, weight, and bone and muscle structure of many champions are averaged, and supposedly significant differences are detected. Some coaches are prone to select their candidates accordingly.

But in most events and in most cases, primary consideration of these factors is misplaced. For example, in the 1948 Olympic 800-meter final at London, one has but to contrast the heights and weights of the five place winners : Whitfield, 5′ 11″, 165 pounds; Wint, 6′ 4″, 175 pounds; Hansenne, 5′ 11″, 150 pounds; Barten, 5′ 8½″, 135 pounds; Bengtsson, 5′ 10″, 155 pounds.

On the other hand, body structure becomes of greater significance as the distance increases. Two-milers and longer-distance men are inclined to be short of stature and leg, slender of build, and gaunt in appearance. Efficiency and economy of action are now primary factors, and weight and size must be trimmed accordingly. For ordinary running in school or college, selection in terms of body type need not be so severe, but if top performance is expected at more than one mile, the big man is undoubtedly greatly handicapped.

Does the greatest development of endurance come from running long distances? Dr. Sid Robinson states that "coaches have found in practice that excellent conditioning work for runners of all distances is the repeated running of short distances at a fast rate with special attention to form. The runs are repeated after short intervals before recovery from the preceding runs has occurred. The scientist has found that a man will accumulate a higher lactic acid in the blood stream in this type of work (one of the effects of fatigue and therefore one of the means to building endurance) than he can in a sustained run of the same total distance. Thus the coach is schooling his men in tolerating higher lactic acid and still having good form". Since one of the basic problems in endurance work is developing a tolerance for fatigue, it seems obvious that repeated speed work can be classified as an excellent and in some ways the best endurance workout.

How can a coach help in building a boy's self-confidence? In general, by asking a boy to perform only what is within his present capacity and what is at least close to the boy's own opinion of his own capacity. More specifically, he can :

1. So arrange workouts that no one individual is always beaten in practice.

2. Occasionally ask a man of lesser ability to set the pace in practice.

3. Urge men to maintain a record of their own progress

and to make comparisons in terms of their own development rather than that of other runners.

4. Encourage group running for run as a part of every day's practice while limiting time trials to only those few occasions when he is sure the individual—not so much the group as the individual—is ready to do better than ever before.

5. Discuss both practice and meet performances with the individual so that he will understand what, how, and when things happen and thereby be better prepared for the next effort.

6. So modify workouts that men are not tired from day to day.

7. The college coach should certainly know what plan of work was followed in high school and with what success. Any changes need to be justified to the individuals involved if self-confidence and confidence in the coach are to be maintained.

8. By comparing the young, athlete's times in practice and in meets with those of former local great runners, indicating the latter's improvement from the freshman through the senior year and beyond.

What does it mean to be "stale" and how can this condition be remedied? Certain writers, as well as Webster's Dictionary, consider "stale" as meaning "impaired in vigour or energy by prolonged activity;—orig. used of overtrained athletes". In over 20 years of coaching, the writer can recall no cases that definitely indicated such impairment of energy for vigour. Obviously, there have been many examples of continued poor performance for which there seemed outwardly to be no reason and to which many would probably attach the adjective "stale"; yet time and again these same men would snap out of the slump and perform as well as ever or better.

In all such cases, something happened that brought a change in mental attitude. Something occurs, perhaps quite unrelated to track athletics, that removes the sense of burden, restores confidence, and re-creates enthusiasm; immediately, the so-called impairment of energy disappears, the "overtraining" is forgotten. Staleness does occur, of course, but it is a staleness of interest and confidence rather than physical incapability.

Through the years, where the big championships at the end of the outdoor season have had little personal attraction to certain athletes, they have quite often gone "stale"; yet time and again, when the informal post-season meets are scheduled, they are anxious to send in their entries and often perform better than ever before.

It seems clear that where symptoms of "staleness" are evident, they can be removed by doing whatever is necessary to revive enthusiasm. To ease up on the amount of work is the usual method. A complete isolation from all contact with and thought of running is one possibility. But, in most cases, nothing will bring a cure so effectively as success. If, somehow, meaningful success can be won or even "arranged", the "stale" athlete will soon take on a warmth and perhaps an eagerness that will quickly bring real performance.

Some coaches almost invariably follow the blanket rule, "Lay the boy off for a few days". And, of course, it is sometimes almost miraculous what a few days rest will do. But if a problem exists, it is seldom solved by being avoided. It will still be there after the rest period, waiting to be solved. Rest is fine, but the wise coach will go further and seek to discover what made the rest necessary.

It should be realized that human improvement in all fields of endeavour does not occur on a consistently straight line upward, but rather by upward spurts interrupted by plateaus and even valleys. Some believe in laying off and resting while in these valleys. Others think continued work with confidence that improvement will soon begin again is the most effective solution.

These periods of failure to improve usually occur at two phases of the long ten months training season. The first comes about four to six weeks after the start of the season, when there is a tendency to crowd in too much work too soon, and when the runner begins to evaluate himself in terms of his teammates or of his first competition and finds himself not quite so talented or well conditioned as he had expected. A period of physical and mental adjustment has to take place, during which improvement is likely to stand still or even fall away. The second period usually occurs toward the end of the outdoor season, when running seems endless and the pressure of competition is more and more exacting. In this case, anything that removes the burden of impending failure or that makes fun of what has now become a drudgery will be most likely to be effective.

As a general rule, an athlete's enthusiasm is likely to be maintained as long as :—

1. His improvement is steady or at least apparent to him.
2. His goals for the coming days and weeks are clear and seem achievable to him, and therefore arouse a minimum of emotional worry and tension.
3. His running conditions are varied to include wood and field running as well as on the track.
4. His practice on the track is varied from day to day and includes a minimum of time trials.

5. His practice each day is varied to include group as well as individual work, and much self-imposed running with a minimum of demands from the coach.

6. There is a close working arrangement between the coach and athlete so that the latter will express his true feelings as well as his honest opinion concerning the best workout.

7. His fatigue does not carry over from one day to the next.

8. His workouts result in fatigue that is primarily physical in nature and include a minimum of nervous stress and uncertainty.

What are the dangers of competitive running at an early age such as 14 or 15? Authoritative studies dealing directly with this problem are exceedingly difficult to carry out and are therefore almost non-existent. However, aurhoritative opinion is almost unanimous in discouraging such early competition. Many sound reasons are given : This is a period of relatively rapid growth, when at least the feelings of both nervous and physical exhaustion appear to be more easily induced. The very newness of the thrills of winning, or of the object sorrows of defeat, the glitter of the gold medal or the self-blame for defeat, all tend to place an exaggerated importance upon winning or losing and therefore call for an almost desperate determination to make an all-out effort. At an early age, this emotional and nervous zeal for victory is more likely to lead to a lack of interests in sports and even to a distaste for them then at any other time. Further, early specialization in a competitive sport is likely to lead to either the broad interest or the broad participation in sports generally that are so important in a sound program of athletic competition.

Even though these are matters of opinion and not

necessarily fact, restriction of regular competition to senior high school age levels and above is undoubtedly a wise procedure. One cannot help feeling that the development of junior high school competitive sports programs, which is prevalent in certain areas of the country, has come about through the selfish interests of adult groups or individuals rather than through a wise concern for the best interests of the youngstes themselves.

How will ultimate and best world's records at the various distances be finally established? This question is far more than academic or the result of idle curiosity, for within its answer lie the fundamentals of good training, correct competitive running, and the best condition for running. One aspect of the total answer, however, lies in the statement that such records will be made only when men's psychological limits of performance are pushed as far back as their physiological limits. The so-called mental-emotional blocks to action—the feelings of fatigue, if you will—must be removed to permit true physiological factors to be wholly effective.

One of the essentials of such an occurrence will be presence of several equally excellent runners in the race. In an unsigned statement released by the Finnish press for use in connection with the planned Finnish celebration of the Olympic games in 1940, this point is clearly illustrated :—

It must have seemed incredible to foreigners how three Finns managed to run under the world two miles record in a single race. The fact is, however, that Finss like company. When one Finn starts smashing records, or making a collection of Olympic medals, other Finns like to join in the fun. Seriously, they realize that only by unselfish cooperation can there be hope of record making.

When Hannes Kolehmainen way back in pre-war days, expressed his scorn for the pronouncements of medical men regarding the limits of human speed and endurance, and bewildered track fans and sports writers into imagining he actually flew, he had his brothers Tatu and Viljam help him identify the Finns with the winged species. When Paavo Nurmi made the world gasp at his record breaking orgies, he had Ville Ritola pay him company. The next great Flying Finn, Lauri Lehtinen, shared the fun with Volmari Iso-Hollo. Gunnar Hockert was not particular; just so long as it was a fellow countryman, he'd do. Ilmari Salminen brought along his pal Askola. Now Taisto Maki has Kauko Pekuri in tow—with Veikko Tuominen, as upstart from nowhere, wolfing into honours; ad he did in the greatest two miles ever run, by beating out Pekuri for second place.

PHYSIOLOGIC EFFECTS OF DISTANCE RUNNING

There are some who tend to discourage young men from entering the distance events because they believe that the effects of prolonged strenuous exercise are harmful.

In view of our own experience and the investigations of others, we believe that distance running is not harmful to young men provided that they are normal in the beginning, that they carefully observe the prescribed process of training and practice, and that they taper off at the conclusion of the season with exercises which are progressively less intense.

The questions raised concerning the effects of distance running are : (1) is it detrimental to health? (2) does it shorten the span of life of the participants?

The most extensive and trustworthy investigation of these questions give negative answers. As compared with similar groups, the athletes participating in endurance events seem to have a slight advantage over those who do not take part in such exercise. The keen interest in the effect of distance and cross-country running on longevity prompted the writers to follow a group of athletes who had participated in these events as long ago as 1905. At the present time these past performers observed number about 130. It is of interest to note that all of them except one, who met with accidental death, are living and are apparently in good health.

That strenuous exercise brings about definite chronic changes in the physiologic condition of the athlete is evident from the following :—

1. The pulse of the trained athlete is as much as 15 per cent below that of the untrained individual.

2. Strenuous exercise brings about a definite increase in heart size. This is due to an enlargement of the muscle cells and not to a dilatation of the heart.

3. The systolic blood pressure falls as much as 25 per cent in the athlete who is physically well trained.

4. There is a definite increase in the number of both the red and white blood corpuscles in those who train strenuously.

5. Exercises of endurance increase the vital capacity as much as 20 per cent.

6. The alkaline reserve is increase as much as 12 per cent through systematic training. The relation of alkaline reserve to endurance has been studied by Hewitt and Callaway. They conducted an experiment in which an attempt was made to increase the alkaline reserve of athletes by feeding them orange juice, tomato juice, and a concentrated alkalizer containing sodium, potassium, and calcium citrates in the form of acid salts. The alkaline treatment apparently bettered performance.

CHAPTER 4

THE IMPORTANCE OF HALF RUN IN RUNNING EVENTS

Any summary of the outstanding performances in the half-mile run can well begin with the wonderful exploits of Lawrence "Lon" Myers of the Manhattan Athletic Club during the years 1865 to 1878 as an amateur and for five years thereafter as a professional. In 1880, he ran seven times in a single afternoon and won the American title in the 100, the 220, the 440, and the 880. In 1886, he defeated the all-time great English runner, W.G.George, in the 880, the ¾-mile, and the mile. Even today, many consider Myers as probably the greatest middle-distance runner of all time. His best time for the 880, 1:55.4, was excellent and remained as the American record for 11 years, despite his tendency to run merely to win and seldom to specialize in a single event. His tendency to stress sprint work and to double in the 440 has set a pattern that by far the greatest percentage of 880 men have followed since that time.

The world's record shifted back to England in 1888 through a 1:54.4 performance by F.J.K. Cross. Again a pattern was created, for of 17 men who have held world's records in either the 800-meter or the 880-yard run, 13 have come from either the United States or England. Both tradition and training methods in these two countries have enabled them almost to monopolize these events.

Italy has held the record but once—E.Lunghi, 1909, 1:52.8—but has had many other find half-milers, including Mario Lanzi who, in 1939, pushed Harbig to his great 800-mete record. In 1928, Sera Martin brought the record to France for a four-year visit. Germany won the world's record on two occasions : in 1926, when Dr. Otto Peltzer broke Ted Meredith's 10-year-old 880-yard record with 1:51.6; and in 1939, when Rudolph Harbig almost shocked the sports world with an unheralded 1:46.6 for the 800-meter, which stands today as one of the greatest of all running records.

Although England has actually held either the 800-meter or the 880-yard world's records on but three occasions, her dominance of international competition in these events gives one an impression of much greater accomplishment. In addition to Cross, Thomas Hampson achieved 1:49.8 for the 800-meter in 1932, and six years later, little Sidney Wooderson, who held the world's mile record at 4:06.4, unleased unexpected speed in posting 1:48.4 for the 800-meter and 1:49.2 for the full 880-yard distance.

America's claim to middle-distance supremacy is based upon 11 record performances. Charlie Kilpatricks, of the New York Athletic Club, arrived some ten years after the great Lon Myers and was national champion in 1894, 1895, and 1896, with a best time of 1:53.4. Ten years later, Mel W. Sheppard won the first of five national 880-yard championships, winning in 1906, 1907, 1911, and 1912, with a best time of 1:54.2. However, he improved on this time and created a new world's record in winning the 1908 Olympic 800-meter championship in 1:52.8. This record held for but one Olympiad, for in 1912, Ted Meredith, an 18-year-old boy just out of Mercersburg Academy, upset the world's best at Stockholm in sending the 800-meter mark down to 1:51.9. Four years later, as a senior at the university of

Pennsylvania, Ted lowered the 880-yard record to 1:52.2.

In 1926, Dr. Otto Peltzer, of Germany, took the 880-yard record, and in 1928, Sera Martin, of France, the 800-meter record. In 1932, Eastman of Stanford ran 1:50.0 for the 800-meter, and in 1934, 1:49.8 for a new record at the 880-yard distance. Two years later, Glenn Cunningham shaved a single .1 second from the 800 mark, and a year later, in 1937, Elory Robinson of Fresno State pinched off another to put the record at 1:49.6. Mal Whitfield completed one chapter of the American record story in 1950 when he won an 880 "match" race and tied Wooderson's record of 1:49.2.

Of these men from various countries who have held records at either the 800-meter or 880-yard distance, four seem to warrant special mention as furthering an understanding of the requirements and the methods of running this race : Ted Meredith, University of Pennsylvania; Douglas Lowe, England; Rudolph Harbig, Germany; and Mal Whitfield, Ohio State University.

Meredith is of greatest interest to this discussion for having set a pattern of combining of 440- and 880-yard distance that many a later 880-yard champion was to follow and find profitable. This 18-year-old Mercersburg Academy runner had made excellent performances in both the 440 and the 880 during the 1912 sprint season, but he had been unable to win either final in the American Olympic tryouts. In running the 440, he habitually took the lead immediately and carried a very fast pace throughout the first half of the race. However in the half-mile, his superior speed gave him an advantage at the finish and he therefore held back until about the final straightaway. In the Olympic final, for example, he was running against Mel Sheppard, the 1908 winner in both the 880- and 1500-meter races, and against Davenport, of the U.S.A., the Braun, of Germany, who were both fine quarter-milers. Sheppard, the strongest but also the slowest of the group, took the lead immediately and hit the 400 mark at the then unbelievable time of :52.4. Meredith was a close second, however, with Braun and Davenport just behind. Not until the final straightaway did Meredith move up and out to take the lead by 2 feet from Sheppard and a new Olympic record of 1:51.9. Sheppard's strategy was to build up as great a lead as possible during the first 440 and "run the sprint out" of his faster quarter-mile opponents. Theirs was to be put at the 660-yard mark and outsprint him at the finish. As has happend since in so many, many races, the man with the finishing kick was the winner.

The next great champion, Douglas G. A. Lowe, of Cambridge College, England, has undoubtedly, by example, teaching and writing, influenced both training and tactics in the half-mile more than any other one person. His first emphasis lay in knowing just as much about the methods and abilities of everyone in the race as he knew about himself. In 1924, Lowe had won the Olympic title by his superior sprint in the last straightaway, and one might have expected him to follow this tactic indefinitely. Yet, two years later, when he became convinced that Dr. Otto Peltzer of Germany had great speed at the finish, Lowe took the place at the quarter post and tried to carry the entire last 440 yards, Peltzer kicked past at the tape, however, in the new world's record of 1:51.6. Probably one consequence of this defeat was Lowe's exclusive attention to quarter-miling and to greater speed throughout the 1927 season.

At the 1928 games at Amsterdam, Lowe knew the abilities and probable tactics of everyone in the field. He knew that Lloyd Hahn, the American miler, would be likely to take the lead and set a fast pace. He knew that Peltzer was not in the best of condition but would be dangerous at the finish. He knew that Sera Martin, the French world's record holder, had a terrific sprint in the final straightaway, and that Phil Edwards, liked to lead the pace but usually had little strength at the finish. Armed with such knowledge, Lowe was content to take second place in his trial race in the slow time of 1:57, whereas Hahn and Martin had to fight hard to win theirs in about 1:53. As expected, Hahn tried to run away fro the field in the final, running about :53 for his first 440. Lowe and Martin, however, stayed at his shoulder, not letting him relax for a moment. Suddenly at the 660, Lowe jumped into the lead, earlier than the others expected, sprinted the entire last 220 yards, and was never seriously challenged.

The greatest performance to date in middle-distance running was given by German, Rudolph Harbig, in 1939. At 26 years of age, Harbig had seven years of extensive running, first as a cross-country man at 19, later as a 220 and 440 man, with best times at the latter distances of :21.8 and :46.0 respectively. In July, Harbig had run 1:49.4 and was therefore matched to run against Mario Lanzi, the Italian holder at 1:49.5. As expected, Lanzi carried a very fast pace, :52 at the 440 mark, 1:20 at the 600, but Harbig stayed close to his shoulder and, in the final stretch, sprinted past to an almost fantasic time of 1:46.6. Unfortunately, the result was so unexpected that no time was taken at the 880-yard mark, which undoubtedly would have been reached in around 1:47.3. All the elements were present here for a great race and great time: Lanzi, the pace-setter, was running a faster pace that is generally considered correct, and Harbig, a fine sprinter and quarter-miler, was following this fast pace closely but was saving strength enough to sprint home. Similar conditions will exist when the ultimate human time for the distance is posted.

The last of these instructive and thrilling races occurred during the 1948 Olympic games. Wint, the 6'

4" Jamaican who had just won the 400-meter Olympic title in :46.2, appeared to be the man to beat. His usual tactic was to outsprint his opponents in the final stretch. Hansenne had lowered the French 800-meter record to 1:48.3, was strong at the 1500-meter, and also had an excellent kick at the finish. Barten, of the University of Michigan, was the miler type but had beaten Whitfield in the half-mile in a May race by outsprinting him in the last 200 yards. The Olympic winner was Mal Whitfield, of Ohio State, perhaps not so much because of his ability, which, in view of his :46.3 400-meter time, was undoubtedly superior, as because he gained his advantage when least expected. Just before the bell at the 400-meter mark, Whitfield jumped to a full 8-yard lead. Each of his opponents gained on him during the final 220 yards but not enough to overcome the lead, and he broke the tape in a fast 1:49.2. Here was a perfect example of right tactics producing the winning margin. Had he taken the lead earlier, his opponents would have had time to recover the distance lost. Had he waited, other races, both before and after the Olympics, indicated that either Wint, Barten, or Hansenne would have outsprinted him. His tactic was exactly right and his winner's honours were well earned.

One of the most interesting and important aspects of half-mile running is proper pace. The more thought the writer gives to the matter, the clearer it seems that the same theory of "maximum pace, minimum deceleration" that was developed in the quarter-mile section, has application here. If trying to make best time, a man should run as fast as he can without having to slow down excessively at any stage of the race. The primary question now is not, "How fast shall I run the first quarter?" but rather, "How fast can I run the first part of the race and continue on with the least possible loss of pace during the later portions?"

At first one might interpret these statements as merely peculiar ways of saying that the half-mile should be run at an even pace, for there would then be no deceleration at all. But this is not the case. For some good reasons—whether it be physical, mental, or emotional is not clear—there seems to be an advantage in speeding up the first part of the race. Of 33 races timed under 1:52 for either 880 yards or 800 meters, for which the writer has statistics, 29 had a faster first quarter. These were all run by champions who had seriously studied their events. To excuse these fast first quarters on the basis of poor pace judgment, of working off an initial excess of energy, or of a belief that a faster pace will be harder on one's opponents than on oneself hardly seems adequate. There must be a sound organic reason for this fact that psychophysiologists have not yet made evident to us.

However, very few times have been taken at the 600 mark and we are dependent upon quarter times only. Of the 33 races mentioned previously, the average total time was 1:50.1; the average time for the first half of these races was :53.4, and for the second, :56.7. This gives an average time difference between halves of 3.3 seconds. This figure is different from the 880-yard and the 800-meter, being 3.7 seconds and 2.9 seconds respectively. Since the 880 is primarily an American race, it should appear that Americans run the first half of their race slightly faster than do Europeans It is also very interesting to note that of 18 races between 1:50 and 1:51.9, the average time difference was 3.4 seconds; whereas of 14 races under 1:50, it was only 2.0. Apparently, the fastest races tend toward more even pace.

Of the races under 1:50, only 2 had a first quarter that was slower than the second: Roscoe Brown's 1:49.3 and Holst Sorenson's 1:48.9. But 9 out of these 15 time differences were under 2 seconds.

It is such a plan as this that a slower but stronger half-miler would follow in beating a speedier but less efficient opponent, or that any man would follow in trying to make best possible time. It should further be noted that this plan places great emphasis upon the third 220, for there must be a minimum of slowing down at this stage of the race. The runner cannot centre his mind and pace upon the 440 time and then relax. Rather, he must view the race as a whole with no physical letdown at any point and with gradually increasing mental emphasis upon relaxation as fatigue accumulates.

Finally, it needs to be stated against that if the race is simply competitive, if beating the other fellow is the primary concern, other considerations may well produce an entirely different plan of attack.

TRAINING FOR THE HALF-MILE

Typical Workout

40 minutes : Group running (preferably off the track. Keep plan flexible but repeat all 6 steps each day. To do this much work requires weeks of graded practice).

1. Easy jogging—5 min.

2. Upper-body exercises—10 min. (arm and shoulder strength; abdominal and back strength; abdominal, back and hip flexibility).

3. Speed work—10 min. (gradually increased and repeated).

4. Walking and jogging—5 min.

5. Speed work repeated—5 min.

6. Restful walking—5 min.

15 minutes : Individualized Work Period (select one for each day's workout).

1. Repeated 220's or 440's (slow pace, little rest

between, for pace endurance).

2. Repeated 220's or 440's (fast pace, long rest between, for speed endurance).

3. Pace work at 440 or 660.

4. Endless relays using 220's for pace and/or speed.

5. Time trial at 660 yards.

5 minutes : Speed Work (always end each workout with speed work).

10 minutes : Recovery Period (restful group jogging and walking. An essential parr of each day's workout).

Daily Variations In Assignments

Monday: Repeated 220's or 440's for pace and/or speed.

Tuesday: Pace work at 660 yards or time trial at 660 yards.

Wednesday: Repeated speed work at 220 yards.

Thursday: 2 or 3 440's at Saturday's pace.

Friday: Rest

Saturday: Competition.

CHAPTER 5

THE MILE RUN

The mile race is one of today's chief attractions in track and field. It holds this position of recognition partly because it is such an exacting test of speed, stamina, and sound judgment in training and racing. Spectators can pick their favourites and have the time to cheer them as they go around the track 4 times. The layman can see the attempts of various runners to use strategy. For the beginning performer in the mile, there are no absolute mechanical principles that must be followed.

Coaches and physiologists have studied and measured the distribution of effort at different stages of the mile run. Although some of their findings have been used by milers in training and competition, running in the most natural and relaxed manner often proves easiest and most economical. This means that the exact procedure for each runner often becomes an individual matter that can be worked out only after a long period of study, self-observation, and determination, supplemented by the advice and help of the coach. This does not mean that the miler will not be affected by the findings of research and experimentation. Some present training and competitive programs have received their initial stimulus from the laboratory. Concepts have to be subjected to study and either accepted or rejected on the basis of results on the track.

There are, however, certain "musts" that apply to most milers which will be presented in the following pages. The ideal miler usually has an average build, long legs, and a natural, loose-striding running action. Of course, there have been many successful exceptions to this body type. Regardless of body build, the miler must have the will to develop the natural talents he possesses. He must also have a nervous system sufficiently high strung and an oxygen consumption system of top ability to enable him to produce a maximum effort far beyond that of the normal individual.

GREAT PERFORMANCES OF THE PAST

Even the general public is aware that distance running times have been lowered with amazing rapidity in recent years. Within the past decade there have been many new world records in the mile run alone. Walter George of England was probably the first great star in the mile and 2-mile distances. In 1882 he set a world mark of 4:21.4 in the mile. As a professional in 1886, he ran a mile in 4:12.8. This mark was not surpassed until 1915, when Norman Taber ran the distance in 4:12.6. Paavo Nurmi, the famous smooth-striding Finn, lowered the record to 4:10.4 in 1923.

The first to break Nurmi's 4-lap time was Jules Ladoumégue, a Frenchman, who ran distance in 4:09.2 in 1931. Jack Lovelock, the speedy New Zealander with a terrific finish kick, ran the mile in 4:07.6 in 1933. Glenn Cunningham, who had the longest competitive career of any American distance star, set a new mile world record of 4:06.8 slender Englishman, lowered it in 1937 to 4:06.4.

The value of much repeat speed work, used by many milers (especially the Americans), and of the Swedish speed play (Fartlek) became evident when two Swedish runners, Arne Andersson and Gunder Hägg, began a fine series of duels that resulted in a new world record by Hägg of 4:06.2 in 1942. Andersson equalled this time a week later, but 2 months later Hägg lowered it again to 4:04.6. The following spring Andersson ran the mile in 4:02.6. The two great runners took turns defeating each other and finally, in July, 1945, running on the fast track at Malmo, Sweden, Hägg lowered the mile record to 4:01.4, defeating Andersson, Rune Persson, and Lennart Strand. Leading all the way, Hägg ran at an almost even pace for the last 3 laps. The prevailing racing concept at that time was that a competitor should run the first quarter of the race faster than the other quarters, then attempt to run the last 3 quarters at even pace.

Andersson and Hägg indicated by their performances that the much sought 4-minute mile was within grasp, but it was not until May 6, 1954, the Roger Bannister, the Great Britain champion, broke the 4-minute barrier with a new world record time of 3:59.4. Then on June 23, 1967, Jim Ryun of Kansas and the U.S. established the present accepted world's record of 3:51.1.

The altitude and a previous illness took much from the efficiency of Ryun during the 1968 Olympics. In one of the finest tactical races ever run in Olympic history, Kipchoge Keino of Kenya ran an unbelievable 3:34.9 for 1,500 meters in establishing a new Olympic record with the second fastest time ever run in this event. Ryun finished second in the excellent time of 3:37.8, well under what he expected to run and, for that matter, what the experts estimated he would need to run to win.

TYPES OF MILES

There has been a variety of body types among the great milers. Nurmi was a rather short man with a smooth stride who lacked native speed and had to depend on his knowledge and constant pace in order to wear down his opponent. Lovelock, the thin, light-footed New Zealander who followed the pace set by someone else, won with his terrific finish kick. Cunningham, the barrel-chested American who took up running to help rehabilitate legs behind in a childhood accident, ran or walked many miles each day. He was the first American to approach the amount of training work for distance running that is employed by most European runners.

Jim Ryun, who is tall and rather heavy in weight for a miler, is an excellent example of one who displays relaxed smoothness in his running style. He wastes no energy with him arm action, his knee life is not exaggerated, and he runs with his chest held out. Ryun is blessed with great natural speed, as his exploseness in the last 220 yards of his races has demonstrated. There seems to be no limit to his ability, and even greater performances can be expected of him within the next few years.

It has been noted that sprinters and quarter-milers strike the ground with the bottom of their toes first, and that half-milers strike the ground with their toes only in the earlier stages of the race. In mile or longer races, it has been found that the ball of the runner's foot will hit first, followed by the heel. The miler performs a rolling motion with his foot against the ground, and does not land flatfooted. A runner who lands flatfooted will tire rapidly because of the consequent pounding action, which is very fatiguing to the legs.

Naturalness in running is one of the most important acquisitions for the miler. He should use a freely moving leg action and have a stride of medium length, making no conscious effort to lengthen or shorten the natural stride. A good knee lift is important, especially when the runner starts his final kick. The feet are not lifted in the rear action much higher than the level of the knee.

The ankles must be relaxed when the foot strikes the ground. The body is held erect, with no body lean. The chest should be thrust out and the shoulders held back but relaxed. This position will allow the runner good chest expansion while running.

The arms are used mostly for balance purposes in distance running. It is important to remember that the shoulders are relaxed, with the forearms carried parallel to the ground. The elbows of the runner are moved back and forth naturally as he runs, but most not restrict the movement of the chest cavity or interfere with the natural swing of the shoulders. An easy, relaxed arm action synchronized with the action of the legs is the goal of the mile runner. Vigorous arm action will fatigue the arms and shoulders and slow the runner.

Each runner has a natural running style which is best suited to his size and build. This principle applies especially to the action of the arms. It would be foolish to say that all milers must have the same style of running. However, from watching champions in action and studying slow motion pictures of their running forms, the athlete may pick up hints that might improves his own style of running. There are certain principles of movement that apply to mile running which may be used by all mile aspirants. These involve pacing, arm and leg action, no body lean, relaxing, and so on.

TRAINING PROGRAM

There are some differences of opinion on the type of training program best suited for accomplishing the desired results for the greatest number of milers. However, it is generally agreed that, primarily, the runner must do a great deal of running over a long period of time. The aspirant who wishes to be at his best during the competitive season must start his training program at least 6 months before the seasons opens.

The great distance coach, Gosta Holmer of Sweden, originated the Fartlek method of training, which means "speed play". This is usually done on grass or in the woods. The runner sets his own pace, running fast or just jogging along as suits his whim. It is thought that he will gradually run faster for a longer period of time as he continues this type of training.

WORKOUT SCHEDULES

A typical workout plan for the fall season, suggested by Holmer, is presented here. The athlete should train from 1 to 2 hours each day, according to this schedule.

Fall Season

1. Easy running on the grass for 5 to 10 minutes (as a warm-up).

2. Steady, hard speed work for a distant of 5/8 to 1¼ miles.

3. Rapid walking for about 5 minutes.

4. Easy running, interspersed by running wind sprints from 55 yards to 65 yards distance, and repeated until runner feels tired.

5. Easy running with 3 or 4 swift step taken now and then.

6. Full speed runs uphill.

7. Fast pace running for one minute following the uphill running mentioned in 6.

This training plan may be repeated many times, but the running should remember that he must feel stimulated, not tired after the daily workout.

Midseason

The following is a typical midseason training schedule as recommended by coaches in the past. This is a so-called Fartlek workout, which not all coaches utilize except during early season.

Monday

1. Do Fartlek for 45 minutes.

2. Run the first 40 yards of a race at competitive speed.

3. Repeat 1, 2, for 3 times. Do easy running for 5 minutes between these runs.

4. Walk and run easy to complete a 2-hour workout.

Tuesday

1. Do Fartlek for 20 minutes.

2. Run 880 yards on the track, 2 seconds per lap slower than time in a competitive race.

3. Repeat 1 and 2 until an hour has elapsed. Run easy on grass between and after each run.

Wednesday

Walk in the woods for 2 hours.

Thursday

Follow same schedule as Monday's, but run uphill 2 to 9×150 yards each time during the Fartlek portion.

Friday

Follow same schedule as Tuesday's but run 4×440-yard laps instead of 2×880 yards. Run each lap one second slower than racing speed.

Saturday

Rest

Sunday

Warm-up and run a mile. Run the first 440 yards and the last 100 yards of the distance at racing speed. Run each lap of the middle of the race 2 seconds slower than racing pace.

Racing workouts are done at the individual athlete's own pace. Work out at the competitive distance once every 10 days.

These schedules are not to be followed as blueprints. Each athlete must use initiative in planning his workouts with the help of his coach.

Other Ideas

In a further interpretation and development of Fartlek, the runners practice Fartlek twice each week during early training, and once each week during competitive periods over the countryside or on a grass sports field. Speed is added by 220-yard bursts being done on the track 2 or 3 times each week. The runner does a series of such bursts at a speed faster than the average speed of his race. For instance, a 4:24 miler runs each 220 yard in 28 seconds. He runs 220 yards, walks back to the starting point and repeats, doing this until he begins feel weary. The training is then finished off with about 30 minutes of easy running on the grass.

The training has been classified into 4 separate periods of progressive activity :—

1. Conditioning period : January to mid-March. Walking, easy running, and indoor gymnastic exercises.

2. Preseason : Mid-March to mid-April. Running work and Fartlek with some speed training.

3. Early competitive season : Mid-April to early June. Training progress is same as that of the persons, except there is one competitive run each week.

4. Competitive season : Early April to late June. The amount of training corresponds to the number of competitive races in which the runner participates. Usually the training is much like that of the preseason

except that much less time is spent.

Interval training. Frank Stampftl, who is now coaching in Australia and has developed some very fine distance competitors in England and Australia, has a theory on training somewhat different from those mentioned above. Two of the sub-4-minute milers he has coached are Merv Lincoln and former world record holder John Landy. Stamptfl strongly believes that the best way to develop stamina is through the "interval training" method. This simply means that the runners run 440 yards, jog 440 yards, and repeat this procedure as many as 20 times in one workout session. These repeat 440's are run at paced time for the distance of the race for which the athlete is training. When the athlete's physical condition is such that he can follow this procedure easily, he then runs repeat 440's with jogs of only 220 yards between.

The authors believe that this interval training plan helps develop some stamina and good judgment of pace, but it does not adequately develop two important phases of conditioning for the mile run-speed and top endurance. Some sub-4-minute milers are not endowed with a great deal of natural speed, but by practicing sprints at distances of 100 to 220 yards at full effort, running with fast leg action and good knee lift, they are able to develop the extra speed and endurance needed in running the mile.

The workload undertaken by today's distance runners is staggering. Every great runner from the mile on up trains on a 12 months basis, and usually twice per day. With high school runners running sub-4-minute miles and sub-9-minute two miles, there is no question that they are following the same vigorous schedules as are the older runners. The normal morning workout consists of from 4 to 10 miles of running, which varies in intensity depending on the level of competition, time of season, and day of the week.

Different kinds of training schedule are given below:—

Preseasonal Workout for Mile Run

Mornings

6 to 10 miles; do not run to the point of exhaustion. You should feel exhilarated as well as a little tired.

Monday: 440-yard runs

1. Start running 440-yard runs at 70-second pace and drop 1 second each week.

2. Run 440's 10 to 14 times, depending on age and strength.

3. Run 440, then jog 440, and repeat (2 minutes for the 440 jog).

4. Run 10×110's.

5. Walk and jog 2 to 3 laps and go to showers.

Tuesday: 220-yard runs

1. Start running 220's at 32- to 35-second pace and drop 1 second each week.

2. Run 220 yards 12 to 16 times.

3. Run 220, then jog 220 and repeat.

4. Run 10×110's.

5. Walk and jog 2 to 3 laps and go to showers.

Wednesday: 880-yard runs

1. Start running 880's at 2.20 pace and drop 2 seconds each week.

2. Run 880 yards 6 to 8 times.

3. Run 880 and jog 880 in about 5 minutes, and repeat.

4. Run 10×110's.

5. Walk and jog 2 to 3 laps and go to showers.

Wednesday: 880-yard runs

1. Start running 880's at 2.20 pace and drop 2 seconds each week.

2. Run 880 yards 6 to 8 times.

3. Run 880 and jog 880 in about 5 minutes, and repeat.

4. Run 10×110's.

5. Walk and jog to 3 laps and go to showers.

Thursday: 1,320-yard runs

1. Start running 1,320's at 3.35 pace and drop 2 to 3 seconds per week.

2. Run 1,320 yards 3 or 4 times.

3. Run 1m,320 and then jog 1,320 (about 8 minutes), and repeat.

4. Run 10×110's.

5. Walk and jog 2 or 3 laps and go to showers.

Friday: combination of distances (breakdown)

1. Run 1 mile, first 3 laps at 72- to 76-second pace, accelerate on fourth lap, trying for a 60-second last lap.

2. Jog 1 mile.

3. Run 1,320, first 2 laps at 68- to 72-second pace, accelerate on third lap, trying for 65 seconds.

4. Jog 1,320.

5. Run 880, first lap in upper 60's and accelerate on second lap, trying for 65 seconds.

6. Jog 880.

7. Run 440, first 220 in 35 seconds, and accelerate on second 220, trying for a 26- to 28-second 220.

8. Run 10×110's.

9. Jog 2 to 3 laps and go to showers.

Saturday

Time trail or early season competition.

Sunday

Cross-country workout away from the track, running 6 to 8 miles.

REGULAR SEASON WORKOUT FOR MILE RUN

Monday

Run 1×1,320 yards, full effort, or 2 to 3×1,320 yards at race pace, with 5 minutes rest intervals in between.

2. Run 220, 440, 880, 440, 220. Performer keeps moving as he run distance at race speed, then jogs distance.

3. Run 10×110's.

4. Jog 2 to 3 laps for cooling down.

Tuesday

1. Run 10 to 12×440's at 1 to 2 seconds below race pace.

2. Jog 440 between, not to exceed 70 seconds.

3. Run 10×110's.

4. Jog 2 or 3 laps to cool down.

Wednesday

1. Run 6 to 8×880's at race pace or slightly below.

2. Jog 880 between, not to exceed 2 minutes.

3. Run 10×110's.

4. Jog 2 or 3 laps to cool down.

Thursday

1. Run 15 to 20×220's at 2 or 3 seconds below race pace.

2. Jog 220 between, not to exceed 60 seconds.

3. Run 10×110's.

4. Jog 2 or 3 laps to cool down.

Friday

Light workout, but do a thorough warm-up.

Saturday

Competition day.

Sunday

Do sprint work, running 20 to 40×200's, or run 5 to 8 miles on cross-country course.

To help combat montony involved with the standard workouts, certain combinations can be used:

4×(110-220-110)

3×(220-440-220)

2×(440-880-440)

These are run as sets, with the jogging intervals between runs brief, and with additional time intervals established between sets.'

It has also been found that placing the miler in an 880-yard race will occasionally help develop speed. Some of the better milers have run on the mile relay team with recorded times of 48 seconds or less for their lap in the relay.

In summary, it might be said that there are 3 major goals for which the miler must train: (1) endurance acquired through the use of Fartlek activities and a lot of running; (2) pace judgment acquired through doing repeated quarter-and half-miles; and (3) speed acquired through participation in wind sprints and repeated 220's.

STRATEGY AND PACE

There has been much discussion in the past regarding the ideal pace to set for running the mile in the time of 4 minutes or less. It is generally agreed that each of the 4 quarters should be run at nearly equal time, with the last half-mile possibly a little faster than the first half. Physiologists tell us that running the first quarter at near the athlete's maximum speed will build up a large oxygen debt which is impossible to overcome. The first quarter should usually be run about 1 to 2 seconds faster than the second quarter, because during the first 50 yards of the race the milers are running for the lead or a position near the leaders.

There are several things that should be considered in planning the strategy for a race.

1. Many races are won by knowing the characteristics of the competing runner. Does he have a good "kick"? How far can he maintain this "kick"? Does he have the ability to sprint at the end of the mile? If it is known that an opponent has a good "kick" during the last 100 yards of the race, then a runner must set a fast pace during the early part in order to build up a lead, or to make his opponent run so fast to keep close that he has no kick left.

2. If the opponent is a strong runner but has no finishing kick, an opposing runner should let him set the pace and then outsprint him in the last 100 yards.

3. It is important that a runner attempt to keep his stride even throughout the race.

4. A runner should avoid running on the pole if there is deanger he might be boxed in by the other runners. It is much better for him to run, in this case, on the outside of other competitors, and to try to avoid the congestion that may cause him to lose ground and force him to change his pace too often.

Physiological and Psychological aspects. There have been may explanations offered as to what causes an athlete to get his "second wind" during the third lap of the mile run, but tolerance to the body stresses involved in running is thought by many to explain why experienced runners seldom seem to get the so-called "second wind".

It is the opinion of the authors that this phenomenon is more psychological than physical. For example, at athlete who has run the first lap reasonably fast thinks, "Can I keep up this pace for two more laps?" Most of the time he will run his last lap at a fast pace because he known by this time that he can run it fast. The third-lap "tired feeling" he experiences must be disregarded; he must run as if he were just starting the race on this third lap. He must convince himself that the others in the race are just as tired as he is, and that his workout schedule has been sufficiently strenuous to train him to run the entire race as well as they. Runners have been able to overcome a "stitch in the side" by simply ignoring it and running as if they had no such pain. Soon they were able to tolerate this "trouble" and run a normal race. Actually, most top runners state that they do not experience this feeling.

The competitive season in the United States is very long and strenuous. Meets begin in early January and continue through June or later. Many runners are required to compete in races almost every Friday or Saturday. The workout schedule should be planned so that the runners will reach their peak of condition at the time of the more important meets in May and June. Acquiring the right mental attitude for these "big" meets in very important. A runner must mentally condition itself in advance for each race but must especially concentrate on winning the big meets.

The workouts should be varied enough to insure that no mental staleness occurs. There must be a feeling of joy and exhilaration in the running during the workouts, and a realization of accomplishment after the competition. Any runner who does not enjoy competing will usually not be a consistent winner.

HELPFUL HINTS

The runner should :

1. Run "his own race", and not be misled by some runner who runs "all-out" early in the race. However, he should stay close enough to the leaders to be able to overtake them at the finish.

2. Be careful not to pick up the running rhythm of an opponent that is entirely unsuited to him. Again it should be said: run at your own speed and pace.

3. Practice long hours in order to be successful. Enough time must be provided for the runner to condition himself properly before competition begins.

4. Remember that it is usually best to run on the pole in a race, especially in long-distance races.

5. Run most of the year in order to be "good" at distance running. Boys who compete in other sports should not forget to do some distance running each week.

6. Plan each particular race with his coach so that he

will have in mind exactly what he must do; be flexible enough to modify plans to meet the situation.

7. Know his liabilities as well as his assets, and plan his training program and racing strategy accordingly.

8. Remember that mile runners have various body builds, and that unless he is extremely large he will have a chance. However, the moderately tall and average weight individuals are usually the most successful in this event.

9. Learn to relax when running by consciously relaxing the wrists and ankles.

10. Not do a great deal of jockeying back and forth when attempting to pass an opponent in a race. Pass him quickly, and, if possible, unexpectedly.

11. Attempt to make it costly in energy for an opponent to pass him, but should not expend too much energy in thwarting his move.

All histories of mile running rightly begin with the exploits of the Englishman W.G.George, who, in 1885, set an amateur record of 4:18.4; then, turning to more lucrative professional racing, which was so prevalent at the time, beat the best of them. W. Cummings, in the amazing time of 4:12.8. In this race, George ran successive quarters in :58.5, :63.3, :66.0, and :65.0. The half first half, 2:01.8, is a little difficult to understand when one considers that a steady pace over long distances was then the common training method. Training articles written at the time emphasize steady running for 2 to 20 miles either once or twice a day. Perhaps it resulted from George's efforts to set records at all distances, from 1,000 yards to 12 miles. In any case, George's success with this first half influenced the attempts of future runners for over a quarter century.

It is of value to note that even during its heyday professional running was hardly an honoured practice and that George succumbed to its lure only when there were no further goals to conquer in amateur running and when he discovered that his attempts to be a combined student-athlete had placed him in debt some 1,000 English pounds. Apparently his debts were soon cleared, for F.A.M. Webster comments that on the day of George's great race with the professional champion, Cummings, such a surge of spectators was on hand—about 30,000—that "George was forced to reach his dressing room at the top of the old grand stand by means of a ladder from an adjoining coal yard".

But, not to be denied, Tabor came back in 1915 with a brilliant 4:12.6, which shattered every mark on or off the books. In so doing, he recorded :58.0, :67.0, :68.0, :59.6 for his four quarters. This is a different pace pattern from that of George, with its slow second quarter, an even slower third quarter, and a blazingly fast final quarter. One thinks of it as being the result of staying up in a large field of runners in which someone always runs the first quarter much too fast, of then simply relaxing with the field for the middle half-mile, and of finally sprinting all-out for the full final quarter. It is a method of running that is still prevalent today. It makes for excellent competition but despite Tabor's success, is hardly conducive to best time.

The next stage in both record making and pace making in the mile was dramatized by perhaps the most famous of all distance runners, Paavo Nurmi, the Phantom Finn. He was not primarily a miler, having established 19 world's records at 11 standard distances during the 11 years of his career; yet he covered the mile distance in 4:10.4 and even held the 1924 Olympic title and world's record at 1500 meters in 3:52.6. The unique emphasis in Nurmi's running was upon even pace. His habit at longer distances of carrying a watch and hitting even pace time for lap after lap was the sensation of the sports world for a full decade. Yet, when he set his world's mile record in 1923, the pace was off. As happens so often, he found it necessary to remain with his opponents regardless of pace. His rival this time and on many another memorable occasion was an excellent runner named Edvin Wide of Sweden, who completed the first lap in :58.6, and the 880 in 2:01.8. However, Nurmi then took over, hitting 3:06.7 at ¾ mile and :63.7 for his final lap. Nurmi is said to have had in mind a 4:08 mile with even quarters of :62 each, but his opponent's pace spoiled these plans and a slower total time resulted. Nurmi's daily practice occurred as he ran 5 miles to and from work. He carried a stop watch at all times, became interested in the relative effects of different pace upon his performance, and thus came to the practice of even pace that has so widely influenced distance running since his time. Running at such an even pace allows no slowing of speed during the third quarter, when men or most aware of the feelings of fatigue. It was here that Nurmi "poured it on", just when others were trying to catch their breath for the final finishing sprint. Such continuous attention to even pace is still today the mark of the mature and experienced runner. The man who can stay mentally and alert and keep the pace going will find his more sensitive opponents dropping back and out of a winning position.

But the flawless Nurmi's mile record lasted only seven years, until 1931, when a rugged little Frenchman, Jules Ladoumègue, became the first man in history to beat 4:10 for the mile, with a best time of 4:09.2. Had he not been suspended from amateur competition. Ladoumègue undoubtedly would have toughened even further the great competition between Jack Lovelock of New Zealand, Glenn Cunningham of Kansas, and Bill

Bonthron of Princeton during the years 1933 to 1936. First, Lovelock, running at the famous Princeton Invitational Meet, beat Bonthron in 4:07.6. A year later, in 1934, Cunningham lowered this record to4:06.8 yet even this fast time had to give way just three years later to the pattering strides of Sydney Wooderson of England. On this occasion a deliberate attempt to break the record was publicized and carried out with almost flawless precision to a 4:06.2 conclusion.

One of the greatest influences upon training for the mile came through the tremendous finishing pace of the champions of this era. Glenn Cunningham, Bill Bonthron, Charles Fenske, and, most of all, Jack Lovelock had tremendous bursts of speed at the finish, and all were capable of excellent quarter-miles well under 50 seconds. For example, in the 1936 Olympic 1500-meter final at Berlin, Lovelock was close to the leader but still in fourth place 300 yards from the finish. Yet within 100 yards he had a 10-yard lead on the field, and his surprised opponents never fully recovered it. The time for his final quarter was :56.0.

The value of such great speed gradually became more evident and athletes in all countries turned to more and more speed work in their practice sessions. Swedish "Fartlek" and American repeated speed work are direct results.

With "Fartlek" came great distance running in Sweden. Rune Persson, Lennart Strand, Rune Gustafsson, Arne Andersson, and Gunder Hägg were all excellent performers, with best mile times under 4:07. The most successful of these were the last two, who by their repeated exploits at many distances surpassed all previous champions. Hägg first attracted attention in August, 1941, by breaking Jack Lovelock's 1500-meter record in 3:47.5. A year later, he also set a new mile record at 4:06.2, with Anderesson only a yard or so behind. Andersson equalled this time a week or so later, but Häg, within two months, lowered it again to 4:04.6. Andersson was not to be outdone, however, and the following spring, in 1942, with Hägg absent, he competed against two of his own countrymen. Arne Ahlsen was third in 4:06.6; Rune Gustafsson, second in 4:05.8; and Andersson, the winner in 4:02.6! Furthermore, to complete his triumph, Andersson took advantage of an American tour by Häg to eclipse the latter's a 1500-meter record in the time of 3:45. To think that the great Nurmi's best was 3:52.6!

The 1944 and 1945 seasons found the four great rivals together again. In a specially arranged match race, Hägg set the 1500-meter time at 3:43.0, the equivalent of about a 3:59 mile. But 11 days later, Andersson returned the compliment by beating Hägg at the mile distance in 4:01.6, running his first half-mile in 1:57.3. Finally, in July, 1945, Hägg Andersson, Persson and Strand were matched on the fast track at Malmo, Sweden. On this occasion, Hägg took the lead all the way. He was :56.5 at the first quarter, :61.9 at the second, and :61.36 at the third; and he hurried home with a sound :61.7 last lap, establishing the present world's record at 4:01.4. Andersson ran 4:02.2 and Persson 4:03.8 in this greatest of all miles. Most unfortunately, Andersson and Hägg were declared professional shortly after this great race, and the much-looked-for 4:00 mile had to wait for other challengers.

It is important to note that almost perfect pace of Hägg during the last three quarters of his race. Andersson was famous for his terrific kick at the finish of his best miles; but on this occasion he either was not at his best or the amazing pace of 2:59.7 for three quarters was just too much for even his great ability. This is one of the few examples in track history in which a strong pace runner has been able to run away from another, almost equally strong, who has a finishing sprint. One can only speculate on how it might have turned out, had these two all-time champions run again.

Post 1952 Olympic performances give every indication of even greater records soon to come. Gunnar Nielsen of Denmark posted 4:04.8; Gaston Reiff, Belgium, 4:03.4 and 4:02.8; Josy Barthel, Luxembourg, 3:44.1 for 1500 meters; Werner Lueg, Germany, 3:43, for 1500 meters; and John Landy, Australia, in January, 1953, 4:02.4 and 4:02.1. These last two times are particularly amazing as they were made in races in which Landy had almost no competition, an "impossible" occurrence. The future for distance-running fans looks bright indeed and the better-than-4:00 mile not far ahead.

PRACTICAL SCHEDULE FOR THE MILE RUN

Typical Workout

40 minutes : Group running (keep plan flexible but repeat all 6 steps every day).

1. Easy jogging—5 min.

2. Upper-body exercises—10 min. (arm and shoulder strength; abdominal and back strength; abdominal, back, and hip flexibility).

3. Gradually increased and repeated speed work—10 min. (mildly fatiguing).

4. Restful walking and jogging—5 min.

5. Repeated speed work—5 min.

6. Restful walking—5 min.

15 minutes: Individualized Work Period (select one for each day's workout).

1. Repeated 220's or 440's.

2. Repeated 220's or 440's (fast pace, long rest between, for speed endurance).

3. Pace work at 440, 880, or ¾ mile.

4. Endless relays for pace and/or speed.

5. Time trial at ¾ mile.

5 minutes : Speed work (always end up with speed work).

10 minutes : Recovery Period (Restful group jogging and walking. An essential part of every day's workout).

Daily Variations in Assignments

(Differences between daily assignments occur primarily during the second period of individualized work).

Monday: Repeated 440's or 880's for pace or speed.

Tuesday: Pace work at ¾ mile or time trail at ¾ mile.

Wednesday: Repeated speed work at 220 or 440 yards.

Thursday: Pace work: 1 or more separate 880's or 440's at Saturday's pace.

Friday: Rest or long walk.

Saturday: Competition.

CHAPTER 6

THE TWO MILE RUN IN RUNNING

Although W.G. George is best remembered for his mile in 4:12.8, his performances extend just as successfully to the longer distances. During five years of amateur competition, George won the English national titles in the mile four times, the two-mile four times, and the ten-mile two times. At the two-mile his best time was 9:17.4.

However, the man whom the English hold up as their greatest champion at these longer distances, and perhaps the greatest of all world's champions, was Alfred Shrubb. During the years 1901 through 1904, he held 14 English national titles at distances from one mile to ten miles and held every distance record on the books from 2,000 yards to eleven miles. As a professional Shrubb ran some amazing races. On one occasion he beat two horses, each going five miles, in a ten-mile race; on another, he won over a relay team of five men, each going two miles while he himself went the full ten miles.

One of the most factual and valuable accounts of training during these early years by the great champions is that written by Shrubb of his workouts during the two weeks prior to the establishment of his two-mile record at 9:09.6 and also his ten-mile record at 50:40.6.

The interesting aspects of this schedule are not merely

in the amount of running done, although this was, of course, tremendous; but also in the number of time trials and the exclusive concern for steady pace running with almost no speed work. When compared with the methods of Emil Zatopek, the current long-distance champion, who is reported to run 60 fast quarters with resting jogs between but with almost no pace work or time trials, the contrast is startling, to say the least.

Shrubb's two-mile record withstood all assaults for 22 years. Even the excellent Jean Bouin of France and the all-time distance man, Hannes Kolehmainen of Finland, were unable to improve upon it. The latter was one of the most famous and enduring of all running champions, winning his first four-mile championship in England in 1911 and the Olympic marathon championship in 1920. He also ran the full distance of the marathon in Paris in 1924.

Only "Chesty" Joie Ray of the Gray Steel Mills and Illinois Athletic Club was able to beat Shrubb's time, recording 9:08 for two miles in 1925, but the race was held indoors and therefore not accepted. Ray, by the way, was another "iron horse", having recorded his first national mile championship in 1915 and his last in 1923. Joie attempted all distances from the half-mile to the marathon, but never with Olympic success. In the 1928 Olympic marathon, he was leading the pack with but two miles to go when leg muscle cramps forced him to drop out.

It was Edvin Wide, the first of a great line of Swedish runners, who officially upset Shrubb's record, posting an amazing time of 9:01.4. But, as happens so often when a long-enduring record is finally broken, a series of better times was soon posted. First in 1931, "Peerless" Paavo Nurmi permitted a slight grin to brighten his impassive face as he heard that he was the first to break 9 minutes, with a clocking of 8:59.6. As in the case of

Alshrubb, American coaches were dumfounded at Nurmi's training methods. The amount of work he took was "inhuman" as compared with that of their college boys. On one occasion he warmed up for an afternoon five-mile race by first jogging a steady two miles. He broke the record—with ease, of course. Later than evening, he appeared for his second race, munching an apple, again warmed up with a full two miles, and again broke the local record. Even today, American distance runners have only partly understood the significance of Nurmi's methods and still tend to work out at minimum and specific distances on the track.

As a matter of fact, the only world's record at distances over one mile that America has held in the past quarter century was made by Don Lash, who, together with his coach. Billy Hayes of Indiana, believed in and practiced Finnish methods of training. The excitement among track fans in America was great indeed as they listened to the results of the 1936 Princeton Invitational Meet and heard 8:58.3 posted for Lash's time in the two-mile.

But just a few months later, Finland resumed the title when Gunnar Hockert lowered the time to 8:57.4. And a year later, in 1937, it was broken again, this time by a Hungarian, Miklos Szabo, in 8:56.0. Again Finland provided the challenger when a great champion, Taisto Maki, recaptured the record in 8:53.2.

The lack of an outdoor program of competitive running for older, post-college men gave no effective opportunity for best running, but an increasing series of indoor meets provided the stimulus for serious training and excellent competition. As a rule the mile was the feature event, but for a period of four years, Greg Rice of Notre Dame stole the show with his remarkably well-paced races and excellent sprint at the end of two miles. His best time, recorded in 1943, was 8:51.0, some 2 seconds better than Maki's official record. One can only speculate concerning what Rice might have been able to do outdoors had a proper competitive program been available. Some feel that indoor facilities provide better conditions for good time, but this is open to serious question. Rice's National Collegiate record of 9:02.6, made at 22 years of age, indicates what he might have been able to do outdoors with four or five more years of training.

Then came Gunder "the Wonder" Hägg, who, in 1942, first recorded 8:47:2. Hägg training methods are adequately described in the section on "Fartlek". Suffice it here to say that it combined the great distances of Shrubb or Nurmi, the repeated speed work of American middle-distance running, and the pleasure of training along wood and meadow paths.

In 1944, Hägg recorded a 2-mile time of 8:46.2 and, a few weeks after, an almost unbelievable 8:42.8. This was considered one of the finest records of all, comparable to Hägg "ultimate" record of 13:58.2 for 5,000 meters. Yet, 8 years later, in August 1952, a supposed "has-been", 31 years of age, Gaston Reiff of Belgium, posted an even greater 8:40.4. In this effort Reiff had little competition and was forced to set his own pace for the entire last mile. Apparently, the ultimate has not yet been achieved.

TRAINING FOR THE TWO-MILE

Typical Workout

40 minutes: Group Running off the Track (keep plan flexible but repeat all 6 steps each day).

1. Easy jogging—5 min.

2. Upper-body exercises—10 min. (arm and shoulder strength; abdominal and back strength; abdominal, back, and hip flexibility).

3. Speed work—10 min. (gradually increased and repeated).

4. Walking and jogging—5 min.

5. Speed work repeated—5 min.

6. Restful walking—5 min.

15 minutes: Individualized Work Period (select one for each day's workout).

1. Repeated 880's, 440's or 220's (slow pace, little rest between, for pace endurance).

2. Repeated 880's, 440's, or 220's (fast pace, long rest between, for speed endurance).

3. Pace work at 880, ¾ mile, mile, or 1½ miles.

4. Endless relays for pace or speed (220's, 440's, 880's each man).

5. Time trial at 1½ miles.

5 minutes: Speed Work (Always end up with speed work).

10 minutes: Recovery period (restful group jogging and walking. An essential part of each day's workout).

Daily Variations in Assignments

(Differences between daily assignments occur primarily during the second period of individualized work)

Monday: Repeated 440's or 880's or pace or speed.

Tuesday: Pace work at 1½ miles or time trial at 1½ miles.

Wednesday: Repeated speed work at 220 or 440 yards.

Thursday: 1 or 2 separate miles at Saturday's pace.

Friday: Rest or long walk.

Saturday: Competition.

CHAPTER 7

LONG DISTANCE RUNNING

Long-distance races are usually considered as those of 2 miles and over. Proper techniques of training for distance running have undergone great changes in the last 10 years. However, Fartlek, interval running, and walking gives distances were also part of the training used by most of the great runners of years ago. Nurmi, the Finn, one of the great distance men of all time, did repeat runs of from 200 to 1,500 meters while training. When the Swedish runners made their world into Fartlek. The great Finnish runners, Salminen, Iso-Hollo, Askola, in the 1936 Olympics used the interval training method. The fabulous Zatopek, who won the 5,000 to 10,000, and Marathon events in the 1952 Olympic Games, used a combination of Fartlek and interval running in preparing for these races.

Kuts of Russia, Thomas of Australia, and Chataway of Great Britain improved their distance running by using training procedures composed of a combination of interval running and Fartlek. Recently, Clarke of Australia, Keino of Kenya, and Lindgren of the United States used Fartlek early in the season, followed by interval training, and climaxed by the use of the "logging miles" technique (simply running a given number of miles in one outing). However, Ron Clarke, the great runner from Australia, reverted to the overdistance or marathon principle of training, and at various times held virtually every record from the 2-mile through the 20,000-meters. In 1968, he simultaneously held world records in the 3-miles, 6-miles, 10-miles, 10,000-meters, 20,000-meters, and the distance covered in the 1-hour run.

On the other hand, Kipchoge Keino of Kenya has developed into a world class distance runner, holding world records in 3,000-meters and 5,000-meters in 13:24.2, while using a system of training completely different from Clarke's. By utilizing some of each method above, he incorporated various systems into one, to serve him, as a miler as well as a distance runner.

The United States enjoyed its greatest day in distance running at the 1964 Olympics in Tokyo, when Bob Shul won the 5,000-meter in 13:48.8, with Bill Dellinger finishing third. In the 10,000-meter run, unheralded Billy Mills of the United States stunned the track word with a brilliant 28:24.4, a new Olympic record. Gerry Lindgren finished an excellent ninth in 29:20.6.

The United States did not fare as well in the 1968 Olympics, as no United States runner placed high in these events. But it is hoped that the future of distance running in the United States will be on the upgrade, as young men such a Gerry Lindgren of Washington State and Van Nelson of St. Cloud State still have many years of competitive running ahead of them.

CHARACTERISTICS OF THE LONG-DISTANCE RUNNER

The ideal distance runner is short and tends to be light in weight, although he may be somewhat stocky. He has a slow pulse rate and likes activities that require endurance. He does not object to continuous practice of the same thing, and enjoys running by himself for hours. What is sheer monotony to others (running for long distances) is fun to him. Boys with these characteristics should be successful at distance running. The essentials of good distance running are knowledge of pace, knowing how to conserve energy, knowing how to relax, and willingness to work very hard to achieve endurance.

RUNNING FORM

Emil Zatopek, the Czech demonstrated good leg action and proper "stride length" in the three races (5,000-meters, 10,000-meters, and Marathon) he won in the 1952 Olympic Games. It was observed that he ran the 5,000-meters with a normal, relaxed, "short" stride, with no effort to lengthen or shorten it as he ran. However, in the 10,000-meter he cut down the length of his stride by dropping the lead foot to the ground sooner through having less knee lift. In the marathon race he used even less knee lift, and thus got a still shorter stride.

The foot in distance running should strike the ground almost directly under the body's centre of gravity. If the foot hits the ground too far in front of the centre of gravity, it will act as a "brake" on the runner's movement, tending to make his body react in the opposite direction. The foot should first strike the strike the ground on the ball or sole, drop lightly down to the heel, then back to the ball of the foot, and not be raised higher than the knee of that leg as it comes up off the ground after the push-off. The contract of the foot with the ground is very brief, as is the time the leg is in the air. The knee of the front leg is not raised very high during the run, but is gently thrust forward to help keep the centre of gravity over the lead foot.

The body should be held rather erect, with the chest pushed out during each stride. The body should be directly above the centre of gravity as the foot contacts the ground.

The arms should be carried up high and across the

chest in a relaxed position. They should move in a short circular action across the body. No undue swinging of the shoulders or rolling of the head should be allowed. However, the head and neck should be to try to conserve as much energy as possible, and this would mean no extra use of the arms and shoulders. The arms are used for balance, moving in coordination with the legs, and the action may differ a little with each individual. Relaxation while running must be one of the distance runner's major physical and mental concerns. Learning to pace himself properly for the entire distance and adjusting to the physiological stress by tolerance are other musts.

TRAINING PROGRAM

Among the things that have been learned about training for distance running is that hard running over a long period of time is necessary for success. Training must be carried on throughout the entire year. The body must be conditioned to perform at close to its peak much of the time. Training must be increased and intensified gradually from early season to late season. An aspirant should not be led to believe that he can follow a champion's workout schedule for three months and hope to break the record. It will take time and hard work over many years for a good runner to emerge as a champion. In fact, most good distance runners currently work out twice a day in order to develop proper endurance.

There seems to be no single training schedule that will insure success for all performers. However, continuous running at a fast pace for long distances appears to be the best final endurance developer.

Training must not be too exhausting or wearisome. Schedules should be changed from time to time. The performer should usually run with others, and train at different places to get a change of scenery. He should run on grass whenever possible—a golf course is an ideal place to train. The performer should take the trouble to develop the entire body. The arms and upper torso of the runner can be developed with weights and by working on the parallel and horizontal bars. The legs can be developed with weights and by running up hills. Running up and down flights of stairs in a stadium is also a good training procedure for distance runners. Running in sand, in shallow water, and as previously mentioned, up hills, helps, in the conditioning process.

WORK-TRAINING SCHEDULE

During Off-Season-Using Weights

1. Warm-up: 1 set of 10 repeats using 100 pounds.

2. Curls: 2 sets of 10 repeats; start with 75 pounds.

3. Leg lunges: 2 sets of 10 repeats with barbell on shoulders; start with 100 pounds.

4. Pull overs (on bench): 2 sets of 10 repeats; start with 75 pounds.

5. The raises: 2 sets of 10 repeats with toes on 3-inch blocks; start with 100 pounds on shoulders.

6. Knee bends: 2 sets of 10 repeats; start with 100 pounds.

7. Step test: Step up on 12-inch bench with 20-pound dumbbell in each hand; continue 3 to 5 minutes.

Initial training each year for the long-distance races to be run from January through July should start the previous September. Cross-country running during the first 3 months in the fall an be used to build strength and endurance for distance running in the winter and spring.

With the advent of a much expanded indoor track season, which includes many highly publicized television meets, conditioning for speed and pace must become part of the workout schedule from the very first week of the cross-country season. The 4 to 8 weeks that may fall between the completion of cross-country and the start of the indoor season can be used to establish race pace and increase the speed intensity of the workouts.

It is imperative that long-distance runners get plenty of rest and sleep and eat well-balanced meals in order to be able to follow these workout schedules. Some men will require more sleep than others, but usually all runners should get at least 8 hours of sleep each night.

There will be some days when the performer does not feel like following his specific training schedule. A day's rest or a change in routine will not affect him adversely as long as he does not deviate from his schedules too often.

A typical weekly training schedule for the 3- and 6-mile runner during the month prior to the season's opening meet is as follows :—

Monday

1. Run 3 to 5×1 mile starting at 5 minutes and gradually lowering time.

2. Jog 7 to 10 minute intervals in between distances run, gradually decreasing interval time as strength and endurance increase.

3. Run 15 to 20×110's.

4. Jog 3 to 5 laps to cool down.

Tuesday

1. Run 20 to 25×440's at slightly below Monday's workout pace.

2. Jog 440 yards in between each 440 at a time not to

exceed 90 seconds.

3. Run 15 to 20×110's.

4. Jog 3 to 5 laps to cool down.

Wednesday

1. Run 12 to 16×880's at pace established at Monday's workout.

2. Jog 880 yards in between, at a time not to exceed 2½ minutes.

3. Run 15 to 20×110's.

4. Jog 3 to 5 laps to cool down.

Thursday

1. Run 30 to 40×220's at slightly faster pace than that established on Monday.

2. Jog 220 yards in between at a time not to exceed 70 seconds.

3. Run 15 to 20×110's.

4. Jog 3 to 5 laps to cool down.

Friday

Warm-up thoroughly, then go to showers.

Saturday

Participate in time trials or in early season competitive workout.

Sunday

Run 10 to 12 miles on cross-country course.

The distance workout combinations are organized in sets, and if performed as such they are considered to be a great deterrent to the development of mental fatigue. Success in running is proportionate to the amount of work done. However, the workload must not become drudgery, which begets mental staleness.

Preseason: 2-mile preparation

Monday

1. Run 2 to 3× mile, starting at 5 minutes and gradually lowering time.

2. Jog a 7 to 10 minute interval between each distance, gradually decreasing time as strength and endurance increase.

3. Run 10 to 15×110's.

4. Jog 3 to 4 laps to cool down.

Tuesday

1. Run 15 to 20×440's at slightly below pace used in Monday workout.

2. Jog 440 yards in between, not to exceed 90 seconds.

3. Run 10 to 15×110's.

4. Jog 3 to 4 laps to cool down.

Thursday

1. Run 20 to 30×220's at slightly faster pace.

2. Jog 220 yards in between at a time not to exceed 70 seconds.

3. Run 10 to 15×110's.

4. Jog 3 to 4 laps to cool down.

Friday

Warm-up thoroughly, then go to showers.

Saturday

Run in time trials or take part in early season

workouts as prescribed.

Sunday

Run 8 to 10 miles on cross-country course.

RACING STRATEGY

Participation in a warm-up program before a distance race is very important. Twenty to thirty minutes should be spent in limbering up and preparing the muscles and circulatory and lymphatic systems for the race. A procedure of jogging 3 to 6 laps, interspersed with a few short running, bursts, then resting and trying to relax for 15 minutes before the race, is recommended by most coaches.

Judgment of pace can be learned by doing repeat runs during the training period. An experienced runner is not often misled by an opponent who goes out too fast or too slow at the start of the race. The distance races should be run at as even a pace as possible, with the times for the various 440's about identical. However, during a given 440 the runner may wish to speed up or slow down a little to relieve fatigue in the arms and legs. Each runner must run his own race; he must run within his own capacity.

It is much easier to follow than lead in running the long-distance races. If possible, and if the pace is right, a runner should follow on of the other runners until he is ready to make his move for the lead. However, he should not follow a slow pace too long or he will not be able to recover in time. Success in the instant when a runner makes his move to sprint for the finish depends on his ability to outsprint the opposition.

A race cannot usually be won by plodding along. A runner should at some stage of the race try to "break" the opposition. If he can maintain a faster tempo than his opponents for half a lap or much longer, some runners may become discouraged. If he does not have the ability to sprint at the end of the race, he must make his move early and try to build up a commanding lead, or take the finish kick out of the opposition by increasing the tempo over a longer period.

A runner should try to avoid running with a group if he is apt to get boxed or bumped in such a way that he will have to change his natural relaxed stride. He should run his own race and stay near the pole on the turns most of the time in order to run and shortest distance possible.

After the race is finished, it is best to keep walking and jogging for 10 to 15 minutes to allow the circulatory system to settle down gradually to normal functioning. The distance runner does not lie down or stand still unless sickness results from the hard running.

SUMMARY

1. Distance runners have a slow pulse rate and usually like activities that demand endurance.

2. Distance runners usually enjoy running alone for hours.

3. These runners easily develop tolerance to the stress of running.

4. Pace is probably the most important factor in this event. This is learned by running many repeat 440's.

5. The runners use a short, easy, quick stride.

6. The longer the race, the shorter the stride, and the lower the knee lift of the leg.

7. In running, the foot should strike the ground almost directly under the centre of gravity of the body.

8. The foot should strike the ground first on the ball or sole, then drop lightly down to the heel, then back to

the ball of the foot, and hence to the big toe.

9. The backward motion of the rear foot should not be higher than the knee of the opposite leg.

10. The body should be held rather erect, with the chest pushed out during each stride.

11. The arms should be carried high and across the chest in a relaxed manner. They should move in a short to-and-fro motion across the body.

12. The head may be so relaxed that it hangs loosely from the body as the runner progresses down the track.

13. Complete relaxation while running is necessary for success.

14. Hard running over a long period of time is necessary in order to be successful at distance running.

CHAPTER 8

TEACHING TACTICS IN RUNNING

Events from the 800-meter race to the marathon are usually considered distance races. Although the elite athlete might consider the 800 meters a long sprint, for beginners this race falls into the category of a distance race.

Training for all races from sprints to the longest distance requires improvement of the athlete's anaerobic and aerobic endurance. Aerobic endurance is controlled by the capacity of the heart, lungs, and circulatory system to supply oxygen to the muscles for a long, sustained effort. Training for aerobic endurance is characterized by long runs at moderate speed. Anaerobic endurance is local muscular endurance, or the capacity of the muscular system to operate using stored fuel. Training for anaerobic endurance is characterized by all-out effort over distances that are frequently shorter than the race distance.

Running places extreme demands on an athlete's anaerobic capacity. As the competitive distance increases, there is progressively less demand for anaerobic endurance and greater demand for aerobic endurance. No distance runner can be satisfied with only aerobic training; the distance runner must be able to maintain as fast a pace as possible and be able to sprint whenever it is required. For this reason, the training of the distance runner is designed to improve both aerobic and anaerobic endurance.

Novices training for long-distance races must begin in the off-season and work progressively toward the competitive season. Stressing volume (long, slow runs) before intensity (repetitive, high-speed runs), a novice approaches the season in the following manner:—

1. Begin training with work on aerobic endurance.

2. After developing a base of aerobic endurance, shift to a mix of aerobic and anaerobic endurance exercises.

3. Complete the program with training that emphasizes endurance and is specific to the event. Tne longer the competitive distance, the less emphasis is needed on anaerobic endurance.

SAFETY SUGGESTIONS

The popularity of distance running—from jogging to serious marathon running—has increased dramatically in recent years. Unlike many other track and field events, distance, running can be practiced virtually anywhere and requires minimum equipment. However, in spite of the simplicity of distance running, both you and the performer must consider many safety factors.

Carefuliy consider safety when planning cross-country, fartlek, and jogging trails. If possible, plot the course so it does not cross other traffic lanes, particularly those used by vehicles. Inform the police if you plane to hold a race that is likely to disturb local traffic patterns. Check the course for potholes, tree roots, and sharp rocks and for trail bottlenecks that might cause the runners to collide.

When running on roads, athletes should run facing

the traffic and wear bright, easy-to-see colours. Runners should be particularly careful at intersections and run with partners during training. Running alone is potentially dangerous—especially on lonely trails.

For both training and competition, you must consider the ages of those taking part as well as the length of the run, the number of participants involved, and the type of weather expected during the run. Excessive heat will demand fluid replacement, and extreme cold will require warm clothing such as hat, gloves, and tights or a track suit. Runners should wear comfortable clothing that will not scratch or chafe the skin. Good quality running shoes are also essential. Tennis shoes are major culprits in causing injury.

The start and finish of a cross-country race must be well marshaled. In particular, the start must be wide enough and long enough so that the runners can separate themselves with the minimum of jostling. The finish must be wide enough to allow exhausted runners to sprint directly to the finish without bumping or spiking each other. Course marshals must be able to position each runner according to finish with the minimum of fuss.

The warm-up is an essential part of distance training and should include loosening activities followed by easy running in which athletes emphasize stretching out and striding. Some accelerative running ("pick-ups") may be used to get the legs moving fast.

The actual sequence and duration of activities in a warm-up will vary according to the preferences of the instructor and the athlete. The intent is to have the body warm and the cardiovascular system working well; for many, the warm-up is as much psychological as physiological.

A distance-running program for young children must be developed slowly and carefully and should emphasize variety and maintenance of interest. Distance running should not dominate a physical education program but should be mixed in with other sports so that children are exposed to a wide selection of activities. Many of these sports can emphasize aerobic development.

Avoid placing excessive demands on young athletes; making them run too often and too far can destroy interest and drive away promising runners. Children who complain frequently of soreness or who try to avoid running may indicate that your approach is wrong. Fun, variety, and progressive development are the keys.

Be aware of what is "enough": what produces a training effect and what is excessive and can lead to injuries. With beginners, use game situations that allow rests or run-walks during which you visually assess participants; red faces and other obvious signs of discomfort are signals to cut back on the demand.

Aerobic workouts should predominate in distance running program for young children. Anaerobic training is particularly demanding for a your developing body and should occupy a minimal part of the programme until the child is in the late teens. Rest and recovery days should occur after demanding training sessions; this is of benefit both physiologically and psychologically.

Athletes concentrating on both cross-country races in the fall and winter and distance competitions in the summer find themselves faced with two competitive seasons. A break should be taken between the two seasons.

TECHNIQUE

The distance runner's technique is characterized by an upright body position, although some slight forward lean may occur during phases of acceleration.

The stride length in shorter distances is moderate to long and in longer distances is somewhat shorter. When the athlete increases speed or sprints, the stride length may be reduced as the tempo of running increases.

Knee lift and leg drive depend upon the distance and the phase of the race. During sprinting phases, the knee lift will be high; during nonsprinting phases, knee lift is minimal. The arm action must balance that of the legs; arm action should be vigorous and powerful during the sprinting phases and moderate to minimal during the nonsprinting phases.

TEACHING TACTICS

Point 1. Lead-Ups

Point 2. Aerobic Endurance Training

Point 3. Power and Resistance Training

Point 4. Mixing Aerobic and Anaerobic Training

Point 5. Anaerobic Endurance Training

POINT 1: LEAD-UPS

Relays, Chase, and Tag

Although these activities do not normally require continuous running (which best produces a base of aerobic endurance), they do help condition the muscles and the cardiovascular system, and the fun of these activities diverts the participant's attention from the amount of running involved.

Games

Sports such as basketball and soccer, which emphasize repetitive running, help prepare novices for more specific aerobic training that will follow later. Repetitive running and passing a ball over selected distances (e.g., the width or length of a soccer field) are also good aerobic lead-ups.

POINT 2: AEROBIC ENDURANCE TRAINING (OFF-SEASON PRECOMPETITIVE PERIOD)

Long Distance Running

Long-distance running is considered the best method for developing an aerobic base and building aerobic endurance. The following examples suggest way for introducing this form of training to beginners. There is no need to introduce these activities in sequence because all develop aerobic endurance. By varying the activity, you will maintain interest.

Long Runs

Long runs are usually performed in a "steady state", in which the athlete works at a rate which oxygen demands and oxygen use are balanced. Athletes can run on trails, fields, roads, and tracks to at slow to moderate speed. Emphasize variety, and instruct athletes to progressively increase intensity by running the same distance at a faster speed or running a longer distance at the original speed.

The recommended distance for beginners is 2 to 3 kilometres.

Timed Runs

The athlete runs continuously for a specific time period rather than for a particular distance. The athlete increases intensity by attempting to run for a long time period. A recommended time period for beginners is 8 to 15 minutes.

Long Runs in Performance Groups

Divide students into groups according to levels of performance; choose a leader for each group. The leaders carry stopwatches and take their groups on 14-minute runs (7 minutes out and 7 minutes back). Faster group will run farther during the 14-minute time period. Increase time periods according to fitness.

Quality Distance Runs

Quality runs are distances run with greater intensity. Use these runs after students have developed aerobic conditioning from long, steady runs and from fartlek. Have students run, with greater intensity, distances that were previously run at an easy pace, and emphasize the maintenance of speed. Quality runs are usually considered the first step toward paced or tempo training, in which the athlete learns to maintain a particular pace over a selected distance. In a quality distance run, an athlete runs a measured route (usually run easily in 15 to 20 minutes) 1 to 2 minutes faster in order to improve the quality of the work.

Handicaped Distance Races

Athletes can also perform a quality run in the form of a handicap distance race. Runners start singly or in pairs with time handicaps so that the fastest runners start last. Attempt to set the handicaps so that all runners arrive at the finish close together. This type of run is ideal for cross-country course and provides motivation for both slow and fast runners.

Fartlek

The objective of fartlek (Swedish for "speed-play") is to provide variation in terrain and running intensity. Fartlek also provides considerable choice in the activities performed, which can range from calisthenics to sprinting. The course is usually varied and interesting and provides opportunity for running fast, for running moderate inclines, and for long periods of slow, easy jogging and walking. For adults, the choice of when to run fast or slow is frequently left to the individual. For beginners, you control the pace and the activity; fartlek should not become a meaningless social excursion. A course lasting 12 to 15 minutes and including walks and calisthenics is recommended for beginners.

POINT 3: POWER AND RESISTANCE TRAINING (OFF-SEASON PRECOMPETITIVE PERIOD)

Power and resistance training actually occurs at the same time of the year as aerobic endurance training—during the off-season precompetitive period. The objective of power and resistance training is to develop muscular power that will assist distance running; this training is not intended to develop needless muscular bulk. This type of training can include light weight training as well as running in sand, in snow, up hills, and in water.

Deep-water running is a popular form of resistance training for distance runners. Using flotation devices where necessary and keeping their bodies upright, distance runners literally "run" circuits in the deep end of the pool, working against the resistance of the water. Normally no contact with the bottom of the pool is allowed. You can also adapt land workouts for use in the pool so that the drills simulate the long runs of aerobic training or the run-recovery-run characteristics of interval training. Pool training is excellent for maintaining the fitness levels of injured athletes while they recover. Exercising in water allows the injured athlete to continue to train and to use joint areas such as the foot, ankle, knee, and hip, which could become more seriously injured (through compression and concussion) if training were to continue on land. Deep-water running also provides diversion, a means of increasing mileage, and an alternative method of training.

Distance runners can also practice various forms of weights (30 to 50 percent of maximum), high repetitions (15 to 30), and short recovery periods (30 to 60 seconds).

POINT 4: MIXING AEROBIC AND ANAEROBIC TRAINING (MIDSEASON PRECOMPETITIVE PERIOD)

Once you have helped the athlete develop an aerobic base through long runs, fartlek, and quality runs, intensify training by increasing the pace or tempo of each run, carefully regulating the length and type of recovery taken between runs, and specifying the length of each individual run and the distance accumulated in each workout.

Achieving the desired training effect is contingent upon the way you design the workouts. You may gradually change the workouts so that more anaerobic training and less aerobic training are included; introduce this change in training by having the group work on intensified fartlek. Thereafter, introduce the group to paced or tempo running, which in itself is a preparation for interval training, which follows.

Intensified Fartlek

In intensified fartlek the terrain is still varied and interesting, and the distance is the same as before, but greater effort is required. Replace walking recovery periods, which jogging, make sprinting sections longer and more vigorous, and intensify and quicken the pace throughout. This activity differs considerably from the more leisurely approach taken to fartlek when it is initially introduced.

Pace or Tempo Training

Pace or tempo training refers to the rate than an athlete must run in order to cover a particular distance in a set time. Students are initially introduced to pace or tempor training through the quality distance runs and intensified fartlek. A feeling for running at the correct speed becomes very important when the athlete begins work on interval training.

Introducing Pace or Tempo Training to Novices

Start a stopwatch and ask the group (or individuals in the group) to estimate when 30 seconds have elapsed. Compare their estimates with the correct time. Then repeat this practice with other times (e.g., 20 seconds, 45 seconds).

Coaching Drills

Close your eyes and imagine the second hand moving on a clock. Say "now" and raise your hand when you think the stopwatch has reached 30 seconds.

Estimate the Duration of a Run

Team members run in a single field. Instruct leaders to take their teams over a random course and bring their teams back to the starting place in exactly 45 seconds. Change leaders and times with each run.

Coaching Drills

Stay together in your teams.

Run any direction you wish; arrive back as a group.

Estimate Pace and Tempo on the Straightaway

Instruct groups to run 50 meters in 15 seconds on the straightaway. Call times as the runners pass the 50-meter mark. Do not allow athletes to suddenly increase speed to arrive at the finish on time. They must try to set the correct pace from the start. Participants walk or jog back to the start. Use the same distance and time requirement two or three times so runners can establish a feel for the required pace. Then use differing times for subsequent occasions so that students can practice faster and slower paces of running.

COACHING DRILLS

Try to get a feel for how quickly you must run to cover the required time.

Do not bound when you run. Keep your stride length the same throughout.

Estimating Pace and Tempo on a Triangular Course

Three groups begin at the corners of a 3×50-meter triangular course laid out on the grass. Tell the groups how long they must spend running to the next corner and that they must arrive as the whistle blows. You blow the whistle at selected times (e.g., 15 seconds for beginners). Those who arrive early must run in place. Those who are slow must catch up and then adjust their paces to be more accurate over the next 50 meters. A short rest period (10 seconds light jogging on the spot) may be necessary at each corner to allow slower runners to recover.

COACHING DRILLS

This is basically the same as repetitively running 50 meters in 15 seconds on the straightaway.

Try to arrive at the corner flag exactly on the whistle blast.

Variation

Participants run a full circuit of the course in 45 seconds. A double blast indicates that athletes must run a circuit in 40 seconds. After one slow and fast circuit, athletes can take a walking recovery period. Later add larger courses (e.g., a square course rather than triangular), jogging rests rather than walking, and faster circuits to increase intensity.

Estimating Pace and Tempo on a 400-Meter Track

Set up flag or traffic cones at 50-meter intervals

around a 400-meter track. Runners must maintain a set pace (e.g., 15 seconds for 50 meters), arriving at the flags on a whistle blast.

Pace and Tempo Training in Groups

Two groups of runners start together but run in opposing directions around the track. Each group must maintain the correct tempo (e.g., 200 meters in 40 seconds) in order to arrive exactly together on the opposing side of the track. They pass each other and continue to run, meeting on the side of the track on which they started. Flags placed every 50 meters around the track, coupled with 10 second whistle blasts, can help athletes pace themselves. Require a faster pace for more experienced athletes.

Pace Training, Varying Distances

Athletes run different distances in the same time period (e.g., 50, 60, and 70 meters, each in 20 seconds), forcing a change in pace for each distance.

COACHING DRILLS

Reduce stride length and tempo for the short distances.

Increase stride length and tempo for the longer distances.

Try to relax as you run, loosening the muscles of your arms, hands, and face.

Swing your arms forward and backward, not across your body.

Keep your vision forward and your head up. Do not roll your head or let it drop back.

Interval Training

There are many variations of this form of training, each type depending upon the balance of aerobic and anaerobic endurance you want to achieve. Interval training systematically varies the following :—

Distance run

Number of times distance is run

Speed of each run

Length of recovery period between each run

Type of recovery (walk, jog) taken during recovery period

Thus, by using recovery periods after each run, the athlete is able to run repetitively at race pace or even faster. No other form of distance training provides this benefit.

Most forms of interval training use an incomplete or partial recovery during recovery periods. This means that the heart is not allowed to fully return to a resting level. By starting the next run when the cardiovascular system has only partially recovered, the athlete progressively adapts to the training, and the cardiovascular system becomes more efficient.

Interval training is usually performed on the track and as a such is highly formal, repetitious, and disciplined, a fact you must take into consideration when working with school-age athletes.

The variables used in interval training (e.g., distance, or number of runs) are interrelated. How much or how many of each ultimately depends upon the athlete's level of fitness and the specific intent of the training, such as the race distance the athlete is training for. These variables are as follows :—

1. Distance. Training distance vary considerably (50 to 1,500 meters) and depend upon the length of race the athlete is training for. The distance the athlete runs is related to the speed of each run, the number of

repetitions performed, and the duration and type of the recovery periods.

2. Number of Repetitions. The number of repetitions depends on the distance of the run, the speed of the run, and the duration and type of each recovery period.

3. Speed. The speed of the run is usually modified so that the heart rate returns to 120 at the end of each recovery period. The speed depends on the distance of the run, the number of repetitions, and the duration and type of the recovery period.

4. Type of Recovery. The type of recovery used by the athlete may be a walk, a slow or fast jog, or a slow run. The type of recovery (and its duration) will depend upon the speed of the run, the distance, and the number of repetitions performed.

5. Duration of Recovery. The recovery period may last from less than 1 minute to 5 minutes or more. As with the type of recovery, the duration of the recovery depends upon the speed of the run, the distance and the number of repetitions performed. The type and duration of recovery period depend upon the speed with which the athlete's heart returns to 120 beats.

Interval Training Designed to Develop Aerobic Endurance

This form of training develops stamina and basic endurance and forms a foundation for the other types of interval training that follow. It is characterized by short distances (50 to 200 meters), short recovery periods (1 minute or less), and a large number of repetitions (10 to 15). Because of the short recovery periods, the athlete is forced to run the next repetition with an incomplete recovery. In this way, the cardiovascular system continuously works under stress and develops the capacity to recover quickly.

Athletes who compete in the long sprints (400 meters) need less aerobic endurance than anaerobic endurance. However, they do train to improve their aerobic endurance.

Introduced beginners or interval training at the same time they work on paced on tempo training. The repetitive runs around the triangular course, although used to develop a feel for paced or tempo running, are also a simplified form of interval training. This triangular course can be expanded to a square course.

Introduction to Interval Training on a Square Course

Groups start at the corner flags and run to reach the next corner flag on the whistle (e.g., 15 seconds). Require a specific recovery period (jogging in place) at each flag. Set the speed of the run, the number of repetitions, and the length of the recovery period according to the levels of fitness of the participants. Recommended time and rest period for novices are as follows: Athletes run each 50-meter side of the square in 15 seconds followed by a 15-second recovery (easy jogging in place). After 4 circuits, assign the groups a circuit of walk recovery.

Introduction to Interval Training on the Track

Groups of novices walk around the track. Group 1 runs at medium tempo to catch up with group 2; at that point group 1 walks again. Group 2 then runs to catch up with group 3, and groups repeat the process around the track. The recovery period is the walk, and the distance is determined by how far the groups are apart. Determine the tempo of running and the number of repetitions according to the fitness levels of the participants.

Interval Training Designed to Develop a Mix of Aerobic and Anaerobic Endurance

Interval training that includes fast to moderately fast

runs builds stamina at a pace close to competitive conditions. Basic endurance improves, and at the same time the muscles become used to working anaerobically. Because the runs are generally fast, the recovery periods are longer. Distances vary considerably. The number of runs depends upon the intent of the training (i.e., aerobic or anaerobic) and the athlete's level of fitness.

There are many ways you can design interval training to develop a mix of aerobic and anaerobic endurance.

Interval Sprints

Students run short distances (50 to 100 meters) at high speed, then have a walking recovery of 50 to 100 meters. The number of repetitions will depend upon fitness. Increase the intensity of the training by changing the walk to a jog.

Equal Distances and Recovery Periods

The athlete sprints for 25 seconds and recovers for 25 seconds by jogging slowly. This sequence is performed for 3 or 4 repetitions.

Interval Relay

Form a team of 3 runners. Runner 1 sprints at top speed to pass the baton to runner 2, then jogs to recover. Runner 2 runs to pass the baton to runner 3 and recovers after the pass. Each runner sprints 5×200 meters to cover a distance of 1,000 meters (3,000 meters in total for the team).

Pyramid (Ladder) Sprints

Progressively increase the sprint distance or duration of the sprint; after the athletes reach the top of the "pyramid" or have climbed the "ladder", then progressively decrease distance or duration. For example, athletes run 50, 100, 150, 200, 150, 100, and 50. Or, they sprint for 10, 15, 20, 15, and 10 seconds.

The type and duration of recovery period will depend on the athlete's levels of fitness.

POINT 5: ANAEROBIC ENDURANCE TRAINING (IN-SEASON COMPETITIVE PERIOD)

Frequently called quality or speed training, the training requires the athlete to run at maximum or close to maximum speed. Although it uses a run-recovery-run sequence, like other types of interval training, quality or speed training is not considered true interval training because it does not work on the principle of partial recovery after each run. Instead, the high speed of each run requires a complete recovery. The types of drills used are similar to those designed to develop a mix of aerobic and anaerobic endurance. However, the difference is that quality or speed training always requires maximum or close to maximum speed, to enable the athlete to develop sheer speed and the stamina to maintain relaxed and controlled form while running flat-out. Because of the high speed, fewer repetitions are used. This type of training adds a final polish to the athlete's preparation and establishes a "feel" for the pace that will be used during the race. This training is performed immediately prior to and also during the competitive season.

COMMON ERRORS AND CORRECTIONS

1. Error

The athlete uses an uneconomical style of running.

Reasons

The athlete's leg drive is too much upward and not sufficiently forward.

Remedies

The athlete practice bounding and hoping, stressing correct leg drive. Emphasize running without rise and fall of the hips.

2. Error

The athlete leans backward while running. The head is back or is allowed to "roll around".

Reasons

The athlete has incorrect chest (torso) and head position, and the vision is not directly ahead. The athlete may have weak abdominal and trunk muscles.

Remedies

The athlete practices running technique activities, running with the head forward and vision ahead. Also assign strengthening exercises for the abdomen.

3. Error

The athlete swings the shoulders (and head) from side to side while running.

Reasons

The arms swing across the chest. The athlete has poor concentration on running technique, and vision is not directly ahead.

Remedies

Stress running technique activities, as with the previous error. Have the athlete practice arm swinging—parallel and in the direction of the run—standing and then while running.

4. Error

The athlete uses poor drive or extension of the leg while running. The athlete has an appearance of "sitting" while running, or "bent-legged" running.

Reasons

The athlete uses no extension or leg thrust during the

run and has poor leg power and hip flexibility.

Remedies

Assign exercises for increasing leg power and hip flexibility: hopping, bounding, and jumping, and hurdier's flexibility exercises.

5. Error

The athlete appears tense while running.

Reasons

Tension results from poor running technique, exhaustion, poor preparation and inadequate flexibility.

Remedies

The athlete must work to relax the face, loosen the lower jaw, and relax the hands (no fists). Arms should be held at an angle of 90 degrees at the elbow. Work to improve the aerobic/anaerobic base, and improve flexibility through related stretching exercises.

CHAPTER 9

RELAY RACING IN RUNNING

A relay race is an event in which two or more men run a specific distance, one relieving the other at some designated point within a fixed zone.

The large number of relay carnivals held each year is an indication of the general favour that this event has met all over the world. This popularity is deserved since a relay race offers spirited team competition and provides places for a large number of athletes. The grouping of distances run also provides competition for almost every type of athlete from the sprinter to the distance runner.

Under former rules, before a relief runner could begin his "leg" of a relay, he was required to touch the hand of the oncoming contestant in a zone of change. However, this method presented the difficulty of judging whether there was an actual hand-to-hand contact. In order to overcome this objection the baton was introduced, and now the oncoming man must hand the baton to the relief runner. Baton exchange furnished a hazard to the relay race, thus making it an exciting and spectacular event. In order to reduce baton-passing hazards to a minimum, rather definite techniques of exchange have been worked out.

Since relay racing requirements and techniques have so many things in common with sprinting, middle distance, and distance running, the chief points which need special consideration in presenting this event are the technical and finesse of carrying and passing the baton.

Relay racing as a form of sports competition had its origins entirely in the United States. As usual, there were certain background activities that might have germinated the idea. For example, there were the relays of horses by which stagecoach transportation was maintained, and the Pony Express, by which news and mail were relayed to distance point in the country. Along more recreational lines, there were the old holiday competitions between fire cart-and-horse teams in which the fastest men "raised the alarm" by sprinting to the cart and touching off the team effort as they crossed a starting line. The Encyclopaedia Britannica credits the Massachusetts Firemen's "bean-pot" race as having been the model for relay racing:

The old method was for the men second quarter of the race each to take over a small flag from relay men as they arrived, before departing on their own stage of the race, at the end of which they, handed on their flags to the awaiting runners. The flags however were considered cumbersome, and for a time it was sufficient for the outgoing runner to touch or be touched by his predecessor.

However, the origin of relay racing as a part of organized track and field athletics is clear, for no one questions that the University of Pennsylvania was the place, and Frank B. Ellis and H.L. Geyelin the "inventors" of the four-man race. Edward R. Bushnell, writing in the 50th-anniversary program of the Pennsylvania Relay Carnival, tells how these two men deliberately searched for something to make track sports more attractive to both contestants and spectators and conceived group effort as providing the answer:

The first experiment was made in 1893, with two teams of four men, each of whom ran a quarter mile. It worked so well in practice that it was decided to add the event to the spring track program and to invite Princeton to send a team. ...Those early runners did not use the flying start, they did not carry a baton nor did they have a 20-yard zone in which to exchange the baton as they do today. In fact, each runner had to remain on his mark until the arrival of the next man. He could not run back to meet a tiring runner and he could not start until his teammate arrived and properly touched him off...

The first race was such a success that it was repeated in 1894, but this time Pennsylvania turned the tables on the Tigers. By this time the new event had aroused so much interest among coaches, athletes and the public that the Pennsylvania committee resolved to expand the idea and hold an invitation meet the following year with outside schools and colleges invited. Apparently the committee was not sure that a meet devoted entirely to relay racing would satisfy the track fans, because only nine races were scheduled for the first meet and they alternated with the events of the University's annual spring games...

In addition to Pennsylvania and Harvard, the other competing colleges in this first carnival were College of the City of New York vs. New York University, Rutgers vs. Swarthmore, Lafayette vs. Lehigh and Cornell vs. Columbia. The Haveford, Episcopal vs. Delancey and Central High vs. Central Manual.

It will be noted that this first carnival includes races at all four levels: university, college, academy and preparatory schools, and high school. The last-named group was slow in organizing and entering its teams but soon became the dominant in terms of numbers of competitors. Estimates have been made that over 115,000 athletes competed in the Pennsylvania relays during its first 55 years, with average numbers in the past ten years exceeding 3,000. In 1952, 328 different high schools entered teams in one or more races.

The original program of only a one-mile relay was soon expanded to include the two-mile and four-mile relays in 1897, the sprint medley and distance medley relays in 1915, the 440 and 880 relays in 1922, and the shuttle hurdle relay in 1926. These now comprise the eight relays given acceptance in official national records books as a part of relay programs throughout this country and other parts of the world. The medley relays were added deliberately to improve the competitive chances of colleges that do not have four good men in a single event, as is necessary in the other races.

From these experiences, the relay ideal has expanded rapidly in all phases of track and field. In 1910, the Drake relays were instituted by Drake University and the Greater Des Moines, Iowa, Relay Committee. These relays have been a distinctively community venture and, in addition to the competitive program, have made the relay week end a time of city-wide holiday, pagentry, and hospitality. The program has been similar to that at Pennsylvania with its emphasis upon numbers of competitors and upon all levels of competition.

This emphasis has made these two great relay meets entirely unique in the sports world in the soundness and the broadness of their basis of competition. In a single afternoon, thousands of athletes compete on the same field and track, though the youngest is still in fifth grade in grammar school and in his first competitive track meet and though the most experienced is several years beyond college and may have one or more world's records to his credit. It is difficult to conceive of an annual event occurring at a single place and time that is a more complete or clearer answer to those who accuse modern sports of encouraging only the few and the talented.

Relay meets have increased in number and influence quite consistently during the past 25 years. In 1930, the National Collegiate Athletic Association Track and Field Guide listed only four such meets: Pennsylvania, Drake, Kansas, and Ohio State. In 1940, the results of eight meets were published. In 1950, sixteen meets were considered large enough to be listed in detail. In addition, there were about a dozen lesser meets and indoor meets sponsored by collegiate institutions throughout the country. As a matter of interest, of these sixteen major relay meets, three were held in the Eastern states; three in the Middle West; four on the West Coast; and six in the South. This last number from the South is relatively new but rapidly growing development they may be influence the track picture in the country as a whole.

The relay meet with its group competition has also increased spectator interest, and the promotion and organization of track has changed accordingly. Time schedules are being revised and accelerated. Pageantry and dramatics are receive more serious consideration and feature events are being highlighted and more widely advertised. The one-mile relay is now an ofticial event on all college dual meets and, in certain areas, such as the Eastern Heptagonal Conference, is supported by a two-mile relay on the indoor program and by a 440-yard relay outdoors. In the Big Ten Conference, relay points count double in the team competition, with increased emphasis upon success there. In 1940, the University of California and Stanford met in a dual relay meet that occasioned much favourable comment but that, for lack of relay teams of consistently equal quality, has not been continued.

In England, relay racing did not attain early acceptance, but is now extended a much wider and more enthusiastic popularity. Douglas Lowe and A.E. Porritt write of its growth up to 1930.

Relay racing was introduced to this country from America; but although a one mile medley was included in the A.A.A. Championships from 1911 onwards, it was only after the Great War that relays attained a popularity in England commensurate with that enjoyed in the United States. In 1920, immediately after the Olympic Games at Antwerp, those two great Oxford and Cambridge athletes, Bevil Rudd and Professor Philip Baker, inaugurated the Achilles Club by staging at Queen's Club, London, the greatest international relay match ever seen—between the Olympic team and the combined teams of the British Empire. At that first meeting the field events were individual; subsequently they were conducted on the team principle as well, by taking the aggregate performance of the several men in each team.

Before an overflowing crowd, which has never since lost its love for good relay racing, a thrilling encounter resulted in a tie...

With such a brilliant commencement and continuance, interest in relay racing has heightened ever since..., and no athletic meeting is complete without one or two relay events.

Present-day English writers such as Ross and Norris McWhirter indicate that this widespread interest has continued to grow, with 4×100-meter and the 4×400-meter relays occurring on almost every important track and field program.

In somewhat similar fashion, relays have become an increasingly important phase of the track and field program of the Olympic games. They were first included in the Lond 1908 games by what would be called a sprint medley relay today. The first two men ran 200 meters, the third 400 meters, and the fourth 800 meters. In 1912, at Stockholm, this medley race was dropped, but both the 4×100-meter and the 4×400-meter relays were added. Of the 16 relay competitions that have occurred in the 8 Olympic games, including those of 1952, the United States has won 12. This predominance of the United States in these events is to be expected because of its great wealth of material in the sprints. But a similar advantage would not be present at longer distances. It is intriguing to speculate upon the great speculator appeal that would be present on an Olympic day devoted exclusively to relay events at, for example, each of the eight distances now commonly contested in the United States.

Wonderful as present world's records in the various relays may seem, times for these events are undoubtedly more vulnerable to improvement than those in any other event in track and field. As yet, no four men of world quality have combined their efforts in any relay, so that it merely requires the necessary talent, competition, and fortuitous circumstances to produce records well below present limits. The little island of Jamaica came very close, however, to presenting just such a combination for the 1600-meter relay in the 1952 Olympics: Wint, who ran :46.5. Their total time of 3:03.9 seems almost unbelievable; yet they beat the American team (Matson, :46.7; Cole, :45.5; Moore, :46.3; Whitfield, :45.5) by only a yard. Wonderful as these individual performances were, and impossible as the final time seems, it is nevertheless true that if one adds the four best times of this race, those of McKenley, Rhoden, Cole, and Whitfield, the total equals 3:01.1. Apparently the ultimate human record has not yet been reached.

TYPES OF RELAY RACES

By agreement, the total length of the race, the length of each leg of the race, an the number of athletes participating, may be set at the pleasure of the games committee. At the present time, the length of relay races varies from 220 yards to any number of miles. However, on the basis of total distance, the relay races which appear most frequently on the track and field program are as follows:

High School

a. 440 yards (4×110)

b. 880 yards (4×220)

c. 1 mile (4×440)

d. Medley, 1650 yards (220, 110, 440 and 880)

e. Shuttle hurdle, 480 yards (4×120)

College

a. 440 yards (4×110)

b. 880 yards (4×220)

c. 1 mile (4×440)

d. 2 mile (4×880)

e. 4 mile (4×1mile)

f. Medley sprint, 1 mile (440, 220, 220, and 880)

g. Medley distance, 2½ miles, (¼, ½, ¾, and 1 mile)

h. Shuttle hurdle, 480 yards (4×120)

International (Olympic)

a. 400 meter (4×100)

b. 1600 meter (4×400)

c. 3200 meter (4×800)

d. Medley, 1000 meter (100, 200, 300, and 400)

Miscellaneous

a. Shuttle (flat) 220 yards (4×55)

b. Shuttle (flat) 440 yards (4×110)

c. Intercity (running the distance between cities)

EQUIPMENT

The only equipment peculiar to relay racing is the baton. Its form and weight are governed by rules which specify that it shall weigh not less than 50 gm, shall be not more than 30 cm. long and shall have a circumference of 12 cm. The baton may be made of either wood or paper composition.

THE TECHNIQUE OF BATON PASSING

The introduction of the baton into the relay has stimulated considerable investigation as to the best method of exchange, and as a result, a number of techniques have been suggested. Some of these methods and their application to various types of races are discussed.

1. Definition of the Baton Pass

The baton is exchanged within a 20-yard zone, formed by lines drawn 10 yards on each side of and parallel to the exchange mark (start and finish line). Within this 20-yard zone each runner must pass the baton to the relief runner, the teammate, may run outside of such zone. The baton must be actually passed, not thrown or dropped by the contestant and picked up by the one succeeding him. Failure to pass the baton shall disqualify the team from competition in the event in which it has occurred. After passing the baton the competitor should jog straight ahead, unless he be in either the inside or outside, in which case he should step off the track as quickly as possible.

2. Methods of Exchange

On the basis of the position of the head and eyes there are two commonly accepted methods of passing the baton. In one, the awaiting receiver keeps the eyes of focused on the baton in the hand of the passer until the transfer is made. This is designated as the visual pass. In the other method, the awaiting receiver keeps the eyes focused on the passer until the latter reaches a designated spot or target on the track about 6½ yards away. Instantaneously the receiver turns the head and eyes to the front and starts running.

The visual method of passing is suitable to all relay races but is more commonly employed in the longer distances where the degree of fatigue of the oncoming runner must be accurately gauged. Therefore, in contests in which an athlete runs a leg of the relay which is 300 yards or more in length, the receiver watches the passer, evaluates his speed, and keeps the extended baton in his vision until it is within his grasp. Meanwhile the receiver gets in motion so that he is underaway when the exchange occurs. The visual method is considered by some authorities to be safer than the nonvisual because both the runner and the baton are in the receiver's line of vision until, and during, the critical moment of the transfer. This method does not permit the speedy exchange offered by the nonvisual method, because the receiver cannot gain optimum speed when the head, eyes, and trunk are turned sideward and backward.

The nonvisual method is universally used in all sprints relays (220 to 880 yards) and in those sections of medley relays in which the passer runs a distance of 300 yards or less. It has already been inferred that there is a greater degree of risk in making the exchange while the baton is out of the range of vision. Insurance against an inaccurate pass must give way to speed in the shorter relay, a factor which adds thrill and uncertainty to the sport, and makes relay racing interesting to contestant and spectator alike.

3. Styles of Arm-Hand Position

On the basis of the position of the arm and the hand, there are five commonly used styles of baton exchange. In all styles, the receiver assumes a stance near the back line of the passing zone. The passer executes the exchange with the left hand, and the receiver in running stride accept it with the right and transfers it to his left hand as soon as possible.

a. The receiver extends the right arm back and slightly below the height of the shoulder. The elbow as well as the palm is up, and the thumb is pointed toward the body (to the left). The passer extends the left arm and aims to synchronize its downward swing with the forward stride of the right leg when making the transfer. The arrow indicates the direction of moving the baton.

b. The receiver extends the right arm back and slightly to the right at a height four or five inches above the plane of the hips. The palm is up and the thumb is pointed toward the rear. The elbow is down.

c. The receiver extends the right arm back so that the hand is at a height approximating the plane of the hips. Some good competitors prefer to hold it below the level of the hips. The palm is to the rear, with the thumb pointing downward. The passer extends the left arm forward, contacting his teammate's hand on the upward rather than on the downward movement.

d. The receiver rests the right thumb on the hip with the fingers extended downward and away from the body. The elbow is pointed to the rear.

e. The receiver places the finger tips on the hip so that the hand is in a cupped position with the thumb pointing toward the front. The passer completes the exchange by a downwars swing of the baton carried in the left hand.

4. Types of Baton Grasp

Frequently little attention is given to the problem of holding the baton by relay runner number 1 when in position on the marks. True enough, relay races have been won, and will continue to be won, by teams whose lead-off competitor gives little heed to the hand grasp. However, teams have suffered disappointment because their number 1 man either left the marks minus the baton or had it knocked from his hand because of either an incorrect carriage or an insecure grasp. The latter hazard is more common to the lead-off athlete than to his three succeeding teammates, especially in races where the start is not staggered. When the starting runner of each team is not placed in a staggered or echelon form, all lead-off men come to the marks shoulder to shoulder on a line across the track.

At the start of the race the number 1 runner grasp the baton in a manner to his liking. It will be noted that the baton is carried in the left hand as a matter of convenience but not of necessity. One reasons for the left-hand hold lies in the fact that the receiver usually takes a stance partially turned toward the outside of the track. In such a stance the backward reach is facilitated by employing the right rather than the left hand. Therefore, to eliminate the necessity of transferring the baton to the left hand, the initial runner carries it in his left hand while on the marks. In addition, since runners pass on the right side, there is less chance of knocking the baton from the grasp if it is carried on the opposite side of the body—in the left hand.

During the main part of a race the baton may be held in any manner that feels comfortable to the competitor.

If the passer allows a considerable amount of exposed surface at the forward end of the baton, he will facilitate passing. To phrase it another way, he gives his teammate “the big end of the stick”.

In the type of pass, the receiver should grasp close to the passer’s hand so that, when (during the first stride) he transfers the baton from the right to the left hand, he will have ample space for the left-hand grasp. In other words, the left hand will grasp the unshaded half, and leave free the shaded portion for the next exchange.

The type of pass requires that when the receiver executes the transfer to the left hand, the shaded portion of the baton be swung outward and forward. At one stage in its movement, while in a plane parallel to the ground, a line drawn through the extremities of the baton forms a right angle to the body. Thus the baton protrudes to the right side. When competitors are closely bunched, there is a possibility of having the baton knocked from the grasp. For this reasons many authorities do not recommend this passing technique.

The receiver may grasp the fore part of the baton and transfer it so that the left hand grasps it at the rear half, again providing ample space for the next receiver’s hand hold.

No matter which type of grasp is employed, the objectives are economy of movement and the exposure of ample surface to permit a substantial grasp by the succeeding teammate. It appears reasonable to assume that time is lost if the athlete, once having possession of the stick, is required to press it against his thigh and slide the hand inward for the purpose of providing a grasping surface for his teammate.

Again the transfer from the right to the left hand should be accomplished with the minimum detraction from sprinting form. To this end, the transfer is usually made when it causes the least interference, usually one the first stride after the baton is taken. Occasionally one sees a fatigued distance relay runner make the mistake of either executing a right hand cross-body exchange or of shifting the baton to the left hand within the last few strides, at a time when his body control is least efficient.

5. Relation of Arm-Hand Position to Visual and Nonvisual Passes

These are utilized in the nonvisual method of exchange.

It was previously pointed out that the nonvisual method was used in races in which the passer covered 300 yards or less in his leg of the relay. Obviously its use is recommended in both the 440- and 880-yard relays. Furthermore, it can be used effectively in medley relays whenever the passer runs less than 300 yards, even though the receiver runs 880 yards. On the other hand, a competitor running a sprint section of a medley relay race should employ the visual method when accepting the stick from a teammate who has negotiated more than 300 yards.

6. Factors to Be Considered When Adopting a Baton Passing Style

When selecting the proper style of baton passing, the coach and competitor make their choice on the following basis:

a. The distance of the relay race. (In sprint relays the nonvisual method is adopted, and in longer races the visual method is used).

b. The mechanical efficiency of the exchange.

c. The adaptability of the style to the athletes.

d. The degree of certainty which a particular style

provides.

e. The amount of free distances gained by the forward reach of the passer and the backward reach of the receiver.

f. The style providing optimum speed for both the receiver and the passer at the instant of exchange.

g. The distance of the receiver's target from the back line of the passing zone, if the nonvisual method is selected. The placement of the target may rightfully vary from the suggested 6½ yards to fit the passer and receiver. If the passer is exceptionally fast, the target may be at 7 yards.

7. Variations in the Nonvisual Method of Baton Exchange

A common procedure in executing the exchange in the sprint relays is as follows: The receiver extends his right arm, and when his teammate reaches the target, turns his head and eyes to the front, and darts away. The right hand is kept well extended backward from the onset of the receiver's getaway until the baton is within his grasp. Obviously the right arm, because of its constrained position, has not provided its share of compensating reaction to the movement of the legs. Therefore, some relay runners vary the procedure as follows: The receiver assumes the customary stance and, when the passer reaches the target, runs at top speed, as in the above described style. However, he uses both arms as in sprinting, counts the strides from the getaway, and as the right arm swings back in the fifth stride, he maintains it in a receiving position until the baton is in his grasp. The latter method offers more opportunity for a speedy exchange because the synchronized arm-leg action during the first five strides is more conducive to acceleration. A disadvantage of this method rests in the fact that the receiver frequently misjudges either the timing, or the direction, or the height of the backward hand swing. The first method described (continuous arm extensions) has the advantage of proffering a target (the receiver's hand) throughout the passing zone.

8. Variations in Baton Handling

The usual admonition of the coach is "receive with the right, pass with the left". It was pointed out earlier that the baton is taken by the receiver in his right hand because he is facing the outside of the track which obviously makes it simpler to extend the right hand.

The omission of the act of shifting the baton from right hand to left is adopted by a few relay teams. Each athlete carries the baton through his leg of the relay in the same hand in which it was originally received. To accomplish this, the second and the fourth runners receive the baton in the right hand in the orthodox manner. The third runner assumes a stance facing the inside of the track and takes the baton in his left hand. Obviously, since runner 1 carried the baton in the left hand, none of the four runners need transfer the stick from one hand to the other. The advantages of this plan are evident, namely, the saving of crossbody arm motions by each of the last three athletes. The disadvantages are twofold: first, the third runner must take a stance at variance with the other competitors and, second the carriage of the baton in the right hand exposes it to interference.

The technique of relay racing, apart from the actual running during each leg of the event, can be considered from two aspects: (1) methods of baton passing, (2) the order in which the four team men are used. The latter consideration is dependent upon many factors: distance to be run, the presence or lack of crowded conditions on the track, the attitudes of each man toward a front or following position, and others, each of which deserves special consideration. The subject will therefore be given a major heading here. The first aspect, methods of baton passing, is still in a somewhat experimental stage, with each coach having his own special details of method, and thus also requires discussion of the more accepted techniques and their relative values. As suggested in the history of the relay racing, the baton must now be exchanged within a 20-yard passing zone, 10 yards on either side of the starting line. Methods of passing can be properly divided into two groups: those involving a "blind" pass and those using a "slight" pass.

"Blind" pass relays. So-called "blind" passes are used in those relays in which the incoming runner is still relatively fresh and therefore moving with steady momentum and complete control of all actions. The outgoing baton taker can therefore relay on his teammate's momentum and control, take his eye off the incoming baton, and move into his leg of the race with all-out speed and abandon. Such conditions are to be found only in the 440-yard relay (often listed as 4×110-yard relay), the 880-yard relay (often listed as 4×220-yard), and in the last two legs of the sprint medley relay. In these races, every tenth of a second means a yard or more and therefore speed of exchange is all-important. To sprint with the eyes turned back to the incoming baton would certainly cut momentum and actually would gain little from a safety standpoint.

All methods of "blind" passes are identical in the means by which the outgoing runner judges the timing of his start and the actual baton exchange. The theory of all sprint relay passing is to utilize the full 20 yards of the passing zone so that the momentum of the outgoing runner is as great as possible. This means, to avoid disqualification for passing outside the zone, that the actual baton exchange should occur between 15 and 18 yards. To effect this end, runner 2 must start as 1 crosses the "Go" mark from 6 to 9 yards before the passing zone. A great deal of study by the specific men involved and the coach as well as repeated drill, must be done to determine the exact placement of this mark and to learn to "go" at exactly the right moment and in the right way. 2 must maintain his eyes on the "Go" mark but concentrate his attention on the incoming runner. Any inattention or uncertainty (and competitive conditions are most distracting) will produce an instant's delay and a loss of vital yards in the exchange and at the finish of the race. Coaches must emphasize again and again that concentration of attention at this point is just as vital as in starting a sprint race. A yard gained or lost here is as important as a yard gained or lost through sprinting ability.

There are those who have criticized the American Olympic sprint delay teams in 1932, 1936, and 1948, first, for using a type of pass that necessarily loses a full half yard on every exchange, and second, for deliberately emphasizing safety against disqualification more then speed of exchange by placing the exchange point at between 10 and 15 yards. Advocates of this practice have protested, "We won and broke the record. What more can be expected?" But opponents protest that better methods and more drill would have produced even great records. However, the point at hand is that few coaches can afford the luxury of such "safety and will strive for every inch, if better methods and increased drill can produce it".

Most coaches depend upon vision only for the "Go" signal. Others combine sight with hearing by having the incoming runner yell "Go" as he crosses the "Go" mark. The danger of miscueing is obvious, and the writer finds it difficult to justify such a procedure.

As the outgoing runner waits for the baton, he should lean well forward, weight on toes, and sight along and under his shoulder toward the "Go" mark. Except for the eyes and body straight ahead, take either 4 or 6 strides (about 10 yards) just as he would when attempting a sprint start, then drop his hand into position to take the baton. Every detail of these procedure needs to be exact and consistently the same. The arm and hand, once dropped, must be held still and steady. The hand must be well spread between thumb and forefigner and yet sufficiently relaxed to permit easy and sure grasping of the baton. If properly drilled, the details will become just as mechanical as the shift of a pole in the pole vault, and just as unconsciously performed. For example, whether to begin with the left or the right foot forward at the start is a matter of importance. Usually the left foot will be forward when taking the baton with the right hand, and the right foot forward when taking it with the left hand. Although a trifle awkward at first, having the opposite hand forward when waiting for the start will give better co-ordination during the first stride. Similarly, dropping the hand into position for taking the baton will come most smoothly after an even number of strides (6 is about right).

There can be no guessing or hesitancy in taking the baton. The outgoing runner must assume that he'll feel that baton at the right moment and will note the 10-, 12-, and 15-yard points slip by with never a doubt of his partner's abilities. If he had timed his start correctly (and an alert man will always know whether he has done this), he should go with confidence and all-out effort.

The amount of time that can be gained by perfect passing over a theoretical relay in which each man begins from a standing start will vary up to a total of about 2.5 seconds. The McWhirters have estimated that the 1936 American Olympic 400-meter team, which set the present world's record at :39.8 gained only 1.5 seconds through their passing. Ralph Metcalfe was slow in getting out, so that Jesse Owens clearly overran him, and the final exchange between Foy Draper and Frank

Wykoff was equally poor.

Methods of exchange. There are three preferred methods of taking a "blind" pass. The arm of the outgoing runner is extended fully backward, the thumb is in, the palm down and to the real in a natural running position. It is possible that a "frozen" hand will be more likely to drop the baton in this position than in others, but such extreme tension is almost never present. On the contrary, the natural reaction of grasping any object that touches the hand is more difficult to resist than the unnatural extension of the fingers. In this method, the action of the hand passing the baton is upward, also an easy and natural movement.

This method has the advantage of placing the receiving palm upward and provides a certain surface on which the baton can be placed. It also involves an extended arm and demands a full forward body Iean, which aids sprint action. However, in the writer's opinion, it places greater responsibility upon the passer to lay the baton correctly across the hand and also uses a downward placement of the baton, which is less natural than the first method.

The method used by the American Olympic team during the past three Olympic games and therefore deserves description, even though there seems little else to say in its favour. The placement of the hand at the hip is awkward and cuts at least 18 inches from each exchange. It certainly does not encourage forward lean and might detract from it. Even the safety its proponents claim for it is questionable, for the thumb is not in a good position for grasping. However, its world's record status undoubtedly makes it worthy of serious consideration.

Handedness in the baton passing. The most widely used practice in sprint passing is to take the baton with the outside right hand, to shift the baton to the left hand either at once or as soon as one is "out of the crowd", and finally to pass the baton with the left hand. Coaches who use this method argue that the right hand is less likely to drop the baton and that there is less danger of either man's running on the lane line.

Certain coaches in the East, notably George Eastment of Manhattan College, have adopted an inside-left-hand pass, which is particularly valuable in distance relays but is claimed to have certain advantages also in sprint passing. In particular, curve running is easier when the outside right hand is free to swing and thereby minimize body centripetal force. Further, the danger of running on the lane line is said to be decreased.

This innovation has led to compromise that was, to the writer's best knowledge, first used by Coach John Keel of the Austin High School, Texas. The first runner starts with the baton in his right hand and, since the second runner in a 440 relay is on the curve, passes it to the latter's left hand. The second man keeps the baton in his left and passes to the third runner's right hand. He in turn keeps it in his right and passes to the anchor man's left hand. (Again the runner is one the curve, where taking with the left is advantageous). The gains made through this method are real in that the momentary loss of arm action as the baton is shifted from one hand to the other, which occurs in the other methods, is no longer present. An appreciable gain in time is therefore made. Further, one of the great dangers in shifting the baton is that one will be jostled at just the wrong moment and the baton will be dropped. The objection raised by some that one is never entirely certain about which leg the various men will run and that therefore they may learn the wrong style of pass is sufficiently valid to cause many coaches to hesitate in adopting this method. However, where plans are relatively certain and there is time for exhaustive drill on passing, this "right-left-right-left" method will prove helpful.

"Slight" pass relays. "Slight" methods of passing the baton are used in those longer relays in which the incoming runner is tired, and uncertain in his strides, his speed, and the preciseness of his hand-eye coordinations. Such relays include the mile (4×440-yard) relay, the two-mile (4×880-yard) relay, the four-mile (4×one-mile) relay, and the distance medley (880, 440,¾, mile) relay. The outgoing runner must therefore maintain his vision and attention upon the baton until it is actually in his own hand. He uses no exact "Go" mark by which to guide his starting, but judges his pace by the momentum of his approaching teammate. Being fresh, he takes—not accepts, but takes—the baton as soon as possible within the passing zone. The incoming runner has but two tasks: to finish his race and to stick that baton up where his teammate can most easily get his hand on it.

All this is not to suggest that either the method or the timing of a "sight" pass is unimportant. On the contrary, a yard or two gained here may make a significance difference in one's lane around the first curve and one's place in the race. This type of passing calls for just as much emphasis upon drill and perfection of technique as in the sprint relays. Men can learn to judge the oncoming speed of their teammates with amazing precision. They can learn to accelerate their own speed, not merely after, but as they take the baton and quickly pick up at least 2 or 3 yards during the first 10 yards of their race. Good coaches get a real thrill out of such a demonstration of skill. The pass is made at full extension and with a perfectly timed acceleration, which is most impressive. In 1941, the writer always looked forward to the baton exchange between Balyeat and Breidenbach on the University of Michigan one-mile relay team.

Breidenbach, the anchor man, seemed to sense his teammate's momentum exactly, moved out with top acceleration at just the right moment, and never failed to pick up a valuable yard or two.

One of the common errors in "sight" passing for the receiver to anticipate the incoming runner by taking a few steps into the passing zone long before this is desirable. Rather, he should wait until the last possible moment and then go out as rapidly as a proper pass will permit.

There are at least a half dozen ways of making a sight pass, but only three seem to warrant description. This style is preferred because it involves natural and safe movements. The incoming runner holds the baton at a downward 40- and 60-degree angle, which is relatively simple and helps him maintain his forward lean at the finish. The outgoing runner can take a forward-facing position both before and during the exchange, with none of the shoulder and hip twisting found in other methods. It is therefore much easier to run straight out in one's lane. Further, since the eyes are directed downward along the shoulder, the lane lines or the curb, if one is taking with the left hand, are within the field of vision and therefore less likely to cause a foul or fall.

It should be stated again that the primary responsibility for the success of this and all "sight" passes rests upon the outgoing runner. He must get or take the baton wherever it may be. He must judge his own outgoing speed in terms of his teammate's speed and be very certain that he keeps his eye on the baton until it is actually in his own hand. Otherwise, a slight stumble or even wavering of the tired passer might cause dropping of the baton and a loss of from 10 to 20 yards.

The style of a "sight" pass has had wide acceptance for many years. It is certainly safe and in the longer-distance relays is probably justified. However, the incoming man sometimes has difficulty in holding the baton vertically and the receiver must twist his body to an awkward running position. Its use is therefore not recommended for relays with legs of less than a half mile.

THE ARRANGEMENT OF A RELAY TEAM

The four members of a relay team usually manifest a range in characteristics and ability. Seldom are they equal in both ability and knowledge of racing tactics. The competitor may be assigned his order of running either at random or after a careful analysis of his strength and weakness. The intelligent instructor balances the factors and decides on the most efficient baton passing and running combination. The points to be considered are:

1. The length of the race. This determines whether the visual or nonvisual method of exchange will be employed.
2. Which athlete runs best when behind?
3. Which athlete runs best when in the lead?
4. Who is the fastest starter?
5. Is the fastest starter cool headed so that he will provide team stability should he be selected as number 1 man?
6. Who are the two best baton handlers? (Obviously the second and the third runners each have two movements to execute, while the first and the fourth runners each perform but one movement).
7. What lane position has the team drawn?
8. Is the competition outdoors with ample room to get around opponents, or is it indoors where the

acquisition of the lead position is very advantageous?

9. In what order of relative strength is the opposing team lined up?

10. What passing-receiving pairs work most effectively together? Adjustments are frequently required when men of varying heights and lengths of arm are to be fitted into a smooth passing combination.

If the four members of a relay team are listed in the order of their ability to cover their respective distances in the shortest interval of time, they may be designated as 1, 2, 3, and 4.

The most commonly accepted arrangement of a team based on the running skill is 2, 4, 3, 1. In such a plan the most efficient team member is placed in the "anchor" position or, in other words, the fourth leg of the race. This arrangement assumes his ability to either retain the lead given him or retrieve any loss in distance that he might have inherited. The second fastest team member is assigned the lead-off position in the hope that he will run on even terms with his competitors or possibly hand over a lead to his teammate. That team member having the least ability is assigned to run the second relief so that should he suffer a loss of distance, there remain two men of fair ability to make up the yardage.

Another order of running calls for placing the men 4, 3, 2 and 1 (in the revers order of their ability). When all members of the team are adept at running a race from behind, this sequence is satisfactory. It has a disadvantage in that frequently the first runner, pitted against relatively faster opponents, suffers a yard age deficiency, which keeps the three remaining teammates in hot water.

Occasionally, in indoor relay competition, the

acquisition of the lead is quite important especially when it is difficult to run around opponents on a track which is either short in length or narrow in width. To meet this condition the members of the team are sent to the marks in the order of 1, 2, 3, 4.

A further deviation consists in placing the runners 2, 3, 4, 1. Here the slowest runner is assigned the third relief in the hope that the first two teammates may turn over a distance advantage to him. In case he should not retain this lead, the heavy-duty work will be assumed by the relay team's best performer (number 1), who will "anchor" the race.

A sound procedure consists of analysing carefully the four runners, determining the most effective order of carrying the stick, emphasizing judgment of pace so that each will run his respective leg at his optimum pace, and then retain this order throughout the season. The confidence and composure of a team is frequently disturbed by a last-minute change in its running order. Needless worry over the possible outcome of the contest is the result.

SPECIFIC ASSIGNMENTS OF THE PASSER AND THE RECEIVER

To be successful an exchange of the baton requires certain definite accomplishments by both the passer and the receiver. An effective pass is defined as one in which the baton is exchanged when the two team members involved are running at an equal rate of speed, this rate being the optimum for each. These tasks imposed vary but slightly when the athlete is required to change from the visual to the nonvisual method. The duties are discussed under: (A) the responsibility of the passer, (B) the responsibilities of the receiver using the visual method, and (C) the responsibilities of the receiver using the nonvisual method.

A. The Responsibility of the Passer

The tasks imposed on the passer are discussed in the order in which they are to completed.

1. He must judge and distribute his strength and effort so as to reach his teammate in the shortest period of time. For example, in the longer races (beyond 220 yards), excess speed at the start may cause him to tie up at the finish.

2. The passer must pick out definitely the teammate to whom he expects to pass the baton so that he may steer his path in the correct direction.

3. He should have a knowledge of where his opponents are going to make the exchange. For example, he should know whether the team wearing blue jerseys, whose runner is just ahead of him, intends to cut to the inside or to the outside of the track.

4. The arm should be extended at the proper time, neither too early nor too late. If it is extended too soon, valuable arm synchronization is lost. The error of an overdelayed extension is obvious. In sprint relays the most effective passes occur 12 to 15 yards from the back zone line. In longer races the pass should occur 5 to 12 yards from this line.

5. When the arm is extended, it should synchronize with the legs.

6. A sufficient amount of the exposed baton should be provided for the receiver. Given him "the big end of the stick".

7. Provided that the receiver holds his hand at the correct height, the passer is responsible for the correct height of the exchange.

8. Likewise the passer is responsible for making the exchange in the correct direction. It should be neither

too far to the right nor to the left.

9. The passer is responsible for applying the correct amount of pressure to the baton in the exchange. He must also retain his grasp of the stick until he is sure that his teammate has a secure hold of it. The baton, laid in the teammate's hand with a moderate amount of pressure, brings about an automatic grasping of the stick by the receiver.

10. The passer should continue in his own lane until he is 'uncovered". He should slow down gradually until the opposing teams have passed the baton, at which time he has a clear path to retire from the track.

11. The passer must not slow up when he approaches his teammate nor should he anticipate the pass. Instead he should run close to his receiver and carry through for several yards beyond the ideal spot of exchange.

B. Responsibilities of the Receiver (Visual Method)

For the visual method of exchange the following tasks are imposed on the receiver:

1. He must be certain that he is in the correct lane. This is especially true when there are six or more teams competing.
2. He must have a correct stance in his lane, namely, one that will permit a fast getaway and give the passer room to run by.
3. The receiver must judge the speed of the incoming runner. Since he is required to watch the teammate coming down the track, he needs drill on running in a straight, forward direction with the head and eyes to the rear. As a safety measure he may glance quickly in the direction of his run, an instant before starting his getaway, so that he may be sure the forward path is clear.

4. Closely associated with speed and judgment, the receiver must gauge the degree of fatigue of the passer. This holds true in legs of more than 220 yards.

5. The receiver must time his getaway correctly, starting neither too soon nor too late.

6. To facilitate an effective exchange of the baton, there are certain definite positions of the hand and arm which are necessary:

a. A wide spread of the fingers, thus providing a sizeable target.

b. A correct degree of height of hand depending on the style of arm-hand position agreed upon.

c. The most desirable lateral position of the arm and hand so that they are neither too far to the left nor to the right.

d. Steadiness of the hand is important. It must move in an even plane with the ground.

e. The response to the touch of the baton must be automatic (in other words, reflex).

7. The transfer of the baton from the right to the left hand should be made at a time when it least affects the running stride. Some athletes make the transfer on the back stretch when the field of runners is not closely bunched, others toward the end of their run, but the majority execute the transfer during the first running stride.

8. After obtaining the baton, the receiver should run close to the left line of his lane thus providing space on the right for his teammate.

C. The Responsibilities of the Receiver (Nonvisual Method)

In addition to the tasks enumerated when the visual method of receiving is employed, the athlete has some further duties to perform when he receives the stick when the head and eyes are to the front.

1. In addition to knowing that he is in the correct lane, the receiver must be sure that he knows the exact location of both the back and the front lines of the passing zones. This applies especially when the entire race is run in lanes.
2. The application of foot drive should be the same as in a start with a gun, provided it is a sprint relay.
3. The receiver must use his own judgment as to the correct moment of initiating the getaway. This means that he should not rely on the verbal signals "go" or "wait".
4. He should accustom himself to running for a period of two and one-half to three seconds before expecting the baton to touch his outstretched hand. An otherwise excellent exchange has been ruined because the receiver became needlessly worried and reduced his speed, fearing that he was running away from his teammate, even though both were well within the passing zone.

RUNNING ORDER OF RELAY TEAM MEMBERS

Time and time again, the deciding factor in losing or winning a relay race is the order in which relay members are put into competition. Here, even more than in individual races, the adages "Know thyself" must be supplemented by "Know thy opponents". How many, many times a good but somewhat inexperienced man will be content to stay with a mediocre field and come home many yards behind his capabilities! How many, many times a relatively poor runner has been matched with excellent runners and has either run himself into the ground on the first half of his race and as a result recorded much slower total time than expected, or, almost equally often, found hitherto unsuspected powers within himself and achieved amazing results. Coaches will therefore find that careful and constant study of all related factors will pay important dividends. Use of personnel is first of all dependent upon the length of the relay race.

The sprint relays. The 440 and 880 relays in college and AAU competition are almost always run in lanes all the way. Therefore, there is no special advantage in having a lead early in the race. Nor, with the exception of the anchor leg, is there an emphasis upon competitive running. The problem, therefore, is relatively simple and is primarily related to baton speed and total income. Factors determining selection of men include:

1. Differing distance each man carries the baton. Because of the method used in the baton-passing zones, the first runner carries the baton 8 yards more than the 110-yard average, and the last runner 8 yards less. This difference might well be an important factor in order assignment, with the stronger man carrying the first, longer distance.

2. Relative abilities to run on curves and straightaway. In general, the shorter-striding individual does a better job on the curve. If the race starts from the middle of track, this factor is nonoperative.

3. Other factors being equal, the most expert starter should run the No. 1 leg.

4. The best competitor might well run the anchor leg. Although the distance he runs is shorter, the ability to keep relaxed despite tough competition might well be the determining factor in the race.

In high school competition, there often are neither

lanes nor staggered starts. In such cases, whenever there are more than four teams in the race, the primary problem is to get out in front, where there'll be a minimum of interference, and to stay there all the way. The best and most experienced starter should run the No. 1 leg, even thought he is a trifle slower at 118 yards than other sprinters on the team. The second-best sprinter should run second; the third-best, third; and the fourth-best, fourth. Once in a while, a coach who does not plan to win an important relay but is hoping to place will run his men in just the opposite order—poorest, and so on. Knowing that the other teams will all be fighting each other on the first leg and that some of them will have to run in the third lane (18 feet farther per curve), he deliberately takes a back position at the start, thus utilizing the inside lane, and reserves his best sprinters for the later legs, when the race will have opened up and they will have a better chance to make their best time. Such instances emphasize the fact that this discussion cannot hope to review all possibilities and that only intelligent and studied consideration of every factor in each race will prove consistently right.

The mile relay. When the mile relay is not run in lanes around at least the first curve, the value of an expert starter who can take the rough going around the first turn and backstretch cannot be overemphasized. This becomes increasingly important as the number of teams in the race exceeds three or four. The practice of using staggered starts and running in lanes around the first run only is of great benefit to everyone and should be strongly encouraged.

Factors that will affect the order of running in the mile relay include:

1. The size and width of the track. Being out in front is a great advantage on an indoor track 220 yards or

less in length, with short straightaway that make passing very difficult. In such a case, men might be run as follows:

A. best starter and, in general, first- or second-best 440 man; B. second-best quarter-miler; C. third-best quarter miler; and D. fourth-best quarter miler, yet one who will protect his position and do his best when the competition is keen and others are fighting for the lead.

2. The number of teams in the race. If more than four, better men must be used on the first three legs in order to stay up in the race. If less than four, best man can be used on the last two legs, when competition is toughest.

3. The order in which the opposition are using their men. This calls for an intimate knowledge of one's opponents. Sometimes in a dual meet, by reversing the normal order and running best men, first, one can build up such a lead that the opponent's strong anchor man will be discouraged or outrun himself on the first 300 yards. In such a plan, one must be rather certain, first, that the team will have at least 25-yard lead at the end of the third leg; second, that the opponent's anchor man is definitely better than one's team understands the gamble and is keen to try it out. Building a lead is not easily accomplished and requires everyone's best effort. Do not permit the gamble to cause your own team to lose faith in your judgment. Let them know the situation and take their own chances.

If your anchor man is better than the opposition's, let the order of running be on a man-for-man basis. Have Jones run against Smith and Brown against Black wherever Smith and Black may run on the opposing team. The knowledge of a superior anchor man will often take one or more half seconds off each team member's time. They need no lead but must merely relax and stay with their opponents.

4. The attitudes of each man toward position in the race. Front runners should be placed where their chances to be in front are increased; followers will do better coming from behind.

5. The lane from which the team starts and in which passes will be made. If it is a good lane, the team may wish to keep it. If a poor one, the team's best man be needed to get the team in a challenging position. Or, on the other hand, they may decide to relax in an inside back position on the first leg and wait for things to open up before using their best men.

6. The method of assigning lanes for passing. Occasionally, although quite unfairly, lanes are fixed for all four legs. Sometimes lanes are alternated—that is, lanes are switched from inside to outside and vice versa on succeeding passes. More commonly today, teams take lanes in the order in which the incoming runners are approaching: first runner in first lane, second in second, and so forth. Where four or more teams are running, a lead is of aid from a yardage as well as time standpoint. Men will be run accordingly.

7. The order in which baton-passing drill has been done. Men learn each other's habits and abilities and can gain yards through such knowledge.

8. Most important factor of all, the order in which the team members have confidence. All the master-minding in the world will prove fruitless if it upsets the poise and assurance of the men doing the running. What has proved best all seasons is probably best today, even though there might be certain detailed advantages in making a change. The best explanation of the innumerable stories of great feats in relay running is always related to lack of tension and doubt. Although the phrase is outworn, confidence really is half the battle.

The two-mile and four-mile relays. In these distance

relay races, the issue can be boiled down to two basic problems: how to stay with the opposition and how to beat the opposition in the closing laps of the race.

How to stay up. If the anchor man is the best half-miler on tne field, the problem resolves itself to staying with the opposition. When one weak runner is present, the coach will be hard pressed to keep his team within "striking range" after this man has completed his leg. Much depends upon the attitude with which this man runs his race. He must know his problem and face it coolly and intelligently. If, in desperation to prove himself, he tries to take the lead or even to stay with the No. 1 man of the opposing teams, both his tension and his bad judgment will drag at his legs on the last laps. If he sells himself short and drops back to last place immediately, he will find the leaders entirely out of reach when he starts his finishing sprint. He must somehow pace himself in terms of his own abilities and yet stay within striking distance of the men he is scheduled to beat. Intelligence and determination often uncover unsuspected talent; desperate "heroism" usually results only in disappointment.

Generally, the best policy is to run this weak man first, then coach the others on just when and how much ground they should attempt to make up. If each tries to get it all back during the first half of his race, he will probably fade during his last quarter and lose as much as he gained. Sometimes it plays to run the third-best man in first position so he can take the brunt of the tough running that often occurs on this first leg, then shift to the weakest man for the second leg. Once in a blue moon, a team will get away with running their weakest man last. When, by so doing, a big lead can be built up during the first three legs, and when the opposition is unaware of how weak the last leg really is, they may be content to clinch their second-place position and not become aware of what they might have done until after the race is over. This is seldom a good gamble, however, for if the first three men are that good, they probably would have been able to make up the fourth man's loss in any case.

In summary, the order of running can be determined only by knowing accurately not only what one's own team can do but, equally important, what one's opponents can do. If there is any such thing as master-minding in track coaching, its opportunities are probably greater here than in any other area, for attitudes affect performance in relay racing more than in any other event.

How to win on the final leg. The anchor man is rightly named only in the sense that he is the steadying influence, the assurance of safety and success by which the less experienced and less able men control their own efforts. Their knowledge that George will take care of things if only they will do what they can do and have done in previous meets puts wings on their feet. But once George has the baton, he must justify their confidence. Of course, every man on the team must run with judgment and racing skill, but he especially must know every angle and device for gaining a yard or discouraging an opponent. A careful study of the section on racing tactics in the chapter on distance running will prove helpful; their intelligent use will pay rich dividends.

In the two-mile relay on an indoor track, the number of team in the race makes a real difference. A good deal of jamming occurs on the first leg and a weak man may wear himself out trying to stay in a "place" position. So many times, good half-milers running the No. 2, 3 or 4 legs of a relay find themselves leading a group of 3 or 4 teams while the 4 or 5 placing teams are running close together in another group that is 20 or 30 yards ahead. A coach and a team will do its utmost to avoid such a situation. A team must maintain direct contact with the place it place it intends to get. The writer has known team members to shift position at the last moment when such a situation develops unexpectedly. The strong anchor man has shifted to the third leg, has brought the team up into contention, and has thus given the last man that "someone to lick" which is so essential to best running.

Shuttle Relay (on the Flat)

This race derives its name from the similarity of the back-and-forth course of the runners to the movement of the shuttle in weaving. These contests may be held either on the cinder straightaway or on the flat enclosure within the oval track. Quite frequently one-half the team takes a position on one goal line of a football gridiron and the other half on the opposite goal line.

This race is popular with youthful competitors since the distance of each leg may be reduced to 50 yards or less. Again, the number of runners on each team is unlimited, being determined by agreement.

The odd-numbered runners (1 and 3) take their positions at one end of the course and the even-numbered runners (2 and 4) at the opposite end. If the number of men is even, both the start and finish are at same end of the course.

Ordinarily, the baton is not utilized in these races, because the runners are going in opposite directions, making it difficult to execute the exchange and alsc to determine where the pass actually occurred. As a substitute for the pass, the relief runner starts when the incoming athlete touches his outstretched hand. As a further aid to the judges in determining a legal touch-off (one in which the relief man remains behind the scratch line until touched), restraining posts for each team are planted on the scratch lines. Therefore, for a given team, the odd-numbered runners, except the first, will use on restraining post, and the even-numbered runners the other at the opposite end of the course. Restraining posts may be either fixed or movable. In meets where portable or movable posts are used, the rules frequently require that they be left standing after the touch-off. The lead-off man starts from the crouch position, and all relief runners start from a standing position, in which the right arm is extended forward at shoulder height, and to the right of the restraining post. At the instant of hand contact the relief runner quickly draws back the right arm and strides out with the right foot. Obviously, his body passes to the left of the restraining post and the incoming runner passes on the opposite side.

The practice schedule, the placement of runners, and the responsibilities of the team members quite closely resemble those of the sprint relay.

Shuttle Hurdle Relay

This event is the same as the shuttle relay except hurdles are placed at the regulation distances. The height cf the hurdles, as well as the distance between them, is determined by the games committee. In collegiate or A.A.U. competition, the obstacles are customarily 42 inches high, spaced according to the rules for the high hurdles. This usually permits 15 yards from the start to the first hurdle and 15 yards from the last hurdle to the finish line. For scholastic meets the hurdles may be either 39 inches or 30 inches high.

It is a common practice to provide two lanes of hurdles for each team. When but one lane is available for each team, a displaced hurdle must be immediately reset. This causes considerable confusion and consequently double lanes for each team are strongly recommended. When two lanes are provided, the athletes should run in the lane to the left. Since most individuals are right handed, such a plan permits the oncoming runner to extend the right arm and touch the relief teammate on the right shoulder. Although a light touch is desirable, in the excitement of the race it may become overemphasized. Since the right-handed man places the right foot back in the crouch position at the start, the body is in better balance for resisting a touch on the right shoulder.

Neither the restraining post nor the baton is employed in the shuttle hurdle relay. The rules suggest (but do not demand) that a touch-off inspector be assigned each runner. It is the duty of the inspector to keep his hand in contact with the relief runner's heel or body until the oncoming hurdle has touched the body of his teammate.

The responsibilities of both the oncoming hurdle and the relief man correspond, in general, to those discussed under relay races when the baton is utilized. The incoming man should finish his race on the correct side of the lane. The touch-off hand must be extended well forward in the correct direction so that it unerringly comes in contact with the teammate. The action desired is not that of a rigid, stiff-arm shove which tends to unbalance the relief runner. The arm should be extended in a relaxed fashion so that the contact is a tap rather than a push.

The relief man is responsible for completing adjustments which include getting on the marks. This should be done shortly after the oncoming runner starts his leg of the race. The set position should be taken as soon as his teammate clears the last hurdle. Obviously the set position must be held until the touch occurs.

In addition to the suggestions made for the order of running in the relays already discussed, the coach takes into consideration such points as the ability of the competitor to run when behind, the ability of the competitor to run when, and the direction and velocity of the wind. Men who perform well, even when behind, are usually placed third and fourth, and those who run better when ahead are ordinarily placed first and second. Of course, it would be ideal if all men ran equally well under either condition. It is customary to assign the best man to run the anchor position.

Generally, the 175-pound hurdler is less affected by a head wind than his 150-pound teammate. The more rugged and taller men are frequently assigned the relief sections which require facing the wind.

In general, the practice schedule for the shuttle hurdle relay is the same as for hurdles. However, in addition to hurdling drills, touch-off practice should be engaged in two or three days each week. These drills may be taken over one hurdle (15 yards from the start, 15 yards to the finish). Three or four touch-off at full effort should suffice for one day's workout.

Perhaps the shuttle hurdle relay is only beginning its popularity, and we may expect more widespread participation in this thrilling contest calling for speed, hurdling skill, and precise timing of the touch-off. Adjustments in both the height of the hurdle and the length of the race provide opportunity for participation by grade school-youths as well as mature athletes.

Shuttle Hurdle Relay

The shuttle hurdle relay is gaining popularity in relay meets generally, both outdoors and indoors. Outdoors, the standard distance is 480 yards; indoors, its length is dependent upon the distance that facilities make available. Its method consists of shuttling four hurdles back and forth, with consecutive men running adjacent hurdles lined up in opposite directions. Thus the starting line is also the finish line.

The major problem of this relay lies in the touch-off. The outgoing runner must not start until he has been touched on the shoulder by the incoming hurdler. Such a correct start is difficult to judge and meet referees have generally been lax in disqualifying protested teams. Consequently, illegal starts have been very common, and some coaches feel the event is too unfair and uncertain to be kept on the track and field program. Responsible and careful officiating is therefore of great importance.

Many meet directors assign an inspector at each end of the course for every two teams and, in addition, assign a touch-off supervisor at each end of the course for each team. This supervisor must keep his hand on the runner's heel until the latter has been touched by the incoming runner. Unfortunately, he is in a poor position to judge whether his man has anticipated the touch-off and can give his opinion to the inspector with little certainty.

In most instances two lanes of hurdles are provided for each team. Where a single lane of hurdles is used, the style of hurdle must be the old-fashioned "T" type, which can be run either way, and overturned hurdles must be righted quickly before the next runner approaches. When using two lanes, hurdles usually run down the left-hand lane and to their own left of the next hurdler. This leaves the right hand free for the light touched-off, which is so important.

This touch of the shoulder must be downward and must not in any way interfere with the forthcoming upward and outward movement of the next runner.

The problem of the proper setting of starting blocks is sometimes a difficult one. Often, team will bring two sets of blocks for each end of the course and adjust each for each individual, simply switching blocks as needed. Where this is impractical, quick-change blocks must be used and managers should be assigned to each team to aid in effecting the change of position of each block.

Usually men will take their marks when their incoming teammate is at his fifth hurdle and get set as he comes off his last one.

The running order of hurdlers is largely dependent upon five factors:

1. Ability. Usually the best men run last.
2. Competitive spirit. Front runners should be placed at that spot where their chances of running in front are best; back runners, where they will be running from behind.
3. Starting ability. The best starter should run first.
4. Use of starting blocks. Where a pair of runners are using a single block, they should start with the same foot back and, ideally, with the same foot-spacing on the block.
5. Direction and velocity of the wind. Some men are more likely to do better against or with the wind than others.

Practice of the shuttle hurdle relay is usually done with three hurdles in each lane. Fewer hurdles provide poor practice in timing the start and touch off; hurdles are too fatiguing.

CHAPTER 10

CROSS-COUNTRY RUN

Cross-country, the sport involving the running of long distance over open terrain, is considered the foundation of successful distance running programs. This activity has enjoyed great popularity for many years in Europe. In England, for example, cross-country is truly run across the country. Races are run from town to town, with the runners obliged to find their own directions. In a sense, the races are run as if there were obstacle courses laid out between the towns.

Cross-country did not gain much prominence in the United States until the late 1930's. On November 28, 1938, the first annual National Collegiate Cross-Country Meet was held at Michigan State University. Since this date, except for the war year of 1943, when it was not held, the number of participants who enter this meet has grown every year. More and more schools have formed teams which run this race competitively. Cross-country is now recognized as an essential part of the over-all track program in most high schools, colleges, and universities in the United States.

The administration of cross-country as an event is included as an integral part of this chapter, even though such an approach is not used in the other chapters. Many cross-country coaches are given this duty as an extra assignment, especially at the high school level, and need help in administering this program. In addition, performers in this event depend on endurance and knowledge of procedures, rather than on speed per set, to gain excellent. Therefore, in order to give them the opportunity they deserve, the meets must be conducted as effectively as possible and in accordance with established rules and regulations.

SCORING

Cross-country is scored similarly to the game of the golf. This means that the team with the low score wins. A team in championship meets is composed of 7 men—5 scorers and 2 so-called pushers. (In less formal meets, more men can be used as possible scorers). The positions of the first 5 runners determine the final score made by a team, with 15 points being a perfect low score. The sixth and seventh men, though they do not affect their own team's score, can influence the score made by the opponents if both finish in front of any of the other team's first 5 men. Therefore, a perfect score would be 158-50, with the winning team's pushers placing sixth and seventh, in front of all of the members of the opposing team. This possibility is a definite inducement for every runner to turn in his top performance.

Collegiate level competition involves the runner traversing any distance from 3 to 6 miles. The NCAA championships are run over a 6-mile distance, while many collegiate conferences set the length of their courses at a distance of 5 miles. At the high school level, 2 miles is the most popular distance, with a few courses being 3 mile in length.

Most races are run over a university- or city-owned golf course. Municipal parks are often made available to city schools which do not have their own facilities. The distance of each course will vary according to its terrain, which may be composed in some cases of flat ground, or a combination of both hills and flat surfaces.

SPECIAL TRAINING AND TECHNIQUES

The coach faces a difficult assignment in designing a workout program to help acquaint his team with the various courses over which they will run during the season. If their home course is hilly and they are to run a race on a flat course, part of the prior week's workouts must be run on a flat surface emphasizing speed. On the other hand, a team used to running on a flat, fast course must get in some hill or grade work during the week's practice before competition on the latter type of course.

Certain special techniques must be used in running over hills. Adequate information about and practice of these techniques help a runner become more effective in running up and down hills, and therefore lessen the psychological tensions which hills may effect in the most effective hill running techniques. A discussion of the different opinions is presented here.

In downhill running, the most important point is that the runner should take advantage of the momentum he can gain from use of the pull of gravity. The conflicting opinions involve the following points of views: (1) the runner should sprint downhill in order to utilize hill slope and downward pull of gravity to the greatest advantage for picking up speed; (2) the athlete should use controlled free running downhill in order to utilize gravity and hill slope properly; very little effort should be made to run any faster than the pull of gravity requires.

The first technique is very effective in picking up distance on the other runners, but involves some difficulty in controlling foot placement. Therefore, its use is more apt to cause injuries. The second technique, the controlled, relaxed running, has many advantages for the runner, but is not as fast. By letting gravity and hill slope pull the body, the runner can conserve energy, and possibilities of injuries and heel jars are lessened.

The runners should shorten stride as they run downhill. The steeper the incline, the shorter the stride that must be used. In this manner, the body's centre of gravity is kept as nearly as possible over the feet.

When approaching a hill, a runner must adjust his stride if he is to navigate such an obstacle effectively. The adjustments a runner must make are as follows: (1) lengthen stride slightly; (2) have some body lean; and (3) increase pace gong uphill. The runner should make these adjustments just prior to starting up the hill, so that he is mechanically correct in his running form and prepared to start up the hill. Upon reaching the top, the runner should return to his race pace.

Analysis of cross-country runner's styles of running reveals that many of them do not use the above techniques. They frequently sprint downhill, using long strides, and prepare for running uphill by using short strides. Because they have superior ability, some runners have succeeded in spite of their using the above wrong techniques.

TEAM STRATEGY

A coach should encourage his team members to stay close together during a race. This does not mean that the front runners should wait for those who are falling behind, but that the back runners be encouraged to stay up with the lead runners. A team whose members run together and have balanced scoring will often upset teams with a few superior front runners.

For effective team running, a small time gap should exist between the first and fifth members. Nevertheless, team members starts to fall off the pace, the others should encourage him to stay up with the group.

Each team member should establish, with the aid of his coach, the pace at which he is going to run a given race. Of course, pace will vary according to the type of course being run. The ideal procedure is to have the runners spread their energy out to last over the entire distance of the race. Some coaches, however, disregard individual pace assignments completely in favour of the establishment of an over-all team pace. Many coaches will also have the members of their team run the first ½ or ¾ of the race together, enabling the back runners to use the team lead runners, as pace setters. After this distance has been covered, the principle of "every man for himself" is adhered to for the rest of the race.

However, a team staying close together can have a dispiriting psychological effect on the opponents. It is very discouraging to sell all the members of an opposing team together and at or near the front of the race.

OTHER RACING COMMENTS

Some runners have the tendency to "fall asleep" during a race; they are simply not as alert as they should be to what is going on in the race. They start the race, establish a pace, and never change it. Every runner should be aware of his position in comparison with members of the other team. If a runner falls into this inattentive state of mind, the coach should instruct him to "check out" (that is, run fast) for 5 to 10 yards every quarter of a mile or so, and then settle back into his race pace. This should "awaken" the runner.

During a race, the runners usually split into competitive groups. A given runner must strive to maintain contact with a group of runners or a single runner of similar ability. Once a runner drifts off from a group, it is extremely difficult for him to regain his contact.

Every member of a team should take the time, with the coach present, to study a strange course prior to participation in the competition. The coach should point out steep hills; loose surface, holes, sharp turns, and any other hazards that could be a potential problem. Obviously, team and pace strategy must be planned around the type of course that is to be the science of the race.

All athletes have a certain amount of reserve energy which they can call upon near the end of the race to help them increase their speed. Since the amount each has no reserve varies, the coach must help each athlete to determine at what point in the race his drive for the finish must begin.

Cross-country races are run in all kinds of weather (sun, rain, sleet, or snow). Consequently, lightweight protective uniforms must be a part of every runner's standard equipment. The running shirt and shorts are the basic equipment. Lightweight long shirts and pants may be worn under this running gear in the event of cold weather. Gloves and stocking caps may also be utilized by the runner in cold and snowy weather.

MEET PREPARATIONS

A coach should make every effort to insure that home meets are conducted in an orderly, accurate, and fair manner. Hosting meet necessitates some very careful preparations by the coach; a checklist of things that should be done follows.

Program. A simple, informative, single-sheet program can be developed and mimeographed for distribution to spectators and competitors.

Course. Each visiting coach should be provided with a layout of the course prior to his arrival for the meet. His team members should also be permitted to jog over the course prior to competition. If possible, a long, reasonably flat stretch should start and finish the race, so as to eliminate any unnecessary congestion and give the competitors every opportunity to perform without hindrance. The course should be marked off in accordance with existing regulations. Every runner should be able to run the course without fear of getting lost or taking a wrong turn.

Some suggested methods of marking off the course include the following: (a) a continuous line, painted, or limed, should be visible along a side of the course; (b) posts should be painted with arrows pointing in the direction the race is to be run; and (c) indication flags should be located at regular intervals and around turns in the following manner: red means left turn; yellow means right turn; blue mean straight ahead.

A combination of these methods is considered the most effective. When a line is used in combination with flags, placement of the flags is very important. Runners are usually allowed to run within 5 yards of the white line, with the flag placed directly on the line. In the "flagging" of the turns, all runners are instructed to go around the flags. Since this is confusing, double "flagging" is recommended around the turns, with 1 set on the line and 1 set used as the curb. During the heat of competition, it is quite possible for a competitor to cut inside of a flag, especially if it is placed on the line. Such an error would make him subject to disqualification, so the use of two flags is recommended to avoid this misjudgment.

Timing. Most athletes are usually interested in the time in which they are running a given distance, whether in practice or during competition. Intermediate and total times should be taken and recorded during practice. This will enable the athlete and the coach to keep a continuous check on progression or change from week to week as various workout distances are run.

In meets, the intermediate times (e.g., 1 mile, 2 miles) should be called out loud and clear by the head timer, in such a manner that every runner is given his own time. In addition, four men may work in two separate groups. One member of one set of partners calls out the time of every runner at every distance, as well as the final time. The other set of partners work so that one man calls out the rank order of each man at each distance and the final order of finishing while the other records this finish order in relation to the time called out by the head timer.

The recording of intermediate and final times can be simplified through the use of time charts. To assure proper recording, 2 men familiar with cross-country times who are quick, alert, and not easily flustered should be selected for this task. One man records as the other reads the times, with no effort made to determine places. The timer simply reads the times as the runners pass the designated places and the finish line; the recorder places a mark at the time indicated by his partner. The time recorded in the chart is later combined with the rank order at which the runners passed the intermediate distances, as well as the order of the finish.

Judging the finish in dual meets is relatively simple. A number is assigned to each competitor and pinned on the front of his shirt. The numbers are read and recorded in order of finish. Two men used for judging and two men used for recording the finish positions can perform their tasks very efficiently.

In larger meets, where more control is required over the competitors as they finish, a quick, effective method of determining scores is essential. The most popular method used to control the competitors is referred to as the finish chute method. The chute can be made of various available equipment, such as park benches, hurdles, narrow fencing, hockey fencing, posts and flagged rope. It does not have to be elaborate in design, as its man purpose is for control of the finishers.

If there are a large number of competitors, a jump-up may occur in the chute. To avoid confusion in this connection, various methods are utilized to assure accurate results and a fair chance for every athlete to be placed as he finishes. One way is to enlarge the chute in width so that it can be divided into 2 sections. When one section fills up, the rest of the incoming runners can be funnelled into the other section. Another method is the utilization of ropes attached to the base of the funnel of the chute. If a jam-up occurs in the chute, the runners are backed up into the funnel; the ropes guide the front line of competitors to the side of the funnel. If the jam-up is large, the next line of competitors can be guided to the other side of the funnel. As the competitors proceed through and out the end of the chute their number, name, and school are recorded on the score sheet by the recorder and scorer.

A much quicker scoring method than described above is utilized in many large meets. As the competitor passes the recorder, he is handed a card with his finish place written on it. He turns this over to his coach, who writes his name, and school on the back of the card. On the front of a scoring envelope, the coach places the runner's number, his name, and his place of finish, and totals his score. Use of this method will help in the accumulation of a quick unofficial team score, and may also serve as a double check on the recorder's official placement of the finishers and the results determined by the scorer. There are many similar methods in use which are quick and effective in helping to determine the winners.

CHAPTER 11

HIGH HURDLES IN RUNNING EVENTS

HISTORY

There is disagreement as to whether the Egyptians or the Greeks were the first hurdlers. In any events, the first hurdles were probably "sheep hurdles" (fences) or solid jagged barriers staked out in a meadow. The main objective was to get over the barriers alive.

Later came the barrier placed across a running track. If the lead runner knocked the barrier down, the other runners had no hurdle in jump. This led to the practice of constructing the individual hurdle in sawbuck fashion, heavy and hazardous on contact. In time much lighter hurdles were made, and hurdlers began to run through them rather than over them. Naturally, this resulted in the adoption of a universal rule (agreed to by all governing bodies) to restore the essential skill of hurdling: if 3 or more hurdles were knocked over, the hurdlers was disqualified. The "L" hurdle brought about a change in this rule.

It is believed that hurdling as a competitive track event began in 1837. The first 120-yard high hurdle event was recorded at an 1864 meet between Oxford and Cambridge, when A.W.T. Daniel ran it in 17¾ seconds.

The earliest hurdling form known is that of the athlete clearing the hurdle in an upright sitting position. Change from this form came about through attempts to maintain momentum by jumping the hurdle and landing on the lead foot. However, the lead leg was kept bent at the knee and the trail leg was not flattened; consequently, the action over the hurdle was more like broad jumping than hurdling. This forms did not help much in saving time over the hurdle. Many national championships before 1860 were won in 19 seconds, which means that it took 5 seconds to go through the air over the hurdles, compared with the 2 seconds or less needed by hurdlers of today to perform the same act.

The major credit for development of the hurdling form using a straight lead leg and a forward trunk lunge is in some dispute. However, in the United States Al Kraenzlein of Pennsylvania is given credit as the innovator. His time in 1898 was: 15.2 Fred Kelley of the University of Southern California ran the high hurdles in 15 seconds flat in 1913, Earl Thompson of Southern California and Dartmouth in :14.8 in 1916, and Robert Simpson of Missouri in :14.6 in the same year. Thompson set a new record of :14.4 in 1920, Percy Beard of Alabama Polytechnic College ran them in :14.2. George Saling of Iowa, 1932 Olympic high hurdle champion, ran them in :14.1, but was not given official credit for this performance.

Until 1935 the inverted "T" type of hurdle had been used, but it was found that it would rise several inches, when hit, causing many hurdlers to fall during a race. The "L" type of hurdle, with weights at the base to meet the newly established requirements of the 8-pound overturning force, was then adopted. This change helped the hurdler to relax while going over the hurdle, and allowed him to run without fear of injury.

The performance improvement evidenced by the faster times recorded was due to such factors as: (1) an attempt to keep goods sprinting action, that is, elimination of the "stagger" as the hurdler landed; the shoulders and hips were not twisted; (2) definite forward body lean as the hurdler went over the hurdle; (3) the semi-straight lead leg; (4) the flattened trail leg and its delayed action; and (5) a conscious effort to keep the feet on the ground and running as much as possible.

Forrest Towns from Georgia, employing what many thought was perfect form, lowered the world record to :13.7 in 1937. Fred Wolcott of Rice Institute, one of the first real sprinter-hurdlers, then entered hurdling competition. Practically all of the great hurdles until Wolcott's time ranged in height from 6'2" to 6'5". Wolcott, not quite 6' tall, ran the high hurdles in :13.7 in 1941. Harrison Dillard, a still shorter man (5'10") and a great sprinter (1948 Olympic sprint champion), lowerd the record to :13.6.

The sprinters all jumped farther over the hurdle with a faster moving trail leg. Because of their great speed and leg drive, they were able to make up for the greater time spent in the air.

The trend to such short sprinters as Wolcott, Dillard, and Allan Tolmich of Wayne caused some coaches to wonder if speed would offset hurdling skill. Then Dick Attlesey of Southern California ran the race in 13.5 seconds in May, 1950, at the Fresno relays, and restored the concept that it takes a tall man to be a hurdler. He was 6' 3½" tall and weighed 178 pounds. Attlesey used what is considered nearforward thrust, a delayed trail leg which he snapped down quickly, descended after clearing the hurdle. His hurdle clearance time was 2 seconds for the 10 hurdles, as compared to Dillard's time of 2.3 seconds.

Jack Davis of Southern California, the so-called "hard-luck kid" of 2 Olympiads (he finished second in the 1952 and 1956 Olympics, both in photo-finish races), climaxed a brilliant career by running the race in 13.3 seconds at Bendigo, Australia, just prior to the 1956 Olympic games, for a new world record. Davis was 6'3" tall and weighed 178 pounds.

In the 1968 Olympics, the United States finished one-two, with Willie Davenport winning in :13.3, thus tying the Olympic record established by Irv Hall in the semi-finals. Hall placed second in the finals, in :13.4. Earl McCulloch was another great hurdler who ran :13.3, but chose not to compete in the Olympics. If a hurdler comes along who can sprint 120 yards in 11 seconds and clear the 10 hurdles in 01.8 seconds, the world record will probably drop to 13 seconds flat or less.

As with every other event in track and field athletics, a sound knowledge of the development of form in the high hurdles portrays if as a smoothly graded evolutionary process. For easier understanding, writers have a tendency to identify radical changes in style with certain outstanding performers: the straight front leg with Alvin Kraenzlein, the forward double-arm action with Earl Thomson, the hurried action of the short sprinter with Fred Wolcott, and so forth. There are obvious advantages in such an association of man with style, and this discussion will undoubtedly be guilty of occasionally using a similar method. Yet it should be recognized as an oversimplification that is actually inconsistent with the facts. Each detail in style development was undoubtedly practiced by many men before its use by some great record breaker attracted the attention of the track world.

For example, Alvin Kraenzlein of the University of Pennsylvania, is generally credited with being the father of modern hurdling through his use, in 1898, of a sprint action and straight first leg over the hurdle. Yet a careful survey of early English and Americans writings on hurdling makes it clear that as far back as 1886, A.C.M. Croome of Oxford, England, used a locked-knee, straight-leg action, and pictures of the American A.F. Copland in 1891, show a bent-knee, straight-ahead leg action that is reasonably consistent with modern form.

There need not be a quarrel between the coaches of different countries or among those of our own country about who should have the credit. As in the case of the crouch start in sprinting or the use of a bamboo pole, the credit must be divided among a large number of men, both coaches and athletes.

Apparently, hurdling as a competitive event goes back no further than the early 19th century in England, for there is no mention in ancient Greek, Roman or European literature of the any similar event. According to some researchers:

There were hurdle races at the tutors and dames houses at Eton College as long ago as 1837, and that is the earliest reference to competition in this kind of sport, but in Bell's Life of 1853 mention is made of a match between two amateurs, one of the events included being a race with jumps over 50 hurdles each 3 feet 6 inches high. The first authentic records of a hurdles time are supplied by A.W.T. Daniel, CUAC. He won the first Oxford and Cambridge 120 high hurdles event, 1864, in 17¾ seconds.

Similarly, Ross and Norris McWhirter write:

Ten flights, ten yards apart, seemed to be the accepted test from the earliest mentions, but the height was merely that of the accepted sheep hurdle of the day, about 3½ feet. In 1866 there was some attempt to standardize the height, for a rule in the first Oxford minute book states "the hurdles shall be 3 feet 6 inches in the ground". It is not recorded how many of the early pioneers were maimed by these crude jagged barriers, which were rigidly staked into the meadown, but it is at least certain that if any of them could now see six rows of zebra striped slats, with their 8 pounds toppling moment, they would wonder if it were the same event.

Although no mention of "sheep hurdles" has been found in American track literature, Comstock suggests a similarly diabolical device that placed a single rope or cross-bar all the way across the track. Although this may seem impossibly dangerous to us now, it was quite a natural evolution from the cross-country obstacle jumping in vogue at the time.

This, however, was found to be impractical for general usage, as one runner would gain an advantage over another by reason of the general hurdle being knocked down by the leading man. The installation of the individual hurdle was the result. This hurdle, made after the style of a sawbuck, was of substantial construction and being a dangerous piece of furniture to strike, the hurdler made an effort to clear it by a good margin.

Yet the writer has in his possession a picture of F.G.Moloney of Chicago winning the first Western Conference hurdles championship in :16.2, in which every hurdle sawback of the first two place winners is flat on the ground. No broken or blood-spattered leg bones are apparent, but of course colour photography had not been invented yet.

Under such conditions, the main consideration was to rise above the hurdle with plenty to spare and yet win. Time was incidental. Exactly measured steps in between the hurdles had not been seriously considered, so that the man who could take off equally well from either foot was thought to have a great advantage. Earliest and crudest form was then as it is in grammar school and intramural races today—a simple hop in which the body remains upright and the legs are drawn up underneath. Undoubtedly some took the event seriously enough to practice it several times, about 1840 in England and 1860 in this country, and were soon attempting a running jump in which they actually landed on the lead leg. This provided much less stopping of momentum after the hurdle than did the earlier jarring hop. However, a lead leg bent at almost a right angle at the knee and approximately parallel to the hurdle, plus a hurried take-off leg still afforded more aesthetics than momentum. National championships in America in the 1870's were often won in time over 19 seconds, which meant that at least 5 seconds was spent sailing through the air, as compared with out greatest modern hurdlers, who take less than 2 seconds more to run the hurdles than to run 120 yards on the flat.

In England, improvements came earlier in 1866, C.N.Jackson of Oxford made the then remarkable time of :16, a mark that was not broken in this country until 25 years later, in 1891, when H.L. Williams (incidentally, the "father of Minnesota"), ran :15.8. According to F.A.M.Webster, England's highly respected National Coach for many years, the major credit for use of the straight lead leg an forward lunge, of the trunk should go to A.C.M. Croome, who ran :15.6 in 1886, some 12 years before America's "inventor" of the straight lead leg, Kraenzlein, achieved prominence.

Although some may thus question Kraenzlein's originality, all must accept his greatness as a hurdler and athlete. Not only did he run :15.2 for the high hurdles in 1898, but he also set a world's record of :23.6 in the lows and another of 24′ 4½″ in the broad jump. Undoubtedly it was his great speed and natural athletic ability that actually produced his running action in the hurdles, even though he may have seen someone else do it first. One of the more interesting and valuable accounts of both the ideas and conditions of hurdling of the period prior to Kraenzlein exists in the comments by Stephen Chase, world's record holder at :15.6 in 1894. The fundamentals of hurdling action apparently were already clear, although the details of actual practice occasionally seem to us slightly askew.

[The hurdler] should be all acting all the way at every instant and by the upward jerk of the rear leg and quick forward inclination of the body, he will anticipate the force of gravity an same time. Every minute detail should be developed perfectly, to the end that the ground be reached in the shortest time, with the body well forward and in the best position for the next stride. Between the hurdles, the three steps should be made with the thought of getting the feet on the ground as soon as possible, instead of reaching out for a long stride. In a race, the 30 feet between the hurdles is divided as follows: 14 foot jump over the hurdles; first step, 5 feet; second, 5½ feet; third 5½ feet. By all means, even when learning, never get nearer than 6 feet from the hurdle when jumping it.

Some of these points are consistent with modern hurdle practice and technique. Others are much less so: for example, his advocacy of a 14-foot jump over the hurdle is hardly consistent with his insistence upon getting to the ground as quickly as possible; or, his belief that "the 15 yards to the first hurdle are run at only a moderate pace, for too much speed causes unevenness and loss of control". Perhaps the following incident is the best mirror of the times. Chase found it just as amusing as we do, but today it would of course be impossible as well as funny.

There was but one other competitor and much was expected of him. Everything went smoothly until the third hurdle was reached. That object presented itself for consideration rather too previous for comfort, while the fourth could hardly be reached with seven league boots, and the writer was compelled to retreat a few steps for another try. Meanwhile the other competitor sailed calmly through, utterly oblivious of everything but his own brilliant success. A protest was made and the investigation showed the hurdles just six feet out of place. After not a little persuasion the winner magnanimously consented to run the race again, but remarked while walking back to the start, in an injured and somewhat sarcastic air, "You must have things down pretty fine to note a little different like that".

A further improvement, which Boyd Comstock considers as important as Croome's or Kraenzlein's straight lead leg lies in the delayed trail leg and increased flexibility of the hips to permit a full forward sprinting action. Like Webster, he credits Forrest Smithson with introducing this change in 1908. Smithson had a serious hip injury that eventually produced unusual hip flexibility. The old side twist of the body, with its off-balance landing position, was now gone, and a man was instantly ready to sprint on to the next hurdle, or "fence", if you prefer. Smithson also placed great emphasis upon getting back to the ground as soon as possible and believed that the best form was the one that most exactly followed sprinting action. Although his extreme emphasis on this point hurried his action and upset his balance and smoothness, he was able to establish a :15 flat record for the 110-meter high hurdles at the 1908 Olympics.

Shortly after 1900, the increasing interest in the low hurdles, combined with the unwieldiness and danger of the old-style sawbuck or "fence" led to a patented hurdle that swung down in the middle either to form a low hurdle or when hit by a high-hurdler. Unfortunately, hurdlers soon took advantage of its light construction and slammed through with no regard for clearance. There followed both a studier hurdle and a rule change that brought disqualification when three hurdles were knocked down.

In general, we "moderns" think of all-out momentum throughout the hurdle action as being a new emphasis. "Thomson may have had good form in his day, but he sacrificed speed for smoothness and balance" is a typical remark today. Yet as far back as 1924, Comstock had a similar view:

Formerly high hurdlers were taught to conserve a portion of their speed as they approached the first hurdle, as most coaches believed that the hurdler would lose his balance if he took the first fence at top speed. This theory can be easily explained, as the extreme body dip was not then in vogue. Nowadays the clever high hurdler takes the obstacle at full speed and converts the upward tendency into forward momentum by cleverly dipping forward as he takes off.

In any case, the general improvement in hurdling time that took place at the turn of the century came about through the more extensive use of five principles, which had thus far been developed: (1) straight-ahead sprinting action with no twist of the hips or shoulders, (2) forward buck or lean of the trunk, (3) the straight, forward lift of the lead leg with more or less knee-bend, (4) the delayed rear leg with flexible hip and positive forward action, and (5) the assumption and momentum comes only through contact with the ground so that hurdling action should get back to earth as soon as possible. F.G. Moloney of Chicago, J.F. McLean and John Garrells of Michigan, all about 1900; A.B.Shaw of Dartmouth in 1908, W.A. Edwards in 1909, Forrest Smithson in 1909, and John P. Nicholson (for many years track coaches at Notre Dame) in 1912, all approached :15 flat. But, except by Smithson's 110-meter hurdle mark of :15, which was never recognized for 120 yards despite its being a greater distance, Kraenzlein's mark of :15.2 was not officially removed until 19136, when Fred Kelly of Southern California ran :15.

As occurs so often when a great record is finally broken, it was smashed several times by different men. A group of fine hudlers came along together on the West Coast: Ward and Kelly of Southern California, Norton and Murray of Stanford, Preble of California, Kirkpatrick of Occidental, Bob Simpson of Missouri, and Earl Thomson, a freshman at Southern California who later became a varsity man at Dartmouth. The last-named pair were undoubtedly the greatest of these.

Thomson, 6' 3" tall and weighing 185 pounds, first broke the old record by running :14.8 in 1916, but Bob Simpson's :14.6 just two weeks later was given official recognition. Continuing his serious-minded efforts. Thomson came back four years later, in 1920, with a remarkable: 14.4, destined to remain as man's best effort for 11 years. Thomson, head track coach at the Naval Academy for many years, seems to have epitomized progress in hurdling form up to 1920 in addition to having perfected a few tricks of his own. To the five principles previously mentioned, which were practiced by Smithson and Kelly, Thomson added a two-arms-forward style that he freely admits he picked up from his rival, Bob Simpson. Yet in this as in all his work, Thomson was a perfectionist, and he gained greater smoothness and easy balance from this and other form details than Simpson or any other previous stylist. Sequence pictures of Thomson are still to be found in many of the locker rooms of American colleges, for, although many later hurdlers have been faster sprinters, few, if any, have surpassed him in hurdling style.

It took eleven years and a man of similar build and perfection of form to break Thomson's record. Percy

Beard, of Alabama Polytechnic, was 6′ 5″ tall, of which by far the greatest percentage seemed to be in his legs. With excellent hip flexibility and good sprinting speed, Beard seemed to be the final word in hurdling potential. Yet within a single year he was out of competition and two men, George Saling of Iowa and Jack Keller of Ohio State, had each established an officially unrecognized :14.1. Within five years, in 1936, his record was officially broken by Forrest Towns of Georgia, and within six years he would have finished a flight of hurdles some 5 yards behind the latest record holder. Towns lacked Beard's height, being a tiny 6′ 2″ tall, but he more than compensated for this through superior speed. The sports world was not surprised that Towns should set a new record, but it was shocked and somewhat incredulous when, in August, 1936, at Oslo, Norway, he was officially credited with :13.7.

The following spring, Robert Osgood of Michigan won the Big Ten Conference high hurdles in :14, and the writer well remembers our hope, even expectation that something would be found wrong with the Oslo performance and the Bob would be credited with an official world's record. But Oslo conditions were as perfect as Towns's hurdle form, and speculation as to whether :14 was a human ultimate was quickly ended.

For several years, attention had been called to the fact that when the inverted-T hurdle, which was then in general use, was knocked down, its base, 26-30 inches wide, first caused it to rise several inches. This was conceded to be an unnecessary hazard to hurdlers. The L-type hurdle, invented by Harry Hillman, of Dartmouth, was therefore adopted. It used weights on its base and thus required an overturning force of 8 pounds. This change, in addition to other practice hurdle devices that decreased the element of danger, greatly aided the confidence, relaxation, and therefore speed of hurdlers generally. This factor needs to be kept in mind in comparing the merits of hurdlers before and after 1935.

Up to this point, in fact up to 1941, concepts of best hurdling requirements and form were well established. Every record holder from Bob Simpson, in 1916, on down—in fact, every champion—had been over 6′ 2″ tall and had followed almost identical methods of form as did Simpson and Thomson. Coaches spoke confidently of the future and knew that only another "skyscraper" with even greater speed could even hope to set new records. But that was before the time of Allan Tolmich of Wayne University, Fred Wolcott of Rice Institute, and Harrison Dillard of Baldwin-Wallace. Three new record holders and all 6′ tall or less! And all violated the sacred laws of proper hurdling as well as the self-assurance of the leading hurdle coaches of the country! First Tolmich beat the great Towns in the 1937 National AAU championships, using a basically sound form that nonetheless included a hurried back leg that displeased the experts. They immediately referred to his excellent :10.5 for 100 meters and suggested disparagingly that he should stick to the sprint events. But in 1938 another shorty, 6′ tall, Fred Wolcott, won the title in :14.5. He placed both arms-forward but failed to achieve a full forward lean. His clearance was high and a hurried back leg straightened the body as the left lead foot touched the ground. Yet two years later, in 1940, and again in 1941, when Wolcott twice equalled Towns's record of :13.7, the coaches began to speak off a new form that was peculiarly adapted to short men with fast action. The important factor was not necessarily smoothness, beauty, or even economy of action, but rather speed of movement. Get those feet down fast from the hurdle as well as in between, and leave aesthetics to the Greeks and the tall boys. They realized Wolcott was the fastest of all hurdlers, having run :09.5 on several occasions for the 100; yet they were not sure this was the entire explanation of his performances. Emmett Brunson, Wolcott's coach, furthered this opinion among college track coaches by recommending that all hurdlers, short or tall, might well follow certain features of Wolcott's style. Specifically, he advocated Wolcott's habits of (1) decreasing the forward lean and keeping it as close as possible to that of sprinting angles, (2) using the lead leg as in sprinting with no unusually vigorous kick upward, (3) maintaining complete relaxation of the lead leg but with no deliberate whip down off the hurdle ("it should come down naturally as in running"), (4) bringing the trail leg through parallel to the hurdle so that "it never rises over the height that it reaches when it goes over the hurdles", and (5) bringing the rear leg through as quickly as possible so that it is in running position. It will be noted that every action is weighed in terms of its relation to sprinting form. "The perfect hurdle form is the form that can get you over the hurdle and down in running position so that you can use your speed". The writer remembers clearly the silence and later words of slight disdain that followed presentation of such opinions. After all, Wolcott was just a sprinter. What should his coach know about the high art of hurdling?

Then came Dillard, whose scant 5′ 10″ and so-called "imperfect" form could never permit him to be a great hurdler! Yet after winning a heat of the National Collegiate high hurdles in :13.9 in 1947, he won 82 consecutive races, indoors and out, and broke Towns's "human ultimate" record of :13.7 by .1 second. Dillard's first leg was locked at the knee, his body was somewhat twisted over the hurdle, his arm action was wide and relatively uncontrolled, and his body lean was upright after clearing the hurdle. Yet he ran :13.6 and to what avoid now was the beautiful style of Simpson, Thomson,

Beard, Keller, and Towns?

The best answer came in 1948, when, after hitting several hurdles in the final Olympic hurdles trials and thereby failing to qualify in the hurdles, he continued on to make the team in the 100-meter dash and to win the Olympic title in the Olympic record time of :10.3. The stylists and the coaches were completely shaken. After all, the champion is the man who gets there first, with no questions asked as to how or in what manner. Shorter men had greater speed and could more than compensate for their lack of smoothness over the hurdle by their great speed between. Perhaps the additional inches of former champions, which made them look so pretty over the hurdles, were actually a handicap in time and hurdling would become the exclusive possession of reformed or sublimated sprinters.

But Dick Attlesey restored the hurdling world to normalcy and mental soundness. At first there was a certain incredulity when, in May, 1950, at the Fresno relays, Attlesey recorded :13.5. There had been no warning that such a time was within his abilities, and some wondered whether the hot California sun had not quickened the timer's finger muscles as well as those of Attlesey's legs. But their murmurs were permanently stilled when Dick was caught under :14 in 12 different races that same year. Dick was 6′ 3½″ tall, weighed 178 pounds, and, although he seldom ran the distance, had been timed in :10.5 for 100 meters while in Europe. He used a modified two-arms-forward style, an excellent forward lean, a nicely delayed trail leg which snapped forward with remarkable speed, and a very relaxed lead leg which snapped quickly down from the hurdles. These assets combined to give him a hurdle-clearance time of only 2.0 seconds for the 10 hurdles, one of the best performances on record. It can be compared, for example, with that of Dillard, who sprinted the equivalent of :11.3

for 120 yards with a best hurdle time of :13.6. The first substracted from the second gives a clearance time of 2.3 seconds. For other comparisons, Wolcott needed 2.5 seconds; Beard, 2.0 seconds; Towns and Osgood, 1.9 seconds; and Thomson, 2.2 seconds. It should be noted that such times are not completely accurate, for hurdler's true speed is seldom tested.

In summary of this short history of form, it seems clear that man's present form in the high hurdles will not change or improve greatly. Certainly little change has occurred from the forms of Bob Simpson and Earl Thomson 30 years ago. If best sprinting time of :11.3 for 120 yards can be combined with best hurdle-clearance time of :01.8, the record can conceivably drop down as low as :13.1. During the winter of 1952, Attlesey seemed likely to improve upon his previous performances, for he was drilling on faster sprinting and faster action to the first hurdle. However, a serious muscle injury postponed his training and kept him off the 1952 Olympic team.

Dillard returned to his first love, hurdling, in the 1952 games and won the Olympic title (:13.7), again putting the short sprinters in the hurdling throne.

CHARACTERISTICS OF THE HIGH HURDLER

Most high hurdlers are tall boys, or at least have long legs. They should have good flexibility in the rear of the pelvis. Since high school hurdles are shorter (39 inches) than college hurdles (42 inches), shorter boys may be successful in high school—to the discomfort of college coaches, who find that they are often unable to become college hurdlers because of the added hurdle height. Speed is necessary, but hurdling skill is as just as important (with some notable exceptions) for success in the high hurdles.

If a boy is not afraid to smash through a hurdle and will not let a fall discourage him, and he has the other requirements, he should become a good hurdler.

MODERN HURDLING FORM

Correct hurdling form should first be thought of as correct sprinting form. Next, the action to and over the hurdle must be smooth and relaxed. In order to get proper speed, the performer must be on the ground as long as possible, maintain proper balance over the hurdle and land with a good forward lean. This means maintaining continuous leg action from takeoff to landing when going over the hurdle. The knee of the lead leg must not be locked, and the trail leg should be delayed to make the action smooth and continuous. The rapid cutdown of the lead leg and the forward pull of the trail leg are phases of a single action, just as in sprinting, and are essential moves.

As the runner approaches the hurdle, he must have his eyes focused on its top. To go over the hurdle, he should: (1) take off from 6′ 10″ to 7′ 2″ from the hurdle; (2) drive his lead knee forward much as in a sprinting stride (the lower leg and foot are then raised to straighten the leg for hurdle clearance; the knee is not locked, but a relaxed, slightly flexed lead leg is used); (3) thrust the opposite arm forward (not above eye level) to keep the shoulders straight and to insure body lean and balance; (4) use the other arm for balance—like the arm action used in sprinting; (5) bend the upper body at the hips so that, when going over the hurdle, the head is never raised much higher than in proper sprinting; (6) drive the trail knee forward as in sprinting (as the trail leg comes up it is flattened out, so that when the thigh is parallel with the hurdle it forms a right angle with the body); (7) snap the lead leg down so that the heel of the foot will land from 3′ 6″ to 4′ 2″ from the hurdle; (8) snap the trail leg forward and down after a slight delay (the foot of the trail leg must be kept flat over the hurdle with the toes turned slightly up to avoid striking the hurdle; the knee must not be raised too high when coming down over the hurdle); and (9) maintain a forward lean so that the lead foot hits the ground with the weight on the toe and ball of the foot.

To summarize the action over the hurdle:

1. Maintenance of proper body lean, accomplished by proper lead arm action, and proper position of the head and shoulders is paramount. Some hurdlers use a distinct dip of the head while clearing the hurdle to help obtain good forward lean.

2. Delayed action of the trail leg insures the accomplishment of a full leg split, and also enables the performer to have a forward lean at the takeoff. A trail leg horizontal (flat) as it comes off the hurdle will aid the hurdler in keeping a continual forward lean and full leg stride beyond the hurdle.

3. A relaxed trail leg with an accompanying rapid pull-through will help in performing a downward snap of the lead leg. A quick, hard cut-down of the lead leg will bring the lead foot down not more than 4 feet from the hurdle, which will get the hurdler on the ground faster and help him in maintaining proper body lean for the next step.

The start and steps to the first hurdle. This is the area in which many hurdle races are won or lost, and much time and practice must be spent on this phase. Momentum must be gained as quickly as possible, but confidence and proper balance over the hurdle are necessary.

The starting position of the hurdler is like that of the sprinter, but the body is straightened up a little sooner during the first 3 strides from the blocks, and the strides must be adjusted in order to accomplish the best approach to the hurdle.

Most hurdlers take 8 strides to the first hurdle, in which case the same foot that the hurdler will use to lead with over the hurdle will be placed in the back block. However, some taller men use only 7 strides, and therefore place the lead foot on the front block. Any chopping of stride necessary to insure that the hurdler has a proper takeoff must be done in the first 4 strides, so that the hurdler may run with confidence. If his steps are off only a very small amount to the first hurdle, this can be corrected by shifting the blocks a few inches closer or farther apart.

It is very important to make the takeoff from the exact and proper spot each time. If the hurdler is too close to the hurdle, it will take him 3 or 4 hurdles to regain his smooth hurdling form, and by then the opposition will be much nearer the finish tape.

Steps between hurdles. Leading hurdlers today take 3 strides between the hurdles. These strides should be approximately the same length each time to eliminate the tendency to "gallop" between hurdles. A typical stride pattern between hurdles would be: first stride, 6′ 3″; second, 6′ 5″; third 6′ 4″.

Length of the hurdle stride. The length of the hurdle stride (distance over hurdle) has varied from 13′ (8′ + 5′) to 10′2″ (5′9″ + 4′5″). One top hurdler took an 11′6″ (7′ 1″ + 4′ 5″) stride, while another used an 11′ (7′ 2″ + 3′ 10″) stride.

The takeoff spot first used by a beginner should be approximately 7 feet from the hurdle. This distance should be adjusted after the coach observes the hurdler and determines what takeoff distance will be best for him to maintain proper body angle and hurdle clearance.

The most important point in connection with hurdle stride is that if the takeoff spot is too close to the hurdle, the hurdler will be forced to throw his lead leg up straight to clear the hurdle, which, in turn, will straighten up his body and eliminate any chance of his attaining a proper lean.

COMMON ERRORS IN HURDLING TECHNIQUE

The novice may already recognize some phase of hurdling in which errors are likely to occur, but for his guidance those most frequently encountered are pointed out.

1. In the Start

Briefly, any divergence from accepted good form in sprint starting is an error. The possible causes of incorrect starting discussed earlier apply to all hurdle races.

2. In the Strides to the First Hurdle

Evidently if the first few strides are too short, the athlete will be required to overstride the succeeding steps so that he may still reach the barrier with the predetermined number. Stepping out with an overlong stride detracts from good performance because the cadence is too slow.

Since the first 13 or 18 yards of either the high or the low hurdle race closely resembles sprinting from during the corresponding section of sprint races, it can be assumed that the potential errors are quite similar. It is obvious that running in a direction which is not straight toward the hurdle detracts from efficiency. If the approach has been properly run, all spike marks made by the right foot will form a line which is straight and parallel to those made by the left. Difficulties in the length of strides are often eliminated by reversing the position of the feet at the start, adding one step if the take-off too far away, or substracting one step if the take-off is too close to the barrier. If the heel-toe direction of the left foot at the instant of take-off is other than straight forward, the effectiveness of the spring is diminished.

3. In Hurdle Clearance

A ball-heel contact of the left foot is permissible at the instant of take-off, although many good hurdlers believe they need not touch ground with the heel, especially when negotiating the last nine hurdles.

The short-legged hurdler requires a more vigorous spring than the long-legged, timber-topping athlete and may have a greater tendency toward committing errors in the execution of the take-off.

Failure to straighten the take-off completely and to follow immediately with the rock-up on the toe is an obvious fault.

Especially in high hurdling, the premature forward bend of the trunk restricts the upward body lift and frequently leads to displacement of the hurdle because of insufficient elevation of the body. On the contrary, if the trunk is carried in an erect position, the competitor experiences difficulty in raising the rear knee sufficiently high when clearance is made. Again, if an erect trunk carriage is maintained to the cut-down stage, the landing is likely to be jarring or abrupt. Even in the low hurdles in which trunk lean form is the least exacting, a moderate forward bend is desirable. However, a full "buck" or chest-to-knee thrust is decidedly a fault in low hurdling and frequently is detrimental to the high hurdler. Another fault is a failure to take advantage of the action-reaction in the buck and clearance.

Occasionally one sees hurdlers spread both arms to the side and soar or sail over the obstacles. Valuable time is lost both because the clearance is too high and because the malposition of the arms makes impossible their use in aiding forward leg action.

In high hurdling the double arm thrust has not been universally accepted because some hurdlers felt this style did not harmonize with their sense of balance. They contend that a sideward and backward sweep of the right arm helps them retain body poise. Further they point out that, if the right arm is to synchronize with the left leg (which has been back), likewise the right arm should be back. In any hurdling style the arm movement is faulty if it does not aid body balance in addition to providing a stimulus to the legs.

Since the eyes are important in guiding the athlete in his course, any deflection of the vision from straight ahead may detract from good hurdling.

Should the athlete get no relaxation when above the barriers, his running and hurdling forms may become stilted. Furthermore, undue tenseness throughout the early phase of the race may result in his tying-up during the later stages of the contest.

Imbalance is clearly a fault and may be caused by improper sideward action of either or both arms, or by an out-of-line swing of the leading leg.

Should the high hurdlers fail to execute the two right angles with the left leg, thigh and foot, the barrier may be either touched or displaced. The downward training of the left toe necessitates spending energy to lift the entire body higher than otherwise is necessary.

In case the high hurdler fails to whip the left knee and ankle across the obstacle a sufficient distance before lowering the foot, he may bruise the ankle on the barrier. Again he may err in whipping the left knee too far forward before straightening the leg. This error causes either a turning of the body from the direction of the run, or a noncoordinated stepping movement.

Some capable low hurdlers vary the left leg technique by trailing the knee until the torso has cleared the hurdle, then instantaneously snapping it across and forward. Therefore, the delayed whipping across of the take-off leg is not a fault in all cases.

It has been pointed out that the cut-down should be anticipated by starting the downward movement of the leading foot some distance before it reaches the barrier. Undue delay in the cut-down causes a prolonged flight in the air thus detracting from sprinting opportunity. The close cut-down is an obvious but infrequent error.

4. In the Strides Between the Hurdles

The athlete may mar an otherwise creditable performance by faulty stride work between the barriers. Here again, any radical departures from good sprinting form tend to reduce efficiency. Frequently, after the hurdle has been cleared, the athlete plants the left foot too rapidly, without gaining the distance needed in the first full stride. If the first full stride (after the landing foot has touched the ground) is too short, the athlete is required to overstretch the succeeding steps to strike the next take-off spot correctly. A pause or a break in the continuity of movement just as the first stride is started is a fault which occurs frequently. It has been pointed out that unevenness of beat is a fault.

Eyes must be kept to the front even when running between the hurdles.

The corresponding strides between the obstacles should be equal in length.

5. In the Finish of the Hurdles

Improper body balance after clearing the last hurdle

is a frequently occurring fault in the finish of hurdle races. Overanxiety to reach the yarn, causing inaccuracy in timing, is mainly responsible for imbalance.

Misjudging distance from the last hurdle to the finish line has been costly to many hurdlers. This is particularly true with indoor competition in which lack of space prevents the full finish distance.

In summary then, a race free from errors is one in which the competitor darts from his marks like a 50-yard dash champion, clears each obstacle with rhythmic, flawless, mechanical precision, instantaneously returning to his sprinter's form, and vigorously dashes to the finish yarn.

To list each of the innumerable faults in high-hurdling would be unduly repetitious, for exaggeration or neglect of any of the many positive statements already made can be considered a fault. However, a review of the major difficulties may help to clarify what has been said. Such faults include the following :—

1. To misjudge effective speed to the first hurdle. Neither overcaution and uncertainty about hurdle clearance nor exclusive concentration upon gaining momentum should be allowed to influence unduly that speed which will bring most effective results. Constant improvement is the real goal.

2. To allow any of several factors to produce a shortened take-off to the hurdle. A poor forward lean, a jump at the hurdle, a hurried trail leg, and a tense and straight lead leg are all likely to result.

3. To fail to keep all actions of the legs, hips, shoulders, and arms in a straight-forward direction consistent with best sprinting form.

4. To extend the arms forward but to fail to lead the

movement into the hurdle with a full forward lean of the upper trunk. Forward lean throughout the entire clearance is probably the most basic element in correct hurdle form.

5. To fail to lead with the knee in approaching the hurdle. To lead with the foot produces a slow swing from the hips, a locked knee joint, a tense leg, a slowed snap-down of the leg, and a lengthened stride over the hurdle.

6. To jump and thus to hurry the action of the back leg so that, as the body is directly over the hurdle, the trail knee is too far advanced and must delay its action. An unduly high knee and an off-balance landing usually result.

7. To permit the backward action of the lead arm to straighten the body and carry the shoulder back with it. This is probably the most common single cause of imbalance.

8. To chop either the lead or the trail foot down too quickly and thus leave too great a distance for the succeeding strides to cover effectively.

9. To practice constantly over three or more hurdles in a set and rather slow rhythm that becomes difficult to break when in important competition. Rhythm is essential to good hurdling, but only as it contributes to greater speed.

10. To assume that a few weeks per season and a half-dozen runs over three hurdles per day will produce proper hurdling style. Hurdling is a complex skill, requiring endless patience, practice, and persistence.

TRAINING PROGRAM

The potential champion will work 9 or more months a year to develop speed, endurance, flexibility, and hurdling skills.

The fall months should be spent running on the grass (using Fartlek) to develop stamina and endurance. Stretching exercises which include the "hurdle exercise" while sitting should be used. The hurdler should stand to the side of the hurdle many times each day, lay one leg on top of the hurdle, and touch the toe of the other foot with the fingers of both hands. All exercises that will stretch the hamstring muscles and loosen the hips should be used. However, these exercises should be done easily at first to avoid straining these muscles.

Since most of the high hurdlers also run the intermediate hurdles, it is good practice for them to do intensive training work with the 440 men during both preseason and seasonal practice. Low hurdler competitions are primarily outdoors (180 yards) in high school, and at 60 or 70 yards indoors in both high schools and in a relatively low collegiate conferences.

Typical schedules of practice are presented for one week each in early season, midseason, and late season with the objective of meeting hurdler's requirements, such as speed, endurance, and form. Plans are made for athletes who compete in both the high and the low barriers, and variations in procedure are appended for those preparing for the intermediate hurdles.

Early Season

The beginner is advised to start his drills on the turf so that cinder burns may be avoided. He is strongly urged to pad the heels with sponge rubber and likewise to protect the knee and ankle of the take-off leg. A padded top bar or a loosely hinged hurdle reduces the chances for abrasions and bumps. A more elaborate practice hurdle is described by Hillman.

Monday

1. Start with jogging, running and walking alternately for 25 yards of each exercise.

2. Spend two or three minutes on exercises chiefly stretching.

3. Set the starting blocks and take three or four starts without the gun, running 40 yards.

4. Set two 30-inch hurdles 15 yards from the starting line. Space the two hurdles 4 or 5 feet apart, and on their top edge lay a piece of lath so that it is in the same lane as the starting blocks. The more youthful hurdler may substitute a 24-inch barrier.

5. Assume your regular starting position and at full speed courageously sprint toward the obstacle. At the end of the eighth stride raise and extend the right leg in a stepping fashion while pushing off with the left foot. The right leg should not be rigidly extended but instead it should be carried partially bent. When the right foot is 12 inches from the top bar execute a sharp groundward movement of the forward foot. Simultaneously the left knee and foot are rapidly drawn up and across the hurdle in readiness for the first full stride. Repeat three or four times.

6. Set a second barrier (lath or crossbar) 30 inches high 10 yards beyond the first obstacle. Run from the start, clear the first obstacle and take three full strides to the second barrier, stepping over it in a manner similar to that described for the first. Repeat two or three times.

7. Continue the use of a readily displaced lath instead of the regulation hurdle until correct form is achieved. Bruises can be eliminated and confidence in oneself gained by this procedure. Add a third barrier 30 inches high, placed 10 yards beyond the second obstacle. Run at top speed, taking eight strides to the

first barrier as before and three strides between the succeeding obstacles.

8. Complete the day's practice with a jog of 300 yards, a tepid shower, and a massage. Record body weight before and after each day's activity.

Tuesday

1. Begin the work with two or three minutes of stationary running, 200 yards of jogging, and 25 yards of running at seven-eighths effort.

2. Execute from three to five minutes of stretching exercises such as the trunk bend, touching the fingers to the ground while keeping the knees rigid, swinging the legs forward and backward and kicking high with alternate legs.

3. Set three obstacles 36 inches high at 15 yards, 25 yards, and 35 yards, respectively, from the starting line. Again use lath or crossbars as substitutes for hurdles. Employ the technique at the top speed over the three barriers. Follow the description of hurdling technique and aim to execute perfect form. Repeat two or three times, always at top speed. The younger hurdler may advance from the 24-inch to the 30-inch barrier.

4. Add two or more barriers as proficiency is attained, until a total of ten are set in the 120-yard course. Run the entire distance two or three times.

5. Join the jumpers and take three or four trials each of the standing broad jump and the running broad jump.

6. End the day's practice with two minutes of the stretching exercises and a 300-yard jog. Take a tepid shower, and follow with a massage.

Wednesday

1. Commence with two or three minutes of bounding,

jogging and running.

2. Execute 20 seconds of inverted hurdling. This exercise is performed by (1) lying on the back and extending the legs, thighs, and trunk upward until the weight of the body rests on the shoulders. Steadinessd in this upright position is maintained by placing the hands on the hips and resting the elbows on the ground. Inverted running is accomplished by moving the legs as in bicycle pedaling. Inverted hurdling requires, first, eight running steps (the eight approach strides). (2) On the ninth stride the left foot, leg, and thigh are dropped into a position of two right angles. (3) The sprinting action between barriers is accomplished by striding out with the left foot (first full stride) then the right (second full stride) and next the left (third full stride). On the fourth stride (taken with the right leg) the left thigh, leg and foot are again dropped so as to form two right angles in the same manner described for hurdle number one. The novice will readily understand that he may simulate the entire hurdle race by performing inverted hurdling. He may count aloud or to himself "one", "two", "three" "A- N- D"; "one", "two", "three" "A- N- D". The above inverted high hurdling exercise may be modified as a drill for the low hurdles by using 10 counts for the approach, "A- N- D" for the clearance, seven counts between the barriers, with the eighth count or "A- N- D" for the clearance of the second and all succeeding hurdles. The beginner will note that the 20 seconds effort represents more than 120 yards of high hurdling and more than 150 yards of low hurdling.

3. Join the jumpers and take three or four trials of the running high jump.

4. Place three or four 39-inch (42-inch for college) hurdles at the regulation distance from the starting line and run through at full effort. Repeat two or three times.

5. Set three or four low hurdles for either the 200-yard lows or the 220-yard lows and hurdle then at full speed. Repeat once or twice.

6. Complete the day's practice with a jog of 350 yards, followed by a tepid shower and a massage.

Thursday

1. Begin the workout by jogging 300 yards, walking 100 yards, bounding 50 yards, and sprinting 25 yards. Spend two or three minutes performing pull-ups on the high bar and dips on the parallel brs.
2. Sit on the ground in a position similar to that assumed when clearing a high hurdle. Vigorously throw the trunk forward so that the chest touches the thigh. Simultaneously the left arm is swung well forward, and the right arm is partially thrust to the front. At the same time the left toe is raised upward. Next swing the trunk upward and repeat the exercise four or five times so that the above movements are speedily coordinated. Be cautious of undue strain when practicing this stunt the first time.
3. Set six high hurdles and step them at full effort. Walk or rest for 10 minutes and repeat. Four-hundred-meter intermediate hurdlers will substitute six 36-inch barriers and rest 20 minutes before repeating.
4. Assume the same sitting position. Call on another hurdler to sit in a similar manner directly in front, so that the right foot of each athlete touches the left knee of his teammate. Extend the clasp left hands. Seesaw back and forth (pull and be pulled) to stretch the muscles of the trunk and thigh. Simultaneously with each forward bend of the trunk raise the left toe. Caution is advised so that

exceptional strain is avoided. Take but three or four trials, rest a few minutes and repeat two or three times. Even though the action seems unnatural, reverse the position of the feet (left leg forward) and repeat the exercises for the purpose of symmetrical body development. In later discussions this exercise will be referred to as "mat hurdling" because this practice is frequently taken on gymnasium mats.

5. Place six low hurdles in their proper position and take them at top speed. Rest 15 minutes. Repeat once.

6. Conclude the day's work with two minutes of hopping and bounding followed by running 330 yards at seven-eighths effort. Again conclude with a tepid shower and a massage.

Friday

1. Prepare for practice with rope skipping, bounding, and jogging.

2. Join the sprinters and take two starts without the gun, then three starts with the gun, running 30 yards in each case.

3. Set one high hurdle 15 yards from the starting line and place the finish yarn 15 yards beyond the hurdle. Take two starts with the gun and at full effort, clear the barrier, and sprint for the yarn. Bear in mind the faults incident to this phase of the race, namely, undue haste in the cut-down, imbalance, and improper carriage of head and eyes. Note the number of full strides taken between the last hurdle and the finish line. Substitute the 36-inch or 30-inch hurdle for the high barrier, place them at the official distance, and repeat the procedure.

4. Place two or three high hurdles at regulation

distances. On the top bar of each hurdle set two 1-inch blocks of wood, each 3 inches from the end of the bar. Take a start with the gun and clear all the obstacles at full effort. Repeat three or four times. Some high hurdlers believe their clearance height is correct if the blocks are displaced and the top bar is not touched. The novice will bear in mind that a slightly higher clearance is a permissible deviation for beginners. The beginning hurdler will recall that the intermediate and the low hurdles are not closely skimmed in the same manner as are the higher obstacles.

5. Prepare for trials the following day (Saturday) over the full distance in your chosen events. End the practice with two or three minutes of stretching exercises followed by a jog of 440 yards. Substitute a sponge bath for the customary shower.

Saturday

1. Warm up in a manner designed to put you in physical and mental readiness for competition. A typical warm-up includes (a) a jog of 350 yards, (b) a walk of 100 yards, (c) one or two minutes of leg and trunk stretching exercises on the hurdle, (d) one or two minutes of push-ups and dips), (e) two sprints of 30 yards at gradually increasing speed, (f) two top-speed trials over one hurdle, (g) two top-speed trials over three to five hurdles.

2. Reassure yourself of heel, ankle, and knee protection so that you can take the obstacles fearlessly.

3. In case your hurdling teammates provide insufficient competition for you, station in the adjoining lane a moderately proficient runner who will sprint the distance without stepping the barriers.

4. Set the starting blocks and make adjustments for the 120-yard high hurdles. Run a time trial the complete distance at full effort. Keep moving after the trial and retain body warmth. Rest 20 minutes.
5. Set a full lane of low hurdles and run a time trial. Sometimes an athlete is aided by giving a teammate a 5-yard handicap. Four-hundred-meter intermediate hurdlers may run but one trial over the full distance and omit the high and the low obstacles.
6. End this week in early season with two or three minutes of calisthenics, a jog of 350 yards, a shower, and a massage. Record the body weight and study your weekly fluctuations.

Midseason

Practice workouts are outlined on the assumption that the athlete is competing in two hurdle events. In case he is engaged in high school competition the events are the 120-yard high hurdles and the 200-yard low hurdles. For the athlete of collegiate grade the races planned for are the 120-yard high hurdles and the 220-yard low hurdles. Variations are indicated where the competitor is called upon to prepare for the 400-meter or 440-yard intermediate contest. Alterations may further be required should the athlete participate in events besides the hurdles.

Monday

1. Begin the day with a jog of 300 yards, a walk of 50 yards, a run of 100 yards, and a sprint of 25 yards.
2. Spend four or five minutes on stretching exercises such as (a) laying the front (right) leg on the top of the hurdle and bending the trunk forward and backward; (b) placing the rear (left) knee atop the

hurdle, forming two right angles as in hurdle clearance, and dipping the trunk forward until the hands touch the ground; and (c) assuming position (b) and extending the arms through the lower crossbars of the obstacles until the hands touch the ground.

3. Stand at the side of the hurdle with the weight resting on the right foot. Lift the left leg to form two right angles and practice whipping the leg across the barrier. Simultaneously rise up on the ball of the right foot to obtain sufficient clearance. Repeat from twelve to fifteen times.

4. Review the correct and incorrect execution of the various phases of hurdle racing as exemplified in the last contest. Set about eliminating faults in form.

5. Take two trials over four high hurdles at top speed, using a gun at the start and a finish line 15 yards from the last hurdle. Note carefully the distance and speed of the approach, the form in hurdle clearance, the evenness of strides between obstacles, and the transformation from hurdling to sprinting in the last 15 yards of the race. Any speed other than full effort alters the timing of hurdle execution. Therefore, whenever less strenuous work is desired, reduce the number of hurdles cleared, or the number of trials taken.

6. Hold yourself in readiness for a time trial over ten high, ten low, or ten intermediate hurdles on the following day (Tuesday).

7. Run over four low hurdles at top speed, and refer to item 5 above for the objectives of this section of the schedule.

8. Take the three or four trials of the running high jump.

9. Finish the day with a jog of 350 yards followed by a sponge bath and a massage is such manipulation has proved beneficial.

Tuesday

1. Warm up as you would for an important competition, keeping your routine definite and fixed once you have determined the type most effective for your races. Extremely strenuous stretching exercises are not recommended on days of either time trials or competition.

2. Run a time trial over ten high hurdles. Compare with the times previously recorded for like distance. Better progress is made by concentrating both mentally and physically on one good practice race rather than by running indifferently through two or three trials.

3. Rest 30 minutes (note the competition day time schedule for the interval between races) and run a time trial over ten low hurdles. If on Saturday low hurdles are contested around a curve, hurdles should be placed similarly in Tuesday's trial. Note carefully the type of warm-up which best suits you for the second race. Ordinarily if body warmth has been retained after running the high hurdles, easy jogging, light calisthenics, and two trials over two or three low hurdles should suffice.

4. Avoid cooling off too quickly by walking and jogging.

5. Dry off perspiration, and, the weather permitting, expose the body to the sun for ten minutes.

6. In case the competitor is preparing for the 400-meter intermediate hurdles substitute one time trial over the full 400-meter distance for the two time trials over the shorter distance. Hurdling drills with both the 42-inch and the 30-inch obstacles are beneficial to the

athlete competing in the 400-meter hurdle race. Have a stop watch held so that time can be read at the 200-meter mark, which is half the distance. The 400-meter hurdle chart depicts a method of running the distance wherein the competitor takes 24 strides to the first barrier, 15 strides between obstacles until the seventh is reached, when he shortens to 17 steps between the last three hurdles. Some good athletes reduce the number of approach strides to 23 and a few taller competitors take but 22. Whenever a competitor utilize the greater number of approach strides, he is able to run in a faster cadence. In addition, he conserves that type of muscular exertion required between barriers, namely, the reaching, or long striding type of leg action. Should the novice encounter difficulty in maintaining 15 strides to the seventh obstacle, he may rightfully shift to 17 strides somewhat sooner. Above all, the running should be even an rhythmical. On the other hand, he may carry 15 strides beyond the seventh obstacle, ultimately gaining ability to carry the 15 strides between all ten hurdles.

7. Finish this, the most strenuous practice day in midseason, with two or three minutes of trunk exercise and a jog of 440 yards. It should be noted, however, that some authorities believe that full distance time trials are too strenuous. They vary the above procedure by running trials over but 7 hurdles on Tuesday.

Wednesday

1. Begin the practice with a warm-up consisting of jogging, rope skipping, squatting, stretching, and running.

2. Join the sprinters and take two or three starts with the gun, going 35 to 40 yards.

3. Perform 20 seconds of inverted hurdling. Repeat twice.

4. Select a teammate, assume the mat hurdling position on the grass and execute 30 seconds of cross-hand bending forward and backward.

5. Vary the procedure by setting the hurdles on the grass but spaced the regulation distance. Take one or two trials over four high hurdles. Rest five minutes. Take two or three trials over three low hurdles. For the 400-meter hurdles, substitute two trials over four hurdles with a ten-minute rest between trials.

6. In case the low hurdles are to be contested around a curve and on a straightaway rather than completely on the straightaway, that portion of the low hurdle schedule in item 5 may well be transferred to the curved portion of the track. Many authorities claim that when running low hurdles counter-clockwise around a curve the competitor who takes off with the right foot (extends the left foot forward) is able to execute a more efficient clearance. It is conceivable that this smoother technique permits shorter running time around the curve.

7. Complete Wednesday's routine with 200 yards at seven-eights effort, resting five minutes, and jogging 300 yards easily.

Thursday

The schedule for Thursday is formulated on the assumption that there is no competition until Saturday. If the calendar calls for competition or trials on Friday, only moderate limbering work should be taken on Thursday. Furthermore, the practice presented for Wednesday should be reduced in both amount and intensity.

Many coaches look upon Thursday's practice in midseason and late season as an optional workout day. The athlete is given leeway in selecting both the type and quantity of physical activity. Coaches frequently judge the morale, tone, and spirit of their track men by the rest and enthusiasm exhibited in Thursday's practice. To be sure, excess activity or engaging in hazardous stunts is out of order on this midseason day.

1. Start the workout with jogging, running, and short distance sprinting.

2. Perform from five to ten minutes of exercises optional to the competitor, such as single and double leg squat, high kicking, trunk bending and twisting, and tumbling.

3. Take a sun bath of ten minutes if the weather permits.

4. Vary the practice activities by participating for a period of ten minutes in stunts or games: forward passing a football for distance, hand or Indian wrestling, tug of war, medicine ball tossing (eliminate from the circle each individual as he fails to catch the ball when tossed at him), or a contest of walking on the hands over a 5-yard course.

5. End the workout by a jog of 440 yards followed by a shower and massage.

6. It should be noted that Thursday schedule is based on the assumption that there are no trial heats run Friday. Obviously Thursday's practice should be reduced to limbering up or should be eliminated entirely in case trial heats are required on Friday.

Friday

1. Take inventory of your personal equipment to make sure than all is in readiness for Saturday's competition.

2. Consult the coach regarding Friday's routine, which may call for complete absence from athletics, or may require suiting up and taking light exercise.

3. Without undue fretting or worrying, outline a plan of attack for use in case the weather becomes rainy or windy. A rain-soaked track may require adjustments of spike lengths. A strong wind may necessitate alteration of striding effort, depending on whether the breeze is from the front, the side, or the back.

4. If your Friday plan call for dressing in athletic garments, limber up, inspect the track layout, and conclude with a sponge bath and massage.

5. Forget the coming contest and divert the attention from athletics by studying, reading, or attending an entertainment selected with the objective of relaxation.

Saturday

1. Warm up with a definite type and amount of exercise, knowledge of which has been gained from previous competition. Refer to hurdles, early season, Saturday, for warm-up suggestions. Time the warm-up so that the peak of your finer physical and mental adjustments coincides with the start of your event. This requires a knowledge of the time schedule as well as the number of your heat and lane. Since ordinarily the high hurdles are contested before the low hurdles, the first consideration is preparation for the former event. In case trial heats are necessary, make no mistake in careless form or loafing merely because it is not a final race.

2. Steel yourself for a supreme effort and with confidence and determination run the high hurdles.

3. Regain composure while walking or jogging for a few minutes. Retain body glow by putting on additional clothing. Rest and relax while awaiting your next competition.

4. Warm up for the low hurdles, bearing in mind that a short but speedy warm-up is required rather than a

slow one of long duration, unless the weather is cold.

5. Adjust yourself for the low hurdles and run the race at 101 per cent of your best effort.

6. Should the athlete compete in the 400-meter intermediate hurdles, he quite likely will omit either or both the high and the low hurdles. The discussion of the warm-up and the adjustments for high and low hurdles applies as well to the intermediate hurdler.

7. End this competition day with a jog of 250 yards, followed by a tepid shower and a massage. Analyse the week's fluctuations in the body weight.

Late Season

In last season the most important contests of the year are scheduled, and ordinarily, the large number of competitors necessitates trial heats on Friday. In midseason, competition usually requires but one day (Saturday), but occasionally two days are needed. With this in view the hurdler must be prepared to compete two days in succession. He may be satisfied with merely qualifying on Friday for the final race, but he will remember that easing up or "running under wraps" in hurdle races is quite different from coasting through a preliminary heat in the sprints. Reduction in speed or effort by the hurdler alters the finer adjustments of spring, clearance, and cut-down. These alterations may result in either striking an obstacle or striding unevenly.

In the preliminary heats in the 120-yard high hurdles very little effort is conserved by taking things easy. Therefore the novice is urged to run the trial heat at full effort. In the low hurdles, the competitor may hold something in reserve by covering the approach and the space between barriers at his best effort, but he may rightfully prolong the short interval of relaxation when atop each low hurdle. Again, he may carry through from the last hurdle to the finish line without "tapping bottom", or summoning all his sprinting ability.

The 400-meter intermediate hurdler who is called upon to run a trial heat on Friday has a more difficult problem in conserving strength than does the high or low hurdler. In case he take things easy during his approach to barrier number 1, his rivals may gain an advantage which will be difficult to overcome. Since this contest is usually run in lanes from a staggered start, he frequently is not aware of his position among the competitors until the head of the home stretch is reached. Therefore he cannot take chances of saving too much effort. In trial heats the competitor may hold something in reserve even though he runs the approach and the distance between hurdles with optimum effort. He may prolong the period of rest or relaxation over each obstacle, similar to the moment of relaxation over the low hurdles.

Some intermediate hurdlers in their trial heats substitute 17 strides for the customary 15 strides between obstacles, on the theory that the shortened stride plan is less fatiguing. In the final race they resume the stride action previously found most effective. The novice is advised to retain his customary stride plan in both the preliminary and final races. This is done on the theory that considerable drill is necessary to gain the ability to make stride adjustments quickly. Between the last obstacle and the finish line (a distance of 40 meters) the intermediate hurdler may adjust his expenditure of energy to meet the conditions of the trial heat.

With the Friday and Saturday competition in mind, the most stenuous workouts are scheduled for Tuesday to allow a two-day period of toning up for the week end.

In the schedule presented, the Tuesday time trials at

full effort call for the use of but seven barriers for the high, the low, and the intermediate hurdles. Seven was decided upon because the distance is sufficiently long to call for a test of both form and endurance. The last three of the ten hurdles are omitted to conserve energy and to help retain a competition edge.

A further variation in the practice indicated for Tuesday in late season calls for reducing the number of hurdles to five in each the high, the low, and the intermediate events. This schedule fits the individual who thrives on short, explosive time trials and who competes better by omitting during late season those workouts necessitate tests of hurdling endurance.

On the other extreme are those who perform better by running time trials over the entire ten-hurdle course. However, these are the exceptional rather than the ordinary athletes.

Earlier in the discussion the novice was advised to experiment with a reversed position of the feet at the start of the race so that he would be in readiness either to add one stride or to substract one stride in the approach. After midseason and some late season experience he may find that a change in the number of approach strides is desirable. This suggestion is an exception to customary late season advice, wherein the athlete is urged to refrain from "shopping around" in search of new styles of hurdle execution. The change in form is justified if the athlete has not "arrived", so to speak, until late season.

The competitor was urged to reverse the position of the feet at the start rather than to reverse the position of the feet when taking off for the hurdle, because the lesser inconvenience is experienced by making but one adjustment at the start rather than 10 adjustments over the hurdles.

Monday

1. Initiate the practice with the customary jogging, walking, running, and sprinting activities.

2. Take four or five trials of the running high jump at gradually increasing heights.

3. Join the sprinters in executing two or three exchanges of the baton.

4. Set the sixth to the tenth high hurdles, inclusive, in their regular stations. Assume your position at the starting line and, starting with a gun, sprint at full effort the 65 yards to the first obstacle, clearing it and the remaining four barriers. Repeat once or twice. This drill has been found effective when emphasizing maintenance of form over the last four or five barriers.

5. Set the sixth to the tenth low hurdles, inclusive, in their regular stations. Sprint at nine-tenths effort to the sixth obstacle, clearing it and the remaining four barriers. Similar to item 3, this exercise is pointed toward form drill in the face of oncoming fatigue. Once trial only may be sufficient for Monday's endurance work because of time trials Tuesday.

6. In case the 400-meter intermediate hurdles, instead of the high and low hurdles, are to be run, set the last five intermediate barriers in a manner similar to that described above. Run on the flat to the sixth barrier at a speed approximating that reached in the first half of a quarter-mile race. Stride the sixth and the succeeding hurdles at optimum effort. This may serve as a drill for the execution of 15 strides between obstacles. If you aim to emphasize the time trial on Tuesday more than the drill on Monday, you may run the flat section (220 meters) at a reduced speed, say two-thirds effort, but stride the five barriers at optimum speed.

7. Terminate Monday's late season practice with a

jog of 440 yards followed by a sponge bath.

Tuesday

1. Begin the day's practice with jogging, bounding, and running exercises.

2. Spend three or four minutes on stretching exercises such as high kicking, running hitch kicking, and mat hurdling stunts. A trainer of wide experience claims that hurdlers are not so susceptible to pulled leg muscles as are sprinters. He believes that the stretching exercises taken by the hurdler prepare the hamstring muscle group for strenuous effort.

3. Prepare for a time trial by completing your usual precompetition warm-up routine.

4. Set seven high hurdles at regulation distance brush the track so that the spike marks are visible and run the 90 yards at full effort.

5. While recuperating, study the distance covered on each stride in the approach, the cut-down, and the finish.

6. After a fifteen-minute rest, set seven low hurdles in proper position, brush the track again, and run this reduced course at top speed.

7. Study the stride action as shown by the visible spike marks, and make the adjustments which appear necessary.

8. Substitute seven intermediate hurdles for either or both the high or low barriers and run a time trial over a 300-meter distance. Study the length of stride.

9. Variations in the distance for each time trial have been previously pointed out. There are individuals who compete better by running the full ten hurdles in each races, while others prepare to better advantage by covering but five barriers in each the high, the low, and the intermediate hurdles.

10. End Tuesday's workout, the most strenuous in late season, by a run of from 300 yards to 440 yards at seven-eighths effort, designed to develop endurance. If speed is to be stressed, substitute 220 yards at nine-tenths effort.

Wednesday

1. Begin the day's work with three or four minutes of easy jogging.

2. Expose the body to the sun for a period of ten to fifteen minutes.

3. Join the sprinters and set one high hurdle in your lane 15 yards from the starting line. Take two or three starts with the gun, clearing the obstacle but paying no attention to the sprinters to the left and to the right. Add two or three hurdles and continue the drill so that you will habitually maintain the focus of the eyes on your own lane. In the final heat of the 110-meter high hurdles in the Tenth Olympic Games several of the competitors displaced their barriers apparently because their attention was diverted from their own race. Possibly the clattering sound made by the first fallen hurdle caused them to shift their vision to ascertain what was going on. This shift even though slight brought about improper variations in form, thus causing them to strike the hurdles.

4. Participate for five or ten minutes on some other track and field event which can have no detrimental effect on your hurdling efficiency.

5. The low hurdler or intermediate hurdler may substitute the 30-inch or 36-inch obstacle in taking the drill.

6. In midseason the low hurdler may have been called upon to run 440 yards in the one-mile relay but the advent of a higher caliber competition during late season

may require that he discontinue this. However, the endurance gained from the quarter-mile running should be highly valuable in running both the low and the intermediate hurdles.

7. Transfer your tapering-off jog of 350 yards to the grass in case the cinder track becomes hard and dry.

Thursday

This day's practice is arranged on the assumption that there are to be preliminary heats on Friday. In case there are no preliminary heats the hurdler may follow the schedule outlined for Thursday in midseason.

1. Limber up lightly, inspect the track layout, and plan your activities for the remainder of the week.

2. Spend five minutes on exercises of your own choice, which are light in intensity.

3. Terminate the practice with a jog of 220 yards, a sponge bath, and massage.

Friday

1. In case you are competing in preliminary heats, begin the practice gradually, and warm up so that the peak of your physical and mental condition coincides with the time of the start of your first race.

2. If you are sufficiently sure of your hurdle clearance and have been wearing knee and ankle pads, remove them if you are unduly conscious of their attachment.

3. Adjust yourself for your trial heat in the high hurdles and run at full effort with your attention fully fixed on your own race.

4. Retain your body glow while walking or jogging to regain composure. Dry off perspiration and keep free from extremes of heat or cold.

5. Warm up for the low hurdles. Run the trial heat in the low hurdles depending upon your rating in the field of competitors. In case you are confident that you do not need to "tap bottom", methods have been described in the midseason schedule of practice for conserving effort. However, the smart athlete does not permit himself to get caught napping by opponents of unknown ability.

6. Should the athlete omit both the high and the low and run the intermediate hurdles instead, he will first ascertain the exact time schedule, adjust his warm-up to meet it and run the trial on a well-ordered plan. He should know the ability of the individuals in his heat and exact number of qualifiers, and he should determine whether he is required to exert optimum effort all the way or whether he can prolong the relaxation over the hurdles and ease up between the last obstacles and the finish line.

7. End the day for qualifying heats by an easy jog on the grass followed by a sponge bath. Avoid a debilitating hot shower.

Saturday

1. Prepare for the most important day of competition by following your well-defined procedure.

2. Adjust yourself mentally for the start of the high hurdles. Think of your opponents simply as aids or stimuli in establishing your best competitive mark. By this time the admonition regarding the fixation of both the attention and the vision should not be needed since proper habits will have taken care of it automatically.

3. Take your position at the starting marks and with a clear-cut pattern of what you expect to do, run the high hurdles at 101 per cent of your best previous effort.

4. Keep moving until partially recovered, dry the body, and stay of the feet until the time to start your warm-up

for the low hurdles. Calisthenics and stretching exercises at this time are not recommended.

5. Again put yourself in the most effective physical and mental poise and run the low hurdles at optimum effort.

6. In case the 400-meter hurdles are substituted for the high and the low hurdles, proceed with the customary warm-up and adjustments for the start of the race. Run the 400-meter hurdles, having in mind that these differ from the high and the low hurdles in that more strength must be kept in reserve during the early stages of the contest. In case the race is run in the usual manner around an oval track, in lanes, with each competitor staggered at the start, judgment of pace is highly important and you must know how fast your are travelling the first half of the race. Better yet, you should know the elapsed time at the 100-meter and the 300-meter marks.

7. Terminate the day with a light joy, sponge bath, and massage. Review the changes in body weight.

HELPFUL HINTS

1. Work with the sprinters at least twice a week to attain speed.

2. Exercise to loosen the hips and leg muscles almost every day for 2 months prior to season's opening meet in order to obtain flexibility.

3. Help avoid injury by using flip board on hurdle (3-inch stride of wood hinged to the top of the hurdle that will flip down when hit) during early season practice.

4. Work often over 1 hurdle to help perfect the step to the first hurdle and to gain speed of leg action.

5. Avoid using 5 steps between hurdles during practice except on occasions when running at ½ speed.

But habits of taking off too close to the hurdle and using an improper body lean may be developed from this procedure.

6. Work over 3 hurdles at near top speed. This can be done many times without fatigue.

7. Be sure the takeoff is not too close to the hurdle.

8. Have no fear of the hurdle; be tough.

9. Maintain the action of the legs, arms, shoulders, and hips in a straight forward direction, as in sprinting.

10. Lead the movement into the hurdle with a full forward lean of the upper trunk. The head during the race should maintain the same level as when sprinting.

11. Be sure to lead with the knee when approaching the hurdle. The leg is straightened out about 2 feet away from the hurdle.

12. Do not hurry the action of the trial leg until on top of the hurdle.

13. Do not lock the knee of the lead leg.

14. The action of the lead arm must not come back so far as to make the shoulders turn to one side.

Essentials of Correct Form

Hurdling action is sprinting action. Correct form in high hurdling duplicates as closely as possible the basic movements of sprinting action. This statement cannot be overemphasized and should be the deciding element in all arguments over the right form for any given individual. To consider the rhythm of a single hurdle to be three strides and a jump is unsound, for it is actually four strides, one of which is merely longer and accentuated in its actions. Speed in the hurdles, as in the sprints, comes through properly balanced contact with the ground so that, assuming control and balance as the landing is made, the best form is the one that spends a minimum length of time in the air. Such details of form as the body angle at the take-off forward body lean over the hurdle, the snap down of the lead leg, or the delayed but quick pull through of the trial leg must be judged on the basis of how they aid the action back to the ground and still give poise and quickness to the succeeding strides.

There are not two types of hurdlers, as some coaches claim. There is not the short type to be contrasted with the tall, smooth hurdling type. There are actually only individual hurdlers, having individual ways of performance. Lloyd Duff was only 5′ 11″ tall, yet he hurdled like Percy Beard, 6′ 5″ or Bob Simpson, 6′ 3″. George Saling, the 1932 Olympic champion, was 6′ 3″ tall, yet his form was closer to that of Dillard, 5′10″, than to that of his taller competitors. Height and speed of action will certainly affect form, but the effect will be determined by individual coaching and individual efforts rather than by the narrow restrictions of type.

Other things being equal, the taller man should be more economical in his clearance form, should require less change from his normal sprinting action, and should get back to earth quicker. He does not need to lift his hips and upper body very much, if at all, and therefore can concentrate on a forward lean into the hurdle, which is so essential to best form and time. It is clearly no coincidence that, of the hurdlers who have bettered :14 flat, only Duff and Dillard have been less than 6′ tall. Yet the short hurdler, through the greater speed of action he has naturally as well as through the greater flexibility of the hips that he can acquire, can offset these advantages and perfect just as sound a style as the tall man.

The importance of continuous action. A further basic point in correct form lies in maintaining continuous leg action from take-off to landing. There can be no locking of the lead leg knee with its delayed cut down beyond the hurdle. There can be no hurried jump with the trial leg with a later hesitation until balance is achieved. As in sprinting, the flow of action in approaching and clearing a hurdle is continuous and consistently fast. Attlesey has denied that he made a conscious effort to cut his lead leg down from the hurdle; yet his excellent forward balance and complete relaxation while over the hurdle forced a quick landing of the lead foot just the same. Nor was he aware of delaying his trail leg as it left the ground; yet, again, his fine forward lean and full striding action with no trace of jump produced the same result. Actually, the cut-down of the lead leg and the forward pull of the trail leg are merely phases of a single action, just as in sprinting the forward pull of the right leg and the driving push of the left foot are phase of a single stride. This concept is tremendously important. It demands complete relaxation and a perfect synchronization of all parts of the body throughout the movement. A locked front knee, a tense arm which pulls the shoulder around and out of balance, or a landing in which the centre of gravity is delayed for an instant behind the lead foot will each destroy poise and momentum.

Action to and over the hurdle. Hurdle form can be properly viewed from two standpoints: directly in front of the hurdle and 10 to 15 yards to the side. When a front view is attempted, the hurdle should be so placed that one-third of its width projects over a lane line. Both the observer and the athlete can then note the extend to which all actions are in a straight forward plane. The lead leg should rise and fall exactly on such a line. May men have a tendency to swing the leg outward in a counterclockwise direction for a right lead leg as it rises, then inward as it lowers to an out-of-line and off-balance position that ruins hurdling form. Sometimes the foot will land as much as 6 inches away from the line.

The coach can next study the head and shoulder level as the hurdle is taken. By sighting along an outstretched arm and hand or against the line of a building, he can note the extent to which the head rises or falls. The head should never be raised higher off the ground when over the hurdle than when only sprinting. To do so is a certain indication of jumping the hurdle, of probably taking off too close, and of failing to achieve a full forward lean from the hips. If the observer were to hold a cardboard in front of his own eyes in such a way as to cut off all view of the hurdler except for the top of his head, he should have difficulty in telling when the hurdle is cleared.

A third observation might well be concerned with the arm and hand placement. Whether a single- or double-arm thrust is used, the actions should be in a forward line throughout, with as little lateral movement as possible. Certainly the backward action of the lead arm—that is, the arm opposite the lead leg—should never draw its shoulder up and around as the trail leg comes through. This is probably the most common and disastrous fault in hurdling. Great hurdlers, such as George Saling of Iowa, the 1932 Olympic champion, have had marked lateral action of the arm, but so long as the forward lean of the shoulder was unaffected, comparatively little harm was done. Insofar as the length of the torso permits, the elbow of the lead arm should be kept in close to the body, where its action most closely compares with that of sprinting. It must never swing around out of sight behind the body, for again its off-balance will throw the entire hurdling action out of line. In most cases, where the elbow or entire arm are wide, or where they twist the body, the primary cause will be found in lack of flexibility around the hips.

While still in front of the hurdle, the coach may well observe the action of the trail leg. Hurdles having but one cross-bar will permit him to view the extent to which the trail foot comes straight from the ground, in a movement as nearly identical as possible to that of sprinting. A toeing-out of the foot will produce a twist of the hips and a less powerful action. As the thigh of the trail leg rises parallel with the hurdle, it should form very close to a right angle with the body. To fail in this implies again that increased exercises for hip flexibility are in order.

An observant coach will also watch the movement of the trail leg as it descends from the hurdle. Many hurdlers, some good and some otherwise, attempt a full stride off the hurdle by raising the knee and dropping the lower leg rapidly. This has a tendency to straighten the body, to delay contact with the ground, and to produce a heel landing, which jars against forward momentum. A better method is to maintain the height of the trail foot until well over the hurdle and then to swing knee and foot naturally and together in a normal sprinting action. Dillard's 5′ 10″ may have forced just such an extreme effort for length of stride, but one wonders whether he did not lose more in balance and momentum than he gained in position toward the next hurdle.

A final observation will watch the centre of gravity as the full weight of the body falls on the lead foot. If it is far over on the foot, time will be lost in shifting the weight to the centre line. Again, the fault probably lies in hips that are too stiff. And again, the criterior is sprinting action, in which the weight is well balanced between the two feet.

The coach will also wish to stand well to the side of the hurdle, where even numerous details can be seen.

Quite naturally, he will first check on the approach to the hurdle. Brushing the track provides the most accurate measure of the point of take-off. Probably the most basic and common fault among beginning hurdlers is to get too close to the hurdle at the take-off and to land too far beyond it. A more distant take-off—at least 6½ feet away—has several advantages: (1) it permits a lower take-off angle, with a quicker landing, (2) it encourages a more extreme forward lean into the hurdle, (3) it provides time in which the lead knee and foot can be raised higher than the hurdle before reaching its plane and thus the downward swing can be started earlier, and (4) it usually prevents the jumping action so abhorred by best coaches and hurdlers.

Actually, hurdlers vary in this detail without too much regard for height or even speed of action. Apparently, Dillard (5′ 10″) took off farthest away of the best hurdlers, varying from 7′ 5″ to 8′ even. Lloyd Duff of Ohio State (5′ 11″) needed 6′ 1″; Sherwood Finlay of Yale (6′ 3½″) used 5′ 9″; Ed Dugger of Tufts (6′ 4″) took off from 7′ 4″; and Dick Attlesey used 7′ ½″. Certainly no pattern of relationship between height and length of stride can be seen here. Rather, the coach should emphasize the four advantages of a distant take-off just mentioned. Is there plenty of space for a free swing of the lead foot above the hurdle? It the hurdle far enough away to permit a full forward body lean at a low take-off angle? Is there freedom for a full striding action rather than an upward and hurried jump? Within the answers to these questions lies the exact distance of the foot placement for the take-off.

The coach will next probably shift his attention to the forward lean of the body. Herein lies the real key to both arm and leg action. The good hurdler will drive forward and incidentally up, rather than up and forward. If the forward lean is sufficient and smoothly done, if it is maintained throughout the entire clearance action and on into the sprint strides between the hurdles, and if it holds the shoulders and hips consistently parallel with the hurdle, the details of arm action and even leg action will be of lesser importance. To be effective, it must be forward enough so that the body almost touches the thigh of the lead leg, and thus requires great suppleness of the hip and leg muscles and tendons. With such a lean, poor arm action in both the forward thrust and the backward pull can be present without destroying the over-all excellent body balance.

However, forward lean is aided by correct and co-ordinated arm action. The summary of form development has indicated differences of opinion as to whether a single-arm or double-arm action is best. It can be argued that a single-arm movement in which the hand of the lead arm is thrust to or even beyond the heel of the lead foot and off arm simply moves in a short circle near the hip is much closer to the arm action when sprinting than is the two-arm thrust. Others contend that the maintenance of forward body lean is so difficult that the aid of both arms is essential. Some coaches believe that the double-arm action is difficult to teach and requires great poise and co-ordination to perfect. Dean Cromwell, for example, does not recommend its use at any time, though some of his best hurdlers, including Attlesey, were adept in this regard. Other good hurdle coaches, such as Johnny Morris, a fine hurdler in his own right, feel that "it is much easier to teach beginners and a hurdler does not have to as much co-ordination using the double-arm action." Apparently personal experience and a certain knowledge of an action determines its teachableness.

In any case, the essential factors in the effectiveness of arm action are: (1) does it precede and aid the forward body lean as the hurdle is approached? (2) does it approximate normal sprint action as closely as possible? (3) in its movement backward, does it maintain the shoulders in a straight line and forward position? This last point needs constant emphasis. Emmett Brunson, coach of Wolcott and other fine hurdlers, always maintained that the elbow should lead in the backward motion—that is, that the hand should come straight back from its forward position, thus forcing the arm to bend and the elbow to lead back as in sprinting. In this way, control of the arm and shoulder is best maintained, and certainly neither will be swept far back and out of balance.

The next factor a coach will observe from his position at the side of the hurdle might be the action of the lead leg. All coaches and nearly all hurdlers agree that one should lead with the knee rather than with the foot. To attempt the latter is to lock the knee joint, to increase the take-off angle, to flatten the arc of the lead foot so that it travels well beyond the hurdle before it cuts down, and in general to increase the length of the hurdle stride. Dillard was the chief advocate of such a style, and it was a major factor in producing his 13-foot clearance. To lead with the knee hurries the lift of the lead foot so that it reaches its highest point some 6 to 12 inches before the hurdle. From this point the extreme forward body lean almost necessarily forces the foot and leg down to a rapid but natural landing will within the recommended 5 feet of the hurdle. A few coaches emphasize pointing the toe forward and down so as to hasten this snap-down, but the more accepted practice is to keep the foot as relaxed as possible and to left is follow its natural path to the ground.

Jess Hill, in writing of Dick Attlesey's hurdling, makes a strong point of the snap-down of the foot:

When the lead leg is about 12 inches from the hurdle

a vicious cut down is started which is aided greatly by a quick straightening up of the trunk to a running position. This lead leg is snapped downward and backward with a pawing-the-ground movement and this should mean that the foot will fight on the ground running at the same speed that the body is moving forward. In Attlesey's fastest races he felt the top and front of the hurdle touch the thigh of the lead leg about 6 inches above the knee, in more or less of a backward pushing action.

Yet in speaking with Attlesey in January, 1952, the writer gained the impression that he thought of the body lean, the rapid pull-through of the trail leg, and the snap-down of the lead leg as being phases of a single movement with no one part being emphasized above the others. It is the co-ordination of the whole action that is important rather than marked emphasis upon any one part of it. Of course, such a point of view is actually not at variance with Hill's statement. Rather, it is the attitude of the experienced performer who has drilled beyond the details of action and is now concentrating upon greater relaxation, greater speed, and greater perfection of the whole.

A second important aspect of the lead-leg action lies in the cushioned contact of the foot with the ground. If the knee is locked or if the foot is extended too far beyond the centre of gravity of the body, the hurdler will land with a jar and loss of speed. The landing should occur on the toes and ball of the foot with no ground contact by the heel. A full forward lean and forward action of the trail leg will prove of help.

From his side position, the coach can recheck on the position of the head and eyes, perhaps even better than from in front. In the writer's opinion, each hurdler, quite naturally and without coaching, will acquire a visual pattern in hurdling. Some coaches say he should concentrate on only one hurdle at a time; others, that he should focus on the entire set of hurdles as a whole, with no wavering from straight ahead. Proper eye focus is a basic element in coaching field events generally; it may well be so in the hurdles as well. Certainly the head must be down and forward. As mentioned earlier, proper balance is the key to proper form in hurdling, and correct use of the head is the key to balance. Although Hill writes that it should lift and the body angle decreases as the hurdle is cleared, the problem with beginning hurdlers is to keep it down. To lift the trail knee over the hurdle while maintaining the full forward lean of the trunk is a difficult task. Assuming good hip flexibility, concentration upon keeping the head forward and down will prove most helpful.

The next aspect of hurdle clearance, second in importance only to the maintenance of forward body lean, has to do with the action of the trail leg. Certain coaches have criticized the styles of the speed-hurdlers Tolmich, Wolcott, and Dillard on the grounds that their hurried back leg has (1) forced a delay of action at the top of the hurdle, and (2) raised the knee and the shoulders to an off-balance position at the landing, which has retarded momentum. They insist that the trail leg must be delayed or held back at the take-off by securing a full split and run at the hurdle with absolutely no hint of a jump. For example, Frank R. Castleman, Ohio State coach of Snyder, Guthrie, Keller, and other fine hurdlers, titled an article, "lead with the left, do not hurry the right", and warned:

A mistake many coaches make is to encourage the boy to jerk the right leg rapidly forward. This tends to raise the right knee and lower the right foot. Often as not, the boy will hook the top of the hurdle...Remember, the right leg should not be hurried. Since it is going to follow anyhow, it should trail as the boy goes forward.

Actually, such trailing is the almost inevitable result of a take-off at least 6½feet from the hurdle, plus a marked forward lean. Where these two factors are present, the second leg will be properly handled. Similarly, where the forward lean is maintained beyond the hurdle, the knee of the trail leg will probably be brought through properly. As Castleman suggests, every effort should be made to bring the trailing foot through flat, with the toe up. To do so will insure a good clearance by the knee as well as the ankle and foot.

We began by stating that the action of the trail leg is second in importance only to forward body lean. This is true because if the trail leg is handled properly, other correct aspects of form will follow quite naturally. A delayed trail leg implies a full split and forward lean at the take-off, and vice versa of course. A horizontal trail leg as is comes off the hurdle—that is, one with a minimum lift of the knee and drop of the lower leg—will aid a continued forward lean and a full stride beyond the hurdle. An extremely rapid and relaxed pull-through of the trail leg cannot help but speed the downward snap of the lead leg, whereas the latter action will not at all insure the former. Attlesey was insistent upon this point and achieved perhaps the fastest rear leg action of any hurdler; yet with no conscious effort he also possessed, as Coach Hill states, "a vicious cut down" of the lead leg, which brought the foot within less than 5 feet of the hurdle. But a hurried back leg, such as Wolcott used, will have to be delayed for an instant and thus destroy over-all smoothness and momentum. Percy Beard felt this fault to be one of the greatest in hurdling.

When the body is immediately on top of the hurdle, the back knee should be well back of the top bar. One of the most common faults is to have the back knee in advance of the top bar and to thus upset the coordination of the legs. In leaving the ground, the back leg has to trail until the front foot is in position to drive and then they act together. If the back leg comes through too soon, the advantage of the scissors action is lost. If they do not act against each other, they are unbalanced and your action is unnatural. The quickest way to detect this is when you see a boy whipping his back leg through real quick and ending up with a stone bruise on his heel. This is most important fundamental in hurdling.

The uses of the horizontal trail leg are important. Primarily, it involves holding the toe up as long as possible. To do so will insure that the toe will not catch the hurdle as it comes through as well as that the knee will not be lifted unduly. This latter fault was Dillard's greatest handicap. It forced a straightening of the body, a wide backward swing of the lead arm and shoulder, and a momentary loss of balance at the landing. One of the most obvious symptoms of this fault is landing on the heel of the trail foot. The body should be sufficiently forward to keep the weight up on the toes, as in regular sprinting. Hurdlers should not need a heel pad in their sprint shoes. Those experiencing heel bruises should look to their form rather than toward the training room.

Finally, the astute hurdle coach will examine the length of the hurdle stride. For many years, 11′ has been accepted as the best clearance distance, yet most champions have varied from this. Dillard averaged 13′ (8′ + 5′) in his races up to 1952. Dugger required 11′ 6″ (6′ 8″ + 4′ 10″) on his first hurdle but 12′ even (7′ 4″ + 4′ 6″) as he achieved full momentum. Duff, who was short like Dillard, used 11′ (6′ 1″ + 4′ 11″). Osgood, who was 6′ 3″ tall, needed exactly 11′ (7′ + 4′). Finley of Yale, 6′ 3½″ tall, strided only 10′ 2″ (5′ 9″ + 4′ 5″). Attlesey took a full 11′6″(7′ 1″+ 4′5″). Smithson, competing in 1908, placed extreme emphasis upon cutting down the lead leg, and was able to place the foot within less than prescribed 4′ , but his critics felt that he lost more in balance and over-all action than he gained in achieving a quicker return to the ground.

Getting to the first hurdle. In general, the positions and actions of starting in the hurdles are the same as in sprinting, so that full instructions can be found. However, because of the importance of concentration upon the hurdle, coaches usually advocate (1) a higher focus of the eyes and therefore a lifting of the head in the "Get set" position, (2) a quicker straightening of the body during the first few strides from the blocks, and (3) adjustment of the strides to accommodate a best approach to the hurdle. Beginning hurdlers will undoubtedly do well to follow these three suggestions. However, as perfection of form and greater confidence are attained, regular sprinting procedures can be followed. Dillard actually focussed his eyes down toward his hands and came out of the blocks with his head down. Of course, he had no problem in overstriding to the first hurdle and therefore could go slam-bang forward with a certain confidence that the hurdle would be just right when he got to it. Hill states that Attlesey focussed about 8 yards down track. An erect head usually creates an upward and then forward leap, which obviously cuts acceleration. Best hurdling will compromise as little as possible and will follow sprinting practice as much is consistent with steadiness, balance and certainty at the hurdle.

The next problem is to determine which foot to place forward in the starting blocks. Most hurdlers take 8 strides to the first hurdle—that is, they make 8 footprints in the track before they take the hurdle. In this case, the same foot must be in the back block that leads over the hurdle. Among hundreds of other good hurdlers,

Tolmich, Wolcott, Dillard, and Attlesey used such a position and method. However, most excellent hurdlers with their long and fast strides have found it best to eliminate one stride. In this case, the lead foot over the hurdle is placed in the front starting block. Among those using this method were Simpson, Thomson, Keller, Beard and Towns, all men over 6′ 2″ tall and with good speed. Eliminating one stride permitted them to burst confidently into the start with full speed and strides; whereas 8 strides forced them to chop and hold back their speed for fear of coming too close to the hurdle on their last stride and thus hitting it or being forced to jump at the hurdle. One might take the case, for example, of Ed Dugger of Tufts College, for it seems typical of such problems. Dugger was 6′ 4″ tall, had been timed in :10 for the 100-yard dash, and normally took off about 7′ 3″ or 7′ 4″ from all hurdles beyond the first. At his first hurdle, however, his long strides brought him within 6′ 8″ of the hurdle and forced a landing some 4″ beyond his normal stride. To the writer, Dugger always appeared to be too upright and slightly off balance at his first hurdle, and he seldom recovered until about the third or fourth. Had he been able to shift his foot position in the starting blocks and to take only 7 strides to the first hurdle, his take-off might have moved back to 7′ 4″ or even 7 6″. He could then have employed the full forward lean and full momentum which he used so well in the later stages of his race. First attempts at doing this are seldom successful immediately, so that many sprinting sessions must be held getting used to the new foot arrangements and to the longer starting strides.

When hurdlers find chopping necessary, it must occur during the first 2 or 3 strides out of the blocks. Then they can move ahead with full assurance. Occasionally a simple backward shift of the blocks, or even of a single block, may cut strides sufficiently. Even though difficulties are encountered, this point should be insisted on. Almost an error or difficulty is better than a close take-off.

With a beginning hurdler, certainty and balance take precedence over momentum to the first hurdle. A few incidences of hitting the hurdles hard, even when no serious injury results, will discourage many a fine prospect. But with average times in both high school and college dropping lower and lower, men will need the momentum to the first hurdle that tends to establish the speed of the entire flight. As in all skill events, form and balance must come first, but momentum cannot be far behind. In keeping with this, the action of the arms during the strides to the first hurdle should not be unduly emphasized. As in sprinting, balance and relaxation come first. To "drive hard with the arms", as some coaches insist, is likely to lessen both.

Action between hurdles. All hurdlers take 3 strides between the hurdles—that is, they hit the ground 4 times. Ordinarily, the length of these strides will increase progressively along with momentum, and will approximate 5′6′, and 7′. However, as perfection in form and balance is achieved, the first 2 strides will tend to lengthen and the third to shorten. Being able to shorten the last stride a few inches greatly facilitates the full forward lean and the momentum with which the next hurdle is taken. Jess Hill seems convinced that this was an important aspect of Dick Attlesey's style:

One of Dick Attlesey's greatest attributes is the ability to enjoy a split-second of complete relaxation at the top of the hurdle. This, no doubt, accounts for his tremendously fast snap-down of his lead leg and effective pull through of his trailing leg. We do not believe it is possible to achieve this sense of relaxation if the hurdler is striving on his third step between hurdles to cover too much ground. Most hurdlers usually take their shorter stride on their first stride over the hurdle, a little longer on the second, and an increasingly longer one on the third. This means that at the moment of take-off over the hurdle the hurdler is at his most tense and strained condition....It is interesting to note that on Dick's :08.2 second 70 yard high hurdle trial mentioned before, his first strides averaged 6 feet 10 inches; his second strides averaged 6 feet 10 inches; and his third strides averaged 6 feet 7 inches.

Such a pattern is consistent with that of strides in the broad jump or high jump, in which men cut their last stride in order to get over the take-off foot and on into the jump. But, as usual, it is an ideal to work toward and not always possible for all competitors. For instance, Jack Keller of Ohio State, one of the greatest of all prospects in the high hurdles, was constantly haunted by a tendency to overrun his hurdles and had to cut all his strides in order to have room for clearance.

Most coaches tend to emphasize the drive of the arms in hurdling more than when just sprinting. Quickened and more forceful action seems to aid balance and to hasten the action of the legs. As in sprinting, however, relaxation, and balance are the essential effects. To consider arm action as directly aiding momentum is undoubtedly false.

The finish. Once the last hurdle is crossed, sprinting techniques take over. Assuming good balance and right position as the hurdler descends. Obviously, finish techniques require special consideration and persistent drill just as in sprinting. Many, many races are won or lost during these last crucial 15 yards.

IMPORTANT QUESTIONS AND ANSWERS

How should candidates for high-hurdling be selected? The problem is not at all a difficult one, even at the college level. The hurdles demand (1) speed, (2) co-ordination and flexibility, and (3) height. Therefore, first run your squad through the 100-yard dash. Secondly, move the fastest of the boys who are over 5′ 10″ tall to a flight of three low hurdles 10 yards apart, and watch carefully for naturalness and ease of action. Your eye can spot the good prospects better than can a stop watch. It is just as simple as this. There is no need for analysing hurdling in terms of its component parts and proceeding through a long routine of high-jumping, broad-jumping, maze running, and so forth. If you're not sure of your own judgment, relax and go ahead just the same. You'll discover before long that your powers of selection are much better than you think. If only the job of creating and maintaining desire in those selected were as easily done, the problem would be simple indeed.

What are the causes of difficult in obtaining 3 smooth strides between hurdles? It may be because:

1. The man's legs are too short or too slow to clear the necessary average of over 6′ per stride.

2. He is chopping the lead leg down too sharply from the hurdle. This is not nearly so likely as the next possibility.

3. The trail leg is not securing a full stride as it comes off the hurdle. This stride must average at least 5′ if the next two strides are not to be overlay long and slow.

4. The body has been straightened as it comes off the hurdle so that an efficient sprinting angle has been lost.

5. The landing on the lead foot has been made on the heel and therefore momentum has been checked.

6. The lead arm has drawn the shoulder back as it is pulled back into running position. Balance and a full

stride off the hurdle are thereby lost.

How should a beginning hurdler start his practice work? First of all, he should not start by hurdling. To begin with hurdling will almost assure a few accidents and setbacks, which might well ruin the man as a hurdle prospect. Instead, there should be several weeks of preliminary work in the form of running and exercises to prepare him for steady progress when the hurdles are finally taken. Read over carefully the written material and illustrations on hurdling exercises and establish a routine of work that will bring flexibility and a toughness of muscle and tendon that can take the stretching and off-balance action of hurdling. Get the legs in shape by running and easy sprints.

When you are certain that the man is ready for hurdling, begin with the lows. Let him run them for several days with a minimum of instructions until he begins to relax a little and feel more "at home". Then work with his form as we have indicated, stressing fundamentals only and passing over the details as quickly as possible. He'll do better if he discovers and works out the details by himself. After all, that's really the track coach's job—to help others to help themselves. Next, shift to a practice high hurdle. There are many type of hurdles, but they should all serve the same purpose of protecting the hurdler against ankle and knee bruises and against unnecessary falls. With a proper device, the athlete will achieve confidence and a more economical clearance that will be very easily transferred to the regulation hurdle.

Some coaches believe that it is better to learn to handle a single hurdle first and then move on to running three or more. To the writer, however, it is better to start with three immediately, so that rhythm and feel of clearing the first hurdle and of proceeding on to the next will be acquired from the start.

Assuming that the man has a certain natural quickness, flexibility, and length of leg, the primary factor for success is patient and persistent practice of the right kind. Hurdling cannot be learned in a few weeks or even a few months. Working out in the fall of the year, when the weather is warm; beginning indoors around the middle of November and continuing on with only a few week's vacation through the indoor and outdoor seasons; hurdling constantly because the event is intriguing and fun—these are the means to success. There is no other way.

What about time trails in high-hurdling? The answer is the same as in the case of all skill events in track and field. As long as a man's mind is on time, he will find it difficult to concentrate on method. Furthermore, few men will run as fast in practice as in a meet and will therefore be disappointed in whatever time is made.

On the other hand, good form in competitive hurdling is inconceivable without having momentum. Therefore, once the essentials of hurdling have been well learned, almost all practice should be at high speed. Much of it can be with competition at odd distances over three or four hurdles. So long as the mind is on "how" rather than on "how fast", competition will help. Yet even such work has its negative possibilities. The writer has had the unfortunate experience on several occasions of having a faster man gradually slow down in practice to the rhythm of a slower teammate and temporarily lose his natural speed. We thought the slower man was getting faster until the watch showed our error. In general, one learns to run faster by being challenged and by trying to run faster.

Should a man lead with the left or right leg? In high-hurdling there is no preference other than personal choice. Normally, a man will swing up the same leg as in the high jump or broad jump. However, if there is any possibility of his also running the low hurdles, he will have a distinct advantage if he leads with the left. The lows (and, incidentally, the 220-yard dash) are increasingly being run around a single curve in order to give the crowd a better view of the entire race. In all fast curve running the natural inclination and therefore the weight of the body is to the inside. Balance is thus achieved more easily when the lead leg is also on the inside, where the weight will fall naturally and easily. The low-hurdler who leads with the right is constantly fighting for better balance around a curve.

What types of practice hurdles are available? The primary purpose of a practice hurdle is to prevent bruises and spills, which always slow hurdling progress and sometimes stop it altogether. There are various alternatives:

1. Place a lath or 5-foot cross-bar between but at the end of two hurdles out on the grass. This will give way easily but has been known to get caught between the legs and thus cause a bad spill.

2. Put finish yarn on which a handkerchief has been hung between two hurdles, again on the grass. This is excellent as a device for beginners.

3. Hinge a 3-inch strip of wood to the regular cross-bar of the hurdle and cover it with whatever rubber is available. This will flip down out of the way when lightly touched. In the writer's opinion, this is the simplest and most effective of such devices. Obviously, the hurdle must be such that it can be lowered the necessary 3 inches.

4. There is on the market a patented hurdle that rolls down easily on a circlet of steel when hit.

5. Another patented hurdle has a divided cross-bar. The two pieces are hinged in such fashion at the uprights that they fall away to each side when hit.

6. In addition, most hurdlers make aluminium, rubber, or plastic protectors for the ankle and knee; these are simply taped to the leg and form an excellent protection. Obviously, a man will need a certain proportion of work without the aid of such protective devices if he is to hurdle without hesitancy or tension in the meets.

How important is relaxation in hurdling? The short and direct answer is, of course, that, once the essentials of form are learned, relaxation is the key to best performance. This can be well illustrated by three examples. In May, 1937, Bob Osgood, of the University of Michigan, had a best time leading up to the conference championships of :14.4. He had trained carefully for this race and was at high competitive pitch—too high, in the writer's opinion, for best efforts. But 30 minutes before the finals, a heavy spring shower left the track partially covered with water throughout the length of the hurdle race. Fast times were apparently out and anything could happen under such conditions. This took the pressure off; Bob was kidding the other hurdlers about wearing rubbers or getting a rowboat. The results? Osgood won in the new American record time of :14 flat.

In 1936, Forrest Towns had gone through a full college season of hurdling, followed by the numerous pre-Olympic trials and Olympic races, which culminated in his winning the world's championship with a best time of :14.1. Yet in a relatively unimportant race is Oslo, one month later, Towns was timed at the then almost incredible figure of :13.7, .4 second faster than he had ever run before.

Up to May 13, 1950, Dick Attlesey had a best personal time of :14.1 for the 120 highs. On that day, he cut .6 second off his time for a new world's record; he was about 5 yards faster than on any previous occasion. In explanation, coaches have mentioned the wonderful Fresno track, the excellent temperature, and favourable wind conditions. Undoubtedly they helped, but the greatest factor, in the writer's opinion, was that the competition was not at highest level and, to quote one observer, that "Attlesey", owing to a slight muscle aggravation, had no thought of pouring it on until after the race was on".

Other examples of similar although perhaps slower performances can be given to indicate that, in a highly skilled event such as the hurdles, the primary coaching problem is to remove pressures rather than to increase them.

What are the relative values of natural speed and of skill in high-hurdling? It seems clear that they are of equal importance. The difference between the best times and the slowest times recorded by hurdlers is approximately 4 seconds (:17.5 — :13.5). The difference between the fastest and the slowest times hurdlers might record in running 120 yards flat is about 2 seconds (:13.3 — :11.3), just half the total difference.

There are several important conclusions to be drawn. First, a man's potential time can be estimated by taking his time for 120 yards flat, substracting a few tenths for improvement in sprinting ability, and then adding about 3 seconds for time over the hurdles. Note that the best hurdlers have needed only 1.8 seconds, whereas less skilled champions have needed over 3 seconds.

Secondly, in selecting candidates, speed and potential hurdling skill should be given equal consideration.

CHAPTER 12

THE LOW HURDLES IN RUNNING

HISTORY OF IMPROVEMENT IN FORM AND TIME

It is believed that hurdling as a separate event was developed in America and adopted by other countries; it was part of the AAU program as early as 1888. Possibly, in the past, obstacles set up as in the steeplechase were used to test men in a combination of jumping and endurance running. The 400-meter hurdles are an event in the collegiate, AAU, and Olympic programs. Low hurdles of 180-yard distance are run outdoors by high school performers. Colleges often include an indoor 70-yard low hurdle race in a dual meet.

In contrast to the high hurdles, the low hurdles have been an almost exclusively American event. F.A.M. Webster, the English track writer, despite diligent search, was unable to discover any record of a race in England over 220 yards and with 10 hurdles 2′ 6″ high until 1922, when W.S. Bristow, of Cambridge, won over Oxford in :26.2. In contrast, in America, the low hurdles were included in the first National AAU championships, in 1887. However, early form in the low hurdles followed the same pattern as form in the highs, with a bent lead leg and a "scattering flowers in May" style that was undoubtedly aesthetically entrancing but athletically impotent. As in the highs, with a bent lead leg and a "scattering flowers in May" style that was undoubtedly aesthetically entrancing but athletically impotent. As in the highs, it was the great Alvin Kraenzlein, of Pennsylvania, who set things right. In 1898, using a straight lead leg and his great natural speed, Krenzlein simply took a long stride over each of the 10 hurdles and sprinted the 220-yard distance in :23.6. This sprinting action was fully understood by Kraenzlein's coach, Mike Murphy, as what he wrote in 1913 clearly shows:

> The stride for the low hurdles is what might be termed an "elongated" stride. Very few hurdlers are able to fully attain this. Naturally, it can best be acquired by a tall man with long legs. A.C. Kraenzlein, the holder of the world's record for this distance, had it mastered better than any man. Kraenzlein could probably sprint 220 yards on the flat in 22 seconds. His world's record for ten hurdles over this same distance is :23.6, consequently the clearing of these obstacles could have added only 1.6 seconds to his time. This sort of speed requires perfection in the art of the clearing the hurdles. In fact Kraenzlein cleared them so easily that, except for a momentary rising and halting as he went over the hurdle, one might have thought that he was running a 220 yard sprint race.

In this section to follow on essentials of good form today, the present writer will find it difficult to improve on Murphy's statement. Only the word "halting" gives a clue to certain limitations in Kraenzlein's form. They could not have been great, however, for the best low-hurdlers during the half century since Kraenzlein have been able to improve on his time-loss in clearing the hurdles by only .6 second, and the present record holder, Dillard, required about the same hurdle-clearance time. It is primarily the modern hurdler's speed afoot that has broken records, rather than their perfection of hurdle form.

It was in the same year in which Murphy was writing, 1913, that Kraenzlein's record was first tied by J.I. Wendell, of Wesleyan University. And not until 10 years later, in 1923, was it reduced to :23.2 by Charles Brookins, of Iowa. Brookins was 6′ tall; he did little in the high hurdles but was a fine sprinter, having run :09.8 for the 100, and could also run a good quarter mile. He therefore had the prime requisities of speed, length of stride, and endurance, which are characteristic of all top performers today. The next year he set a second record at :23 flat.

In 1925, Edward Spence, of what is now Wayne University, won the National Collegiate low hurdles in the college record time of :23.5. Although slower than Brookins record, this performance was remarkable because it was actually better time than Spence had ever recorded for the 220-yard flat race. Of course, he had done very little sprinting for time in either practice or meets; but his coach, David L. Holmes, insisted and Spence agreed that the hurdles helped him to relax sufficiently to permit better time than when they were not present. Certainly, one was convinced of the plausibility of this statement when watching Spence run over the hurdles. His legs actually seemed to move faster than when sprinting between. The writer had a similar impression nine years later, in 1934, in watching the work of Heye Lambertus, of Nebraska, who had a best time of :23.1. These men did not jump in any sense of the word, nor did they seemingly employ any special form such as consumes so much attention in the high hurdles. They sprinted the full distance and would have laughed at the very thought of the hurdles as being obstacles. They were not high-hurdlers who also run the lows as a means of gaining additional points. Nor were they sprinters who took a little time off occasionally to run a few lows. They were specialized low-hurdlers who had as great a pride in their own event and in perfecting their hurdling forms as can be had in any other track event.

Dean Cromwell tells at some length and with deep satisfaction of the similar 1939 performances of Earl Vickery, who made a best time of :22.7, although his fastest 220-yard-dash time was :21.7. That is, it took him merely one second longer to run over the 10 hurdlers. In contrast to Spence and Lambertus, Vickery devoted a good share of his time to sprinting and therefore probably achieved sprinting ability close to his true maximum.

The interesting part of Earl's improvement is that during his last two seasons at Southern California he was given speed work almost entirely in training. He had perfected his hurdling form as a sophomore and therefore the only way to improve his time was to make as fine a sprinter as possible out of him. In preliminary work and during the first few weeks of the 1939 season, Vickery was put through the sprinter's training program and for a time we just forgot that he was a hurdler. In fact, even when he began to run the low hurdles in meets, we'd ignore the barriers in returning to the practice field the following Monday and would go back to the sprint training again.

On the evidence of these three men, and of others whom it is not necessary to mention, it can be assumed that a single second is all that is needed to take the low hurdles and that, assuming excellence in form, performances in the future will be determined by sprinting speeds.

In 1929, R. C. Rockaway, of Ohio State, came from obscurity and, incidentally, out of officially unrecognized starting blocks to run a surprising :22.8. Like Spence and Vickery, he was almost exclusively a low-hurdler. In contrast, the next record breaker, Jack Keller, also of Ohio State, was known as a great high-hurdler. Had Keller concentrated his efforts on the longer distance, his great speed and ease of stride might well have bettered his time of :22.7.

In 1935 the sprinters took over, as they must continue, to do from now on. We must mention again the great Jesse Owens, who, for the fourth time on May 25, 1935, set a world's record of :22.6. Jesse never claimed to be a great hurdler. Movies still demonstrated to us that he jumped the hurdles and was not entirely on balance as he reached the ground. But his ability to run :20.3 for the 220 was sufficient to win over the finest of hurdlers. It should be noted that on this day he took 2.3 seconds longer to clear the 10 barriers. Even admitting that he was somewhat tired from his previous record performances, 2.3 seconds does not compare favourable with Vickery's single second. It also implies that, had he Vickery's or Spence's perfection of style, the record might now be well below :22, an almost shocking thought.

But now the combination sprinter-hurdlers assumed control. First Fred Wolcott, in 1940, combined a :13.9 high-hurdle performance with that of :09.5 for 100 yards and produced :22.5 for the 220-yard lows. He was a fine low-hurdle stylist and ran many races under 23 seconds. Then Harrison Dillard came along with the even greater combination of :13.6 in the highs and :09.4 for the century dash. First, in early June, 1946, he equalled the :22.5 record. Then, in the National Collegiates at Minneapolis, two weeks later, he covered the 10 hurdles around a turn in :23, a world's best mark although not officially recognized. Finally, in June, 1947, at the National Collegiates in Salt Lake City, he established an officially accepted record of :22.3. Some estimate of Dillard's form can be gained from comparing this performance with :20.9, which is his best recorded time for the 200-meter race. This implies that clearing the hurdles consumed approximately 1.4 seconds.

ESSENTIALS INGREDIENTS OF CORRECT FORM

Correct form in the low hurdles can be best described as being both a modified high-hurdle action and an elongated sprint stride. Although the latter statement was used and understood a half century ago, it is actually the former concept that has predominated in coaching and hurdling circles since that time. An excellent example of this is to be found in the point of view presented by Wolcott's coach, Emmett Brunson, at the National College Track Coaches Association in June, 1940, two weeks after Wolcott had run :22.5.

In contrast to such a point of view, the best low-hurdlers, regardless of their time on the stop watch, specialize in this event and develop a form that, although similar to both high-hurdling and sprinting, is identical with neither. Such form, through its perfect smoothness, relaxation, balance and efficiency, demands as much in thoughtful study and persistent practice as the highs themselves. It is simpler in action, to be sure, but who can say that the simpler actions are easier when done perfectly than those more complex?

Form in the low hurdles should be as similar as possible to that of sprinting. For the taller man, with a leg length of 34 to 36 inches, there will be no change in sprinting angle and very little increase in the height of head or hips; nor will there be an effort to skim the hurdles with the frequently mentioned "dime-tipping" clearance. Arm action will not change at all in rhythm and very little in the slight lift of the elbow of the lead arm. The lead leg will, of course, need to be lifted high enough to clear the 30-inch barrier, and the trail leg also; but neither should change the sprint timing or coordination. Best hurdling will actually consume a single tenth of a second longer over each hurdle than flat running.

For the shorter man who yet has enough speed to permit seven strides between the hurdles, each of these factors will be slightly increased. He will rise a little higher to give clearance and to provide the length of stride required by the 20 yards between each hurdle. If his speed is equal to that of his taller competitor, he will take a small fraction of a second longer, which must be regained in the strides between.

Whereas in the high hurdles use of either leg as the lead leg is a matter of personal preference, in the lows there is a definite advantage in lifting the left leg first. An increasing tendency to run the 220-yard distances around the curve, so that both the start and the finish can be seen by the crowd, is a boon to left-footed hurdlers. There is a natural tendency to lean to the inside on any curve, and this throws the weight toward a leading left leg but away from a leading right leg. In addition, the left-footed low-hurdler finds it simpler to cling to the inside edge of his lane, which is, of course, the shortest distance around. Smart coaches will have this in mind when instructing beginners, for when habits are once formed, changes are seldom justified.

Sprinting to the first hurdle

The position and action in the starting blocks for low-hurdling is identical to that when sprinting. Since the distance to the first hurdle is 20 yards and the change in action over the hurdle is very minor, there is plenty of time and space to rise to a hurdling angle and guage the exact location of the hurdle. Needless to say, the learning hurdler will use a little discretion in his speed to the first hurdle, but as skill and confidence increases, he will work on securing all possible speed as soon as possible.

Almost invariably, low-hurdlers take 10 strides to the first hurdle; accordingly, they take their position in the starting blocks with the same foot back that will lead in clearing the hurdle. A very few will find an additional stride necessary and will therefore reverse the feet. But such men will find it almost impossible to carry the full 10 hurdles in 7 strides each and will be fortunate to place in decent competition.

Sprinting between the hurdles

For the tall man whose balance off the hurdle has been performed, sprinting action between hurdles will be identical to that when running a flat race. When balance has been lost through improper body or arm carriage or through too short or too long a stride over the hurdle, men may need to exaggerate arm action or consciously to lengthen strides between in order to reach the next hurdle comfortably. When a deficiency in length of leg or stride is present, men will have great difficulty in maintaining the normal seven strides between after they have cleared the first five or six hurdles. In those cases where a full stride has never been learned, much can be done to aid the athlete. Correct sprint practice will increase speed and therefore the length of stride. But, in addition, an emphasis upon higher knee action, upon the development of bounce and quickness of the feet and ankles, and upon the 2- or 3-inch extension of the foot as it is placed on the track will in time gain as much as 5 or 6 inches in each stride.

But where the nature has simply failed to provide more than about 30 inches between foot and crotch, certain adjustments must be done. One is to concentrate upon sprinting and sprint relay racing, and to hope that the right character development will occur there rather than in hurdling. Another is to alternate lead legs over successive hurdles. Through diligent practice men have learned to take the hurdles with either food forward and have become valuable point gainers in college meets of lesser caliber or even in high school championship meets. Each coach and athlete will need to consider his own situation and what will bring both points and personal satisfaction. No excellent times have been made in the 220-yard hurdles by men using such a method.

Sprinting at the finish

This phrase tells its own story quite adequately. As in the last yards of a 220-yard dash, a speed faster than one's best is somehow discovered and carried through and beyond the finish line. It should be emphasized, however, that many a race is won or lost in these last few yards and that skill in their full use requires as diligent practice as does skill in hurdle clearance itself.

Organization of Practice

The practice organization of the usual combination high- and low-hurdler as already described : further consideration must be given to the low-hurdle specialist. In general, his work will be as follows :

Preliminary work. After the usual jogging and easy wind sprints, there should be 10 to 15 minutes of general body exercises. Flexibility is not so vital a factor in the lows as in high-hurdling, but it must not be underestimated and should be stressed in the all-round body-condition work this period involves.

The workout. In contrast to the high-hurdler, the low-hurdler can do serious sprinting practice before hurdling. After a few increasingly fast wind sprints, the hurdler should report to the starting blocks with the sprinters. Once again, drill is the key to excellence of style and ease of action, and 6 starts are certainly not enough to learn even the rudiments of skill in sprinting.

Since the purpose of this phase of practice is increased speed, such sprints should be kept under 100 yards, and 25 yards is usually sufficient. The hurdler should try to lick somebody, even though he needs a handicap to do it. Only by having greater efforts demanded from them are muscles likely to improve in power and speed.

Now the man should shift to the low hurdles and drill, drill, drill. As many competitive situations as possible should be set up; not only are they fun, but only that form which involves top momentum is best form. The low hurdles cannot be truly learned by a few easy runs down through three or four each day. The more low-hurdling is done, the more interested the athlete will become and the more he will find to do. Increasingly he will take a deep pride in the ease, smoothness, and quickness with which he sprints over the lows as though they were not there at all. Only when he has that pride and that perfection of style can he say he is a real low-hurdler.

The low-hurdler has now worked on sprinting for speed and hurdling for skill. Only endurance remains. Endurance comes best for hurdlers by repeated speed work over 220 yards or less. An occasional 300 or even 350 yards is worth while. Best of all, a serious effort should be made to qualify for the mile-relay team. It'll be fun and the best endurance training in the world.

TECHNIQUES OF GOOD FORM

Most 440-yard hurdlers take off about 7½ feet from the hurdle and land about 4½ feet beyond. The normal number of strides to the first hurdle will be 23, with 15 strides used between hurdles. These strides must be accomplished in a smooth and relaxed manner, using good hip swing. Unless the athlete is very tall and has a naturally long stride, he will find it almost impossible to use 13 strides between the hurdles (yet champions use 13 strides part of the distance).

Knowledge and judgment of pace is very important in the 440-yard hurdle race, much as it is in the 440-yard dash. This knowledge is gained by having times checked at the 100-meter, 200-meter, and 300-meter marks to see at what pace a runner is capable of running these distances, and how closely he is able to determine his speed. He must learn to run at the predetermined pace.

The 440-yard hurdle is a tough race. Endurance is absolutely necessary. Many races are lost by the runner's striking the last few hurdles because his legs have tied up and he is unable to get over the barriers. Thus, training to be both a quarter-miler and hurdler is necessary.

TRAINING PROGRAM

Many of the same general training comments that have been made previously about quarter-milers apply here.

Monday

1. Warm-up by running and jogging 1 mile.

2. Work vigorously 15 minutes on stretching and hurdle exercises.

3. Run ½ mile of wind sprints and first 3 hurdles.

4. Run 1× 550 pace speed, running first 440 at 52 seconds.

5. 10 to 15 minute rest interval.

6. Run 1×660 at pace speed, running first 440 at 53 seconds and finishing strong.

7. Run 10×110 yards.

8. Jog 2 to 4 laps as cool-down.

Tuesday

1, 2, 3. Same as Monday.

4. Run 3×220's at pace speed, 23 to 25 seconds.

5. 4 minute interval.

6. Run 10×110 yards.

7. Jog 2 to 4 laps as cool-down.

Wednesday

1, 2, 3. Same as Monday.

4. Run 3×330's at full speed.

5. 5 to 8 minute interval.

6. Run 10×110 yards.

7. Jog 2 to 4 laps as cool-down.

Thursday

1, 2, 3. Same as Monday.

4. Run 5 to 8 hurdles 4 to 6 times.

5. 3 to 5 minute interval.

6. Run 10×110 yards.

7. Jog 2 to 4 laps as cool-down.

Friday

1, 2, 3. Same as Monday.

Saturday

Run time trials or participate in early season competition.

1, 2, 3, 4. Same as Monday.

5. Run 20 to 30×200 yards.

440-yard Intermediate Hurdles: Midseason

Monday

1. Warm-up by running and jogging one mile.

2. Work vigorously 15 minutes by doing stretching and hurdle exercises.

3. Run ½ mile of wind sprints. Run over just 3 hurdles several times.

4. Run 3×330's at full speed.

5. 5 to 7 minute interval.

6. Run 10×110 yards.

7. Jog 2 to 4 laps as cool-down.

(110's listed in 6 may be modified by placing hurdles on track and running over them as the 10×110 distance is covered. This is of special benefit when you are tired).

Tuesday

1, 2, 3. Same as Monday.

4. Run 3×5 to 8 intermediate hurdles at 23 to 25 pace for 220 yards.

5. 5 to 7 minute interval.

6. Run 10×110 yards.

7. Jog 2 to 4 laps as cool-down.

Wednesday

1, 2, 3. Same as Monday.

4. Run 220-330-220 full speed.

5. 5 to 7 minute interval.

6. Run 10×110 yards or modify by use of hurdles.

7. Jog 2 to 4 laps as cool-down.

Thursday

1, 2, 3. Same as Monday.

4. Run 5 to 8×gun starts and first 3 hurdles.

5. Run 3×(110-220-110) at race pace.

6. Run 5×110 yards or modify by using hurdles.

7. Jog 2 to 4 laps as cool-down.

Friday

1, 2, 3. Same as Monday.

4. Jog 10 to 15 minutes.

Saturday

Competition.

Sunday

1, 2, 3. Same as Monday.

4. Run 15 to 20×150 yards on grass.

LOW HURDLE FORM

Form in the low hurdles should be as similar to sprinting as possible. There is no need for the runner to change the sprinting position when the hurdle is taken. The head should be maintained at the same height, the arms should swing in the same manner, and it is not necessary to settle down over the hurdles just to make a close clearance. The only change is that the foot of the lead leg is shifted to clear the hurdle and the trail knee and foot are flattened out slightly as they go over the hurdle. Usually, in clearing the hurdle, the trail leg is carried much farther forward and more under the runner's body than is true in high hurdling.

Good low hurdle form is characterized by uninterrupted smoothness and quickness of movement as the hurdle is taken. There must be no sense of sailing or of a break in the continuity of leg and arm action.

Length of stride over the hurdle. The length of the stride over the hurdle may vary from 10 to 13 feet, depending upon the leg length of the hurdler. The taller hurdler often has trouble cutting down his strides between hurdles in order to avoid getting too close for a proper takeoff for the next hurdle. In such cases it is important that he make an effort to land not more than a 3½ feet beyond the hurdle.

The start and steps to the first hurdle. The start of the low hurdles should be exactly like that of the sprints. Most hurdlers take 10 strides to the first hurdle in the 180-yard event. It may be necessary to alter the length of the first 4 strides in order to insure a proper takeoff. Some men may want to change the position of their feet in the blocks so that what would customarily be the front foot is the rear foot. This will enable them to go over the first hurdle using the preferred takeoff foot. They then would take either 9 or 11 steps to the first hurdle.

Steps between hurdles. All of the outstanding low hurdlers use 7 strides between hurdles. The short-legged hurdler may have difficulty getting close enough to the hurdle to go over it in good sprinting form. It may then be necessary to work on increasing stride length by having more vigorous arm action, lifting the knee higher, swinging the hips more, and increasing the landing position of each foot by 2 or 3 inches.

On the other hand, the taller man may have the difficulty of overrunning the hurdles. He must get the lead foot on the ground as near the hurdle as possible after clearing it. Each stride may be shortened 2 or 3 inches by constant practice.

The low hurdler in high school who also runs the high hurdles should practice running over from 3 to 5 low hurdles 4 to 6 times once a week. He should also follow a workout schedule that combines some parts of the sprinter's and high hurdler's training program.

The low hurdler who also runs the sprints should add 2 days per week practice over the low hurdles to the sprinter's schedule, in order to perfect form and gain confidence in approaching and running between the hurdles.

WORKOUT SCHEDULES

Low Hurdles: Preseason

Monday

1. Warm-up by running and jogging 1 mile.

2. Work vigorously 15 minutes on stretching and hurdle exercises.

3. Run ½ mile of wind sprints and run over the first 3 low hurdles.

4. Run 3×220 yards, ¾ speed. Increase speed as conditioning improves.

5. 5 to 7 minute interval.

6. Run 10×150-yard sprints.

7. Jog 2 to 4 laps as cool-down.

Tuesday

1, 2, 3. Same as Monday.

4. Take 8 to 10 starts and run over first 3 hurdles.

5. Take 2 to 3 starts and 5 to 8 hurdles (depending on whether indoors or outdoors).

6. Run 10×150-yard sprints.

7. Jog 2 to 4 laps as cool-down.

Wednesday

1, 2, 3. Same as Monday.

4. Run 20×150-yard sprints, concentrating on form and relaxation.

5. 2 to 4 minute interval.

6. Jog 2 to 4 laps as cool-down.

Thursday

1, 2, 3. Same as Monday.

4. Take 3 to 5 preliminary starts for warm-up.

5. Take 4 starts, concentrating on first 15 yards.

6. Take 4 starts, concentrating on first 30 to 50 yards.

7. Run 10×150-yard sprints.

8. Jog 2 to 4 laps as cool-down.

Friday

1, 2, 3. Same as Monday.

Saturday

Participate in time trials or early season competition.

Sunday

1, 2, 3. Same as Monday.

4. Run 20 to 25×200 yards.

Low Hurdles: Midseason

Monday

1. Warm-up by running and jogging 1 mile.

2. Work vigorously 15 minutes on stretching and hurdle exercise.

3. Run ½ mile of wind sprints and first 3 low hurdles.

4. Run 3×220 yard full speed.

5. 5 to 7 minute interval.

6. Run 10×150-yard sprints. (May be modified by placing 2 or 3 hurdles on track and running over them when tired).

7. Jog 2 to 4 laps as cool-down.

Tuesday

1, 2, 3. Same as Monday.

4. Take 2 or 3 starts and 5 to 8 hurdles (depending on whether indoors or outdoors).

6. Run 10×100-yard sprints.

7. Jog 2 to 4 laps as cool-down.

Wednesday

1, 2, 3. Same as Monday.

4. Run 1×330 yards, full speed.

5. 7 to 10 minute interval.

6. Run 1×220 yards, full speed.

7. Run 10×150-yard sprints.

8. Jog 2 to 4 laps as cool-down.

Thursday

1, 2, 3. Same as Monday.

4. Run 3 to 5 preliminary starts for warm-up.

5. Take 4 starts, concentrating on first 15 to 20 yards.

6. Take 4 starts, concentrating on first 60 to 100 yards (progression from 50 to 100 yards).

7. Run 10×110-yard sprints.

8. Jog 2 to 4 laps as cool-down.

Friday

1, 2, 3. Same as Monday.

4. Jog 10 to 15 minutes.

HELPFUL HINTS

1. In addition to speed and flexibility, the 180-yard low hurdler must have endurance. The 70-yard hurdler needs speed and rhythm. If he is to specialize in low hurdles, he must run repeat 200's and an occasional 300-yard dash as part of his workout schedule.

2. The low hurdler must learn to sprint through the entire 180 yards. This event is not a hurdle-jumping contest.

3. He should be sure to keep the shoulders square and maintain proper balance when coming off the hurdle.

4. Best form in low hurdling is attained by running at full effort during practice. Competitive runs with teammates over 5 fights of hurdles are good practice.

5. The hurdler should practice taking off without being too close to the hurdle.

6. He should learn to run over the hurdle, not to jump or float over it.

7. He should keep a smooth, relaxed sprinting stride throughout the race. He should not gallop.

CHAPTER 13

TEACHING TACTICS AND TECHNIQUES IN HURDLING

Modern hurdling requires a tall athlete who has excellent hurdling technique combined with tremendous sprinting ability. This is particularly the case in the men's 110-meter hurdles, where the hurdles are 3 feet 6 inches tall. In other hurdling events (women's 100-meter hurdles and men's and women's 400-meter hurdles), the lower hurdles allow for a less exaggerated technique and greater variation in body size. In all cases, sprinting ability is absolutely essential.

SAFETY TIPS

Novices should begin by clearing low obstacles that are 6 inches to 1 foot in height. They can then move to low practice hurdles (at approximately knee height) using short distances between each hurdle and can progress slowly to competitive standards. Once familiar with competitive hurdling over 100/110 meters (where hurdles are all in a straight line), the athlete can then attempt sprint endurance hurdling lover longer distances. This will demand the ability to hurdle around curves, to hurdle with either leg, and to alter the tempo of running and stride length between hurdles.

Hurdle height and distance must also be varied

according to seasonal levels of fitness. In the offseason, reduce heights and distances between hurdles, particularly with the 400-meter hurdles. A simple guide is to check the stride pattern of the athlete and position the hurdles accordingly. Set the hurdle low enough so that an easy clearance is possible and adjust distances and heights as performance improves.

The ability to hurdle cannot be improved solely by clearing hurdles. The closer that the hurdle approaches competitive height, the greater the demand placed on hurdling technique. This technique is improved by related stretching exercises, most of which are aimed at increasing flexibility in the hip area.

Teach novices that hurdles are normally cleared in one direction only, although this does not apply to bamboo canes balanced on traffic cones or to hurdles specifically designed to be hurdled in either direction.

TEACHING POINTS

Drill 1: Lead-Ups

Select hurdles substitutes that are below hip level for the participants. This will require several lanes of obstacles set at varied heights. Initially, emphasize simply running and clearing the obstacles. Later teach participants to use a 5-pace and thereafter a 3-pace rhythm between the obstacles. Once this is achieved, use low hurdles and emphasize the technique of clearing the obstacles. Progressively increase hurdle height and distance between the hurdles.

Jumping Low Obstacles

Participants run and clear low obstacles. Obstacles can be bamboo canes balanced on traffic cones, elastic high-jump crossbars, or mats laid cross-wise. All obstacles are low and easy for the participants to clear.

Clearing Low Obstacles in Shuttle Relays

Include low obstacles (mats) in shuttle relays. The runners clear each mat and tag their teammate for the return run. Do not emphasize technique or the number of paces taken between the obstacles.

Developing a Stride Pattern

Mark pairs of lines on the ground. Distances between pairs of lines and from one pair to the next vary from one lane to the next, which allows for differences in stride length. Students run along a lane and jump the gaps between the pairs of lines, trying to run 3 paces between each pair of lines.

COACHING POINTS

For the selection of the leading leg when clearing the obstacle

1. Standing with your feet together, lean forward until you overbalance and take a place forward. The leg that you place forward is your leading leg; clear the gap leading with this leg.

2. If you find it too difficult to achieve the 3-pace rhythm in one lane, move to the next where the lines are closer together.

3. Use a rhythm of "over-1-2-3-over-1-2-3-over" to help you as you clear the gap between the lines and run the 3 paces in between.

Developing a Stride Pattern and Clearing Low Obstacles

Set up low obstacles between each pair of lines, placing the obstacles 2/3 of the distance from the first of each pair of lines. Obstacles may be low hurdles, bamboo canes balanced on traffic cones, or ropes held lightly by members of the group. Initially set the height of the obstacles at 6 to 12 inches. Each participant takes off from the line to clear the obstacle and runs 3 paces to the next obstacle. Emphasize that each athlete must try to run moderately fast, keeping each clearance low and maintaining the 3-pace rhythm, but do not emphasize clearance technique. This practice teaches an estimation of the takeoff and rhythm between obstacles.

COACHING POINTS

1. The obstacles are very low, so avoid making your hurdle clearances like 3 high jumps.

2. If you find it difficult to maintain the 3-pace rhythm and clear the hurdles, move to another lane where obstacles are closer together.

3. As you gain confidence and run faster you may want to move back to a lane where the obstacles are farther apart.

Drill 2: Introduction to Hurdling Technique

Many of the drills used to introduce good hurdling technique are similar to those used to develop correct sprinting technique. The close relationship between hurdling and sprinting occurs because a successful hurdler must be an excellent sprinter and because the emphasis on high-knee lift, lower leg extension, and vigorous arm action is essential for both sprinting and hurdling.

Some of the following drills will be tiring for beginners. A recommended distance for each drill is 8 to 10 meters.

High-Knee Marching

Each athlete marches forward slowly, driving the thigh of the leading leg forcefully up to horizontal. The arms are bent at 90 degrees at the elbows, and the supporting leg extends fully up onto the toes as the opposing knee is lifted. The athlete works the arms as vigorously as possible, pulling the elbows back and up. Begin the drill by emphasizing one leg only; thereafter, the athlete elevates each thigh in sequence.

COACHING POINTS

1. Be sure to lift each thigh to horizontal.

2. Push up onto your toes with each step.

3. Work your arms vigorously forward and backward, not across your body.

High-Knee Marching With Extension of the Lower Leg

Each participant practices high-knee marching with extension of the leading leg in the following sequence. The right leg steps forward normally, and the left thigh is raised and the lower leg extended. Next the left leg steps forward normally, and the thigh is raised and the lower leg extended. With each successive step, the right thigh and then left thigh is raised to horizontal, with the lower leg extended each time. The athlete takes each step precisely and slowly, kicking out the lower leg after lifting the thigh to horizontal.

COACHING POINTS

1. Keep your vision directly ahead, and relax your shoulders.

2. Keep your arms at 90 degrees at the elbows, and swing them back and forth vigorously.

3. Lift your thigh as close to horizontal as possible. When the thigh is in the air, kick the lower leg forward and step down to repeat.

High-Knee Running

Each member of the group practices high-knee lift while moving forward at a slow jog. The thighs are raised to horizontal or above, and the knees remain flexed throughout. Students work their arms vigorously throughout. This drill was be quite strenuous for novices.

COACHING POINTS

1. Look forward and try not to lean backward.

2. Concentrate on raising your thigh at least to horizontal.

3. Keep your arms moving strongly back and forth to balance the leg action.

High-Knee Running With Lower Leg Extension

This drill, which is quite exhausting for novices, simulates the prancing motion of a horse. The performer can begin with simple high-knee running and then include the lower leg extension once the rhythm of the high knee lift is established.

COACHING POINTS

1. Set up rhythm while running in place and then try to move forward at a slow jog. Slowly increase the speed of your legs.

2. Use a rhythm pattern of "up-step out, up-step out".

Simulated Hurdling Action

The basic hurdling action is best demonstrated in a mechanical fashion, phase by phase, and as slowly as possible over low hurdles. The participants follow behind and copy your actions. To start, emphasize leg actions.

The sequence of movements is as follows: the left (leading) leg is elevated, the lower leg kicked out forward, and the foot then placed on the ground. As the left leg is elevated the right arm reaches forward to counter-balance it. The right (trailing) leg is turned outward, flexed, at the knee, rotated upward and forward at the hip, swung around and forward, and placed down on the ground. To counterbalance the right leg, the right arm will swing backward. At high speed, arm action will be more vigorous to counter-balance the more powerful leg action.

COACHING POINTS

1. Lift the knee of the leading leg to above horizontal, kick out the lower leg, and step down.

2. Turn the trailing leg out to the side, bend (flex) it at the knee, and bring it forward up and under your arm. Rotate the leg to the front, lower the foot, and step forward.

Leading-Leg Action—No Extension of Lower Leg

Participants walk along the side of low hurdles. If the leading leg is the right, the participant walks on the left side of the hurdles, and vice versa. The participant lifts the thigh of the leading leg so that the foot clears the hurdle; no lower leg extension occurs. The performer places the foot of the leading leg on the ground and moves on to the next hurdle; no trailing-leg clearance of the hurdle occurs. Participants walk to the next hurdle and repeat the sequence over 3 low hurdles.

COACHING POINTS

1. Be sure to flex your leading leg at the knee as you lift your leg upward.

2. Lift the leading leg directly forward and upward; do not swing it sideways and up.

3. Concentrate on the action of the leading leg only. Do not worry at this point about the action of your arms or the trailing leg.

Leading Leg—High-Knee Lift With Lower Leg Extension

Participants jog very slowly with high-knee lifts along the side of the low hurdles. Each participant lifts the thigh of the leading leg to horizontal, extends the lower leg over the hurdle, and brings the trailing leg around the side of the hurdle. The athlete maintain high-knee lift throughout the jog.

COACHING POINTS

1. Lift the thigh of your leading leg above horizontal and kick the heel forward to extend the lower leg.

2. Position yourself so that the leading leg can be extended without hitting the hurdle.

Partner Practice for Trailing-Leg Action

Participants work in pairs. The performer stands on his or her leading leg at the side of a low hurdle, and a partner holds the performer's outstretched arms. The performer brings the trailing leg slowly over the hurdle and down to the ground, then repeats the action.

COACHING POINTS

1. Concentrate on bringing the trailing leg around, forward, and up under your arm.

2. Perform the action slowly and mechanically at first, and then slowly increase speed.

Trailing-Leg Action Only

The athlete walks, then jogs, along the side of low hurdles so that only the trailing leg clears the hurdle. The athlete raises the leading leg to clear an imaginary hurdle; the thigh of the leading leg is raised to horizontal, but no lower leg extension occurs. When the performer places the leading leg on the ground, the trailing leg is brought over the hurdle.

COACHING POINTS

1. Imagine you are clearing a low hurdle with the leading leg. Reach forward with the opposite arm.

2. Lift the thigh of the trailing leg upward and outward to clear the hurdle.

3. Raise the heel of the trailing leg so that your heel does not hit the hurdle.

4. Bring the knee of the trailing leg up and forward, simultaneously swinging the arm on the same side to the rear.

Walking Hurdle Clearance With No Leading-Leg Extension

The performer approaches the hurdle directly from the front at walking speed. The hurdle is set low enough so that full leading-leg extension is not required. The leading leg crosses the hurdle and is placed down on the ground. The performer then brings the trailing leg quickly over the hurdle and walks to the next hurdle to repeat the action. Eact performer should get close enough to the hurdle so that the leading leg can easily clear the hurdle and be placed on the ground. You can increase the intensity of this activity by having the performer move from one hurdle clearance to the next with a prancing, high-knee lift. This is a strenuous activity for beginners; 2 to 3 hurdles in sequence are recommended.

COACHING POINTS

1. Lean your upper body forward as you raise the leading leg. Maintain this lean, because it will make the clearance of the trailing leg easier.

2. Place the foot of the trailing leg on the ground directly ahead of where the leading leg lands.

3. Work your arms vigorously during the hurdle clearance to counter-balance leg action.

Walking Hurdle Clearance With Leading-Leg Extension

The performer walks between the hurdles, raising and extending the leading leg for the hurdle clearance and bringing and trailing leg quickly over the hurdle. You can increase the intensity of this drill by requiring a high-knee lift at jogging speed between the hurdles.

COACHING POINTS

1. After raising the thigh of the leading leg, kick out the heel of the lower leg.

2. Aim for fast, snappy actions during the hurdle clearance.

3. Move slowly between the hurdles, concentrating on the actions needed to clear the hurdle.

Hurdle Clearance From a Running Approach

Students use the normal hurdling action, approaching the hurdle at a jog. Over low hurdles, participants will not need to incline their upper bodies excessively. As participants gain confidence, progressively increase the speed of approach. Use only 1 hurdle for this drill.

COACHING POINTS

1. Begin with fast leg actions and moderate knee lift during the approach to the hurdle.

2. Initially, move slightly faster than walking speed. With each approach, increase your speed.

3. The faster you approach, the farther back your takeoff must be. Work your arms and legs vigorously during clearance.

4. Make the clearance as fast as possible and sprint for another 8 to 10 meters. Do not slow down immediately after clearing the hurdle.

Clearance of 2 Hurdles

Set up 3 or 4 lanes (containing 2 hurdles each) that alternate with lanes containing no hurdles. Each line with hurdles has them set progressively farther apart, at distances ranging from 6 to 10 meters. In the empty lanes, athletes test their approaches and their pacing alongside the hurdles, and partners mark the takeoff positions for the first and second hurdles. Judging from the takeoff marks, participants choose the lane in which they are able to perform 3 paces between each hurdle. Challenge the athletes to see if they can progress to the lane where the hurdles are farthest apart.

COACHING POINTS

1. If you find yourself on top of the second hurdle with no room to take off, move to a lane where hurdles are farther apart.

2. In an empty lane sprint fast, putting in 2 simulated hurdle clearances with 3 paces in between. Your partner checks your takeoff spot for the 1st and 2nd hurdle.

3. Drive low and hard at the first hurdle and sprint to the next.

4. Avoid high-jumping the second hurdle.

5. Do not jump the hurdle: get over it and back to sprinting. Work your arms and legs vigorously.

Step 3: Sprint Start and Approach to the First Hurdle

A sprint start for hurdling may require the performer to place the trailing leg forward in the blocks and set the leading leg to the rear. Therefore, if the hurdler uses 8 strides to reach the first hurdle, he or she should position the trailing leg forward and the leading leg back in the blocks. Some long-legged athletes use 7 strides, in which case the leading leg is put forward in the blocks. Using 9 strides is also acceptable for beginners.

The performer accelerates throughout the drive to the first hurdle and over the next 2 to 3 hurdles. The body becomes upright after the 5th and 6th stride in the approach to the first hurdle.

Clearance of 1 Low Hurdle From a Standing Start

Set up low hurdles in lanes that alternate with lanes containing no hurdles. Vary the distance between hurdles 11 to 13 meters from the starting line. The participant begins by running in a vacant lane along the side of the hurdles. The participant uses a standing start with the left foot forward if the right leg is the leading leg. You or a partner counts the number of strides and marks the 8th stride, which will be the takeoff spot for the hurdle clearance. The distance of the takeoff spot from the hurdle should be approximately 2/3 the total distance taken to clear the hurdle. If you find during these preliminary practices that the hurdle is too far away, use the following options.

Move the hurdle closer until the participant's confidence improves and speed increases. Then shift the hurdle progressively farther back. or, instruct the performer to switch legs at the start and use 9 strides to the first hurdle. The performer can revert back to 8 strides as confidence improves and speed increases.

COACHING POINTS

1. Aim for good acceleration from the standing start.
2. Drive aggressively toward the hurdle.
3. Do not slow down as you approach the hurdle.

Clearance of 2 Hurdles From a Sprint Start

During practice with 2 hurdles, you can vary the distance of the second hurdle from the first, and also set the second hurdle lower in height than the first hurdle. As speed and confidence increases, the athlete works toward taking 8 strides to the first hurdle and 3 strides to the second.

Competition Over Two Hurdles

Competition helps to develop an aggressive approach

to the hurdles. For this practice, vary hurdles in distance from the start in each lane: set some hurdles at 11 meters from the start, some at 12, and others at 13. The second hurdle in each lane may also vary in distance from the first. The total distance to the finish (25 meters) is the same for each lane.

COACHING POINTS

1. Get the leading leg down to the ground as fast as possible after clearing each hurdle.

2. Be aggressive with arm action, and bring your trailing leg past the hurdle as fast as possible.

3. Drive hard between the hurdles and through the finish.

4. Aim for continuous acceleration.

Increasing the Number of Hurdles

As the performer's abilities improve, progressively increase the number of hurdles from 2 to 5. Initially reduce the height of the hurdles and the distance between each hurdle, although urge students to work toward competitive distances and heights. Further improvement in hurdling technique will occur through repeated hurdle clearance, sprinting, practice, and improved flexibility.

400-METER HURDLES

The 400-meter hurdles event is an extension of the sprint hurdle races and is usually considered as event for more mature athletes. Occasionally, 200-meter and 300-meter hurdle races are held, but these distances are now more commonly used as training for the 400-meter distance.

The 400-meter hurdles event demands excellent hurdling ability combined with a high level of sprint-endurance. As such, it is an event built upon a foundation of long sprints (i.e., 400-meter sprints) and sprint hurdling (i.e., 100- and 110-meter hurdles). Coaches normally introduce young athletes to the 400-meter hurdles after building a background in endurance training, sprinting, and sprint hurdling. Because of this, the 400-meter hurdles tends to be a specialist event for the more senior of school-age competitors.

TEACHING TECHNIQUES

Drill 1: Lead-Ups

Review lead-ups and drills for the 100/110-meter hurdles; review lead-ups and drills for sprinting and sprint starts.

Drill 2: Hurdling With a Right- and Left-Leg Lead

Review drills for 100/110-meter hurdling.

Hurdle Clearance at Walking Speed

Set 3 to 4 hurdles 6 to 9 inches below competitive height, arranging them so that only the athlete's leading leg crosses the hurdle. Participants walks and step over each hurdle, leading with the right leg over the first and the left leg over the second, or vice versa. On each occasion, the participant brings the trailing leg around the side of the hurdle.

COACHING POINTS

1. Be slow and precise in your actions to begin with.

2. Try to get comfortable leading with your non-favoured leg.

3. Mimic the action of the trailing leg, but concentrate more on the actions of the leading leg.

Hurdle Clearance at Jogging Speed

Set up hurdles as for hurdle walking. The performer

slowly jogs toward each hurdle, emphasizing high-knee lift. The leading leg crosses the hurdle, and the trailing leg is brought around the side.

COACHING POINTS

1. Use the high-knee lift only as you get close to the hurdle.

2. Lift the thigh and extend the lower leg to cross the hurdle.

3. Your favoured leg will feel comfortable crossing the hurdle.

4. Work on lifting your nonfavoured leg directly toward the hurdle. Kick the heel forward to extend the lower leg.

Hurdle Clearance With Even Strides Between Hurdles

Set up hurdles so that students take 4 to 6 easy running strides between each hurdle. Only the leading leg crosses the hurdle; the trailing leg is brought around the side of the hurdle. The even number of strides between the hurdles will require an alternate leg lead.

COACHING POINTS

1. Be sure to lead with an alternate leg each time. Do not alter the stride pattern so that you lead with the favoured leg throughout.

Hurdle Clearance With Two Strides Between Hurdles

Reduce the distance between low hurdles so that student take 2 easy strudes between each hurdle. This will demand good coordination and an alteration leg lead over each hurdle. Only the leading leg crosses the hurdle; the trailing leg is brought around the side.

COACHING POINTS

1. Concentrate on the nonfavoured leg. Clearances

with the other leg will cause no difficulty.

2. Use a rhythm of "drive-1-2-drive-1-2-drive-1-2" as you cross the hurdles.

3. Reach forward with the opposing arm to balance the leading-leg action.

Lead Leg Clearance Only—2 Strides Between Hurdles

Adjust the distance between 2 hurdles so that students can run 2 strides in between at greater speed. Only the leading leg crosses the hurdle.

Trailing Leg Clearance Only—2 Strides Between Hurdles

Have students repeat the previous 4 drills with only the trailing leg crossing the hurdle.

COACHING POINTS

1. Walk up to the hurdles and lift the trailing leg slowly and mechanically over each hurdle. Concentrate on developing the correct action, particularly when using the nonfavoured trailing leg.

2. When running faster, use strong arm actions and good body lean over the hurdle. This will help the trailing leg clear the hurdle.

3. Simulate the action of the leading leg even though it is not crossing a hurdle.

Hurdle Clearance—Alternate Leg Lead

Place the hurdle in a line; the athlete crosses them directly from the front (i.e., both leading and trailing legs cross the hurdle). Arrange the hurdles to give the athlete 4 or 6 strides in between with an alternate leg lead. Initially reduce the hurdle height, and later increase it. The athlete can also practice over hurdles that are set up to allow 2 strides in between each hurdle.

Alternate Leg Lead Over Hurdles Set on the Curve of the Track

In the 400-meter hurdles, 5 of the 10 hurdles are set on the curves of the track. To prepare for this situation, arrange hurdles as in the previous drill, but place them on the curve of the track. Students practice taking 6 or 8 strides between each hurdle.

COACHING POINTS

1. This drill will show you that it is more efficient (and comfortable) to have a left-leg lead over hurdles set on the curve, particularly when running on the tighter inside lane.

2. The inward lean to the left as you run around the track will help to clear the right (trailing) leg.

3. A right-leg lead is awkward but frequently has to be used, particularly on the last curve, when you are tired. Be sure to run directly at the hurdle so the leading leg crosses the hurdle well toward the outer edge of the hurdle. If you do this, the trailing leg (and foot) will completely cross the hurdle. If they do not cross the hurdle, you will be disqualified.

4. As a beginner, you will find it easier to run directly at hurdles set on the curve of the track for at least 2 strides prior to the hurdle and run straight at least 2 strides after the hurdle. This will help you avoid disqualification.

5. When you are more experienced, you will be able to cross the hurdles at more of an angle.

Alternate Leg Lead With 10 to 14 Strides Between Each Hurdle

Progressively increase distances between hurdles so that students take 10, 12 and 14 strides between each hurdle. The even number of strides demands an alternate leg lead over each successive hurdle. The athlete can begin with hurdles set in adjacent lanes and arranged for leading-leg clearance only. As the athlete's confidence increases, place the hurdles in the same lane so that both the leading leg and trailing leg cross the hurdle.

Hurdle Clearance Using Uneven Strides Between Hurdles

Set distances between hurdles so that the athlete takes an uneven number of strides (9, 11 or 13) between each hurdle. This will require the same leg lead over each hurdle.

Drill 3: Establishing a Stride Pattern for the First Hurdle (And Between Subsequent Hurdles)

The number of strides taken to the first hurdle (competitive distance is 45 meters) varies considerably for each athlete. The number of strides the athlete takes will depend on which leg is forward in the blocks and the stride length taken to the first hurdle. The athlete's natural stride length and level of fitness will determine the number of strides taken between hurdles throughout the race. The stride pattern and tempo of approach to the first hurdle will determine the number of strides taken between the next 5 to 6 hurdles. Fatigue during the remaining 4 to 5 hurdles will require changes in stride pattern, normally an increase in the number of strides taken between hurdles. For example, at the 5th hurdle a 15-stride pattern may be changed to a 17-stride pattern; in this case the stride length must be shortened to include the additional 2 strides. It is not uncommon for athletes to change their stride patterns 3 times within a race.

The stride patterns that elite athletes take to the first hurdle vary from 21 to 24 strides. These athletes then use stride patterns ranging from 13 to 17 strides to the next 5 to 6 hurdles and thereafter up to 19 strides for the remaining hurdles. The stride pattern depends upon the athlete's level of sprint endurance and other factors such as tempo and stride length.

Approach to the First Hurdle

The method for teaching the approach to the first hurdle is the same as for the 100/110-meter hurdle race. The number of strides the athlete uses will depend on the individual. An even number of strides in the approach to the first hurdle will require the starting blocks to be set with the trailing leg forward.

The athlete runs by the side of the first hurdle, noting pacing and takeoff position for the first hurdle and deciding the number of strides to use (e.g., if a 22-stride rhythm is too difficult, the athlete switches to 23 or 24 strides). Starting blocks are readjusted accordingly.

Approach and Clearance of 2 Hurdles—Competitive Distance (35 Meters) Between the Hurdles

Initially place the second hurdle in the adjacent lane. The athlete clears the 1st hurdle (e.g., 22 paces) and runs past the second hurdle, noting the pacing and deciding on the number of the strides to use (e.g., 15) prior to takeoff for the second hurdle. The second hurdle is taken placed in the lane, and the athlete repeats the start and attempts both hurdle clearances. A partner can assist in assessing the stride pattern and determining the number of strides to take between hurdles.

Stride and Tempo Variation Using 2 Hurdles

The athlete uses varying stride patterns (e.g., 17, 18, and 19) while running between the hurdles. This familiarizes the athlete with the "change-up" to a shorter stride length, faster tempo, and increased number of strides between the hurdles.

Approach and Clearance of 3, 4, and 5 Hurdles Set at Competitive Distance

Set 5 hurdles at competitive distances and add 15 meters after the last hurdle. The distance of 45 meters to the first hurdle, 35 meters in between the hurdles, and 15 meters at the finish totals 200 meters. Repetition of this distance, with specific controls set on the speed of the run, the number of repetitions, and the rest period becomes an excellent form of interval training.

Variation

Elite athletes will frequently set 3 to 4 hurdles on the straightaway facing one direction, and in the adjacent lane 3 to 4 hurdles facing the opposing direction. In repetitions using a flying start athletes run up one lane and immediately down the other. Placing the hurdles in adjacent lanes reduces the amount of labour required to place hurdles around the track.

Combinations of Hurdles and Distances

Variations in distance and the number of hurdles help the athlete develop stamina and a feel for pacing and rhythm between the hurdles. The athlete practices changes in the rhythm of running, as well as change up in tempo to diffeiing stride patterns, over distances in which hurdles are included in the latter part of the run. Assign the number of repetitions of each run and the rest periods taken in between according to the level of fitness.

CHAPTER 14

3,000 METER STEEPLECHASE IN RUNNING

The steeplechase was popular at the 2-mile distance in the late 1800's, but was not permanently placed in AAU competition until 1919. In 1932 it was changed to the 3,000-meter steeplechase (total distance 1 mile, 1520 yards, 2 feet, 8 inches). This was an Olympic year, and the 3,000-meter distance conformed to international rules.

In 1948 it became one of the events scheduled every 4 years in the NCAA championship meets, when they were held during an Olympic year. In 1959, it became a permanent part of the NCAA meet schedule. The first NCAA record holder was Pat Traynor, Villanova, whose time of 8:48.6 was set in 1962.

In world class competition, Horace Ashenfelter won the 1952 Olympic Games race in Helsinki, Finland, with a time of 8:45.4. Since this date, the United States has not fared too well. Gaston Roelants of Belgium dominated this event during the mid- and late 1960's winning the 1964 Olympic Games. The present world record holder is Jouko Kuha of Finland, who ran this distance in the outstanding time of 8:24.2. George Young, the top United States prospect and fifth in the 1964 Games, set an American record of 8:30.6 during the pre-Olympic training session. Young ran an exceptional race in the 1968 Mexico City Olympics, placing third in this event.

In recent years, the 3,000-meter steeplechase has become a very popular track event in this country. In fact, it is now an integral part of several intercollegiate conferences and dual and championship meets. Many excellent distance runners perform well in this event. It is a very demanding physical experience, as the performer must clear 4 wooden barriers (3 feet high) and 1 water jump (from a 3-foot barrier) that is 12 feet long. This is done every one of the 7 complete laps of the 400-meter track which is run in this race (a total of 28 jumps over the hurdle and 7 over the water hazard).

The steeplechaser's training program must be two-fold, embracing both distance running and hurdling. The training needed for proficiency as a hurdler is the less exacting. The 3-foot barriers are not much of an obstacle, yet the steeplechaser must display good hurdling form, utilizing the same mechanics of movements used by the intermediate hurdler. One key to successful hurdling of the barriers is for the steeplechaser to "charge" the hurdle; hesitation causes problems. Failure to clear the hurdle through jumping rather than hurdling will temporarily slow or stop all forward momentum. The idea is to get over the barrier and return to a running stride as quickly as possible without loss of forward momentum. This means that the steeplechaser must hurdle rather than jump the barriers.

On the other hand, clearing the water barrier does take a lot of practice, as there are definite techniques to be used in the effective accomplishment of this task. The length of the water hazard jump (12 feet) makes it necessary for the steeplechaser to jump to the top of the 3-foot barrier placed immediately prior to it. He then pushes off from the barrier with his feet in order to clear or go over as much of the water hazard as possible. The steeplechaser's intent should be to clear the hurdle barrier and the water jump area without any appreciable loss of his forward momentum. (He lands on one foot in a stride position).

Steeplechase, which is derived from cross-country running and obstacle course races, is a combination of distance running, hurdling, and water jumps and as such combines the training necessary for the distance runner and the hurdler. At present steeplechase is a track event for males only.

The laws of the event allow the athlete to jump on and off the water-jump barrier and to use the same technique in clearing the steeplechase hurdles. The athlete is also permitted to vault over the barriers, although this method is seldom used because it is extremely inefficient. The hurdles and the water jump barrier used in the steeplechase are solid, heavy barriers designed to support the weight of several athletes at the same time. The barriers are not designed to fall or to be knocked over in the manner that occurs in the 100-110-meter and 400-meter hurdles.

Clearance of the water jump requires a technique similar to that used in jumping on and off steeplechase hurdles. The two types of obstacles differ in that the water jump not only has a barrier but also a 3.66-meter (12-foot) water pit, which the athlete must jump across or run through. The common practice is to jump up onto the 91.4-centimeter (3-foot) barrier with one leg and use the same leg to drive across the water. Occasionally an athlete will jump from the barrier and totally clear the water, but most athletes land with 1 foot in the water and step out with the other.

For athletes over 19 years of age, the competitive steeplechase distance is 3,000 meters with the water jump most frequently on the inside of the track. Each lap is slight less than 400 meters (approximately 390 meters). At the senior level, a 3,000-meter race contains 28 hurdles and 7 water jumps. A 2,000-meter steeplechase race has 18 hurdles and 5 water jumps, and the 1,500-meter race 12 hurdles and 3 water jumps. The latter two races are usually run by athletes below senior age level.

An athlete who concentrates on steeplechase needs to be an excellent distance and cross-country runner and a good hurdler and must be strong enough to perform efficiently over the water jump. One of the biggest difficulties that the steeplechaser will face is estimating takeoff positions for the hurdles and the water jump throughout the race relative to an increasing level of fatigue. All steeplechasers jump on and off the water-jump barrier. Some use the same technique on the hurdles, whereas others use a hurdle clearance similar to a 400-meter hurdler. Whatever the method, the athlete must cross the barriers as efficiently as possible and with minimum wastage of energy.

HURDLE PRACTICE

The steeplechaser should practice his hurdling form at every practice session, during either the warming-up or "warming-down" running periods. Regular hurdles set at the height of 3 feet should be placed on the track at the official locations; as the steeplechaser runs his laps he also hurdles these barriers. Use of proper hurdling form in these practice session is essential to the development of proper hurdling mechanics needed in a competitive race. In most instances, the hurdle should be taken with the dominant leg. That is, if the steeplechaser is right-handed, he would normally lead with his right leg, and therefore take off from the ground with his left foot.

WATER JUMP TECHNIQUE

The water jump, as can be imagined, is the most difficult part of the race. Fortunately, it only occurs one during each lap of the race. The reason for its difficulty is that the steeplechaser must clear the 3 foot wooden barrier as well as the 12-foot water jump. As has been stated, continuous momentum is essential for successful clearance of all of the barriers. To insure attainment of sufficient distance in the jump, and in order to maintain continuous momentum, the steeplechaser should spring to the top of the hurdle and jump the water barrier in one motion. If he is right-handed, he should probably plan to land on the top of the hurdle with his left foot, as does the long-jumper on the takeoff board. This will put him in position to use the so-called "springing leg" for jumping the 12-foot distance, and to keep the strong (dominant) leg available for landing purposes.

In practice, a marker placed a few strides from the hurdle for foot striking purposes will enable the runner to adjust his stride in order to assure proper foot placement up to and on top of the hurdle. If these last few steps and the move up to the top of the hurdle are taken smoothly, and executed rapidly, the runner can push off the top of the barrier with confidence that he has the strength and momentum to clear much or all of the water hazard. Most steeplechasers attempt to land at approximately the 11-foot mark. Some top performers land beyond the water hazard. Since the landing position of the runner is important for proper subsequent action, it is necessary that he land and reach with the opposite leg for the next step in one continuous movement. Consequently, he should not land with a stiff leg, but with one which is slightly bent and ready for a quick extension. If the runner lands in a straight, stiff-legged position, he will tend to "brake" his momentum and disturb the rhythm. Therefore, mastery of the technique of negotiating the water jump is of paramount importance.

A water jump can be simulated by placing one of the hurdles near the long jump area. The stride patterns could be marked off and the 12-foot water jump measured out, using the long jump pit as part of the area. The runner can run, hit this stride pattern, jump onto the hurdle, push off, and land in the sand. This is the safest procedure and also makes use of much drier material than is contained in the regulation water jump.

Confidence is every phase of the water jump technique can be gained through practice in this type of simulated area. Ability to hurdle the barriers, clear the water hazard, and run the 3,000-meter distance with assurance characterizes the champion steeplechaser.

TRAINING PROGRAM

As has been stated earlier, the steeplechaser must first be a distance runner. The training program that he should follow would be almost identical to that designed for a 2-miler.

PRECAUTIONS

Steeplechase is a demanding distance race. In terms of fatigue, a 1,500-meter steeplechase race is generally considered equal to a 3,000-meter race on the flat. Young athletes are usually introduced to steeplechase by way of cross-country running. Their initial experiences with steeplechase should be short competitions that have the minimal number of hurdle and water-jump clearances.

It is particularly important that the young athlete learn to jump on the jump off the barriers before learning to hurdle. In addition, the athlete should develop a good aerobic base through the long runs and interval training. The stamina that the athlete develops with this kind of training will mean that fatigue will take longer to affect the quality of the clearance technique used. Part of the young athlete's training will be to recognize and guage the onset of fatigue and to decide when to switch from actually hurdling steeplechase hurdles to the easier technique of jumping on and off.

To maintain a high level of safety, check all steeplechase hurdles and the water-jump barrier to make sure that they are stable and capable of withstanding the force applied by several athletes jumping on and off the same time. Replace the tops of barriers when they become splintered, and be sure the floor of the water-jump pit is smooth and covered either with the same rubberized surface used on the track or with a mat. This cushions the athlete's landing when he jumps down into the water. Empty the water from the water-jump pit when it is not in use.

Competitors should wear well-fitting spikes that drain well and are comfortable to run in when wet. A good safety practice is to have athletes walk into the water-jump pit with their spikes on, totally immerse their feet (and shoes), and then retighten the soaked laces. Nylon shoes stretch when they become wet, and this precaution prevents shoes from becoming loose and uncomfortable during a race.

In physical education classes in which students to not wear spikes, it's best to use a simulated water jump: students jump onto a steeplechase hurdle and then into the sand of the long-jump pit. Even though the surface of the hurdle is likely to remain dry, be aware that wet grass or sand on top of the hurdle can cause an athlete not wearing spikes to slip. When students wear rubber-soled shoes, all surfaces should be dry and the hurdle surface brushed clean of sand and dirt.

The preparation for clearing the hurdles and the water

jumps is an important part of steeplechase technique. Elite athletes become accustomed to occasional bumping and jostling and to maneuvering and adjusting their approach for each of the barriers. Even though bumping occurs, athletes are expected to respect the rules and avoid cutting in and disrupting the approaches of others. The first barrier (hurdle) in a steeplenchase race is purposely made longer so that at the start of the race, athletes who are bunched close together can clear the hurdle without incident.

Teach the athletes to approach all barriers straight on so that the contact of the foot with the barrier is at a right angle. This becomes even more important when the barriers become wet on top. When the water jump is on a curve of the track, the athlete should run wide so that the approach to the water jump is in a straight line.

The athlete must not run closely behind an opponent when approaching the barriers. It is better to shift away from the opponent and get a clear view of the barrier, so that if the opponent trips and falls, the athlete behind is not involved in the same incident. Also, teach athletes to avoid pausing after landing in the water at the water jump. Other athletes will be following and preparing to jump down from the barrier.

For indoor training, vaulting boxes safely substitute for steeplechase barriers providing that spotters stabilize the boxes. Outdoors, a steeplechase barrier set in front of the long-jump pit provides a good substitute for the water jump, particularly as landing in the sand simulates the drag of the water.

When you work with young athletes, the most important feature of training is careful and progressive development. Increase of the competitive distance and the number and height of the barriers as fitness and maturity develop. For beginners, 1 or 2 vaulting-box sections 30 to 60 centimetres tall set in front of the long-jump pit substitute adequately for a water jump.

TECHNIQUE

At about 10 to 15 metes prior to the water jump, the athlete accelerates in order to jump up onto the barrier and then clear the water. The takeoff usually occurs 1.5 to 2 meters prior to the barrier. The upper body leans forward, and the free leg is flexed so that the instep can be placed on the barrier.

Once on the barrier, the supporting leg flexes to approximately 90 degrees and the upper body is kept low so that the athlete passes low over the barrier, rather than jumping upward.

When the athlete's body has passed over the supporting leg, the spikes grip the forward edge of the barrier in preparation for the drive over the water. The athlete drives forward and downward with the leading leg, aiming at landing 30 to 40 centimetre before the end of the water jump. The athlete extend the arms sideways on the landing to maintain balance.

TEACHING TIPS

Drill 1. Lead-Ups

Drill 2. Steeplechase Hurdle and Water-Jump Clearance

Drill 1: Lead-Ups

All lead-up drills used for distance running and for hurdling are excellent preparation for the steeplechase, because a steeplechaser is in essence a cross-country runner competing on the track. Lead-ups that develop stamina, hurdling ability are excellent preparation for the steeplechaser. Flexibility exercises will improve hurdling technique, and weight training leg exercises and rebound jumping (plyometrics) are excellent for improving leg strength and assisting in the clearance of the water jump.

The developmental sequence for teaching steeplechase consists of combining endurance training with drills that teach the young athlete to jump on and off the steeplechase hurdles.

Because the steeplechase hurdle has the same dimensions as the barrier in front of the water jump, a common practice is to use a hurdle as a substitute for the water-jump barrier and the long-jump pit as a substitute water jump. Once accustomed to landing in the sand, the athlete then progresses to clearing the actual water pit. Throughout these practices, the athlete can work to develop a reasonable hurdling technique over low sprint hurdles. When the athlete can easily clear 91.4-centimeter sprint hurdles, he can apply the same technique to steeplechase hurdles.

Drill 2: Steeplechase Hurdle and Water-Jump Clearance

Jumping on and off a vaulting box

The vaulting box is progressively built up in sections to the competitive steeplechase height of approximately 3 feet. Students can initially practice in the gym, starting with lower the heights and using a mat to cushion the landing. The athlete jumps onto the box and, using the same leg, drives forward onto the mat (the takeoff leg from the floor is not the same leg used to drive from the box). Each athlete should learn to lead with either leg and to judge the takeoff position relative to the approach speed. The athlete must drive forward and upward with the arms and free leg to help jump onto the box. Once on the box, the athlete rotates forward over a flexed supporting leg keeping the body low and the torso inclined forward during the clearance. The athlete uses a strong drive forward with the leading leg to jump from the box and uses the arms to maintain balance during the landing. Bounding and hopping activities used in triple jump are useful preparatory exercises for steeplechase hurdle and water-jump clearance.

Use spotters to assure that the vaulting box is stable and will not tilt when the performer jumps onto it. The athlete must approach and jump onto the box at a 90° angle; any other angle may cause the athlete to fall when jumping onto a wet steeplechase barrier. The athlete must approach the box at right angles.

COACHING POINTS

1. To begin with, use your favoured leg to jump up onto the hurdle from the ground.

2. Run wide from the curve and line up directly at the centre of the vaulting box.

3. Swing the thigh of the leading leg upward and drive strongly from the jumping leg.

4. Swing both arms forward and upward to assist you in jumping up onto the box.

5. Stay low over the box; do not straighten up.

6. Jump long and low down to the ground.

7. Put your arms out sideways to help maintain balance in the landing.

8. Keep moving forward; do not pause at the landing. In a race other competitors will follow.

Inclusion of a Vaulting Box and Two Low Sprint Hurdles in a Circuit

This practice is for the athlete who can hurdle over low hurdles and adjust the approach for takeoff to the hurdles.

Variations in the size of the circuit and the position

of the box and hurdles develop the athlete's abilities to assess the distance of the jump takeoff and to clear the hurdles. At least 15 meters should be available for acceleration toward the box. Use check marks set at 6 to 8 strides prior to the box to help beginners judge the approach distance for takeoff. You can also set the box low and then progressively move it higher. Initially set the hurdles well below 91.4 centimetres.

COACHING POINTS

1. Try to lengthen your stride rather than shorten it when assessing the distance for the takeoff to the box.

2. Accelerate toward the box; do not slow down.

Jumping On and Off a Steeplechase Hurdle

The steeplechase hurdle substitutes for the barrier in front of the water jump, because both are the same height and width. Draw a line on the ground to indicate the 3.66 meters of the water jump.

COACHING POINTS

1. Be sure to accelerate toward the hurdle.

2. Contact the hurdle with your instep; allow your foot to roll on the top of the hurdle so that the instep of the foot grips the far side of the hurdle.

3. Lean forward and flex the supporting leg on the hurdle so that your body rotates low over the hurdle. (Do not try standing up on the hurdle).

4. Drive low and forward for the landing.

5. Use the swing of the leading leg to assist in driving your body outward for the landing.

Combining a Steeplechase Hurdle and the Long-Jump Pit to Simulate a Steeplechase Water-Jump Clearance

Place a steeplechase hurdle at the edge of the

longjump pit, and include other steeplechase hurdles or sprint hurdles in a circuit. Athletes jump up onto the hurdle and jump down into the sand of the long-jump pit.

COACHING POINTS

1. Concentrate on driving low and forward into the landing.

2. Do not relax in the landing; try to keep moving forward.

Jumping Onto the Water-Jump Barrier and Clearing the Water Jump

The performer jumps up onto the barrier and aims to clear all but the final few centimetres of water. One foot lands in the water and the other steps forward out of the water to continue running. Teach the performer that the single-legged landing in the water is an active landing from which the athlete quickly moves forward.

COACHING POINTS

1. The single-legged landing in the water is an active landing: do not relax when you land, but keep driving forward. The next stride should be clear of the water.

Improvement of Steeplechase Hurdle Clearance

Remember steeplechase hurdles cannot be set at a height lower than 91.4 centimetres. They are built to support several athletes jumping on them at the same time. Consequently, the novice should continue to jump on and off steeplechase hurdles until an adequate hurdle clearance technique is developed over sprint hurdles. It is an advantage to be able to hurdle with either leg leading, although this is not absolutely necessary. For greater confidence in clearing the 91-centimeter steeplechase hurdles, the athlete must be comfortable in hurdling sprint hurdles set at 98 centimeters.

Clearing a Steeplechase Water Jump and Steeplechase Hurdles in Distance Training

Place the steeplechase water jump and steeplechase hurdles in various sections of middle-distance training runs. By varying the positions of the barriers, you force the athlete to adjust approach and stride pattern relative to various levels of fatigue. If several athletes train together, this drill forces each athlete to asses stride patterns for takeoff under competitive conditions. The level of fatigue will vary according to the run.

ENCYCLOPAEDIA OF TRACK AND FIELD
(In 3 Vol.)

YOGRAJ THANI, RACHNA
& DEEPAK JAIN

Vol. 3

SPORTS PUBLICATION

Delhi-110 052

Published by:

Lokesh Thani

SPORTS PUBLICATIONS

H.O. 4264/3, Ansari Road, Darya Ganj, New Delhi-110002
B.O. WP-474, Ist Floor, Shiv Market, Ashok Vihar, Delhi-52
Phones: 3246532, 7241050, 7562163
Website: *www.sportsbookshouse.com*

I.S.B.N. –.81-7879-56-4

PRINTED IN INDIA 2003

Laser Typeset by:

JAIN MEDIA GRAPHICS

B-4/40-A, Lawrence Road, (Keshav Puram),
(Near Chandni Restaurant),
New Delhi-110035

Printed by:

CHAWLA OFFSET PRINTERS

Delhi-110052

Price: Rs. 3000/- (3 Vol.)

ENCYCLOPAEDIA OF TRACK AND FIELD
(In 3 Vol.)

YOGRAJ THANI, RACHNA
& DEEPAK JAIN

Vol. 2

SPORTS PUBLICATION

Delhi-110 052

Published by:

Lokesh Thani

SPORTS PUBLICATIONS

H.O. 4264/3, Ansari Road, Darya Ganj, New Delhi-110002
B.O. WP-474, Ist Floor, Shiv Market, Ashok Vihar, Delhi-52
Phones: 3246532, 7241050, 7562163
Website: *www.sportsbookshouse.com*

I.S.B.N. – 81-7879-56-4

PRINTED IN INDIA 2003

Laser Typeset by:

JAIN MEDIA GRAPHICS

B-4/40-A, Lawrence Road, (Keshav Puram),
(Near Chandni Restaurant),
New Delhi-110035

Printed by:

CHAWLA OFFSET PRINTERS

Delhi-110052

Price: Rs. 3000/- (3 Vol.)

VOL. II

PART 3

JUMPING

CONTENTS

PART 4

THROWING

CONTENTS

PART 3
JUMPING

CHAPTER

THE IMPORTANCE OF COACHING IN JUMPING EVENTS

ORGANISATION OF COACHING

The organisation of coaching, for athletes is based on a three-tier system consisting of a first, second, and third tier, as follows:

First Tier

Two principal National Coaches and the Coaching Administrator.

The two principal National Coaches are responsible for all technical development including the organisation of coaching for the national track and field teams and the overseeing of all groups of event specialisation.

Second Tier

All National Coaches together with other senior coaches specifically nominated for event responsibility.

Their duties are concerned with event specialisation and responsibility at all national levels and also with the development of selected top-class athletes in the events for which they are responsible. National Coaches also have regional and area responsibilities.

Third Tier

All senior coaches, club coaches, assistant club coaches and teachers holding the appropriate qualification. Their duties include coaching or assisting with coaching at area, region, country, club and school level.

Within the senior coach structure, appointments have been made to staff coach. Such appointments are made by areas or regions in consultation with the national and event coaches. Staff coaches have an important role in the event responsibility aspect of the scheme.

Any young athlete who requires coaching would be advised to contact the coaching department of his area or national organisation and they will be able to put him in touch with the coach who lives nearest to his home.

THE COACHING SESSION

Coach and athlete should meet either once or twice a week. On one of these occasion the coach will be involved in actively coaching the athlete and on the other he may just watch him in training. A club coach has to divide his time among a number of athletes and it is not always possible to coach every athlete at each club practice.

The session can begin with a mass warm-up at the track for all the athletes and this can be taken by the club coach with assistant coaches to help him. It will begin with jogging, running and slopping exercises, followed by striding and some sharper bursts over about 80 meters. The track suit should be worn in cold weather for all this preliminary work and taken off only when the more technical work begins.

The club coach should come to the track with a clear plan in his mind for all the events under his control. His assistants can each be given groups to help or supervise by timing, measuring or recording. In some cases they will be coaching specific skills under the direction of the coach. Some clubs may be fortunate and have several coaches capable of looking after events to a higher level. In this case, each one could be given a specific group of events to look after for the season, e.g., jumping, sprinting, hurdling, throwing etc. Assistant coaches can often be recruited from amongst the mothers and fathers who come to the track to watch their youngsters perform. An enquiry by the club coach may unearth a father or mother who was at one time a good performer and who still knows something about one or two events. In this case they should be encouraged to take up coaching at the club. The club coach and club secretary can do a lot to persuade these people to give a hand rather than sit in their cars waiting for the session to end.

WAYS IN WHICH THE COACH CAN HELP THE ATHLETE LEARN TECHNIQUES AND TECHNICAL SKILLS

By Personal Demonstration

If the coach happens to be a good demonstrator then this can be useful. However, if the coach is young enough to demonstrate well, he is seldom old enough to have experience.

Getting an Expert to Demonstrate the Event

This can be extremely valuable if the coach can talk about the event and outline the technique which is being exhibited by the demonstrator. This also has an inspirational value which has a big part to play in the early instruction of the young athlete.

Putting athlete in position and guiding

This is all right in the beginning because it gives the athlete some idea. However, all movements are performed at speed, and therefore, this method has its limitations.

Verbal Instruction

The coach must spend a certain amount of time on each session instructing the athlete verbally. There are, however, certain pitfalls into which the coach can be drawn, even with the best of intentions, therefore:

(A) What he says must be brief and to the point. Coaches tend, by the nature of their profession, to become verbose. Too much instruction is both tedious and confusing to the athlete. It is far better to say too little than too much because the short sharp instruction will at least be put into effect because it will be heard and understood.

(B) In cold weather, outdoor instructions should be given 'on the move'. Run with the athlete as he jogs back up the runway and tell him quickly what happened and how to correct the fault. In all cases be quick and decisive; do not come back and have second thoughts, explaining all over again something which you are not sure about.

Asking the athlete to report back his sensations after each jump

For instance, if the athlete has just cleared the bar with a 'Fosbury Flop' ask him to explain his sensations during the run-up, take-of and clearance. It is better to be specific and say something like, 'Where were your hips in relation to the rest of your body as you crossed the bar?' After the athlete has explained briefly to the coach what he thought happened, he may be surprised to be told by the coach that his sensations were wrong. The athlete must then go back and try again until he gets the feeling the coach requires. This is an important aspect of coaching and in this way the coach also learns and builds up a mental picture of what it feels like to the athlete.

Getting the athlete to explain the techniques of his event to others

In the club hut during the winter months this can be an interesting and profitable exercise. Also, on the track, an experienced athlete can sometimes help the coach instruct beginners because he has had the feeling of certain situations himself. The coach cannot have experienced every event himself to high level and, therefore, the experienced athlete can be of assistance to him at certain times.

MENTAL PRACTICE

The coach should give the athlete a true picture of the event and the sensations experienced on each successive movement. He should then ask the athlete to go through the whole skill over and over again in his mind. This form of mental training has been shown to produce an immediate improvement in performance.

CINE FILMS

This is a first rare method of instruction. Take film of the athlete both in competition and training and show it to him many times with comments and criticisms. The coach should let him sit down by himself, watching it and comparing it with champion in the same event. All the time he will be learning.

VIDEO TAPE

This is better than cine film in that the athlete performs his event in training and can then walk straight across and see exactly what he has done. His sensations are still with him as he watches his every movement on the television screen. Although this is the ultimate in training aids, it is inevitably very expensive to hire.

DRAWINGS, PHOTOGRAPHS, STRIP PICTURES AND TECHNICAL ARTICLES

These are ideal for the club coach - easy to obtain and inexpensive. They should be pinned round the walls of the club hut both for their instructional and inspirational value. Young boys and girls should be encouraged to read about top athletes, get to know what they look like and how they perform and train. The club should buy suitable magazine and make them available to club members. The first requisite of the coach is that he should be available. The athlete should be able to see him at least once a week at the track and he should be available for advice at other times. The coach must also be on time; if the athlete knows the coach will be on time, there is far less likelihood of him cutting a session or being late. The coach must be the driving force behind the athlete and the onus must always fall on him.

The coach must have sufficient technical knowledge to teach the athlete the fundamentals of his event. He must also be capable of imparting this knowledge to the athlete in terms that he can understand and interpret into physical movement. Many people can learn and understand the technical skills underlying an event, but not so many can 'get it over' in a way which will get results. It is only by experience that the coach can understand the feelings of the athlete on the end of a pole and formulate phrases which mean anything to a boy in this situation. Hence it is essential that the coach gets experience by coaching and not just by reading technical books. Reading is important but it is more important to see and appreciate physical movement.

BASIC EQUIPMENTS FOR THE CLUB COACH

Clip board with pencil attached, preferably with waterproof cover and metal clip to hold a watch.

First aid kit (small).

10 meter tape measure.

One pair of flat training shoes.

Pair of pliers for removing spikes.

Pair of wooden clappers to use instead of a starting pistol.

Penknife.

Safety pins (various sizes).

Scissors.

Short steel tape measure for block spacing and stride length measurements.

Spare shoelaces.

Starting pistol and ammunition.

Stop watch.

Talcum powder, useful for shoes and checkmarks.

Whistle.

Stop watches vary - for sprinting, a 10-second dial sweep with a split hand is preferable. For middle distance, a 60-second sweep measured in 10ths, with a split hand for lap times, is essential. The coach should remember that he will be standing out in all weathers, so warm waterproof clothing and footwear is necessary throughout the winter and spring. Remember, also, that the head needs protection when one is standing still in cold winds for several hours; the waterproof jacket should also have a hood to cover the head.

CHAPTER 2

THE HISTORY OF HIGH JUMP

When the final history of improvement in form in the high jump is written, it is quite likely to take a circuitous route from emphasis upon the run and take-off through rather exclusive attention to the method of clearing the bar and finally back to the full development of all phases of the event—the run, take-off, and clearance.

More exactly stated, this event is a run, jump and lay-out over a bar. Earliest scissors jumpers thought, or at least performed, entirely in terms of the run and jump. They soon discovered, however, that a fast run did not help the upward leap and therefore adopted a slow approach, which to this day, with very few exceptions, has been universally followed. For these jumpers, form then was in terms of take-off—the approach, the crouch, the vertical lift of the body as a whole, and the vertical driving kick of each leg in turn. Jumping high, driving all parts of the body as high as possible, was their entire concept of good form. Using this form with only a slight backward lay-out, W. Byrd Page, of the University of Pennsylvania, only 5′ 6¾″ tall, was the first to clear 6 feet officially and, in 1887, established the world's record of 6′ 4″. It is essential, in understanding the relative importance of the various phases of form, that this height be considered and compared with the world's record of today. The greatest high-jumpers of the past 65 years or more, with their perfection of lay-out over the bar, have been able to add only about 7 inches to Page's record with his "poor" form. This is undoubtedly the smallest percentage of improvement in any event on the track and field program. A full explanation of this fact should develop as the discussion continues. It is sufficient at this point to emphasize that the least economical style in terms of clearance must yet have possessed the essentials of performance, and that, despite our present almost exclusive concern for layout, it is actually a matter of less importance than the other phases of form.

This concern for lay-out was initiated primarily by Michael Sweeney, of the Xavier Athletic Club, who, in 1895, set the record at 6′ 5$\frac{5}{8}$″. Sweeney's style was distinctly a two-part action: first the upward leap, then the snap of the upper body into a more horizontal position. His run was from directly in front at a 90-degree angle to the bar. He first threw up his right leg, then the left, but in contrast to scissors jumpers, he brought the left leg under the right and down to the ground first. This brought him around on his left side as he cleared the bar and made it possible to lower the great weight of the shoulders and head to the left and down to the bar. Lowering the centre of gravity of these body parts lifted the hips and buttocks, which had formerly been the cause of dragging off the bar.

This Sweeney, or "Eastern" form, as it is commonly called today (probably as a means of distinguishing it from the Western roll but also because jumpers in the East of the United States persisted in its methods until well into the 1930's), had certain definite assets. The primary problems in high-jumping is to convert the forward momentum of the body to a vertical direction. This is best done by crouching slightly during the last two or three strides, by sticking the take-off foot well ahead of the body, causing a backward lean, which "brakes" the forward speed and converts it upward. This direction is made more vertical by the vigorous throw of the lead leg directly upward and not sideward, the upward drive of the leg shoulder and arm, and the straight-upward lift of the chest and head. All these actions are an inherent part of both the scissors and the Eastern style, and for these sound reasons the Easterns style is still the accepted method in all other countries of the world. In fact, the 1948 Olympic games winner, John Winter of Australia, used this style in clearing 6′ 6″.

However, despite these advantages and its present-day use, the writer is convinced that the Easten style of jumping does not have either the potential or the immediate value of the Western and straddle forms. Suffice it to say that men who used this style properly and successfully (Wesley Oler, Yale University, 1916, 6′ 4½″; George Spitz, New York University, 1933, 6′ 8½″) placed great emphasis upon the run and take-off. Few better statements of their more effective use have been written than this by the great athlete:

Most of the spring in high jumping starts from the heel of the foot and not from the ball as is commonly supposed. It is always remembered that he used to compare his jumping with pole vaulting—imagining his take-off leg as the pole—and just as the vaulter jams his pole into the hole at the take-off board, so he jammed his foot down; then keeping the leg stiff, rose on it as the vaulter rises on his pole, getting his upward swing just as he does, by kicking up the other leg.

An even greater emphasis upon full utilisation of the run was expressed by Clinton Larson, of Brigham Young University, national champion in 1917, who cleared 6′ 9½″ in an exhibition meet in 1924. This is an amazing record, considering Larson's short height—5′ 9½″—and his very poor efficiency of clearance.

Many excellent Easter-style jumpers have demonstrated remarkable ability to utilize its advantages as emphasized by Oler and Larson and also to minimize its weaknesses. The extreme contortions by which they lowered their shoulders and raised their hips were truly amazing. I.K. Baxter, Richard W. Landon, LeRoy T. Brown, Clearance T. Flahine, and George Spitz, were all great stylists. Probably the greatest of these was the last named, George Spitz (New York University '33), who cleared 6' 8½" off the boards indoors, and 6' 8½" unofficially outdoors. Spitz's greatest asset in clearance lay in his straight second, or take-off, leg, which he whipped vertically upward in such vigorous fashion as to lift his hip up and away from the bar.

The next great innovation in style came in 1912, 17 years after Sweeney's record, when George Horine, of Stanford University, startled the world and the East in particular by clearing 6' 7". Horine describes the discovery of his new style as a chance circumstances of right-footed jumping companions and a tiny jumping area that forced him to run from the "wrong" side. Like those of Oler's, the fundamentals of his form as he describes them are as sound today as when written in 1920:

The run is made from the left side and the take-off from the left foot. I used a short, slow preliminary run—really a walk—except for the last three or four steps. It was therefore necessary that I hit the exact spot on the ground without getting overbalanced or out of line with my foot. When my condition was right, I invariably hit my take-off to an inch. I never measured my run and never marked my take-off.

I always used two handkerchiefs on the bar. I watched these and tried to clear between them. I never took my eyes off these two cross-bar markers. I paid a great deal of attention to this point and also kept my mind on the take-off problem when actually competing, that is, during the jump.

Getting the take-off squarely under the body is quite a factor in the jump. Leaning forward too far shoots one into the bar and leaning back will tend to drop a jumper on the bar. My spring was made from the heel of the foot. I always used a modified running shoe without heel spikes but with a small pad inside to prevent bone bruises. I crouch slightly at the time of the foot stamp. The legs are not held together, nor is the body thrown forward to any great extent. The right leg is immediately kicked up hard and as high as possible, slightly to the right of the line of approach.

The left leg is snapped up against the right as the ground is left and almost instantly the body is turned toward the bar. By the time the maximum height is reached, the turn has been continued until I am facing the ground. This turn in the air has given the "form" its name, for it is often referred to as the "roll". The position going over is nearly parallel with the ground, with the head raised a trifle. As the right leg is kicked up, the left arm is also extended and generally follows the right leg by a few inches across the bar.

Since Horine's record in 1912, the world's record has been broken by seven men. Five of these men—Ed Beeson, Harold Osborn, Walter Marty, Cornelius Johnson, and Mel Walker—jumped a style that, with individual variations of course, was very similar to that of Horine. The other two—Dave Albritton and Les Steers used a variation of the Western roll, the straddle jump. Of the 47 men whom Potts and Quercetani have listed as having jumped higher than Horine's record of 6′ 7″, only 12 have used the Eastern style of clearance. Two of these have bettered 6′ 8″—George Spitz and Kalevi Kotkas. Despite the prevalence of Eastern-style jumpers abroad, the record seems clearly in favour of the Western style and its variation, the straddle.

Probably the most perfect style of clearance in the Western roll was made by Harold Osborn, of the University of Illinois, in 1924: 6′ 8¼″. Osborn, who was only 5′ 11½″ tall, was able to judge the height of the bar exactly and consistently jumped just high enough to make an economical clearance. Through this skill and his manner of rolling around the bar, he was able to push it against the uprights of the standards and, according to his critics, hold it on the supporting pegs even though his body was at a slightly lower height. On occasion, the bar did bounce but it stayed on. Through the general criticism of the Western roll, with its tendency toward diving, new rules were established making diving subject to disqualification and new standards constructed that placed the cross-bar on top of the uprights as they are today.

Osborn claims that his development of style was entirely without knowledge of the form of Horine. He had come upon an article in the American Boy by Walter Camp:

In this article, Mr. Camp described Alma Richard's form and I tried to imitate his style. Instead of doing this I actually thrust my foot further to the left and developed more of a layout. In a great many respects my form resembles the Western form although it is my own style, and aside from the stimulus I have mentioned it is original. Prior to this time I had no opportunity of seeing any of the best jumpers in action and had no knowledge of the "roll" form that has been made famous by Horine and Beeson.

Osborn's style of clearance, was extremely efficient. As he approached the height of his jump, he extended his lead leg and his body along the bar, lying out on his left side and rolling around the bar. It is difficult to conceive of a more efficient clearance with a side and back position.

However, by introducing a prone position, a new style, the straddle, produce what must be considered the ultimate in economy of clearance. Disregarding other aspects of the high jump, there is no possible improvement in clearance, except in small details of course, over the prone bar-hugging position of Dave Albritton, Les Steers, or J. Lewis Hall.

This style of clearance was first jumped in big-time competition by Jim Stewart, of the University of Southern California, National Collegiate champion in 1930. Dean Cromwell gives a tongue-in-check explanation of how Stewart invented this form:

Like other users of this form, Jim could jump with either of the Western rolls. Jim picked up the roll so quickly that I asked him if he had ever tried it as a youngster. He said that he had been raised on a ranch and had needed considerable agility at the fences whenever the cattle went rampaging. At first he took the barbed wire fences with the scissors high jump form, but he found this dorsal clearance both destructive for the seat of his trousers and unpleasant anatomically. Finally, he said, since the cattle did not get any more peaceful and the fences did not get any lower, he was forced to use the technique of the belly roll, for with this form he could hold down the barbed wire as he rolled over it. I never believed Jim's yarn either.

The great advantage of this straddle style lies in its completely prone lay-out; only the thickness of the body must rise above the bar, rather than its width as in the Western roll and perfected Eastern style. In addition, the eyes are toward the bar at all times, where they can judge its height and make clearance of all body parts accordingly. It seems clear, to the writer at least, that despite its weaknesses at the take-off and despite its demand for great agility and co-ordination, the ultimate and perfect human record in the high jump will be made with a style of jump that uses this method of clearing the bar.

It is therefore reasonable to assume that if improvement in form in the high jump is to take place, and of course it will for many years to come, the thoughts and actions of coaches and athletes must circle back to the much neglected run and take-off. It is the considered opinion of the writer that a man can learn to handle greater speed at the take-off than has heretofore generally been the case, and that some means of suddenly bracing against horizontal momentum can be acquired, thus catapulting the body into the air with a straddle style of clearing a bar well over the now "ultimate" 7 feet. The jumper will have Les Steers's ability to take work, developed through years of effort, but he will have Clint Larson's speed and gather up to the bar. Only by combining the two will the best-ever performance be forthcoming.

The running high jump, like the running broad jump, dates back to antiquity. It was probably introduced as a competitive event in the American track and field program in 1868, the year of the founding of the New Year Athletic Club. It was placed on the Amateur Athletic Union program in 1876, when H. E. Ficken of the New Year Athletic Club took first place with a height of 5 feet 5 inches.

Among the contributors to the development of form in the running high jump was Michael F. Sweeney, who set the world's record of 6 feet 4½ inches in 1892. Three years later he bettered his own performance by jumping 6 feet 5⅝ inches. His record stood for eighteen years. The style of jump employed by Sweeney is referred to by many authorities as the Sweeney form, and resembles somewhat the eastern style.

In 1912 George Horine, of Stanford University, broke Sweeney's record when he cleared the bar at 6 feet 7 inches. This is of historical interest since it was the first time that an athlete, using what is now called the western form, became the record holder. It should be recalled that a contemporary of Horine's, a fellow California, Edward Beeson, surpassed Horine's mark, also using the western form, with a jump of 6 feet $7\frac{5}{16}$ inches.

The mark of 5 feet 5 inches made by Ficken in 1876 is exactly 1 foot 4¾ inches less than the height attained by champions sixty years later. The marked improvement in performance is worthy of analysis. It can be accounted for partly by a change in form from the old-fashioned scissors, in which the jumper cleared the bar in a sitting position, to the eastern and western forms in which the body layout is employed when crossing the bar. Improvement in the type of footing from which the take-off is made is another factor contributing to better performance. Such refinements as improved jumping shoes, well-marked crossbars, and shock-proof pits add to the efficiency of the jumper.

As times goes on, more and more athletes become interested in the running high jump. The widespread scheduling of the event on both the indoor and outdoor programs, ranging from the sand lots to the Olympic Stadium, has served as an incentive for increased participation. In addition, it should be mentioned that instruction in the running high jump is now more intensive, and advantage is taken of knowledge of body mechanics, physiologic responsiveness, and psychologic reactions.

Obviously, point winners in various grades of competition must acquire height, depending on the class of the field of opponents. The height required to place is give for the high or preparatory school aspirant.

There have been 4 basic high jumping forms used in the past. First came the scissors, used by most athletes up to 1895. This form required the jumper to concentrate on the run and takeoff, with very little thought of the clearance or "lay-out" over the bar. He went over the bar in a sitting position. The jumper could transfer the speed of the run to a vertical lift quite effectively, as proven by the record of 6′ 4″ established in 1887 by W. Byrd Page (who must have used some type of backward "lay-out" as he cleared the bar).

The eastern form, thought to have been initiated by Michael Sweeney in 1895, was a type of scissors jump, but a definite "lay-out" over the bar was added. Sweeney's record of 6′ 5 5/8″ proved that the position over the bar was an important factor. This form was used in the United States with a few variations until 1930, and by most foreign performers until 1948. Using this style, John Winter of Australia jumped 6′ 6″ to win the high jump in the 1948 Olympic Games. However, since he used almost a 60° approach, as compared to most other jumpers approach of 45° or less, he had the advantage. The takeoff place was wet and muddy during this competition, and the more a spot was used the worse it became. He was one of the very few who utilized a takeoff spot not previously used.

The western roll was introduced by George Horine of Stanford University in 1912. He jumped 6′ 7″ with this style. A description of this style by Horine seems to demonstrated that he jumped in the same manner as modern jumpers.

This method of clearance was an important over the 2 previous forms of jumping. The body was placed flat over the bar, horizontal, to the ground, and on the side. Walt Davis of Texas established a new world record of 6′

11$\frac{5}{8}$" in 1953 using this form.

The straddle or belly-roll form was first used successfully in competition by Jim Stewart of the University of Southern California in 1930. The advantage of this straddle style lies in the fact that the body is in prone "lay-out" position over the bar, and only the thickness of the body must rise above the bar (in contrast to the width that must be above the bar in the western roll).

Most top high jumpers use this form or a variation of it which involves the addition of a dive to the straddle roll (Valery Brumel, the present world record holder, used this variation). However, for several years track scientists have predicted that the high jumper must also be able to tumble in order to gain greater height. Dick Fosbury, United States 1968 Olympic champion, uses a backward layout tumble over the bar from a scissors takeoff style to corroborate this prediction.

CHAPTER 3

THE ESSENTIAL INGREDIENTS OF HIGH JUMP

The essentials of form in the high jump should be considered from two equally important points of view, jumping high and economy of clearance. The first of these has been somewhat neglected during the past 25 years in out concern for correct position while over the bar.

There are more individual variations in the high jump than in any other event on the track and field program. The last Olympic games saw advocates of each of the generally styles—the Eastern, the Western, and the straddle forms—as well as great variations in the details of each of these. Not only were there differences in the styles of clearance but also in the length, speed, and direction of run and in body position at the take-off.

Consequently, textbooks and lecturers generally are prone to refrain from any hard and fast rules of procedure. A personal preference for this or that aspect of form is suggested, but the general conclusion is to work out one's own style in terms of one's own experience and peculiarities. However, it is difficult for the writer to conclude that the high jump is a permanently uncertain or multiform event. The cause of this variation does not lie in differences in individual build or co-ordination, which all too often serve as excuses for careless coaching. Rather, it has occurred almost entirely because neither the rules nor the nature of the event places any limitation upon the direction, length or speed of the run. In the broad jump and pole vault, one can hardly conceive of any approach other than at right angles to the take-off board or cross-bar, and, of course, runways have been constructed that fix such an approach. In contrast, the high jump presents a full 180 degrees within which to run, and it was inevitable that each of these degrees should be tried before a final form could be adopted. Each variation in run produces a somewhat different style of clearance; needless to say, they have all been thoughtfully tried. However, 75 years of experimentation should be more than enough time in which to discover and utilize every aspect of form and understanding its value and shortcomings. Certainly we should now be approaching that stages in the evolution of style when a "best" form can be universally adopted as producing maximum results. Other forms may continue, of course, because of their advantages in certain ways—ease of learning, for example, or low requirements in flexibility or co-ordination. But these logical reasons should be given for their use rather than the lame excuse of "individual differences".

Form in the high jump is not merely a differences in the position of the body while clearing the bar. Rather, form begins with the first step of the run and involves every succeeding action. Proper bar clearance is essential to best heights, but in practical coaching work, careful consideration to each phase of the run and take-off will pay greater dividends than will efforts deaiing with later phases of form.

Traditionally, all discussions of form in the high jump begin with the various aspects of the run, move through the take-off, and end up with a major concern for the method of clearance. From a time standpoint, this is very logical. Yet it tends to break up the action into separate parts and encourages separate decisions regarding each aspect of form that are not necessarily well integrated with the form as a whole. Although extremely difficult, each phase must be considered in relation to what comes after and what went before. This dilemma cannot be entirely avoided, for talking about action requires a stopping of action, as in the projection of a single slide rather than of a continuous motion picture.

But we can at least discuss first things first. In the writer's opinion, such first things do not lie in the method of clearance, important as that is to successful jumping. All the improvements in clearance methods have added but 7 inches to the world's record in over 50 years of effort. Rather, they lie in the take-off and in the actions that immediately precede it and proceed from it. Which style of clearance should one use? The answer lies, in large measure, in how one is able to get off the ground, at what angle, with how much lead-leg drive, and with what shoulder and arm position. How fast and far should one run? Again, that depends upon how momentum can be utilized in the take-off. If in the take-off the initial body position is near to or forward of the vertical, if the take-off is merely under the body weight, and if the lead leg is bent and has little vertical force, then speed in the run will produce a broad jump and greatly reduce body height. It would be better to use a bouncing slow jog.

The take-off. The take-off must be regarded as including the last two or three steps of the run as well as the actions of all body parts as they assist the upward leap. Its many essentials of action should include the following:

1. Take-off efficiency should be judged by the velocity with which the body drives vertically from it base,

the ground; not by its preparation for a proper lay-out over the bar.

2. The last three steps must be smooth, quick, and progressively longer, so that the take-off foot is well ahead of the body weight, strongly braced against its horizontal momentum and forcing an upward leap. The body's centre of gravity is lowered and, at first, well back of the take-off foot, driving the heel hard into the ground. It is this bracing action with its backward lean and with the weight on the heel that causes jumpers to prefer a heelless track shoe despite the constant danger of a painful stone bruise to the heel. It also leg Les Steers to construct a special having the no-heel feature of the ordinary track shoe but including a protecting steel heel plate and a single spike to aid the conversion from forward to upward motion.

3. Further, the last two steps include a settling or lowering of the body. This is a natural accompaniment of the backward lean and aids not only the action just described but also the leap into the air. In a sense, it compresses the body springs or, more literally, places the leg muscles in positions where they can be most effective.

4. If the jump is properly executed, as just suggested, the right leg (assuming a left-footed take-off) must come through somewhat bent. Most men who high-jump properly and vertically have difficulty with this foot, since its spikes drag through the ground and throw off their timing.

5. Throughout these movements, the line of the body, if viewed from behind, is vertical. That is, there is no anticipatory lean of the body or the head to the left or toward the bar.

6. The eyes should be upward, even if the height of

the bar is below the eyes. This will aid the backward lean and emphasize the important principle that all jumps should be made as though the bar were higher than one's head.

7. The lead leg should be thrown vigorously with as little knee-bend as possible in a nearly vertical direction. The foot should point straight up and should begin its turn toward and over the bar only after it is high in the air. It is extremely difficult to do this effectively and still achieved a good jump from the take-off leg. Most jumpers give up in despair after a few trials, for it destroys all their feeling of jumping off the ground. Yet not only can a definite gain in upward lift be made from the inertia of this leg throw, but it also keeps the body over the take-off for as long a time as possible, a very important consideration. Certain jumpers, such as Gill Cruter of Colorado (6′ 8¾″), have failed to use this lead leg almost entirely. Yet its value is certain and its use should be strongly emphasized and persistently practiced.

8. The inside shoulder should aid this vertical jump by being hunched vigorously upward with as little inward and forward lean as possible. The greatest objection to the straddle form lies in the tendency to anticipate the bar clearance and to lean forward and toward the bar early in take-off action.

9. The arms should aid this vertical effort, but in a natural and co-ordinated fashion, working for control and later bar clearance. To throw them high in the air is probably to lose more in control than is gained in impetus.

10. The head should start its movement vertically as though the bar is at least 6 inches higher than the head. This is true even though the bar is actually

much lower. Always try to jump high first. Then worry about clearing the bar.

The run. Problems in the run are concerned with how far, how fast, in what direction, and with what method. How far should one run? Certainly no specific conclusion can be drawn from observing the world's best jumpers. Wilson, of Southern California, who cleared 6′ 10″, ran less than 25 feet, whereas Albritton, of Ohio State, took more than 60 feet on most occasions. Even a single individual may vary his length of run. Les Steers varied his approach as much as 5 steps, or about 20 feet, under different take-off conditions. He had no definite check marks and preferred to "feel" his way up to the bar. In contrast, Osborn, one of the event's greatest stylists, measured his approach exactly, using two check marks at 24 and 12 feet respectively from his take-off.

How fast should be run? Here again there are differences in practice among even the best men. Mel Walker and Dave Albritton, of Ohio State, both cleared 6′ 9¾″ and were both coached by Larry Snyder, and excellently coached, too; yet Mel approached at little more than a walk, whereas Dave achieved a good momentum during his last 4 strides. Osborn writes of his run as being a "dog trot", whereas Larson gradually increased his speed during a 60-foot run "so that by the time I hit the take-off I am running at full speed".

How far and how fast, should one run? Certainly the examples given us by the experts provide almost no final answers. Perhaps one should accept this simple dictum: run far enough and fast enough, by simple trial and error, to clear the highest possible heights. And that appears to be the best advice of most professional coaches. Cromwell seems to accept as something final the fact that the athletes approach the bar with varying speeds and recommends that the approach should be at a reasonable speed because the momentum is wanted upward and forward but also because a run that is too fast might cause the jumping leg to give way at the take-off instead of taking on added spring.

Tom Jones, Wisconsin's long-time and honoured coach, wrote that "the length of the run varies from 7 to 12 yards" and that "speed in the approach is not an important factor. There is an optimum speed for each jumper determined by experimentation. In a fast approach, the jumper must possess enough leg strength to covert the forward momentum into an upward lift. Too fast a run will tend to carry the high point of the jump beyond the cross-bar whereas lack of sufficient speed will cause the jumper to come down on the crossbar. The front approach usually requires greater speed.

Bresnahan and Tuttle assume that both the length and the speed of the run are largely individual matters, although different styles of jumping have different speed requirements. In the Western form, "a competitor will not go far wrong in running at one-third his maximum effort between check marks 2 and 1, and at an increasing speed up to two-thirds his maximum effort between check mark 1 and the point of take-off".

Perhaps such statement as these are about as far as coaches can safely go and still cover all cases. Certainly, the beginning jumper will do well to run slowly and smoothly up to the bar and to place major emphasis upon a proper take-off and bar clearance. Coaches agree that beginning jumpers have a tendency to run both too far and too fast. Not only is their speed sometimes too great for even the expert to use effectively, but their muscular resiliency and skill in making the take-off are too undeveloped to permit a proper use.

Admitting the merit of all these statements and the attendant dangers of diving and broad-jumping, it is still true that, after the fundamentals of the take-off have been learned, the values of momentum in the run should be carefully studied and persistently practiced. To continue permanently to run slowly is to limit the values that can be derived from the run. If beginning jumpers run too fast, most "expert" high-jumpers run too slowly. Keeping primary attention upon maintaining a proper take-off, a man's speed in the run should be as fast as possible—that is, as fast as he can use effectively. In many cases this will still mean a slow, easy jog to the bar no matter how long or faithfully he may work on speed, but at least the jumper will have been given his chance to reach his greatest potential. To do less is to admit defeat before the contest.

It would be well at this point to read again the comments of both Larson and Oler just quoted. Written 25 years ago, their emphasis upon this aspect of form is as valuable now as then. How fast and how far should a high-jumper run? The answer must always be in terms of the individual jumper. Yet it is a clear and certain answer. He should run as fast as his perfection of the take-off will enable him to jump high. He should run as far as is necessary to co-ordinate smoothly and momentum of the run and take-off. Such a coaching emphasis will win the dual meet this month and even this week and at the same time will establish a proper pattern for making the Olympic team some years hence.

Obviously, momentum in the run cannot be learned in a few practices, any more than a vigorous throw of the lead leg can be easily co-ordinated with the jump from the left foot. Such learnings require consistent practice throughout the entire school year. One can no more learn to high-jump properly during the meet month of March, April and May alone than one can acquire endurance in distance running or mastery of a foreign language or skill in playing a musical instrument by a few weeks of effort. To do such a complex skill correctly and at one's best level inevitably requires consistent, prolonged, and intelligent effort.

An equally important question lies in how momentum is gained in the run. Should it come from a short run rapidly accelerated, from a long run slowly accelerated, or from a medium to long run that starts slowly but places great emphasis upon the last 3 or 4 strides? Accepted practice by great jumpers usually follows the third method. This brings momentum and muscular quickness where it is most needed. Further, the last 2 strides are thus naturally longer and produce a lowering of the centre of gravity, a backward lean, and a bracing action of the take-off leg, which are essential to a vertical effort.

Check marks should be used when first learning to jump so that they become natural and almost unconsciously a part of running procedures. The run will thereby become quite mechanical in its rhythm and method, and not merely the take-off but the co-ordination of the entire action will be consistently exact. One check mark at the start of the run is usually sufficient, although beginning jumpers may be aided by a second mark at one-third the distance and a third mark at which to start the last 3 fast and longer steps.

The clearance. Although the high-jumpers of the world, other than in America, continue to use the Eastern cut-off style, and sometimes very effectively, it appears clear to the writer that its effects and difficulties more than offset its advantages. In brief, its advantages lie in its take-off style, which furthers an excellent gather and a more vertical jump than in any version of the Western style. Its defects lie in its method of clearance, for despite the remarkable agility and perfection of movement of certain jumpers, the width of the hips and usually the shoulders, rather than their thickness, must clear the bar. Its advocates argue that the value of a two-leg throw more than compensates for this weakness. But very few men can actually use the second leg lift effectively and it is not, in any case, more useful than the second leg throw of the straddle form.

It is interesting to note that in the 1952 edition of Athletics, by the famous English Achilles Club, A.W. Selwyn expresses the opinion that the victory of John Winter, Eastern stylist from Australia, in the London Olympics "may well prove to have been the swan-song of the cut-off".

Technique of the western roll. Clearance of the bar in the western roll is made with the side next to the bar. This discussion assumes a left-footed jumper, who would clear on his left side. In such a case, the run is made from the left, the take-off from the left foot, the clearance on the left side, and the landing on the left foot and hands.

The run is usually at an angle of about 45 degrees. To use less is to encourage a broad jump, a sliding along the bar. To use more gives the jumper a feeling of being cramped or restricted at the take-off. However, this has the advantage of being cramped or restricted at the take-off. However, this has the advantage of forcing a vertical jump. Both the planting of the take-off foot and the vigorous swing of the lead leg are made in line with the direction of the run. This straight-ahead and vertical throw of the right leg seems most logical in terms of take-off and upward propulsion. Yet many successful jumpers prefer to throw it outward toward the right standard. They thereby have more freedom of action for the clearance and also are able to make a take-off that is closer to the bar. Some jumpers compromise by starting the right leg straight ahead and upward but then shifting its direction toward the upright. They then gain the double advantage of a correct take-off and freedom for clearance. It will be later explained that the writer believes it best to begin all jumpers with the Western roll rather than with the straddle form. However, in so doing, the later probable change-over should be kept in mind and a form of

Western roll developed that will be consistent with the straddle and involve the least possible change in action.

It is essential that this action be accompanied by a vertical hunch of the inside left shoulder and arm. This insures a vertical jump and prevents a premature lay-out before the jumping action is completed. Some jumpers throw the entire left arm high in the air and secure good results by keeping the arm above the head during the clearance. In general, however, the action of the arm is more easily co-ordinated if it is in close to the body.

The head should be kept vertical during the take-off. There is a strong tendency to incline the head toward the bar and to the left, in anticipation of the clearance. This precludes a full upward jump and places clearance before height in the air. It should be constantly emphasized that all jumps should assume that the bar is higher than the head and that therefore one must jump up before attempting to lie out. Walter Marty, of Fresno State, was outstanding in this respect. Very few pictures of him show an economical clearance, for his shoulders are high in the air, but without exception, he made maximum use of the take-off regardless of the height of the bar. In the writer's opinion, if Marty had been able to drop his head and shoulders more quickly, although no sooner, he would have been the greatest of all Western-rollers in combining maximum height with efficient clearance.

The position of the body while directly over the bar will depend upon the earlier actions in the take-off. The 1952 Olympic champion, Walter Davis, jumped this style. If the lead leg is directed toward the right standard, a clearance form like that of Harold Osborn is more likely. This position not only affords good clearance but is consistent with the action of the straddle form and may later be converted to that form. The lead leg at this point serves as a balancing weight, permitting the second leg to come through well bent, as close as possible to the lead leg, and to continue on down toward an easy landing. Except for a turn horizontally and then downward of the right toe, which aids the body to turn over the bar, the right leg holds its high position, and even increase it, throughout the remainder of the jump and the landing. A straight right leg is thus the steadying point for equilibrium and the main key to an economical and properly timed clearance.

After the full benefits of the take-off have been achieved, the head is dropped quickly forward and sideward down toward the bar. If the bar is more than 4 inches above the head, this dual role presents no problem. There is time in which to jump up first and then lie out. What, however, should be the form of a man 6′ 2″ tall whose best height is 5′ 10″ or 5′ 11″ ? To the writer, the emphasis should still be upon jumping up. Doing so assumes that 6′ 2″ or higher will be cleared some day; not to do so makes such higher heights more difficult. This sudden dropping of the head and shoulders is effective in lifting the hips, the most common point of contact with the bar in this style of jump. The hips should be the focal point of coaching attention when considering clearance. The details of clearance will vary somewhat with each athlete, but if they are effective in raising the hips and rolling them around the bar, the form is undoubtedly sound.

Harold Osborn, famous athlete is generally credited with being one of the closest students of form in the high jump. Certainly his clearance was about as efficient as one can imagine from a side-to-the-bar style. He described his form as follows :

I approach to an angle of about 45 degrees and use a long easy bounding step, a little faster than a dog trot. On the last step I settle for the spring, then swing the outward leg up and over the bar with considerable force, then I snap the jumping leg in close to the first (lead) leg and straighten the body with a snap or jerk, just before the body appears to hit the bar. After this action and before the body gets over the bar the lower arm is snapped down, the lower shoulder is jerked or lifted up and the lower leg is involuntarily drawn down to raise the body along with the lower arm movement; the leg is then kicked upward and outward, and also backward, toward the rear of the jumping pit. This twisting leg kick serves to turn the body in the air, supplemented by the arm action, and it concludes the action, as the body has no started on its downward drop. The lower leg is snapped down to catch the body and the athlete lands on this same jumping leg, assisted by both hands so that the landing jar will be broken.

In addition to the important details of this description, the primary impression the writer gains is one of deliberate and conscious timing of each stage of the action. This is not a nicely rounded curve of action from take-off to landing, but rather a series of sequence actions: (1) the take-off with its forceful upward "swing" of the lead leg; (2) the "snap [of] the jumping leg in close to the first"; (3) the "jerk" with which the body is straightened and the hips lifted; (4) the downward "snap" of the lower arm and the upward "jerk" of the lower shoulder; (5) the "twisting leg kick", which turns the body toward the ground, combined with the snap down of the lower leg for the landing. All this is a story of perfected timing, of trained co-ordination, and of assiduous and carefully considered practice.

Advocates of the Western roll want to praise its simplicity of action, and rightly so. But the careless jumping one sees constantly, often by men of great ability, in which the almost exclusive thought is for lay-out and landing, is an insult to the very word "form". Each phase of the high jump has its contributions and its problems; only as all phases are studied, used most effectively, and integrated into an intelligent whole should a jumper be referred to as a stylist or as having good form.

Technique of the straddle form. Both the discussion and the practice of the straddle style of high-jumping must simultaneously evaluate its great assets and weaknesses. To place either above the other is to misunderstand the form and reduces its effectiveness. The straddle style of high-jumping is undoubtedly the most perfect form yet devised; in fact, it is probably the ultimate and final form in terms of economy of clearance of the bar. On the other hand, it is the poorest of all forms in its tendency to lessen the effectiveness of the take-off and of all actions related to jumping high. With few exceptions, straddle jumpers anticipate later action by leaning in toward the bar at the take-off, by taking the weight of the body on the whole foot rather than on its heel and then rocking forward and up on the toes, by turning the take-off foot in to the left and toward the bar, by bending the lead leg and cutting its vigorous upward action, and, speaking generally, by turning the whole body down and forward toward the bar rather than first jumping upward and then, afterwards, lying out efficiently.

Most students of this form strongly urge that all jumpers should first learn the Western roll. They argue that the primary aspects of the take-off, will then be properly learned and firmly fixed. Attention can be shifted later to a more perfect method of clearance as is found in the straddle form. All of the early straddle jumpers—Stewart, Albritton, Steers, Canham—followed this pattern, found it effective, and quite naturally advocate such a practice for others. On the other hand, they had little or no choice. They first learned the Western roll because the straddle style had not been invented, or at least not accepted. Their advice is undoubtedly sound. Yet it is illogical to assume that coaches and athletes will follow such a circuitous route in learning form. The youngest grammar school jumpers are already using the straddle style and will resist a change back to the Western roll.

Rather, the weaknesses of the straddle should be repeatedly and clearly emphasized and coaching techniques constantly applied to forestall and overcome these weaknesses as well as to utilize the more obvious values of the form.

Assuming that the fundamentals of a correct take-off, are being given proper consideration, the form over the bar in the straddle style should approximately the following:

The pendulum, semi-straight action of the lead leg is toward the right standard at an angle of from 40 to 10 degrees to the bar. Such an outward kick helps to prevent the natural tendency to lean to the left and forward at the take-off and to keep the weight of the body over the take-off foot. The toe of this lead foot starts vertically but turns inward across the bar as the height of the kick is reached, thus beginning the body turn and lay-out.

After the jump for height has had it full effect and after the head and shoulders have risen well above the height of the bar (particularly on lower heights), they are turned quickly downward and to the left toward the bar. This snap of the head around and down is a potent factor in achieving a full body twist, which pulls the left leg over and away from the bar.

The left arm should aid in this turn to the left and should be thrown from its position at the side or above the head and to the left.

Last of all movements in the clearance and the one that is likely to give greatest difficulty is the quick movement upward and to the left of the left hip, leg and foot. The most generally effective method is the twisting snap outward and upward of the toe of the left foot. If quickly and fully done, it will pull the knee and hip with it so that all three will be moved at once. Some jumpers, however, may find that concentrating on the roll of the hip or of the knee many produce better results.

The primary force of the landing will fall on the right leg but, if the leftward turn has been properly executed, the body will roll over to the left shoulder and back. This should break the fall without an unusual jar.

Stress on the straddle form. One of the most valuable and interesting discussion ever to occur in connection with high-jumping took place in 1941 when the coaches of the National Collegiate Track Coaches Association questioned Les Steers just two weeks after his 6′ 11″ performance.

IMPORTANT QUESTIONS AND ANSWERS

How hard should a man work and how often should he jump in the high-jump? The answer is almost irritatingly uncertain. The traditional answer is simply and quickly, "very little work and very few jumps". Cromwell warns that "after the season is underway, the jumper must remember that the spring in his legs must be developed and conserved. He must not jump too much because it is asking a great deal of a leg to lift the body higher than the head and too many leaps will wear out the spring". Other textbooks and other coaches in general support this advice.

On the other hand, there does not exist the fact of Les Steers with his 20 or 30 jumps at high heights in practice after practice and his habit of taking many jumps in practice with only one day's rest before important events. Most coaches brush him off as being superhuman or the exception to the rule. In contrast, the writer believes his superhuman qualities lie primarily in his assumption that learning proper high-jump technique is a problem that must be worked at 10 or 12 months a year. Over a period of many months and years, he built up his body and leg muscles to withstand a great deal of jumping.

Not every man, and probably not many men, can develop Steers's resistance to muscle soreness and deadness. But almost all men can improve their ability to take work and in so doing will improve the technique and the height of their jump. Steers mentiones a period of one or two weeks at the beginning of the year's practice when the muscles are "dead". The writer's personal experience, as well as what he observed with other jumpers, indicates that this may be prolonged, but a persistent development program of jumping and exercise will restore spring and quickness and gradually increase working capacity. The intricate and difficult movements of the high jump simply cannot be perfected except through several thousand jumps for form. The more jumps a learner is able to take, the more perfect the form is likely to the higher the heights that can be cleared.

The answer to this question, then, must always be an individual answer. But the starting assumption should be that within a period of months, or even years, the ability to take many jumps and still maintain muscle resiliency can be developed. Obviously, experimentation and development should begin in October rather than in March. To start practice in March with a first meet in April is to think in terms of minimum developmental and learning.

How much jumping for height should be done in practice? The answer is somewhat paradoxical. Jumping for height should be done very seldom, but jumping high for form should occur at every possible opportunity. Jumping for height in practice, with the exclusive aim of clearing the bar, should occur not more than once a week. The strongest argument in its favour is that it if fun, and fun in practice is an important factor. Yet it actually accomplishes little. Certainly it is not a real test of jumping ability, for the good competitor will almost always do better in the meets.

On the other hand, jumping high for form is essential to correct style on two counts. First, a man should always attempt to jump high, and especially so when the bar is low. A low bar is the greatest hindrance to good form and should be merely a guide for jumping action on those occasions when it seems necessary to use it. The action of the head and shoulders and the lead leg should always be made as though the bar were above the height of the head. This point cannot be overemphasized.

Secondly, the co-ordination and timing of a jump at high heights are essentially different from those for one at lower heights. Only by practising toward, if not actually at, these highest heights can correct rhythm and co-ordination of movement be established. The crux of this problem lies in the attitude of the jumper. As long as his attention is upon form and technique, and as long as there is a reasonable possibility of clearing the bar, the higher it is placed in practice the better.

All coaches agree that the weakness of both the Western and the straddle styles lies in their tendency to anticipate the lay-out. Sometimes men who can clear good heights will lean forward and to the left even before the left foot hits the take-off mark. Yet, ideally, the lay-out should not begin until after the left foot has the left the ground. From this standpoint, the short man has a great advantage over the jumper who is 6' 2" or 6' 4" tall. He naturally must jump up first, before lying out. Interestingly enough, this could be one explanation of the rather puzzling fact that many of our greatest jumpers have been under 6 feet in height. Their form in jumping high is thus necessarily better.

What are the important physical characteristics of the champion high-jumper? Certainly height is not essential in clearing bars under 7 feet in the air, as a glance at the list in Table 24 of the world's record holders will show. Only four of them champions—Johnson, Albritton, Steers, and Walker—are over 6 feet in height. Larson, although he cleared 6′ 9½″, was only 5′ 9½″ tall; this is the greatest difference between personal height and height cleared of any jumper. Similarly, W. Byrd Page, only 5′ 6½″ tall, was yet able to clear 6′ 4″, and Walter Marty, 5′ 11½″ tall, cleared 6′ 9½″, both with styles that were certainly several inches less efficient than that of Steers or Albritton.

On the other hand, it would be difficult to argue that height is not an asset. Certainly from every logical standpoint save that of quickness and co-ordination, it is so. Further, a glance at all the great high-jumpers who have cleared 6′ 7″ or better will reveal their average to be over 6 feet tall. Cromwell states that "high jump fans who have wondered if a 7 foot jump will ever be attained can be sure that it will be. It awaits only a stream-lined athlete who is about 6 feet 6 inches in height and who combines with his altitude the spring and co-ordination of the present record holders. Actually, such a height as 6′ 6″, desirable as it may be, is not at all necessary to clear over 7 feet. Steers, at 6′ 1½″ cleared 6′ 11″. In the writer's carefully considered opinion, there have already been several jumpers of under 6′ 3″ in height who could have cleared more than 7 feet. Had Albritton or Gil Cruter, of Colorado, achieved a take-off as perfect as their lithe and sinuous style of clearance; had Bill Stewart supplemented his fast approach with a later perfection of take-off and clearance; had Clint Larson and Bert Nelson attempted the straddle form rather than their on-the-back position; had Willis Ward, who cleared 6′ 7⅛″

as a freshman with only a fair Eastern style but who preferred to play at sprinting, broad-jumping, hurdling, and incidentally football--had he cared to specialize in the high jump; had these things happened, not merely one but several men would have cleared this "superhuman" height. And all were less than 6′ 4″ tall.

Certainly weight is an important although negative factor. The small-boned, long-muscled individual under 170 pounds obviously has an advantage in load to be lifted. On the other hand, Steers, just over 6 feet tall, weighed over 190 pounds when he cleared 6′ 11″.

Apparently the only essential quality is ability to jump high and clear the bar. Certain ideal physical characteristics can be established, of course, but where these are not present there are always compensating factors, such as greater spring or quickness, which make the desired result possible.

Undoubtedly most champion high-jumpers have been good athletes—that is, they either did or could have done well in other events or other sports. Yet, without a possibly embarrassing mention of names, it is the writer's definite impression that there have many exceptions to this rule. It is true that few high-jumpers have been outstanding in other events. (Harold Osborne held the world's record in the decathlon), but in this era of specialization, this is to be expected.

In summary, the importance of certain physical characteristics is generally exaggerated and is more an academic and theoretical problem than one of practical selection of candidates. When looking for high-jumpers, place a cross-bar on the upright, and watch 'em jump. The boys with spring will come in all shapes and sizes, but there'll be no difficulty in recognizing their talents.

Which form should beginners be taught? The advice of the experts (those who have jumped both styles) is to begin with the Western roll and later, when a proper take-off has been learned and after several years of experience, shift to the straddle form. In any case, whether one begins with the Western or the straddle, first emphasis must be placed upon jumping high. No matter how low the bar, men should always take off as though the bar were higher than the head. Learn to jump up first. Then—and this will take months, perhaps many months—make lay-out and economy of clearance a primary concern. Men jump over 6 feet through a proper run and take-off; they gain only an additional 5 to 7 inches through lay-out. Coaches will do well to insist that jumpers should follow in practice the old competitive rule that "a fair jump is one in which the head of the jumper does not cross the bar in advance of either foot". A head that leads the clearance action is almost certain evidence that the take-off and the vertical jump have not been properly performed.

What specific techniques can be used to aid the trail leg in clearing the bar in the straddle form? Speaking generally, the correct timing of this action is depending upon a well-balanced and upward take-off. If the take-off is one-third lay-out before the second foot leaves the ground and if the body weight is poorly balanced off the take-off foot, all work on clearing the second leg will be largely wasted. But if the body moves up, over, and down in an inverted "U", there will be balance and time with which to clear all parts of the body. Assuming these are present, attention can be given to any one of the following, their relative effectiveness being a largely individual matter:

1. Evert the toe of the left foot outward and upward. If done vigorously and explosively, it will carry the knee and hip with it and make special action by these parts unnecessary.

2. Twist the left knee outward and upward. Some men

combine the action with the eversion of the left toe; others perform one without the other.

3. Lift and rotate the left hip away from the bar.

4. Throw the left shoulder and arm upward and backward away from the cross-bar.

5. Turn the head quickly to the left toward and above the cross-bar.

The question of which attempt is most likely to produce the desired result will find a slightly different answer with each individual. All should be encouraged by the coach. In any case, the action of lifting the trail leg is an unusual one and requires specific practice. To lie on the edge of a bench or table and throw the leg, foot, and toe repeatedly in the desired manner should be an important part of each day's exercises.

ORGANIZATION OF PRACTICE

High-jumping requires an extremely high degree of co-ordination, quickness, and elasticity of all parts of the body. Although the ability to jump many times at each practice can and should be increased, such practice must be augmented by many other activities and exercises.

The high-jumper should also hurdle, sprint, put the shot, or even pole-vault. It must be emphasized again and again that the complexities of high-jumping require careful and repeated practice and that every major attention and activity must be concentrated there. But added events will increase both interest and over-all ability.

The warm-up. The usual pattern of jogging, repeated wind sprints, and stretching exercises is effective here. However, special concern should be given to the jumping muscles and tendons.

1. Easy vertical bounding into the air from the jumping leg can be combined with a gradually increased swing of the lead leg.

2. From a standing position, the lead leg should be kicked more and more forcibly until, when fully warmed up, it extends straight at the knee and high above the head. This is a dangerous exercise for the muscles and tendons of both legs and should be approached very gradually.

The usual hurdle exercises taken at the hurdle and on the ground are excellent, although of course with the usual precautions against overstretching. Keep in mind that all this activity is merely preliminary and for warm-up purposes. Exercises for strengthening and development of the muscles and tendons should follow the jumping period, not precede it.

High-jumping. As soon as possible, raise the bar to the highest height that can be cleared at least some of the time. Jump high but jump for form. If the jumper can ignore the height of the bar altogether and continue t make a proper take-off with a low bar, then its height is of no concern.

But if a low bar means taking off down to the bar with a predominant concern for economy of clearance, then a faulty habit is being learned that will negate all the benefits of a proper lay-out. Run with as much speed as can be used effectively, jump high, and then do a proper lay-out.

Deliberately attempt to increase, from month to month, the amount of jumping that can be done in one day and on consecutive days.

Jump for form, but also jump for greater endurance. Be concerned about loss of spring, but not overconcerned. After all, work at jumping is the only means to excellence in style.

Post-jumping exercises. The order in which these are taken will vary with individual preference and with the conditions of each day's practice.

It is strongly recommended, however, that as soon as actual high-jumping is completed, a sequence of regularly practiced exercises be followed. Their purpose is to strengthen and develop all the muscles and tendons of the body that relate to high-jumping.

Warm-up exercises should do little more than their name implies; these later exercises after jumping are much more strenuous.

The following list is merely suggestive of a long list that might be devised or selected.

1. Repeated high bounding, particularly from the take-off foot, in which the body drops as low and bounds as high as possible.

2. Sprinting from the starting blocks, emphasizing a high knee action and an exaggerated bounce from the feet and ankles.

3. Actual high-hurdling as well as the many exercises related to hurdling.

4. Hip-twisting exercises, from a standing position, a sitting position (such as the hurdle exercises), or an inverted bicycle-pedalling position. Several excellent hip exercises can be devised from this back-on-the-ground-and-feet-in-the-air position.

Also in this general category could be included that squat thrust so prevalent in late years: start at erect position. Squat with hands on ground, head up, on "1." Legs fully extended behind on "2". Legs back to squat position on "3". Up on "4". Do it rapidly many times.

5. Put the shot from either a stand or from across the circle. Work for good form and for improvement in

distance, but use it as an exercise for high-jumping. Make many puts in a short period of time.

6. Devise exercises related specifically to the actions of the high jump. For example, a high kick of the leading leg accompanied by a high bound from the take-off foot. Or, in anticipation of the straddle form, even though the jumper is not yet using it, lie prone on the edge of a bench or table and throw the trail leg high from the hip, up and down repeatedly.

Concentrate on the toe to see that it is thrown outward and high.

CHAPTER 4

THE TECHNIQUE OF HIGH JUMP

The running high jump, like the running broad jump, dates back to antiquity. It was probably introduced as a competitive event in the American track and field program in 1868, the year of the founding of the New York Athletic Club. It was placed on the Amateur Athletic Union program in 1876, when H. E. Ficken of the New York Athletic Club took first place with a height of 5 feet 5 inches.

Among the contributors to the development of form in the running high jump was Michael F. Sweeney, who set the world's record of 6 feet 4½ inches in 1892. Three years later he bettered his own performance by jumping 6 feet 5⅝ inches. His record stood for eighteen years. The style of jump employed by Sweeney is referred to by many authorities as the Sweeney form, and resembles somewhat the eastern style.

In 1912 George Horine, of Stanford University, broken Sweeney's record when he cleared the bar at 6 feet 7 inches. This is of historical interest since it was the first time that an athlete, using what is now called the western form, became the record holder. It should be recalled that a contemporary of Horine's a fellow California, Edward Beeson, surpassed Horine's mark, also using the western form, with a jump of 6 feet 7$\frac{5}{16}$ inches.

The mark of 5 feet 5 inches made by Ficken in 1876 is exactly 1 foot 4¾ inches less than the height attained by champions sixty years later. The marked improvement in performance is worthy of analysis. It can be accounted for partly by a change in form from the old-fashioned scissors, in which the jumper cleared the bar in a sitting position, to the eastern the western forms in which the body layout is employed when crossing the bar. Improvement in the type of footing from which the take-off is made is another factor contributing to better performance. Such refinements as improved jumping shoes, well-marked, crossbars, and shock-proof pits add to the efficiency of the jumper.

As times goes on, more and more athletes become interested in the running high jump. The widespread scheduling of the event on both the indoor and outdoor programs, ranging from the sand lots to the Olympic Stadium, has served as an incentive for increased participation. In addition, it should be mentioned that instruction in the running high jump is now more intensive, and advantage is taken of knowledge of body mechanics, physiologic responsiveness, and psychologic reactions.

Obviously, point winners in various grades of competition must acquire height, depending on the class of the field of opponents. The height required to place is given for the high or preparatory school aspirant.

A study of successful competitors in the running high jump leads us to the conclusion that they do not conform to any set type. In general, they are rather tall with well-developed lower extremities. They usually weigh approximately 165 pounds. It is of interest to note that there have been but few champions under 5 feet 10 inches in height. Furthermore, men weighing more than 175 pounds are the exception among running high-jumpers.

PHYSICAL QUALIFICATIONS

Many of the physical qualifications of the running high-jumper are so similar to those of the running broad-jumper that further discussion would be repetition. There are, however, a few differences which are worthy of note.

In the running high jump, for obvious reasons, the taller individual has an advantage, provided he possesses the requisite native ability. Since the objective of the running high jump is to gain maximum height, leg spring is of supreme importance. Due to the fact that the participant in this event is called upon to execute body position changes while in the air and in the face of a hazard, the crossbar, neuromuscular coordination and rhythm are extremely important. Speed in the running high jump is relatively unimportant since only sufficient momentum is required to insure transit across the bar. The degree of speed necessary for the various forms of jump must be considered and thus presents a problem for the competitor. This phase of the jump is discussed later.

TECHNIQUE OF THE EVENT

The running high jump is an event in which the objective is to attain a maximum height through a process of transferring the body from a vertical to a horizontal position. In order to accomplish this, there must be a synchronization of successive events which follow a running approach from which sufficient momentum is acquired to insure crossbar clearance.

In discussing the techniques in the running high jump, the event is divided into its component parts. Each part is discussed separately so far as the nature of the event permits. An attempt is made to show the relationship of these various parts to the whole procedure. The logical approach to a description of this event seems to be from the standpoint of the various types of crossbar clearance which are the western form, the eastern form, and the modified scissors form. The discussion is based on the assumption that the jumper drives off the ground with the left foot.

THE WESTERN FORM

This form of jump probably had its origin on the Pacific Coast and received world-wide recognition about 1912, when George Horine and Edward Beesn, exponents of this form, were successful in excelling the accepted world's mark in the running high jump.

1. The Approach

The angle of approach is approximately forty-five degrees. The number of strides employed varies with different competitors, eight strides being the average. The total distance from the initial stance to the crossbar ranges from 37 to 41 feet.

To insure accuracy in the approach, two checkmarks are commonly used, four strides and eight strides, respectively, from the point of take-off. The point of take-off is determined by addressing the bar at an angle of 45 degrees and finding a spot from which, when the right foot is swung forward and upward, it barely misses the bar. This distance, for the average jumper, is approximately 3 feet 4 inches.

Checkmark 1 is found by measuring off a distance of approximately 25 feet (four running strides at two-thirds speed) from a point directly under the crossbar. With this spot marked as temporary checkmark 1, set temporary checkmark 2 approximately 12 feet (four strides at one-third speed) directly back of temporary checkmark 1. Brush the approach so that spike marks are visible. Standing with the feet together on temporary checkmark 2, stride off easily with the right foot striking temporary checkmark 1 with the front spike of the leg shoe. With speed increasing from one-third to two-thirds effort, continue the run with the elastic strides of moderate length, running through without jumping. Now observe the relationship between the spike marks of the left shoe at the eighth stride and the previously determined take-off spot. Repeat the run a number of times until the relationship of the eighth stride and the take-off spot is constant. Next, adjust temporary checkmark 1 so that it is exactly four running strides from the take-off spot. This new mark is designated as permanent checkmark 1. Move temporary checkmark 2 so that it is exactly four running strides back of permanent checkmark 1. This becomes permanent checkmark 2. This procedure is known as standardizing the stride. It is worthy of the attention of the competitor that, as he develops his technique, the checkmarks have to be further adjusted. It should be borne in mind that the component materials used in constructing the runway may require additional checkmark adjustments. More specifically a competitor who has made his original plan on a cinder approach may be required to compete on one consisting of turf, clay, or loam. It is not uncommon to compete on a gymnasium or armoury floor.

A further consideration of approach adjustments is the direction and velocity of the wind. If the wind is at the back, the length of the approach must be increased, and conversely, the approach is shortened if the contestant is called upon to run against it. It should be remembered that, whether seven, eight, or nine strides are used, the number should remain fixed, but the length of the strides must be varied to meet the conditions of competition.

The western form of jump requires a rate of speed which is less than that demanded in the eastern form, but slightly greater than that employed in the modified scissors jump. While it is difficult to prescribe definitely a rate of speed between checkmarks, a competitor will not go far wrong in running at one-third his maximum effort between checkmark 2 and checkmark 1, and at an increasing speed up to two-thirds his maximum effort between checkmark 1 and the point take-off. After all, it is necessary for the jumper to learn by experience the most effective speed relationships during the various parts of the approach. Let it be remembered that in approaching the high jump bar, emphasis is placed on conserving effort rather than on generating speed. During the approach in the running broad jump, the competitor rises on the toes in an effort to generate speed, while in the running high jump he may let down lightly on the heels in an effort to conserve energy for an explosive spring.

2. Addressing the Bar

As the jumper approaches the take-off spot, he gathers himself or settles down in preparation for an explosive spring. He accomplishes this by driving less vigorously, thus approaching a semicoasting forward effort. The last stride is lengthened in order to provide a greater arc for the right leg swing. The lenghtening of the last stride tends to bring the centre of gravity over the left foot rather than ahead of it. At the same time, the last stride adjustment provides for a more complete settling down which permits a moderate flexion of the left knee.

After the jumper gathers himself, he springs. The left foot beats the ground flat-footed. The angle of the left foot remains the same as in the run, at a 45 degree angle with the bar. As the left foot strikes the ground, the right leg is thrown vigorously forward and upward. In executing the forward leg swing, some jumpers throw the right leg forward in a straightened manner, while others perform this part with the right knee slightly bent. Those who use a forceful straight right leg action assume a position in which the left knee is only slightly bent (at the start of the spring), while those who place less emphasis on the right leg swing take a position in which the left knee exhibits a greater degree of flexion (at the beginning of the spring). This is an individual characteristic of jumpers, and the athlete, through experimentation, determines the degree of left knee bend which is most effective.

As the right leg is swung forward, the left arm is synchronized with it as in walking or running. It is thrown vigorously forward and upward. The right arm aids in maintaining balance and in generating "lift".

Near the end of the right leg swing, and closely coordinated with it, the jumper straightens the left knee vigorously, and forcefully rocks up completely on the toe. The centre of gravity is directly over the take-off foot. The right arm has been thrust upward and forward and now both arms are forward.

At this point in the event, the jumpers is on his left toe, his right leg having been swung forward and upward, and he is ready to leave the ground. This is a crucial moment in the jump. In order to make the effort most effective, there must be perfect synchronization of the run, the right leg swing, the arm action, the body lean, the spring, and the rock-up on the toe. Since the leg swing adds impetus to the upward force of the body, the rock-up on the toe must be blended into it so that the forces generated by these phases of the technique are added together. Should the rock-up on the toe occur too soon, much of the added impetus due to the leg swing is lost.

A study of a series of action of champions using the western form of jump reveals the fact that some of them delay the rock-up on the toe until the right foot is swung as high as the cross-bar, while other equally good jumpers execute the rock-up on the toe when the right foot is at a height several inches below the crossbar. These action pictures also show that jumpers using the delayed rock-up on the toe usually swing the right leg forward and upward nearly straight, while those employing an earlier rock-up on the toe usually swing the right leg forward and upward with considerable knee flexion.

The body angle necessarily varies during the course of the jump. During the run the jumper assumes a body position in which the trunk is bent forward, approximating his position while sprinting. During the last stride, and while the jumper gathers himself, he bends the trunk backward, thus throwing the centre of gravity behind the take-off foot. At the instant of take-off, the body is erect with the centre of gravity directly over the take-off foot. Although during the run, the gather, and the take-off, the frontback body angle necessarily changes, it is important to note that the lean should be neither to the left nor to the right.

At the end of the rock-up on the toe and the leg swing, the jumper leaves the ground. As he does so, he begins to flex the left leg and thigh so that when he reaches a point equal to the height of the bar, these members of the body are in an extremely flexed position. During the course of the flexion of the left leg, the right remains straight (with the toe pointing upward) and is kept high. The main objective in this phase of the jump is to lift the left leg as high as possible, just touching the right. The arms are still extended in front of the body.

3. Crossbar Clearance

The force of the right leg swing is the impetus for the body turn. The jumper must acquire a position in which a line drawn through the shoulders is nearly perpendicular to the crossbar, while the left toe, the left knee, and the left hip are in the same plane. This is commonly called the layout. When the jumper reaches a position where his right leg is straight and as high as possible and his left leg bent at a right angle, the body should be at the highest point in the jump. The left leg is brought up close to the right. The clearance is initiated by sweeping the right foot across the bar followed or accompanied by the left arm and left shoulder clearance. As a result of the preceding movements, the hips are raised, aided by the reaction of the dropping of the left shoulder, thus completing the roll across the bar. The jumper is then in a position for cross-bar clearance. Since the left hip is the lowest point of the body and the greatest hazard to clearance, a more nearly perfect clearance is attained by simultaneously snapping the left arm backward and downward, and the head backward to the left, in a conscious attempt to lift the left hip higher. If there has been proper sychronization of the events preceding the layout, the force of the run will carry the body across the bar.

Many jumpers, attempting the western form, clear the bar with the belly rather than the left side toward the bar. Some have achieved fair success with this form. However, the majority of champions employ side clearance. Those who attempt the belly type of clearance may sacrifice spring because the earlier body turn detracts from the application of upward force. A properly timed execution of the various phases of the jump will bring the body in a side layout at the crest of the leap.

As the body reaches its greatest height the execution of the following simultaneous movements completes the transit across the bar:

a. The left knee is snapped across the bar.

b. The left arm, which has cleared the bar, is thrust

downward.

c. The right arm is swung to the right.

d. The extended right leg is swept across the bar to provide impetus for the roll.

The result of these movements is that the body is brought into a position with the jumper facing the pit. The landing is made on the left foot and hands.

4. The Landing

Although the landing is an aftermath of the jump proper, self-preservation still remains an important phase of the event. The ability to relax and the power to maintain body balance are the factors which make for easy landing. A properly constructed and well-conditioned pit materially reduces the hazards in falling. It should be added that a pit can be too loose as well as too hard. Extremely loose shavings have resulted in turned ankles in the high jump as well as in the pole vault. Either sand or a mixture of sand and sawdust provides a satisfactory pit.

The novice frequently experiences a sprained wrist at the instant of landing in the western form of the jump. This can be avoided by relaxation and a properly constructed pit.

5. The Head and Eyes

The sequence of visual concentration is an important phase in all forms of the running high jump. For the experienced jumper, the general procedure is as follows:

a. He assumes a position a short distance back of check mark 2, where he spends more time gaining poise and confidence for the jump, with the eyes in the general direction of the bar, yet not sharply focused on it.

b. As he steps off slightly, he looks at checkmark 2 to strike it accurately with his left foot.

c. Similar attention is paid to checkmark 1.

d. From checkmark 1, the eyes are sharply focused on the bar until it is cleared.

e. After the crossbar has been cleared, the eyes are focused on the pit.

Jumpers who are novices at the western form frequently make the mistake of consistently taking off too far away from the crossbar. For them it is sometimes recommended that the ideal take-off spot be marked and that vision be focused on this spot until the foot is planted. The vision must then be quickly shifted to the crossbar. This is a practice upon which authorities are not agreed.

THE EASTERN FORM OR JUMP

This form of jump antedates the western style, and, although its exact origin is unknown, Michael F. Sweeney in 1892 brought world-wide attention to it. It is so called because for many years its exponents were chiefly in the eastern section of the United States. However, at the present time it is practiced all over the world. Although there are many variations of this form of jump, a commonly used method is described.

1. The Approach

The approach is made directly from the front and about opposite the right standard. However, in the course of the approach, during the last two strides, the jumper swerves to the left at an angle of approximately 60 degrees to the bar and takes off from the left foot. The usual number of strides is eight, but this varies among competitors. As in the western form, the length of the run varies from 37 to 41 feet. Likewise, two checkmarks, four and eight strides, respectively, from the take-off spot, are used.

The point of the take-off is determined by addressing the bar at an angle of 60 degrees and finding a spot from which, when the right foot is swung forward and upward, it barely misses the bar. This distance, for the average jumper, is 4 feet 3 inches. The take-off spot should be located so that it permits clearance at the lowest point of the crossbar. This is recognized as fair competition, since the measurement of a record jump is made from the ground to the top of the bar at its lowest point.

Checkmark adjustments are made in a manner similar to that described for the western form of jump.

If a jumper using the western form were to shift to the eastern style, he would employ the rate of speed between checkmarks 2 and 1 which is approximately one-third his best sprinting effort. However, between checkmark 1 and the take-off spot, the speed in the eastern form is greater than that employed in the western style, that is, approximately three-fourths his best sprinting effort. Here, also, experience the jumper his optimum speed during the approach. Obviously the eastern form requires a faster run since the body goes over lengthwise and the take-off spot is farther back, thus requiring a longer transit.

2. Addressing the Bar

As the jumper approaches the bar, he swerves to the left during the last two strides, for the purpose of being in a position for the initiation of the body turn. Furthermore, this turn in the run permits the jumper to take off closer to the bar than if he continued a straight run. One of the variations of the eastern form of approach is the straight run, which necessitates a take-off still farther away from the bar.

A part of the technique involved in addressing the bar is essentially the same for both the western and eastern forms of jump. Where this is true, a repetition of description is omitted. This sameness holds especially for the gather, the last stride, the centre of gravity, the spring, the rock-up on the toe and the focus of the eyes. The angle of the left foot with the crossbar is approximately 60 degrees, as contrasted with 45 degrees in the western form.

In the eastern form of jump, greater emphasis is placed on the forward leg swing. Here the jumper exerts greater force with the free leg, swining it higher and straighter. Acting pictures of champions show that great emphasis is placed on the free leg swing: the left knee is but moderately bent at the instant of initiating the swing. One should avoid the impression, however, that in the eastern form the left knee bend is not an important factor.

This phase of the jump is also an individual characteristic, and only by experience can the beginner learn the optimum amount of knee bend.

During the free leg swing, both arms and thrown upward. The force of the left arm should be great enough to maintain body balance, yet not vigorous enough to hinder the beginning of the body turn. Usually, the hands reach a position which is well over the head, thus contributing their bit to the lift.

At the instant of take-off, the jumper sets as his objective a position in which the right leg has been swung vigorously toward the crossbar (an angle of approximately 60 degrees) and straightened so that the right toe has attained considerable height. The left leg has been forcefully straightened so that only the toe is touching the ground. Both arms have been thrown high and in such a manner as to maintain balance. The body has been brought to an erect position so that the centre of the gravity is over the left foot. There is no body lean either to the left or to the right at this instant.

3. Crossbar Clearance

At this point the force of the spring is added to the forward right leg swing. The right leg continues its upward flight in a straightened position. The next movements to be executed are the most difficult to master as well as the most important in the eastern style of jump. These are known as the "snap-up" and the "undercut" The snap-up and undercut consist of speedily snapping the left leg to a height almost equalling that of the right in a straightened position, nearly parallel with the bar. The snap-up of the left leg is aided by the reaction resulting from a downward, backward thrust of the right leg. This is followed immediately by a vigorous backward and then downward cut or swing of the straightened left leg after it has cleared the bar. A correctly performed snap-up permits an ideal layout in which the component parts of the left side of the body (left heel, left knee, left hip, and left shoulder) are bowed over the crossbar. At this instant the trunk is bent forward and is at about right angles to both the left leg and crossbar.

The continuation of the right leg swing has carried it across the bar so that the greatest height of the body, the right heel, the right knee, and right hip, and the right shoulder are arched over the crossbar. The left leg executes a vigorous rotary backward swing in a plane above and parallel to the crossbar, thus drawing the left hip away from the bar and resulting in a half turn. The right leg is thrust backward and then upward. The momentum of the run has carried the jumper across the bar, and he is now facing the approach.

4. The Landing

Because of the half turn, the jumper lands facing the crossbar, the left foot touching the pit slightly in advance of the right. The hands may be used to break the fall.

Throughout the jump, the right leg swings up at the take-off, then down to aid the hips in clearing the bar, and then up as the shoulders clear the bar. The left leg performs three well-defined actions: the spring, the snap-up, and the undercut. It is in the later stages of undercut that the left leg comes in advance of the right, thus striking the pit first.

5. The Use of the Arms

There is a wide divergence in the matter of arm movement among competitors. The object of the arm movement is, first, to aid in the spring from the ground, second, to maintain body balance, and third, to assist in completing the half turn of the body. Shoulder clearance is aided by the reaction from the downward movement of the right leg.

The position of the arms is dependent on the position of the body in the flight. As the body changes its position, the jumper likewise adjusts the arms. Additional lift is obtained by throwing the arms upward and forward. As the forward leg swing is nearly completed, the right arm is well extended upward and sideward. The right leg and right arm swing up together. The right arm swings, backward and sideward, then slightly forward. The purpose of this arm action is to give a lead to the right shoulder which must proceed in a forward-upward direction. A continuation of this motion leads to the body turn. The left arm is kept in synchronization with the right leg until the right leg is as high as the bar. At this point, a sweeping action, a downward and backward movement of the left arm, aids in completing the turn, but, more than that, it adds altitude to the left hip. Coincident with the backward left arm sweep, the undercut is forcefully executed. The successful execution of the undercut and backward arm swing differentiates the champion from the mediocre jumper. As the left arm is swept backward, the right arm is carried forward. The jumper has cleared the bar and is ready for landing.

The relaxation and sequence of vision holds for all forms of jumps.

THE MODIFIED SCISSORS FORM OF JUMP

One of the early exponents of the modified scissors form was Clinton Larson, Brigham Young University, who became American champion in 1917 and Inter-Allied Games Champion in 1919.

The particular method described is one which is often seen and is one of the modifications of the old scissors form in which the jumper takes off from the outside foot. In the scissors form the right leg is kicked forward and upward over the bar; the left leg is forcefully drawn up. The jumper now in a sitting position, at the crest of the leap, whips the take-off leg across the bar and lands on the right foot. This form is inefficient because the absence of a layout causes too great an expenditure of energy in lifting the head and trunk upward. The term "modified" is used in this discussion to indicate the inclusion of a layout in the scissors form.

1. The Approach

For a left-footed jumper the approach is made from the right side at an angle of approximately 45 degrees. The commonly accepted number of strides is eight, but, as in other forms, individuals may require more or less. Two checkmarks, four and eight strides, respectively, from the take-off spot are employed. The take-off spot is closer to the bar than in either the eastern or western forms of jump. The average distance back of the bar is 3 feet 2 inches. The take-off spot is located in the same manner as in the western form. Checkmark adjustments are made in a manner similar to that described for the other forms of jump. The speed between checkmark 2 and checkmark 1 is the same as for the eastern and western forms of jump, namely, one-third the best sprinting effort. However, between checkmark 1 and the take-off spot the speed should be greater than that for the western form, but less than for the eastern form, that is, five-eighths the best sprinting effort. Here, also, experience teaches the jumper the optimum speed between the checkmark and the take-off spot.

2. Addressing the Bar

As the jumper approaches the take-off spot, he settles down or gathers himself during the last two strides. The last stride is lengthened to permit a greater free leg swing. Furthermore, a longer last stride permits time for the adjustment of the centre of gravity so that it is directly over the left foot at the time of applying the foot-stamp. The stamp and the rock-up on the toe do not differ in this type of jump from that employed in the other forms. The right leg is kicked upward as high as possible at an angle of 45 degrees with the bar. Simultaneously, the force of the stamp and rock-up on the toe is applied. The trunk is thrown into the air in an upward position.

3. Crossbar Clearance

As the body is lifted toward the crossbar, both legs are extended, the hips are lifted high, and the shoulders and the head are snapped backward. This is the start of the layout in which the body tends to straighten. Since the take-off was made at approximately a 45-degree angle with the crossbar, the right foot is slightly ahead of the rest of the body and is first across the bar. The raising of the left leg and hip is accomplished by the continued upward swing of the left leg and is materially aided by the reaction from the downward thrust of the right leg. This is a scissorlike action of the legs from which the jump receives its name.

The left leg, now higher than the crossbar, continues a swing carries the leg over the bar. The body is now bowed over the crossbar. A downward sweep of the left leg, coupled with the upward raising of the right arm, provides sufficient height for shoulder clearance and results in a half turn. The speed of the run has been sufficient to carry the body across the bar in the layout position. As soon as the bar is cleared, the left leg arm and shoulder are dropped. These movements cause the body to turn toward the bar. Most jumpers using this style clear the bar face upward, with the back to the crossbar. There are some, however, who make the clearance with the left side toward the bar.

4. The Landing

The landing is made on the left foot and left arm. The right foot, together with the hands, is used to maintain balance and break the fall. It must be remembered that there are successful jumpers who vary the landing technique so that they turn their bodies away from the bar and land on the right foot and right arm.

It might be added that there are some prominent jumpers using the modified scissors style who float across the bar and land on the back in a flattened manner. The chief objection to a flat landing is the shock to which the jumper is subjected.

5. The Use of the Arms

In the modified scissors form of jump both arms are thrown forward and upward to facilitate the spring and to maintain balance. They are kept high during the body lift and the clearance of the crossbar. After the bar has been cleared, the arm action depends on the type of laning employed. When the body drop is to the left, toward the bar, the left arm is thrown sharply backward and downward to help break the fall. The right arm swings upward and forward to maintain balance.

Those who drop the body to the right, away from the bar, snap the right arm downward simultaneously with the right leg so that the landing is made on the right arm and right leg. The left arm must necessarily be swung over and downward to maintain balance. This form is very difficult to master because of the physical principles involved. It requires that, with the right shoulder and right heel as an axis, the entire body be rotated. Such a rotation calls for a specialized movement technique. Those who turn toward the bar when landing seemingly float across the drop the left side rather than lift it. This makes for economy and simplicity in clearance.

COMPARISON OF STYLES OF JUMP

Some coaches have fixed opinions on the effectiveness of the various forms of high jumping, and their pupils are usually schooled in but one particular form. Many critics feel that the western form borders dangerously close to a diving activity and thus claim that it is not a clear-cut jump. Coaches who fail to emphasize the eastern form do so because they believe that it requires a technique so difficult and exacting that the brief period allotted to collegiate and scholastic coaching does not permit its mastery by the average jumper. Those who reject the modified scissors do so because of the difficulty which they experience when inserting a layout into the old scissors style.

For the average beginner, the western form is recommended because it is quite efficient, since it requires less expenditure of energy in body lift, readily permits a well-defined layout, and provides a landing relatively free from shock.

THE RELATION BETWEEN THE TIME SPENT IN EXECUTING THE SPRING AND THE HEIGHT OF THE JUMP

The importance of the relationship between the time spent on the ground in executing the spring and the height of the running high jump has been recognized for a long time. There were no experimental data available concerning this question until Lance conducted a controlled experiment in an attempt to solve it.

The procedure used in collecting the data consisted of measuring the time spent in executing the spring and comparing this time with the height to which the athlete was attempting to jump. The results were quite conclusive. An examination of all the trained running high-jumpers available showed that the higher the jump attempted, the shorter the period of time spent on the ground in executing the spring. In fact, the data seemed to fit into the formula for inanimate elastic objects, such as the bouncing of a rubber ball.

One of the important contributions made by Lance's investigation was that untrained jumpers exhibited the same characteristics as the trained. The high-jumper should be taught to place emphasis on speed in completing the spring, once the jumper foot strikes the ground.

DAILY SCHEDULES OF PRACTICE

In presenting the daily schedule of practice for the running high jump, repetition to some extent is necessary. However, special exercises and procedures are suggested which apply especially to this event. It may be found by experience that the intensity of the schedule must be varied to meet the needs of the individual.

Early Season

Monday

1. Start by jogging 250 yards, walking 25 yards, and sprinting 25 yards.

2. Execute three minutes of exercises including half squats, full squats, forward leg swings, and high kicks.

3. Run 100 yards at three-fourths effort.

4. Brush the approach so that spike marks are visible and jump five or six times, gradually increasing the height of the crossbar. Analyse the approach for direction (angle), number of strides, placement of checkmarks, and length of each stride.

5. With the crossbar at a moderate height, jump three or four times with emphasis on correctly striking the checkmarks and the take-off.

6. Finish the day's practice with a jog of 300 yards, a tepid shower and massage. Record body weight before and after each practice.

Tuesday

1. Limber up with a jog of 200 yards followed by 50 yards of hopping and bounding. Alternate the effort from the right foot to the left.

2. Join the sprinters and prepare for starting practice. Sprint 35 yards and rest three minutes; repeat once.

3. Sit on the ground with the legs extended forward, feet together. Execute forward and backward body bends for one or two minutes.

4. Brush the runway, set the crossbar at a height sufficient to call for seven-eighths effort, and jump five or six times. Reassure yourself of the most desirable rate of speed, the length of your strides, and above all the distance of your take-off spot from the crossbar. An observer standing in line with the crossbar can tell you at what point you reached the greatest height.

5. Take three or four trials with the bar at the same height, with attention focused on springing vigorously.
6. Complete the workout by running 200 yards at seven-eighths effort, and follow with a shower and massage.

Wednesday

1. Begin with a jog of 250 yards, a walk of 25 yards, a run of 25 yards, a walk of 25 yards, and a sprint of 25 yards.
2. Skip rope for two or three minutes.
3. Execute three or four minutes of gymnastic stunts of a type designed to develop the arms and the shoulder girdle, such as chinning, walking on the hands, and tumbling.
4. Set the crossbar at a height slightly below your best performance and jump six or seven times. Concentrate on forward leg technique, including the degree of knee bend, the direction of the leg swing, the force of the swing, and the timing of the leg swing with the rock-up on the toe. One should know the height of leg swing which best coordinates with the rock-up on the toe.
5. Set the bar at a height equal to your best performance and jump three or four times. Make a conscious effort to use the arms effectively. Refrain from needless worry in case the crossbar is displaced. Obtain form precision first, because successful clearance will be a later reward.
6. Join the running broad-jumpers and take two or three trials.
7. Terminate the day's activity by running 100 yards at seven-eighths effort and walking 50 yards; repeat

once. Finish with a tepid shower and massage.

Thursday

1. Initiate the workout with a jog of 150 yards, a walk of 50 yards, and a spring of 50 yards.

2. Execute seven or eight trials of the standing broad jump to develop spring.

3. Set the crossbar at a height just below your best effort and emphasize the hip lift while in the layout position a fraction of a second prior to the crossbar clearance. In the western form the part played by the left arm and the head is illustrated by the following exercise. Stand erect with arms at the sides. Swing the left arm forward with moderate effort until the hand is head high and then jerk it immediately sideward and backward with considerable vigour. Simultaneously thrust the hips upward and forcefully tilt the head backward to the left. Jump seven or eight times practising these movements.

4. Perform three minutes of hopping and bounding exercises off the left leg and then the right. Vary the practice by standing erect, bending the trunk forward to touch the toes without bending the knees. The intensity of this exercise should be moderate at first, then gradually increased.

5. Finish the practice by a jog of 250 yards, followed by the usual bath and massage.

Friday

1. Commence with a jog of 200 yards, followed by five minutes of body-building exercises, such as trunk twists, full squats, push-ups from the front leaning rest position, and high kicks.

2. Refrain from tiring practice today because of jumps

for height tomorrow. Reassure yourself of the length, direction, and speed of the approach.

3. Try five or six standing broad jumps.
4. Complete the workout by jogging easily 300 yards. Omit a prolonged bath, since sponging only will suffice.

Saturday

1. Warm up with exercises of the type and intensity which your past experience has found most suitable to your requirements. The amount and quality of warm-up should by this time become standardized and be used on those days when you are called upon to extend yourself, whether in team trials or in competition. A typical precompetition warm-up includes:

a. A jog of 250 yards.
b. A walk of 50 yards.
c. A spring of 25 yards.
d. Two minutes of leg exercises such as high kicking, hopping, and bounding.
e. Two minutes of arm- and trunk-developing exercises such as handstands, walking on the hands, front leaning rest and push-ups, and tumbling.
f. Two or three high jump trials to prove correctness of the details of the approach.
g. Two or three high jump trials to reassure your-self of accurate timing of the forward leg swing, the spring, the body turn, and the layout. The crossbar in these trials should be raised to a height barely sufficient to require moderate jumping effort. If the crossbar is too low, the task imposed is insufficient to require a fully executed spring and layout. If the crossbar is too high, energy is unnecessarily expended.

2. Set a limit of nine or ten trials. Develop the knack of complete relaxation between jumps. Raise the

crossbar to successive heights just as in competition. The catch phrase, "one height, one jump" applies equally well to the high jump and the pole vault. An observer or an instructor should witness each trial to aid in correcting form.

3. Raise the crossbar 1 inch beyond your best previous effort and take two trials. Get accustomed to steeling yourself for 101 per cent performance. In aeronautical terms, set a high ceiling.
4. Complete the day's workout with a jog of 150 yards followed by a run of 100 yards at seven-eighths effort, a shower, and a massage. Record body weight, and study your weekly weight fluctuations.

Midseason

A characteristic of this season of practice is a reduction of drill on such exercises as pertain to the arms and shoulders and the elimination of fatiguing calisthenics. The emphasis is placed on the acquisition of skill in crossbar clearance. In general, the athlete will jump at full effort on but two days a week, usually on Wednesday in practice and Saturday in competition. For the jumper who requires three days rest, the hard jumping can be changed to Tuesday.

Monday

1. Limber up with a jog of 150 yards, a walk of 25 yards, and a run of 25 yards, followed by a sprint of 25 yards.
2. Spend two or three minutes on exercises such as rope skipping, leg swinging, hitch kicking, and squatting.
3. Lie in the pit in a position approximating the layout and practice the leg movements used in crossbar clearance. Adapt the exercise to the form of jump

used.

4. Review the faults of Saturday's competition and work on their correction.
5. Join the sprinters and take two 35-yard dashes.
6. Spend five or ten minutes on both the speed and the angle of approach. Checkmarks should be corrected at the same time. The jumper must bear in mind that spring must not be sacrificed to attain speed.
7. Jog 220 yards as a final exercise, then have a shower and massage.

Tuesday

1. Jog 150 yards, walk 50 yards, and stride 100 yards at three-fourths effort.
2. Perform two minutes of inverted running.
3. Practice stretching exercises, including the hitch kick, for three or four minutes.
4. Join the running broad-jumpers, and jump for distance twice. If the foot-stamp in the broad jump interferes with the efficiency of the high jump spring, another event may be substituted at the discretion of the coach.
5. Expose the body to the sun for five or ten minutes.
6. Tuesday's work is varied in nature, yet sufficiently light to permit the building up of body tone. Get set both mentally and physically to jump for height on Wednesday.
7. Conclude the day's work with light jogging, followed by a sponge bath.

Wednesday

1. Warm up as on a day of competition.

2. Set the crossbar at the same height at which the competition will start in the next meet. Set a limit of eight or nine jumps. Gradually raise the crossbar so that the last height is 1 inch above your record jump.

3. Participate for five or ten minutes in a game or contest which requires only moderate exertion. This may be hand wrestling, leapfrog relay, sprint relay (each man running 25 yards), and putting the 12-pound shot with first the left and then the right hand. The shot put may be scored by adding the distance attained by both hands.

4. If weather permits, take a sun bath for five or ten minutes.

5. Complete the practice with a jog of 200 yards.

Thursday

1. Take an optional amount of jogging, walking, sprinting, and calisthenics.

2. Spend two or three minutes verifying the different phases of the approach.

3. Set the crossbar at a moderate height and jump five or six times, emphasizing form.

4. Join the javelin-throwers and participate in their workout for ten minutes. This is an event at which the jumper may become adept.

5. Taper off by jogging an optional distance, then analyse your weekly body weight changes.

Friday

1. Jog 220 yards easily.

2. Make a study of the consistency of the approach and pit. Adjust the shoes and length of spikes to meet the conditions. Be your own cheer leader in

keying yourself for Saturday's contest. Decide in your own mind just how you are going to compete, set an objective, and think in terms of better heights than you have attained heretofore.

3. Refrain from jumping but take light exercises of a varied nature which you have learned are best suited to your present needs.
4. Omit sun baths for the sprinting. Substitute a tepid sponge bath for the customary shower.
5. Keep off the feet from now until competition. A well-known athlete, as the story goes, climbed the Statue of Liberty on the day preceding an important meet. All he has to show for his competition is his contestant's linen number.

Saturday

1. Remember that the event can be won only on the field. Therefore, go about your daily routine in the regular manner. Conserve both nervous and physical energy.
2. By now the contestant knows the type and amount of warm-up that he requires. He also knows whether he should allow 20, 30, or 40 minutes to elapse between the warm-up and the starting of the event.
3. An alert contestant is always ready for his competition. He has checked the order of jumping on the official roster.
4. Maintain body glow between jumps. Take advantage of this time for physical and mental relaxation.
5. Remember "one height, one jump".
6. Conclude the day's activities with a shower and massage. Has your body weight fluctuation been ideal?

Late Season

The late season schedule of practice is lighter in intensity and designed to smooth the form and point toward further improvement in body tone.

Monday

1. Open the day's practice by jogging 220 yards, walking 10 yards, running 25 yards, and sprinting 25 yards.
2. Discuss both the correct and incorrect execution of form in the previous Saturday's meet. A competitor's enthusiasm for the event is increased by having his own exemplification of correct technique pointed out.
3. Jump four or five times at a moderate height to eliminate any errors which may have been discovered.
4. Take part in a game for five or ten minutes. Obviously the competitor will not participate in any contest or event that may seriously jeopardize his high jumping accomplishments. The game should serve the purpose of variety and relaxation in the workout, but in no sense should be horseplay. A friendly scuffle has proved costly when a good athlete received an incapacitating spike wound.
5. Finish the day's work by jogging 220 yards at an easy pace.

Tuesday

1. Begin by jogging 100 yards, and walking 10 yards; repeating twice. Jogging precedes calisthenics as a protective measure since injuries occur in executing vigorous movements when the athlete is unprepared, just as in jumping vigorously when one is unprepared.

2. Spend from three to five minutes on exercises, completing the entire repertoire of gymnastic stunts which have proved of value in perfecting jumping ability.
3. Work on another event such as the shot-put or the javelin throw.
4. Reassure yourself of the optimum speed, direction, and length of the run toward the bar.
5. Do not jump today.
6. Conclude the practice by jogging 100 yards, running 100 yards, and sprinting 50 yards. This means 250 yards of continuous effort, starting slowly and culminating in a burst of speed. Substitute a tepid sponge bath for the tepid shower.

Wednesday

1. Limber up with a jog of 200 yards, a run of 50 yards at three-fourths effort, and conclude with 25 yards at nine-tenths effort.
2. Try three or four standing broad jumps.
3. Spend five to eight minutes on light gymnastic stunts of special benefit to the high jumper.
4. Jump for height and not to exceed eight times, but emphasize form.
5. Finish the practice with a run of 200 yards, followed immediately by a sprint of 25 yards.

Thursday

1. Take a warm-up, optional both as to type and quantity.
2. Prepare for javelin throwing and participate in four or five trials with the javelin-throwers.
3. Execute four or five trials of the running hitch kick.

Since this event taxes the energy of some jumpers, good judgement must be used in the degree of effort applied.

4. Spend two minutes in bounding and bending exercises. If the approach is of cinders, shifts this workout to the turf. Variety aids in improving body tone.
5. Taper off with a jog of 300 yards at an optional pace. Conclude with a shower and massage; the check your body weight.

Friday

1. There are two schools of thought relative to Friday's work. One school prefers that the competitors dress in competition, suits and, after light jogging, sponge the body with tepid water and call it a day. The other contends that complete absence from the practice field is more desirable. This group further believes that nervous and physical energy are best conserved by avoiding contact with the event or its environment.

Saturday

1. The suggestions presented for Saturday's competition during midseason are applicable to late season. Conservation of energy during the day, relaxation between jumps, and alertness at all times are factors with which the competitor is already familiar.
2. Aim at 101 per cent your best effort, and make a mental resolution to clear each height on the first jump.
3. End the day with a jog of 200 yards, a shower, and a massage. Analyse the week's fluctuation in body weight.

CHAPTER 5

COMMON ERRORS AND THEIR CORRECTIONS IN HIGH JUMP

When a jumper fails to clear a height, his attempt should be analysed in order to isolate his shortcomings. There are certain faults common to the execution of the various parts of the jump which are pointed out and discussed.

1. In the Approach

An obvious error in this part of the jump is a run which is either too long or too short. A run which is too long calls for a needless expenditure of energy. One which is too short fails to permit the acquisition of sufficient momentum for crossbar clearance. If excess speed is generated, insufficient time is permitted for the execution of the gather, the foot-stamp, the rock-up on the toe, and leg swing. In general, only a moderate amount of speed is required for this event.

Any wide variation from the angles of approach should be avoided. The technique prescribed in each style of jump requires a rather close adherence to the proper angle of approach.

Errors in checkmarks adjustments are reflected in a misplaced take-off spot. Even though the checkmarks are correct, a mis-judged last stride may lead to the same error. Even the novice will understand that, if the take-off spot is too close, the crossbar will be displaced on the upward flight; and conversely, if it is too far back, the maximum height will be attained in advance, and the crossbar will be displaced on the downward flight.

To avoid vagueness, definite and measurements have been given for the length of run, the number of checkmarks, the speed of the run, and the distance of the take-off spot from the crossbar. It must be borne in mind that these figures are only a starting point from which to work. The experience of the individual and also the advice of the coach or observer will lead the jumper to the most effective approach adjustments.

2. Addressing the Bar

Although the gather is executed during the last two strides, it is considered here as a part of addressing the bar. Some jumpers fail to gain height because they have not settled down during the last two strides and have not permitted themselves the semirelaxation prior to the explosive spring action. In other words, they are too tense.

Even though the take-off spot is accurately struck, if the last stride is too long, a loss of power results because the centre of gravity is too far back at the time of the beginning of the spring. Conversely, if the last stride is too short, the centre of gravity is too far forward, thus detracting from the free leg swing.

If the foot-stamp is executed at an angle other than that prescribed for a particular form of jump, the direction of the flight is impaired correspondingly. Obviously, a partially completed or half-heartedly executed spring is an error. It is a hard, vigorous stamp that sends the jumper into the air.

Many jumpers make errors in the degree of knee bend which they employ. Different forms of jumping call for varying degrees of knee bend. Errors in the amount of knee bend are fatal to good performance, yet the proper amount for the individual cannot be accurately described. Generally speaking, the error leans toward the side of insufficient knee bend.

Some jumpers, while addressing the bar, make a mistake by leaning to the left or to the right. In the western form of jump, for example, a lean to the left tends to throw the left shoulder into the bar. The right lean in the western form hampers the layout because the left shoulder is too far away from the bar. Furthermore, the jumper is not in the most desirable position to execute the undercut of the left leg.

In the eastern form, if the lean is too far to the left, the jumper has an extra task imposed in turning the trunk back at the instant of layout and crossbar clearance. If the lean is too far to the right, the body is brought too close to the bar for the execution of the jump.

The following errors are to be guarded against in the forward leg swing:

a. Incorrect direction.

b. Insufficient height.

c. Incorrect degree of knee bend.

d. Lack of vigour in the swing.

There are jumpers who detract from their effort by failing to achieve a complete rock-up on the toe. Closely associated with this point is the forward leg swing. These actions must be so timed that their combination gives maximum height to the body. Obviously, inaccurate timing is a serious error.

The vigorous use of the arms is an aid to the forceful use of the legs, and it is obvious that dangling arms are merely appendages rather than effective working parts of the body.

In addressing the bar, the chief faults are insufficient spring and lack of virour in the leg swing and the arm action.

3. In Crossbar Clearance

After addressing the bar, the jumper begins his flight upward, climaxing his effort in the layout and the clearance, and terminating in the landing. In the order of execution the first possible error is a failure to snap up rapidly the take-off leg. If this movement is delayed, the forward flight has brought the jumper to the crossbar before the leg is up.

Any motion which keeps the body from attaining a bowed position (the layout), just prior to crossbar clearance, is an error. An observer standing near the bar is in a position to note the parts of the body which are lowest. The left hip causes more grief than any other part of the body in the western form. A low left hip may be raised by snapping the head backward and to the left.

In the eastern form of jump the left hip is also the offending member. In this form of conscious upward hip lift coupled with a vigorous downward sweep of the leg leg during its backward movement together with a fully executed body turn aids in correcting this fault.

A fatal error in the crossbar clearance is a lack of coordination in the snap-up and the undercut.

Whenever there is a movement to execute, there is a possibility of error. The jumper must make use of the knowledge of body mechanics and physiologic principles in perfecting the form which is especially fitted to him.

Common Errors and Corrections

1. Error

The athlete leans forward toward the bar at takeoff.

Reasons

The last two strides of the run-up are too small.

Remedies

The athlete practices the run-up with the last strides marked on the ground. Emphasize placement of the jumping foot with the heel placed down first and good backward body lean prior to takeoff.

2. Error

The athlete leans the upper body sideways towards the bar at takeoff.

Reasons

The takeoff foot is placed parallel to the bar at takeoff.

Remedies

Mark the run-up with a line and draw the position of the takeoff foot on the ground (diagonally toward the crossbar).

3. Error

The athlete takes off with the back already rotated toward the bar.

Reasons

The athlete is anticipating the back-layout position. The takeoff foot is pointing back toward the run-up. The curve of the run-up is too tight.

Remedies

Mark the correct position of the takeoff foot. Use visual cues ("Look along line of the crossbar") to control body position. The athlete should reduce the "tightness" of the curve.

4. Error

The jumper has difficulty getting into a back-layout

position over the bar.

Reasons

The athlete has insufficient curve in final part of run-up and does not lean into the curve of the run-up. The jumper has poor rotary action of the leading leg.

Remedies

Make the correct position of the takeoff foot. Instruct the athlete to increase the curve of the run-up and lean into curve. Have the athlete emphasize the upward thrust and rotation of the free leg back toward the run-up at takeoff.

5. Error

The athlete crosses the bar in a sitting position, knocking the bar off with the seat.

Reasons

The athlete lifts the thighs or shoulders too early during the bar clearance. The head is lifted to look at the bar during the clearance.

Remedies

After the takeoff, the athlete must drop the leading leg downward and press the hips upward. The athlete should drop the head back and use sideways vision toward the use sideways vision toward the crossbar to give timing for the elevation of the legs.

6. Error

The athlete crosses the bar with the side of the body nearest the bar rather than with the back.

Reasons

The athlete uses insufficient rotation around the long axis of the body and insufficient rotation of the leading leg back toward the run-up.

Remedies

Instruct the athlete to use a 3-stride run-up emphasizing the upward and inward rotation of the leading leg. The athlete should emphasize strong lean into the curve when using a longer run-up. A tighter curve in the run-up may be necessary.

7. Error

The takeoff foot placement varies with each jump.

Reasons

The stride length in the run-up varies with each approach. The run-up is poorly established, and the athlete does not know the correct stride length.

Remedies

Measure the run-up and use control markers. Work on building uniform acceleration throughout the run-up.

8. Error

The athlete slows down before takeoff.

Reasons

The athlete is anxious about the takeoff. Stride length is incorrect in final phase of run-up.

Remedies

Have the athlete practice run-up and takeoff without using a crossbar. Use markers for positioning the last 3 strides.

9. Error

Run-up speed is not translated into height.

Reasons

The run-up is too fast. The athlete uses no backward body lean at takeoff or inward lean into curve. The takeoff foot is incorrectly placed. Leg power may be poor.

Remedies

The athlete should start the run-up slowly and accelerate throughout, tighten the curve of the run-up, and/or lean more into curve. The athlete should point the takeoff foot diagonally toward the crossbar and lean back at takeoff. The athlete can also improve leg power to assist in takeoff.

Assessment

1. Assess the following theoretical elements as taught during instructional sessions.
   - a. Fundamental rules governing the high jump.
   - b. Good safety habits for use in the high jump.
   - c. Basic elements of high-jump technique.
   - d. Basic elements of training for the high jump.
2. Assess the performance of technique during the following stages of skill development.
   - a. Backward jumping and flop bar clearance (elastic crossbar is used).
   - b. Flop high jump from a 3-stride noncurved run-up.
   - c. Flop high jump from a 5-stride curved run-up.
   - d. Flop high jump from 9- and 11-stride curved run-ups.

Critical Features of Technique to Observe During Assessment :

- a. Measurement of the run-up and positioning of check marks.
- b. Acceleration through the run-up and inward lean into the curve of the run-up.
- c. Shift of the hip ahead of the upper body in the final

strides of the takeoff. Backward rotation of the arms.

d. Positioning and alignment of the takeoff foot immediately prior to takeoff.

e. Upright trunk and elevated head at takeoff.

f. Upward drive of the arms and knee of the leading leg during takeoff.

g. Rotation of the thigh of the leading leg back toward the run-up at takeoff.

h. Lowering of the leading leg and the elevation of the hips over the bar.

i. Rotation of the body to a layout position.

j. Vision along the line of the crossbar.

k. Flexion at the knees and hips to clear the bar.

l. Relaxed landing on the shoulders with the arms spread.

3. Hold graded competitions to help develop motivation and technique.

a. Jumpers use a backward jump and flop clearance to clear an elastic crossbar.

b. Jumpers compete in a flop high-jump competition using a straight 3-stride run-up.

c. Jumpers compete in a flop high-jump competition using a curved 5-stride run-up.

d. Jumpers compete in a flop high-jump competition using a run-up with stride length chosen according to individual preference.

CHAPTER 6

TEACHING TACTICS IN HIGH JUMP

In recent years the Fosbury Flop technique of high jumping has superseded the straddle, and the world records for both males and females are held by flop jumpers. The preference for the flop technique also exists in the multidiscipline competitions of the decathlon and the heptathlon. Although a few athletes still use the straddle, most prefer the flop. Most athletes find the flop technically less demanding than the straddle and considerably easier to learn. Youngsters tend to grasp the fundamentals quickly and find the flop's dramatic method of bar clearance more attractive than that of the straddle.

SAFETY TIPS

The drop from height and the backward rotation in the Fosbury Flop frequently cause jumpers to land on their shoulders and then roll backward. Landing pads that have insufficient depth and are too low to the ground allow too much backward rotation in flight, which, combined with drop from a height, cause compression injuries in the neck and shoulders. You should use landing pads that are specified by the manufacturer to accommodate the flop. Such pads are noted for their absorbency and large landing area (5 meters by 4 meters). The landing surface is at least 1-1/2 meters above the ground, which is essential in stopping athletes from overrotating backward while in flight.

Flop jumpers also tend to have flight paths that cause them to cross the landing pads diagonally and land in the corners, so the corners should have as much support as the centres. Do not use any landing pad that might allow the athlete to "botton out". Nor should you try to create a landing area out of a stack of gymnastic crash pads. Even when the mats are tied together, an athlete could fall into the separation between them.

Surgical tubing or elastic rope is an excellent teaching aid and is preferable to competitive crossbars for training. Take care to ensure that the high-jump standards are well anchored at the base and that the rubber "crossbars" can stretch adequately so the standards do not pull in toward the athlete during a poor jump.

Run-ups should be firm and give good traction and support for each successive jumper. Grass and artificial surfaces may become slippery and dangerous when wet unless spikes are used. The design of high jump spikes is critical for good traction on the takeoff. The shoe on the jumping foot normally has 6 spikes on the sole and more on the heel to prevent slipping during the last stride prior to takeoff. Many athletes use short spikes or none at all on the leading (swing-up) leg.

One of the most important factors in successful flop high jumping at the elite level is an extreme back arch during bar clearance. This high degree of flexibility is developed slowly and systematically over a long period. It is unnecessary for novices and recreational jumpers; they can achieve good performance with minimal hyperextension of the back during bar clearance. It is important that instructors who work with young athletes realize that the back arch is not a natural position for the body and that extreme spinal flexibility is not a prerequisite to enjoying high jumping at the elementary level.

TECHNIQUE

The athlete leans into the final curve of a fast, long run-up. At takeoff the athlete drives directly upward off the jumping foot, simultaneously forcing the leg nearest the bar both upward and back toward the run-up. This action helps to rotate the athlete into a back layout position.

The arms, which assist in takeoff, may be brought into the sides of the body, or one arm can reach out along the line of the bar. When the jumper's shoulders cross the bar, the back is hyperextended and the hips pressed upward. Once the athlete's seat has passed over the bar, there is a powerful flexion at the hips as the legs are brought toward the chest. The head and shoulders lift upward and assist in clearing the legs over the bar. The athlete relaxes to land on the back and shoulders.

TEACHING POINTS

Drill 1: Lead-Ups

All jumping, bounding, and sprinting activity are excellent preparation for the high jump. Lead-ups used for the long jump, the triple jump, and sprinting can also be used for the high jump.

High-Knee Marching

With each step the athlete drives the thigh of the leading leg up to horizontal or above. The athlete drives up onto the toes of the supporting foot, works the arms vigorously, and drives the knee upward as powerfully as possible.

High-Knee Running

Each participant runs slowly, concentration on raising the thigh of the leading leg to horizontal or above.

The athlete drives up onto the toes of the supporting foot throughout.

Long Bounding Strides

With each stride the athlete drives both forward and upward to cover as much ground as possible. The athlete drives the thigh of the leading leg up to horizontal and works the arms of vigorously throughout. The driving leg extends powerfully and vigorously throughout.

Coaching Points

1. Swing your arms forward and upward with each bounding stride.

2. Try to achieve a wide stride position at the midpoint of each bounding stride.

3. Try to get a feeling of "floating" at the midpoint of each stride.

Jumping to Head a Suspended Volleyball or Soccerball

Suspended balls 30 to 60 centimetres (1 to 2 feet) above the heads of the participants. From a run-up of 3 to 5 strides, each athlete jumps to head the ball, using a 1-footed takeoff.

Coaching Points

1. Try to lean slightly backward prior to takeoff.

2. Jump directly upward.

3. Swing your arms and leading leg upward as vigorously as possible.

A Stride Jump Over the Bar

Substitute surgical elastic tubing for a competitive crossbar. Participants approach directly from the front and stride-jump over the substitute crossbar to land on both feet in a standing position. This drill encourages the athletes to jump directly upward and also develops the correct rolling action from the heel and toe on the takeoff (jumping) foot.

Coaching Points

1. Drive up vigorously with the leading leg and your arms at takeoff.

2. Stretch up and extend your body at takeoff.

3. Keep your head up; do not lean forward in the jump.

Marking a Takeoff Line for a Stride Jump Over the Bar

Set the elastic crossbar 2 to 3 inches above the top of the landing pads. Mark a takeoff line on the ground at approximately one arm's length back from the bar. Participant are not allowed to jump from farther back than the line; this forces them to high jump rather than long jump.

A Stride Jump Using a Three-Stride Approach

Set the takeoff spot 1 arm's length back from the bar. Starting with the feet together, each participant measures 3 running strides from the takeoff spot at an angle of 35 to 40 degrees to the bar. This angle allows the athlete to rotate onto the back for the bar clearance and will be required later for a curved run-up. Use traffic cones to guide the run-up. A jumper approaching from the left begins with the feet together and starts the run-up with the right foot. The jumper will use a right-left-right run-up and take off with the right leg.

Coaching Points

1. Use a powerful bounding jump to "stride" up onto the landing pads.

2. Drive the thigh of the leading (left) leg up to horizontal or above.

3. Hold your head high and keep your upper body

straight.

4. Swing your arms to help you jump upward.

Drill 2: Flop High Jump Using a Short (3-Stride) Run-Up

Each participant jumps backward to land flat-backed on the landing pads. The jumper's heels are no more than 2 foot lengths away from the base of the landing pad at takeoff. No elastic crossbar is used in this drill.

Coaching Points

1. Lift the hips upward during the jump so that the body lands flat on the landing pad.

2. Spread your arms to cushion the landing.

Backward Jumping With Leg Elevation

The starting position is the same as for the previous drill. Each athlete now lands on the back with legs elevated. The performer must jump upward, and the back, then flex at the hips to lift the legs upward. No elastic crossbar is used.

Coaching Points

1. Think of this drill as a jump followed by a sit-up in the air.

2. Jump upward, drop your shoulders and head back, and then pull your knees to your chest.

Backward Jumping With Leg Elevation—Elastic Crossbar Set at Hip Height

The athlete performs the same action as in the previous drill but uses the elastic rope as a crossbar. Initially set this substitute crossbar just above the height of the landing pad. For better performers in the group, raise the elastic beyond hip height to shoulder height.

Use of Minitrampoline by Experienced Jumpers

Experienced athletes often use minitrampolines to gain additional height and time in the air in the backward jumping drill. This drill enables the jumper to concentrate on visually timing the bar clearance. Position the minitrampline to slope toward the landing area. This drill is not recommended for novices.

Coaching Points

1. Look across your shoulder at the bar to time the bar clearance of your legs.

2. Arch your back above the bar, and when your seat has crossed the bar, pull your knees toward your shoulder to clear your legs.

3. Be sure to flex the legs at the knees.

Elementary Flop Using a Straight Three-Stride Run-Up

Initially set the takeoff at 1/4 of the crossbar's length in from the nearest standard, and 1 arm's length away from the bar. Use an angle of 35 to 40 degrees for the run-up. Starting with feet together the jumper runs back 3 fast strides from the takeoff spot. A partner marks the third stride. The jumper begins the run-up from the left side starting with the right foot (i.e., "right foot, left foot, right foot, jump"). Use markers to guide the foot positions.

Coaching Points

1. Accelerate toward the bar during the run-up.

2. Place the takeoff foot down quickly (directly in line with the run-up) and drive the knee of the leading leg vigorously upward.

3. Once the knee is as high as possible, turn it back toward the centre of the run-up.

Drill 3: Flop High Jump Using an Extended (Curved) Run-Up

Technique

The run-up for the flop is straight to start with and curved prior to takeoff with the greater part of the curve usually occurring in the last 5 strides before takeoff. The number of strides taken in the run-up varies greatly, ranging from 9 to 15 or more. Frequently elite athletes use 2 check marks, the first positioned where the first stride falls in the approach to the bar and the second frequently placed 5 strides prior to the takeoff. The run-up is characterized by continuous acceleration.

Body Position During the Run-Up

The athlete leans forward at the start of the run-up and accelerates toward the bar. During the curved part of the run-up, the athlete leans in toward the centre of the curve but straightens again at the takeoff. The penultimate (second to last) stride is usually longer than the last stride before takeoff. The characteristic curve in the run-up used by the flop jumper helps the jumper to assume a good takeoff and an optimal layout position over the bar.

Drills

Curve Sprinting

This activity is a preparation for the curved flop run-up. Participants sprint a figure eight, alternately curving to the left and then to the right. Each runner leans the body weight (centre of gravity) well into each curve. The curves are moderate and should not slow the running speed.

Coaching Points

1. Be sure to lean into the curve of the run-up so that the body weight is on the inside of the curve each time.

Orientation to a Curved Run-Up

Mark a circle of 6 to 7 meters in diameter on the ground. Jumpers who approach the bar from the left side and take off with the right foot run clockwise. The speed of the run should be sufficient to give the athlete a feel for the outward pull of centrifugal force and the need to lean in toward the centre of the circle. The amount of lean will depend on the speed of run.

Coaching Points

1. Run fast and lean well into the curve.
2. Place each foot parallel with the curve of the run-up.

Elementary Curved Run-Up

This run-up is adequate for young novices (12 to 15 years of age) attempting the flop from a curved run-up. Measure the takeoff for an athlete approaching from the left in the following manner.

Set the takeoff 1 arm's length from the bar and 1/4 of the crossbar's length in from the left high-jump standard. Take 1 large stride to the left from the left high-jump standard, and take 2 strides from this point back into the run-up. Mark this position, which will be the third to last stride in the run-up. Measure out the strides, making allowance for the ages and sizes of the participants.

Measure a 5-stride run-up from the takeoff spot. When the athlete is approaching the bar, the first 2 strides will be straight and the final 3 strides will be curved. The run-up will resemble an inverted *J*. Each run-up will differ slightly according to individual stride length. Increasing confidence and faster approaches will necessitate a longer run-up.

Increasing the Length of the Run-Up

As participants develop confidence, they will need to enlarge and adjust the run-up to allow for greater approach speed. The takeoff spot will still be 1/4 of the crossbar's length in from the nearest high-jump standard. The following sequence will assist in setting up a 9-stride run-up. Adjustments will have to be made relative to individual stride length and speed of approach.

The take-off spot is 1/4 of a crossbar length in toward the centre of the crossbar, measured from the nearest high-jump standard. The takeoff spot is shifted back from the bar to just beyond 1 arm's length. This allows for an increase in the speed of approach.

Measure 3 to 4.5 meters directly to the left from the left standard and 6 to 9 meters back into the run-up. This marks the start of the curved part of the run-up. Measure 4 more strides in a straight line back from the 5th stride to give a 9-stride run-up.

An athlete will begin a 9-stride run-up from the left side with the right foot (starting with the feet together); one or two check marks on the run-up assist in making the run-up accurate. If 2 check marks are used, place the 1st where the first stride falls in the approach to the bar. Place the 2nd check mark 5 strides prior to takeoff. With improved technique (and leg strength), the athlete can lengthen the run-up in order to gain additional acceleration.

Developing the Arm Action and Stride Length During the Last Three Approach Strides

This action closely resembles the technique used in the last three strides by the straddle jumper.

Lead the group through the required movement pattern of the last three strides, which the students then practice freely on grass. The actions are performed slowly and mechanically to begin with and then progressively increased in speed to a slow run.

The sequence of actions for jumps approaching the bar from the left side (and jumping from the right foot) is as follows:

1. The jumper stands with feet together and the arms extended at the side of the body.

2. The jumper steps forward 1 medium-size stride with the right foot, keeping the arms at the side of the body.

3. Next is a step forward, using one long stride with the left foot and allowing the hips to "slide" ahead of the shoulders.

4. Both arms move in a circular fashion (similar to breaststrokes arm action) ahead of the body.

5. The jumper steps forward 1 short stride with the right foot, emphasizing a backward lean, and at the same time rotates the arms backward.

6. Finally, the athlete jumps directly upward from the right foot, driving the thigh of the left leg up to horizontal and simultaneously swinging the arms upward.

Coaching Points

1. Stretch forward into the penultimate stride.

2. Place the jumping foot down on the ground for the last stride as quickly as possible.

Skipping Backward With a Rope While Moving Forward

One difficulty for jumpers in learning the last 3 strides of the flop run-up is rotating the arms backward while simultaneously moving the body forward. Skipping backward with a rope while moving forward is an excellent method to teach the backward rotation of the arms.

Coaching Points

1. Start skipping in place with the rope rotating backward, then slowly move forward. Keep the rope rotating backward.

Long Bounding Strides With Arm Swinging

If skipping backward while moving forward is too difficult, the athlete can practice bounding forward with long strides, swinging the arms forward on one stride and backward on the next.

Arm Action and Stride Length Adjustment During the Run-Up

This drill does not use a crossbar. Place marks on the run-up or use traffic cones to indicate the size of the last 3 strides. The performer "slides" the hips forward in the penultimate stride, maintaining the backward lean into the last stride. The arms are shifted from forward to backward as the athlete steps quickly forward for the last stride.

Coaching Points

1. Step well forward in the penultimate stride and lean back.

2. Push your hips ahead of your chest and swing your arms backward.

3. Put the jumping foot down quickly for a short stride, and swing your arms and nonjumping leg forward and upward for takeoff.

CHAPTER 7

THE HISTORY OF BROAD JUMP

Lack of such complicating factors as an unspecified direction of run in the high jump or as a pole in the pole vault has permitted the development of forms in the running broad jump to follow a rather simple, clear and steady pattern. Basically, performance in this event is dependent upon only three factors: momentum secured from the run, height in the air attained from the take-off, and efficient placement of the feet in the landing. All the controversies about the relative values of various forms while in the air, which were so prevalent during the first quarter of the present century, have been reduced to this simple statement. Form in the air is important almost entirely as it results from a proper take-off and as it is related to balance and correct position in making the landing. Except for a simple forward thrust of each leg, every kick of the legs or throw of the arms must necessarily be accompanied by a compensating backward action by some other body part, which nullifies the benefits of the former. To expect a running stride in the air to increase momentum is comparable to trying to lift one's self by one's bootstraps.

In any case, action by the legs while in the air is not a recently developed style. Every broad-jumper who attempts relaxation and balance while in the air quite naturally moves his legs in some manner similar to the hitch kick and it seems certain that even the earliest jumpers attempted such a style. The picture of Myer Prinstein, of Syracuse, national champion in 1900 with 24′ 7½″, which appears in Lawson Robertson's College Athletics, clearly shows a continuous running action style. Undoubtedly there were others at the time.

Of course, broad-jumping goes back far beyond the present era and was a natural part of living as well as of recreation in man's earliest history. The universal actions of the chase and flight over fallen trees and streams certainly carried over to the play and competitions of ancient man. It was inevitable, therefore, that the running broad jump should be a part of the ancient Olympic games. E. Norman Gardiner states that this was probably the only jump in the ancient games and that there is no evidence of either the high jump or the pole vault in Greek athletics. A pole or spear was used for vaulting to the backs of horses, but not for jumping itself.

His description of the ancient methods is both interesting and valuable as showing the close similarity to modern equipment and methods:

For the long jump a firm hard take-off was provided called the Threshhold. We do not know whether it was of wood or stone. [Without shoes and modern rubber heel protection, either must have caused many a stone bruises.—J.K.D.] In vase paintings the take-off is marked by spears stuck in the ground or by stone pillars similar to those used to mark the start of a race... The ground in front of the take-off was dug up and levelled to a certain distance. This was called the Skamma. "To jump beyond the skamma or the dug-up" was the proverbial expression for an extraordinary feat. Phyllus, the hero of a fabulous jump of 55 feet, is said to have jumped 5 feet beyond the skamma, and we are not surprised to hear from one commentator that he broke his leg in the performance...

The Greek always used jumping weights, halteres, in the long jump. These jumping weights, which somewhat resemble and were probably the origin of our dumb-bells, were made of metal or stone and varied in weight from 2¼ to more than 10 pounds...The jumper with weights depends for his impetus partly on the swing of the weights, partly on the run. The run is short and not fast...As the jumper takes off he swings the weights forward, so that in mid-air arms and legs are almost parallel. Before landing he swings them backwards, a movement which shoots the legs to the front and so lengthens the jump.

Little is known of the true distance made by the Greeks, for they paid more attention to style than to records. But a few professional sprinters and jumpers in England during the 19th century and 5-pound dumbells as a part of certain trick jumping acts. Gardiner appears to accept the statement of one of the them that "J. Howard jumped 29 feet 7 inches at Chester in 1854" and that use of the weights "added at least 8 feet to his jump".

There is, of course, the Nibelungen story of how Siegfried threw a huge stone over 12 fathoms and then leaped far beyond it, incidentally carrying King Gunther with him en route; but there are certain unrealities about the tale which shed some doubt that it would hold water if submitted to the IAAF as a world's record.

It is certain that the broad jump has been included in the track and field program since its modern beginnings. The McWhirters state:

Jumping for distance has been a standard event since the revival of athletics in the early Victorina era. The prospectus of the inaugural "Grad Annula Games" of 1860 at Oxford University invited entries for a "wide jump", though, when the programme came to be printed, the event was designated a "running long jump". The winner was Powell of Oriel with a "length of 17 feet 4 inches", which, incidentally was the same distance at which the first American championship was won 16 years later.

Of course, pits were undoubtedly very poor at these early dates and the use of a take-off board did not occur until 1886, when M. W. Ford, of New York, reached 23′ 2″. During the next 15 years, the world's record was broken 10 times by 3 Irish and 4 American jumpers. The most consistent and long lived of the latter was Myer Prinstein, of Syracuse University, who won national championships in 1898, 1902, 1904, and 1906, with a world's record of 23′ 8 7⁄8 ″ in 1898 and another of 24′ 7″ in 1900. The best of the Irish was Pat O'Connor, who cleared the remarkable distance of 24′ 11¾″ in 1901, a record that stood for 20 years.

Webster states that O'Connor "did not use the 'hitch-kick' but simply drew the knees up toward the chin and trusted to his initial velocity to carry him sailing through the air...Had he known the modern 'hitch-kick' method, he might well have exceeded 26 feet instead of just failing to reach 25 feet". This last statement, written in 1929, indicates that belief in the efficacy of the hitch kick was prevalent at the time; it is no longer generally accepted.

The first man to make the long-awaited more-than-25-foot jump was Ed Gourdin, of Harvard, who, on July 23, 1921, first beat the 1924 Olympic champion Harold Abrahams in the 100-yard dash and then leaped 25′ 3″ in the broad jump. Pictures of Gourdin indicate that he also used a "float" style, with little leg action while in the air. In commenting on his style, Robertson suggests that we "note that the athlete is in position to complete the action without have to resort to any expedient to gain body control". The implication that leg action is a means to balance and control is important.

Various photographs of Legendre indicate a delayed action of the legs in what is now called a delayed hip swing. The drive for height comes primarily from the take-off leg, an upward lift of the head and chest, and an arch of the back. Balance is maintained through the swing of the hips rather than of the lower legs, and only at the last moment are the legs swung forward to an efficient landing position.

The day before this startling performance, the American champion, DeHart Hubbard, from the University of Michigan, had won the regular broad jump with a disappointing 24′ 6″, but within less than a year, on June 13, 1925, Hubbard cleared 25′ 10 7/8″ and thus assured the world that 26 feet was but a matter of time. Hubbard actually cleared 26′ 2″ in 1928, but the record was not accepted on the grounds that the level of the take-off board was one inch higher than that of the landing pit! At best, this could make a difference of 1½ inches. Hubbard's style include a short run of less than 100 feet, remarkable acceleration of speed, good but not unusual height, a single but fast kick of the lead leg, and an excellent forward placement of his feet.

Hubbard's successor, Ed Hamm, of Georgia, never had his record actually on the record books, for only 2 months after he leaped 25′ 11 1/8″ in 1928, Silvio Cator, of Haiti, became the first man officially to clear 26 feet, exceeding it by a mere 1/8 inch. Ed Hamm, with Lutz Long, of Germany (25′ 11″ in 1936), demonstrated most effectively of the great jumpers the delayed hip and leg swing style. Their excellent spring into the air with the head and chest up but with the legs trailing gave great body height. Yet there was time in which to bring both legs, forward together in a good sit-down landing.

Three years later, in 1931, Chuhei Nambu, of Japan, established a new record of 26′ 2 1/8″. Stocky of build, yet a good high-jumper, a :10.5 100-meter man, and world's record holder in the hop, step, and jump at 51′ 7″, he combined speed, good height in the air, and excellent co-ordination.

Then came a marvellous performance of 26′ 8¼″ by the great Jesse Owens, of Ohio State, who on that single day of May 25, 1935, at Ann Arbor, Michigan, established three world's records and tied a fourth. The writer was fortunate to be meet director of this Conference championship, and he remembers with some pride how the broad jump pit was deliberately placed directly in front of the stands, even though a new grass runways was thus made necessary, and of how all other activity was stilled while Jesse made his try. The announcer had the delightful effrontery to suggest that Owens would attempt a new world's record and a white handkerchief was boldly placed at 26 feet. All eyes were concentrated upon this one event and went wide with amazement to see Jesse sail beyond the cloth marker. Surely no other world's record has been so obviously planned or made with such concentration of attention.

Jesse appeared simply to run off the board. There was no obvious foot stamp at the board, no striving for unusual height. He used a simple kick—more of a swing, perhaps, than a kick—of the lead leg; this seemed to be a matter of balance rather than of gaining momentum. His balance was excellent; his sit-down position with feet well extended at the landing was also very good. His greatest asset was certainly his tremendous speed, which surpassed that of any other broad-jumper before or since. Only Eulace Peacock, who cleared 26′ 3″ and beat Jesse on three different occasions, might dispute this statement.

Owens brought nothing new to the broad jump, despite his great performance. Nor have there been suggestions of important improvements in style in the methods of other great jumpers. Lorenzo Wright, of Wayne University (25′ 11″ in 1950), did not permit a full knee-bend during the landing but stiffened his knees in such a way as to produce a bounce up and forward out of the pit. However, to the writer, this seemed to force a slightly quicker dropping of the feet, a higher position of the buttocks, and a loss of best distance. A small yet imposing number of jumpers, including Bill Brown and Willie Steele, tried to prevent their buttocks from touching the pit by sliding off to the side after the feet had landed. However, this method seems to offer no advantages and holds the danger of dropping one foot too soon.

It may well be that this same Willie Steele was an even greater broad jumper than Owens. His career was plagued by injuries and interruptions. He reportedly cleared 27 feet several times in practice and was measured at 26′ 10″ on a fractional foul in the 1948 final Olympic trials. However, greatness is never judged by near misses.

CHAPTER 8

THE ESSENTIAL INGREDIENTS OF BROAD JUMP

The broad jump is relatively simple event: a fast run, a high jump, a little extra momentum gained from a simple leg kick, and finally an extended foot landing. Fortunately, there is time in which to achieve each of these four elements separately and completely.

1. The run is long enough and accelerated enough to gain maximum momentum.

2. Attention shifts in the last 4-strides of the run to jumping—not running, but jumping—as high as possible.

3. A single forceful kick of the take-off leg does slightly increase upward and forward momentum.

4. Both feet are raised to a sit-down position and the body is balanced in order to keep the buttocks from touching the pit.

No extended discussion of the details and problems of the event should remove from either the coach's or the athlete's mind this basically simple and natural action.

The run. Men vary in the length of their run from 100 to 150 feet. Jesse Owens, with his small size and tremendous acceleration, used a short run of about 100 feet, whereas Willie Steele, of about equal ability, ran over 140 feet. The length of the run, then, is determined by the shortest distance within which a man can achieve maximum speed and still be prepared for the jump for height at the toe-board.

The studies of Henry are very valuable in determining this point of maximum velocity. One conclusion he reaches is that 95 per cent of peak velocity is attained at 22 yards. Further results indicate:

The place at which a sprinter running a 100 yard dash reaches peak velocity...turns out to be a function of his speed, but is reached in almost exactly 6 seconds regardless of the speed if he is running at full effort. The runner will be within 1 per cent of his greatest speed at 50 yards if he runs a 10.5 hundred, at 53.7 yards for 10 flat, 57.0 yards in the case of a 9.5, and 60.6 yards in a hypothetical 9 flat.

Note that these conclusions are based on the assumption that the sprinter is making an all-out effort for top speed from the start of his run. This is not ordinarily done by broad jumpers and means that the latter attain maximum velocity at some imaginary point beyond 180 feet. Either broad jumpers must be satisfied with a velocity which is only about 95 per cent maximum or must lengthen their runs beyond what is now customary.

A consistent method of run in the broad jump is of vital importance, and therefore a second mark and in many cases a third will be needed. In finding these marks, the following method is suggested as being simple and sound:

Be sure to warm up thoroughly. Following figure, the distance A-C should correspond to that in which the desired degree of velocity can be obtained. Point C is placed about 26 feet from the toe-board and A-C measured back from that point. The jumper should start at A with the left foot, assuming he jumps from the left foot, in the same manner as in the track run, and should attempt relaxed all-out acceleration at once. The coach should stand about 25 feet to the side from point B and watch the fall of the left foot on the seventh stride at about 30 feet. Repeat until certain of the exact mark. The runner is not attempting to hit a certain mark but is simply running through. Now that mark B is secured, however, he does becomes conscious of it and does hit it exactly as he goes through. Then the coach moves all the way to the board and the process is repeated. The jumper again does not try to hit the board but merely runs through. After three full runs, the coach averages the footmarks and moves the other two check marks either forward or back so that the take-off foot will now hit the board. Only by actually jumping can these marks be double-checked and made exact. The last four strides before the board will differ slightly from those preceding. The first two will be slightly longer as the man relaxes for the jump; the third will probably be as much as 6 inches shorter; and the fourth, from 6 to even 12 inches shorter.

In running through without jumping, the take-off foot should naturally go a few inches beyond the board. Then, when jumping begins, the important shortening of the last one or two strides will bring the foot exactly on the board.

Perhaps it is only a delusion, but the writer feels that his men have had comparatively little difficulty with fouling in the broad jump. If true, he would credit the fact primarily to an insistence that the run be kept as simple as possible. The confident assumption that steps and check marks are not a problem is the best safeguard against the problem. Except in very unusual instances, two check marks are enough. Perhaps even more important, the run should be considered a unit with constant acceleration throughout. There is no change of pace at point B. As a matter of fact, after several years of experience, the B check mark can be eliminated. Few actually do this, for it gets to be a habit; but its purpose is primarily psycholgoical. For this reason, there should be no looking down at mark B to see that it is hit exactly. Certainly there should be no gradual approach to B followed by a sudden all-out effort, although this method is used quite often. The run should be even all the way.

Point C, also marks no deliberate change in the run. Rather, the attention shifts away from the increased momentum and toward the approaching jump upward. At first, a marker may be necessary at this point to remind the jumper to relax a little more and to gather himself for the jump, but this will soon become a habit. During these last four strides to the board, the athlete's eyes, chin, and chest will lift somewhat. At the same time, if his attention is now on jumping high, he will naturally crouch a little.

This use of a third check mark at the start of these last four strides is strongly advocated by H.E. Askew, who found through 14 years of competitive experience that it aided both rhythm and relaxation:

Another help in getting into the air is to count the strides in the coasting section, working up to, and feeling the climax, as the take-off foot comes down on the last number. This enables the athlete to get the rhythm into his system, and it helps the timing of the take-off foot on the board. For example, the writer coasts over the last 4 strides, so he counts in a rhythm of 5. Coming down the runway, as his leg (which is the same as the take-off leg) hits the last check-mark, he begins to count his strides—one, two, three, four, five—with his whole being concentrated on the upward drive as his foot comes down on the board on the count of five.

This practice would probably have the result of overemphasizing the gather and jump, and of slowing down the run during the last four strides. But a beginner, or a man having difficulty in gaining height, might find it very advantageous.

The take-off. The all-consuming purpose of the take-off is to attain maximum height with as little loss of forward momentum as possible. Although somewhat obvious, it is still important to emphasize that the take-off begins at least as far back as point C. Unless the proper preparation has been made, the jump itself cannot be successful. The last four strides must be sufficiently controlled and relaxed to provide four adjustments:

1. The slight lateral shift of the body weight to the left over the left foot. The right foot will naturally toe out and may even shift a little out of line to the right in order to accomplish the lateral shove. Jesse Owens achieved this same result by shifting the left take-off foot an inch or so the right, a way even more efficient and likely to provide excellent balance.

2. The body will settle slightly from the hips down, just as a high-jumper settles on his last stride. This must be done exactly right. A fraction too low means the knees will give way and be unable to drive up into the jump. A fraction too high and there will be no springs to decompress. In short, the major key to proper height lies here, and much careful practice must be done to achieve exact timing and co-ordination. Broad-jumpers are, of course, both born and made. They are born with speed; they are made primarily by perfecting this aspect of the event.

3. A lift of the eyes, chin, and chest places the take-off foot ahead of the body weight as its heel first contacts the board, where it becomes a partial brace against the forward momentum of the body. This bracing action is very minor as compared with the high jump, yet it drives

the heel hard into the ground and forces a flexion of the left ankle, knee, and hip. The natural reaction into extension is a primary factor in gaining height.

4. The last stride to the toe-board will normally be from 4 to 12 inches shorter than those preceding it. This again is a natural phase of the effort to attain height. It should be noted that the word "natural" has been used throughout. No wise coach would attempt to teach each of these actions, for the athlete would be lost in confusion as to which part to use next. If the over-all movement of securing height while moving near maximum speed is understood, the parts will fall into place quite "naturally" without special attention. It is desirable, however, that the coach should understand how things occur so that he can offer suggestion where such naturalness is not present.

William Watson, of the University of Michigan, primarily a shot and discus man, weighing 196 pounds, was yet able to clear 25′ 5½″ through perfection of the gather and take-off and the excellent height that resulted. His crouch seemed excessive at times, yet he was able to rise out of it. We found the answer on the day he cleared 6′ 5¼″ in the high jump.

Larry Snyder, coach at Ohio State University and of Jesse Owens, emphasizes, along with many other good coaches, that "the centre of gravity must be ahead of the take-foot off. The shorter last stride helps in attaining this position. A 'reaching' last stride kills the jumper's speed". A similar puzzling statement is made by Dean Cromwell: "On the other hand, if the body leans backward to any extent, it will lose much of the momentum of the run and spring. A backward lean causes the athlete to be far off balance when in the air". These statements raise the question of when they are true. They are not and should not be true as the heel of the foot touches the toe-board, for at this point the centre of gravity is behind the foot. They are always true, of course, as the toe leaves the board.

It seems clear, then, that the often repeated phrase, "Get the body weight over or in advance of the take-off foot", refers to the instant when the foot is driving off the board. If at this point the centre of gravity is directly above the take-off, the effect will be upward only with a loss of forward momentum, as in the high jump.

The landing. A well-timed landing can be defined as one in which the lowest point of the buttock is but a fraction of an inch above the level of the extended heels at the moment the latter first touch the ground. Such a position requires quick and well-timed action to prevent an actual sit-down in the pit. In general, this means a forward and downward thrust of the heavy head and shoulders, which pulls the buttocks upward. The chin drops quickly down between the knees. The knees themselves are completely relaxed and bend quickly and fully in most instances. In such cases, the jumper falls directly forward in a compact tuck position very close to the landing on his hands and knees.

Some jumpers, such as Lorenzo Wright, bend the knees only slightly and use the forward momentum of the body in lifting the buttocks high above the feet and in leaping forward beyond the pit. This form has a tendency to drop the feet too soon, an unforgivable sin in broad-jumping.

Other jumpers, such as Bill Brown (National Collegiate champion, 1941) and most of the Southern California jumpers, relax one knee and stiffen the other after the heels have hit and then fall off to the side and slightly forward. This method holds the danger of anticipating the turn and of dropping the one foot too soon. In almost all cases, a straight-forward action throughout the entire jump is much to be preferred. But if the heels are extended together and high, all following actions are of little significance. Theoretically, for every inch that the heels are kept up, a gain of 1½ inches results in the jump, a very important point to emphasize in coaching broad-jumpers.

Keeping the feet high is the most difficult aspect of the broad jump to learn. It requires strong abdominal muscles, a willingness to sit down in the pit occasionally, and a persistent concentration upon this phase of the jump in practice. This is best done with a short run and a dirt take-off. Constant jumping off the board involves danger to the heel and, of course, a full run means fewer jumps. It is important to avoid bringing the head and shoulders down toward the knees until just before the heels touch the ground. Rather, the legs should be held up to an almost horizontal position with only a slight bend at the knees.

The use of the arms throughout the landing depends upon their position during the jump. If thrown high above the head, they should be brought quickly down and forward at the last moment, aiding the forward action of the shoulders. If carried low, they can be thrown downward, backward, and then upward, thus forcing the shoulders forward and downward; the action is similar to that of a man jumping with weights and casting them behind him at the last moment. In most cases, the first of the two methods will prevail.

IMPORTANT QUESTIONS AND ANSWERS

What hints can be given for competition in the broad jump? The key to competitive broad-jumping lies in effective concentration of effort. From every standpoint, it is wise to make extremely careful preparation for the first jump and to plan to do one's best on the second and third efforts. After such efforts, the runway is almost certain to be less firm and the jumper less effective. This is especially true when, as so often happens, the jumper is also competing in other events. For many years, the writer has encouraged his broad-jumpers to emphasize a fair jump on the first effort. That is, they should try to get a fair jump that will at least qualify them for the finals and possibly place them in competition. In most cases, this means a concentration of attention upon not going over the toe-board, upon chopping the last two strides slightly, and upon relaxing somewhat more than usual throughout the run. Sometimes it means moving the check marks back 3 or 4 inches to guard against fouling. Once this qualifying jump is made, they can go all-out. The second jump can now be taken as though it were the last. Maximum momentum is taken for granted. Attention, which normally can be concentrated on only one detail in any given action, should be directed upon relaxing during the last four strides and jumping high. Many men make the serious error of "trying hard" to do something at this point. They stamp the floor hard on the board. They throw the arms vigorously to gain greater height. Actually, the problem is just the opposite. Once momentum is achieved, how can it be most easily and smoothly directed upward and outward? In almost every instance, jumpers state that the best jumps are the easy ones.

Careful preparation is vital before the first jump. Check marks should be measured by a steel tape, and certainly not by striding through and guessing at the board. An experienced jumper or coach should aid in the first runs through the board. By standing 25 feet to the side from the board, he can get a quite accurate impression of whether the jumper is reaching or chopping at the board. If at all uncertain, take two unofficial trials before the competition begins. Confidence in one's run is essential to good jumping, and every effort should be made to secure it before the official jumps begin.

What can be done to prevent heel bruises? The coach can work to change the rule concerning board dimensions so that the toe-board will be at least as wide as the foot is long—that is, at least 12 inches.

Always jump with a wide-heeled sprint shoe that has a thin strip of resilient rubber on the outside and a piece of fine-grained foam rubber on the inside covering the entire flat of the heel. A few jumpers use the regular field shoe with a wide heel and two spikes in the heel. It is certainly safe and extremely unlike to produce a stone bruise. On the other hand, it is heavy and, through its thick heel, tends to throw the jump forward rather than upward. A painful stone bruise may force the use of such shoes in practice or even in a meet, but they are not likely to aid best performance.

Do only enough jumping with the full run and off the board to insure confidence and consistency in meet jumping. To do more may improve performance but is certainly dangerous, not only to the heel but to the jumping muscles as a whole. The board jump places greater stress on leg muscles than any other event in track and field. In this one event, it is better to accept less than your best and be unhurt than to work for perfection and take the chance of serious injury.

When jumping off the board, insist that the ground in back of the board be higher than the board itself—nor merely even with it, but higher. Further, it must be firm, lest it give way and drop the heel on the edge of the board.

Do most jumping with a short run and from a firm dirt take-off. The fundamentals of form of getting in the air and making the landing can be best learned in this manner. Such form is not the same as when taking a full run, however, and therefore the latter cannot be ignored.

Can proper broad jump form be learned with little practice? No, certainly not, for excellence in any event, no matter how apparently simple, requires endless practice. Those coaches who, year after year, have the best broad jumpers, concentrate their personal attention and practice time upon the broad jump. Their jumpers work hard at broad-jumping, in most instances with a full run and take-off from the board. There is no easy event, and no easy road to excellence in anything.

Without question, the reason hard work in the broad jump is minimized by most coaches is dual in nature: (1) it is dangerous to leg muscles and heels, and (2) its first requirement is speed and therefore the best sprinters are encouraged to enter the event. Coaches argue that it is far better to get two high places in the sprints and a lower place in the broad jump than to try to win the broad jump and get nothing. One answer lies in having the secondary sprint candidates specialize in the broad jump. They can then practice as assiduously as any high-jumper or hurdler. Larry Snyder, Jesse Owens coach at Ohio State, writes that "athletes who have the broad jump as their only competitive event may jump daily. After the athlete has attained top condition by running, hurdling, and jumping, he can still improve his jumping technique. A typical daily workout might include three full-speed jumps plus eight or ten short jumps".

Should a foot stamp be coached in the broad jump? Analysis of the contrasting statements of coaches indicates the problem is merely one of degree. For example, in his book, Dean Cromwell states:

The jumper aims for a pronounced upward drive at the moment of leaping. At this point it is common fault to overemphasize the foot stamp on the board. Naturally, with the body gathered for the jump in the closing approach strides and with all the weight carried over the take-off leg there is a tremendous strain on the jumping foot. It comes down firmly on the board but if athletes concentrate on the main elements, which are speed and lift, they won't need to be bothered with stressing a stamp of the foot".

Yet, in another talk, Cromwell said: "It seem to me that a great many runners are thinking of running instead of jumping and a great many jumpers are just thinking of the sprinting. There is actually a tremendous foot stamp given to the jumping foot as the take-of is made."

Admitting a very forceful foot action, it can better be thought of as a heel-ball-toe roll than as a stamp. As the heel first touches the board, the toe is up off the board and the leg is backward at about a 30-degree angle. As the body moves forward, the foot rolls with it in a heel-ball-toe action, which, although solid and vigorous, has more resiliency than a foot stamp implies. No height can be secured from taut, tense muscles. Rather, quick, relaxed jumping action is what is needed.

The answer probably lies in emphasizing the over-all action. The coach may talk about the importance of attaining height in the air but should leave the means as much as possible to the athlete. The good jumper will necessarily exert a forceful pressure and rebound on the take-off foot. But to call his attention to it as a "foot stamp" may exaggerate the point and make the entire jump tense and dead.

What about teaching a jump for height by stretching wool yarn at a height of 3 or 4 feet in front of the board? This method has been and still is very extensively used, particularly at the high school level. Some coaches believe it is definitely worth while, especially with the beginning jumper. Others vehemently condemn the practice as teaching a very artificial style in the air as well as in the take-off. None of the accepted texts in track and field recommend such a method. General opinion seems to be that, in the long run, a more natural and effective action will come without the use of such devices. However, when a boy seems to have little natural aptitude in gaining height, temporary use of the yarn will sometimes prove very beneficial. As soon as the "feel" of securing height has been gained, however, continued use of the yarn will probably do more harm than good.

What can be done for the broad-jumper who continually fouls regardless of how his check marks are moved back from the board? Every experienced coach has had men who continue to step beyond the board in practice and in meets. Their marks can be moved even 3 feet backward, yet somehow these men will reach out during their last few strides and again step over. Continued changes of check marks simply confuse the jumper until he begins to hit the board with the wrong foot and loses all consistency. The difficulty in such instances usually lies in the last four strides, when the jumper's eyes and attention have shifted away from the board and toward a more vertical effort. Somehow the eye-foot co-ordination has miscarried and the jumper has developed the habit of placing his foot beyond the board, no matter how he must stretch to do so.

Several suggestions that should prove helpful can be followed. First, assure the boy that his problem is not at all unusual, that many other jumpers experience this same difficulty, and that with a little careful practice it will be overcome. Second, shift his practice to the low hurdles, in which even strides are essential; or to sprinting adjacent to hurdles so placed that every fourth step on the left foot will come exactly opposite the hurdle. Third, go back to the short run in the broad jump, in which the eyes look above and beyond the board but the attention is upon cutting the last two strides so that the board is hit exactly right. Drill on this point until good confidence and consistency are achieved. The jumper should concentrate his attention upon the board and upon the idea of jumping even though he does not actually take off. Encouragement, patience, and careful drill are certain to produce the right result.

ORGANIZATION OF PRACTICE

The primary requirements in the broad jump are speed, violent stress upon the leg, abdominal, and back muscles, evenness of stride, jumping high, and of course the form of the event itself. The second item demands first attention and calls for long and consistent preparation of the musculature before the formal training season opens. Active games and gymnastic events related to broad-jumping action, combined with informal wind sprints, will be of value during the fall. Sit-ups, leg-raises, and similar exercises from a horizontal bar, parallel bars, or stall bars are important throughout the year, with decreasing emphasis as the season progresses. The feet and ankles are under particular strain and therefore require special pre-season attention. Rope skipping, an exaggerated bounce while walking and running, hurdling and hurdle exercises, and repeated bounding in the air from both feet will prove helpful.

Speed is gained, of course, only through doing speed work, preferably at from 30 to 100 yards with the sprinters and out of the starting blocks. Repeated winds sprints at the end of practice will bring both speed and endurance. Evenness of stride is learned, if it does not seem to come naturally, by running low hurdles, or by repeated full runs with exactly placed check marks. Ability to jump high is best learned at the broad jump pit itself and without artificial aids. Regular high-jumping is interesting and may help, especially if the old scrissors style is used. A straddle style, in which lay-out begins before the take-off is completed, will prove harmful. But to take a short run, to leap as high as possible with head and chest up, and, incidentally, to make a proper landing is the best practice of all for gaining height in the jump.

If an athlete intends to specialize in the broad jump to the exclusion of all other events, he should make very early and unusual efforts to build up his leg and body muscles to withstand the strain of jumping practice four or five times a week. Only by so doing can he perfect all the aspects of form. But only by using months of preparation in attaining such conditions can he expect to avoid muscular deadness and injury.

If, on the other hand, broad-jumping is an even added on to sprinting, high-jumping, or hurdling, as is so often the case, practice will be at minimum levels. Once a man's check marks are certain, he will usually confine his practice to short runs with jumps for height, for proper action in the air, and for an efficient landing. Jumps with a full run off the toe-board will occur only in meets or not more than once a week, on either Tuesday or Wednesday.

The warm-up. Preliminary work consists of the usual light exercises and wind sprints. When fully warm, report to the starting blocks for work with the sprinters. Take six to eight starts at 20 yards and then a series of three or four sprints at from 30 to 70 yards.

Jumping. Warm up further by running through the check marks beyond the board. Check the pit first for softness so that you will not lose your balance or twist an ankle as you run through. Then take a few jumps for form, using a short run. If it is the early season and you are in good condition, take three or four jumps with a full and fast run. If it is the late season, or if the broad jump is merely an extra event, confine the work to short-run jumps. In any case, intelligent practice is essential. Learn the effects of a following wind, a head wind, and a side wind, as well as differing track conditions. Learn to gather during the last four steps before the take-off, to jump high with good balance, and to make a proper landing.

Work in related events. Unless an unusual amount of work has been done in the broad jump, shift efforts to the sprints, the high jump, or the hurdles. Remember that the broad jump is a real strain on the legs and that a slight soreness or ache after jumping may become a serious injury later when sprinting or jumping. Work for form and relaxation rather than for all-out performance. Always finish up with a longer run of from 220 to 350 yards.

CHAPTER 9

THE TECHNIQUES OF BROAD JUMP

The running broad jump as an event on the track and field program can be traced to ancient times. No doubt its appearance in early competition can be attributed to its use by man in his search and pursuit of food and in escape from his enemies, both man and beast. In the development of the warrior the running broad jump took its place along with spear throwing, running, weight, casting, and wrestling. The reason for the inclusion of the running broad jump as a military exercise for the combatant is clear when we recall the need for jumping ability even in the World War where trenches and barbed wire fences were employed as agencies of defence.

History tells us that the running broad jump was one of the first regular events in the ancient Olympic games. It probably had its inception in the track and field programs of America in 1868, the year of the founding of the New York Athletic Club. The first performance recorded by the Amateur Athletic Union as an American championship was in 1876, when I. Frazier, of the Yonkers, New York, Lyceum, won first place with a leap of 17 feet, 4 inches.

The date of the introduction of the broad jump into the preparatory schools is somewhat uncertain. However, after the organization of the annual Interscholastic Track and Field Meet by the University of Chicago in 1901, it became a standard preparatory school event. The University of Pennsylvania, through the Penn Relays, which were organized in 1895, afforded preparatory and high school relay competition. The Chicago Interscholastic Track and Field Meet was the most important event which provided national preparatory school competition in the running broad jump up to this time.

When the record of I. Frazier is compared with present performances bordering on 27 feet, it is at once apparent that there are some underlying factors responsible for the differences in performances. Can it be that the competitor of sixty years ago had less native ability than the athlete of today? Is it a question of improvement of the technique? Does the present-day running broad-jumper analyze himself more completely? Is the instruction more thorough now than then? Is the present-day equipment chiefly responsible for greater distances, or is it the inspiration of our times and the desire to emulate?

A comparison of the present-day athlete with his predecessor is time worn but even now is capable of precipitating debate. No one thing can account for the improved performance in the running broad jump, but rather a combination of a number of factors is responsible for it. There is much doubt that the present-day athlete has more native ability than the competitor of years gone by. Increased interest in the running broad jump has caused the entrance of more contestants, thereby inspiring greater efforts. The desire for improved performance has led the athlete to a more thorough study of the event and a more complete analysis of his own strong and weak points. The inspiration of the times and the enthusiasm for the running broad jump have spurred us on to improved technique and instruction.

Paralleling the advances in technique and instruction, more equipment, which makes present performances possible, has been developed. When all these things are added together, the answer to the question, "What is responsible for the steady improvement of performance in the running broad jump?" Is at once apparent.

With a knowledge of the distances which are likely to place in the various classes of competition, the next thing to which the running broad-jumper should give his attention is the question of equipment.

EQUIPMENT

Every jumper should know the type of equipment conductive to his best performance. It should be realized, however, that the quality and the type of equipment are not entirely under the control of the jumper, and circumstances may arise where he will have to adjust himself to conditions as he finds them. In spite of this, the responsibility for certain items in the equipment falls chiefly upon the contestant. In this discussion the most acceptable equipment is described. Such element as money, space, and labour may prohibit the establishment of an ideal layout. Under these conditions the resourcefulness of the competitor is called upon to make adjustments to meet the local situation. Only equipment peculiar to the running broad-jumper is mentioned here.

1. Shoes

The shoe is the most important item in the personal equipment of the running broad-jumper. Some competitors favour a shoe with a high, stiff counter and one or two spikes in the heel. Others prefer the ordinary sprinting shoe with or without sponge rubber in the heel. Still others use a lighter weight shoe having a high counter of soft leather with sponge rubber glued or sewed inside the heel, but without heel spikes.

The shoe having a high, stiff counter with spikes in the heel affords protection from bruises, prevents slipping at the instant of the take-off, and retains its shape well. This type of shoe has the disadvantage of being heavy, and does not permit maximum foot leverage because the heel is elevated. The ordinary sprinting shoe without a counter and without heel pads is the lightest footgear available. A sprinting shoe without heel pads does not afford sufficient protection against bruises. It is also important to remember that the addition of inner heel pads to the ordinary sprinter's shoe makes the counter too shallow, and because of this shallowness the athlete may cast the shoe during the event.

The shoe which is recommended is similar to the ordinary sprinting shoe except that it has a counter sufficiently high to permit the insertion of a sponge rubber pad and at the same time to insure a snugly fitting heel.

2. Protective Heel Pads

Another important item in the personal protective equipment of the running broad-jumper is the type of pad for the heel, especially for the take-off foot which must stand up under the strain of vicious driving or pounding. Pads are made of felt or rubber. The rubber pads are made of coiled rubber tubing, solid rubber, bath-sponge rubber, and flat sponge rubber. The flat sponge rubber is most desirable because it has sufficient resiliency to afford protection, is readily fitted, and is easily held in position by glue or stitching. The solid rubber does not absorb enough of the shock, and the bath-sponge type compresses too readily, absorbing even less shock. The rubber tubing type absorbs sufficient shock but does not hold its position in the heel of the shoe. Felt is not widely used because it lacks cushion qualities.

TYPES OF COMPETITORS

There are three types of jumpers: (1) the highly coordinated type, (2) the "lift" type, and (3) the speed type.

1. The Highly Coordinated Type

This type of athlete is endowed with a fair amount of speed plus a certain amount of leg lift. He has great ability in combining his speed and lift. In the flight through the air he is able to use his arms to good advantage for balance. More outstanding than this is his timing of the forward thrust of both legs to attain maximum distance and at the same instant making use of the forward thrust of the arms to prevent falling backward when landing. This type of athlete is usually an exponent of the walk-in-the-air style of flight.

2. The Lift Type

This type of competitor accentuates a vigorous foot-stamp combined with a powerful rock-up on the toe. He may have already shown proficiency in events requiring an elastic spring, such as the high jump, the pole vault, or the hurdles. Very frequently the lift type is not a fast sprinter and therefore requires a longer run in order to gain his maximum momentum. He may resort to either the walk-in-the-air or the knee-tuck style of flight.

3. The Speed Type

This type of jumper depends on his sprinting ability and is often counted on to win points in the dashes. He relies chiefly on his high rate of speed rather than on his left lift. He is able to gather momentum quickly and does not require as long a run as an individual who gathers speed more slowly. The speed type, also, may be an exponent of either the walk-in-the-air or the knee-tuck style of flight.

There are certain qualifications which are common to all good running broad-jumpers.

PHYSICAL QUALIFICATIONS

The points to be considered in discussing the physical qualifications of a running broad-jumper are (1) age, (2) endurance, (3) height, (4) spring, (5) neuromuscular coordination and rhythm, and (6) speed.

1. Age

There is no physiologic reason, as far as is known, why boys should not participate in the running broad jump at an early age. An examination of the record holders in the broad jump shows that they became champions between the ages of twenty-two and twenty-five years. However, learning the broad jump is like learning to play the piano. Both diligence and patience are needed to bring about perfection of movement.

2. Endurance

The running broad jump is an event which, in the minds of average individuals, does not require endurance. The contestant should be fortified, however, with sufficient reserve to meet the demands of the most strenuous competition, which includes several practice runs without jumping, several practice jumps, and eight competitive jumps. The amount of effort expended in other events before the jump also must be considered.

3. Height

Although short men have attained proficiency in the running broad jump, the tall man has an advantage. Experience teaches us that, as a rule, the tall man is able to lift his body and legs higher in his transit across the pit and to reach farther with his feet on landing. By so doing, he is able to utilize to the maximum his forward leap and to permit a full extension of the legs an instant prior to landing, thus attaining greater distance. A short man must compensate for his lack of stature by generating greater speed and by developing a more powerful spring.

4. Spring

In order to acquire distance in the running broad jump, one must combine momentum with height. Momentum is gained by the speed of the run, while height is obtained by the spring from the take-off board. The power of the spring depends on the strength of the foot, leg, and thigh muscles and their ability to respond efficienctly and quickly.

5. Neuromuscular Coordination and Rhythm

One may be an excellent sprinter possessing a powerful spring and yet fail to gain distance in the running broad jump. This, no doubt, is due to a lack of neuromuscular coordination. A fast sprinter in executing the running broad jump may attempt to carry a speed which is too great to permit him to gather or collect himself just prior to the instant of the foot-stamp on the take-off board. This lack of the co-ordination results in a jump of insufficient height. As opposed to this, an excellent high-jumper who undertakes to execute a running broad jump may attempt a spring with such emphasis that he attains a height out of proportion to his speed, thus incorrectly making a high jump of the event rather than a broad jump. In order to attain maximum distance the movements of the arms and legs must be properly synchronized for forward and upward movement during and at the end of the flight.

The execution of the running broad jump requires proper co-ordination and rhythm, which are evident in the following phases of the jump: the rock-up on the toe coordinated with the run; the timing of the upward swing of the forward leg with the spring from the take-off board; the timing of the first kick or stride in the walking-the-air; and the timing of the extension of both feet forward at the instant of landing, coupled with the forward thrust of the arms.

6. Speed

The importance of speed in the running broad jump is obvious. The additional distance gained in this event over the standing broad jump is due to the speed of the run. A running broad-jumper should strive to acquire speed comparable to that of the best 100-yard sprinter in his competitive class.

TECHNIQUE OF THE EVENT

After one or two weeks of jogging, running, and calisthenics, the candidate for the running broad jump is ready to receive instruction in the technique of the event. This is discussed under four divisions in the sequence of their execution: (1) the approach, (2) the foot-stamp, (3) the flight, and (4) the landing.

1. The Approach

The approach is discussed as follows: (A) definition of types, (B) comparison of types, (C) method of adjusting checkmarks, and (D) speed between checkmarks.

A. Definition of Types

The type of approach taught the beginner depends on whether momentum is gained slowly, fairly fast, or extremely fast. There are three plans for stride adjustment and a number of variations from them. For the sake of simplicity, these plans are discussed as the 2-4-8 stride plan, the 2-4-6 stride plan, and the 2-4-10 stride plan.

B. Comparison of Types

The first question which naturally arises is, "What stride plan shall use?" The answer to this question depends on the ability of the jumper to gain proper momentum when striking the take-off board.

The individual who gathers speed slowly usually requires a greater number of strides to reach his optimum speed when striking the take-off board. For this type of jumper, the 2-4-6 stride plan is recommended for him. The majority of jumpers gather speed at a rate which falls between the relatively slow and the extremely speedy jumper. The 2-4-8 stride plan is recommended, therefore, for most running broad-jumpers.

It must be remembered that the fewer strides a jumper takes, the easier it is to keep the checkmark adjustments accurate. For accuracy and for conserving effort, a jumper should use the least possible number of strides which will permit him to gain optimum speed at the take-off board.

C. Method of Adjusting Checkmarks

Painstaking care in the adjustment of checkmarks amply rewards the running broad-jumper. If the approach (checkmark adjustment) is incorrect, the jumper will do one of two things, either step over the front edge of the take-off board, resulting in a foul which nullifies the performance, or step back of the board, depriving himself of the full measure of his leaping effort, since measurement is made from the front edge of the take-off board to the nearest break in the ground. The importance of proper checkmark adjustment was illustrated in the Tenth Olympiad where a number of famous jumpers fell short of their best previous performances because of inaccuracy in checkmarks adjustments. For sake of illustration, adjustments for the 2-4-8 stride plan are described.

The method of adjusting checkmarks is as follows: on a runway which has been brushed so that the spike marks from the shoes of the jumper are visible, measure exactly 50 feet up the runway from the front edge of the take-off board. Place checkmark 1 here temporarily. Always place the checkmarks on the side of the runway next to the take-off foot. Scratch a line across the runway from the checkmark at the side. Temporarily place checkmark 3 approximately 35 feet up the runway from checkmark 1, and likewise scratch a line across the runway. Standing with the toe of the take-off foot on checkmark 3, run down the runway, striking checkmark 1 with the toe of the take-off foot, running through the pit, paying no attention to the take-off board. The run should be gradually accelerated so that when the take-off board is reached, the jumper will be at 95 per cent of his best speed for 100 yards. An observer locates the position of the take-off foot at the end of the eighth stride from checkmark 1 and measures its distance from the front edge of the take-off board. The above directions should be repeated until there is uniformity in the position of the toe of the take-off foot at the end of the eighth running stride. The procedure is termed "standardizing the stride". Next, move checkmark 1 so that the toe of the take-off foot will be 5 or 6 inches beyond the front edge of the take-off board at the end of the eighth stride from checkmark 1. This overstride is the allowance which should be made for the cut-down in the beginning of the spring. After these adjustments have been made, checkmark 1 is marked and measured. This completes the standardizing of the eight-stride section. You are now ready to locate checkmark 2, for the four-stride section.

In order to locate checkmark 2, the jumper runs through the course again, being sure that the toe of the take-off foot strikes checkmark 1. An observer then marks the spot four strides back of checkmark 1. This is temporarily marked as checkmark 2. With the runway brushed, the jumper repeats his trials, running through the path, over the board, and through the pit. In order to prove checkmark 2, the jumper runs through the course a number of times, being sure than the toe of the take-off foot strikes checkmark 2, checkmark 1, and a point 5 or 6 inches beyond the front edge of the take-off board. The next step is the adjustment of checkmark 3, for the two-stride section.

With the runway brushed, the jumper starts his run with the toe of the take-off foot on temporary checkmark 3 and run through the path as before. The correctness of checkmarks 2 and 1 should be retested each trial run. The observer marks the spot where the toe of the take-off foot strikes two strides back of the checkmark 2 and marks this spot checkmark 3. This checkmark, together with the other two, is proved by repeated trials. Accuracy is paramount in every case. This procedure completes the checkmark adjustment.

The checkmark adjustments for the 2-4-6 stride plan and for the 2-4-10 stride plan and for variations are made in a similar manner.

D. Speed Between Checkmarks

The speed of the jumper is gradually accelerated from the initial stance to the take-off board. Between checkmarks 3 and 2, the jumper should be exerting about one-half his effort; between checkmarks 2 and 1, he should exert about three-fourths his effort; and between checkmark 1 and the take-off board, a speed should be gathered which represents about ninety-five one-hundredths of his effort.

The question immediately arises, "Why should a jumper not be running at 100 per cent of his speed for 100 yards?" When the individual sprints 100 yards and later competes in the running broad jump, he has different objectives. In the sprint the objective is to stride the cinders in the shortest possible time. In the running broad jump, in addition to speed attention must be given to striking the checkmarks, striking the take-off board, and gathering for the leap. Speed must be slightly reduced during the last two or three strides for the sake of accuracy and spring. If the speed of the run is too great, the jumper will suffer in the effectiveness of his spring.

Three checkmark flags or distinctive pegs and a measuring tape should be a part of the equipment of the jumper.

The next factor to consider is the foot-stamp on the take-off board.

2. The Foot-Stamp

This phase of the running broad jump is also called "the take-off" "beat the board", or "pound the board". In any case, these synonyms indicate that the jumper strikes the board flat-footed and then applies vigorous effort to the board. In no case is the take-off board to be slapped lightly. The take-off consists of a number of very definite movements, each of which is discussed in some detail.

If the foot is to be in the proper position for the maximum spring, the jumper must pay particular attention to the length of the last stride. If the last stride is too long, the centre of gravity is back of the point of application of power. If the last stride is too short, the centre of gravity is too far ahead of the point of the application of the power. For the proper take-off the centre of gravity should be slightly ahead of the point of the application of the power. If the centre of gravity is directly over the point of application of power, the jump would be upward rather than upward and forward. If the centre of gravity is back of the point of application of power, the jumper will fail to get height and will have a tendency to sit back on his haunches when landing. The speed-stamp force must be combined in both upward and forward propulsion with the emphasis on the stamp. The relation of the centre of gravity to the point of application of the force must be changed by the jumper so that he gets sufficient height to utilize his forward speed to the best advantage. In our experience this adjustment of the centre of gravity is made most effectively by shortening the last stride 5 or 6 inches. This represents the distance the jumper oversteps the take-off board when running through the approach without jumping.

When an athlete sprints, he "beats the track" with approximately the same force with each foot. However, if the same individual were executing the running broad jump, he would accentuate the beat of the take-off foot by a vigorous stamp on the take-off board. This necessarily curtails the speed slightly because some time is required for the physical adjustment in settling down or gathering. The more forceful the stamp, the greater will be the height and forward motion.

The jumper should strike the take-off board flat-footed. This is accomplished principally by shortening the last stride. It is an advantage since he is in a position to begin the rock-up on the toe. It must be remembered that the rock-up cannot be started until the heel touches the ground. Therefore, a flat-footed landing is speedier and more effective than a ball-heel landing.

The next movement which occurs after the flat-footed landing is "settling down", or gathering oneself, which results in a slight bending of tine knee of the take-off leg. This gathering oneself is comparable to the crouching of a cat before it springs. The jumper should avoid an extreme bend of the knee because this results in a loss of forward motion. If he fails to bend the knee sufficiently, the spring will suffer. The jumper must lean by experience the proper degree of knee bend in relation to his speed and spring.

From the flat-footed position with the knee bent, the following movements should be executed simultaneously: (a) the forward swing of the free leg, (b) the straightening and backward thrust of the take-off leg and thigh, and (c) the rock-up on the toe. Advantage should be taken of the free power by swinging the free leg well out and up in front. The guiding factor in the extent of the swing of the free leg and arms is the amount of force that can be controlled and coordinated. Another important item is that the timing of the movements should be synchronized with the downward and backward thrust of the jumping leg.

The straightening of the leg and thigh must begin simultaneously with the stamp on the board. The leg-straightening process must be vigorous in order to turn the resistance of the board into upward and forward motion. If the take-off leg is not completely straightened, valuable power in the spring is lost.

The rock-up on the toe, executed simultaneously with the extension of the leg and thigh, likewise must be complete.

Arm movements are synchronized with the movement of the legs. The hands should be cupped or semiclenched, and the arm muscles should be slightly tensed.

3. The Flight

The flight through the air is defined as that part of the jump which begins when the contact with the take-off board is broken and ends at the instant the heels touch the pit. Up to this point there is uniformity among all trained jumpers in the execution of the jump. However, there are two distinct types of flight through the air: (a) the walk-in-the-air type and (b) the knee-tuck type.

A. The Walk-in-the-Air Type

The majority of good jumpers use this type of flight. The characteristic of this technique is a walking motion in the air for the purpose of aiding in forward propulsion. The first stage of the walk-in-the-air flight is taken with the free leg. The timing of the step in the walk is highly important. The walk-in-the-air should not begin until the jumper is well on his flight. It should not be started until the speed-stamp force has been partly expended. The reason for this is that the jumper must maintain his balance in the air by bringing the take-off leg forward. With the take-off leg partially flexed and coming forward, he is ready to begin the execution of the step with the free leg. The characteristic of the step in the air is that it consists of a downward backward drive with the free leg accompanied by a knee lift of the take-off leg as in sprinting. The take-off leg is brought forward. After the step in the air is taken, the knee of the free leg is brought even with the opposite knee as a first preparation for the landing. As the jumper approaches his landing, the legs and thighs tend to straighten out as they touch the pit.

At the instant of leaving the board, the take-off leg is inclined forward at an angle of approximately seventy-five degrees, with the trunk erect. An erect trunk carriage is maintained until shortly after the crest of the leap is attained. From this point on, the trunk is gradually inclined forward until, in the landing position, its angle is about forty-five degrees. The movements of the arms are synchronized with the movement of the legs as in ordinary walking. The trunk is carried in an erect position until the walk-in-the-air is concluded because leg action is curtailed by any other trunk position. After the walk-in-the-air has been completed and the legs are being extended, the trunk is bent forward and the arms are swung backward. As soon as the heels touch the pit, the knees are bent and the trunk and arms move forward. As the knees bend and the body moves forward, the flight the centre of weight moves downward and forward along the line of flight. The buttocks may rightfully reach a position so low that they almost touch the pit. As soon as momentum has carried the centre of weight in front of the feet, the body falls forward. Recovery is accomplished in a variety of ways, any of which is correct as long as the jumper does not break ground nearer the take-off board than the marks made by the heels.

B. The Knee-Tuck Type

In this type of jump, the knees are drawn up in a sitting position and the jumper depends chiefly on the speed-stamp force for his propulsion, getting little aid from leg movement while in the air. Although this jump lacks some of the advantages of the walk-in-the-air type, it is more simple to execute.

Most jumpers using the knee-tuck style leave the tack-off board with the trunk and legs at an angle of approximately seventy degrees. The body is inclined farther forward than in the other style of flight. The free leg swing in the knee-tuck style is slightly more pronounced than in the walk-in-the-air type for the reason that the free leg is not called upon in the initiation of a backward-downward drive. The thigh of the take-off leg is brought parallel to that of the free leg and the knees are drawn up in front with the trunk bent slightly forward. It is obvious that there is no treading action in the transit over the pit. The knees are kept in a tuck position until the loss of altitude begins, at which time the first preparation for the landing is made.

The preparation for the landing for any type of jump consists of the extension of the legs, the forward inclination of the trunk, and the backward swing of both arms.

4. The Landing

There are but few fundamental differences in landing between the walk-in-the-air and the knee-tuck types of flight. The objective in the either case is to touch the ground with the legs extended as far forward as possible with the balance maintained at the same time. In a proper landing the ground is touched with the heels in line but far enough apart to maintain lateral balance. Besides, the centre of gravity of the body should be in such relationship to the feet when they strike the pit, that the jumper will not fall backward. For instances, the centre of gravity should not be so far forward that it impedes the forward leg reach, thus causing the jumper to lose well-earned distance. The centre of gravity may be brought forward by a vigorous trunk lean, and forceful forward swing of the arms. This completes the technique of the execution of the event.

CHAPTER 10

COMMON ERRORS AND THEIR CORRECTION IN BROAD JUMP

For purposes of ease in following the discussion, common errors are pointed out in chronologic order: (1) in the warm-up, (2) in the run, (3) in the foot-stamp, (4) in the flight, and (5) in the landing.

1. In the Warm-Up

Many jumpers make the mistake of entering competition without sufficient warm-up, especially of the active type. This means sufficient bodily exercise such as jogging, running, and sprinting. A passive warm-up, consisting either of massage or heat from wet towels or a lamp, is not sufficient. Once the warm-up has been completed, the body glow should be maintained by adequate clothing.

2. In the Run

A common error in the run is the improper acceleration in approaching the take-off board. Some jumpers reach their maximum speed too far up the runway and have less speed when the take-off board is reached. The opposite error of too little speed in the beginning is obvious.

Inaccuracies in striking the checkmarks are also common and result in uneven strides. The uneven strides cause improper striking of the take-off board. If the successive checkmarks are carefully hit, the jumper is relieved of doubt concerning the striking of the take-off board. Therefore, he is able to concentrate on the most important phase of the event, the speed-stamp and spring.

The semicoast is defined as the reduction of effort during the last two strides. This phase of the event is comparable to the idea of freewheeling in automobile language because it is desirable to maintain as much speed as possible with a reduced application of sprinting power. This adjustment permits the jumper to shift from speed power to lift power. The omission of the semicoast detracts from the efficiency of the spring, while an overaccentuated coast results in a loss of speed. Excessive speed prohibits a jumper from properly shortening the last stride.

3. In the Foot-Stamp

Some jumpers do no attain their best performances because they fail to strike the take-off board flat-footed. The jump may be further hindered by erroneously setting the foot in a direction which is not straight down the path. Failure to hit the board with a forceful stamp is a common error among beginners. An insufficient knee-bend does not permit the jumper to settle in preparation for his supreme effort. The head and eyes should not be directed at the pit; they should be directed forward and upward.

Another common error in the take-off is the failure to straighten the leg and thigh, depriving the jumper of some of the available power. Likewise, an incomplete rock-up on the toe and failure to utilize fully the power of the free leg swing will detract from maximum performance. The chief fault in body carriage occurs when the centre of gravity is not ahead of the take-off foot. This results from carrying the trunk too erect at the take-off.

4. In the Flight

The essential differences between the walk-in-the-air and the knee-tuck types occur in the flight. The common errors are discussed for each type of jump.

A. In the "Walk-in-the-Air" Type

One of the common faults is the extreme outward throw of the forward leg. This causes a turning of the body out of line with the jump and a subsequent loss of distance. The body should always be kept facing in the direction of the jump. Some jumpers make the error of describing a sideward swinging motion of the take-off leg when bringing it forward, thus throwing the body out of alignment. There is a natural tendency toward a more forceful pawing with the take-off leg than with the free leg. This is a source of imbalance at the very beginning of the flight.

It is a common error for beginning jumpers to start the treading motion almost immediately upon leaving the board, causing a bommerang effect because forward progress is retarded. Furthermore, there is a tendency for many jumpers to continue the walk-in-the-air too far through the flight. The causes of this fault are that the jumper either executes the treading motion too slowly or attempts to get in an extra step, both of which prevent a proper preparation for the landing. The walk-in-the-air should cease soon after the onset of the loss of altitude.

The natural arm action is reflex and parallels the action of the legs. For example, when the left knee comes forward, the right arm comes forward, this movement being similar to actual walking.

The most common error in the body carriage is a pronounced forward lean in the early stages of the flight. When this occurs, the proper amount of knee elevation is hindered. However, the extreme forward lean is very essential in the preparation for the landing in order to keep the centre of gravity forward.

B. In the Knee-Tuck Type

There are many errors which are common to both the walk-in-the-air and the knee-tuch types of flight. (Obviously, the treading action errors do not occur in the latter form). A pronounced mistake in the knee-tuck style is a lateral spreading of the knees. They should be held fairly close together. A moderate lateral spread is permissible as an aid in landing, but it is obviously an error in technique to fail to draw the knees sufficiently upward and forward as a preparation for the forward thrust of the feet in landing. If the trunk is carried too erect, the jumper will be unable to obtain the maximum reach forward with both heels and at the same time maintain his balance. Theoretically, the arm action is synchronized with the legs as in the walk-in-the-air type of flight, but many times the arms are extended sideward in a winglike manner for the purpose of correcting an unbalanced condition arising at the take-off.

5. In the Landing

A common error in landing is an overemphasized extension of the legs which results in sitting back in the pit at the completion of the jump. However, if the feet are not carried far enough ahead, valuable distance is lost. In order that the legs may be carried well forward, the trunk should lean at an angle of approximately forty-five degrees.

Many jumpers fail to get maximum distance because they do not execute a forceful backward thrust of the arms just before the heels touch the pit. The tendency to sit back in the pit may be overcome by swinging the arms sideward and forward when landing.

CHAPTER 11

THE RUNNING HOP, STEP AND JUMP IN TRACK & FIELD

The running hop, step and jump is one of the more complex events in track and field athletics. It begins with a full run and take-off as in the broad jump. However, the first landing, at the end of the "hop" phase, is made on a single foot, the same one used for the take-off. A second jump, the "step", ends on the opposite foot, from which a full "jump" occurs as in the broad jump, with an orthodox two-footed landing. For example, a man might "hop" on his left foot, "step" over to the right, then "jump" from the right to a regular broad jump landing.

One of the mysteries of track and field athletics is the great neglect and lack of interest in this event by American college and school athletes and coaches. It is not a recently introduced event, such as the javelin; it has no serious difficulties or dangers, such as exist in the 400-meter hurdles or the hammer throw. And, on the positive side, it is a more interesting event to watch than the broad jump and for more intriguing in its many aspects of form. Yet, the fact is that although America has produced the greatest sprinters, broad-jumpers, and high-jumpers in the world for the past 50 years or more, she has not won a single Olympic title in the triple jump since 1904. In the last 8 Olympiads, the United States has achieved a single second place, 4 fifth places, 3 sixth places, and has twice gone unplaced, including the games at London. This is hardly a record to call for national rejoicing.

To achieve a commendable jump in this event, one must carefully study and perfect all its phases: the length and speed of the run, the length and height of the hop, the extent to which a jump is made on the step, and finally the full form of the final broad jump. Each phase has its unique problems and the co-ordination of the whole presents a challenge that is quite comparable to the form difficulties of the pole vault or the discus.

The present world's record of 53′2 5/8″ by A. F. da Silva, of Brazil, excellent as it may seem, is asking to be broken, for one would hardly select da Siliva's qualifications as being ideal for maximum human jumping. He is 5′ 10″ tall, weighs 143 pounds, is considered "slow" in the 100-meter dash, and has broad-jumped 23′ 7½″. Even more tempting is the fact that during only three years has the American championship been won with distances over 50 feet and that in the past ten years a jumper has been crowned champion on three different occasions with a performance under 46 feet.

The explanation of this mystery probably lies in the early acceptance of the broad jump as a regular part of the school and college track programs and in the difficulties involved in practising and competing in both the broad jump and the hop, step, and jump. There is already present a tendency for the broad jump to be just one more event for overworked sprinters. To add another has not been considered wise.

However, those favouring the hop, step, and jump point out that this event requires more specialized training than the broad jump, that ordinary sprinters can achieve championship jumps, and that it therefore tends to produce its own specialists, quite apart from sprinters. Da Silva is certainly a case in point. When Mikio Oda, of Japan, toured this country in 1949, he pointed out that present-day Japanese hop, step, and jump men were achieving distances well over 49 feet although running only :11.5 for the 100-meter. For these reasons, consideration is being and should be given to the adding the event to the school and college program, or, if more feasible, to substituting it for the running broad jump.

HISTORY OF IMPROVEMENT IN FORM AND DISTANCE

According to F. A. M. Webster, the hop, step, and jump originated in Ireland and was dominated by men of Irish birth and ancestry throughout its early history. The Ahearne brothers, of Ireland and the Irish-American Athletic Club of New York, were the most famous of these, but P. J. O'Connor and Con Leahy were first and second in the Hellenic Festival in 1905 and many other Irishmen achieved marks.

However, strange as it now seems, America dominated the hop, step, and jump during the first three Olympiads. J. B. Connolly was the first Olympic winner with 45 feet in 1896 at Athens. Myer Prinstein of Syracuse, won in 1900 and 1904 with 47′ 4½″ and 47 feet even, despite the fact that the event was dropped from the American National AAU championships from 1893 to 1906. This ended American Olympic victories, but in 1911, Dan Ahearne, of the Irish-American Athletic Club of New York, established the amazing world's record of 50′ 11″. This distance remained the American record until 1941, when Billy Brown, of Louisiana State University, beat it by only ½ inch; and it remained the world's record until 1924, when A. W. Winter, of Australia, won the Paris games with 50′ 11¼″. Dan Ahearne's durability in a tough event was just as amazing as his record. He won the American championships on eight different occasions from 1910 to 1918, and in 1924, at something over 40 years of age, was still expert enough to represent America in the Paris Olympic games. Incidentally, his younger brother, Tim, won the 1908 hop, step, and jump event in the London Olympics while Dan was trying to get settled after his emigration to America. According to Richard Ganslen, the breakdown on Ahearne's jump was 20 feet for the hop, 11' 3" for the step, and 19' 1½" for the jump. This proportion was characteristic of early jumpers, who took a relatively short step compared with the full jumping stride of later competitors.

Following the comparative monopoly of the Ahearne brothers, North European jumpers dominated the event, G. Lindblom, of Sweden, won in 1912 at 48' 5 1/8"; and V. Tuulos, of Finland, in 1920, at 47' 7". But in 1928, Mikio Oda, of Japan, 5' 6" tall and weighing 130 pounds, began a 12-year period of victory for Japanese jumpers. After winning the 1928 Amsterdam games with 49' 11", he continued on in 1931 to set a new world's record at 51' 1 3/8". In 1932, he expected to repeat his earliest Olympic triumph with a new record, but leg injuries forced him to retire. However, the world's record broad-jumper at 26' 2", Chuhei Nambu, came through for the East with the title and a record of 51' 7". In 1936, the triumph of the Japanese was even greater. Naoto Tajima won with a world's record of 52' 5 7/8", Masao Harada was second with 51' 4 3/8". and Kenkichi Oshima was sixth with 49' 5 1/8", a truly remarkable dominatin of the event by a single nation. Incidentally, Harada had 6 jumps over 51 feet in this competition, the best series of any jumper up to that time.

The explanation, as usual, lies in the combination of natural talent found in the fast, sturdy, and resilient legs of the Japanese, the seriousness with which they studied the event, and the nationwide enthusiasm with which the Japanese specialized in this aspect of track and field.

In 1949, the Japanese Olympic coach, Mikio Oda, toured this country, seeking information on track and field athletics and imparting it with equal frankness and candor. The author spent some time with him and gained the major share of his present knowledge of the hop, step, and jump at that time. With most pleasant honesty, Oda admitted his debt to the 1924 Olympic jumpers, Winter of Australia and Tuulos of Finland, who tried to get maximum distance and continuous momentum out of each phase of the event—first the hop, then the step, and finally the jump. At first he had little success in copying their method, but in 1926 he found that by bending deeply at the knees and springing suddenly he could accentuate each jump and still maintain his over-all momentum. In this, he and his Japanese followers were able to develop their form beyond that of their teachers. The Japanese custom of sitting on the floor might well have strengthened the knee joint for this strenuous action.

Today, the best jumpers throughout the world are following the methods of the Japanese. In particular, the Swedish jumpers carefully studied the 1936 Olympic movies and adopted the Japanese methods. There may have been no direct relation, of course, but the fact remains that A. Ahman, of Sweden, won the London games with a fine jump of 50′ 6¼″. Like the Japanese, Ahman was but 5′ 8″ tall, well muscled, and thus able to handle the difficult co-ordination and muscular stress of the event.

The performances are remarkably consistent,

indicating that da Silva has perfected his own method to a marvellous degree. The lengths of all phases of his triple jump are more nearly equal than those of the any other great jumper, and only the Russian, Shcherbakov, has used a longer step, 17′ 2¾″, in clearing over 51 feet.

Da Silva and Brazil's disappointment over his foul on a 52′ 6¾″ jump were assuaged a year later, when he recorded 52′ 6¼″ for a well-earned exclusive title, and again in 1952 when he won the Olympic title with a new record of 53′ 2⅝″. This is even more amazing when one considers his "slow" sprinting ability and his relatively poor 23′ 7½″ in the broad jump.

Future improvement in the event seems likely to come through increased natural ability and greater perfection of the form than is now generally accepted. Nambu, of Japan, was a great athlete, ran the 100-meter in :10.5, and broad-jumped over 26 feet. Only a very few men in history have better marks in these events. However, Nambu, despite his world's record, never really liked the hop, step, and jump and failed to perfect all its phases as did his less talented countrymen. Oda seemed to feel that, with increased speed, jumps well over 53 feet were entirely possible.

ESSENTIALS OF CORRECT FORM

There are six fundamentals of form in the hop, step, and jump that should be kept clearly in mind at all times:

1. The event demands complete co-ordination and unity of action. To stress any one phase with a resultant loss in another will certainly produce a lesser total jump. In one sense, the history of development of form has been an attempt to discover the right emphasis that should be placed on each aspect of form: the length and speed of the run, the height and reach for distance in the hop, the degree of jump as contrasted with a short step in the

second phase, and so forth. Each aspect has its value, but it must always be assayed in terms of the whole action.

2. The event is actually a triple jump, per Dreisprung, as it is more correctly called in German. The "step" is therefore a misnomer, for good distance demands a full gather and upward leap as in the first and third phases. Although 50-foot jumpers commonly clear about 13 feet on their step, a full 15 feet has often been recorded. Such distances certainly require an effective jump, not a mere step as commonly practiced in this country.

3. Body angle is very important at all points of the action. It must be far enough behind the jumping foot to provide adequate height, yet not so far as to check momentum and lessen the distance of succeeding jumps. To say that the centre of gravity must be ahead of the feet is incorrect; yet the over-all feeling during the triple jump is that this is the case.

4. Speed in the run must be developed gradually in practice. At first, the demands of balance, rhythm, and co-ordination will force a slowing of momentum.

5. However, full momentum is essential to best performance. If new world's records are to be established, performance must be at ever increasing speeds. The height and length of each jump must not check momentum unduly.

6. Few events demand as great a degree of relaxation as does the triple jump. The knee must give—in fact, the whole body must settle slightly at each landing. Yet an immediate rebound or upward spring must occur. Even ordinary tension would make such resiliency impossible.

The relation between jumps. The primary coaching problem in the triple jump has lain in the degree of emphasis that is rightly placed upon each phase. This is, as always, an individual matter; yet, as always, it is also a matter of physics and of the anatomy of human structure. One can safely assume, as in other events, that there is a right form and a right distance ratio for each jump, within which there is sufficient range and flexibility for individual differences.

F. A. M. Webster, in his study of Japanese methods in the 1936 games, advocated as a general rule a ratio of 3:2:3 between the lengths of the hop, the step, and the jump. That is, a 48-foot jump would include an 18-foot hop, a 12-foot step, and an 18-foot jump.

Yet there has been much variance from this rule. In 1932, Mikio Oda, of Japan, after ten years of topflight competition, was striving for a 21-foot hop, a 14-foot step, and a hopeful jump of 17 feet or more. But, writing in 1949, Oda admitted the unreasonableness of such a long hop for a man of his comparatively slow speed: "If one hops that far, unless one is endowed with super-human leg power he is unable to continue the other two parts of the jump with maximum efficiency". On his world's record 1928 jump of 51′ 1″, Oda actually achieved 21′ 4″ on the hop, but then dropped to a mediocre 11′ 6″ on the step.

During the past 20 years, there has been a growing tendency to increase the relative length of the second jump, the so-called steps. For example, in Japan, where the most thoughtful experimentation has been done, a 6:5:6 ratio is being attempted. Oda reports that when Hasegawa, an :11.6 100-meter man, achieved 51′ 3″ in 1948, he hopped 18 feet, stepped 15′ 5″, and jumped 17′ 10″.

In commenting on the implications of such performances as these, Oda was very much impressed with the over-all distance achieved by relatively slow sprinters. He felt that if an :11.6 man could record over 51 feet by such methods, a :10.5 sprinter such as Nambu could have cleared a much greater distance. His current plans for continued improvement, which he felt the Japanese would need to make if they were to continue their long supremacy in this event, therefore, included increased emphasis upon the length of the step, and the increased use of momentum in the run and in all aspects of the triple jump.

The run. The run is almost identical to that used in the broad jump. The length of the run, the securing and use of check marks, the smooth but early achievement of momentum, and the relaxation and gather for the take-off are all of equal importance.

There is a greater tendency to slow down during the last three or four strides, but this should lessen as form and performance improve. In America, runways are constructed for the broad jump only. When the takeoff board is moved back about 25 feet, only about 95 feet of prepared surface remains for the run of the triple jump. It is inevitable that decreased performance will result.

The take-off. As in the broad jump, the last three or four steps of the run must maintain full momentum and yet be sufficiently relaxed and smooth to permit a balanced and well-co-ordinated take-off. There is an even greater need for shifting the body weight over laterally to the take-off foot. Otherwise, balance will be lost and later phases of the jump shortened. To accomplish this, there will be a natural outward twist of the last foot before the take-off. No coaching is required.

Most jumpers agree that the take-off for the hop should be made from the stronger leg—that is, from the same leg used in the broad jump. In the following discussion, it is assumed that this is the left leg, that the step is made over to the right, and that the jump made from the right. This is a matter of individual choice, however, and should be studiously tried both ways.

As in the broad jump, there is a heel-ball-toe roll of the foot at the take-off, with an upward and vigorous drive of the right knee to hip height, which is of great aid in elevating the hips and the body as a whole.

The problem of just what angle should occur in the take-off is an important one. However, for present purposes, experts seem to agree that the best take-off angle in the triple jump is somewhat less than the optimal 45-degree angle recommended in the broad jump.

The hop. The length of the hop has varied in recorded over-50-foot jumps from 18 feet to 21′4″. Oda, who made the latter record, feels that this was too long a hop, but at the same time believes that hops of over 20 feet are entirely feasible if the jumper has excellent speed in his run.

In landing, there should be no effort to extend or reach with the leg and foot. Rather, the momentum of the action should produce distance. Yet there should be a waiting "for the ground to come up" so to speak, rather than too hurried a placement of the foot. This implies that the foot, ankle, and knee "gives" in a relaxed action as the landing is made and yet reacts with a vigorous foot stamp and upward knee extension, which will produce reasonable height on the next jump.

The body should be erect, although slightly forward, if balance is to be correctly maintained. The arms will be used naturally, as an aid to balance only and not as a driving force. They should therefore be kept relatively close to the body, where they will aid the over-all co-ordination.

The step. The relative length of the step seems to vary even more than that of the hop, with a range from 11′6″ to 17′ 2¾″. The usual beginner has a tendency to chop his step in order to maintain balance and momentum, but modern experts are placing increased emphasis upon greater and greater length. Oda found that leaping with legs spread far apart helped him to increase his step. He achieved this by swinging out consciously and strongly with the knee of the right leg, thus getting forward drive, yet without placing the foot in a disadvantageous position.

The longer the step, the greater the strain thrown upon the right leg and the greater the need for strengthening muscles and tendons of this leg during the pre-season and early-season practice.

The jump. All aspects of the jump should parallel those of the broad jump. The drive for height througha take-off angle of 45 degrees, the use of the arms and legs achieve balance and an economical landing, the maintenance of the feet at the highest possible level until the last moment—all these are the same as in the broad jump.

ORGANIZATION OF PRACTICE

The strain placed upon most of the muscles and tendons of the body places unusual emphasis upon early-season and strenuous conditioning. This is particularly the case with the knee and leg muscles. Conditioning should therefore begin some months before competition. Deep knee-bends and upward leaps, standing broad jumps from both right and left feet, and many hop, step, and jumps from a stand should all take place very early. When one considers that American experts in pole vaulting or javelin throwing work on about a ten-month basis, it should be clear that this triple jump demands at least equal specialization.

Sprinting should be just as basic to this event as to the broad jump. Low-hurdling, with its speed and rhythm of action, is excellent. High-jumping, especially scissors style, with its erect position and excellent take-off position, is worth while for both conditioning and form. Even shot-putting and weight swinging, if not actual throwing, should be of help in strengthening the leg and back muscles.

Each athlete will establish his own routine in terms of what he enjoys and what he does well, but every man must make proper preparation. Without question, the poor performances of American triple jumpers in international competition are entirely caused by lack of preparation in practice as well as in meets.

No exact week-by-week and day-by-day program of activity is needed here. But it cannot be overemphasized that much jumping in practice must be done if proper strength and form is to be achieved. The Japanese and North Europeans work with shortened runs so that less strain is placed upon each effort. Yet the relative timing and co-ordination of the event are basically the same. Generally speaking, the more even the rhythm and equal the timing for each of the event's three phases, the better the form and the performance are likely to be.

CHAPTER 12

THE TRIPLE JUMP

The tripe jump was on the program from the very beginning of the modern Olympics. The triple jump, composed of a hop, step, and jump, is one of the most complex and highly coordinated events in track and field. It begins with a full run and a takeoff such as is used in the long jump, but the landing is made on the same foot executing the takeoff. This is called the "hop" phase. A so-called second jump, one "step", is made immediately and in sequence by the performer's landing on the final "jump" by taking another jumping step and landing on both feet, as in the long jump.

It has been stated that the triple jump originated in Ireland, and men of Irish birth and ancestry dominated this event in its early history. However, during the first three Olympics, Americans won this event. J.B. Connolly was the first Olympic winner in 1896 at Athens, Greece, with a "jump" of 45 feet. Myer Prinstein won the event in 1900 and 1904 with a best "jump" of 47 feet 4½ inches. In 1911 Dan ahearne of the Irish American Athletic Club of New York set a world's record of 50 feet 11 inches. This remained the American record until 1941, when Billy Brown of Louisiana State University "jumped" 50 feet 11½ inches.

No one country consistently provided top performances for the event through the years. During its early history (1896-1928), Europeans dominated the event. From 1928 to 1940 Japanese performers set many records and won the Olympic hop, step, and jump (now called the tripple jump).

The distances achieved in this event fell off after World War II until the 1950's, when A. F. da Silva of Brazil began setting new records. He was the first competitor to jump over 54 feet and was Olympic champion in 1952 and 1956. Certainly da Silva has done more than any single person in recent years to perfect the form and to create world-wide interest in the event. One of the authors has an opportunity to watch him perform and to talk with him during some practice sessions held in the United States. A study of his form was included in the preparation for writing this material.

CHARACTERISTICS OF A TRIPLE JUMPER

The characteristic of a triple jumper are about the same as those of a long jumper. He must possess good speed, strong legs (especially strong knee and ankles), and have good spring. He is usually of average height and slim in build. He must be highly coordinated in leg and foot action and possess good rhythm in jumping and hopping movements.

Triple Jump Form

The triple jump performer should be concerned with five basic factors: (1) a run long enough to insure good speed; (2) a proper takeoff to secure maximum distance in the hop with as little loss of forward momentum as possible; (3) a long unhurried step; (4) a good balanced position in the air to help in making a proper final landing; (5) as much relaxation as possible while executing the hop, step, and jump movement.

The run. The length of the run depends upon the distance it takes the individual to gain near maximum speed. A distance of about 130 to 150 feet is used by most jumpers today. It is most important that the jumper maintain a consistent stride throughout the run. He must run under control. This means he is not running at quite full speed as he approaches the takeoff board.

The method used for securing the proper run is the same as that used by long jumpers.

The takeoff. The accomplishment of proper takeoff is basic. It insures making a good long hop and maintaining proper balance and momentum for the step. In long jumping, when there is only one explosive effort to be made, the distance a man travels through the air is determined by his takeoff velocity and angle of projection. He should strive to obtain maximum speed and takeoff from the board at an angle as great as possible (25 degrees or more, depending upon the speed of the jumper at the takeoff). However, in the triple jump there are other things to be considered. A takeoff angle of 20 degrees or even less will case much lower loss of velocity, which is very important to the execution of the remaining actions.

There must be a definite effort to obtain distance on the hop, but no so much that the step and the distance of the jump are shortened, causing a decrease in total distance. Therefore, the jumper strives to take off at a relatively low angle of projection. He also shifts his body weight over his takeoff foot during the last stride before striking the board (as does the long jumper).

At the insant of pushoff from the board, perfect balance is essential. If the jumper is off balance his leg may collapse at the end of the hop. To insure proper balance, the jumper should keep his line of vision straight ahead by looking at a spot beyond the pit. He must not look up or down as he jumps, for this will upset his balance. The arms aid in maintaining good balance and forward velocity. The arms should be thrust forward and upward at the takeoff.

Upon landing after the hop, the jumper prepares himself immediately for the "step" portion of the event. He must absorb the shock of the landing and in turn be prepared to take the step. The performer must keep under control during his hop, and never allow his takeoff foot to get very far in front of his body. In landing from the hop, the body's centre of gravity must be only slightly behind the landing foot, but it moves in front of the body before the preparation for the step is complete. The body is held erect, but the leg "gives" during the landing. If there is conscious effort to extend the leg, balance will be lost.

The step. Proper action in the step is very important, for this is the portion of the event in which most inexperienced jumpers have difficulty. Most poor jumpers take a quick, short step, which partly accounts for their inability to get good over-all distance. Balance and momentum are also important in the step. The performer coming downs to the ground from the hop may be in good position for the step, but he must make a maximum driving effort with the landing foot in order to make a good step. After the jumper has made a forceful spring off his landing or hop foot, his "step" leg must swing up vigorously, with the bent knee raised waist-high and the upper leg held parallel to the ground. This must be an unhurried action coordinated with the arms in order to help maintain balance and get good body lift upward.

The body should be leaning slightly forward at the waist. The jumper must get as much distance as possible without overextending the lead leg. If the lead leg is overextended forward, the jumper will find that his centre of gravity is far back of his jumping takeoff foot, and he is then in a poor position from which to execute the jump. The step may be described as a floating motion that is done slowly and very deliberately.

The jump. The techniques employed and the form

used in the "jump" portion of the event should be the same as those used in the regular long jump. The performer should endeavor to obtain as much height as possible by driving the arms upward and swinging the lead leg forward and upward. The chest is raised and held high, and the head thrown backward. The feet should be held at the highest possible level until the last moment before landing.

One of the most important things to try to achieve in the triple jump is an event, rhythmic movement throughout the entire event. Each portion must be considered separately, but the 3 parts must be coordinated into a smoothly integrated performance. Each action should be deliberate and rhythmical.

It is generally agreed that the ratio of the hop to the step to the jump should be 6 to 5 to 6; in other words, in a total jump of 51 feet the hop would be 18 feet, the step 15 feet, and the jump 18 feet. This relationship is not a strict rule, but it gives an indication of what many better performers try to achieve.

TRAINING PROGRAM

Since speed and leg strength are so vital to the triple jumper, it is essential that he practice sprinting and low hurdling frequently and constantly. The abdominal and back muscles must also be strengthened in order to accomplish the action in the air and land properly. The following schedule assumes that 3 months have been spent in a weight-training program and leg strengthening exercises. Hopping on alternate legs on the grass as the performer circles the field is considered an essential exercise to be done every week. This can also be done with light weights strapped on the shoulders.

WORKOUT SCHEDULES

Four weeks prior to meets

Monday

1. Jog ¼ mile.
2. Do stretching exercises:
   a. Hurdle exercises from sitting position.
   b. Touching the toes from a standing position, keeping the knees stiff.
   c. Situps, raising the feet and touching the toes in a jackknife action.
   d. Inverted bicycle riding.
3. Run ½ mile of wind sprints.
4. Go through the run-up 5 times at full speed.
5. Take 10 triple jumps, using a short run.
6. Run 3 flights of 70-yard low hurdles.
7. Do horizontal bar-leg raises for 10 minutes.

Tuesday

1. Jog ¼ mile.
2. Do stretching exercises.
3. Run ½ mile of wind sprints.
4. Take 5 triple jumps, using a short run each time.
5. Run 3 flights of 70-yard low hurdles.
6. Take 5 starts from the blocks, running 50 yards each time.

Wednesday

1. Jog ¼ mile.
2. Do stretching exercises.

3. Run ½ mile of wind sprints.
4. Take 5 triple jumps, using a short run each time.
5. Take 10 triple jumps, using a full run-5 at half speed, 5 at ¾ speed.
6. Do horizontal bar-leg raises for 10 minutes.

Thursday

1. Jog ¼ mile.
2. Do stretching exercises.
3. Run ½ mile of wind sprints.
4. Take 6 starts from the blocks, running 50 yards each time.
5. Run 3 flights of 70-yard low hurdles.

Friday

1. Jog ¼ mile.
2. Do stretching exercises.
3. Run ½ mile of wind sprints.
4. Run through the full distance to the takeoff, checking accuracy of the stride with the check marks 3 times.
5. Take 10 triple jumps, using a full run-5 at half speed, 5 at full speed.

After Meets Start

This schedule is made to account for Saturday meets. If meets are held on Friday, the schedule be altered accordingly.

Monday

1. Jog ¼ mile.
2. Do stretching exercises.

3. Run ½ mile of wind sprints.
4. Go through the full run 5 times at full speed.
5. Take 5 triple jumps, using a short run.
6. Take 5 triple jumps, using the full run at ¾ speed, work on gather for the takeoff, and be sure to take a long, unhurried step before the final jump.

Tuesday

1. Jog ¼ mile.
2. Do stretching exercises.
3. Run ½ mile of wind sprints.
4. Run 3 flights of 70-yard low hurdles.
5. Take 3 starts from the blocks, running 50 yards each time.
6. Do horizontal bar-leg raises for 10 minutes.

Wednesday

1. Jog ¼ mile.
2. Do stretching exercises.
3. Run ½ mile of wind sprints.
4. Take 5 triple jumps with a short run—work on a long "step" and on proper landing.
5. Take 5 triple jumps, using full run at full speed each time.

Thursday

1. Jog ¼ mile.
2. Do stretching exercises.
3. Run ½ mile of wind sprints.
4. Take 5 starts from the blocks, running 50 yards each time.
5. Do horizontal bar-leg raises for 10 minutes.

6. Go through the full distance to the takeoff 3 times.

Friday

Rest and study movies of previous action made in practice and in meets.

Weight-Training Program

This is the same as that used in the long jump.

Helpful Hints

1. Be sure to get into proper physical condition before starting to practice jumping.
2. Work consistently on the run to gain confidence and to help minimize fouling.
3. Prevent heel bruises by wearing proper shoes and by using heel cups.
4. Practice good form in jumping, spending much time on rhythm and attempting to get proper step distance.
5. Be sure the surface back of the board is not below the level of the board.
6. Be sure that the runway is smooth and firm enough to help prevent sprained ankles and knees.
7. Practice on the grass to help prevent shin splints and heel bruises.
8. Work on maintaining proper ratio of the hop, step, and jump—approximately 6 to 5 to 6.
9. Check arm action in the air, as seen by film, to insure maintainance of proper balance.
10. Check carefully the measurements for the run, the type of runway, and the wind conditions before competing.
11. Run and triple jump in a relaxed manner.

CHAPTER 13

TEACHING TACTICS IN TRIPLE JUMP

The triple jump was included in the Olympic Games of 1896 and until recently was a men's field event. Today, triple jump competitions are held for men and for women.

Like the long jump, the tripe jump demands great speed and spring; however, the 2 events differ in that the triple jump involves three jumps in sequence, all of which are interdependent. To achieve the greatest possible distance, the athlete must balance the distribution of effort between the three jumps. Another unique feature of the triple jump is tremendous demands on rebound ability (i.e., the ability to jump, land, and jump again). This means that the triple jumper must not only be an excellent sprinter but must have the muscular power and resilience to rebound for three successive jumps.

SAFETY PRECAUTIONS

Although the triple jump is an attractive and fun event, you must be aware of the intense physical demands that training for this event places upon the athlete. The triple jump places considerable stress on the heel, knees, hips, and joints of the feet. Consequently, the intensity of training should be increased slowly and progressively. No instructional period should be devoted solely to triple jump until the participants develop sufficient muscular power and endurance. During the introduction, keep repetitive jumping and rebounding to a minimum, and limit sequences of jumps to 3 or 4. To ease the shock of repetitive jumping and bounding, have athletes perform on surfaces that provide adequate cushioning, such as grass or mats. During indoor training, gymnastic floor-exercise mats are excellent for this purpose. Heel pads provide additional protection.

TECHNIQUE

The technique of triple jumping has changed very little over the past 20 years. Some variations have occurred in the use of arms in gaining lift during each jump. But the main elements of the technique have remained basically the same.

The Hop

After a fast run-up, the athlete takes off with a strong forward drive from the jumping leg. The body is upright during takeoff, and a flat horizontal trajectory conserves takeoff speed for use in each of the jumps. The athlete drives the leading (nonjumping) leg up to horizontal and then swings it back to the rear. The thigh of the jumping leg is lifted upward so that a wide stride position exists at the midpoint of the hop.

At the end of the hop, the athlete brings the jumping leg forward and reaches out for distance. As the jumping leg lands, it flexes in preparation to drive the athlete forward in the step. The arms work vigorously to balance the body and assist in driving the body forward. The hop is approximately equal in length of the jump.

The Step

The step is usually shorter than the hop or the jump. The body is upright in the takeoff for the step, and the leading leg is flexed and vigorously swung forward to become the active leg at the end of the step. At the midpoint of the step, the athlete has a wide stride position.

The Jump

The athlete vigorously swings the leading leg forward from the step into the jump, aiming for distance and a good landing position (feet together well in front of the body).

TEACHING POINTS

Drill 1: Lead-Ups

Training for the triple jump is excellent preparation for the high jump and long jump. Likewise, all the lead-up activities and run-up practices for long jump are excellent preparation for the triple jump. The demands of triple jump training improve leg power, muscular endurance, and coordination, which benefit not only the jumper but the thrower as well. Repetitive bounding, jumping and hopping activities are excellent preparation for the triple jump.

Repetitive Bounding

Participants bound with long, reaching strides (3 to 4 strides in total) from a standing start and from a short relaxed run-up (3 to 5 strides). Methods for measuring a run-up and choosing the jumping or favoured leg are taught during instruction in long jumping.

Coaching Points

1. Drive forward vigorously with the jumping leg.
2. Swing the leading leg up to horizontal with each bounding stride.
3. Try to hold a wide stride position at the midpoint of each bounding stride.

4. Swing your arms forward as powerfully as possible at the takeoff for each bounding stride.

Hopping for Distance

The athlete performs 3 to 4 hops for distance on the right leg, then on the left leg.

Coaching Points

1. Swing the leading leg and the arms forward and upward to assist with each hop.
2. Drive as powerfully as possible with the hopping leg.

Rabbit Hops

Each member of the groups performs 3 to 4 repetitive 2-legged jumps (rabbit hops).

Coaching Points

1. Extend both legs as powerfully as possible for each jump.
2. Lean forward and swing your arms forward and upward to assist the legs.
3. Do not collapse into a full squat position at the end of each hop.
4. Allow the legs to flex to about a 1/4 squat position, no more.

Standing and Running Long Jump

The performer practices standing and running long jumps (from a short 3-stride run-up) using a takeoff from the nonfavoured leg. Because the triple jump is 3 jumps in succession, 1 of the jumps occurs from the nonfavoured leg. This practice familiarize the performer with this action.

Coaching Points

1. Drive powerfully with the jumping leg at takeoff.

2. Lift the thigh of the leading leg to horizontal.
3. Swing your arms forward and upward as strongly as possible at takeoff.

Combinations of Hops, Jumps, and Bounding Strides

The step (the second element in the triple jump) is really a bounding stride. Participants practice combinations of hops, jumps, and bounding strides, initiated from a standing start and then from a short controlled approach of 3 strides. The step is used in the following combinations:

a. hop, hop, step;

b. step, step, jump;

c. hop, step, hop, jump; and

d. hop, hop, step, step, jump.

Distance and Time Competition

Instruct students to practice the previous 4 sequences and award points for the greatest distance achieved. For the latter contest, require a minimum distance of all participants, determine combinations to be performed, and require all jumps to be performed from a standing start. A time competition forces the participant to drive low and forward as powerfully as possible with the legs and arms throughout all jumps.

Repetitive Bounding and Jumping Over Low Obstacles

Place mats short distances apart and use low obstacles, such as bamboo canes on traffic cones or elastic crossbars. Students perform combinations of jumps. Increase distances between mats to make the athlete reach out with each jump. The low obstacles require a minimal height to be achieved with each jump.

Drill 2: The Triple Jump

Learning the Sequence and Rhythm of the Triple Jump

On grass or mats, participants practice the sequence of jumps in the triple jump by hopping (left to left), stepping (left to right), and jumping (both feet and together). All sequences begin by the athlete's placing the foot behind a line and attempting a triple jump. You provide a verbal count: "left, right, together". Then change the starting foot to accommodate those who wish to begin with the right foot.

Coaching Points

1. Try to make each of the three jumps in the hop, step, and jump equal in size.
2. Take off into each of the three jumps with a powerful leg drive.
3. Swing the thigh of the leading leg to horizontal at each takeoff and simultaneously swing your arms forward and upward.

Standing Triple Jump Into the Jumping Pit

Using starting positions that vary in distance from the side of the pit, athletes practice the triple jump to land in the sand. Participants attempt to "graduate" to the takeoff line, which is farthest from the pit. Each jumper should still attempt to make the hop, step, and jump more or less equidistant.

Coaching Points

1. Lift the thigh of the leading leg to horizontal on each of the three jumps.
2. Swing your arms forward and upward as vigorously as possible on each of the three jumps.
3. "Claw" back at the ground with the foot of your supporting leg at the end of each jump.

4. Think of jumping long and low rather than up.

Triple Jump Using a Run-Up

Each participant attempts a triple jump using a run-up and jumping from a takeoff area. Place the takeoff area 5 to 8 meters from the sand pit. The selected distance will depend on age and ability. A run-up of 9 to 11 strides together with check marks is worked out in the same manner as in long jump.

Coaching Points

1. Drive long and low at the takeoff. Concentrate on horizontal rather than vertical movement (i.e., do not hop high in the air).
2. Aim for equal distances in each of the jumps.
3. Listen to the rhythm of the footballs during the triple jump; the cadence should be regular ("da—da—da").
4. Lift the thigh of the leading leg to horizontal at the midpoint of the hop and the step and for the takeoff in the jump. Aim for a wide stride position on each occasion.
5. Land flat-footed at the end of the hop and step.
6. Pull the body forward with the foot of your supporting leg using a clawing or pawing action at the end of the hop and the step.

Double Arm Action

Participants attempt double arm action during the three jumps as an alternative to the more natural alternating arm action (i.e., left leg forward, right arm forward). The double arm action is used by many élite jumpers and is easy enough for young athletes to attempt.

Coaching Points

1. At the takeoff from the hop and the step, swing both arms forward, sideways, and upward together, to a point where they are horizontal and parallel to the ground; this will help to lift your body forward and upward.
2. Keep your arms flexed at the elbows (approximately 120 degrees).

Note: The following exercises are extremely demanding and are recommended only for mature and experienced athletes, not for novices. They are usually practiced in the off-season and only after an athlete's leg strength has been developed in other less demanding activities. Increase height and distance between obstacles in the same manner as with a weight-training schedule. Participants should become well accustomed to landing from low heights before trying to land and rebound from greater heights. All of the following examples are variations of rebound jumping.

Repetitive Bounding Over Obstacles Varying in Height and Distance

The performer bounds or strides from one floor to the other over various obstacles. Carefully select obstacles according to the maturity and ability of the athlete. You may choose one or two sections of vaulting box, mats placed lengthwise or crosswise, elastic high jump "crossbars", or low hurdles. Whatever you choose, the athlete should be both challenged by and capable of leaping the obstacles.

Place the most challenging obstacles first. Place last easier obstacles that fatigued athletes can knock over without risking injury.

Coaching Points

(Applicable to all types of rebound and depth jumping)

1. Cushion the landing on the full foot, not on the ball of the foot or on the heel. (This action transfers the shock of landing through the bones to the joints of the body rather than to the muscles).
2. To absorb the shock of landing, partially flex at the knees and hips.
3. Be sure to roll forward and push off the ball of the foot for the rebound.
4. Initially practice from low heights of 15 to 30 centimetres (6 to 12 inches). Increase heights gradually.

Combination Hopping and Bounding Over Obstacles

To increase the work load placed on the athlete, add repetitive hopping to bounding over high obstacles.

Rebound Jumping

The performer jumps down from one vaulting box onto a mat, immediately rebounding up onto the next box. Boxes are varied in height.

Repetitive Two-Leg Jumps Over a Series of Hurdles

This activity allows no momentary pause, as can occur on top of a vaulting box. Hurdles are varied in height.

TWO-LEG JUMP UP ONTO A VAULTING BOX, FOLLOWED BY A SINGLE-LEGGED LANDING AND AN IMMEDIATE REBOUND

The athlete must have sufficient power to control the single-leg landing and then immediately drive up onto the next vaulting box. Elite athletes frequently increase the demand on the legs even further by wearing weight belts are weighted jackets! This level of power takes a long time to develop and is achieved only after years of hard training.

COMMON ERRORS AND CORRECTIONS

1. Error

The athlete uses stutter steps in the run-up. The run-up is irregular.

Reasons

The athlete is unsure of the run-up. Check marks may be incorrect, and the athlete may be tense and anxious prior to jumping.

Remedies

The athlete practice the run-up, assessing positioning of check marks on the run-up.

2. Error

The jumper uses too much backward lean at takeoff.

Reasons

The penultimate and final strides are too long, and the athlete overemphasizes height in the hop. The leg is too straight during the takeoff, and the head falls back as the athlete (incorrectly) concentrates on height in the takeoff.

Remedies

The athlete practices run-up and takeoff, aiming for a fast, flat takeoff. The takeoff leg is slightly flexed, the upper body erect, and the vision ahead. The athlete concentrates on a low, flat trajectory in the hop.

3. Error

The hop has too much height and distance. The jumper "collapses" at the end of the hop and has no momentum for the step and the jump.

Reasons

The athlete leans backward at the takeoff. Strides prior

to the takeoff are too long. The athlete overemphasize the hop and forgets that two more jumps follow.

Remedies

The athlete practices repetitive jumps, hops, and bounding strides with upright or slight forward lean at takeoff. The athlete practices hops and steps with the distances well defined by cones or markers.

4. Error

The jumping leg is allowed to hang or drag during the hop.

Reasons

The athlete relaxes the jumping leg after extension for the step.

Remedies

The athlete practices sequential hopping, jumping, and bounding on grass or mats, emphasizing forward and upward drive with the thigh of the jumping leg.

5. Error

The athlete performs the triple jump with stiff legs throughout.

Reasons

The athlete does not flex the legs at the midpoint of the hop or the step or on landing at end of the hop and step.

Remedies

Correct as for the previous error.

6. Error

The athlete lands on the toes at the end of the hop or step and complain of painful landings at the end of the hop and step.

Reasons

The athlete is reaching out with the toes for distance instead of with the heel followed by a flat footed landing.

Remedies

Correct as for the previous 2 errors, emphasizing a heel-flat-footed landing throughout. The athlete should aim for a pawing or clawing action with the foot and should "drag" the ground backward with the supporting leg at the end of the hop and step.

7. Error

The athlete's arm action is poor and haphazard during each of the 3 jumps.

Reasons

The athlete is unsure of the technique.

Remedies

Have the athlete repeat standing triple jumps, emphasizing strong upward arm swing at the takeoff of each of the 3 jumps. Decide on alternate or double arm action.

8. Error

The step is extremely short, and there is no drive for distance.

Reasons

The athlete has too much height and distance in the hop, and the jumping leg "collapses" at the end of the hop. The athlete is unable to drive forward with the leading leg in the step. Arm action is weak and ineffective.

Remedies

The athlete practices repetitive jumps with emphasis on vigorous arm action and powerful leading-leg action (i.e., the thigh driven forward and upward to horizontal on each occasion). Assign hop and step practice over low obstacles and require specific distances.

9. Error

After the hop and step the jump is weak and achieves poor distance.

Reasons

The athlete loses momentum in the hop and the step, the speed throughout the hop and the step drops off dramatically. Errors in hop and step culminate in a poor jump.

Remedies

The athlete practices sequential hops and steps on grass and mats, using a short run-up. Emphasize maintenance of horizontal speed throughout. Have the athlete practice long jumps from short run-ups, taking off from the nonfavoured leg.

ASSESSMENT

1. Assess the following theoretical elements as taught during instructional sessions.

a. Fundamental rules governing the triple jump.

b. Good safety habits for use in the triple jump.

c. Basic elements of triple-jump technique.

d. Basic elements of triple-jump training.

2. Assess the performance of technique during the following stages of skill development.

a. Repetitive bounding, hopping, and jumping.

b. Various combinations of bounding, hopping, and jumping.

c. Triple jump using a short run-up (3 to 5 strides).

d. Triple jump using a full-length run-up.

Critical Features of Technique to Observe During Assessment:

1. Ability to use a run-up and 2 check marks.
2. Achieving a strong forward drive with a flat trajectory in the takeoff for the hop.
3. Driving the leading leg back and stretching out with the takeoff leg in the flight of the hop.
4. Pawing or clawing backward with the foot of the supporting leg in the landing at the end of the hop.
5. Driving upward with the arms to horizontal at the takeoff for hop, step, and jump.
6. Pawing or clawing backward with the foot of the supporting leg in the landing at the end of the step.
7. Swinging the thigh of the leading leg up and forward in the takeoff for the jump.
8. Reaching out with the legs well in front of the body for a good landing position at the end of the jump.
9. Achieving a distance ratio of 35 percent-30 percent-35 percent between the hop, step, and jump.

3. Hold graded competitions to help develop motivation and technique.

a. Jumpers compete for distance from a standing start using a jump from a single-legged takeoff and then a jump from a double-legged takeoff.

b. Jumpers compete for distance using these sequences: 3 bounding strides from a standing start, 3 hops from a standing start, 2 bounding strides and a jump taken from a standing start, and 2 hops and a jump taken from a standing start.

c. Jumpers compete for distance from 3- and 5-stride run-ups using a selection from the sequences listed under b.

d. Jumpers compete against each other and the stopwatch by jumping a series of hops, bounds, and jumps that you designate. Who can compete the series covering a specified distance or more in the shortest time?

e. Jumpers compete for distance in a triple jump from 3- and 5-stride run-ups.

f. Jumpers compete for distance in a triple jump from an extended run-up of 9 to 13 strides. Takeoffs can occur from a takeoff area rather than a takeoff board.

g. Jumpers compete under full competitive conditions.

CHAPTER 14

THE LONG JUMP

The long jump seems to be one of the oldest events in track and field. The Greeks carried weights in the hands and used a short run; thus they were able to jump almost as far as our best jumpers of today.

The earliest United States records reveal that a leap of 17′4″ won the first AAU national championship. Ellery H. Clark of the United States won the 1896 Olympic title in Athens with a leap of 20′ 9¾″. Chronologically, the following men are among those who have helped to improve performance in this event: Alvin Kraenzlein, Pennsylvania; Myer Prinstein, Syracuse; Ed Gourdin, Harvard; Robert Legendre, Georgetown; DeHart Hubbard, Michigan; Edward Hamm, Georgia Tech; Jesse Owens, Ohio State; Eulace Peacock, Temple; Robert Long, Southern California; Lorenzo Wright, Wayne State University; Willie Steele, San Diego State; Jerome Biffle, Colorado; George Brown, UCLA; John Bennett, U.S. Army; Greg Bell, Indiana University; Peter O'Connor, Ireland; Sylvio Cator, Haiti; and Chuhei Nambu, Japan.

A particularly outstanding performance occurred on May 28, 1935, when Jesse Owens set a world record of 26′ 8¼″. His greatest asset was probably his then world record speed of 9.4 seconds for the 100 yards. He jumped with great ease, and his speed was so great that, according to a film of his action, he did not seem to kick up his lead leg as high or attain as great an altitude as some of our jumpers do today. He often used the "float" style while he was in the air. Of course, he had good landing position.

Many early jumpers used some of the same styles of jumping used today, although the distance of the run has increased through the years from 90 or 100 feet to a minimum of 120 feet. It is thought that pits in the early period were very poor, and a takeoff board was not used until 1886. Undoubtedly, more impressive records would have been made in these earlier attempts if the facilities had been better.

Greg Bell of Indiana, the 1956 Olympic long jump winner, combined what some coaches believe and the ideal essentials for correct long jumping. He had a relaxed run to the takeoff, good lead leg swing, arched back with chest and head up to assure proper hip swing, and good landing position.

Recently, Ralph Boston, Lynn Davies of Great Britain, and Igor Ter-Ovanesyan have dominated this event, all being able to project themselves beyond 27'. However, probably one of the greatest feats in track history was the 29'2½" distance jumped by Bob Beamon of the United States in the 1968 Olympics. (It has been calculated mathematically that man could long jump 35'). Beamon approached the board at near maximum speed. His centre of body mass was behind his takeoff foot. His takeoff foot was on the board long enough to generate force and give him upward thrust at a reasonably high angle. He arched his back in flight and extended his legs as far as possible.

CHARACTERISTICS OF A LONG JUMPER

The characteristics of a long jumper are the same as those of a sprinter, low hurdler, and quarter-miler, but he may possess more spring in his legs than the average competitor in these events.

LONG JUMPING FORM

The long jumper should be concerned with 5 factors: (1) a run long enough to gain optimum speed; (2) a good lift off the board to gain height; (3) a forceful kick or swing by the lead leg at the takeoff to project the body upward; (4) a good balanced position in the air to insure proper landing position; and (5) a full leg-extended position upon landing.

The run. The length of the run depends on the distance it will take the individual to gain maximum speed. A run of about 135 feet is the average used by most jumpers today, although a 160-foot run might be ideal. It is most important for the jumper to use a consistent stride during the run. He must also be able to run under control. This means he is running at not quite full speed, but in a fast, relaxed manner.

In order to insure a legal or fair jump each time, it is necessary for the performer to use at least 2 check marks. The following method of securing these marks is suggested: (1) measure off approximately 130 feet (or more) on a smooth portion of the running track. (2) Start with both feet on the first mark, and, stepping forward with the takeoff foot, attempting to run in a relaxed manner down the runway. (3) At the midpoint of the run, or about 65 feet, the coach should check the spot where the takeoff foot hits as the run is continued through the entire 130 or more feet. (4) Alter a second runthrough it made to verify this foot near the end of the runway distance. (5) Measure the distance of these check marks from the start of the practice runway and transfer these measurement points to the site of the long jump runway. As the jumper runs through, the takeoff foot should land a few inches beyond the board to allow for the few shortened strides that occur when many men actually jump. However, it is best not to shorten the last few strides.

Usually the jumper strides to the first check mark, tries to reach near maximum speed by the time he reaches the second check mark and then runs under control, but at near top speed, to the takeoff board in order to prepare for the "gather".

It is important that the jumper hit the second check mark with the toe of the takeoff foot. The runthrough must be practiced continuously so that the jumper will be able to hit the broad accurately without "eyeing" it. He must concentrate on the path of his flight and the place in the pit at which he will land, rather than keep his eyes and head down looking at the board. He usually looks at a spot some distance away, observing this possible landing point through peripheral vision.

The takeoff. This part of the jump is probably the most important in determining the distance attained. The jumper is trying to transfer his forward momentum to upward and forward momentum.

During the last 3 or 4 strides before takeoff, the runner "settles" into a relaxed, controlled run. For average to good jumpers, the last stride to the toe-board is usually from 4 to 8 inches shorter (only 2 to 4 inches shorter for top jumpers) than the preceding one. This shorter stride helps the jumper to place his weight over the takeoff foot, and prevents him from having too much backward lean at the takeoff. The latter would cause him to lose some forward momentum. The great sprinter could probably use a longer last stride if he had gained enough forward momentum to carry his body to beyond his foot at the takeoff. (The body would be behind the takeoff foot as it is placed on the board). This would enable him to keep his foot longer on the board, and therefore exert more force with it. Most 26- and 27-foot jumpers have good speed and use a relatively long last stride.

As the takeoff foot strikes the board in a heel-ball-toe motion, the eyes, head, and chest are held in an erect position. The lead leg is swung vigorously forward and up, with the knee flexed as much as in a running stride. The back is arched to enable the jumper to use a hip swing. The takeoff leg then comes up and body assumes a sitting position in preparation for the landing. The arms are raised at the takeoff to aid in elevating the body, and thereafter used for balance.

Action in the air. One of the most important things to have in mind at the takeoff is to get height in the jump. Any action done by the jumper in the air will not add distance to the jump, except that the spot where the feet land determines the distance attained. To assist in getting the feet in the best landing position, the jumper will need to put his legs out in front as feasible just before landing. Many of the best jumpers today take one full stride while in the air so that their legs can be in an extended position upon landing. The 2 most commonly used kinds of movements in the air are the "hitch-kick", or "running in air action", and the "hip swing" or "hang". The running in air form is accomplished by driving the lead leg forward and upward, and then back in a clawing movement. The takeoff leg is simultaneously brought forward in a running action and extended forward into a horizontal position for a proper landing. The lead leg is then brought forward and extended horizontally alongside the takeoff leg in preparation for a landing.

The hang style is accomplished by dropping the lead leg after the takeoff so that both legs appear to drag in the air. At the same time the back is extended and the chest thrust forward. At the top of the arc, the legs and feet are violently swung forward and outward in an attempt to touch the now extended arms and hands. It becomes difficult to hold the legs in any one position while in the air, so several moves in midair are used by jumpers.

The landing. An effective landing is accomplished by holding the feet high as the landing begins. The legs are kept extended as far as possible until the buttocks nearly strike the ground. Then the head, chest, and shoulders are thrust forward and the knees are relaxed just as the heels touch the pit. The jumper should fall directly forward into a compact tuck position and onto his hands and knees. Keeping the feet high is very difficult and will take strong abdominal muscle action. The jumper will need a great deal of practice on this phase of the jump, which can consist of doing short runs jumping into a pit of foam rubber or other shock-absorbing material. Another type of landing used by some jumpers is to relax one knee upon landing and then stiffen the other after the heels hit, causing the jumper to fall off to one side as the landing is completed.

The three most important factors in the running long jump are speed at the board, upward spring at take-off and a good landing with the feet well up forward in relation to the centre of gravity of the body. The most difficult part of the event is to obtain height after a fast approach and most of a long jumper's training should be devoted to this aspect of the event.

THE APPROACH RUN

The total distance of the approach generally varies between 90 feet and 130 feet. However, some jumpers have utilised approaches considerably in excess of 130 feet. This means the jumper will be taking between 17 and 23 strides. The odd number of strides is sometimes used with beginners because they may start the run, hit the check marks and the board all with the same foot. However, many jumpers walk, jog or run on to a starting mark; in this case consistency of the early strides is very important. The novice might be advised to commence the run with the feet together toeing the starting mark and step off with the foot with which he or she wishes to hit the check marks and the board. However, if there appears to be tension building up in the run, it would be better to start with a walk or trot on to the mark. This method is conducive to more relaxation at the beginning of the approach.

THE TAKE-OFF

The jumper should have reached maximum possible speed some distance from the board. During the last four strides the necessary adjustments to the body carriage should be made in order to allow the athlete to make an effective spring and obtain height. This will means a drop in tension, a more erect carriage of the upper body and lowering of the hips on the penultimate stride. The jumping foot is planted in front of the body weight and slightly towards the centre line. This will allow force to be applied against the ground for long enough and also directly underneath the body mass. As the jumper comes over the take-off foot, the opposite leg, knee bent, is swung rapidly forward and upward to gain momentum; so also is the opposite arm to this leg.

STYLE IN THE AIR

Once a jumper has broken contact with the ground there is nothing further that can be done to gain distance apart from obtaining a good landing position. Although the jumper can leave the board with forward rotation, backward rotation or no rotation at all, generally speaking there will be forward rotation in the body after take-off. If this is allowed to continue, without being slowed prematurely and a consequent loss of distance. In order to assist with obtaining a good landing, one of two styles is used by most jumpers, either the hitch-kick or the hang.

In the hang technique the jumper swings the non-jumping leg back, straightened at the knee, after take-off, to join the take-off leg in an extended position. The body remains in this position until both legs are brought through together, bent at the knees, and then straightened and extended forwards for the landing. The first part of the hang has a hitch-kick effect as the straightened leg swings back and the extension of the body slows down the forward rotation. The arms are swung back, round, over and forwards working in unison and this also has some effect in temporarily interrupting the forward rotation set up at take-off.

The hitch-kick has become more popular with the world's best long jumpers in recent years. Here the running action is continued in the air, the legs performing either $1\frac{1}{2}$ or $2\frac{1}{2}$ running strides before coming together and forwards for the landing. The beginner will only have time to manage the $1\frac{1}{2}$ stride technique; the expert jumping much further will manage $2\frac{1}{2}$ strides before completing the landing. All backward movements of the legs are done with the leg straightened at the knee; all forward movements are made with the leg bent and snug about the axis at the hip. The greater moment of inertia of the straight leg moving back creates a backward displacement of the body, allowing the legs to come well forward for the landing. The arms generally work independently rotating forwards but some jumpers work them together as in the hang. Either way they have a slightly beneficial effect.

IMPORTANT POINTS OF TECHNIQUE

(1) Drive in at take-off, hit the board at speed.

(2) A slightly bent knee position just prior to take-off.

(3) An explosive jump upwards.

(4) Trunk erect during the early part of the jump.

Coaching position (1) — standing well back at right angles to the approach run.

Common Faults

(1) Erratic approach to the board.

Correction

(1) Adjust the starting mark and check marks.

(2) Regular sprinting and low hurdling.

(2) Slowing down in the approach run.

Correction

(1) Ensure that the approach run is correct.

(2) Ensure that the jumping leg is strong enough to work at speed.

(3) Put a flagpost in at 20 metres from the board and another at the board.

(4) Stand well back and time with a good stop watch. Check this time against the jumper's speed over 20 metres on the track without a jump.

(5) Insert a mark 6 strides from the board and make the jumper think of acceleration and drive into the board from this point.

(6) Correction (2) is very often the ultimate answer because a sudden increase in speed at the board will mean the jumper is without sufficient strength and skill to obtain height. This will mean re-thinking the weight training schedule for the following winter.

(3) No height from the board.

Correction

(1) Corrections (2) and (6) for major fault (2).

(2) Jumping off a short approach and bounding exercises with and without a weighted belt out-of-season.

(3) Drive up with the knee of the non-jumping leg.

(4) Accentuate arm drive at take-off.

(4) Completing the $1\frac{1}{2}$ stride hitch-kick too soon and 'collapsing' on landing.

Correction

(1) Delay the hitch-kick action off the board. Hold the leading knee high briefly before going into the hitch-kick.

(2) If the distance covered is in excess of 23 feet consider the use of a $2\frac{1}{2}$ stride hitch-kick.

(5) In the hang technique, the trunk coming forward to the legs, resulting in a poor landing position.

Correction

(1) Emphasis a powerful take-off, hold the position momentarily and then swing back the leading leg straightened at the knee.

(2) Ensure for the landing. If they are brought through straight, or straightened too early, the trunk will be dragged down to the legs in reaction.

Coaching position (2) — at the end of the pit and in line with the approach run

Common Faults

(1) Swerving on the runway.

Correction

(1) An unusual fault but sometimes evident with the

beginner. Transfer the approach run to the track and have the athlete running down a line. This can take the form of 8×50 metres with a walk back recovery. Check each run from the front.

(2) Exaggerated lateral movements during the last three strides to the board, leading to loss of speed.

Correction

(1) The beginner may be attempting to drop the hips deliberately on the penultimate stride. In this case he will splay the feet and knees, passing through a position which is too low and so will lose speed. The correction lies in short approach work off 7-11 strides (not less than 7 strides). Too much very short approach work in training (3-5 strides) can often lead to faults being built into the technique, the lowering of the hips being exaggerated at slow speed and the limbs splaying to achieve such a position.

WORKOUT SCHEDULES

Four weeks prior to meets

Monday

1. Jog ¼ mile.
2. Do stretching exercises:
   a. Hurdle exercises from sitting position.
   b. Touching the toes from a standing position, keeping the knees stiff.
   c. Situps, raising the feet and touching the toes in a jackknife action.
   d. Inverted bicycle riding.
3. Run ½ mile of wind sprints.
4. Go through the "run-up" 5 times at full speed.

5. Take 10 triple jumps, using a short run.
6. Run 3 flights of 70-yard low hurdles.
7. Do horizontal bar-leg raises for 10 minutes.

Tuesday

1. Jog ¼ mile.
2. Do stretching exercises.
3. Run ½ mile of wind sprints.
4. Take 5 triple jumps, using a short run each time.
5. Run 3 flights of 70-yard low hurdles.
6. Take 5 starts from the blocks, running 50 yards each time.

Wednesday

1. Jog ¼ mile.
2. Do stretching exercises.
3. Run ½ mile of wind sprints.
4. Take 5 triple jumps, using a short run each time.
5. Take 10 triple jumps, using a full run-5 at half speed, 5 at ¾ speed.
6. Do horizontal bar-leg raises for 10 minutes.

Thursday

1. Jog ¼ mile.
2. Do stretching exercises.
3. Run ½ mile of wind sprints.
4. Take 6 starts from the blocks, running 50 yards each time.
5. Run 3 flights of 70-yard low hurdles.

Friday

1. Jog ¼ mile.
2. Do stretching exercises.
3. Run ½ mile of wind sprints.
4. Run through the full distance to the takeoff, checking accuracy of the stride with the check marks 3 times.
5. Take 10 triple jumps, using a full run-5 at half speed, 5 at full speed.

After Meets Start

This schedule is made to account for Saturday meets. If meets are held on Friday, the schedule be altered accordingly.

Monday

1. Jog ¼ mile.
2. Do stretching exercises.
3. Run ½ mile of wind sprints.
4. Go through the full run 5 times at full speed.
5. Take 5 triple jumps, using a short run.
6. Take 5 triple jumps, using the full run at ¾ speed, work on gather for the takeoff, and be sure to take a long, unhurried step before the final jump.

Tuesday

1. Jog ¼ mile.
2. Do stretching exercises.
3. Run ½ mile of wind sprints.
4. Run 3 flights of 70-yard low hurdles.
5. Take 3 starts from the blocks, running 50 yards each time.

6. Do horizontal bar-leg raises for 10 minutes.

Wednesday

1. Jog ¼ mile.
2. Do stretching exercises.
3. Run ½ mile of wind sprints.
4. Do 5 to 10 pop-ups.
5. Take 5 jumps, using full run at full speed each time.

Thursday

1. Jog ¼ mile.
2. Do stretching exercises.
3. Run ½ mile of wind sprints.
4. Take 5 starts from the blocks, running 50 yards each time.
5. Do horizontal bar-leg raises for 10 minutes.
6. Go through the full distance to the takeoff 3 times.

Friday

Rest and study movies of previous action made in practice and in meets.

WEIGHT-TRAINING PROGRAM

Use 1 to 4 sets of 5 to 15 repetitions with near maximum weight that can be handled. It is best to start with about 75 pounds and work up to the athletic maximum over a period of 3 weeks to a month.

1. Do partial squats and heel raises, jumping off floor.
2. Do 2-arm military press.
3. Do leg lunges with barbell on shoulders.
4. Do toe raises with barbell on shoulders.

5. Do situps with the knees flexed. Start with 25, progress to 200.

6. Do leg raises slowly. Progress from 10 to 100.

7. Run and hop up stairs with and without weighted vest.

HELPFUL HINTS

1. Be sure to get into proper physical condition before starting to practice jumping.
2. Work consistently on the run to gain confidence and to help minimize fouling.
3. Prevent heel bruises by wearing proper shoes and by using heel cups.
4. Practice good form in jumping by using pop-ups at the takeoff.
5. Be sure the surface behind the board is not below the level of the board. This condition could cause heel bruises.
6. Practice some full runthroughs. It is necessary on occasion to jump using a full run in order to get the proper timing for taking off.
7. Concentrate on jumping off the board. It is not necessary to emphasize a hard "foot stamp", but an effective jump will mean that a forceful jumping action was used.
8. Concentrate on the lift off the board with the lead leg swung up, the chest kept high, and the spring being made fro the big toe.
9. Hold the feet up high for as long as possible.
10. Check carefully the measurements for the run, the type of runway, and the wind conditions before competing.

CHAPTER 15

TEACHING TACTICS IN LONG JUMP

For many decades long jumping was an event that sprinters enjoyed as a diversion from sprinting. Today, athletes specialize in long jumping, although it is still common for sprinters to be great jumpers, and vice versa.

Two major techniques are used in long jumping: the hang technique and the hitch-kick technique. The hitch kick is the more popular, but both techniques have been used by elite athletes to reach distances in excess of 8.83 meters.

The hang and the hitch kick are patterns of movements used by the athlete while in flight. Each technique is intended to counteract the unfavourable forward rotation imparted to the athlete at the moment of takeoff. If the hang or the hitch kick were not performed, the athlete's feet and legs would contact the sand earlier than necessary and the resultant distance would be shorter.

Both hang and hitch kick require the same fast run-up, similar body positions at takeoff, and similar actions for the landing in the sand. Most your athletes will have difficulty performing the hitch kick, because it requires considerable speed and spring to perform well. However, an elementary long jump and a rudimentary form of the hang technique are well within the reach of young athletes. Remember that the most important requirements of long jumping are speed and spring and that an athlete does not have to perform a hitch kick to achieve excellent distances.

SAFETY PRECAUTIONS

The sand in a long-jump pit should be fine, well raked, level, and slightly wet to avoid dust. It should be deep enough (i.e., no less than 38 centimetres, or 15 inches) to prevent jarring and should be frequently searched for debris. It should be covered when not in use. The edges of the pit should be designed so as not to injure the athlete, although they must be well defined so that sand does not scatter onto the grass. The pit should be surrounded by a wide grass area or open area that is well clear of the walls, trees, fences, and other obstacles. The pit should be positioned so that athletes are not in any danger from throwing events.

Brooms, rakes, and spades must always be stacked well clear of the pit, not left lying around. You as well as officials should ensure that no jump is made while the pit is being raked or dug. The takeoff board should be firmly fixed to the ground and should lie flush with the surface of the run-up. The run-up should provide a firm but comfortable approach and should be kept clean and swept clear of dirt, sand, and other debris. Depressions near the takeoff board should be filled in and made level, and takeoff boards narrower in width than 20 centimetres should not be used, because these are likely to cause foot injuries. Another consideration is that grass and certain types of artificial surfaces can become slippery when wet and can be dangerous unless the athletes wear spikes.

Elite athlete in the long jump and the triple jump prepare in the off-season by practising sprinting, sprint endurance training, and a variety of dynamic jumping activities that develop the explosive elastic quality of the legs. In these activities, variously called rebound activities, depth jumping, and more commonly "plyometrics", the athlete simulates the rebound of a bouncing ball. These activities place considerable stress on the joints and muscles of the legs and are not recommended for the young and physically immature athlete.

TECHNIQUE

The following descriptions of the hang and hitch kick give the main elements of each technique. Elite athletes will perform the techniques with some individual variations. Nevertheless, the main elements remain the same.

The Hang Technique

After a first run-up, the athlete drives up powerfully at takeoff, extending the leading leg and driving it backward to join the trailing leg. Both arms circle downward, backward, and then forward in clockwise rotation, and the athlete momentarily "hangs" in the air. The legs are flexed and driven forward, and as the legs extend for the landing, the arms reach forward and rotate backward again at the shoulders. As soon as contact with the sand is made, the legs flex at the knees and the upper body moves forward and over the feet.

The Hitch-Kick Technique

After a first run-up, the athlete drives up powerfully at takeoff. The leading leg, which is flexed at takeoff, is extended so that the athlete assumes stride position in flight. The leading leg is rotated back in an extended position, and both legs are flexed and brought forward for the landing. The arms rotate clockwise, balancing the action of the legs; this characteristic cycling action of the legs is called the hitch kick. The athlete extends both legs for the landing, as the arms circle forward and then backward. Upon contact with the sand, the knees flex and the upper body moves beyond the feet.

TEACHING POINTS

Drill 1: Lead-Ups

Long jump and triple jump use similar lead-up and preparatory activities, and both events require excellent sprinting ability and explosive leg power. Following are some demanding activities that develop leg power. For beginners, 3 to 4 repetitions with short rests between each are recommended. For activities that develop sprinting ability.

Hopping for Distance and Finding the Favoured Jumping Leg

Measure the distance each participant can achieve in 3 successive hops from a standing start with the right leg only. Measure the distance gained from the same action performed with the left leg only. Which leg hopped the longer distance and is therefore the preferred jumping leg?

Coaching Points

1. On each hop drive the thigh of the leading leg (i.e., nonjumping leg) to horizontal.

2. Jump for distance with each hop, not height.

3. The leg with which you jump farther is your favoured leg.

4. Remember whether it is the right or the left leg.

Bounding for Distance

In this lead-up activity, the thigh of the leading leg is lifted to horizontal with each bounding stride. The performer should strive for long strides, reaching for distance.

Coaching Points

1. Swing your arms up and forward with each bounding stride.

2. Try to achieve a wide stride position at the midpoint of each bounding stride.

3. Try to get a feeling of "floating" at the midpoint of the stride.

Standing Long Jump Using a Two-Legged Takeoff

The athlete uses a strong swing of the arms coupled with a double-legged drive to cover as much distance as possible.

Coaching Points

1. Extend your leg as powerfully as possible and combine that action with a strong swing of the arms.

2. Pull the legs forward underneath your body to cover as much distance as possible.

Standing Long Jump Using a Single-Legged Takeoff

This is similar to a bounding stride except that both legs are brought together for the landing. Participants jump using their favoured and nonfavoured legs for the takeoff and then compare distances.

Coaching Points

1. Extend the jumping leg as powerfully as possible.

2. Swing the leading leg up to horizontal.

3. Use your arms in the same fashion as with the two-leg jump. Swing both of them up and forward in unison with the leading leg.

Distance Jumping Competition

From a line, participants see how far they can jump in total with 3 successive two-footed jumps (rabbit hops).

Who can go the farthest?

Coaching Points

1. Do not put everything into the first of the 3 jumps.

2. For optimal distance, all 3 jumps must be fairly equal in length.

3. Avoid jumping upward. Jump low and forward.

Variation

The first member of a team completes 3 two-footed jumps (or 3 bounding strides). The next member of the team adds 3 more jumps to increase the distance achieved. Which team can accumulate the greatest distance?

Circle Jumping

Lay a series of hoops (3 or 4) on the grass in front of each team. Each team member hops or bounds as required from hoop to hoop. Initially place the hoops close to each other, then set them progressively farther apart to demand long reaching strides and explosive leg action. The hoops should not slip if an athlete lands on them. If there is any likelihood of this occurring, use traffic cones; the participants attempt to land next to the cones.

Coaching Points

1. Use a forward and upward swing of the arms to help with each jump.

2. Drive forward as vigorously as possible from the jumping leg.

3. Concentrate on lifting the leading thigh to horizontal with each successive jump.

4. Keep your vision forward, do not let your head drop backward.

5. Do not relax when you land; try to "claw" the ground backward immediately upon landing with the supporting foot.

6. Experiment by starting the series of jumps from the right foot and then from the left. Which gives you the greatest distance?

Hopping and Bounding Over a Series of Low Obstacles

Each participant hops, bounds, or jumps over a series of low obstacles. The arms are driven upward and the thigh of the leading leg is driven up to horizontal with each jump.

Heading Suspended Volleyballs or Soccer Balls

Suspend volleyballs or soccer balls from ropes at various heights. Participants use a 3-stride run-up to head the ball. If they are successful hearing 1 ball, they shift to the next highest.

Coaching Points

1. Work out a 3-stride run-up so that you jump from your favoured leg.

2. Lean back slightly prior to takeoff.

3. Swing your arms and the leading leg upward to help in gaining height.

4. Keep your trunk upright at takeoff and extend the jumping leg as powerfully as possible.

Jumping From a Beat Board and a Low Box

Participants pace a 3-stride run-up from the beat board. They step from the beat board onto a low box and take off from the favoured leg to land on mats or in sand. Athletes practice different types of flight patterns (e.g., tuck, straddle, or stride).

Coaching Points

1. Approach the beat board and box at the same speed

that you "measured" your run up.

2. Start your run-up from the other leg if your find yourself jumping from your nonfavoured leg.

3. Drive up strongly from the box so that you have time to complete the required maneuver.

4. Use your arms and the leading leg as before. Swing them upward as strongly as possible.

Drill 2: Elementary Long Jump and Run-Up

Technique

At takeoff, the athlete fully extends the jumping leg and flexes the leading leg with the thigh raised to horizontal. The upper body is perpendicular, the vision is ahead and upward, and the arms complement the action of the legs.

When the athlete is in flight, the leading leg extends and the jumping leg trails behind so that the jumper is momentarily in a stride position. For the landing, the jumping leg is brought forward and both legs are extended. The arms and upper body reach forward, and the legs flex at the knees on contact with the sand.

Elementary Long Jump From 3 Bounding Strides

The athlete takes 3 bounding strides in sequence. On the third, the jumper takes off from the favoured leg, holding the thigh of the leading leg at horizontal through to the landing in the sand pit. The jumper lands in a one-legged kneeling position with the leading leg forward and flexed at the knee. Be sure the pit is well dug for this drill.

Coaching Points

1. At takeoff, swing (drive) the thigh of the leading leg to horizontal and hold it in this position through to the landing. Do not be tempted to lower it while you are in the air.

Standing Jump Over a Mound of Sand

Build up a mound of sand lengthwise down the centre of the long-jump pit. Fashion the mound of sand to become progressively higher along the length of the sand pit. The mound forces the jumper to flex and pull the legs up and under the seat and then extend them forward for the landing. Participants jump from the side of the pit. If they are successful in jumping a higher section. Each participant jumps taking of with both feet together, then taking off from a stride position with the jumping foot placed forward.

Coaching Points

1. Extend your legs strongly at takeoff, then flex them quickly.

2. Pull the legs up under your seat and extend forward into the landing.

3. Flex at the knees and hips on the landing.

4. Reach forward with your arms in order not to sit backward on the landing.

An Elementary Long Jump From an Elevated Takeoff

The performer uses a short run-up (3 strides), steps onto a low box (1 section), and takes off from the box to jump into the sand. Those who prefer jumping off the left foot will start with the right foot forward. The run-up sequence for a left-footed jumper is as follows: left foot, right foot, left foot, jump. The elevated takeoff allows time in the air in order to achieve a good stride position and bring both legs forward successfully for the landing.

Beat-Board Takeoff

Athletes repeat the previous drill but from a lower elevation (e.g., substitute a gymnastic beat board for the top section of the vaulting box).

Ground Takeoff

Remove the gymnastic beat board and have athletes repeat the drill from ground level.

Measuring a Run-Up

A sequence for determining a run-up for beginners is as follows:

1. Each jumper stands in stride position, facing back down the run-up with the toes of the non-jumping (i.e., nonfavoured) foot placed against the leading edge of the takeoff board.

2. The jumper runs 9 strides down the long-jump run-up, with the 1st stride taken by the jumping foot.

3. You or a partner counts each football of the jumping leg, in a sequence of 1, 3, 5, 7 and 9 (this is easier and less confusing than counting every stride).

4. Mark the 9th stride, which gives an approximate starting point for the run-up. The athlete then places the nonjumping foot on the mark and takes the 1st stride toward the pit with the jumping foot. The uneven number of strides in the run-up will put the jumping foot on the board for the takeoff.

5. You can use check marks at the 1st and 5th strides of the run-up for additional accuracy.

Variation

You may use the following variation to determine an approximate run-up for beginners.

1. Lay out a 100- to 150-foot tape next to the curb of the track straightaway.

2. Starting at the zero end of the tape, the athlete sprints down the straightaway.

3. Approximate the position where the athlete reaches top speed, and mark the distance.

4. Before sprinting the athletes calls out "right" or "left" to indicate the jumping foot, and then sprints down the straightaway a second time.

5. Note the placement of the jumping foot nearest the top speed marker as a partner counts the athlete's strides. The partner tells the athlete the number of strides used to reach the top-speed marker.

6. Transfer the distance to the long-jump run-up. The athlete counts the number of strides while accelerating down the run-up and jumps from a takeoff area.

Using a Takeoff Area Instead of a Takeoff Board

It is recommended that beginners jump from a takeoff area rather than from a takeoff board. Using a takeoff area helps make beginners more relaxed during the run-up and less concerned about hitting an exact spot for takeoff. The competitive takeoff board is 20 centimetre (8 inches) in width and is 1 meter from the edge of the pit. A takeoff area can be a chalk-marked area or a large board 80 centimetres to 1 meter in width, set flush in the runway with the position of a regular takeoff board marked on it in a central position. For competitive purposes, all jumps taken from within the takeoff area are valid.

9-Stride Run-Up

As each participant attempts the 9-stride run-up, you stand by the takeoff area and note the relationship between the position of the takeoff foot and the takeoff board. Help the athlete adjust the start of the run-up to bring the takeoff as close to the board as possible.

Shortening the Last Stride in the Run-Up

Long jumpers must learn to lengthen the penultimate stride and shorten the final stride prior to takeoff. This lowers the body, tilts it backward, and places it in an optimal position for takeoff.

TEACHING THE RHYTHM AND PLACEMENT OF THE LAST TWO STRIDES

A mark positioned on the run-up used with a beat board and the top of a gymnastic vaulting box can help teach athletes to stretch the penultimate stride and reduce the length of the final stride before takeoff.

Position the marker by the side of the run-up to indicate the start of the penultimate stride. Place the beat board a sufficient distance from the marker so that the athlete must stretch to reach the beat board. Position the box top beyond the beat board half the distance of marker to beat board. The athlete uses a short 5-stride run-up. Direct the athlete with vocal cues from the previous drill. Jumping from the box top will give height in the flight of the long jump.

Coaching Points

1. Stretch your body upward immediately prior to takeoff.

2. Look forward, not downward, at takeoff.

3. Reach out with your stride onto the beat board, then shorten the last stride into the box top for the takeoff.

Increasing the Length of the Run-Up

Place a check mark to indicate the first stride and another to indicate the 5th stride prior to the board. Elite athletes will use 19 strides or more for their run-ups. For a 19-stride run-up, use check marks in the same fashion, placing them at the 1st stride and at 5 strides prior to the board. After hitting the 1st check mark, the elite athlete sprints 13 strides to gain maximum acceleration. When the athlete reaches the 2nd check mark, the trunk is upright and the body begins to sink a little. The shorter last stride is used in preparation for the upward drive of the takeoff.

Drill 3: The Hang Technique

Learning to Drive the Hips Forward

Each performer runs, takes off as for an elementary long jump, and attempts to drive the hips forward toward a bamboo cane that is held by a partner or by you. For a variation, 2 partners stand 1 meter away from the takeoff with their arms outstretched to form a double "gate"; the jumper must open the gate.

Coaching Points

1. At takeoff, lift the thigh of the leading leg up and forward as normal.

2. Drive powerfully with the jumping leg.

3. Once in the air, lower the leading leg and push the cane forward or open the gate with the stomach or hips.

Learning the Arm Action of the Hang Technique

The performer jumps upward, and a partner assists by holding the performer's waist and lifting upward from the rear. As the performer jumps he or she practices the clockwise circling of the arms.

Emphasizing the Arm Action in the Hang Technique

The participant stands in stride position with the leading leg on a box top and the favoured or jumping foot to the rear, a stance that simulates the position that the jumper assumes after driving upward from takeoff. The athlete places both arms forward and pushes off with the leg that is on the box top. The arms simultaneously circle clockwise (downward and backward and then forward, and the athlete lands with feet and arms forward.

Practising the Complete Hang Technique From Height

Place two vaulting boxes (using 2 to 3 sections each) lengthwise, one behind the other. Performers step along the top of the boxes, taking off from the end. The additional height provides time to attempt the hang technique

Coaching Points

1. After takeoff, drop the leading leg backward and push your stomach forward.

2. Circle your arms backward and then forward.

3. As your arms come forward and downward, lift your legs up to meet them for the landing.

Practising the Hang Technique From Reduced Height

Set a beat board 1 stride away from 1 or 2 sections of a vaulting box set crosswise. Using a slow 3-stride approach, the performer steps onto the beat board with the jumping foot, then up onto the box top with the leading leg to attempt the hang technique. The extra height will give the performer time to "hang" the legs and pull them through for the landing.

Coaching Points

1. Be sure to measure the 3 strides so that your favoured leg land on the beat board. The step onto the vaulting box simulates the position of the leading leg in the air at takeoff.

2. Walk through the approach to begin with, then gradually speed up your run-up.

3. Circle your arms forward and down from beat board to box top, then backward from box top to the sand.

4. Try to complete the whole action before landing in the sand.

Variation

Using the favoured leg, the jumper takes off at the top of an incline. The extra time in the air provides better opportunity to complete the leg and arm action of the hang technique.

Attempting the Hang Technique From Reduced Height

The performer attempts the hang technique from a single section of a vaulting box (or from a beat board). The performer uses a 3- to 5-stride run-up and takes off from the favoured leg.

Hang Technique With Extended Run-Up

The athlete performs the hang technique from the ground into the pit using an extended run-up.

Drill 4: The Hitch-Kick Technique

Swinging the Leading Leg Up and Forward

Using a short run-up, the participant jumps from the edge of the sand pit, holding the leading leg forward throughout. The participant lands in the sand in a flexed stride position (i.e., kneeling, with 1 leg forward and 1 leg back).

Coaching Points

1. Swing (drive) the thigh of the leading leg to horizontal and hold the leg in that position through the landing.

Practicing the Hitch-Kick Leg Action

Using a 5-stride run-up, the jumper takes off from a beat board or a single section of a box and while in the air pedals backward (i.e., kicks backward) with the foot of the leading leg. The jumper tries to kick a bamboo cane that is placed approximately 1.5 to 2 meters (5 to 6 feet) beyond the takeoff and .5 to .75 centimetres from the ground.

Coaching Points

1. Lift the leading thigh to horizontal, then straighten the leg and pedal backward. Try to kick the cane backward.

2. The leading leg should end up in a stride position to the rear of the jumping leg when you land.

Variation

A partner holds the cane in position and the jumper practices the same action.

Completing the Hitch-Kick Action

The jumper takes off from a beat board, "cycling" the leading leg to the rear and bringing it forward again in a flexed position for the landing. The arms rotate and balance the actions of the legs. The bamboo cane can still be used if it helps the jumper initiate the backward rotation of the leading leg.

Coaching Points

1. Begin by concentration on the leg action during this drill. Do not worry about your arms to begin with.

2. Lift the thigh of the leading leg, then straighten it and pedal the foot backward.

3. Then flex your leading leg and bring it forward for the landing.

Practicing the Hitch Kick Without Additional Takeoff Height

Because the hitch kick must be performed without assistance of any type at takeoff, jumpers now attempt the hitch kick without any additional height and using an extended run-up. If the athlete does not have sufficient speed and spring, the hitch kick can easily dissolve into an aimless wriggling of the legs and can detract distance from the jump. Most jumpers at the elementary level will find that they cannot complete a full hitch-kick action and that they have more success with the hang technique.

CHAPTER 16

POLE VAULTING

The history of the development of form in the pole vault is one of relatively clear and early insight into the best style of vaulting but, of course, a much slower general acceptance and general practice of these best methods. Unlike the high jump, in which there is a "new" straddle form and the relative merits of various styles are still being argued, the essentials of good form in the pole vault as taught by today's best coaches are little changed from those expressed by Henry F. Schulte or F. A. M. Webster over a quarter century ago. This, of course, is a natural outcome of the event itself, in which it is inherent that all actions should be along a single runway and on a single plane of movement.

In summary, development over the past 50 years has been primarily in increased utilization of body momentum in the run, the swing, and the final action in the air. Furthermore, continued future development will be along this same line. The ultimate record holder will be a tall sprinter of record speed who, through great gymnastic and jumping ability, can maintain high momentum through the take-off, swing, pull-up, and fly-away. These statements summarize the writer's basic concept of pole-vaulting from it earliest days to its future ultimate record of well over 16 feet.

Cromwell writes of the ancient history of pole-vaulting

from the angle of its foreign equivalents:

The Greek word for pole vaulting is translated literally as "spear high jump". The German word Stabhochsprung means "staff high jump".

From the Greek word it is easy to visualize the soldiers of the constantly warring Hellenic States using their spears to hurdle hedges and jump streams as they pursued one another with homicidal intent. From the German word one is taken back to the days when boys and young men of Teutonic tribes tended their flocks and used their staffs as an aid in jumping stone fences or other obstructions. Through the use of the spear and staff in clearing heights or making jumps, a vault technique was developed.

More directly related to modern vaulting is the story of vaulting in Ulverston, England, as related by F. A. M. Webster in his interesting book, which emphasizes the history and development of track and field athletics:

But in 1874, E. Woodburn of the Ulverston Cricket Club, came south and improved Mitchell's championship record of 10 feet 6½ inches by half-an-inch. From that day onwards the lads of Ulverston might be seen any summer evening after their day's work vaulting among the cinder heaps of the Lancashire town.

The upper hand was shifted a foot up the pole and the lower hand brought up to it. The climbing continued until the pole had passed the vertical position. As it began to fall forward, the athlete drew up his knees and went over the bar in a sitting position, a last backward push preventing the pole from following through to remove the bar.

The Ulverston method obtained until 1889. The American athletes contended that the performance of Ray and Stones were nothing but acrobatic balancing feats, requiring neither strength nor endurance, and a new rule was passed prohibiting the athlete from shifting the grip of the upper hand and from placing the lower hand above the upper hand after the feet have left the ground. About this time too, several men suffered death by impalement, through their wooden poles snapping transversely, and the pole vault began to disappear from the programmes of British school sports.

The origin of the Ulverston method is suggested by Hugh H. Baxter as derived from Ulverston's located in England's fen country. "This country is bisected by numerous dykes and canals, and it has been the custom from time immemorial for the inhabitants to use long poles, by means of which they negotiated these obstacles". This undoubtedly accounts for the early popularity of pole-vaulting for distance rather than for height. In the trophy cases at the University of Pennsylvania, for example, there is a beautiful 18-inch figure won by C. Hoffman at the 1895 World's Fair at Chicago for his effort in the event called "vault for distance". In 1910, Platt Adams held the record at 28′ 2″.

Elimination of the hand-over-hand style concentrated attention upon increased momentum of the run and some means of increasing the swing. The heavy wooden poles made real speed impossible and a wide handspread in the pole carry necessary. Quite naturally, earliest vaulters maintained this wide spread of the hands throughout the vault, and therefore had almost no effective swing. Hugh H. Baxter, who held the world's record at 11′ 5″ from 1887 to 1898, states:

Up to 1879, American pole vaulters used various styles, all of them crude and unscientific. The upper grip on the pole was in all cases at least 3 feet higher than would be used by a modern pole vaulter for the same height. Some carried the thumb of the right hand up, and that of the left hand down, and all pulled with the upper hand alone, using the lower hand simply as a prop.

In 1879, W. J. Van Houten of the Scottish-American Athletic Club, New York, won the American championships with 10 feet 4¾ inches, using the same style as the record holders of to-day except that he did not some of the fine points which have developed in recent years. He knew nothing about the shift, but being a very light man and using a very light pole he was able to carry it with both hands close together, thus obtaining the two hand pull which is the essential difference between the new and old styles and mainly accounts for the differences in records....

It is impossible to say just when or where the Van Houten style of pole vaulting returned and came into general use, but it is certain that R. G. Clapp of Yale used it when he made a record of 11 feet 10½ inches in 1898, and all subsequent records were made in practically the same style.

Use of the bamboo pole became more general just after the turn of the century, faster runs were used, hands were shifted so that a faster swing resulted, and greater momentum throughout the vault was established. From 1904 to 1912, six new world's records were established, beginning with Norman Dole, of Stanford, at 12′ 1¼″ (the West Coast's first great vaulter), and ending with a rather startling vault of 13′ 2¼″ by M. S. Wright, of Dartmouth.

By this relatively early date, 1912, the main elements of modern vaulting had been established. Pictures and descriptions of Wright's vaulting, for example, indicate a run of about 100 feet, a straight-forward hand shift, a reasonably prolonged swing, a good pull, an extreme arch position over the cross-bar, and finall a single hand (first left, then right) release. Of these elements, only the arch has been abandoned. This style involved a curl of the body over the bar, with the feet starting down immediately after they clear the bar and release of the pole occurring after the arch had been formed. Its theoretical advantage lay in its prone, "hollow stomach" position over the bar.

Some experts claim that modern vaulting really began in 1919 with Frank X. Foss, of Chicago. Possessing good speed in the run and with excellent early training in gymnastics, he confused the pole vault authorities with his high leg position and jackknife over the bar and a single-hand release, (first lower, then upper) that was very similar to the great Cornelius Warmerdam's some 30 years later. Foss's record of 13′ 5 1/16″ was truly remarkable, but was soon broken, in 1932, by perhaps the greatest potential vaulter of all time, Charles Hoff, of Norway.

Hoff was 6′ 2″ tall, weighed about 165 pounds, had run the equivalent of under 10 seconds for the 100-yard dash, had high-jumped over 6 feet, had broad-jumped over 23 feet, and had unofficially broken the world's record for the decathlon. His vaulting style was extremely simple, almost careless—a fast run and a long relaxed swing that had startling momentum and carried the feet and body high in the air with a beautiful fly-away finish that had no resemblance to the old arch or jackknife styles. By no means a stylist, if style refers to the precise details of vaulting, he possessed the all-important qualities of height, run momentum, and a natural, relaxed maintenance of momentum throughout the action in the air. Most unfortunately, a broken ankle kept him out of vault competition in the 1924 Olympics, but he still managed to qualify for the semifinals in, of all events, the 400-meter dash. Hoff's best official effort was 13′ $11\frac{3}{8}$″, in 1925, but after turning professional as a dancer and exhibition pole-vaulter, he made over 14 feet on several occasions.

Although Hoff startled the pole vault world with the ease of his swing and fly-away, his method was a natural result of his speed and height rather than a deliberately chosen form. In contrast, Lee Barnes, Olympic champion in 1924, while still a California high school boy, recognized the limitations of his jackknife form and studiously perfected the greater momentum of the fly-away. In consequence, he showed consistent improvement throughout his college career at Southern California and ultimately, in 1928, established a world's record at 14′ 1½″. To Barnes and to his coach, Dean Cromwell, should undoubtedly go a major share of the credit for clearly demonstrating the value of this style. In passing, it is of value to note the great and sometimes heartbreaking uncertainty of the pole vault, as illustrated by Lee Barnes, who won the 1924 Olympics and yet, at the peak of his career in 1928, was able to place only fifth at Amsterdam. Many other examples are available, notably George Varoff, the world's record holder in 1936 at 14′ 6½″, who failed to qualify for the United States Olympic team in that same year. Real consistency in vaulting is a rare quality and comes, if at all, only after many years of careful practice and competition.

It was in 1927 that the much discussed "ultimate height" of 14 feet was officially broken by Sabin Carr, of Yale University. A few "experts" now figured that the perfect vault had been made, but, on the contrary, best heights were just beginning, for the next decade was the most prolific in vaulting records in track's entire history. New marks were established on nine different occasion, the climax occurring in the remarkable duals in 1937 between Southern California's "Heavenly Twins", Bill Sefton and Earle Meadows. In two meets within three weeks, they tied for new world's record heights, first 14′ 8½″. then 14′ 11″. Further, to emphasize the ascendancy of this great year of 1937, four men—Sefton, Meadows, Varoff, and Warmerdam—tied for the National AAU championships at 14′ 7⅝″.

Surely this was the all-time tops. And well it might

have been for some years, had it not been for the continued effort over a period of seven years of Cornelius Warmerdam, of Fresno State College, unquestionably the pole vault's "best ever" athlete. No athlete in any event on the track and field program has been so consistently superior to his predecessors. On over 50 occasions, he cleared 15 feet or better, and finally reached his outdoor peak in 1942 at 15′ 7¾″, and in 1943, his indoor record, using a board runway, of 15′ 8½″.

Yet even Warmerdam contributed nothing really new to vaulting technique. Rather, the consistent development throughout the quarter century from 1925 to 1950 was brought about through increased perfection of all aspects of the vault rather than through the discovery of new techniques. Warmerdan simply did everything right that others had been trying to do for years. Possessing good speed and excellent rhythm, and 6′ 1″ tall, he moved through all stages of the vault with an ease and perfection of form that brought gasps from spectators and sighs from coaches and other vaulters. Much more will be said of his style in the later discussion of correct form.

Although given little publicity, two changes in vaulting equipment had almost as favourable effect upon both form and height as the change to the bamboo pole. The first occurred in 1924 with the adoption of a uniform vaulting box, which made the placement of the pole for the jump certain, safe, and fixed. The earlier spike on the end of the pole sometimes failed to hold in the soft earth and caused many a bad spill. Further, its position on the ground was often not just right for greatest height over the bar. In contrast the box, with its cushion of sand or shavings to break the jar of the pole and its V-shape to insure a safe plant of the pole, was exactly fixed and could be located relative to the cross-bar by moving the standards. Vaulters therefore moved with more confidence and relaxation.

The second change occurred in the landing pit and proved even more beneficial. Early pits were only 12′ × 10′ in size and merited their low-level name; they were merely turned-over loam or sand, which did little to cushion the drop from a 12- or 13-foot height. In contrast, the modern "pit" is actually a mound of fine shavings 15 feet wide, 14 feet deep, and from 3 to 4 feet high. All fear of injury or painful jar is removed, and men are able to concentrate on going higher with no concern for the when and how of making a proper landing. Dean Cromwell states that the early use of such pits is a basic reason for America's supremacy in vaulting. Certainly the few European vaulters who have come to this country of late years have been delighted with the conditions here and are advocating the use of similar pits at home.

ESSENTIALS INGREDIENTS REQUIRED FOR CORRECT FORM

Although there are certain disagreements among coaches concerning the details of pole vault form, there can be none concerning the over-all unity of the event. For discussion purposes, it is necessary to set apart certain phases of the vault and consider each as though it were a unit in itself. Actually, nothing could be more misleading. These essentials, as well as shall call them here, are merely aspects of a single movement, which begins with the first step of the run and continues smoothly through the shift, swing, pull, push, and landing. Correct execution of any one phase is dependent upon equally correct execution of the preceding phase. In coaching and in learning, first movement must be learned first, and at all times, special attention to any one phase must keep clearly in mind the entire action.

Disagreement concerning the details of each phase of form is undoubtedly the result of the almost exclusive use of individual trial and error as a basis for judgment. There is a tendency to assume that what the champion does is probably right and to forget at least part of what works best for him is merely compensation for incorrect methods learned early in his career. These individual variations are used as arguments against a general acceptance of what constitutes "best form" and as supporting the contention that "after all, form is an individual matter". Obviously, the latter statement is partly true, for no two vaulters are likely to duplicate all the details of form; but at the same time it is true that a perfect form can be contrived and universally accepted as a goal toward which all individuals should guide their efforts, no matter how imperfectly or desperately.

The most thorough efforts to discover the nature of such a form are to be found in the work of Richard Ganslen and Cornelius Warmerdam, who, in preparing their master's theses and in subsequent studies, greatly clarified the mechanics of the pole vault event. The writer gratefully acknowledges the influence of their findings upon his own viewpoints, and upon what is written here. There is general agreement among coaches or athletes that the pole vault is the most complex event and the most difficult to learn of all the events in the track and field program. A champion must combine the speed of a sprinter during the run with the strength, balance, and agility of a gymnast throughout the actions in the air. Perhaps even more important is the fact that the exhausting demands of each vault seriously limit the number of trials and thereby the amount of learning in any one practice period. Ingenuity in providing means for learning related actions is one of the keys to increased development as a vaulter.

But the very complexity of the event places unusual emphasis upon a clear understanding of its fundamental mechanics and upon as simplified a coaching method as possible. Basically, the problem is to convert to a maximum extent the horizontal momentum of the body, gained through a run, to a somewhat less than vertical direction through the aid of a portable pole. After a run of unfixed length and speed, forward momentum and weight of the body is then transferred to the pole and is swung and pulled upward in a complex lever-pendulum movement. First, there is the lever of the pole swinging upward, with its point in the box as its fulcrum, with the body as its weight, and with the body's momentum from its grip on the pole, shortening its length by bending at the knees, hips, and shoulders and swinging rapidly to a high position, where it can be further raised by a pull of the arms along the stable length of the pole. Finally, there is the upward extension of the body and upward push by the arms and hands from the vertical pole in a fly-away and landing.

Holding the pole. The body as a whole is facing straight ahead, that the arms are bent, and that the grip is relaxed. The left forearm is approximately parallel with the ground and at more than right angles to the pole. The arms and shoulders are thereby given freedom to swing somewhat with the rhythm of the run while still holding the pole steady. The spread of the hands varies somewhat from 2½ to 3½ feet, depending upon the height and strength of the vaulter. A wider spread "lessens" the weight of the pole but increases the tension of the arms and shoulders during the run and makes the shift of the hands at the take-off more difficult. The upper hand, with the thumb toward the upper end of the pole, should hold the pole firmly between the thumb and forefinger throughout the entire run and vault. The other three fingers can be allowed to relax out the entire run and vault. The other three fingers can be allowed to relax during the run, thus giving greater freedom to the elbow and shoulder. They will, of course, take a tight grip during the shift. The left hand should be loose, with the weight of the pole resting primarily on the thumb. Such looseness in the hands will aid greatly in the smoothness and rhythm of the run.

The angle of the pole during the run. The greater the angle at which the pole is held during the run, the more compact its weight and the lighter it feels to the vaulter. On the other hand, the higher the angle of the pole, the straighter the running angle of the vaulter and the lesser the momentum he can gain during the run.

As part of his research, Ganslen timed 50-foot dashes with a pole by 4 subjects, each of whom took 16 trials at each of 3 types of carry: a low horizontal carry, a medium-angled carry in which the pole tip was at eye level, and a high-angled carry in which the pole tip was above 8 feet in the air. Although Ganslen's method of timing was not as accurate as it might have been, and although he does not mention the influence of other related factors such as handspread on the pole, his conclusions are clear and apparently justified. The medium-angled carry is between 2 and 3 feet faster at 50 feet than the horizontal carry and between 4 and 5 feet faster than the high-angled carry. This conclusion is substantiated by the methods of the majority of our greatest champions, including Warmerdam, Meadows, and Sefton. Others, such as Guinn Smith, Morcom, Richards, and Ganslen, used the lower carry and the somewhat forward body lean that accompanies it.

An additional factor in this problem of angle of carry lies in the ease and smoothness of the pole shift and the exactness of its plant in the box. Here again the argument favours the lower carries, for the pole is already pointed at or close to the box. Those who make a smooth shift from a high carry usually lower the tip of the pole gradually during the last 40 feet of the run. Those who attempt to lower the tip at the last moment are less likely to be co-ordinated in the action and are often caught short at the take-off.

A few excellent vaulters—notably Laz, of Illinois—carry the pole across the body and the line of run. They argue that the forward position of the hips and shoulders is thus made easier during the run and greater speed gained. However, such a position necessitates a gradual swinging of the pole to the right and in line with the box during the last 40 feet of the run, so that the actual gain in speed is questionable and the loss in simplicity of action is of real concern.

A third consideration in this matter of holding the pole is grip height on the pole, determined by placing the pole in the box vertically and measuring the height to be cleared by the upper hand. In general, good vaulters are able to clear at least 18 inches higher than the height of their grip. Beginners, however, and others trying low heights, should place their right hand at approximately 10 feet on the pole, for this will provide both a chance to swing and a minimum of shock at the take-off. As soon as they have learned the rudiments of form, this should be raised to 10′ 6″ or 10′ 9″. Holding at a lower height cuts the swing and generally develops poor timing habits. Most men about 5′ 10″ in height who have good speed of run and reasonable smoothness in the take-of and vault will hold the pole at about 11′ 3″ when attempting to clear from 12 to 13 feet.

The exact location of this hold on the pole is of great importance, for it seriously affects the efficiency of the vault. Obviously, additional height of the grip is an assent above 12′ 6″; yet each raise of 3 inches or so changes the timing and the "feel" of the vault and demands practiced adjustment. There is a good deal of truth in the statement that each time a man raises his grip he loses his old form and must learn a new one. Recently, the writer worked with a boy who had cleared 13 feet with a poorly balanced style, a 12′ 3″ grip, a late shift, an early pull, both pole and vaulter falling off to the left, and so forth. Using an 11′ 6″ grip, the boy worked carefully on correcting these various faults and showed definite improvement in form. Later, however, in an intramural competition, he raised his grip in his desire to win, and immediately reverted back to his old form. This is a very typical experience. Eventually the grip of such a boy can be raised to at least 12 feet, but only after the new style has become firmly fixed.

The run. Assuming that the vaulter has learned an effective take-of, the greater his momentum at this point, the higher he can vault. However, as in all field events, only as much speed as can be controlled and used is likely to prove of effective value. The more speed in the run, the more difficult the timing of the take-off and of form in the air. Conservative coaches, or those primarily interested in what happens this week and this month, will therefore place control and smoothness above momentum.

But those working toward maximum efforts will encourage greater speed and will work through the problems that attend it. In an important and careful study of many aspects of the approach in pole vaulting. Warmerdam found that greater heights cleared were almost invariably accompanied by increased speed in the run: 22 men who cleared 12′ 6″ averaged a speed of 11.3 seconds per 100 yards; 18 men who cleared 13 feet averaged 11.4 seconds; 9 men who cleared 13′ 6″ averaged 11.01 seconds; and 8 men who cleared 14 feet averaged 10.7 seconds. The slowest of the first group ran at a 12-second pace; of the second group, at 12.3; of the third, at 11.52; and of the last, 11.1 Warmerdam concluded not only that faster men clear greater heights but that great vaulters gradually speed up their run as the height of the bar is used. This is not to state that slow runners cannot clear good and even championship heights in the pole vault, but does emphasize the great importance of securing as much momentum as can be smoothly and efficiently used.

Directly related to this problem of generating momentum in the vault is the length of the run. With only one exception, the champions all use runs of 11.5 feet or more in length. This is consistent with Warmerdam's findings, which indicated that length of the run was directly related to momentum: "Only 3 men out of 14 using a run of 120 feet or less were faster than 11 seconds, while 7 out of 10 using a longer run were under this figure. Seven of the 10 vaulters who cleared 14 feet used a longer run". Warmerdam also found that length of the run was related to the man's height and that short, quick-starting individuals tend to take a shorter run than long-legged vaulters.

Such studies confirm coaches opinions that the run should be long enough to build up maximum speed at least three strides before the take-off. This early gathering of top speed permits a concentration of attention upon a smooth pole shift during these last strides and aids a co-ordinated transfer of momentum and body weight to the pole.

The problem of deciding just what length of run is necessary to achieve maximum momentum is not easily solved accurately. Sprinters attain 95 per cent of top velocity at about 75 feet and full speed at 180 feet. But vaulters are held back by the vaulting pole. The most common, although inaccurate, method is to observe the length of strides on the runway. Once top speed has been achieved, the length of the strides should be constant.

First work on the regular track straightaway. Carefully brush a 150-foot length of track. Have the vaulter stand on a definite mark with both feet; then, in a consistent and rhythmic pattern of movement, let him attempt to accumulate as much speed as soon and as smoothly as possible. Have him move out with assurance. There is no need for "feeling his way" or waiting for a second check mark before sprinting. After sufficient trials have been made to establish a definite and satisfactory pattern, carefully measure the length of strides. When three consecutive strides of the same length are observed, it can be assumed from the first of these three strides to the starting point and transfer it to the pole vault runway so that the farther mark falls exactly four strides from the take-off. This should insure sufficient length to give maximum momentum. Adjustments will need to be made for exact check marks, of course, but the total length of the run should be correctly established. The experiences of other vaulters indicate that this distance will vary with different individuals from 100 to 135 feet.

Securing check marks. The next problem is securing check marks for the run. Unfortunately, this is not always a simple procedure. A consistent length of stride is often lacking, especially when the man is burdened by a five-pound pole and is consciously striving for form and rhythm. Until stride consistency is achieved by many trips down the runway or down the track, attempts to get check marks are likely to prove very frustrating. Further, once a measured run is secured, attention to form in the shift and vault will often unbalance the rhythm of the run. Patience and continual rechecking of marks is the only solution. In the beginning little attention should be drawn to an exact and full run. It is better to take a shorter and slower run and to learn the rudiments of the shift. Once the over-all feeling of things has been learned, stride consistency will follow more naturally and easily.

Methods of securing check marks vary a great deal, but the writer has found the following both simple and accurate. First, brush the full runway. Then start with a definite mark at about 110 feet from the box. Do not get back and skip up to it, as is so often done, for this will encourage variation. Stand on the mark with both feet and start with the take-off foot. Only one more mark is needed, checking the take-off foot at about 40 feet from the starting point. This second mark merely checks smoothness and regularity in the first phase of the run. It does not establish a point where greater speed is suddenly attempted. The entire run, from the very first step, is a unified and smooth effort to attain top usable momentum. Occasionally, where steps are very uncertain, a third mark can be tried, but the attitude of hesitancy that it implies may do more harm than good. Normally, it is better to use just the two and drill on consistency on the runway as well as on the track.

Now the vaulter should take a full-length run, using the two check marks but making no attempt to hit a take-off point. He should run right on through the pit, keeping the strides as natural and even as possible. The coach, standing some 25 feet to the side, can note the placement of any selected left footmark as well as the smoothness of the run. The distance of this footmark from the correct take-off point will guide the coach in moving the temporary check marks either forward or back. Certain adjustments will need to be made later, of course, but not too often. The assumption that the check marks and the run are correct is the best guarantee of consistency. Changes should be made only when necessary and when the new marks are certain.

Of course, the exact location of these marks on any given day will vary in accordance with wind and runway conditions as well as with the athlete's physical condition. Every vaulter will need to test his marks carefully before competition and later, as well, when runways become soft and strides shorter.

The pole shift. Throughout the run and shift, the eyes

are concentrated upon the vaulting box. During the last three strides of the run, the pole is shifted smoothly into take-off position. There must be no slowdown at this point, merely a relaxed preparation for the take-off. The actual point at which this shift begins varies somewhat, even with excellent vaulters. However, pictures of Warmerdam show clearly that he started his shift while still two and one-half strides from the take-off. Richards started on the third stride, so that by the time the take-off foot landed, the pole was already in the box and starting upward. In any case, the shift must be started soon enough to permit an unhurried and co-ordinated placement of the pole, the hands, and the arms, so that the weight of the body can be transferred to the moving pole with a minimum of jar and deceleration. It can be done quickly, but it must be done without loss of momentum.

The shift itself is a simple pull and forward thrust of the pole by the right hand exactly along the plane of the run and vault, and in line from the carrying point to one directly in front of the eyes, a so-called underhand shift. The arms are not fully extended, in fact are flexed about 90 degrees just before the body weight is transferred to them. The left hand is now either adjacent to the right or not more than four inches below it. Cromwell permits a spread of not more than six inches. Sefton contends that two or three inches provides good lateral balance, sufficient swing, and a strong pulling position. Warmerdam, who greatly emphasized the importance of swing, advocated a hand position as close together as possible; yet actually his hands were often separated as much as four inches. First efforts should be toward bringing the hands close together; then, if they slip a little, no harm will result. Certain excellent vaulters, notably Meadows and Smith, use the overhand shift, in which the right hand starts up before starting forward. However, the upward movement necessitates an outward and out-of-plane swing, which tends to bring the take-off position of the hands and the pole to the left and off balance. Such an out-of-line position of the hands and an off-balance angle of the pole are among the most common and most vicious faults connected with vaulting. Being off balance at this point inevitably means being off balance and lacking timing throughout the vault. Therefore, the direct underhand shift is strongly recommended.

The pole should definitely not be thrown quickly forward and upward but rather be an integrated part of the entire forward and upward movement. The primary problem now is to use and maintain the accumulated momentum of the run, not to increase it. Further, the pole should not be thrust so far ahead as to produce straight arms at the start of the swing. Rather, the arms should be flexed (Ganslen states at 90 degrees), and should thereby absorb the shock of the take-off with a minimum loss of speed. As the full weight and force of the body shifts to the pole, the right arm will extend almost completely, aiding a full swing. The left will remain somewhat more flexed through the lower position of the left hand on the pole. Both details are extremely important. The 90-degree flexion of the arms provides muscular force and flexibility at the moment of greatest impact. The almost full extension provides a maximum swing with readiness for the pull-up.

The take-off. The correct location and method of the take-off is one of the most important aspects of vaulting. It also comprises one of the greatest points of variance among vaulters and coaches. All agree than the placement of the take-off foot should be exactly in line with the run and with the position of the hands at the take-off. The linear placement of the foot is usually described in terms of a plumb line dropped from the upper edge of the upper right hand. Coaches who emphasize a full swinging action at the take-off—e.g., Dean Cromwell—recommend that this plumb line should drop down past the back of the head to the back of the heels. Those at the other extreme, who stress a strong spring from the ground, believe that the toe of the take-off foot should be on, or even two or three inches back of, this plumb-line point. Most good vaulters are in between, with the consensus favouring the ball of the foot. A variation of three inches or more will definitely make a difference in the effectiveness of the vault. Once the extent of swing or spring is fixed in the vaulter's habits, the take-off point becomes equally fixed and must be carefully planned for each condition of runway, wind and limb. Exactness here is just as important as in the broad jump and should be as carefully planned for each competition.

Even more important than linear foot placement is that of lateral position of the foot. Almost no vaulters put the foot to the left of the centre line, but all too many place it from one to four inches to the right. Such a position to the side will almost certainly throw the entire vault off balance—the swing, the pull, and the landing—so that there is danger of landing out of the pit or even on the standards. The cause is usually to be found in a shift to the pole, which starts out to the side rather than straight up and ends to the left of centre. Maintenance of a straight-forward shift will produce a pole position that splits the body, so to speak, and will force a correct foot placement.

In the final analysis, the amount of spring that is desirable in a vault is determined by the extent to which it can be integrated into the action as a whole.

The swing. The all-important function of the swing is to maintain the body momentum that has been attained during the run and take-off. To delay all action deliberately and to permit the momentum already attained to run its full course are essential. Only when the inevitable deceleration, which naturally occurs as the body swings against gravity, becomes too great is the pendulum shortened and are new forces brought in. The athlete should look straight ahead and keep his chest exactly behind, not around, the pole. Although the elbows are flexed at approximately right angles at the take-off and during the initial movements of the swing, they will be almost fully extended throughout the swing if the full pendulum effect is to be achieved from them. Those who are primarily concerned with the swing as against the pull-up—Warmerdam, for example—shift the left hand up tight against the right and thereby aid the full arm extension and increase the tendency to prolong the swing. Of all aspects of the vault, beginning vaulters tend to neglect most the full swing. Quite naturally, they tighten their hold on the pole, pull and turn over immediately, and thereby destroy the momentum gained by the run. To extend the body full, to wait until the centre of gravity is along the pole, to pull only after the pole is approaching the vertical and becomes a stable support—these are difficult lessons and require patience and much practice.

If the left hand should be two or more inches below the right, the left arm will necessarily be slightly flexed. Those advocating a separation of the hands argue that this is an advantage. The full swing will be insured through the full extension of the right arm (their opponents disagree); lateral balance will be aided and the left arm is in better position for the pull. In any case, a full swing with extended arms or arm is essential and must be deliberately practiced.

It is believed that the swing is the most important part of the vault and that the difference between a good and a poor vaulter is the ability to swing correctly. The secret lies in holding your pull-up until the legs have gone by the pole. If this movement is correctly executed, the centrifugal force generated by the swing and the power of the arms are blended harmoniously and complement each other in such a way that the utmost power is achieved.

Shortening the pendulum. As deceleration inevitably occurs, the long pendulum of the body becomes unduly inefficient and a shortening of the body pendulum takes place. The head drops back, the back arches, the legs bend at the hips and knees into a roll-back or half-tuck position. The arms remain extended so that the shortened swing action occurs from the shoulders. As becomes readily apparent if a small weight is swung around the finger on a string, the shorter the pendulum, the less the force that is required to bring it up toward a vertical position. This reason alone would justify the action. However, it also is planned in order to pull the legs and the body weight generally in toward the pole and hands, where the pull-up can be made more effectively.

Exactly how soon this bending at the knees and hips begins depends upon earlier factors and whether the athlete emphasizes the swing or the pull-up. Sefton, in speaking of experienced vaulters, suggests that the swing should be eliminated and that the vaulter should try to get in position for the pull-up as fast as possible. Apparently such a practice worked for him. Few vaulters or coaches would agree. Certainly, beginning vaulters do not swing enough and pull much too soon. Some athletes and coaches aid this body tuck by dropping the head back so that the eyes are toward the top of the pole. Properly co-ordinated, this action is effective. With many vaulters, however, it seems to destroy balance and timing.

In any case, there is no separation of swing, body shortening, and pull-up, as the paragraph headings here might suggest. They are, rather, a smoothly co-ordinated unity of movement flowing toward its objective. Let one aspect be lessened, eliminated, or too greatly emphasized and the vault will fail. If the swing is too free or prolonged, there will not be time in which to pull the legs back into pulling position. If the pull begins before the weight of the body is along the length of the pole, momentum is lost. Of all aspects of the pole vault, timing is the most important.

The pull-up. If all preceding movements have been efficiently made, the pull-up can now be truly effective. It has been delayed until the hips are about as high as the shoulders. The legs, especially the right leg and foot, are high in the air in a half-tuck position and reaching toward the vertical. The shoulders are on one side of the pole and the hips and legs on the other, so that the body is almost wrapped around the pole. The vaulting pole is at an angle of about 75 degrees and forms a stable support along which an effective pull can be made. The arms are now parallel with the pole. In summary, the run momentum has been well conserved and has placed the body in a compact position close to the hands and the pole, where a new force, the pull-up, can be applied. Up to this instant, conservation of momentum has been primary; now a new means for accelerating the vertical shoot upward is brought into use.

The pull is made equally with both arms, so that at first no turn of the body is produced. However, the naturally greater pulling power of the upper arm does produce a smooth body turn. By the time the right foot reaches full height, both the pull and the turn have been completed and the head faces back toward the runway. Needless to say, the pull-up must be fast, even explosive. It is not so much power as quick force that is wanted. If the take-off and swing have been straight and exactly along the plane of the run, and if the feet, especially the right foot, have been swung upward, with no action off to the left, then the effect of this explosive pull will be to straighten the entire body and to thrust the right foot some four feet above the bar. This high right foot is the key to good balance, to an effective pull, to a well-timed turn, and even to a smooth landing. Its importance can hardly be over-estimated. Some vaulters bring both legs up simultaneously and almost together and achieve excellent results. If this occurs naturally without coaching, there should be no objection, but direct concern should be only for the lead foot.

The turn. The turn actually occurs simultaneously with the pull-up. However, because of a natural tendency for vaulters to turn over too soon, the coach and vaulter will do well to consider it as beginning during the later stages of the pull-up. A hurried turn, as might occur in swinging the right hip ahead of the left during the body swing, will usually pull the entire body off angle and ruin the vault. Howeverm, once the pull and turn begin, they should occur rapidly and completely.

Researchers observed that the turn as resulting from a 180-degree twist of the right foot with no lateral movement at all. Just the right foot is turned high in the air, with the other parts of the body following afterward. Such a concept permits the vaulter to concentrate on the high foot position first, prevents any tendency to swing the legs out of line with the vault, and places the body in excellent position for the push-up. Warmerdam speaks of the turn as "a twisting shoot upward rather than a mechanical rollover of the body", a very clarifying distinction.

The often described scissors action of the legs in producing a turn is a poor coaching emphasis, for it complicates the action and weakens good balance. It does occur, but should be done naturally rather than through deliberate coaching. As a matter of understanding, however, this scissors action should occur as much as possible along a vertical plane and should not destroy either balance or momentum. Even Warmerdam shows a slight lateral spread in certain pictures of his good vaults, but the less said on this point, the clearer a learner will visualize what he is trying to do.

The push-up. The more commonly used terms for this phase of the vault are "push-off" or "push-away". However, the important emphasis at even this late point is upon going up rather than off or away. The pole is now close to the vertical in a good vault and forms a firm base for downward thrust. The pole has been pulled in close to, even against, the right shoulder and neck. The biceps are fully contracted, so that the bent arms can be fully extended. The bent right knee places the right foot almost directly above the head, thus putting the full weight of the body over the hands and making a forceful puch-up very effective. A still picture of this position shows an excellent handstand with the body apparently will balanced over the hands. However, to speak in coaching of a handstand position is deceiving and destroys the all-important concept of maintaining momentum and action. Throughout this discussion it has been emphasized that the so-called separate movements of the vault are merely aspects of a single movement and of a single effort to maintain vertical momentum. This needs re-emphasis in speaking of the push-up. The push-up does not begin as the pull-up ends. Rather, the two are part of a single unified movement. There can be no waiting at this point for an arch or jackknife. The action is one, rather, of using whatever momentum still remains from the swing and pull-up, which should be considerable, and increasing it through a combined thrust straight down the line of the pole and drop of the right leg, or of both legs, as the case may be. The combination should produce considerable upward movement, adding as much as a foot to a man's clearance.

To the observer this will appear as an arch, and some coaches actually teach such a position. However, continuous action is the wiser concept, and all thinking and teaching should work toward it. Through such action, men have cleared as much as 39 inches higher than their hold on the vaulting pole. Warmerdam's previously mentioned study found that 6 men clearing heights of 14′6″ or better averaged 2′6″ higher than their hold on the pole, whereas 5 men clearing heights between 12′ 6″ and 13′ 6″ averaged only 1′ 3″ higher. Although other factors such as physical height influence such clearance, the maintenance of momentum is the primary factor. Properly executed, it will lift the hips and chest in truly remarkable fashion.

At lower heights it will appear as a rather spectacular fly-away, but even at top heights there should be continuous and definite upward action. The quick dropping of the high right leg is a definite aid in the push-up, producing a sort of "teeter" effect on the centre of gravity of the body, which shifts the head and shoulders. Coaching emphasis on this point, however, should be upon keeping the legs up until after the pole is released. The natural tendency is to drop them too soon and thereby diminish the push-up effort.

Some coaches speak of the push-up as being merely an upward lifting of the arms, shoulders, and head away from the pole and over the bar. This is an error, for it indicates that the body weight has dropped and that the push from the pole has come too late to have an upward effect. This is the primary objection to the old arch and jackknife styles. Ganslen's studies found that in 26 successful vaults, the average angle of the push-up was 76 degrees, whereas in 20 unsuccessful vaults, it was only 48 degrees.

An essential aspect of the push-up is utilization of the forceful kickback of the vaulting pole. The pole has been kept well bent by the body weight throughout the swing and by the constant force of the pull-up and push-up. As this force and weight are decreased toward the end of the push-up, the pole springs back, producing an effective action of which good vaulters take full advantage. Other than the safety and weight factors, this is the primary element in a good vaulting pole and is sought by top vaulters as carefully as a member of the feminine sex selects her Easter hat. The consistency of the modern steel pole has cruelly limited the chief topic of locker-room conversation for pole vaulters, so that occasionally they are actually forced to listen to men in other events! Few studies are available of the exact degree and timing of the bend of the pole or of the timing and effects of its straightening. Ganslen states that "the pole bend of the better vaulters studied...seldom exceeded four or five inches.

About half the world's best vaulters keep both feet fairly close together at the top of the vault. In most cases this produces a fly-away style that differs in several important respects from that described here and used by Warmerdam and many others. The lower left leg, in Warmerdam's style, dropped down below the bar level and formed on open "V" of the body while over the bar. In contrast, the push-up in the fly-away style occurs while both feet are still high in the air. The natural result of this position and action brings a simultaneous release of the two hands and a flying "U" body position or inverted arch in which the back is arched and the feet are well balanced and well controlled; it certainly makes an easy landing more difficult. Ganslen argues strongly that all vaults over 14′ 6″ have been made with a fly-away form, but he fails to distinguish between the form of Warmerdam and Richards on the one hand and that of himself and Morcom on the other. True, all fly up from the pole and maintain upward momentum throughout; but the backward-upward folding of the legs and throw of the arms that characterizes the latter is not an easily timed or easily co-ordinated movement that the ordinary vaulter can handle without some years of practice.

The pole release. If all previous actions have been well executed, the pole release is incidental. Those using Warmerdam's style will release the lower hand first, then the upper. Both styles, however, stress a balanced, two-arm push-up. Both styles should continue the important emphasis upon keeping all action on a single plane. Warmerdam turned away from the runway at the last moment of release and landed facing away from the bar. Yet there was little lateral movement throughout. Wise coaching will insist upon maintaining the face toward the runway position until all aspects of the straight action of vaulting have been firmly fixed. After that, no harm can be done.

The landing. Concern over the dangers of an improper landing is often the primary reason for a poor vault. The pull-up and turn are hurried, the feet are not swung high over the head but make for a landing as soon as they cross the bar, and the push-up is impossible. Time, patience, and an insistence upon a simple, well-balanced form are most important. Add a mound of fine shavings (not sawdust or heavy curls of wood) at least 36 inches high, and the problem may be solved.

Balance and timing in the air are essential to a good landing. If this two-hand release comes too late and after the feet and body have dropped, it will throw the vaulter backward to a heavy landing. If the single-hand release comes as the result of the body swinging around the pole, control has been lost and anything can happen in the pit and sometimes, unfortunately, out of it as well.

With the soft built-up pits of modern vaulting (incidentally, they are just as important to high school as to college vaulters) men can plan deliberately to relax during the landing and take up some of the shock on the hips and shoulders. Meadows and Richards were unusually adept at this. The practice of making a tumbler's roll cannot be encouraged, however. It is extreme, unnecessary, and often ends up out of the pit entirely.

IMPORTANT QUESTIONS AND ANSWERS IN POLE VAULTING

What about the vaulting pit? Get ride of the pits and replace them with mounds of fine shaving at least 36 inches high, 15 feet wide, and 14 feet deep. A pit of turned-over sand or sandy loam is the best possible guarantee against good vaulting. According to Cromwell and vaulters who have toured abroad, hard and small pits have been one of the major handicaps of foreign vaulters, just as soft grass runways have been one of the primary deterrents of American javelin throwers. Certainly a similar situation exists in high schools generally. Such carelessness is usually inexcusable. Shavings are inexpensive and available almost everywhere. A canvas 15'×15' in size and well anchored will prevent the wind from scattering the shavings and the rain from getting them wet, and, incidentally, it will discourage the small neighbourhood boys from decorating the landscape.

One can judge quite accurately the success a particular school or coach has in pole vaulting by observing the type and condition of the vaulting pit, as well as of the runway itself. To remove an athlete's fear of the landing is a major step toward greater heights.

Is the use of gymnastics apparatus and exercises of value? Most certainly, as long as they supplement vaulting and are directly related to vaulting movements. It is true that the best and, in the final analysis, the only way to learn how to vault is to vault and vault and vault again.

Third, to what extent does he spring from the ground? Although a quick spring from the take-off foot tends to decrease the swing, it does aid the take-off and makes a higher hold possible. And perhaps most important of all, how well does he cushion the shock of the take-off? How smoothly does he makes his hand shift on the pole? How perfectly does he hit exactly the right spot for his take-off? How flexible is the condition of his arms and shoulders to absorb the transfer of weight to the pole and to maintain a minimum of deceleration during the swing? The combined answer to these questions is actually the only determinant of how high a particular man can grip.

On the other hand, we do have the records of great vaulters to aid us in our answer. Warmerdam leads all vaulters in the height of his grip. For heights under 15 feet he held at 12′6″. It should be noted once again that measurements of this height is secured by placing the pole vertically in the box and noting the height cleared by the right hand. A few writers, Richard Ganslen, quote hand grips that are actually measured on the pole and therefore appear about 8 inches higher than those stated here. For vaults above 15 feet, Warmerdam gradually moved his grip up to 13′ 3″. At the time, this was about 10 inches higher than any previous vaulter had ever used effectively. Sefton and Meadows gripped at 12′ 2″ for their record height of 14′ 11″, a clearance of 2′ 9″ above their grip compared with Warmerdam's 2′ 5½″ (15′ 8½″ minus 13′ 3″). Richards held at 12′ 10″ when he cleared 15′ 4¾″, Don Laz at 12′ 10″ while clearing 15′ 1¾″, Morcom at 12′4″ when making 14′9″, and Varoff at 12′ 2″ for 14′ 7⅝″. Of these men, Varoff is generally credited with being the first to use a grip above 12 feet when clearing record heights.

To state that a higher grip multiplies the problems of the vault is not to accept it as impossible. Rather, it implies greater momentum in the run, greater perfection of the various aspects of form, and more years of training. As vaulters reach heights of 16 feet and beyond, as they certainly will do, the major improvement will come through the effective use of greater momentum in the run and take-off, which will permit a higher grip on the pole. Warmerdam used 13′ 3″ in his best vaulting; yet it was his opinion that greater speed and perfection of form would make a 14-foot grip possible. If such a vaulter can achieve Warmerdam's increase of 29½ inches above his grip, one can conclude that 16′ 6″ is a practical possibility. Meadows and Sefton cleared heights that were 33 inches above their upper-hand grip, thereby making 16′ 9″ within reason and even 17 feet conceivable.

Since the grip height is allied with run-momentum, wind and runway conditions may force a slightly higher or lower grip. These should be carefully studied before and during the competition.

How should a vaulting pole be selected? It now seems clear that this will soon be no problem at all, for the Swedish steel vaulting pole, or its American equivalent, seems well on the way to supplanting both bamboo and aluminium alloy. The latter has never proved very satisfactory because of its stiffness and is now used largely for beginning vaulters and under certain practice conditions. The steel pole, in contrast, is being used by top vaulters with great success and over-all satisfaction. In action and flexibility it is very similar to the bamboo pole and requires only a slight change in timing at the top of the vault. Its advantages for transportation, weathering, and consistency of weight and strength are obvious and important. If the time should come when the local Games Committee at each meet can provide steel poles to meet the requirements of all vaulters, a great load will be lifted from the minds and shoulders of vaulters, managers, and coaches. The writer can remember many unhappy experiences of carrying a 16-foot pole over the heads of a Broadway crowd on the way to Madison Square Garden, in New York, or of being unable to secure a taxi driver who would disregard the local transportation regulations and therefore being forced to carry the pole from Broad Street station at 15th Street, in Philadelphia, to Franklin Field at 34th Street.

If critical material requirements or other considerations should eliminate the steel pole, we shall undoubtedly return to the bamboo, which has served so well although so inconsistently for so many years. The selection and maintenance of a bamboo pole are serious problems requiring careful study and proper conditions.

Bamboo varies in many respects. It varies in the length of its joints and the thickness of its walls. Longer joints and thinner walls give greater flexibility but less strength. It varies in greenness when cut and in the time and method of its drying. When overly green, it lacks resiliency; when overly dry, it cracks and breaks. Poles vary in the care with which the joint ridges have been planed and rubbed down and in the amount and manner in which tape has been applied. The degree to which each of these details is important or needed depends upon the individual vaulter and the stress he places upon the pole.

Once a satisfactory pole or poles are secured, proper care is tremendously important. When poles are plentiful and of good quality, most top vaulters will change their best pole each year. However, proper care will permit a pole to be used for several years. Rain, heat, prolonged sun, or rapid changes in temperature will ruin a pole. Dropping it to the ground when vaulting will crack it in a very short time. Removing tape from joints will hasten weathering and cracking. Standing it in the corner or laying it horizontally on only two end pegs will certainly bend it. Throughout the lay-off periods, especially during the hot summer months, a cool, slightly moist place is best, especially if the pole can be hung from its tip, as is done with javelins.

What about placement of the vaulting standards? In general, vaulters place the standards too close to the line of box. In a particular meet, the cross-bar should be located at the point of greatest height of the body. But, unfortunately, until full consistency has been gained, this point will vary from meet to meet and from vault to vault. It is better to keep the cross-bar from 12 to 18 inches back of the vertical vaulting pole and thus permits a full swing, pull-up, and push-up. Obviously, the push-up should occur as the pole approaches, a vertical and stable position. The body weight should be over the hands, of course, but inevitably will be at an angle away from the pole. This angle will be about 20 degrees on best vaults and as small as 80 degrees on poor vaults. Vaults at lower are usually made with the body at a greater angle to the pole during the push-up. For these reasons, the standards should always be placed 12 inches back of the vertical pole and should be as much as 2 feet back for low heights and for inexperienced vaulters.

Warmerdam kept his standards well back but moved them in closer after the bar reached 14′ 6″. Don Laz, of Illinois, placed the cross-bar from 2½ to 3 feet back of the take-off box on his jumps over 15 feet. From this position there is less need for hurry. The vaulter can take full advantage of the swing and still feel no urgent need for getting rid of the pole before it hits the cross-bar.

What causes a vaulter to hit his pole? In every case the cause is related to improper balance at the take-off. Most probably the shift is out of line, so that the pole starts outward rather than forward and upward. This will bring the hands to the left of the centre line upon completion of the shift, where they are incapable of taking on the weight of the body. The pole is brought in close in an effort to recover balance and comes in hard contact with the body. In most such cases, the take-off foot will be found to be the right of the centre line, thus increasing the imbalance. To coach a proper foot placement is not likely to prove successful; to coach a proper shift will be much more so. Ask the vaulter to exaggerate the forward shift so that it ends to the right of the centre line. He may not follow the suggestion completely but is likely to end up in a correct position.

What are the characteristics of a pole vaulter? Any specific and final statement of the qualities necessary to a successful pole vaulter would be folly, for a glance at the chart of pole vault records would reveal men of every height, weight, speed, and high-jumping ability. Sefton, who cleared 14′ 11″, was 6′ 3″ tall and weighed 180 pounds. In contrast, Morcom, who cleared 14′ 9″, was but 5′ 10″ tall and weighed 145 pounds. Sefton's next-best event was the discus, which he threw over 140 feet. Morcom, despite his height, cleared 6′ 7¼″ in the high jump.

Truly, this is an event of balanced compensations. To be tall has certain advantages in the take-off and push-up; but height is a disadvantage during the roll-back and pull and must be balanced by gymnastic quickness and dexterity. Speed in the run is very important, but effective use of such speed demands perfection in the shift, take-off and swing as well as quickness in the later phases of the vault. The world's greatest ultimate vaulter will be tall, extremely fast, wonderfully co-ordinated, catlike in his balance and quick control of the body while in the air, and a natural athlete in many events. But there is only one such athlete in a hundred years, and all the other thousands can clear championship heights with almost any combination and degree of the desired physical characteristics.

Speaking generally, however, every good vaulter must be an even better athlete then men in other track and field events. Not only must he be physically able to run, jump, and co-ordinate difficult stunts of balance and dexterity in the air; he must, perhaps even more vitally, have the mental traits of intelligent persistence, courage, and psychomotor poise and control beyond those required in any other event.

The need for persistence is almost painful when one considers the complexity of the event, the few attempts (perhaps 15 vaults in an afternoon) in which learning can occur, and the all-important unity of the event, which forces a complete vault even when only a single phase is being studied. In any one beginner's practice session, the wrong method is used to much more often than the right one that one wonders how any correct learning occurs at all. Yet persistent effort day for many years (Warmerdam had vaulted 16 years before he made his final world's record) does produce results. The twin of persistence is intelligent practice. There should be a clear and deliberate purpose before every vault: "My shift must come earlier on this vault", or, "My pull must come later". And there must be an immediate and intelligent reaction after each vault: "That was right that time, and it felt this way".

A man should have but three grips: one grip for warm-up jumps, one for all regular vaults including his best height, and one some two or three inches higher to be used when attempting new personal record heights or when wind and track conditions are favourable to such a high grip. If the wind is helpful and the track fast, a higher grip may be very desirable; if otherwise, the grip should probably be lowered a little. Correct placement of the grip is of great importance and calls for careful judgment.

2. Having completed all preparations some 15 to 30 minutes before competition and perhaps an hour or even

more before your first vault, either watch the other competitors in order to pick up new and worth-while ideas or, probably better, inform the pole vault official of your intentions and go back to the dressing room for complete relaxation. The event will take from one hour to four or even five hours. The less time you spend on the bench, the better. This is particularly true when weather conditions are fatiguing—too hot, too cool, too wet. Have someone you can trust watch the event and warn you when the bar approaches your vaulting height.

3. Assuming that your confidence in your check marks is well-founded, do not waste energy on low heights. Start at the greatest height you are certain to clear. In general, plan to attempt only four or five heights before your maximum efforts.

4. Be sure to warm up well before each effort. The wait between vaults is usually too long to permit constant muscular readiness.

5. In competition, do not think of the details of form. To do so might correct the detail but will probably throw off the co-ordination of the whole. Once plans are set, assume that all is well and that only the relaxation and smoothness of the action as a whole is important. This is not to imply that the vaulter should be blind to certain factual details, such as proper placement of the standards on each vault. Rather, such placement should be in accordance with a plan and with the vaulter's experience in many practice and meet vaults, and should not be shifted back and forth with the variations of each vaults.

6. Take a positive attitude toward each vault, with a quiet confidence that you will clear it the first time. To take pride in being able to clear the bar on the third and last trial, "when the chips are down", is a silly attitude. The first vault is the important one, from every competitive standpoint.

7. Tenseness and uncertainty are the greatest deterrents to best efforts. Every successful vaulter knows that the finest vaults are the easiest vaults and that after a "missed" vault at highest heights there is a memory of tenseness and poorly timed effort.

ORGANIZATION OF PRACTICE

A proper organization of practice in the pole vault is probably more important than in any other field event. The relative complexity of the vault, combined with the limited number of trials that are possible in any one practice, requires thoughtful organization of what and how much should be done.

First of all, it is essential that practice carried on consistently throughout as many months of the year as possible. Since so little can be learned in any one session and since only three practice sessions per week on vaulting is generally the limit for best progress, only months and years of vaulting will produce results. Those who state that vaulters are borne and not made are speaking only a half-truth. Obviously ability is necessary, but only that ability which is specifically trained by intelligent and consistent practice, day after day and month after month, will produce the athlete's best performances. Like distance running, a man must "live" pole vaulting if he's going to conquer it. Without question, the emphasis on year-round practice is the primary secret of the Far West's success in the pole vault, as well as of the success of those institutions, such as Yale University, that have warm indoor fieldhouses for practice throughout the winter months. Contrarily, vaulters are handicapped who must vault outdoors during the winter months, or who, indoors, have hard, unsafe mats for landing. There is a serious question as to whether such vaulting with mats does not do more harm than good. His mind is so certain to be upon a safe landing that a vaulter cannot possibly achieve the full swing, pull, and push-up with the feet high in the air, which is essential to good form.

Assuming months of practice time, the vaulter and the coach must consistently place first things first. No man can pull up properly unless his swing has had momentum, smoothness, and full length. Such a swing depends upon a balanced and correctly timed take-off; the take-off, upon the shift; and the momentum of the whole vault, upon the length and relaxed speed of the run. In reverse, emphasis must first be placed upon the run and then upon the shift, the take-off, and so forth. Men such as Hoff, of Norway, or Laz, of Illinois, have cleared record heights with little exactness of technique in the later stages of the vault, but none done so who have violated the essentials of form in the early phases.

Secondly, it should be re-emphasized that the vault is a unified movement from the first step of the run to the landing. One can therefore learn to vault only by vaulting, by practicing as a single action the full movements of the event. The use of gymnastics, of climbing ropes, and of special exercises will probably prove of great value, but it is no substitute for learning the event itself. Vault at every opportunity and with the rhythm, timing, and co-ordination of the full movement. Southern California vaulters, notably Meadows and Sefton, have made extensive use of a short run of about 50 feet in practice. It permitted them more trials and a maximum emphasis upon relaxation and ease of effort. For them such practice was worth while; perhaps it would be for others, also.

The third principle regarding practice methods advocates vaulting at close to highest heights for form. Vaulting for heights—that is, where concern is exclusively upon clearing the bar—is of little value in practice. It disrupts proper form and is or should be no criterion of what height can be cleared in the meets. A good competitor who has consistent good form will always vault higher and better in competition. Without good form, even the best competitor will be frustrated.

But the form needed in vaulting at 13 feet or more has a different timing from that needed at lower heights. Vaulting at low heights for form is therefore just as inefficient as vaulting for height.

The answer lies in putting the bar up as quickly as possible in practice to heights that are within about 6 inches to a foot of one's best height, and then in vaulting with the techniques of form clearly in mind. To make a decent vault at such a height will require full momentum in the run and in all phases of the vault. This is as it should be, for the efficient and co-ordinated use of just such momentum is the major problem to be solved in learning to vault.

Of course, individuals will vary in their reactions to such practice. Some men will lose their confidence and general co-ordination if they fail to clear the bar somewhat consistently. The least suggestion of a change in style throws them "all off", and they will need to lower the bar to a height that can be ignored. As confidence returns perhaps the greater bar height can be restored; then again, perhaps not. Humans are queer that way, sometimes.

Most coaches advocate vaulting on only three days per week during the competitive season. Some competitors like two days of rest before the meet and thus do no vaulting on Thursday or Fridays; others take their days off on Wednesdays and Fridays. In both cases, the athlete works out on Wednesday and Thursday but confines his practice to work on sprinting, running, with the pole, hurdles, or perhaps high-jumping.

On those days when vaulting is a part of the practice, the order of activity is often as follows:

1. Warm-up. Easy wind sprints, and stretching exercises that loosen muscles and tendons but do not

tire them. Several starts from the blocks at distances under 60 yards at about $\frac{7}{8}$ speed.

2. Pole vault. After two or three warm-up vaults at any height or even without a cross-bar, push the bar up rapidly. Take a full run at full vaulting speed.

Once the vaulter feels ready, he should carefully review what he hopes to accomplish in the vault today. Perhaps it is the early and smooth shift of the pole at the take-off. Perhaps it is a longer delay of the pull-up or a faster break at the hips into the roll-back position. In any case, he should get the problem clearly in mind and concentrate intelligently upon its solution. In any one practice session, only one or two details can be worked on effectively; but a practice without such specific and planned attention to form is largely wasted.

From the coach's point of view, there are two aspects to such intelligent practice. First, it helps the athlete gain a verbal understanding of best form; but much more important and difficult, it helps his muscles to understand and feel best form. "There, that vault was right. What did you do? How did it feel? Think about it, now. How did it feel?" Such methods will bring muscular understanding, which is the only kind that is really effective in motor learning.

Almost constant attention should be paid to the correct location of the take-off. The relative dependence upon a spring and a swing at the take-off will determine its exact position; but once located, it should be habitually watched to see that track and wind conditions do not change it and thereby ruin a good vault before it has a chance to get started. Practice under all weather and track conditions. Learn to handle a cross wind, a trail wind, a front wind. Know how to adjust your marks for a very hard track or for a track that is hard at first but softens rapidly under repeated vaults. You'll certainly face these problems in meets.

Vaulters should attempt constantly to channel or "groove" their vaults. That is, once the fundamentals of form have been learned, it is the sense of rhythm and relaxation and "rightness" that affords maximum momentum at the top of the vault, where it is most needed. It has been rightly said that Warmerdam contributed nothing new to vaulting other than the perfection of all aspects, of the "wholeness" of the vault from the first step of the run to the landing. What must be deliberately practiced by the experienced vaulter is this sense of a flowing rhythm and ease of movement that produces and maintains momentum naturally and easily. One can compare it to the development of distance running through pace work, which is a major key to running success.

Coaches and individuals vaulters disagree about the value of continuing on one's "bad" days or after one is tired and form has deteriorated. In most cases, it will be found best to shift to other easy work for the day, get a good night's rest, and come back refreshed tomorrow. However, it often happens that the warm-up period and early vaults go badly, whereas later vaults are excellent. Suddenly the vaulter seems to get the feel of things and a series of very valuable trials occurs. Do not assume incompetence too soon.

COMMON ERRORS AND THEIR CORRECTIONS

Since the pole vault is a gymnastic stunt involving a series of coordinated movements, errors in technique detract not only from the grace of the event, but also from the height attained. In order that they may be avoided, some of the most common errors are pointed out.

1. In the Handhold and Pole Carry

If the vaulter grasps the pole too high, he fails to generate sufficient momentum to bring the pole to an upright position. If he grasps the pole too low, he fails to gain optimum height even though he executes the event properly. One of the prerequisites to good vaulting is a knowledge of where to grasp the pole correctly in relation to the height of the crossbar. A vaulter may be inefficient in carrying the pole because he grasps it too tightly. Tenseness in the arms and shoulders is an error which prevents freedom of movement in the carry.

2. In the Approach

Common errors in the approach are excess speed, insufficient speed, inaccurate checkmarks adjustments, and a devious run. The correction of these errors is obvious from the discussion of the approach.

3. In the Pole Plant

The chief mistakes in planting the pole are lack of concentration of vision on the target, which is the centre of the stopping board, failure to hit the apron of the trough properly, and inaccuracy in combining the run and the plant.

4. In the Hand Shift

A failure to shift the left hand against the right is the most noticeable defect in this phase of the technique. As previously pointed out, this error prevents the most advantageous pull-up.

5. In the Foot-Stamp

One of the imperfections to be guarded against in this part of the vault is an incorrect position of the foot. The possibilities are planting it too far to the right or to the left, too far back or in front of that spot previously determined as correct. It is obvious that a plant in which the heel and toe are not in a line and at right angles to the crossbar detracts from a straight forward lift.

6. In the Swing-Up

Extreme muscular tension of the arms tends to retard the swing-up, and a premature pull-up checks the forward-upward momentum. If the body swing too far away from the pole, the movement becomes sideward and upward rather than forward and upward. A lack of continuity of momentum detracts from the height of the vault.

7. In the Pull-Up

Costly miscues befall the vaulter who delays his pull-up too long. The late pull-up does not permit the body to assume a position from which to make the turn, since the pole has attained a vertical position too soon. On the other hand, a premature pull-up reduces the efficacy of the pole erection. A jerky pull-up contributes to imbalance and obviously is to be avoided. An incomplete pull-up detracts from attaining height with the body, which is the major objective in vaulting.

8. In the Body Turn and Leg Scissors

Some athletes are victims of imbalance because they permit the right leg in its upward flight to rotate too far before checking it with a vigorous scissors action of the left. Others fail to keep the feet high, even though they have sufficient speed and lift to do so. Still others fail because of an incomplete turn to get the body squared away for the push-up and the throw-away. The chief method for correcting this defect consists of kicking the left leg vigorously upward and outward. The legs may then appear in a V-shaped position.

9. In the Crossbar Clearance

Vaulters who have successfully executed the pole plant, swing-up, pull-up, and body turn sometimes fail at the crisis, that is, the crossbar clearance, because they do not keep the feet at a height already attained. This means that they bend at the hips too soon. As a result, the dropping feet bring the chest against the bar, thus displacing it.

Another glaring inefficiency is a failure to extend the body to a proper handstand position. True enough, the feet and legs may have been propelled sufficiently high but may not have been used to best advantage in the leg-hip trunk momentum, which should almost straighten the arms.

10. The Push-Up, the Throw-Away, and the Landing

In case the vaulter's arms are completely straightened before the application of push-up force, proper leverage is not provided. If he should reach the push-up stage with extremely flexed arms, he is in a position to exert ample force when straightening them, but the body height suffers. The time required to extend the arms from an extremely flexed position is sometimes so long that the forward-upward momentum of the body and legs may be spent, thus causing them to displace the bar. Frequently the effectiveness of the push-up is lost because it is incomplete or is executed with less than full effort.

Among vaulters using the shoot form one notices a tendency to hasten unduly the push-up and the throw-away before the pole attains a vertical position. It is obvious that with the pole in a position other than vertical the direction of the force of the push-up is sideward rather than downward. In the jackknife form vaulters frequently permit the feet to drop considerably below the level of the handhold before the release. Thus, they put themselves in a predicament which is costly in two ways: first, the force of the push-up is effective only in lifting the shoulders rather than the whole body; and, second, this precarious position hinders the push-up and compels a hasty throw-away. A most obvious fault is a failure to lift the hands sufficiently high to clear the crossbar. The transgressions of form in the straight forward movement of the pole, the swing-up, and pull-up and the body turn manifest themselves very definitely in a faulty push-up and throw-away. The crossbar can be more easily avoided if the eyes are focused on it.

In conclusion, a properly executed vault consists of a blending of a number of movements, each depending on the one which preceded it. This can only be attained by practicing correct technique.

1. Error

The upper arm is bent during takeoff.

Reasons

Grip is incorrectly positioned in the pole. The speed of the run-up and the body position below the pole at takeoff vary.

Remedies

The athlete practices swinging on the pole with the upper arm extended, taking off from a vaulting box. Have the athlete remeasure the run-up and swing on the pole from a 5-stride run-up. Hold the pole ready in the takeoff position. The athlete should emphasize a fully extended upper arm.

2. Error

The chest hits the pole during takeoff.

Reasons

The left arm collapse and does not keep the body away from the pole. The pole does not flex.

Remedies

Use a pole that the novice can bend easily. The athlete should hang with the right arm and push with the left.

3. Error

The athlete takes off with the body too far to the side of the pole.

Reasons

The athlete is afraid of swinging on the pole and raising the legs and is not directly to the rear of the pole at takeoff.

Remedies

The athlete should work on "riding the broomstick" - swinging with one leg on each side of the pole. The athlete should be directly behind pole at takeoff.

4. Error

Legs are not elevated during the swing.

Reasons

The athlete is trying to raise the legs by pulling with the arms. The legs are raised without any flexion at the knees. The athlete may have poor abdominal strength.

Remedies

The athlete should leave the upper arm extended and raise the legs by dropping the shoulders back and bending the legs at the knees. The athlete should practice abdominal exercises.

5. Error

The swing and 1/2 rotation are not completed. The athlete performs a 1/4 rotation or none at all.

Reasons

The legs are not raised at all, there's no pull and turn action from the arms, and the head is not turned back toward the run-up. The athlete may have poor abdominal and shoulder strength.

Remedies

Instruct the athlete to practice the swing and 1/2 rotation on a rope, also the underswing dismount with 1/2 rotation on the low horizontal bar. The athlete should practice general upper body and abdominal exercises.

6. Error

The run-up is inaccurate and varies each time. The athlete slows down during the run-up.

Reasons

The athlete's ability to run with the pole is poor. The athlete is afraid of the takeoff and riding on the pole. Measurement of run-up and check marks is incorrect, and the run-up may be too long.

Remedies

Have the athlete remeasure the run-up. The athlete should practice sprinting with the pole and should work to improve sprint endurance. To improve accuracy of the approach, have the athlete practice at lower heights from a shorter run-up.

7. Error

The takeoff foot is not directly below the upper handhold at takeoff. The pole jerks in the athlete's hand at takeoff.

Reasons

The run-up is poorly measured, or the speed of the run varies with each approach. Upper arm may not be extended at takeoff.

Remedies

Have the athlete remeasure the run-up, making sure that speed used running back from the takeoff spot is same speed as the approach run. The athlete should work for smooth, regular acceleration in each run-up.

8. Error

The takeoff foot is too far to one side at takeoff.

Reasons

The athlete overemphasizes the swing to the side of the pole. The body is not directly behind the pole at takeoff.

Remedies

Instruct the athlete to practice the pole plant from a short run-up. Place orientation marks on the ground to assist in foot positioning.

9. Error

Legs and hips are poorly elevated after takeoff.

Reasons

The athlete is afraid of dropping the shoulders back and lifting the legs and has sufficient abdominal power.

There is no upward drive with the thigh of the leading leg at takeoff.

Remedies

Assign power exercises for the upper body, arms, and abdomen as well as gymnastic, rope, and pole activities in which the lower body is lifted upward.

10. Error

The athlete extends the body too early. The legs are driven toward the bar, not upward and parallel to the pole.

Reasons

Timing of the extension of the body is incorrect. The athlete is hurrying the extension of the body instead of waiting for the completion of the swing. The shoulders do not drop backward.

Remedies

Assign rock-back and extension activities using ropes and poles. Instruct the athlete to drive the feet up parallel to rope and pole. Provide verbal assistance on timing of extension.

11. Error

The pole does not bend sufficiently, and no energy is stored in the pole.

Reasons

The pole is too stiff for the weight and strength of the vaulter. The athlete's grip is too close or too low on the pole, and the lower arm is not extended and driven forward into the pole. Run-up speed prior to pole plant is too slow.

Remedies

Check pole specifications relative to athlete's body weight. Check grip height and grip width. Have the athlete practice the plant and pole bend from a short run-up.

12. Error

Vaulter and pole slow down and fail to reach a vertical position.

Reasons

The vaulter runs too slowly during the run-up, and the grip is too high on the pole. The legs and hips are elevated too early.

Remedies

Help the athlete improve sprinting ability with the pole. Check grip height and lower if necessary. Instruct the athlete to wait until the pole begins to straighten before driving upward. Provide verbal assistance on timing.

13. Error

The athlete has too little time to complete vault and knocks the bar off on the way up.

Reasons

The grip is too low on the pole, and the legs and hips are elevated too late. Extension of the body above the handhold occurs too late. The athlete's centre of gravity is not directly below the upper handhold at takeoff.

Remedies

The athlete must raise the grip on the pole. Have the athlete practice the complete vault, working to correct the timing for the elevation and extension of the body above the handhold.

14. Error

The athlete crosses the bar on his back and never achieves the facedown position over the bar. The athlete uses no rotation.

Reasons

The athlete's feet are not close together or close to the pole during the upward pull. The legs and hips drop away from the pole.

Remedies

Have the athlete practice with the rope and pole, pulling and rotating with the feet as close to the rope and pole as possible. Work to improve abdominal and upper body strength.

Assessment

1. Assess the following theoretical elements as taught during instructional sessions.
   a. Fundamental rules governing pole vault.
   b. Good safety habits for pole vault.
   c. Basic elements of pole-vault technique.
   d. Basic elements of training for pole vault.
2. Assess the performance of technique during the following stages of skill development.
   a. Vaulters run to swing on the pole, which you hold ready for them.
   b. Vaulters run to swing and perform a 1/2 turn on the pole while you hold it.
   c. Vaulters perform the plant action with the pole, using a 5-stride approach on grass.
   d. Vaulters perform the run-up, pole carry (pole at the side of the body), plant, and swing. They do not elevate the hips and legs, and no 1/2 rotation is required.
   e. Vaulters perform a run-up, pole carry (pole at the side of the body), plant, swing, and elevation of the hips and legs. No 1/2 rotation is included.
   f. Vaulters use a short run-up, plant and flex the pole without taking off.
   g. Vaulters perform the complete vault from an extended run-up.

Critical Features of technique to observe during assessment (right-handed vaulter)

a. Gripping and carrying the pole.

b. Accelerating through the run-up.

c. Pushing the pole forward and upward and taking off below an extended right arm.

d. Flexing the pole from the forward push of the left arm, combined with the downward pull of the right.

e. Flexing the legs and hips during the ride on the pole.

f. Pulling with the arms and extending the body upward close to the pole as the pole straightens.

g. Rotating 180 degrees and flexing at the hips to achieve a picked position above the bar.

h. Hyperextending and pushing away from the pole for the release and landing.

3. Hold graded competitions to develop motivation and technique.

a. Vaulters compete for height using an elementary swing and 1/2 rotation on the pole. (You assist with the pole at takeoff).

b. Vaulters compete for height using a run-up, swing, and 1/2 rotation on the pole. The vaulters carry the pole in plant position above the head during the run-up, and you assist with the pole at takeoff if necessary.

c. Vaulters compete using full competitive conditions.

PART 4
THROWING

CHAPTER 1

FUNDAMENTAL OF THROWING EVENTS

Organization

There are at least five different field events and seven different places where a track coach ought to be at any given moment of an afternoon during the winter or spring. His legs may be long and active, his eyes sharp, and his voice loud and far-carrying; but even a coach with the magical powers of Houdini finds it impossible to fulfil the requirements of such a situation. Wise coaches will recognize their personal limitations, will do what they can to organize the practice lay-out of events, and, equally important, will establish a realistic coaching method.

First consideration in the lay-out of field events should be given to meets and to the best interests of both contestants and spectators. However, it is only slightly less important to have a lay-out that provides good organization in practice. Ideally, a coach should be able to work with his sprinters and hurdlers and still be within easy seeing as well as calling distance of the shot-put, high-jump, pole vault, and perhaps other events as well. The shot circle is easily laid out. Modern jumping pits can be set almost anywhere, since they do not need to be dug but can be built above ground level with sawdust-filled burlap bags and shavings. Runways require care, of course, but the time and effort involved will pay excellent dividends. Of the hundreds of fields visited by the writer, few indicate that planning has been done along these lines. Yet a little planning would save numberless steps by the coach and help to lessen that sense of frustration which is the bedfellow of every track coach.

Secondly, a coach should seriously consider and organize some system of event captains. Every track and field situation has a captain, whether the coach likes it or not. Any time three men work together in a given event, one will assume leadership in advising the others. The question is whether this is done willy-nilly, without planning, or whether a carefully worked out method grasps all the values that are there. One successful high school coach uses the following plan: a captain for each event, track as well as field, is selected by a committee (the coach, the captain, and the manager). The coach spends special time and uses special materials in educating this captain. The captain works with and coaches all the men in his event. A period of time is agreed upon (September to January) during which there is competition on a basis of improvement within each event-group. Performances at the beginning and at the end of this period are scored on the regular international Decathlon Score Charts. The problem of having different numbers of men in each event is solved by taking an average improvement score. The members of the winning group are rewarded by a scrumptious Sunday dinner at the coach's house, and the event captain is given a very nice small cup. Other equally effective methods can be worked out, but planning in this area is essential to effective organization and coaching.

Other aspects of this matter of organization should be read and studied in the paragraphs dealing with getting and keeping the boys out.

Personal experience in field events. Personal experience is absolutely essential to a sound knowledge and to effective coaching in the field events. Actual competitive experience is desirable. Few coaches can have this privilege, but all good coaches must handle the implements and gain a feeling, both mental and muscular, for every event. Good coaching presupposes a true understanding of and insight into the fundamentals of an event as contrasted with its nonessentials. Such insight can occur only through thoughtful direct contact.

Coaching fundamentals of form. In every field event there are certain fundamentals of form and action that govern the range within which every athlete who is achieving his maximum must perform. For example, one such fundamental in the weight events is that all body positions and actions that directly affect the impetus of an implement should be along a single plane in the direction of the throw; another, in the jumps, is that a man should use to the fullest extent at all the momentum that is potentially available in the run. It is such fundamentals as these about which the coach should do his hardest thinking and on which he should do his hardest hitting in his coaching work. To spend time and wear out the patience of both coach and athlete in teaching nonessentials is wasted effort. Every time a coach calls the attention of the athlete to a "defect" in any detail of form the learner suffers a temporary loss of over-all co-ordination and confidence.

One of the leading advocates of this emphasis upon "fundamentals only" in Frank Ryan, assistance coach at Yale University in charge of field events (Fuchs in the shot, Frank in the discus, Appel in the pole vault, and many others). Ryan calmly accepts the minor idiosyncrasies his men naturally develop in their actions, but he is adamant in his emphasis upon the essentials of form. Fuchs could shake his head just before starting across the circle as much as he pleased, so far as Ryan was concerned; but let his head get out of line or balance with the action as a whole, and he'd hear about it in a hurry.

A corollary of this whole idea is distinguishing between symptoms and causes in correcting errors in form. Certain aspects of form errors are readily apparent and therefore are likely to be called to the attention of the athlete. Actually, however, these errors are merely symptoms and the real cause must be sought further back in the action. For example, a coach quickly notices that the throwing hand of a shot-putter or javelin thrower carries off to the left after the implement leaves the hand. Often the coach will then emphasize a proper follow-through and suggest that the hand should continue in the exact direction of the throw. Actually, this action is but a symptom; the true cause of the fault probably lies in the position of the feet or in the action of the right hip. Or again, in the high jump, an easily apparent dive over the bar might bring suggestions from the coach about use of the head and arms while over the bar. Yet the true cause of the dive undoubtedly goes back to the angle of take-off and the method of foot placement. To deal with causes is to teach efficiently; to coach symptoms is, reminding us again of the bit of verse, to distract the centipede unnecessarily.

Practice alone does not make perfect. Only correct and thoughtful practice can produce best results. Modern psychologists are agreed that learning does not occur by experience alone, but by experience and the insight that accompanies it. It is entirely conceivable that a correct action can be taught by coercing a man to follow exact instructions again and again and again, thus wearing a pathway through the neuro-muscular system much as a river deepens its channel and eliminates loss of water into other streams. But intelligent practice, in which the performer is stimulated to think through the how and the why of his event and his practice, will produce a better result more quickly.

Deciding which form to teach. The proper answer to this problem can be given only in terms of the particular event concerned and of the interests, plans, and abilities of the individual athletes. In general, interest and plans for the future take precedence over ability in this matter. Where determination, intelligence, and adequate time for practice, both in hours per day and in months per year, are present, a potentially "best" form can be selected. When these are lacking, that form which produces quick results most easily will be most worth while.

Often in coaching clinics coaches slight the question of why a certain man performs in a certain way by pleading "individual differences". One sometimes wonders whether it is not their own uncertainty or, worse, their own carelessness of thinking and coaching that produces their answers. It is true that there is a range of deviation (called "tolerance of error" in industry) from what might be called "perfect" forms within which great performances may result. For example, both Fuchs and Fonville put the shot about the same distance, over 58 feet. If force can be assumed to result from a combination of power and momentum and 58 feet is assumed to equal 10 units of force it can be logically stated that Fuchs accumulated his 10 units through combining 6 units of power with 4 units of momentum, whereas Fonvile totalled 10 by combining 4 units of power with 6 units of momentum.

In similar fashion, there can be a certain deviation from all aspects of correct form, yet always within the range of tolerance. To state another example, the toe of the left foot can be placed against the toe-board exactly in line with the centre line of the circle, where it provides maximum bracing effect and maximum power, or it can land about 15 inches to the left of the centre line where it permits the hip to come through with maximum speed. It is entirely conceivable that new world's record in the shot can be made in which the left foot is at any point within this range of tolerance. If far to the left, momentum will be a major factor; if on the centre line, power will be the major factor. Both 6 plus 4 and 4 plus 6 are equal to 10. To argue, as some coaches do, against the establishment of correct form on the basis of individual differences is to indicate a misunderstanding of these considerations as well as of the basic similarity of all human beings.

Relaxation and co-ordination. These two words express almost the same meaning, although with a slightly different emphasis. Co-ordination is more generally understood than relaxation. It is the harmonious and efficient working of muscles to produce a given action. The flow or timing of muscular contraction, the degree of contraction of each muscle group, the exactly timed relaxation of opposing muscles, and the complete relaxation of unrelated muscles are all essentials to a well-co-ordinated movement. Similarly, a relaxed action in sports involves these same essentials but emphasizes the last two, the relaxation of opposing and unrelated muscles.

Certainly relaxation does not in any way imply a less forceful effort. On the contrary, force can only be created at a maximum level when complete relaxation of appropriate muscles is present. To relax is to concentrate action within those muscle groups that produce the wanted movement. It is a channelling of effort rather than a lessening of effort.

Perhaps the simplest illustration lies in the biceps and triceps of the arm, the actions of which are opposed to each other. The biceps pull objects toward the body; the triceps push away. If, in attempting a chinning exercise, both muscles contract equally, no action can occur. If an effort to pull up as quickly as possible includes any concentration of the triceps (the "push away" muscles) or, incidentally, of the facial or neck muscles, a tense action results that is relatively slow and fatiguing. In contrast, a relaxed all-out chinning effort involves complete and immediate contraction of the biceps and complete relaxation or inaction of the triceps and all unrelated muscles. Only relaxed efforts are best efforts.

For an athlete to understand these matters verbally or mentally will not insure his understanding them organically or muscularly, but in almost all cases it will help. Attempts at clearer understanding will pay dividends.

Teaching momentum. Until an athlete has gained a little skill in the basic co-ordinations of his event, the momentum with which he performs should be either ignored or restrained. For example, in the javelin throw, until a man knows how to hold the shaft, or to pull it straight through over the shoulder so that its flight is high and smooth and ends in a one-point landing, the momentum of the run preceding these actions is entirely secondary.

On the other hand, the teaching of momentum during the early phases of the form should not wait until the various parts of the action have been perfected. An athlete may perfect the co-ordination of an event while moving slowly and then discover, when he speeds things up, that his balance and skill are upset and that he must learn things over again. In the discus, for example, balance is so precarious that coaches and athletes tend to cut down momentum whenever it seems to interfere with balance. From the standpoint of immediate results, this practice is usually effective. But when greater performances are needed and greater momentum in the turn is attempted, balance again is lost and must be learned all over again. Each time a new level of performance is sought, each time a faster run is attempted, the same difficulty is encountered.

It is the carefully considered opinion, which gains in certainty with each year of coaching experience, that momentum should either be allowed to take its natural course (which almost always means high momentum) or should be deliberately introduced into the learning process as early as possible. That is to say, once the basic co-ordinations are reasonably well established, movement with momentum should be a regular part of the daily practice schedule. Best possible performances will thereby be achieved most efficiently and most rapidly.

This point of view is consistent with the findings of time and motion studies in industry and psychology. For example, Viteles summarizes such findings as follows:

On the whole, it seems well to insist that the initial emphasis in training should be upon good habits of work. This should be followed quickly by an emphasis upon fast work. In this way it is possible to profit from a joint stabilization of correct and fast movements into a fixed habit of work embodying the advantages of speed and accuracy in production.

Practising for form versus practising for distance or height. Every recognized authority on this question agrees that the emphasis in practice work should be placed upon form rather than upon height or distance. Cromwell, for example, believes that "in training for the event the athlete should work for a long time on form only, letting distance come gradually as technique is perfected".

Similarly, Miller summarizes the opinion of various athletes by writings:

Emphasis on maximum performance causes the boy, especially the beginner, to forget form. This both retards the learning process and increases the chances of injury. An occasional maximum effort in practice may be needed to decide team places or as a motivating device. But in general, the high school practice sessions should be devoted to perfection of form with only occasional near maximum or maximum performance.

Nor does the writer wish to disagree basically with this point of view. On the contrary, athletes and other coaches have accused him many times of harping on form to the exclusion of distance and even gold medals. "Do it right and the gold medals will take care of themselves" is a reasonably safe point of view in coaching. Until a fair mastery has been gained of the basic co-ordinations of field events, the speed with which they are executed should not be emphasized. But this is not to say that momentum and distance should be consciously reduced. On the contrary, they are an essential part of good form and as such should be encouraged along with right position and right balance. The important element in all such question is attitude and attention. As long as the athlete's attention is upon learning, upon method and position, and upon the how of performance, the distance to which the implement may go in practice is a matter of secondary concern. The emphasis then should never be upon holding back distance but rather upon keeping the mind on forms. It may be argued that we have merely run around the question rather than answering it; but the difference indicated here is an important one. It places a positive emphasis upon from where it is needed, but it removes the negative approach to distance, which is the best of all incentives to practice. The difference in approach will permit pegs to be placed in the landing spots in practice and a steel tape to be present at all times. The athlete will be aware of how far the throws or puts are going, but it will be what might be called in psychology an associate and secondary awareness, whereas consciousness of form and method will be primary. "Put it as far as you can, as long as your mind is on putting it right" combines sound learning and good fun.

In summary, then, the case might be stated as follows:

Correct form is basic to successful performance in the field events so that, if a choice must be made, right position and good balance should precede momentum and distance in both time of learning and emphasis.

However, approached realistically, proper form includes both momentum and explosive force and cannot be separated from them. In the weighing of emphasis upon whole versus part learning methods, part learning must form the basis for understanding and development, but only actions of the whole event and the whole body can be considered true learning. Both body momentum and explosive force require practice just as much as position itself, if not more. The value to a 50-foot shot-putter of a practice put under 47 feet is limited. To practice on so-called form—that is, right position of all body parts—on Monday, Tuesday, Wednesday, and Thursday, and then to expect competitive spirit to pull momentum and explosiveness out of nowhere is completely to misunderstand the elements of motor learning.

The final answer, then, does not lie in a negative approach to throwing for distance, but rather in a continuous and positive emphasis upon form, with distance simply taken for granted.

Work. The related problems of how much work is excessive, of how many throws of any kind can be productively taken in practice, or of how many throws for distance are possible day after day are increasingly coming to the attention of athletes and coaches today. One athlete is reported to be working longer and harder than ever before. Somehow the others cannot let him outdo them, so they work even harder and longer than he does.

Many wise and well-balanced coaches believes there are limitations on both time and work established by the demands of more important factors, those of academic studies and preparation for a lifework. They insist that a high school or college student has neither the time nor the energy to do justice to his schoolwork and still practice on a maximum basis. Further, they believe that amateurism is not merely of not being paid for one's efforts but also of keeping sports in their appropriate place, a place that is secondary to mental achievement and to service to one's associates and society. For them—it would be honoured to be included in their number—the problem of work is not so much one of physical capacity as one of relative social and personal values. In the writer's opinion, this, and not the question of subsidization and scholarships, is the crucial problem in college athletics today.

However, in extra-academic circles and, unfortunately, in those educational institutions that have lost their sense of values, the pros and cons of physical capacity will be uppermost. Entirely apart from what should or should not be, one is convinced that we have only begun to work. The demand for an ever greater degree of excellence is a primary one in human affairs and it has certainly not run its course. That we can work harder and longer seems self-evident. The modern dance, for instance, which involves intricate and rapid movements, demands from 30 to 40 hours of rehearsal each week for many weeks. Professional gymnasts and acrobats often work twice a day for several hours each time in perfecting their acts, many of which involve strength and fatiguing exercises. How, then, can we assume there is danger that we are overworking, or that we may become muscle bound? In every event on the track and field program, one can conceive of improvements in either form or momentum in even our greatest champions. As long as that is true, better records are possible and will be achieved through longer hours of more intense work.

Obviously, relatively poor physical condition places limitations upon both intensity and length of effort, but the final answer lies not so much in doing little work as in gradually improving body condition and being able to do more work.

The statement has been made here that increased emphasis upon momentum is the greatest reason for present-day improvement in the weights. But proper use of momentum, so that it includes balance and smooth integration of all movements, presupposes regular practice on an eight- or ten-months basis. Only by such practice can a man gain the exactness of form and the perfect consistency of action that are absolutely essential to best efforts. Only where consistency in all the phases of action has been established with a minimum of deviation; only when the right foot always comes out of the back of the circle in exactly the same way or when the left foot always hits the toe-board at exactly the same spot and in exactly the same position can a shot-putter concentrate his explosive energies on maximum distance.

As long as the emphasis is upon fast actions and explosive power rather than slow strength, there is no danger of becoming muscle-bound in the weight events or of losing one's spring permanently in the jump events, any more than there is danger of losing one's speed through ten months of "speed-play" in the case of distance running. Further, as long as the athlete keeps his mind on his objective clearly and certainly, there is no danger of going stale. Some coaches will accuse the writer of taking all the fun out of track and of overemphasizing its values. Yet the drive toward excellence knows few if any reservations or limitations. More than that, enthusiasm and fun are not the exclusive possession of the dilettante or the "take it easy" specialists. There is not fun like work if you enjoy the work.

This is written in the full knowledge that few writers and coaches take so positive an attitude toward work. The tendency for weight men to play football means that the shot is likely to be done on a minimum basis. Coaches have therefore toward the weight men an attitude quite different from their attitude toward the distance runners. Yet the problem is basically the same.

In a very real sense, the important question is not, "How hard should I work in the field events?", but rather, "How much does excellence in performance mean to me?" Coaches, therefore, should devote at least as much attention to establishing incentives and motivating practice as they do to form itself.

For example, the following methods have been used with good results in creating proper incentives:

1. See that men in field events get as many chances for trips and for competition as do the runners—that is, that not merely the one best man but two or three or more be included if they have a chance to place.
2. Work actively toward the inclusion of all field events in all meets and toward the placement of such events directly in front of the spectators. Thirty minutes spent filling the holes made by the shot in the football filed in May or June will completely hide them in September.
3. Encourage the scheduling of dual meets in which the combined distances of three or even four men in each field event decide the team score.
4. Place a special "Progress Chart" for each field event on the team bulletin board or even on the general school record board. Select improvement records of appropriate local starts for comparison.
5. Set up special medals for the most improvement or for outstanding performance in all field events.

In creating fun in practice the following measures have proved effective:

1. Be enthusiastic about each event yourself. As a rule, wherever one finds a series of outstanding performers in any given field event, one also finds a coach who is especially enthusiastic about this

event. Enthusiasm, of course, must be based upon sound knowledge and a certain personal experience with the event.

2. Permit as much trying for distance as the demands of good form will permit. Only the very exceptional athlete will be happy when forced to work on form only. As a matter of fact, there is a serious question, in the light of present-day emphasis upon momentum, whether any such restriction on distance is desirable.

3. Encourage competition in practice between shot-putters, on a handicap basis where necessary. Have a 48- or 5-foot arc drawn before they arrive on the field. Keep a chart of wins and losses for the season and then have a little celebration for fun—a party, with special pie or cake or ice cream for the winner. Betting should be kept out of the picture entirely, but a special prize "for fun" will work wonders.

4. Keep the men working together. Not only will they have more fun, but they will get more done as well.

5. Have the men work in spurts. "Work fast and hard for a while, make as many jumps or throws as you can; then rest for a while, and start in again".

6. Have a workout plan each day, as you would for distance runners. There is much to be done and little time in which to do it. Therefore, there is no reason for standing around, watching other performers, or wondering what to do next. Such practices are always a sign of poor motivation and probably of poor coaching.

The Weight Events

A proper understanding of the weight events must be based upon five fundamental aspects of form: (1) the building of greatest usable body momentum, (2) the co-ordination of this momentum with (3) the greatest possible body force acting through (4) a maximum time-distance, and at (5) the most productive trajectory.

In addition, coaches and athletes must understand certain matters common to all weight events, such as how much and what kind of work is desirable, the meaning of explosive power in human action, or the significance of individual differences in form. It is the intent of this section to further such understanding.

Body momentum. The accumulation of body momentum occurs during the early stages of a weight event. It occurs during the run in the javelin, during the glide in the shot, and during the turn in the discus. Its importance cannot be overestimated in achieving best performance, even in an event like the shot, where a tiny 7-foot circle places body momentum at rather minimum levels. In the javelin, achieving momentum is no problem at all; the difficulty here is in making proper use of it.

It is the carefully considered opinion that the great progress that has been made in weight events during the past quarter century has occurred primarily through increased momentum and its more efficient use, and that future progress will occur along similar lines.

Momentum is not something to be added to good form after balance and co-ordination have been fully achieved; it is an essential part of it. Good form in the field events can be considered only in terms of the correct actions with momentum.

It is not a series of proper positions such as one sees in sequence pictures of form. It cannot be demonstrated by doing all the phases of form "perfectly", although at slow speed. Correct form implies "form-with-speed" as a single indivisible concept.

The co-ordination of body momentum with body force. For convenience of understanding and discussion, we may think of body force as beginning from a stationary position, and equalling that speed-power or explosive power which the muscles of the body, acting with maximum efficiency, can generate. The problem of co-ordinating body momentum with such force is fundamentally the same in all weight events, subject of course to their particular limitations and elements. Basically, it is a matter of stopping momentum of the lower parts of the body so that their accumulated power can be concentrated toward the upper extremities and the implement involved. The whip concept is valuable to understanding. The velocity of the tip of the whip is dependent upon four factors: (1) the forward momentum of the stock or handle, (2) the shortness of time and space within which this momentum is stopped, (3) the length of the whip, and (4) its flexibility.

Similarly, these four factors are active in each of the weight events. In the javelin, the basic advantage of the Finnish cross-step style lies in the shortness of space and time within which body momentum is stopped. It occurs within the short length of a single stride, a simple placement of right and left feet, and a throw.

In contrast, the stopping of forward momentum in the now discarded back-cross-step style involved the space of three full strides, thereby making momentum almost useless. In the shot put, the traditional emphasis upon a somewhat closed stance, with the left foot hard against the toe-board and stopping the forward motion of the lower body, is an effective device.

This same device is present in the discus despite its use of a turn. In all three events, body height is an aid to implement velocity, and of course flexibility of the throwing arm, wrist, and fingers is an important factor.

The whip concept is only partially in point, for the body has force within itself by which to accelerate velocity. In general, early attempts to learn right form emphasized this factor. Proper placement of feet, right use of the hip, back and abdominal muscles, and a full follow-through were of almost exclusive concern. Exercises that produce an increase in muscle power were stressed, and body momentum across the circle was seldom permitted to interfere with good balance and co-ordination. The problem today is different. Performances in nearly all meets are now at such a high level that only a combination of both maximum momentum and maximum force will prove effective.

Maximum time-distance. The velocity of a shot or other implement is determined by the acting force multiplied by the time-distance through which it acts, divided by the mass of the subject. The factor of time-distance in which force can be applied and thereby made to accelerate a given implement is therefore extremely important.

Hence the development of a straight-forward action and a full follow-through. Hence the great value of the form of Jim Fuchs in the shot put, with his extreme backward lean and very low position. As compared with other putters, he thereby increased by at least a foot the distance within which force could be applied. Again, this is the advantage that the American hop style in the javelin possesses.

The hop permits a greater turn of the body to the right as well as a greater backward reach with the javelin. The problem here is whether this advantage is not more than offset by the resulting loss in body momentum.

Trajectory. In general, the science of ballistics states that 45 degrees is the most effective angle for propelling an object such as the shot or javelin. The shape of a discus, however, introduces the problem of wind resistance, and the difficulty of obtaining such an angle of release without meeting such resistance. For many years, coaches and athletes have assumed that 45 degrees was too high an angle for the human body to use effectively.

The construction of our joints and tendons did not make such a high put or throw of practical use. Yet, today, the greatest champions are throwing at exactly 45 degrees in both the shot and the javelin, and, when wind conditions are right, in the discus as well. Further, in all three events, it is agreed that acceleration occurs best when applied along a single line or plane of action. There are no longer any dips, crouches, or lifts that are out of line with the throw.

CHAPTER 2

IMPORTANT TESTS FOR FIELD ATHLETE

Available tests which may be applied to field athletes are numerous. Generally speaking, they fall into two classes: first, those which measure an individual's condition at the present time, and, second, those which predict what one may expect of him in the future. An examination of these tests reveals the fact that many of them are questionable as practical instruments since their reliability as measuring sticks has not been definitely established. On the other hand, many of them, even though they have been definitely proved to be reliable, are so complicated that they are not practical. Many useful tests cannot be employed in an applied way since they require expensive apparatus and highly technical procedures. There are, however, some representatives of both general classes of tests which are planned for practical use by coaches. Those tests which are described and discussed in our judgment simple enough and sufficiently reliable to merit use.

Soon after the coach calls the squad for practice he begins to concern himself with the physical efficiency of the group. No doubt, rules, regulations, and suggestions have been made relative to diet, sleep, rest, and the daily schedule of practice. For this particular phase of the coach's work, he makes use of whatever available tools he has at hand. For the most part, objective measures are lacking, and he must resort to subjective observations.

In addition to knowing the physical condition of the athletes, as the practice schedule proceeds, a coach is often in a quandary as to whether certain members of the squad are in condition or if they are up to par as an important meet approaches. Perhaps a high-point man reports with symptoms of illness; the question may arise as to the feasibility of using him in an event. Up to now, the coach has had to answer these questions more or less on the basis of subjective observations.

A Test for Physical Efficiency

Wide use and study of the pulse-ratio test has demonstrated that it furnishes an objective method for answering, quite satisfactorily, many of the questions about physical efficiency. In view of this fact, it is described in some detail.

1. Definition of the Pulse-Ratio Test

The pulse-ration test is based on the ability of the heart to compensate for exercise. The pulse ratio is defined as the ratio of the pulse rate after exercise to the normal sitting pulse rate. It is found by dividing the pulse rate for two minutes immediately following exercise by the normal sitting pulse for one minute. For example, if the normal sitting pulse is 70 per minute and the total pulse for two minutes immediately following exercise is 210, then the pulse ratio is 210/70 or 3.00.

2. Why the Pulse Ratio is an Index to Physical Efficiency

It has been conclusively demonstrated that physical training has a marked effect not only on the normal resting pulse rate, but also on the time required for the heart to return to normal after exercise. As physical training progresses, the heart rate becomes slower. Heart rates of 50 or less are not at all uncommon among trained athletes. It has been proved also that with the cessation of training, the athlete's heart returns to its pretraining level. On the basis of these facts, a failure of the athlete's heart to return to a pretraining level is a sign of lack of compensation.

In addition to the rate change, it has been shown that physical training shortens materially the time required for the heart rate to become normal after exercise. It is upon this principles that the pulse-ratio test depends. For example, an athlete with a pretraining pulse ratio of 3.00, after a prescribed exercise, will experience a decrease in this ratio as training progresses and as he becomes physically more efficient.

By use of the pulse-ratio test, it is obvious that the progress of physical efficiency can be followed throughout the season of competition. In addition, alterations in efficiency brought about by breaking training or by approaching disease can be detected readily.

3. How to Measure Physical Efficiency with the Pulse-Ratio Test

In order to find the physical efficiency of an individual, the amount of a standard exercise required to produce a pulse ratio of 2.50 is determined. The pulse ratio 2.50 is an arbitrary figure adopted solely for purposes of comparison. This value was selected since experience with the test showed that in most healthy individuals 2.50 fell somewhere between that resulting from the light exercise and that produced by the more strenuous exercise. This requires (1) a standard exercise, (2) efficiency in counting the pulse, and (3) a method for finding the exercise corresponding to a 2.50 pulse ratio.

1. The Standard Exercise—Considerable investigation has been carried on to find a standard

exercise suitable for the pulse-ratio test. Experimentation led to the adoption of stool-stepping. This is an exercise which can be performed almost equally well by all normal individuals. For sake of uniformity, a stool 13 inches high has been adopted. For testing purposes, the act of stepping on the stool is described as follows: The athlete is seated in such proximity to the stool that when he stands, he is in a position to begin stepping. At the count of one, the right foot is placed on the stool; at the count of two, the individual steps up with the left foot. Now, he is in an upright position on the stool. At the count of three, he steps down backward with the right foot, and at the count of four, the left foot is placed on the floor. Now, the athlete is standing in front of the stool ready to repeat the stepping. Of course, the footedness of the individual may make it desirable to start with the left foot, in which case the foot sequence is reversed. The exercise should be continued for exactly one minute.

The stool-stepping must be carried our in regular cadence. This can be maintained by counting or by following the beat of a metronome. The latter method is preferable since advantage can be taken of calibration, and the movements can be synchronized better.

Flexibility in the amount of exercise is one of the requirements of the pulse-ratio test. Stool-stepping meets this requirement, since by varying the rate of stepping, the amount of exercise done per minute can be changed.

2. Efficiency in Counting the Pulse—Although counting the pulse, at first thought, seems to be a simple procedure, investigations have shown that practice, together with care and uniformity of procedure are necessary for reliable determinations. For the pulse-ratio test, normal sitting pulse is recommended. This may be obtained by counting the heart beats at the wrist or by placing a stethoscope over the heart. Perhaps the latter

is preferable since our hearing is more sensitive than our touch. Time should be recorded by a stop watch. The sitting pulse is considered normal when, in three full one-minute counts, with one minute elapsing between each count, the same values are obtained. Of course, a variation of a beat or two may be disregarded.

The determination of the pulse rate for the two minutes after exercise should begin the instant both feet are on the floor after the last trial of the prescribed exercise. The beginning of the count is important since compensation begins very shortly after the cessation of exercise.

3. A method for Finding the Exercise Which Corresponds to 2.50 Pulse Ration—It is obvious that considerable difficulty would be encountered if an attempt were made to fit an exercise to any given pulse ratio by the process of experimentation and elimination. However, it is easy to find the exercise corresponding to any pulse ratio by combining experimentation and calculation.

It has been proved that for normal hearts the response varies directly with the intensity of the exercise and that this relationship is rectilinear, that is, follows a straight line. This being true, it follows that by establishing two pulse ratios corresponding to two standard exercises of different intensities, the exercise corresponding to any pulse ratio falling between those experimentally established can be mathematically calculated.

To determine the amount of exercise necessary to produce a 2.50 pulse ratio, using the number of stool-steps as the exercise, the procedure is as follows: An exercise of, say twenty stool-steps per minute, is selected; it will produce a pulse ratio slightly but definitely above 2.00. Then a more strenuous exercise, say thirty steps per minute, is performed; this will produce a pulse ratio greater than the first but well within the physiologic limits of the heart. Now, by plotting the pulse ratio corresponding to each exercise against the exercise in steps per minute, two points are established and are connected by a straight line. This curve forms the basis for calculating the pulse ratio for any exercise, or the exercise corresponding to any pulse ratio, falling between the points established on the curve.

After the pulse ratios are established for the light and the strenuous exercises, either of the following methods for calculating the number of steps equivalent to any intermediate pulse ratio may be employed.

A. The data may be plotted on graph paper. The pulse ratios are plotted on the ordinate and the number of steps on the abscissa. Now, by dropping an ordinate from any point between those points experimentally established, the number of steps for any intermediate pulse ratio can be found.

B. A more accurate method for calculating the number of steps corresponding to an intermediate ratio consists of substituting in the formula:

$$e = \frac{e_2 - e_1}{r_2 - r_1}(r - r_1) + e_1$$

Where e equals any desired exercise; e_1 the less intense exercise in number of steps; e_2 the strenuous exercise in number of steps; r_1 the pulse ratio corresponding to e_1; r_2 the pulse ratio corresponding to e_2; and r the ratio corresponding to e.

In both methods of calculation, the pulse ratio should be carried to two decimal places.

Eighteen steps for one minute in recommended as the light exercise, since for most individuals it produces a pulse ratio slightly but definitely about 2.00. Forty steps for one minute is recommended for the strenuous exercise, since in most cases it produces a pulse ratio well above 2.50 but within the limits of normal cardiac response.

The flexibility of the pulse-ratio test permits the shifting of the exercise in number of steps so that it may be more or less strenuous. For example, if eighteen steps per minute fail to raise the ratio definitely above 2.00, then twenty steps may be substituted. If forty steps per minute fail to raise the pulse ratio above 2.50, then fifty steps may be used. This latter figure is approaching the upper limit of stool-stepping ability, since sixty steps per minute is the maximum speed at which the exercise can be correctly performed.

The Interpretation of Physical Efficiency on the Basis of the Pulse-Ratio Test

If one wishes to set up a program for following the physical efficiency of the members of the squad through the season of training and competition, the first procedure at the beginning of the season is to determine the amount of exercise required, in terms of steps, of each individual to produce a 2.50 pulse ratio. These values then should be charted and the test repeated at weekly intervals or at any time that the coach desires.

As the athlete improves in physical efficiency through training, the amount of exercise required to produce a 2.50 pulse ratio will become greater. Any marked decrease in the number of steps necessary to produce a 2.50 pulse ratio may be interpreted as meaning that the athlete has broken training, is suffering from the approach of sickness, or has grown stale. Such discoveries prepare the coach for remedial measures.

The success which one attains in the use of the pulse-ratio test depends in a great measure on the adequacy of the technique involved in securing the values. Such items as counting the pulse and uniformity in stool-stepping have been mentioned. In addition, the test should be given at some uniform time when the athlete is free from undue fatigue and when his daily routine is free from outstanding deviations. Loss of sleep or undue exertion before a test will give misleading results.

The Detection of the Abnormal Heart

Good practice recognizes the importance of the physical examination. Perhaps, if this procedure is followed, the abnormal heart will not be a problem. However, although this procedure is highly recommended, it cannot be practical everywhere. In view of this fact, a simple method, designed for detecting noncompensated organic lesions, that is, those which demand restricted exercise, has been devised.

1. The Basis of the Test

It has been demonstrated, as previously stated, that the response of the normal heart, whether in the grade school child or the adult, varies directly with the strenuousness of the exercise and that the relationship is rectilinear.

It has been just as conclusively demonstrated that the abnormal heart does not conform to this law. Since this is true, by testing the heart and determining whether its response to exercises of graded intensity is rectilinear, we have a means for detecting the decompensated heart.

2. Technique for Detecting the Abnormal Heart

The basis of this method is the pulse ratio which has been described. The procedure is as follows: An exercise, for example, eighteen steps per minute for one minute, is performed on a stool 13 inches high, the resulting pulse ratio being distinctly above 2.00. Then a more strenuous exercise, say forty steps per minute for one minute, is performed, which gives a pulse ratio materially greater than the first, but well within the cardiac limit. Now, since the increase in heart rate in the normal individual varies directly with the intensity of the exercise and the relationship is rectilinear, one can mathematically determine the pulse ratio corresponding to any exercise between eighteen and forty steps. This is done by the formula

$$r = \frac{r_2 - r_1}{e_2 - e_1}(e - e_1) + r_1$$

Where r is the ratio required; r_1 the ratio corresponding to e_1; r_2, the ratio corresponding to e_2; e, the number of steps corresponding to r; e_1, the less intense exercise; and e_2, the more intense exercise.

Suppose that eighteen steps of the standard exercise gave a pulse ratio of 2.18 and that forty steps increased it to 2.66. By the formula, one can calculate the pulse ratio for any number of steps between eighteen and forty. Let us take twenty-five steps. The ratio corresponding to this amount of exercise is 2.33. The next procedure is to find experimentally the pulse ratio corresponding to twenty-five steps by having the athlete actually perform the exercise. Now, if the heart is normal, the calculated and experimental ratios will coincide. If the two ratios vary more than 0.05, a decompensated organic lesion is suspected. A person with this type of ration should be reexamined and, if the difference persists, should be thoroughly examined by a physician. If the discrepancy between calculated and experimental ratios is 0.1 or more, there is but little doubt that the athlete has a heart disease and should be eliminated from the squad. The pulse-ratio technique for detecting abnormal hearts holds for grade school children as well as for adults.

The success which one meets in using the pulse-ratio test for detecting abnormal hearts depends entirely upon the proficiency of one's technique. The acquisition of good technique can be proved by applying the test to a few individuals known to have normal hearts. As soon as one is able consistently to establish calculated and experimentals values which closely coincide, the technique is evidently mastered.

A Method for Evaluating Endurance

Everyone recognizes the importance of developing

endurance in those competitors who are to participate in athletic competition, especially the longer races. During the training period and season of competition, it is very convenient, as well as essential, that the coach be provided with a test which is reliable for evaluating endurance. Such a test furnishes a means by which one can follow the development of the endurance of a team and evaluate it at any resulted in the development of an endurance index which has been proved sufficiently reliable to warrant its use.

1. The Endurance Index

The endurance index is based on the responsiveness of the heart to exercises of graded intensity and was determined by correlating a test of endurance with the number of stool-steps required to produce a 2.50 pulse ratio. It was sponse of the heart to exercises of graded intensity was sufficiently great to indicate a very high degree of relationship.

2. The Interpretation of the Endurance Index

For predicting endurance on the basis of the pulse-ratio test, indices are given for individuals varying in endurance from very poor to excellent. For example, a competitor who requires only seventeen steps, endurance index 3.80, to produce a pulse ratio of 2.5 has poor endurance, while one who requires forty-five steps, endurance index 3.20, to produce a pulse ratio of 2.5 is in very excellent condition as far as endurance is concerned. The competitor who requires twenty-eight steps, endurance index 3.55, to produce a 2.5 pulse ratio shows average endurance.

The procedure for making practical application of the endurance indices is as follows: first, determine the number of stool-steps required to produce a 2.5 pulse ratio. Should a member of the squad fall above 3.55, he is below average, while if his index is lower than this figure, he has better than average endurance.

It is obvious that by keeping a continuous check on the squad, information is at hand at all times relative to the development of endurance during training and the maintenance of it during the season of competition.

A Method for Estimating Track and Field Ability

When the track coach for prospective candidates for the various events on the program, the first question which presents itself is, which of these candidates possesses the greatest potential ability for this type of sport? An immense amount of time can be saved in selecting prospective candidates for training for varsity competition, if one makes use of a reliable test for estimating potential ability. Persons interested in this problem have carried on a vast amount of research in an attempt to provide such a test. The results of these investigations have given us a test for the purpose of estimating potential track and field ability, which has proved sufficiently reliable to deserve use as an aid in selecting prospective candidates.

The principles and techniques used in the development of this index are too complicated and involved for consideration here. However, the information necessary for making practical use of the test is presented.

1. An Index for Estimating Track and Field Ability

In order to score a prospective candidate, the following computations are made: 20×age in years + 6× the height in inches + weight in pounds + 10×sargent jump in centimeters. If a candidate seventeen years old has an index of 1,580, the prediction is then that he is in the upper 5 per cent on the basis of potential ability and should turn out to be among the best track and field performers. If this same candidate scores only 1,249, he is in the lower 10 per cent on the basis of potential track and field ability and will probably never attain much success. By the use of the formula, a good estimate as to what to expect from candidates as far as potential ability is concerned can be obtained.

The only technique involved in this test which requires practice is the Sargent jump.

2. The Sargent Jump

The technique for scoring the Sargent jump is simple. The competitor to be tested stands erect in an 18-inch circle close to a wall upon which is a centimetre scale. He is instructed to swing his arms downward and backward with the body inclined slightly forward and the knees bent to about a 90-degree angle. This approximates the body position assumed preceding a standing high jump. From this position the competitor jumps upward as high as possible, swinging his arms violently upward and forward to a vertical position. Then the individual is instructed to swing the arms downward and forward just before the highest point of the jump is reached. The end of the downward swing of the arms is timed to coincide with the end of the upward jump. At this moment the body is straight and the top of the head has reached its highest point.

With the competitor in an erect position close to the scale on the wall, his height is measured in centimeters. The highest point which the crown of the head reached during the jump is recorded. The difference between standing height and the height jumped is the Sargent jump score.

It is recommended that before the individual jumps for height he be permitted to practice for a few times so as to sure of the technique of the jump.

The Importance of the Testing Program

Some coaches have the idea that tests are more or less playthings for research and are of no practical use to them. It cannot be denied that there is some ground for such an opinion, since in the past many coaches have sacrificed the time of their squad for test validation and have realized nothing in return. It might be pointed out also that many times the impression is left that the use of tests involves complicated mathematical manipulations, technical complications and time consumption which are not warranted on the basis of value derived. All of these things may be true regarding many tests. However, the coach owes it to himself to become familiar with tests which are simple to administer and at the same time reliable. One may make successful use of tests, even though he cannot sacrifice time from coaching and other duties to master the theories and procedures which were involved in their development.

A test which requires the hand of the expert to administer and interpret is beyond the reach of the great majority simply because such experts are not available. This is not a legitimate reason for the coaching profession to misjudge the whole testing program, because there are many useful tests which are reliable and not time-consuming and which fill well into the practice schedule. The importance of the testing program cannot be denied and is worthy of the consideration of all those interested in efficiency in the development and maintenance of a track and field team.

CHAPTER 3

THE HISTORY OF SHOT PUT

The story of improvement in shot-putting can be rather clearly developed by dividing its history into five periods: 1896-1910, typified by Ralph Rose; 1910-1920, period of little progress and no great performances; 1920-1930, typified by Houser and Hirschfeld; 1930-1940, Torrance and the 1939 National Collegiates; 1940 to date, featured by Fonville, Fuchs, and O'Brien.

1896-1910. Throughout this period there was undoubtedly extensive experimentation by the comparatively few athletes and coaches who were interested in the shot. The event was new and limited in style only by the small 7-foot circle. Most progress was made by a very few men who worked hard on style for many years. For example, G. R. Gray, of Toronto and the New York Athletic Club, first set the world's record at 43′ 11″ in 1887, raised it to 47 feet in 1893, and continued to compete, winning his last American title at 46′5″ in 1902, after more than 15 years of continuous competition. Similarly, Denis Horgan, of Ireland, continued to compete until the age of 43, winning his first English title in 1893, his last in 1912, and establishing a new world's record of 48′ 2″ in 1900. The greatest putter of this period, both in performance and in physical size, was Ralph Rose, of California and the University of Michigan, who began his competition in

California as a school boy in 1898, set his first world's record of 48′ 7″ in 1904, and competed in his last Olympics in 1912, placing second to the great Pat McDonald by less than an inch, with a 50′ 3 1/8 ″ put. Rose's greatest official performance, 51 feet in 1909, stood for 19 years as the world's record. Because of his great size, his natural speed, and his apparent mastery of the event, many thought his record was to last for all time. Templeton, Stanford's great weight coach, stated that he saw Rose perform many times and that Rose took a position about 45 degrees to the right of the front of the circle. He started with the left foot well back, combined its forward throw with a twisting hop, and landed in the centre of the circle facing to the side at 90 degrees to the front of the circle. Such a form would necessarily produce a strong hitch of the shoulders and a definite hesitation in the middle of the circle before making the put. Momentum across the circle was a very negligible factor.

1910-1920. Perhaps because of Rose's pre-eminence, perhaps because of the World War, little apparent progress took place during this time. No great champions controlled the event, nor were numbers of competitors very evident. Although written in 1926, the following statement by Lawson Robertson is characteristic of this decade:

Shot putting form has been practically at a standstill for a great many years, having registered but a few slight changes in the initial leg swing. This unfortunate adherence to a poorly conceived style is responsible for the generally mediocre performances of the past twenty years...Shot putting today admits of but little variation in the manner of delivery, and if almost any champion were asked for the best method of putting, it is more than likely that the answer would be similar to that of nearly every other titleholder.

1920-1930. This was a period of tremendously increased interest and growth. Probably "Bud" Houser, of Southern California, was its greatest hero. Although weighing only 180 pounds and just 6 feet tall, Houser was the first of this era to hit over 50 feet. Houser possessed great speed, remarkable co-ordination, and a flawless style. But if he could do that well with his small size, others could do better. Immediately, a new group of men pushed to the front: Hills of Princeton, Hartranft of Stanford (whose form, although much slower, was remarkably similar to that of Fuchs, of present-day fame), and Liversedge of California were among the leaders. Professional coaches in America began to take the event seriously. Dick Templeton, of Stanford, one of the foremost of these, made an exhaustive study of the details of good form. In many respects, present-day form is very little changed from that advocated by Templeton a quarter century ago. True, he would not have approved the form of either Jim Fuchs or Parry O'Brien.

But his extreme emphasis upon proper use of the hips, proper and simultaneous placement of the feet, and the importance of momentum across the circle is just as sound today as when spoken 25 years ago.

The decade was climaxed during the Olympic year, 1928, by the breaking of Rose's record through a startling 51′ 9½″ by Emil Hirschfeld, of Germany, just prior to the games. This was rapidly followed by a new Olympic and world's record of 52′ ¾″ by John Kuck, of the United States and Kansas State Teachers College. Two weeks later, Kuck's record was surpassed by Hirschfeld with a 52′ 7¾″ performance.

1930-1940. But the boys were just beginning to get serious with the little round ball.

And there it stayed—57′ 1″! How could this be? In 1928, the world's record was 51 feet even and had been that for 19 years. Now suddenly, in the space of 6 years, the record was broken by 9 different athletes and improved by 6 feet. The answers are plural, of course. First, many more good big men were trying the event. According to the valuable record book put out by Potts and Quercetani, 70 puts of more than 51 feet were recorded between 1928 and 1940. None for 19 years, but then 70 in 12 years. Secondly, the careful studies of the technique of the event and the continuous hard work toward perfecting those techniques were paying off and men were achieving marks truly commensurate with their potential abilities. In 1939, at the National Collegiate championships at Palo Alto, California, first place was won with 55′ 11″ by Hackney, of Kansas; but, more significant, fifth place was 51′ 11″ by Anderson, of Stanford. The great "human ultimate" performance of Ralph Rose would have taken sixth place that day in a college championship meet. Lastly—the boys believed they could do even better and such belief permitted them to relax just enough and forced them to work hard enough to reach their goal.

However, it may be that the greater significance of this remarkable day lav in the putting of Hackney and of second-place Bill Watson (national decathlon championship, 1940), of the University of Michigan. Both these men were remarkable in the speed with which they hopped, not glided, across the circle. Both men landed "too close" to the toe-board, with their left foot far "in the bucket" to the left of the centre line and with their hips and shoulders well forward. "Poor form", the experts said; "if only they would get better position and use their power with all that speed". For four years the coaches at Michigan had insisted that Watson should carefully consider the placement of his left foot and had emphasized the importance of delaying the right-hip action. Watson followed such instructions perfectly as long as the situation called for 50 or 51 feet. But as soon as the big meets came up, all interest in balance and position was gone. "Zoom" he would go across the circle, slamming his left foot hard against the toe-board but far to the left, bringing his hip through fast like a discus thrower, but above all concentrating his momentum in a desperate drive upward and out into the put. "Too bad", we all intoned sadly, until of course we looked at the steel tape with its 54-foot measurements. Watson never learned all that his coaches had to teach him; but, on the other hand, it was not until years later that they learned what Watson had to teach them, namely that body momentum is as essential to great distances as are proper position and explosive power. In a very real sense, Hackney and Watson were the teachers of Fonville and, through him, of Fuchs.

1940 to date. This period opened quite auspiciously with a series of fine performances by the late Al Blozis, of Georgetown University. Several puts of more than 56 feet indoors were climaxed by a splendid 56′ 6 1/8″ on June 15, 1941. Certain doubts began to arise concerning Torrance's all-time "perfect" performance. Big Al was 6′ 6″ tall, weighed 240 pounds, and was very fast in basketball and football—just the type of superhuman who might beat the 57′ 1″ record. Blozis secured excellent position throughout all stages of his put, but never acquired the momentum necessary to real records. Most tragically, his career was cut short by his death in the second World War.

As was to be expected, performances fell off during the war period, so that after Anderson, of Stanford, achieved 55′ 3¾″ on May 4, 1940, no puts exceeded 55 feet outdoors until the Olympic year, 1948. Fonville achieved 54′ 10 7/8″ in winning the National Collegiates at Salt Lake City in 1947, but there was little warning, to the general public at least, of his 1948 record. Within the space of 2 months, he bettered 56 feet 9 times, with a second-best put of 56′ 10¾″ and an amazing new world's record of 58′ 3/8″.

Few world's records have been more shocking or unbelievable than this. Torrance, who held the record, was an exceptional giant of 6′ 5″, weighing 260 pounds when in best shape, who seemed to combine all the prerequisites of an all-time record holder—size, certainly, but with it remarkable speed and co-ordination. When, in 1935, Brutus Hamilton attempted to list human ultimates in all events, he could not think beyond Torrance's performance and assigned 57′ 1″ as an example of human perfection. Yet here was a college junior, 20 years old, 6′ 2″ tall and weighing only 195 pounds, and merely breaking the "perfect" record but surpassing it by a full foot! In a list of the world's 20 best shot-putters, Fonville was the lightest in weight of them all. What special element did he have? Was there a new technique, a more powerful position of the body, a more rapid means of gaining momentum? How much better can he get?

As his coach, but it is his certain belief that Fonville was far from reaching his best effort. His steady improvement in both practice and meet performances gave definite indications that 58 feet was only the beginning and that 60 feet was a distinct possibility. Most unfortunately—and a world of heartache for everyone concerned is contained in that phrase—Fonville aggravated an old and hitherto unknown injury to his lower spine and was unable to complete the Olympic year. Following an operation and a year's complete lay-off, he tried the shot again and made amazing progress, but he lacked the necessary confidence and incentive to approach his potential greatness.

What were Fonville's special assets? First, an amazing degree of explosive power and quickness of muscle action. Second, and equally important, an unparalleled desire, which made play out of drudgery and every "vacation" period or hour a chance to work. Third, a perfection of all the aspects of form as then approved by the experts, not merely as to proper position but in the momentum he achieved across the circle and in the high efficiency with which he co-ordinated this momentum with great body force. And fourth, an ability to concentrate his energies in competitive performances that, to the writer, is still somewhat beyond the level of understanding.

But was Fonville the last word in shot-putting? Not at all. Within 16 months, Jim Fuchs, of Yale, had a new world's record of 58′ 4 3/8 ″, and within another 2 years, he made 8 puts of more than 58 feet and a best effort of 58′ 10¾″. Fuchs was also far from being a big man as great shot-putters go—6′ 2″ tall and 224 pounds, which places him about twelfth in size among the world's 20 best putters. In addition to Fuchs, Chandler, of Stanford, in 1950, and O'Brien, of Southern California, in 1952, each cleared 57′ 4 3/8 ″; Hooper, of Texas A. & M., cleared 57′ 2/3 ″ in 1952; 2 other men cleared 56 feet, and 3 more cleared 55 feet. One cannot help being reminded of the 1928-1934 era. Once the magic mark is broken, a surge of aspirants for new records comes forward, and who can predict the new level?

What was Fuch's contribution? In addition to natural explosive power and a great competitive spirit. Fuchs, with the important aid of his coach, Frank Ryan, developed a style that achieved unusual body force with little loss of body momentum. First, the backward-pointing right foot made a forward rotation of the right hip impossible and forced an upward and straight-outward action, which is so important for greatest power. Second (and the two are closely allied), a fully stretched left side and extreme sideward bend toward the back of the circle increased the potential power. Fuchs bent so far sideward and back that the line of his backbone was almost horizontal as he started his glide and when he was in the centre of the circle. His shot was off the neck as he started his action and only very lightly touching the neck when his put actually began. This, combined with his backward lean, lengthened the distance through which he could apply body force by about a foot over that of most putters. Again, this extreme backward lean, added to his upward and outward action produced a trajectory angle of 45 degrees, which was higher and therefore more productive than that of any previous putter. Fuchs's shot, before the upward drive in the middle of the circle began, was actually not so low as that of Fonville, whose knee-bend was very deep, but his backward lean seemed to give him greater power and a slightly greater angle of delivery.

Of the putters who have copied Fuchs's unusual style, O'Brien, of Southern California, was the first to become outstanding. He began by surprising everyone and beating Fuchs in the 1951 National AAU meet with 55′ 9¼″. In 1952, Fuchs made a determined effort, but leg injuries held him back and O'Brien won the national title with a fine 57′ 4⅜″ and the Olympics with 57′ 1 4/10″. O'Brien differed from Fuchs primarily in the position of his eyes, head, and shoulders throughout the put and in his foot position at the start of the put. At the back of the circle as well as during the glide. O'Brien focused his eyes on a spot about 10 feet behind the circle, leaned far back and down and pointed his right foot directly back of the circle. In a conversation during June, 1952, O'Brien compared his action with the letter "J" and state he came around and up into his put. But extreme eversion of his right foot made such an action very difficult, and close observation indicated that he definitely came "up and out", as did Fuchs and Fonville. In 1952, O'Brien was not able to maintain the low backward lean as he glided across the circle, which was such a feature of Fuchs's form. But he was working toward this position and undoubtedly gained power and distance in his later competition.

The future in shot-putting. The ceiling is still unlimited at all levels—high school, college, and world. The first essential that needs empnasis is desire—desire that considers 8 to 10 months of practice as an opportunity rather than a hardship, desire that says, "Oh, let's take a few more, coach", as did Fonville, desire such as that which caused O'Brien, after returning from a track meet at 1:00 A.M., to turn on the lights in his backyard and practice on a detail of form before going up to bed. But supporting such desire, there must of course be ability. If an ultimate world's record is wanted, size such as that of Torrance or Blozis must be combined with Fonville's explosive power and momentum across the circle and with Fuchs's maximum use of the body force. It is certain that 62 feet is not impossible. The prodigy may need 15 years of practice and competitive experience such as that of G. R. Gray or Consolini, of Italy, in the discus. But that is merely a matter of maintaining proper incentives. Let use hope such an all-time champion is able to maintain a truly amateur spirit—"the game for the game's sake"—and is not a subsidized work-horse who does it for monetary gain, whether from college or club for "outstanding achievement" or from his country for maintaining its place of honour in international competition.

CHAPTER 4

THE TECHNIQUE OF SHOT PUT

This is a contest in which the missile is pushed rather than thrown. Impetus is added to the push by a body shift across the circle. From the beginning to the end of the put there are a number of well-defined body movements. These movements are discussed in the order in which they are executed: (1) the handhold, (2) the initial stance, (3) the leg swing, (4) the shift, (5) the delivery, (6) the release, and (7) the recovery.

1. The Handhold

There are three generally accepted types of handhold based on the spread of the fingers. These are shown in figure. In the illustration A represents the type in which the first, second, and third fingers are back of the shot. The little finger is bent and aids the thumb in maintaining lateral support. Handhold B is more frequently used. The first, second, and third fingers, slightly spread, are likewise back of the shot and again the thumb prevents sideward movement of the missile. Hold B differs from A in that the little finger not only aids in maintaining balance but also contributes force to forward and upward propulsion. The novice must remember that these are holds employed by experienced putters, and he will note that the shot is carried well up toward the fingertips. Beginners are advised to carry the shot lower down in the palm until the musculature of the hand is sufficiently developed to carry it higher. Finger development, it will be noted, is a highly important practice objective.

The type of handhold shown in figure is that employed by men with smaller hands and shorter fingers. Here it is necessary to maintain a wider finger spread. The little finger is placed farther back of the shot so that it may be used for adding impetus to the put. The thumb is used to maintain lateral balance. With this type of hold the shot is ordinarily carried farther down in the palm of the hand.

Scan Fig. 44, page no. 317 of track and field athletics by George T. Bresnahan

2. The Initial Stance

It is assumed that the putter is right handed. A position is taken in which the right foot is close to the back edge of the 7-foot circle and the left foot is from 10 inches to 16 inches away. The angle, the direction, and the distance of the placement of the left foot in relation to the right are a matter of convenience since the left leg is to be lifted and swung at the initiation of the shift.

The shot is carried slightly above and directly in front of the shoulder with the elbow away from the body. In the initial stance the right knee, supporting most of the body weight, is slightly bent. The left hand is extended upward and outward in order to maintain balance. Except the hand grasping the shot, body musculature, is, in general, relaxed. The novice is urged to study the series of form in order to see the relationship of the shot to the right foot. It is seen that a plumb line dropped from the shot to the ground touches a spot to the right of the right foot. From this position the leg swing begins.

3. The Leg Swing

For the purpose of securing poise and balance for the shift, the putter performs three (more or less) preliminary leg swing. These swings may be executed by swinging the left leg forward and backward in line with the right leg; or forward and backward in front of the right leg; or forward and backward to the rear of the right leg. The type of preliminary swing employed rests with the putter. As the left foot reaches the farthermost point back in the last swing, the shift begins, the swinging leg contributing momentum thereto.

4. The Shift

Naturally, the last preliminary swing becomes the start of the shift.

At the beginning of the shift the body weight is obviously on the right foot, with the right knee moderately bent. As the left foot reaches the most forward point in the swing, the right leg is vigorously straightened and a moderate push is given by the right thigh, leg and foot. Many good competitors swing the left arm downward at the start of the shift and vigorously upward during its execution, an activity which they feel adds impetus to the body glide across the circle. The word "shift" is used rather than "leap" because of the latter term frequently designates a high bounding action. The movement desired is, in fact, a low glide. During the shift the trunk is carried so as to maintain balance. The position of the shot in relation to the body remains unchanged. At the conclusion of the hop on the right foot, the left foot is from 6 to 10 inches from the ground. As the left foot comes down, the trunk and shot continue their movement in the direction of the put, and the legs and trunk gather for the delivery. This rocking forward is important in order that the momentum of the body acquired during the shift be maintained.

However, there are competitors who execute the shift by planting the left foot simultaneously with the right. Athletes who use this method successfully believe that since the right shoulder has been drawn back during the shift and the right hip slightly relaxed, they are in position to execute a double leg drive rather than a rocking movement over a single leg shove. This method is criticized because of an apparent pause in the forward progress of the shot.

The left foot lands near the toe board, the distance ranging from 3 inches to 8 inches. The feet are fairly well spread, from 34 inches to 39 inches. In this position the body weight rests chiefly on the right foot, and the right shoulder is drawn well back. A quite drop of the right hip is claimed by some shot-putters to be an advantage. The trunk is aligned with the left leg. From this position there is the beginning of the consummation of all the forces of the body to provide forward propulsion of the missile. It should be noted that at the release, the trunk is aligned with the right leg.

5. The Delivery

As soon as the feet are planted after the shift, the delivery begins. An effective put is one in which there is no pause between the shift and the delivery. A good putter gains distance by concentrating on speedy rather than forceful movement. During the course of delivery the following movements are rapidly executed: (a) the straightening and rotating of the right leg, which produces a movement that looks like a thrust of the right hip, (b) a quick twist of the trunk to the left, (c) forceful push of the right arm upward and forward, (d) a forceful swing of the left elbow to the left side and backward, and (e) a push-off from the right toe. Coincident with this last movement the arm is vigorously straightened, and the body weight is transferred to the left leg. It should be remembered that form and speed are the important factors in gaining distance.

6. The Release

The total of all the forces generated in the shift and the delivery has been transmitted to the wrist and fingers. Added to these factors is an instantaneous forward snap of the wrist and flip of the fingers which provides added impetus to the shot. Good form requres that the major force contact be kept directly behind the centre of the shot in the line of flight. This imparts a slight backward rotation to the missile.

The most effective angle for the release of the weight depends on the velocity with which it leaves the competitor's hand. The range of angle is from 37 to 42 degrees.

There are two theories with reference to the direction of the head and eyes during the release. Some coaches contend that the head should be inclined downward and to the left, thus permitting a freer right arm and shoulder action. Others think that the head and eyes should be kept in the direction of the put, thus aiding in a complete and effective follow-through.

The action of the right arm at the release varies among putters, the chief difference lying in the direction of the follow-through. Those competitors who employ what is known as the crossfire style, lay more emphasis on a trunk twist and a rapid cross-body action of the arm. With this type of release the missile usually falls to the left of a line drawn through the centre of both the circle and the toe board. Another type of release is one in which the shot leaves the hand from a point above and directly in front of the right shoulder. With this type of release the missile usually falls to the right of the centre line. The novice should observe that regardless of the type of arm action, the right foot retains contact with the ground until the shot has left the hand. So long as correct body mechanics are adhered to, both styles are effective.

7. The Recovery

The right foot is flush against the toe board while the left leg is swung backward and sideward. This is accomplished by the speedy interchanging of the position of the feet, commonly known as the revere. In the shot-put event the toe board is by official rule, included as a part of the equipment for the purpose of checking forward momentum. But in the discus throw, for which the circle is larger, no provision is made for similar equipment.

The carriage of the right arm indicates that the follow-through has been completed. The downward bend of the wrist reveals that excellent use has been made of the wrist snap and finger flip. The left arm, following the release, has been swung backward and downward to maintain balance. To avoid even the appearance of a foul, the competitor is urged to retire from the circle by way of the rear half, and then only after a signal from the official indicating that the put has been marked.

CHAPTER 5

TEACHING DRILLS OF SHOT PUT

The shot put is contested as a separate event for males and females and also as part of the decathlon and heptathlon. Over the years, the event has come to be dominated by big, powerful athletes.

A major advance in the technique of the event occurred in the 1950s, when Parry O'Brien began his throw facing the rear of the ring. This method, known as the O'Brien technique or more commonly as the glide technique, is used by the majority of modern shotputters.

A technique gaining popularity is the rotary shot-put technique, which employs a discus-style rotation across the shot-put ring rather than the backward shift or glide that characterizes the O'Brien technique. Both glide and rotation have been equally successful in achieving long throws.

The rotary technique is more difficult to master than the glide technique, because the rotation has to be performed in the confines of the shot-put ring and because the rotary action makes the control of the shot more difficult.

First teach beginners the glide technique. Once the young athlete has worked seriously with this technique and can perform the footwork for rotational discus throws, the athlete can experiment with the rotary shot-put technique.

Teaching Points

Drill 1: Lead-Ups

Preparatory activities for shot putting can begin with all forms of throwing using soccer balls, basketballs, or light medicine balls. Initially, throwing is two-handed (e.g., from behind the head, between the legs, and around the side of the body). Then require one-handed or two-handed throwing in a "pushing" or "putting" fashion, which simulates the action required in shot putting.

A Push-Throw With a Medicine Ball

Students throw medicine balls against the wall using a pushing or putting action. The throwers catch the balls on the rebound.

Coaching Points

1. Push forward into the throw with your body, making sure your legs are extended.
2. Keep your chest high and your head up.
3. Extend your arms as vigorously as possible and be sure to push with your fingers.

Push-Throws in Pairs

Pairs face each other and use one- and two-handed push passes with a medicine ball.

Coaching Points

1. If you are throwing with your right arm, be sure to step forward 1 long stride (before you throw) with the left foot. This will give you a good throwing stance.
2. Keep your elbow of the throwing arm at shoulder level; do not let it drop down to the side of the body.
3. Keep your chest up and extend your legs as you

throw.

Putting the Medicine Ball for Distance

Individuals put the medicine ball for distance. Distance lines are marked on the ground.

Coaching Points

1. Try to make your throwing action as long as possible. Push from as far back to as far forward as possible.
2. Drive up onto your toes and push forward with your body. Use your whole body in the throw, not just your arms.
3. To obtain the longest distance, a trajectory of about 40 to 43 degrees above horizontal is necessary. Release the medicine ball so that your arms are fully extended in front of you and just above head height.

Putting a Medicine Ball for Height and Distance

This practice emphasizes both height and distance. Surgical tubing is suspended between 2 high-jump or pole-vault standards 2 to 3 meters above the ground. If the student can throw the medicine ball over the crossbar, the thrower takes 2 paces back. Who ends up the farthest away from the standards? (Be sure than the elastic will stretch sufficiently when hit. It is also a good idea to weight down the bases of the high-jump or pole-vault standards).

Coaching Points

1. This lead-up will test whether you are achieving the best trajectory.
2. Remember to extend your legs and lift your chest upward as you throw.
3. Use the big muscles of the legs, back, and chest before using the arms, not afterwards.

Passing Relay

Students push-pass a medicine ball in zigzag fashion from one end of a team to the other. Which team is quickest in passing the medicine ball? Make sure than the medicine ball is light enough to catch easily.

Coaching Points

1. Be alert and ready to catch the ball.
2. Reach out to catch the ball and absorb its momentum by drawing your arms and body back the moment your hands contact the ball.
3. Throw the ball accurately and with the correct amount of force so that your partner can catch the ball easily.
4. Whoever drops the medicine ball has to pick it up, so be accurate when you throw.

Drill 2: Shot Put From a Standing Position

Technique

The athlete begins a standing put facing away from the direction of throw, keeping the vision to the rear, and cradling the shot under the chin. The athlete flexes the right leg and reaches back with the left leg into the putting stance, lowering the upper body at the hips. The shoulders at this point remain square to the rear. The athlete drives upward and rotates toward the direction of the throw by extending the legs and thrusting the hips and chest forward. A powerful thrust of the throwing arm and the vigorous snap of the fingers complete the putting action.

Drills

The Correct Handhold for Cradling and Shot

Each participant raises and lowers the shot from the shoulder to full arm's length several times. This develops a feel for the manner in which the shot rests between the fingers and the thumb.

Coaching Points

1. Hold the shot between your fingers and thumb; do not let the shot drop into your palm. If you can only hold the shot in your palm, the shot is too heavy and you need to use a lighter one.
2. Raise and lower your arm slowly. This will give you a feel for the support given to the shot by the combined action of the thumb and the fingers.

Standing Put—Initial Stance Facing the Direction of Throw

Participants stand facing the direction of throw and holding the shot in the correct hand position. The thrower steps forward with the left foot (right-handed thrower) and then puts the shot.

Coaching Points

1. Keep the elbow of the throwing arm high (at shoulder height) during the put.
2. Begin the putting action by moving your body forward. Move the hips forward and keep your chest high and square (at right angles) to the direction of throw.
3. Extend your legs and be sure to put the shot from your fingers (not from your palm).
4. Finish the putting action with the throwing arm extended in front of your body and with your hand raised to just above head level.

Standing Put—Shoulders Rotate 90 Degrees From the Direction of Throw

The thrower steps toward the direction of the throw with the left leg (right-handed thrower), rotating the shoulders 90 degrees to the right (i.e., away from the direction of throw). The put begins with the right leg extending and driving the hips and the chest toward the direction of throw. The extension of the arm and the thrust of the fingers complete the putting action.

Coaching Points

1. Be sure to begin the putting action by extending your legs.
2. After your legs are extended, turn your hips and chest toward the direction of the throw before using the throwing arm.
3. Be sure to keep the elbow of the throwing arm at shoulder level. Do not let it drop downward, otherwise the shot can bend the fingers backward. Think of the putting action as a bench press in the weight room!
4. Finish the put with a thrusting action from the fingers toward the direction of the throw.

Standing Put—Initial Stance Facing the Direction of Throw

The performer begins facing the direction of the throw with the feet together, then takes 1 pace forward (slightly wider than shoulder width) with the left leg. This provides the correct foot positioning for the final throwing stance. The thrower then rotates 180 degrees on the balls of the feet and faces directly away from the direction of the throw, shifting the body weight back over the right foot. From this position the athlete simultaneously lifts upward, turning the hips and chest toward the direction of throw. The put is completed with a strong extension of the throwing arm.

Coaching Points

1. Lift upward with your legs and back and simultaneously rotate toward the direction of the throw.
2. Do not be in a hurry to use the throwing arm; wait

until your body has lifted up and rotated toward the direction of the throw.

3. Try to keep the sequence in the correct order: legs extend and rotate simultaneously, followed by the hips and chest, and finally the throwing arm extends.

4. Keep the elbow of the throwing arm at shoulder level throughout.

Standing Put—Initial Stance 180 Degrees From the Direction of Throw

This is the complete action of the standing put. The thrower begins facing 180 degrees from the direction of throw (i.e., facing the rear of the shot-put ring). There are 2 acceptable methods for performing the standing put: the athlete begins with both feet already positioned in the putting stance; or the athlete begins with both feet together, then initiates the standing put with the left foot reaching back into the putting stance.

For a right-handed thrower the standing put occurs in the following sequence. The athlete begins by lowering the upper body downward and flexing the right leg to approximately a 1/4 squat position. The right leg rotates and extends upward, forcing the hips around and toward the direction of throw. The chest is thrust forward by the action of the hips, and both legs extend fully. The extension of the throwing arm completes the standing put.

When the left foot is positioned in the putting stance, the foot must be "offset" correctly.

The Putting Stance

The foot positions used in the putting stance allow the body to rotate and move forward toward the direction of the throw. For a right-handed thrower facing the rear of the ring, the left foot is placed approximately 1 foot width to the thrower's right of a line indicating the direction of throw. If the left foot is positioned to the left, it will block the thrower's efforts to drive forward into the throw. The distance between right foot and left foot in the putting stance is slightly more than shoulder width.

Drill 3: Shot Put Using the Glide Technique

Learning the Glide With Partner Assistance

A partner holds the performer's hands, making sure that the performer's upper body remains low and the shoulders are "square" or facing directly to the rear. As the performer glides backward, the partner moves in the same direction, making sure at the same time that the performer's upper body stays low throughout. The thrower concentrates on the following actions, which are performed simultaneously. One action is a low backward thrust of the left leg, with the left foot landing in the correct throwing position each time (i.e., offset to the right). Another important action is a backward drive with the right leg, which after extension is flexed and immediately pulled in directly below the upper body. The right foot and knee should also rotate approximately 45 degrees toward the direction of throw. The performer must be sure than the right and left legs perform their separate actions almost simultaneously. Both feet should land in the putting stance at the same time.

Repetitive Glide Practice Without Partner Assistance (No Shot Used)

The performer assumes an initial stance similar to the standing put position. After lowering the upper body and flexing the right leg, the performer drives backward for each glide.

The athlete should concentrate on each glide individually, making sure it is completely correct. This drill should not become a series of aimless backward hops.

Coaching Points

1. The backward gliding action is not an upward jump. Do not raise your back or jump up in the air.
2. Keep your feet close to the ground throughout.
3. After extending the right leg, pull it in so that it ends up in a flexed position directly below the upper body. (If this is not done, the right leg will be unable to provide

Glide and Shot Put Using a Short Glide and Light Shot

The initial stance in this drill is the same as for the standing put. A short glide allows the thrower to concentrate on the rhythm of both glide and put. In this way the performer is not concerned about the distance that must be covered in a normal glide.

Coaching Points

1. Keep your upper body low until the glide is complete; then lift into the putting action, not before.
2. Extend and flex the right leg so that it is pulled in directly below your upper body at the end of the glide. Do not leave the right leg "behind" you, otherwise you'll land with both legs extended and with no leg power available.

Glide and Shot Put Using a Full-Size Glide

This is the complete putting action using the glide technique. The rhythm of glide and put must be smooth, not jerky. A controlled glide takes the athlete from the back of the ring to a putting stance in the centre. A full-size glide requires the athlete to shift backward approximately 60 centimetres. The glide is then followed by an explosive putting action. The momentum of the body driving the shot toward the direction of throw and the vigorous extension of the legs should force the athlete to step forward with the right leg and so perform the reverse.

Coaching Points

1. A longer glide will demand more effort from the right leg. Think of the action as a push and a pull-in with your right leg.
2. Thrust your left leg backward to its rotation in the putting stance the same time that you extend your right leg.
3. Remember to stay low until both feet are in position.
4. Thrust forward into the throw as powerfully as possible, and perform the reverse only after the shot has left your hand.

The Reverse

Athlete use the reverse to keep from falling out of the front of the ring and fouling the throw.

Coaching Points

1. Make sure your hips and chest move forward beyond the left foot before initiating the reverse.
2. Do not get into the habit of performing the reverse without extending your legs fully and driving your body well forward into the throw.

Drill 4: Shot Put Using the Rotary Technique

The rotational technique uses a discus-style rotation across the shot-put ring in place of a glide. Once the athlete has completed the rotation, all else in the throw is basically the same as with the glide technique. However, the addition of the rotary action causes control problems that do not exist in the glide technique, problems due to the centrifugal force generated in the rotation. Quite simply, the shot "wants" to fly out sideways, and the athlete must generate the additional force to hold the shot in position. The timing required in the rotary action into an essentially linear action.

Athletes who have not mastered the rotary technique will find that they may throw the shot out of the sector (right-handed throwers tend to throw the shot outside of the sector on the right side); lose control of the shot during the rotation across the ring; or land in a poor (narrow) throwing stance at the end of the rotation, (usually caused by using a "discus-size" rotation across the shot-put ring, which is 37 centimetres, or 14.5 inches, smaller than a discus ring).

It is strongly recommended that you teach only the glide technique as a class activity. The rotational technique should be taught to advanced throwers only as an alternative and experimental method after they have mastered the glide technique.

Participants Learn the Discus Rotation

Teach the rotary action used in the discus throw to all participants attempting the rotary shot-put technique.

Simulating the Position of the Shot During the Rotary Technique

With the throwing hand held at the neck, but without using the shot, the athlete practices the rotary technique in the shot-put ring.

Coaching Points

1. Be sure to make the rotation at the back of the ring tight enough to allow sufficient room in the front of the ring for a wide throwing stance.
2. Concentrate on rotation only in the rear half of the ring. A linear (nonrotary) thrust in the direction of the throw must predominate after both feet have landed in their final positions at the front of the ring.
3. Put your left arm out to the side during the rotation to help maintain balance.

A Rotary Shot Put Using a Light Shot

Choose a shot that is 1 to 2 kilograms (approximately 2 to 4 pounds) lighter than the shot used by the performer in the glide technique. The athlete rotates slowly into the putting stance, using the outward swing of the left arm to help initiate rotation from the rear of the ring. The athlete must hold the shot firmly in the neck. Once the rotation has been completed, the final part of the put is performed in essentially the same way as with the glide technique.

Coaching Points

1. Squat down at the rear of the ring as though sitting on a stool.
2. Look forward and pivot on the balls of both feet to initiate the rotation.
3. Keep pivoting on the balls of your feet until facing the direction of throw.
4. Continue the pivot on the left foot, meanwhile bringing the right leg around to be positioned in the centre of the ring.
5. Land with the toes of the right foot pointing out toward the right side of the ring.
6. Shift the left leg as quickly as possible into its position in the final putting stance.
7. Try to keep your body weight to the rear of the ring, so that when you land in the putting stance, your upper body will be over a flexed right leg.
8. Throughout the rotation, hold the shot tightly against your neck and keep the elbow of the throwing arm at shoulder level throughout.
9. Complete the putting acting with a linear thrust at the shot. This action is similar to that used in the glide technique.

Rotary Shot Put Using a Competitive Weight Shot

The thrower selects a shot that is the correct weight for his or her competitive age level and attempts the rotary shot put, slowly at first. Control over the shot during the rotation (or a good throwing position at the end of the rotation) must not be forfeited for increased rotary speed at the back of the ring.

Common Errors in Technique

In the description of the shot-put technique an attempt was made to show correct execution, and by inference some of the imperfections were point out. At the risk of repetition and for the purpose of emphasis, faults in execution are discussed.

1. In the Handhold

Should the weight be grasped too low in the hand, the value of the finger propulsion is lost. If the hold is too far toward the fingertips, insufficient purchase on the shot may result in its slipping backward off the fingers. This miscue frequently causes pain and necessitates a brief period of rest before resuming hard putting exercises.

The faults of imbalance caused by inaccurate placement of the thumb and the little finger are obvious, in that the missile may fall ineffectively too far to the right or to the left. Deviation from a previously determined ideal finger spread decreases the possibility of exerting maximum force.

By carrying the shot in the left hand until ready for the initial stance, the competitor averts possible fatigue of the putting hand. This may seem trivial to some athletes, but let them recall that in professional baseball, where unnecessary fatigue costs in dollars and cents, the catcher, when making a return throw to the pitcher, relieves him of unnecessary effort by directing the ball to his gloved hand held shoulder high at the side.

2. In the Initial Stance

Shot-putters frequently make mistakes in the initial stance by attaining a position of extreme body tension instead of moderate relaxation. The placement of the feet both as to their direction and spread can contribute to low-grade performance if it differs to any great amount from the predetermined style. Imperfections in the knee bend may be corrected by the time the shift has been completed. Therefore, knee flexion variance at the initial stance may or may not be faulty.

3. In the Leg Swing

Detraction from good effort may be traced to extreme delay in starting the leg swing once the putter has taken the initial stance. The competitor who is trying to reach the peak of mental and physical poise has "ridden past his stop". A leg swing out of alignment or improperly timed will be reflected in malposition of the feet after the shift has been completed.

Balance, ever of prime importance, must be maintained. This being the case, any movement in the leg swing which causes imbalance obviously is an error.

4. In the Shift

A shot-putter may have failed to gain creditable distance because his execution of the shift was harmed by:

a. Overspeed or underspeed.

b. Inclining the trunk too far forward or sideward.

c. Overdistance or underdistance.

d. Changing the plane of the shot. It should move first forward, then forward and upward. It should not fluctuate upward and downward.

e. Twisting the trunk to the left or failing to draw back the right shoulder.

f. Failing to straighten the right leg effectively.

g. Aligning the feet improperly.

h. Failing to distribute the body weight correctly (mainly on the right foot).

i. Failing to swing the left arm and leg vigorously.

j. Failing to take advantage of an effective rock-over in the shift.

The method of correcting these faults together with those indicated later in the discussion should be evident to the novice, after he has studied the description of the shot-putting technique, the drawings illustrating form, and the schedules of practice.

5. In the Delivery

Failure to attain maximum distance because of the technical defects during the period of delivery may be attributed to:

a. A lack of elbow height.

b. A failure to begin the right hip thrust soon enough.

c. The incorrect timing of the trunk twist with the arm push.

d. The improper coordination of the leg drive with the above actions.

e. An insufficient or too deliberate straightening of the right leg.

f. The starting of an arm push which brings the shot to an improper angle (37 to 42 degrees is correct) when the release is executed.

g. A deficiency in the complete rock-up on the toe.

h. A carriage of the head and eyes in a position at variance with the direction of the body.

i. An ineffective use of the left arm in aiding a forceful

trunk twist.

j. Failing to keep the hand directly in line with the elbow.

6. In the Release

Lack of distance may be traced to the release if the tasks just preceding it have been completed satisfactorily. The arm movement determining the angle of release begins in the delivery but ends in the release. Obviously the lowering of the forearm decreases this angle, and the raising of the forearm increases it.

Puts falling too far to the right or to the left may be caused by either a premature release or an ill-timed trunk twist.

Failure to complete a timely and vigorous wrist snap and finger flip will detract from performances otherwise technically sound. Distance is lost if there is an incomplete coordination of the sources of power just as the shot leaves the hand. If the follow-through is not fully concluded, quite likely there were untapped sources of power which were not behind or under the missile.

7. In the Recovery

By the time the shot has broken contact with the fingers nothing more can be done to help or harm its flight. The sole concern of the athlete is the prevention of fouling. The rules prohibit him from touching both the circle and the top of the circle or the toe board is likewise a foul. During the release he has been losing balance by completing the follow-through. If he expects to have his put ruled fair he must regain balance. Otherwise, the effort will be declared a foul. These are the main factors contributing to foul puts:

a. Failure to bring the right foot to the toe board immediately after the hand has ceased contact with the shot.

b. A lack of a speedy subsequent backward swing of the left leg.

c. The omission of the backward-downward sweep of the left arm.

d. An incomplete bend of the right knee preventing a lowering of the centre of gravity.

e. A careless or slipshod mental attitude after the release indicating a lack of determination to save the put. Careless practice habits when executing the recovery frequently are responsible fore competition penalties.

Common Errors and Corrections in Shot Put

Standing put

1. Error

The performer has no thrust from the fingers during the put.

Reasons

Handhold is incorrect; the shot is put from the palm of the hand.

Remedies

The athlete should support the shot with the pads of the fingers and thumb. Have the athlete practice standing puts, emphasizing extension of arm and thrust of fingers (use under-weight shots). Or, the athlete can practice the action of the hand and fingers without the shot.

2. Error

The shot is thrown rather than put. The novice complains of the shot "bending" the fingers backward during the put.

Reasons

The shot is not cradled under the chin. The elbow of

the throwing arm drops below the shoulder in the putting stance.

Remedies

Correct the handhold and the position of the shot in the neck. The athlete must hold the elbow high, keeping the thumb of the throwing hand down and the little finger uppermost. Have the athlete practice the standing put after these factors are corrected.

3. Error

The athlete's seat goes backward as the shot is thrust forward.

Reasons

There is no extension and thrust from the legs, and the hips are not driven forward. The left foot is in the wrong position in the putting stance, and the left leg blocks the athlete's rotation toward the direction of the put.

Remedies

Have the athlete practice the standing put, emphasizing leg thrust and hip movement toward the direction of throw. The left foot in the putting stance must be offset.

4. Error

The left side of the body "collapses" during the final phase of the put.

Reasons

No extension or "resistance" is provided by the left leg and the left side of the body during the put. Vision is not toward the direction of the throw.

Remedies

Have the athlete practice the standing put, emphasizing upward thrust of the left leg and left side of the body. The chest should rotate toward the direction of throw around the axis of the left side of the body.

5. Error

The shot is put with the body sideways to the direction of the throw. The shot is released over the top of the head.

Reasons

There is no rotary drive from the right leg, and the hips are not turning toward the direction of the put. The rear leg is not extending toward the direction of put and the left foot is incorrectly positioned.

Remedies

The left foot must be in the correct position in the throwing stance. The athlete should practice (without shot) the positioning of the left foot, followed immediately by the lift and extension of the legs, chest, and throwing arm. The athlete can then practice this action using light shot.

6. Error

The shot has no height, released with a low trajectory.

Reasons

The athlete does not extend the body upward during the put. Both the throwing arm and line of vision are too low.

Remedies

The athlete should practice a standing put over a high jump bar set high enough to emphasize extended legs, lifted chest, and forward vision.

7. Error

The sequence and timing of actions are incorrect (i.e., the throwing arm performs its thrust on the shot prior to the thrust of the legs and chest).

Reasons

The athlete is too eager to throw and has poor understanding of sequence and timing of actions.

Remedies

Have the athlete practice a standing put without the shot, then a standing put without extending the arm without neck. The athlete can practice using the action of legs and chest alone to drive the shot forward.

Glide Technique

1. Error

The athlete swings the left leg back and forth in pendular fashion before initiating the glide.

Reasons

The athlete relies on the swing of the left leg to help shift the body across the ring and uses insufficient drive from the right leg. The left leg should be thrust backward.

Remedies

Have the athlete practice repetitive glides using correct leg action.

2. Error

The athlete jumps upward instead of gliding low and close to the ground, and the left leg is kicked high in air at the start of the glide.

Reasons

The drive from the left leg is upward instead of backward and across the ring. The left leg is swung upward instead of thrust backward at the start of the glide.

Remedies

Have the athlete practice glides without shot, emphasizing powerful backward thrust of the left leg followed by a similar drive from the right leg.

3. Error

The athlete is upright at the end of the glide; body weight is not over the rear (right) leg at the end of the glide.

Reasons

The upper body is raised at the start of or during the glide, then the athlete falls backward during the glide. The right leg is not pulled in under the body at the end of the glide.

Remedies

The athlete should practice glides while maintaining low upper body position, making sure both feet hit the ground at the same time with the body weight over the right leg throughout.

4. Error

The athlete turns prematurely toward the direction of the throw.

Reasons

The left foot is incorrectly placed. The athlete rotates at start and during the glide, turning the head and shoulders prematurely toward the direction the throw.

Remedies

Have the athlete practice on glide, keeping the vision to the rear throughout. Mark on the ground the final foot positioning at the end of the glide. The left arm should extend and point to the rear throughout the glide.

5. Error

The athlete's hips move backward as the throwing arm and shot are driven forward.

Reasons

The athlete's weight remains over the rear foot during the final phase of the put. The athlete does not extend the right leg or move the hips and chest toward the direction of the throw.

Remedies

The athlete should practice the standing put, emphasizing upward lift and forward motion of the body over the left foot while keeping the body moving forward toward the direction of the throw.

6. Error

The athlete extends the throwing arm in the putting action before the legs, hips, and chest drive forward into the put.

Reasons

The athlete is overeager to complete the throw. Timing and sequence of actions are incorrect.

Remedies

Have the athlete practice action of the standing put, emphasizing action of legs, hips, and chest. The athlete should practice with and without shot.

7. Error

The athlete performs the reverse before the shot leaves the hand.

Reasons

The athlete is afraid of making a foul put and is not moving the body weight toward the direction of the put. The athlete extends the left side of the body too soon.

Remedies

Instruct the athlete to practice the standing put without a reverse. The athlete should push forward beyond the left foot position during the put and delay the extension of the left leg and left side of the body.

Rotary Technique

1. Error

The athlete uses too much rotation and has no linear thrust on the shot. The athlete loses control of the shot, and the shot lands outside of the sector. The hips "open" up (i.e., rotate too far) by the time the throwing stance is achieved.

Reasons

Rotation continues too long. The athlete fails to achieve a strong throwing stance.

Remedies

Have the athlete practice rotation and putting action without a shot, then slowly with a light weight shot, emphasizing a good throwing position. Slow down the rotation.

2. Error

The thrower is upright before assuming the throwing stance and achieves no power in the throw.

Reasons

The upper body is elevated and legs are fully extended at back and in the middle of the ring. The athlete lifts upward when performing the rotation.

Remedies

The athlete must practice keeping low during rotation, lifting upward only out of the final putting position.

3. Error

Rotation across the ring is not toward the direction of the throw.

Reasons

The time spent rotating at the back of the ring is either

too long or too short.

Remedies

Use lines on the ground and a rhythm count to assist with directional control.

4. Error

The athlete loses control of the shot, which flies away from the neck before the final putting action is complete.

Reasons

The throwing hand is not holding the shot firmly enough in the neck. Timing of the final thrust is incorrect, and rotation across the ring is too fast.

Remedies

Instruct the athletes to practice slow rotational puts, waiting until the throwing position is fully assumed before initiating final thrust on the shot.

CHAPTER 6

THE DISCUS THROW

The history of the development of form in the discus throw is primarily one of taking old, discarded styles and making them effective. More than two turns will some day be used in the discus. Yet the use of two and even three turns was attempted and discarded as being impractical even prior to 1910, when the circle measured only 7 feet. In 1949, Fortune Cordien established a world's record of 186′ 10 $\frac{7}{8}$″. The "falling with balance" form he used, in which one often wondered whether the balance factor would ever catch up with the falling factor, is certainly similar to almost any beginner's style and undoubtedly was used and discarded over a quarter century ago as being ineffective.

Therefore, to outline a clear-cut, step-by-step evolution of style would be untruthful and an injustice to those intelligent and resourceful pioneers of style prior to 1925. For example, Lawson Robertson edited a book in 1926 which stated that the use of "2 and even 3 turns preceded this single-turn style" but was discarded "because the weight of the discus is not sufficient to steady the whirling advance, as is done in the hammer throw". Robertson then describes the single-turn style and emphasizes that "the basis of this form is speed" that the right arm should be held "at full extension to the right and rear of the body" at the end of the turn, that "the thrower leaves the ground (hops) during the turn, and that a full "reach-over finish" is very desirable.

It seems evident that an understanding of at least the fundamentals of good form was possessed even at this relatively early date. Yet we would be mistaken if we assumed that little has been learned in the past three decades. The words may be little changed, and the general concepts of form may be about the same; yet the significance of those words and the degree to which those concepts have been developed has undergone tremendous growth. Momentum undoubtedly was an element of good form in 1920, but it was "horse and buggy" speed compared with the present-day form of either Gordien or Consolini.

Before proceeding with this development of style and momentum, some background of the early history of the event is of value. Homer mentions throwing the quoit (discus) in the games held at the funeral of Patroclus, and it was an accepted part of the pentathlon competition in the ancient Olympics. However, there has been a difference of opinion concerning the method of throwing employed by the Greeks. Theories are based upon a description of the event given by Statius and upon a reconstruction of Myron's statue of a discus thrower (discobolus). The form adopted at the modern games, in 1896, placed the thrower upon a pedestal, permitted no turns, and required him to leap from the pedestal as the throw was made. However, the restrictions of this method were so impractical that a change to a 7-foot circle took place immediately upon introduction of the discus event in America in 1897. Although Robert Garrett, of Princeton, had surprised everyone by taking the event at the Athens games with no prior practice. America's first national champion and record holder was C. H. Henneman, of the Chicago Athletic Association, with 118′ 9″. But the real star of this early period was Martin J. Sheridan, a powerful Irish-American New York City policeman. During a 10-year period (1901-1911), he broke the world's record 7 times, was national champion in 1904, 1906, 1907 and 1911, and Olympic champion in 1904, 1906 and 1908. His best distance came in his last year, 1911, at 141′ 4$\frac{3}{8}$″ from a 7-foot circle.

The constant difficulty in preventing fouls when working in this small circle finally produced an increase to 8′ 2½″ and a new world's record by James H. Duncan in 1912 of 156′ 1$\frac{3}{8}$″. Duncan's style began with the discus high above and behind the head, from where it followed a down, up, down, up, and out motion. A single turn was used in which at least one foot was on the ground at all times.

With the adoption of new ring, the discus event grew rapidly in popularity. In 1915, G. L. Walker, of Passaic High School, New Jersey, achieved 158′ 2¾″ with a junior-size discus that was not adopted by high schools generally until many years later. It was not until 1925 that Duncan's 1912 record was broken by Glenn Hartranft, of Stanford, and, a year later, by Bud Houser, of Southern California. In this respect, at least, the history of the discus is similar to that of the shot put, in which Rose's 1909 world's record of 51 feet was not broken until 1928 by Hirschfeld, of Germany. Undoubtedly the first World War and the general lack of organization in sports were contributing factors.

The period 1915 to 1925 was primarily one of experimentation in styles. The writer was coached by David L. Holmes, of Detroit City College, a real student of field events. Yet he can remember that each year we were trying a slightly different style in the discus. We began by throwing from a stand, as should every beginner today. We then moved to a single step forward with the right foot, a pivot to the right into throwing position with the right shoulder and hip, and the actual throw with a reverse of the feet. The next stage brought a full turn. The thrower faced in the direction of the throw. He stepped forward with the left foot, swinging the discus behind his back in an inverted position so that the palm and the discus were uppermost. A slow pivot on the left foot was somewhat aided by the opening arc of the discus as it was gradually turned over. At times we were coached to swing the discus in a wave-like motion, up, down and up again into the actual throw. Sometimes it followed a rather horizontal path with just a minor dip during the gather for the throw. Only when both feet were on the ground and a firm balance secured was the upward and outward drive made. Finally, in 1925, after having watched Tom Lieb, of Notre Dame, win the National Collegiate meet in the preceding year with a "new" form, Coach Holmes taught a full one and one-half turns. This form was described by Tom Lieb in a very interesting article on discus throwing written in May, 1925.

This form, with individual variations in momentum of the turn, method of carrying the discus, and extent of crouch while making the turn, won almost universal acceptance until about 1935. Cromwell states that Houser used such a form during his great career from 1920 to 1928.

As a matter of fact, a few coaches of today still advocates just such a style. Bresnahan and Tuttle, in the 1950 edition of their very exhaustive text on track and field athletics, recommend a pivot-rotation style in which momentum is quite obviously not a primary factor. The jump-rotation style is given very minor attention and the full one and three-quarters turn is not considered at all.

However, since about 1929, when Eric Krenz, of Stanford, set a world's record of 163′ 8¾″ by dropping very low at the back of the circle and hopping high up and then down for the final pull, there has been a steady adoption of the hop as a standard form. A hop, of course, does not necessarily mean an up and down movement. Rather, it can be defined as a form in which, during the middle of the turn, both feet are definitely off the ground together. In contrast, the now almost entirely discarded pivot style maintains at least one foot on the ground at all times. To the writer's knowledge, the last excellent discus thrower or use this style was Hugh Canon, of Utah, who won the National AAU meet in 1943 with a fine throw of 174′ 10⅛″. Andersson of Sweden, Schroeder of Germany, Dunn and Fox of Stanford, and Consolini of Italy were all great throwers and all used a hop. The Europeans tend to keep the hop very close to the ground because of their emphasis upon momentum, but it is nevertheless a hop rather than a pivot.

The next important change in style was the use of one and three-quarters turns as a means of gaining additional momentum. The right foot is placed in the same spot at the back of the circle, but the left foot is allowed to shift with the backward swing of the right shoulder and arm to a point near the ring, about 15 to 20 inches from the right. This permits a full rotation of the body to the right, so that the back is facing in or even beyond the direction of the throw. A full hop or whirl brings the right foot into its usual position in the centre of the circle. Many throwers attempted this style earlier in the game, but Phil Fox, of Stanford (172′ 4½″ in 1939), was the first to master its difficulties and convince others of its merits.

With minor changes produced largely by individual differences, this form described by Fox is the most commonly used style in America today. Only one new approach or modification of this style has been suggested by an outstanding thrower—the style developed by Minnesota with Fitch as its chief proponent and carried to a somewhat extreme but remarkably successful degree by Gordien. Fitch's style, first of all, emphasized momentum and centrifugal drive through an extreme leading of the turn with the left shoulder and entire upper body. He permitted the great weight of the upper body to "fall" around the circle, with the feet trying desperately to catch up and only succeeding after the reverse and after the right foot had landed at the front of the circle. All other successful throwers have used the left leg as a firm brace against which they could stop the momentum of the lower body, accelerate momentum in the upper body and especially in the right arm and hand, and still remain in the circle without fouling. Fitch did brace against the left leg, yet carried his upper body momentum right on over the left foot with no hesitation for bracing and drove his right shoulder on into a very quick reverse, which was an actual part of the throw rather than a consequence of it. Gordien was even more extreme in this respect. The momentum and extreme shoulder lead of the opening movements usually carried his right foot well to the left of the centre line of the circle, so that the area in which he had to finish the throw without fouling was very limited. Unquestionably, this style produced greater momentum in the turn and greatly increased the arc of circle traversed during the entire action. Some excellent coaches believe, however, that Gordien certainly and Fitch perhaps lost more in body position and explosive force than they gained in centrifugal force. Severan more years and many thousand more throws, will need to pass we have any final answers concerning the merits of their form.

Essentials of Discus Throwing

It is the general viewpoint that teaching of form in field events should place emphasis upon the whole action as soon as possible and that part learning should be done at minimum levels. However, the unusual difficulty of maintaining balance while in the turn and of controlling the scale of the discus forces a special approach to this event and a much greater stress upon part learning of each phase than is normally necessary. Such a step-by-step method might be approached as follows:

Learning to handle the discus. For some time—perhaps days, perhaps weeks, depending upon the individual's quickness in learning—emphasis should be placed on throwing from a stand and getting the "feel" of the discus. As it is thrown, it rotates clockwise, leaving the index finger last, in such fashion that it travels almost parallel with the ground. The shape of the discus and the slight upward tilt of its forward edge increases the air pressure on the lower surface and decreases that on the surface, thus producing a lift effect identical to that on an airplane's wings. It is this lift plus the angle of delivery plus the upward drive of the right leg, hip, and back muscles that produces the actual trajectory and height of the throw.

The first difficulty will lie in maintaining control of the discus in the hand as it swings back and forth during the preliminary movement. These preliminary swings should be taught in such a way that they will be consistent with the form that is ultimately desired. They should therefore keep the discus away from the body, and beneath the palm of the hand at all times, using a forward and backward swing at an angle as close as possible to that of the throw itself. Keep the eyes horizontal at all times, for they are the best means of maintaining balance. At first, there should be little twisting of the body from the hips, but as learning progresses, a full twist around and down into the accepted starting position as shown in drawings should occur. This starting position places the feet about the width of the shoulders apart. More than this will make a proper start and control of the turn more difficult. The top of the head should drop down about 12 inches; to get lower will make a later whirl less well balanced; to stay higher will remove the power drive of the right leg and hip.

As the throw is made, emphasize the upward drive of the right leg while the discus is still behind the body. This action is similar to the upward drive in the shot and is the best method of securing a high trajectory and a flat discus at the same time. A trajectory of more than 30 degrees is necessary to good distance, at least if the wind is low, but if it is secured by tilting the forward edge of the discus up, the flat surface encounters wind resistance and throwing distance is lost. Such a method will bring the discus not more than 6 inches below shoulder height as it reaches the mid-point of the throw when the arm is at right angles to the direction of the throw. Many throwers neglect this procedure, bringing the discus through much lower and closer to the hip. They must then attempt either a low-angled throw or greater height by tilting the discus, either of which brings a loss in distance.

As soon as good judgment permits, there should be an awareness of the effect of the wind upon the discus. Most of the time, throws should be made against the wind, for circles are usually placed in that position. Steady winds up to about 6 miles per hour are helpful, for they increase the difference in pressure on the lower and upper surfaces of the discus and thereby provide more lift. The stronger the wind, the flatter the position of the discus should be while in flight.

At the very back of the discus swing, while still making the preliminary movements, the right foot will be in a rather flat-footed position with about one-third of the weight on the heel. However, from the point the body weight will move upward to the ball and toes of the right foot. Similarly, when the left leg braces against the drive of the right, the left foot will be rather flat against the ground, although with only a little weight on the heel. As the throw is made, the body weight shifts up and over to the toes of the left foot, with a full follow-up and follow-through in the direction of the throw. In throwing from a stand, there should be no reverse. The body momentum is not so great as to make a reverse necessary; and, since the reverse is but the consequence of momentum and follow-through rather than a part of the power action itself, it should not be taught until later.

The discus gains a much greater proportion of its force from the momentum of the body turn than is secured by the shot from the momentum of the travel across the circle. However, this fact does not justify the conclusion that one can neglect the slightest fraction of power from the body drive. Throwing from a stand should demand the highest attention to every aspect of body action that will bring greater explosive power. Only about 30 or 40 feet can be gained from the momentum of the turn, while the remaining 100 or 150 feet comes from the power of the body drive.

This drive begins from the right foot, which is solidly planted on the ground. The right knee and hip push upward first and then outward in the direction of the throw, but forward only enough to permit the hips to come through. In the beginning, it is more of a shot-putting action that a forward twisting of the hips and legs. The back begins to arch, and the chest and chin lift, but only to the point of aiding a forward drive to the toes of the left foot. If the head lifts up and back too far, the weight will shift to the left heel, the discus will be pulled across the chest to the left, with a great loss of the final whip action of the hand and fingers.

Throughout all this action, the left arm should be put in correct position as shown in the drawings and then forgotten. It will naturally accompany the action of the right arm and aid balance during the throw but should not be thrown outward and to the left in an effort to increase shoulder momentum. Such an attempt pulls the body forward too soon and diminishes the drive of the right leg and hip.

Learning to step forward and throw. This action is an extension of the process of throwing from a stand and is one more step toward learning the rhythm of the turn. The thrower faces the direction of his throw and swings the discus in an identical manner to that already learned. As it reaches the extreme left position over or close to the left shoulder, the thrower takes a short step about 15 inches forward with the right foot, smoothly pivoting and accompanying the discus to an extreme right position identical to that taken when throwing from a stand. From this point the throw is made. The additional momentum and force generated by such an action will add from 10 to 20 feet to the throw.

This method affords an excellent opportunity to practice natural recoil and bounce from the extreme position to the right, which Fox emphasizes and which be felt aided him greatly in getting an increased early body momentum. This results, as he states, from anchroing the right foot. Fox further suggests that the backward turn to the right, which uses a pivot on the right foot, should be supplemented by a very short twisting hop into the throwing position. Such a hop increases momentum and the effect of the bounce.

Learning the turn. The turn in the discus is probably the most difficult phase of any weight event to teach or learn. The problem is not merely how to learn correct form, balance, and momentum, but how to learn them as quickly as possible. The great majority of coaches attack the problem very cautiously and take each phase step by step. However, 25 years of enthusiastic discus coaching has convinced that a little daring pays dividends. Since 1940, our discus throwers have all used the one and three-quarters turn and have permitted momentum to come as it would even during the first week of throwing. There have repeatedly been times of discouragement and no progress, of course, but all in all, if one is reaching for best possible performances, this "nothing held back" method has been economical of time and productive of success.

Perhaps one of the reason for this has been the use of the device which has a cloth belt or strap is tacked to an old discus so that the hand can be easily slipped under it. This strap prevents the discus from being dropped while turning or from being released at the end of a "throw". Consequently, many more turns can be taken in a short period of time and without tiring the throwing muscles. Without question, discus throwers do not make enough thousands of turns. Consider the perfect balance of ballet dancers, which is acquired only by endless turning. Discus men should and can do likewise.

When beginning with this "Fox" style, the writer has emphasized the whole action and ignored momentum. That is, do not try for speed, but do not try to hold back either. Think through and then call out the rhythm of a long "turn-n-n-n-n and throw". Just let the discus go as you call "throw", no matter how much off balance your body is or in what direction the discus may go. Of course, the coach and all other contestants might well hide behind a brick wall during these first efforts, for few men know which way is up or out while they are turning. Keep your eyes on the horizontal, hold your right shoulder and the discus back just a little, and then go right into the "turn-n-n-n-n and throw" with confidence.

This method, thus simplified as much as possible, produces relatively quick and sure results, and is most certainly faster than teaching and perfecting one and one-hald turns first and then increasing he arc later.

To complete the description of the essentials of modern form, the so-called "Fitch" style requires explanation beyond that already made in the section on form development. First it should be emphasized that Fitch leads not only with the hips but with the entire upper body. Only the discus and discus arm are held back. The momentum established is thereby increased beyond what can be secured from a more simple hip lead. However, the problem of catching up with balance is increased tremendously, and even such an experienced thrower as Gordien, who used this style, had his balance troubles. Second, Fitch used a very fast forward throw of the right shoulder, making the reverse somewhat more a part of the throw and landing rather hard on the right leg. Fitch, however, did use the left leg as a brace by which the lower body momentum could be accelerated and transferred to the upper body and right arm and hand. Gordien carried this emphasis several degrees further by throwing through the right shoulder and off the left leg even more quickly. He was able to stay in the circle only through a hard landing on the right foot and series of rather desperate hops for balance around the left edge of the circle.

It can be argued of course that the style used by Fitch and Gordien is merely an extension of that used by Fox. If so, it will be learned automatically as increased confidence, relaxation, and perfection of form and balance tend to encourage ever greater momentum. In any case, it seems clear at the present time that attempts to teach this style early in the learning process will prove unwise and wasteful of time and effort.

Important Questions and Answers

How important is size in the discus throw? The importance of size is dependent upon how far and how soon you want to throw the discus. Great size complicates an already complex event and makes quick mastery extremely difficult. If the important event this year is only ten weeks away and all the candidates are new to the discus, it would be well to depend upon the smaller and more easily co-ordinated men. This is particularly true with the smaller 3-pound-9-ounce high school discus, with which quickness and explosiveness are more important than power and either height or weight.

On the other hand, size is essential to best distances in the discus. Of the best 25 throwers in history, only 2 could be classified as small men—Vic Frank, of Yale, and Phil Fox, of Stanford. But even they had sufficient power to loss the shot over 50 feet. An interesting contrast can be made between Frank and Fuchs, both of Yale. Undoubtedly Fuchs had the greater size and ability of the two men, but because of greater attention and effort given to the discus by Frank, he was able to win over his teammate quite consistently.

Perhaps the greatest of all discus prospects was Al Blozis, the fine shot-putter from Georgetown University. He was 6′ 6″ tall, weighed 240 pounds, and was very quick and well co-ordinated; he might have thrown the discus over 200 feet. But his activity in football and his primary interest in the shot meant that only a small proportion of his time and study was given to the discus. Consequently, Blozis best toss of 173′ 10¾″, though well beyond his average, was probably not near his potential best.

The only common-sense answer to this question, of course, is simply to get the best material you can and then make the most of what you have.

How should the discus be held? The discus should be held in a way that is as natural and easy as possible but that still provides the last-minute whip of the wrist and hand that drives it on its way. This requires a clawlike grasp of the fingers, so that the discus will be whirled out of and around the first finger rather than from the second finger. Release from the second finger is quite likely to tilt the discus while in flight and often causes it to wobble. Such wobbling increases air resistance and reduces the lifting power of the difference in air pressure upon the two sides of the discus. However, a "clawlike grasp" does not mean tense and widespread fingers. With practice, complete control of the discus can be secured by relaxed fingers that are only about ½ inch apart. Proper maintenance of centrifugal force will keep the discus in the hand without difficulty.

How hard should a discus thrower work? The answer is clear and certain: as hard and as long as the thrower's ambition and available time will permit. This is true not only for the number of throws per day, but for the number of days per week and weeks per year as well. There is no danger of going stale physically, of becoming muscle-bound or overdeveloped. Most throwers do become tired after about 30 minutes of steady work and do have a tendency then to lose form. However, a short rest of 10 or 15 minutes will restore energy, and practice can then be resumed. Or, if preferred, a session of throwing from a stand or of whirling without actually throwing the discus will condition the body so that next week more throws can be taken without fatigue.

A recent excellent article on discus throwing quoted an "authority" in motor learning as stating that 30 minutes of practice on any one motor skill was sufficient for greatest progress. This might be true for extremely simple motor skills but certainly has no significance for the discus. If a man's schedule permits, three times this amount of time will hardly suffice for accomplishing all the things that need to be done. Not only longer but more that as little time as possible will be wasted in running out after them. Throwers should work in pairs, if possible. Having more than two men working together wastes time and greatly increases the danger of being struck by the discus. Practice, practice, practice, and then be patient with slow progress.

How much momentum is needed in the discus? The answer to this question lies with each individual. If his time and interest are at rather minimum levels, momentum is similarly a minimum concern. In such a case, it is better by far to stress proper control of the discus, to learn a sound throwing position and style, and then simply to walk across or around the circle. About three-fourths of maximum distance can be secured by such a method and that may wins a few dual meets. Again, perhaps interest is high but only two or three years are available for practice before graduation. Fitch's shoulder throw would undoubtedly be difficult to learn thoroughly in this short length of time.

On the other hand, if ability, time and interest are all at high levels, there is almost no limit to ultimate momentum of the body. Ryan, of Yale, speaks of "critical" momentum, a very useful concept. He contends that each man has a right momentum, beyond which the loss in balance and power more than compensates for the gain in speed of the turn. This is undoubtedly true for each man at any given time. Yet such "critical" speed is actually a challenge to the athlete and the coach to raise its level to new heights. A greater relaxation, a slightly different sense of balance, and a slightly increased "off-balance" action will all raise the "critical" momentum beyond what is now possible. The answer to new records at both the high school and the college level lies in the utilization of increased momentum in the turn. We are likely to improve very little in our fundamental position and throwing action.

Certainly we have not begun to reach maximum momentum in our discus throwing as yet. Watch the speed with which modern dancers or acrobats whirl. True, the discus is an added factor, but that merely means more thought about the method and more practice in its perfection.

At what angle should the discus be thrown? The generally accepted angle is 30 degrees. However, the ability to throw the discus higher with no loss in throwing power is a most valuable one. Its accomplishment lies in a slightly lower position during the turn and a greater emphasis upon the upward drive of the right leg and hip at the start of the throw. In line with such an emphasis, the discus should be lifted at the start of the throw rather than just before its release. Keep the discus from the hip and at shoulder level as it reaches the halfway point of the throw. When throwing from a stand, practice throwing the discus as high and as parallel with the ground as possible; an angle of 60 degrees is not too much. This will give the sensation of driving upward with the legs and lifting at the start of the throw. When there is a strong following wind or no wind at all, such a method is invaluable.

A strong head wind requires a flat discus, and, unless the thrower is very clever in handling the discus, a low one as well. A head wind gives additional "lift", to a discus just as it does to an airplane, and the angle of tilt of the discus needs to be less than normal. The discus that climbs high with the wind and then turns half over has lost distance. The 174′ 8¾″ world's record throw of Archie Harris (Indiana ′42), which he deliberately threw well to the right and low in order to gain the advantage of a strong wind and which appeared to hang forever only about 40 feet off the ground. Obviously, the good discus thrower will experiment with the wind, throwing at all angles until he knows its whims, its dangers, and its values.

Common Faults and Their Correction

Faults in the discus result exclusively from the conflict between efforts to achieve a high degree of momentum in the whirl and efforts to preserve maximum explosive power in the throw itself. Basic throwing position has not changed since 1912. It is the degree of emphasis upon momentum that has aroused all the uncertainties, created all the arguments, an upset all the balances of the past half century.

1. Permitting momentum to become a problem before a sound knowledge of all other aspects of the discus has been established. This refers particularly to attempts to increase momentum but also to efforts to slow down the natural speed of the whirl. Wise coaches will ignore the problem entirely and never mention momentum at all until late in the learning process. They will teach a style which presupposes high momentum and from which such momentum will inevitable result without special emphasis in coaching. After a highly developed sense of position and balance has been achieved through years of throwing, this rule can be ignored and increased

momentum can be a matter of deliberate effort and coaching.

2. Permitting the eyes to drop below the plane in which the throw is being made. Eye position is primary in all actions involving balance. To permit the eyes to drop toward the ground near the circle will almost certainly bring the body forward unduly and make balance precarious. A style such as that used by Fitch violates this rule and thereby makes balance extremely difficult. At the other extreme, a pivot-step turn such as Houser or Cannon advocated maintains an erect position at all times and a horizontal eye focus throughout the turn. Continued horizontal focus of the eyes implies, of course, that the line of the shoulders will also be close to the horizontal.

A related fault lies in lifting the eyes unduly as the actual throw is made. This lifts the head too far back, pulls the weight back to the left heel, throws body power off to the left, and usually results in a loosened and wobbling discus off to the right.

3. Permitting the discus to aid the turn. Body momentum must precede discus momentum. The whole theory of the discus turn is that body momentum must first be established and is then accelerated and transferred to the right arm, wrist, hand and fingers in an explosive concentration of energy. It is an though one were cracking a whip that contained springs or units of force within itself. The first inertia to call into play would be that of the heavier handle. Obviously, the tip would lay back or drag behind; the more drag, the greater the potential time in which force can be applied. An extension of this analogy reveals that it is the handle of the whip which must stop first and that the more sudden the stop, the more force is generated. Herein lies the importance of the left leg as a bracing unit.

4. Permitting the upper body to move too far forward and around at the start of the turn. This always creates

too long a hop either forward or to the left of the circle, and makes balance questionable, application of power difficult, and fouling certain. Again, it is necessary to note that the Fitch style utilizes just this means of gaining momentum. However, to copy Fitch is to gamble ultimate greatness against more immediate results. More conservative methods will hold the weight of the shoulders back, drag the arm and the discus, and place the right foot close to the diameter of the circle.

5. Hopping up rather than hopping around. The hop is an essential part of accepted discus from today. It implies that for an instant (very short with Consolini, much longer with Gordien) both feet are off the ground. However, the effect of such a hop should be to increase horizontal momentum and should lift the body upward as little as possible. The drive off each foot, which creates the hop, should push the already falling body even faster in its whirl. It must therefore occur after the weight of the body has passed beyond the foot, rather than when it is over the foot. In this respect the purpose of the hop in the discus is similar to that in the shot put. To understand its effect in one event is to understand it in both.

6. Failure to use the left leg as both a brace and a power unit when making the throw. The primary value of the left leg in making the throw itself is to stop suddenly the whirling momentum of the lower body and to permit concentration of force in the upper body and right arm. A left foot that is "in the bucket" has little value for this purpose or for the final upward and outward drive up on the toes that accompanies the final wrist flick of the discus. Gordien used his left leg, of course, but with almost minimum effect and in minimum time. His form in this respect still does not have general acceptance, however, and caution would argue for more orthodox methods.

7. Hesitating near the end of the whirl in order to

gather for the final throw. Such hesitation is contrary to modern practice and to the full use of body momentum, but if immediate results are important, it may afford just enough balance to make immediate efforts more effective. Usually, however, such hesitation is the result of an extreme loss of balance. Correction of the fault which caused the loss of balance will eliminate the hesitation.

8. Permitting the right hip to rotate forward too soon. The hip should come through much faster in the discus than in the shot. But, faster should not be interpreted as sooner. To hold the right side, shoulder, and arm, and the discus well back throughout the turn will prove helpful. Or one can emphasize the right leg's upward drive and thereby lift the right arm and discus rather than simply swinging them around at a low-angled arc. This will help to delay the start of hip rotation.

9. Failure to follow up on the toes of the left foot. This is particularly in point when throwing from a stand, for if the correct procedure is not learned there, a similar fault will probably occur when whirling. Such failure usually means a poor follow-through and a strong tendency to fall off to the left and away from the throw. It is sometimes caused by an attempt to impart rotation to the discus by pulling across the body at the end of the throw. In fact, some coaches advocate just such a method. It is inevitable that the hand and arm will move quickly to the left after the discus is in flight; but for them to do so before a full follow-through in the direction of the throw has been made is definitely to shorten the throw.

10. Permitting the discus to wobble in flight or to slide off to the right. Usually such a fault results from a failure to maintain the pressure of the first finger. The discus slips through around the second finger, and control of both discus tilt and rotation is lost. Occasionally a more basic cause can be found in the tendency to pull the

discus through close to the right hip. This brings the discus up on a concave curve and releases it at a rather vertical plane. The natural pull of the hand causes a wobble instead of giving the usual impetus. In contrast, a more horizontal plane of pull provides a flat discus and a smooth release. Sometimes, of course, the fault can be corrected simply by taking a slightly larger "bite" on the discus with the first finger or by moistening it just before throwing. The concept of a "talon" grip throughout the entire action should be helpful.

Organization of Practice

Organization of practice is of course dependent upon the individual, his ambition, and his available time. Perhaps he is throwing the discus on time left over from football practice or from the shot put. Practice will be apportioned accordingly. However, assuming that discus throwing is a primary concern, efficient practice will be organized about as follows:

1. Preliminary period. This will include easy sprinting, warm-up exercises, and throwing from a stand. This last is not a mere warm-up but an essential part of learning to throw. Experiment with wind directions. Try for very high throws and low ones. Keep the discus off the hip and get height by lifting the discus at the start of the throw rather than by tilting it. Exaggerate the low crouch at the start of the throw to develop leg and hip power. Be conscious of using the first index finger in the release of the discus. The latter must roll around it, not through it.

2. Throwing from within the circle. Think in terms of the whole action rather than of details. Strive for over-all balance and rhythm. Gradually increase momentum as confidence and co-ordination increase. Toward the end of this period, take a number of throws from which excellent distance

results but in which the attention is upon the whole form and upon the how of the action. Take as many such throws as seem to be worth while. However, as fatigue develops and co-ordination begins to slip away, shift to the next activity.

3. Throwing from the circle for condition and with greater concern for the details of form. Even here, try to minimize details and stress fundamentals. Always throw from within the circle, always keep the ground brushed, and always be aware of how your feet are travelling across the circle. Try for greater angle of throw. Shift the circle so that throws are going both with and against the wind. Shift your starting position in the circle so that you can throw either to the left or to the right of the 90-degree arc.

4. Throwing from a stand. Have three or four discuses and a manager present so that you need only to reach down in order to be ready to throw again. Make repeated throws for condition as rapidly as possible and as far as possible. Be sure than none of the fundamentals of correct form are being neglected, but emphasize the repetition of form so that it becomes automatic and involuntary. Some throwers may prefer to use this final period in continuing the whirl. If balance and co-ordination have not been lost, this is, in fact, preferable. Without question, the main reason discus throwers have so much trouble with the turn is that they simply do not turn often enough.

5. Shifting to other events. Sprinting, high-jumping, standing broad jump, and low hurdles are all worth while.

DAILY SCHEDULES OF PRACTICE

The amount of practice permissible in the discus throw is similar to that in the shot-put. Many throws in daily practice may be taken without fear of injury. Like the shot-putter (and a man may well compete in both events) the discus-thrower who understand the mechanics of the event and who diligently pursues simple daily exercises the year round will be in readiness for early season schedules of practice. In addition to the large muscle groups of the legs and trunk, he must develop strength in the fingers and wrist. Agility in footwork is as essential for him as for the boxer.

By the time early season practices are called, the discus-thrower is presumed to have completed the preliminary season workouts.

The attention of the discus-thrower is called to the fact that he may not find his achievements progressing steadily onward and upward. There may be days when his advancement may be at a standstill, or the distance of his throws reduced by several feet. He must take heart and try to solve the difficulties which may be but temporary faults in technique.

Schedules are presented for early season, midseason, and late season, based on a discus-thrower competing in this event alone. If additional events are assigned the athlete, changes in the amount and character of the schedules will necessarily have to be made. The discus-thrower may find certain coaching points in the shot-put valuable, and is referred to the schedules of practice for that event.

Early Season

Monday

1. Start the workout by jogging 200 yards, walking 285 yards, and jogging 150 yards.
2. Execute from six to eight minutes of exercises, such as handstands, squats, running in place, and vigorous bending.
3. Familiarize yourself with the various types of

discuses: (a) wood-centered, (b) rubber, and (c) all-metal.

Experiment with the different styles of grasp. Note that the grasps vary with the size of the hand and length of the fingers.

4. From the standing position release the discus so that it describes a clockwise spin as it is pulled by the first finger. Adjust the wrist turn and the pressure applied by the little finger so that the missile spins cleanly, offering minimum resistance to the air. The angle of flight may vary slightly from 30 degrees. Repeat the efforts from twelve to twenty times or until the knack of sailing the discus has been mastered.
5. Throw from the standing position from ten to fifteen times, emphasizing the power developed from the right leg and initiated by a forceful upward-forward movement of the right hip.
6. End the day's practice with a jog of 300 yards and a sprint of 20 yards followed by a shower and a massage.

Tuesday

1. Begin the day's work with a jog of 150 yards, a walk of 50 yards, and a run of 25 yards, and a sprint of 25 yards.
2. Perform from six to eight minutes of body-building exercises which may include stunts with the 25-pound weight, trunk or leg raising while lying on the back, and vigorous high kicking, both forward and backward.
3. Throw the discus from the standing position (without pivot or jump-turn) ten to sixteen times. Study your effort for height, discus angle, angle of flight, and direction of throw, bearing in mind that

throws falling outside the 90 degree sector are not recorded.

4. Skip rope for two minutes.
5. Join the sprinters and take two dashes of 25 yards.
6. Assume the initial stance which seems best fitted to you. Without the discus, go through the consecutive steps, pivot or jump-turn, in traversing the circle. Repeat from eight to ten times.
7. Grasp the missile in a manner to your liking. Experiment with the various styles of grip even though you have found one that seems effective. Throw four or five times using the turn and final delivery. Ask the coach or observer to note the propulsion obtained from the right leg.
8. Complete the practice with a jog of 200 yards, a sprint of 20 yards, a shower, and a massage.

Wednesday

1. Initiate the practice with jogging, running, and walking a total distance of 440 yards.
2. Perform from five to ten minutes of stunts such as weight lifting, vigorous arm swinging, medicine ball passing, or tumbling.
3. Experiment on a discus made of lead but meeting all standard specifications except weight. Obviously it will weigh more than 2 kilograms. Note the effect on balance when you again throw the regulation missile. Has the use of the heavier discus been an aid or a hindrance?
4. Throw the discus from fifteen to twenty times (using moderate effort) from a position near the front of the circle without employing the body turn or the foot reverse. On succeeding trials and before the final pull, vary the amount of knee bend employed. What degree of bend do you find

produces the greatest leg drive? What degree of bend produces a leg drive that can be best imparted to the discus?

5. Throw with moderate effort from the standing position from ten to twelve times, half of them with the implement held at arm's length, high and to the back, the other half low and to the back. Note the height of the throws resulting from the extremes of arm elevation and draw your own conclusions.
6. Join the broad-jumpers and take two or three trials.
7. Finish this practice session by jogging and sprinting; then take a tepid shower and a massage.

Thursday

1. Limber up with jogging, walking, and sprinting.
2. Execute from five to ten minutes of diversified exercises designed to develop the large muscle groups. Perform as many pull-up and chinning exercises as you feel capable of doing. Remember that the discus is an arm-pulling event. Develop the pectoral and deltoid muscles by swinging an ordinary window sash weight in each hand simultaneously.
3. Smooth out any faults in the release by delivering from ten to fifteen times at seven-eighths effort, from the standing position. Summon an observer, if the coach is not available, to note the location of your right foot at the instant the discus leaves the hand. If the right foot has been lifted too soon, enlist the aid of a teammate in holding it on the ground until the discus leaves the hand. An alternate drill consists of delivering the discus and omitting completely the reversing of the feet. The right toe may be dragged forward after he missile is released. This type of footwork is regularly employed by a number of European discus-throwers.

4. Eliminate the teammate's assistance and throw the discus six or eight times with conscious effort placed on the right leg drive.
5. Join the high-jumpers and take five or six trials.
6. End the practice by jogging 300 to 350 yards and taking a tepid shower and a massage.

Friday

1. Start the day with jogging, hopping, and bounding.
2. Brush the surface of the circle smooth so that your spike marks are visible. With the discus in hand, traverse the circle, noting the distance covered in each foot movement. Again brush the circle and repeat from fifteen to twenty times until you are convinced you have found the most efficient distribution of distance. Retain a mental pattern of your new discovery.
3. Experiment with various methods of traversing the circle, i.e., the pivot-rotation style the jump-rotation style, and their variations. Throw four or five times with each style. Aided by an observer, critically analyse your own application of these various forms. In early season, experimentation with different methods of crossing the circle is desirable. In the midst of the competitive season such shifting of form is undesirable. Increase gradually the power behind each succeeding throw.
4. Vary the practice procedure by joining the broad-jumpers for six or eight jumps.
5. Conclude the day's practice with three minutes of exercises which are needed especially in the discus throw, a jog of 200 yards, and a sprint of 50 yards. Substitute a sponge bath for the shower, and obtain a massage.

Saturday

In early season we have assumed that no contest has been scheduled for Saturday and that the athlete will have six days available for practice.

1. Warm up thoroughly, having in mind your individual requirements for efficient throwing. Jog 200 yards, walk 25 yards, hop and bound 10 yards, and sprint 25 yards.
2. Perform from five to eight minutes of moderate exercises, such as trunk bends, trunk twists, wood-chopping exercise, or complete body spins from the standing jump.
3. Skip rope for two minutes.
4. Throw from six to ten minutes, applying three-fourths effort from the position at the front of the circle. Concentrate on coordination of power from the foot to discus. Emphasize the follow-through and the whip of the arm across the chest. If the discus is sailing smoothly and at the correct angle, you are then ready for throws using the complete form including the progression across the circle. Note carefully the footage made in each successive throw so that you can judge the correct amount of warm-up.
5. Throw six or seven times, employing the complete form. Analyse your turn or pivot to see whether optimum speed is generated and whether the correct amount of distance is covered. Throw with increasing vigour until your last heave represents nearly full effort.
6. Rest momentarily and acquire physical and mental poise as though you were entering an important contest.
7. Throw with full effort six or seven times, carefully

observing the rules on fouling. As observer or coach will advise you after each throw or your correct and faulty executions.

8. End Saturday's practice with three minutes of vigorous exercise for the wrist and fingers, such as the wall push-away and wrist roll. The jog 250 yards followed by a shower and massage. Analyse your weight chart for the week.

Midseason

Schedules for midseason are planned to meet a program calling for competition on Saturday. Like those for the shot-put, midseason schedules in the discus event indicate reduction in throwing at full effort and provide for light activity on Thursday and Friday.

A majority of coaches agree that very little discus tossing for distanced should be prescribed after Wednesday. There is a division of opinion on the most desirable days for strenuous practice. One group favours throwing for distance Monday and Tuesday, with tapering-off practices on Wednesday and Thursday. The other group advises throwing at full effort on Monday and Wednesday, using Tuesday as a light practice period.

Since excellent results have been obtained with both plans, the competitor and coach will arrange this detail to fit individual needs. The first plan is described in the succeeding paragraphs.

Monday

1. Adjust yourself for a day of vigorous throwing by jogging, hopping, and sprinting. Take from three to five minutes exercises on the side horse, such as single and double leg swings (the weight being supported by both arms).

2. Observe the direction of the wind and the temperature of the day. Then determine the type and quantity of warm-up you require. Execute five

or six minutes of calisthenics.

3. Sprint 15 yards at top speed and skip rope for two minutes.

4. Simulate unfavourable weather conditions by immersing the discus in muddy water and make use of recommended aids such as resin, compound tincture of benzoin, or balsam of fir, to hold the implement. Experiment with these accessories on practice days rather than during important competition, tossing the discus three or four times with the aid of each substance. These substances may be removed from the discus and the hands with alcohol.

5. Throw five or six times, employing the entire form at full effort. Make use of your teammates so that an accurate report is available to you after each effort. Note the distance of each throw so that you may judge when you have reached the crest of your warm-up. Remember the desirability of getting your best throws early in the preliminary round.

6. Lean to relax completely between trials. Throw three times with full effort to conclude the strenuous section of Monday's practice.

7. Jog 300 yards before ending the day with either a sponge bath or a tepid shower of short duration.

Tuesday

1. Begin the practice with a jog of 200 yards, a walk of 25 yards, a run of 100 yards, and a sprint of 50 yards.

2. Arrive at a definite procedure in your warm-up which will be adhered to whenever preparing for intensive throwing. Vary it only to meet exceptional weather conditions.

3. Skip rope for two minutes. Engage in three to five minutes of brisk exercises, such as chinning on

the high bar and dip-swinging on the parallel bars to bring into action the deltoid and pectoral muscles which play a major part in discus throwing.

4. Throw six or eight times from the standing position, noting the plane of the discus itself and the angle of its path shortly after the release; the drive of the legs, the trunk, and the arms; and the intensive wrist snap at the finish.

5. Throw from six to ten times employing the turn, the release, and the recovery. Duplicate your predetermined ideal from on the distance of footspread, the amount of knee bend, the speed of body rotation, the timing of the final heave, and the follow-through. Increase or diminish the number of preliminary throws so that you feel primed to give your best performance quite early in the next section of the workout. In other words, make certain that you have properly timed your warm-up.

6. Deliver four times as in competition. Compare trial by trial your Tuesday efforts with those of Monday. With this background adjust or retain your daily routine.

7. Finish the practice with a sun bath (weather permitting), a jog of 300 yards, and a tepid shower. Avoid a debilitating hot shower, especially on days preceding throwing for distance. Obtain a massage.

Wednesday

1. Start practice with jogging, sprinting, and calisthenics.

2. Practice from three to five minutes on the footwork and turn without carrying the discus.

3. Take five or six moderate throws with an overweight missile.

4. Spend from five to ten minutes with the regulation implement, throwing for form only and polishing the rough points of execution. The number of trials and the amount of effort expended on each are left to the contestant.
5. Participate in stunts or a game to vary the practice routine.
6. Take four or five trials of the running high jump.
7. End the workout with a 250-yard jog, a shower, and a massage.

Thursday

1. Jog 300 yards, dry off perspiration, and expose the body to the sun for five minutes.
2. Make use of action photographs of yourself to visualize proper and faulty execution.
3. Spend from three to five minutes on gymnastic stunts such as handstands, walking on hands, and tumbling.
4. Deliver the discus eight or ten times at moderate effort. Emphasize handling it under various conditions of windage. Become accustomed to throw from any type of footing, either clay, cinders, grass, or loam—dry or soggy.
5. Conclude the strenuous section of this week's practice with two or three dashes of 50 yards. Substitute a sponge bath for the usual shower, and follow it with massage. Note the change in your body weight.

Friday

There are two methods of dealing with Friday's activities, one calling for complete absence from the athletic environment and the other recommending light limbering up. If the competitor chooses to appear suited-up, he may investigate the type of circle he is to use

Saturday, thus affording opportunity for adjusting length of spikes. Take cognizance of the prevailing winds as well as the weather forecast. Check on all personal equipment, especially the weight of the discus.

1. Jog and walk alternately for two or three minutes.
2. Perform three or four minutes of light calisthenics.
3. Jog in for a sponge bath, but omit the customary shower bath. Massage or manipulation of the throwing muscles is recommended for those who believe it benefits athletic performance.

Saturday

Since this is a day of competition, the athlete will adjust the routine of rest, meals, study or work so that he will be in readiness both mentally and physically for the contest. Arrange your preliminary exercises so that you allow from five to fifteen minutes between the end of the warm-up and the beginning of competition. If this rest period is unduly shortened, the athlete will have insufficient time to acquire physical as well as mental poise. If the rest period is extremely long, the thrower may lose the benefits derived by a well-calculated warm-up. This situation parallels that of the manipulator of the hammer and forge who must be accurate in heating the metal and precise in timing the blows which determine its shape.

1. Complete your warm-up, by this time a ritual on days of throwing at full effort.
2. Competition: if your practices have been fruitful so that your sequence of movement is automatic, you may concentrate on an explosive delivery.
3. Analyse your throws after the competition is over. If you made a brilliant toss, retain the formula so that you may duplicate it in future contests. In other words, be muscle-minded. On the contrary,

if your performance was substandard, analyse the activity so that faulty parts may be corrected in future practice sessions.

4. Take two or three throws after the competition is over when nothing is at stake. Carefully note the degree of body tension employed, together with the distance thrown. If these nonscoring throws are better than the scoring marks, the competitor may well recheck his warm-up procedure and his mental and nervous control.
5. End this week in midseason by two or three minutes of exercise for the fingers, wrist, and arm, followed by a shower bath and massage. Study your fluctuation of body weight during the week.

CHAPTER 7

THE TECHNIQUE OF DISCUS THROWING

To obtain maximum distance in throwing the discus, a sequence of movements involving forward acceleration acquired through body rotation with the discus held at arm's length must occur. There are several methods of approach practised in order to achieve this end. There are two styles used extensively, the pivot-rotation and jump-rotation. In Europe a style is used which is at considerable variance.

Since the technique of the pivot-rotation style lends itself better to teaching beginners, it is described in more detail than other forms. After this form has been mastered, a competitor may either continue its use or make such variations as lend greater distance to his throw. In the description which follows, it is assumed that the athlete is a right-handed thrower.

The Pivot-Rotation Style

The throw is described by following a sequence of movements based on the successive position of the feet, so far as the event permits. The divisions of the discussion are as follows: (1) the handhold, (2) the initial stance, (3) the preliminary swings, (4) the left foot pivot, (5) the right foot pivot, (6) the delivery, (7) the release, and (8) the recovery.

1. The Handhold

The method adopted for grasping the discus depends to a large extent on the size of the hand. The discus is held flat against the palm with the first joint of each finger over the edge. The fingers are slightly and evenly spread and grasp the edge firmly. The thumb is flat against the discus, extending in a straight line with the forearm. The grasp is such that the hand is behind the centre of weight of the discus. This type of hold provides for balance and lends impetus to the spin as it leaves the hand. The extended thumb serves as a supporting rather than a grasping member.

It is obvious that shorter fingers detract from a firm hold on the discus rim. In this form of grasp the centre of the palm falls more nearly over the centre of the discus.

This method of grasping the discus is described by Hamilton of the University of California as follows: "In grasping the discus the athlete's hand resembles somewhat the talon of the eagle. The hand is arched or cupped so that the lobes at the base of the fingers do not touch the discus, the back of the discus resting lightly on the wrist and the lobe of the thumb. With the exception of the fingers over the edge and the thumb lightly on the face of the discus close to the index finger, no other parts of the hand except those mentioned touch the discus. It is impossible to cup the hand properly for this style if the thumb is extended to the left as far as possible. It must be relaxed and carried reasonably close to the index finger. As the hand is set in the talon grip, the hand should be turned slightly to the right. This serves a double purpose—it allows for a little more wrist snap at the conclusion of the throw and it will place the weight of the discus slightly in front of the fingers". This method provides for greater hand flexion, more force, and less friction on the implement.

2. The Initial Stance

The competitor stands at the back of the circle with the feet at approximately a right angle to the direction of the throw. The feet may or may not be parallel. The distance between them varies from 16 inches to 20 inches, depending on the requirements of the thrower.

In the initial stance the body weight is evenly distributed between the feet. The trunk is almost erect with varying degrees of knee bend. In general, the musculature of the body is relaxed. The initial stance is flat-footed.

As soon as the competitor assumes his initial stance, he grasps the discus in preparation for the beginning of the preliminary swings. At the start of the preliminary swings, the left hand may be used as a support.

3. The Preliminary Swings

Usually, a competitor swings the discus from front to back three times for the purpose of establishing proper balance, reassuring himself of his grasp, and adding impetus to his body for the beginning of his turn. The swings are performed in a relaxed manner. During the arm swings the body weight shifts from foot to foot.

As the discus reaches the rear, in the last preliminary swing, the body turn begins.

4. The Pivot on the Left Foot

When the last preliminary swing reaches the farthest point back, the competitor's body weight is on the right foot while body balance is maintained by the contact of the ball of left foot with the ground. The left arm is usually extended and synchronized with the swinging of the right. The knees are slightly bent. As the discus is brought forward, the trunk is turned sharply to the left and body weight is shifted from the right to the left foot. From this position a half turn is executed by pivoting on the ball of the left foot.

5. The Pivot on the Right Foot

Maintaining the impetus gained in the half turn, the competitor continues the turn by shifting the body weight to the right foot, and executes an additional half turn by pivoting on the right foot. During the turn, the left foot reaches ahead toward the front of the circle and establishes contact with the ground rather earlier than would be expected for a pivot turn, so that the thrower is enabled to gather himself for the final throw without losing any of the essential angular or turning velocity. He simply turns into the position for the final effort. Both feet are then planted on the ground. This completes the turn and marks the beginning of the delivery.

6. The Delivery

As the movement described above is completed, the thrower is set for the final effort. Both feet are on the ground with the body weight chiefly on the right foot. He then throws himself into the final heave which involves the execution of the following synchronized movements: (a) a vigorous forward and upward thrust of the right hip, (b) a straightening of the right leg, (c) a rapid twist of the trunk to the left, (d) an explosive whip of the arm, and (e) a fast, powerful snap of the wrist, which has previously been "set" or "cocked" for this movement.

The knees are slightly bent with the body weight resting chiefly on the right foot. The trunk, while nearly erect, is inclined neither forward not backward. The discus is being carried at about the same angle as at the release. From this position the right hip thrust is begun. As the movement continues, the right leg is straightened. The thrower is well along in the execution of the delivery. As the throw is continued, the body weight is shifted to the left foot. The angle of the discus during the flight has been determined by the time this stage of the throw has been reached. From this position, the release is executed.

7. The Release

The discus is released with the plane of the throw at an angle of approximately 30 degrees. The discus is released from a point about opposite or slightly ahead of the shoulder. It leaves the hand, spinning in a clockwise direction. The spin is brought about by the follow-through of the arm and is given additional impetus by the vigorous snap of the wrist to the left. As the discus is released, the momentum of the body tends to carry the thrower forward, and, since he must stay within the circle, he must gain body balance. The position of the feet is then quickly reversed, the left being brought sharply backward and the right snapped to the front.

8. The Recovery

After the discus is released the body weight is totally on the right foot. Balance is gained by synchronization the bending of the right knee and the backward swinging of the left leg and left arm.

Jump-Rotation Style

In this style of throw the handhold, the initial stance, and the preliminary swings may be executed in the same manner as described in the pivot-rotation form. The chief variation comes in gaining momentum across the circle.

An initial stance is taken in which the feet are placed at right angles to the throw. The right foot is close to the edge of the circle and the left foot from 10 to 14 inches away. In this style the feet are closer together than in the pivot form, since one jumps to a better advantage from this position. Continuous with the last preliminary swing the competitor drives vigorously from both feet, jumping in the air and making a complete turn of the body, landing on both feet. The distance of the jump usually varies from 36 inches to 42 inches. In landing after the jump, the feet are fairly well spread, the customary distance being from 32 to 36 inches.

The discus is delivered from the stance which the competitor assumes at the completion of the jump. From this position the thrower adds more impetus to the power gained from the jump and body turn by a vigorous thrust of the right hip, a straightening of the right leg, and a snap of the right arm. Discus throwers are warned not to rely too heavily on momentum gained in the turn at the expense of neglecting the leg drive.

The release is made at arm's length from a point about opposite or slightly ahead of the shoulder. The angle of the discus flight may be somewhat less than 30 degrees.

In order to gain balance, the position of his feet is reversed, but not until the discus has left his hand. If the reverse is executed prematurely, valuable driving force from the right foot is lost.

Variations and Errors in Discus Throwing Technique

In the description of discus throwing, numerous points of interest to the student of this event were omitted in order not to break the continuity of the different phases of the throw. These phases of discus throwing are discussed separately as they apply to (1) the handhold, (2) the initial stance, (3) the preliminary swings, (4) traversing the circle, (5) the delivery, (6) the release, and (7) the recovery.

1. The Handhold

The first consideration in the grasp of the discus is that the athlete must decide on the style which permits him to have the weight of the discus in front of the fingers. A discus cannot be thrown by grasping its front edge any better than a javelin can be thrown by grasping it at the point. Obviously, the size of the hand and the length of the fingers determine the position of the discus. A man with long fingers should use such type of handholder in which the fingers are evenly spread, is an effective method, but here the major pull is made with the first finger. The individual with a smaller hand will adjust the fingers to the best advantage for applying power to the missile. His grasp of the discus will be less firm if the first joint of each finger does not extend will over the edge.

It is claimed by some that the talon grip lends more power to the discus throw because it gives better leverage and provides for less friction. One reason advanced is that all four fingers are placed well in the rear half of the discus. A further advantage may be accounted for in the extreme hand abduction. This is also known as the "wrist cock", a term commonly used in golf. The vigorous pull of the hand toward the left adds several feet in distance.

Since a competitor is forbidden by rule to cut notches or make indentations in the rim of the discus, weather conditions frequently interfere with smooth handling. There are devices which are legal and even in fair weather the competitor should become accustomed to their proper use. Among the aids are the use of compound tincture of benzoin swabbed on the fingers, powdered resin dusted on the hand, and balsam of fir spread thinly on the discus rim. These help to maintain the grasp during wet weather. Experimentation is necessary in order to know when and how much of the aids to use. Such experience may be acquired by wetting a discus and trying the various substances.

2. The Initial Stance

There are effective variations from the form of the initial stance. Among them are: (a) facing backward, (b) facing forward. Good competitors are found who use these types of stance. However, the majority favour standing facing the right half of the circle because it requires one less operation in footwork.

If the feet are too close together in the initial stance, the pivot is less effective. However, for the jump turn it is desirable to have the feet moderately close together because an evenly distributed lift from both feet is more readily executed. It should be added that an extremely wide foot plant in the pivot form may result in covering too much of the circle. The detrimental effects of covering too much of the circle are (a) the speed of the turn will be appreciably reduced, (b) forward momentum will be lost, and (c) the competitor will land so close to the front edge of the circle that he may either foul or experience a cramped delivery style.

During the initial stance the question of tension in all its phases must be given consideration. The heels and toes are on the ground, and the knees are bent to a degree which the thrower has found most effective. Usually the tall man bends his knees but slightly while the extremely short competitor uses a pronounced knee bend. The trunk, although, erect, is not stiff. The handhold is neither a death clutch nor is it a limp grasp. It is during the initial stance that the competitor acquires a condition of mental poise, body tonus, and a clear-cut mental picture of what he hopes to do.

3. The Preliminary Swings

There are three variations in the preliminary swings based on the arm action. These are independent of the type of footwork. One method of arm action consists of carrying the discus in the palm of the hand, palm down, during the entire swing. Another method frequently used consists of grasping the discus in the palm of the hand, palm down at the beginning of the back swing. As the extended arm swings backward, the hand is turned so that when it reaches the farthest point back the edges of the discus are approximately perpendicular to the ground. A third way of carrying the discus through the preliminary swings consists of grasping the discus in the same manner as previously described, but, as the extended arm swings back, the hand is rotated medially until it is palm up. Simultaneously the forearm is bent so that when if just reaches the back it is at an angle of 90 degrees with the upper arm. In this form of preliminary swing, as in the case of all others, the forward movement is just the reverse of the backward movement.

The advantage claimed for the first form of swing described in the simplicity of movement in that the hand and discus are swung in the same plane both forward and backward. However, it has the disadvantage of requiring a firmer grip in the backward phase of the movement. In applying the firmer grip there is a tendency toward overtension in the arm and fingers.

In the palm vertical type of swing the advantage claimed is that as centrifugal force subsides when the arm is swung back, the turning of the hand aids in the support of the discus without undue tension. For some competitors this form appears disadvantageous since it requires a change of the plane of the discus during the swing. The advantages claimed for the palm-up method are that it affords a more certain grip in that the weight of the discus is flat on the palm, and, since the swing starts from a position farther back, the arm describes a greater arc, thus developing greater angular or turning velocity. Some authorities further claim that this type of arm swing is more readily adapted to an extremely fast jump or pivot. The only apparent disadvantage of the palm-up form of the swing lies in the fact that the arm swing is complicated since not only the plane of the discus is changed but also the arm is bent and straightened in the swing.

4. Traversing the Circle

Of the two methods most commonly used for traversing the circle, the pivot turn has been widely accepted because of its relatively simple technique of footwork. Many authorities consider this style conducive to a throw in which the competitor does not foul. This is due to the fact that it lends itself to a greater security in maintaining balance after the throw has been made.

Many competitors using the pivot form begin their turn slowly and gradually accelerate until the greatest speed is obtained at the instant of delivery. However, this does not mean that discus-throwers using the form must initiate the turn of the body slowly. The optimum amount of speed is determined by the ability of a competitor to coordinate throwing activity with forward movement and spinning activity. The discus-thrower must adjust his speed of body rotation to his ability to gather himself and to deliver.

Numerous authorities state that the pivot turn assures the competitor of better balance since at least one foot is on the ground at all times during the passage across the circle.

Those athletes using the jump-rotation form feel that they can generate speed of two types more rapidly, namely, body rotation and forward propulsion. It might be added that in this style, body balance is harder to maintain. Men of smaller stature take to this form more readily than taller individuals who frequently encounter difficulty in blending the spin and the throw.

Excess speed in the jump-rotation form of discus throw offers the same difficulty that it does in the running broad jump. It prevents the competitor from getting set or gathering himself for the final effort.

Although it is desirable to keep the discus in an even plane during the body turns, there are successful discus throwers who carry it through a wavy circle. Some coaches contend that during the turn there should be continuous shoulder pull exerted on the discus throughout the turn. Others feel that after the initial pull there should be sufficient relaxation to permit a so-called freewheeling of the discus. This does not mean that the discus ever leads the shoulder but that it is carried slightly farther forward than at the initiation of the turn.

5. The Delivery

The position of the feet both as to distance apart and

their relation to one another is of vital importance. If the feet are too close together, it is more difficult to maintain proper balance, and, if they are too far apart, there is a loss of power.

The planting of the left foot with respect to the right must be considered in the delivery. If the left foot is planted too far to the right, the twist of the trunk and the swing of the arm are hampered. If the left foot is planted too far to the left, the discus will be carried beyond the point where the greatest power can be applied to it.

It is obvious that insufficient knee bend causes a loss of leg drive. In case the knee bend is too pronounced, the arm completes its share of the work prematurely. As a result, the discus has already left the hand before the legs are straightened.

If the final swing of the discus is started too low, the delivery will be too high an angle. In event that the discus is held higher than the shoulder, the plane of delivery will quite likely be too low.

The final pull on the discus should be started immediately after the left foot has been planted and the arm supporting the discus is still held back of the body. In other words, many discus-throwers permit the discus to proceed too far in its arc before applying a forceful pull to it.

The right hip is apparently brought into the throw before the right arm on the theory that leg action is slower than arm action. If they are to execute concurrent force, the slower leg action must be started in advance of the faster arm action. American discus-throwers are accused of failure to use the large muscles of the legs to best advantage.

During the delivery the head and eyes should be in the direction of the throw.

Although we believe that more force can be applied to the discus if the right foot maintains contact with the ground until after the missile has left the hand, yet it is recognized that these actions occur almost simultaneously. However, a motion picture study of champions shows that in many throws, the delivery is completed as instant after right foot contact with the ground has been broken. Many discus-throwers, in their effort to execute the foot reverse, prematurely lift the right foot from the ground. By so doing, throwing power, especially the drive from the right leg, is lost.

6. The Release

The angle of release and the plane of the discus during its flight depend on the velocity of the prevailing wind. With little or no wind, the angle of release and the plane of the discus should be about thirty degrees. However, when the velocity of the wind is greater than 14 miles per hour, the problem of anglès becomes difficult. According to Taylor, when there is a strong head wind, the thrower should elect a direction quartering into it and should release the discus at a flat angle of elevation. If the wind is following, the thrower should use a nearly vertical angle of inclination and throw well up in the air so that the discus remains along as long as possible in order to neutralize the directly following wind.

The findings of Taylor were based chiefly on observations made on a discus suspended in a wind tunnel. Scientific data are meager as to the best angles to employ when actually throwing the discus.

The sideward movement of the discus to the left is accomplished by pressure on the thumb or by twisting the wrist. The sideward movement to the right is accomplished by twisting the wrist.

The front of the discus is raised by increasing the pressure on the forefinger and decreasing the pressure of the little finger. The wrist also plays in controlling the plane of the discus. The front of the missile is lowered by increasing the pressure on the little finger. Again, the wrist participates in this adjustment.

The importance of the snap of the hand at the release has been previously mentioned. This is made possible by cocking the hand far to the right during the early stages of the throw. At the instant of release the hand is forcibly snapped to the left. The force exerted by the finger is applied to the discus at a point directly behind the centre of the missile, that is, exactly opposite the intended line of the flight.

7. The Recovery

That phase of discus throwing, known as recovery, in which the athlete regains balance, is in reality an aftermath of the throw proper. Generally speaking there are two types of recovery, depending on the habits acquired. Some reverse the feet and then recover by a continuous spin or hop on the right foot. The left leg is extended backward and the left arm swings wide and to the rear. Other throwers recover by reversing the position of the feet and maintain balance with both feet on the ground. Bending the right knee, thus letting the body down, is a partial insurance against fouling.

Let us again point out that American discus-throwers, as contrasted with Europeans, commit errors of technique by lifting the right foot too hastily from the ground.

Some Europeans vary the type of recovery by employing neither the body pivot on the right foot, nor the speedy reverse of the feet. Instead, they initiate the delivery with the thrust of the right hip, immediately followed by a twist of the trunk and whip of the arm, and maintain balance by casually bringing the right foot near the front of the circle. For the lightweight athlete, this form is inadvisable since it does not permit him to throw a sufficient amount of body lean into his final effort.

CHAPTER 8

THE TEACHING DRILLS OF DISCUS THROWING

The discus throw is included in the Olympic Games as an individual event for males and females. It is part of the decathlon (men) but is not included in the heptathlon (females).

The tremendous increase in distances thrown by modern athletes has resulted from improvements in technique employed by athletes who have also spent years in weight training specifically related to the event. Today, athletes use a common technique of throwing, and little variation is seen from one thrower to the next.

The modern thrower begins the throw facing to the rear of the 2.5-meter ring. Using approximately 1-3/4 rotations, the athlete is able to accelerate the discus through two full rotations during the throw. Some athletes have attempted to add an additional hammer-style spin to the 1-3/4 rotation across the ring, but this has proved to be ineffective because it gives no additional acceleration to the discus.

Of all throwing implements, the discus resembles an airfoil. Spin is essential for stability during flight, and a head wind gives lift to the discus and assists in producing the longest throws.

For a right-handed thrower, a quartering wind of about 10 to 15 miles per hour approaching the thrower from the left front produces the most favourable conditions for the longest throws. Under these conditions, the wind combines with the aerodynamic shape of the discus to give it lift. The rules of the event allow records to be set in any wind conditions.

Teaching Points

Drill 1: Lead-Ups

The use of a small rubber ring (quoit) or hula hoop as a substitute for the discus eliminates handhold problems that a novice commonly experiences with the discus. The young athlete grips the ring normally and then concentrate on other parts of the throw, such as the footwork. Once the athlete learns the footwork, practice than begins with the discus itself.

These substitutes are useful because they

- are safe to use and can be thrown both indoors and outdoors;
- are easy to grip and light enough to be held at arm's length;
- have a certain amount of drag that forces the throwing arm into a good trailing position; and
- cannot be thrown far, which means that novices can repeat throws more often.

Slinging a Small Rubber Ring

Each participant steps forward and slings a small rubber ring, keeping the throwing arm straight throughout and swinging it around the body just below shoulder level. A right-handed thrower steps forward into the throw with the left foot, extending the legs powerfully and driving the hips and chest forward into the throw.

Coaching Points

- As you swing your arm back, step forward with your left foot into the throwing stance.
- Thrust your hips and chest well forward ahead of the throwing arm.
- Keep the throwing arm below shoulder level, and release the ring ahead of your body and at eye level.

Accuracy Competition With Small Hoops

Set up a pole-vault standard to use as a target. Individuals or teams compete against each other for points, which are awarded for hitting or dropping the hoop on the standard. The slinging action used earlier is repeated in this lead-up activity. Combining height and distance requirements teaches the performer to lift the body upward into the throw.

Slinging a Vollyeball, Basketball, or Light Medicine Ball for Distance

Use any slinging activity with volleyballs, basketballs, or light medicine balls as an introduction activity for the discus throw. Particularly beneficial are two-handed slinging activities, which teach the twist or windup of the shoulders relative to the hips. Throwers use various throwing positions (e.g., standing, sitting, or kneeling).

Coaching Points

- Concentrate on thrusting your chest forward into the throw ahead of the arms and the ball.
- Extend your legs vigorously toward the direction of throw when you use the standing throw.

Drill 2: Standing Throw Using a Discus Substitute

Standing Throw Initiated With the Side to the Direction of Throw

A right-handed thrower stands side-on to the direction

of the throw (i.e., with the left shoulder toward the direction of the throw). The feet are shoulder-width apart with the left foot offset correctly in the throwing stance. (The offset position allows the athlete to drive the body fully into the throw. Any other stance effectively blocks this action. This is also true for the shot put and the javelin).

The ahtlete swings the hoop (and shoulders) back and around to the right side of the body and rotates on the balls of the feet toward and right, shifting the body weight over the right leg. The standing throw begins with the hips turning vigorously toward the direction of throw. The hips lead the chest and throwing arm, and the body drives upward and forward.

Coaching Points

- Swing your throwing arm back as far as possible to the right and rotate your shoulders as far as you can in the same direction. This will generate a windup or muscular stretch that you will use to pull on the discus.
- Start the standing throw by turning your knees toward the direction of the throw and extending your legs.
- Thrust your hips and chest forward before your throwing arm swings around.
- Keep the throwing arm just below shoulder level, and release the hoop in front of your body, just below eye level.

The Step-Back Standing Throw

The performer begins with the back toward the direction of throw. As the performer rotates the hoop and shoulders to the right for the windup, he or she simultaneously places the left foot back in the throwing stance. The thrower's body weight remains to the rear over a flexed right leg during this action.

The rotation of the knees drives the hips and chest toward the direction of throw, and the throwing arm is subsequently dragged around by the action of the chest. The arm completes the throw with a whiplike action, releasing the hoop as far ahead of the body as possible.

Coaching Points

l Keep your weight over a flexed right leg as you shift the left foot back into position.

l Be sure to step back into the correct offset position with your left foot.

l Initiate the throwing (slinging) action from "the ground up" (i.e., rotate the knees toward the direction of throw, followed by the hips, chest, and finally the throwing arm).

Drill 3: Rotational Throw Using a Discus Substitute

A rotary throw using a substitute for the discus (i.e., a rubber ring or small hoop) requires the same footwork and body actions as a throw with the competitive implement).

Rotational Throw Initiated Facing the Direction of the Throw

Mark foot positions on the ground to guide the athlete through the rotary steps of this drill. The athlete begins facing the direction of the throw with the left foot placed one step forward. The athlete gently swings the throwing arm (and the implement) back as far as to the right as possible for the windup and then holds the arm in this position.

The thrower begins by pivoting on the left foot and rotating forward and around onto the right foot. The right foot is positioned one pace forward with the heel now pointing toward the direction of the throw. The thrower's weight remains to the rear. The remaining part of the throw is a repetition of the step-back standing throw, taught previously.

Coaching Points

l Step directly back into the correct throwing position

with your left foot. Do not swing the foot out and around into position, because this takes too long.

1 Initiate the throwing action by rotating your knees toward the direction of the throw.

1 Follow the rotation of the knees by turning your hips and chest toward the direction of the throw.

1 Last, bring the throwing arm around just below shoulder height to complete the throw.

Rotational Throw Initiated With the Side to the Direction of the Throw

Mark foot position on the ground to guide the athlete through the rotation. The athlete begins with the left side of the body toward the direction of the throw. This adds a further 90 degrees of rotation to the previous drill. The hoop is gently swung around as far as possible to the right for the windup and remains in this position. The athlete pivots on the left foot and steps forward and around on to the right foot, continuing to pivot until the heel of the right foot points toward the direction of throw.

The remaining part of the throw is a repetition of the step-back standing throw.

Coaching Points

1 Always keep your weight back toward the rear of the circle (i.e., do not shift it forward) as you pivot and step forward to position the right foot.

1 Continue to keep your weight to the rear as you thrust your left leg back into the throwing stance. This will put you into a powerful throwing stance in which your right leg is partially flexed and your upper body is tilted toward the back of the circle. From this position you can now drive up and rotate around into the throw.

Rotational Throw Initiated With the Back to the Direction of the Throw

Mark foot positions on the ground to guide the athlete

through the rotation. The athlete begins with the back toward the direction of the throw, adding yet another 90 degrees of rotation to the previous drill. The hoop is gently swung back as far as possible to the right for the windup and is held in this position. The athlete begins to rotate, shifting the body weight over the left foot, and pivots on the balls of the both feet until the left foot points toward the direction of the throw. The athlete continues the pivoting motion while bringing the right foot around and placing it down with the heel pointing toward the direction of the throw. The remaining part of the throw is a repetition of the step-back standing throw.

Coaching Points

l This drill simulates the competitive discus throw.

l Flex your knees slightly and "sit" as though squatting on a stool during the rotation at the back of the ring.

l Pivot on the balls of both feet until you face the direction of the throw.

l Continue to pivot, placing your right foot 1 pace ahead with the heel facing the direction of the throw.

l Keep your body weight to the rear.

l Step back with your left leg into the throwing stance (body weight still to the rear of the circle).

l Make sure the left foot is offset correctly in the throwing stance.

l Drive around into the throw, working from the ground up (i.e., extend and rotate the legs, followed by the hips, chest, and finally the throwing arm).

Rotational Throw in the Discus Circle (Initiated With the Back to the Direction of the Throw)

Mark foot positions in the discus ring, and have athletes repeat the action of the previous drill. Using this drill, the athlete will become accustomed to rotating within the discus ring. The athlete begins in a shoulder-width stance, straddling the line of throw.

Coaching Points

l Swing the hoop as far to the right as possible, and maintain this position throughout the rotation across the ring.

l Shift your weight over your right foot as you swing the hoop to the right.

l Enter the rotation by shifting your weight back over the left foot.

l Pivot on the balls of your feet until the left foot points toward the direction of the throw.

l Step around the left foot with the right, placing the right foot in the centre of the ring (heel toward the direction of throw).

l Place the left foot approximately 6 inches from the front rim of the discus ring, offset to the thrower's right.

l Complete the forward rotary drive of your body into the throw, as before.

Drill 4: Standing Throw With the Discus

Technique

The athlete stands with the back toward the direction of the throw. The athlete swings the discus back to the right, and steps back with the left foot, keeping the body weight over a flexed right leg.

After the left foot is in position the athlete vigorously rotates the hips toward the direction of throw. The hips are followed by the chest and the throwing arm, which is swung around the body just below shoulder level. The squeeze of the hand on the discus gives it a clockwise rotation (right-handed thrower). The index finger of the throwing hand is last to contact the discus.

Drills

Gripping and Discus

The athlete holds the discus on the pads of the fingers, resting the thumb against the side of the discus and flexing the hand slightly inward at the wrist. Some variation in grip can occur (e.g., the index and second finger can be placed close together rather than spread apart).

Coaching Points

1 As your throwing arm hangs beside your body, the discus will rest on the last pads of your fingers (i.e., nearest the fingertips).

1 Your thumb does not hook around the edge of the discus but rests against the side of the discus.

Swinging the Discus

Participants swing the discus lightly forward and back at the side of the body (i.e., 20 degrees either side of perpendicular) with the arm acting as a pendulum. This provides a feel for the pressure of the discus against the pads of the fingers. The discus is not released in this practice.

Coaching Points

1 Use your left hand to help control the discus at the apex of the forward swing. Squeeze the discus between the left and right hands at the top of the swing.

Learning to Spin the Discus

This drill teaches the spin that is given to the discus when it is released from a rotary throw. Place participants 3 to 4 meters apart along a line. Each thrower steps forward with 1 foot (right-handed throwers with the left foot). Each participant swings a discus forward and backward beside the body and then gently tosses it forward and up in the air so that it hits the ground 3 to 4 meters ahead of the performer. A squeezing action initiated from little finger through to the index will cause the discus to roll out of the hand and rotate with a clockwise movement during flight. Participants throw at the same time or in sequence according to the command of the instructor.

Coaching Points

l Squeeze the discus out of your hand like a bar of soap, starting with the back of your hand and completing the action with your index finger.

l The index finger is the last finger to be in contact with the rim of the discus, not the little finger!

Bowling the Discus

Participants bowl the discus along the ground a distance of 5 meters. The discus rolls off the index finger in a clockwise direction. On a flat surface the discus should roll directly ahead.

Coaching Points

l Right-handed throwers step forward with your left feet.

l Swing the discus back gently and then bend forward and release it with your hand almost touching the ground.

l Squeeze the discus out of your hand, pulling your fingertips toward your palm in sequence from the little finger to the index. Perform this action quickly and vigorously.

Standing Throw With the Discus (Initiated With the Side of the Direction of the Throw)

The initial attempt at this type of standing throw using the competitive implement must be performed with minimum effort and with little to no windup (backswing). A right-handed thrower begins in a shoulder-width stance with the left side toward the direction of throw and the left foot offset to the left in the throwing stance. The performer swings the right arm and the discus loosely back and forth around the body with the discus at hip level (no higher) and no more than 30 centimeters away from the side of the body during the swing. When the discus has swung back and around the body as far as possible, the performer rotates on the balls of the feet toward the direction of throw, pushing the hips and chest ahead of the discus arm. The performer throws the discus only 3 to 5 meters. In subsequent attempts with this type of standing throw, the performer will use more windup and throw greater distances.

Coaching Points

l Start the throw by turning on the balls of your feet and pushing your chest and hips toward the direction of throw immediately after you swing the discus back for the windup.

l Do not try swinging the discus a long way out from your body.

l As your throwing arms swings toward the direction of throw, your throwing hand will be above the discus with the thumb leading.

l Do not be tempted to turn your hand sideways to the direction of throw or turn your hand palm up so it is underneath the discus.

l Squeeze the discus out of your hand.

l The index finger is in contact with the rim of the discus last of all.

Step-Back Standing Throw With the Discus

The athlete begins in a shoulder-width stance with the back toward the direction of throw, loosely swinging the right arm and discus back and forth. Using a strong backswing with the discus, the performer immediately places the left foot backward into the throwing stance, keeping the body weight over the right leg as the left is thrust back into position. Legs, hips, and chest then drive around and forward into the throw. The throwing hand is on top of the discus with the thumb leading. With the exception of gripping the discus, all actions replicate those performed earlier with the rubber ring or hoop.

Coaching Points

l Do not try to swing the discus far out from your body. Keep the discus at hip level and about 30 centimeters from your body.

l Try to make your body move ahead of your throwing arm.

l Thrust of the legs, hips, and chest toward the direction of the throw.

l The pull on the discus arm is the last action that you perform.

Rotary Discus Throw Initiated Facing the Direction of the Throw

Although this drill was performed earlier with a rubber ring or hoop, the use of the discus will present some control problems. Students can overcome these in the following manner:

The performer swings the discus back gently for the windup with the discus kept low (at hip level) and 30 centimeters from the body. When the discus can be swung back no further, the athlete immediately rotates into the throw. Carrying the discus low coupled with immediately starting the rotation will stop the discus from falling out of the throwing hand.

The performer swings, the discus back at hip level and then presses it against the seat, holding the discus in a pseudo windup position. This allows the novice to rotate more slowly and concentrate on the correct footwork.

Coaching Points

- Trail the discus behind your body throughout the rotation. When the rotation is complete, drive your body forward into the throw ahead of your throwing arm.

- Keep your throwing hand on top of the discus, and remember that the index finger touches the discus last of all.

Rotary Discus Throw Initiated With the Side to the Direction of the Throw

The thrower begins with the left side of the body toward the direction of the throw, using the same methods as used previously for controlling the discus. The footwork replicates the rotary throw initiated with the side to the direction of throw when using a substitute for the discus.

Coaching Points

- Try to keep the complete throw flowing and continuous, which will help you keep the discus under control. The more fluid the motion, the easier it is to hold the discus in the correct position.

Rotary Discus Throw Initiated With the Back to the Direction of the Throw

This is the complete rotational discus throw. The athlete begins with the back toward the direction of the throw, then either swings the discus back low and close to the hip, using rotational speed to hold it in position, or swings the discus back and holds it on his or her seat during the rotation across the ring. The footwork replicates the same action practised earlier using a substitute for the discus.

Coaching Points

- Keep the discus arm trailing to the rear of your body during the rotation across the ring.

- Try to increase the speed of rotation and run into the throwing stance with the discus trailing behind.
- Work on getting both feet into the throwing stance almost simultaneously.
- The instant your feet land in the throwing stance, thrust forward into the throw with your hips by turning your knees as fast as possible toward the direction of the throw. Think "knees, hips, chest, arm, discus" to help you remember the sequence.
- Make the right side of your body and the discus arm rotate around the left side of your body and the left leg. Imagine the left side of your body as the axle of a wheel.
- Once your throwing arm swings forward and releases the discus, bring your right leg forward for the reverse.

Variations in Starting Position at the Back of the Discus Ring

Many athletes begin their throws with a stance in which the feet straddle the line of direction of the throw. Others shift the starting position farther to the right (right-handed throwers), attempting to add more rotary pull to the discus at the back of the ring. Members of the group experiment with each starting position.

Coaching Points

- The farthest you shift your starting position to the right, the longer you must pivot on the balls of the both feet at the beginning of the rotation across the ring. Pivot, do not fall backward, across the ring.

Common Errors and Corrections

Step-Back Standing Throw

1. Error

The novice steps back with the wrong leg.

Reasons

The athlete is unsure of the correct action.

Remedies

Right-handed throwers step back with the left leg, not the right. The athlete should practice the correct actions without the implement.

2. Error

As the athlete steps back into the throwing stance the body weight is shifted the same direction.

Reasons

The athlete is too eager to throw with the arm. The athlete lifts the upper body or falls backward into the throwing stance.

Remedies

The body weight must stay over the right leg as the athlete steps backward into the throwing stance, and the right leg must remain partially flexed until the left leg is in position. The throwing sequence is hips, chest, and arm.

3. Error

The athlete turns prematurely toward the direction of the throw as the left foot is placed into the throwing stance.

Reasons

The hips rotate prematurely toward the direction of the throw.

Remedies

Instruct the athlete to practice the step-back action of the left leg with seat toward the direction of the throw. The athlete should begin the rotation of the hips toward the direction of throw only after the left foot is in position on the ground.

4. Error

The left leg blocks the thrower from turning fully toward the direction of throw.

Reasons

The left foot is not offset correctly during the step back into the throwing stance. The left foot is too far to the left.

Remedies

The athlete should practice shifting the left foot back into the correct throwing position without using the discus.

5. Error

As the throwing arm and chest move forward into the throw, the hips and seat move backward.

Reasons

There is no leg or hip action during the throw, and the chest drops forward during the throw.

Remedies

Instruct the athlete to practice pushing the hips forward and elevating the chest during the throw. The left foot must be offset correctly in the throwing stance.

5. Error

During the release the body falls to the left or right.

Reasons

Foot positioning is incorrect, and the body weight does not shift toward the direction of throw. The throwing arm is above shoulder level during the release, and the head and shoulders are dropped to the opposite side.

Remedies

Mark correct foot positions on the ground. Have the athlete practice stepping back into the correct foot positions, driving the body ahead of the discus toward the direction of throw.

6. Error

The athlete releases the implement with the throwing hand close to the hip.

Reasons

The throwing arm is too low.

Remedies

The throwing arm must be swung around the body just below horizontal (or the line of the shoulder). The athlete should practice this action without the implement.

7. Error

The discus has no spin but flutters in flight.

Reasons

The discus is not squeezed out of the hand; the fingers release the discus simultaneously. The palm is toward the direction of throw.

Remedies

Have the athlete practice bowling the discus. The athlete should also practice standing throws, with the back of hand uppermost and the thumb leading. The discus must be squeezed out of the hand beginning from the little finger, with the index finger touching the rim of the discus last.

7. Error

The athlete releases the discus out of the back of the hand.

Reasons

The performer is unsure of the hand action to be used when releasing the discus. The throwing arm is flexed at the elbow immediately prior to release.

Remedies

Have the athlete practice bowling and tossing the discus forward, keeping the throwing arm extended. The thumb should lead the throwing hand and the index finger touch the discus last of all. The athlete should practice easy standing throws with the discus.

Rotary Discus Throw

1. Error

The discus does not trail behind the body during the rotation across the ring.

Reasons

The discus is not held back at the end of the backswing.

Remedies

Instruct the athlete to practice rotary throws with the discus held on the seat. The athlete should also practice the rotation without the discus or using a light substitute for the discus.

2. Error

The athlete "dives" of falls backward across the ring.

Reasons

The athlete's vision is not horizontal, and the left foot does not pivot toward the direction of throw at the start of the rotation at the back of the ring. There is no flexion in the knees.

Remedies

The vision must be up and forward, and the head and left knee must lead into the rotation across the ring. The athlete should practice the footwork using a discus substitute. The athlete should sit and pivot as though squatting on a stool.

3. Error

Rotation across the ring is not toward the direction of the throw.

Reasons

The athlete uses too much or too little rotation at the back of the ring. The athlete's weight does not move across the ring, and the line of vision is incorrect.

Remedies

The athlete should practice rotational throws without the discus or with a substitute discus. The athlete should concentrate on legwork and direction of rotation across the ring.

4. Error

When the athlete is in the throwing stance, the athlete's body weight is prematurely over the front (left) leg.

Reasons

The upper body continues to move toward the direction of the throw during rotation. The athlete's weight does not stay over the flexed right leg as the left leg is pushed back into the throwing position.

Remedies

Instruct the athlete to practice the step-back standing throw, emphasizing body weight over the right leg as the left steps back. Repeat with slow rotational throws.

5. Error

When in the throwing stance, the athlete has no windup and is unable to pull on the discus. The athlete is unable to use the power of the hips and chest on the discus. The discus is swung ahead of the thrower.

Reasons

The athlete does not hold the discus back during rotation, and the legs and hips do not rotate ahead of the hips do not rotate ahead of the shoulders and throwing arm. The left leg is swung around to its position at the front of the ring instead of driven straight back into the throwing stance.

Remedies

The athlete should work on step-back standing throw, emphasizing straight backward thrust of the left leg.

Using a discus substitute, the athlete practices running the legs around ahead of the shoulders, placing the feet into throwing position simultaneously.

CHAPTER 9

THE HISTORY OF JAVELIN THROW

The javelin, like the discus, had its place in the pentathlon of the ancient Olympic games, and quite naturally, in addition to its uses in war, has been a regular event in most sports competitions since that time. In the German story of Siegfried, it will be recalled the Queen Brunhild named the javelin as one of the trials of strength and skill during the suit of King Gunther. King Henry VIII of England is reported to have been adept in its use, and in the 16th century, Rabelais recommended its value in the development of the young Gargantuna.

The history of modern javelin throwing, from the combined standpoints of the development of style, of championships won, and of world's records, is an almost exclusively Scandinavian story. First introduced into the 1906 Hellenic games at the request of Sweden, the javelin has been won in all but 2 Olympic games by the athletes of either Finland or Sweden. Incidentally, these two losses were keen disappointments to the Finnish people. In 1936, Matti Jarvinen, sometimes called "Mr. Javelin" because of his long-time dominance of the event, had just set a world's record of 253′ 4½″. He was universally admitted to the unbeatable, but injury to a back muscle prevented his best effort in the Berlin games and Gerhand Stoeck, of Germany, won with a toss of 235′

8 5/10". The second disappointment came in 1952, when, after waiting 20 years from the time the games were first awarded to Helsinki, the Finnish people were unable to produce a single champion in any event. In the javelin, their champion, Hyytianene, could do no better than third to the surprising American throwers. Young and Miller. Of a total of 54 individual places awarded in the javelin during the 9 Olympiads (1908-1952), 36 have been won by Scandinavian countries. All the other countries of the world have succeeded in taking only 2 first places, 3 seconds, 4 thirds, 4 fifths and 5 sixths.

Of the 2 countries, Finland has the better record. Of the 12 best throwers of all time, 7 have been Finnish and have achieved 244 feet or better. Further, the only 3 men to achieve over 250 feet have been Finns—Jarvinen, Nikkanen, and Autonen. This is particularly amazing considering that Finland's population has been less than 4,000,000 and that her cold climate is one that would certainly not be thought by Americans to be conducive to pleasant and safe practice conditions. Reasons for such dominance lie, first, in the national interest in the event with a resulting training of young boys and the continued practice by veterans until beyond the age of 30, and second, in the early adoption of a style of throwing that leads to best results. Jonni Myrra was already using what is now called the Finnish front cross style when he won the 1920 Olympic title at 215′ 9".

According to the McWhirters, "the first mention of a javelin being thrown in the modern era of athletics was in 1886, when a Swede by the name of A. Wigert pooped off a throw of 117 feet 6 inches for an inaugural national record which was to last 6 years." Its introduction, internationally, occurred in the special 1906 games at Athens, when Eric Lemming, of Sweden, won with 176′ 10". Lemming dominated the event for 6 years, finally clearing 204′ 5 5/8" and winning both the 1908 and 1912

Olympics. However, in 1920, Finland took the first 3 places with Myrra, already the record holder at 216′ 10 $\frac{3}{8}$″, as the new champion. Sweden cam back in 1925 with a world's record by Gunnar Lindstrom of 218′6 $\frac{7}{8}$″ and with the 1928 Olympic title by E. H. Lundquist. But Finland retailiated with Eino Penttila's 229′ 3 $\frac{1}{8}$″ and the greatest Olympic and world's champion of all time, Matti Jarvinen.

Jarvinen first caught world attention when he established a world's record in 1934, at the age of 21, of 234′ 9¾″. Born into the greatest of all Olympic families, which brought 4 Olympic place winners to Finland's athletic glory, Matti learned the event at a very early age. It is lightly rumoured that "Mr. Javelin's" teething ring was held by a javelin cord and that he just managed to clear the crib on his first javelin toss. But it is an undeniable fact that by the time he was 27 he had established 8 world's records and that he was still throwing over 220 feet at the age of 40. An enthusiastic teacher, he found a certain solace for his 1936 Olympic defeat in watching 2 of his pupils take second and third positions behind Stoeck. On several occasions he has freely given of his knowledge and vast experience to American coaches and athletes travelling in Finland.

Two years after his greatest effort, however, Jarvinen was defeated by a Finnish newcomer, Yrjo Nikkanen, with a new world record of 258′ 2 $\frac{3}{8}$″. It is interesting to note that a heavy rain had forced officials to use burning gasoline as a means of drying the runway and that the temperature was an impossibly cold 43 degrees. Nikkanen injured himself on the record throw, as who would not under such conditions, but 14 years later his performance was still as good as ever.

Acceptance of the javelin by the United States has

been slow and somewhat precarious. It first appeared in the National AAU championships in 1909, when Ralph Rose won the event with 141′7/10″. Webster comments, "and it has been said that he got this distance through brute force and beastly ignorance. Still he was a grand shot-putter". Yet it was not adopted into the ICAAAA program until 1922. Further, because of the possibility of injury to both the thrower and to other persons on the field, it has not been accepted as a part of all high school programs, and, in fact, was cut from the Big Ten College Conference program in 1943.

Even today, throws over 175 feet in high school and over 200 feet in college are considered exceptional. Perhaps the primary cause of lack of interest lies in the fact that javelin throwers are the only track and field men who have no competition during the long indoor season. Discus men are likely to put the shot, and hammer men the 35-pound weight, but javelin throwers are seldom able to find another event in which they can compete. Only on the West Coast, where javelin men have an opportunity for competition, as well as warm weather for early-season practice, is there widespread, enthusiastic interest.

Fortunately, the event is a fascinating one to both contestants and spectators, so that as better form is more widely taught and as methods of avoiding dangers are more universally followed, it should grow in both number of competitors and in the success with which the United States will meet international competition.

The history of the development of style in the United States is one of persistent emphasis upon the techniques of baseball, which stress the throw itself; of the very gradual adoption of Finnish methods, which stress the value of body momentum as a factor in throwing force; and of the consistent failure of college champions to continue their throwing more than a year or two beyond graduation. Introduced into National AAU competition in 1909, the event was won with distances under 180 feet until 1916 and under 200 feet until 1928, when Creth B. Hines, of Georgetown, achieved 202′ 1¾″. However, in 1930, James DeMers, of tne Los Angeles Athletic Club, achieved 222′6¾″, using an orthodox hop style. Not until 1948, when Steve Seymour, of the same club, won with 230′ 5″ did a National AAU champion use the Finnish style.

College men followed similar methods. In 1936, Alton Terry, of Hardin-Simmons College, using the hop, established an excellent mark of 226′ 2¾″, which was not broken until 1952. But Bob Peoples, of Southern California, used the Finnish style when he won the National Collegiates at 220′6½″ in 1939. Since that year, all but three National Collegiate champions have used the Finnish style.

This shift in style has produced a steady increase in distance in the NCAA meets during late years. All winning throws since 1947 have been over 209 feet; 4 have been over 215 feet, and the record throw of Roseme, of the University of California, in 1952, was 229′ 8⅜″. Similarly, National AAU champions have exceeded 230 feet, and Dr. Steve Seymour's championship record effort in 1947 covered a most respectable 248′ 10″. In 1952, the American record was held by Franklin Held, of Stanford, made in August, 1951, at Stockholm, Sweden, with 249′ 8½″, thus establishing Held as the fourth-best performer in world history.

CHAPTER 10

THE TECHNIQUE OF JAVELIN THROW

The javelin throw has been evolved into its present form from an ancient practice of throwing a spear for either distance or accuracy. When distance was the objective, the weapon was made with a blunt and equipped with a metal ring to give it weight. When it was thrown at a target, the end was sharp. Frequently when accuracy was being practised, the javelin was thrown from horseback at a target.

In the beginning, the missile was provided with a leather strap, 12 to 18 inches long, known as thong. This aid was bound around the shaft near the centre of weight so that a loop was provided for the first and second fingers. The javelin was carried between the thumb and first finger, over the shoulder. It was delivered by a terrific whip of the right arm, the force being applied to it through the leather strap. As the javelin left the hand it was not only propelled forward with great force, but also sent whirling through the air as a result of the unwinding of the leather strap. The forward propulsion and its whirling motion made it a deadly weapon.

The revival of javelin throwing at the Olympic games in 1906 where E. Lemming, of Sweden, threw the missile 175 feet 6 inches was responsible for the introduction of this event in America. Javelin throwing first appeared on the National Amateur Athletic Union program in

1909, when Ralph Rose, of the San Francisco Athletic Club, won the champion with a throw of 141 feet $\frac{7}{10}$ inches.

Types of Competitors and Physical Qualifications

Champion javelin-throwers are found among all types of men. The slender, wiry, long-muscled individual has been in the winning column and likewise the short, stocky, well-muscled man and the large, powerful type of competitor. All things being equal, the large, strong man has an advantage.

Although authorities differ on the importance of strength, we believe it to be an important asset to the javelin-thrower. Since the javelin weighs less than 2 pounds, the weight of the competitor is not so important as in putting the shot and in throwing the discus.

In any type of competitor coordination of movement is one of the most outstanding characteristics which contributes to success in casting the spear. In fact, many good javelin-throwers have been skilled gymnastic performers.

Speed is of some import, but the ability to transfer speed into force against the javelin is far more important.

Equipment

The chief item in the equipment of the javelin-thrower which needs special attention is the javelin itself. The international rules prescribe that the spear shall be of wood with a metal point. It must be constructed so that the space between the foremost point and the centre of gravity is no greater than 110 centimetres or less than 90 centimetres. A whipcord binding, 16 centimetres broad, around the centre of gravity is required. No other throwing aid is permitted. The circumference at either edge of the binding must not exceed the circumference of the shaft by more than 25 millimetres. The over-all length of the shaft as thrown must be not less than 260 centimetres, and its weight not less than 800 grams.

Although the metal javelin is prohibited by international rules, its use is accepted under the joint rules of the National Federation of State High School Athletic Associations and the National Collegiate Athletic Association as long as it complies with all other specifications.

It should be added that a javelin of reduced size and weight is legal for use by women. A junior javelin has also been adopted for grade school competition.

Javelins are made of hickory, second growth ash, or birch. It is of interest to note that in Finland, Sweden, and Germany manufactures utilize birch. The objective in making the spear is to produce one which is moderately rigid, to maintain its shape at all times. If the shaft is too rigid, it may break when it hits the ground. If a javelin is too limber, or crooked, it will develop a tail spin which offers resistance to the wind and detracts from the distance of the throw.

The adjustment of the whipcord binding, either forward or backward on the shaft, moves the point of balance. It should be noted that the rules permit a whipcord adjustment of 20 centimetres, approximately eight inches. Some competitors prefer a centre of balance at a position farthest from the metal point, while others prefer it centered in the whipcord. Perhaps the majority like the centre of gravity at a place in the whipcord as close to the metal point as the rules permit.

In selecting the javelin, a competitor should look for one with the following characteristics:

a. Straight shaft.

b. Clear, straight grain.

c. Correct degree of resiliency, neither too stiff nor too limber.

d. Size. A javelin of diameter that fits the hand. Some prefer the fat shaft and some the slim shaft.

e. Proper balance. One with the centre of weight so placed to meet the desire of the competitor.

f. Type of point. The point should be rather long. Provisions should be made so that the wood shaft may sway slightly, once the point has been fixed in the ground at the end of the throw. An absolutely rigid union of the wood shaft and the metal tip frequently causes the shaft to break at the junction. Cushioning devices of cord or rubber bands have been employed to keep the point in place firmly and to offer protection against breakage.

g. Specifications. Make certain that a javelin meets the rules requirements.

Those who are experts on wood claim that the javelin should be stored in a cool and moderately dry room. It should be suspended from the point. This is readily accomplished by slipping over the point of the javelin a leather washer about the size of a dollar with a half-inch hole in the centre. It is then suspended from a rack provided with notches 2 inches deep and 1 inch wide.

Because there are but few types of metal javelins manufactured, the athlete has a limited range of choice. The metal javelin, still in the experimental stage, has served the needs of practice rather than of competition. Some metal shafts have little or no resiliency, a quality which many throwers claim adds distance. They believe that the bow imparted to the spear. Although at the present time wood javelins are more generally used, research may produce a metal spear which will ultimately supplant the wood.

Field event shoes are commonly a part of the equipment of the javelin-thrower. Some athletes prefer those which lace moderately high; thus for dry weather they wear either a weight-thrower's or a baseball player's shoe and for wet weather a football player's shoe.

Technique of Throwing the Javelin

Grasping the Javelin

The type of handhold which an individual selects depends on the length and strength of the fingers, the size of the javelin shaft, and the athlete's personal choice. There are three methods of holding the javelin. First method, the Finnish hold, consists of grasping the javelin at the rear of the binding so that the second finger encircles the shaft, and barely touches the extended thumb. The first finger is approximately in line with the wrist and curls slightly around the shaft. The Finnish grasp finds ready acceptance among throwers since the shaft lies in the natural cradle of the palm of the hand, thus giving a feeling of security. The pull is exerted mainly by the second finger which rests on the wood shaft and against the back of the binding.

The second method of holding the javelin is American grasp, the spear is held with three fingers encircling the whipcord and the thumb resting lightly along the shaft. The chief difference between this style and Finnish grasp lies in the fact that the pull is exerted by the first finger. Here the javelin is held at a greater angle to the forearm.

The third style of holding the javelin is the Hungarian form, was given prestige by the excellent results obtained with its use by Szepes, of Budapest. The shaft lies in the hand hammock in a manner similar to the Finnish style. The chief variation from the Finnish style is that the first finger is extended to the rear along the underside of the shaft. The pull is exerted by the second finger, and the thumb provides lateral support. The third and fourth fingers encircle less of the whipcord in third style.

In all forms the amount of finger tension is practically the same, in that there is only a moderate degree at the initial stance and during the approach, but a high degree of tension at the start of the delivery. Good results have been obtained by the use of all the styles. There are, no doubt, deviations from these basic types of grasp which prove successful.

Carrying the Javelin

It should be remembered that the handholds are not only ones which may be employed.

The type of carry selected by a competitor depends on the ease with which he can fit it into the run, the drawing back of the arm, and the delivery. Usually carry 3, is associated with the Finnish form of throw. Carry 1 is usually employed in the hopstep style and carry 2 is ordinarily used with the rear cross-step form.

The Finnish Form of Throw

The outstanding success of javelin-throwers from Finland has attracted the attention of all the world to the Finnish form. For sake of clarity in presenting this style an action series for form, together with a stride plan of approach, is included.

1. The Approach

The competitor grasps the javelin and assumes a front carry, point down.

The run is started from a spot which is located a distance of 100 to 110 feet from the stop board, also known as the scratch line. This spot is designated as A. Point B is set five strides toward the scratch line. Point A is then set eight strides from point B. The distance from points A to the scratch line should receive the greatest attention because the delivery is completed during four of the last five strides. The fifth stride is the recovery step.

During the approach, the competitor strikes the points in the order of C, B, and A, but in locating them the order is A, B, C.

It should be noted that between points C and B, which is the first section of the run, the athlete exerts only one-half effort. Between points B and A he gradually accelerates so that by the time he reaches point A, he is running at seven-eighths speed.

During the approach the javelin is carried to the front. The thrower does not hold it in a stationary manner but moves it up and down, synchronizing the right arm action with the left leg action. Neither the body nor the hand grip is extremely tense during the approach.

2. The Delivery, the Release, and the Recovery

As the left foot strikes point A, the competitor begins preparing for the heave. The movement involved are described, first, according to foot position, and second, on the basis of the carriage of the javelin. As described by Runar Ohls, the Finnish competitors count 1, 2, 3, 4, and 5 for the five steps involved in the delivery and recovery. The count is either silent or audible. On the count of 1 the right foot strikes the ground in the direction of the board. On count 2, the left foot, pointed to the right, strikes the ground. On count 3, the right foot executes a front cross-over step landing which the toe pointed to the right and the right cross-over parallel to the board. On count 4, an extremely long step is taken, the left foot landing in the direction of the throw. When the right foot touches the ground on the step preceding the throw, the whole body is inclined backward about 35 to 40 degrees, and the centre of weight (at the level of the belt) is travelling forward at the rate of 15 to 25 feet a second. When the feet stop momentarily on the ground, the centre of weight continues forward, forcing the top of the body practically to double its forward speed, thus materially aiding the whipping of the javelin arm forward. The position of the feet during the throw and immediately after the javelin leaves the hand. At the count 5, the thrower brings the right foot close to the stop board for the purpose of checking body speed. In order to secure balance, the athlete may hop on the right foot with the left leg extended backward and sideward.

On count 1, the javelin point is tilted upward. On count 2, the arm is straightened and thrust forward. The javelin is lowered and is approximately parallel with the ground. At this particular phase of the throw the javelin apparently stays in place while the body catches up with and passes it. At count 3, the throwing arm is drawn completely back, and at count 4 the initiation of the throw occurs. It should be noted that the elbow leads the hand. The arm action is such that the shaft when released forms an angle of 35 degrees with the ground. The arm position assumed just previous to. The javelin is released just above and slightly in front of the right shoulder. In the recovery, the use of the arm in maintaining balance is an individual characteristic.

The Hop-Step Form of Throw

The hop-step form of throw has been quite popular in developed countries among high school, colleges and Olympic preforms. A series of form of approach is presented.

1. The Approach

A stride plan for the run in the hop-step style are organised as per the calibray of the athlete. The athlete grasps the javelin in a manner that will match his body language and with the norms.

The thrower begins his run a distance ranging from 80 to 90 feet from the stop board. This point is designated as point 3. From this point a seven-stride run is executed at one-half effort, the end of the seventh stride being marked as point 2. From point 2 the speed is increased so that at the end of six additional strides three-fourths of the best effort is being exerted. The end of the thirteenth running stride (six strides from point 2) is marked as mark 1. The distance from point 1 to the stop board varies from 12 to 15 feet. It is during the third segment of the run that the all-important hop, gather, and throw are made. As in all forms of carry, the javelin need not held rigidly. In both the over-shoulder and the underarm carry the javelin position tends to restrict the arm in aiding the run. Only natural body tension is maintained during the run, but the spear is firmly grasped at the first application of throwing power.

2. The Delivery, the Release, and the Recovery

As the right toe strikes point 1, a hop coupled with a quarter body turn, is executed. The foot spread and is moderately wide. From this position the throw is made with the same body whip described for the Finnish form. The footwork at the instant of release consists of swinging the right leg swiftly forward so that the right foot lands close to the stop board. The sudden planting of the right foot well forward serves as a brake to prevent fouling. The right foot should be set as close to the scratch line as possible, yet sufficient room should be allowed to permit the left foot (during the recovery) to touch the ground in fair territory. Balance is gained by a backward swing of the left leg after the right has been planted close to the toe board.

At the start of the hop, the initiation of the draw-back of the throwing arm causes a quarter body turn. As soon as the right foot is planted, the throwing is drawn well back. Now, the weight is resting chiefly on the right foot but is transferred to the left as the javelin is carried forward. The right elbow precedes the hand in its forward progress. The left arm is carried sharply backward. Good form in all types of javelin throwing calls for a delivery in which the javelin path is close to the head. The action is an over-shoulder whip as contrasted to a side arm swing. The release occurs just above and slightly in front of the right shoulder. The angle of release is approximately 35 degrees.

The arm action in the recovery is solely for the purpose of gaining balance and depends on the method of foot action employed.

The Rear Cross-Step Form of Throw

This style of throw has been effectively used in American schools and colleges.

1. The Approach

The hand grasp is optional, but the majority select the Finnish hold. The carriage of the javelin also is at the discretion of the thrower.

The distance and speed of the run and the method of adjusting the points are similar to these activities described in the hop-step form of throw.

2. The Delivery, the Release, and the Recovery

When the right toe strikes point 1, the left foot is brought forward and planted. From this position the right foot executes a rear cross-step. From here, the left foot is planted a considerable distance forward so that the leg spread is quite pronounced. The spear is delivered from this stance. The body whip is also important in this style of throw. The competitor saves his throw by shifting his feet in a manner similar to that described for the hop-step form and the Finnish style.

As the right foot strikes point 1, the right arm is gradually drawn back. It should be noted that the body makes a half turn as the right foot is brought quickly back of the left. The left leg is planted a long step from the right. Simultaneously with the planting of both feet, the delivery of the shaft begins. At the initiation of the delivery the right knee is moderately bent, and the trunk is aligned with the left leg. The javelin and the left arm are pointing in the same direction. The greater part of the weight is on the right foot. A slightly bent right arm is conducive to better throwing than a locked arm. The forward propulsion of the missile is initiated by a forward-upward thrust of the right hip and a sharp twist of the trunk to the left. Simultaneously with these movements the arm is whipped forward with the elbow leading the right hand. The javelin is carried forward in a straight line, close to the right ear. It is released just above and slightly in front of the right shoulder, with the forearm flexed at an angle of 80 degrees with the upper arm. As the spear is released, the wrist whips it forward. The movements have been such that the angle of release is approximately 35 degrees. As the shift is whipped forward, the competitor rocks-up on the right toe, so that all forces generated culminate in a powerful release. Body balance is maintained by bringing the right foot parallel and moderately close to the scratch line. The weight is on the right foot, and the left is swung backward and to the left for the purpose of maintaining balance.

Comparison of Styles of Throw

Now developments are constantly being made in form so that the athlete may expect more changes in the javelin throwing style than in any other weight event. A majority of champions favour the hand grasp on the theory that the second finger provides more power than the first. In addition, this hold permits placing the shift in the natural groove or cradle of the hand and gives the athlete a feeling of firmness of grasp.

The first finger, curved lightly around the shaft in grasp A, provides lateral support during the overarm whip. There are athletes who claim that a clockwise spin, or rifling, of the javelin is imparted by a first finger pull at the instant of release. Other competitors believe that a premediated attempt to spin the javelin may result in too much downward pull on the missile at the expense of forward propulsion. The type of hand grasp which a given thrower selects should be one that fits his style of carry and with which he can get the farthest throws.

The chief consideration of the thrower in choosing the style of carry is the selection of one which will best permit him to cock the arm for the delivery and at the same time allow him to generate speed in the run. The underarm carry readily permits the arm draw-back in preparation for the throw.

The hop-step method of delivering the javelin comes quite natural to many throwers. Possibly if provides for ample potential throwing power once the competitor is set for the delivery, but there is bound to be an abrupt checking of running speed by the execution of the hop. The sideward turn of the body may allow the use of the trunk-rotating muscles to provide power, but the turn frequently is accomplished with an ineffective utilization of power from the muscles that flex the trunk forward.

Less running speed is lost at the start of the delivery in the rear cross-step style than in the hop-step method. However, the same extreme body turn that was shown in the hop-step form may result in a side arm rather than an overarm delivery.

Because of its greater possibilities for transferring running speed to throwing momentum, the advantage seems to rest with the Finnish style. The javelin movement is synchronized with the footwork during the delivery to better advantage in the Finnish method than in other forms. The large muscles that flex the trunk function more readily in this style because the body is carried more nearly to the front. This technique of squaring off in the direction of the throw serves to prevent arm injury, because, by promoting the overarm whip, the tendency toward the perilous side arm release is diminished. In addition, the overarm method prevents the loss of time (used in rotation) in getting the arm motion added to the body whip.

Because of the above reason and the proof given by championship records, many competent authorities favour the Finnish method of throwing the javelin.

Common Errors in Technique

In the discussion of the techniques of javelin throwing an attempt was made to present effective methods. It should be obvious to the beginner that any radical departure from accepted forms will quite likely detract from the throw. There are, however, some errors which in our experience are frequently encountered.

1. In the Handhold and the Carriage

In brief, any grasp of the javelin which fails to provide a firm hold at the instant of delivery, and any carry which inhibits moderate speed in the approach, or offers impediments to the drawback of the throwing arm is obviously bad form.

2. In the Approach

Disproportionate amounts of speed during the various sections of the run are contributing factors to a poor throw. The beginner must bear in mind that varying rates of speed are recommended for different forms. This means that the speed generated should fit the style which the athlete adopts.

Should the speed in the approach be too slow, power is detracted from the release. If the speed is too great, the thrower has insufficient time for blending the life action of legs with the forward movement of the trunk and arm.

It should be apparent to the beginner that, if the points are a bit too close to the scratch line, he will foul, and conversely, if the points are too far back, the distance from the point of recovery to the board is lost.

3. In the Delivery, the Release, and the Recovery

Regardless of the style of delivery, there are mistakes which are common to all forms. Some of them are as follows:

a. An improper amount of hand tension when starting the delivery.

b. Unduly applying the brakes when fusing the run into the delivery.

c. An arm draw-back in which the javelin is out of alignment.

d. An incomplete arm draw-back.

e. Delivering with a side-arm swing rather that with an over-shoulder whip.

f. Imbalance during the delivery.

g. Releasing at an angle which is too high or too low.

h. Releasing before the full body power is applied to the spear.

i. Taking too short a stride when getting set for the delivery.

j. Failing to have the right elbow lead and hand. This precaution helps to avoid injury to the throwing arm.

k. Failing to keep contact with the ground until the javelin has left the hand.

l. Failing to make use of the right hip thrust coupled with an instantaneous straightening of the right leg.

Essentials of Correct Form

As in the other field events, the complete action of the javelin throw (the full run, preparation for the throw, and the throw) should be taught as a single unit of action as early and consistently as possible. However, the nature of the javelin throw does permit a step-by-step approach, which is economical of time, muscles, and javelins. The details of such an approach can be outlined as follows:

1. Learn a proper handhold. Whatever style is chosen must provide flexibility and relaxation of the fingers, hand and wrist; control of the javelin in both the vertical and horizontal plane of flight; and sufficient grip to utilize the concentration of force that is so marked in the javelin.

2. Learn control of the flight of the javelin by throwing from a stand or from a walking hop. The following order of points of emphasis will prove efficient and safe:

(a) Keep the point down and in, and the tail up and out. Point the javelin at a close object. Bring the elbow and the javelin tail through high. Practice such spot throwing until a reasonable degree of accuracy is achieved. This will take several days at least. A high point or low tail will mean that the tail will land first and a broken javelin result. Keep the fourth and fifth fingers relaxed, yet on the cord, pulling the point in and down until the moment of release.

(b) Throw at more distant objects by following methods similar to those already learned, but throw a higher javelin. Pulling back the javelin so that the right elbow is almost straight will aid distance. Height will be achieved by lifting on the tail of the javelin as the hand comes through and not by allowing the point to lift. In later throwing, the point does lift, but it should not do so at this early stage.

Herein lies a second failure of American throwing. Such an action requires a firm brace and solid ground in which to fix spikes or cleats. When laying out the event consists simply of placing a toe-board on the football field, as is usually the case, proper footing and good throwing are impossible. Only when proper surfaces, comparable in firmness to high-jump take-offs, are provided will American throwing realize its potentials.

If the throwing action is to be straight up and over with no side-arm action, this left foot should be well out in front and cannot be "in the bucket". It is true that great throwers, such as even Jarvinen himself, did at least occasionally have this fault. A widely used movie of Jarvinen, taken from in front, shows his left toe about 15 inches back of the line of the right heel. Such a position is consistent with the side-arm action Jarvinen uses in this series. In fact, one can draw almost a straight line from the right hand down through the arm and along the left leg. It is the writer's opinion that in Jarvinen's best throws this line would approach the vertical and that his left foot would approach within 10 or 12 inches of the line of throw. If this opinion is incorrect, it merely demonstrates again that human perfection has not been reached and that even "Mr. Javelin" had his faults.

This use of the left leg is one of the essential factors in proper throwing and must be carefully considered and perfected, regardless of particular styles in other aspects of form.

Mechanics of the throwing action. The acceleration of momentum and its concentration in the upper body, arm, hand, and fingers could, of its force alone, result in a passable throw. As a matter of important practice, the intelligent javelin thrower will constantly try to feet and to learn this whiplike action. It places emphasis upon the left leg, upon the complete relaxation of the body muscles, and upon flexibility of the arm and wrist. It does not try to throw or to augment action but rather to utilize and concentrate all the potential impetus of the stopping of lower-body momentum. Such practice will include full speed in the run and a resultant learning of the correctly timed rhythms and co-ordinations, but does not involve danger to the right arm and elbow. The whole form is identical to that of throwing for distance, but the right shoulder and arm simply let things happen. Such throwing will double the number of full-action throws that can be made in practice and will greatly further effective learning.

However, no, one can question that primary power comes from the throwing action itself. Such action begins with the body erect, the weight well back of the right leg, and the right arm reaching back although not fully extended. It involves a straightening of the right hip and leg, an upward pushing of the right foot and ankle, a forward explosive pull of the abdominal, back, and shoulder muscles, and then a relaxed yet forceful snap of the right arm, wrist, and fingers. One of the major factors in producing propulsive force lies in the vigorous upward and forward extension of the right leg and hip. Seymour and Finnish throwers generally stress a forward-facing style and a conscious vigorous forward thrust of the hip before the arm pull begins. There is some question, however, as to whether this is a point of coaching and of deliberate learning or whether it is a natural and inevitable result of proper position and style of throw. In most cases, the writer believes the second assumption is the better.

The path of the javelin should be along the line of the run and the throwing action. If the right hand has been drawn straight back and if the left foot has been placed properly, the javelin will quite naturally be pulled directly along the line of action and up over the right shoulder. The arm should be quite straight so that, as the elbow reaches the line of the shoulder, it is at a definitely higher level than the shoulder. In this manner, a minimum of strain is placed upon the elbow and the chances of injury are greatly reduced. Further, this action lengthens the whip of the arm and increases the energy of the throw.

To make this over-the-shoulder action easier, there will be a natural inclination of the head to the left, which gets the head out of the way of the shoulder and aids the body weight in moving up and over the left foot. It is important, however, that this head action should not be directly taught. To attempt to teach it will probably result in either an excessive or a premature action and will produce a falling off to the left, which is fatal.

The importance of relaxation of the arm, wrist, and fingers throughout the throw can hardly be overstressed. A valuable comparison can be made with the limp and completely flexible action of the tip of a whip. Any resistance or tension at this point reduces the crack of the whip and similarly the impetus of the javelin. There are many opinions in support of this statement. Seymour states that "the javelin must be held so lightly it can drop to the ground". Cromwell mentions a relaxed arm many times, emphasizing that almost any style of carry is acceptable "as long as it creates no tension in the arm".

Proper alignment and trajectory of the javelin. Once again the problem does not change with the form that is used. As mentioned above, the line of the javelin throughout the run, throw, and flight must be exactly along the line of the body action itself. To pull across the length of the javelin in any manner or at any time is a very common early fault. It occurs when the javelin is pulled too far around to the right as it is dropped back into throwing position; it occurs again when the point is allowed to rise unduly as the throw is made; and finally it occurs when an improper follow-through causes the hand to pull down on the javelin rather than along its length.

The other aspect of alignment have commonly regarded the proper trajectory of throw. American procedures have commonly regarded the proper flight angle as being definitely below the "ideal" angle of 45 degrees. However, as the emphasis upon throwing over the shoulder with a fairly straight arm has gained acceptance, angles of throw have increased. Seymour states that "the Finns release is about 40 degrees; the Swedes generally at 45 degrees along with most USA men. My thrusting style is at 50 degrees. Ganslen and Jarvinen are very detailed in a discussion of this point:

The angle of delivery is of particular interest. In 15 different efforts of world ranking throwers, not once the javelin delivered at an angle of less than 42 degrees; and in nine throws, equally divided between Rautavaara and Jarvinen, this angle of delivery ranged from 46 to 50 degrees.

The explanation for this seems to be aerodynamical in character. With the javelin's centre of gravity forward of centre, as soon as the javelin is released the nose tends to fall toward the ground as the forces of gravity go to work.

In order to counteract this and get peak elevation which, coupled with velocity, also gives peak distance, it is necessary to throw the javelin at such an angle that it will be parallel to the ground at its peak of elevation. Any deviation from this flight plan must materially affect the path of the javelin. The optimum angle from this film data seems to be a departure angle of nearer 50 degrees than 40 degrees.

Any premature dropping of the javelin tip will permit the wind to exert a maximum deflecting force on its upper surface and greatly handicap the throw. European throwers on the whole tend to throw at higher angles of elevation than American throwers. This possibly explains their greater success.

In an accompanying chart, Ganslen and Jarvinen advocate a javelin angle at the start of the throw which is above that of the angle of flight, arguing that this is necessary to counteract the action of the wind and the fact that the centre of gravity is forward of the centre of the javelin itself. This reason does not seem justified and, compared with the danger of pulling across the javelin when such a position is taken, the advantage is certainly unimportant. On the contrary, one of the best means of securing javelin height is through the upward and then outward left of the right leg and hip, the relatively straight right arm, and, very important, the maintenance at all times of a javelin angle which is not above that of the flight itself. Such a method, sometimes aided by a finger lift at the time of release, will drive the javelin as high as desired at a full 45-degree angle if properly done.

A major aspect of the problem of alignment in both the hop and the front cross styles lies in a smooth and rhythmic drawing back of the javelin during the first four steps after hitting the second check mark. The exact method of doing this is relatively unimportant. Some great throwers drew straight back along the line of the shoulder; others first drop and then pull it back. The essential factor is smoothness, rhythm, and the assurance that it will be in just the right place before—not after or even as, but before—the throwing position is reached.

It is very important that the throw be made from a wide stance with the left leg being thrown well ahead where its bracing action can be effective. This brace of the left leg against the forward momentum of the body is the most effective means for utilizing the potential force of the run. If well done, it will drive force toward the upper body and the javelin itself, and will also serve as the most effective means against fouling. In fact, a correctly used left leg will entail the allowance of only a few feet of space between the final landing on the right leg and the foul line. In contrast, lacking such a braking action, some throwers waste from 10 to 15 feet to prevent fouling. Obviously, this distance is substracted from the measured throw.

Styles of throw. There are only two acceptable methods of co-ordinating body momentum and force: the American hop and the Finnish front cross step. In terms of potential effectiveness, the great bulk of fact and opinion unquestionable supports the latter. To the writer's knowledge, no thrower using the hop style has bettered 230 feet, whereas over 30 men using the Finnish style have done so. Further, opinion seems almost unanimous that the hop style simply will not permit sufficient momentum to make maximum distances possible.

On the other hand, for American boys, the hop has produced much quicker and reasonably satisfactory results. Cromwell states tersely, "About the best thing that can be said about the American javelin-throwing style is this: do not use it". But Cromwell's position as coach of America's greatest college track teams made him place a premium upon ultimate and maximum performances. Further, weather conditions in California permitted work on the details of javelin throwing the year round. Where time and weather are less favourable, and where ordinary throwing will still win dual meets and occasionally important meets, there is sound reason for coaching the American hop style.

The American hop style. As with the Finnish method, the second check mark in the hop style is hit exactly with the left foot. In preparation for the hop and the final throwing position, this foot is turned slightly to the right, thus initiating a smooth and gradual drawing back of the right hip, the right shoulder and the javelin itself. This is the first of six steps or counts before the actual throw is accomplished. The second and third steps place the right foot and then the left in a more extreme turn to the right and accompany a more complete backward position of the javelin. This rhythmic movement is completed on the fourth count with the right foot reaching a position that is about at a 60-degree angle to the direction of the run and with the javelin reaching a full backward extension. The fifth count involves a hop on the right foot, which accentuates the action of the earlier four steps. The right foot is now at right angles to the direction of run and throw, and the body is erect but bending fully back to achieve maximum power. The sixth count occurs when the placement of the left foot within a few inches of the line of run, where it can brace against the forward momentum of the lower body and thereby concentrate momentum and power in the upper body, arm, wrist, hand, and fingers.

When speaking of the throwing position, reference is made to the position during the fifth and sixth counts. In general, this position is more powerful than that achieved in the Finnish style and approaches that secured in the shot put and discus. If the action is properly executed, the right foot, hips, and side of the body generally are well around and back, in what is termed a closed stance, permitting an upward drive of the right leg and hip and a fully braced left leg, which forces an acceleration of action in the upper body and drives it straight over the left foot in a full extension and in the exact direction of the throw.

As in the shot put, the expression "hop" is seriously misinterpreted if it is considered to mean an upward movement. To hop up would of course imply a slowing of action, which would render best efforts impossible. On the other hand, good momentum in the run will produce a long but low hop in which both feet are simultaneously off the ground. For example, Seymour speaks of Mikola, of Finland, as achieving 3 metres on his hop to position.

The Finnish front cross style. It should be emphasized again and again that fundamentally the hop and the front cross style have much more in common than in contrast. For example, in describing the Finnish style, one must repeat exactly the method used in the hop style of approaching the first check mark and of taking the first steps and counts. The javelin and the body can and should be pulled back and around in identical fashion in both styles. In both forms, the feet gradually swing to the right and the javelin drops smoothly back into position before the fourth count.

Actually, the term "front cross" is a misnomer that arose from incidental observation of the form. There is no deliberate crossing of the right leg in front of the left. Rather, the thrower simply drops his right side and shoulder around and back into throwing position during the first four steps and then makes him throw. Turning to the right in this manner necessarily gives both the thrower and the observer the impression of crossing the right over the left leg, but actually it is the attempt to secure a proper throwing position that is important.

The fundamental differences occur during the four-five count. In the Finnish style, after the right foot has achieved its placement angle of 62 degrees to the line of run, the left leg is swung well forward into a fully stretched position, thus bracing against the forward momentum of the run, and the throw is made. Any loss of momentum occurs at the last moment after the left foot has landed on the fifth count. In the hop style, loss of momentum is not quite so instantaneous, occurring during the hop and after the left foot reaches its extension on the sixth count.

The other inherent difference between the two styles lies in the fact that, in the Finnish style, it is very difficult to plant the right foot at more than a 60-degree angle to the throw. This forces a relatively forward-facing position, which, according to generally accepted theories of weight throwing, is not a most powerful position. In contrast to the Finnish style, the American hop, which occurs after this 60-degree placement of the right foot, is capable of producing a position comparable to that of the shot put. Opponents to this suggestion argue that to do so is to nullify all the speed of the run and that the loss in momentum more than offsets the possible gain in power.

Further, they believe that the light weight of the javelin permits the effective use of muscles that would not prove adequate for a 16-pound shot.

In another most interesting and valuable article, Dick and Matti Jarvinen, 10 times world's record holder in the event, advocate a forward facing position that places the left foot at about a 20-degree angle or about a foot to the left of the line of run. This position necessarily means a quick forward rotation of the hips so that they are at right angles to the throw very early in the throwing action. If the javelin has been drawn straight back and has been pulled straight through over the shoulder and the right ear, the body power will have to come through a bowing forward, as Seymour describes it, and predominantly through the action of the abdominal muscles. If, on the other hand, there has been any side-arm movement in the throw, the open stance of both the right and left feet will certainly contribute to a circular action, which means a pull across the length of the javelin and a reduced distance.

Regardless of the pros and cons of this matter, the facts are that Finnish javelin throwers, the greatest in the world for half a century, have generally followed the pattern described by Ganslen and Jarvinen. It would seem that little more would need to be said.

However, it is extremely interesting to note that the great American thrower Held, of Stanford, throwing Finnish style, achieved a more extreme turn of the right foot, a full 90-degree angle, and a closer placement of the left foot. A more effective bracing action is thereby possible, as well as a more powerful action of the tremendously strong muscles of the left side and back. If Held, or anyone else, is able to achieve this position while still maintaining maximum momentum until the last possible moment, all records will be endangered.

Important Questions and Answers

How can javelin throwing be made safer? The dilemma in the javelin is that it is fascinating event that can attract and maintain the attention of a large number of throwers but that its dangers to both the throwers and those nearby place as high a premium upon the organization and safeguarding of practice as it does upon proper coaching of the event itself. Further, the javelin throw requires great skill in its execution, so that the best candidates are not always apparent immediately. The importance, then, of allowing time before screening candidate is obvious. Yet the danger of numbers forces an early decision. A partial solution to this dilemma lies in the following procedures:

1. Demand early practice and excellent body conditioning. Early practice emphasizes javelin throwing throughout the

fall, during the winter (when in any way practicable), and certainly during the very early spring. Such practice permits a more careful screening of candidates, having fewer throwers on the field at any one time, greater perfection of the many aspects of right style, and over-all conditioning work, which is essential to personal safety as well as to best efforts.

2. Enforce safety devices and safety methods around and in the throwing area. Such effort include:

(a) A continuously roped-off area in which only the regular javelin throwers may go. "Danger" signs on the field and warning notices in the locker room are helpful. No field event should be held within 100 feet of the outer limits of such an area.

(b) Provision of as much space as possible for throwing but maintaining organized practice regardless of space conditions.

(c) Organization of practice so that safety always comes first. Men should work together and throw in any given direction together. They should get the fixed habit of calling out "Javelin" before throwing, even though no one is very near the landing spot. Anyone within 100 feet of the landing spot can get to it between the time the javelin leaves the hand and the time it lands. Further, even the javelin temmate who is looking "directly" at the thrower may actually have his eyes focused on some distant point.

(d) Enforcement of a demand that only "official" javelin throwers touch the event. The only exceptions should be with the direction permission and in the presence of a coach.

(e) Separation of the time at which throwers practice, thus decreasing the number on the field at any one time.

How can injuries to elbow, arm, and upper body be avoided? Apparently the honest answer to this question is that they cannot be entirely avoided with any degree of certainty. Most javelin throwers of any years of experience have their personal stories of injury and disappointment.

Yet, as indicated in previous discussion, these can kept at minimum levels by careful planning and ever watchful practice.

First, there should be an insistence upon early conditioning of all muscles of the body but with particular emphasis upon those related to javelin throwing. Ordinarily, the writer believes that the best exercise for any given event is the event itself; but in the case of the javelin, the almost irrepressible desire to "let one go" as soon as the man gets to the field on the first day of practice makes a preliminary period of training in other activities and with other implements a necessity. Among such activities should be handball, paddleball, ropeclimbing, throwing and medicine ball, tumbling, wrestling, and swimming. This last-named sport is traditionally taboo for track men, of course, but the over-all body conditioning and arm exercise involved in swimming is actually excellent for an event such as the javelin. For many years, the writer has noted with great interest that varsity swimmers who attempted the javelin event after the swimming season was over were able to make an amazingly consistent good performance. Their upper-body development with special emphasis upon shoulders, combined with a looseness of action, seemed to make the javelin natural to them.

The use by earlier champions of woodchopping as an early-season exercise was very effective, for its action is very similar to that of throwing and develops those back and abdominal muscles that are weak in present-day American boys. The absence of wood today is a deterrent, of course, but exercise with a light maul or sledge hammer would be equally effective.

A special exercise developed some years ago proved very effective. He cut off the last 2 feet of a javelin, placed a large hook in the cut end, and caught it in the eye on the rope of a wall-pulley weight. He could then reproduce javelin action almost exactly, pulling, letting the weight pull him back into position, pulling again, and so on repeatedly. By snapping into position, he developed explosive force as well as protection against later strain.

Throwing a javelin into a pit or bales of straw is excellent exercise but has the disadvantage of teaching a bent arm and a downward pull.

Further, after reporting on the track, a period of time in which the shot is substitured for the javelin will prove beneficial. There is little danger of injury and the great similarity of action of the two events means there is an actual carry-over of good form from one to the other. To put the shot throughout the indoor season is excellent.

Of course, where training facilities permit, there is not adequate substitute for javelin throwing itself, and this can be done profitably throughout the winter season. Where warm and dry weather exists, there is of course no problem. Where fieldhouses are available, throwing into nets has certain advantages. A device for making such work possible is illustrated here. However, the comparatively low height of most fieldhouses may lead to low throwing and a bent-arm style, which will preclude best performances later and make elbow injury more probable.

A second essential to prevention of injury is a meticulous attention to proper warming up. The extreme strains of the event demand that every body part by ready. Such readiness involves at least 20 minutes of time and gradual preparation. A few quick throws and easy sprints are certainly not enough. Unfortunate indeed is the athlete who must discover this fact for himself and thereby lost important weeks of competition and perhaps a whole season.

The third means of preventing injuries lies in achieving a style of throw that avoids undue stresses upon any one part of the body. Insistence upon an over-the-shoulder and fairly straight-arm throw will help. A foot placement that brings the body around to the right and puts the left foot in a strong bracing position is essential. A constant striving for relaxation of the javelin arm and shoulder will act as a safeguard as well as produce better throwing. And finally, increased use of high momentum should occur very gradually. Only when the body is in top condition and the weather is warm should maximum momentum be attempted.

A fourth important source of injury lies in taking too many throws for distance in a single practice or in consecutive practices. To go all-out when tired in explosive events such as the javelin or the 100-yard dash is to court danger and is seldom justified. This does not mean stopping practice when tired. On the contrary, better condition can come only through more practice. But it does mean to stop throwing for distance.

Perhaps most basic of all the means of preventing injuries is the presence of a well-kept and smooth surface for javelin throwing only. The common practice of using just any place on the football field, regardless even of the turf's being wet and slippery, is a definite hazard. If a carefully prepared area, covered regularly by canvas, is justified for other field events, why not in the javelin?

What style of shoe should be worn in javelin throwing? If the throwing surface is consistently hard and firm, field-event shoes with long spikes will be best. Where the surface is soft or uncertain, baseball shoes or even football shoes may prove worth while. Cromwell recommends that the baseball cleats be moved toward the rear of the shoe for better grasp of the sod or earth. During the early spring, when weather conditions are uncertain, it will be found worth while to take both types of shoes to the meets. Obviously, adequate practice under all ground conditions, using both styles of shoes, is essential.

How fast should the run be? A quick answer—e.g., as fast as body momentum can be effectively utilised by the athlete's natural co-ordination and his style of throwing—is not very satisfactory. Should he be making the mistake of using the American back cross step, the run must be very slow if it is to contribute to the throw. At the other extreme, if he is using the Finnish front cross, which is so dependent upon body momentum for distance, he must still have worked sufficient months and years to have learned to get well back into a strong throwing position. Such position does not come easily. The form's greatest asset, body momentum, naturally throws body weight forward to the left leg and ahead of the powerful right leg and hip. No man, regardless of talent, can start a good throw from this position. Somehow he must learn to reach back with the javelin arm and thus pull the entire body into a 20-degree backward angle with the entire weight momentarily on the right leg.

An inevitable corollary to this question is at what stage in the learning process momentum of the run should be taught or attempted. Traditional and more conservative present-date methods teach that increased momentum should only be taught after a relative high degree of perfection of form has been reached. This is, in the long run, a wasteful and inefficient method. Each time that momentum is increased, the thrower must acquire a new balance and co-ordination, must almost learn a new form. True, this conservative method does permit a good competitive performance at all stages of the learning process; there is a relatively short period of "lost form" and complete lack of co-ordination. Where meets are only a few weeks away, such an approach is probably justified.

On the other hand, when this month's performances are unimportant, most efficient learning will occur when momentum is considered as much a part of right form as balance and position and is used as early in the learning process as possible. Obviously, momentum places a greater strain on all relevant body parts and the danger of injury is increased. Two conference champions working under the writer lost the major part of a season because momentum was attempted too early in the training period, before muscles and tendons were in condition to take the strain. The answer in these cases does not lie, however, in avoiding momentum, but rather in a longer and more graded period of preparation.

Again, when momentum is used early, there is certain to be a longer period of uncertainty and imbalance, which will try the athlete's confidence and sense of progress and cause many a worry for even the experienced coach. Yet, in the long run, desirable performance will come sooner and maximum performance be achieved more certainly when momentum is given its proper emphasis early in the stages of learning. Had American coaches made this decision 30 years ago, Cy Young's splendid victory in the 1952 Olympics would not have been America's first in this event.

How important is body size in throwing the javelin? Since the weight of the javelin is less than 2 pounds and the length of run in unlimited, body size is not an essential factor for any but the very best efforts. Most of the world's best throwers have been about 6 feet tall and have weighed from 180 to 190 pounds. For example, Matti Jarvinen in his best years was just 6 feet tall and weighed 180 pounds. However, by way of contrast, Matti Sippala and Eino Pentilla, Finnish throwers who achieved over 231 feet in 1934, were 5′10″ tall and weighed only 160 pounds. Even more startling was the Japanese champion, Sumiyoshi, who threw 226 feet despite his height of 5′4″ and weight of 140 pounds.

Good musculature is certainly important to produce the necessary force as well as to withstand the strain of the throw without injury, but such muscle development can be achieved with time and consistent work.

The main essentials are explosive force, sufficient co-ordination to utilise body momentum effectively, and the desire and determination to make the most of what one has.

How long and hard should a javelin thrower work? Traditionally in America the ordinary javelin thrower does less work than any other track and field athlete. Competing outdoors only, he has little incentive for indoor workouts. Then, because of cold and rainy spring weather and the uncertain footing of grass runways, he is advised to take it easy during the early weeks. By the time warm weather has arrived, the competitive season is under way and he can do only as much work as his poor physical condition and the danger of injury will permit. Either mediocre performances or injuries, if not both, are the all-too-common result.

On the contrary, the very nature of the javelin throw, which places utmost stress upon muscles and tendons, requires better body condition than any other field event. Obviously, such condition comes not from weeks, but from months and even years of consistent training and throwing.

Daily Schedules of Practice

The schedules of practice for each day may of necessity be modified to meet either conditions of weather or special form requirements of the individual. An attempt is made to avoid needless repetition but at the same time to provide specific recommendations for the development of the javelin-thrower.

It must be remembered that the javelin throw is one event requiring a minimum of trials at full effort because of the peculiar stress on the elbow. The utmost caution is recommended so that painful arm injuries may be prevented. Unusual care in the duration and type of warm-up, as well as in the protection of the throwing arm between trials, is urged. Just as some baseball pitchers, even on a hot day, wear long woolen sleeves, so likewise do some javelin-throwers. This practice is recommended especially on cold days.

In conformity with the plan for other events, weekly schedules are suggested for early season, midseason and late season.

Early Season

Monday

1. Begin the practice by jogging 250 yards, hopping and bounding 25 yards, and sprinting 25 yards.
2. Spend from five to ten minutes on exercises designed to develop the large muscle groups. Include the push-ups, from the front learning rest position, half squats, full squats, trunk twists, hand-stands handsprings, tumbling and wood-chopping exercise. The latter stunt

is performed by jumping to a stride stand, clasping the hands with arms fully extended above the head, and then vigorously swinging the arms downward while bending the body at the hips. The arms may be swung to the left, to the right, or between the legs with an abundance of energy. The above exercise is so named because of its resemblance to the handling of an ax. According to some authorities on javelin throwing, wood chopping is a profitable exercise for developing muscle groups used in this event.

3. Experiment with the various methods depicted for grasping the javelin.
4. From a standing position deliver the javelin six or seven times into the vaulting or jumping pit from a distance of fifteen feet. Your chief objective is to see that the throwing arm is well extended to the rear (not locked, however) and that the javelin point and tip when delivered are in a plane at right angles to the javelin scratch line (stop board). The angle of elevation at the time of the release is necessarily ignored. A more desirable exercise which permits delivery at the correct angle consists of throwing into stacked bales of straw.
5. Assume the position of the javelin-thrower but substitute for the spear a bag of sand weighing from 3 to 5 pounds. Run through and deliver in the usual manner. This exercise develops throwing muscles.
6. Increase gradually the force applied to eight or nine jabs into the pit or straw from a distance of 20 feet and add the following three item of form: (1) keep the javelin point in close to the head and above the shoulder; (2) make an effort to have the right elbow lead the right hand as it passes the right shoulder; and (3) attempt to develop the wrist snap. By employing these actions, the thrower avoids a rotary or sidearm movement. The possibility of elbow injury is appreciably reduced when the elbow leads the forearm. In addition, this procedure invites cooperative effort

from the flexor muscles of the trunk. The novice will bear in mind that javelin throwing is an activity requiring infinitely more than mere arm action. Baseball pitchers depending on the arm alone cannot hope for success. They know that the legs and the trunk must coordinate to produce effective pitching. For similar reasons the trunk and legs must become a part of successful javelin-throwing form.

7. Jab the javelin nine or ten times into the pit or straw from a distance of 25 feet, drilling particularly on a smooth release.

8. Complete the day's practice with a jog of 200 yards, followed by a tepid shower and a massage. Record body weight both before and after practice.

Tuesday

1. Warm up effectively by vigorously whirling the arms, jogging 150 yards, walking 25 yards, and running 50 yards.

2. Jab the javelin seven or eight times into the pit or some straw at a spot 25 feet distant. Note the change of tension of the grip on the shaft, during the period of delivery.

3. Spend from five or ten minutes on the approach and checkmark adjustments.

4. Deliver the javelin a distance of 40 or 50 feet, making a special effort to have the right hip lead the right arm at the onset of the delivery. Repeat six or seven times.

5. Verify your checkmark adjustments by running through and releasing the javeling with about one-half your full effort. Make sure that you are perfecting the following:

a. The full rear extension of the throwing arm.

b. The straight forward alignment of the point of the spear during delivery.

c. The javelin is brought forward, close to the head and directly above the shoulder.

d The right elbow comes forward in advance of the right hand (grasping the spear).

e. The right hip is thrust forward and upward to initiate the propulsion of power from the legs and trunk in advance of throwing arm.

Since the above schedule calls for throwing at only half effort, the beginner may repeat eight or nine times.

6. Jog 250 yards followed by a 10-yard sprint, thus ending the day's practice.

Wednesday

1. Limber up with jogging, walking, and sprinting. Experiment with the warm-up, so as to find one that best meets your personal requirements.
2. Perform five minutes of stretching exercises.
3. Join the sprinters and sprint 35 yards at top speed.
4. Jab the spear into the pit or straw ten or twelve times, starting easily, and gradually increasing the power applied. Stress the application of the laws of body mechanics on each trial.
5. Run through the approach (carrying the javelin) with the idea of adjusting speed between checkmarks. Repeat six or seven times.
6. Release the javelin with about two-thirds your best effort, making use of the knowledge gained in practice on the approach. Repeat eight or nine times.
7. Finish the day's work with three minutes of gymnastic stunts such as handstands, walking on the hands, tumbling, and handsprings, followed by a shower and a massage.

Thursday

1. Jog 200 yards, walk 50 yards, and run 100 yards.
2. Join the high-jumpers and take five or six trials at gradually increasing heights.
3. Prepare the arm for throwing by swinging it in a circle and jabbing the javelin into the pit without the run. The previous warm-up experience of the novice should guide him in the number of trials required and the amount of power applied to each succeeding trial. Usually from ten to fifteen trials are sufficient.
4. Run through for checkmark adjustment four or five times, releasing the javelin with a minimum of effort. The objective is confined temporarily to speed and accuracy of the run rather than to the delivery of the spear.
5. Throw the javelin six or seven times with the run, but deliver it at about three-fourths your best effort. An observer or coach will be able to tell whether you are getting a proper extension of the body at an instant just before the release. Action photographs of champions show a straight line from the right toe through the right knee, right hip, right shoulder, and right elbow immediately after the release.
6. Cease throwing just as soon as arm fatigue appears. When the arm begins to feel dead or begins to lose snap, substitute an activity other than throwing. Injuries occur more frequently after the onset of fatigue. When the thrower is tired, he tends to become careless in adjusting his throwing stance. Maladjustment of body mechanism in throwing leads to improper stress on the throwing arm, thus increasing the hazard of elbow strain.
7. End the day's routine with a jog of 200 yards and at the conclusion sprint 25 yards.

Friday

1. Begin with a jog of 150 yards, a walk of 25 yards, a run of 25 yards, and a sprint of 25 yards.

2. Refrain from hard throwing today because you are scheduled to throw Saturday at seven-eighths your best effort.
3. Join the broad-jumpers and take the trials of the standing broad jump and three trials of the running broad jump.
4. Verify the approach and checkmark adjustments by running through five or six times while carrying the javelin. You may release the javelin easily at the end of the run since it is difficult to execute the delivery strides without actually throwing.
5. Finish the day's practice with a jog of 300 yards followed by a sponge bath.

Saturday

1. Initiate the practice with a jog of 200 yards, a walk of 50 yards, a run of 50 yards, and a sprint of 50 yards.
2. Analyse the length of time you require in the various phases of the warm-up, as well as the amount of energy put into each phase. Execute five to ten minutes of exercises, including arm swinging, trunk twisting, trunk bending, and bounding.
3. Jab the javelin into the pit or some straw, from a position 25 feet distant, taking one step with the left foot while delivering. Exert but little effort at the beginning, and make each successive jab more vigorous until the last jab approximates the amount of force applied to your best throws with the run. Draw your own conclusions as to the amount of jabbing required, since you will have to rely on this storehouse of experience at a later date. In early season, if the weather is cool, from fifteen to twenty trials at jabbing may be necessary. A woolen football stocking pulled on the throwing arm and pinned to the shoulder loop of the jersey has proved effective as an aid in the warm-up and a protection from cool winds.

4. Run through the approach at a predetermined rate of speed (one that meets your personal needs) and at the same time have an observer note how you strike the checkmarks. Repeat twice.
5. Throw the javelin at one-half effort, then two-thirds effort, and then three-fourths effort so that you are gradually increasing the vigour applied in preparation for harder throwing. A total of six to eight trials should suffice.
6. Throw the javelin not to exceed four times at seven-eighths your best effort. Your objective should be the improvement of your form during the approach and the furtherance of coordination during the delivery strides and the final release. Master the niceties of form at this stage of your training.
7. Conclude this day's workout with three minutes of vigorous calisthenics, a sprint of 100 yards, and a jog of 150 yards. After the shower and the massage analyse the weight chart for the week.

Midseason

1. Begin with a jog of 250 yards, a walk of 50 yards, a run of 25 yards, and a sprint of 25 yards.
2. Execute from five to ten minutes of gymnastic stunts such as trunk bends, trunk twists, hand-stands, handsprings, and wood-chopping exercise, the thumbling.
3. Begin with easy jabbing into the pit or into the ground at a spot 20 feet away and gradually increase the force applied with each succeeding trial. A total of fifteen to twenty trials is indicated.
4. Run through the approach three times to verify the speed of the run, the accuracy of the checkmarks, and the timing of the delivery. Release the javelin but apply only one-half your best throwing effort. An observer or your coach will note whether or not the actions in the javelin carriage coordinate with the

leg movements. In practice, vary the type of footing in the approach, so that you will become accustomed to a runway of either long turf, short turf, firm cinders, loose cinders, or loam. The better constructed athletic plants are including an approach of cinders, although closely clipped turf is the type most frequently provided.

5. Throw the javelin six or seven times using the running approach, but exert only one-half effort on the early throws. Gradually increase their intensity to three-fourths your greatest effort. An observer or your coach will report on the path of the javelin during the delivery, especially noticing the angle formed by the javelin and the ground at the instant of release. Furthermore, the thrower should keep in mind the part played by the legs and the trunk during the final effort. Since Tuesday's practice will include a few throws at nine-tenths effort, Monday's work should not be strenuous.

6. Conclude the workout with a jog of 300 yards and a sponge bath.

Tuesday

1. Warm up as you would on the day of competition. In case your past experience is insufficient to guide you, the following exercises are suggested in preparation for a day of vigorous throwing.

a. Jog 250 yards, walk 50 yards, and run 100 yards at gradually increasing speed.

b. Spend from five to eight minutes on varied exercises, including moderate stretching, bending, trunk twisting, leg swinging, and arm swinging.

c. Stand 20 feet from the pit and jab the javelin into it from ten to fifteen times. The feet are not together when the delivery is made since one forward stride is taken with the left foot. Try to achieve good form in your jabbing practice. This means to duplicate the arm, the trunk, and the leg action, and to maintain the same javelin path that you would when throwing for distance.

d Remove with a towel any excess body perspiration which has been induced by exercising in a training suit. This prevents a rapid cooling of those parts of the body exposed to the wind, especially the throwing arm.

e. Run through the approach to assure yourself of the correct distance of your checkmarks and the proper amount of speed between them. Repeat twice while carrying the javelin, but without throwing.

f. Throw the javelin at two-thirds effɔrt, using the recommended type of running approach. Repeat twice. The competitor should feet out the timing of the footwork with the action of the throwing arm. He should get the sensation of an effective delivery stance conforming to the laws of body mechanics, and a release that includes the summation of power developed by legs, trunk and arm.

g. Throw the javelin two or three times at three-fourths effort, using the running approach. These exercises should produce a feeling of body warmth, relaxation and tone, so that the athlete is in readiness to add power to his throw

2. Throw the javelin for distance, applying slightly less than full effort. Repeat three or four times. The coach or observer assigned to specific activities will report on the accuracy and speed of your run, the timing of your delivery strides, the backward extension of the throwing arm, the path of the throwing elbow, the leading action of the right hip, the height at which the spear is released, and its angle of trajectory. Bear in mind, do not throw with maximum vigour today, nine-tenths to ninety-five one-hundredths effort being sufficient. Champion javelin-throwers report that their longest heaves, seemingly are achieved with little effort. This statement bears out the contention

that a throw which properly coordinates the sources of power will be devoid of shock, yet most effective. Compare the distances made in each trial and draw your own conclusions as to the amount and intensity of the warm-up performed that day.

3. Throw the javelin four or five times at seven-eighths effort, measuring the distance. Experiment with various angles of the javelin at the instant of release. Note the most effective angle when throwing into a head wind, a wind, a wind quartering from the right, a wind quartering from the left, or a wind at the back.

4. This completes the most strenuous throwing of any day during a week in midseason with competition schedules for Saturday. It is pointed out, however, that there are some successful javelin-throwers who vary this plan by throwing moderately hard on both Monday and Wednesday and lightly on Tuesday and Thursday.

5. End the day's schedule by jogging 150 yards, walking 50 yards, and sprinting 100 yards. Take the usual shower and massage.

Wednesday

1. Limber up with a jog of 250 yards.

2. Join the sprinters, and after a thorough warm-up take two gun starts of 35 yards. Speed is definitely a factor in the javelin throw, especially in the Finnish style.

3. Take six or seven trials in the running high jump at gradually increasing heights, taking off alternately from the left foot and then the right foot. Note the amount of leg drive exerted in the javelin throw.

4. Expose the body to the sun for ten minutes.

5. Jab the javelin into the pit or straw from eight to twelve times, increasing the effort with each succeeding throw. Vigorous jabs without the run may be executed without fear of arm injury, because the thrower usually has correct balance at the instant of

release. The addition of the run presents a hazard to perfect poise at the onset of the delivery. It has been previously stated that imbalance of the body at the instant of starting the throw results in an incorrect stress on the arm, frequently causing strain.

6. Deliver the javelin at three-fourths effort, experimenting with various rates of speed during the approach. Again note the amount of power supplied by the muscles of the trunk. One authority, after watching both American and European javelin-throwers, significantly remarked, "The American throwers immediately after each trial obtained relief by rubbing the right elbow; the Europeans obtained relief by rubbing the muscles of the trunk".
7. Finish the day's practice with two minutes of calisthenics followed by a jog of 300 yards.

Thursday

1. Begin by jogging 220 yards, hopping and bounding 25 yards, running 50 yards, and sprinting 35 yards.
2. Prepare for the running broad jump by adjusting checkmarks and take two or three jumps for distance. Latent ability in this event may be uncovered. Frequently, javelin-throwers are proficient jumpers; both the high jump and the broad jump combine well with javelin throwing.
3. Experiment with javelins which balance at varying points. Some throwers prefer the centre of gravity at a point in the grip farthest from the metal tip. Others select shafts whose balance is midway of the corded grip, and still others, perhaps the majority, will give first choice to that spear which balances at a point in the corded part well toward the metal tip. The competitor will bear in mind that the thickness (diameter) of the shaft is not flexed, thus offering considerable range in selection. Some prefer a slender shaft, others a fat shaft.

Release the javeling four or five times, applying approximately one-half your best effort.

4. Become accustomed to the feeling of a substitute or a reserve javelin. Champion throwers familiarize themselves with two or more spears, labelling them in order of first, second, and third choice. In competition, such as the Olympic games and the National Amateur Athletic Union track and field championships, the athlete must use only those implements provided by the games committee. Therefore, the smart athlete will know how to select his implement and how to test it out speedily, and will be in readiness when called on to compete. Although a javelin-thrower should take pride in, and give care to, his shafts, he should not become so wedded to one particular spear that its loss would shock him to the degree of lowering his morale. Throw five or six times at two-thirds effort, testing out two or more javelins.
5. Vary the practice by participating in a contest such as medicine ball passing, wheelbarrow race, walking on the hands, sprint relay (50 yards each), or the standing broad jump.
6. Conclude the day's schedule by swinging through 200 yards, negotiating the last 30 yards at nine-tenths sprinting effort.

Friday

1. Check your implements to make certain that they conform to the specifications found in the rule book. Of greatest importance is the minimum weight (800 grams) and the minimum length (260 centimetres). Good competitors upon presenting their javelins at the implement inspection booth have been surprised to see their shafts rejected because of underweight or underlength. Force continually applied to the point when striking the ground frequently jams the metal tip farther onto the wooden shaft, thus reducing the

overall measurement. A javelin, once weighing 800 grams, at a later date may weigh less for a number of reasons, chiefly, the evaporation of moisture in the wood. Become a handy man to the extent of being able to remedy such imperfections. Underweight in the javelin may be corrected by removing the metal point, by inserting bird shot, or lead foil to the required amount, and by replacing the metal point accurately.

2. Study the conditions under which you will compete the Saturday. Note the composition of the approach and the direction and velocity of the prevailing winds.
3. Do no javelin throwing today.
4. Follow the advice of your coach on the matter of Friday's routine. Some prefer to dress in competition suit and limber up lightly. Others recommend complete absence from the practice field.

Saturday

This being competition day, adjust your program, including meals and rest, so that your efficiency is at its highest point. Conserve both physical and nervous energy, but otherwise carry on the usual daily routine.

1. Present the implements to the official responsible for their inspection.
2. Warm up according to a plan which, in the light of past experience, has proved the most effective.
3. Begin the arm exercises with easy jabbing, then firm jabbing, and then forceful jabbing, repeating until the body is toned.
4. Throw the javelin (with full run) at one-half effort, then two-thirds effort, and finally seven-eighths effort. Repeat until you feel in readiness for vigorous action.
5. Set an objective in distance and, with your thought on executing a smoothly coordinated delivery, unleash your supreme effort.
6. Protect the arm between throws. In case your throw

was creditable, indicating a proper warm-up, omit intense practising during intervals between your official trials. In case you find that your warm-up was insufficient, you may safely increase the intensity of a few more practice throws. Select an observer to note your sequence of movements from the initial stance to the recovery stride. Should you lead the field in the first round, figure out how you can improve. Should you trail the field in the first round, constructively map out a plan that will place you among the leaders in the second round. Concentrate on the early throws. A survey of officials scoring charts for the javelin throw reveals the fact that the winning effort was made on the second trials more frequently than on any other of the four preliminary and three final trials. Next in the frequency distribution came the first trial, and next in prevalence came the third trial.

7. Regardless of the fact that one is permitted four preliminary and three final throws, he need not avail himself of this privilege. Since he is credited solely with the one best effort, there are times when good judgment calls for no more than three or four throws applying maximum vigour. We do not wish to discourage the athlete, who on his seventh trial says, "I'll heave it farther this time". True enough, javelin contests have been dramatically won on the very last throw in the final round. However, such achievements are the exception, and it is strongly recommended that the athlete set himself mentally and physically to deliver the spear the maximum distance in the early trials. Furthermore, injuries are less prevalent when the arm and trunk muscles are not fatigued. The thrower is more susceptible to injury during the fifth, sixth and seventh trials than during the first, second, and third. These precautionary measures should not cause the athlete to become a javelin-shy or induce a phobia that he is a "brittle bone".

CHAPTER 11

TEACHING DRILLS IN JAVELIN THROWING

Javelin throwing has been in the Olympic Games since 1908 as an individual event for men and women; it is now also part of the decathlon and heptathlon competitions.

Two developments have affected the conduct of competitive javelin throwing. The first was an attempt to use a discus-style rotation to throw. Although this method produced great distances, it was subsequently banned, and the rules now prohibit the athlete from turning the back toward the direction of throw.

The second development resulted from the tremendous increase in distances (over 100 metres) thrown by men. Worried rules makers subsequently changed the configuration of the javelin, substantially reducing the distances thrown with the men's implement. No such changes have been made in the women's event.

Teaching Points

Drill 1: Lead-Ups

The following lead-up activities will involve throwing. They culminate with modified ball-throwing activities that are based on javelin-throwing technique.

Team Competition

Two terms used on lines 20 metres apart, with a basketball placed on the ground equidistant from both teams. Each team throws volleyball at the basketball, attempting to drive it over their opponents line. Allow one-handed and two-handed throws from above the head only.

Accuracy Competition

Basketball are placed on a box top and must be knocked off by group members throwing tennis balls or softballs. Throwing distances are appropriate for the ages of the participants. All participants throw the same direction.

Two-Handed Throw With a Basketball

While sitting, the athlete uses both hands to throw a basketball from behind the head. This activity forces the thrower to lean back and pull the basketball vigorously over the head and helps the thrower of experience of stretch-pull action of the muscles of the chest and shoulders.

Coaching Points

1. Reach back as far as possible behind your head with the basketball.
2. Without overbalancing backward, let your elbows drop as far as possible.
3. Pull the ball forward and throw it as far as possible.
4. Flex your arms at the elbows and lead the pulling action with your elbows.
5. Extend the throwing action as far in front of your head as possible.

Two-Handed Basketball Throw From a Kneeling Position

This activity is similar to the previous drill except that the thrower is in kneeling position. This drill simulates the pull of the javelin over the thrower's head.

Coaching Points

1. Tilt back to a position that you can comfortably control.
2. Pull the ball forward as vigorously as possible.
3. Contract your stomach muscles to help pull your chest forward.

Two-Handed Throw from a Standing Position

Each participant begins in a standing position with the feet together. The participant takes one stride (left foot forward for a right-handed thrower) and immediately performs a two-handed throw over the head. This practice simulates the thrower's forward body movement and the pull of the javelin over the head.

Coaching Points

1. Step out into a wide throwing stance.
2. When you throw, make sure that you move your body forward and past your front foot (left for right-handed throwers).
3. Make the throwing action last for as long as possible. Pull from as far back as you can drive the ball forward as far beyond the front foot as possible.

Running Two-Handed Throw

Add to the previous drill a short 2- to 3-stride run-up to simulate the approach of the javelin throw in the run-up. This practice is also similar to a soccer throw-in.

Coaching Points

1. The addition of the 2- to 3-stride run-up will let you lean back farther as you shift into the throwing stance.
2. Step forward in the run-up quickly, then lean back a little more as you shift into the throwing stance.

Two-Legged Jump and Throw

This practice is quite difficult and demands good coordination and quick explosive muscle actions. It simulates the pull on the javelin and in doing so strengthens the abdominal muscles. Novices should begin with a small jump and a push-throw from above the head. The action then progressively builds so that each performer jumps higher and throws the ball from behind the head rather than pushing it from in front.

Coaching Points

1. First practice the action without the ball.
2. Think of jumping and then contracting the abdominals to pull the shoulders forward.

Lift, Turn, and Throw

A lift, turn and throw simulates the hip rotation that occurs in the javelin throw. This drill should be performed slowly until the required actions are well learned. Thereafter, it can be made more vigorous and explosive.

Coaching Points

1. A right-handed thrower will turn the hips to the front by rotating the knees first in the same direction.
2. Imagine a corkscrew action, with your knees turning to the front followed by your hips, chest, and arms.
3. Practice the action slowly to begin with, and do not concern yourself with distance.
4. As the action becomes more fluid, increase the distances.

Drill 2: Three-Stride Throw With a Ball Using Javelin Technique

Technique

The thrower stands facing the direction of the throw with the feet together. The shoulders are turned 90 degrees with the left shoulder toward the direction of the throw and the right shoulder back. The athlete extends the left arm in the direction of throw and the throwing arm to the rear. The ball (tennis ball or baseball) is gripped in the right hand with the palm uppermost.

The left foot steps one stride forward, and the shoulders remain rotated with the throwing arm fully extended to the rear. The right foot steps across and ahead of the left foot, and the body leans backward (the cross-step or impulse step). The throwing arm remains fully extended to the rear, palm uppermost. Next, the left foot steps forward into the throwing stance, with the heel placed down first. The thrower's body weight begins to shift forward.

To begin the throw, the hips and chest rotate toward the direction of the throw and, thrusting the chest forward, the athlete pulls the throwing arm forward with the hand passing above the shoulder. The throwing arm flexes, and the elbow leads the throwing hand in the throw. The left leg and left side of the body straighten, and the left side of the body moves forward and rotates around the left side. The athlete releases the ball above and in front of the head. After the ball is released, the right leg steps in front of the left to arrest further forward motion.

Drills

Reaching Back to Throw

Place several tennis balls or baseballs (4 to 5) on a box top to the rear of the thrower. The thrower stands in a wide stance (slightly wider than shoulder width). The thrower reaches back, grasps a ball, turns to the front, and completes a standing throw.

The balls must be placed for enough back to ensure that the thrower reaches well back with a straight arm, shifting the body weight well over the right foot and partially flexing the right leg.

As a variation, a partner offers balls individually on an open palm to the thrower. The thrower must be forced to reach well back to get each ball.

Coaching Points

1. Once you grasp the ball, turn your right knee (right-handed thrower) vigorously in the direction of the throw, forcing your hips toward the direction of the throw.
2. Your hips will pull your chest around.
3. Your chest will then pull your throwing arm; be sure that your arm flexes and your elbow leads your hand in the throwing action.
4. Release the ball well ahead of you and above shoulder level.
5. Concentrate on the action of each throw individually; do not rush.

Throwing at Targets

Suspend hoops from soccer goalposts or draw circular targets on a wall. Students throw tennis balls at the targets from various distances. All throwers throw the same direction, and each begins the throw with the body weight well to the rear and with the throwing arm extended. The targets force throwers to throw both forward and upward. You can award scores for accuracy.

Coaching Points

1. Reach well back with an extended throwing arm, and make sure your weight is well over the rear leg.
2. Move your weight forward and rotate your right knee (right-handed thrower) toward the direction of the throw.
3. Finish the throw with your body extended upward, an step with your right foot 1 more pace ahead of

the left foot. This action will make sure that your body moves forward into the throw.

Practising the 3-Stride Throw

Participants practice the 3-stride throw using the technique explained previously. A right-handed thrower begins a 3-stride throw with the throwing arm fully extended and takes the 1st stride with the left foot. All actions are initially performed slowly and mechanically so that they are fully understood.

Coaching Points

1. Keep your throwing arm extended as you walk forward into the 3-stride throw.
2. Tilt your body backward as your right leg steps forward in the cross-step (right-handed thrower).
3. Step out into a wide throwing stance with the heel of your left foot.
4. Initiate the throwing action from the ground up by hips, then chest, and finally the throwing arm.
5. Keep your body moving forward all the time.
6. Release the ball well ahead of your body at an angle of 30 to 40 degrees above horizontal.

Increasing the 3-Stride Throw to a 5-Stride Throw

The performer adds 2 additional strides at the start of the 3-stride throwing sequence, making it a 5-stride throw. The thrower walks through the sequence with the throwing arm extended.

A right-handed thrower begins the 5-stride throw in the same manner as the 3-stride throw (i.e., taking the 1st stride with the left foot). The thrower keeps the throwing arm extended throughout the approach and turns the shoulders 90 degrees away from the direction of the throw until the actual throwing action occurs. A 5-stride throw is as follows:

Sequence: Left-right-left-right-left-throw

The cross-step (impulse step) occurs on the penultimate stride, and the throw occurs after the last stride has been completed.

Coaching Points

1. Remember that this drill is similar to the 3-stride throw. The only difference is the addition of 2 strides in the approach.
2. Be sure to keep the palm of the throwing hand uppermost and the throwing arm extended so that it is parallel to the line of throw.
3. Turn your shoulders 90 degrees so that your right shoulder is directly to the rear, but walk through the approach with your hips facing the direction of throw.

Extending the Throwing Arm During the Approach

This drill teaches the thrower to extend the throwing arm during the approach. Participants repeatedly rotate their shoulders 90 degrees and extend their throwing arm as they jog. The ball is not throw.

Coaching Points

1. Rotate your shoulders a full 90 degrees so that your left shoulder is forward and your right shoulder is back. Then bring your shoulders square to the front, and repeat the complete action again.
2. Extend your throwing arm each time so that it is parallel to the direction of throw and directly to the rear of the your body.

A 3-Stride Walk and Throw With the Throwing Arm Extended on the First Stride

The thrower begins with the throwing arm flexed and the ball held at chest right in front of the body. On the 1st stride, the thrower rotates the shoulders 90 degrees from the direction of throw and extends the throwing arm. The remaining portion of the 3-stride throw is performed as before.

Coaching Points

1. Be sure to turn your shoulders a full 90 degrees, no less! Keep your hips facing the front until you complete the cross-step.
2. Extend your left arm and point it toward the direction of the throw. This will keep the left shoulder in front and your right shoulder to the rear.

A 5-Stride Walk and Throw With the Throwing Arm Extended on the First Stride

The performer adds 2 strides to the 3-stride walk and throw, extending the throwing arm during the 1st stride, as before. The throwing arm stays extended until the throwing action itself is performed. Once the athlete extends the arm, he or she performs the remaining part of the 5-stride walk and throw as before. Stress the same coaching points as in the previous drill. Once the 5-stride walk and throw has been learned well, the speed of approach can increase from a walk to a jog.

Drill 3: Standing Throw With the Javelin

Technique

The performer places the left foot forward in a wide throwing stance, keeping the throwing arm fully extended, palm uppermost, tip of javelin at eye level, and vision forward. The left shoulder and left arm are forward and the left arm points in the direction of the throw.

The right knee rotates in the direction of the throw, forcing the hips and chest in the same direction. The left arm swings to the left to help pull the chest forward. The athlete pulls the javelin over the shoulder. The throwing arm flexes at the elbow. The left leg and left side of the body extend upward.

The sequence of actions is fast and explosive. Beginners initially practice slowly, thereafter increasing the speed of movement.

After the javelin has left the hand, the forward movement of the body will cause the thrower to step forward with the right leg ahead of the left. This action is used to arrest further forward motion.

Drills

Learning to Grip the Javelin

Member of the group try 3 javelin grips, each of which is described here. Of all the methods of grasping the javelin, Index-finger grip is most commonly used and is the one you will probably want to teach. Second-finger grip is often called the Finnish grip and is moderately popular. V grip is used least.

Securing the Grip on the Javelin

The participant sticks the javelin in the ground and slides the throwing hand down the javelin from the tail to the grip.

Coaching Points

1. Each javelin must lie along the "lifeline" in the palm of the hand.
2. The index finger (for the index-finger grip) wraps to the rear of the binding, and the thumb lies along the side of the binding.
3. The remaining fingers of the hand wrap around the binding.

Throwing the Javelin Forward Into the Ground

Once the athlete secures the grip, and beginning with a flexed throwing arm, the athlete slowly takes the javelin back to arm's length. The palm of the throwing hand is uppermost. Stepping forward with the left leg (right-handed thrower), each participant throws the javelin down into the ground 3 to 4 meters directly in front.

Coaching Points

1. Keep the point of the javelin just below eye level and directed down at the ground
2. Pull on the javelin as though pulling a rope past your ear.
3. Flex your throwing arm at the elbow as you pull the javelin forward.
4. Pull your throwing arm forward, keeping the elbow of the throwing arm close to the javelin and well ahead of the throwing hand.

Preparation for Standing Throws

Participants work in pairs without throwing or releasing the javelin. The partner stands to the rear of the thrower, holds the tail of the javelin, and provides gentle but mobile resistance. Beginning in a throwing stance with the javelin arm fully extended, the thrower practices rotating the right knee, hips, and chest "under" the javelin and toward the direction of the throw, producing the "bow" position that the body passes through during the throw. Led by the elbow of the throwing arm, the thrower pulls the javelin forward over the head. The partner holding the tip of the javelin moves forward, still providing gentle resistance. Note: The javelin is not released or thrown in this drill.

Coaching Points

1. Aim for smooth, nonjerky actions, beginning with the rotation of the right knee, hips, and chest under the javelin.
2. Keep the elbow of your throwing arm close to the javelin throughout.

3. Perform the action slowly and precisely at first.

The Standing Throw With the Javelin

The athlete throws the javelin from a wide stance with the throwing arm fully extended to the rear. Participants no longer throw down at the ground, but perform 8- to 10-metre throws.

Coaching Points

1. Begin the throw by rotating your hips and chest toward the direction of the throw. Remember to initiate the hip rotation by the forward movement of the right knee.
2. Keep the palm of your throwing hand uppermost.
3. Pull the javelin forward, with your elbow leading the hand, and release the javelin above and in front of your head.

Drill 4: Javelin Throw Using a Run-Up

Technique

The thrower faces the direction of the throw, holding the javelin in the carry position. The body is square to the direction of throw, the throwing arm is flexed at the elbow, and the palm of the throwing hand is uppermost.

The athlete steps forward with the left foot and begins to take the javelin back to arm's length. By the second step, the thrower has extended the javelin arm and rotated the shoulders 90 degrees from the direction of the throw. The hips are still square to the direction of throw. On the third step, taken with the left foot, some backward lean is apparent.

The cross-step and fifth step occur in quick succession. The cross-step will put the thrower into a backward lean with the right knee slightly flexed and turned outward. The shoulders remain rotated 90 degrees with the left shoulder toward the direction of throw. With the fifth stride, the left leg steps out into a wide throwing stance with the heel of the left foot contacting the ground first. Once the athlete is in the throwing stance, he or she rotates the hips and chest toward the direction of the throw. The body resembles a bow with the javelin being pulled whiplike over the shoulder. The body rises up, forward, and over an extended left leg. A sixth stride occurs when the athlete performs the reverse, bringing the right leg in front of the leg in order to arrest any further movement forward.

Drills

Extension of the Javelin Arm

The athlete practices extending the javelin arm directly backward, initially at a walk, then at a jog, and then at sprinting speed.

Coaching Points

1. Hold the javelin just in front of your head and parallel to the direction you will be running.
2 Keep your body square to the front, your shoulders relaxed.
3. Rotate your shoulders and take the javelin back to arm's length.
4. Keep the palm of the throwing hand uppermost.
5. Look to the front and keep your hips square to the line of the run-up.
6. Keep the tip of the javelin at eye level when you extend the throwing arm.

A 3-Stride Javelin Throw at Walking Speed—Throwing Arm Extended on the First Stride

The performer extends the javelin arm directly backward on the 1st stride of the approach, keeping the javelin parallel with the direction of the throw. As the right foot steps forward into the cross-step, the upper body tilts backward slightly. The left foot steps well out into the throwing stance.

Once the athlete is in the throwing stance, the right knee pushes the hips and chest toward the direction of the throw. This action must occur before the thrower pulls the javelin arm forward over the shoulder.

A 3-Stride Javelin Throw With the Throwing Arm Extended Throughout the Run-Up

When the approach speed approximates a fast run, the performer must try to shift both feet into the throwing stance as quickly as possible. This fast shift of the feet can be practised using a 3-stride approach. With this approach, the performer should try to use a rhythm pattern in which both feet land in the throwing stance almost simultaneously. Immediately when the feet have landed, the thrower must concentrate on driving the hips and chest toward the direction of throw before pulling forward on the javelin with the arm.

Coaching Points

1. Listen to the sound of your feet landing, and try to make them land simultaneously in the throwing stance.
2. Drive your hips and chest into the throw as soon as your feet land.
3. Keep your body moving forward.

A 5-Stride Javelin Throw With the Throwing Arm Extended Throughout the Approach

A 5-stride throw at walking speed will add 2 more strides to the start of the 3-stride throw. The athlete begins with the javelin arm extended. The sequence of action is schematically laid out.

A 5-Stride Javelin Throw With the Throwing Arm Extended During the First 2 Strides

The thrower starts the approach with the javelin held in the carry position. The thrower then takes the javelin directly back to an extended arm position during the first and second strides of the approach, which is practised at walking speed.

Coaching Points

1. Keep the javelin parallel to the direction of the throw as you extend your throwing arm.
2. Keep the tip of the javelin just below eye level.
3. Aim for a fast shift with both legs into the throwing stance.
4. As soon as you place your left leg down in the throwing stance, "strike" forward with your right knee, then hips, and chest toward the direction of throw.
5. Brace your left leg and the left side of your body.
6. Make the right side of your body move forward, upward and around the "post" formed by the left leg and left side of the body.

Increasing the Approach to 9 to 11 Strides

Add additional strides to the approach. For beginners, a 9- to 11-stride approach is recommended. Elite athletes frequently use a 25- to 30-metre approach, in which 10 to 15 strides are devoted to a smooth acceleration into the throwing stance. Elite athletes also use one or two check marks, the most important of which is commonly placed at the 5th stride prior to throwing. Thus the most important phase of throwing is accurately positioned. The recommended teaching sequence for increasing the size of the run-up is as follows:

1. The athlete repeats the 5-stride throw, extending the javelin arm during the first and second strides. The athlete begins with a walking approach, counting out the strides, then attempts the same actions using a slow jog.

2. Add 4 strides for a 9-stride throw. The athlete begins with a walking approach, using a verbal count and check marks to indicate where to extend the javelin arm and where to enter the throwing stance.
3. Add 2 more strides for an 11-stride throw. The athlete increases the speed of the approach and adjusts check marks accordingly. Using javelin-thrower's spikes will help the thrower obtain a good backward body lean without fear or slipping.

Coaching Points

1. Drive your right foot forward into the cross-step and tilt your body backward.
2. With the heel of your left foot, step out long and low into the throwing stance.
3. Drive your hips and chest ahead of the throwing arm.
4. Think of your body as the handle of a whip and the javelin as the tip of the whip; strike forward with the handle and "crack" the whip.

CHAPTER 12

THE HAMMER THROW

The first Olympic hammer competition was held in Paris in 1900. Only five athletes took part and the winner was John Flanagan of the USA, who threw a hammer with a wire and wooden handle 51.01 m. Flanagan won the event again four years later in St Louis. The St Louis Games were fairly disastrous—only nine countries took part in the athletics and the contests were spread over four and a half months. In London, 1908, Flangan, who had held the world record for thirteen years, won an incredible third Olympic gold medal with a 51.92 m throw.

Pat O'Callaghan, a mighty Irishman, dominated the event in Amsterdam, 1928 and Los Angeles, 1932 winning two gold medals. During the 1930s and 1940s, the hammer was dominated by Europeans, notably Imre Nemeth of Hungary who won gold in London, 1948, with a 56.07 m throw. He took the bronze medal four years later in Helsinki, behind his protégé and fellow Hungarian Jozsef Csermak, and German Karl Storch.

The gold medal returned to the USA in 1956, thanks to Hal Connolly.

Connolly's left arm was severely withered as a result of the numerous fractures he had received playing American football and wrestling. Connolly claimed this actually helped him to wrap his arm across his chest when throwing the hammer. His winning throw of 63.19 m - a new Olympic record - proved he knew what he was talking about. Before the Games, the hammer would record had been hotly contested between Connolly and Mikhail Krivonossov of the USSR.

By Munich 1972, the Olympic record was extended to a massive 75.50 m by Anatoliy Bondarchuk of the USSR. His victory marked the start of the Soviet domination of the hammer event. Montreal, 1976, marked the beginning of one particular athlete's domination - Yuri Sedykh.

Sedykh is one of the greatest-ever hammer throwers. He was born in Nova Cherkass on 11 June 1955. In 1973, he set a world junior record of 69.04 m and became the European junior champion. Sedykh was a supreme technician and had immense body strength. He won the Olympic gold medal on two occasions - Montreal in 1976 with a 77.52 m throw and Moscow, 1980, with an incredible world and Olympic record of 81.80 m. The Eastern bloc boycott of the Los Angeles Games denied him another certain gold medal. Sedykh returned to Olympic competition in Seoul in 1988 to collect a silver medal with a 83.76 m throw.

The Soviet hammer throwers would almost certainly have won gold, silver and bronze medals in the Los Angeles Olympics. The contest was eventually won by Juha Tiainen of Finland with 78.08 m. The Soviet athletes returned to Olympic competition in Seoul, 1988, and made the clean sweep that had been denied them in 1984. Winner Sergei Litvinov hurled his missile 84.80 m to collect the gold medal.

The hammer throw has been traced back in history as far as 2000 B.C., when competition was held during the Tailteann Games at Tara, Irelan. This event is related to log and stone throws used by other nations earlier than 2000 B.C. The hammer throw was introduced into the United States by Irish immigrants during the late 1800's. These Irish-Americans dominated the hammer event in the United States from about 1890 to the 1920's.

The 7′ diameter circle was standardised in 1907. The hammer weighs 16 pounds and is attached to a 48-inch wire chain. Most throwers in the early 1900's were using 1 or 2 turns while spinning on the toes and heels, and even becoming airborne during the turns. Now the throwers turn 3 times while spinning from the heel to outer edge of foot, keeping the pivoting foot in contact with the ground throughout the turns.

Irish-Americans John J. Flangan, Matt McGrath, and Pat Ryan held either the world's record in the hammer throw and/or were world champions from 1900 to 1920. For example, Flanagan was Olympic hammer champion 3 times, in 1900, 1904 and 1908. His all-time best was 172′ 11″, which was a world's record. McGratch bettered this record twice and won this event in the 1912 Olympics. However, his world record of 187′ 4″ was set during 1911.

For about 8 years after this, Pat Ryan dominated the hammer throw, setting a world record in 1913 of 189′ ½″. Ryan held the world record for 25 years. Then European throwers dominated the event from 1924 to 1956.

During 1956, Cliff Blair of Boston University set a new worlu record of 216′ 4½″. The former record was held by Russia's Mikhail Krivonosov, who later that year reclaimed that the world record with a mark of 217′9½″. That same year, Harold Connolly of the United States set a new world's record of 220′ 8″ and also won the 1956 Olympics. Connolly fought off challenges by the Soviet throwers during the next 10 years. In September, 1965, Connolly bettered his own 1962 world record of 231′ 10″ with a mark of 233′ 9½″. Connolly generally dominated the hammer record for about 10 years, but he was defeated in the 1960 Olympics by Vasiliy

Rudenkov of the Soviet Union and in 1964 by Romuald Klim, also of Russia, with an Olympic record of 228′ 9½″.

During September, 1965, Gyula Zsivotsky of Hungary bettered Connolly's world record with a throw of 241′ 11″, and again set a new record of 242′ just a few weeks prior to the 1968 Olympics.

Zsivotsky (Hungary) won at the Mexico Olympics with a throw of 240′ 8″, defeating Romuald Klim (U.S.S.R.) by only 3 inches. The following are the first 5 winners at the 1968 Olympics in the hammer throw:

1. Gyula Zsivotsky (Hungary)	240′ 8″
2. Romuald Klim (Soviet Union)	240′ 5″
3. Lazar Lovasz (Hungary)	228′ 11″
4. Takeo Sugawara (Japan)	228′ 11″
5. Sandor Eckschmidt (Hungary)	227′ 10½″

Interest in and popularity of the hammer throw in the United States has increased greatly in recent years because of the efforts of Hal Connolly, Sam Felton, Jr. Fred Wilt, and other concerned Americans. Manufacturers are also producing "training hammers" with shorter wires, and underweight hammer which allow the beginner to progress gradually to the official 16-pound hammer.

Fundamentals of the Hammer Throw

Starting position. The thrower starts with his back to the direction of throw. The feet are placed shoulder width apart, with the legs flexed and the body in a sitting position. The back is straight, head upright, and eyes focused horizontally, The hammer rests on the ground directly in front of the thrower. The handle is held loosely in the right hand (right-handed thrower). When the throw is started, the hammerhead is swung to the rear of the right leg, while the head and shoulder simultaneously rotate about 90 degrees to the right. The gloved left hand is then slipped under the right hand, gripping the handle with the middle pads of the fingers. The left arm should remain straight as the hammer is pulled into orbit in a series of over-the-head swings.

Preliminary windups. Generally 2 preliminary windups are used to build up the hammer head velocity. However, beginners often need 3 windups to build momentum. The windups are the foundation of the throw and must build up hammer head speed gradually in a controlled manner. The body (hips, back, and legs) are the main source of power countering and accelerating the hammer during the windups. The arms must be kept straight and the shoulders relaxed, allowing the hammer to sweep through the widest possible orbit that can be controlled.

The turns. The purpose of the turns is to build up maximum peripheral velocity in the hammer head by increasing turning speed and the length of the radius through which the hammer head is swept. If maximum speed is to be reached at the time of release, it must be a gradual, controlled acceleration. This requires excellent technique, rhythm, balance, strength and quick reflexes. The following are techniques which should be practised and observed:

1. Work for a gradual increase of speed by sweeping the hammer smoothly and controlling it in the widest possible arc while keeping the arms extended and shoulders relaxed.

2. While turning, keep the left foot in contact with the ground. The left foot moves down the middle of the circle in a straight line, keeping contact with the ground from the start of the turn until the release. Rotate around the heel of the left foot to the outside of the foot toward the ball and toes, continue on to the heel of the other foot, and repeat in a series of continuous movements. The right foot remains grounded until the hammer is moved well

to the left and is at shoulder height. The feet set the tempo of the throw and should work and drive hard to the left and ahead of the hammer.

3. To control the turns the right foot and leg must be shifted quickly, keeping the right foot low and close to the left leg. A loss of control and balance will occur if the shift of the right leg is too high or wide. The ball of the right foot should complete each turn well ahead of the hammer. Upon landing quietly, the right foot quickly but firmly presses on into the next turn. During the turns, both legs must be well flexed until the ball of the right foot is in place, starting a strong lifting and pressing effort to the left.

4. The hammer's high pint should not be forced. The hands should rise naturally to about eye level as the hammer reaches its high point. The hammer's low point should be kept well to the right because of the tendency of the low point to creep left during each turn. The correct low point can be achieved by making quick, tight turns while increasing torque from turn to turn.

5. The role of the arms and shoulders in the buildup is to increase the effective radius through which the hammer is swept. Since, in essence, the straight arms are an extension of the wire, the arms and shoulders must be relaxed and as passive as possible during the turns. The hammer head hangs directly in front of the chest during the turns.

6. The head plays an important role during the turns. The head and eyes should be kept up, particularly, as the turns are completed. The head and hips lead the action to the left, but the head should not get ahead of the hips. A proper lead with the head makes it easier to hang from the hammer and leave the arms and shoulders behind. Beginners should

not emphasise the head lead until they have mastered the fundamentals.

7. The throwing action begins after the completion of the last turn and just before the hammer reaches its low point. The thrower should be in a strong finish position, with the left shoulder down and legs flexed in a powerful lifting position. The thrower's arms remain extended as the legs straighten and the body extends upward and backward. The release takes place at shoulder level at an angle of 42 to 45 degrees. After release, recovery is made by completing another turn while staying in the ring.

Training Program

It must be remembered that it is impossible to judge whether each individual should follow any training plan to the letter. Allowances must be made for those who may have a very heavy work and study program in school. The age and maturity of each athlete should also be considered. Some of the older, stronger men may need more work than is contained in most schedules. The coach and the athlete should determine the exact workout program needed. The schedule presented below is suggested for the 4-week period prior to participation in the first meet.

Workout Schedules

Four Weeks Prior to the First Meet

Monday

1. Jog ¼ mile.
2. Run wind sprints for ½ mile, sprinting 50 yards and walking 50 yards.
3. Do stretching exercises involving the large muscles of the back, shoulders, and arms, always including 10 or more hip twists while hanging from chinning bar.

4. Do 10 push-ups (repeated 3 times) executed from the fingertip position.
5. Do 10 throws, concentrating on gradual build-up of hammer head speed.
6. Do 20 throws, working on form.
7. Take 6 to 10 starts from the blocks, running 25 yards each time.

Tuesday

1. Jog ¼ mile.
2. Run wind sprints for ½ mile.
3. Do stretching exercises.
4. Do 10 push-ups (repeated 3 times) from the fingertip position.
5. Do 10 throws, working on keeping arms extended and shoulders relaxed.
6. Do 10 to 20 throws. Work on proper form and getting into effective throwing position.
7. Take 5 starts from the blocks.
8. Train with weights.

Wednesday

1. Jog ¼ mile.
2. Run wind sprints for ½ mile.
3. Do stretching exercises.
4. Do 10 push-ups (repeated 3 times) from fingertip position.
5. Throw 10 times, working on gradual acceleration and relaxation of arms and shoulders while sweeping hammer through widest possible radius.
6. Take 20 throws for form at near maximum, but not all-out, effort for the first 4 weeks.

7. Execute a high jump at reasonable height, or a standing long jump and vertical jump attempting to touch basketball rim or football goal cross support with one hand.

Thursday

1. Jog ¼ mile.
2. Run wind sprints for ½ mile.
3. Do stretching exercises.
4. Take 10 throws for form and position.
5. Do 10 to 20 throws at near maximum, working on gradual accelerating of hammer head speed.
6. Train with weights.

Friday

1. Jog ¼ mile.
2. Run wind sprints for ½ mile.
3. Do stretching exercises.
4. Do 10 push-ups (repeated 3 times) from the fingertip position.
5. Take 10 throws, working on proper form and position.
6. Take 20 throws at near maximum effort, working on acceleration and getting good lifting action from legs.

Saturday

Train with weights if time and facilities are available.

After Meets Start

This schedule is set up in preparation for Saturday meets. When meets are held on Friday, the schedule should be altered accordingly.

Monday

1. Jog ¼ mile.
2. Run wind sprints for ½ mile.
3. Do stretching exercises.
4. Do 10 push-ups (repeated 3 times) from the fingertip position.
5. Take 10 throws, working on proper form and position.
6. Take 15 to 20 throws, working on weak points in your form.
7. Take 6 to 10 starts from the blocks, running 25 to 50 yards each time.
8. Check action pictures taken of your performance the previous Saturday

Tuesday

1. Jog ¼ mile.
2. Do stretching exercises.
3. Do 5 push-ups (repeated 3 times) from the fingertip position.
4. Take 10 throws for form and position.
5. Take 10 throws at all-out effort, in competition with teammates.
6. Take 6 starts from the blocks, running 25 to 50 yards each time.

Wednesday

1. Jog ¼ mile.
2. Run wind sprints for ½ mile.
3. Do stretching exercises.
4. Do 5 push-ups (repeated 3 times) from the fingertip

position.

5. Take 10 throws, working on weak points in your form.
6. Do 20 throws at maximum effort.
7. Train with weights.

Thursday

1. Jog ¼ mile.
2. Run wind sprints for ½ mile.
3. Do stretching exercises.
4. Do 5 push-ups (repeated 3 times) from the fingertip position.
5. Take 5 throws for form and position.
6. Take 7 throws under meet conditions.
7. Take 6 starts from the blocks, running 25 to 50 yards each time.

Friday

Study motion pictures of yourself and others in action. Get plenty of sleep and rest. Prepare yourself mentally for a great performance on Saturday. Be confident!

Saturday

The day of track meet. Be prepared to compete at your best.

1. Arrive at the stadium in plenty of time to dress slowly and get properly warmed up for competition.
2. Jog 1 lap.
3. Do stretching exercises.
4. Take 3 starts and run 25 yards each time.
5. Take 10 throws, working on form and position. Throw with near maximum effort, working on form

and attaining best possible throwing position.

6. Do your best on each throw after competition begins. It is unwise to save up for any one all-out effort.

Weight-Training Program

The hammer thrower, like the shot putter and discus thrower, must make use of weight-training in order to develop into a top performer. Such performers often train as much as 4 out of every 5 days with weights. Perhaps this is too much effort expended in weight-training. A more reasonable approach might be to participate in weight-training 2 out of every 5 days.

Coordination in throwing the hammer should have top priority in the schedule in the other 3 days of training. It is recommended that the hammer thrower do 1 to 5 sets, repeating each set 1 to 8 times. The starting weight should probably be around 75 pounds. This may be gradually increased to the maximum that can be handled 2 to 4 times.

Standing Position

1. Two-arm barbell military press: The lifting action should be done rapidly to help develop explosive power.
2. Two-arm barbell snatch: Make very quick lifts with only average weight.
3. Curls: Be sure to start with arms extended and lift to a complete flexion.
4. Deep knee bends (not more than 90° bend): Be careful to bend the knees only to the position in which the thigh are parallel to the floor.
5. Combined deadlift and shoulder shrugs: Raise shoulders as high as possible and lower weight to floor after each shrug.

6. Upright rowing: Pull barbell up under chin.
7. Heel raises: Place toes on 2-inch board and raise up as high on toe as possible with weight on shoulders.
8. Bench press: Do with the back horizontal and on incline.
9. Twisting situps: While holding weight of 10 to 30 pounds behind neck, situp while sitting on incline board with feet and legs up.
10. Simulations of hang position: Using rubber stretch hose attached to base of goal post or other structure, simulate hang position and do 2 or 3 sets of 10 to 20 repetitions.

CHAPTER 13

THE TEACHING DRILLS IN HAMMER THROWING

The hammer throw was first contested in the Olympic Games in 1900 and since then has become one of the traditional field events for males. At track meets it is frequently contested by females as well, and it is likely that the hammer throw will soon join shot put, discus, and javelin in the Olympics as a throwing event for women.

The hammer throw is considered one of the most technical and complex of throwing events and unique in that the athlete repeats similar movements more than once (i.e., through 3 or 4 turns). Used correctly, the turns successively increase the velocity of the hammer; however, if errors are committed, they are progressively magnified from 1 turn ot the next.

Although athletes claim it to be one of the most satisfying of throwing events, hammer throwing suffers from being confined to relative obscurity on waste tracts of land. To a large degree, this "rejection" stems from the fact that the event can be dangerous and requires the most rigorous of satety precautions. In addition, the impact of the hammer with the ground is such that the area cannot safely be used for other activities (except throwing events).

In recent years Soviet athletes have revolutionized the technique of hammer throwing, changing the footwork and the plane that the hammer follows. For the beginner, however, the traditional technique is more than adequate. After gaining some experience, the athlete can attempt the more advanced technique.

You can teach the fundamentals of hammer throwing with a variety of training implements. Athletes can use 3-to-4-foot broom handles or wooden poles for simulating the extension of the hammer while concentrating on the footwork. A basketball or medicine ball in a net with a handle attachment is also excellent training implement. Using this equipment, the athlete can safely practise preliminary swings, turns, and the delivery (release) of the hammer both indoors and outdoors.

Teaching Points

Drill 1: Lead-Ups

All two-handed slinging and swinging throws are good lead-up activities for the hammer. These simulate the delivery (final throwing action and release) in the hammer throw.

Two-Handed Throws With the Medicine Ball

The athlete throws a medicine ball in two-handed fashion for height. This activity resembles the upward thrust of the hammer thrower's body during the delivery (release) of the hammer.

Coaching Points

1. Extend your legs and lift up onto your toes.
2. Throw your head back and lift your torso.
3. Use both arms to throw the ball as high as possible.

Two-Handed Overhead Throw With a Medicine Ball

An overhead throw for distance emphasises not only the upward thrust of the body but also the backward lean required in the delivery of the hammer. Participants can compete for distance and height in this activity.

Coaching Points

1. Use your legs and back as powerfully as possible to drive the ball backward and upward as far as possible.
2. Lift up high onto your toes.

Two-Handed Overhead Throw With the Medicine Ball Against a Wall

Participants throw the medicine ball in overhead fashion against the wall and then quickly rotate to catch it on the rebound. This activity combines an extension of the body with quick reaction and rotation of the body.

Coaching Points

1. As soon as you throw the ball backward against the wall, pivot on the balls of both feet for a 1/2 rotation to catch the ball again. This pivoting action is used both in the hammer turns and in the delivery of the hammer.

Two-Handed Slinging of a Medicine Ball Over the Shoulder

This lead-up drill emphasises the upward rotary lift of the body during the delivery of the hammer. The legs and body extend upward and the extended arms sling the medicine ball over the shoulder. The two-handed slinging action simulates the two-handed motion used in the hammer throw. Participants can compete in this activity for distance.

Coaching points

1. Extend your legs and back simultaneously and pivot on the balls of your feet toward the direction of throw.
2. Release the ball high over your left shoulder (right-handed thrower).

Drill 2: Hammer Swings

Technique

The athlete grips the hammer handle with the left hand inside the right (right-handed thrower). The swings begin with the hammer laid back on the ground to the right rear. The athlete rotates the shoulders to the right and fully extends the left arm, forming a straight line with the hammer wire. The legs are flexed.

The athlete begins by pulling the hammer upward to the left so that the plane of the hammer has a high point to the left rear. When the hammer has rotated as far to the left as possible, the athlete rotates the shoulders quickly toward the right, shifts the body weight in the same direction, and pulls the hammer down to its low point on the right side. This completes 1 swing. The athlete repeats the sequence for 1 or 2 more swings, increasing the hammer's speed each time.

When the hammer passes in front of the right foot in the final swing, the athlete shifts the body weight above the left foot in preparation for entry into the turns.

Drills

Hammer Swings Using a Pole

Introduce the hammer swings with the use of a 3- to 4-foot broom handle or pole. The left hand grips the near end of the pole, and the right hand grips the pole just beyond the left. Both arms are extended.

Coaching Points

1. Make sure your arms are extended in front of your body.
2. Flex your legs slightly and look forward.
3. Swing the pole as far to the left as possible, and at the same time move your hips to the right.
4. Swing the pole upward on your left side so that the

arc of swing has a high point to the left rear and a low point to the right front of your body.

5. When the pole is swung as far to the left as possible, drop your head underneath your arms and rotate your chest and shoulders to meet the pole on the right.

Hammer Swings Using a Basketball in a Net

A basketball or light medicine ball in a net with a string extension is an excellent substitute for the competitive hammer. Swings that are practised with this equipment will be much faster than those performed with a pole. It is very important to establish the correct body positions first, using the slower actions of the pole. Participants can then work on the swings using the following sequence: (a) with both hands gripping the net handle, (b) with the left hand only gripping the net handle.

Coaching Points

1. Stand in a shoulder-width stance.
2. Place the ball (in the net) on the ground to the right rear.
3. A straight line should extend from your left shoulder down the string extension to the ball itself.
4. Drag the ball upward to the left by extending the legs and body and pulling with the shoulders. This initiates the first of the swings.
5. As soon as you have swung the ball as far to the left as possible, duck your head under your hands and the string and turn to meet the ball again on the right side.
6. Throughout the swings, think of the ball and net as an extension of your arms and shoulders.

7. Avoid bending your arms when the ball is in front of your body.

Hammer Swing and Delivery (Release) Using a Basketball in a Net

The athlete adds a delivery (release) to 2 to 3 hammer swings using a basketball in a net.

Coaching Points

1. Perform 2 or 3 swirgs, setting the high point of the ball's arc over your left shoulder.
2. Shift your hips to the right when the ball rotates to the left.
3. Begin the final pull on the ball for the delivery 2 tc 3 swings when the ball is at its low point in front ol your body.
4. Extend your legs and back vigorously and throw your head back.
5. Pivot on the balls of your feet toward the direction of throw, and release the ball over your left shoulder.

The Grip on the Hammer Handle

Throwers become accustomed to the grip on the hammer handle. A right-handed thrower (who will release the hammer over the left shoulder) wears a protective glove on the left hand. The left hand grips the hammer handle, and the right hand is wrapped over the left. The reverse arrangement occurs for left-handed throwers.

Coaching Points

1. When you grip the hammer, avoid making a tight fist with your hands.
2. Form a long "hook" with the fingers of both hands and use this hook togrip the handle of the hammer.

Hammer Swings and Delivery (Release) Using a Light Hammer

Throwers practise hammer swings and delivery using a hammer that is approximately 1/2 of the competitive weight for their age range; in most cases a 4-kilogram hammer is adequate. The hammer is placed on the ground to the right rear of the thrower, who tows it into the first swing in the same manner as with the ball in the net. The high point of the hammer's arc is to left rear of the thrower, whose hips are shifted to the right to counterbalance the pull of the hammer. When the hammer is to the left, the athlete shifts the hips to the right, and vice versa. With each swing, the high point of the hammer is raised in preparation for the delivery.

The delivery is performed through an upward extension of the legs and back. The athlete pivots on the balls of the feet toward the direction of throw and releases the hammer over the left shoulder. Throwers practising the drill can compete against each other for distance.

Coaching Points

1. Keep the high point of the arc to the left rear of your body.
2. Fully extend your arms when the hammer is in front of you.
3. Drive up with your legs and chest in the delivery.
4. Keep your arms extended during the delivery.

Drill 3: Hammer Turns

Technique

After completing 2 or 3 swings; the athlete enters the turns with the hammer "fixed" in front of the body, the arms extended, and vision toward the hammer. The athlete (right-handed thrower) begins the 1st turn with rotation on the heel of the left foot (180 degrees) and the ball of the right foot (180 degrees). The right knee is turned inward to the rear of the left knee during the rotation to the left.

The athlete rolls along the side of the left foot and then rotates 180 degrees on the toe of the left foot, simultaneously lifting the right foot off the ground and bringing it fully around so that the body rotates 360 degrees. As the athlete enters each of the turns, the hammer is raised on the left side and lowered on the right. This establishes a high point and low point in the arc that the hammer follows and also sets the angle of trajectory for the hammer when it is released.

With each turn the athlete attempts to rotate the lower body ahead of the upper body. By doing this, the athlete "winds up the body" like a coil spring. Because the feet are on the ground ahead of the torso in each turn, the unwinding of the spring progressively accelerates the hammer.

Drills

Rotation With the Arms Extended

Participants rotate on the spot with the arms outstretched in front. No implement is used and no specific footwork is demanded.

Variation

The athlete performs the same action, gripping the end of the 3- to 4-foot pole.

Coaching Points

1. Squat down, look forward, and extend your arms, holding them out horizontally in front of your body.
2. Do not worry about footwork; shuffle around in a circle, turning on the same spot.

Footwork for Hammer Turns

Throwers practise the footwork used in hammer turns.

Practising a Sequence of Hammer Turns

Draw 2 parallel lines shoulder-width apart on the ground to assist the performer in the alignment of the feet during the turns. The athlete performs 1, 2, and then 3 turns in sequence.

Coaching Points

1. Squat down and look forward.
2. Pivot a full 180 degrees on the heel of your left foot and the toe of your right foot.
3. Press the knee of the right leg in behind the left leg.
4. Keep your legs close together.
5. Pivot 180 degrees on the toe of the left foot, simultaneously picking up the right foot to rotate around and complete the turn.
6. Do not swing your right let out wide. Keep the legs close together.
7. Make sure that your feet line up parallel at the end of each turn.
8. Look forward throughout the whole action.

Hammer Turns Using a 3- to 4-Foot Pole

Athletes perform the same action as in the previous drill, but using the 3- to 4-foot pole. Each performer squats down and holds the pole at arm's length and directly ahead of the body throughout each turn.

Coaching Points

1. Look forward and keep your arms fully extended.
2. Do not raise or lower the pole during the turns.
3. Concentrate on completing each 180-degree turn and ending up with both feet on the parallel lines.

Hammer Turns Using a Basketball in a Net

Each thrower uses a basketball in a net instead of the 3- to 4-foot pole. The performer passes the ball around the body to give it some initial rotary momentum, then enters the 1st turn holding the basketball in the net in extended position in front of the body. Providing that the 1st turn is completed correctly, the performer then moves immediately into the second turn.

Turns using a basketball in a net will be much faster than with a pole. If the athlete gets confused and performs the footwork incorrectly, the slower movements with the pole should be practised again.

Coaching Points

1. Complete each turn so that your feet land on the parallel lines.
2. Maintain a balanced squatting position throughout.
3. Look forward.
4. Concentrate on completing a full 180-degree rotation on the left heel, and then repeat it on the ball of the left foot.
5. Keep your arms extended and the implement directly in front of your body.
6. Make the first 180 degrees of the turn slow and precise, then finish the last 180 degrees of the turn quickly.
7. Keep your knees close together during the turn.

Adding a High and Low Point to the Turns

In order to release a hammer at the correct angle of trajectory (called a high point), the performer must correctly angle the arc of the hammer during the turns. An elite athlete will progressively increase the angle through each turn. A right-handed thrower will lift the hammer high to the left rear and low to the right rear of the body. A novice can practise this action with the arms extended, holding a basketball or volleyball between the hands. An alternative is to use the 3- to 4-foot pole.

The athlete raises the ball or pole upward to a high point to the left rear during the first half of the turn, then lowers it to a low point to the right front during the second half of the turn.

Coaching Points

1. Keep your arms fully extended during the turns.
2. Raise your arms for the high point as you complete the first 180-degree rotation on the heel of your left foot. Lower your arms for the low point when the final 180 degrees is completed.
3. Keep your legs flexed and knees together during the turns, and squat down (as though sitting on a stool) and look forward to maintain balance.

Combinations of Swings and Turns

Put swings and turns together in various combination to familiarise the athlete with the transition from swings to turns. This practise stresses the importance of the shift of body weight to the left for the entry into each turn and also the shift of the hips to counteract the pull of the hammer during the swings. Use a light hammer for this drill. Examples of combinations of swings and turns are: (a) 2 swings followed but 1 turn; (b) 2 swings followed by 2 turns; (c) 2 swings, 1 turn, 2 swings; (d) 1 swing, 1 turn, 1 swing, 1 turn; and 2 swings, 2 turns, 2 swings, 2 turns.

Coaching Points

1. Establish a high point and a low point during the swings, and maintain these positions through the turns.
2. Shift your weight over the left foot in the transition

from swings to turns.

3. Keep your knees close together in each turn.
4. Keep your left foot in contact with the ground, and shift your right foot through the last half of each turn as fast as possible.
5. Keep the implement "fixed" at arm's length in front of your body during the turns.
6. Shift your hips away from the hammer in the swings, and squat down and lean away from the hammer in the turns.

Drill 4: Combining Hammer Swings, Turns, and Delivery

The Complete Throw

The complete throw combines preliminary swings, followed by 1, 2, or 3 turns, and finally the delivery or release. Participants slowly practice this action using the 3-to-4-foot pole, then practise faster using a basketball in a net or a lightweight hammer. Thereafter, the athlete practises with progressively heavier hammers until working up to the competitive-weight hammer.

A typical practise sequence is as follows: (a) 2 or 3 swings, followed by 1 turn and the delivery; (b) 2 or 3 swings, followed by 2 turns and the delivery; and (c) 2 or 3 swings, followed by 3 turns and the delivery.

Coaching Points

1. Do not rush; perform the swings fairly slowly and increase speed in the turns and delivery action.
2. Be sure to keep your arms extended and the hammer in front of your body.
3. Try to bring your right leg around your body as fast as possible to complete each turn.
4. Make sure your feet line up parallel to the direction of throw at the end of each turn.

Delivery and Reverse

The delivery (i.e., the actual release of the hammer) at the end of 3 turns demands extremely fast actions and precise timing. The rotation of the legs and hips in the third turn must occur at great speed so that both feet are on the ground well ahead of the upper body (and hammer). In this way, the athlete can exert tremendous pull on the hammer.

The pull on the hammer begins with the hammer head passes in front of the body. The athlete rotates on the balls of the feet toward the direction of throw, lifting the chest up and extending the legs and back. The action simulates an upward spiral. The athlete's body is fully extended when the hammer is released over the left shoulder.

The athlete avoids a foul throw by performing a reverse, withdrawing the left leg from the rim of the hammer circle and flexing on rotating on the right foot.

Coaching Points

1.. Begin the throw slowly and accelerate from swings to turns to the final release.
2. Make the acceleration smooth throughout.
3. Start with the plane of the hammer fairly flat, then successively raise the high point in each turn.
4. Straighten your back and extend your legs as powerfully as possible in the delivery. Spiral upward toward the direction of throw.
5. Throw your head back and deliver the hammer over your left shoulder.

Practising the Reverse

The athlete practises the reverse (or recovery after releasing the hammer), at any time that the hammer is released.

Coaching Points

1. Complete the delivery, release the hammer, and then consciously pull your left foot back from the inside edge of the rim of the circle.

2. Flex your right leg and lower your weight backward.

Alternative Technique for Performing the Reverse

In an alternate technique used to prevent fouling, the athlete continues to rotate on the balls of the feet after releasing the hammer and rotates back toward the centre of the circle.

Coaching Points

1. After you release the hammer, rotate another 1/2 turn on the balls of the feet so that you face the direction of throw.

2. Flex your legs simultaneously to lower your weight backward toward the centre of the ring.

Common Error and Corrections

1. Error

The athlete bends the arms in the swings.

Reasons

The thrower is fighting the hammer. The thrower fears loss of balance and uses no leg flexion. The athlete lowers the head and bends forward.

Remedies

The thrower should allow the hammer to "hang" as an extension from the shoulders and should flex the legs and squat as though sitting on a stool. Instruct the athlete to practise one-handed, and two-handed swings, stretching the arms out in front of the body during the swings.

2. Error

The athlete loses balance during swings.

Reasons

The athlete uses no leg flexion and looks downward. There is no shift of the hips in opposition to the pull of the hammer. The arms may be flexed when the hammer is in front of the body.

Remedies

Instruct the athlete to practise the swings slowly using a pole. The athlete should also practise "sitting" and shifting the body weight in opposition to the movement of the hammer. The faster the swings, the more emphatic the hip shift.

3. Error

No high or low point occurs during the swings. Or, the low and high points are in the wrong position.

Reasons

The athlete does not take the hammer to the left as far as possible during the swings. The arc of the hammer is not elevated to the left side of the body.

4. Error

No high or low point occurs during the swings. Or, the low and high points are in the wrong position.

Reasons

The athlete does not take the hammer to the left as far as possible during the swings. The arc of the hammer is not elevated to the left side of the body.

Remedies

Have the athlete practise establishing the correct plane of the hammer using a pole and then a basketball in a net or a lightweight hammer. The athlete should sweep the implement upward the left with each swing.

5. Error

The athlete swings the arms and hammer like a windmill or propeller in front of the body. The hammer does not rotate to the rear of the thrower during the swings.

Reasons

The thrower stands too erect and is afraid of swinging the hammer to the rear of the body and losing balance. The arms are flexed, and the hammer is not swept for enough to the left and rear during each swing.

Remedies

The athlete should squat down, look forward, and sweep or "tow" the hammer upward to the left. The athlete must also shift eh hips to the right and rotate the shoulders to the right as the hammer moves from left rear to the right rear. The athlete should work to flatten the plane followed by the hammer (still keeping the high point on the left side of the body).

6. Error

The thrower lands heavily on the right foot at the end of each turn.

Reasons

The athlete's body tilts toward the right. The body weight is not shifted over the left foot during the transition from swing during the transition from swing to turn.

Remedies

The athlete must consciously shift the body weight to the left and over the left foot when entering the turns. The athlete should practise the turns without the hammer and then with a pole. The right leg action must be fast with both knees tight together during the turns. The athlete must avoid falling to the right as the right foot is placed on the ground at the end of each turn.

7. Error

The thrower loses balance, particularly during the second and third turns.

Reasons

The thrower does not counteract the increasing pull of the hammer by leaning away from the hammer. The legs are not flexed, and the arms may be flexed or the vision directed downward.

Remedies

Instruct the athlete to practise the turns, progressively increasing speed. The athlete must "hang" on the hammer with "long arms", flex the legs, squat, and shift the hips away from the hammer to maintain balance as the rotational speed increases.

8. Error

The hammer and thrower appear to rotate as a block. The legs do not shift ahead under the upper body during each turn.

Reasons

The movement of the hips below the torso is slow. The knees are not pressed together during the turns, and the non-supporting leg is allowed to swing outward during the turns.

Remedies

The athlete must rotate the right leg around in each turn as fast as possible. Have the athlete practise rotating the legs and hips ahead of the torso without the hammer. Then the athlete can use the hammer substitutes and finally the hammer.

9. Error

The thrower is unable to make the transition from swings to turns. The thrower attempts to perform a swing while entering the first run.

Reasons

The thrower does not hold or "fix" the hammer at arm's length in front of the body when entering the turns.

Remedies

Instruct the athletes to practise swings plus 1 turn using a pole. At the end of the second swing, the athlete holds the pole at arm's length in front of body and performs a turn. The athlete can work with a basketball in a net or with a lightweight shortwire hammer.

9. Error

The thrower rotates on the spot or travels sideways during the turns. There is no movement across the ring in the direction of the throw.

Reasons

The heel-toe pivot is poorly performed. The thrower may be pivoting continuously on the toe of the left foot.

Remedies

Have the athlete practise the turns without the hammer, accentuating heel-toe action with each turn. The athlete should pivot on the heel of the left foot 180 degrees and then rock over the side of the front to the ball of the foot to repeat the next 180 degrees. Use parallel lines to help establish correct footwork.

10. Error

The plane of the hammer is incorrect—either too flat or too high. The hammer hits the ground.

Reasons

The upper body is tight, not relaxed. The angle of the arms at the shoulders is varied and not held constant.

Remedies

Have the athlete practise turns slowly using a 4-foot pole to establish the correct angle of the arms. The athlete should progressively raise the hammer's plane in each turn to the correct angle for the delivery of the hammer.

Hammer Delivery Following 3 or 4 Turns

1. Error

The athlete flexes the arms during the delivery.

Reasons

The athlete feels that by flexing the arms, he or she will direct more pull to the hammer. The legs are extended too early.

Remedies

The pull on the hammer comes from a powerful extension of the legs and back. The athlete must think of "long" arms and "loose", relaxed shoulders and must maintain flexion in the legs during the turn. The athlete should practise the correct action slowly using a pole.

2. Error

The athlete loses balance and falls over during the delivery.

Reasons

The athlete does not shift the body weight over the left foot during delivery. The pull during the delivery is not directed down the length of the hammer wire to the head of the hammer. The timing of the pull is incorrect.

Remedies

The athlete should shift the body weight over the left foot during the delivery. The pull on the hammer occurs when the hammer head passes in front of the body. The athlete then extends the legs and back and rotates toward the direction of throw.

3. Error

The athlete does not generate any power in the

delivery.

Reasons

The legs and back are already extended prior to the delivery. The plane of the hammer may be too flat immediately prior to the delivery. The timing of pull on the hammer in the delivery is incorrect.

Remedies

Have the athlete practise the swings and delivery action with no turns and without the implement. The athlete must raise the high point progressively through the turns and emphasize throwing the head back and extending the legs and back in the delivery. The upward thrust of the body should pull directly along the wire of the hammer, not at an angle.

4. Error

The hammer head hits the ground during the delivery.

Reasons

The upper body drops forward during the final turn and during the delivery. The high point of the hammer is too high in the last turn, or the high and low points are in the wrong.

Remedies

The athlete should work on the correct action using a pole. The athlete lowers the high point a little but maintains the high point over the left shoulder. The athlete must flex the legs and keep the upper body perpendicular.

5. Error

The thrower is "thrown" or pulled out of the ring during the delivery.

Reasons

The thrower initiates the delivery with far too much backward upper body lean. The timing of the extension of the legs and the position of the hammer head during the pull of the delivery are incorrect.

Remedies

Have the athlete practise swings and delivery using 1 turn. The athlete pulls on the hammer by extending the legs when the hammer passes in front of the right foot. The athlete then extends the body in an upward spiral and performs the reverse immediately after the hammer is released.

6. Error

The hammer flies out of the sector boundary (right-handed thrower).

Reasons

The movement of the right foot into position for the delivery is too slow.

Remedies

Have the athlete speed up rotation of the right leg and placement of the right foot, keeping the knees close together in the turns. Using a pole, the athlete can practise rotating the hips and legs around and ahead of the shoulders and hammer.

CHAPTER 14

THE IMPORTANCE OF NUTRITIONAL DIET AND WEIGHT CONTROL IN THROWING EVENTS (WEIGHT EVENTS)

BASIC NUTRITIONAL PRINCIPLES

There are three basic rules of nutrition. First, the body requires essential nutrients: carbohydrates, proteins and fats (the energy-supplying nutrients) and the vitamins, minerals, trace elements, and water that are necessary for the utilization of that energy. Second, these nutrients are contained in four basic food groups: the meat, fish, and meat-substitute group; the fruit and vegetable group; the milk and diary produce group; and the bread and cereal group. Third, items from these basic food groups should be eaten in the following portions each day: meat and fish, two portions; milk and dairy produce, two portions; bread and cereal, four portions, and fruits and vegetables, four portions.

Let us consider these three principles in greater detail.

THE SIX BASIC NUTRIENTS

Carbohydrate

The following points emphasizes the value and

functions of carbohydrates for the athlete:—

- The body has limited carbohydrate stores.
- These carbohydrate stores are utilized at rates proportional to the intensity of exercise.
- The larger the carbohydrate stores before exercise the better the performance.
- The extent to which the body carbohydrate stores are filled depends on the carbohydrate content of the diet and can be increased by the carbohydrate-loading diet.

These are the theoretical considerations. The practical questions that arise are these: What foods comprise mainly carbohydrates? How much carbohydrate should be eaten when training? How does one carbohydrate load? Are there any dangers involved in this practice?

CARBOHYDRATE-CONTAINING FOODS

Some high-carbohydrate foods, all of which comprise at least 90% carbohydrate with less than 5% protein and 5% fat. These are the types of carbohydrate-containing foods that should be eaten during heavy training and when you are carbohydrate-loading.

Thus, a high-carbohydrate diet consists almost exclusively of fruits, vegetables, and cereals (bread, pasta, rice, potatoes, and breakfast cereals). Sweets, chocolates, and other confectioneries may have relatively lower carbohydrate contents because of high fat contents. It is best to eat more natural high-carbohydrate foods, in particular potatoes, during carbohydrate loading.

The Carbohydrate Content of the Diet During Heavy Training

The work of Costill and Miller showed that muscle glycogen levels in athletes eating normal mixed diets

(40% carbohydrate) fell progressively when these athletes exercised for up to 2 hours a day. This fall was prevented when the athletes ate a high-carbohydrate diet in which 70% of the dietary energy was provided by carbohydrate (70% carbohydrate diet).

In practice, few athletes eat diets that contain as much carbohydrate, largely because such diets are extremely bland and unappetizing. Unfortunately, it is the protein and fat content of foot that increases its palatability.

The Carbohydrate-Loading/Carbohydrate-Depletion Diet

Highly trained athletes should not undergo the carbohydrate-depletion phase and should rather ingest adequate amounts of carbohydrate during prolonged exercise, especially exercise that lasts more than 4 hours. By avoiding the carbohydrate-depletion phase, they also avoid some potential dangers that will be described subsequently.

Less well trained athletes may benefit from the carbohydrate-depletion phase. Using this technique, they may store more muscle and liver glycogen than they would be only eating a high-carbohydrate diet for the last 3 days before competition.

First, it was originally thought that complex (unrefined) carbohydrates such as potatoes and bread induce more complete carbohydrate storage during carbohydrate loading than do simple carbohydrates (Costill et al., 1981). This is no longer believed to be the case (Roberts et al., 1988). The optimum strategy is to eat simple carbohydrates for the first 24 to 48 hours of carbohydrate-loading diet and thereafter to eat determined by the carbohydrate content (in grams) of the diet and is maximum on a diet providing 500 to 600 g of carbohydrate per day. Athletes eating 25 g of carbohydrate per hour resynthesize glycogen at a rate of 170 mmol per kilogram of wet muscle every 24 hours and are therefore able to completely restock their muscle glycogen stores within 24 hours of being totally carbohydrate depleted. Athletes involved in prolonged (4 to 6 hours) daily exercise, like cyclists in the Tour de France, can restock their muscle glycogen stores each day only if they ingest high-carbohydrate solutions both during and after exercise.

Probably the safest way to carbohydrate load before a race is simply to modify your diet in the following ways:

- Eat cereals, bread (with honey), fruit, and fruit juices for breakfast. Use skim milk in place of whole milk, because skim milk has a lower fat content.
- Substitute pasta (e.g., macaroni and spaghetti) for meat, and eat more potatoes.
- If you are still hungry, eat sweets, but not to the point of gluttony.
- Supplement the diet with 200 g of high-carbohydrate "carbo-loading" athletic drink.

Note that the carbohydrate-depletion diet is no longer considered to be an essential method for optimum carbohydrate loading, at least for well-trained athletes.

The best sign that sufficient carbohydrate has been stored during the loading phase is an increase in body weight. For every 1 g of carbohydrate that is stored, approximately 2 to 3 g of water are also stored. If the body carbohydrate stores were completely empty before carbohydrate loading commenced, body weight should increase 2.0 to 2.5 kg (equivalent to a total carbohydrate store of 600 g) during the loading phase.

Are any other food supplements necessary during carbohydrate loading?

Clearly, fluid intake needs to be increased during the loading phase so that sufficient water can be stored with glycogen. The best guide to the adequacy of fluid supplementation is urine colour. A light-coloured urine indicates an adequate fluid intake.

Potassium is also stored with glycogen. Thus, potassium requirements must also increase, and you can best meet these by eating oranges, tomatoes, and bananas, which are good sources of both potassium and carbohydrate. There is tentative evidence to suggest that the requirements of the B-group vitamins thiamine and niacin may be slightly increased during the loading phase.

One should never take vitamin-B-complex tablets immediately before exercise, particularly those containing nicotinic acid. When present in high concentrations in the blood, nicotinic acid prevents the mobilization of free fatty acids. Thus, if taken in high doses shortly before exercise, nicotinic acid will impair endurance performance by increasing the rate of muscle glycogen utilization during exercise.

Are there any dangers in the carbohydrte-depletion/ carbohydrate-loading diet?

Carbohydrate loading does not suit everyone. Although most will probably run better after loading, a few runners may be adversely affected and will curse the day they ever heard about this diet.

The main risk is that the high content of carbohydrate in the loading diet may cause intestinal distress, in particular with the diet by initially deviating as little from your normal diet as possible. With time you will learn which carbohydrates to avoid and how much you need to eat to achieve maximum benefit.

The second major problem of the diet is that during the carbohydrate-depletion phase, physical performance capacity falls steeply. After about 24 hours without carbohydrates, any physical effort much greater than a walk becomes very tiresom. Worse, after 36 hours of carbohydrate depletion, even the most docile, congenial runner becomes an irritable, aggressive, short-tempered monster of impossible proportions.

In addition, it seems that the long depletion run originally advocated by Scandinavian researchers, coming as it does only 7 days before a major race, must be detrimental. For this reason, it is probably better to run relatively short distances on the 3 days of carbohydrate depletion rather than a single long run. In addition, there is no evidence that the depletion run by itself increases muscle glycogen storage.

Other medical risks that have been described include acute kidney failure, induced by the depletion phase in two athletes who almost certainly suffered from obscure muscle cell metabolic abnormalities. Although the high-carbohydrate diet would be expected to affect blood fat levels adversely, causing blood cholesterol and triglyceride levels to rise, this has not been found. In general, even the carbohydrate-depletion phase of this diet appears to be very safe.

It is generally held that carbohydrate loading should be undertaken two to three times a year and only before major races. However, you certainly should not try it for the first time before a major race. In addition, the diet should be gradually adapted to the individual's needs and should certainly not be followed blindly without modification. Elite athletes should probably avoid the depletion phase altogether.

Food Intake During Races Lasting Between 7 and 24 Hours

Prolonged exercise lasting more than 5 hours, because it is performed at less than 75% VO_2 max, does not affect the rate of gastric emptying. Furthermore, such exercise has no effect on digestion. Thus, during prolonged exercise you can ingest essentially whatever you choose, although such food should have a relatively high-carbohydrate content.

Protein

There are few dietary myths greater than those surrounding the protein needs of people who exercise vigorously. Most people are aware that strength-trained athletes, in particular power lifters and weight lifters, have an ability to eat protein in the form of eggs and mean that defies description.

Less well known is that in the 1860s, the Oxford University rowing crew, training on underdone beef and mutton without vegetables, completed a string of nine consecutive victories over Cambridge rowers, who trained only on vegetables, fruit, and bread. The natural, but incorrect, conclusion was that the Oxford rower's success was due to their diets; thus, the importance of protein in the athlete's diet received unwarranted public credibility. One wonders how the Oxford team might have performed with a little carbohydrate loading! The early pedestrians also ate a great deal of protein.

Protein is a relatively minor fuel during exercise; only during prolonged exercise in the carbohydrate-depleted state ao proteins become more important. Even then, protein supplies only about 10% of the total energy requirement and is used as a substrate both for new glucose production in the liver and for oxidation in the Krebs cycle. Nevertheless, the increased use of proteins during exercise may be sufficient to increase the daily dietary protein requirements of athletes and cyclists to about twice (2 g/kg/day) those of sedentary persons.

The main function of the body protein stores is to provide the basic structure of most body tissues, in particular the muscle proteins acting and myosin, as well as other essential components such as hormones, cellular enzymes, and genes. In all these structures, proteins exists in a dynamic state, that is, they are continually being broken down and replaced by new proteins absorbed from the intestines. This continual protein replacement is known as the protein turnover rate and equals about 25 g of protein per day for a 70-kg person.

Stresses such as physical training, severe illness, or major surgery all lead to an increased protein turnover rate. In athletes, this increased rate of protein turnover acts mainly as a noncarbohydrate source of new glucose, especially when the rate of carbohydrate utilization during exercise exceeds the rate of dietary carbohydrate ingestion so that body carbohydrate stores fall. In addition, it seems likely that during the recovery phase after marathon and ultramarathon races, the rate of protein turnover is increased, in part to repair the muscle damage that such events cause.

It is apparent that these demands for more protein arise from within the body. It is not possible to increase the body's protein metabolism artificially and thereby stimulate muscle growth simply by eating larger amounts of protein in the diet.

The question that we needs to ask is this: By how much does exercise, particularly the "muscle sports", increase the protein turnover rate? This is where each expert has a different opinion.

One review referred to a number of studies that showed that although the protein requirements of athletes involved in intensive training do indeed increase, these requirements exceed 1.7 g per kilogram of body weight, a value that will be met by the increased energy intake of the athlete in training. Thus Haymes calculated that a 70-kg athlete who eats a diet containing 12% protein and who begins exercising and increases his or her energy intake from 3,000 kcal to 4,000 kcal per day will increase protein intake relative to body weight from 1.3 to 1.7 g per kilogram of body weight.

Support for this conclusion comes from a study of Laritcheva and his colleagues from the Moscow Institute of Nutrition. They studied a group of top Soviet weight lifters and found that during periods of very intensive training, the protein requirements of some of these athletes went as high as 2.3 g per kilogram of body weight. But even this value was met by a well-balanced diet adjusted to the higher caloric requirements of the athlete's increased daily energy outputs. The authors concluded that excessively high-protein diets were useless, because as the protein content of the diet increased, proportionately less protein was absorbed from the intestine. The study of Tarnopolsky et al. showed that protein requirements of body builders were, in contrast to those of distance runners, only marginally greater than those of the sedentary individuals.

This conclusion brings us to a statement made by an American weight lifter who religiously followed a high-protein diet until a scientific colleague showed him where his money was actually going.

Fats

The fat in the diet provides a convenient, palatable, and highly concentrated source of energy. Triglyceride is the form in which fat occurs both in foods and in the body's fat stores.

The principal foods contributing fat to the diet are vegetable oil, salad dressing (in particular mayonnaise), meat, the visible fat of meat, the skin of the chicken, egg yolk, nuts, olives, avocados, and daily produce such as milk, cream, cheese, and butter.

These fats may be either saturated or unsaturated. Saturated means that most of the chemical bonds in the free-fatty-acid component of the triglyceride molecule are occupied by hydrogen; unsaturated fats have fewer of these bonds occupied by hydrogen.

Animal fats, particularly those found in red meat and dairy produce, are predominantly saturated, whereas vegetable fats are predominantly unsaturated.

Unsaturated fats are mostly liquid at room temperature (such as oils); in order to increase the solidity of these fats (so that they can be used to spread, for example, on bread), some of the unsaturated bonds in the free-fatty-acid molecules have hydrogen added in a chemical process known as hydrogenation. Polyunsaturated margarines are therefore partially hydrogenated vegetable oils, which contain free fatty acids that are nevertheless more unsaturated than those found in dairy produce, butter in particular.

Dietary fats pose at least three problems:

1. The fat in the diet is largely "hidden". In addition, fat is a highly concentrated energy source providing more than twice as much energy per gram than does carbohydrate. Thus, a few smears of butter or margarine or a few glasses of whole milk constitute many calories of energy. This high-energy source may be of value to those living on a subsistence diet, but in the developed countries of the world, many of whose citizens are already overfed, the high energy content of fat makes it an undesirable food.

2. There is a relationship between the fat content of the diet, the blood cholesterol levels of persons living on that diet, and their risks of developing coronary artery disease. The risk of colon cancer in both sexes and breast cancer in women is also increased in those who eat a high-fat diet. Thus, the persons and nations with high dietary intakes of saturated fats have an increased incidence of coronary artery disease and cancer; those with a lower intake have reduced incidences of these diseases. On the other hand, the intake of the fats of fish, especially eicosapentantaenoic acid, is associated with a reduced incidence of coronary heart disease.

3. The thermic effect of fat is very little. Thus, weight gain in far greater from a fat-rich diet than from an equicaloric, carbohydrate-rich diet.

Thus, the practical problems posed by the fat found in the diet are that fat is a high-energy source, it is appetizing and readily satisfies hunger, and its storage in the body is more efficient that is the storage of carbohydrate. The result is that too much fat in your diet may suppress your appetite before you have ingested sufficient carbohydrate to restock your body carbohydrate stores. This is especially important during carbohydrate loading. In addition, it seems that a high-fat diet increases the risk of gaining weight and of developing coronary artery disease and certain cancers.

Vitamins

The vitamins make up a group of unrelated organic compounds that are needed only in minute quantities in the diet but are essential for specific metabolic reactions within the body and for normal growth and development. Thus, vitamins regulate metabolism; they are essential for the metabolic processes that convert fat and carbohydrate into energy; and they assist in the formation of bones and other tissues. Clearly, they are an essential dietary component.

Vitamins fall into two main groups: those that are fat soluble and those that are water soluble. Fat-soluble vitamins are absorbed with dietary fats; they can be stored to some extent in the body and are not normally excreted in the urine. In contrast, water-soluble vitamins are not normally stored within the body, and any excess intake over daily bodily needs is excreted in the urine.

The differences in solubility of the vitamins is therefore important, because solubility determines the extent to which vitamins can be stored in the body. Because fat-soluble vitamins are readily stored in the body, deficiencies of this group are far less likely than are deficiencies of the water-soluble vitamins, which must be replaced daily. For similar reasons, overdose or intoxication is far more likely to occur with fat-soluble vitamins but may still occur with water-soluble vitamins.

Practical Considerations

One of the most frequently asked question about nutrition is whether athletes require increased intakes of vitamins.

Very little evidence supports the practice of supplementing, a nutritionally balanced and adequate diet with additional vitamins, even though exercise may increase the requirements of certain vitamins, in particular riboflavin and also probably vitamin C. Interestingly, the evidence that vitamin C requirements are almost certainly increased by exercise comes from the polar expeditions of Amundsen, Scott, and Shackleton. Although members of all three expeditions ate rations that were totally vitamin C deficient, members of only the latter two expeditions, both of which hauled their own sleds, developed symptoms of scurvy. Thus, despite eating essentially identical diets, none of the members of Amundsen's group developed symptoms of scurvy, almost certainly because their sleds were pulled by dogs and the members consequently exercised considerably less than did members of Scott and Shackleton's expeditions.

With the possible exception of folate deficiency, vitamin deficiencies are extremely uncommon in athletes, and the only vitamin deficiencies that have been shown to impair performance are those of thiamine and vitamin C. In addition, no study, including those undertaken by Lindsay Weight at the University of Cape Town, has yet shown that supplementation with any particular vitamin increases athletic performance in persons eating a normal diet. The studies of Weight et al. found that blood vitamin and mineral levels were high in a group of marathon athletes and did nor raise greatly during 3 months of treatment with a powerful vitamin/ mineral supplement.

However, a possibility that cannot be ignored is that at the high doses taken by some athletes, vitamins no longer work in their vitamin roles but act as drugs in other currently undefined ways. It is possible that those actions could improve athletic performance, but this has not been scientifically proven.

Although, in theory, vegetarians are prone to vitamin deficiencies, in practice, few develop clinical evidence of such deficiencies. Those that do almost always follow the more extreme forms of vegetarian diets.

Minerals

The most important minerals in the diet include sodium, potassium, magnesium, calcium, iron, zinc, and copper.

Sodium

Sodium is stored mainly in the body fluids with much smaller amounts inside cells. Sodium plays a number of important physiological roles: It maintains the normal water balance and distribution within the body; it determines the blood pressure; and it maintains osmotic equilibrium, acid-base balance, and normal muscular irritability. The total body sodium content is about 80 g.

Two important myths that have developed concerning sodium chloride (salt) are that athletes need to increase their salt intakes when they start training hard and that salt is an important cure for cramps. Let us consider these two questions.

The daily food intake of persons living on typical Westernized diet has a sodium chloride content of 5 to 20 g. Of this, 3 g occur naturally in the food, 3 to 5 g are added to the food during processing, and the rest is added by the consumer (i.e., from the salt shaker) either in cooking or at the table. Salt is added to the diet largely because it improves the taste of food but also because it acts as a preservative.

Current evidence shows that the body's daily salt requirement is about 0.2 to 0.5 g, about one tenth of what we actually consume. The excess that is ingested is lost in the urine. Even vigorous and prolonged daily exercise increases salt requirements only very slightly, because sweat has a low-salt content that decreases as one becomes more fit and heat acclimatized. Thus, the sweat of heat-acclimatized runners has a very low salt content, so that its composition approaches that of distilled water.

The salt content of sweat in an untrained subject is about 3.5 of salt per litre of sweat, whereas the sweat of a trained, heat-acclimatized subject contains about 1.8 g of salt per litre of sweat. This means that untrained subjects would have to sweat a minimum of 3 L/day and trained, heat-acclimatized athlete up to 6 L/day just to ride themselves of the excess salt in their diets. To induce salt deficits, they would need to exercise even more. But even then, the body has conservation mechanisms that are activated if there is a risk of salt deficiency developing.

On the other hand, there is at least some evidence that a high-salt intake may increase the risk of high blood pressure (hypertension), especially in some subjects who are genetically prone to this condition. For this reason most nutritional authorities advise that daily salt intake in the general population, especially in those with high blood pressure, should be reduced with the ultimate goal of a daily salt intake of 3 g. Their argument is that the taste for salt is an acquired taste and is reversible if the amount of salt added to food is reduced, especially during processing. Adding salt via the salt shaker is, of course, quite taboo. Some authorities even feel that 3 g per day is probably still too high.

Where does this leave the runner? Obviously, we are fortunate that our daily exercise rids us of some of the excess salt in our diets and may therefore protect us against the subsequent development of high blood pressure.

Interestingly, most of the scientific literature on muscle cramps during exercise in the heat (heat cramps) was written in the 1930s and early 1940s; little work has been done subsequently.

Potassium

Potassium is stored in the body mainly inside cells and is found in the diet in citrus fruits, bananas, and tomatoes. The daily potassium requirement is about 2 to 4 g, which is about 4 to 8 times more than the daily salt requirement. The total body potassium store is about 90 g.

During exercise, potassium is lost in urine and sweat, but these losses are trival. Thus, the sweat potassium content is only 0.1 to 0.2 g/L; even when eating a low-potassium diet (2 g/day), subjects exercising at 50% VO_2 max for 2 hours a day in the heat (dry bulb temperature 47° C) showed no evidence of developing potassium deficiency.

The major factor for runners is that potassium is stored with glycogen in the body; hence, potassium requirements are increased during carbohydrate loading. The ingestion of fruit during carbohydrate loading will adequately cover the additional potassium needs.

The potassium stored with glycogen is released into the bloodstream as exercise progresses and as the intramuscular glycogen stores are utilized. The extra potassium is then lost in sweat and urine in place of sodium chloride; thus, potassium excretion during exercise helps to conserve sodium.

Magnesium

In some countries, magnesium levels in the soil and therefore also in the drinking and irrigation water are low. Persons living in these areas may well have mild magnesium deficiencies, symptoms of which may include impaired exercise tolerance.

We at the University of Cape Town have found that blood magnesium levels in our local runners are usually in the low-normal range. These findings are suggestive, but not diagnostic, of magnesium deficiency. Whether increased magnesium intakes in these runners would improve their performances is not yet established. Interestingly, magnesium levels are inversely related to VO_2 max and are lowest in individuals with the highest VO_2 max values. The reason for this is unclear, but it does suggest that low blood magnesium levels may not be altogether bad.

Although this is not proven. Magnesium losses in urine and sweat are, like those of potassium, trival. Thus, the cause of any magnesium deficiency in athletes is almost certainly inadequate dietary intake, nor excessive sweat or urine losses.

Calcium

Most of the body's calcium stores exist in bone, and the major complication of calcium deficiency is reduced bone strength due to inadequate bone calcification.

The only athletes likely to be at risk of calcium deficiencies are those females whose diets are abnormal, in a particular those whose eating patterns preclude them from eating an adequate amount of dairy products, the major source of dietary calcium. The important practical point is that a woman who does not menstruate should increase her calcium intake by eating high-calcium foods, in particular dairy produce, and should seek the opinion of a gynecologist regarding the need for estrogen, progesterone, and calcium supplementation.

Iron

Evidence shows that exercise, running, particular,

causes increased iron losses from the body. Because the daily intake of iron, especially in females, is only marginally above the levels needed to balance normal daily iron losses, the additional iron losses caused by running may cause iron deficiency.

The distance runners most likely to become iron deficient are those who run high weekly mileages, women runners who lose large amounts of blood when they menstruate each month, and those (of either sex) who eat iron-poor diets. Foods that have a high-iron content include liver, red meat, egg yolk, legumes, dark green leafy vegetables, molasses and whole grains. Vegetarians who eat no meat or eggs are particularly prone to iron deficiency. All at-risk runners could benefit by eating more red meat, liver, or the dark levels are found to be sufficiently low to indicate iron deficiency anemia.

Daily iron requirements of heavily training runners might be as much as 2 mg, but because only 10% of ingested iron is actually absorbed, one should aim to ingest about 20 mg of iron per day. The diet normally provides about 6 mg of iron per 1,000 kcal of energy. Thus, a normal dietary intake of 3,000 kcal will provide 18 mg of iron, which should be sufficient to balance daily iron losses. Problems arises when the daily calorie intake is restricted or the daily iron losses exceed 2 mg. Evidence shows that many elite women runners restrict themselves to as little as 6,300 kJ per day, which provides only 9 mg of iron per day.

Only if the athlete is found to have an iron-deficiency anemia should iron therapy be considered. Total body iron stores are between 3 and 5 g, so an iron-deficient runner taking 200 mg of element iron per day would, assuming 10% absorption, require 150 to 250 days (5 to 8 months) to repeat his or her iron stores.

A drawback to iron therapy is that iron tablets tend to cause indigestion and constipation. Of the commercially available iron tablets, those least likely to cause these problems are the "slow release" forms and the iron chelates.

Iron is best absorbed when taken with foods high in vitamin C. Tea and coffee greatly diminish iron absorption, as do the oxalates, phytates, and phosphates found in whole-grain foods. By simply drinking orange juice and not tea or coffee with meals, one can increase the iron absorbed from a meal fivefold. Similarly, animal protein increases iron absorption from beans and peas.

Zinc

The possibility that distance runners may be zinc deficient was raised by a study in which blood zinc levels were found to be low in a group of runners and lowest in those who trained and hardest.

The symptoms of zinc deficiency are fairly nonspecific (loss of taste and smell, loss of appetite, loss of hair, and skin lesions). We do not know whether zinc deficiency adversely affects athlete's performance, although one study showed increased muscle strength and endurance after zinc supplementation. Nor do we know whether the low blood zinc levels measured in long-distance athletes indicated that the athletes were truly zinc deficient. Zinc is found mainly in protein foods, and its content is low in high-carbohydrate food such as fruit, vegetables, grains, and pasta; thus, vegetarian athletes are more likely to be zinc deficient. Freeland-Graves et al. showed that zinc deficiency may indeed occur in vegetarians.

Copper, Chromium and Other Trace Elements

There is no published evidence of copper, chromium, or trace element deficiencies in runners, even though exercise alters the metabolism of these elements and increases their losses in sweat, urine, and feces.

Other Nutritional Additives

Studies confirm this observation and show that the findings of Pipes, which claimed a miraculous 28% increase in VO_2 max in athletes taking this substance, water in error and that this vitamin, also known as pangamic acid, has no effect on metabolism or performance during running.

In a report in New Scientist, Dr. Stephen Fulder introduced the Western world to the newest wonder drug, the exact of the thorny creeping plant related to the ginseng root and known botanically as Eleutherococcus senticocus. The extract of the plant, we are told, has been extensively tested in Russia—thus the popular name "Siberian ginseng"—and has become an official medicine in the Soviet Union. The evidence that this drug improves performance apparently comes from studies conducted in 1,500 athletes at the Lesgraft Institute of Physical Culture and Sports in Moscow.

Alcohol

Ethyl alcohol (etthanol-C_2H_5OH) is formed in nature by the fermentation of sugar and is used for several purposes. As a source of fuel for the body, ethanol differs from carbohydrate and fat in three respects.

First, ethanole is essentially foreign to the body and unlike fat and carbohydrate cannot be stored in the body. Second, the metabolic products of ethanol are utilized by muscle only to a limited extent and are almost entirely metabolized in the liver. Third, ethanol is metabolized in the liver at a fixed rate that is unaffected by the ethanol concentration in blood. The rate of metabolism varies widely in individuals and ranges from 60 to 200 mg per kilogram of body weight per hour (mg/kg/hr). The average rate is usually about 10 mg/kg/hr. This means that a 65-kg person drinking a 30-g dose of ethanol (equivalent to about 70 ml spirits, 180 ml sherry, 250 ml wine, or 850 ml beer) will require 4 hours to metabolize the ethanol. In addition, alcohol provides 7.0 kcal of energy per gram and therefore falls between carbohydrate and fat in its energy content.

Many runners have the mistaken impression that alcohol can provide a rapid source of energy exercise. This is clearly incorrect. Ingested ethanol must first be metabolized in the liver to acetaldehyde and then to acetate before it can be used by either the liver or muscles to produce mitochondrial ATP. But a muscle's capacity for acetate metabolism is extremely low and not of the same order as its ability to burn glucose. Thus, alcohol ingestion during exercise will nor have any special benefits, and it is certainly not as beneficial as is the intake of glucose polymers or other carbohydrates.

Alcohol has important negative metabolic effects. The metabolism of ethanol to acetaldehyde in the liver causes the accumulation of hydrogen (protons) in the liver. For various reasons, the accumulated hydrogen impairs the liver's ability to produce a new glucose (gluconeogenesis) from lactate and other substances.

Also, ethanol in a moderate dose reduces both the amount of glucose released by the liver during exercise and the amount of (blood) glucose used by the active muscles. Thus, the rate of muscle glycogen utilization during exercise after ethanol ingestion is probably accelerated, and this could compromise endurance during prolonged exercise.

But alcohol is not all bad and is probably of value after competition, because it is a pleasant change from the cola drinks during the race. In addition, alcohol will stimulate urine formation after exercise, which may be important in the prevention of kidney stones.

In addition, some evidence shows that a moderate daily alcohol intake may play a beneficial role in the prevention of coronary artery disease. One study found that persons who drink no alcohol had the highest mortality from coronary artery disease, whereas heavy drinks, ingesting more than 31 ml of alcohol per day, had the lowest heart disease mortality rate. Unfortunately, the beneficial effects of alcohol ingestion on heat disease mortality were largely negated at alcohol intakes greater than 10 ml/day because of a steep rise in mortality from strokes and cancers in persons ingesting more than 10 ml of alcohol per day. The result was that total mortality was lowest in persons ingesting 1 to 10 ml of alcohol per day. However, the risk of breast cancer is increased in women who drink even this relatively small amount of alcohol.

Dietary Practices of Athletes

We have now completed a theoretical consideration of the athlete's diet. But what do athletes actually eat in practice, and are they guilty of any common dietary malpractices that could affect their performances?

Surprisingly, few scientific studies have examined the dietary practices of athletes. Before we consider the studies that have been completed, let us begin by considering the dietary ideas of Alec Nelson and Arthur Newton.

Nelson emphasized that "all food must be of the freshest and best—English meat, fresh fish, and eggs, vegetables straight from the garden and cooked the same day, new milk and butter—and everything only when it is season". He also advised that the menu should be varied as much as possible.

Newton came to two main conclusions about diet: Vegetarianism is not appropriate for athletes, and with heavy training, a craving for sweet, carbohydrate containing foods becomes apparent. He observed that the initial tendency at the onset of training hard is to eat more, but that as one becomes fitter, this tendency disappears. It has observed this but can offer no proven explanation for it. Possibly, increased fitness improves metabolic efficiency and reduces energy losses through the various forms of thermogenesis.

Γhe only other dietary comments made by Newton concern vitamins, which were finally isolated only sometime after Newton began running in 1922.

Scientific Studies

One of the first scientific studies of what athletes actually eat was reported by Barry et al., who studied 108 Irish Olympic hopefuls and identified a number of dietary malpractices.

The diets contained too much fat (40%), too much protein (15%), and too little carbohydrate (45%). The optimum athletic diet, especially for endurance athletes, should contain up to 70% carbohydrate with about 15% fat and 15% protein. Also, the intakes of the vitamins thiamine and nicotinic acid were suboptimal, and the female athletes's iron and folate intakes were well below their requirements. The authors offered a number of explanations for these malpractices.

- The high intake of dietary protein indicated that the athletes still believed that a high-protein intake is essential for strength development.
- The high intake of dietary fat was a result of eating energy-rich foods, in particular animal and dairy produce, fried foods, cakes, and other confectioneries, all of which contain large amounts of hidden fat.
- The suboptimal intakes of thiamine and nicotinic acid were caused by a tendency to eat concentrated energy sources like refined carbohydrates (sugar and white flour and its products) and fat (fried foods, butter or margarine, and confectioneries), all of which have very low contents of thiamine and micotinic acid.
- The low-iron intakes of the female athletes

occurred because they ate less meat (especially kidney and liver) than men. They also ate fewer green leafy vegetables such as broccoli, brussels sprouts, and spinach, which together with kidney and liver are the main dietary folate sources. The authors found a direct relationship between the body folate stores and blood hemoglobin levels in the women athletes; those with the lowest body folate stores also had the lowest hemoglobin levels. The authors suggested that inadequate dietary folate intakes might be one explanation for the low hemoglobin levels in these female athletes.

Other similar studies have shown essentially the same, albeit less severe, dietary errors. The outstanding observations from these studies point out that although athletes have higher caloric intakes, the percentage contributions of carbohydrate, fat, and protein to athlete's diets are generally not greatly different from those of nonathletes. Certainly there is no evidence that athletes have carbohydrate intakes as high as those recommended by David Costill and his colleagues.

These studies indicate that the female runner requires a daily energy intake of 8,500 to 10,000 kJ, whereas the male requires an intake of 12,000 to 14,500 kJ. Many elite female athletes eat severely calorie-restricted diets that place them at risk of developing menstrual dysfunction and osteoporosis. How they can continue to run when eating so little is mystery that no one has yet explained.

The optimum athletic diet should include 55% of energy from carbohydrate, 30% from fat, and 15% from protein. Ideally, 350 to 500 g of carbohydrate should be eaten daily. Such a diet corresponds to the healthy or prudent diet advocate the U.S. Select Committee on Nutrition and Human Needs and to the American Cancer Society diet to reduce diet-related cancers.

Relatively few studies have looked specifically at

vitamins and mineral intake of athletes. The only important mineral and vitamin deficiencies that have been reported commonly among athletes are of iron and folate. These can be corrected by taking appropriate vitamin and mineral tablets and by eating iron- and folate-rich foods.

Kirsch and Von Ameln studied the feeding patterns of athletes and found that endurance athletes ingesting 14,000 to 26,000 kJ per day followed "nibbling" patterns characterized by frequent (8 to 10 times per day) eating and drinking. Of particular interest was the finding that 45% of the total fluid intake occurred after 8 p.m., suggesting that fluid intake follows a circadian rhythm. This study showed that athletes should always have ready access to food. Fluids, in particular, must be available in the evening.

Diet-Related Idiosyncrasies

Not everyone can eat all foods. Milk intolerance may cause specific problems, in particular diarrhoea and irritable bowel syndrome, in susceptible persons. Sheehan described essentially the same findings in persons unable to absorb gluten, a protein found in all grain foods except corn and rice. This condition, known as colic disease or gluten enteropathy, is completely cured by avoiding all gluten containing foods.

So the paradox is that the staple food of life—bread and milk—may be just the food that some athlete should avoid.

There are other food to which certain individuals may be allergic and that can cause bizarre symptoms.

The chocolate caused this runner's problem would only be proved conclusively if his symptoms were completely absent as long as he stayed off chocolate and if the reintroduction of chocolate into his diet, without him knowing it, caused the identical symptoms, whereas the introduction of an inactive substance did not. This type of testing is known scientifically as a crossover reintroduction trial and is the bet basic scientific technique used to determine if a food allergy explains the symptoms present in a particular individual.

Food allergies do indeed exist and should be considered by any athletes with persistent problems, especially exercise-related diarrhoea and effort migraine, that are not helped by conventional medical or other advice.

Exercise and Weight Control

Human weight control is a very complex problem, far more complex than the conventional idea that being overweight is simply due to an imbalance between daily food intake and energy expenditure. Consider, for example, the following studies:

- In 1902, R.O. Neumann performed a 725-day study of himself. During that time he varied his energy intake over a wide range. His weight refused to change.
- In 1961, G.A. Rose and Williams studied groups of people who eat a lot and people who eat very little. From each group they were able to select pairs of individuals who did the same amount of exercise and who were of the same mass but whose daily intakes of food differed by a factor of 2.
- Sims and his colleagues invited a group of Vermont state prisoners to eat as much as they could for 6 months. The prisoners gratefully responded, increasing their daily food intakes by an average of 75% with some gluttons eating as much as 9,500 kcal daily, or almost 4 times the average daily intake of 2,500 kcal and nearly twice the daily intake of competitors in the Tour de Franc.

Sims reported the following. First, the prisoner's

weights increased for the first few weeks of the experiments and then syabilized.

Second, the equilibrium weights achieved by the prisoners were independent of how much extra food energy each ate; some prisoners were relatively resistant to gaining weight, whereas others who overate to the same degree put on considerably more weight. Miller and Mumford reported in a similar study that some subjects lost weight when eating an extra 10,000 kcal per week.

Third, even those most gluttonous prisoners who ate 4 times their normal daily requirements increased their weights by only between 20 and 25%.

Sims et al., also investigated two heavy subjects who had voluntarily dieted so that they were equally as overweight as the prisoners. To equalize their weights with those of the prisoners who ate the most, the two subjects could eat only 1,200 calories of food energy per day. This study showed that individuals whose daily energy intakes differed by a factor of 8 could have the same body weight.

Sims et al., also showed that when nonobese subjects are made to become obese by overeating, they require more energy in relation to body surface area for maintenance of the obese state than they require at their natural weight, and they also require more than spontaneously obese subjects. Other studies suggest that this may be because the obese have blunted thermogenic responses to feeding: They heat up less and therefore waste less of the energy contained in the food they eat. These people are said to be more "fuel efficient" or "thrifty". Not all studies show this, however.

- Miller and Parsonage, incarcerated 29 volunteers, all of whom claimed to be unable to lose weight on rigorous slimming diets, in an isolated country house for 3 weeks. On arrival, the subjects luggage was searched for hidden food, and their car keys were confiscated. All the volunteers were placed on the same 1,500-kcal diet, and their weight losses were determined after 3 weeks. Nineteen of the subjects did actually lose weight on this diet, but nine maintained their weights, and two actually gained weight on what for many people would have been a starvation diet. Those subjects resistant to losing weight were found to have low basal metabolic rates.

- Studies in identical (monozygous) twins showed that genetic; not environmental, factors play the predominant role explaining their body weights and their body fat contents. Similarly, Mayer found that in the absence of parental obesity, the incidence of obesity in children was 14%; if one parent was obese, this incidence rose to 40%, and if both were obese, the incidence was 80%. An adoption study showed that the body compositions of adopted children resembled those of their biological parents, not their foster parents, suggesting that hereditary factors are more important than environmental factors in determining body composition.

- Contrary to popular belief, there is absolutely no valid scientific evidence that the obese eat more than lean individuals. In fact, some evidence shows that obese females may actually eat less than lean females. Rothwell and Stock concluded that "it is difficult to support the contention that food intake is the primary determinant of body weight in man or experimental animals".

- A growing body of evidence suggests that the body "defends" its weight, in part by maintaining a certain size of fat cells—large in obese subjects, small in thin people. Diet and exercise can reduce

> fat-cell size only up to a point. Once a certain fat-cell size is reached, further weight loss becomes impossible. Reversion to a normal diet and sedentary state causes the fat cells to return to their previous sizes. Interestingly, those fat cells that remain in the body after surgical removal of other fat cells do not enlarge to compensate for the reduced body for content. Thus, surgical removal of fat may be the only effective method by which a sustained loss of body fat can be achieved.

One mechanism by which the body defends its weight may be that in the face of a reduced energy intake, the body becomes more "fuel efficient", as did Sim's prisoners. That is, the amount of food energy required to maintain a certain body mass is reduced. Brownell et al., noted the remarkable fuel efficiency of female athletes with amenorrhea and reduced bone density and questioned whether exercise training may enhance food efficiency.

The logical explanation for these anomalies is that either of two mechanisms must be operative. Humans must differ either in the amounts of energy that they can actually store from the food they eat or in the amounts of energy they need to maintain a constant body weight (i.e., their basal metabolic rates). In addition, body weight—in particular the size of the body fat stores—must be carefully controlled within certain genetically determined limits by a regulator, sometimes referred to as the adipostat.

Most current obesity research centres on the possibility that certain metabolic processes, so-called futile cycles, exist that effectively waste energy by turning the excess energy ingested in food into heat in a process known as dietary-induced thermogenesis or the thermic effect of feeding. The theory is that the adipostat regulates the activity of these futile cycles, which are less well developed in the obese than in lean subjects.

Most of the evidence to support this thermogenic control of body weight comes from rat studies. Two British researchers, Nancy Rothwell and Michael Stock, made use of the discovery (previously also known to keepers of rats and not to scientists who lack such practical experience) that rats can be enticed into gross obesity by a "cafeteria diet" that includes such delicacies as pasta, pizza, cake, chocolate, liver pâté, ham, bacon, and hamburgers.

As they become fatter, such rats develop increased masses of specialized fat cells, so-called brown adipose tissue, which is specifically adapted to lose heat. In response to a meal, the brown adipose tissues of these obese rats heat up under the influence of certain hormones released in response to the meal, thereby losing some of the excess energy elevated, levels. In addition, if the fat rats exercise, their capacities for dietary-induced thermogenesis are increased, so that their weight gains on the cafeteria diet are less than those of sedentary rats fed the same diet. Once the cafeteria diet is removed, the fat rats rapidly lose the extra weight they have gained, their brown adipose tissues shrink, and their increased capacities for dietary-induced thermogenesis return to normal.

Unfortunately, although this mechanism is clearly established in rats, its role in humans who probably lack sufficient brown adipose tissue is unclear. Furthermore, exercise training may reduce, rather than increase, the capacity for dietary-induced thermogenesis in humans, at least in the highly trained athlete. The thermogenic response to caffeine ingestion is also lower in trained then untrained subjects.

Other factors that are known to be thermogenic and therefore aid weight loss include caffeine, alcohol, nicotine, and certain drugs and hormones, in particular thyroxine. The action of thyroxine is to "uncouple" respiration so that when substrate is oxidized in the mitochondria, greater amounts of heat are released and less ATP is produced, hence a thermogenic effect. Obviously a safe thermogenic drug would have enormous potential for aiding those who wish to be thinner.

The thermogenic effect of nicotine probably explains why persons who stop smoking tend to put on weight and why smokers are generally thinner than nonsmokers despite their eating more. The thermogenic effects of cigarette smoking and caffeine intake probably also explain the tendency of some people wishing to lose weight to live on diets of coffee and cigarettes.

Practical Relevance

Generally, the society is excessively concerned about weight, and this concern is particularly evident among endurance athletes like runners who must carry their unsupported weight with them. It is quite true that, up to a point, the less fat we carry, the faster we will run. But each of use has a certain safe body weight that we can reasonably achieve, and even with a superhuman effort we can only reach a shade lower than this weight.

The only way to reduce genetically determined optimum body weight is to exercise as much as possible and to diet within reason. Weight loss is increased if breakfast rather than dinner is the main meal of the day and if the foot eaten at breakfast is fixed (and dislike) rather than freely chosen (and liked).

Unsubstantiated observations, confirmed in discussion with other athletes, suggest than 2 hours of running a day causes body weight to level off, presumably at or near the genetic limit, which may be anything between 3 and 25% body far for males, with higher values for female athletes. Koplan et al. found that weight loss in athletes equalled about 1.2 kg expect his or her body weight to stabilize at a weight 5 times

1.2 kg, that is 6 kg lower than prior to exercise. The athlete who ran 100 km/week could expect a total weight loss of 11.2 kg.

The particular benefits of exercise in weight control are as follows:

- The exercise session, particularly if it is intense and prolonged, may cause the metabolic rate to be elevated for some time after exercise. Furthermore, prior exercise may increase the thermogenic effect of food eaten for some hours thereafter. Thus, additional energy is burned up free of effort.
- Unlike dietary restriction, which causes a loss of water, muscle, and fat, the weight loss caused by exercise training comprises a loss only of body fat, with increases in lean body mass and body water content.
- The increased lean body (muscle) mass that results from exercise training should increase the basal metabolic rate, at least in men; no such effect has been reported in women. Thus, a higher food intake will be needed to maintain a lower body weight in trained men. In contrast, weight loss by dietary alone causes a loss of lean body mass. Therefore, the basal metabolic rate falls, and progressively less food must be eaten to maintain the reduced body weight. In contrast, exercise may even prevent the fall in resting metabolic rate that accompanies severe caloric restriction. Unfortunately, there is no scientific evidence that exercise of the legs, for example, can cause a specific reduction of the fat overlying the leg muscles.
- The resting metabolic rate may be chronically elevated in those who train 12 to 16 hours a week.
- Apptite and therefore food intake may fail to adapt immediately to increased physical activity. Thus,

there is a period in the beginning of an exercise program when extra weight is lost as food intake fails to meet requirements.

In contrast to a widely held belief, exercise does not appear to stimulate appetite even in the obese. And, not all activities are equally effective in inducing a weight loss. Walking, cycling, and running appear to be the most effective, whereas swimming may be without effect. The reason for this is unclear.

Growing evidence suggests that genetic factors control the extent to which many of these variables alter with training. Research shows that 40% of the differences in resting metabolic rate between individuals are genetically determined, whereas 81% of the variation in the response of this variable to training is genetically determined.

Thus, just as there are high and low adaptors to exercise training, so there are those in whom exercise training has no effect on resting metabolic rate (low adaptors) and others in whom a marked effect is found (high adaptors).

The same has been found for the effects of exercise training on the thermic effects of feeding; 72% of the variation in the response of this variable to training is genetically determined.

Women are at a disadvantage in terms of weight loss; even the leanest, most highly trained female athletes have about 12 to 15% body fat. Regrettably, one consequence of this modern obsession with weight control and being thin (especially among female gymnasts, ballet dancers, and models) may be the increasing incidence of anorexia nervosa and bulimia among adolescent females in Western society.

ANOREXIA NERVOSA

Anorexia nervosa is a condition in which a person

basically stops eating and starts starving to death. The term is misleading, however, because it literally means "loss of hunger on a psychological basis". In fact, there is no loss of hunger in this condition; the person with anorexia nervosa suffers from intense hunger and food preoccupation but will not eat.

The typical person likely to suffer from anorexia nervosa is an adolescent female from a higher socioeconomic class. Probably she is industrious, introverted, and self-denying; of above average intelligence; a perfectionist; and highly active in sport.

The reason such an intelligent and talented individual would choose to flirt with death is obviously extremely complex, and probably no single theory can explain all aspects of the disease. Some of the most interesting insights into the disease have been provided by medical historian Janet Brumberg.

In her search for the original description of the condition, Brumberg discovered that anorexia nervosa was first described simultaneously in 1873 by a British physician, Sir William Gull, and a French psychiatrist, Charles Lasegue. Whereas Gull concentrated on the medical features of the condition, Lasegue sought a psychological explanation for its development. Lasegue linked the onset of anorexia to a broad set of frustrations arising in the daughters of the 19th century European middle class as they approached adulthood. These frustrations included parental pressures that their daughters should marry "appropriately" and blocked educational or social opportunities.

Brumberg suggests that 19th century middle-class parents were the first to use love rather than authoritarianism to cement family relationships. The danger was that this expression of love could become suffocating or manipulative and prevent the growth of the individual self-esteem necessary for separation from the family.

Victorians often expressed their love in the form of gifts, the most basic of which was food. At the same time, the culinary standards were improving rapidly, and food and eating habits were increasingly taking on special social significance. Women were not to be seen eating, as food and eating were connected to gluttony, sexuality, aggression, and bodily "indelicacies" such as urination and defecation. Brumberg notes that for these reasons, constipation was incorporated into the ideal of Victorian femininity.

In addition, the adolescent Victorian girl was not allowed the freedom to express her emotions. Thus refusing food was a silent but potent form of expression:

> Refusing to eat was not as confrontational as yelling, having a tantrum, or throwing things; refusing to eat expressed emotional hostility without being flamboyant...Food refusal, while an emotionally charged behaviour, was also discrete, quiet, and ladylike in keeping with the Victorian notion that women were expected to carry reserve further than the male.

By the turn of the century, slimness had become a sign of social status: "A thin frail woman has a symbol of class and an object of beauty precisely because she was unfit for productive (or reproductive) work...A thin woman signified the idle idyll of the leisured classes". The result was the appetite had become less of a biological drive and more of a social and emotional instrument.

At about this time, psychoanalyst Sigmund Freud turned his attention to this condition and proposed that anorexia nervosa developed in adolescent girls who wished to keep their bodies small, thin, and childlike, thereby retarding normal sexual development and forestalling adult sexuality. The legend of Wilgefortis incorporates this interpretation.

Wilgefortis, who lived sometime between A.D. 700 and A.D. 1000 was the seventh daughter of the King of Portugal, a tyrannical man known for his cruelty and grossness. Wilgefortis was horrified to hear that her father hand arranged for her to marry the King of Sicily. She had already made a vow of virginity and had planned to give her lift to God, not man.

She prayed to God for help. She became ascetic, and overcoming her appetite, she begged the Lord to deprive her of all her beauty. God granted her prayer by causing her to develop a hairy body (the lanugo hair of the anorectic) and to grow a beard. Her father was so angry that he had Wilgefortis crucified. While on the cross, Wilgefortis prayed for all to remember the passions that encumber all women, and she prayed that any woman who used her as a medium of prayer would be blessed as she had been.

Brumberg suggests that factors that have influenced the incidence of anorexia nervosa since the end of the World War I include the evolution of the basic institutions of the American beauty culture, including the fashion and cosmetics industries, beauty contests, the modeling profession, and movies, all of which promote the ideal of the slender woman. Thus women increasingly desired slim bodies:

The body of the new women was a sign of modernity that marked her for more than traditional motherhood and domesticity. With the introduction of birth control, sexuality and reproduction could be separated so that a slender body and willingness to wear more revealing clothes were taken as signs of increased sexual confidence, freedom and enjoyment. A svelte female figure became, for the first time, the ultimate sign and symbol of heterosexual interest and success.

Additional factors that have come into play since the end of the World War II include medical concerns with the dangers of childhood and adult obesity; the growth of the diet industry to multibillion-dollar status; and the added emphasis of physical fitness and athleticism as criteria for perfection so that "compulsive exercising and chronic dieting have been joined as twin obessions". One result has been that the female role models—beauty queens, fashion models, and Playboy centerfolds—are getting thinner, whereas women are tending to get fatter. The weight of anorexic girls has also become progressively less in recent years.

But Brumberg concludes that the evolving overemphasis on diet and athléticism cannot adequately explain the recent rise in the incidence of anorexia nervosa. Rather she suggests that modern attitudes toward food and the expectations between the sexes must have played a role.

She suggests that food has become increasingly more available and desirable at the very time when our "obeseophobic" society demands that we eat with restrain. Food has become associated with sociability, status, and sexuality and has been identified as an analogue of the self; Brumberg cites the example of the hippies of the late 1960s who stopped eating the foods associated with their "bourgeois" upbringing and turned rather to grains, unprocessed foods, and the avoidance of meat. Brumberg identifies a conflict between the cultural imperative to control appetite and the all-pevasive stimulus to eat.

The second factor that may contribute to increased incidence of anorexia nervosa relates to the stress imposed by the breakdown of family structure. Brumberg suggests that the young woman of today must view heterosexual relationships with ambivalence as so few such relationships have happy endings. In addition, AIDS poses sexual uncertainities. The young woman of today is therefore forced to develop a professional career to ensure her future security in the event of divorce without forsaking the ideas of marriage and a family.

The result is that young women must fulfil an impossible role, and the demands are extreme and unrelenting. Just as these young women are being challenged and their expectations raised, so there is no coherent support system or philosophy to guide them. The cult of diet and exercise comes closest to a "coherent philosophy of the self...of all the messages they hear, the imperative to be beautiful and good by being thin, is still the strongest and most familiar".

Brumberg concludes her book with the following:

Anorexia nervosa ultimately expresses the predicament of a very distinctive group, one that suffers from the painful ambiguities of being young and female in an affluent society set adrift by social change...Intelligent, anxious for personal achievement, and determined to maintain control in a world where things as basic as food and sex are increasingly out of control, the contemporary anorectic unrelentingly pursues thinness as a secular form of perfection. In a society where consumption and identity are pervasively linked, she makes nonconsumption the perverse centre piece of her identity. In a sad and desperate way, today's fasting girls epitomize the curious psychic burdens of the youthful daughters of a people of plenty.

Anorexia and Running

One of the main reasons of anorexia is an interesting article that appeared in the world's leading medical journal, the New England Journal of Medicine, in February 1983.

The article, written by three running doctors, Alayne, Yates, Kevin Leehey, and Catherine Shisslak, from the department of psychiatry at the University of Arizona, carried this dramatic title: "Running—An Analogue of Anorexia?"

The article began by noting that the 1970s were characterized by two major social events: (a) increased incidence of anorexia nervosa among adolescent females to the extent that this illness is now regarded as a major public health problems in Western countries and (b) an almost simultaneous increase in the number of joggers and runners in the same countries. The possibility that the two conditions might be related first occurred to the authors during a research project in which they interviewed 60 athletes who regularly ran more than 50 miles a week. During these interviews, the authors noted similarities between the characters, lifestyles, and backgrounds of some runners whom they labelled obligatory runners and of the anorectic women they were accustomed to treating in their psychiatric practices. The similarities they noted were the following:

Singular Dedication

Although the anorectic person's goal is physical attractiveness and the obligatory athlete's goal is physical performance, the authors contend that both subjects pursue their different goals with degrees of dedication that are alarming and potentially dangerous.

Personality Characteristics

Anorectic females are usually model children reared in middle- to upper-class homes, often in families that are overtly concerned with achievement, diet, and exercise. These children tend to be introverted, intensely active, and liable to depression. Some 24% of anorectic women are said to be "very athletic". Typically, anorectic women had a hazy sense of self as children, and they depend on others for opinions of their own self-worth. Successful dieting reduces the anorectic patient's anxiety and introversion and may produce a "high" similar to that experienced by athletes.

VOL. III

PART 5

ATHLETIC TRAINING

CONTENTS

PART 6

ATHLETIC CONDITIONING

CONTENTS

PART 7

INJURIES IN ATHLETICS

CONTENTS

PART 8

PHYSICAL EDUCATION—A HANDBOOK FOR TEACHERS

CONTENTS

PART 5
ATHLETIC TRAINING

CHAPTER - 1

INTRODUCTION TO ATHLETIC TRAINING

In the last few decades sports have gained tremendous popularity all over the globe. The popularity of sports is still increasing at a fast pace and this happy trend is likely to continue in the future also. When one looks at the history of the modern Olympic games one sees that the number of sports for which competitions are held at Olympic games has increased steadily. The total number of participating countries and sportsmen has also increased steadily.

In addition to Olympic sports, indigenous sports have also become popular in each country. Several new sports like sky-diving, skating, motor-racing have also come into existence and are quite popular with the masses.

The television and press are giving much more coverage to sports and have become effective medium to carry sports to millions and millions of people around the world. Sports have become an important social and cultural activity of the modern world which is being given the rightful place it deserves by the nations and societies of the world.

Sports serve vital social and cultural functions the importance of which can hardly be exaggerated. The contribution of sports towards the overall welfare of the human society may be capsulated in the following points;-

- Sports serve vital social and cultural functions the importance of which can hardly be exaggerated. The contribution of sports towards the overall welfare of the human society may be capsulated in the following points:-
- Provide ample and healthy means fore recreation and relaxation of human mind and body.
- Are effective for rehabilitation and social adjustment of the injured, sick and handicapped.
- Provide opportunities for social interaction thereby fostering peace and understanding among different people, nations, races, religions etc.
- Perform preventive and curative functions for several diseases and ailments inflicting human body and mind.
- Provide healthy and socially acceptable opportunities for the people and nations to compete against each other thereby touching heights of excellence of human endeavour and attainment.

Keeping in mind the aims, organisation and means of sports activities the sports are classified into several areas e.g., performance sports, physical education, rehabilitation sports, fitness and leisure sports, adventure sports etc. Each area of sports caters to the requirements and demands of a particular section of the society. The are of performance sports has gained mist more publicity and importance than the other areas. It has it's own structure and organisation, cadre of functionaries and a science which exclusively deals with this area. The principal aim of performance sports is to prepare sports persons for giving high sports performances.

The area of performance sports is not merely a glamourous area of sports, it also fulfils certain valuable social functions due to which it has been accorded high importance all over the world. It contributes towards the all round development of personality and enhances the horizons of awareness among the competing sportsmen with regard to the fact that they are representing particular states or countries of their origin. It inculcates in the youth a fervent desire to excel. For this they have to discipline themselves for carrying out rigorous training over a number of years. International champions becomes models to be emulated by their people especially by the youth. They are considered national heroes and the nation feels proud of them. Television has added new social dimension to performance sports as millions of people watch their chosen representatives taking part in international competitions. People rejoice at their victories and feel sad when they lose. Victory or defeat of their sportsmen/ teams is perceived as the victory or defeat of the nation.

Performance sports aim at high sports performances and for that the physical and psychic capacities of sportsmen are developed to extreme limits. This normally does not happen in other areas of human activity. As a result, performance sports yield valuable knowledge about the limits to which human performance and various performance factors can be developed. It also leads to discovery of means and methods for improving various physical and psychic capacities (performance factors) to exceptionally high levels. This knowledge can be fruitfully applied to other areas of sports and human activity.

Sports performance is indeed an aspect of complex human performance which has several aspects or dimensions. Hence several disciplines of sports science are required to work in a co-ordinated manner to explore the nature of sports performance and the process of improving sports performance. In the last few decades several disciplines of sports science have been established e.g., sports medicine, sports physiology, sports training, sports bio-mechanics, sports psychology, sports pedagogy, sports nutrition and so on. The sports science is still in its state of infancy and in the near future more sports science disciplines are likely to emerge, some of these disciplines have already emerged, e.g., sports statistics, sports biochemistry, sports neuro-physiology, sports cybernetics etc.

All the disciplines of sports science have their own areas of study which in all cases is a certain aspect of sports performance and sports training. Each discipline has its own qualified cadre of workers as well as means and methods of investigation. Except the training science, all other disciplines have the cadre/workers who are taken from their respective mother sciences and they then specialise in the concerned sports discipline. This is not the case in science of training in which the cadre is recruited from the sports itself. This is for obvious reasons. Science of training, unlike other disciplines, studies sports performance and sports or athletic training in totality and not just one aspect of the whole. This discipline carries the most important responsibility of creating knowledge and assimilating and collecting knowledge from all sports disciplines and on its basis to formulate theories, principles etc., to determine how the athletic training should be planned, organised, implemented and regulated.

Training science is further divided into two separate but highly interrelated and interdependent areas. One is the general theory and methods of *athletic training.* It is also called *science of training* or *training methods. Second,* area comprises of theories and methods of training of different sports. The main task of athletic training is to study the principles and fundamentals of athletic training for all sports. The subject matter of TMT is also the same but it is limited to only one sport. It operates at the specific level whereas athletic training operates at a general level.

Science of athletic training is a recent entrant to the field of sports science. Earlier only the theories and methods of individual sports existed. The reasons for the emergence of athletic training as a separate sports science discipline are several. TMT by it's very nature is limited to a single sports. Hence it is not in a position to investigate and formulate theories and principles of training applicable to all sports. Moreover, TMT is preoccupied with the specific technical aspects of a sport. It's cadre i.e., coaches/trainers have no time to study important fundamental aspects of training e.g., training and competition load, talent, motor development etc. To formulate valid theories and principles one has to study the training process in all sports i.e., from a general aspect.

The sports science disciplines have improved at a very fast pace in the past few decades. The knowledge gained by these disciplines has to be understood by the coaches and trainers to apply it correctly to the training process. But majority of the coaches do not have sufficient scientific background and training to make full and effective use of the knowledge acquired by the sports science disciplines. This creates a gap between scientists and coaches. The science of training, with its workers having sufficient background of science and sports, are able to fill this gap and can become mediator between the scientists and the coaches.

Science of training also fulfils an important didactical task for the professional preparation of coaches. The students after studying athletic training are in a better position to comprehend the theory and methods of training of their sport. With this objective in mind in many countries the curriculum for the study courses for coaches contain this subject and due weightage is given to it. The subject of athletic training has proved to be of high utility to the students and is also very popular among them.

Science of training is relevant not only in performance sports, it is equally important for other areas of sports also e.g., physical education, rehabilitation, fitness and leisure sports, physical training of military etc. In these areas the training is mainly, directed towards the development of fitness and health. Science of training contributes tremendously towards the achievement of such aims of these areas of sports. The recent trends in the further development of sports science indicates that in the near future the subject matter of athletic training will be expanded to include the problems and tasks of training in all the areas of sports.

CHAPTER - 2

HISTORY OF SCIENCE OF ATHLETIC TRAINING

THEORIES AND METHODS

Of training have existed since time immemorial. One finds mention of these in the history of mankind. The Egyptian, Greek, Roman, Chinese, Indian and other ancient civilisations used special methods of physical preparation for training soldiers and sportsmen. Some basic principles of training like continuity, progression of load, specificity were recognised and widely practised in ancient times. But these theories and methods were generally for the physical preparation only. A distinct scent of sports training however, did not come into existence till the latter half of the twentieth century.

The modern Olympic movement brought recognition to the cultural and social functions of sports. Sports once again became a respectable activity and several popular sports acquired organisational infrastructure at national and international levels. The physical education also gained strength from the modern Olympic movement and it acquired the status of an important science in the beginning of the present century. As sports are the principal means of physical education, therefore, in the initial stages of its development, the discipline of *athletic training* was developed as a part of physical Education. With the rapid increase in the popularity of modern Olympics and alongwith it of performance sports the discipline of *athletic training* also assumed more importance leading to its further development.

Science of *athletic or sports training* as an independent sports science discipline is hardly 30 years old. Before this we find theories and methods of training scattered in different sports and sports science. Physical education and theory and methods of some popular sports like track and field, football, boxing, swimming etc., are principle sources out of which the science of *athletic training* developed as a scientific discipline. Sports medicine is another science which contributed significantly towards the development of *athletic training.*

A very powerful impetus for the development of *athletic training* came from the performance sports. The process of preparing athletes for winning world level competitions led to the emergence of a new profession in sports i.e., the profession of coaching.

In several countries, especially Europe, it was realised that coaching is a highly complex and scientific job and, therefore, coaches must undergo special courses for this purpose as is the case in respect of physical education teachers. As the principal objective of coaches is to train sportsman for high level performance, therefore, all available knowledge about theory and methods of training must be brought together in a systematic and integrated manner in order to impart it to the coaches. This task was accomplished in many East European countries by establishing a separate sports science discipline of *athletic training* as a research and teaching subject in the sports colleges and universities. It is interesting to note that *athletic training* got established as a separate subject only in those countries in which we find professional courses being run by sports colleges & universities for coaches. In countries like England, U.S.A., Canada etc., the subject of *athletic training* has still not clearly emerged as a separate entity as there we still do not have proper professional courses for coaches. But in the near future, there are indications that such courses will be started in these countries also and *athletic training* will emerge as a separate sports science discipline.

As pointed out earlier, till the first half of 20th century the subject matter of *athletic training* lay scattered in different sports, physical education and sports medicine. In the late forties and early fifties there were some attempts to formulate systematic and complete theories of different components of training e.g., strength, endurance, technique etc. But still no attempt was made to put forward a body of knowledge systematically covering all the aspects and components of *athletic training*. The year 1957 is important in the history of *athletic training* (AT) and sports science as in this year a book on *athletic training*. This was the first book to present all aspects of training in a systematic and scientific manner. This book, since then, has undergone several revisions and is considered a classic in the classic in the field of *athletic training*.

In the sixties the pace of development of *athletic training* picked up momentum. The contributions came mainly from GDR and USSR. In GDR another important book titled "Bewegunqslehre" written by Kurt Meinel was published in 1960. This book did not cover all the aspects of training but confined itself to the problems of co-ordination, technique training, movement assessment and motor development. This book has also been revised several times. The Soviet sports scientists also made significant contributions towards the development of *athletic training*. They limited their efforts to specific areas or elements of *athletic training*. In the early sixties in USSR the book "Periodisierung des Sportlichen Trainings" written by L.P. Matweyew was published. This book revolutionised the concepts of planning and perodisation of *athletic training*. Like

Harre's book on sports training the book of Matweyew is also considered as a landmark in the development of *athletic training.*

In the early seventies more books on different aspects of *athletic training* were published in USSR. Verchosanskij wrote a book on special strength, Zaciorskij on motor abilities, Farfel on movement control and Kusnezov on strength. It was only in late seventies that a book dealing with all the aspects of *athletic training* was published in USSR. This book titled, "Grundlagen des Sportlichen Trainings" written by L.P. Matweyew was published in 1977. In the same year in F.R.G. a book "Grundlugen der Trainingslehre" written by D. Martin was published. The second part of this book, however, was published in 1980 and deals with the problems of periodisation, planning, regulation of training etc. Another book on GTMT written by M. Letzelter of FRC was published in 1978.

The contributions to the development of *athletic training (AT)* in the seventies and eighties are still coming from mainly two countries i.e., GDR and USSR. In addition to revising the earlier books, the sports scientists from these tow countries have written several books on the subject matter of *athletic training* and have thereby further developed the subject. In addition to the publication of books on GTMT the sports scientists of GDR and USSR have also been publishing numerous articles and paters on different topics of *athletic training.* The total amount of literature produced by GDR and USSR on *athletic training* is several times more than the one produced in all the countries of the world put together.

The development of *athletic* or *sports training* in U.K. North America, South America, Africa, Asia and Australia is lagging far behind. GDR and USSR have become the leaders and the other countries are trying to follow them. But unfortunately, still majority of the countries have not realised the importance of this subject and, therefore, this subject till now not been established as a separate sports science discipline. In English language there is hardly any book dealing with all the aspects of training. The English translations of German or Russian books are the exceptions in this regard. Most of the books in English on *athletic training* only deal with the motor abilities. Important among these are given below:-

1. Scientific Basis of Athletic Conditioning. By Jenson and Fischer. 1979.
2. Athletic Training and Physical Fitness. By J.H. Wilmore. 1977.
3. Sports Training Principles. By F.W. Dick. 1979.
4. The Scientific Aspects of Sports Training. By A.W. Taylor. 1975.
5. Towards Better Coaching. By F.S. Pyke. 1980.

In India, *athletic training* was first introduced as a teaching subject by the Netaji Subhash National Institute of Sports, Patiala in the early seventies. In the various colleges of physical education and university departments of physical education the subjects of *athletic training* has still not been introduced as a separate subject. It is mostly taught as a part of science of coaching for a particular sports.

From the above discussions it becomes amply clear that *athletic training* is a new science and is developing at a very rapid pace. In view of the ever increasing popularity of sports, especially performance sports, the *athletic training* will continue to develop further at a fast pace. *Athletic training* in the past had mainly devoted itself to performance sports. But at present with the sports fast becoming a part and parcel of daily life activity of humans of different ages, professions and by serving different aims and objectives of different sections of human society the *athletic training* has to widen its field of study. There are new challenges and tasks for *athletic training* to face and in future *athletic training* is bound to gain in stature and significance.

SUBJECT MATTER OF THE SCIENCE OF ATHLETIC TRAINING

Every science has to very clearly define and delimit the subject matter which it purports to study. This is essential in order to justify its existence as a science. Physics studies energy, chemistry studies the matter as a physical entity and biology studies the vital functions of life of plants and animals. It is difficult to pin point what is the real object of study of ST. This problem is there because *athletic training* focuses on sports training which is a complex biological, social and psychological process.

Athletic training is a distinct type of human activity and like all human activities it is multi-dimensional and this problem is further aggravated by the fact that its object of study is also a direct concern of theory and methods of various sports. As a result the borders of the subject matter of *athletic training* as a practical necessity overlap the borders of the subject matter of several sciences and practically all sports.

The *athletic training* studies the theory and methods of *athletic training* from a general aspect. It studies all the components or parts of *athletic training* as well as the *athletic training* in its entirety as a complex process of preparation of sportsmen and human beings for better sports performance or physical performance. In doing so it does not limit its study to *athletic training* for one sport only but for all the sports. The *athletic training* does limit its study of theory and methods of training to any one aspect of training e.g., psychological, physiological etc., but attempts to integrate all such aspects into the actual and practical phenomenon of *athletic training.* Other sports sciences do not go beyond a certain aspect of training i.e., they tend to study only one aspect of complex multidimensional human activity of athletic training.

The *athletic training* also distinguishes itself from other sports science disciplines by its characteristic of studying theory and methods of training from a practical point of view. It studies the actual planning, implementation, assessment, and regulation of athletic training in its totality. The sports science disciplines focus their attention on studying their own aspects of the components of the training but these disciplines do not study or describe in which way the knowledge discovered by them should be used effectively in the planning, implementation, assessment and regulation of sports training. This task is the subject matter of *athletic training.*

Athletic training is a conscious human activity. Also, it is a goal oriented activity. Therefore, it is obligatory for *athletic training* to include in its subject matter the study of sports performance and performance capacity. Without an understanding of sports performance and performance capacity no effective and meaningful theories and methods of training are possible. As a consequence, *athletic training* provides high weightage to studying the nature and genesis of sports performance in training and competition.

Similarly, a large portion of *athletic training* is devoted to the study of performance capacity which further comprises of physical condition, technique and co-ordinative abilities, tactics, physique and psychic factors.

Sports performances are to be achieved in sports competitions. It is, therefore, logical to include competition as a subject matter of *athletic training*. The relationship between competition and performance is well known. Hence, here the *athletic training* endeavours to study the effect of competitions on sports performance and to use it for better training and for better preparation of sportsmen for competitions. The competition theory in *athletic training* has a very high relevance for performance sports. But for other areas of sports it is not of much relevance.

The study of sports performance, performance capacity, *athletic training* and competitions form the actual subject matter of ST. The other topics which are also to be studied by *athletic training* are there because without studying these the above mentioned objects of study can not be properly studied. These topics are: motor development, training load, talent identification and its development, education through sports, regulation of *athletic training* and so on.

RELATIONSHIP OF ATHLETIC TRAINING WITH SPORTS AND SPORTS SCIENCE DISCIPLINES

Science oi *athletic* or *sports training* has emerged as a discipline of central importance in physical education as well as sports science. It is an integrative science which attempts to collect relevant information and knowledge about the various aspects and components of *athletic training* from the actual process of training in different sports and also from various other sports science disciplines. Its function is not limited to collecting of information and knowledge but goes much beyond it. It analyses and synthesises this information in the light of actual practise and applicability of these into the training process. It formulates theories and methods for the planning, implementation, assessment and regulation of *athletic training*. These theories and methods as such or in the form of principles, fundamentals, rules, guidelines etc., are given over to the various sports for application in their specific fields.

It relationship with the sports and sports science disciplines is a two-way-traffic. On the one hand, it is collecting information and knowledge about *athletic* or *sports training* from sports and sports science disciplines and on the other hand it is also giving back information and knowledge back to these sports and sports science disciplines after analysing and synthesising these in the form of theories and methods etc.

FUNCTIONS OF SCIENCE OF ATHLETIC TRAINING

Science of training is fast emerging as an independent research and teaching discipline in the field of sports science. It has multifarious functions to perform which are presented below in brief:-

It studies sports performance, *athletic training*, sports competition from a general view point. For this purpose it has its own methods of investigation. It works in close combination with individual sports and other sports science disciplines to achieve its objectives. The knowledge gained by *athletic training* is given back to the sports and sports science disciplines for their use. It also acts as a medium of conveyance of information from sports to sports science disciplines and *vice versa*. It acts as a filter and interpreter for the exchange of knowledge between sports and sports science disciplines.

Athletic Training plays an important role in the development of theories and methods of sports. It provides technical assistance and guidance to the sports coaches and sports teachers to study and develop their sports. To the sports science disciplines it contributes by helping them to understand the vital aspects and details of various aspects of theories & methods of training thereby enabling them to focus on problems of real practical importance.

The knowledge about theory and methods of training, gained by *athletic training* in the area of performance sports, forms the basis of training in other areas of sports and physical education. In the recent past this function of *athletic training* has gained immense importance because of increasing popularity of sports and physical activities for health, recreation, rehabilitation, prevention and cure of diseases and so on. The physical education is fast being applied as an obligatory. Subject in schools and colleges all over the world. For achieving its aims and objectives physical education is now increasingly taking the help of *athletic training.*

The terminology of sports and physical education was facing the problem of being not clear, precise, uniform and universally accepted. The absence of a standard and universally accepted terminology is a serious draw back and limitation for the science of sports. *Athletic training* because of its close proximity with sports and sports science disciplines is attempting to evolve a uniform and standard terminology for use in *athletic* or *sports training,* competitions and other aspects of sports.

As a teaching discipline *athletic training* helps the students of sports, physical education and sports science disciplines to get a better and clearer view of the theories and methods of training. This has proved to be very helpful to the students in order to understand their own fields of study with greater depth.

CHAPTER - 3

THE IMPORTANCE OF ATHLETIC TRAINING IN PHYSICAL EDUCATION

The word 'Training' has been a part of human language since ancient times. It denotes the process of preparation for some task. This process invariably extends to a number of days and even months and years. The term 'Training' is widely used in sports. There is, however, some disagreement among sports coaches and also among sports scientists regarding the exact meaning of this word. Some experts, especially belonging to sports medicine, understand athletic training as basically doing physical exercises. Several terms used in training e.g., strength training, interval training, technical and tactical training reflect this line of thinking.

The regular and systematic use of physical exercises, however, does not guarantee maximum improvement in performance. The effect of these exercises is increased or decreased by a multitude of factors. Some of these factors, if ignored, lead to a drastic reducation in the efficacy of physical exercises. Most important among these are sports equipment and implements, verbal instructions, means of recovery, means of assessment of performance capacity, nutrition, psychological means and so on.

In order to achieve best results, all these factors or means are to be used in addition to or along with physical exercises. The physical exercises and the other means or factors are to be judiciously applied in a systematic manner. The process of preparation of a person for improving his performance, therefore, should not be confined only to physical exercises.

The complex nature of *athletic training* involving physical exercises alongwith other means becomes obvious when one looks at the training of advanced sports persons. The training of advanced sports persons is significantly supported by means and measures from several sports science disciplines e.g., sports medicine, sports physiology, nutrition, physiotherapy, sports psychology, sports biomechanics and so on. It can be stated as a principle that higher the level of sports performance, more is the involvement of sports science disciplines.

It, however, does not mean that the role of a coach becomes less but that the help taken by the coach from the sports scientists increases. The planning, implementation and control of training is still the sole responsibility of the coach.

Athletic training is performed for improving sports performance. The sports performance, as any other type of human performance, is not the product of one single system or aspect of human personality. On the contrary, it is the product of the total personality of the sports person. The personality of a person has several dimensions e.g., physical, physiological social and psychic. In order to improve sports performance the social and psychic capacities of the sports person also have to be improved in addition to the physical and physiological ones.

In other words the total personality of a sportsman has to be improved in order to improve his performance. Athletic training, therefore, directly and indirectly aims at improving the personality of the sportsman. No wonder, therefore, sports training is an educational process.

Athletic training is a systematic process extending over a long period. For best results the system of training has to be based and conducted on scientific facts and lines. Where it is not possible to do that, the training has to be based on the results of successful practice which has withstood the test of time. Sports science has still not been able to provide a scientific base for all the aspects and elements of training. Many things are still based on the results of successful practice which on deeper analysis is also a method of science to prove or disprove a theory. Moreover, the principle characteristic of a science is the existence of a systematised body of knowledge.

The science of *athletic training* has its own systematised body of knowledge and hence is a science in itself. "Athletic training, based on scientific knowledge, is a pedagogical process of sports perfection which through systematic effect on psycho-physical performance ability and performance readiness aims at leading the sportsman to high and the highest performance. Through active and conscious interaction with the given demands in *athletic training*, the sportsman's personality develops according to the norms and standards of socialist society".

Athletic training is a scientifically based and pedagogical organised process which through planned and systematic, effect on performance ability and performance readiness aims at sports perfection and performance improvement as well as at the contest in sports competition."

Now, it is quite obvious that various endeavours have been made at different levels to advance acceptable definition of the vital process of *athletic training*. After considering the nature of *athletic training* as viewed by some eminent authorities on this subject, the following definition of sports training is proposed:-

Athletic training is a pedagogical process, based on scientific principles, aiming at preparing sportsmen for higher performances in sports competitions.

CHAPTER - 4

AIMS OF ATHLETIC TRAINING

Athletic training aims at improving the performance of sports persons. The sports performance depends on several factors. The performance of a sports person primarily depends on his performance capacity which is a complex of five groups of factors. All these factors, therefore, are the principle aims of *athletic training.* The constitution or physique is almost completely genetically determined and hence cannot be improved by training. But the other four groups of factors are trainable to a greater or lesser extent. These four, therefore, are generally considered to be the aims of *athletic training.*

PHYSICAL FITNESS OR CONDITION

The physical fitness or condition is the sum total of five abilities namely strength, speed, endurance, flexibility and coordinative abilities. These five motor abilities and their complex form are the basic pre-requisites for human motor actions. Therefore , the sports performance in all sports depends to a great extent on these abilities. The improvement and maintenance of physical fitness or condition is perhaps the most important aim of athletic training. Each sport requires a different type and level of physical condition and as a result a different type of fitness training or conditioning is required for different sports. Some like distance running require a very high level of endurance but a low level of other motor abilities. Sports like shooting and archery do not require a high level physical condition.

TECHNICAL SKILL

Sports performances are possible only through sports motor actions or movements. The performance of a sportsperson is significantly affected by the skill with which these actions or movements are executed by a sports person. The acquisition of sports technical skills, therefore, is an important aim of *athletic training.* In all sports one or more skill have to be acquired by doing technique training. The role of technical skills in different sports, however, is different. In sports, in which only one or two simple movements have to be learnt the role of technical skills is less. But in sports in which several difficult movements and their variations are to be mastered the role of technical skills increases manifold e.g., gymnastics, football etc. In team games, combat sports etc., the technical skills serve as basic elements of tactical actions which are indispensable for good performance in these sports. Even in sports depending largely on fitness or condition the technical skills are important for economy and efficiency of simple movements like running, swimming, jumping, lifting and throwing.

TACTICAL EFFICIENCY

The tactical efficiency consists of three elements: Knowledge of competition rules and possibilities of exploiting various internal and external factors for achieving best possible results; tactical abilities and tactical skills. Tactical efficiency is important in all sports but its role is different in different sports. Tactical efficiency is of paramount importance in team games, combat sports and racket sports. These sports, therefore, are also called *tactical sports*. The role of tactics in individual sports is limited e.g., throws, gymnastic, weight lifting etc. The contribution of tactics towards sports performance increases with the improvement in performance. The total volume of tactical training, therefore, also increases with the increase in the level of performance.

EDUCATION

Sports performance is the product of the total personality of the sports person. It is highly erroneous to think that sports performance is determined exclusively by the physique and physical qualities. Sports performance is a psychomotor performance and for its improvement through training as well as for achieving it in a competition. The sports person depends heavily on his qualities of head and heart. These qualities or abilities can be classified into five groups given below:-

(1) Beliefs, values, motives, interests, attitudes etc.

(2) Cognitive abilities e.g., perception, thinking, memory etc.

(3) Emotional abilities e.g., control of emotions.

(4) Personality traits e.g., regularity, sincerity, hardwork.

(5) Habits e.g., habits of eating, sleeping, hygiene, spending of leisure time etc..

The above mentioned five groups of qualities and abilities enable the sportsperson to compete successfully in a competition. It is also of equal importance to realise that these qualities also enable a sportsperson to do training effectively and systematically for a number of years.

The *athletic training* aims at improving these qualities through proper selection and implementation of various means and methods of training. In other words, is an educational or pedagogical process. Without understanding this aspect of a sportsperson has a very low chance of achieving high sports performance.

CHARACTERISTICS OF ATHLETIC TRAINING

Athletic training is not mere physical activity involving physical movements or actions. Such type of physical is common to several type of human activities e.g., play, dance, physical or manual work like household work, work in industries and factories. In addition to physical activity the *athletic training* possesses more characteristics which are explained below in brief:-

(i) Performance in a Sports Competition

Athletic training aims at achieving high performance in sports competition. It is a process which is spread over a long period of time. It is a competition and performance oriented process. It is not just play or recreational activity, but a serious activity.

(ii) Planned and Systematic

In order to achieve high performance *athletic training* is performed in a planned and systematic manner. Athletic training is always planned in the form of shorter and bigger training cycles e.g., microcycle, meso-cycle and macro-cycle. The planning of the process of *athletic training* cannot be haphazard or unsystematic. A system most suitable for achieving high performance has to be first made on the basis of which *athletic training* is planned.

(iii) Scientific

Modern age is the age of science. Different sciences are exploring different dimensions of human nature and human performance. In order to achieve best results the knowledge from these sciences has to be incorporated in the process of *athletic training.*

In other words *athletic training* is based on scientific facts and principles. Where science is silent it is based on results of successful training/practice which has repeatedly withstood the test of time. Theories and methods of training are, therefore, either supported by science or by time tested practice.

(iv) Coach as a Leader

Athletic training is always assessed, planned, organised and implemented by a coach or a sports teacher or some other person. A coach controls everything. He bears the overall responsibility for the effectiveness and success of training. As the performance level of a sportsman improves the coach has to take the help of sports scientists more and more. But at no time does his responsibility as a coach decreases. The dominant position of the coach is not an indication of total dependence of sportsperson on the coach. Sportsperson, with the passage of time, should become more and more independent. He should assume more responsibilities and should be involved in planning, implementation and assessment of training. But the responsibility of the coach to guide and help him in achieving high performance remains intact.

(v) Development and Exploitation of Reserves

A person, in spite of his best intentions and efforts, cannot fully use his psychic and biological capacities to the maximum. Some reserves are always left untapped. This is particularly evident in sports. Many times the sports person is not even aware of the limits of his performance. The *athletic training* aims at finding these hidden reserves and makes the sportsperson aware of it. Athletic training also aims at further development of these reserves. This characteristic of *athletic training* is unique as in other areas of human activity a person is rarely pushed to the ultimate limits of his performance i.e., super human efforts.

(vi) Controlled Daily Routine

Athletic training is not play or recreation. It is hard and exacting. Besides, in order to do training regularly with best effects, the sportsperson has to adjust his other activities i.e. training should take precedence over other activities. As a result the sportspersons control their day-to-day routine in such a manner that they are able to do training once or twice a day with high effect. When we look at this important and vital characteristic of training, we realise that sportspersons must possess a high sense of self discipline, a quality shared by all champions.

(vii) Educational Process

As explained earlier *athletic training* is basically an educational or pedagogical process. It strives to develop all the aspects of personality. Without developing the personality *athletic training* and high performance are not possible. Therefore, personality development and performance development are two interrelated and interdependent aspects of *athletic training.*

(viii) Process of Perfection

Athletic training is a planned, systematic and scientific process of preparation of sportspersons for high performances. To achieve this aim different means and methods are used. These means and methods are not static in nature. These are being constantly improved, modified and new ones being discovered by the sports science disciplines. Valuable contributions are made by implementing these means and methods in different forms and under different conditions. The process of scientific observation, experimentation, analysis and synthesis is an important characteristic of *athletic training* in modern age. Athletic training, therefore, is a continuous process of perfection, improvement and creation of means and methods of improving sports performance and factors of performance.

TRAINING STRUCTURE

Athletic training is a complex process of preparation of sportspersons. It consists of various parts, phases, cycles, proportions of training elements, load dynamic etc. Thiess and Schnabel define training structure as follows:-

> "Structure of internal interdependence of important aspects, parts and phases of training process, their lawful relationship and interaction as well as their general sequence". The training structure is based on the laws and principles of sports training and aims at systematic development of sports performance.

Training structure is primarily characterised by the following:-

- Parts of training based on the performance structure and demand profiles.
- Parts of training based on the performance structure and demand profiles.
- Purposeful order of training parts.
- The proportions and interrelationships of training parts, e.g., proportion of general and special preparation, conditioning and technical training.
- Temporal sequence and change in the training parts with respect to training state, age, periodisation etc.

Load dynamic e.g., volume, intensity.

The structure of *athletic training* can be studied and analysed either from its cross-sectional or longitudinal aspect. The training plan for a training session is an example of training structure depicting the cross-sectional view of training on a particular day.

The structure of training basically comprises of training elements/parts and their interrelationships. But it is important to note that structure of training is in fact structure of long term process covering several years. With the passage of time the training structure also undergoes change.

It is also important for the students of *athletic training* to understand that the principle aim is always to study the process of training in its entirety. For pedagogical reasons the various elements/parts of training are discussed separately. For example, strength and strength training has been discusses as a separate element; but in reality strength training is always a part and parcel of the total structure of the training. Hence, the study of strength and strength training is incomplete till we learn how to integrate strength training effectively with the actual process of training over short and long periods. This applies to all elements, parts, aspects phases of the complex training process.

MODEL OF ATHLETIC TRAINING

The starting point of *athletic training* is the determination of aim of *athletic training*. This is primarily done by the coach after a thorough analysis of various factors. The sports scientists and the sportsman are also involved in the fixation of the aim. It is not sufficient to determine the general aim only. It is also essential to set aims for different factors on which performance depends. It is preferable to split the aim into sub-aims to be achieved after definite periods of training. While determining the aims the coach must set aims for personality as well as for performance.

On the basis of set aims and objectives for personality and performance development the coach makes shorter and bigger training plans to achieve these aims and objectives. On the basis of these plans he organises the actual training process. Under his direct guidance, supervision and help the sportsman does the training.

In the planning and implementation of training the sports scientist, physician and sportsperson are also involved. The quality and extent of their involvement depends on the judgment, experience, and knowledge of the coach.

Society plays an important role in the implementation of the training process. It contribution is direct as well as indirect. The coach, sportsman, sports scientists and other persons involved in training are part and parcel of society. They are all subject to social influences through family members, friends, colleagues, associations, press, T.V. etc. Besides, the infrastructure required for *athletic training* and sports competitions, is directly or indirectly provided by the society. Social recognition, praise, criticism, apathy have all pervasive effect on the training process. Society provides the basic prerequisites for successful implementation of training and competition system. It is not an exaggeration to say that training and competitions satisfy social needs and hence society provides for the implementation and success of this system.

Different nations or societies of the world, in the process of their Development, have evolved different sports systems. The sports systems of socialist countries are vastly different from the sports systems of European and American systems. Each country has a system which suits its social, political and economic conditions.

System of one country may not prove to be good for another country. These systems have to be gradually evolved and cannot be changed in a short span of two or three years.

In the end it must be pointed out that the success of *athletic training* process depends on several factors particularly social, political and economical conditions. A coach or sports teacher alone cannot guarantee its success. This does not mean that the coach can be absolved of his responsibility. He has a very crucial and pivotal role to play. He should be a scientist and an artist both to train the sportsman. His job is to coach, and coaching is the art of successfully training the sportsman for higher performance and better results.

GENERAL PRINCIPLES OF ATHLETIC TRAINING

Principles of *athletic training* are the guidelines for coaches, teachers and sportspersons for the formulation, implementation and control of *athletic training*. These principles are valid for all aspects and elements of training. These are formed on the basis of knowledge gained from various sports science disciplines and successful practice. The principles of training can be general or specific.

General principles are valid for the process of *athletic training* as a whole. The specific principles, however, are applicable to a limited part or aspect of training only e.g., principles of periodisation; principles of technical training etc. Principles are not applicable to specific situations or actions. These have regulative function for a whole class or groups of actions. The principles, however, can be further split into rules which are more specific in nature.

It is human nature to formulate principles and serve an important didactic function of helping the humans to regulate their activity in order to achieve their goals.

The history of the principles of *athletic training* is as old as the history of sports and *athletic training*. However, with the establishment of *athletic training* as a science the formulation and development of training principles also became a topic of scientific interest. Sieger discusses the history of training principles in GDR in the previous two decades and points out that with the rapid increase in knowledge about training and it's various elements and aspects the principles of training have also been undergoing change.

Schnabel and Muller review the present state of principles of *athletic training* and conclude that the state is not very satisfactory. They point out the following reasons for such a state of affairs:-

(1) A very large number of principles have been formulated. In German sports literature alone there are 70 general principles and about 20 special principles.

(2) There is lack of understanding of the concept of principle.

(3) Several principles are in reality the principles relating to human activity in general and hence can not be called principles of training in true sense e.g., principle of consciousness.

(4) There is much overlapping gegarding the nomenclature and contents of the principles of training.

(5) The present level of knowledge about the science of training is not adequately reflected in the principles. This is particularly true regarding the functional interrelationship between training performance prerequisites—competition performance.

(6) A stable concept of a system of principles of training is still not available.

(i) Principle of Formulation of Training on the Basis of Prognostic Performance and its Structure

Athletic training aims at achieving high performance in future. Therefore, the structure of prognostic sports performance should form the basis of formulation of training. All aims, objectives, means, methods and measures for different stages of training are to be derived from the performance capacity essential to achieve the prognostic sports performance. The performance structure, in combination of other factors like motor development, age, training state, periodisation etc. Determines the training structure.

(ii) Principle of Continuity of Training

This principle states that sports training should be a continuous and regular process. Continuous and regular training leads to improvement of performance capacity. But when the training is stopped for some period or there are too long intervals between training sessions the performance capacity starts decreasing. It is, take pre-cautionary measures to neutralize the effect of factors which can result in shorter or longer training breaks. For proper implementation of the principle of continuity the following rules have to be observed:-

(1) The sportsman must be educated about the importance of continuity of training by convincing him about the negative effects of training breaks and irregular training on his performance capacity. He should not only be informed and educated but should also be helped and encouraged to continue his training regularly without training breaks. He should be enabled to carry out his training programmes independently event when the coach can not be physically present. For periods of vacations etc., the sportsman should be supplied with training programmes which he can follow without any problem.

(2) The principle of continuity of training extends to all factors of performance. A performance factor developed by training over a period of time needs to be maintained when the stress is shifted to other performance factors. Therefore, in the complex process of training some amount of training, either for development or maintenance, should always be there for all factors of performance. It is, however, important to note that much larger volume of training is required to develop a performance factor as compared to its maintenance.

(3) The state of overload always results in markedly low training volumes or even worse long training break. Therefore, proper measures should be adopted to prevent the occurrence of over-load.

(4) In case the sportsman is sick or injured the coach should try to find out, in consultation with the physician, ways and means by which the sportsman can continue his training even though with low load intensity and volume e.g., with leg injury the sportsman can do some exercises with his arms or upper body from sitting or reclining position.

(iii) Principle of Progression of Load

Training load is the principle stimulus for starting the psycho-physiological processes of adaptation which eventually lead to increase in performance capacity. A certain quantum of training load forces the organism to adapt to a certain level of psychic and physical demands. If the same load is repeated again and again, then it gradually loses its value as a stimulus for adaptation. The organism adapts to this load and is in a position to tackle this load effectively and easily. It is no longer adequate to force the organism to adapt to a higher level of functioning. In simple words this load is just good enough to maintain the achieved level of adaptation or the achieved level of performance. Higher performance will be achieved when the organism adapts to a higher level of functioning.

This is possible only by increasing the load. In *athletic training* we want continuous improvement in performance. Therefore, we have to keep on increasing the training load from time to time or periodically.

The training load in *athletic training* can be increased by two methods:-

(a) Linear Method

In this method the load is increased in every training session. This method is possible only during the initial days of training.

(b) Step Method

In this method the load is increased in steps i.e., after an increase in load it is maintained for some training sessions before increasing it again.

The step method of increasing load is most commonly used in training as it results in stronger stimulus to the organism for adaptation. A combination of linear and step method, however, can also be used under special circumstances. With the passage of time and improvement in performance capacity the magnitude of 'step' for increasing load becomes lesser and lesser. There is no fixed formula to determine what should be the magnitude of load 'step'. It depends on several factors like training state, load tolerance, age etc. One things, however, is certain: the load increase must be enough to constitute a strong stimulus for adaptation and it should be strongly felt by the sportsman.

The means and measures which can be used to increase training and competition load are numerous. The important ones mentioned below:-

(a) *Factors of Load:* Change in load intensity or load volume or both is the most frequently used means of increasing the load. Change of physical exercise is also sometimes used for increasing the load. Stress on movement quality coupled with an increase in the degree of difficulty of the movement execution is the principle means of increasing load for technical and tactical perfection.

(b) Number and difficulty of competitions.

(c) Inclement weather conditions e.g., hot and humid weather, cold weather, strong wind, rain or wet conditions, higher altitude etc.

(d) Organisation and methods of training e.g., single or group training, continuous or interval method.

(e) Ground or surface e.g., rough terrain, uneven ground, hard, soft or fast surface etc.

(f) Increase in psychic load through audience, spectators, element of rivalry, unaccustomed conditions generating tension and anxiety.

Training and competition load, as stated earlier, is most frequently increased by changing one or more factors of load. Therefore, the coach must know which way this can be accomplished. Following hints are given regarding the general sequence of changing load factors:-

(a) To start with the training frequency i.e., number of training sessions should be increased.

(b) After an optimal increase in training frequency the training volume of each training session should be increased.

(c) Load density in a training session should be increased.

(d) *Lastly,* the load intensity should be increased.

From the above given sequence of change of load factors, it is clear that volume gets preference over load intensity. Load volume creates the necessary psychic and biological base for the organism to tolerate higher load intensities.

The change of load factors for increasing the load is of cyclic nature. In the initial days of a training cycle the load volume is increased while maintaining the load intensity. In the final days or second half of the training cycle, the load volume is maintained or reduced to some extent while at the same time increasing the load intensity. This is followed by a period of recovery after which the next training cycle starts.

(iv) Principle of Uniformity and Differentiation

In order to achieve best results, the *athletic training* should be formulated uniformly but allowing for individual differences. To start with the training should be predominantly uniform for all in order to spot talent. Uniformity also means that training for all should be based on the same principles and system which have been worked out to achieve the prognostic sports performance in stages. The goals, means, methods and organisation of training should be uniform. With the passage of time, however, the training should become increasingly individualised. The training of advanced sportsmen must be formulated in consideration of following individual factors:-

(a) Age, biological and chronological.

(b) Sex, training age and training state.

(c) Talent.

(d) Psychic factors e.g., personality, temperament etc.

(e) Nature and volume of training in the past.

(f) Performance and rate of performance improvement.

(g) Total load and possibilities of recovery.

(h) Social and economical factors.

For proper implementation of the principle of uniformity and differentiation Muller formulates the following rules:-

(1) Go from differentiated formulation of group training of youth to predominantly individualised training in high performance training stage.

(2) Determine the individual prerequisites and development situations of sportsmen and consider these for planing and formulation of training.

(3) In the initial years of training, emphasise the removal of individual weaknesses and concentrate increasingly on the long term performance development and the development of individual strengths.

(4) Ensure accelerated performance development of talented sportsmen and sports women through differentiated as well as individualised formulation of training.

(v) Principle of Progressive Specialisation

The term specialisation in sports training means use of specific means and methods for improving performance in a particular sport. Logically speaking specific means and methods lead to faster improvement in sports performance. But in real training process, which starts in childhood and can continue upto 25-30 years of life, the predominant use of specific means and methods throughout the long term process of training does not give good results.

On the contrary, it can lead to negative results. This is due to the following reasons:-

(1) Highly specialised is not suitable for children and youth who are still in the stage of growing. Their organism is incapable of tolerating the demands of highly specialised training for too long. It frequently leads to premature 'burning out' drop out' effects.

(2) High performance can he achieved faster by adopting highly specific means and methods but these performances are not stable and cannot be maintained for a sufficiently long period as is required in the high performance training stage.

(3) Sportsman will achieve high performance before the start of the age of high performance if highly specialised training is used in childhood. It means he will not be able to achieve his maximum potential performance. Therefore, it is essential that sportsmen should achieve high performances only in the age of high performance and in which they have the best psychic and biological prerequisites for high performance in a sport.

(4)The high performance depends on the totality of sportsman's physique and personality. Specialised training will result in the improvement of only the selected systems, organs and capacities of the sportsman. This will also result in inadequate development of other systems, organs and capacities, which will sooner or later act as limitation for further improvement of performance.

It is now universally accepted that the *athletic training*, in all stages and phases, should be a judicious mixture of general and specific means and methods of training. To start with the training should be highly general development oriented but with the passage of time should give way to gradually increasing specialisation.

The high proportion of general preparation in the initial years of training ensures all round development thus creating the base for future performance. It also helps to secure maximum 'transfer of training' effect which at later stages of training is not possible. General means of training in childhood are also important for developing the various components of sports talent which can be then identified and selection for a sport can be made.

There is a general misconception among sportsmen and coaches that the total volume of general preparation decreases with the advancement in sports performance. This is not correct. In fact the total volume of general as well as of special preparation increase with the improvement in sports performance but their proportion to one another changes in favour of special preparation.

(vi) Principle of Planned and Systematic Training

This principle, as its name suggests, actually consists of two training principles which are interrelated. Athletic training is a scientific and pedagogical process and for best results each and every part, phase and stage of training must be properly planned. As a result in training we have short and long term plans which form the basis of implementation and assessment of training.

It is however essential to realise that planning has to be done on the basis of a system, which has been worked out in consideration of the present available knowledge regarding best ways and means of achieving high performances through *athletic training*. In other words correct planning of training is impossible without a thorough understanding of training systematics.

Training system means the goal oriented arrangement of all training elements, parts and processes. This arrangement has to be based on the following:-

(1) The ultimate goal of *athletic training.*

(2) The interrelationship among performance structure, performance capacity and training structure.

(3) Principles of improvement of sports performance over a long time period.

(4) Principles of motor development.

(5) Principles of periodisation.

In consideration of the above mentioned factors the various elements, parts and processes are to be arranged in such a manner and sequence that the long term goal of sports training is achieved or even surpassed.

The major aspect of systematic training is the correct proportion and sequence of various training elements, contents and tasks. This should enable optimum rate of development of various performance factors and performance capacity. It should also ensure stabilisation of previous achievements/improvements and should create base for ensuring further continuous improvement.

There can be a fixed or stable system of training for all sports and sportsmen. The training system required for best results, will be different for different persons and sports. Nevertheless there are certain rules which are universally applicable. Important among these rules are given below:-

(1) General preparation should always precede special preparation. General means and methods of training and general factors of performance are used/developed earlier than the special means, methods and factors.

(2) The less effective physical exercises should be used before more effective exercises.

(3) The interdependence and inter-relationships existing among various performance factors should be fully exploited to achieve faster and better results.

(4) Condition and skill should form basic elements for tactical training.

(5) Technical skills depend, to a greater or lesser extent, on the level of one or more motor abilities.

(6) The previously learnt skill help in the learning of new skills.

(7) A good level of basic endurance is a basic prerequisite for the development of other performance factors.

(8) There are 'sensitive phases' during growth and development for the improvement of various performance prerequisites.

(9) Each stoke if training must consist of optimum periods of training and recovery.

(10) High load volume should precede high load intensity.

(vii) Principle of Cyclicity of Training

The process of *athletic training* is formulated in shorter and longer cycles. The reasons for carrying out training in form of cycles are given below:-

(1) In training the different tasks can not be tackled simultaneously. This has to be done in a definite sequence determined on the basis of a training system.

(2) Certain tasks of training have to be tacked again and again after certain time periods in order to achieve the desired results. This has to be based on the proper sequence of load and recovery phases.

(3) The sportsman has to participate in competitions and for successful participation he must achieve top form. Top form is developed in phases which have to be repeated after certain time period. Besides important competitions repeat themselves yearly or after definite time periods.

A training cycle basically consists of a load phase and recovery phase. But the principle of cyclicity goes beyond the cyclic nature of load dynamics. It extends to repeated occurrence of same or similar training tasks, means, methods, contents etc., after certain time intervals. In other words, the training structure is characterised by its cyclic nature. There is, however, a definite hierarchy of training cycles. The shorter training cycles are based on the bigger cycles by at the same time the shorter cycles give rise to bigger cycles.

In sports training we have three types of training cycles: macro-cycle, mesocycle and micro-cycle.

(a) Macro-cycle

This is considered the longest cycle of training. Its duration can be from 3-4 months to 12 months or even longer. Macro-cycle is formed by a certain arrangement of meso-cycles. Macro-cycle can have two aims:-

(1) Achievement of top form at a particular time.

(2) Increase of performance capacity to higher level.

In a macro-cycle the last meso-cycle is formulated to ensure recovery and relaxation and for effective transition to the next macro-cycle.

In high performance training stages the macro-cycle has both the aims and as a result it is formulated on the principles of periodisation. The various mesocycles are so formulated and arranged that the macro-cycle is clearly divided into three periods i.e., preparatory, competition and transitional period. Macro-cycle, in case of single periodisation, is an yearly cycle of training. But in case of double or triple periodisation there are two or three macro-cycles in a year. Macro-cycles, in high performance training stage, are usually arranged in certain manner to form longer cycles of training e.g., Olympic cycle of training.

In initial stages of training the macro-cycle aims at systematic development of performance capacity in order to achieve high performance in the high performance training stage. It's training structure does not depends on the principles of [periodisation but on the principles of developing performance over a long period. The motor development principles have a strong determining influence on the formulation of Macro-cycle in basic and advanced training stages.

(b) Meso-cycle

Meso-cycle is a training cycle of medium duration. It is composed of a definite arrangement of 3-6 micro-cycles or weekly cycles. The last micro-cycle or weekly cycle of a meso-cycle primarily aims at recovery and relaxation.

A meso-cycle aims at tackling of definite training tasks as part of the total process of development of performance capacity or top form. Generally, a mesocycle has one or two aims which can logically be achieved in 3-6 weeks. Depending on its position in a macro-cycle and on the aim of macro-cycle the meso-cycle can have a variety of aims e.g., learning or perfection of technical skill or skills, improvement of motor ability or abilities, maintenance and stabilisation of performance factors improved in the previous meso-cycle, achievement of top form or direct preparation for a competition, recovery and relaxation and so on.

Due to a wide range of aims which a meso-cycle can have there can not be a single model structure of a meso-cycle. But there are possibilities of having model structures of meso-cycles having definite aims. A thorough understanding of the nature and application of various types of meso-cycles is indispensable for correct formulation of a meso-cycle. Some important hints for the proper formulation of meso-cycles are given below:-

(1) For improvement of performance factors the minimum duration of a meso-cycle should be 4 weeks as this is the minimum period needed fro psychic and physiological adaptation.

(2) In a meso-cycle, aiming at improvement of performance capacity, stress should be laid on one or two factors while maintaining the other factors. In the next meso-cycle the stress can be shifted to some other factor of factors while ensuring the maintenance of others.

(3) In a meso-cycle, aiming at direct preparation for a competition, the training should aim at achieving top form and not at improving the performance factors in an isolated manner.

(4) In a meso-cycle, if not otherwise required, the volume of load should be increased in the first half of meso-cycle while maintaining or slightly increasing the load intensity. In the second half of meso-cycle the load intensity should be increased while maintaining or decreasing the volume of load.

(c) Micro-cycle

It is the smallest training cycle and consists of 3 to 10 days. When the duration of micro-cycle is seven days it is called *weekly cycle*. The duration of a micro-cycle in case of trained sportsman is normally from 5-10 days. The last training session or day of a micro-cycle aims at recovery and relaxation. The training structure of a micro-cycle is determined by its position within the meso-cycle and also on the aim of the meso-cycle.

The duration of a micro-cycle is not enough to ensure effective tacking of most of the training tasks. This is achieved in the meso-cycles. But the micro-cycle form indispensable units or steps in the process of tackling training tasks. As a result the effective formulation and implementation of micro-cycles determines the effectiveness of meso-cycles and in turn that of macro-cycle. A micro-cycle, is much closer to the day-to-day training process and hence enables optimal loading of the sportsman.

(viii) Principle of Regulation of Training

Athletic training is a goal-oriented long-term process of preparation of sports men for higher performance. It involves use of training means and methods for improving various performances prerequisites. Sportsmen, like other humans, are bio-social entities. During the long term period of training, different factors, in addition to training, affect sportsmen. These factors also have influence on sports training and its effects. It is, therefore, highly unwise and unscientific to lose track of the process of performance development at any point or time of the long term training process.

A coach should always know what effect the training is producing on the performance of the sportsman. If necessary the *athletic training* should be changed or modified to ensure proper and effective development of performance. This is possible through continuous regulation of sports training.

Regulation of *athletic training* is a goal-oriented process of training and performance assessment for controlling the process of performance development through training. For effective regulation of sports training the following three things are essential:-

(a) Training plans giving the aims, sub aims, load dynamic, means, methods etc., of different phases and periods of training.

(b) Training documents containing in a precise form the informations about load, means, methods etc., of training. Competition protocols and documents are also essential.

(c) Information about the level as well as rate and direction of improvement of performance and performance prerequisites.

On the basis of the three factors mentioned above a coach can, at any given moment, asses the effect of training on performance and performance pre-requisites and can thereby keep adjusting or modifying the training process in order to achieve good results.

It is, therefore, very important to prepare proper and detailed plans for various phases and periods of training. The training documents, like training diary, enable the coach to compare the training plan with the training done in reality in the light of the results achieved in terms of changes in performance and components of performance capacity.

The assessment of performance and performance prerequisites is indispensable for regulation of training. The sports performance can be adequately assessed from the competition results or results achieved in training. But it is better if the part performances are also measured/recorded and assessed. The performance capacity and the various performance prerequisites/ performance factors can be measured and judged effectively through sports motor tests, training controls and standardised training programmes.

In addition the investigation procedures of sports physiology, sports biochemistry, sports, psychology and sports bio-mechanics can be used to get additional informations regarding performance capacity, performance prerequisites. These can also be used to diagnose sports performance in some sports like track and field, swimming, weight lifting etc.

CHAPTER - 5

THE SIGNIFICANCE OF CO-ORDINATIVE ABILITIES IN ATHLETIC TRAINING

In the past, five motor abilities were recognised as components of physical fitness. These were strength, endurance, speed, flexibility and agility. But since one and a half decade the term agility has been gradually replaced by the term co-ordinative abilities. The reasons for this replacement are explained below:-

1. There was no agreement regarding the nature and definition of agility.

2. Though the term agility was used but it was explained as a complex of several coordinative abilities. Different experts explained agility to be composed of a different number of coordinative abilities.

3. Because of lack of unanimity about the nature and definition of agility, it was difficult to adopt a uniform methodology to explore and study agility. It lead to considerable confusion and chaos.

4. It was difficult to provide a systematic and logical basis for the improvement of agility as it was not possible to clearly determine its nature and component factors.

It was increasingly felt that if the concept of agility can be discarded and replaced by the concept of coordinative abilities, it will be more scientific and practical and will help in cleaning the confusion. Blume in his path breaking effort suggested that in place agility there should be even co-ordinative abilities which are important in sports. This will help in formulating the guidelines for improvement of each co-ordinative ability separately and will also help in better understanding of the role of co-ordinative factor in sports.

The theory of co-ordinative abilities is still in a stage of infancy. Though there is rapidly increasing acceptance of the term co-ordinative abilities yet there is no agreement regarding the number of co-ordinative abilities important for sports. The methodology of improving different co-ordinative abilities is also yet not available in full detail. But in the near future it is expected that a clear cut system of means and methods for improving each and every co-ordinative ability will be evolved.

NATURE AND DEFINITION OF CO-ORDINATIVE ABILITIES

Co-ordinative abilities are primarily dependant on the motor control and regulation processes of CNS. The theory of motor co-ordination, therefore, is the basis for understanding the nature of co-ordinative abilities. For each co-ordinative abilities the motor control and regulation processes function in a definite manner. When a particular aspect of these functions is improved then the sportsman is in a better position to do a certain group of movement which for their execution depend on this type of CNS functioning pattern.

This also explains the difference between a co-ordinative ability and motor skill. For a co-ordinative ability the control regulation processes are required to function in a particular manner whereas in case of a skill these processes are automatised to a great extent.

Motor co-ordination is a part and parcel of action regulation and is hence closely linked with the processes of regulation of cognitive, psychic and movement execution aspects of an action. *Hirtz* and *Meinel* and *Schnabel* point out the these aspects of action regulation are important determinants of co-ordinative abilities.

Co-ordinative abilities have also important and strong links with the motor skills as motor co-ordination forms the basis of both. Co-ordinative abilities become effective in movements only through the motor abilities activity determined drives and cognitive processes.

In the end the important characteristics of co-ordinative abilities are summarised in the following points:

1. The motor co-ordination processes from the basis of co-ordinative abilities. Hence, co-ordinative abilities belong to the performance factor Technique/Co-ordination.

2. As the control and Regulation processes of motor co-ordination can only be influenced through the process of afference and reafference, therefore the various sense organs involved in motor co-ordination are the necessary biological prerequisites for the improvement and perfection of co-ordinative abilities. The functional capacity of these sense organs determines the level of co-ordinative abilities to a great extent.

3. Co-ordinative abilities find expression in the quality of movement as well as in the ability to learn movement. The movement on the other hand are essential for the improvement of co-ordinative abilities.

4. Co-ordinative abilities always appear in a complex combination with one another as well as with the conditional abilities, and processes of will, cognition and other psychic factor involved in the process of action or behaviour regulation.
5. Co-ordinative abilities have general and specific aspects both.

IMPORTANCE OF CO-ORDINATIVE ABILITIES

Co-ordinative abilities are an expression of motor co-ordination which is of crucial importance in sports movements. The importance of co-ordinative abilities is discussed below in four points:-

1. The movement quality depends to a great extent on co-ordinative abilities. The rhythm, flow, accuracy, constancy, amplitude etc., of a movement are expressions of motor co-ordination and hence highly dependent on co-ordinative abilities. In technical sports beautiful and graceful movements are a product of well developed technical skills and co-ordinative abilities.
2. The speed of learning of skill and its stability is directly dependent on the level of various co-ordinative abilities. Motor learning ability is a product of co-ordinative abilities. In all sports lesser or greater number of motor skills have to be learnt. Besides, the sportsmen are also required to learn the exercise needed for training and for recovery, relaxation etc., well-developed co-ordinative abilities, therefore, assume high importance in all sports. Their importance assumes very high significance in sports in which sportsmen are required to continuously keep learning more and more new movements with higher degree of difficulty e.g., gymnastics. The

success of re-learning, frequently needed in many sports, depends on motor learning ability.

3. Co-ordinative abilities are also needed for maximal utilisation of conditional abilities, technical skills and tactical skills. Without the adequately developed co-ordinative abilities, a sportsman can not make maximum use of his psycho-biological capacities and reserves.

4. The co-ordinative abilities, to a great extent, determine the maximum limits to which sports performance can be improved in several sports especially the sports which depend largely on technical and tactical factors. Because of this reason assessment of co-ordinative abilities and the possibilities of their further development form an important part of the process of talent identification in sports.

BRIEF DESCRIPTION OF CO-ORDINATIVE ABILITIES

In sports seven co-ordinative abilities are important. In different sports the relative importance of these abilities is, however, different.

1. Differentiation Ability

It is the ability to achieve a high level of fine tuning or harmony of individual movement phases and body part movements. It finds expression in high degree of accuracy and movement economy. Differentiation ability depends on conscious and precise perception of temporal, dynamic and spatial parameters of movement execution and their comparison with the similar parameters of movement concept at different levels of control and regulation. The high level of differentiation ability depends on movement experience and the degree of mastery over motor action. It enables the sportsman to perceive micro-differences regarding the temporal, dynamic and spatial aspects of movement execution.

Differentiation ability is to be particularly stressed when the aim is to achieve high level of mastery over sports movements and their effective application in competition. High level of differentiation ability is expressed in different sports as a feeling or sense of an implement or movement e.g., ball sense, movement sense, water feeling etc. The ability to execute highly skilful, movements with hand, feet or head is also a special type of differentiation ability. Muscle relaxation ability is also a type of differentiation ability.

Differentiation ability appears in different forms in different sports as each sports puts different types of demands on the control and regulation processes. In gymnastics differentiation ability enables highly precise and accurate movements according to a given model of movement.

In football it finds expression in dexterity of feet and head. In different sports, therefore, different means and methods should be adopted for the improvement of differentiation ability.

2. Orientation Ability

It is the ability to determine and change the position and movements of the body in time and space in relation to a definite field of action. The perception of position and movement and the motor action to change the body position should be understood as a unity for the ability for space-time oriented movement regulation.

The demands on the orientation ability are vastly different in different sports e.g., team games, combat sports, technical sports. In gymnastics the position and movement of head and eyes is important for orientation. In wrestling, on the other hand, kinesthetic sense organs assume importance for orientation. In team games vision, especially peripheral vision, is decisive for orientation.

3. Coupling Ability

It is the ability to co-ordinate body part movement with one another and in relation to a definite goal oriented whole body movement. Coupling ability is especially important in sports in which movements with a high degree of difficulty have to be done e.g., gymnastics, team games.

In a team game like football the foot movements for ball control or dribbling have to be coupled with the whole body movement of running, jumping etc. In gymnastics and also in wrestling the movements of hands, legs, trunk and head have to be successfully combined to achieve a certain goal. In sports, depending on the nature of activity, the movement coupling can be either successive or simultaneous.

The coupling ability primarily depends on the functional capacity of kinesthetic and optical sense organs. Orientation, differentiation and rhythm abilities are also closely related with the coupling ability.

4. Reaction Ability

It is the ability to react quickly and effectively to a signal. Reaction ability has been discussed in detail in the chapter on speed and hence it need not be discussed here again.

5. Balance Ability

It is the ability to maintain balance during whole body movements and to regain balance quickly after the balance disturbing movements. Balance ability can be of two types:-

(i) Ability to maintain balance during stationary position or slow movements. It depends primarily on kinesthetic, tactile and to some extent on vestibular sense organs.

(ii) Ability to maintain or regain balance during large range movements and during rapidly changing positions of the body. It depends primarily on the functional capacity of the vertebral sense organ.

Balance ability is a necessary pre-requisite for all types of movements. Static balance is required for the execution of all movements whether slow or fast, part body movement or whole body movement. Static balance ability develops to a significant extent through various activities in childhood. Dynamic balance ability is important in sports in which frequent and rapid change of body position is required e.g., gymnastics, ski jump etc. In these sports the performance has positive relationship with dynamic balance.

6. Rhythm Ability

It is the ability to perceive the externally given rhythm and to reproduce it in motor action. It also denotes the ability to reproduce a rhythm, existing in motor memory, in motor action. In some technical sports like gymnastics, figure skating the sportsman has to perceive an external rhythm, given in the form of music, and to express it in his movements. In many sports rhythm is not given from outside. In these cases the sportsman has to make use of the rhythm stored in his motor memory. This is essential for effective motor learning as well as for high quality of movement execution.

The rhythm ability, like balance ability, is of fundamental importance in sports. This ability is not limited to the movement of the sportsman himself but extends to the perception of rhythm of other's movements also e.g., group rhythm. The ability to perceive the rhythm of movement of others is the basis for sound perception of technical errors by coaches. It also finds expression in the tendency to 'flow alongwith' the rhythm of some one else's action.

7. Adaptation Ability

It is the ability to adjust or completely change the movement programme during the movement on the basis of changes or anticipated changes in the situation. The situational changes may be expected ones or may suddenly take place. The movement adjustment in cyclic sports takes place primarily by the adjustment of the spatial, dynamic and temporal parameters of movement e.g., in running, cycling etc. This type of adjustment is possible when the changes in situation are not of large magnitude. But in team games and combat sports the changes in situation can be considerable enough to stop the movement and to start a new one.

The adaptation ability depends considerably on the speed and accuracy of perception of changes in situation. It also depends heavily on experience. For starting a new movement the sportsman must be able to select an alternative programme and to execute it without breaking the movement continuity. The adaptation ability is closely linked with reaction and orientation ability. The playing ability needed in team games depends heavily on adaption ability.

IMPROVEMENT OF CO-ORDINATIVE ABILITIES

It is not possible here to discuss the improvement of all the seven co-ordinative abilities separately and in detail. In addition to the limitation of space, the unsatisfactory level of methodology for the improvement of these co-ordinative abilities is the principal reason for this. The principles for the formulation of training for coordinative abilities are presented below:-

(i) The Principle Method is Varied Practice and the Principle Means are Learnt Physical Exercises

Inspite of the fact that co-ordinative abilities are determined by the control and regulation processes, the best method for effective development of these abilities is practising physical exercises. The control and regulation processes are the processes of motor co-ordination and hence are best affected by doing gross motor movements. The movements, however, should be practised with enough variation. For best effects the movements to be used should have already been learnt to a sufficient degree by the sportsman. Unlearnt movements cannot be used for the training of co-ordinative abilities. During practice the movement should be done with several variations. The more variable is the movement execution the more effective it is for the development of co-ordinative abilities.

(ii) General and Special Exercises Should be Used

Each co-ordinative ability has a general and special aspect. In the initial stages general exercises for the development of general co-ordinative abilities should be dominantly used. But later on special exercises should be used more and more to ensure best effect for performance improvement in a sport. For example, for gymnasts in the beginning general balance exercises are to be use but later balance exercises on the balance beam are indispensable to develop the special balance ability needed in gymnastics.

(iii) The Movements Should be Done Correctly and Consciously

The execution of movement is made possible by control and regulation processes. Incorrect execution of movement will force the control and regulation processes to take place differently and hence to give a different sort of sensations and feelings to a sportsman. As a result he forms wrong associations between movement image and movement sensations and consequently is unable to correctly grasp and understand the verbal instructions of the coach or the teacher. It is, therefore, essential that movement is executed correctly. Each time the movement is to be done it must be done consciously with the required concentration. It enables the sportsman to consciously involve the psychic, volitional and cognitive processes, in the control and regulation of the movement. As a result these are also positively affected by movement practice. The net result is more effective training.

(iv) Additional Means for Improving Motor Sense Organs Should be used

The co-ordinative abilities depend heavily on the functional capacity of various sense organs e.g., optic, acoustic, tactile, kinesthetic and vestibular. The functional capacity of these organs can be improved by doing exercises during which the sportsman remains comparatively physically passive. For example, exercises to improve peripheral vision from sitting or standing position; exercises on the turn table to improve vestibular functional capacity; exercises to improve tactile or kinesthetic perception by use of various types and intensity of touch signals or through use of tensiometer or dynamometer respectively. These exercises, however, should be used as additional exercises only. These serve to improve only the functional capacity of motor sense organs which is only a part of the total control and regulation processes determining coordinative abilities. Improvement of the functional capacity of a single motor sense organ will have a positive effect on several co-ordinative abilities as each co-ordinative ability depends, to a lesser or greater extent, on several motor sense organs.

(v) Accentuated Development of Co-ordinative Abilities

A physical exercise always has a complex effect. It will lead to improvement of several conditional and co-ordinative abilities. For instance, typical obstacle runs or agility runs are good for improving a number of co-ordinative abilities alongwith speed and strength. But a faster and effective improvement of a coordinative ability is possible if the exercise is modified to ensure the improvement of a single co-ordinative ability. Therefore, it is advisable to devise special exercises to ensure effective development of each co-ordinative ability. Obstacle runs or agility runs, however, are effective when used with children as they ensure effective development of a number of co-ordinative abilities.

(vi) There Should be a Rich Variation of Exercise

For the improvement of co-ordinative abilities a limited number of exercises do not give desired results. Each set of exercises have their effect for a certain period of time. Therefore, the exercises should be changed frequently. A rich and continuous variation of exercises used is of utmost importance to ensure continuous development. As a principle sportsman should be continuously doing new and unaccustomed exercises for best effect. The use of same exercises seriously limits the generalisation of control and regulation processes-the basis of coordinative abilities.

(vii) There Should be a Systematic Increase in the Difficulty of Co-ordination

To ensure continuous improvement in co-ordinative abilities the degree of difficulty of physical exercises should be systematically increased. There are unlimited possibilities of doing this. The important methods of increasing the degree of difficulty commonly used in sports are described below in brief:-

(1) Variation in Movement Execution

The variation in movement execution can be achieved by bringing some change in the phases of movement or changing the complete movement to some extent. The temporal and spatial parameters of movement execution are changed more frequently e.g., doing the movement with slower or faster rhythm, increasing the movement amplitude; change in the starting position or end position.

(2) Variation in External Conditions

Here the possibilities are practically unlimited. The change in external conditions to increase degree of difficulty is frequently achieved by (a) changing the weight, size, shape or height of apparatus/implement/ball (b) changing the surface (c) changing the partner (d) changing the distance between the equipments, players etc. (e) changing the ground dimensions.

(3) Combination of Movements

Combination of two or more movements is very frequently used to increase the difficulty of co-ordination. Movement combinations can be successive or simultaneous combinations. Most common movement combinations are running and jumping, catching and throwing, running and throwing, running and dribbling and so on. Combining three or more movements is also possible and that too with some task of accuracy e.g., running, jumping, turning in the air and shooting at a target.

(4) Change in Information Uptake

The co-ordination performances depend on the information uptake and synthesis. The sportsman receives information about the movement from his different motor sense organs. If these pieces of information from the important sense organ/organs are reduced, changed or completely stopped then the degree of difficulty increases manifold. The possibility of using this method in sports training is, however, limited. But it can be done in some exercises e.g., practice before a mirror, exercising while looking up or with closed eyes.

(5) Practice Against Time

If the exercise is required to be done with high speed then the difficulty of co-ordination increases considerably. But, for effective use of this method the sportsman should use only those exercises the technique of which he has already mastered. For effective use of this method the exercises should be done against time. The decreases in the duration to complete the exercise indicates an improvement in co-ordination.

(6) Practice Under Fatigue

Fatigue, whether general or specific, has a deteriorating effect on motor co-ordination. Hence co-ordinative abilities training under conditions of fatigue can be effective. But, like in the earlier method, only thoroughly learnt exercises should be used. According to this method exercises should be done after some sort of strenuous training e.g., endurance training.

Exercises can also be done after producing specific type of fatigue of some motor sense organ. For example balance exercises after doing several forward or backward rolls or after spinning around for few seconds. The forward/backward rolls or spins produce specific fatigue of vestibular sense organs thus making balance exercise far more difficult. Similarly, several maximal muscle contractions can be done to fatigue the kinesthetic sense organs which make exercises demanding high accuracy or precision much more difficult.

CHAPTER - 6

THE IMPORTANCE OF TECHNIQUE IN ATHLETIC TRAINING

Sports activity consists of sports movements. A sports movement is a motor action complete in itself. The efficiency or effectiveness of these sports movements determines the sports performance. All factors of performance capacity are ultimately needed to increase the efficiency of the sports movement/movements during training or competition. As a result the sports performance in sports depends to a great extent on the efficiency or effectiveness of sports performance in sports depends to a great extent on the efficiency or effectiveness of sports movements or motor actions. In other words the factor technique/co-ordination is of high importance as it is through technical actions that the given tasks in sports training or competition are effectively tackled. Technique and technical training, therefore, is an important part of the total process of training.

The technique and technical training in sports is based on four basic considerations:-

(1) In each sport tasks have to be fulfilled or tackled during competition. Each task can be tackled in one or more ways. The best motor procedure of tackling the task has to be determined and

consequently taught to the sportsmen. This becomes the aim of technical training.

(2) After determining the technique or motor procedure to be taught it is essential to know in which way this motor procedure is realised into actual motor action by the sportsman. For this we have to study the control and regulation of the motor action by the central nervous system. In other words, motor co-ordination as determinant of motor action has to be studied.

(3) The third step/consideration is to find out ways and means by which motor co-ordination is perfected and refined. This is essential for improving the effectiveness of the motor action. The process of improving and perfecting the motor co-ordination is called the motor learning process.

(4) After studying the motor learning process we have to study and explore the ways and means of organising and implementing technique training in such a way that motor learning takes place faster and effectively.

These four considerations or steps give rational and scientific basis to technical training in sports. The science of sports training is mainly concerned with the organisation and implementation aspect of technique training. But, for this it has to depend heavily on the knowledge about motor co-ordination and motor learning though these aspects are not its direct concern. The present chapter on technique, therefore, does not aim directly at motor co-ordination or motor learning. Basically, its aim is to provide fundamentals and guide lines for proper formulation of technique training in sports.

As discussed earlier motor co-ordination also forms the basis of co-ordinative abilities. The training for co-ordinative abilities is, therefore, basically aimed at affecting the motor co-ordination through motor learning process. Co-ordinative abilities are, therefore, considered to be a part of the performance factor technique/co-ordination.

TECHNIQUE, SKILL AND STYLE IN ATHLETIC TRAINING

Technique is defined as the *motor procedure* for tackling a motor task. Motor procedure should be understood as a system of movements of body parts in a definite sequence. Many of these movements, however, may take place simultaneously. The motor procedure or technique is always task or goal oriented. In different sports sportsmen have to tackle different types of motor tasks. Therefore, different motor procedures or techniques are required in different sports. In shotput, for example, the motor task is to put the shot as far as possible; whereas in weightlifting, in clean and jerk, the motor task is to lift as much weight as possible. In team games, the sportsmen are required to tackle a variety of tasks under different conditions. Therefore, in these sports the sportsman has to learn a number of techniques with possible variations.

Technique or motor procedure is basically a model. It symbolises the motor procedure which should be followed to tackle a certain motor task. The model of technique is presented in verbal, mechanical or physical mathematical form. The most common form of presenting the technique is verbal and physical. The physical aspect of technique is conveyed through demonstrations and audio-visual aids. The technique does not say anything about the capacity of the sportsman to realise it in the actual movement. It just tells us in what way the movements should be done in order to effectively tackle a given motor task.

Techniques in sports have evolved over a long period of time. Each technique has its own history. On the one hand it means that techniques are not static but dynamic in nature as these change with the passage of time. On the other hand it means that technique cannot be created in laboratories though it can be effectively studies there giving rise to information which can be used to further refine and prefect the technique for better tackling of a motor task.

Models of technique are based on the actual motor procedures followed by top level sportsmen. These individual motor procedures are studies and generalised to form a model of technique which can then be presented for acquisition by other sportsmen of different levels. But history has exhibited that sometimes a highly successful motor procedure used by an outstanding sportsman can suddenly change the model of technique. But in these cases the new technique must be carefully studies and analysed before being accepted as a model of technique.

SKILL

A motor skill is acquired through a long process of motor learning. Skill denotes the level of effectiveness with which a movement or motor action can be done. Skill is defined as automatisation of motor procedures. A sportsman tries to learn a technique or motor procedure and through continuous and systematic process he is able to acquire the skill i.e., automatisation of the motor procedure. In other words, one can say that skill is the capacity of the sportsman to realise technique in actual motor action.

Technique training aims at the development of technical skills and not at the development of technique. As the process of skill acquisition is the process of motor learning, therefore, technique training is essentially purposeful manipulation or exploitation of motor learning for best results through organisation of training means and methods.

In sports, we come across sportsmen with varying degree or level of skill who are attempting to follow the same motor procedure or technique. Their skill or lack of skill does not convey much about the effectiveness or correctness of the technique. Skill can be assessed and evaluated by the use of different procedures e.g., bio-mechanical procedures of skill assessment.

Skilful movement are made possible by highly advanced control and regulation processes of motor co-ordination. To understand skill and to derive guidelines for its improvement, therefore, motor co-ordination has to be first understood in all its relevant details.

STYLE

Style is individual expression of technique in motor action. No two sportsmen are alike in different factors which determine motor action. Therefore, each sportsman, because of his peculiar psychic, physical and biological capacities realises the technique in a different manner. This is his style. Several sportsmen may follow the same technique in order to tackle a definite task, but the motor action of each will be different from that of the others. Technique model, therefore, should be flexible enough to allow for individual difference. It is wrong and unproductive to try to copy each and every minute detail of technique model or the technique of outstanding sportsmen.

In actual practice, we come across individual styles of technique. The analysis of individual styles of top level sportsmen is the basis for preparing a model of technique. This model may not tally cent percent with the style of any sportsman. Sportsman tries to do the movements according to the technique model; but at the same time the individual style, of top sportsmen, of doing the movements forms the basis of technique model.

In the end, it is important to understand that the model of technique is a generalised model of successful motor procedures of tackling motor tasks. These models are to be followed by sportsmen of all levels. But the children and sportsmen of lower qualification are normally not in a position to effectively adopt this technique model in all the required details. Therefore, it is essential to prepare separate models of technique or technical demand profile for lower stages of training. Needless to say these profile must be based on the technical model high performance training stage with due modification in consideration of possible changes in the model in the near future.

MOTOR CO-ORDINATION

Previously, it has been stressed that skill is the product of motor co-ordination automatised to a great extent. An understanding of the basic mechanism of how motor actions are controlled and regulated is essential for effective formulation of motor learning process. For this purpose motor co-ordination is described briefly in the following paragraphs.

The control and regulation processes involved in motor co-ordination takes place at different levels of CNS. Some of these processes are conscious bound and some are not conscious bound. Hacker states that there are basically three levels with definite tasks of co-ordination: (i) intellectual level which is responsible for the general plan of action (ii) perceptive-cognitive level responsible for the motor action programme (iii) senso-motor level responsible for fine programming of the musculo-skeletal system. In motor co-ordination almost all parts of the nervous system are involved in an integrated manner.

As soon as the sportsman decides to tackle a certain task, a movement programme for accomplishing this is formed at all the CNS level which are to be involved. The forming of movement programme is considerably affected by motor memory and the perception of the prevailing situation. On the basis of this programming the required nerve impulses from the different levels go to the concerned muscles which respond by contracting as directed by the nervous system. With the action of the muscles the motor action starts. During the movement execution the various motor sense organs send the informations back to the nervous system. This information do not come from the working muscles and joint only. Information about the changed situation is also taken up by the nervous system through eyes etc.

Vast amount of information regarding movement, environment etc. is continuously reaching the nervous system. All this information is analysed and synthesised to arrive at conclusions regarding which way the movement is taking place. During information uptake and synthesis motor memory plays an important role as it helps in quick identification of signals, thereby helping in movement perception.

The actual picture of the movement being done is then compared with the movement programme according to which the movement should take place. This vital process is called comparison and takes place at all levels at which the movement programme was formed. The comparison allows to detect differences and discrepancies between the between the movement programme and the actual movement. On the basis of this correction impulses are sent to the muscles to correct the movement. In this manner, in a cyclic form, the movement execution is controlled and regulated till the end.

The above given description of motor co-ordination is a highly simplified description of a process which in reality is very complex. It is important to realise that the quality of motor co-ordination primarily depends on the effectiveness of three key mechanisms: programming, information uptake and synthesis and comparison. In technique training, therefore, we have to primarily aim at improving these three mechanisms. Programming and comparison, however, cannot be affected directly. This can be only done through information uptake and synthesis. Therefore, giving of timely and correct movement feedback forms the basis of technique training. With the improvement in these mechanisms qualitative/quantitative changes take place in the movement execution. Alongwith this there is progressive shifting of functions and responsibilities to lower levels of control i.e., automatisation.

AIMS OF TECHNIQUE IN SPORTS

In different sports different types of tasks have to be tackled. Therefore, technique aims at different things in different sports. The aim for which a technique is to be used is important for proper formulation of technique training as well as for correct assessment and evaluation of technique. There are numerous techniques which are used in sports. It is, therefore, impossible to discuss the aim of each and every technique. But in the following paragraphs general aim of technique in different groups of sports is discussed in brief.

(1) Endurance Sports

In these sports technique aims at ensuring high movement economy or reduction in energy expenditure. In endurance sports, normally one or two techniques have to be learnt. The movements to be learnt are usually simple and can be learnt in a short period. Examples: long distance running, cycling, rowing etc.

(2) Sprints

The aim of the technique in sprint events is to ensure high movement frequency with high generation of force for short duration. In these sports also one or two movements are to be learnt. These movements are usually simple but as these have to be done at high speed therefore the role of technique is moie as compared to endurance sports. Examples: track and field sprints.

(3) Power Sports

In these sports the technique aims at generating maximum force for imparting maximum speed to the body or to an implement. The movement must be performed with high co-ordination so that the force generated by different muscle groups/body parts can be effectively simulated to achieve the principal aim of technique. In these sports normally one or two technique have to be learnt. The movements are usually complex requiring much longer period of training for perfection. Examples: shotput, high-jump, weightlifting.

(4) Technical Sports

These sports are characterised by a large number of techniques with a very high degree of difficulty. The technique aims at executing a movement or combination of elements with high quality combined with grace and beauty. Because of several techniques, their high degree of difficulty and constant introduction of new and more difficult exercises the role of technique in these sports is very high. Examples: gymnastics, diving, figure skating.

(5) Regulatory Sports

In these sports technique aims at regulating a system consisting of sportsman and some equipment/ automobile/animal. The force for movement is external and the sportsman has to control and regulate it to get best results. Examples: sailing, motor sport, equestrian.

(6) Combat Sports

In combat sports the aim of technique is to execute

learned movements for tackling a task in consideration of the situation and tactics. In these sports technique is mostly used as a tool for effective tactical action. A large number of techniques are required to be learnt and mastered alongwith their variations. Examples: boxing, judo, wrestling.

(7) Team Games

The technique aims at tackling a task in consideration of situation, opponent, team mate and tactical aim. Like combat sports, in team games also technique is normally subordinated to tactical action. Large number of techniques and their variations have to be mastered with the aim of applying these under different conditions from tactical aspect.

It is difficult to determine the relative importance of factor technique/co-ordination in different sports. But the extent of importance of this factor in sports depends on the following three things:-

- Number of techniques.
- Degree of difficulty technique.
- Variable applicability of technique and its variations.

RATIONAL TECHNIQUE

A motor task can be solved or tackled by different techniques. But out of these one technique will be the most effective for a sportsman. This technique can be called the rational technique for him It will enable him to tackle the task with best results. A technique which is best or rational for one sportsman may not be the same for the other. The rationality of a technique cannot be determined by bio-mechanical analysis of the technique alone. More factors must be taken into consideration to decide whether a technique will suit a sportsman or not

All the external and internal factors which can have a significant effect on the motor procedure during action have to be carefully judged. Some of the important factors are:-

- Bio-mechanical factors.
- Energy expenditure.
- The role of ground, equipment, opponent etc. during the course of movement execution.
- Height, weight and body dimensions.
- Tactics.
- Psychological considerations.
- Motor habits.

Motor Learning

Learning is a fundamental activity in human life and is instrumental in the development of personality. Learning can take place through play or work. But in addition to these two, there is also learning activity which directly aims at acquiring knowledge and capabilities. Learning activity is basically of two types: mental learning and motor learning. Both are interrelated and interdependent. In sports, both the types of learning are common though motors learning takes precedence over mental learning.

Motor learning is the process of acquisition, refinement and stabilisation of motor actions. Motor learning is a conscious activity and includes elements of mental learning. The process of acquisition of motor skill is normally a long process. It is not a uniform and smooth process as the nature and rate of learning changes with the learning of a movement. Motor learning in adults is basically a restructuring of basic and fundamental movements which are learnt during childhood. Therefore, the beginning of motor learning of sports movements in reality is in early childhood.

The process of skill acquisition is essentially a process of refinement and stabilisation of motor co-ordination. This process, however, is influenced by a number of factors which if properly managed can make motor learning more effective and faster. Important among these are discussed below in brief:-

(1) Information Essential for Learning

The motor learning starts with the giving of information about the movement which has to be learnt. Moreover, information as feedback is also essential for effective control and regulation of motor action. A constant, timely and systematic flow of relevant information before, during and after the movement execution is obligatory for motor learning i.e., unity of mental and motor learning. The role of information in motor learning points to the fact that motor learning is a conscious activity in which for best effects the sportsman must be mentally and physically active. It also brings into focus the role of language and motor sense organs in motor learning.

(2) Training State

Motor learning is further dependent to a great extent on the training state. The level of conditional and co-ordinative abilities for effective motor learning is self explanatory. In addition, the already acquired skills have an important role to play in the learning of new skills. The already learnt skills can hinder or help motor learning through transfer or interference effect. Moreover, certain psychic factors like mental capabilities, personality traits etc. enable the sportsman to do motor learning in a much better way.

(3) Motivation and Interest

Without the required motivation and interest, the learning activity cannot be done effectively. It is, therefore, essential to cultivate positive interest and attitude for motor learning. On this basis the sportsman can be easily motivated to put in his best in the activity of motor learning. This enables him to do technique training with the required concentration and attention.

The above mentioned three factors which influence motor learning in reality represent three groups of factors. In addition to these factors, the social factors also have an effect on motor learning. Last, but not the least, the proper formulation and implementation of motor learning activity in the form of technique training can have a highly positive effect on motor learning.

The process of motor learning in sports training is normally a long process. As the nature of motor learning is not uniform throughout, therefore, different types of means and measures are adopted to affect it positively at different times. The motor learning process is normally divided into three phases described below:-

(i) Phase I

It begins with the introduction of a sportsperson to the movement/technique which he/she has to learn. It ends with the achievement of rough co-ordination i.e., the sportsperson is able to do the complete movement but with several errors and mistakes. Depending on the complexity of the movement this phase can be short or long. In the case of complex movements or technique e.g., pole-vault this phase can last several weeks. But in the case of simple techniques like dribbling in basketball it is much shorter.

(ii) Phase II

This phase starts with the acquisition of rough co-ordination and ends with the acquisition of fine co-ordination i.e., the sportsperson is able to do the movement nearly perfectly under normal conditions; but he/she is unable to do so under changed or difficult conditions. In this phase motor co-ordination undergoes vast changes. This phase is normally much longer than the earlier one and is also more hard on the sportsperson.

(iii) Phase III

This phase starts with the achievement of fine co-ordination and ends with the mastery of the technique. As a sportsperson cannot master a technique cent percent, therefore, this phase never ends. Moreover several factors like growth, periodisation, change in technique model etc. keep affecting the skill level negatively and as a result the technique training in the third phase never ends. Mastery of technique denotes the ability of the sportsman to do the movement nearly perfectly under all types of conditions: normal, changed or difficult.

The division of the motor learning process is arbitrary because, in reality, it runs unbroken and continuously. But as this process is not uniform in nature, throughout, therefore, it is divided into three phases for the purpose of understanding it and for deriving guidelines for effective formulation of technique training in the different phases of motor learning.

TECHNIQUE TRAINING IN THE FIRST PHASE

The aim of technique training in the first phases of skill acquisition is to achieve rough co-ordination i.e., to enable the sportsman to do the complete movement, under easier conditions. The movement has several errors and mistakes but effort should not be to achieve perfect movement but a complete, though largely imperfect movement.

The control and regulation processes in the first phase are too inadequate to allow perfect movement execution. The movement programming is not complete. It mainly consists of a visual image of the movement formed by seeing the demonstrations and through verbal explanations. It lacks kinesthetic elements of programming. Moreover, the movement programming does not include all the details of the movement. Therefore, to start with the programming is inadequate and incomplete.

Because of imperfect programming, the motor commands to the muscles are imperfect. Moreover, there is irradiation of excitation among the motor centres which leads to innervation of muscles not needed for the movement. This results in undue tension in the body in general. As in programming the kinesthetic elements which pertain to control and regulation of muscle actions with the required tension and sequence are largely absent, therefore, this function has to be performed by the higher centres which are ill equipped for this task. The result is imperfect movement with conscious control by higher centres.

Information uptake and synthesis is also inadequate for the task. Foremost short coming is the lack of awareness and utilisation of information coming from the kinesthetic, tactile and vestibular sense organs. Sportsman, due to this reason depends heavily on his optical sense and verbal information from outside for feedback about the movement. He lacks the 'feel of the movement'. Short-comings in the motor memory because of lack of required experience seriously hamper the process of information synthesis and movement perception. All these things lead to poor feedback about the movement.

The process of comparison which forms the basis of movement correction cannot take place effectively because of poor programming, unsatisfactory feedback and inadequate motor memory. The result is that the sportsman normally does not become aware of movement errors himself and hence cannot correct these.

The poor state of motor co-ordination in the first phase finds expression in poor movement execution. When one looks at the movement execution, one can notice several draw backs in it. Some of the important drawbacks which characterise rough coordination are given below:-

1. The movements are usually tense and cramped. The undue muscle tension, however, enables the sportsman to do the movement by ruling out movement of other body parts. But muscles tension also ensures more energy expenditure and faster onset of fatigue.
2. The movement execution lacks proper rhythm. The application of force is incorrect and is either too much or too less. This makes the movement unrhythmic, jerky and edgy.
3. Because of wrong force application the movement flow is not smooth. There are sudden changes in the speed of movement significantly lowering the movement flow and continuity.
4. The sportsman is unable to meaningfully the movements of different body parts i.e., coupling of movements. This results in undue wastages of force generated by various body parts as it cannot be added to the force generated by other body parts.
5. The movement amplitude is either too less or too much. Generally, because of undue muscle tension and body rigidity, the movement amplitude is lesser than required. This results in ineffective force generation.
6. The movement execution is highly inconsistent. Each repetition of the movement differs significantly from the previous one.

7. There is low movement accuracy and precision.

IMPLICATIONS FOR TECHNIQUE TRAINING

On the basis of the nature of motor co-ordination in the first phase of skill acquisition, the following suggestions are presented for effective formulation and implementation of technique training in the first phase.

1. Analysis of the Present State

Technique training is a long term process, therefore, before its start a general strategy or plan of technique training for all the three phases must be worked out. For this purpose first the present state of the sportsman must be analysed. Among other things, it is important to find out the label of co-ordinative and conditional abilities, the technical skills learnt in the past, motor experience, motivation, interest and other mental and psychological qualities and traits which are important for learning the intended movement. If it is needed then effort should be made to improve certain things e.g., conditional or co-ordinative abilities, motivation etc., without which technique training cannot be effectively started.

Special stress should be laid on improving the motivation and interest of the sportsman since without these technique training is not possible. This can be done by different means: demonstrations, explanations, discussions etc. The sportsman must be convinced about the importance of the technique to be learnt.

On the basis of the analysis of the present state, the teaching procedure, including teaching steps/stages, sequence of exercise to be use, means and methods to be followed etc., should be planned.

2. Practice Under Easier and Favourable Conditions

In the first phase, as a rule, technique training

should be done under easier and favourable conditions of learning. The movement execution can be made easier by adopting several means: breaking the movement into parts; by practising with lighter/smaller equipment; by doing the movement at a slower speed, by giving external help and so on. By favourable conditions were also mean technique training should be done in an atmosphere in which a sportsman can practise without any external disturbance or discomfort. Practise under conditions of fatigue should be avoided.

Stress should be laid on enabling the sportsman to do the movement optimum number of times, because only by doing the movement he will learn it. Therefore, it is important that sportsman is enabled to get a feeling of the complete movement as quickly as possible.

3. Development of Movement Concept

Movement concept or movement image is a vital part of movement programming which forms the basis of movement execution. Therefore, a lot of effort should be made to enable a sportsman to have a clear movement concept of the technique which he is to learn. In the first phase all the details of movement concept should not be given. Only that much is needed which can be grasped by the sportsman. Moreover, the stress should be on the visual aspect of the movement and not on the dynamic and temporal. Development of movement concept should be mainly achieved through demonstrations, explanations, by showing pictures, diagrams, etc. The basic rhythm of the movement, however, should be stressed right from the beginning of technique training.

4. Less Stress on Kinesthetic Perception

In the beginning of motor learning a sportsman cannot consciously discriminate between the informations coming from his kinesthetic, vestibular and tactile sense organs. This is because of the lack of requisite movement experience as well as due to the absence of link between these sensations and his consciousness. Therefore, during practice less stress should be laid on this information i.e., kinesthetic perception. On the contrary, more stress should be laid on the visual and verbal information. Lack of discrimination of kinesthetic perception, however, does not mean that the sportsman cannot feel the movement. He can feel the movement but he is unable to determine the quantitative and qualitative aspect of the movement through kinesthetic perception. He should be asked to consciously feel the movement but should not be asked to correct or refine the movement on its basis.

5. Less Correction

In the first phase of skill acquisition, too much stress on movement correction is not advisable. This is because of two main reasons. *Firstly,* he is not in a position to have a good movement perception and hence is unable to effectively correct his movement. *Secondly,* because the aim of technique training is rough co-ordination and not fine co-ordination. Movement correction should be limited to major and basic errors in the main phase of the movement. Alongwith correction is a good amount of encouragement should also be given to the sportsman. This should take place in the form of pointing out the progress he has made in learning the technique. Encouragement in this sense is a positive means for further refinement and stabilisation of movement concept.

6. Competitions

Formal competitions during the first phase of skill acquisition should be avoided because of poor level of motor co-ordination and also because of higher chances of stabilisation of incorrect control and regulation process under high psychic stress. But in team and combat sports informal competitions, with changed rules etc., can be used with positive effect on motor learning as these afford opportunity to sportsmen for variable applicability of the technique being learnt.

TECHNIQUE TRAINING IN THE SECOND PHASE

The second phase of technique training begins with the achievement of rough co-ordination and ends with the acquisition of fine co-ordination. The second phase is characterised by high training volume, increased amount of movement correction and erratic progress in motor learning. All these factors tend to make technique training very stressful and uninteresting for the sportsman resulting in loss of interest motivation and decrease in the quality of learning activity.

In the second phase the motor learning is not smooth. It is characterised by phases of stagnation. These are the phases in which, inspite of continuing technique training, no significant improvement takes place. There can even be deterioration. But after these phases of stagnation there is normally a sudden increase in performance. It may also happen if during stagnation the technique training is stopped for some training session. It seems that during stagnation phase the further refinement of motor co-ordination continues though it does not find any expression in the movement execution till it reaches a certain level.

By the end of second phase motor co-ordination reaches a satisfactory level for good movement execution under normal conditions. The movement programming is to a great extent complete and adequate. It has both the gross programming and the fine programming. The movement programming therefore, takes place at all the level of motor control. It includes elements of anticipation also e.g., goal and situation anticipation. The sportsman is in a position to imagine the movement in great detail.

The information uptake and synthesis improve to a considerable extent by the end of second phase. Due to increased amount of experience of the movement the sportsman is now able to discriminate with high degree of accuracy the information about movement coming from kinesthetic, vestibular and tactile sense organs. He learns to associate these with verbal signals and hence is able to better express his movement feeling. He is also better able to correctly grasp the verbal information given from outside. Because of the increased role of movement perception, the information uptake and synthesis take place with higher speed and accuracy. The role of visual and acoustic sense organs for motor co-ordination, as a result, progressively decreases. As a consequence of all these changes, a sportsman becomes highly aware of qualitative and quantitative aspect of the movement during the movement execution.

The process of comparison, as a result of better programming and information uptake and synthesis, takes place in a highly effective manner, with high speed and accuracy. This holds true for all levels at which programming and comparison take place. All the concerned levels do the comparison as per their role and due to this the total comparison is characterised by a high degree of differentiation accompanied with high speed and accuracy. As a result even minor deviations from the original programming are quickly detected and corresponding corrections take place.

The above described level of motor co-ordination is valid only when the movement is done under normal conditions. The motor co-ordination is not yet properly stabilised and as a result if the movement is done under different or difficult conditions the motor co-ordination is unable to cope with the demands, with the result that the movement execution is done with errors and mistakes.

A good level of motor co-ordination achieved by the end of the second phase of technique training finds expression in good quality of movement execution. The important characteristics or qualities of this are presented below in brief:-

1. The movement is done without undue muscle tension. This is made possible by the contraction of only the concerned muscles. Hence the movement is done in a relaxed manner only with the required force and speed.

2. The movement is now done with the required rhythm.

3. The sportsman is able to effectively combine the movements of different body parts. This enables the sportsman to do the movement with higher force and speed if it is so desired.

4. Movement execution is characterised by good movement flow. The jerky movements and erratic changes in movement speed are no longer there.

5. The movement amplitude is optimum. This is specially true in the preparatory movements for the main phase e.g., preliminary swings in discuss throw.

6. The movement is now characterised by a high degree of accuracy and precision.

7. There is increased degree of movement consistency. The fluctuations in movement quality from one repetition to another are reduced to a great extent. In other words, there is a high degree of constancy of movement parameters as well as of movement result.

IMPLICATIONS FOR TECHNIQUE TRAINING

1. Help and Encouragement

As pointed out earlier, the motor learning in second phase is not smooth. It is characterised by phases of stagnation. Besides, it involves high amount of movement correction, high training, volume and high level of concentration and attention. All these things tend to make motor learning stressful and frustrating for the sportsman. Unless the coach adopts certain means for constant encouragement, help and motivation the sportsman can gradually loose interest and motivation for technique training.

2. High Volume of Technique Training

The volume of technique training in second phase is much more than in the first phase. This means higher number of repetitions in a training session. The technique training, therefore, should be carefully planned and organised so as to enable the sportsman to do the needed number of repetitions with proper attention and concentration.

3. High Concentration and Attention

The technique training in second phase aims at fine co-ordination and as a result there is increased amount of movement correction and increased stress on movement perception and conscious execution of movement. Therefore, each repetition of movement must be done with a high degree of concentration and attention. In a systematic manner the sportsman must direct his attention and concentration to different parts, details and aspect of movement execution. He should also strive to consciously perceive and understand the movement sensations.

4. Practise Under Normal Conditions

As a rule the movement should be practised under normal and standard conditions. But this rule may have to be modified in sports like team games and combat sports. In these sports, because of the nature of sports and also because of subordination of technique to tactics, the technique training in second phase has to be, to some extent, done under different changing conditions.

5. Refinement of Movement Concept

In the first phase only a gross movement concept is conveyed to the sportsmen. In the second phase the movement concept has to be further refined and enriched with more details. Now the movement concept should not be limited only to the visual aspect of the movement. It should be gradually extended and refined to include dynamic and spatial aspects of the movement. For this purpose, in addition to verbal explanations and instructions, the teacher should increasingly make use of other means by which the internal structure of the movement can be made clear to the sportsman e.g., use of graphs, diagrams, bio-mechanical procedures etc. Accurate and timely feedback is of high value in this regard.

Tasks of movement observation and description are valuable means for further refinement of movement concept. These tasks, however, should be carefully planned and the activity of the sportsman must be properly supported and guided to get the best results.

The use of language has a double to play in the development of movement concept. Firstly, it is used as a means for conveying the information. Secondly, it is used to build association between movement perception and awareness. The second function of language is the basis of making the sportsman conscious about movement perception, and thereby helping in fine programming. The effect of verbalisation of a technique, which takes place consciously or unconsciously to some extent in advanced sportsmen, depends on the link between language and movement sensations.

The development of movement concept runs parallel to the advancement in motor learning. The development of required conditional and coordinative abilities also runs parallel to motor learning process.

6. Stress on Kinesthetic Perception

The kinesthetic perception should be given high priority in the second phase. The sportsman must be enabled to correctly perceive it. The role of language in this regard has already been pointed out in the preceding point i.e., point No. 5. In addition to facilitate kinesthetic perception movement feedback should be used. The feedback during the movement or immediately after the movement execution is very helpful in this regard. To make the sportsman aware of kinesthetic sensations the movement can also be done with minor variations in speed, force etc. It helps the sportsman to differentiate between sensations he receives while doing the movement differently. The aim of improving kinesthetic perception should not be limited to mere awareness but it should extend to differentiation and precision in movement perception.

7. High Movement Correction

In the second phase the movement execution has to be continuously corrected till it is possible to execute the movement without error under normal conditions. All possible means and methods of movement correction should be used to achieve this target. But all this must be done in a systematic and organised manner. Major errors must be removed first. Moreover, at one time the stress should be laid only on one or two errors and not more.

8. Competitions

Sports in which technique is to be realised under standard and unchanging conditions competitions should be avoided during the second phase. In other sports in which technique is realised under constantly changing conditions the competitions are advisable. In these sports competitions, by the end of second phase, should be increasingly used as effective means of technique training as these allow for meaningful technical actions coupled with tactical aims.

TECHNIQUE TRAINING IN THE THIRD PHASE

The third phase of motor learning starts with the achievement of fine coordination and leads the sportsman to achieve mastery over the technique. Mastery of skills is considered to have been achieved when the sportsman is able to do the movement successfully under different and difficult conditions. It denotes the variable applicability of movement. The important criterion to judge skill mastery is the ability to do the movement correctly and effectively in competition.

The third phase of motor learning never ends. Complete mastery over the technique is never achieved, and as a result a sportsman has to continue training for this purpose. The continuity of technique training is also necessary to effectively maintain the level of skill acquired and to avoid deterioration due to discontinuity. In addition to this, there are other factors which can lead to deterioration in skill. Most common among these are the effects of periodisation, growth in height and weight and change in body proportions in childhood and adolescence, changes in rules and regulations of competition, introduction of new equipment, surface etc., necessitating relearning, introduction of new technique and so on. All this makes it imperative to continue technique training without any end in sight.

In the third phase motor co-ordination achieves a very high level of perfection. The movement execution is characterised by a high degree of automatisation. Movement programming is highly perfect. It takes place in a highly differentiated manner at all levels of CNS involved in motor co-ordination. There is a highly advanced fine programming containing the detailed programme of dynamic, temporal and spatial aspects of the movement. The programming is now combined with anticipation of goal, movement and situation. Programming is not limited to a single movement programme but it essentially includes several alternative programmes of the movement and its variations. At any moment during the movement execution the CNS can switch over to an alternate movement programme with ease and speed.

The muscle innervation is highly differentiated and accurate due to high level of movement programming. Different muscles are made to contract at the right time, with right force and speed and in correct sequence most appropriate for achieving the goal. The irradiation in motor centres is practically not there.

Information uptake and synthesis also achieve a very high level. Sportsman is acutely aware of the various sensations coming from different sense organs especially from the kinesthetic, vestibular and tactile sense organs. There is high level of differentiation, filtering and selection of information signals which takes place at high speed and with high accuracy. Sportsman, if he so wants, can attend to the minutest details during the course of the movement and even immediately after the movement. A high level of association between movement perception and language is a unique characteristic of the mastery of technique. Verbal description or mental imagination of the movement calls forth corresponding movement sensation. The control and regulation of the movement is now achieved through the internal circuit which is best equipped for this task. There is a vast store of motor experience in the memory which helps strongly in the information uptake and synthesis.

Because of the high level of programming and information uptake and synthesis the comparison of intended and actual movement takes place very fast and accurately. This enables anticipation of movement errors and corresponding movement correction which is difficult to be observed by another person. This results in smooth and graceful movements. Sportsman is in a position to perceive minute deviations from the intended movement programme. He also perceives the speed of deviation. This enables him to correct the movement with high speed and effectiveness.

A high level of motor co-ordination in the third phase of motor learning is characterised by several movement qualities mentioned below:-

1. The movement can be done with high degree of precision and accuracy.

2. There is a high degree of movement constancy. The important parameters of movement change very little from repetition to repetition e.g., speed and force values or indices.

3. There is also a high degree of movement consistency or result consistency. Irrespective of the changed conditions the sportsman is able to achieve fairly constant results.

4. The movement is also characterised by a high level of other qualities e.g., movement coupling, movement flow, movement rhythm etc.

5. The movement execution is accompanied by feelings of joy, pleasure and satisfaction. Sportsman

enjoys doing the movement which he can do with high results and with great ease and comfort.

IMPLICATION FOR TECHNIQUE TRAINING

The technique training in the third phase is continuation of the technique training in the second phase. There is only qualitative difference. In many respects it resembles the second phase e.g., help and encouragement, training volume, high concentration and attention, stress on kinesthetic perception and high amount of movement correction. In addition the following guidelines are given:-

1. Practise Under Difficult and Different Conditions

Mastery of skill can only be achieved by practising the movement under different and difficult conditions. The application of this principle takes place in two ways depending on the nature of sports.

(i) Standardised Sports

In these sports the technique is realised under more or less standard conditions e.g., in swimming, gymnastics, weightlifting, track and field. In these sports technique training should aim at stabilisation of movement execution under different difficult conditions. This is achieved mostly by practising the movement under higher psycho-physical load e.g.,

- Practising the movement with different rhythm, higher resistance, higher speed etc.
- Practising the movement under different external conditions e.g., ground, surface, weather conditions, changed ground dimensions etc.
- Practising the movement with minor changes in the movement execution.

- Practising the movement under higher psychic stress caused by competition, spectators etc.
- Practising the movement under conditions of fatigue.

(B) Non Standardised Sports

In these sports the technique is realised under constantly changing conditions e.g., team games, combat sports. In these sports technique training should aim at variable applicability of skill. The movement should be practised under considerably different conditions. The important possibilities are mentioned below:-

- Practising the different variations of technique.
- Practising the movement in combination with other movements.
- Practising the movement from tactical aspect.
- Practising the movement different partners and opponents.
- By changing the external conditions for movement practise e.g., size of ball or other equipment, difficult weather conditions, change in rules, change in ground dimensions.

2. Development of Movement Concept

The movement concept must be further developed in the third phase of technique training. All the aspects and details of movement execution need to be conveyed to the sportsman gradually and systematically. For this purpose one should not limit the movement concept only to diagrams or pictures of the movement. But it should extend to the kinetic and kinematic aspects of the movement. The effort should be directed to enable the sportsman to understand the internal structure of the movement.

Along with the refinement of the movement concept effort should be made to develop the required conditional and co-ordinative abilities still further.

3. Accurate and Precise Feedback

High amount of movement correction is an important characterstic of the third phase of technique training. For this purpose the sportsman must be given very accurate and precise feedback about the movement execution. For this the coach or teacher should not depend on his subjective judgement only. He should increasingly use various equipments and apparatus which can give accurate information about the movement execution e.g., video films, timing devices, cinematography, force platform etc. Quick and timely feedback is essential for achieving mastery of a skill.

4. Increased Use of Competitions

In the third phase competitions should be used as means of technique training. Competitions involve higher degree of psycho-physical demands and, therefore, help in skill acquisition under different and difficult conditions. Role of competitions for achieving stabilisation of movement execution as well as for variable applicability of learnt movement can hardly be exaggerated.

5. Ideo-motor Training

In the third phase because of highly strong link between language and movement perception ideo motor training can be used with positive results. Ideo-motor training, also called mental practise, is helpful for the precision and stabilisation of temporal and spatial aspects of movement execution.

Best results by ideo-motor training are achieved when it is combined with actual movement practise. Ideo-motor training has also proved to be effective for maintenance of skill during periods when technique cannot be done e.g., training break due to injury or illness.

Ideo-motor training is a complex psychological procedure and should be learnt under expert guidance before it can be effectively used by a sportsman independently.

RELEARNING

In sports, sometimes it becomes necessary to change the already learnt movement. This is called relearning. Relearning is basically restructuring of a skill to a lesser of greater extent. Relearning is normally more difficult than new learning because of high degree of interference of already learnt movement. It also does not always lead to good results. In sports, relearning becomes necessary due to any of the following two factors:-

- Introduction of a new and more effective variation of technique.
- Presence of a few or a large number of errors in the movement execution which have been automatised.

The necessity for learning a new variation of technique mostly arises due to introduction of new implement or equipment, introduction of new playing surface, or change in rules and regulations of competition. In technical sports like gymnastics, diving etc. there is a continuous change in the movements to increase their degree of difficulty, thereby necessitating new learning or relearning. In case of children and adolescents, rapid growth in height, weight or change in body proportions can lead to adoption of a new variation of technique.

In India relearning is a common problem faced by sportsmen due to automatisation of incorrect movement execution in the initial stages of training or due to non-availability of standard equipment/implements or playing surface.

The process of relearning according to Harre can be divided into the following four phases:-

I. Phase

The old variation of skill is highly dominant and strongly hinders the new variation. It is not possible to successfully execute the new variation.

II. Phase

The old variation is destroyed but the new variation has not yet been adequately learnt. There is still a strong interference.

III. Phase

The new variation is gradually acquired, but it is not yet stable and can be easily disturbed if the movement is done under different and stressful conditions. During competition or under stress the old variation asserts itself over the new one. The performance with the new variation is still less as compared with the performance with the old variation.

IV. Phase

The new variation achieves stability and reliability. The performance starts improving. But if care is not taken the old variation can again assert itself. In this phase mastery of new variation is achieved only after some tome.

Relearning is a long strenuous process and often does not yields desirable results. Regarding relearning following suggestions are made:-

1. It is best to avoid relearning, and it can be possible if the correct variation of technique is taught from the very beginning. It is helpful to teach a basic variation of technique in initial stages of training and on the basis of this in later stages the other variations can be learnt. It is also important not to go in for a high degree of automatisation of a technique in the initial stages as it will make relearning, if required, more difficult later on.
2. If relearning cannot be avoided it should be planned on a long term basis. During the process of relearning, competitions should be avoided. The old variation should not be used at all in training or in competition.
3. The process of relearning is very hard on the sportsman. For best results his full co-operation and willingness is required. To achieve this coach must convince the sportsman about the importance of relearning for his performance improvement. He should also constantly encourage and motivate the sportsman to ensure high level and volume of learning activity.
4. The process of relearning must be continuously controlled and regulated.
5. Ideo-motor training should be used as an additional means of technique training. It helps in checking interference and in facilitating positive transfer.

TRANSFER OF MOTOR LEARNING

Motor learning does not begin from a scratch. There is always some amount of co-ordination patterns existing which affect motor learning. In childhood, and also later on, we acquire certain basic and fundamental movements which serve as a base for learning other movements. According to Roleb the motor learning in later phases of life is essentially a reorganisation and restructuring of the basic movements learnt in childhood.

The already learnt movements or movement patterns can help or hinder the learning of new movements. This effect is called transfer of motor learning. When the transfer helps in learning a new movement it is called positive transfer of motor learning. But when it interferes or hinders new learning it is referred to as negative transfer or interference.

INTERFERENCE

In sports interference can take place in two forms or ways: (i) old skill or coordination pattern hindering the learning of new skill. Relearning falls into this category. (ii) a skill being learnt hindering the learning of another skill or vice versa.

Interference does not only take place when the movement to be learnt is similar to an already learnt movement. But it can also take place when the two movements are directly opposite to each other regarding the coordination mechanisms.

For an effective tackling of the problem of interference following things should be performed:-

1. Several movements should not be learnt simultaneously, especially those movements which are similar to each other.

2. Correct variation of technique should be learnt to avoid relearning at a later stage.

3. Interference is considerably reduced or totally stopped when the sportsman is able to adequately differentiate the movement programmes of the skills concerned. Therefore, the coach must adopt means and measures to clarify the movement

concepts of the movements. Ideo-motor training or mental practice can also be used effectively for this purpose.

POSITIVE TRANSFER

The positive transfer can take place in two ways (i) from an already learnt skill (ii) from a skill being learnt at the same time. The basis of positive transfer is the similarities between co-ordination mechanisms of the two skills. *Bernstein* found that for positive transfer the similarities between the senso-motor co-ordination of two skills is decisive and not the similarities in the external aspect of movement execution.

Motor learning process should be consciously planned and implemented to ensure maximum possible positive transfer. To achieve this the following steps should be taken:-

1. The movement should be learnt in a definite sequence. For this purpose the various exercises and technical skills should be hierarchically organised and systematised on the basis of the co-ordination mechanisms. On the basis of this system learning of a class of exercise/technical skills is faster because of the positive transfer from the exercises previously learnt. Such a systematisation of exercises laying down the sequence of learning of various exercises is highly desirable in all sports.

2. The development of required co-ordinative abilities is a necessary prerequisite for effective positive transfer as the development of co-ordinative abilities ensure generalisation and stabilisation of co-ordination mechanisms for a group of exercises or technical skills. E.g., balance ability for learning exercises depending primarily on balance. But care should be taken to develop

special co-ordinative abilities with specific exercises for best results.

3. The positive transfer is desirably affected by practising the movement with opposite side, hand or foot. Both sided practise has been found to have a positive effect on positive transfer.

METHODS OF TECHNIQUE TRAINING

Method of technique training essentially concern the regulation of the activity of the teacher and the taught for the purpose of enhancement of motor learning. There are three method of technique training. These are used in different forms in technique training.

(I) PRESENTATION METHOD

In this method the teacher is active and the student is physically passive but mentally receptive. The main task accomplished in this method is the presentation of information and knowledge about the movement to be learnt by the student. In sports the presentation method is used in three forms which are described below:-

(A) Demonstration

Demonstration of the technique to be learnt is normally one of the first steps is technique training. The complete movement may be demonstrated by the teacher or some student. Technique is also demonstrated through films, video, diagrams etc. For the proper utilisation of demonstration in technique following suggestions are given:-

1. Correct variation of technique must be selected for demonstration. The demonstration of this technique should be correct otherwise the students will form a wrong movement concept. The movement should be demonstrated several times

during the practice if needed. The demonstration by actually doing the movement before the students must be further supplemented by showing the movement in picture, figures etc. to clarify important aspects of the technique. Showing films or video recording of the movement execution of famous sportsmen serves the additional purpose of creating positive motives and interests for learning the concerned technique.

2. The technique to be demonstrated should be suitably modified to correspond with the level of the students. Highly advanced version of technique is normally beyond the ability of children and beginners to realise it in their movements.

3. During demonstration observation tasks should be set for the students so that they can properly and systematically observe the important and finer points of technique.

4. Demonstration can be done in slow movement to effectively illustrate the fast and complex phases of movement. For the sake of clarification important phases, therefore, should be 'stretched' or even done exaggeratedly.

5. To facilitate observation, the class formation should be correct. All students should be able to clearly see the complete movement. Demonstration should also be done at an optimum distance from the students. If needed, the demonstration should be done in such a way that the students can observe the movement from different angles e.g., front, back, side or from above.

6. Demonstration and explanation normally should not be given simultaneously especially to the beginners. For best results the demonstration and explanation should be in a definite sequence. But while demonstrating the movement in slow motion

or when using films, figures etc. explanation and demonstration can be given simultaneously.

(B) Lecture

In sports lectures are not commonly used on the field during movement practise. These are mainly used in theory sessions. The contents and method of lecture must correspond to the level of the students. It must ensure optimum attention and receptiveness on the part of the students. Long lectures containing difficult words and ideas should be avoided. For the purpose of technique training the lectures must depend considerably on the use of audio-visual aids.

(C) Explanation

Explanation consists of a few lines, sentences or hints. An explanation should never become a lecture. Explanation in technique training should be used for making the movement concept clear, for correction and for motivation and encouragement. It is also used to compare the two movements as well as to generalise the important aspects of the movement. For effective explanation in technique training following suggestions are offered:-

1. It should be short and simple containing only the information needed for the time being. It should last for a few seconds only.

2. In an explanation simple language should be used which can be understood by the students. The extent to which difficult scientific words and concepts should be used depends on the knowledge and mental maturity of the students. They should be prepared for this gradually through separate theoretical sessions.

3. Explanation should be used to enable the students to learn and internalise standard terms and expressions and to associate these with the actual sensations they receive during the movement execution. The use of correct and effective examples is of immense value in this regard. It also helps to avoid interference and to facilitate positive transfer.

4. In an explanation the vital and crucial aspects of movement execution should be repeatedly stressed.

5. Explanation should be given in a loud and clear voice with a tone which is optimistic and motivating. Explanation should never be depressing and demoralising.

II. CO-OPERATIVE METHOD

In co-operative method the student and teacher are both active. The most common variation of co-operative method is movement practise. In movement practice the student does the movement for optimum number of times while the teacher is constantly supervising, helping and correcting him. There is a high degree of interaction between them, mental as well as physical. There is a constant flow of information between the two.

(A) Movement Practise

The manner in which the movement should be practised in the three phases of motor learning has already been discussed. Here some more helpful suggestions are given:-

- The movement to be learnt should be done, with the required concentration and attention, for optimum number of times. As the absence of fatigue is a necessary prerequisite for motor learning therefore, repetitions should be done in such manner that fatigue does not accumulate to a significant extent. It is preferable to arrange the repetitions in series with pauses of optimum recovery in between. During the pauses exercises should be done to accelerate recovery as well as for removing mental tension.

- The pauses should be utilised to give additional information and hints about the movement, for giving demonstrations and also for motivating and encouraging the students.
- Each repetition of the movement should be done with the aim of doing the movement in a better way i.e., repetition without repetition.
- Stress should be laid on conscious movement perception. Use of language during movement execution is very helpful in this regard. To start with it should be done loudly but progressively with lower voice till it becomes just a mental activity.
- In case of complex movements, the movement should be broken into parts for the purpose of learning. Later on with the advancement in learning the parts should be gradually combined till practice with the complete movement is possible.

During movement practise certain more measures are adopted. Due to the importance of these measures for the effectiveness of movement practise these are discussed below in more detail.

HELP AND SAFETY

Measures for providing necessary help or assistance or ensuring safety of the sportsman are not needed for learning of all type of movements. But in some sports, due to the nature of movement or technique these measure have to be adopted.

Help in the form of physical support or assistance should be given in cases where the students cannot do the movement on their own e.g., swimming, pole-vault, gymnastics etc. External help or assistance enables the students to get a feeling of the complete movement, thereby enabling better movement concepts. It is also motivating to the student when they are helped to do the complete movement. The external help however should be provided only to that extent to which it is required. It should not lead to habit formation, thereby hindering the learning process. Gradually and progressively, the external help should be reduced till it is no more required by the students.

Safety measures have to be adopted during movement practise when there is a risk of injury or mishap. The safety measures should be adopted, if the situation so warrants, even if the student does not feel the necessity of it. On the other hand these have to be adopted if the student thinks he can get injured though the situation does not warrants this. Use of protective equipment like pads, mattresses etc., are commonly used. Much more important is, however, the physical presence of the coach or helpers to give a feeling of safety to the student and to induce confidence in him.

HINTS AND IMPULSES

It is quite common during movement practice to remind the student about various aspects of movement execution which have been already explained to him. This is done through hints and impulses. Hints are short phrases or incomplete short sentences which are loudly said by the coach to the student while he is doing the movement e.g. head up; look forward, trunk straight, high knee action etc. The hints help the student to correct the movement during the movement execution.

Impulses are special sounds or words to draw the attention of the student about the application of force during definite phases of movement execution. There are, for example, such words or signalled; Now! Hup! Ya! Go! Jump! etc. These help to do the movement with correct rhythm. Impulses can also be given in forms of counts. The impulses, to be effective, must be given at the right time otherwise these tend to disturb the motor co-ordination. As a rule impulses should be given fraction of a second before the required application of force. It is always better if the impulses are preceded by some sort of a sound so that the student prepares himself for the coming impulse and can effectively make use of it.

ENCOURAGEMENT AND CORRECTION

Encouragement during movement practice is as important as correction. Encouragement means informing the student to what extent and in which respects he has made progress. On the one hand it helps in further development of movement concept. On the other hand it helps in motivating the student, thereby positively affecting the learning activity. Encouragement and correction, therefore, should be judiciously combined and used during movement practice.

Correction is the process of removing errors in the movement execution. Error should be understood to be a deviation in the movement execution from the technique model. Movement correction is of central importance in technique training. Therefore, it needs to be discussed here from three practical aspects: Location, causes, and methods of correction.

LOCATION OF ERROR

It is always easy to locate error. This is the job of the coach or the teacher. The most important precondition for error detection is the movement concept of the teacher/coach himself. It must be correct and clear. The next important prerequisite is the knowledge and clarity about the various aspects of the movement execution of the student. If needed the teacher should make use of necessary equipments and apparatus to exactly grasp the movement execution of the student. A detailed and systematic comparison of the movement execution with the movement concept of the teacher should from the basis for the location of error. In order to be precise and accurate in error detection the coach or teacher should consider several repetitions of the movement and that too from different angles and aspects. The ability to perceive the rhythm of the student's movement is usually very helpful for the teacher to determine if there is some thing wrong in the movement execution. It is advisable for the coach to adopt a scientific and systematic procedure for error detection. He should not depend on his subjective observation only.

CAUSES OF ERRORS

There are a number of reasons which, separately on in combination, lead to errors in movement execution. Some of the common causes are listed below:-

- Wrong or incomplete movement concept.
- Lack of awareness about the movement execution.
- Poor level of required conditional and co-ordinative abilities.
- Anatomical or physical factors.
- Incorrect coupling of head movement with the movement of the other body parts.
- Interference or negative transfer of motor learning by already learnt movement.
- Emotional factors e.g., fear, anxiety, nervousness etc.

- Inadequate motivation, attention and concentration.
- Fatigue, injury, stiffness etc.

It is of utmost importance to detect the real cause of movement error as this will determine the means and methods of correction as well as their effectiveness. In detecting the cause or causes of errors the coach should not limit his effort to just external symptoms of the cause or causes of error. He must probe deeper.

METHODS OF ERROR CORRECTION

There are two methods of error correction which are discussed below:-

Direct Method

In this method the error is explained to the student and effort is made to correct it in the following ways:-

- By explaining to the student about the negative effect of the error on his performance and by convincing and encouraging him to correct it.
- By making him aware of the error by demonstrating the wrong and the correct movement. An effective use of audio-visual aids should be made for this purpose.
- By making him aware of the error by demonstrating it in an exaggerated manner.
- By trying to direct his attention towards the real cause or causes of the error, and thereby helping him to over come it.

Indirect Method

In this method the sportsman is not informed about the error. To remove the error, however, appropriate measures are adopted.

1. The cause or the causes of the error are removed e.g., by removing fear, anxiety, improving the necessary conditional and co-ordinative abilities.
2. Practising the movement under easier conditions to remove the error.
3. Changing the external conditions e.g., surface, equipment, partner etc.
4. Setting additional tasks during the movement execution.
5. Directing the student to do the movement in contrast to the error or to do it exaggeratedly.
6. Reverting back to the earlier stage of learning.
7. Using means for providing additional objective information.

The actual process of movement correction should be well planned and organised on the long term basis. For effective movement correction the following suggestions are given:-

1. Location of errors and determination of their causes should be correct.
2. Movement correction should be started at right time. An automatised error is very difficult to remove.
3. Only one error should be corrected at one time. Several errors should be corrected one after the other.
4. Major errors, especially in the main phase of movement execution, should be corrected first.
5. Correction and encouragement must run parallel to each other.
6. Both the direct and indirect methods should be used in harmony for error correction.
7. The ability of the sportsman to observe errors and correct these should be systematically developed.

8. The group correction and individual correction should be done in appropriate proportion.
9. After the use of a corrective measure the sportsman should be made to do the movement a few times in order to remove the error.

(B) Discussion

This is the second variation of co-operative method of technique training. The discussions between the teacher and the taught are important means of education. Discussions for the purpose of positively affecting the motor learning must aim at the following:-

- For further clarification and refinement of the movement concept. Through questions and answers, the teacher should also try to get the feedback from the students to find out the quality and content of the movement concept they have formed.
- For making the students aware about the errors, the causes of these errors and the possibilities of error correction.
- For providing encouragement to the students and for motivating them for putting in more effort for motor learning.
- For getting a feedback from the students about the effect of means and methods being used for motor learning.

The discussions should be planned and interestingly organised by stimulating the students to actively participate in it. A discussion should take the form of a free and interesting dialogue between the teacher and the students. Discussion can be held at any time. After a technique training session a short discussion of 10-15 minutes is always advisable.

Task Method

Task method serves important purposes in sports training. It is primarily effective as a method of education. In technique training it is normally used as an additional method for stabilising the learnt movement and to enable the student to work independently for gaining better knowledge and insight about the movement being learnt.

In the task method the teacher gives different types of tasks to the students which they must fulfil on their own. From this angles the teacher is passive and the students are active. But the task method involves use of presentation method for giving and explaining the task to the students. Moreover, it also involves the helping and guiding role of the teacher to enable the students to complete the task successfully. For Effective use of the task method, the following points must be kept in mind:-

1. The necessary prerequisites for the effective use of the task method are (a) ability of the students to work on their own (b) motivation and interest of the students. The students should be gradually and systematically developed to tackle the tasks independently.
2. Task must be presented clearly and precisely alongwith the importance of tackling the task.
3. The teacher must provide the necessary help and guidance to the students in tackling the task effectively with the desired results.
4. The accomplishment of each task must be properly asscssed and evaluated by the teacher and results and suggestions convincingly conveyed to the students.

In technique training, most commonly, the following types of tasks are given to the students:-

- Practice task
- Performance task
- Study task
- Observation task
- Assessment task

TEACHING PROCEDURES

In technique training the three methods of technique training are used in combination. When these methods are used in a definite combination it is called a teaching procedure. The following two teaching procedures are commonly used in technique training:-

I. Deductive Teaching Procedure

In this procedure the methods of teaching are arranged as follows:- Presentation methods, co-operative method and task method. This is the most commonly used teaching procedure. It is more effective, less time consuming and also simpler to plan and organise.

II. Inductive Teaching Procedure

This procedure is used less commonly. In this procedure the methods are arranged in the following sequence:- Task method, presentation method and co-operative method. This method is more time consuming and requires a lot of effort and experience on the part of the teacher to effectively plan and organise it. But on the other hand this method is good for increasing motivation and self activity of the students. Children especially enjoy learning by this teaching procedure.

CHAPTER - 7

THE TRAINING ROOM

One of the most significant developments in the medical supervision of athletes has been the expansion of facilities in the training room. Once it was a room furnished sparely with a long treatment table, adhesive-tape wall rack and antiseptic solutions, distinguished by a pervasive odour of oil of wintergreen.

Now it is replete with modern equipment and supplies, and in some instance rivals hospital emergency-room set-ups. Formerly, trainers massaged the athlete, did some taping, and rendered some crude first aid. Presently, the most scientific methods of conditioning, training, and emergency care are given by highly qualified trainers under the direct supervision of the team physician. The training room is usually the first medical facility to receive the injured or ill athlete. The physician, coach, trainer, and athlete should have an intense interest in this facility, which should be provided with the best equipment.

PLANNING A TRAINING ROOM

Location

Modern architectural designs for sports stadiums and buildings, high school and college gymnasiums make adequate provision for training and first-aid room facilities. The training-room area is an important component of the total architectural sports design, which also includes the playing area, squad locker room, shower and toilet facilities, and coaches' quarters. Unfortunately, most athletic areas currently in use were not designed to include training-room facilities, so the trainer must find appropriate space. Because he must start somewhere, the trainer modifies and rearrange the available space to suit his needs.

The following basic prerequisites may serve as a guide in locating a training room:

1. Convenient location, accessible to both outdoor and indoor playing areas.
2. Adjacent to but separate from the team dressing room.
3. Has facilities for central heating, hot and cold water, adequate lighting, electrical outlets, and ventilation.
4. Allows the maintenance of scrupulous cleanliness.
5. Provides adequate storage space.

Determination of Size

The ideal training room allows 3 feet of working space around each piece of equipment. A minimal room size of 15 × 20 feet is recommended for high schools, although smaller rooms have proven adequate. Rooms measuring 20 × 22 feet or larger are recommended for colleges and universities. The following guidelines may be used in determining the size of the training room:

1. The number of athletes to be accommodated.
2. The type and quantity of equipment and supplies that can be purchased or improvised within the existing budget.

Efficient Utilization of Space

Proper utilization of space for the equipment and supplies aids the trainer in rendering maximal service.

1. Place the training tables at the front of the training room; this discourages excessive traffic.
2. Locate the work tables and therapy equipment near electrical outlets. Establish good overhead lighting.
3. Keep sensitive electrical instruments against the wall and away from the flow of traffic.
4. Equipment should not be located in drafty areas.
5. Locate the training room cabinets near the taping and treatment tables.
6. If the room is small, space can be conserved by hanging cabinets and shelves on the wall. Also, taping tables may be shorter than treatment tables.
7. Place the wash-up and whirlpool areas toward the back of the room, out of the way of normal traffic.
8. Keep whirlpool baths near wall outlets and drains.

EQUIPPING THE TRAINING ROOM

A training-room budget depends upon many factors, including the following:

1. Whether the team is amateur, semiprofessional, or professional.
2. Whether it is a high school, college, or university team.
   - (i) Geographic location.
   - (ii) Role of the Department of Athletics in the total educational program.

3. The space, equipment, and supplies that are available.
4. The quality of the coaching staff and the awareness of its members of the importance of the training room.

Obviously, the training room of a professional team with the most modern and sophisticated medical and physical therapy equipment and supplies will bear little resemblance to a training room set-up in a college or even a large university, because their budgets are thousands of rupees apart. Some high schools and college have to build and improvise part of their equipment. Other small schools might depend on donated equipment from neighbouring and patronizing colleges and universities. Many high school teams have no training-room facilities.

Inasmuch as training-room set-ups vary with the size of the budget, only general guidelines can be stated. The most important allocation must be for a qualified trainer with an excellent pair of hands who is also knowledgeable in the techniques of physical therapy. Depending on the budget, the trainer must select the equipment and supplies that will enable him to render the best care to the athlete.

The initial outlay required to establish a training room may be large, but much of the equipment purchased will have a long life expectancy. Later, most of the expense is incurred for expendable items, such as medications and supplies.

Each training room must have a treatment table, physical-therapy equipment for heat application, and a first-aid dressing cart on casters that contains sufficient instruments, medications, and dressing supplies to provide a sterile dressing for an injured part. A refrigerator with a freezer cc ıpartment for biologic supplies and ice cubes and a file cabinet are necessary.

The treatment table is the most important piece of training room equipment because it can be used for a variety of purposes. This table may be use for examining, treating, taping, and massaging athletes.

The athlete may use this table himself to exercise joints and muscles, as well as for resting from the day's activities. Because of its multipurpose functions and its reasonable price, the treatment table should be the first piece of equipment installed in the training room. One long table per 20 athletes is sufficient. The dimensions recommended for a table are 78 inches long, 24 inches wide, and 30 inches high; however, individual trainers may prefer other sizes. It is wise to get a table with which the trainer is familiar and with which he functions best. When the budget is increased, additional, shorter-sized table may be installed primarily for taping.

The ability of heat to improve circulation and aid resorption of swelling, induration and relief of pain in traumatized soft tissues of the musculo-skeletal system by increasing tissue metabolism is well-documented. This modality is enhanced when local swelling is first minimized by compression dressings, ice packs, and elevation of the injured part when feasible. Therapeutic heat for training room purposes may be produced by various types of apparatuses. In each instance, the attending physician prescribes the type and amount of heat therapy to be used.

Infrared and microwave units are not recommended for training room use. There is no proof that these apparatuses produce any better results than other forms of heat therapy. The proper application of these devices demands the experience and knowledge of a trainer skilled in their use and the ease with which they may be self-administered makes them, in our opinion, undesirable in a training room. Ultrasound units should not be placed in a training room unless the trainer is thoroughly qualified and experienced in the use of such machines. Ultrasound therapy must never be self-administered by an athlete.

A whirlpool bath is an excellent therapeutic device that also affords psychological benefits in the treatment of an injured athlete. If funds are available, a large whirlpool bath should be purchased, to enable treatment of several athletes at one time. If there is no monetary provision for a whirlpool bath, substitutes can be improvised.

From the athletes' point of view, the ultimate in training-room facilities is the sauna bath. This is quite popular but is found mainly at the collegiate and professional levels. The trainer also has available other therapeutic modalities outside the training room but within the school environs that can be used effectively to rehabilitate the injured athlete. For instance, a swimming pool is excellent for providing exercises by eliminating the effects of gravity. Gymnastic equipment, such as stall bars, are useful for stretching. The presence of a nearby weight room with free barbells, isotonic and isokinetic equipment can be used to increase the strength, power, and endurance of an injured part as well as non-injured parts of the body. This equipment is equally useful in reaching and maintaining condition.

When a budget is particularly limited, donations of training-room equipment and supplies should be actively solicited. Potential contributors of such items include doctors, hospitals, pharmaceutical houses, and manufacturers of physical-therapy equipment. As soon as the budget is expanded, we recommend purchasing new equipment to replace second-hand items. Some items, particularly storage units, work tables, benches, and stools, may be built in school or home workshops, allowing considerable savings. Also, government surplus materials may be bought at discount. Access to complicated and expensive equipment often results in the fitting of the athlete to the equipment, rather than *vice versa*.

More modern and sophisticated equipment and supplies should be purchased as the demand arises and the budget allows. However, high-school training rooms have no need for expensive paraffin bath units, electrical muscle stimulators, or progressive resistive exercise units. Moreover, the experience, training, and qualifications of the trainer bear a direct relationship to the type and amount of equipment ordered and used in the training room. A trainer must beg, borrow, build, and improvise to make his work area the most complete, efficient, and inviting place for the conditioning and training of athletes. The success or failure of a training room is mainly the trainer's responsibility.

Each trainer must carry a trainer's kit at all practice sessions and scheduled contests. This kit should contain sufficient training-room equipment, medication, and supplies to enable him to cope with emergency situations that may occur with athletes in competition. It must be inclusive, practical, yet not bulky. Each coach and trainer may have favourite supplies, especially for such sports as gymnastics, wrestling, boxing, and swimming.

RATIONALE AND USE OF THERMOTHERAPY EQUIPMENT IN THE TRAINING ROOM

Thermotherapy equipment being considered for purchase for use in a training room should satisfy many of the following prerequisites:

1. Relieves pain.
2. Stimulates circulation.
3. Relaxes muscle spasm.
4. Helps soften adhesion.

5. Aids absorption of waste products.
6. Offers some psychological benefit in its application.
7. Its projected use warrants the expenditure.

Hydrotherapy

Hydrotherapy has become the most popular and effective modality in the treatment of clinical conditions encountered in athletes. Hydrotherapy techniques may range from the simple application of a warm, moist towel for a contusion to a sauna bath for generalized muscle soreness. Other forms of hydrotherapy include immersion baths, with water temperatures ranging from lukewarm to hot, sitz baths, contrast baths, salt glows, steam cabinets, whirlpool baths, and hot packs.

Hot Packs

Every training room should have moist heat-pack equipment, because it is the simplest and most economical way to apply moist heat for the relief of pain and muscle spasm. The packs are contoured to fit different parts of the body and are especially good for necks, shoulders, backs, and the musculature of the arms and legs. Wrapping the hot pack in a heavy Turkish towel before applying it diminishes the risk of injuring the skin. The heat penetrates 3 cm, compared to the 0.1 cm penetration of infrared heat. A 20- to 30- minute treatment is sufficient; the steam packs maintain effective heat for at least 30 minutes. A master unit with an 8 or 12 pack capacity is a real time saver because it allows a trainer to handle several athletes at one time. After 10 minutes, the trainer must check the skin to avoid burns.

Whirlpool Bath

The whirlpool bath is a popular piece of equipment for giving hydrotherapy, and is probably the apparatus most familiar to athletes. Training room scenes in books and newspapers invariably include the whirlpool bath. Most athletes consider a whirlpool bath a necessary part of a well-equipped training room. A whirlpool bath should definitely be purchased if funds are available; otherwise, the trainer can use substitute methods to accomplish similar results. After the initial investment, the cost of the operation is low.

Benefits of Whirlpool

The whirling water has the effect of gentle massage, which helps reduce swelling, relieves pain, and relaxes muscles. Tissues become soft and pliable and joints move with less difficulty. The whirlpool action provides certain psychologic benefits; it is a type of therapy that may be seen, heard, and left by the athlete, and it has a sedative, comforting, soothing effect.

As with any form of physical therapy, the treatment of specific conditions with the whirlpool must be prescribed by the physician. The use of warm water in the whirlpool stimulates circulation through the dilatation of superficial blood vessels. The average water temperature is best held between 101° to 105° F for 30 minutes. A warm whirlpool stimulates phagocytosis and helps to reduce inflammation. It usually reduces pain, relaxes certain muscle spasm due to trauma, and aids absorption of waste products. It is also an excellent debriding agent for open wounds. Mobility of a limb is increased as a result of decreased swelling and pain. Cold water constricts superficial blood vessels. It may be used in the whirlpool to reduce swelling in acute sprains, but other methods exist.

The following conditions may be treated by the whirlpool method in the training room when prescribed by the attending physician:

1. Adhesions;

2. Ankle swelling;
3. Arthritis;
4. Before applying electrical treatments;
5. Bone bruises;
6. Bromidrosis;
7. Burns;
8. Bursitis;
9. Circulatory disturbances-water temperature usually should not be higher than 99° to 100° F;
10. Cleansing wounds, lacerations, etc;
11. Contusions;
12. Hyperhidrosis;
13. Myalgia;
14. Periostitis;
15. Postfracture care;
16. Postoperative care;
17. Scars;
18. Sprains;
19. Strains;
20. Tenosynovitis.

The whirlpool is an efficient form of therapy. It saves treatment time and prepares muscles and joints for massage and manipulation. Moreover, it is easily applied and handled by someone trained in its use, and the temperature and duration of treatment may be regulated at will. Depending on the model, it may be a mobile unit and have a self-emptying tank.

Prevention of Adverse Effects

A few adverse effects may occur with the use of a whirlpool bath. A dirty tank becomes a carrier of disease; several cases of dermatitis and spread of infection have been reported. Occasionally, a person may faint if the water is too warm. If a person with an acute condition is unwisely treated too long in hot water, with too much agitation, and a high temperature, his ailment may become worse. Transient swelling may occur.

To keep the tank clean, and Betadine, according to manufacturer's direction, to each tank of water. When the tank is drained, spray the inside of the tank, rim, and seat with an aerosol germicide. Do not depend on the heat of the water to kill bacteria. Athletes should be instructed to use the whirlpool only after they have thoroughly showered with soap. Persons known to have a skin infection should not be allowed to use the whirlpool unless they use it alone and the water is drained and the tank disinfected afterwards. Frequent use of the whirlpool dictates frequent draining and disinfecting; used water should not be allowed to stand overnight.

If the water is hard, a detergent may be added, but one should check with the athletes for possible allergies to such chemicals.

Tips From the Trainer's Table

1. Keep the hydrotherapeutic equipment grounded by running a ground wire from the chassis to a nearby faucet. Use a alligator nose on the wire, which is easy to remove and hook up.
2. Use hydrotherapy to prepare for massage, and range-of-motion exercises. The whirlpool bath can be quite soothing to the athlete.

Substitute Methods for Whirlpool Bath

1. *Epsom Salt Soak:* Use an empty bucket of 2 to 5 capacity. Dissolve 2 tumblerfuls or 4 cups of Epsom salts to a gallon of hot water from the faucet and soak the following injured parts: ankle, foot, toe, calf of leg, hand, finger, wrist, forearm, elbow.
2. *Shower:* A hose attached to a shower connection can direct warm water on an injured part, wrapped in a towel, to accomplish the same purpose as a whirlpool. Adjust the nozzle so that there is a forceful direct spray on the following injured parts: shoulder, neck, back, knee, thigh, hip, arm, ribs, groin muscles.

There are many forms of hydrotherapy. The type to use depends mainly on the attending physician's prescription and the training, experience, and ingenuity of the trainer.

MASSAGE

Massage is an ancient and well-documented therapeutic modality useful for the treatment of athletic injuries and as part of a preliminary warm-up for an athlete prior to competition. In his book, How Ancient Healing Governs Modern Therapeutics, Kleanthos A. Ligeros, a physician from Athens, Greece, states the following: "Naturally, such practices as laying one's hands over the patient's head and manipulating his forehead for relief of headaches or other pain or massaging the spine or the entire body and thus relieving the sufferer of his affliction have been known to man from remote times. All ancient records point straight to the fact that these methods were instinctively practices in the stone age and have been transmitted and transplanted by man everywhere. Dr. Allan Ryan, Editor-in-Chief of the Journal of the Physician and Sportsmedicine, bemoans the fact that massage, one of the oldest and time-proven methods of treatment, is being neglected by the modern trainer therapist. He further emphasizes the fact that massage is an excellent warm-up exercise modality prior to athletic competition that is not practiced by most athletes. He further states that, in American athletics, the masseur has been given a back seat, unlike the masseur in European athletics. He recommends that the practitioner of the art of massage be given a specialty within the framework of the training profession.

Massage can be beneficial for many of the soft-tissue and joint injuries suffered in athletics. This includes sprains, strains, contusions, as well as other injuries. Massage is used to assist in removing edema and facilitates recovery after the initial inflammatory reaction due to the athletic trauma has subsided. In clinical conditions in which there is muscle spasm or painful muscular contractions due to prolonged tension, strenuous exercises, or immobilization, deep-stroking or kneading massage are useful in relaxing muscle spasm and in relieving discomfort by increasing the athlete's pain threshold.

In regard to adhesions and scars, friction massage is often used in combination with stretching to help free the tissues and gain mobility. In giving massage for adhesions, it should be remembered that only the thumbs massage over the adhesions or scar tissue, gently giving friction massage in the hopes of lessening the scar without any lubricant.

Massage should be used along with other forms of treatment as soon as bruising and swelling have ceased; this may take 24 to 72 hours post-injury depending on the severity of the trauma. Massage is only one part of the total treatment and does not replace other modalities, such as immobilization, cryotherapy, heat, and exercise.

Massage and therapeutic exercises are also used following cast or dressing removal for dislocations, fractures, and operations. Following the massage, the injured limb should be elevated for 10 to 15 minutes to encourage further drainage of the injured part using the force of gravity. Isometrics of the muscles of the elevated limb further encourage drainage, which results in reduction of the swelling as well as improved muscle strength. Range-of-motion exercises of the surrounding joints lessen the potential for adhesions and assist the total rehabilitation of the injured athlete. Massage is indicated when the following are sought:

1. Relief of pain.
2. Improvement of circulation.
3. Improvement of circulation of the skin and underlying soft tissues.
4. Accelerated removal of waste end products.
5. Dissolution of adhesions.
6. Reduction of swelling and induration of tissues.
7. Loosening and stretching of contracted tendons.
8. Soothing of the central nervous system and peripheral nerves.

Contraindications to massage are the following:

1. Inflammations due to bacterial action.
2. Skin eruptions, infections, abrasions, and varicose veins.
3. Calcifications of soft structure such as the quadriceps muscle, medical collateral ligament of the knee, and others.
4. Rheumatoid or gouty arthritis.

5. Traumatic arthritis of the elbow.

6. Acute bursitis.

7. Pressure on nerve as in a carpal tunnel syndrome.

8. Phlebitis and cellulitis.

Effleurage

Effleurage, or stroking, is accomplished by passing the hands slowly, gently, and rhythmically over a portion of the athlete's skin. This is a superficial type of massage usually affecting the subcutaneous level. It is the type of massage most frequently used for athletes. It is usually performed with the palm of the hand.

To obtain maximal benefits from superficial effleurage, the movement of the hands must be deeper centripetally. The movement is slow, rhythmic, continuous, and in the same tempo, with the hands always remaining in contact with the athlete. Approximately 15 strokes per minute is the usual rate. The movement must be gentle because this is essential in obtaining the desired effect.

Petrissage

This is a kneading and/or compression type of technique. The tissues are picked or lifted off the bones by the thumb and fingers and kneaded, compressed, or wrung. This type of massage assists arterial and venous circulation and accelerates lymphatic flow and hastens the removal of waste products from the muscle. This technique also stretches retracted muscles and tendons and assists in breaking adhesions. One or both hands may be employed. In addition to improving circulation it is frequently used to relive muscle spasm.

Friction

Friction massage is a deep, circular, rolling movement employed around body prominence or joints. It is used in loosening adhesions and promoting absorption of exudate. Friction massage may also be useful in lessening scar tissue. The finger of the trainer-therapist remain on one point of the skin, and the skin is rolled over the underlying tissue. This movement tends to loosen superficial scars and adhesions. Most of the motion is carried out with the thumbs over the treated area. Friction movements are usually followed by effleurage.

Tapotement

This type of massage is not recommended for athletes. It consists of sudden, blow-like contacts by the ulnar side of the hands to the patient, such as in clapping, hacking, and cupping. It is used to encourage drainage from lungs with patients afflicted with bronchitis, emphysema, and chronic pulmonary disorders. There are potential, harmful effects with its use.

Vibration

This type of massage is also not recommended for athletes. It is an inward, trembling pressure exerted by the hands and fingers to any part of the body to stimulate nerve activity.

Therapeutic Cold

The use of ice has been used as an immediate therapeutic agent for many years, principally for arresting and reducing swelling. It can also be used to interrupt the pain-spasm cycle, which is present in a wide variety of injuries to the neck, shoulders, or lower back. The changes observed in the muscle during ice therapy are the firm hardness at the onset and jelly-like consistency at the end of the treatment. The local application of cold decreases neural activity locally and studies have shown that cold raises the threshold stimulus of the muscle spindles, thereby greatly enhancing the relaxation of muscle spasms. Along with the visible relaxation, ice produce a mild anaesthetic effect on the area being treated. This effect provides the athlete with the opportunity to perform exercises with a minimal amount of pain and if he exercises are too strenuous or cause more damage to the injury, enough pain will be exhibited by the athlete that the limits will be known.

Physiologic Effects:

1. Superficial anesthetic effect.
2. There is a depressing effect on the stretch reflex allowing the muscle-spindle threshold to rise. This decreases the spasticity that usually accompanies injury, and that then causes some loss of range of motion in the area.
3. Initial vaso-constriction, then secondary vasodilation, which may last from 30 minutes to an hour.

For muscle injuries, cold facilitates increased blood flow via two mechanisms: by cold vasodilation and by allowing use of the injured muscle by light exercise. These two processes have a greater effect on increasing muscle blood flow than heat has, and they allow the athlete to perform exercises with less pain.

ULTRASOUND

Ultrasound is the deepest form of heat currently available for therapeutic use. Ultrasound waves are of the same nature as sound waves but have such a high frequency that they are inaudible. After experimental work, it was found that waves 700,000 to 1 million cycles per second were desirable for therapeutic application. The electrical energy produced by the generator is converted into mechanical vibrations by means of a quartz crystal.

The mechanical vibration produced by the ultrasound must be propagated through a coupling agent between the transducer head and the patient's skin in the form of an oil, cream, or water. The mechanical vibrations produce a liberation of heat in the body tissues, which is greatest at interfaces between heterogeneous tissues, such as bone and muscle or muscle and tendon. There also seems to be selective heating of bones, joints, tendons, and nerves.

Though the thermal effects of ultrasound account for the majority of its use, there are mechanical, chemical, and biologic effects that add to the versatility of the apparatus.

Clinically, ultrasound produces a mechanical effect of dispersion and agitation of the deep cellular tissues, which may be referred to as the micro-massaging effect. In addition, electron microscopy studies have shown ultrasonics capable of separating collagen fibres from each other.

Certain effects of ultrasonic energy can be considered chemical, such as acceleration of enzyme activity and the increase in cell-membrane permeability.

Studies on tendon extensibility have been conducted revealing that ultrasonic energy can produce changes in frog tendon that make for greater extensibility; thermal denaturation of proteins of the tendon is offered as a possible explanation. Ample evidence exists to demonstrate that ultrasound affects the nervous system, including the autonomic portion, which produces a vasomotor response.

PART 6
ATHLETIC CONDITIONING

Chaptér-1

INTRODUCTION

The approach to rehabilitation after injury must include an accurate appraisal of muscle strength to determine areas of local weakness. The results of muscle testing are evaluated in terms of muscle strength on opposite sides of the body. A full range of motion is equally important and limitations when compared to the opposite side give rise to the possibility of further injury. Unless strength and range of motion are accurately determined the athlete is not fully protected against further difficulty.

The cause of the weakness or limitation may be a medical condition requiring further attention. If so, it is brought out for the athlete's own well being. Where correction of the weakness involves further exercises of a special type, these exercises have been detailed.

For easy reference this section starts with a listing of individual testing areas. This is followed by an evaluation of the equipment necessary and a survey of the methods for determining limited motion at any particular joint. Individual strengthening exercises and weight-lifting are then given. Individual stretching exercises and cardiovascular exercises complete the list.

Getting into condition or "shape" for a sport is the athlete's goal. The athlete reaches this goal when he can make specific musculo-skeletal movements repeatedly and efficiently without becoming unduly fatigued, and when fatigue does set in, a quick recovery is anticipated. Such bio-efficiency results from the interrelated development of the musculo-skeletal, respiratory, and circulatory systems coordinated by the central and autonomic nervous systems. All body functions contribute to the quality of the athlete's performance. Only the athlete in the finest condition can stand the wear and tear of a competitive season.

The main features of a conditioning program are:

1. Stretching/flexibility training.
2. Strength training.
3. Speed training.
4. Endurance/stamina training.
5. Equilibrium.
6. Agility training.
7. Reaction training.
8. Percent body fat.

Since the first edition, flexibility/stretching training is a prime effort in the training and conditioning program. This type of training not only prepares the athlete for maximum performance, but also prevents many types of musculo-skeletal injuries. Examples of this will be states later. Too flexible a knee joint in sports such as football, soccer, and hockey should be strengthened if possible.

Strength, speed, stamina, and endurance are developed by the physiological overload principle, which utilizes graduated muscular exercises, and interval and circuit training. All of these should be achieved in off-season programming and maximized during pre-season and seasonal activities. Physicians, coaches, trainers, and athletes have become increasingly aware that only through strenuous exercises and play can an athlete reach his best playing form: that when the arms and legs begin to hurt, you know they are being strengthened. The heart muscle also benefits from overloading by beating more slowly and more efficiently, delivering a greater volume with each stroke. The capacity of the lung increases by utilizing many dormant alveolar sacs as well as developing accessory muscles of respiration, thus supplying larger amounts of oxygen to the blood and removing waste metabilities more efficiently. Getting the cardiovascular and respiratory systems in shape should be the first order of business; the best way to do this is by running.

Each sport has its own patterns, muscle loads, tempo, and duration. The skills and the conditioning necessary to participate in one sport are not interchangeable with another sport. For example, a well conditioned football player might run out of steam quickly in a boxing match, and a high-scoring bowler might be a duffer at golf. Participation in the particular sport is the best way to become proficient and conditioned for the athletic activity. However, despite the differences among sports, some generalizations can be made about getting into condition and maintaining it.

Although we now recognize that keeping in condition is a year round objective, it may be divided into pre-seasonal, seasonal, and off-seasonal activities. During off-seasons, bicycling, running, and rope jumping are excellent exercises for maintaining tone of the muscular and cardio-respiratory systems. Supervised weight training based on weight-pushing, pulling, lifting, and pressing is an excellent activity for maintaining condition. Weights of varying sizes may be attached to various parts of the anatomy to develop general muscle tone, or to a specific group of muscles used in a particular sport. During the season, these off-seasonal activities are generally relegated to a lesser role in the training program. Progressive overloading is carried out through one or a combination of interval, circuit, or weight training techniques.

INTERVAL TRAINING

Interval training originated in Europe as a scientific method of developing speed and endurance in treatment. It is a method of overloading the athlete by the use of aerobic and anaerobic exercises, thus developing a high oxygen debt. A quick recovery of the cardiovascular and respiratory systems is sought for and expected.

In this method, an athlete runs a prescribed course in a specified time for a prescribed number of times. Fast runs are interspersed with short recovery periods of jogging. The athlete becomes fatigued many times in a single training session, depending on his fitness and his ability to handle many states of high oxygen debt. In this manner he is able to progressively increase his endurance by increasingly stressing the cardio-respiratory system. Besides developing endurance and strength, interval training has the added advantage of allowing large numbers of athletes to train at the same time.

CIRCUIT TRAINING

A scientific arrangement of proven exercises are performed systematically and repeatedly as a circuit, the repeated twice more as a circuit. Circuit training is designed to elicit maximal overall balanced development. A circuit may consist of the following exercises:

1. Steps on and off chair.
2. Trunk curls.
3. Hops 25 yards on alternate legs.

4. Dips between chair backs.
5. Squat jumps.
6. Press-ups.
7. Situps and twists.
8. Squat thrusts.
9. Shuttle run.
10. Dorsal lifts, supported by a partner.

Because of the strenuous nature of the exercises, circuit training is usually done at the end of a training session. The entire session should not last more than 20 minutes. Sebastian Coe, gold-medal winner for than 1500 meter in the 1980 Moscow Olympics, is a devotee of circuit training.

WEIGHT TRAINING

Today the people of our country are more concerned with physical fitness than ever before. Each year, manufacturers of fitness equipment introduce to the coaching and training professions and to the public new apparatus that can be used to build strength and improve cardiovascular endurance. Weight training is used by many athletes to get into top condition for a particular sport; it is an integral part of every athlete's training program. It is physiologically and psychologically sound.

A general program of weight training for conditioning must include exercises that will develop muscular power and muscular endurance. Muscular strength is the ability to work against a specified resistance without injuring the muscle; it is best developed by using high resistance with a low number of repetitions. Muscular endurance is the ability of a muscle to respond repeatedly for a long period of time; this is best developed by using low resistance with a high number of repetitions. The athlete tries progressively to exceed his limits in lifting, and also stresses movements that must be done repeatedly with enough weights to make the muscle work. All lifting motions require timing, snap, and explosive power, which are desirable in athletic training.

Weight training for athletes is not the same as lifting weights for body building. In body building, isolated muscles or muscle groups are exercised to produce large muscle mass and strength-reaching total conditioning is not the goal. Generally, conditioning is not enhanced when body building is the main concern, although some body builders achieve total conditioning through the intelligent application of weight lifting exercises.

Isotonic and isometric muscles exercise programs with and without apparatuses are popular because of their time saving features. When finances are a problem the same routines can be used without apparatus, although the desired results may take a little longer to attain. In isotonic exercises, the muscle is contracted under constant tension. Performed with full range of motion of the adjoining joint and using the power rack, isotonic exercises provide an efficient means of achieving general bodily development.

In isometric exercises, one muscle or one part of the body is pitted against another or against an immovable object. The pushing, pulling, pressing, and fleshing activities are strong but motionless. Isometric exercises are valuable only if the athlete expends 100% effort to develop strength in specific muscles or to maintain general muscular strength. The isometric rack may be used, and the exercises may be done daily at the beginning of football practice.

The most popular muscle-strengthening program is performed by using isotonic apparatuses. We refer to the

Nautilus and others. The Cybex and Orthotron machines are isokinetic devices used therapeutically to strengthen and rehabilitate injured limbs. Isometric exercises have lost favour with the strength programs for athletes. However, they still play a significant therapeutic role in the rehabilitation of the injured athlete. If budgetary deficits preclude those apparatuses, isometrics are still useful.

Only through hard work can an athlete develop his strength potential from a weight-training program. The athlete should start off with a general body-building program during the off-season. During the pre-season, he must focus on those muscle groups that are most involved in his sport. However, the athlete should not overdevelop one set of muscles to cause an imbalance with the antagonistic muscle groups, since this could cause an uncoordinated joint movement. Experience has shown that there is a need to place more emphasis on strengthening the shoulder and upper extremities, although this should not be done at the expense of strengthening the legs. The amount of weight to be used is somewhat a matter of trial and error, and each athlete must experiment to find the baseline from which his weight training program is launched.

The best results in a weight training program can only be realized when the program is fitted to the individual's need and he is conscientiously involved in it. If an athlete is presently working on a weight training program and getting good results, there is not need to experiment with a new method until its advantages and disadvantages have been evaluated. Records should be kept of the individual's progress, and adjustments in the program made in accordance with the athlete's newly acquired strength. An individual progress chart-much like a diary-should be kept by each athlete.

Weight training is no replacement for running in the conditioning program. During the season, weight training should be used sparingly; however, it has a place as a supplement to regular work-out activities to maintain strength and endurance that might be lost during a season. If a coach insists on weight-training exercises during the season, they are best done after stretching/flexibility exercises.

Weight-training exercises are also useful as therapy following injuries to athletes. This completely differs from conditioning routines and is prescribed by the team physician as rehabilitative therapy.

FLEXIBILITY TRAINING

One only has to watch a football game to see the unusual positions in which a joint may be placed in the course of a game. Flexibility allows uninhibited joint motion and perfection of movement, giving an added margin of safety to the joint and its surrounding connective tissue structures when it is needed most, without tearing, which could lead to sprains, subluxations and dislocations, or fractures. Flexibility training is designed to increase the range of motion of joints; this requires stretching of the tissues, especially connective tissues, beyond their normal limits. Connective tissue periodically shortens with aging, and unless it is actively stretched, it will remain shortened, thus cutting down on the range of motion of the joint. This is especially noticeable in the shoulders and low back, as well as other joints.

Flexibility is best achieved with slow, controlled movement, as is seen in ballet, rather than with ballistic or bouncing type movements. Since pain is a factor in inhibiting movement, controlled movements are not likely to exceed the extensibility of muscle tissue and cause injury. A simple way to maintaining a full range of motion, and even slightly more, is for the athlete to go through those motions associated with his sport daily and even during the off season. Each sport has its own particular activities that help in obtaining suppleness of the joint. For example, the golfer and the batter should practice swinging; the boxer shadow boxing; the hurdler and the punter, leg and groin stretching. The following sketches are examples of stretching/flexibility exercises that can be used by the athlete in his sport.

REACTION TRAINING

Reaction training is designed to shorten the delay between the perception of a stimulus and the athlete's response to it. The objective is to make the musculo-skeletal system move almost automatically, in a reflex manner, thus bypassing the decision-making functions of the brain. In effect, each muscle has its own "mind." Automatic response in anticipating the stimulus reduces reaction time. Continuous training of this type will improve performance. Reaction training and agility training are combined to increase mobility in the quickest possible time.

FLUID BALANCE AND WEIGHT CHARTS

Coaching and conditioning athletes demands complex skills that go far beyond the teaching of offensive and defensive plays. The coach must correlate and utilize large amounts of personal and environmental data to get his charges into condition. He depends on information from his assistants, trainer, and the physician as well as his own daily observations to determine the level of conditioning that an athlete has reached.

The weight of the athlete is an important indicator of his physical state. The training room should have a scale, and daily weight records should be kept for each athlete. Weight loss or gain is related to environmental conditions as well as bodily conditions. Therefore, weather facts such as temperature and humidity, as well as the type and severity of the work-out, should be noted along with the daily weight record: the coach uses all this information to form an educated opinion of the athlete's state of conditioning.

FLUID AND ELECTROLYTE BALANCE

Maintenance of adequate body fluids and proper balance between extra-cellular and intercellular fluid volume is a complex concept, often neglected, yet indispensable for an effective conditioning program because it affects weight loss, and the musculo-skeletal, cardio-respiratory and neurologic systems. An understanding of these relationships by the coaching and training staff will reduce the casualties that occur from water, electrolyte, and acid-base disturbances.

Water comprises about 70% of the adult body, i.e., 46lb. in a man weighing approximately 154 pounds. Obese people have relatively less water than thin people, and their water content may be as low as 45%. Some of this water lies outside the cells, as in blood plasma, and also between the cells, and some lies within the cells. Dissolved in this water are electrolytes, which are ions that carry an electric charge and are involved in the chemical reactions that occur within the body. In order to function properly, the body must maintain a proper balance in the amount and distribution of water and electrolytes. Haemostatic mechanisms regulate this balance.

About 86% to 90% of weight loss from muscular activity is due to water loss and only about 10 to 15% is from heat and caloric dissipation. The increased heat produced escapes from the body. It is dissipated mainly through the skin and the lungs and a small amount through the kidneys. As the superficial blood vessels dilate, heat is lost from the skin by way of radiation, convection, and conduction, except when the external temperature is high. In addition, the sweat glands excrete a fluid composed mainly of water and salt although it also contains other minerals, including potassium,, which is important. Evaporation of perspiration allows cooling of the skin surface. Rapid breathing also allows evaporation of water from the lungs thus reducing heat. Evaporation cannot take place effectively in a humid atmosphere.

Therefore, the water and electrolyte balance is affected by heat, such as that generated by muscular activity, and by the external temperature, humidity, and environment. Reducing the amount of clothing, which tends to insulate body heat, and lessening the physical activity also help to stabilize the body temperature.

Losses of water and electrolytes, as occurs in dissipating increased heat, must be compensated by fluid and electrolyte intake. Since heavy perspiration causes a loss of water and salt, both must be replace. An average adult required 1500 to 2000 ml of water a day; he needs an additional 500 to 1000 ml to compensate for slight to moderate sweating and anywhere from 1500 to 3000 ml for heavy to severe sweating when playing football on a hot, humid day. A football player may lose 3 to 4g of salt in addition to other electrolytes daily, under hot, humid playing conditions, that must be replaced to established electrolyte balance. Many electrolyte replacement solutions available commercially are too concentrated to be beneficial. They need dilution by 1 part electrolyte solution to 2 parts of water. The temperature of the fluid offsets the rate of absorption and therefore, its effectiveness; cooler is better.

HEAT STRESS

Coaches, trainers, and team physicians must be able to train their athletes to become acclimatized to high temperatures and humidity; they must be able to recognize and cope with conditions of heat stress when they occur.

No one can study the deaths from heat stress as correlated with the climatic conditions for the time and place and type of activity involved without the firm belief that 98% of all such reactions are avoidable. A heat stroke is not a chance proposition like being struck by lightning. It is a predictable phenomenon.

HEAT STROKE

Heat stroke is an acute medical emergency, the onset of which may be sudden or delayed. It requires heroic emergency measures once it appears.

Excessive heat is produced in the body by exercises that cause the body temperature to rise. If a heat balance cannot be obtained by loss of heat to the surroundings because of atmospheric or other reasons, the hypothalamus becomes excessively heated by the rise in blood temperature. The heat-regulating ability of this structure becomes depressed and sweating is diminished.

The athlete may develop an abnormally high rectal temperature. Characteristically, he does not sweat despite the high environmental temperature. His face is flushed and his skin is dry and hot because of capillary dilatation. His pulse is elevated and strong, but his breathing is increased and laboured. He may complain of weakness, headaches, nausea, and dizziness, and experience convulsions, projectile vomiting, and shock. The absence of sweating despite exposure to high environmental temperature should make one suspect heat stroke rather than heat exhaustion.

Emergency measures designed to reduce the athlete's temperature must be undertaken while preparations are made to transport him to the hospital.

Place him in a shady and cool spot. Strip him of all clothing and apply cold compresses to his head. Give him cold sponge baths or place him in a tub of water with ice. Vigorous skin massage of trunk and limbs to dissipate body heat. Frequent sips of cool liquid are recommended. However, do not waste time playing doctor on the field or in the dressing room. Get him to a hospital where he can have an air conditioned room, hypothermic blankets, intravenous therapy and a laboratory work-up as quickly as possible.

HEAT EXHAUSTION

In this condition, there is excessive sweating and associated loss of salt in the sweat. Because cell membranes are freely permeable to water and there is constant to-and-fro filtration between compartments, equilibrium is quickly established between the extra-cellular and intercellular fluids when some of the intercellular water passes into the extra-cellular by osmosis. However, if there is not adequate fluids and salt replacement, the osmotic pressure of the extra-cellular fluid is lowered, causing it to flow into the intercellular compartment. This leads to diminished extra-cellular volume, including plasma volume, and results in a decreased circulating blood volume, decreased venous return, tachycardia, and poor cardiac output leading to a state of shock.

Clinically, the athlete complains of fatigue, headache, muscle weakness, and muscle cramps. His face is pale and perspiring; his mouth is dry; the skin of his lambs is cols and clammy; he has absent or collapsing peripheral pulses. The urinary volume is low, as are the sodium and chloride concentrations. Strangely enough, thirst is frequently absent. This condition may go on to nausea, vomiting, diarrhoea, and even fainting. Treatment is directed to the replacement of water and electrolytes, especially sodium, to increase the osmotic pressure of the extra-cellular fluids. Water replacement alone only aggravates the sodium loss. In marked exhaustion, get the athlete to the hospital as soon as possible for clinical and laboratory control

Athletes, coaches, trainers, and physicians are well aware of the necessity of taking electrolyte supplements during physical activity and liberally salting meals during meal times. Obviously, water replacement alone in the face of mineral depletion would aggravate the latter by further diluting the mineral content of the blood. The need for a proper proportion of minerals and fluids in the form of a drink has become an accepted conclusion. There are a number of broad-spectrum mineral drinks with a relatively high potassium content along with sodium, chloride, magnesium, zinc, and calcium available.

HEAT CRAMPS

Heat cramps are painful contractions of the voluntary muscles characterized by twitching, cramps, and spasms of the arms, legs, and abdomen. They are caused by a loss of salt and possibly potassium through heavy sweating. High external temperatures are not necessary for their occurrence; any prolonged period of sweating without replacing essential electrolytes, especially salt, might cause them.

Treatment consists of resting and replacing electrolytes, especially sodium chloride and potassium, with an oral solution. Even salt tablets taken orally with water can be irritating to many people, but they are used even though they lack some of the other minerals, particularly potassium. Severe cases might require hospitalization and intravenous administration of normal saline solution. Salt tablets are contrain-dicated on the field. They are likely to cause undesirable fluid shifts unless taken with appropriate amounts of free water. Heat cramps might be prevented by prior acclimatization, liberal intake of salt with foods, and proper use of an electrolyte solution during activity.

PREVENTION OF HEAT STRESS

Warm weather, heavy uniforms, and prolonged play without a prior period of acclimatization may lead not only to a loss of weight, but to a loss of life. This is especially true in September football, when all these variables are mixed together indiscriminately. Warm weather induces perspiration, which is further augmented by physical activity. An athlete working out in temperatures of 65° F or less in light gear sweats little if there is little humidity. However, with humidity up to 70% he will perspire much and even chill. If the external temperature goes over 70° F and the humidity remains high, he will sweat significantly. A coach must be watchful in early season workouts when the temperature is above 80° F and the humidity is 50% or more. Prolonged workouts in moderate heat cause excessive perspiration and electrolyte loss. When the water loss is about 2% of the body weight, the athlete develops a thirst. When an athletes loses 6% of his body weight in water loss daily, he develops a marked thirst, dry mouth, and oliguria, and is on the way to heat exhaustion if not promptly treated appropriately with water and electrolytes.

Higher percentages of weight loss with accompanying physical weakness, fatigue, mental changes, and others will lead to heat strokes and eventually death, if immediate steps are not taken. These conditions can be prevented if adequate water and electrolytes are available and consumed.

Although the coach is unable to control, the weather, he must be able to handle such variables as scheduling and type of workouts, clothing, gear, climate-controlled housing and play areas, and food and drink. In hot weather, the coach must acclimatize his athletes to the heat, to avoid heat stress reactions. Acclimatization, or heat training, causes the following changes in the body:

1. Increased circulation to the skin and dilatation of the blood vessels in the ski.
2. Increased extracellular fluid volume.
3. Increased ability to produce large volumes of dilute sweat. The same degree of exertion produces less of a rise in body temperature and pulse rate compared to the unacclimatized individual.

Acclimatization requires that the athlete work out in the heat, perhaps for an hour the first day, gradually increasing the length and the severity of the practice. Adequate electrolyte and fluid replacement must be maintained. In this manner, an athlete is almost fully acclimatized after 5 to 7 days; full acclimatization occurs after 2 weeks of training. It must be remembered, however, that 50% of this acclimatization may be lost after 1 week if exercise in the heat is stopped, and it disappears completely after 2 weeks without exercise, requiring complete retraining to prevent illness.

Interscholastic and intercollegiate football practices are mandated to practice specified periods of time in early season football to acclimatize the athlete and avoid heat stress reactions. Football players should start off in hot weather with shorts and T-shirts only. In hot weather, it may be advisable to schedule practice sessions during the cooler morning and early evening hours. Coaches should be liberal with rest periods, water, and electrolytes during hot weather. While thirst is a good guide for the replacement of fluids for athletes, weight loss per unit of time is more exact.

The coach and trainer should regulate the adjust practices when the temperature and humidity are so great that practising is dangerous. Two methods have now been developed to determine levels of heat and humidity. A wet-bulb globe temperature index, developed by the United States Marine Corps, is calculated from three thermometer readings: (1) a wet bulb thermometer; (2) a dry bulb thermometer, and (3) a black globe thermometer. An apparatus containing these three devices may easily be built, and is placed on the playing field.

The wet bulb is a standard thermometer with the bulb wrapped in a gauze wick that is in contact with a water reservoir. Temperatures recorded by this thermometer reflect the moisture content of the air. A low external moisture content allows evaporation of water from the wick, which lowers the thermometer reading. The dry bulb measures air temperature without being affected by the humidity. The black globe thermometer consists of a standard thermometer with the bulb encased in a copper tank float ball that has been painted with non-reflective flat black paint. This measures the radiant heat from the sun, which may be considerable even on cloudy days.

The heat index (HI) represents the sum of 70% of the wet bulb reading, plus 10% of the dry bulb reading, plus 20% of the black globe reading.

The HI may be adapted to guiding football practice as follows:

HI	*Precaution*
Below 80	None necessary
80 to 85	Cancel drills in full uniform during first weeks of practice. Limited drills in full uniform after heat acclimatization is complete.
85 to 90	Cancel all drills in full uniform. During first week of practice, use indoor sessions.
Above 90	Stop all training. Skull sessions and demonstrations.

Calculations of indoor heat are made from 70% of the wet bulb reading plus 30% of the dry bulb reading; the black globe is not used.

The sling psychrometer is an instrument containing both wet and dry bulb thermometers in a rotating arm attached to a handle; the handle has a built-in slide ruler that correlates the two temperature readings to give the percentage of relative humidity. The rotating arm containing the thermometers is twirled to allow air circulation around the wet bulb thermometer. If over 60° F, the coach should insist that electrolytes and water be available. Below this temperature, use weight loss as a guide as previously determined under similar conditions so that fluids and electrolytes may be replaced accordingly. The following recommendations have been made in reference to football players:

Wet Bulb Temperature	*Precautions*
Under 60° F	None necessary.
61° to 65° F	Alert observations of all squad members, particularly those who lose considerable weight.
60° to 70° F	Insist that salt and water be given on field.
71° to 75° F	Alter practice schedule to provide rest period every 30 minutes in addition to above precautions.
76° F and higher	Practice postponed or conducted in shorts.

Coaches should use the daily weight of their athletes to prevent heat-stress reactions. For a 188-pound athlete, temperature and humidity could induce a 3% weight loss, which would be over 5 pounds, the upper limit of safety. The athlete would have a 5% weight loss if he is suffering from frank heat exhaustion, so coaches and trainers take heed.

Overseeing the training program of athletes could be done more scientifically if various laboratory procedures, such as urinalysis, blood volume, electrolytes, and a host of others, could be done on the field. However, on the field and in the gym, the coach, trainer, and team doctor must depend on what they know about the weather, strenuousness of play, and clinical appearance of the athlete to guide them in the training program as well as the prevention of untoward mishaps of heat cramps, heat exhaustion, heat stroke, and water exhaustion.

Although the body is fortified with homeostatic regulators, such as anti-diuretic hormone and aldosterone as well as electrolyte balance, the athlete himself may undo inborn protective mechanisms and expose himself to a serious disturbance.

On the intercollegiate level with full-time trainers, the Wet Bulb-Globe Temperature Index is used. The sling psychrometer is also useful for the same purpose at a much lesser expense. When neither the WBGTI nor a sling psychrometer are part of the equipment, the coach should call the local weather station for the humidity index reading. Some locales even have radio stations that give this information in the public interest.

KEEPING AND INTERPRETING WEIGHT CHARTS

The daily use of a training room scale before and after a workout, and the recording of these weights on a weekly chart marked "in" and "out" for each day will help a coach and his staff to note weight fluctuations and to follow the progress of an athlete's conditioning. Weight charts may also be used to prevent immediate or delayed clinical states of water loss, heat exhaustion, and heat stroke. Also noted daily on the weight chart should be the daily environmental temperature, humidity, and the severity of the workout.

On the first day of practice, the coach instructs the members of the team to record their weight daily before and after a workout wearing the same attire—a genital supporter is sufficient. Systematic, honest recording of weight gain and loss should be done by a trainer or manager if such help is available.

The athlete's daily weight loss will be greatest early in a training program, ranging from 2 to 8 pounds, with the average around 5 pounds. Most of this is water. As the program continues, foodstuff are oxidized, contributing to the loss of body protein, carbohydrates, and fat depots. A balanced diet provides the athlete with necessary operating calories. The water loss is replaced daily.

Eventually, the daily fluctuations on the athlete's weight chart start to level off; at this point he has reached his best weight for maximal efficiency. However, he may still continue to show a daily weight loss owing to sweating, but this weight is regained overnight. The less physically fit an athlete's body is, the longer it takes for him to reach his best playing weight. Obese athletes may take longer than a thin person to reach a satisfactory plateau.

Interpretation of weight records as an index to the level of conditioning requires judgment, experience, and training. If an athlete continues to lose weight beyond his expected levelling off period, the physician should be suspicious of illness, inadequate diet, emotional problems, drug use, lack of sleep, or other problems. It could also indicate a state of being over-trained, or "stale." The reason should be found and appropriate remedies instituted. In the case of staleness, a vacation or break from the monotony of training for one or two periods is especially therapeutic.

The objective of getting into condition is to achieve maximal physical efficiency for a sport. This entails a loss of excess weight and the development of firm, elastic muscles. If the athlete is overweight, it is necessary to eliminate layers and rolls of fat that result from overeating. This demands hard work and self-discipline. The body gives up stored fats slowly and reluctantly, and this type of weight is the hardest to lose.

A persistent, continuous reduction of an athlete's weight within 1 or 2 weeks by use of a "crush" diet, steam baths, and drugs is easily discernible on a weight chart. Boxers and wrestlers frequently resort to these measures in order to participate in a lighter weight class. It is a dangerous procedure.

The use of diuretics by an athlete may have serious consequences. The faking of a weight-loss record when in fact no obvious weight changes appear in the athlete's build is inexcusable. The coach must act quickly to stop these practices. When a squad of players continues to lose weight or displays symptoms such as irritability, sleepiness, nausea, cramps, and cardiac palpitation, the coach may be driving his men too hard or is overemphasizing a game or games. Such coaching practices need review and modification because they are not in the best interest of the team.

The training-room scale is a simple and important mechanical aid that can impart valuable information if used daily and honestly by the athlete and if the coach correlates his knowledge of the athlete and the external factors of the training program.

Conclusions drawn from the daily weight record may help prevent fatalities arising from water and electrolyte imbalance. Under to circumstances should a coach or trainer make a medical judgment based on weight-chart records. They should call in the team physician whenever there is any suspicion of an irregularity noted on the weight chart or impending stress to the athlete as a result of the training program, especially when the athlete is subjected to heat stress. Although this is a valuable parameter for athlete surveillance, an institution needs a large staff to implement for effectiveness.

Chapter-2

PHYSICAL CONDITIONING EVALUATION FOR ATHLETICS

INTRODUCTION

When developing physical conditioning programs for sports, one of two basic objectives must be chosen. Either the program must be designed to *develop* conditioning or it must be designed to *maintain* conditioning. The maintenance program, of course, is followed during the season, and is determined by the results of the program designed to develop condition.

This program to develop condition consists of three phases. Phase one would be an individual muscular evaluation of each player immediately at the end of the season so that the effects of the season's play, from the standpoint of muscular deficiencies, can be determined. It has been found that many times severe bruises, which do not hinder the capability of the athlete, may be responsible for more severe injuries in the future. This is caused by the athlete inadvertently substituting other muscle groups for the injured group and, by so doing causing a pronounced muscular weakness to occur. A muscular evaluation at this time permits the development of a special off-season exercise program which may prevent the occurrence of such injuries.

Phase two would be an individual muscular evaluation each player at the start of the preseason conditioning period in order to evaluate the effects of the off-season work and to determine present exercise needs.

Phase three would be an individual muscular evaluation each player during the preseason training period to ascertain whether the desired results are being achieved from the prescribed program or whether adjustments must be made. This final phase is highly advisable if the athlete is to begin the season in the best possible condition.

SCREENING TESTS

In order to achieve the optimal benefit from any individual exercise program, it is imperative that a battery of screening tests be used to determine the special exercise needs of each individual. Such tests must be capable of pinpointing deficiencies which may lead to injury. Therefore it is important to include both strength evaluations and range of motion evaluations among these tests.

The tests of any screening test battery must be directed primarily toward diagnosis, not correction. In cases where there is evidence of past injury, it is suggested that the individual be careful re-examined by the team physician or, if possible, by an orthopedic surgeon to determine if he has any structural problems, prior to the application of a special exercise program.

SCREENING TEST FORMS

General Screening Test Forms for the strength tests, the range of motion tests, and for the recording of past injury history are presented here for the benefit of the reader. It should be noted that on the strength testing, the machine settings used on the initial test should be used on all the following tests. The squares under R and L are used to record the strength scores of the right and left lower limbs respectively, and the "Diff" column is for any variation between the two scores. Under "Machine Setting" are recorded the settings for the Testing Table:< for the angle of the test arms, B for the cross bar position on the test arms, and A for the angle of the activator on the cross bar.

When using the range of motion test form, the "1" column is used to record the initial reading of the instrument, the "2" column is used to record the final reading of the instrument after completion of the movement, and the "Diff" column is used to record the total range of motion score for each movement. S or F represent Structural or Functional, should the subject have a deep hollow back. In using the cardiovascular endurance test form, merely circle the number which corresponds to the pulse count after each 15 seconds. The count is begun 10 seconds after the completion of the exercise and is continued for 1 minute.

SCREENING TEST INTERPRETATION

The Strength Tests

Knee Extension

It there is a difference greater than 10% between the right and the left strength scores in any of the knee extension movements, it is suggested that the individual be fully examined by the procedure outlined for *Evaluation of Knee Injuries.* If still further differences are noted after the application of these additional tests, if is suggested that the individual be thoroughly examined by an orthopedic surgeon.

Knee Flexion

Any individual who has a score difference greater than 10% in this area should be further evaluated. This series of knee flexion tests should also be used for all individuals who have had serious or frequent injuries to the hamstring muscle group. If the additional testing produces a difference greater than 10% between the right and left side for any of these movements, if is suggested that such individuals be placed on a complete program of exercises designed to strengthen the knee flexion groups.

Hip Extension

If a difference of 10% or more is noted between the right and left for any of the hip extension movements, the individual should be further evaluated. If these additional tests also indicate differences of at least 10% between the right and left hips, and the individual has been thoroughly examined by an orthopedic surgeon, he should be placed on a special exercise program designed to strengthen the hip extension muscle groups.

Additional Strength Tests

The tests listed in this section combine both strength and endurance factors, so a failure may be due to either a lack of muscular strength or muscular endurance. Therefore, for the most efficient correction of this deficiency, it is advisable to use the tests as an endurance type activity in conjunction with the proper strengthening exercises.

Slow Push-Up

It thee athlete fails this test at the beginning of the push-up. If failure occurs during the final half of the upward motion, exercises related to it should be beneficial. In addition, exercises pertaining to slow push-up should be used to increase the muscular endurance of these areas.

Slow Pull-Up

It the athlete cannot begin the pull-up, the strength deficiency is probably in the upper back and shoulder area. Therefore, exercises pertaining to it should be beneficial. If failure occurs during the final half of the upward motion, a strength deficiency may exist in the upper arms as well as the upper back.

THE RANGE OF MOTION TESTS

Wrist Ranges of Motion

If there is a difference greater than 5° between right and left wrist range of motion scores, or if the individual has a very limited range of motion in any of the wrist areas tested, a restricted range of motion is indicated in the area involved. It is suggested that stretching exercises for the wrist be used to correct these deficiencies.

It should be noted that best results are usually obtained from any stretching exercise if heat is applied to the area immediately prior to the stretching. In addition to is applied to the area immediately prior to the stretching. In addition to the stretching exercises, strengthening exercises for the antagonistic muscle group involved in the stretch are quite beneficial in restoring normal ranges of motion.

A program designed to correct restricted wrist ranges of motion would include wrist stretching exercises as well as wrist strengthening exercises are quite beneficial to baseball players because of the action necessary when swinging a bat or throwing a baseball. This again illustrates the necessity of being specific in exercise, both in diagnosis of the strength deficiency and in diagnosis of the strength need.

SHOULDER RANGES OF MOTION

Dropped Shoulder

Through continual of one limb rather than the other, such as in throwing with the right hand, one shoulder will usually become lower than the other. In the case of the right handed thrower, the right shoulder will be lower than left. It Test 26 indicates a dropped shoulder, Exercises 122, 123A, 123B, and 141 may be used to correct this deficiency.

Raised Hip

Because of past injury or improper posture mechanics, an individual may have one hip higher than thee other. This will usually indicate a weakness in the abduction function of the muscles involved. Any athlete who exhibits this imbalance may be more vulnerable to back or knee injuries than the normal athlete, because extraneous muscles are often used to accommodate for the weak ones. It test 17 indicates a raised hip.

Shoulder Movement

Many athletes who have concentrated on team sports for several years are very apt to have a restricted shoulder range in motion. This is probably due to the predominately forward motion of the arms which is necessary in most team sports. In this event it is suggested that he be carefully examined by the team physician or an orthopedic surgeon to determine whether there is some structural difficulty involved. It the physician indicates that there is no structural difficulty the above exercises may then be followed.

Deep Hollow Back

If tests indicate that an individual has a deep hollow back which is structural in nature, he should be closely examined by an orthopedic surgeon before any corrective exercises are given. If the condition is functional in nature, it is probably due to foreshortened hip flexor muscles. Therefore, exercises may be used for correction.

Trunk Range of Motion

The tests for the deep hollow back and for trunk ranges of motion should be used in conjunction with each other. This is quite obvious when one considers that any structural condition or tightness of the back will very definitely influence the amount of trunk range of motion possible.

Another area which is closely related to trunk range of motion measurements is the measurement of the ankle range of motion. A tightness in the heelcords can inhibit the degree of trunk range of motion, especially when it is measured by means of test. Therefore, the ankle range of motion tests should also be used in conjunction which the trunk range of motion tests.

If, when using test, the subject's low back has flat rather than a rounded appearance, he should be examined by an orthopedic surgeon to determine whether this is caused by a structural condition. If no structural condition is indicated and the subject cannot touch his elbows to his knees the condition may be due to tightness in the back, lower limbs, or the heelcord. He should then be given test. If he can touch his toes but cannot pass test, there is probably a tightness in the low back. If so, exercises would be quite beneficial. If he cannot touch his toes in test but can pass test, there is probably a tightness in either the lower limbs or heelcord. If test indicates no restricted ankle range of motion, exercises should be used to stretch the hamstring group. It should be remembered, however, that these tests are not foolproof. An athlete who has tight hamstrings may still be able to touch his toes due to very good back flexibility.

When testing trunk range of motion one should very carefully observe the subject's knees on both test. If the knees have a tendency to flex, it is probably due to a tightness in either the hamstring group or in the heelcords. It, when performing test, the athlete cannot lean forward while the heels remain on the stool, a tightness is almost certain to be present in the heelcords.

Ankle Range of Motion

If, when measuring ankle range of motion, there is a difference of more than 5° between the right and the left ankle, a range of motion deficiency exists which should be corrected. A highly restricted range, such as one less than 10°, in the dorsiflexion movement is also indicative of a deficiency in the ankle range of motion. This is very apt to be present in the right ankle of right handed pitchers or the left ankle of left handed pitchers. A normal ankle range of motion should be at least 60° or 70°. If a range of motion deficiency is evident in the ankle area, Exercises 161 to 164 should aid in its correction and in possibly preventing future injury.

KNEE EVALUATION TEST FORM

A sample Knee Evaluation Test Form is included which may serve as a guide to the reader. It also illustrates the very essential point that prior to any strength testing, the team physician or an orthopedic surgeon must approve a medical clearance for the testing. This is extremely important in injury cases.

Again it is emphasized that the machine settings used on the initial testing should be the settings used on subsequent tests. This enables the tester to remain more objective in his testing while still using a concrete guide line. It should also be noted that a space for the notation of pain is provided in each test area. The tester should check with the subject on all movements and make appropriate entries in this column. He will find these entries very useful and interesting in future testing.

KNEE EVALUATION INTERPRETATION

If there is a difference greater than 10% between the right and left strength scores in any of the above test movements, a strength deficiency is indicated. However, in the areas of the hip extension, hip flexion, and hip abduction and adduction, the comparison must include the scores obtained by testing at the ankle as well as those scores obtained by testing above the knee.

The knee extension and knee flexion tests, of course, primarily indicate strength deficiencies in thee large muscle groups involved in these movements. But in the hip extension movement a difference of 10% or more between the two limbs which is found when testing at the ankle but not found above the knee, may indicate posterior laxity of the knee joint.

In the hip flexion testing, such differences may indicate anterior laxity of the knee joint. For the hip abduction test, this may indicate lateral instability of the knee joint and for hip adduction it may indicate medial instability of the knee joint.

In cases where there is a strength deficiency and in which the orthopedic surgeon give a medical clearance for corrective exercises, an appropriate special exercise program should be designed for application to those areas which have the strength deficiencies. This program will probably include Exercises 111 to 113 and 143.

EVALUATION OF GROIN INJURIES

In cases of groin injury occurrence the athlete should be very thoroughly evaluated in the areas listed below in order to determine thee exact point of strength loss. Once the loss is pinpointed, corrective exercises can be properly administered with the most effective results.

Groin Injury Test Form

No Groin Injury Test Form will be presented here because of its great similarity to the Knee Evaluation Test Form. However, the reader is cautioned to include the essential points in any test form he may use to evaluate groin injuries. The most important point, of course, is the inclusion of a section for medical clearance prior to the testing.

Groin Injury Evaluation Interpretation

If there is a difference greater than 10% between the right and left strength scores in any of the above test movements, a strength deficiency is indicated. This strength difference is usually accompanied by pain in the area of injury. In the hip extension movements, strength loss will usually appear on the uninjured side. This is due to the stabilization action of hip flexor muscle groups on the side *opposite* the movement.

In all of the above tests, the athlete should exert as much force as possible. He should indicate the beginning and degree of pain on any movement. This must always be recorded. The testing should be performed as soon after thee injury as the team physician indicates is feasible.

After determination of the exact point of injury, and after clearance from the team physician or the orthopedic surgeon, an appropriate special exercise program may be initiated. This may be conducted as is outlined in the following section, *Heat and Exercise Program. The* exercises used for an injury of this nature must be very precise, and can only be prescribed after proper testing.

Because of the difference in individual body mechanics, no general exercises for this injury will be recommended here.

HEAT AND EXERCISE PROGRAM

Recent work in the area of strengthening and rehabilitation seems to indicate that a muscle will not develop in strength, especially after injury, unless it is specifically stimulated. Furthermore, there appears to be evidence that in cases of injury different motor units or portions of the injured muscle may be strengthened very rapidly so that the individual may function without loss of efficiency. This enables an athlete to be returned to duty much sooner than previously thought possible. Work with the Pittsburgh Pirates that was initiated by their trainer, Danny Whalen, and which utilized this technique appears to have produced excellent results in returning players who had suffered muscular pulls and strains to activity at a faster rate than the normal techniques. This technique consists of the following procedures.

1. When the injured player receives a muscular strain, especially in the groin, hamstring, thigh, or ankle areas, cold is applied immediately to limit the degree of edema.
2. The next day, hot packs or a whirlpool are used in the following manner:

   a. Twenty minutes of heat is applied;

   b. After the heat, isometric strength exercises for the appropriate position or movement are used. These depend upon the type and area of the injury;

   c. The isometric strength exercises are followed by appropriate isotonic exercises. These will vary as to duration and type depending upon the nature of the injury involved;

d. The isotonic exercises are followed by appropriate stretching exercises. These are probably more effective if they are of the self-stretching rather than the manual-stretching type;

e. After the isometric, isotonic, and stretching exercises are performed, heat is again applied to the injured area;

f. Following the heat, the exercise procedure is re-applied;

g. This sequence should be performed no more than three times each exercise session.

These procedures, which are accomplished with the testing instrument, are continued until the player shows signs of fatigue. It is a sign of fatigue when the strength score begins to decrease or reaches a plateau rather than continues to increase. When fatigue becomes evident, the heat and static program is stopped for that particular session. These sessions should be accomplished twice daily for optimal results. The player should not be returned to competition until the strength scores indicate that he has fully recovered.

CONCLUSIONS

Due to the keen competitive spirit in present day athletics and to the relatively small difference in skill levels of the athletes or teams within a given league, special exercises and special exercise programs are extremely important. The approach to such a program, however, must be based upon sound exercise aims and principles if maximum effectiveness is to be achieved. To instituted a haphazard program merely because of excessive publicity or current popularity may actually be more harmful than beneficial. This would be especially true if a specific type of exercise were being unfairly exploited by individuals primarily for the purpose of personal gain.

Any athletic conditioning or special exercise program, whether it is isometric or isotonic, should be carefully evaluated prior to application. It must be capable of fulfilling specific exercise needs without creating deficiencies in other areas. An example of this would be to increase strength without foreshortening of motion. This implies an exercise program which is specific in nature, yet general in scope. The only practical means of achieving such a difficult aim is by use of an individualized approach.

In order to incorporate this type of special exercise program into the overall athletic program, the following steps are recommended.

1. All athletes should have a thorough medical examination with the physician carefully evaluating the nature and extent of previous injuries or areas of disability. This examination should include the "drawer sign." Thus, in cases of knee injury, there is an established reference point.

2. The muscular strength of athletes should be tested periodically to determine thee existence of any weakened muscular areas, so that these areas can be strengthened. Past data have indicated that few new injuries occur, but that many old injuries recur. This recurrence can often be prevented by finding the weakened area and applying the proper exercise.

3. A supplementary program of strengthening and exercising should be used not only during the

season, but also in the pre-and post-athletic seasons.

4. To be of optimal effectiveness, a supplementary exercise program must be based upon an individualized muscular evaluation, and the exercise recommendations must be performed exactly correct.

Without the above safeguards, an exercise program is apt to exercise only the strong muscular groups and allow very limited use of the weak muscles. This creates a muscular imbalance which can lead to injury, as well as limit the functional ranges of motion of the sound muscular groups. But if based upon these safeguards, a special supplementary exercise program can be a valuable asset to any well organized athletic program.

Chapter-3

CONDITIONING OF ATHLETES

Competitive sports make a tremendous demand on the physical condition, vitality, endurance, and mental powers of the participant. Only athletes in the finest condition can withstand the wear and tear of a competitive season; only the fittest can play to the best of their ability. Athletes not in condition are prone to injury or "going stale," and might never make the team. Thus, proper conditioning not only is necessary in preparing for sports participation, but is of great importance in preventing injuries. The athlete who is properly trained and conditioned will sustain a lower incidence and severity of injuries and a higher level of performance.

Individuals who are obese, awkward, considerably underweight, or ill-trained suffer the greatest number of injuries. The athlete who is well muscled and properly conditioned rarely requires medical treatment for injuries. Proper conditioning requires the joint effort of the physician, coach, trainer, and athlete.

PRE-SEASON PHYSICAL EXAMINATION

The conditioning of an athlete is based upon well established physiological principles, but results can only be expected if the athlete is of sound mind and body. This is determined by a detailed pre-season history and physical examination; sometimes, a pre-contest examination is indicated. Preferably, the examination iş performed by a physician who understands sports medicine and is sympathetic to athletics. Although personal experience in sports on the part of the examining physician is advantageous, it is not a prerequisite.

A family physician familiar with a candidate's prior medical history may contribute information that has a bearing on the athlete's fitness for a sport, but he may also be less thorough and objective in his examination. Nevertheless, in the best interest of the athlete, the beam physician and family physician should be in communication about the athlete's past and present state of health.

PURPOSE OF THE EXAMINATION

The basis for sound medical care of the athlete is the pre-season and in some instance, the pre-contest medical examination. School administrator, athletic director, coach, trainer, or team doctor should not presume an athlete to be physically fit merely because he "came out for the team." A complete medical examination is mandatory prior to all participation to prevent potential tragedies. The pre-season examination has several purposes:

1. To determine the physical fitness of the athlete and eliminate candidates who are unfit for a sport.
2. To screen out silent diseases, congenital abnormalities, and residuals from injuries, of which the athlete and even the parents may be completely unaware. This is an important part of an athletic-injury prevention program.
3. To establish a baseline profile of the athlete's state of health, which is especially useful to a physician in the treatment and follow-up care of injury or

illness. This information should be available to the athlete, the doctor, and the athletic supervisory personnel throughout his athletic career.

4. To demonstrate the school's concern for the candidate's health and welfare.

The physical examination of athletes prior to participation is a medical, legal, and moral obligation of the administrators, athletic directors, coaches, and physicians. It is not subject to the whims, interference, or control of the coach or others.

EXTENT OF THE EXAMINATION

Before any conditioning program begins for an athlete, a medical examination is performed, which includes a history of past illness and injuries as well as emotional and psychiatric difficulties. In addition, all indicated laboratory and electro-diagnostic adjuncts are performed. If a history or medical examination reveals evidence of potentially disqualifying medical conditions, the athlete must be referred to an appropriate consultant for an opinion on his fitness to participate in a particular sport. Dental, visual, and auditory surveys are also an integral part of the examination.

The following conditions might be causes for disqualification depending on the sport:

1. Medical

a. Uncontrolled diabetes myelitis.

b. Hypertension.

c. History of/or active heart disease.

d. History of/or active nephritis and other renal disease.

e. Tuberculosis, if active or arrested for less than 5 years.

f. Asthma, emphysema, bronchiectasis.

g. Syphilis, active or untreated.

h. Other active venereal disease.

i. Narcotics addiction.

j. Blood discourses, haemophilia, sickle cell disease or trait.

k. Athletes with one organ, such as an eye, kidney, or testicle, or severe deafness in one ear.

l. Prior cardiac surgery for acquired or congenital heart disease.

m. Enlarged liver or spleen.

n. Acute infections, respiratory, genitourinary, infectious mononucleosis, and rheumatic fever.

Some recent judicial decisions have permitted an athlete with one eye to participate in basketball and an athlete with an undescended testicle to play football. In such cases, appropriate protective equipment must be used. A boxer possessing sight in only one eye, an epileptic, and a deaf-mute are disqualified from international amateur boxing under International Amateur Boxing Association auspices.

Primary aortic disease or a combination of aortic and mitral disease, unusual rhythm changes, conduction disturbances, and coronary artery disease are sufficient reasons for disqualification. "Functional" heart murmurs must be thoroughly investigated to determine whether or not they are disabling. This can be done by using non-invasive techniques, such as an exercise tolerance test using a bicycle speedometer, treadmill, or radio-nucleotide stress testing with thallium 201, or technetium. The use of echocardiography is extremely valuable for evaluating murmurs. Of course, the conventional electrocardiogram and determination of heart size clinically and by x-ray should be done first when heart disease is suspected. This can be followed by the more expensive, sophisticated, and time-consuming non-invasive technique noted earlier.

Diabetic teenagers and adults are encouraged to participate in athletics and exercise programs such as calisthenics, baseball, basketball, golf, and tennis. Diabetics have been known to play varsity college football. The diabetic must be instructed in regulating his food and insulin intake in the proper amounts because strenuous exercises result in an increase of endogenous insulin. The athlete must learn to neutralize anticipated episodes of hypoglycemia with extra carbohydrate intake during athletic activity.

2. Neurologic

a. Convulsive disorders not completely controlled by medication.

b. Tremors, tics, fasciculations, and other abnormal involuntary movements.

c. Ataxic, spastic, or cerebellar gaits.

d. Cerebral haemorrhage, concussion, or history of serious head injury.

e. Labyrinthine disturbance.

f. Chorea.

Candidates with a history of convulsive disorders require individual evaluation, but should be barred from participation in those sports where chronic recurrent head trauma may occur. History or clinical findings of injury following a fractured skull or brain concussion indicate electroencephalograph to rule out the presence of intracrannial damage. An athlete who sustains a head injury in a contact sport other than a minor concussion should be disqualified for the rest of the season. In the case of boxer, who has been knocked out with a loss of consciousness, two months' rest is mandatory, and if he has suffered three or more such injuries within a year, he should be disqualified for life from the sport. Athletes who sustain head injuries require follow-up by frequent clinical examinations, brain scans, CAT scans, and electroencephalograms.

Athletes with latern jaws are easy prey to knock-out blows in football and in boxing, and should be discouraged from participating in sports in which the chain is especially vulnerable.

3. *Ophthalmology*

a. Severe myopia.

b. The presence of only one eye or useful vision in only one eye.

It is extremely important that both normal peripheral vision and central visual acuity be present. The need for corrective lenses is not in itself disqualifying, but is determined by the extent of visual deficiency and the type of sport. In recent years, the soft lenses are commonly used in athletic pursuits. They are even worn in contact sports in which glasses are not commonly seen.

4. *Orthopedic*

a. Klippel-Feil syndrome.

b. Myelomeningocele.

c. Instability of the atlantooccipital joint.

d. Anomalies of the odontoid process.

e. Incapacitating clinical conditions of the axial or appendiceal skeleton.

A physical examination is directed to the musculoskeletal system to check out the muscles, joints, and bones of the athlete. Balance, gait, and coordination ability during the performance of certain exercises in the examination are noted. Muscle strength and weaknesses are tested. Girth measurements of extremities are taken if atrophy or hypertrophy is suspected. Joints are examined for range of motion, restrictions, and laxity. Leg lengths should be measured when shortening is suspected. Extremities showing residual weakness or imbalance, joint restrictions or laxity from prior injuries, disease, disuse, or overuse may be prone to recurrent injury.

Athletes with long necks should not be encouraged to play football or box unless they can build up strong neck and shoulder muscles. An athlete may be unaware of congenital anomalies of the vertebral column until he has been injured. Such backs heal less satisfactorily than spinal columns with normal bony architecture. Unless the restoration proceeds normally and fully, the athlete should be directed to a less-demanding sport.

A consultation must be requested whenever the examination causes the examining physician to suspect a clinical condition beyond the scope of his training and experience. This also applies to mental and emotional difficulties.

• Physicians must not be restricted by inflexible rules in determining the fitness or unfitness of an athletic candidate. Individuals vary considerably in their capacity for adjustment and achievement. Sports lore is replete with stories of severely handicapped men and women who have competed with non-handicapped players, often winning prominence in highly competitive sports.

A great deal of psychological damage can be done to an athlete who has been unnecessarily restricted. When the physician forbids a candidate to participate in sports, the reasons must be made clear to the candidate and to all those concerned with the program. Much misunderstanding and resentment will be avoided if the team doctor maintains a policy of frankness and clarity in his dealings with the coaches and players.

When a candidate is a minor, the parents must be advised of the reason for the disqualification. If the candidate is in need of medical care, the instructions must be imparted to those concerned. On occasion, parents may insist that their child is capable of playing a sport in spite of medical disqualifications. At no time may the coach take it upon himself to set aside the doctor's decision. In such a situation, the coach should direct the athlete and his obstinate parents to the athletic or school administrators, who should refer the matter to their legal representative. It may be necessary to adjudicate legally.

However, a candidate with physical conditions that disqualify him from one sport is not automatically disqualified from all sports. For instance, a youth with mild mitral insufficiency may be permitted to participate in a sports program that does not require constant strenuous effort or body contact. Rigorous sports, such as swimming, track, tennis, football, boxing, wrestling, soccer, and hockey should of course be forbidden; but golf, baseball, and volley ball, in which effort alternates with relaxation, may be permitted.

SETTING UP A PHYSICAL EXAMINATION

Step One

Obtain the services of a licensed physician who is interested in and sympathetic towards athletics and athletes. Spell out in precise terms the exact medical coverage you expect from the doctor. The doctor must know whether he is to be the examining physician for the pre-season or pre-contest examination, the game physician, or the team physician. A financial arrangement for the doctor's services must be arranged in advance.

The physician in charge of attending the medical needs of the team must have free rein in the choice of consultant. However, if a parent insists upon a different consultant or examining physician for the child, this request must be honoured, but a note of it should be made on the athlete's medical file.

Step Two

Provide a satisfactory examination area. Doctors prefer conducting examinations for a large number of athletes in a large are, such as a gym, rather than in a private office. A satisfactory area may be arranged by providing a few examining tables, screens, weighing scale, and eye chart.

Step Three

Provide the doctor with assistants, such as a nurse and perhaps a trainer who can take height, weight, temperature, pulse, and respiration reading. Blood pressures may be taken by nurses. Student managers and stenographers can record the observations and facilitate the working of the project. Scheduling the examinations over several periods of time instead of crowding them all into one afternoon would alleviate pressure on the doctor and perhaps allow a more thorough, unhurried examination of each athlete.

Record-keeping

All medical records should be typed in triplicate. The physician, coach, and athletic director each keep one copy.

It is absolutely essential that a candidate for an athletic team sign an athletic participation form, wherein he states he is familiar with the eligibility rules and believe he is eligible to represent the team. He also agrees to abide by rules and regulations of the school authorities as well as the training rules established by the coach and his staff. Parental consent is necessary for minors, and a parental consent section may be incorporated with the physician's examination certificate on a single form, such as that used by Highland Park High School Athletic Department.

At this time, no standard physical examination form for athletes is available. In general, the form should include all past and parent medical history that might have a bearing on the physical fitness of the candidate. Any injuries or illnesses, old or new, and the degree of restoration are significant data to a physician in assessing an athlete's fitness to play. The athlete must be thoroughly and completely examined from head to toe, front and back. Normal and abnormal findings must be recorded.

The short but comprehensive physical examination form included here is especially useful in assessing the physical fitness of an athlete. It not only includes all body systems, but also covers those parts of the body that have special significance in athletics. General practitioners and specialists will find this form easy to handle and informative in evaluating an athlete's physical fitness. In drawing up an examination form, it may be advisable for the physician to consult a lawyer familiar with state and school regulations.

Chapter-4

PHYSICAL CONDITIONING FOR FOOTBALL PLAYERS

PRE-SEASON CONDITIONING

Many sports allow ample time for proper conditioning after school opens. In football, however, the time available for preliminary training and conditioning is woefully short. Each day taken to develop strength, endurance, and speed reduces the available time for teaching the fundamentals and complexities of the sport. No less than 6 to 8 weeks of conscientious hard work are required to get an athlete into tiptop shape for intensive football competition.

Therefore, the football player must follow a carefully planned program of training that includes spring football when possible, and hat is followed during the summer. This enables him to report at he opening of the playing season in good physical trim, and prepares him sufficiently to participate in the strenuous work necessary to develop fundamentals and teamwork within a week after the opening of the training season.

A summer exercise and conditioning program will aid in heat acclimatization, so that heat-stress reactions are less likely to occur as the training becomes intensified during the regular season. The more graduated, intensive, and persistent the training routine, the more efficiently the body responds to the increased demands upon it. Pre-season conditioning is now being stressed as an absolute necessity to lessen the frequency of serious injuries. It is practically indispensable in football.

COACHING INSTRUCTIONS

As we mentioned in the beginning of this section, running provides an excellent means of building general strength and endurance in order to avoid injuries early in the season that could affect the player for the entire season. Football squads should get extensive practice in running during the early season. Moreover, all participants in contact sports should learn techniques of falling, rolling, and changing speed and direction. Since most shoulder and arm injuries occur when a player falls and strikes the arm or shoulder, football players in particular should learn to fall when tackled by tensing themselves, bringing their arms in close to their bodies, and flexing their heads and bodies into a fetal position.

Most adolescents tend to be "awkward" when they first participate in contact sports in high school. Therefore, they should receive instruction in tumbling, agility, and leg action during pre-season practice and throughout the season. Learning proper running techniques helps a player to avoid overreaching on pivot plays or plays that require abrupt changes in direction. All these methods help to improve coordination, equilibrium, and prevent joint, muscles, and ligament injuries.

At the end of spring football practice, the coach should call a meeting of the varsity players and newcomers to talk about the importance of the team's reporting in good condition at the opening of the following season. He may emphasize the fact that players who do not take time to stay in good condition might have to take time out—i.e., if they go stale or become disabled with injuries—and that their chances of making the team are bettered or worsened by their physical fitness. The coach may also point out that his athletic life of a youth is a rather short one and that he may as well make the most of the span.

Before the departure of the athletes, the coach should obtain their summer addresses. As the summer progresses, the coach should drop them occasional "reminders" covering pointers noted below.

HELPFUL SUGGESTIONS FOR SUMMER CONDITIONING

1. Use electrolyte solutions before, during and after workouts.
2. Loosen up well before doing sprints; stretch the leg muscles.
3. Take good care of your feet. Use plenty of foot power. Use two pairs of socks cotton socks next to the skin and a pair of wool socks over these. If you feel a hot spot on your foot, apply petroleum jelly over the area between the two pairs of socks.
4. The player should not wait until the last moment to start a balanced diet.
5. Strengthen the muscles of the thigh and foreleg for knee and ankle problems, respectively.
6. Take short sprints to develop speed. Do distance running to develop endurance. Run in circles and figure-eight's to strengthen ankles, knees, hips, and back.
7. Exercise 15 to 30 minutes, depending on your physical condition.
8 Do a general toning up of all muscles with special emphasis on those muscles important in your sport. Do not perform violent or excessive exercises.
9. Take a short rest period between exercises.

10. The player should not perform exercise immediately after a meal or when fatigued.

Players should be warned against going to extremes. Some youngsters are so anxious to make a good showing that they report too "fine," so that the coach has a problem keeping them from going stale when the strenuous workouts start.

PRESEASON CONDITIONING PROGRAM.

This program is designed to get an athlete in excellent physical condition for the practice sessions and the season ahead. Speed, strength, endurance, flexibility, agility, balance, and neuromuscular coordination must be developed.

Most athletes do not know how to condition themselves when they are on their own. The following conditioning program is for high school or college football prospects. This program can be done 6 days a week during the month of July; on August, the tempo should be increased.

The following exercises are included in the preseason program:

HURDLE POSITION

The player should sit in hurdle position with left leg forward. Bend trunk forward and touch left foot with both hands. Repeat 10 to 15 times; then extend right leg and repeat 10 to 15 times. This is a great exercise for stretching hamstring muscles; however, it may pose some problems for a heavily muscled linesman.

REACTION DRILLS IN CRAB POSITION

Face down, weight on hands and feet. Move crab-like on command in a forward, backward, and sideward manoeuvre rapidly about 10 yards. This exercise not only quickens reflex reaction to changing football situations, but enhances agility. It also stretches groin muscles.

ROCKING CHAIR POSITION

Lie flat on back, bring knees to chest, place hands around shins and rock back and forth 20 times. This exercise stretches the back muscles.

Push-Ups

Lie flat on stomach with hands on the ground at sides and near shoulders. Legs are extended and toes pointed. Push down with hands and push body off the ground. Do a series of five push-ups in less than 5 seconds. Relax for a couple of seconds and repeat four additional series, totalling five series. This exercise strengthens arm, abdomen, chest, and leg muscles. Two additional series of five push-ups can be done using finger tips as support. This latter exercise strengthens the fingers and hands.

Chin-Ups

Grasp a chinning bar, a cross bar, top of door or a tree limb. Pull your body upward until chin passes bar. Lower your body to complete extension of the arms and repeat six times. This is a good therapeutic exercise following shoulder injuries.

Stomach Drill Position

Lie flat on back with hands on chest, legs straight together, and toes pointed. Raise feet slowly with a slow count of 10 until the legs are perpendicular to the ground, then lower legs slowly counting from 10 to 1. When the number 1 is reached, the feet should be about 6 inches above the ground. Hold position for the count of 10. Repeat 10 times. This is a good exercise for the abdominal muscles.

Calf-Raises

Performed on a 2-inch board with toes pointed and heels placed on the ground.

Most running in the games consists of quick, short bursts, and the athlete must condition himself for these. The 20-yard burst is really important, and the first three steps are crucial. The entire preseason program should be repeated until the season begins.

The football player who fails to condition himself during the summer is at a distinct disadvantage when he reports for the season's opening. He soon realize that he has wasted valuable time that not only impedes his progress, but also makes him vulnerable to injuries. The coaches does not have time to wait for the athlete to get into physical condition after reporting for practice or to recuperate if he is injured because he is not in shape. The time between the season's opening and the first game is generally short. The athlete who reports in good physical condition will find that the game of football can be beneficial if he has prepared himself properly for the coming season.

The best criterion for coaches is how fast you can run 40 yards with full uniform. Timing for speed is big with coaches. There is no substitute for speed and power.

Practice Sessions

Because there is no short cut to experience, every practice session counts. In most secondary schools and college, there are only 3 to 4 weeks of practice time between the opening of the season and the first game. In this short period, the football coaches has the herculean task of getting his team into peak physical condition and teaching them fundamentals, skills, strategies of offence and defence, and protective manoeuvres. He must build up a high morale and esprit de corps among his athletes. He knows that although each player has received a written set of exercise instructions to be followed during the summer, the athletes will come back in different states of conditioning, requiring individual attention.

Since early sessions are usually held twice a day until the first game, the coach and his staff must check out each athlete's condition of readiness for the season's rigors by questionnaire and interview. Only in this manner can the coach avoid overtaxing his players, which would set them back and seriously hamper their conditioning program. It is in the early days of the season when the temperature is hot and the players are not yet in shape that coaches can wreck their athletes by being overzealous. Although muscle soreness is to be expected following the first days of practice, working an athlete too hard during the first days may result in a major problem that may seriously hamper the progress of a team, particularly if key players are slowed down by it.

Although most athletes usually recover in a few days, valuable time has been lost and their activities limited. Muscle pulls, particularly in the groin and hamstring areas, are also quite frequent among athletes during early season practice; effort must be made to avoid these troublesome injuries.

An already mentioned, the coach should schedule the practice sessions in the cool hours of the early morning or late afternoon to avoid the hottest hours of the day. Practising at these times helps to prevent heat-stress reactions and fatigue states, provided the athletes take salt and water as needed. When an athlete tires, the reaction time of his reflexes is slowed down and he is more prone to injuries. Twice-a-day practice sessions should be spaced as far apart as possible. This interval allows the athlete to rest and recuperate, so necessary when maximal efforts are expended. Be liberal with rest periods during a practice session.

Each practice session should begin with 10 minutes of stretch/flexibility and/or agility drills designed to warm up all the major muscle groups and stretch ligaments. Coaches are now relying more heavily on agility drills such as crabouts, carioca drills, monkey rolls, and others of this nature than old-fashioned calisthenics. However, the coach must not overdo or dwell too long on this phase of the program; it hardens muscles and helps to prevent injuries, but does not teach the players anything about football. After the warm-up sessions, the athletes should go to their respective groups where specialty coaches teach them football and give them exercises designed to strengthen the muscles associated with their respective positions in the line-up.

OFF-SEASON CONDITIONING

Training is not only a seasonal affair; it should be carried on throughout the year. After the season is over, the athlete should continue exercising to keep his body in good condition. Since he has worked hard to attain top physical condition, he should not stop suddenly. He should follows a program of exercises designed to keep his muscles toned and provide recreation simultaneously. The following activities are good to accomplish such a purpose: badminton, basketball, bicycle riding, bowling, touch football, golf, handball, cross-country running, squash, racquet ball, roller skating, paddle-ball, swimming, tennis, and just plain walking several miles daily. Weight training is the most important off-season activity; boxing, handball, squash, and tennis are the best agility activities.

Chapter-5

PHYSICAL CONDITIONING FOR BASKETBALL PLAYERS

Basketball is a team sport with a great deal of body contact. Rule changes have speeded up the game offensively, and increasing emphasis is being placed on using, tall, large-sized athletes. These aspects have made the sport increasingly more rugged.

Today's well-muscled basketball players move with almost incredible speed and agility and are constantly running into, bumping, pushing, and elbowing their opponents voluntarily and involuntarily. Consequently, basketball players are subjected to tremendous pounding and roughness during a game.

The athlete must him down excess weight and harden flabby muscles to withstand these hazards. A tall player without sufficient muscle mass may not be able to stand the rigors of this sport.

Basketball players are continually running, interspersed with abrupt stops and starts. Basketball is similar to track, in that only by running can strong legs and adequate cardio-respiratory endurance be developed.

The heart and lungs must reach a degree of efficiency to supply sufficiently oxygenated blood to meet muscular demands and remove waste metabolites.

The player with sufficient cardiovascular reserve may be able to put on enough extra pressure in the last 5. minutes of a game to win a close one or ice a near-win. Unless the basketball player does a lot of preseason running conscientiously, he will fatigue easily during the season.

Basketball players should follow a running program to aid preseason conditioning. They should run up hills, multiple short sprints including running backwards and angular run to three spots at 10 yard intervals at top speed with another person pointing to the next designated spot is a variation of a running pattern to assist in fitness for basketball. This can be followed by 20 minutes of stretch/flexibility training. Weight spats or sneakers with lead in the soles have been used in running programs in the past.

Spectacular jump shots and rebound efforts place a tremendous strain on the antigravity muscles of the back, hips, and legs. Well-conditioned basketball players exhibit great muscles elasticity and joint flexibility. Jumping ability can be increased by mechanical resistance equipment, but they should be used only under expert supervision.

A simple and revolutionary method to improve jumping ability is by jumping in shoulder-height water dipping below the water and exploding straight up in sudden violent contraction without the resistance of weights. Repeat 10 times in rapid succession. Wrist weights to increase the strength of the arms have been use in the past. The amount of weights can only be determined by experience and experimentation.

Basketball conditioning starts in earnest with the beginning of the fall season, and the player should be thoroughly conditioned when the season opens officially in October. A combination of the following constitutes a sound basis for basketball conditioning program.

1. Running
2. Conditioning drills
3. Flexibility
4. Weight training

The summer conditioning and the preseason exercise programs mentioned for football may also be used by basketball players. Great athletes work on their sport 12 months a year.

Chapter-6

PHYSICAL CONDITIONING FOR BOXERS

ABOUT BOXING

Fighting is a natural sport of man. Boxing is an individualistic combative sport that requires courage and skills not possessed by average men in the general population. Thus, a thorough toughening process is necessary; boxers spend years hardening their bodies. Blows do not affect them as they would an unprepared male, who no doubt would be easily battered and bruised.

A fighter's legs, along with his endurance, enable him to avoid and to withstand the rigors of this rough sport. His legs must be agile and quite strong; manoeuvrability helps him to avoid hit and brings him to his target at the appropriate time. The boxer's legs must be strong enough to "stand up"-in the boxing ring, there are no substitutions or doors. As *Joe Louis,* former heavyweight champion of the world, once said, "In the ring you can run but you can't hide."

Every muscle from head to toe is developed in the training and conditioning of a boxer. Every fighter needs a different training routine tailored to his particular physical and emotional needs. However, some basic requirements of training are expected of all fighters to prepare them properly for the rugged career they have chosen. Boxing, gym work, roadwork, and mental discipline are essential. There rounds of boxing are equivalent to ten rounds of gym work. Gym work encompasses small and heavy bag punching, rope jumping calisthenics, shadow boxing, and wall weight pulleys. *Angelo Dundee,* trainer of many world champions, doesn't use wall-weight pulleys for his boxers. *Cus D'Amato,* trainer of two world champions, recommends them, if used properly, because they use muscles used in boxing. However, they are obsolete in most gyms. Generally a boxer must train per day a minimum of double the number of rounds he is scheduled to box.

Punching the small bag aids in speed, rhythm, timing, and coordination of the hands and eyes. The heavy bag helps a fighter to develop leverage to get the most effect from his punches. He practices his various manoeuvres and develops muscle control on the bags. A relaxed arm does not hurt anyone; snap, shoulder movements swivelling of hips, and turning of feet are responsible for the strength of a punch, and these skills can be developed with light-and heavy-bag punching.

To become an excellent boxer, one does not just wake up one morning and decide to be a champ. Boxing is an art that takes years to master. A boxer must be toughened up from childhood, eating simple, nutritious foods, leading a clean, wholesome life, and getting sufficient rest and sleep.

To be a boxer, you cannot burn the candle at both ends-you must maintain physical fitness at all times through various types of exercises and calisthenics designed to build the stamina and endurance needed to move in, out, and around your adversary. It is most important to box often in competition before large crowds. A "boxer" might box well in a gym, but get "stage fright" when he hears the roar of a crowd and see the ring lights, and may lose control of his boxing ability.

All the gym work in the world cannot supplant actual boxing.

A workout starts with limbering and loosening up exercises, to get the links and stiffness out of the muscles and joints. This takes about two to three rounds. All parts of the musculo-skeletal system are put through their ranges of motion, especially the neck, shoulders, trunk, upper and lower extremities. The head and neck and rolled around several times, first in a clockwise and then in a counter-clockwise direction.

The shoulder ridge muscles are shrugged and the shoulder joints are put through a range of motion. A few deep knee bends are done. The trunk is rotated in all planes, including a few toe touches and alternate toe touches. The boxer jumps and bounces around in small circles with his hands and arms held high. From this position he throws a few punches as if he were shadow boxing, and then he goes into the shadow boxing routine.

Shadow boxing is done for two to three rounds before a body-size mirror or in the ring. Offensive and defensive moves are planned and executed against an imaginary opponent. Following the shadow boxing, the fighter boxes with a sparring partner for an appropriate number of rounds. Boxers need sparring practice while training.

The frequency and number of rounds depends on his state of conditioning. Every new punch or manoeuvre must be practices in shadow boxing and with sparring partners. Boxing often with different partners also acquaints the fighters with various styles of boxing and adversaries. Instruction is usually given during round breaks, but occasionally the bout may be stopped to emphasize a point.

The sparring is followed first by heavy-bag punching for a minimum of two rounds to develop leverage, strength, and execution of manoeuvres. This is followed with two to three rounds of little-bag punching to develop speed, rhythm, timing, and strength to keep the hands high. Rope skipping is done for about three rounds to develop footwork, co-ordination, strength and flexibility of arms, wrist, and legs. This exercise keeps the muscles from stiffening up and assists in developing cardiovascular-respiratory endurance. The training session is concluded by floorwork consisting of exercises to strengthen the abdominal muscles, the neck, and the legs. Dundee eliminates shoulder push-ups for his charges. The boxer then dries off and gets a rubdown.

Massages and rubdowns are still an important part of the training program. Massage varies with the size and physique of the fighter, but the rubdown must not be done too vigorously, or else the muscles may go into spasm. Massage reaches those muscles that some exercises miss and loosens up those muscles that may become sore or tighten up from exercise. Heat liniment can be used for some areas, as well as infrared lamps.

Each trainer prefers a particular brand or mixture of rubdown material, which ranges from Omega oil, wintergreen, and alcohol to various combinations of these ingredients. These helps evaporate the water from the skin giving a cooling effect. Dundee doesn't believe in massages for his young boxers. He says" everything natural is better."

Roadwork helps develop stamina and endurance; it "cleans out the lungs." It is essential for all boxers from the 3-round amateurs to the 15-round professionals. The amount of roadwork depends on the number of rounds of the upcoming bout as well as the importance of the match. Some fighters jog the entire distance. Some fighters break up the roadwork with footwork moving the hands and trunk simultaneously. Roadwork is the best single conditioner in the training program for boxers. This, of course, depends on the boxer's needs and what helps him most.

If a boxer is overweight, water and caloric intake must be counted. He should dress in heavy clothing and be encourage to sweat. Thin boxers should be dressed in light clothing. The boxer must be weighed every day before and after his workout, to enable the trainer to assess the degree of conditioning. The trainer must keep the boxer at the weight at which he achieves a competitive edge and at which he functions best.

The trainer must be able to dry out the fighter without weakening him. Approximately 2 to 3 pounds daily can be lost in the drying-out process. However, if the fighter becomes too drawn or tight, he may be on the verge of going stale, i.e., reaching a state of boredom. At this point, eliminate a day of running of boxing. Two days before a contest, all training is stopped except for light roadwork.

FIGHT CAMPS

Many boxers who compete in main events and championship bouts do their training in a fight camp. Although this is the ideal place to train for a bout, fight camps are losing their importance because most fighters cannot afford them. Training starts 4 to 6 weeks before the contest, depending upon when the boxer had his last bout or training period and his state of conditioning. The fighter starts his day by arising between 6:00 and 6:30 A.M. and does 2 to 3 miles of roadwork, which includes sprints, jogging, and various forms of footwork. It is best to run with company.

Following the roadwork, the fighter lies down and rests for 1 to 2 hours until he is completely sweated out. Some trainers rub their fighters down at this time. At 10:00 a.m., he has breakfast, consisting of cereal, three eggs, toast, and tea with lemon. He then walks for one half mile and rests again until the afternoon.

Fighters usually do not have lunch. The gym routine starts between 2:00 and 3:00 P.M. The boxer weighs in, and starts with a few rounds of shadow boxing. Six rounds of boxing are done with three fresh sparring partners. If enough sparring partners are not available, the amount of heavy-bag punching is increased. He skips rope for three rounds, followed by a complete floorwork routine. The boxer takes a hot shower, follows with a cold shower, weighs himself, and gets a rundown by his trainer.

The boxer lies around until dinner time-and 6:00 P.M. Steak, chicken, or lamb chops make up the main fare. Salad and tea with lemon complete the meal. Water and caloric intake is watched if he has to make a certain weight. Following dinner, he takes a walk in the woods or on the road for about 1 hour. He may then write letters, play cards, or see a movie. He goes to bed about 10:00 P.M. The time-honoured traditions of wood chopping and sawing have proven too strenuous for modern fighters, and are not even shown toady for publicity purposes.

Chapter-7

PHYSICAL CONDITIONING FOR SOCCER PLAYERS

Soccer is truly an international sport, being played before crowds of 100,000 and more in stadiums in Latin America, Europe, Asia, Africa, and Australia.

Its international popularity has influenced the tremendous growth of this sport in the United States. This is especially true with the establishment of the North American Soccer League established in 1971 with international starts such as American-born Kyle Rote, Jr. over 70,000 people have come to see the Cosmos at Giant Stadium in the Meadowlands with such famous names as Pele, Franz Beckenbauer, Giorgio Chinaglia, and others. The inherent physical mental, and social factors that have made the game so popular throughout the world have inspired physical educators to include soccer in the physical education curriculum and in interscholastic programs from the grade-school level up through college.

The conditioning of the soccer athlete is similar to that for an athlete who participates in other contact sports that require running, speed, agility, neuromuscular coordination, and endurance. In addition, soccer players must develop the ability to accelerate instantly in forward, backward, and lateral directions. Therefore, the soccer player must develop especially strong legs, ankles, feet, abdominal and neck muscles. Running, running, and more running is necessary. The strong "educated" feet of a soccer player can only be developed by coordinating the kicking and running skills of the athlete.

The soccer field, stadium, and cross-country terrain may be used to develop the strong legs necessary for soccer players. A practice session starts with 10 minutes of loosening up. This is followed by 10 to 15 minutes of sprint drills on the soccer field. The athletes are encouraged to run around the field any number of times, depending on the condition they are in. Jogging once around the field is followed by an all-out sprint of 30, maximum 50 yards, with and without the ball. Training with the ball should be emphasized. This is followed by a ¾ sprint for 50 yards, another jog, an all out sprint for 50 yards, and another jog. To avoid the boredom of always sprinting about a soccer field, cross-country running for 2½ to 3 miles, accelerating up the hills and coasting downhill, is substituted. All out sprinting is encouraged on the flat. Alternate jogging and sprinting may also be done on a large, flat field.

Strength and power in the muscles of the legs can be gained by running up rows of stadium seats in sneakers. The athlete runs up a complete level of about 100 feet at full speed, walks down and runs up again. This exercise is done on a progressive basis until ten ascents can be done. Insight acceleration is also developed by this type of running. Running is done 6 days a week.

When practising, a soccer player should not only run in a forward direction, but must also practice running in reverse and lateral directions. This helps him to recover his position if beaten to it by his opponent; recovery is essential, since failure can be to the opposition's advantage.

Individual skills and game situations are developed next. Work on the weak-side extremities is stressed.

Goalies also need training in gymnastics, in addition to the usual skills of soccer players.

Before the start of each game, the players should run onto the field and do short wind sprints in all directions, alternated with jogging, with or without the ball. These should take place in an area of 5 to 10 yards. The timing of the wind sprints and jogging should be approximately 2 to 5 minutes. After this, the players should do "stretch-out" exercises. For example, the player spreads his legs and touches his toes, both in an erect and supine position, turns his head in different directions and jumps up and down, and moves his head up and down practising head balls. Fifteen minutes of kicking and heading should be practiced before each game. The player should work up a light perspiration just before the start of the game.

The day following the game, relaxing exercises with no physical contact are encouraged, such as groups of four players practising head balls, trapping the ball, and so forth.

In the winter season, indoor running and exercises should be done at least every other day. Dribbling with short passes should be practiced during these months. Indoor swimming is recommended to increase vital capacity. During the summer, running on sandy shores, hiking, and mountaineering are useful in building up stamina.

The regularity of exercises and running is the key to building of stamina. This sort of intensive program develops agility, speed, strength, neuromuscular coordination and instant acceleration, which are so important for a soccer player.

Chapter-8

PHYSICAL CONDITIONING IN SWIMMING

As a sport, swimming provides, fun, health, and fitness. It is an excellent therapeutic modality for many musculo-skeletal injuries. It also develops a feeling of security in handling oneself in water. Few sports contribute as much as swimming to total-body conditioning by means of strengthening the cardiovascular system, stretching, and coordination techniques. Swimming can build muscular strength, power, and endurance.

During the summer months, the athlete should work on long-distance swimming and exercise in a well-planned and supervised program that will help build arm strength, leg strength, neuromuscular coordination, and increase lung volume.

Cross-country running and the preseason condition guide given for football players may also be recommended for swimmers. It is suggested that the swimmer work on weights during the season to develop his shoulder, arm, and leg strength. Recreational swimming at the beach during the summer months is not sufficient for competitive swimmers, who should train in pools. When the season begins, the athlete should be in such top physical condition for competitive swimming that he could participate in a race if necessary.

GENERAL SWIMMING TRAINING SCHEDULE

A. Calisthenics

1. 55 days; 2. 30-minute; 3. 5 day weekly.

B. Weight Training

1. 55 days (Mini-Gym); 2. 30-minute sessions (Nautilus); 3. 5 day weekly (Nautilus).

C. Pulley Work (Light Weights with Repetition)

1. From beginning of school; 2. Maximum each time; 3. 3 days weekly.

D. Pull-Ups (Chinning)

1. 55 days; 2. Maximum each time; 3. 3 times per week;

These should be performed about 90% of the time with an overgrasp to bring the back of the neck to the bar. This is done to develop the triceps. The other ten per cent of the time, an undergrasp is used to bring the chin to rest on the bar. This develops the biceps.

E. Running

1. 1 month; 2. 1 mile distance; 3. 3 times per week.

F. Water Work (Swimming, Kicking and Pulling)

1. From beginning of school; 2. 1 hour daily; 3. 5 days practice per week

G. Workout Procedures

1. Swim all distances with repeated swims at varied intervals of 25, 50, 75, 100, 125, 200, 500, 1,000, and 1,650 yards; 2. General guidelines for total distance per

daily workout are as follows:-

Sprinters: 4,000 to 6,000 yards daily

Middle distance: 6,000 to 8,000 yards daily

Distance: 10,000 to 12,000 yards daily.

These should be performed in two sessions. The swimmer should set up his own daily schedule and uses those distances that suit him best, varying them daily to improve his performance. Success is spelled w-o-r-k. Whenever in doubt, swim more distances.

Chapter-9

PHYSICAL CONDITIONING FOR TENNIS PLAYERS

Tennis has always appealed to both sexes, both young and old. Although it is more of a participant's sport than a spectator's sport, it is an exciting game to watch when played by top-ranking performers.

The conditioning of the athlete is similar to that of an athlete who participates in any other sport that requires running. Speed, agility, neuromuscular coordination, and endurance must be developed to play a good game of tennis.

One must have strong legs; cross-country running and bicycle riding are excellent ways to condition the leg muscles. Special attention is performing calisthenic exercises should be placed on strengthening the ankle, knee, wrist, arm, and shoulder joints.

In order to keep the feet from getting sore and blistering, the player should wear two pairs of socks, especially when playing on hard courts such as asphalt, cement, composition, or wood. Playing during the summer months is an ideal way to condition the body and improve the tennis game.

Chapter-10

PHYSICAL CONDITIONING IN TRACK AND FIELD

The most significant change in track is the increasing number of females going into these events as competitors and coaches, the use of the coordinated staff of coaches and the change from the English to the metric system. *Traditionally,* men coached male and female track athletes, although there have always been a number of female coaches who coached female athletes. However, with increasing numbers of women going into coaching, the philosophy of the coordinated staff is now being employed; here the coach, regardless of gender, will coach athletes of both sexes depending, of course, on what specific talent the coach has to offer. This is an efficient way of utilizing coaching talents maximally for the benefit of the athlete.

Although female athletes have traditionally accepted male coaches, the reverse is not true, but attitudes are changing. More time is necessary to effect this change. Therefore, it behooves coaches who train female athletes to be conversant with those problems attendant with the breast, menarche, and conception.

Although the coach must be able tó speak with some degree of understanding about these matters, the right of privacy of the athlete must always be respected, and the coach must be able to refer the troubled athlete to the proper physician.

Track and field is a demanding sport that requires speed endurance and strength. This requires strict adherence to a training and conditioning program so a constant output of energy over a certain period of time can be generated and maintained. Such conditioning requires that the athlete progressively push his body to the limits of exhaustion and fatigue, learn to tolerate the pain and discomfort resulting from such training to a safe level, and expect full recovery when the event is over. Conditioning is essential because events can be won and lost as a result of it.

In track, the athletes must be in the right frame of mind for the task ahead. Above all, athletes must believe in themselves and in the coach and trainer and be willing to pay the price to get into proper condition through the vigorous training schedule outline.

The coach and trainer must understand and be aware that their athlete will be nervous before the meet and especially the event. Applying the right motivation is crucial for a coach in readying the athlete for an event. The wrong motivation can be as unrewarding as lack of proper conditioning. The coach and trainer must know the individual personalities of their athletes, which comes only from experience with athletes. The coach must also be patient.

Most of the general training and conditioning techniques stated in the first edition of this book are still valid. For instance, the first few weeks of practice employ conditioning techniques such as cross-country running, easy jogging, interval training, and warm-up including stretching/flexibility exercises that relax the ankle, knee, and hip joints, and the adjoining musculature. During the first month, endurance, speed, and distance are progressively increased. By this time, exercises should include rhythmic jumping on both feet to develop flexor and extensor muscles that control bending of the hips, knees, and ankles. Every athlete should have some background in distance work.

It will serve him well in competition. In distance work, endurance and stamina are developed with distance rather than speed.

The following are applicable for sprinters, hurdles, and middle-distance runners:

1. ***Jogging.*** Jogging is important in beginning warm-ups and conditioning. Mixing striding and walking over a distance is better than jogging all the way.

2. ***Warm-Up.*** Warm-up is important before practice and before participation in different competitive track events. A runner is not ready for hard work until the athlete has thoroughly warmed up.

3. ***Starts.*** In similar, although augmented fashion, reaction time and training are essential to good starting. The start is the most important part of racing.

   a. ***"On your marks."*** Starting blocks should be used for all sprint starts. The runner takes a place on the starting line. Before the runner gets on his mark, he should take three deep breaths and think of reaching the finish line first. The runner must be completely relaxed when the command "On your marks" is given.

   b. ***"Get set."*** The hips are elevated according to which start is used. This position should make the back level and thrust the weight forward. The runner is now ready for the gun. A faster reaction to the gun will be made if the runner reacts to the gun automatically.

   c. ***"Go."*** The runner should aim for quick action of the right foot, first hand and arm movements, and tremendous push from the left foot. The runner should keep in mind that the legs will go only as fast as the arms. Therefore, the sooner the arms get going, the faster the legs will go. The focus of the eyes rises to a point further down the track. The runner must strengthen up gradually as the runner races down the track.

d. ***The Finish.*** The body should be pressed forward. The head should be well forward. The eyes should be kept straight ahead. Maintain proper running form. Keep the speed until 5 yards beyond the finish line and slow down gradually after passing the finish line.

All cross-country runs are from 4 to 5 miles and the routes are of the athlete's own choosing. They are varied to keep the workout from becoming boring, dull and monotonous and are usually done after school.

Weight-training programs vary with the philosophy of the coach and the available equipment. Some coaches do it daily, others on alternate days, but generally, arms and legs are done on different days. Regardless of the philosophy of the coach, weight training must be done throughout the season if the athletes are to benefit from it.

Since the first edition, the progress made by our female track-and-field athletes has been extraordinary and bodes well for future international competition. Women should be encouraged to wear supportive, custom-made bras as well as other appropriate, protective equipment for the sport.

When a female athlete complains of menstrual pain, menstrual irregularity, or other gynecologic symptoms, the coach should refer the athlete to her personal physician.

Chapter-11

PHYSICAL CONDITIONING FOR BASEBALL PLAYERS

When winter is on the wane and the baseball season is not far off, an urge to play baseball grips many athlete. Professionals go off to training camps conducted by the major league clubs; here they train vigorously for 6 to 8 weeks to get into condition for a rigorous season of approximately 200 ball games of which 162 are regulation. The sunny climes of Florida, California, and Arizona are a welcome relief from the wet, cold, snowy weather of winter and are conducive to getting in shape.

The majority of the baseball aspirants in high school and college are not blessed with such ideal training weather and have a much shorter time to get in condition for 15 to 30 games of the season, which generally begin in early April and finish in May or early June. Regardless of the sponsorship and the variations accorded to players by virtue of the position they play, certain fundamental training and conditioning practices are used by most managers, coaches, and trainers for all baseball athletes. Notwithstanding the tremendous press coverage devoted to the throwing arms of pitchers, catchers, and fielders, and to the batting power of hitters, strengthening the legs, developing flexibility, aerobic and anaerobic power have primary importance in the conditioning program. As veteran managers and coaches state it, "get the legs and lungs in shape and the arms will come around. "Conditioning also improves agility, timing, speed of foot, reflexive movements, and eye-hand-ball coordination.

The foundation upon which conditioning in baseball is built is running; this applies to all baseball players regardless of the position they play. It is best accomplished by running a prescribed number of laps as well as by wind sprints of varying lengths in the early weeks of training. Some managers run their athletes up to 2½ and perhaps 3 miles daily. As part of the running program, fielders shag flies in the outfield, participate in infield drills, run and slide into bases. A conditioned young ballplayer should be able to run from home plate to first base in about four second. As the ballplayer ages, it may take him 5 or 5½ seconds to run the same distance.

During the competitive season, most of the ballplayers, except the pitchers, get enough daily work to keep them in condition. It is between seasons that many ballplayers get woefully out of shape. If a baseball player can run a specified distance either cross-country, in a gymnasium, or in a park, he could keep some balance of condition.

Swimming and bicycle riding would benefit him as well. If he could also play some handball, volleyball, squash, racquet-ball, and basketball, he could arrive at training camp reasonably physically fit. A surprisingly large number of professional players conduct their winter fitness programs and report to training camp in near "ready-to-go" condition. To do otherwise, they would risk their jobs. On the other hand, there are just as many top baseball players who go on rubber-chicken circuit.

In addition to running, the surest and most reliable method of getting these muscles in condition is static stretching exercises. These exercises are performed to stretch the ligaments and adjoining muscles of the larger joints, such as the shoulder, back, hips, knees, and ankles, in an effort to make the ballplayer supple and loose. Emphasis is then placed on those special exercise routines that stress bending of the trunk, throwing, and running. These are necessary physical attributes of a successful ballplayer who moves frequently in quick, graceful, fluid motion. One has only to bring to mind a spectacular fielding of a sharply hit ground ball by the short-stop as he flips or throws the ball for a double play or a put-out. Many of these activities are done in a manner to simulate actual baseball moves. These bending and stretching routines are best done in a group for 15 minutes at the beginning of each practice session and are varied to prevent monotony and boredom. They are continued until the player is quite loose and limber and his stamina is improved. Usually the player enjoys increased physical well being. The feeling of suppleness can be maintained by engaging in games of pepper.

Players generally combine flexibility and conditioning exercises, and light throwing from the start of training. As the player's muscles become stronger and his stamina improves, he progressively throws the ball harder. After a ballplayer has reached a maximal level of conditioning, he should throw the baseball hard only after his arm has been sufficiently warmed up. The length of the warm-up varies with each player.

Although the optimum warm-up time is still a matter of research, we know empirically that some ballplayers require just a few pitches and some may need as much as 10 to 15 minutes at varying paces. Each player knows when he is ready, usually when his arms and shoulders feel loose.

Weight work has now become an accepted method of preparing players for a season of baseball. For years, professional baseball pitchers have strengthened the muscles of forearms, wrists, hands, and fingers by squeezing hard rubber balls on and off the field. Babe Ruth developed calluses on his hands by gripping the handle of his bat as hard as he could in an effort to hit home runs. He said "When I am after a homer I try to make mush of this solid ash handle." His calluses explain his home-run records. Most hitters now wear hand gloves to prevent calluses. Now more scientific methods are used to develop muscle strength.

The time devoted to baseball is divided into a preseason and competitive season. The preseason weather of March in most locales is hardly fit for outdoor training for high school and college teams, so the program begins in a gymnasium with the athletes wearing sneakers. Indoor sessions should last no more than 1 and 1½ hours and should be evenly divided between running exercises, light throwing exercises, light batting with a hard rubber ball and/or batting machines, infield drills, and teaching of skills. Running should include a prescribed number of laps around the gym floor and 10 and 20 yard sprints. Some weight work can also be incorporated in the preseason conditioning program.

As soon as the weather permits, the baseball aspirants are taken out doors, where the same fundamental conditioning practices are continued. However, more time is devoted to batting. Playing pepper makes the players bend and become more agile and sharpens their reflexes. Fielders shag flies in the outfield, run and slide into base. Infield drills are continued. Players become conditioned by gradually increasing the amount of play associated with their position. Athletes who have used sneakers in the gym must now change over to spikes; this should be a gradual process to get the feet and legs accustomed to the change and to prevent blisters. Drills for teaching fundamentals of the various positions may be modified to assist in achieving top condition, e.g., drills that stress running for pitchers and outfielders are used. A specific number of laps around the field as well as some wind sprints ranging from home to first base; first to second; first to third, and from second base to home plate. Pitchers should do their running near the end of the practice session. The other ballplayers may do their running at the beginning, during or at the end of the practice.

THE PITCHER

The conditioning and care of the pitcher's arm differs from the care extended to other ballplayers. Since the effectiveness of a pitcher may amount to 60 to 70% of his team's defence, it is understandable why pitchers merit more attention than other ballplayers. In a professional baseball game, the pitcher is physically the most active man on the team. He delivers as many as 150 or more pitches during the course of a game, and perhaps 50 to 70 in warming up.

One has only to watch a pitcher to appreciate the tremendous total bodily effort that goes into each delivery; he may lose up to 9 pounds in a game. In the early days of the live ball, the pitcher was at a disadvantage against hitters like Babe Ruth, Lou Gehrig, Ted Williams, Johnny Mize, Mickey Mantle, Hand Aaron, and others; he had to bear down on each pitch in an effort to get it past the batter. Today the pitcher is better able to control the aggressive effort of the batters such as Reggie Jackson, Chris Chambliss, Rod Carew, Pete Rose, Mike Schmidt, Carl Yastremski, George Brett, or Craig Nettles. The pitchers are coming up with more no-hitters, shut-outs, and generally reducing the batting averages and home run records of the baseball players. They do it with blazing fast balls, curves, screw balls, sliders, and other breaking stuff at their command. These unnatural motions in pitching, plus the tremendous braking forces to the momentum of the follow through, put great strain on the shoulder, arm, and elbow and may cause abnormal clinical conditions at these sites.

Differences in training begin in the preseason program. In professional baseball, the pitchers and catchers go to camp about 5 to 10 days before the regular squad. This gives the pitchers an opportunity to get their legs and arms in condition before the remainder of the squad arrives. While the legs are getting into shape, the pitchers are gradually strengthening their arms, at first by light throwing to the catchers.

As the arms unlimber from a winter sleep, they can throw harder or spin depending on the individual's progress. Premature spinning of the ball can injure an arm unless it is in excellent shape; it takes a minimum of 2 weeks of conditioning to reach this stage. Many trainers with professional baseball clubs like to stretch the muscles of the shoulders, arms, back, and legs of the pitchers before they go on the field and start throwing so they can more easily bend down and follow through. These parts of the body must be made strong as well as loose. In some camps, the same result is accomplished by 15 minutes of calisthenics at the beginning of each session. Some of these exercises simulate game situations. Pitchers then follow up with pepper to improve bending, agility, and reflex action. After the remainder of the squad shows up, the pitcher is called on to pitch in batting practice.

Although a certain amount of stiffness, soreness, and discomfort is expected before the arm is fully conditioned, hard throwing in the early days of camp will lead to an unusual amount of pain and soreness that will not respond to rest, heat, massage, or gentle passive stretching. A pitcher must be cautioned against allowing this to happen since it may also lead to tight, sore arms and shoulders. If it does happen, the following procedure is recommended: The sore arm to above the shoulder is placed in a whirlpool bath at 105 to 110° F for 5 minutes. After the arm is removed, a cold wet towel is placed about it, and the arm is massaged through the towel for one minute. The athlete is then placed on the table on his back. The wrist of the affected arm is grasped by the trainer and the player's arm is flexed forward in the anterior sagittal place from 0° to 180°. Slow, steady traction is exerted by the trainer's hand. The trainer then takes his other hand and places it on the upper edge of the scapula; his fingers grip the shoulder-ridge muscles and extend to the supraclavicular area. The elevated arm is then drawn to the side of the thorax while a slow, steady pull is still exerted on the arm. Some trainers combine these exercises with adduction of the arm across the body towards the other shoulder and with rotary movements of the arm at the shoulder. This procedure passively stretches and relaxes the tight muscles about the arm shoulder, and shoulder blade. The manoeuvre is applied for 1 minute and usually causes these muscles to relax. If the trainer feels a point of resistance accompanied by pain during this manipulation, additional traction with a quick jerk of the arm is applied. This usually releases the tightness. Then the arm is returned to its neutral position. It relief is accomplished, the manoeuvre need not be repeated; if only some relief is afforded, it may be repeated 2 or 3 times. Catfish Hunter's shoulder was salvaged into a winning season after manipulation under general anaesthesia.

When a player is scheduled to pitch, the trainer should immerse the pitcher's arm to above the shoulder in a whirlpool at 105-110° F for 5 minutes a half hour before game time. Following removal from the whirlpool a cold wet towel is placed about the entire arm to close the pores, and the arm is massaged with the towel in place for about one minute. The athlete puts on his uniform to maintain the heat and protect the arm and shoulder from the cold.

This kind of pregame care improves the muscle tone of the arm and makes arm movements easier and more effective. A pitcher must be warmed up well and feel loose before a pitching stint. The importance of keeping a pitcher's arm warm when he is not using it cannot be overemphasized. It may seem old-fashioned to expect the pitcher to wear a long-sleeved undershirt and jacket between innings or when he gets on base, especially in hot or warm weather, but it is an effective practice, necessary to protect his arm from cool or cold air.

If a pitcher has warmed up sufficiently to become loose and perspire, but is not going to be the game pitcher, he should change to a dry sweat shirt. After pitching, it is good to sit around the dressing room and cool off in a dry sweat shirt. Some pitchers like to have their arm "milked" after a game: the arm is held elevated and the blood is drained from the finger tips towards the shoulder. The trainer facilitates this drainage by "milking" the arm with his hands; this increases the venous and lymphatic circulation and reduces swelling. It is also recommended that the trainer ice massage the pitching arm for 15 minutes prior to showering. This technique rids the pitcher of the heavy feeling in his arm following a pitching stint, although some pitchers and trainers prefer only a massage following a game.

Most ballplayers, managers, coaches, physicians, and trainers agree that a conditioning program based on the general outlines discussed here will ready all ballplayers for a season of play and prevent sore or pulled muscles.

Chapter-12

PHYSICAL CONDITIONING IN WRESTLING

Although great muscular strength is desirable in a wrestler, he must also develop cardiovascular and respiratory endurance, as well as timing, balance, agility, flexibility, and coordination. A wrestler can reach top condition by strictly adhering to a program that includes running, calisthenics, weight training, fundamental wrestling techniques, and actual competitive wrestling. Proper nutrition and diet play a significant part in this program. Superb physical condition is absolutely essential for success in wrestling.

A coach should begin training under the assumption that no one on his squad has worked out since the final wrestling practice of the preceding year. Wrestlers should not be hurried in the first few weeks of formal practice. Some coaches make the mistake of starting the first practice sessions as though the athletes are well-conditioned-this causes pain, pulled muscles, and other injuries that may plague a wrestler for much of the season.

The conditioning program should be a gradual one. The early practice sessions should be adequate to challenge those who are going to participate, yet not so strenuous that the athletes suffer extreme exhaustion and contemplate leaving the squad. Many fine, potential wrestlers are lost in this "washing out" period before they have an opportunity to develop their abilities. The first few weeks should be devoted to conditioning the cardiovascular and respiratory systems and developing muscle strength, flexibility, balance, timing, agility, and coordination. The practice session should be long enough to include a warm-up period of stretching, calisthenics, conditioning drills, instructional period, drilling of moves, and actual competitive wrestling. Of course, the routine should be changed occasionally to allow a change of pace, which will renew the team's interest in the conditioning program.

Daily running is necessary to strengthen the wrestler's cardiovascular and respiratory endurance. Running distance range from one-half to one mile during the first and second weeks of training. If a track is available, the athlete runs one lap at top speed and jogs one lap at half speed. The running distance is increases to two miles or more depending on the athlete's response and the coach's conditioning practices.

Usually, if the athlete experiences some difficulty, he continues on the one-half to one mile course until he can run it easily. Some coaches recommend running for 15 minutes before practice without regard to the number of laps circled. Whether or not daily running is encouraged depends on the training program established by the coach. We recommend daily running throughout the wrestling season because it maintains the condition of the athlete and keeps the legs strong. Running up and down stairwells during inclement weather provides an alternative and serves the purpose of developing wind along with leg strength. Running keeps the body loose, but coaches recommend that the athletes loosen up before running to avoid muscles pulls.

The development of strength in the muscles of the neck, shoulders, chest, arms, back, trunk, abdomen, hips, thighs, and legs is important in the training and conditioning of a wrestler. This can be achieved by overloading the muscles of these regions by conventional, buddy, and other types of exercises, either done individually or as part of a circuit drill. Eight to 12 of these exercises are done daily for 35 to 45 minutes during the first month of the season.

As the conditioning program progresses, these muscles are progressively overloaded by increasing the number and severity of the exercises. Conventional exercises, such as front and back neck bridging and sit-ups for abdominal and hip muscles, push-ups for chest and shoulder muscles, and back jacks for back muscles, are all excellent muscle strengtheners. In addition, stretch exercises are designed to loosen up the muscles of the limb, trunk, back, groin, and abdomen; they are extremely important and must be stressed because they prevent muscle pulls.

Many wrestlers are lost for a good portion of the season because of neck injuries or pulled hamstring or back muscles, which could have been prevented with proper training and conditioning. Some buddy exercises include floating, in which each wrestler floats with a partner in each position usually for 1 or more minutes; and two-man stand-ups, in which a partner is draped over the shoulders of his buddy.

When the wrestlers are fairly well-conditioned, many coaches reduce the calisthenics' period to about 20 minutes. Ten minutes of stretching and calisthenics seem to be the ideal combination to prepare for practice once the season gets underway. These exercises should not cause strain or tiring and should be organized to work several muscles at one time.

Calisthenics should help build agility, conditioning, and endurance. Exercise drills should produce coordination, balance, timing, and precision in the execution of holds. Spinning, floating, and other innovations of the coach may be used at this time.

Calisthenics should be followed by an instructional period, in which experienced wrestlers assist the neophytes with holds and moves. This is the testing period before actual competition. In actual competition, some coaches usually have a wrestler go 9 minutes. However, some prefer multiple short shots of wrestling, in which the wrestlers start from a referee's position and wrestle hard for periods of 10 to 15 seconds with a 2 to 3 minute interval, with the wrestlers changing positions at the end of each wrestling period.

The number of competitive periods depends upon the time element, available space, and level of conditioning sought. Before securing the wrestling room for the evening, the wrestlers should have a final round of calisthenics and some running. A coach should change the practice routine occasionally to avoid team boredom.

The workouts should be challenging even to the most conditioned wrestler on the squad. The workout the day before a wrestling meet should be one that will get the wrestlers loose and break a sweat. It should not be long and tedious; we have found that wrestlers do not operate effectively the next day in a varsity match if they have had a gruelling weight-losing session the previous day.

The coach should discourage excessive weight reduction. Most physicians recommend a maximal weight loss of 5%. Many wrestlers believe that the lower the weight class in which they participate, the better their chances for success. This might be true in some cases; however, the athlete can lose too much weight, suffer illness, and lose strength.

The coach should check the weight of his wrestlers daily before and after practice. If one of his wrestlers is several pounds over his weight class the day of the match, he should not be permitted to lose the excess weight in the gym, during study halls, or physical education classes. In many cases, a wrestler who loses 4 pounds between 9:30 A.M. and 4:00 P.M. is weak and will not perform up to his ability. Most wrestlers normally lose 1 to 2 pounds during the day in calorie metabolism and the natural process of elimination.

Once the season is over, many wrestlers gain too much weight. The athletes should be encouraged to participate in other sports, e.g., football, cross-country, track, and soccer. This helps keep their weight down and provides conditioning. Those who participate only in wrestling should be encouraged to work out on their own in the off-season.

Weight training and running should be encouraged, and the coach should assist in establishing a positive weight program. For example, the athlete could lift weights on Monday, Wednesday, and Friday, and run, play basketball or handball on Tuesday and Thursday. However, some time must be taken off. A holiday away from home base will break the monotony, but at the end of the holiday the athlete must returns to his workout program.

It takes a well-conditioned wrestler to perform effectively. Proper dieting, social activities, and conditioning programs are imperative. Athletes find it difficult to be successful without the proper programs and guidance from the coach. Success is measured in the win/loss column, and the success of the season depends on the training program and instructions formulated by the coach.

Chapter-13

PHYSICAL CONDITIONING IN JUDO

Traditional jujitsu, the precursor of judo, has it roots in ancient Japan where it is difficult to separate fact from legend. Judo was first introduced into the United States by Jigoro Kano, a Japanese professor of physical education who came here on a lecture-demonstration tour in 1938 following a trip to Cairo, where he attended an International Olympic Committee meeting. Kano changed the ancient martial art of jujitsu by eliminating some of the dangerous techniques and retaining some of jujitsu's best techniques. He combined these with some of his own ideas, improvements, and improvisations and developed a modern martial art now known as kokodan judo, which is the type of judo practiced in our country.

Kano developed a sport that not only was a system of self-defence, physical fitness, and self-discipline but also a spiritual experience in which one's opponent was held in high regard. In judo, the body and mind are trained together to attain a moral goal for modern life. A major principle of judo is embodied in the expression "gentle" way."

Judo pupils and experts are ranked by the colour of their belts: one starts with a white belt and moves upwards to green, brown, and finally, the coveted black belt, which has its own various degree. Higher rankings are earned by five dans. Beyond these five dans, there are five more that are purely ceremonial.

Judo is now one of the fastest growing sports in the United States and includes male and female participants. Judo was a subcommittee of the Wrestling Committee of the Amateur Athletic Union until 1953, when it became an independent AAU Committee. In 1981, in accordance with the recent law enacted by Congress giving each sport separate jurisdiction over its own affairs, judo left the AAU and formed United States Judo, Incorporated, which is the sport's national governing body.

In 1974, the United States won its first Olympic medal when a Plainfield, New Jersey, athlete won a bronze in the heavyweight classification.

The judoka aspirant should join a club with a good coach who will initiate the athlete into the world of judo; self taught judo is poor at best and lacks the spirit of the sport. The coach will start with the basics, for mastering the basics will protect the athlete from injuries.

TRAINING AND CONDITIONING

All judo players must start with a warm up including stretching, flexibility, and joint-loosening exercises. The judo player moves his head and neck and all the major joints of the upper and lower extremities including the back and foot. The participant does a number of stretching exercises for the various joints. Fifteen minutes is usually sufficient for the warm-up.

The judo instructor places great stress on *ukemi* as a means of limiting the potential of injuries, such as fractures, sprains, strains, and cerebral concussions. The following is a list of ukemi:

1. Sidefall.
2. Backfall.

3. Frontfall.

4. Forward roll.

The neck is particularly vulnerable to injury because of its proximity to the spinal cord. Fracture-dislocations of the neck can be catastrophic. The neck is protected by flexing the head and neck forward and then the judo players roll over onto the mat. Exposed joints such as the shoulders, elbow, and knees can be protected by the judo player landing on the overlying soft-muscle mass. The object is to land on the side of the body and thighs to protect the knees.

In backward breakfalls, slap the mat with the arms and forearms to absorb some of the energy when hitting the mat. To prevent the head from striking the floor, bend the neck directly forward so that the eye can focus on the knot of the belt. Coaching and mastering the protective mechanisms does not take long. This is done for about 5 minutes before the player proceeds to other techniques.

A student must be proficient in ukemi before he can proceed to *randori*, which consists of free movement around the mat while working with a partner under the condition of an actual contest, and *kata*, which is a formal system of prearranged exercises designed to teach and perfect the techniques, or *waza*.

In judo, the player's opponent's strength is used to defeat him through speed, movement, and feinting. Three elements make up throws: breaking balance; getting yourself in position and throwing.

In choking, the hands use the opponent's collar in a pulling, twisting motion that somewhat resembles the motion of wringing out a towel. Choking is accomplished by pressure of the forearm radium bone against the carotid artery in the neck, shutting off blood to the brain. It has nothing to do with air passages to the lungs.

Careful rules set up the procedures for chokes and arm bars; great care is exercises to ensure that these rules are learned and followed explicitly to guard against injury. The loser must tap the mat without delay. With choking techniques, unconsciousness comes with surprising suddenness. In a good choke, the loser simply "goes to sleep." In arm locks, great care must be taken by all concerned; the loser should tap the mat, and the winner must watch constantly.

In judo mat techniques, fairly frequently the winner may be at the bottom and seem to be losing.

COMPETITION

All judo players who desire to achieve any degree of proficiency should compete against different clubs and participate frequently in tournaments. This is an entire daily program of roughly 2 hours 3 times weekly; however, many clubs meet twice a week for about a 2 hour workout.

COMMON INJURIES

In addition to contusions and abrasions of the face, trunk, upper and lower extremities, judo players sustain a wide assortment of orthopedic injuries, including sprains of all the major joints and especially of the shoulders, knee, and ankle. Dislocations of the shoulder, elbow, and patella, and fractures of the clavicle, ribs, humerus, forearm bones, and wrist are not uncommon. Strains of muscles and of the groin are also encountered. All of these injuries are treated by conventional methods.

Chapter-14

PHYSICAL CONDITIONING IN ICE HOCKEY

Scottish settlers in Canada brought a version of field hockey to the New World and called it "Shinty." Their children changed the name of the game to "Shinny" and began hitting stones with broomsticks on ice-covered ponds, lakes, and other waterways. Thus, Canada is the birthplace of this exciting sport.

Because of its popularity, ice hockey became a major organized sport by 1855 in Kingston, Ontario, although sport historians claim it was already well established in cities such as Halifax, Montreal, and other Canadian cities. By 1893, Lord Stanley, then Governor-General of Canada, established the Stanley Cup for the best amateur ice-hockey team. Since the turn of the century, this coveted ice-hockey trophy goes to the best professional ice-hockey team.

Ice hockey soon achieved popularity beyond its national borders. American universities such as Yale and Johns Hopkins fielded ice-hockey teams and the sport spread quickly to many other colleges and universities. The first American amateur hockey league was formed in New York in 1896, and soon a Baltimore hockey league was formed. In 1920, ice hockey became an official sport at the Amsterdam Olympics, where Canada won the first Olympic Ice Hockey Gold Medal; they continued to dominate the sport in the 1924, 1928, and 1932 Olympics. At the 1936 Olympics, however,

Great Britain's team ended the Canadian winning streak. The Russian team claimed Gold Medals in the 1956, 1964, 1968, 1972, and 1976. An American team triumphed over the highly favoured Russians in the 1980 Olympics Games in Lake Placid.

Ice hockey is a violent, exciting hard-hitting collision sport that requires speed, agility, endurance, balance, maneuverability, and neuro-muscular coordination. It is an aggressive sport in which players are constantly running, bumping elbowing, and pushing their opponents voluntarily and involuntarily. They body-check their opponents and are frequently slammed into the boards that line the rink. Players must harden their bodies to withstand the physical shock of this forceful contact. They must also develop and use carefully coordinated skills such as skating, controlling a puck at the end of the blade of a stick by dribbling it, passing quickly and accurately on the move to team-mates, and scoring on the move.

Eye-hand-stick coordination as well as co-ordinated movements of the upper and lower extremities and the trunk are also essential. Hockey blends individual skills and teamwork.

Hockey players skate in abrupt starts and stops. Occasionally, players are able to break away from opponents and pass the puck to a moving team-mate or shoot the puck at speeds up to 100 mph for a goal. Speed and agility are most important especially in breakaway situations. Because ice hockey is essentially a stick and ball game with the players on skates, the skaters must be able to change direction quickly and faultlessly. They must feel comfortable on skates and possess full body control for balance and movement. This necessitates strong legs, ankles, and feet.

Ice hockey is a team sport that requires many skills. Because these skills take years to master, it is best for the hockey players to start training early and progressively to perfect the various skills. Those youngsters who start before the age of 8 are called "mites"; ages 8 to 10, "squirts"; ages 11 to 12, "pee wees"; ages 13 to 14, "bantams"; ages 15 to 16, "midgets"; ages 17 to 20, "juniors"; and the rest, "seniors." The sooner the hockey aspirant starts, the better the opportunity to advance and develop skills. The player must develop power, speed, endurance, and mobility on skates and be able to stop, turn, cut to left and right, and skate backwards. Pushing off forcefully helps develop speed. Coaches have a difficult time trying to incorporate all of the many basic techniques and advanced components of a training and conditioning program for a hockey player. A regimen would include:

1. Warmups.
2. Individual skills and tactics.
3. Small groups skills and tactics.
4. Total team strategy and tactics.
5. Aerobic or anaerobic conditioning or training.

Some of these must be accomplished by players practising on their own under the previous direction of the coach. In order to save ice time, each coach should instruct his players to engage in the following activities 6 to 8 weeks before team assemblage.

OFF-ICE TRAINING

Off-ice training activities should include stretching and flexibility warm-ups for about 10 minutes, and interval or circuit training to build up the athlete's cardiovascular-respiratory status. Interval training should be composed of all out sprinting for about 2 minutes, followed by 25 calisthenic exercises as prescribed. Take a 1-minute rest and repeat the entire interval training cycle and exercises.

The time for this is approximately 1 hour. This is done 3 times weekly. On alternate days, the athlete engages in about 1 hour of weight training. This will build up maximal muscular strength and endurance.

ON-ICE TRAINING

All training sessions begin with 15 to 20 minute warm ups. These warm ups include flexibility/stretching exercises; leg drags while skating for groin, hamstring, and heel stretching; sit ups; push ups; knee pull and knee bends for knee and leg muscle balance; windmills to loosen up neck, shoulders, back, and abdomen; and power-skating drills.

The warm-up is followed by agility and skating drills. The agility drills require the player to do leg kicks with the hockey stick held horizontally at shoulder level with alternate toe touches while skating; alternate knee touches while skating; jump over obstacles; forward rolls; and dive to ice and recover.

Skating drills to develop endurance and skating skills should last for 10 to 15 , minutes and include the following: long strides with knees apart, body leaning forward and half squats; sprinting in both circular and straight fashion at coach's whistle; power-skating drills to enhance endurance and performance in backward and forward motions; and simple puck and stick drills to enhance passing and shooting skills, using wrist shots, slap shots, and backhand shots.

Some coaches eliminate pucks during the first week to encourage players to develop skating skills. As the season progresses and the player become better conditioned, the warm-ups are decreased to 10 minutes

The second week if for simple stick-and-puck drills. Stick handling and passing drills are emphasized. Toward the end of the second week, the forward perform stick-handling and puck drills defensive players. As the stick-handling becomes more advanced, passing drills are practiced under simulated game conditions. Players are taught to react automatically and appropriately to constantly changing game situations.

During the third week and thereafter, the skills of skating, stick-handling, shooting, and checking are integrated for offensive and defensive strategies. These skills are applied to simulated and actual game situations. At the end of the third week, a controlled scrimmage is held for the coaches to correct any problems that have become evident during the pressure of a game situation.

In the fourth and fifth weeks, the team continues to practice with more emphasis on coordinated skills such as the various shots and body-checks. Advanced passing and skating drills are started and gradually integrated into the practice schedule prior to scrimmages with outside clubs.

In the sixth week, the team should be conditioned and trained for an outside schedule.

Special techniques are required for face-offs, power plays, and penalty-killing situations. Goal-tending is a key position requiring a great deal of agility, coordination, flexibility, strength, maneuverability, and courage. Protective equipment, especially the face mask, is very important to the goal-tender.

This is a suggested training and conditioning program that can be modified or augmented depending on the coach's philosophy and the player's age and experience.

The following minimal protective equipment is essential and must fit properly and comfortably:

1. Skates that are comfortable yet close-fitting when laced correctly over one pair of socks.
2. Shin guards with knee pads.
3. Plants to provide protection for thighs, hips, and ribs.
4. Shoulder and elbow pads.
5. Gloves to protect against bruising and slashing.
6. Helmet.
7. Mouthpiece.
8. Genitalia cup.

For Goalies

1. Helmets with a cage-type face mask, throat protector and internal mouthpiece.
2. Chest protector.
3. One-piece shoulder and upper-extremity pad.
4. Leg pads.
5. Heavily padded pants.
6. Catching glove and waffle-shaped pad.
7. Genitalia cup.
8. Specially padded skates.

All of the goalie's equipment is heavily padded in order to withstand the impact of the puck. His stick must be of proper length and lie.

All equipment, including skate blades, should be aired and dried after every use.

The ice hockey injuries listed on page 122 are common.

Head

1. Facial lacerations and eye injuries.
2. Loss of teeth.

Shoulder

1. Acromioclavicular separations.
2. Shoulder dislocations and subluxations.
3. Rotator cuff tears in older players.

Upper Extremities

1. Elbow: Olecranon bursitis.
2. Forearm: Contusions and fractures.
3. Wrists and Hands: Sprains and fractures, especially of the carpal navicular bones.

Trunk

1. Rib fractures.
2. Contusions and strains.
3. Low-back sprains and strains.
4. Hip pointer.

Lower Extremities

1. Groin strain.
2. Hip and thigh contusion and myositis ossificans.
3. Knee sprains and internal derangements.
4. Lower leg contusions.
5. Ankle sprains and fractures.
6. Ingrown toe nails.
7. Fractures of the feet, especially metatarsals.

Chapter-15

NUTRITIONAL NEEDS OF THE ATHLETES

INTRODUCTION

Interest in the relationships between the athlete's diet and his performance is probably older than organized sports. Many of the dietary superstitions of primitive tribes are based on the idea that certain foods-in-particular the meat of certain animals-endowed the consumer with thee qualities of strength, endurance, and courage with which his prey was identified. Perusal of the daily press leads one to believe that some special nutritional factors are responsible for the preparation of and success of members of professional or Olympic teams. Proper nutrition all too often loses out to food fads, quackery, and superstitions among athletes. Special properties are ascribed to specific foods and food supplements that have little scientific merit. Evaluating the effect of a single food on motivation, differences in experimental conditions, types of works performed, and the wide range of individual response.

The practices being followed may have potentially harmful effects (e.g., megavitamin treatment) or may reinforce eating habits or attitudes about food that may be detrimental in later life (e.g., inappropriate high calorie intake leading to obesity). The implications of dietary practices for future health should be carefully considered, especially when dealing with the young athlete whose growth and development must be protected.

The athlete's nutritional needs are similar to those of non-athlete; he requires calories, protein, water, vitamins, and minerals in quantities determined by his age, body size, and activity level. These requirements can be met by a basic, well-balanced diet.

IMPORTANCE OF CALORIE NEEDS FOR AN ATHLETE

The calorie of energy requirement of a person is determined by his basal energy expenditure and the energy expended in physical activity. Basal energy expenditure is relatively constant and includes energy required for maintenance of muscle tone, body temperature, circulation, respiration, and other glandular and cellular activities, including those related to growth.

The primary determinants of basal metabolic energy requirement are body size, age, and sex. With these determinants, basal energy requirement can be determined from a nomogram, or can be estimated from the formula; basal energy needs equals one kilocalorie per kilogram of body weight per hour.

In general, the basal energy requirement increases as body size or surface area increases, is higher in young people than in older persons, and is higher in males than in females.

Physical activity is the major determinant of variation in energy expenditure among individuals. Whenever muscular work is performed, energy is used, and the amount required is proportional to the work performed. Estimates of energy needs are: for extremely light or sedentary activity, such as writing at a desk or standing in one place, add 30% of the basal metabolic energy needs; for light activity, such as fling or other office work, 50%; for moderative activity, such as that allowing for little sitting, 75% or more.

The non-athlete can, therefore, estimate his daily energy requirement by determining his daily basal energy requirement using 24 kilocalories by determining his daily basal energy requirement using 24 kilocalories per kilogram of body weight and adding to that the appropriate percent of the basal calorie needs for the level of activity selected by the person as most typical of his daily routine.

The athlete also uses this method of determining calorie needs but must determine the additional calories required for his athletic activity by considering thee frequency and duration of his participation in the activity. The amount can be approximated by knowing the caloric cost per minute of the activity. The athlete's daily energy requirement will change depending on whether the day is the day of competition, a training day, or a day during off-season. The duration of activity will differ in each of these situations. For the runner, the approximate calorie cost of cross-country running is 10.6 kilocalories per minute; and of marathon running, 20.7 kilocalories per minute.

Estimates of energy expenditure in running are made more difficult by variations in terrain and air resistance. Various investigators have shown that the variations in terrain and air resistance. Various investigators have shown that the total energy expenditure in running on a level surface is constant and independent of velocity for a given person; pace has little effect on the caloric cost of running. Running up a hill with an incline of 6% requires 35% more energy than running on level ground. Running down a similar grade reduces the effort by only 24%. Studies of running in still air and against the wind suggest that in distance running about 5% to 8% of the energy spent is needed to overcome air resistance. Of more importance, perhaps, is the energy cost based on the weight of the runner.

Because the work of exercise, as measured by oxygen consumption, increases as body weight increases, it is easy to understand thee advantage attributed the runner who has small bones and minimal body fat. The less nonpropulsive weight or fat, the greater thee efficiency of movement. Anatomically, marathoners are usually small and thin. A weight chart may give a false impression of overweight for the muscular athlete for the muscular athlete, however, because muscle tissue is heavier than fat tissue. A more accurate method to assess an athlete's excess weight is to measure thee percent of body fat by use of calipers designed to measure the thickness of a fold of skin. Buskirk advocated measuring the skin over the triceps muscle and advised that a skinfold less than eight millimetres thickness indicates a "lean" body build, eight to fifteen millimetres is "acceptable", and greater than fifteen millimetres (about one-half inch) is "over-fat." These measurements apply to highly trained athletes in top condition whose ideal fat content is 5% to 8%, the figures must not be broadly applied. When skinfold estimates of body fat were made on 114 competitions at thee 1968 U.S. Olympic Marathon Trial, they showed that the marathon runners had about 7.5% fat or about 9% less than normally active men of comparable age. Several of the top finishes were found to have less than 5% body fat.

Additional weight was found to decrease significantly maximal oxygen uptake (expressed relative to total weight carried), maximal treadmill run time, and 12-minute run distance. An increase of 5% additional weight was found, on the average, to decrease maximal oxygen uptake by 2.4 ml, the treadmill run time by 35 seconds, and the 12-minute run distance by 89 meters. These decreases were direct consequences of thee increased energy cost of running at submaximal speeds.

The determination of and adherence to daily caloric intake appropriate for body size and activity needs are, therefore, of great importance, because if thee runner's caloric intake exceeds his needs, his total body fat will increase. The increase in body fat resulting from caloric intake exceeding caloric needs will not only decrease thee runner's performance by increasing the work of his exercise but also may create eating habits and attitudes about food that may contribute to thee development of obesity in later life.

Caloric balance is especially important for athletes during the off-season and in the post-competitive years. Many athletes develop weight problems at these times because they fail to realize that when competition and training stops, habitually high calorie intakes must be lowered for adaptation to decreased energy demands.

PROTEIN

Proteins are more complex molecules than either fats or carbohydrates. The molecules are similar in that they all contain oxygen, and carbon, but proteins (unlike fats or carbohydrates) also contain nitrogen; many contain sulphur, phosphorus, iron, and other minerals as well. Proteins are made up of great number of relatively simple units, the nitrogen-containing compounds called *amino acids.*

The major roles of proteins in the body are for building new tissues in growing children, in athletic training, and after injury; for maintaining tissues already built and replacement of regular losses; as regulatory substances for internal water and acid-base balance; as a precursor for enzymes, antibodies, and some hormones; and as energy. If more protein is eaten than is needed for essential functions, thee extra protein is oxidized to supply energy or is converted to body fat if the total energy intake is excessive. If the content of the diet is inadequate (i.e., if sufficient carbohydrates and fats are not supplied to meet the energy needs of the body), proteins are burned for energy because energy needs have a higher priority than does maintenance of some of the tissue proteins. In this event, building or repair processes will suffer. Nitrogen, which is indispensable as long as protein is used for tissue building, becomes a liability when protein must be used for energy. The nitrogen-containing substances (primarily urea) that result from amino acid oxidation must be excreted by the kidneys. Because energy is more economically supplied by carbohydrates and fats, the consumption of protein greatly in excess of body needs is usually disadvantageous.

The requirement for protein in the diet has been set at 0.8 grams per kilogram body weight per day for adults. Because of thee additional need for protein for growth in children, thee requirement decreases gradually from 2.0 grams per kilogram at ages 0.5 to 1 year to 0.8 gram per kilogram at age 18 years.

Increases in lean body mass, enzymatic proteins, and haemoglobin, all typical effects of training, may temporarily require greater than normal intakes of protein. Athletes who develop proteinuria, hemoglobinuria, or myoglobinuria as a result of high-intensity exercise may also require greater than normal levels of protein until these conditions subside. One recommendation has been that during training and competitions the mature athlete needs 1 gram protein per kilogram body weight per day, and the growing athlete may require up to 1.5 grams protein per kilogram per day to meet his greater demand for amino acid retention and protein synthesis.

The recommendations for increased protein intake during athletic training vary, however. Consolazio and Johnson believe than an increased dietary protein above normal intake for men in athletic training is not necessary.

Although early workers thought that protein was the primary source of muscular energy, the work of Voit and Pettenkofer, as Mayer and Bullen pointed out, refuted this theory, and this refutation has been well confirmed. Nitrogen excretion has been shown repeatedly not to increase during muscular work. As Consolazio and co-workers mentioned, Atwater showed that nitrogen excretion was not above that in the resting conditions, even when metabolic rate was nearly doubled by physical work. Astrand cited data showing the combustion of protein was not higher during heavy exercise than during rest, even after glycogen depots have been depleted. Pitts, Consolazio, and Johnson examined the effect of variation in the level of dietary protein on the physical fitness (i.e., treadmill runs of various speeds and grades, followed by pulse counts, of three subjects studied under both temperate and tropical conditions while reclining, standing, and marching). There was no change in performance attributable to dietary protein level under any of these environmental conditions, although improvements due to training and acclimatization were observed.

More recently, it has been proposed by Evans and co-workers that, in addition to carbohydrates and fats, amino acids can contribute to whole body energy metabolism. The availability of amino acids results from a substantial decrease in the rate of protein synthesis during exercise. These researchers estimate that protein can provide up to 5.5% of the total calorie cost of the exercise. According to this study, estimates of the extent of amino acid oxidation indicate that current recommendations for maximal protein requirements may not be adequate for physically active individuals.

Excess protein intake increases water requirements of the body because additional fluid is required to eliminate nitrogen by-products in the urine. Not only is excess protein unnecessary, it can be harmful, particularly when ingested during times of intense athletic competition, when it can compromise body hydration.

VITAMINS

Vitamins are organic compounds that occur in small concentrations in foods; they are necessary in small amounts in the diet for normal growth, maintenance, and reproduction. Their absence in the diet or improper absorption results in specific deficiency diseases. They differ from each other in physiologic function, in chemical structure, and in distribution in food. The vitamins are classified into two groups based on their solubility. The solubility characteristic is important in determining whether the body can store the vitamin or whether the supply must be replenished daily. Solubility also has implications for the vitamin's toxic potential when taken in excess of body needs. The four vitamins A, D, E, and K are soluble in fat and fat solvents and are therefore known as the fat-soluble vitamins. They can be stored in the body to some extent, mostly in the liver, and as a result manifestations of deficiencies are likely to be slow. The water-soluble vitamins include vitamin C and the B complex vitamins.

The body has limited ability to store water-soluble vitamins, except water-soluble vitamin B12, which is stored extensively in the liver. Tissues are depleted of their normal content of these vitamins in a relatively short period if the diet is deficient, so supplies are needed regularly to maintain tissues levels. The tissues take up only as much as is needed, and because water-soluble vitamins are freely soluble in water, most of the intake of these vitamins not required for day-to-day use is excreted in the urine. However, excessive intakes of some of the B complex vitamins may cause side effects.

Most B complex vitamins act as an organic catalyst or as a part of a catalyst. A catalyst is a substance that speeds up a chemical reaction without itself taking part in it. The special types of organic catalysts that promote these reactions in living tissues are known as enzymes and co-enzymes, which aid enzymes in their tasks. Many of the vitamins occur in the body as co-enzymes responsible for promoting some essential chemical reaction. For example, the cell gets much of the energy it requires through oxidation of the carbohydrate glucose. This oxidation takes place in many intermediate steps, so that energy is gradually set free. Several of the B complex vitamins are co-enzymes that catalyse specific steps in the oxidation of carbohydrates. The absence of any of these enzymes means a failure of some link in the chain of tissue oxidations. Therefore, the lack of a vitamin that is an essential part of such an enzyme can inhibit oxidative processes in cells.

As in the case of caloric undernutrition, the impairment of the ability to perform work efficiently in cases of frank vitamin deficiency is well known. No conclusive evidence, however, supports thee theory that once vitamin requirements are met, supplementation will enhance athletic performance. Greater attention should be directed to the possible detrimental effects of their indiscriminate use.

Easy fatigability, loss of appetite, irritability, and apathy are signs of vitamin B complex deficiency; the ability to perform work efficiently is impaired in this state. Review of the studies done on work efficiency of persons receiving diets adequate in B complex vitamin versus B complex vitamin supplements indicate that supplementation does not enhance performance. In normal men, in experiments lasting 10 to 12 weeks, intakes of the B-complex vitamin thiamine at four different levels, from 0.23 mg per 1,000 kcal daily up to 0.63 mg per 1,000 kcal, exerted no beneficial effect on diets otherwise considered adequate. Muscular, neuro-muscular, cardiovascular, psychomotor, and metabolic functions tested were in no way limited. Clinical signs, subjective sensations, and state of mind and behaviour were likewise unaffected.

Nicotinic acid, or niacin, is another of the B complex vitamins. It has been shown, in exercising men, to decrease mobilization of fatty acids from adipose tissue, resulting in increased utilization of muscle glycogen stores for energy. The effects of large doses of niacin on myocardial metabolism in men, either at rest or during exercise, have been documented as undesirable on the metabolism of heart muscle. Because fatty acids are important fuels for the heart, excessive consumption of niacin is contraindicated before endurance events.

Vitamin C supplementation is especially popular among athletes, because of is known role in collagen synthesis and the poor quality of tissue repair associated with vitamin C deficiency. The reasoning is that the athlete has perhaps a greater need for collagen synthesis and tissue repair, and thus athletic performance would benefit from supplementation. It has been found that vitamin C supplementation has a negligible effect on endurance performance, of on severity or duration of athletic injury.

Excessive vitamin C supplementation increases vitamin C destruction in the body. Scurvy has been noted in persons who have had a history of taking excessive amounts of vitamin C and who returned to a diet containing normal amounts. Seventeen subjects consuming 1 to 3 grams of vitamin C per day over a period of three to 36 months were studied to determine the serum ascorbic acid levels. The subjects' intake was first standardized to 2 grams vitamin C supplement per day for ten days. The serum ascorbic acid level was found to be 1.45 mg per 100 ml. The serum ascorbic acid level of 16 normal controls not receiving supplemental vitamin C was 1.20 per 100 ml, and increased to 2.75 mg per 100 ml after the administration of 2 grams vitamin C supplement daily for eight day. Therefore, the serum ascorbic acid levels initially increase, reaching a maximum value after about eight days supplementation. The continued use of supplemental vitamin C leads to a gradual decline of thee serum levels that cannot be compensated by increasing the dosage.

Because adequate saturation levels of ascorbic acid may be maintained on recommended dietary sources of vitamin C, the habitual intake of larger amounts is not advantageous, while posing the risks of causing the ascorbic acid deficiency on termination of the regimen.

On the basis of these data, one can no longer presume that excessive intake of a water-soluble vitamin will simply result in excess quantities being excreted in the urine with no possibility for toxic effects. At high does, vitamins stop acting as vitamins and act instead as pharmacological agents. While nontoxic at recommended allowances for vitamins, impurities in vitamin preparation when vitamins are taken in megadoses can far exceed thee limits of safety.

Vitamin E is a fat-soluble vitamin. There is no evidence that the healthy human is susceptible to vitamin E deficiency; supplementation has, likewise, not proved to be advantageous. Vitamin E toxicity in humans has not been confirmed. An oxidation product of vitamin E has been thought to be an inhibitor of vitamin K and, therefore, responsible for a prolongation in blood clotting time. Large doses of vitamin E potentiate the affect of warfarin. A study conducted by the National Institutes of Health on persons who had been ingesting up to 800 IU of vitamin E for more than 3 years did not find evidence of toxicity.

Although some athletes have taken vitamin E in hopes of improving athletic performance, vitamin E taken at a level of 900 IU daily for six months did not improve athletic performance in well-trained swimmers.

MINERAL

Sodium, potassium, and iron are the minerals most often affected by heavy exercise. While mineral losses may be incurred during strenuous exercise, athletes must be aware of the potentially toxic side effects of the inappropriate use of minerals. Because sodium and potassium are intimately related to the athlete's of minerals. Because sodium and potassium are intimately related to the athlete's state of hydration, these minerals will be part of the discussion of water requirement.

Iron is distributed through the body as a component of essential metabolic enzymes in every cell. About 65% to 70% of the body is present in the blood as haemoglobin in the red blood cells. Haemoglobin is essential for oxygen transport in the blood. The remainder of the iron stored in the body is found in combination with protein in the liver, bone and bone, and bone marrow or found in other tissues such as myoglobin in muscles. In all sites, the iron-containing compounds are involved in thee vital processes of cells and tissues.

The body guards its iron stores carefully and reuses any iron that is broken down in the body over and over again. Only small amounts of iron lost in thee urine, sweat, hair, sloughed-off skin, and nails and by menstruation needs to be replaced normally only about 1 or 1.5 mg a day. About one-tenth of the iron in the diet is absorbed, which means that about 10 times the amount of iron must be eaten than the 1 or 1.5 mg a day that the body actually uses in its tissues. The 1980 National Research Council's recommended dietary allowances are 18 mg of iron per day for women and 10 mg day for men.

Iron needs are greater during of growth, including pregnancy, lactation, and infancy through adolescence. Iron deficiency is the most common nutritional deficiency in the United States.

Bunch states that low or low-normal haemoglobin or hematocrit values commonly found in runners or other endurance-trained persons seldom reflect true anaemia and do not indicate a need for folate or vitamin B12.

In the past decade, interest has increased among athletes in thee use of iron to improve performance. Low serum iron values and subnormal haemoglobin values have been demonstrated among athletes who are involved in intense physical activity. That finding has been looked on as a possible factor responsible for sub-optimal oxygen transport and hence lower capacity for physical performance. The relationship between performance and serum ferritin was evaluated by Martin *et al.* In the nine elite male distance runners studied, this relationship suggested that iron depletion state may be significant in these runners, even in the absence of anaemia.

The iron status and the possible effect of training on iron metabolism of a group of extremely hard-training long-distance runners has been reported from Sweden. A depressed absorption combined with an increased elimination were thought to explain these runners' sub-optimal iron state. Reports of anaemia and sub-optimal haemoglobin levels in athletes have generated much speculation regarding the possible causes of sports anaemia. One or more of the three mechanisms could result in the development of anaemia. *First,* a relative anaemia could develop through a hemodilution effect of an expanded plasma volume. This increase in total blood volume is thought to be a positive adaptation to increase stroke volume of the heart and maximal cardiac output.

Second, reduced haemoglobin synthesis and/or erythropoiesis could result in an actual decrease in total haemoglobin. Since endurance trained athletes tend to manifest a high total haemoglobin it seems unlikely that the rate of haemoglobin synthesis and red blood cell production are depressed in athletes as a group. However, it is possible that sports anaemia could result from reduced or inadequate rates of haemoglobin and/or red blood synthesis in affected athletes.

Third, an increased rate of destruction of red blood cells and degradation of haemoglobin could decrease the concentration of haemoglobin in circulating blood. Ehn *et. al.*, have reported high rate or iron loss, which was not explained by intravascular hemolysis or hemoglobinuria. It was suggested, however, that loss of iron through heavy sweating could have been a factor. Iron loss via sweat is usually considered to be negligible in humans. Vellar showed, however, that in cases of extreme sweating as much as 40 mg of iron per 100 ml sweat, resulting in perhaps an extra iron loss of 0.4mg to 1.0 mg peer day. The increased elimination rate or iron found in the runner could be explained by the profuse sweating that occurs.

It has been suggested that hemolysis is a possible cause of low iron storage and sports anaemia. A high rate of intravascular hemolysis may be a transient condition resulting from the breakdown of fragile red blood cells at the onset of heavy training. Runners and joggers may inflict trauma on red blood cells circulating through the capillaries in the feet. This may be manifested as hemoglobinuria, the presence of free haemoglobin in the urine. This condition has been reported in some athletes, but its incidence does not appear to be high.

Heavy menstrual blood losses may combine with other previously mentioned factors to increase the female athlete's risk of developing iron deficiency and/or anermia.

Many possible causes of sports anaemia and sub-optimal haemoglobin have been suggested, but few have been studied in depth. Sports anaemia, as distinct from sub-optimal haemoglobin, seems more likely to be associated with dietary deficiencies and/or high rates of iron loss through menstruation, sweating, and hemoglobinuria.

From the physical standpoint, the runner should be advised to include adequate quantities of iron in his diet. To advise oral iron therapy for women runners is appropriate because of menstrual loss. As recommendation for individuals in the general population, greater attention to good sources of iron in the diet seems reasonable. The best dietary sources of iron are meat, especially organ meats, fish, poultry, and eggs. Green leafy vegetables, potatoes, dried fruits, and enriched bread and cereal products are the best plant sources.

WATER

Humans can live for about 30 days without food, but will die in 5 to 6 days if deprived of water. Water is lost from the body constantly from the skin as perspiration; from the lungs as water vapour in expired air; from the kidneys as urine; and from the intestines in feces. A minimum of 800 ml of water is lost daily through the skin and lungs and this amount may increase in hot, dry environments. The kidneys eliminate about 1,000 to 1,500 ml of water in urine; fecal losses approximate 200 ml., daily.

Fluids are replaced by the ingestion of liquids and foods containing water. To ensure sufficient water, adults should drink 2,000 to 2,500 ml of water or other liquids daily.

Body water serves may function. Nutrients, hormones, waste products, and antibodies are all transported in the water of the blood plasma. All of the body's chemical reactions are carried out in water and are significantly less efficient when an adequate amount of body water is not available.

The role of water in regulating body temperature is of particular importance to the athlete. The excessive heat generated by exercise must be dissipated, and the most effective way is through evaporation of sweat. This mechanism fails to function effectively, however, if the water supply is inadequate to meet the needs of the sweat glands.

When fluid losses exceed supply, dehydration follows. Dehydration is characterized by loss appetite and limited capacity for work. Physiological changes that impair performance are detectable with losses no greater than 3% of body weight. When losses are 5%, evidence of heat exhaustion becomes apparent and at 7% hallucinations occur. Losses totalling 10% are hazardous and lead to heat stroke, sudden collapse, and loss of consciousness. Persons in excellent physical condition can perform adequately until body water equal to 4% to 5% of body weight is lost. Generally, with the loss of water amounting to 4% to 5% of body weight, the capacity for hard muscular work declines by 20% of body weight should be lost.

During exercise and muscular work, changes take place in the distribution of body water. When exercise begins, water is immediately transferred from the extracellular fluid space to the intracellular space within cells. This transfer facilitates the utilization of energy. The extracellular fluid that moves into the muscle cells is rapidly replaced by water from blood plasma, thereby reducing the volume of circulating blood. The amount of blood plasma that is available to flow to the kidneys is thus reduced, and urine production is decreased.

Once exercise begins, the water is lost through sweating and increased breathing, this reduced excretion of urinary water provides a control mechanism that helps to conserve body water. Mechanisms for increased water intake ate not nearly as effective.

After of exercise and resulting dehydration, the average thirst response will not in itself cali for complete replacement of body water for a considerable time, often up to several days. The need for a prescribed schedule for water intake to maintain hydration is important for the athlete.

The athlete who is well conditioned will voluntarily drink more often than one who is not well trained. The well conditioned athlete will also sweat more profusely and will thus more effectively dissipate his body heat.

The athlete who is well acclimated replaces water and salt losses in sweat and urine by diet. There should be no need for an increased salt intake, just greater amounts of drinking water. Non-acclimatized athletes may sweat excessively and have salt losses that greatly exceed dietary intake.

Graduated physical activity should be scheduled for one week to allow for acclimatization and permit the kidney and endocrine glands to adjust to sodium conservation. Even the well-conditioned athlete, who drinks more and more nearly compensates for his water losses, may spontaneously replace the one-half to one-third of his sweat losses within 24 hours of a vigorous work-out or competition id weight loss is not considered, along with thirst, in water needs.

Distance runners may lose 8 to 13 pounds of water during a marathon run. That loss causes dehydration of 13% to 21% of plasma water and 11% of muscle water. All athletes should weigh-in before and after each event or practice.

The difference in weights before and after the event or competition represents water loss, and the proper amount of water replacement required can be determined. Weight loss should be a guide to water replacement. The athlete should take 2 to 3 cups of water or liquid supplement for each pound of weight loss.

In addition to their role in maintaining acid-base balance, sodium and potassium exert a primary influence on the distribution of body water.

Sodium is concentrated primarily in thee extracellular fluid, whereas potassium is concentrated in the intracellular fluid. Any salt ingested in excess of salt losses will cause a trapping of water between cells and deplete the intracellular supply.

When water is an short supply in the body, the most critical need is to maintain the metabolically active water within cells.

Sweat is hypotonic compared with the body fluid, so that relatively more fluid than salts, such as sodium and potassium, is lost from the body during sweating.

Athletes in training do not require electrolyte supplements to replace perspiration losses because healthy kidneys automatically compensate by conserving sodium and potassium.

Clearly, the body has highly effective mechanisms for regulating its supply of sodium and potassium.

Specific salt replacement is rarely needed during athletic activity, even if excessive sweat loss occurs. About 20 to 30 milliequivalents of sodium are lost per 1,000 ml of perspiration. Excessive sweating can lead to sodium losses of 350 milliequivalents per day in the acclimated person.

The usual dietary sodium intake of the adult is 100 to 300 milliequivalents per day. Americans eating a varied diet generally get more than enough sodium in their daily foods to meet even the extraordinary needs of vigorous athletic activity. As a general guideline, however, Smith recommends that, if water loss exceeds 5 to 10 pounds in a given workout, some consideration may be given to specific salt replacement.

This replacement can be made by liberally salting a normal diet or it can be provided by a highly dilute salt-containing fluid, whose concentration should not exceed 1.5 grams of salt per litre of water.

Smith states that the use of slat tablets is inappropriate because they provide a high concentration of salt and may complicate thee state of dehydration.

Williams believes that salt tablet may not be necessary to restore lost electrolytes if the weight loss is less than 6 pounds per day.

The person who is not acclimatized to heat will lose about 4 to 5 grams sodium with a 6 pound loss; the acclimatized person will lose only about 3 grams.

Because the average meal contains as much as 3 grams of sodium, normal food intake should suffice. Williams recommends that one salt tablet should be taken per pound of weight loss over 6 pounds and that a pint of water be taken with each 7 gram tablet. This dosage is consistent with the Food and Nutrition Board of the National Research Council recommendation of a 2-gram salt replacement per litre of extra water lost in sweating.

Potassium losses in sweat are negligible under any but the most extreme conditions, and potassium depletion is not a primary concern. The need for potassium has been suggested because of the low serum levels found in some athletes after exercise.

Now, however, it is thought to be due to hemodilution rather than actual depletion of body potassium. Muscle weakness could result from excessive potassium losses. If additional needs do exist because of exercise losses, potassium may be increased in the normal diet by the inclusion of foods high in potassium, such as oranges, grapefruit, pineapples, apricots, bananas, and dried fruit.

BASIC DIET

Optimal nutrition is one of the basic conditions necessary to maintain top performance for the athlete and non-athlete alike. As the previous review indicates, the athlete, aside from possible increases in caloric intake necessitated by increased energy expenditure and in water intake to ensure adequate by increased energy expenditure and in water intake to ensure adequate hydration, does not need additional nutrients beyond those in a balanced diet.

The diet recommendation for the athlete, and for the population in general, is one in which about 15% of calories are derived from protein, 30% to 35% from fat, and 50% to 55% from carbohydrates.

This distribution of nutrients will allow for a moderate intake of protein, which easily meets requirements during training and is reasonable in terms of thee athlete's appetite for meat. It provides a fat intake that is less than that currently consumed in this country but meets the recommendations of the American Heart Association.

No single food or category of foods contains all of the nutrients in amounts sufficient to maintain life. The key to balancing the diet is combining different foods so that nutrient deficiencies in some foods are made up for by nutrient surpluses in others.

Each nutrient performs specific functions in the body and each needs to be present for the body to be in peak condition. Eating a proper variety of foods at each meal is the secret.

An adequate guide on which an athlete should base his food selection is the use of food groups. These food groups include milk products; meat and meat substitutes; fruit and vegetables; and cereals and grains-the Basic Four Food Groups as established by the United States Department of Agriculture in 1956.

For a diet selected to meet high energy needs, such as the athlete's diet, additional groups such as fats and oils, desserts, and sugars and sweets are also appropriate.

Foods are classified into groups on the basis of similarities in nutrient composition; foods in a group are comparable in calories, protein, minerals, and vitamins, and can be interchanged if taken in the suggested serving sizes.

There is a vast leeway in the choice of the foods within each of the groups. The diet is flexible enough to adapt to an almost unlimited range of condition and circumstances.

A reference runner, male, 29 years old, 170 cm in height and 61 kg in weight, would require about 1,500 kcal for daily basal needs.

Calorie needs on a day when he is engaged in light activity would be met by the addition of 50% basal needs or about 2,200 calories.

As the calorie level of the diet is adjusted depending on the daily calorie demands for activity, the distribution of protein, fat, and carbohydrate should remain relatively constant so that the diet remains well balanced, nutritionally.

That is, the intake of calories should not be increased by merely adding more meat or decreased by eliminating bread or potatoes.

Optimum body weight is important for the runner. If the reference runner weighs 70 kg and wishes to reduce to 61 kg at a comfortable rate of about 1 kg per week, he must reduce his daily calorie intake by 1,000. Because 0.5 kg body fat equals 3,500 calories, a deficit of 7,000 calories a week would result in 1 kg of body fat.

To maintain this rate of weight loss, on light activity days, the reference runner's calorie intake should be about 1,200 and 2,100 on days when he runs about 60 minutes.

In the weight-reduction diet plan, less emphasis is placed on foods from the desserts and sugars and sweet food groups, because they tend to be higher in calories and lower in essential nutrients than are appropriate at low calorie intakes.

The percent of calories derived from protein is likely to be greater to meet the person's protein requirement of 0.8 gram per kilogram body weight.

Weight reduction efforts by means of starvation or fad diets that emphasize the omission or encourage the increased use of a particular group of foods are never appropriate.

Fat diets are usually nutritionally inadequate and will compromise not only athletic performance but general health. Weight loss from starvation involves loss of protein, glycogen, potassium, sodium, phosphorus, sulphur, enzymes, and other important cell constituents. Fifty percent or more of weight loss induced by total starvation involves fat-free protoplasm. The result of these responses is diminished body reserves for athletic demands. Weight reduction efforts should include increased physical activity and a calorie-controlled, nutritionally well balanced diet.

If the athlete eats a varied diet that meets but does not exceed his calorie, protein, vitamin, and mineral requirements, he need not take protein, vitamin, or mineral supplements; his nutrient requirements will be met by food. A dietitian should be consulted if there are questions about the formulation of the diet.

CARBOHYDRATE LOADING

The key role of carbohydrate in exercise performance has been emphasized for several decades. The main source of carbohydrate was thought to be local glycogen stores in muscle tissue, which was confirmed by Bergstrom and co-workers by direct determinations of glycogen content in human muscle tissue during exercise.

In 1967, Bergstrom and co-workers and Hermansen *et. al.,* reported studies in young men of the effect of muscle glycogen levels on physical performance and endurance. The results indicated that performance time to exhaustion averages 59, 126, and 189 minutes after three days on a high fat-high protein diet, a mixed diet, and a high carbohydrate diet, respectively.

Muscle biopsy measurements indicated that the nutrient composition of the diet could affect the muscle glycogen stores.

These stores were observed to be reduced during strenuous exercise, and when the muscle glycogen drops to a critical level, work usually stops or thee physical activity rate is decreased.

In this instance, an increased energy yield from free fatty acids results. These studies show that the working muscles have a requirement for carbohydrate as an energy source and that carbohydrate is obtained directly from the muscle stores of glycogen.

In the well-trained athlete, in brief high-intensity exercise the size of the glycogen store is not a limiting factor, provided that it is not grossly subnormal at the beginning of the exercise.

On the other hand, with high-intensity exercise of long duration, glycogen stores can be a limiting factor for the endurance capacity, especially considering that, at the end of the competition, a capacity to increase thee performance may be decisive for winning.

Such long-duration, high intensity exercise includes long-distance running, cross-country skiing and possibly some team sports, such as soccer and ice hockey. The amount of glycogen stores must also be considered when athletes perform repeatedly during one day.

Bergstrom *et. al.,* observed that, after the muscle glycogen stores had been depleted by previous exercise, a high-carbohydrate diet for one to three days greatly enhanced the synthesis of muscle glycogen. They also showed that, when carbohydrate was given without any previous exercise, muscle glycogen stores only moderately increased.

Slovic confirmed that carbohydrate loading does improve performance, with the improvement most pronounced in the final stages of the event.

The available information indicates that the glycogen content of the working muscle is one of the most important factors for prolonged exercise.

The carbohydrate loading technique has been published in many forms, but essentially consists of three phases: phase I, the depletion phase, consists of days 7 to 4 before the event; phase II, the glycogen synthesis phase, days 3 to 1 before the event; phase III, the day of the event.

In phase I, the specific muscles to be used must be exercised to exhaustion by thee same type of activity as performed during the event, to deplete them of their glycogen stores. Phase I is done about six to seven days before the day of thee endurance event. So that the muscles can be rested before the event. The diet during this phase is crucial. While depleting the muscles of glycogen, a high-fat, high-protein, low-carbohydrate diet is followed for three days.

The glycogen content of the muscles is kept low during this time. One possible problem during phase I is a feeling of fatigue, irritability, nervousness, or nausea, due to the low carbohydrate intake. During this phase, many athletes will refuse all forms of dietary carbohydrate and eat only protein and fat, resulting in ketosis. Intake of carbohydrate should be kept at about 100 grams per day.

After three days on the low-carbohydrate diet, the athlete begins the high-carbohydrate diet of phase II. This diet is adequate in protein and fat but the major source of calories is carbohydrate. A minimum of 250 to 525 grams of carbohydrate is needed each day in phase II.

During this period, glycogen synthesis is enhanced and is localized to the muscles that were depleted during phase I. Exercise is not recommended at this time, because if depletes the glycogen stores. Diets during phases I and II should be similar in caloric value and should be designed to meet thee athlete's protein and energy needs.

Phase III is the day of the athlete may eat anything he wishes. If an athlete thinks any one food will help his performance, he should eat it. The pre-event meal should be eaten tree to four hours before the event, so that,the stomach is empty at thee time of competition. Intake of food or fluid is necessary during an endurance even, to maintain hydration and blood glucose.

A shorter method of carbohydrate loading would consist of the exhausting exercise on day 4 before the event, followed by three days of high-carbohydrate diet. Many misconceptions exist about diet for carbohydrate loading.

Many equate carbohydrate with foods containing simple sugar, such as candy, soft drinks, and honey, neglecting the complex carbohydrate sources such as vegetables, breads, and cereals.

Several investigators believe that the carbohydrate loading technique should be used with caution and done at most two to three times a year. In addition to glycogen, water is also deposited in muscle in amounts equal to about three times thee amount of glycogen deposited.

While this deposit of water may contribute to a sensation of muscular heaviness and stiffness, some believe that it partly compensates for the evaporative water losses experienced during thee event. It does, however, result in increased body weight. For example, with glycogen storage of 700 grams, there is an increase in body water amounting to about 2 kilograms. In activities in which the body weight must be lifted, an excessive glycogen store should be avoided.

Carbohydrate loading should be used very selectively for high school and college athletes, and rarely, if ever, for early adolescent or pre-adolescent athletes.

Athletes with diabetes or hypertriglyceridemia or who are at risk for cardiovascular disease should consult their physicians about endurance exercise or carbohydrate loading.

Although carbohydrate loading appears to enhance performance, its use has been questioned. Mirkin reported ST-T wave changes and chest pain in a 40-year-old man who followed an extreme version of the carbohydrate-loading diet. Blair *et. al.,* monitored possible electrocardiogram and blood lipid changes in a group of 14 well-trained runners who engaged in carbohydrate loading. Ten of these runners followed thee classic carbohydrate-loading procedure and four runners followed their usual diets.

No changes were noted for any variables in the non-loading runners. Runners who used thee carbohydrate loading had higher triglyceride values after the race, and may have exhibited slight decreases in R-wave height after carbohydrate loading.

It has also been suggested that athletes using carbohydrate loading may be destroying muscle fibres, due to the high glycogen stores or to the heavy exercise. Because no evidence supports this theory, no definitive statement can be made concerning possible muscular breakdown.

The purpose of carbohydrate loading is to supersaturate with glycogen the muscles to be used in competition. The competition should be longer than 30 to 60 minutes, to fully utilize the glycogen stores.

The complete technique of carbohydrate loading should be used only for endurance events and, because of the demands of the muscles, it should be used sparingly, possibly two to three times a year. For shorter events, phase I can be omitted and phase II can be followed to fill but, not supersaturate, glycogen stores.

The effects of using the technique over a competitive lifetime are unknown. Adverse effects are suspected, but full knowledge of possible dangers in lacking at this time because of the limited duration of use. If this dietary manipulation is practiced by many athletes to enhance their endurance and achieve better performance, the nutritional adequacy of the diet should be carefully considered.

PRECOMPETITION MEALS

Unfounded beliefs have probably places greater restrictions than necessary on food choices for the precompetition meal. The rigidity of some well-known recommendations is obviously extreme and limited in the light of what is known about food its digestion.

There is no reason that an athlete should not enjoy his pre-event meal and have the privilege of selecting the customary food he enjoys at other times during training. Probably more important than the foods consumed during this meal is the psychologic significance ascribed to foods or combination of foods by the athlete.

The relative composition or size of the meal preceding an event of short duration has little influence on improving performance. The main concern is that the meal be consumed at a reasonable time, usually three hours before thee competitive event, which allows for digestion and absorption but is not long enough for feelings of hunger to develop.

In long-duration events, the meal should also be consumed about three hours before the event. The fat content of the meal should be kept at a minimum, however, because fat in any form slows stomach-emptying time.

Protein intake should also be limited because most protein sources contain fat. The athlete will want digestion in the stomach to be complete before the competitive event begins. Protein also yields the nitrogen by-products of digestion, which can only be eliminated by urinary excretion, therefore requiring fluid loss.

The carbohydrate content of the meal should be higher than normal, because it is easily digested and readily absorbed and will ensure adequate glycogen stores. The meal should exclude foods that are likely to cause flatulence and discomfort. To compensate for sweat losses, the athletes should drink 2 to 3 cups of water to insure adequate hydration.

An additional cup of water should be taken 1½ hours before competition. Ingestion of bouillon, broth, or consomme at least three hours before the event will ensure adequate salt intake. Because of its potentially detrimental effect, alcohol should be avoided.

Caffeine in coffee and tea should also be avoided because it has a diuretic effect, causing a depletion in body water and because it is a central nervous system stimulant that may impair the athlete's awareness of fatigue.

Some athletes are more sensitive than others to the effects of caffeine. With the ingestion of 4 to 5 mg per kilogram body weight some claims have been made that caffeine prior to exercise stimulates the release of free fatty acid, thus sparing glycogen.

Costill believes that an experienced runner will generally learn when and what to eat during precompetition. For a race that begins at noon, the runner generally eats his major meal about 6 o'clock the night before, followed in four hours by a snack.

Breakfast should be taken about 4 hours before the race. All of these meals and snacks should be high carbohydrate, defined by Costill as being 60% to 70% of calories as carbohydrate.

A study analysing the training methods and racing techniques of 12 athletes who have completed 100-mile runs was reported. A wide variation in thee ways athletes prepare for and run a 100-mile race was seen.

Moreover, thee results suggest that an average marathoner can finish a 100-mile race without modifying his training program. Requisites for optimal performance in the 100 mile run remain ill-defined.

These data show no consistent correlation between finishing times and a runner's age, sex, height, weight, running experience, weekly mileage, frequency and intensity of workouts, diet, use of vitamins and other supplements, or nourishment during the run.

To maintain energy and prevent dehydration in long-duration events, runners need to drink during competition. Excess amounts of glucose, dextrose pills, sugar cubes, honey, or hard candy should be avoided because they draw fluid into the intestinal tract and may add to the problem of dehydration. A concentrated sugar solution may also cause distension of the stomach, cramps, nausea, and diarrhoea.

These proportions are recommended as sufficiently dilute to allow for rapid gastric emptying. Commercial solutions ate generally more concentrated than the recommended solution. The role of the electrolytes, sodium, and potassium in the recommended fluid is primarily to improve absorption; these electrolytes do not appear to need to be replaced during exercise.

The addition of glucose increases the blood glucose level and thus increases the insulin level, which may increase the utilization of glucose. The ingestion of glucose may decrease the rate of utilization of glycogen and thereby improve endurance.

The position paper also states that runners should be encouraged to ingest fluids frequently during competition and to consume 400 to 500 ml of fluid 10 to 15 minutes before competition. In races of 16 km or more, fluid should be consumed every 3 to 4 km.

SUMMARY

Aside from heredity and training no single factor plays a bigger role in the quality of athletic performance than diet. Physical training by the athlete requires that appropriate adjustments in the diet be made in total calories, proportion of carbohydrates, water, salt, and iron to maintain optimal performance.

A varied diet, coefficient in amount to satisfy the energy needs of an athlete, will provide adequate vitamins and minerals. The energy cost of a sport depends on the intensity of the physical activity demanded, the length of time exertion, and the total time of participation.

Eating habits that promote obesity, semi-starvation, dehydration, and excess vitamin supplementation are counterproductive to physical training and optimal performance.

Chapter-16

A DISCUSSION OF ISOMETRICS

Recently, great popular emphasis has been placed on the use of isometric exercises for the development of strength. Due either to commercialism or to an attempt to get on the publicity band wagon, many persons have produced methods, gadgets, and exercises to extol the huge benefits that can be derived from isometrics. Unfortunately, many of these methods, gadgets and exercises are based more on fantasy than on fact.

The purpose of this chapter is to present some basic facts so that through proper use, isometric exercises can be capitalized upon as a highly desirable procedure. It should be definitely recognized, however, that no exercise or exercise method can be a panacea for, nor can it necessarily solve, all exercise problems.

CRITICISMS

Some of the commercial products available have based their sales literature upon the extreme usefulness of the isometric contraction. This usefulness has been established unquestionably by some of the fundamental research that has been conducted in isometrics. In stressing the benefits of isometrics, however, the commercial literature usually has failed to note the following points.

1. When a scientific study was conducted, muscle groups were isolated as much as possible, so that little or no substitution of other muscles could take place.

2. A method of measuring the force being exerted was used.

3. Summaries from textbooks describing the physiological effects of exercises have been taken out of their proper context. The original scientific investigators have frequently published material which was based only upon isotonic work, but the new copied summaries claim that isometrics will develop the same physical capacities or produce the same physiological effects. This has not been proved up to the present time.

CONDITIONING NEEDS

It is well to note that in both physical education and athletic programs there are four distinct types of conditioning needs.

1. Cardiovascular efficiency, or the adaptive response of the heart to exercise.

2. Muscular strength, or the ability to accomplish an activity at peak performance without injury. Strength is the ability to work against a specified resistance.

3. Muscular endurance, or the ability of the muscle to respond repetitively for a relatively long period of time.

4. Flexibility, which is defined both as the elasticity of a muscle group and the effective use of the muscle group throughout its maximum range of motion. The maximum effective range of motion varies among individuals. When this definition is

used, it should be noted that flexibility is closely allied to strength.

Each of these four areas of response must be developed in accordance with an individual' needs. Some activities stress one or two areas more than they do the others.

An athletic fitness program, for example, must differentially develop the areas proportionately to the needs of the individual rather than span all fitness categories. It has long been recognized that participation in sports does not, of itself, necessarily produce the optimal benefit that should accrue to the individual.

Thus, special conditioning programs have arisen to make the individual more proficient in the activity in which he is to participate. These special programs point to the necessity of using the proper type of conditioning activity to fulfil an individual's specific conditioning needs, rather than to use the same general program for all participants.

VALUES AND LIMITATIONS OF ISOMETRICS

Isometrics can develop strength and, if used properly, can offer a great deal to any physical education or athletic program. The studies using practical application of isometrics, which were undertaken at the Southern Illinois Laboratory of Applied Physiology and the Laboratory of Physical Education, thus take on a timely and special significance. These studies have led to the following conclusions.

1. The greatest value found so far in the use of isometrics has been in the elaboration of a method to evaluate the strength of various movements surrounding joints. This method of strength evaluation is extremely effective after because the

exact area or areas of weakness can be determined and the proper rehabilitation technique applied. Moreover, the testing allows evaluation of the effectiveness of the applied corrective method or of any applied conditioning program.

2. An isometric contraction can develop muscular strength at any point of stimulation throughout a range of motion. The literature contains electromyographic studies which indicate that in muscular activity about a joint, certain muscles act only in parts of the range whereas other muscles are active in another part of the movement.

   For example, in knee extension, which is mainly an act of the quadriceps femoris muscle, the rectus femoris and vastus intermedius are primarily responsible for thee movement beginning with full flexion and ending at approximately 125° extension.

It therefore seems to be pertinent that there is available a Multiple angle Testing Method which readily measures the strength of muscle groups at various points in the range of movement.

This method of testing has permitted the conduction of isometric strength studies which test the claims made above. The results of the necessity of strengthening more than one point in a range of motion if sufficient benefits are to be obtained.

3. The isometric contraction must be highly controlled if proper strength development is to be achieved.

   The above strength studies, using athletes in various, have indicated that when a weakness exists in muscles ordinarily used in a normal movement, other muscles adaptively take over to a varying extent.

4. Evaluation of the effect of isometric exercises is necessary if strength gains are to be realized. It must be recognized that no external work takes place during an isometric contraction.

   Therefore, there is no way to know whether or not a particular individual is actually exerting the force necessary to gain strength without some form of measurement available. Studies have indicated that individuals will not exert pressure to develop strength.

   These reasons may include (a) lack of motivation, (b) lack of belief in the benefit of isometrics, (c) lack of kinesthetic sense to exert full power, and (d) the individuals may be malingerers or have other psychologic complications.

5. Isometric exercises are not the whole answer to the conditioning needs of most individuals. Isometric exercises are extremely effective for the development of strength, but their effectiveness is increased if they are used with proper adjunctive isotonic and stretching exercises.

6. An isometric conditioning program using gross exercises is often more detrimental than beneficial. This would include exercise programs such as pressing the whole body against a bar or applying gross resistance with ropes or straps and without the benefit of measurement. Such programs may develop the wrong muscles, partly through unwanted muscular substitution and partly because the full ranges of motion about joints are not being taken into consideration.

It is suggested that such activities can often do more harm than good and should be eliminated.

RECOMMENDATIONS FOR ISOMETRICS

The recommendations that follow are based upon isometric exercise programs which have been conducted by the Southern Illinois University Laboratory of Applied Physiology and the Laboratory of Physical Education.

In Physical Education Classes

1. Isometric testing and strengthening can be beneficially applied to children and adults who need a corrective program, as well as to those who have insufficient strength to handle their body weight in such activities as chinning, dipping, and push-ups.

2. Isometric testing and strengthening can be used appropriately in activities such as postural work, sports, and dance if the students cannot properly perform the activity.

3. In general, isometric exercises can be used if the development of strength is necessary or desired.

4. An isometric exercise program should be individual rather than general in nature.

In Athletics

1. All members and prospective members of a team should be tested by isometric methods to determine what muscle groups of their body need strengthening.

2. A muscle strengthening program should be designed for each athlete on the basis of the testing.

This program should include isometric, isotonic and stretching exercises.

3. Muscle testing is necessary after athletic injury to determine the optimal time when the athlete can return to competition without a high susceptibility to injury.

   An athlete with a severe knee injury one season will start the next season with the same injury unless specific remedial exercises have been applied to the injured areas.

In a study involving 12 high schools in the Southern Illinois area, boys who had been injured one year still had significant strength losses in that same bodily area the following year, despite continual physical activity.

Additional data have indicated that unless a very specific kind of corrective exercise is applied, re-injury is apt to occur.

Many college and professional athletes, as well as individuals who discontinue athletics beyond high school, are often plagued by an injury which has occurred in high school sports.

It is therefore of utmost necessity they injured boys be tested for strength by isometric methods to determine whether or not the injury has been corrected.

PART 7
INJURIES IN ATHLETICS

CHAPTER-1

THE EXTENT OF ATHLETIC INJURIES

It is worthwhile noting that in a large medical centre drawing athletic injuries in particular, injuries that occur on the backyard swing or tree are treated much more frequently than are injuries from any type of sport activity. And, if one considers only the older age groups, many more injuries are treated every day that arise from the use of the automobile than are brought to the attention of the orthopedic surgeon following college football or professional baseball games. If one is going to be active at all in life, it appears less hazardous to be on the playing field than on the street or even in the home.

National magazines highlight articles on athletic injuries. Parents debate whether junior should play Little League Baseball in the light of elbow injuries. A death in athletics will make front page reading in daily newspaper. People are interested in athletic injuries, either as parents, trainers, coaches, physicians, or as proponents or antagonists of sports.

If the statistical results of cataloguing injuries at a prominent college are reviewed, the distribution of various types of injuries is fairly typical. The injuries were catalogued from 1950 to 1955. Of 920 athletes, 448 were involved in injuries that disqualified the athlete for one or more participations in all sports—a rate of 48.7%.

There were 10 injuries and 1 illness that ruled out any further participation in athletics. In the various sports, 9 of these occurred in football, 1 in hockey, and 1 in basketball. Two injuries involved the neck, there were 2 concussions, 3 shoulder dislocations, 1 bilateral leg pain with spondylolisthesis, (incomplete dislocation of a vertebra in the lower spine, not strictly an injury), 1 repeated injury to a gastrocnemius tendon with calcification, and 1 illness.

That the knee takes the brunt of athletic activity is shown in this series as in others; 44 of the injuries involved the knee. In second place but still prominent was the ankle, with 34 cases. Concussion, severe but not disqualifying, occurred 10 times. There were 8 neck injuries and 6 acromioclavicular separations. Fractures of all types involved 10% of the series—equal to the knee injuries when treated as a group, but still a much smaller group than the soft tissue injuries. One abdominal contusion occurred, but no ruptured spleens, although some statistical studies report one or two.

Creighton J. Hale, Research Director for Little League Baseball, reported on injuries among 771,810 Little League Baseball players. The pitched ball caused the greatest number of injuries; the children faced approximately 148,000,000 pitches. In relation to the number of exposures, the batted ball actually caused more injuries.

One half of all the injuries were found to be abrasions and contusions.

The usual injury is abraded skin from sliding or falling (the so-called "strawberry"). Only 1% of the players sustained fractures, sprains, contusions, and dental injuries, and most of these were minor. Forty per cent of the fractures involved the finger. The incidence of brain concussion was 0.6%. Sliding and catching behind the plate appeared to be the most hazardous occupations.

Interestingly enough, despite the wide circulation given to reports of epiphyseal injuries in this age group, no such injury was reported by physicians treating this group of 771,810 boys. Although the author has been several involving the medical epicondyle of the distal humerus, is by no means common.

Over-all 2% of the players received some form of reportable injury, no matter how minor. The head and upper extremity was most often injured in this group.

No matter what the age group or sport, the incidence of various types of injuries reveals that ligamentous tears of various types far outweigh the incidence of fractures. The knee and ankle are the most vulnerable areas. The head injury is a problem in itself, resulting in occasional serious injuries and even fatalities. Neck injuries are more prominent than most sports enthusiasts might suppose.

With the emphasis on sports participation for everyone, it is well to examine how physical education and intramural-type activities fare so far as injuries are concerned.

It should be noted that of 81 injuries that occurred in physical education activities at one college in 1960, only 27 required the services of a physician. These 27 constituted only 1.6% of the total number of student injuries that were treated that year.

In one report, the injury rate per 1,000 participants for all intramural activities was 7.2. The information regarding injury rates in the various intramural sports is summarized in Table II. Ice hockey, wrestling, and touch football lead the list.

In physical education activities, wrestling led the list with an injury rate of 26.0 per 1,000 participants. Double tumbling had a similar rate. Boxing, squash, apparatus stunts, individual tumbling, handball, ice skating, and soccer were above the usual rate. In these activities, sprains accounted for 24% of the total number, bruises and cuts made up 30%, and fractures represented only 10% of the total. The distribution of injury type is very similar whether the sport is intra-or extramural. The knee; face, ankles, eyes, and shoulders were the most frequently injured areas. Dislocation principally involved fingers and shoulders.

From these reports one learns which sports are most likely to lead to injury, and that the most frequent sports injuries are contusions and sprains.

Measures can be taken to assure that the participants are in a safe situation to compete. These measures should include medical supervision with provision for first aid treatment. The manner of handling a casualty should be defined ahead of time and the referral route for their care arranged prior to embarking on a program.

The participant should know the game. There should be instruction, supervision, and officiating with observation of the rules to the letter. Playing fields and gyms should be clean of irrelevant material: this includes clothing, gear, and maintenance equipment. The playing surface must be smooth. Now if participants are in good condition and the sports are played with good protective equipment, injuries will be kept to a minimum.

T. B. Quigley has had a lifetime interest in athletic injuries. His ideas concerning the relation of the athlete to protection and care has prompted him to compose a Bill of Right for the college athlete. This is essentially a statement of how to do things right, and is valid for any organization embarking on an athletic program.

CHAPTER-2

EXERCISE FOR ATHLETES

The correlation between what is known about muscles scientifically and what is good practice is not easy to determine. The better a person is trained, the higher will be his peak oxygen utilization. But what kind of training achieves this? And it is not just a question of muscle contraction in a laboratory sense, but the achievement of a given task with speed, strength, and agility. Any one of these factors might be more important than the others in a given athletic feat.

Many athletes, particularly professionals, become way of exercises as a means of increasing their prowess or of staying at a high level of proficiency as age advances. Everyone is familiar with the paradox of the weight-lifter who can't run; the loss of efficiency is called being "*muscle bound.*" Exercises will not produce this result if a new fundamental principles are observed.

Athletics generally require a wide range of joint movement. The athlete who prides himself on speed and ability is well aware of his powerfully built friends who have neither. If the reader prides himself on his ability to throw, he can make a simple test. Hold both arms straight out from the side, with the palms down and even with the shoulders, and then rotate the arms externally. The throwing arms will rotate 20° more than the other arm.

The fundamental principle underlying athletic exercise is based on maintaining full joint excursion while increasing strength and endurance. Some types of exercise can do harm or limit prowess.

CONTRAINDICATED EXERCISES

There are two general types of exercises which can limit the prowess of the athlete attempting to stay physically fit. The first are those that stretch ligaments with muscles protection eliminated. The most common example is the deep knee bend. During the Second World War, this exercise was used as part of the physical fitness preparation of para-troopers in some areas; one regularly sees it used as part of the training for football teams. Done for a series of ten it has value in maintaining full stretch of the quadriceps and excursion of the knee. Unfortunately, deep knee bends frequently become a competitive thing in a group of men. The champion can do several hundred without halt. On examination, the champion has abnormal mobility of his knee forward, backward, and to either side. This gross instability results in loss of speed and agility.

Principle

Repetition to the point of exhausting the muscles, if done against a constant load, will result in stretching of joint ligaments.

The second form of harmful exercise is that done against a fixed or limited resistance which moves not at all or only through a very limited range. This results in the short muscle of great cross-sectional area but little athletic use. For demonstration purposes such a muscle can support an inordinate amount of weight, but the agility and speed necessary to get the weight into a position of mechanical advantage for the muscle is often lost when this type of exercise is the sole type of stress that the muscle has received in training.

Principle

Exercise against a resistance which is fixed or has a limited range of reaction will result in functional shortening of the muscle.

One might feel that a case could be made for this form of exercise for certain functions in certain sports, such as line blocking in football. If one could depend on the opposing lineman to merely charge straight into the limited range of these muscles and maintain the pressure, this would be true. Pushing against a post fixed in the ground will not develop the ideal lineman, even though it may develop somebody who can break the post.

ENDURANCE EXERCISES

In general, endurance building consists of repetitious exercise against a light load, and the result is increased vascular function. In a trained individual the pulse rate is slower for any given level of exertion than in an untrained person. The amplitude of heart contractions increases during exercise; the stroke volume of the heart increases. These things are possible in the trained person because his heart has larger muscle fibrils and increased blood supply. In either the trained or the untrained individual, the response to exercise is an increase of pulse rate and pulse pressure. The trained individual will get much more return for this increase, however.

An oxygen shortage occurs in the body during periods of intense exercise. The ability of the lungs to aerate the blood in any individual is definitely limited. When muscle metabolism enters an oxygen starved phase there is an increase in lactic acid accumulation. The removal of lactic acid requires increased oxygen consumption, and is a slow process.

The rate of removal can be influenced by continued exercise at less than peak effort. It is possible to have a strenuous effort without a corresponding lactic acid increase in the early phase of a muscular effort. During this period, there is a considerable rise in oxygen debt. Training alters these responses through its effect on the cardiovascular system.

Repetition against light resistance appears to increase endurance. Running is the most prominent form of this type of exercise. Whatever the take required for any particular sport, it can be simulated with a light enough load so that repeated endeavours are possible. The load must be sufficient to create a demand in terms of oxygen utilization, but not so overwhelming that the response of heart and lungs cannot rise to meet it by increased efficiency of operation. Daily repetition of this demand will result in changes in the heart such as stronger muscle fibrils and increased blood supply, so that challenges are overcome with progressively greater efficiency.

FUNCTION AND CONDITION EXERCISES

The general principle underlying all exercises for general conditioning or specific function is that the joint must be uninhibited in carrying out a full range of motion. When resistance is applied it should exist to some degree throughout the range, increasing as mechanical advantage for the muscle increases. Stretching is another type of exercise which will insure that a full range of motion is maintained. Stretching exercises should be done with an exercise partner. At the extremes of motion the position of the joint is sometimes awkward and the mechanical advantage of the muscle protecting this range is small. A partner, usually in a position of great mechanical advantage, can exert pressure beyond his comprehension, resulting in torn ligaments.

As athletes age, the usual incapacity limitation involves the legs since these are carrying a more or less constant load. The function of arms and trunk will far outlast the legs, which are doing more work and tend to do this work in a more limited range. Stretching exercises for the legs, such as hamstring stretching, are very important in prolonging athletic life. The second phase is maintenance of the player's full range of joint motion. It has already been pointed out that certain joints will have developed a range greater than normal to aid an athletic function.

A scientific record of athletes and their condition should include these accurately measured ranges of motion, and the same range which was achieved at the end of a season should be regained by the start of the following season.

Principles

Enduring athletic ability depends on maintaining a full range of the joint motion peculiar to a particular athlete in all joints. One of the simplest ways to maintain this range is to go through the motions required in a particular sport each day during the off season. Light throwing, fielding, and swinging a bar would be helpful in baseball, and other sports would have their particular activities.

A more formal program of stretching is worthwhile in addition. For anyone who must throw, a full range of shoulder motion with particular attention to external rotation is important. All stretching exercises should be done actively by the athlete, not passively by a device or partner. For the legs, ten deep knee bends daily, done both upright and while lying on the back with thighs fully flexed on the abdomen, increase full stretch in the most significant plane.

ISOMETRIC EXERCISES

It is helpful to know the reaction of muscle in humans to a training period which consists solely of isometric contractions at maximum effort. The result have been tested by evaluating the level of strength that can be achieved in an isometric contraction.

Daily muscle contractions of short duration have no effect in increasing muscle strength. In order to get an effect that increases strength, at least two thirds of the maximum possible force must be exerted for 4 to 6 seconds. The duration should be at least 15 to 20% of the maximum time a contraction could be held by the individual.

One training stimulus a day under these circumstances is all that is necessary, and it has been shown that increasing the training periods by five failed to increase the training effect. If only one period a week is used, the training effect is reduced by 40%. No effect occurred when the interval was increased still further. The training effect is also reduced as the individual's maximum normal strength is approached.

Dr. Bender has developed isometric exercises as a means of testing the strength of an individual in various movements necessary to a particular sport. In Multiple Angle Testing as developed by *Bender*, various points in the range of movement are evaluated. This procedure has pointed out that often in injury, full strength may be recovered in one portion of the range of joint motion while weakness lingers in another portion. Such lingering weakness obviously predisposes to injury.

Bender has also exhibited that in athletes there is a strong tendency to adapt to a muscle weakness by substitution of an uninjured muscle in the same plane. As a result, the weak muscle falls into progressive disuse and the strong muscle increasingly exerts its effect. The essence of a program to overcome this once it is discovered is to position the athlete so that only the weak muscle can be used. In such a position, maximal effort is excited using isometric contractions at various points to achieve a training effect.

STRENGTH BUILDING EXERCISES

Different muscle groups increase at different rates. The time of the year has an effect, with muscle training appreciably better in the sunlit months and lowest in December, January, and February. Immobilization decreases strength, one week in a plaster cast reducing strength by 13%. Strength was regained by training after a 10-day exercise period. Roughly, one can count on 20% of the strength being lost with immobilization week by week. Muscle strength is related to the cross sectional area of a muscle and its relative length.

Trained muscles accumulate less lactic acid than untrained muscles. Men are stronger than women and age decreases the ability to train. These things are obvious, perhaps, but the surest fact of all is that strength will increase only when an effort greater than the normal daily activity occurs.

So far in this discussion, we have been concerned only with those things that will maintain the maximum strength of a given muscle. An isometric contraction has been used as the test. If hypertrophy is desired in addition to fitness, weight lifting through a full range should be substituted for maximum stress against a fixed resistance. The growing youngster can keep his strength at a high level by daily isometric stresses, but he will not increase his potential.

CHAPTER-3

USE OF PHYSICAL AGENTS AFTER ATHLETIC INJURY

APPLICATION OF COLD

Cold is used to produce ischemia to contract blood vessels and thereby diminish the possibility of further hematoma due to hemorrhage following the injury. Cold brought to the point of skin application should be at the temperature of ice water. The use of an ice peak invites the possibility of secondary damage due to frostbite.

Parts that are swollen and tender do not welcome pressure from heavy apparatus. Compresses may be dipped in ice water and applied. These may be reinforced by ice water filled bags laid against but not on the part. Limbs may be immersed for short periods in ice water containers but the dependent position frequently invites edema and is therefore disadvantageous. Wrappings that are extensive on the limb, although cold to start with, shortly become in reality a hot pack.

The most advantageous time for the use of cold is immediately after an injury, and in such cases the cold application should always be accompanied by compression with an elastic wrapping that begins on the most distal part of the extremity and encompasses the injured part. Elevation of the limb is equally important.

APPLICATION OF HEAT

Heat is used to bring about an increase in the circulation. Vasodilation occurs, leading to more efficient removal of fluid and consequently increasing rapidity of healing. As a side effect, heat tends to relax muscles and sedate the injured individual.

All forms of heat are dangerous when used in the presence of circulation that is not normal. Such a situation in an athlete should result in hospital care where treatment can be given to relieve the condition.

Radiant Heat

Heat may be applied in several forms, the safest of which is infrared radiation. Radiant heat comes from any hot object whether it is luminous or not. The commonest device used is the "baker." A reflector is filled with several luminous bulbs which produce more of the most penetrating of the various infrared radiations. Infrared lamps should be kept at least several inches away from the skin and, if large, even further away. The skin becomes warm and reddened and with heat sweat occurs. The reddened skin should rapidly resume normal colour after treatment or the treatment has been too long or too intense. Abrasions and wounds should be covered by dressings and not exposed to the direct effects of the radiation.

Direct Heat

Whirlpool

The water in the whirlpool bath is usually kept in the range between 110° and 115° F. As an application of heat, it is efficient and is accompanied by a sort of massage due to the motion of the water. This may be of great aid in reducing edema quickly but is hindered by the fact that the non-active limb is held down in a position favouring the accumulation of edema.

Wool Packs

Wool blanket pieces are dampened and spun dry so that they can be applied without burning the skin. Their application requires great expenditure of time on the part of personnel, but they appear quite efficient in relieving muscle spasm and pain in an injured limb.

Hydrocollator Packs

These packs are designed to hold heat for long periods. They are an aid but cannot be laid directly on the injured part if it is tender, because of their weight.

Contrast Baths

A container of hot water at 105° F and one of cold water at 60° is used in alternating fashion to stimulate circulation. If 5 minutes in the hot water is followed by 1 minute in the hot water is followed by 1 minute in the cold for four cycles, a reddening of the part will be produced.

Penetrating Heat

Short Wave Diathermy

High frequency current is supplied by means of an induction cable to create an electromagnetic field. It tends to spread as it contrast the tissues and causes a rise of temperature to a depth of about 1 inch in 30 minutes. Although its safety margin is greater than microwave or ultrasound diathermy, there is not good evidence that it has benefits over single superficial heating devices in the treatment of athletic injuries. Because the greatest increase in heat occurs in the subcutaneous fat, its effect can be judged by skin tolerance.

Ultrasound Diathermy

There is a possibly very destructive agent which penetrates sufficiently to heat bone. In our opinion, this agent is not indicated in the treatment of athletic injuries. The energy generated at the source is measured, but the amount delivered to the deep tissues is subject to many variables. Variation in water content of the tissue affects its transmission even more than with microwave therapy. Heating of the deep tissues such as bone may occur to an extent not appreciated.

Microwave Diathermy

As with ultrasound, the intensity of the temperature rise in the deep tissues cannot be judged by skin sensation. There are too many variables to justify the use of this agent or ultrasound in the treatment of athletic injuries.

Neither agent should be used in youngsters still growing since the area of injury so often is near the epiphysis of a long bone. Neither agent should be used around the face, or head, or in the early treatment of fractures, or where there is embedded metal. Large nerve trunks may be susceptible to damage.

Both ultrasound and microwave therapy are better left out of the treatment of athletic injuries.

MASSAGE

Active exercise is an efficient form of massage, self applied. Massage applied to an injured area aids in fluid displacement on both the vascular and lymphatic side. Blood flow in this area is increased with a secondary renal effect in terms of fluid loss. If fluid is steadily being allowed to accumulate, than the injured limb is aided in its flow. As the fluid is removed there is a theoretical diminished likelihood of protein breakdown and fibrosis. This theory is very poorly understood at the moment, however.

Areas that seem tight and bound down appear to be aided in their mobilization by massage. The skin becomes reddened and it is assumed that this vascular dilation also occurs in muscles. Tender areas appear to gradually subside as the intensity of the massage is increased. It is a valuable aid in treating athletic injuries, but is also time consuming. The whirlpool acts as a partial substitute.

Stroking is one form of massage. Done superficially it dilates the blood vessels by reflex action. Deep stroking aids in pushing fluid along through the tissues. Deep massage must be done toward the heart for maximum efficiency in moving fluid out of the injured area.

Kneading with compression is used to mobilize tissue that appears bound down and tight. The rotation of the hand on the skin aids in mobilizing the area. Such motions are usually circular.

Percussion of tissues by tapping or hacking at them produces motion of the tissues down to bone, but does not appear to have any aid in recovery from injury.

Since one of the aims of massage is the relaxation of protective muscle spasms, all motion should be rhythmic and slow, covering the same course usually without removing the hand. Lubricants are often used to aid in the production of continuous slow motion. Since the object is relief of pain, its use should not produce painful reactions or muscle spasm will increase. Heat is usually applied prior to massage.

EXERCISE

Active Exercise

Isometric Contractions

Static or isometric contractions occur when a muscle is applied in force against a resistance but does not move it. Thus the muscle is kept at a fixed length while the contraction is going on. This type of exercise builds strength in the particular position that the limb or trunk is placed in when the contraction occurs. It is a good means of testing strength since many other variables affecting the force that can be exacted are kept at a minimum.

Isotonic Contractions

Isotonic contractions occur when the muscle moves the resistance to the contraction; the force generated must be maintained until the motion is complete. This type of contraction is performed with a resistance which calls for maximum effort to complete the motion. Isotonic exercises lies at the heart of progressive resistance exercises and is very useful in athletics. Increased muscle power is gained throughout the range of motion.

Passive Exercise

Passive exercise performed by the therapist has little in athletics. If maintenance of a full range of motion is desired, or even an increased range, the chances of success are much better when the individual uses active exercise. This is because of Sherrington's Law of reciprocal innervation, which states that when a muscle is voluntarily contracted this contraction is accompanies by a simultaneous relaxation of its antagonist. Voluntary motion is greater than passive motion since the individual instinctively guards against the passive stretch being initiated by the therapist.

Stretching can be actively done by the athlete and is safer the when it is done by a partner where non-stretching may occur.

The athlete can gain endurance by performing repetitious motions against less than maximal resistance. This type of exercise has not only a local effect, but a general effect over the cardiovascular system, with development of increased efficiency of heart muscle and increased development of the vascular bed. Running is an excellent example of this type of exercise.

SKIN PROTECTION

Skin abrasions can be a troublesome entity in athletics due to the fact that they occasionally become infected and lead to loss of time from the sport. So-called "strawberry" abrasions of the thigh in baseball and lesions on the back of the hand in football are typical examples.

Exposed areas of the skin can be protected by taping. A dry sterile dressing should be applied over the skin to be protected before the tape is applied. It is better not to cross a joint with the tape if it is not necessary for support. In areas of skin lesions this may lead to further chafing. If the skin is actually broken, fine wrist gauze is a useful wrapping before the tape is applied.

When the skin has been freshly abraded as in the typical sliding injury in baseball or the mat bruise in wrestling, the area should be thoroughly cleaned with cotton swabs and warm soapy water. When all possible dirt is removed, the area may be painted with a non-alcoholic antiseptic agent. A sterile dressing is then applied. Such lesions readily form a deep crust or scab beneath which the skin heals. Infection leads to a troublesome and prolonged course and also runs the risk of spreading troublesome bacteria in the locker room.

Frank cuts occurring on the field of play should result in the athlete's removal from the game and immediate treatment of the laceration. A dry sterile dressing should be applied immediately to cover the wound and the athlete should be moved to a sterile area—preferably a hospital outpatient department.

The skin about the lesion is thoroughly washed using warm soapy water while keeping the laceration itself covered with a sterile dressing. Hair is shaved off about the area. The laceration itself is then thoroughly irrigated with isotonic saline solution from the depths of the wound outward. In the process shreds of tissue may be seen waving in the irrigating solution. These are removed by shard dissection. If the wound is absolutely clean, it can then be approximated with skin sutures.

If dirt has been ground into laceration, it is best to excise the edge continuously so that the lacerated area is lifted from the wound like a pocket, leaving a clean area to sew. Healing takes place readily except in the presence of infection. The most important deterrent of infection is prompt and complete cleaning, with debridement converting the laceration to a surgical wound.

Athletes sometimes employ commercial products for toughening the skin, but many agents which toughen the skin also dry it. The simplest is ordinary rubbing alcohol. The best skin protection is a covering of either athletic clothing or gauze and tape.

CHAPTER-4

THE SCIENCE AND BIOMECHANICS OF RUNNING

Introduction

The biomechanics of running are somewhat difficult to discuss because of the great variability of the activity, i.e., from the slow recreational jogger to the world class sprinter. In the biomechanical studies "normal" human walking, subject variability is minimal and the speed of gait is constant, as are the range of motion of the joints of the lower extremity, phasic muscle activity, and forces.

In running, there is a broad spectrum of speed resulting in extreme variability in the range of motion of the joints, phasic muscle activity, and ground reactions.

GAIT CYCLE

The gait cycle is a useful framework by which the various events that occur during human locomotion can be expressed. The gait cycle begins and ends with heel strike of the same foot. That sequence also constitutes a stride, which consists of two steps, In the case of a person running on his toes, the gait cycle will obviously be from the time of initial ground contact until the same extremity once again comes into contact with the ground.

The cycle is further divided into a stance phase and a swing phase. During walking the stance phase occupies about 60% of the gait cycle and the swing phase 40%. Two periods of double-limb support occur during the first 12% and the last 12% of the stance phase, and a period of single-limb support occupies about 35% of the walking cycle.

ANGULAR ROTATION OF THE LOWER EXTREMITY

During normal locomotion, motion occurs in the lower extremities in the transverse, sagittal, and frontal planes. In walking, this motion has been well documented and has been measured by many laboratories. The results of the measurements basically agree with one another.

BIOMECHANICAL PRINCIPLES

Several basic principles should be kept in mind when evaluating the changes in the biomechanics of the lower extremities as the speed of gait increases. The transverse rotation that occurs in the lower extremity during walking gait has been documented both quantitatively and qualitatively, but quantitative data of running have been difficult to obtain. Qualitative data obtained from high-speed motives exhibit that the same basic type of rotation occurs during running, and the rotation seems to be of somewhat greater magnitude than that observed during walking.

FUNCTIONAL BIOMECHANICS

Thus, far some of the biomechanics principles of the lower extremity have been presented. Needless to say, the function of the lower extremities is a dynamic one, and as the speed of gait increases, not only is the speed by which each of these mechanisms occurs increased but, the magnitude of the force involved increased greatly. At the time of initial ground contact, internal rotation occurs in the lower extremity, and as the foot is loaded, concomitant eversion occurs in the calcaneus. The eversion of the calcaneus starts a series of movements that results in pronation of the longitudinal arch. The eversion of the calcaneus results in a flexible transverse tarsal joint, which permits a certain degree of collapse of the longitudinal arch as the foot is applied to the ground.

This mechanism of eversion of the calcaneus, along with flexibility of the longitudinal arch, is purely passive and is not under any muscle control, *per se*.

ELECTROMYOGRAPHY

The electromyographic data of the phasis activities of the muscle in the lower extremities also change as the speed of gait increases. Generally speaking, by percentage, the muscles have a longer period of stance phase activity than that normally seen in walking.

The muscle function about the hip joint demonstrates that, during walking, the gluteus maximum is active from the end of the swing phase until the foot is flat on the ground. It is probably functioning to help decelerate the swinging thigh and to provide stability at the hip joint at the time of initial ground contact.

PRONATION

Pronation itself is a passive event brought about by the weight of the body against the lower extremity and the subsequent loading of the subtalar joint, which will normally collapse into an everted position at ground contact, due to the configuration of the joint. The constraints of pronation are the shape of the joints of the subtalar joint complex, along with their ligamentous support, and, to a lesser degree, the muscle support. As pronation occurs, the tibia rotates internally, which, again, is secondary to the eversion movement of the subtalar joint.

Runners develop problems mainly because of the repetitive stress imparted to the lower extremity. An average 150-lb man who is walking with a step length of 2½ feet and taking about 2,110 steps to walk a mile will absorb at initial ground contact, considering an impact of 80% of the body weight, a total 2,53,440 lbs. (127 tons) or 63½ tons per foot. If the same person were running a mile, taking a step of 3½ feet and taking about 1,175 steps, he would absorb at initial ground contact, considering an impact of 250% of body weight, a total of 440,625 lbs. (220 tons) or 110 tons per foot.

EFFECT OF ORTHOTIC DEVICES ON HINDFOOT MOTION

In a small percentage of runners, an overuse syndrome can occur as a result of the repetitive stress of running. Such persons generally tend to have a more pronated foot than the average population, but a few may also have a cavus type of foot. Other malalignment problems, such as genubvarum and valgum, and toeing-in and toeing-out, can also lead to clinical problems secondary to the stress of running. Various types of orthotic devices have been used by runners, and the question that always arises is: what, if anything, does an orthosis do, from a biomechanical point of view? One of the problems in making such a determination is the actual measurement of tibial and subtalar joint rotation during running. Unfortunately, no reliable method is available at this time, but a fairly good estimate of subtalar joint motion can be obtained by placing a series of dots along the posterior aspect of the calf, the heel, and the shoe. By a photometric method of analysis, a general quantitation of the motion of the subtalar joint has been obtained. By careful laboratory study of high-speed motion pictures of runners, we have been able to demonstrate a qualitative decrease in pronation, as well as medial deviation of the inner border of the foot and ankle, with increased support along the medial side of the foot.

An orthosis providing a medial arch support, therefore, appears to play a role in the control of the foot, by decreasing the total numbers of degrees, as well as the rate of pronation of the foot. This type of device would be clinical benefit in a certain select group of symptomatic runners.

CHAPTER-5

THE IMPORTANCE OF DIAGNOSIS IN ATHLETIC INJURIES

INTRODUCTION

Injuries that result from athletics predominantly involve the musculo-skeletal system. Sprains, strains, contusions of joints and muscles, and fractures and dislocations of bones and joints make up the bulk of these injuries. Head, face, neck injuries and internal injuries of the thorax and abdomen statistically play a minor role, but they can be quite serious and even fatal. The attending physician must be aware of his limitations and should call in a consultant when an injury is beyond his training and experience.

Abrasions and lacerations of the skin and bruises of the subcutaneous tissue are so commonplace that they represent red and then black and blue status badges of body contact. These injuries present no great difficulty in treatment unless they become infected.

It is not within the scope of this book to discuss in detail the diagnosis and treatment of all the clinical condition that result from athletic injuries. Only some basic principles can be noted for some of the more common injuries of the connecting and supporting structures of the body. The following discussions cover only that treatment that can be rendered up to and excluding surgical intervention or procedures requiring the use of an operating room.

Some of the terms used in this chapter to describe clinical conditions have been either discarded by the Advisory Panel on the Standard Nomenclature of Athletic Injuries of the Council on Scientific Affairs of the A.M.A. or found unacceptable to the same committee. We have retained these terms because, at the present stage in the development of athletic medicine, most coaches, trainers, and athletes are more familiar with these terms than with specific anatomic and pathologic terminology. The anatomy and pathology of these clinical conditions are explained in the text and in the glossary.

THE PSYCHOLOGY OF ATHLETIC PERFORMANCE

Any attempt to separate the psychologic from the physical in athletic performance is an artificial one. The two are inseparably and intrinsically entwined. It behooves the medical, coaching, and training staff to be cognizant of this, because dealing with athletes depends on an understanding of this relationship.

Various personality types, which carry their own psychologic nuances, confront these professional. These professionals must deal with the athlete; this task is best accomplished in caring for the athlete and is based on a mature understanding of both themselves and the athlete.

The varied personality types may be catalogued as they reflect the athlete's motivation and his response to pain. First, it cannot be emphasized too often that pain is nature's way of alerting the performer that something is wrong and needs attention. Though it is not the purpose of this chapter to classify the types of pain, it should be known that the athlete's personality will affect his perception of pain, particularly the degree to which he will accept or deny its presence. Then there are the psychologic factors, which will determine the athlete's perception of pain. For example, the excitement of the competition, the thrill of victory, the exhilaration of a good play, a winning score, an outstanding performance-all may contribute to the absent perception of pain in the heat of the contest. However courageous the athlete is, he must ultimately pay the piper in the various forms of injury or illness, if his pain is neither perceived by him nor detected by the medical and training staffs. Recent studies have also shown that within the excitement of the competition, the body may pour out its own natural pain antidotes, known as endorphins, which conceal the pain by the euphoria they bring about.

Thus, the team physician and trainer must appreciate that the peak-performing athlete may be razor-edge close to a state of injury or illness: One of the psychologic manifestations of peak performance is a certain euphoria or feeling of well-being, above and beyond the athlete's base-line personality mood. Conversely, signs of irritability, depression, and loss of interest should be detected, for these are signs of impending staleness, injury, or illness.

Whatever the status of the athlete, he must be treated as an equal. At the same time, it must be realized that each athlete is an individual and must be handled as such. The goal, therefore, of the physician and trainer now intertwine. The main goal should be prevention. How does one approach this?

In terms of prevention, the coach and trainer in getting the athletes ready, is also teaching certain lessons in life. Take for example, the warm-up. It is essential that the warm-up be adequate, for muscles that are literally warm and joints that are flexible are less liable to be injured. Here the lessons is that things must be worked at; you cannot obtain what you want immediately, and slow and steady often is what wins the race. The same is true of injury in a converse way in that you cannot always have your wish to be healed immediately. Injuries take time to heal, but what is necessary for proper healing is both a realistic and optimistic attitude. The trainer must assist the athlete, therefore, in using his time fruitfully during the range of time in which he cannot compete. It may be necessary to recommend an alternate form of conditioning during that lag period.

Though the trainer need not have any formal course in psychology, what is needed is a mature judgment on his part. He cannot let his own ego intrude, for if it did, he may be unrealistic either in getting the athlete back too soon, or may have unrealistic, even grandiose, conceptions of his influence. The trainer, hopefully, has gained the trust and rapport of his athlete so that he will freely come to him and tell him of pain, loss of interest, or any of the manifestations of impending danger as mentioned above. Total honesty on the part of the trainer, both in his dealings with his athletes and in his dealings with himself, is necessary to obtain the rapport which will not only prevent injuries, but provide the touch needed for the rapid and complete healing of injuries already sustained. This information is in time conveyed to the attending physician.

Finally, the athlete, coach, physician and trainer, must understand the principles of training and conditioning. This in turn involves the application of moderate amounts of stress for which the body compensates, making the person stronger and stronger. If the stress, however, is too much and the body cannot respond, injury and illness are the results. Stress comes not only in the form of measured stresses imposed by the athletic situation, but within the total stresses of everyday life. Awareness of this and of the athlete as an individual subject to the pressures of his everyday work, be it schoolwork and/or vocation, home life, or other personal stresses-all these contribute to the total need for adaptation on the part of the organism. This only underlines, therefore, the Athletic Advisory Personnel ability to know their athlete and have the rapport, trust, and understanding of him which is engendered by their own simple, honest, and open attitude.

THE USE OF ADHESIVE TAPE

Proper equipment is an important safeguard against injury in all sports. The athlete must be uniformed so that the vulnerable parts of his body are protected without unnecessarily limiting freedom of action. Each sport has special requirements for protective equipment. There are rules that prohibit the use of certain so called "protective" devices. The team physician, the coach, and the trainer should know about the fashioning and fit of protective pads, uniforms, and shoes. The use of protective and therapeutic wrapping and strapping affords some protection to the musculo-skeletal system, which bears the brunt of athletic injuries. Because of anatomy and physiology, some parts of the musculo-skeletal frame are better protected than others. Elastic bandages, non-elastic bandages, and adhesive tape are the materials used, but the latter is vastly superior to the other two in most circumstances providing they are used properly.

In athletics, the use of adhesive tape is a way of life. A trainer is not experienced unless he knows how to apply adhesive tape expertly. This requires not only manual skill, but also an understanding of the anatomy and the mechanism of injury in order to apply the tape for maximal preventive or therapeutic benefits. Thus, the application of adhesive tape is an art as well as a science, which can only be developed with considerable practice. Its primary function is to support ligaments and thereby prevent joint injury or re-injury. It can also be used therapeutically to reduce pain and discomfort, and to permit more rapid healing by pulling injured parts closer together and promoting repair. Adhesive tape is also used to hold protective pads and dressings in place. Once a trainer has learned the fundamentals of taping, he can determine the taping requirements best suited for the athlete and incorporate his own variations.

Some general rules for adhesive taping follow:

1. Clean the area with soap and water, shave and dry thoroughly. Oily or sweaty skin is difficult to tape.
2. Cover any laceration or abrasion with sterile dressing.
3. Spray area with a skin protectant such as tincture of benzoin or a similar agent. Such agents not only keep adhesive from slipping or becoming loose, but also reduce the incidence of tape dermatitis.
4. Place the part to be taped in the proper anatomic position for maximal benefits.
5. Select tape size that best conforms to the contours of the injured part.
6. Tape from roll.
7. A thin underwrap is also used preparatory to taping to prevent skin irritation.
8. Apply tape neatly and smoothly, moulding with palm of hands.
9. Apply tape snugly, but never so tight that it causes constriction of the blood vessels.
10. Avoid circular taping when possible, since this may constrict and cause circulatory impairment. If it is used, circulation should be checked frequently.

11. Each strip of tape must overlap the preceding strip to avoid leaving exposed skin, which may cause skin irritation.

12. Following strapping, if movement of the part causes undue tension and/or pain, the strapping may have been incorrectly applied. Remove the tape and apply correctly.

13. Leave the tape in place long enough to promote healing; 5 days is sufficient. The strapping should then be removed, the skin cleansed with tape remover, alcohol, or ether, and the part re-taped if indicated medically.

14. Do not retape an irritated area unless it is properly prepared.

15. If an athlete is sensitive to tape to a skin protector, then and underwrap is necessary prior to taping.

16. Remove all circular strapping following a game or practice.

17. Remove all adhesive taping about a part if injuries suspected.

18. As much care should be exercised in removing the tape as was used in applying it. Never tear, rip or pull adhesive tape off the skin. Use a tape-cutter and gently push the skin away from the adhesive by exerting a little tension on the tape.

19. Removal of ankle strapping is facilitated by vertical and horizontal cuts with bandage scissors previously coated lightly with a skin lubricant. Following removal, the area should be cleansed and a light bland oil massaged gently over the skin to replenish the natural oils and to stimulate circulation.

20. Avoid taping any area immediately after exposure to a whirlpool bath, hot shower, or other physiotherapeutic modality in which heat is emitted from the skin. If taping of this part is necessary, first apply a cold towel to reduce the dilatation of the skin vessels and close the pores; then apply the tape.

21. *Adhesive tape* is best stored in a dry, cool place with the container standing upright. If stored on its side, the rolls of tape may sag on their spindles and make it difficult to unwind upon application.

CHAPTER-6

TREATMENT AND CARE OF JOINT INJURIES

Contusions and sprains of joints constitute a large group of athletic injuries. Of the major articulations, the ankles, the knees, and the acromioclavicular joints—in that order—are injured most frequently. Although the majority of joint injuries involve ligamentous sprains, there also occur, to varying degrees, rupture of the blood vessels in the surrounding areolar tissue, the formation of hematomas, ecchymosis, and tears of muscles and tendons, depending on the severity of the trauma. These may also be complicated by injuries of the synovium, meniscus, and bursa. The degree of injury is revealed by pain, swelling, tenderness, ecchymosis, limitation of motion, and joint laxity.

Joint injuries present a greater challenge to the physician because of the anatomic and kinesthetic complexity of joints and their tendency to adhesions. Joint injuries may also lead to a late disabling osteoarthritis.

Obtaining maximal restoration from treatment with a minimum of residuals requires a coordination of the skills and judgment of the physician and the trainer, the cooperation of the athlete, and the patience of the coach.

Sprains of joints result from a sudden twisting, wrenching, or external force applied to the bones that constitute a joint. This results in a mild ligamentous stretching or tearing, or a moderate to severe partial tearing or complete rupture of one or more ligaments. The joint may subluxate and reduce itself spontaneously if an isolated ligament ruptures.

A joint dislocation occurs when more than one ligament and its capsule are ruptured. Sprains have been classified as first, second, and third degree, or mild, moderate, and severe, but there has never been any unanimity or wide acceptance of this classification.

Although this chapter is addressed to physicians, coaches, and trainers, we assume that, in most instances, the trainer is the first paramedical person on the scene to survey the injured athlete. After taking a history, the trainer performs a cursory examination and initiates the proper first-aid measures. He makes clinical notations of his observations of injured athletes in a permanent training-room record, which is available to the team physician at all times.

The appropriate first-aid measures for an athlete with an injured joint consist of applying a pressure bandage and cold compresses, resting and elevating the injured part, and administering analgesics.

In fact, the trainer's first rules of action for most musculo-skeletal injuries are set forth in the acronym ICE, which stands for (1) the application of ice, (2) the application of compression, and (3) elevation of the injured part, if possible. Cold compresses may be elastic bandages immersed in ice water, ice bags or towels containing finely cracked ice, or sponge rubber compression bandages wrapped about the injured part, which is then immersed in ice water.

Another excellent method for cold compression is the use of towels and/or wash cloths previously frozen and stored in thermal picnic bags, which give a half hour of cold. Many commercial chemical cold packs are also on the market. When applying cold, avoid direct contact with the ice on skin. This can cause frostbite and burns. Compresses or compression reduces hemorrhage and edema about the joint. Although it is not necessary to make an accurate diagnosis immediately after the accident, one should be made before pain, swelling, and spasm of muscles surrounding an injured joint prevent a comprehensive examination. Abnormal motion at a joint due to a ligament tear or rupture is more easily diagnosed at the time of the accident, before muscle spasm prevents joint laxity.

Effective, definitive treatment must be started within 24 hours. This depends on the physician's analysis of the mechanism, nature and extent of injury. Supportive measures include giving analgesic and anti-inflammatory medication, strapping, heating, massaging, and exercising.

These measures improve circulation, hasten healing, minimize adhesions, and return muscle tone and strength. Infrequently, hospitalization with surgery and/or cast application may be indicated.

CHAPTER-7

TREATMENT AND CARE OF ANKLE INJURIES

The ankle joint, despite its relatively small size, has the huge job of transmitting the body weight to the foot in standing, walking, and running. The ankle is subjected to frequent violent high-speed movements peculiar to athletics, which makes it the most frequently injured joint. Although its primary function is dorsiflexion and planter flexion of the foot, the ankle is not the simple hinge joint that it is usually described to be.

Actually, it is an arrangement of three joints that work in concert. The distal tibia, fibula, and talus, enclosed in a capsule supporting ligaments, tendons, and muscles, are connected at the ankle and form the tibiofibular, talotibial, and talofibular joints. As with all mechanisms having multiple moving parts, the ankle is vulnerable to injury when unusual forces are exerted on its structures, especially with sudden changes in body speed and direction, as in dodging an opponent, pivoting or cutting away from or into an athletic situation. This is so because the ankle is largely a joint having hinge motion, and motions of the ankle-foot complex such as rotation, eversion, and inversion are considerably less. Because of the lack of "universality" of the ankle joint, tremendous mechanical stress is placed on it that may result in a sprain or other injury.

The ankle joint has connecting ligaments on all its surfaces. The ligament most commonly injured is the anterior tibiofibular; injury results from excessive external rotation of the foot on the leg or from internal rotation of the leg when the foot is fixed.

The next most frequently injured ligament is the calcaneofibular portion of the lateral ligaments of the ankle. This injury occurs when there is a forcible inversion of the foot. If the foot is inverted while plantarflexed, the anterior talofibular ligament will sprain. Sprains from the reverse direction involve the medial ligament, and are infrequently seen. If this does occur, one should also suspect a fracture of the fibula and tear of the anterior tibiofibular ligament.

FIRST AID MEASURES

Step 1. The trainer questions the athlete as to when, how, and where the accident occurred. Was the ankle ever hurt before? Did the athlete hear any snap, crack, or tear at the time of trauma? He carefully inspects the bony and visible soft-tissue landmarks about the foot and ankle, looking for deformity, swelling, and ecchymosis and carefully testing range of motion. He questions the athlete to localize the pain. Some gentle palpation of these areas may be done to localize the injury. After rendering appropriate measures to control hemorrhage and extravasation of hemorrhagic exudate into the surrounding tissue, he notes all his observations in a permanent training-room record.

Step 2. An elastic bandage is first immersed in ice water and the applied to the ankle and the foot in a figure-eight technique, extending it down to the base of the toes. Following this an ice bag or towel filled with finely cracked ice is applied to the site of the injury and held in place by a second elastic bandage. This should be kept in place for 30 to 60 minutes; then a sponge rubber donut is held in place at the site of the injury by an elastic bandage. The duration of the ice compress is determined by the severity of the injury. In mild sprains, one application may be sufficient. In a moderate sprain, it may be necessary to apply cold compresses for 2 to 3 hour intervals until swelling is controlled. If the sprain is severe, continuous application of cold compresses for 48 hours is necessary; this occasionally requires hospitalization of the athlete. To prevent frostbite, ice and skin should not be in contact with each other.

Another method of compression is the open basketweave strapping, provided the injured ankle is properly prepared. The application of an open basketweave strapping to a sprained ankle is only indicated when the anticipated swelling is minimal or nil. Physicians who are not as adept at taping as trainers may prefer to use elastic bandages for injured joints to allow for swelling. The attending physician will decide whether elastic bandages or open basketweave adhesive strappings are to be used for acute ankle sprains.

Step 3. The athlete is provided with crutches of proper size and instructed in their proper use. He is not to bear weight on the injured foot. He is instructed to elevate the injured leg above the him during waking hours and during sleep, to place the injured foot and ankle on two pillows, which aids gravity in the drainage of the swollen ankle. He is also to apply a cold compress to the injured ankle.

The athlete is referred to the doctor the same day and instructed to see him before going to bed. The attending physician examines the athlete and decides whether or not an x-ray picture is indicated.

DEFINITIVE TREATMENT (FOLLOW-UP CARE)

The following day the doctor reappraises the ankle. He looks for pain, swelling, tenderness, ecchymosis, joint restriction, and laxity. Even with the most adequate first-aid measures to control hemorrhage, some does occur. However, within 24 to 48 hours, the attending physician will be able to pinpoint and diagnose the pathologic condition and prescribe proper therapy.

Mild Sprains. Mild ankle sprains with minimal swelling, tenderness, ecchymosis, and limitation of motion.

First Day

1. Immerse foot and ankle in ice water for at least 20 minutes. If ice water is not available, an ice bag with finely cracked ice may be secured to the site of injury with an elastic bandage.
2. Apply open basketweave strapping with 1½-to 2-inch adhesive tape or an elastic-bandage dressing to the injured ankle depending on the amount of objective and anticipated swelling.
3. Continue with crutches and no weight bearing on injured leg.
4. Keep leg elevated above hip during waking hours and on two pillows while asleep. The athlete must be instructed to remove an elastic bandage at bedtime if he is wearing one. To not do so would be to invite increased pain and swelling one. To not do so would be to invite increased pain and swelling as the result of the pooling of the blood as the circulation slows down during sleep.
5. Take analgesics for pain if necessary as prescribed by the attending physician.

Second Day

Morning

1. Repeat first day treatment.

Afternoon

1. Repeat morning treatment.

2. Encourage athlete to do isometric exercises of muscles of the entire leg as well as active motion of the hip, knee, ankle, and foot.
3. The athlete should be trying protective progressive weight bearing to pain tolerance.
4. Keep leg elevated.
5. Continue with analgesics as occurrence arises.

If by the beginning of the second day post-injury hemorrhage has stopped and exudate is under control, contrast baths can be started. If not, contrast baths can be started on the third day post-injury. The technique stimulates circulation, aids lymphatic drainage, and facilitates healing. The procedure consists of applying alternating hot and cold applications to the injured areas. The first and last applications are always with hot water. The time interval varies with the trainer's or therapist's choice. It runs from 4 to 10 minutes for hot and 1 minute for cold. The most frequently used variable is 4 minutes to 1 minute. The entire treatment runs about 20 minutes. As noted before, a sock shall be worn to increase the athlete's tolerance for ice water. Buckets or plastic, rectangular wastebaskets may be used for the contrast bath.

Third Day

Morning

1. Contrast baths as described before.
2. Repeat second day's afternoon treatment.
3. Soreness can be relieved by adding 2 cups of epsom salts to every gallon of hot water.

Afternoon

1. Immerse leg in whirlpool between 105 to 11° F for 15 minutes.

2. Follow with light, gentle massage of foot, ankle, and lower leg for 5 to 10 minutes.
3. Apply a 2 inch elastic bandage using figure-eight and locked heel.
4. Discard crutches if pain is minimal and there is no limp with full weight-bearing.
5. Keep leg elevated when not weight-bearing
6. Encourage walking and active exercises of the entire leg to aid in milking out the residual exudate.
7. Analgesics and other medication should be stopped.

The athlete can return to his sport in less time depending on his response to treatment.

Sprains with moderate tearing of the ligamentous fibres or severe sprains with definite rupture of one or several ligaments are best treated by flexible, removable casting, or surgery respectively; however, early appropriate first-aid measures to reduce hemorrhage are also necessary before casting or surgery.

MODERATE SPRAINS

Sprains with moderate swelling with or without ecchymosis, local tenderness, and painfully guarded ankle mobility are treated with a removable type of plaster immobilization. Supportive measures such as bed rest, continuous cold compresses for 48 to 72 hours, elevation, elastic bandaging, and analgesics are instituted. A sitrrup-type removable plaster splint is applied after hemorrhaging has ceased and preceded by cotton padding material. Commercially prepared stirrups air splints, such as devised by Stover, are also available. The instep and Achilles-tendon are left uncovered. Isometric exercises for the splinted leg are encouraged. The athlete uses crutches with no weight bearing on the injured leg. Keep leg elevated when not on crutches. The ankle is examined frequently, active and passive ankle motion is done, and contrast baths for the injured ankle and permitted. When there is no longer any appreciable tenderness on palpation of the injured ligament, progressive and protected weight bearing of the injured foot to pain tolerance is permitted. Approximately 1 week post-injury, pain, discomfort, and swelling should have lessened considerably. Physical therapy efforts should now be actively implemented to facilitate the removal of the remaining traumatic exudate and swelling. Modalities such as cryotherapy, hydrotherapy, ultrasound massage, therapeutic and isokinetic exercises by use of cybex and other muscle-strengthening equipment should be used in their proper sequential manner to effect maximum benefits from treatment. This requires the coordinated efforts of the athlete, trainer-therapist, and physician. It may take as much as 2 or 3 weeks of rehabilitation for an athlete to recover sufficiently to return to competition.

SEVERE SPRAINS

Severe sprains with rupture of one or more ligaments produce abnormal motion at the ankle joint. These athletes should be hospitalized and the ankle treated with continuous cold compresses, elevation, and analgesic medication. The joint laxity should be confirmed with comparative stress x-ray films. Some authors have shown that arthrographic determination of the ligament rupture prior to surgery is helpful. The ligaments are then repaired surgically, after which a short leg cast is applied. The initial cast is removed in 4 weeks and a walking cast applied. Therapy directed to other parts of the musculoskeletal system should be encouraged throughout the complete care of this athlete.

An athlete treated for an injured ankle is functionally ready for competition if he can perform simulated rope skipping or hopping without undue pain, limp, or supportive strapping.

The healing time, the duration of treatment, and the athlete's response vary with the severity of the sprain, the immediate first-aid measures, and the definitive therapy employed. The use of heat and massage and resumption of full weight bearing too early may start additional hemorrhaging and minimize the effect of early first-aid measures to reduce swelling. If the athlete still has a perceptible limp, he should not be discharged from treatment. The use of a protective wrapping or strapping to support an injured ligament until the athlete can walk and run without a limp is recommended. Returning an athlete to competition before maximal benefits have been gained may result in a chronically painful and disabled ankle. With this type of sprain, the mutual coordination of the physician's and trainer's skills and the cooperation of the athlete in most cases brings about excellent results. The axiom "once a sprain", always a sprain" should not apply here.

STRAPPING THE ANKLE

Anatomically and physiologically, the ankle is best suited for the benefits of protective strapping and wrapping. Adhesive-tape strapping aids considerably in the prevention of ankle sprains, and also reduces the severity of sprains that might occur despite the strapping. The tape is applied so that the athlete is capable of complete dorsiflexion and planter flexion of the ankle joint, it practically eliminates completely inversion, eversion, and rotation of the ankle.

Prophylactically, in an uninjured ankle, 1½ inch adhesive tape is applied with the foot at a right angle and the heel in slight eversion; a heel lock is added to stabilize the heel and the talus. This strapping prevents the heel from rolling under and takes the strain off the lateral ligaments. The ankle strap makes the ankle mortise snug by bringing the tibia and fibula together at the ankle joint. This allows full hinge motion of the joint and at the same time provides effective protection against external rotation, which causes a sprain of the anterior tibiofibular ligament, the most commonly injured ligament of the ankle.

Adhesive strapping of the ankle is also used in the treatment of sprains and the prevention of re-injury. In sprains, the ankle must be strapped in position so that the strain is taken off the injured ligament. A small wedge placed on the appropriate side of the heel of the shoe continues to protect the ligament off the field.

Many excellent methods of taping are available to give protection to the ankle. Moreover, since many trainers devise their own variations of taping methods, we will illustrate only one classic form of taping the ankle.

The Gibney adhesive-tape strapping gives effective support and may be applied closed or open. The closed basketweave is an excellent support and when properly applied, practically eliminates rotary and side-to-side motion of the ankle while permitting full planter and dorsiflexion of the foot.

Closed Basketweave.

1. Use skin protectant.
2. Use pre-taping underwrap.
3. Anchor meets in the front.
4. Stirrup is applied from the medial side of ankle, close to edge of Achilles tendon.
5. Horseshoe applied as far down on the side of foot as possible.
6. Second anchor applied.
7. Second stirrup, second horseshoe, fourth anchor.

8. Third stirrup, third horseshoe, fifth anchor.
9. Fourth and fifth horseshoe, sixth anchor.
10. Second, third anchor around arch.
11. Start figure-eight from inside of foot.
12. Figure-eight under arch and back over ankle front.
13. Figure-eight completed and an anchor applied around other anchors on top of tape.

After the ankle and foot are sprayed with a skin protectant, blisters and other skin irritations can be prevented by use of an underwrap.

The closed Gibney basketweave is best indicated for practice, games, and the prevention of re-injury in moderate, severe, and complicated ankle sprains. It is especially useful when the anterior tibiofibular ligament has been sprained, which may lead to a permanently weakened and widened mortise.

The open basketweave may be used therapeutically for an acute ankle sprain. This type of strapping not only helps to reduce the swelling, but allows some swelling to occur.

In addition, the ankle is supported, which reduces the pain felt by the athlete. If the ankle presents a moderate amount of swelling or a moderate amount is anticipated, do not use any type of adhesive strapping, since this may cause circulatory impairment with ensuing pain and discomfort. Apply in elastic bandage and refer the athlete immediately to the doctor, who is in the best position to prescribe what type of strapping or wrapping is indicated.

When there is a question as to whether or not a collateral ligament of the ankle has ruptured, x-ray pictures of the ankle should be taken, with the hindfoot held in forced inversion or eversion, depending on which side of the ankle the ligament rupture is suspected. The degree or lack of talar tilt helps determine the diagnosis. Using local procaine or sedating the athlete before manipulating the ankle reduces the pain and anxiety usually associated with this stress testing.

ANKLE WRAPPING

There are as many different methods of preventive ankle wrapping with elastic and non-elastic bandages as there are adhesive strapping technique. Elastic wraps are better used to treat ankle sprains than for prophylaxis. Although adhesive taping is superior in the prevention of ankle injuries, fabric wraps have materially reduced the incidence of ankle injuries because the same anatomic and physiologic fundamentals are followed in their application. Wraps may be used successfully for prevention of injury for athletes without prior ankle injuries and for those who are sensitive to tape. They are applied smoothly over the athletic sock around the foot and ankle with two figure-eight turns incorporating a heel lock. This also prevents blisters and skin irritation. The wrap is secured either with a few small pieces of adhesive tape or a few turns of adhesive tape in a figure-eight. Obviously, ankle wrapping is easily applied by the athlete, inexpensive, and easily laundered.

If the athlete has an ankle that has been injured, adhesive tape is the strapping of choice. For all games and contests, adhesive taping, even though more expensive, is recommended.

CHAPTER-8

TREATMENT AND CARE OF KNEE INJURIES

The knee joint is the largest articulation in the body and one of the strongest for the normal activities of daily living and working. Yet, it is the joint most vulnerable to athletic trauma because of its construction, function and location. Nature has endowed the knee with a system of intricately designed and ingeniously arranged ligaments which, in harmony with powerful muscles, maintain the stability of the knee at any point of motion. However, the knee is structurally deficient to withstand the tremendous forces to which it is subjected in athletics. The femur, tibia, and patella articulate in such a manner as to allow two basic types of motion-flexion-extension and rotation. The anatomic make-up that allows these motions in what is basically a hinge joint also makes the knee more subject to injuries in athletics.

This is because the slightly concave surfaces of the tibial condyles and their loosely-held menisci give an insufficient repository for the convex, dissimilar-sized femoral condyles against the direct, lateral, and rotary forces to the knee. The patella moves up and down between the femoral condyles and lifts the tendon of the quadriceps muscle away from the axis of motions of the knee joint.

The quadriceps muscles are the main extensors of the knee; this extensor apparatus is mainly responsible for man's ability to stand, walk, and run. Unfortunately, because of its delicate mechanism and late evolutionary appearance, it is unstable and easily deranged by any injury severe enough to restrict activity. A loss of muscle volume, tone, and control may follow restriction of activity, resulting in quadriceps weakness and inadequate joint protection. The forces required of the quadriceps mechanism during activity are large. In stair-climbing, a force three to five times that of body weight is necessary to maintain knee equilibrium. Similar forces are needed in kicking a football. The knee is most stable in extension. The bulk of knee injuries involve the medial structures because most traumatic forces are directed from the lateral to the medial aspect with the knee in a bent position.

As noted before, there is a rotary component to knee-the tibia rotates medially in flexion, and in extension, it rotates laterally in the so called "screw home" mechanism. Associated and controlled motions of the menisci place them in position to distribute the load on the joint. With the many synchronous movements of the component parts that occur in the moving knee as well as its anatomic deficiencies, it is understandable why this joint is so easily injured in its exposed position. It is difficult to protect the knee from sudden blows and from the rotary forces of turning and twisting quickly when the foot is fixed to the ground while running at high speeds. The knee must also be stable in extremes of motion. The collateral and cruciate ligaments cannot accomplish this stabilization alone-there must be a harmonious working relationship of all muscles and ligaments to enable the knee to function efficiently.

The detailed anatomy and physiology of the knee is beyond the scope of this book and the reader is encouraged to read works by Kaplan, Clancy, Kennedy, Slocum, Larson, James, Nicholas, Noyes, Palmer, Smillie, O'Donoghue, Helfet, Frankel, Nardin, Hughston, MacIntosh, Marshall, Rockwood, Green, and others to enhance his understanding.

FIRST AID MEASURES

Step 1.

The trainer questions the athlete about where, how, and when the accident occurred. Was the knee ever hurt before? Was the knee struck by another player or by the ground? Did it happen while running and then twisting the knee to avoid another player or to "cut back" into a play situation? Did it happen during a tackle, block, or pile-up? Was the knee struck from the medial or the lateral side, or from front or behind? Was the knee injured when it was straight, bent, or turned medially? Was the foot fixed to the ground? Did the knee "give way?" Did the athlete feel two bones slipping over one another in the joint? Was he unable to straighten the knee because it felt locked? Was the inability to stand or bear weight associated with a tearing sensation or "giving way" of the knee accompanied by excruciating pain or a snapping, painful pop.

The trainer carefully inspects the bony and visible soft-tissue landmarks, looking for deformity, swelling, and ecchymosis. He questions the athlete in order to localize the pain. Some gentle palpation of these areas may be done to detect tenderness and swelling. The trainer tests range of motion of the knee, but does not test for ligamentous instability.

Step 2.

An elastic bandage first immersed in cold water is applied in a figure-eight fashion about the knee. Then an ice bag or towel filled with crushed ice is applied to the knee and secured to the knee with another elastic bandage; this is kept in place for 1 or 2 hours. After the cold compress application, a felt padding shaped to the anterior contours of the knee is secured to the knee to compress the exposed joint capsule, thus preventing the collection of blood, lymph, and synovial fluid in the intra-and extracapsular tissues. The athlete may go home with this wrap, but the trainer must check that it is applied snugly but not tightly.

As with ankle sprains, the duration of the ice compress is determined by the severity of the injury. In mild contusions and sprains of the joint, one application may be sufficient. In a moderate contusion or sprain, it may be necessary to apply cold compresses in 2 to 3 hour intervals until swelling is controlled. If the injury is severe, the athlete should be hospitalized and swelling checked with cold compresses continuously for 48 hours and with analgesic and anti-inflammatory medication if necessary.

An alternate method is to immerse the injured knee is ice water for 30 minutes. After removal, thoroughly dry the skin and wrap the knee in underwrap for a distance of 4 inches above and below the joint. Then apply a 6 inch square of soft sponge rubber with space for the patella cut out; secure to the knee with an elastic bandage. Weight-bearing is forbidden until the athlete is seen by the physician.

Step 3.

The athlete is supplied with appropriately sized crutches and cautioned not to walk on the injured leg. He is instructed to keep the leg elevated above the hip during waking hours. During sleep, place the injured leg on two pillows. This aids gravity in draining the swollen knee.

The athlete is referred to the doctor and instructed to see him immediately. The attending physician examines the athlete and decides whether or not an x-ray study is indicated.

DEFINITIVE TREATMENT

The earlier a physician systematically examines an acutely injured knee, the sooner a diagnosis can be established and definitive treatment started. The presence or absence of joint laxity can be determined more reliably when the physician examines the injured knee immediately after the injury. The examination must be done carefully and under ideal conditions that allow privacy. All clothing, taping, and wrapping is removed. The uninjured knee is used for comparison.

Inspection

The doctor looks for the presence or absence of a limp. He observes the position of the knee with the athlete in erect and supine positions. He notes whether or not deformities are present. He notes the location and degree of swelling, determining whether it is in the joint, bursa, or soft tissue surrounding the knee, and whether it is synovial effusion or hemorrhage. Rapid swelling in a knee joint suggests hemorrhage. He must decide whether the intra-articular effusion, which causes increased articular pressure and distention with or without risk of serious infection.

Palpation

The doctor palpates the bony and soft-tissue landmarks. Tenderness and swelling along the course or at the tibial or femoral attachments of the collateral indicate ligament injury. Tenderness over the medial-joint space with inability to extend the knee completely suggests an associated damaged meniscus. Ballottement of the patella indicates effusion into the knee joint.

Range of Motion

The physician tests the range of motion of the knee joint, being fully aware that intra-articular effusion limits motion at the extremes of flexion and extension. Most athletes maintain an injured knee in slight flexion because the capacity of the joint is greatest in this position. Spastic hamstring muscles may also keep the knee flexed. Inability to extend the knee completely does not always signify a torn cartilage, but a torn cartilage should be suspected if the condition persists after considerable treatment, provided the history and other findings corroborate such a diagnosis. The appropriate rotary motions of the femur and tibia must be observed during the range-of-motion, tests, which include the Helfet, Lochman, MacIntosh lateral pivot shift, Slocum tests and others. Eliciting a click in the knee during the McMurray test suggests a cartilage injury.

Ligament Stability

We are primarily concerned with the collateral and cruciate, ligaments and capsular structures. The medial collateral ligament is the knee ligament most commonly sprained, usually from a blow to the lateral side of the knee when the foot is fixed to the ground. This same type of blow may also lead to a torn anterior cruciate and medial meniscus, resulting in the "unhappy triad of O'Donoghue." Hyper-extension and hyperflexion forces can cause multiple ligamentous injury.

The lateral aspect of the knee is less frequently involved than the medial side, and the lateral collateral ligament is infrequently injured. However, a tremendous force to the medial aspect of the knee may cause a tear of the lateral collateral ligament, along with injuries to the biceps femoris tendon, peroneal nerve, and popliteus tendon. Posterior cruciate ligament tears are most commonly injured in severe hyperflexion and hyperextension injuries, and also in conjunction with injuries of the anterior cruciate and collateral ligaments. It has also been shown that the posterior capsule is one of the main stabilizers of the knee and is frequently injured with ligaments of the knee.

The physician should examine the injured knee within 30 minute after the accident, before pain, swelling, muscle spasm, and the athlete's anxiety make the examination difficult. If this is not feasible, the trainer performs a cursory examination and follows with the appropriate first-aid and supportive measures to relive pain and swelling. When the physician finally does get to examine the athlete, repeated examinations should be done, including stress testing of the knee under x-ray control if a ligament tear or rupture is suspected. The use of local anaesthetic and sedation before stress testing reduces the pain and anxiety usually associated with this procedure. Stress testing of both knees is done to check out any physiologic laxity of the ligament of the uninjured knee. Knee-joint stability is tested while the knee is held in terminal extension, in 30 or 90° of flexion, and the lower leg positioned in neutral, or internal or external rotation. Valgus (abduction) or varus forces are then directed to the flexed or extended knee. Push and pull forces are directed to the upper tibia in the positions of the lower leg as noted. The nature and extent of the instability is noted. The extent of the joint laxity ranges from <0.5 cm., which is 1+<0.5 cm to 7 cm is 2+ and > 1cm, which is 3.

However, Marshall states that in spite of the disagreement on this concept in the knee literature, it will serves as a useful and practical guideline for physicians testing a knee for stability. It helps in the understanding of the laxity of the knee joint and its pathologic correlation with the suspected ligaments and capsular tissue causing this joint instability. The reader is encouraged to read authors such as Hughston, Hoppenfeld, Netter, Larson, and others who have made great contributions to knee testing.

After taking his own history and physical examinations, and reviewing the x-ray findings and the information noted by the trainer, the physician should be able to pinpoint the pathologic condition and prescribe the proper treatment in 24 to 48 hours after the injury.

ARTHROGRAM AND ARTHROSCOPY

Until recently, a detailed history, physical examination, and conventional x-ray films were all that was available to the attending physician to assist him in arriving at a diagnosis and rendering appropriate care. Now we have arthrography and arthroscopy, which aid the physician in pinpointing the pathologic condition.

With an arthrogram, a special radio-opaque dye is injected into the knee joint under local anaesthesia. A series of x-ray pictures are taken in multiple projections to follow the flow of the dye in the joint. Although the arthrogram provides fairly accurate information about whether or not the meniscus is torn, it is not that accurate about ligament tears unless there is a complete rupture of the capsule and ligament. Popliteal cysts are also visualized in arthrograms of the knee. Arthrograms are useful with musculotendinous cuff and capsular tears of the shoulder.

Although arthroscopy has been around quite a while, the advancement of fibre optics and the smaller-size arthroscopy tube have led to its popular use among orthopedic surgeons. It has resulted in a significant reduction in major surgery of the knee with its attendant postoperative morbidity, prolonged hospitalization, increased expenses, and loss of income for the professional and recreational athlete and the working man.

The arthroscope is inserted into the knee joint through a less than 1 inch surgical incision with the patient under local anaesthesia. Its major benefit is its ability to diagnose meniscal, ligament, and capsular tears, floating loose bodies, and chondromalacia of the patella. It also helps to identify malalignment subluxation. With this added information, unnecessary surgery is avoided, leading to other forms of therapy, such as conventional casts, fabric immobilizer splint with velco fasteners, and rehabilitation for partial ligament tears of the knee.

If arthroscopy reveals a slight tear of the meniscus, it can be repaired through the arthroscope, leaving most of the meniscus intact. Complete menisectomy, when indicated, via the arthroscope tube has been reported by Cavanough of Colorado. Intra-articular shaving through the arthroscope of the cartilaginous surface of the patella in chondromalacia is also performed. Floating loose bodies and debris are easily washed out through the arthroscope. Retinacular releases can also be done through the arthroscope.

If the arthroscope confirms significant tears of the ligament, these are best repaired by a conventional surgical approach and repair with its attendant, increased postoperative hospitalization and longer rehabilitation program. Although most arthroscopy procedures are done in a hospital setting with a 1 or 2 day stay, outpatient arthroscopy is now being done by Pevey and others under local anesthesia. However, it is reported that, with outpatient arthroscopy using general anesthesia, arthroscopy accuracy is above 90%.

According to Tongue and Larson, arthrography and arthroscopy used together have a 98% accuracy for meniscal lesions and an 82% accuracy for medial collateral ligament disorders.

Contusion

Contusion of the knee with minimal synovial effusion, pain, swelling, tenderness, limp, and limitation of motion, usually following a direct blow to the front of the knee.

First 48 Hours

1. Repeat ice and compression treatment if swelling has not been checked.

2. Apply a knee immobilizer to keep knee straight and discourage bending.

3. Quadriceps setting exercises to pain tolerance are started immediately. The athlete tenses his quadriceps muscles as hard as he can for 5 seconds, relaxes the muscles momentarily, and then repeats the exercises for as many times as he can in a 5 to 10 minute period. For total leg strength, the athlete should do 300 quadriceps contractions daily in the intervals best suited for himself.

4. In conjunction with quadriceps setting exercises, the athlete should also do straight-leg raising exercises following such series of quadriceps sets. The knee must be held in full extension throughout the straight-leg raise.

5. Hip abduction exercises while side-lying on the uninjured side with the injured knee held in full extension to maintain the strength of the hip abductors of the injured leg.

6. The muscles of the lower leg on the injured side are included in the total leg program of resistance exercises using a towel or belt or on isokinetic equipment designed for dorsiflexion, inversion or eversion, and plantar flexion, both with knees flexed or extended.

7. Keep leg elevated above hip during waking hours and on two pillows while asleep.

8. Continue with crutches and avoid weight-bearing on injured leg if limp is present.

9. Analgesics for pain and anti-inflammatory medication is prescribed when necessary by the attending physician.

After 48 Hours

1. Discontinue knee immobilizer.
2. Use moist hot packs for 20 to 30 minutes or immerse injured leg in a whirlpool between 105 to 110° F for 15 minutes; still others have their athletes immerse their full bodies in the whirlpool between 105 to 110° F for 15 minutes. Some trainers use the contrast baths routine.
3. Next the athlete places himself in a supine position on the treatment table and elevates his injured leg for about 10 minutes to allow swelling to drain from the injured knee.
4. This is followed by 5 to 10 minutes of massage to disperse the remainder of the intra-articular swelling.
5. Then perform range-of-motion exercises for the knee to pain tolerance.
6. Progressive resistance exercises for the quadriceps, hamstrings, hip and lower leg muscles using isokinetic equipment if available to achieve total leg strength beginning with short arc knee movements. If such equipment is not available, ankle weights or aluminium sandals and a metal handle with removable collars can be used starting at 5 pounds and going up to 10 and 20 pounds and then switch over to an isotonic knee-strengthening machine to full range, first starting with short are movements.
7. Swimming can also be used for knee-exercise therapy.

8. Dry the knee and apply a dry elastic bandage.
9. The athlete continues his exercise program at home.

Fortunately, most effusions are small and resorb in a few days if immediate measures of cold application, compression bandaging, and restriction of knee motion to check swelling are instituted. Although an elastic wrap for the knees for practice or games gives safe psychologic support, it is not wise or necessary to apply preventative adhesive tape strapping for this condition. The athlete may discard his crutches and bear weight as soon as there is no limp and he able to extend his knee easily against a resistance of 10 to 15 pounds. Normally is usually achieved in about 1 week.

Aspiration of the knee is indicated only when there is a large accumulation of intra-articular fluid and capsular distention. Significant accumulations of blood in the effusion should be aspirated to relieve pain and prevent adhesions. The technique of aspiration must be done with strict asepsis, preferably in a hospital or doctor's office.

Sprains

The knee is more vulnerable to ligament sprains than any other kind of injury. Injury to the medial collateral ligament is the most frequent knee injury of any type. A mild sprain results in either ligamentous stretching or mild tearing or both without any impairment of ligament strength. A moderate sprain results in the ligament being partially torn. A severe sprain follows complete rupture of one or more ligaments which may results in some degree of separation or even dislocation and the knee's giving way. The pathologic and clinical findings vary with the nature and extent of the external force to which the knee is subjected. Clinically, mild and moderate sprains are differentiated by the amount of pain, swelling, ecchymosis, tenderness, limp, limitation of motion and joint laxity. In the severe type, joint laxity also is observed. All three conditions are treated differently. An injured athlete walking off the playing field unaided may still have a serious knee injury requiring surgery.

IMMEDIATE TREATMENT

1. Examine the athlete carefully to determine the nature and extent of the injury and how to remove the athlete from the playing field.

2. Treatment in athletic training room:

   a. Have athlete take a shower.

   b. Apply a 4 inch elastic bandage previously immersed in cold water. Elevate the injured leg. Apply an ice bag or cold pack to minimize swelling and secure to injured knee with another elastic bandages. This is kept in place for at least 1 hour.

   c. Remove cold compresses, dry skin thoroughly, and wrap injured knee with a fresh, dry elastic bandage.

   d. Apply a knee immobilizer.

   e. The athlete is provided with proper sized crutches with instructions in crutch-walking and cautioned to avoid weight-bearing on the injured leg. The athlete is instruct to keep the injured leg elevated above the hip during waking hours. During sleep, the athlete is instructed to remove the elastic bandage and knee immobilizer and place the injured leg on two pillow. Leg elevation aids gravity in draining the swollen knee. The duration of the cold compresses for overnight treatment is determined by the severity of the injury.

f. As soon as possible, the athlete is referred to the attending physician who examines the athlete and determines the nature, extent, and treatment of the injury.

Mild Sprains

Mild sprain of the medial collateral ligament with minimal pain, swelling, tenderness, limp, and limitation of motion.

First Day

Morning

1. Repeat ice and compression treatment if swelling has not been checked.
2. Continue with elastic bandage and knee immobilizer.
3. Continue with crutches and avoid weight-bearing on injured leg.
4. Keep leg elevated above hip during waking hours and on two pillows while asleep.
5. Analgesics for pain and anti-inflammatory medication as prescribed by the attending physician.

First Day

Afternoon

1. Repeat morning treatment.

Second Day

Morning

1. Repeat first day's treatment.

2. Encourage athlete to do quadriceps setting exercises-about 300 during day at intervals most suitable for the athlete. Straight-leg raising exercises follow quadriceps sets.

3. Hip abduction exercises in a side-lying position on the uninjured side with injured knee held in full extension.

4. Active range-of-motion exercises for the hip, foot, and ankle; guarded exercises for the injured knee.

5. Continue exercise program at home.

Second Day

Afternoon

1. Repeat second day's morning treatment.

Third Day

Morning

If swelling is still present, repeat second day's treatment. If swelling has subsided, exudate is under control, and pain and discomfort are lessened, the following can be used:

1. Immerse injured leg in whirlpool bath between 105 to 110° F for 15 to 20 minutes. Some trainers use a contrast bath routine.

2. Remove from whirlpool bath, dry and follow with gentle massage of the upper foreleg, knee, and thigh for 5 to 10 minutes.

3 Begin with resistance short-arc extension and gradually progress to repetitions and range-of-motion exercises.

4. Place elastic bandage about knee.

5. Apply knee immobilizer.
6. Keep injured leg elevated when not ambulating.
7. Continue with crutches until limp, pain, and swelling are no longer present and progress onto weight-bearing activities, while periodically testing with protective weight-bearing to grade degree of recovery.
8. Encourage walking as long as it does not increase exudate. Walking and exercise of the leg help milk out traumatic exudate.
9. Continue exercise program at home.

Third Day

1. Same as morning treatment.
2. Discontinue knee immobilizer.

Fourth Day

Pain and discomfort should have lessened considerably by now and should not impede intensified efforts to facilitate removal of the traumatic exudates and reduction of swelling and rehabilitation of the quadriceps, other leg muscles, and joints for total-leg strength.

1. Remove elastic bandage support and immerse leg in a whirlpool bath for 20 to 30 minutes.
2. Remove leg from whirlpool, dry, and follow with gentle massage of the upper foreleg, knee, and thigh for 15 minutes.
3. Progressive resistance quadriceps exercise routine is best accomplished with isokinetic and isotonic exercise equipment if available. Otherwise, it is done in the following manner:

a. Use an aluminium exercise sandal weighing about 2½ pounds, metal handle with removable collars, and iron discs weighing 2½, 5, 10 and 12½ pounds.

b. The strength of the uninjured leg must be used as a guide in the rehabilitation of the injured leg. The athlete sits at the edge of the examination table and a weighted sandal is applied to the foot of the uninjured leg. He is asked to straighten his knees 10 times. Then iron discs in 2½ or 5 pound increments are added to the sandal. The greatest amount of weight he is able to lift while straightening the uninjured knee is the maximal strength that the injured leg must achieve. This testing can be done while the injured leg is recovering from the immediate symptoms and signs of the injury.

c. The injured leg is now tested by applying the weighted sandal to the foot; in a similar manner, the maximal weight that can be lifted 10 times is noted.

d. The athlete must exercise his injured leg daily by extending it 10 times with 50% of the maximal weight.

e. The athlete should be encouraged to increase the maximal weight established in "c" whenever he can; he follows the same pattern of exercise, making appropriate increases in 50 and 75% of the new maximal weight.

f. When the treated leg is able to extend the same weight as the uninjured leg 10 times, the maximal benefits of treatment have been gained and normal strength achieved. Extending the knee 10 times with 50 pounds attached to the exercise sandal is not an unusual feat for college and professional football players.

4. Keep leg elevated when not weight-bearing.
5. Discontinue crutches and bear weight as soon as there is no limp and the athlete is able to extend his knee easily against a resistance of 10 to 15 pounds.
6. Encourage walking and active exercises of leg to help milk out traumatic exudate.
7. Analgesics and other prescribed oral medication should be discontinued when there is no longer any pain.

Fifth Day

1. Same as fourth day's treatment.

This type of injury may take 5 to 10 days of treatment. Whirlpool treatment may be alternated with moist hot packs followed by a light, fingertip massage twice daily for the duration of the treatment. An elastic-bandage support for the knee should be continued until all the swelling has been resorbed and full range of knee motion and maximal strength of the musculature that activates the knee have been achieved.

MODERATE SPRAINS

With a moderate sprain of the medial collateral ligament with pain, ecchymosis, swelling, limp, and painfully guarded motion, treatment depends on whether or not there is slight joint laxity. With no joint laxity, the athlete is placed in a knee immobilizer and on crutches for 3 weeks. In addition to cold compresses, elevation, analgesic and anti-inflammatory medication, elastic bandages, and restrictions on weight-bearing, a knee with marked effusion or distention should be aspirated under strict aseptic precautions. The aspiration is repeated if necessary. By the third or fourth day, with pain, tenderness, and swelling lessened, continuous hot moist packs are applied to the knee and the athlete is started on isometric exercises. No weight bearing is permitted on the injured leg. The knee is rehabilitated with whirlpool, massage, and progressive resistance exercises in the same manner as described for the mild sprain. It takes a minimum of 3 weeks of intensive rehabilitation efforts to reach a competitive edge. Knee braces with single-or double-sided hinged splints made of plastic or metal material forming a bridge over the knee are useful to prevent reinjury.

If a knee is moderately sprained and also shows some minimal or slight laxity along with effusion, this joint laxity may be associated with sub-clinical tears of the anterior cruciate or medial collateral ligament and associated meniscus tears. Because a further workup, such as an arthrogram, examination of the knee under general anesthesia, and an arthroscopy may be necessary to ascertain the knee joint pathologic condition, hospitalization is indicated. If the workup indicates surgery is unnecessary one of us waits until pain, discomfort, tenderness, and swelling have lessened considerably and applies a plaster cylinder cast on the third or fourth day with a knee held between 20 to 30° in flexion. Some physicians use removable, variable-position knee immobilizers or commercially prepared plaster splints. The athlete is discharged from the hospital on the same day following cast application. The athlete continues with crutches and does not bear weight on the injured leg. Isometric exercises are reinforced along with other rehabilitation efforts. The cast is removed 3 to 4 weeks post injury. If a variable-position knee immobilizer is used instead of a cast, physical therapy and rehabilitative measures can be started much earlier. The knee is rehabilitated with whirlpool baths, massages, progressive-resistance exercises, and other exercise modalities.

SEVERE SPRAINS

Severe sprains of one or more of the collateral or cruciate ligaments are responsible for abnormal laxity at the knee joints. These athletes are best treated in a hospital with continuous cold compresses, elevation, anti-inflammatory and analgesic medication, and other supportive measures. After a diagnosis has established the extent of the damage, surgical repair of the injured structures should be done soon thereafter. A padded, long-leg plaster cast is applied with the knee flexed between 20 to 30° ; the cast remains on for 6 to 8 weeks. During the wearing of the cast, therapy to other parts of the musculoskeletal system must be encouraged to render complete care to the athlete. Whenever plaster-cast immobilization is used, no weight-bearing is permitted because synovial reaction is usually present. As this reaction subsides, weight-bearing is started.

MENISCUS TEARS

The semilunar cartilages move backward during flexion, pressing the posterior halves between the posterior surface of the articulating femoral and tibial condyles. The menisci move forward in extension, and the anterior halves are snugly held between the opposing femoral and tibial condyles. The medial meniscus, in addition to its tibial attachments, also is attached at its periphery with the deep layers of the medial collateral ligament. A traumatic force directed to the lateral aspect of the knee that is strong enough to separate the medial aspects of the femoral and tibial condyles also places the medial collateral ligament and capsule under strain. If the force is great enough, it may also damage the medial meniscus because of its attachments and position. The medial meniscus is most frequently injured when a partially flexed knee is struck by a sudden blow on its lateral aspect as the femur rotates medially on a tibia that has been secured by the foot fixed to the ground. The same injury may also occur without any external force when the knee is quickly turned inwardly with the foot fixed to the ground while running or cutting at high speeds.

Tear of the medial meniscus under the circumstances described above is characterized by the knee giving way, pain, swelling, tenderness, limitation of motion, and a true history of locking. In questionable cases of cartilage or ligament tears, the recent use of arthrography and arthroscopy in experienced hands has proven to be a valuable diagnostic procedure in determining the integrity of these structures.

Treatment varies with the age of the athlete, his response to treatment, the number of recurrences, and his desire to continue in athletics. Junior high, high school, and college athletes who suffer torn semilunar cartilage for the first time and are confirmed to the undisplaced by arthroscopy are treated operatively or conservatively depending on the size of the tear. Conservative care includes hospitalization, leg traction, plaster cylinder, crutches, and no weight-bearing for 1 month. During the cast immobilization, quadriceps setting exercises are strongly emphasized, as well as isometric exercises of the other leg muscles. After the cast is removed, local moist heat, massage, and progressive resistance exercises for the quadriceps and hamstring muscles are started. The player can return to the game only after a full range of knee motion and maximal thigh muscle strength have been achieved. Recurrence of meniscus injury is usually an indication for surgical removal of the meniscus if the athlete intends to continue in the sport that caused the injury. Bucket handle and some other less complicated meniscal tears can be surgically removed by operative, arthroscopy. Athletes who have suffered several recurrent meniscal injuries in a sport have not required surgery because they finally discontinued the sport, concentrating instead on one that did not subjected their knees to such trauma.

The rehabilitation of the injured knee that has been operated on and/or casted requires a considerable amount of coordination of the skills of the attending physician, trainer, and physical therapist. The athlete and the coach also play an important role. The athlete must show patience, determination, and motivation to achieve maximum benefits from treatment. He must not try to hurry along his return to competition before recovery has been reached. Most young athletes are too impatient to allow nature to heal in its own time. They may actually retard full recovery if they pressure the medical personnel to allow them to get back to competition before its time.

In addition to the personal equation and whirlpool baths, there is some isokinetic equipment that can be used to help recovery along, such as Cybex II, Nordic Ski track, treadmills, and bicycles. Swimming is another useful modality in the rehabilitation of the injured knee. However, this equipment must be used properly and sequentially in the athlete's recovery. The trainer-therapist's ingenuity and skill allows the rehabilitating athlete to benefit from this equipment. In addition to equipment, active exercises must be used to keep muscles distal and proximal to the traumatized joint active throughout the rehabilitation process. Flexibility/stretch exercises also play a role in the injured athlete's total rehabilitation.

STRAPPING THE KNEE

The application of an elastic bandage with or without a sponge rubber or felt pad or strapping with adhesive tape, aids considerably in supporting the sprained knee. This support enables the athlete to move the knee with less pain. The bandaging or taping is applied in a figure-eight manner, so that the loops cross directly over the injured ligament, which has been placed in a relaxed position. This gives a feeling of support, strength, and security to the knee. Slocum limits adhesive taping to convalescent treatment in knee sprains, but questions its value for the prevention of injuries. Thorndike disagrees and recommends a Duke-Simpson tape strapping to prevent reinjury of the knee ligaments. In some parts of the country this tape job is still being used. This topic is just as controversial among trainers-many do not tape knees for preventive purposes for practice or games. We do not subscribe to the practice of routinely taping a knee post-injury to prevent a reinjury. If, in the judgment of the medical staff, a protective knee strapping is indicated, however, the tape job indicated in Figure 9-8 can be used, despite its psychologic implications. Many trainers use their own versions of this basic knee strapping technique.

Unfortunately, some physicians permit trainers to ply their knee-strapping technique and skills on players with "floating cartilage," or chronically unstable and weak knees in the mistaken belief that this will help the knee to withstand the rigours of a sport. This should not be permitted; rather, the player should be disqualified from the sport that is wrecking his knees and transferred to one that does not expose the knee to such trauma. It is doubtful whether any braces, devices, or strapping or wrapping methods can protect the knee against the violent forces of some body-contact sports.

Maximal development of power and strength of the musculature that moves and stabilizes the knee is an absolute prerequisite for sport participation. Formulation of new safety rules and better enforcement of existing rules to prevent knee injuries are necessary to reduce the incidence of injured knees in contact sports such as football, soccer, and ice hockey. Artificial turf is being used with the expectation of reducing the incidence and severity of knee injuries. As yet there is insufficient evidence to warrant any definite conclusions.

ARTIFICIAL TURF

In the summertime and early fall, artificial turf's characteristic of retaining heat makes playing difficult and causes a skin burn of the elbows and knees on contact. It is great for upkeep and maintenance, but its medical benefits are far from conclusive, and the "jury" is still out concerning its applicability on the high school level. Its suitability for use in the pros is another matter.

CHONDROMALACIA

It is most frequently seen in adolescents and young adults. It is only occasionally seen in oldsters. In chondromalacia, the gliding patellofemoral joint motion that we take for granted becomes painful and disabled because of the tremendous amount of bio-mechanical strains and stresses placed on this joint in running and jumping sports such as basketball, jogging, running, tennis, and volleyball. The undersurface of the patella is somewhat protected from the body condyles of the femur by the interposition of the fat pad. When the knee flexes repetitively, as it does in athletic activity, however, the patella loses the protection of the fat pad. Therefore, as the knee cap descends distally, the articular surface of the patella makes increasingly more bony contact with the distal end of the femur as the patella moves in the groove between the femoral condyles. At the same time, the patellar tendon is placed under greater tension causing a compressive force directly on the patella within the patellofemoral articulation.

Other anatomic and biomechanical factors affecting the tracking mechanism of the patella between the femoral condyles add to the patho-physiologic changes of the patellofemoral articulation, which lead to increased biomechanical pressure on the articular surface of the patella. Some physicians usually refer to imbalance of the musculature on the lateral and medial sides of the patella as well as the lateral and medial retinacular ligaments and iliotibial band. These muscles and ligaments play a role in keeping the tracking of the patella on the cartilage-covered groove between the femoral condyles during the constant flexion and extension of the knee during athletic activity. These are other anatomic conditions that lend themselves to pathophysiologic movements that aid in the development of chondromalacia causing pain and disability of varying degrees in the athlete. The malicious malalignment syndrome starting at the hips with an increased femoral neck anteversion, increased Q angle, hypermobile patella, increased external tibial torsion, and pronated flat feet are all causes leading to chondromalacia. Essentially, the causes of chondromalacia are traumatic-malalignment of the patella and resultant maltracking between the femoral condyles -and idiopathic. Pathologically, there is an early softening, then roughening, and subsequent fibrillation of the articular of the patella. These pathologic changes cause a disruption of the normal gliding motion of the patellofemoral articulation. Pain and discomfort may be only minimal. As the athlete continues participating on the involved knee, increasing degeneration sooner or later causes the athlete to become sidelined. This is a difficult condition to treat unless it is recognized and treated in its earliest stages. At this early level, medical help can be instituted to curb its progression.

The diagnosis is not usually difficult to establish. It is important that the athlete describe to his doctor the disability, the site, as well as the time of occurrence of the pain. The pain may be described as peripatellar or even retropatellar. The most frequent site of pain is along the medial border of the patella. In some runners, the pain may lessen during a run only to worsen near the end of the run. Going up and more frequently, going down stairs causes pain. Stiffness of the knee with prolonged sitting or the knee "giving out" may cause the athlete to seek out his doctor's help. Joint-line tenderness is frequently present but not associated with meniscal tears.

The clinical examination leaves no doubt as to the diagnosis. Tenderness of one or both patella facets may be elicited. Flexion and extension of the knee usually produces crepitus that can be felt by the examiner's hand. If the degeneration is marked, the crepitus is even audible to the athlete. Passive motion of the patella laterally may produce anxiety or an apprehension sign. Compression testing of the patella manually against the femoral condyle with the knee extended or pushing the proximal pole of the patella distally as the athlete is asked to contract the quadriceps muscle with the knee extended produces pain with a chondromalacic condition. Extending the knee from 30° of flexion against resistance is used to elicit patellar pain. If pain is produced with the aforementioned tests, chondromalacia is probably present. Other signs confirming chondromalacia would be atrophy of the thigh and even the calf, and perhaps effusion.

Conventional x-ray views of the involved knee may show no bony or periosteal pathologic condition. However, tangential may reveal an increased femoral sulcus angle with an inadequately developed lateral femoral condyle and perhaps a "jockey cap" appearance of the patella. If there is some accompanying arthritic spurring, it may be picked up on the anterior, posterior, lateral, or tunnel views.

The management and care of chondromalacia patella is best handled in a conservative manner using rest, physical therapy, which includes a combination of cryotherapy and moist heat, isotonic and progressive resistance isometric exercise routine, and in some cases, infrapatellar restraining braces and straps. Occasionally, because of the intense pain and discomfort exhibited by the athlete, it may be necessary to temporarily immobilize the involved knee of the athlete with a plaster cylinder cast or a commercial knee immobilizer, along with the use of crutches and partial weight-bearing until the knee becomes manageable, for the remainder of the conservative therapy. Pain can be reduced by rest and early cryotherapy for 3 or more days, followed by moist heat. The knee can then be built up with an isotonic and progressive-resistance isometric exercise program as formulated by De-Haven, et al. His 82% recovery rate in athletes from contact as well as recreational sports who sustained this condition speaks well for his program. Brody, in his monograph on running injuries, is equally emphatic on a conservative program for runners with chondromalacia. He further adds that an orthotic may correct excessive rotation and pronation, thereby correcting the tracking problem. If the temporary orthotic is helpful, it can be replaced by a well-tolerated shoe orthotic, obviating the need for wraps, horseshoe braces, infrapatellar straps, and derotation braces about the knee. Surgery for chondromalacia is rarely recommended or performed.

JUMPER'S KNEE

Although this pathologic entity was described by Sinding-Larson and Johansson for adolescents and by Smillie for adults as patellar or quadriceps tendonitis, it was Blazina who popularized it as the "jumper's knee," aided by the publicity extended to a big time basketball players who suffered this clinical disorder. Clinically, it is a tendonitis of the quadriceps tendon insertion at the superior pole of the patells and/or the inferior pole of the patella. It is brought on by repetitive jumping athletic activities with sudden decelerating forces, active or violent, active extension of the knee such as is seen in rebounding or in trying to stop quickly in basketball. These activities cause maximal stresses and strains of the knee leading to microruptures of the quadriceps tendon at superior and inferior attachment sites to the patella. Basketball and volleyball are classic athletic activities that bring on these abnormal stresses. It is also seen in high jumping, long-jumping, platform diving, triple jumping, cross-country running, figure skating, tennis, and other recreational and competitive athletic activities.

Clinically, the history brings out the abnormal forces to which the quadriceps tendon attachment sites are subjected during an athletic activity. At first, an aching pain is felt that disappear with varying amounts of rest. As the disorder progress, the athlete may experience a sense of fullness about the tendon-attachment sites, which will be described as swelling. With further progress, the athlete may even describe a feeling of "giving way" momentarily, which is quite different than true locking or catching.

The athlete is best examined in supine position with the entire leg exposed. In most cases, a tenderness can be elicited at the inferior pole of the quadriceps attachment. Effusion of the knee is usually absent. Although signs of ligamentous or meniscal damage are not present, it is not uncommon to find other patellar disorders, such as patellar subluxability, patellar chondromalacia, genu recurvatum, genu valgum, and others.

Although x-ray films of the knee in multiple view, including intercondylar and skyline views of the patella, may initially be negative or perhaps show a radiolucency at the involved patella pole, a number of radiographic abnormalities have been described, such as a periosteal reaction of the patella, elongation of the involved pole, fatigue fractures of the inferior pole or other radiographic abnormalities.

Treatment of this condition depends on the stage of the disorder when the athlete seeks medical help. If pain or discomfort is experienced only after the activity has ceased, we are usually dealing with a mild form. Ice compression is applied immediately to the knee, and it is followed by elastic bandaging and more ice compression the same evening. A felt horseshoe conforming to the patella and secured by the elastic bandage can be helpful. The best treatment is rest from the sport and the athlete is advised to stop playing until the acute symptomatology disappears.

In mild cases, the athlete is put on a hip-flexion and abduction exercise program. As the acute pain lessens, the athlete is put on an isometric exercise program for his quadriceps to increase his tolerance to pain. No knee-bending exercises are permitted. Moist hot packs to the knee are helpful prior to competition when the athlete is ready to return to his activity. A scout x-ray film of the knee should be taken. The young athlete with only a mild case finds it difficult abstaining from his sport even though participating will aggravate it.

Clinically, the athlete. experiences pain and disability during and after cessation of the activity. Even though the athlete is advised against continuing in the sport, he usually elects to continue. Despite the use of medication, ice compression, rest, wet heat, exercises, and a patella-restraining brace, the athlete may experience no relief. At this point, the attending physician may elect to inject a corticosteroid at the sit of the pathologic condition. If he does, the athlete must be advised that injection of this material has led to weakened tendons and in some cases, to tendon ruptures. Multiple injections should not be done. The physician must monitor the gastrointestinal status and periodic blood counts if certain medications are prescribed that require such surveillance.

If none of the recommended treatments help and the athlete persists in playing the sport, there is a surgical option available. Removal of the inferior pole of the patella or surgical removal of the degenerated quadriceps and patella-tendon site with supplemental reefing can be done.

CHAPTER-9

TREATMENT AND CARE OF SHOULDER INJURIES

The shoulder is a complicated structure of multiple bones, joints, muscles, ligaments, nerves and vascular structure whose main function is to move the arm on the trunk. Because the shoulder has relatively little inherent bony stability, it is suitably designed for producing large ranges of motion of the arm, which are so essential in athletics. In fact, it is the most mobile joint in the body. This mobility is achieved through the harmonious working of strong ligaments and powerful muscles. These muscles also provide bulk, and together with the ligaments ensure a firm anchoring of the component parts.

The shoulder is best known for its functions in ball throwing in such sports as baseball, football, and basketball. However, the shoulder also plays an important role in throwing a left, stroking a tennis ball swimming, driving a gold ball, throwing a shotput, flinging a javelin, hurling a discus, and thrusting a foil. In addition, the shoulder may be used to protect a boxer's chin or head from a punch, perform a rugged block or tackle, or form a line of resistance to a forward moving opponent. The offensive and defensive use of the shoulder complex varies with the size of the object that has to be moved bodily or propelled by a piece of equipment, as well as the demands of the competition. This usage is most effectively realized with proportionate assistance from foot, leg, hip, trunk, and contralateral upper extremity movements in a coordinated and integrated manner.

The bony components of the shoulder include the clavicle, the heat of the humerus, the sternum, the scapula, and that portion of the thorax over which the scapula moves. These bones and accompanying ligaments form four separate yet interdependent joints. These joints are listed in the order of frequency of injury:

1. Acromioclavicular.
2. Glenohumeral.
3. Sternoclavicular.
4. Scapulothoracic.

The muscles of the shoulder contribute to the size of this region, making it quite prominent and more easily injured in contract sports because of its exposed position and usage. The shoulder is also prone to injuries because of the tremendous leverage forces to which it is subjected. Slocum, Bateman, Brewer, Neer, Cox, Rowe, DePalma, Allan, and Stewart, have described and analysed the mechanism of throwing as well as the stresses and strains to which the structures of the shoulder are subjected as a result of it. The unnatural motions of throwing a baseball, including the tremendous forces, braking the momentum of the follow-through, make pitchers more prone to shoulder, arm, and elbow injuries, especially those pitchers who depend on curve and screw balls. The reader is encouraged to read these informative articles to understand the anatomy, physiology, and the mechanisms of injury that lead to these clinical conditions, which a times are difficult at diagnose.

Additional protection is also provided with protective equipment. In addition, shoulder and arm conditions that are seen frequently in baseball players are discussed.

FIRST-AID MEASURE

Step 1.

The trainer questions the athlete as to how, when and where the injury occurred. Was the shoulder ever hurt before? Did the injury result from a blow, fall, or twist? Did it happen during a tackle, block, pile-up, or throwing motion of the arm? If he fell, did he land on his hand, elbow, arm or shoulder? If he fell on his hand, was his body weight moving forward, causing his elbow to bend? If he fell on his elbow, was the arm flexed and internally rotated or extended and externally rotated? If he fell on his arm, what was its position on impact? If the arm was struck a blow, what was its position from the trunk? If the athlete heard a clicking noise, had a sensation of something "catching," or felt bones slipping over one another in the shoulder, at what point and in what position was the arm from the trunk? If he fell on his shoulder, what aspect of it took the brunt of the force? Is he able to move his arm or does he have to support the arm and shoulder because of the pain? Answers to these questions help in understanding the mechanism of the injury and the probable clinical conditions resulting from it.

The trainer carefully inspects the bony and visible soft-tissue landmarks, looking for deformities, deltoid flattening, position of the arm to the trunk, swelling and ecchymosis. He questions the athlete to locate the site of pain. Some gentle palpation of these areas may be done to elicit tenderness and swelling. The trainer then tests the range of motion of the arm on the trunk, immediately stopping if the pain is great with any attempted motion.

Step 2.

If the history of trauma suggests acromioclavicular joint injury, the trainer must take steps to check swelling and immobilize the injured shoulder with an elastic compression bandage and ice therapy before referring the athlete to the attending physician. This is done in the following manner:

1. The shoulder and arm are immobilized with a sling.
2. The lower arm is placed diagonally across the chest and the entire upper extremity is tied high in a sling to elevate the scapula.
3. An ice compress is applied to the injured area to check swelling.

If the trainer suspects a separation or dislocation of this joint, he must immediately contact the team physician for further instructions. In any event, the injured athlete is referred to the doctor and instructed to see him immediately. The physician decides whether an x-ray study is indicated. If the history suggests a glenohumeral-joint dislocation, the athlete's arm is placed in a sling and the attending physician is immediately contacted. This is an emergency that needs immediate care by a physician, who will tell the trainer to send the athlete either to his office or to the hospital emergency room, where a closed reduction is done. If this is unsuccessful the athlete can be admitted to the hospital and he reduction performed under general anesthesia. In the interim, the trainer applied ice therapy to the shoulder and the shoulder is protected from further injury.

DEFINITIVE TREATMENT

The mechanism of injury and subsequent pathologic condition of the acromioclavicular or glenohumeral joints are usually quite apparent, unlike clinical conditions resulting from the act of throwing, which usually require more extensive investigation to make a diagnosis. This attending physician takes his own detailed history and makes a careful examination under ideal conditions in privacy, with clothing taping and wrappings removed. The uninjured shoulder is used for comparison. The doctor should have no difficulty in arriving at an accurate diagnosis and starting proper treatment.

ACROMIOCLAVICULAR JOINT

This is the most frequently injured joint in the shoulder complex. Contusions, sprains, separations, and dislocations of this joint result most frequently from a sideway fall onto the lateral aspect of the shoulder. This injury may also occur from a direct blow to the acromion during a hard block, by a shoulder striking another shoulder during body contact, or by a direct downward force on the shoulder. A player who is "piled on" from behind while rising from a prone position may suffer an acromioclavicular injury.

The degree of injury varies with the nature and extent of the traumatic force. The term "shoulder separation" is commonly used when the trauma is great enough to produce a separation or dislocation at this joint, with an accompanying deformity. A separation may be severe enough to warrant a closed reduction and immobilization with slings, elastic bandages, adhesive dressings, strappings, or bracing; this may be difficult to achieve dressings, strappings, or bracing; this may be difficult to achieve, because of the small size, large range of motion and anatomic relationship of the acromioclavicular joint to the chest and shoulder girdle. The attending physician must use that method by which he can best restore the joint to its normal position and keep it there until the torn ligaments have fully healed.

CONTUSION AND MILD SPRAIN

Contusion and mild sprain of the acromioclavicular joint following minor trauma is usually associated with pain, local tenderness, swelling and limitation of arm movement. This condition is best treated with ice therapy to the injured joint the use of a sling for 24 to 48 hours. The upper limb is tied high in a sling and ice therapy applied to the injured joint. The immobilization is removed after 48 hours, and if pain and swelling have been controlled, physical therapy consisting of ice therapy, and range-of-motion exercises of the shoulder are done, at first passively and then actively, to pain tolerance. If early return to athletics is warranted, additional protection to this joint can be provided with a sponge rubber pad placed over the acromioclavicular joint and adhesive strapping. A novel protective device by D'Andrea to reduce direct trauma to the injured acromioclavicular joint can be fashioned with an inflated appropriately sized bicycle inner tube taped on the under surface of the shoulder pad which keeps the shoulder pad off the acromioclavicular joint. The valve stem is covered with foam rubber and positioned beneath the shoulder pad and not externally exposed.

SEPARATION

Second degree sprain of the acromioclavicular joint with incomplete tears of the acromioclavicular joint capsule and ligament can be recognized when the out end of the clavicle is prominent and shows a joint laxity with the inferior surface of the clavicle at or just below the superior surface of the acromion accompanied by pain, local tenderness, and restriction of arm movements. The joint separation can be demonstrated by x-ray examination done while the athlete holds 10 to 15 pound weights in each hand to produce downward traction.

The attending physician can perform a reduction with the trainer acting as an assistant. A properly fitting Kenny Howard brace is applied. This maintains the reduction be depressing the clavicle and elevating the acromion to insure a properly reduced acromio-clavicular joint. Analgesic and anti-inflammatory medications are prescribed when necessary. The athlete is instructed to keep an ice bag on his injured shoulder for the next 48 to 72 hours. One of us uses only a sling as prescribed by his attending physician.

The following day the athlete is examined by the doctor, who checks the pulses, nerve function, and the status of the immobilization. He also starts the athlete on isometric exercises of the shoulder-girdle muscles on the injured side as well as the muscles of the immobilized limb. This immobilization remains for 3 to 4 weeks. X-ray picture are again taken on the second week and after the immobilization has been removed.

Following removal of the immobilization, physical therapy consisting of Hydrocollator heat, massage, and exercises facilitates recover. This can be hastened if done twice a day. A program for rehabilitation is described on page 205, following the discussion of glenohumeral dislocation.

DISLOCATION

In dislocation of acromioclavicular joint, a deformity is noted, with the distal end of the clavicle elevated above the acromion and the presence of a marked separation of these bones equal to the depth of the lateral end of the clavicle or more. Dislocation results from ruptures of the acromioclavicular joint capsule and ligaments and the coracoclavicular ligaments. X-ray films show widening between not only the acromion and distal end of the clavicle, but also the coracoclavicular distance. Pain, tenderness, deformities at the acromioclavicular joint and restricted arm movement make the diagnosis easy. Physicians vary in their approach to this problem; some prefer surgery, others recommend more conservative measures, such as the Kenny Howard brace.

If conservative measures fail and the adult athlete wants a cosmetically more attractive shoulder, surgery is indicated, even though the recent trend is not to operate on this condition. The surgeon can select from many operative procedures is this is his judgment. A primary repair of the ruptured capsule and ligaments without any bone work is an acceptable method. The literature suggests that excision of the distal end of the clavicle is an excellent procedure provided no more than 1 to 1½ cm of the bone is resected and the trapezius, deltoid, periosteum, and capsule are sutured to their origins to contain the bone end of the clavicle in its proper place. The distal end of the clavicle must be bevelled.

Some surgeons, after excising the distal end of the clavicle, use a Dacron Velour graft ligament reconstruction. Early mobilization and, as a rule, no special taping or pads are necessary postoperatively. The same type of physical therapy is given as for separation of the acromioclavicular joint. After sufficient physical therapy including an intensive program of resistance exercises has produced a normal range of motion, muscle strength-athletic activities may be resumed. Post-operative care lasting up to 3 to 4 weeks or more must be anticipated.

GLENOHUMERAL JOINT

This is the most mobile joint in the body because of its loose, relaxed ligaments and the lax articular capsule that binds the large round head of the humerus into the shallow oval cavity of the glenoid fossa and its attached labrum. The arm is moved about at the shoulder joint by the deltoid, pectoral, biceps, triceps, and latissimus dorsi muscles in a coordinated manner with the rotator cuff muscles, which also contribute strength and stability to this joint by firming the position of the head of the humerus into the glenoid fossa. Anteriorly, the deltoid protects the shoulder joint well against direct trauma, but the subscapularis muscle is now regarded as a prime protector against a dislocation. Inferiorly, the capsule is vulnerable; superiorly, it is protected by the acromion.

CONTUSIONS

These are common occurrences in athletics and usually cause pain, tenderness, and restriction of shoulder motion. A careful history of the injury and the basic examining procedures of observation, palpation, and joint-function tests make the diagnosis obvious. If a fracture or dislocation is suspected, a roentgenogram should be taken. Treatment is with ice therapy and limitation of shoulder motion for 24 to 48 hours. Wearning a sling for a day or two helps, followed by local moist hot packs, light massage, and active exercises to pain tolerance.

SPRAINS

The ligaments of this joint are seldom sprained because they are loose and allow a great range of motion.

DISLOCATION

This joint dislocates more frequently in athletics than all other major articulations considered together. Pan, deltoid flattening and inability to move the arm are characteristic of dislocation. The large head of the humerus slips out from the shallow respository of the glenoid fossa and its attached labrum, contusing, stretching, and tearing through supporting soft tissue in its path, most frequently as a result of indirect trauma. The humeral head is moved out of its normal articulating position by forces that cause the humerus to act as a lever or by forces that are transmitted through the shaft of the humerus. As the shoulder is placed in abduction and external rotation, the subscapularis muscle moves upwardly exposing the unprotected anterior capsule through which the humeral head dislocates an teriorly. This causes a flattening of the side of the shoulder because the humeral head is normally positioned under the deltoid muscle. This dislocation is confirmed by palpation. Moseley adds that most anterior dislocations follow an anterior-inferior direction because the tendon of the long head of the triceps affords strong support to the inferior capsule when the arm is in full abduction. In addition, the greater portion of the head of the humerus projects anteriorly to the biceps tendon, which further predisposes to an anterior-inferior dislocation. The head of the humerus is most commonly in a subcoracoid position following dislocation; this can be confirmed by inspection or palpation. Subclavicular and subglenoid dislocations have been noted, but these are rare. With the anatomy to distorted, shoulder motion is practically nil and any active or passive attempt to move it causes severe pain. Usually, with an anterior dislocated shoulder, the athlete is unable to place the hand of the arm of the injured shoulder onto the uninjured shoulder. Some of the more common histories associated with anterior dislocations are the following.

1. Fall on outstretched hand as body lungs forward, causing the elbow to flex and exerting maximal stress on shoulder capsule.
2. Fall backward on the point of elbow with the arm in backward extension.
3. Movement of the arm into a position of abduction, horizontal extension, and external rotation.
4. A blow on an abducted and externally rotated arm during a poorly executed tackle, when the momentum of the runner forces the tackler's abducted arm backward into horizontal extension, levering the head out of the joint.
5. Direct blows to the posterior aspect of the shoulder can cause anterior dislocation.

No athlete is immune to this clinical condition. I have reduced shoulder dislocations in boxers that occurred following the delivery of a blow, in tennis players as a result of a serve, and in basketball players who have crashed into a wall. Although posterior dislocations of the glenohumeral joint are rare, they do occur as a result of direct blows or a fall anteriorly on the shoulder as well as forced internal rotation of the abducted arm.

The doctor's examination includes determining the status of the axillary nerve, since this is frequently injured in shoulder dislocation. The ulnar nerve can also be injured but rarely the radial. Hypoesthesia of the lateral aspect of the shoulder or a weakness of shoulder abduction by the deltoid strongly suggests an injury to this nerve. However, the presence of nerve injury does not alter the immediate treatment. The x-ray pictures must be taken of the shoulder to confirm the diagnosis as well as the possibility of associated fractures.

The best treatment is immediate closed reduction of the dislocation on the field of play if the athlete is seen within minutes of the injury. The athlete is placed supine on the ground or floor. The doctor kneels on one knee and then exerts straight traction on the dislocated arm by grasping and pulling the athlete's hand and wrist while the trainer exerts counter-traction. An audible thud in the region of the shoulder as well as a normal rounding out of the flattened deltoid signals a successful return of the humeral head to the glenoid.

If straight arm traction is unsuccessful after a few minutes, take the athlete off the field. Appropriate pre-reduction analgesic and/or muscle relaxant are given; then use the Kocher method of reduction. In this method, with the elbow held in flexion and the arm adducted and externally rotated, traction is exerted on the arm as it is carried into forward flexion and then internally rotated.

If the injury is not seen within minutes of the trauma, it is usually necessary to use general anesthesia to relax the powerful shoulder muscles of the athlete, which resist reduction, especially when muscle spasm, pain, and anxiety are also present. The reduction must be as gentle as possible to prevent further soft-tissue damage.

After a traumatic dislocation of the shoulder has been reduced, immobilization in adduction and internal rotation in a wrap-around sling for 3 weeks have been shown to reduce the high incidence in recurrent dislocation up to 40 years of age as much as 10 to 15%. Post-reduction x-ray films must be taken. The neuro-vascular structures are checked periodically.

There are significant differences of opinion concerning postreduction management and treatment for high school, collegiate, and professional athletes. However, there is agreement that high school and collegiate athletes must have full recovery of normal strength in all the muscles of the shoulder before they resume play. For high school and intercollegiate athletes, one shoulder dislocation per season is sufficient to ban the athlete from further competition that season. These primary reduced shoulder dislocations are immobilized for no less than 3 weeks followed by a period of physical therapy including progressive resistance exercises.

Under 20 years of age, the recurrence rate is 94%; at 20 to 40 years of age, there is a 74% recurrence rate; and over 40 years of age the recurrence rate is 14%. In a football player, a recurrent dislocation should be repaired and football disallowed until this is done. In the 40 years old and over group, 2 weeks of immobilization are sufficient. Protective harnesses for reduced dislocations are available but are ineffective and not recommended.

The professional athlete is in a class by himself, often being permitted to return to active competition in 7 to 10 days with a restrictive harness limiting abduction, extension, and external rotation; the harness is worn for about 4 weeks while a rehabilitative program progressive resistive exercises is simultaneously carried out. This traditional program of limited immobilization has led to increased incidence of redislocations. If the dislocation recurs, a surgical repair is performed followed by the usual rehabilitation.

Whenever a shoulder is to be immobilized with either a sling or Velpeau type of dressing for a period of time exceeding a week, a program of rehabilitation of the muscles must begin at the onset of the immobilization to prevent muscle atrophy. Isometric exercises of the shoulder and arm should begin as soon as pain permits. If the forearm muscles are also included in the immobilization, the muscles of this part must also be exercised

Following removal of the immobilization, Codman exercises are encouraged. These are both isotonic and stretching exercises that are aided by the force of gravity. Some muscles need more strengthening than others; this is determined by testing. The following inexpensive equipment is useful for exercising; rubber ball, finger exercisers, bouncing putty, finger ladders, shoulder wheels, metal handle with removable collars, and iron discs weighing 2½, 5, 10, 12½ to 50 pounds. Klein recommends a reconditioning program of seven specific progressive resistance exercises that produce significant functional gains in chronic shoulder injury, dislocations, and instability. Isometric exercises following termination of the regular exercise program are done to maintain the strength of the shoulder-girdle muscles.

SHOULDER LESIONS IN BASEBALL

Baseball players are plagued by the same clinical conditions of the shoulder, arm, and elbow as anyone else in the general population. However, the constant wear and tear and great strain placed on these parts are responsible for the more frequent occurrence of injury in professional baseball players and especially pitchers. Professional and Little League baseball pitchers can each claim a distinctive yet different lesion in the shoulder that may result from pitching. The shoulder is most frequently the cause not only of sore and tight shoulders, but also of sore and tight arms. Some of the more common ailments are strains of frequently used muscles or their tendinous insertions, subacromial or subdeltoid bursitis, bicipital tenosynovitis, osteoarthritis of the shoulder joint, loose bodies in the shoulder joint, exostosis at posterior-inferior rim of the glenoid, luxation of the biceps tendon from the bicipital groove, supraspinatus tendon fraying, nonspecific inflammation and others. Elbow conditions are considered elsewhere.

Since a variety of clinical conditions may be responsible for a disabled shoulder and arm, an effort must be made to locate the source of trouble. It is important to take a detailed history. In addition to the usual examination techniques of inspection, palpation, range of motion, and muscle testing, it is absolutely necessary to observe, study, and analyse the player's throwing motion from stance to follow-through. Slocum has divided the act of throwing into four steps or phases:

1. Initial stance.
2. Wind-up preparatory phase.
3. Initial forward action of arm.
4. Follow-through.

In order for a physician to pinpoint the pathologic condition responsible for the ballplayer's ailing arm, he must have a thorough understanding of the mechanism of throwing. He will then be able to observe, study, and analyse the layer's throwing or pitching pattern, thereby enabling him to arrive at an accurate diagnosis. He does this by correlating the appearance of the symptoms with the anatomy and the phase of the throwing mechanism in which these appear. Routine and special x-ray views including the West-Point view and including arthrography, as well as arthroscopy help considerably in visualizing any bony, periosteal, or soft tissue pathologic condition.

The protracted "sore arm" that is the bane of pitchers may be due to a variety of causes. As noted before, the pathology may be in the shoulder, arm or elbow. Only the most frequent clinical conditions of the shoulder responsible for the sore arm are discussed here.

PERIOSTEAL-TENDINOUS AND MUSCLE TEARS

During the preparatory phase of the wind-up, the anterior deltoid and pectoralis major muscles are stretched as the arm is drawn back and into abduction and external rotation. The insertions of these muscles may be injured by tension. During the follow-through phase, the scapular insertions of the posterior deltoid, rhomboid major and long head of the triceps are fully stretched. These muscles can be easily injured as a result of an overload.

These lesions cause local pain and discomfort. They are easily localized by palpation as well as by studying the throwing pattern. An injection of local diagnostic and therapeutic. The injected area is treated by cryotherapy for 24 hours. Ultrasound may be helpful and is instituted the day after an injection. The pitcher uses a 5 pounds steel ball, the exact size of a conventional baseball, in a series of exercises carefully designed to strengthen and rehabilitate sore arms. The exercises simulate the various motions, including wind-up and follow-through in the act of throwing. It is also recommended the pitcher rest for 1 to 2 weeks following the injury depending on the extent of the injury. This applies equally to swimmers, tennis players, and other who sustain similar injuries.

EXOSTOSIS ON POSTERIOR INFERIOR RIM OF GLENOID

As a result of the tremendous throwing and braking forces to which the capsule and its coverings at the shoulder joint are subjected in the follow-through phase of pitching, pathologic changes occur in the posterior capsule and adjacent triceps tendon. Bony deposits may form at the posterior-inferior rim of the glenoid following excessive strain and overuse. This condition is a distinctive lesion of professional baseball pitchers. These deposits cause local pain and discomfort posteriorly in the shoulder. Tenderness can commonly be elicited in the posterior axillary fold, yet pain may be felt anteriorly in the deltoid because of pain referred by way of the circumflex nerve when it has been irritated. Pitching causes increased pain and discomfort. After a couple of innings of hard pitching, the pitcher may find it difficult to continue.

Routine A-P or P-A x-ray views of the shoulder may not reveal the lesion; it may be necessary to x-ray the shoulder while positioned in external rotation with the x-ray tube tilted 5° cephalad. The best and quickest way to manage these lesions is by injections and physical therapy. The point of maximal tenderness is injected with a 1 or 2ml combination preparation of local anesthesia and corticosteroid. If the athletes gets relief, he may continue to perform. The injection may be repeated if pain recurs after a suitable interval.

If no relief is experienced after three injections plus physical therapy, it may be necessary to have the pitcher change his pitching style from overhead to a side arm or ¾ style, provided he is young enough to make such a change. Operative treatment for this condition has a poor prognosis for returning the athlete as a successful pitcher.

BICIPITAL TENOSYNOVITIS

Suspect this condition when the athlete complains of local pain and discomfort over the front of the shoulder in the region of the tendon of the long head of the biceps when there is marked tenderness with palpation over this tendon in the bicipital groove, or tenderness on rolling the tendon under the examiner's fingers. The diagnosis is firmly established when testing of the biceps muscle against resistance produces pain in the region of the bicipital tendon.

If the pitcher is not a professional, the arm should be placed in a sling and painful movements avoided. Daily physical therapy, consisting of moist heat and ultrasound, is indicated and nonsteroidal anti-inflammatory such as aspirin. If the condition does not subside in 1 week, then an injection of a corticosteroid and local anesthetic should be considered at the site of maximal tenderness under strict aseptic precautions. Resumption of pitching duties, of course, depends on the athlete's response to treatment and is usually allowed in a graded manner.

In the professional pitcher, this lesion is best treated early with an injection of a corticoid combined with a local anesthetic, the injected area is treated by cryotherapy for 24 hours. Following this ultrasound may be used. In this manner, the pitcher is relieved of the pain and kept active but probably misses his regular rotation. However, repeated injections of corticosteroid into a tendon are not without the risk of inducing subsequent tendon rupture.

The doctor must be alert to the fact that, if this clinical condition goes unrecognized, it may lead to a rupture of the long head of the biceps with characteristic deformity of the biceps. This complication is best treated surgically upon early recognition.

FOCUS OF INFLAMMATION.

Infrequently, a ballplayer will have a sore and disabled arm or shoulder that is difficult to diagnose. Because many team physicians are orthopaedically and surgically oriented, the diagnosis remains an enigma after their examination. A complete medical check up by a physician oriented in internal medicine is then indicated. Various medical conditions such as arthritis, gall-bladder disease, kidney infections, cardiac conditions, and other may be the cause of his pitching difficulties. Rarely, a dental problem may be responsible for the ballplayer's wretchedness and poor performance.

LITTLE LEAGUER'S SHOULDER

This is a fracture of the proximal epiphyseal cartilage of the humerus in Little League pitcher. It is usually accompanies by sharp pain in the shoulder region and a marked reduction in pitching efficiency. Localized tenderness, painful shoulder motion that become intensified with testing of the various shoulder muscles against resistance, and radiographic widening of the translucent line of the epiphyseal cartilage in a Little League pitcher usually establish the diagnosis.

Treatment of these athletes is the use of a sling for several days and discontinuance of all participation until symptoms are resolved. The prognosis is excellent. According to Torg, this translucency may take 8 to 12 months to reossify.

Anterior Instability and Transient Recurrent Subluxation of the Shoulder. Periodically, a physician is consulted by an athlete who has a disabling shoulder condition that causes recurrent episodes of pain and disability. Because the condition has not improved, the athlete has decided to see his doctor. The patient's history and complaints strongly suggest glenohumeral joint instability. Vigorous, and sometimes violent, repetitions of overhead athletic activities of the shoulder and arm, as are used in racquet, throwing, and swimming sports, can lead to this disabling entity. Blazina and Satzman highlighted this syndrome in a 1969 report, which caused practising orthopaedists to give more attention to this clinical entity. They added that following an injury, the entire upper extremity may be limp, feel numb, or tingle. Rowe and Zarins stated that following a transient subluxation, the athlete may complain of a sudden sharp, stabbing, paralysing pain. The arm may "go dead", which prevents the athlete from using the arm above shoulder level. Rowe and Zarins named this the "dead arm syndrome.

According to Protzman, may West Point cadets, whose training includes hand-walking by grasping the rungs of overhead ladders as well as large amounts of pull-ups, have sustained anterior shoulder instability disorders and subluxations. Rockwood adds that even a minor fall or such minor activities as swinging a badminton or tennis racquet can lead to transient subluxation.

The clinical disorder may also appear in non-athletes, especially in those who do heavy overhead work.

The physician must may particular attention to the patient's history because at times that may be the only guide available for selecting proper therapy. The patient usually describes a sensation of looseness and instability in the shoulder. Patients may say, "My shoulder comes out," My shoulder is about to come out,"

"My shoulder slipped out," or "My shoulder voluntarily slipped back in." Other may say, "My shoulder hung up and then went back into place." It is important for the doctor to ascertain what the shoulder position had been when the symptoms commenced. The majority of these disorders occur as a result of abduction, extension, or external rotation of the shoulder. Here, the head of the humerus transiently subluxes over the anterior rim of the glenoid, causing anterior shoulder pain. The pain lessens when the humeral head relocates itself. Pain is also felt posteriorly because of the checkrein function of the shoulder's posterior structures, which prevents further subluxing of the humeral head. Knowledge of prior trauma or operations is important since it can help the physician make an appropriate judgment for treatment.

A careful examination is done with the patient standing, sitting, or lying in a supine position. Testing for anatomic contours, muscle strength, and range of motion is best done with the patient standing. More precise testing of the shoulder is done with the patient in a sitting or supine position and the elbow of the involved upper extremity on either the examiner's hip or a pillow. Tenderness and instability can be elicited. Anterior pain is almost always present with anterior-inferior instability.

A clicking, snapping, or clunking noise may be hear during range of motion of the shoulder. These noises may be related to movement of the head of the humerus as it subluxes over the rim of the glenoid or returns to its normal position.

External rotation and abduction of the shoulder produce in the patient a positive sign of apprehension, indicative of anterior shoulder instability and subluxation. If an athlete starts guarding or resisting external rotation when the shoulder is in 90 degrees or less of abduction, then a subluxing shoulder must be suspected. A comparative examination of the non-injured shoulder and arm must also be done.

The physical examination should be followed by an x-ray examination that includes anteroposterior views of the shoulder in internal and external rotation, lateral axillary views and a West Point view. Although an acute anterior subluxation of the shoulder may not show any demonstrable bony disorder chronic anterior subluxations may reveal an avulsion fracture of the anteroinferior rim of the glenoid, irregularity of the glenoid rim, calcific deposits anterior to the rim of the glenoid, and defects of the humeral head.

Treatment of the patient depends on the type and degree of subluxation. Rockwood classifies subluxation caused by trauma, voluntary and involuntary atraumatic, respectively.

The surgeon performs the shoulder reconstruction operation with which he is most familiar. For a type II subluxation, if the athlete has a history of one or multiple dislocations interspersed with intermittent subluxing episodes, a standard shoulder reconstruction operation is indicated. Anterior redundant capsular pouches must be eliminated surgically.

The causes of the patient's disability must be accurately established. A rehabilitation program is always beneficial. Surgery should not be performed if there is a neuro-psychiatric component. It may be helpful to send such patients to a psychiatrist for consultation and therapy.

Determining the type of atraumatic subluxator prior to treatment is important. Rockwood emphatically states that whenever surgery is indicated, the anteroinferior redundant pouch must be eliminated.

IMPINGEMENT SYNDROME

Neer's pioneering research on the shoulder led to our present understanding of painful disorder of the shoulder seen in athletes, such as the impingement syndrome. He demonstrated that the shoulder's functional arc of elevation is forward, not lateral as was commonly believed. He also showed by cadaver dissection how the overhead motion of the shoulder could produce the impingement syndrome. Impingement occurs when the greater tuberosity impinges the soft tissue against the anterior edge of the acromion and the cora-coacromial ligament. Cadaver dissection of older persons showed marked degenerative changes and osteophyte formation on the under-surface of the anterior acromion. In other cadaver specimens, thickening and even osteophyte formation was noted in the coracoacromial ligament.

Rathbun and McNab's microvascular research on the subclavian artery provided additional etiologic evidence of the impingement syndrome. Injection of a micro-opaque substance into the subclavian artery, which carries the blood supply to the rotator cuff, revealed an vascular pattern in the supraspinatus tendon and intracapsular portion of the biceps tendon when the arm is held dependent at the side of the body. Accordingly, these tendons are more vulnerable to degenerative changes. Since these relatively avascular tendons course together over the humeral head, McNab suggested that this avascular pattern is conducive to development of the impingement syndrome.

This syndrome gained wider clinical recognition and acceptance from Hawkins and Kennedy's cross-Canadian letter survey, conducted on 2496 Canadian swimmers of major swimming clubs following the 1976 Olympic Games. Fifteen percent of the swimmers that specialized in freestyle and butterfly strokes were discovered to have shoulder disability of the impingement type. Johnson, in a more recent report, found that between one half and two thirds of the world-class swimmers surveyed have had significant shoulder problems. Johnson adds backstroke swimmers to the category of freestyle and butterfly swimmers.

Kennedy's cadaver dissections of the shoulder confirmed Neer's finding. Impingement was also shown to occur at the acromioclavicular joint, subacromial bursa, infraspinatus, and long head of the biceps. Johnson states that a rigorous training program that involves as much as 16,000 strokes per week or 660,000 strokes per season produces over use syndromes as a result of the subdeltoid bursa's inability to keep pace with the lubrication demands of the shoulder.

Accordingly, inflammation results. When examining athletes with shoulder complaints, physicians must be aware of the close anatomic relationships of the important shoulder structures that exist within a small area, and they must consider that one or several of these structures may be the cause of pain and disability. This clinical disorder is also seen in such competitive and recreational athletes as tennis and racquet-ball players, baseball pitchers, quarter-backs in football, and other athletes who participate in predominantly overhead sports.

The impingement syndrome occurs in all age groups, from teenage swimmers to geriatric tennis players. Repeated loading of the shoulder as the arm is brought vigorously into a forward flexed position above the horizontal plane causes repeated impingements and progressive wear and tear of the bony and soft tissue structures. In addition to the bony and soft tissue changes that take place, rotator cuff tears do occur in later stages.

Neer and others divide the progressive development of this syndrome into the following three stages.

STAGE I-EDEMA AND HEMORRHAGE

The first stage results from over use-overhead activities in such sports as baseball, tennis, and swimming and typically affects athletes under age 25. Pain is usually minimal and occurs with activity, although it is sometimes described as resembling a toothache and occurring primarily at night. Tenderness may be elicited at the anterior acromion and greater tuberosity, the biceps and supraspinatus tendon may be tender and may cause bicipital groove pain, and crepitus may be present. A test for impingement syndrome is done in the following manner: The arm is flexed forcibly against the anteroinferior surface of the acromion; if 10 ml of a local anesthesia injected into the patient's subacromial impingement area causes relief of pain, the diagnosis is confirmed. Stage I is reversible.

Conservative care consisting of rest, oral anti-inflammatory medications, and physical therapy is recommended for treating this stage of the condition. When the pain lessens, additional measures are instituted, such as stretching of the muscle and capsule, muscle strengthening, and corrective measures to eliminate faulty athletic movements and the produce proper biomechanical moves. The athlete must warm-up properly to ensure loosening and flexibility of the joints, muscles, and tendons and activation of the lubrication mechanism. Training programs must include flexibility and strengthening exercises to help prevent shoulder problems. Subluxing shoulders, frozen shoulders, and acromioclavicular arthritis must be ruled out.

STAGE II-FIBROSIS AND TENDINITIS

As impingement continues without relief, the disorder becomes chronic and more difficult to treat.

Additional inflammatory scarring occurs in the subacromial bursa, supraspinatus tendon, and biceps tendon. Tenderness is frequently elicited over the biceps and supraspinatus tendons as well as other areas of the shoulder. The shoulder joint becomes progressively stiffer. Although this condition is seen more frequently in the 25 to 40 year old age group, it is also seen amount 50 and 60 year olds. Clinical testing must be precise to ascertain which structures are causing pain and disablement.

In this stage, it is important to either confirm or rule out the presence of coracoacromial ligament involvement. This can be done in the following manner. The humerus is forcibly flexed to 90 degree and the forcibly rotated internally, which causes the greater tuberosity to impact the supraspinatus tendon against the anterior surface of the cora-coacromial ligament. The previously described impingement injection test is then performed.

One of the characteristic signs of this stage is the athlete's reluctance to bring his arm down vigorously from an abducted, overhead position, such as that used in serving a tennis ball, or in executing an overhand stroke in racquet-ball, or in performing a swim stroke. Soon the patient avoids all athletic activity because of the anticipated pain and weakness. The patient has now reached a stage of irreversibility, in which either surgery or complete avoidance of the offending activity is indicated.

The type of surgery indicated depends on what pathologic process is responsible for the patient's condition. A chronic subacromial bursa may have to be removed, or a coracoacromial ligament may have to be resected. In any event, the patient must be told to expect a lengthy rehabilitation program to recover a normal range of motion and strength. A return to competitive athletics at the same level of proficiency should not anticipated, but a return to recreational athletics can be.

STAGE III-BONE SPURS AND TENDINITIS

The third stage is characterized by continuing shoulder problems, running a gamut of minimal to severe pain, weakness, and limitation of motion of the shoulder-arm complex in patients over age forty. Chronicity can be punctuated by recurrent attacks of tendinitis that may be severe enough to awaken the patient from sleep. Progressive degeneration of the tendon leads to partial or complete rupture of the rotator cuff and the biceps tendon.

A complete cuff rupture is evidenced by tenderness over the greater tuberosity, atrophy of the infraspinatus and supraspinatus muscles, and weakness of abduction and external rotation. Crepitus and the impingement sign aid in diagnosis. Bony excrescences of the coracoacromial ligament and of the acromion's anterior and undersurface help the physician to localize the pathologic process responsible for this stage of the disorder. If conservative care fails and surgery becomes necessary, anterior acromioplasty and/or repair of the rotator cuff tear may be indicated. Cervical radiculitis and neoplasm must first be ruled out.

In all three stages, a thorough history must be taken, followed by a meticulous examination. An x-ray examination and impingement injection test should be conducted. Rest, oral anti-inflammatory medication, and physical therapy must be utilized in all three stages. Ice applied after activities is usually beneficial. Limited use of corticosteroid injections into the subacromial bursa may be helpful. Ultrasound and TENS have also been effective in chronic, refractory cases. Arthro-games are best reserved for stage III.

Such preventive measures as muscle stretching and strengthening must be practiced by athletes prior to competition, as part of a training and conditioning program. If a Stages II and III an operation is planned, the athlete must be advised that rehabilitation is important for his total recovery. He also must be advised that following surgery he might not be able to reach his former competitive level. If the athlete follows the reconditioning program conscientiously, however, he should be able to reach a satisfactory recreational capability.

CHAPTER-10

TREATMENT AND CARE OF ELBOW INJURIES

The elbow is an interesting anatomic arrangement of three joints formed by the articulating surfaces of the distal humerus, proximal radius and ulna and adjoining muscles, ligaments, synovium, nerves, and vascular structures. Its primary function it to move the forearm to and from the arm as well as to rotate it. The hand, by virtue of its connection to the forearm, moves with it. The forearm can also act as an extension of the arm. Flexion and extension movements of the elbow occur at the capitellum-radial head and the trochlea-ulna articulation. These motion are done with a reasonable degree of inherent mechanical stability because of the accurate adaptation of the trochlea to the semilunar notch of the ulna. The biceps and brachialis muscles that run anterior to the joint produce flexion of this joint. The triceps muscle, which runs posterior to the joint, produces extension of this joint. These are strong muscles that also aid the ulnar and radial collateral ligaments in stabilizing the joint. The distal humerus just proximal to the condyles, anteriorly and posteriorly, has been adaptively thinned to accommodate the coronoid and olecranon processes of the ulna. Because of the bony weakening, this part of the humerus is not infrequently fractured when the curved beak of the olecranon recesses into the olecranon fossa when the elbow is fully extended.

The proximal radius and ulna are bound together by a strong annular ligament. These articulate with each other as well as with the capitellum and trochlea, respectively, to produce pronation and supination of the forearm. These movements are produced by muscles that originate from bony processes of the distal humerus, the medial and lateral epicondyles. At the medial epicondyle, flexor and pronator muscles originate. The pronator teres muscle produces forearm pronation; the flexor muscles produce wrist and finger flexion. The origin and the muscles of this epicondyle may suffer a painful disabling condition seen in baseball pitchers. At the lateral epicondyle arise the supinator and extensor muscles. The supinator muscle produces forearm supination; the extensor muscles produce wrist and finger extension. The disabling "tennis elbow" involves the origin of muscles at this epicondyle.

In athletics, the shoulder and elbow work in concert to produce one or a combination of the fundamental movements of flexion, extension, pronation, or supination of the forearm. This movement is seen in sports in which throwing is dominant, such as a baseball, javelin, and in boxing with the proper execution of a left jab, when the forearm and hand are flung forward at the elbow. The elbow not only is contused and sprained in a manner similar to other joints, but is also subjected to powerful repetitive hyperextension movements and rotary forces of the forearm, such as occur in baseball pitching, javelin throwing, golf, tennis, jai alai andothers, which can result in pathologic changes in the joint and structures about it.

Any trauma to the elbow that causes swelling may be serious, especially if swelling occurs in the antecubital fossa, which is tightly bounded by the bicipital aponeurosis. The lack of "give" in this space may cause an unyielding tightness and pressure on the nearby blood vessels, leading to arterial impairment.

Although the median, radial and ulnar nerves course about the elbow, only trauma to the ulnar nerve has practical implications in athletic injuries. This nerve is superficially placed in the ulnar notch and is not infrequently contused, causing a sharp momentary pain, tingling or numbness to radiate down the inner side of the forearm to the ring and small finger.

The elbow joint is frequently threatened with a marked loss of function because of development of myositis ossificans and adhesive capsulitis following muscle contusion, fractures, and dislocation of the bones of this joint. The reader is encouraged to read the anatomy, physiology, and kinesiology of the elbow.

FIRST-AID MEASURES

Step 1.

As with other injuries to joints, the trainer takes a complete history, placing special emphasis on the mechanism of the injury? Did the injury result from a blow, fall or twist? What was the position of the part at the time of the injury? Did it happen during a tackle, pile-up, arm lock, hitting the boards or gym floor, throwing motion, or during a tennis match? Is he able to move his elbow or does he have to carry this injured upper extremity by holding the wrist of the injured limb? Did he feel an electric-like momentary pain, tingling or a numbness radiating from the inner side of the elbow to the ring and pinky finger?

The trainer makes a careful examination of all surface of the injured elbow, inspecting the soft tissue and bony landmarks looking for deformities, swelling, and ecchymosis. He looks for the points of the olecranon and both epicondyles and palpates them, looking for a triangular outline formed by these bony prominences when the elbow is held flexed at 90°. Unnatural depressions and prominences must be noted. He palpates the radial pulse. He gently tests for range of motion and immediately stops if the pain is too great. He tests for finger approximation, spread, and extension.

Step 2.

If the trainer feels reasonably certain that there are no fractures or dislocations, he renders first-aid care similar to that for other injured joints, the emphasis being directed to checking hemorrhage and extravasation of fluid into tissues by applying cold water or ice packs and compression bandaging. The injured athlete is referred to the doctor and instructed to see him before going to bed.

If the trainer suspects a fracture or dislocation, the athlete's arm is placed in a sling and the physician is immediately contacted. This is an emergency, and the physician will instruct the trainer about splinting and referring the athlete to his office or the hospital emergency room. Closed reduction is performed either with appropriate medication or with general anesthesia after the athlete has been admitted. A cold compress is applied to the elbow during the interim. Delay in appropriate treatment can lead to disastrous complications such as Volkmann's contracture.

DEFINITIVE TREATMENT

Contusion

Because the back of the elbow is superficial and exposed and has practically no protective muscle padding, it is frequently contused from blows to it or falls in football, wrestling, basketball, tumbling, and ice hockey. Since the point of the elbow and its overlying soft tissues are prominent, reaction to trauma is rapid and readily observable. Subsequently, serious prolonged disability in contused elbows is infrequent because early and effective first-aid measures to check hemorrhage and extravasation of fluid into the joint can be started. The use of ice compresses, sponge rubber padding, and elastic compression bandaging for 24 to 48 hours materially reduces swelling. This is followed by ice, massage and guarded active exercises. A sponge rubber pad should be worn in competition to prevent re-injury.

If the superficially placed olecranon bursa has become distended, the same type of treatment is rendered. However, some team physicians may prefer to aspirate the bursal sac, which must be done under strict aseptic precautions. Although this may reduce the recovery time, it does carry a risk of infection.

If chronic or recurring bursal effusions appear or the bursa becomes thickened, a search must be made for the chronic or repetitive source of trauma, which will be removed. It may even be necessary in such cases to remove the bursa surgically if the pathologic condition continues.

SPRAIN

Elbow sprains rank low in the incidence of joint injuries. Although twisting of the elbow in any direction can produce a sprain of this joint, sprains occur in athletics most commonly when the back of a fully extended elbow is struck a blow while the athlete's hand and shoulder are held in a fixed position, as in a football pile-up. This injury occurs also in a basketball game when a player's arm is forced into hyperextension when caught between two players. The elbow may also be sprained when a player strikes a gym wall, floor, or earth with his outstretched hand and braced elbow to keep his body from colliding with the immovable mass. Acute onset of pain, tenderness, swelling, and marked restriction of elbow function should make one suspect a sprain of the elbow joint.

In our experiences, sprains of the elbow are due mainly to hyperextension injuries and involve the anterior capsule. Some authors disagree, stating that the pathologic condition is predominantly a tear of one or both origins of the flexor and extensor muscles at the medial and lateral epicondyles of the humerus. This can easily be determined by careful palpation to localize the greatest point of tenderness, followed by testing of various muscles against resistance. Contraction of an injured muscle group causes pain at its point of origin. If there is significant pain, an x-ray study will determine whether an avulsed chip of bone from the epicondyle is present. A nondisplayed fracture of the radial head can mimic this condition and may not appear on x-ray films for up to 2 weeks.

The immediate treatment is the application of cold compresses, elastic bandage compression and support of an arm in a sling until seen by the doctor. The doctor applies a bivalved padded plaster cast for the upper extremity with the elbow held in 90°; this is worn for 7 to 10 days, depending on the severity of the injury. Joint aspiration has little to offer in the treatment of this condition.

Following cast removal, whirlpool and massage of the area are started. Active exercise is done during the whirlpool therapy. Progressive-resistance exercise is started as the range of elbow motion increases. Following each treatment, the elbow is wrapped with an elastic bandage. A program of isometric and isotonic exercises of the upper extremity is performed at home by the athlete hourly for 5 minutes. The use of a sponge rubber or tennis ball for the hand aids in the restoration of muscle strength. Avoid forceful flexion or extension of an injured elbow of muscle strength. Avoid forceful flexion or extension of an injured elbow to increase range of motion.

The athlete may return to participation after a full range of painless motion and muscle strength have been regained. A protective tape strapping is applied that allows flexion beyond 90°, but limits extension to 20° less than the zero starting position. This is worn for 1 to 2 weeks following return to competition.

JAVELIN THROWER'S ELBOW

Although the configuration of bones that articulate to form the elbow joint are suitably structured for flexion and extension, the humerus-ulna articulation is not anatomically suited for some of the lateral and medial movements of the ulna of the elbow that occur in the javelin throw. The ulna abducts when the radius crosses it in pronation; the ulna adducts when the radius returns in supination to its parallel position with the ulna. The movements of the ulna at the trochlea are not generally well known and may be the reason for many obscure cases of elbow pain.

However, these proximal ulnar movements are considered the mechanism of injury in the "javelin thrower's elbow." There is a coordinated movement of powerful forearm pronation and elbow extension as the javelin is hurled on its way. As the olecranon moves medially during forearm pronation, it exerts tremendous pressure on the medial side of the joint, placing the ulnar collateral ligament under great strain. Although gradual in onset, pain may be acute after a violent throw. It disappears with rest and reappears with effort. On physical examination there may be nothing to see except perhaps some tenderness and slight swelling or fullness along the medial aspect of the elbow. There is usually a full range of painless motion. Muscle testing is usually normal as are x-ray studies. However, the history is a give-away. The best treatment is prevention, that is, the use of correct throwing techniques.

Another, rarer type of javelin thrower's elbow follows a hyperextension injury to the tip of the olecranon, including a fracture. This more difficult to treat because of recurrence and may eventually necessitate surgical removal of the olecranon tip.

ELBOW INJURIES IN BASEBALL PLAYERS

Certainly a majority of our readers are familiar with the scene of a baseball pitcher on a mound, rearing back, and firing a baseball towards the batter at a velocity in excess of 100 miles an hour. He may have to pitch inning after inning with such power because a "no hitter" is within his grasp. Or he may have to bear down exceptionally hard because of a game situation. The power of each pitch is generated in the large area of the shoulder and arm and is transmitted through the narrower elbow with an increased limb velocity to effect maximal transmission of energy through the forearm and hand.

With an understanding of the anatomy and physiology of the shoulder and upper extremity and the biomechanics of the complicated act of pitching, which may average between 100 to 140 pitches in a regulation nine innings of a baseball game, the reader should be able to appreciate why the elbows of pitchers are so frequently injured. The repetitive throwing stresses the medial reinforcing soft tissue restraints for the same reason that the capitellum is compressed. Therefore, attenuation of the medial ligament system from valgus strains occurs, which leads to pain, instability, and loss of function. Such was the case of Tommy John, a veteran left-handed hurler of the Angels team. His pitching arm was salvaged by Dr. Frank Jobe, who replace a withered and torn medial collateral ligament with a palmaris longus tendon from high right forearm. The forearm is repeatedly subjected to the powerful extension force of the contracted triceps muscle at its insertion in the olecranon. This causes it to be flung forward at the elbow prior to the release of the ball and the follow-through. The elbow in particular is subjected to a great deal of stress in pitching; this stress, according to Elleman, causes compression of the radial head and may be partly responsible for osteochondrosis of the radial.

In addition, rotary forces of the forearm and flexion and extension of the wrist are powered by muscles that arise from the medial and lateral epicondyles of the humerus. The muscles that predominate depend on whether the hand is supinated with a snap or flexed sharply at the wrist to accomplish a desired curve, hop, sinker, or slide of the ball. These pitchers are more prone to elbow injuries than those who depend on a fast straight ball. Muscle ruptures, medial collateral ligament sprains, and ruptures in the elbow have also been described.

Pitchers who throw breaking stuff-curves, sliders, sinkers, and screw balls-cause the upper extremity and its joints to move unnaturally, thus placing great strain on the arm, elbow, and shoulder. This causes degenerative changes of the hyaline cartilage at the tip, margins, and articular surfaces of the olecranon, medial surface of the coronoid process of the ulna, and the adjacent surfaces of the condyles of the humerus. Such changes result in synovial thickening, hypertrophic arthritic changes, spurs, osteochondritis, and loose bodies. Although most frequently seen in veteran professional pitchers, degenerative changes are also noted in adult pitchers who regularly take their stint on the mound and in other players. Olecranon fractures have been described in baseball players as well. All of these conditions can cause pain, swelling, restricted and painful elbow motion.

Loose bodies caused by cartilage and/or bone are most frequently located in the olecranon fossa, at the tip of the coronoid process, and about the radial head.

They may mechanically obstruct extension in the elbow to varying degrees. Loose bodies have also been noted in the ligamentous tissue and tendinous attachment in the region of the medial epicondyle of the humerus beneath the ulnar nerve. They may produce a paresthesia of the ulnar distribution of the hand by irritating the ulnar nerve in its vicinity. It is not unusual to find loose bodies in the olecranon fossa of pitchers in their late teens who have been pitching regularly for a number of years. This is the end result of a chronic Little Leaguer's elbow or aseptic necrosis involving the capitellum, radial head, or both. Yet some authors state that the incidence of aseptic necrosis of the radial head or capitellum or both is rare or low.

Treatment of elbow injuries when joint changes are suspected requires the taking of comparative x-ray pictures of the injured and uninjured elbows. The injured elbow should receive physical therapy consisting of local heat and massage. Physical therapy to the elbow in a whirlpool bath is also beneficial. Injections of a combined corticosteroid and local anesthesia should be tries for points of tenderness. Intra-articular injections may also be given when indicated, and certainly should be tried before surgery is contemplated.

However, the benefits must be weighed against the risk of joint destruction, which may follow intra-articular corticosteroid injections. This has been aptly termed "steroid-induced arthropathy." Surgical removal of an isolated but symptomatic spur, exostosis, or ossicle may have a favourable prognosis. However, when surgical removal of loose bodies is performed because they cause the elbow joint to lock, the prognosis for the resumption of a pitching career is uncertain. Treatment of olecranon fractures is well documented in other texts.

Another type of Little Leaguer's elbow has been described for some young pitchers who develop pain, tenderness, and swelling in the medial epicondylar area following maximal pitching effort in Little and Poly League baseball. These clinical findings stem from an avulsion fracture of the epiphysis of the medial epicondyle, which occurs as a result of an extremely vigorous contraction of the flexor-pronator muscles. This produces forearm pronation and wrist and finger flexion to propel the ball on its way to the batter. The epiphysis and attached muscles are displaced downward, away from their normal anatomic site in various degrees of displacement. Inadequate preliminary warm-up, inexperience, and a poorly coordinated pitch may contribute to the incience of this injury.

In elbow injuries of children in which a fracture or dislocation is suspected but not obvious clinically, comparative x-ray pictures are taken of both the injured and uninjured elbow. Special care must be exercised by the attending physician in the interpretation of adolescent elbow radiographs because of age-related normal variants of the ossification patterns of epiphyses in children.

A definite separation and wide displacement of the epiphysis of the medial epicondyle is best treated with open operation and internal fixation followed by application of a padded long arm cast with the elbow positioned at a right angle. If the epicondylar fragment with its attached muscles can be replaced and reattached satisfactorily by a heavy suture material, this should be done. If the reduction cannot be maintained by a suture materialm, it should be fixed with Kirschner wire, which is incorporated into a padded cast with the elbow held at a right angle. This cast is worn for about 1 month. If the postoperative course has progressed satisfactorily clinically and radiographically, the arm is placed in a sling with resumption of graded activity for approximately 2 more weeks. Active elbow motion is encouraged. Passive elbow motion should be avoided.

In some cases the player is also advised to take up another sport.

A slight separation of the epiphysis can be adequately treated by resting the arm in a posterior padded splint for 3 weeks. Preliminary cold packs and elastic compression bandaging are started and continued for 48 hours to check the swelling. The elastic compression bandage is removed after all swelling has ceased, but the arm is maintained in the splint with the elbow positioned at a right angle. Graded activity of the muscles and elbow joint is started when all acute pain, tenderness, and painful motion have disappeared. These active exercises and joint motions are continued progressively until full return of joint mobility and muscle power have been obtained. These athletes are also directed to take up another sport.

Pitchers subjected muscles about the elbow to a tremendous strain which causes them to develop a painful localized condition of "tendino-myositis." The flexor-pronator group of muscles that arise from the medial epicondyle are most commonly injured. However, injuries of muscles that arise from the lateral epicondyle have also been described.

It is not unusual for a young pitcher to develop an acute episode of tendinomyositis, which may cause these muscles to go into spasm from fatigue or other reasons after a number of innings of pitching. The player is unable to extend the elbow completely because this tightened muscle spans the elbow joint. With early adequate ice therapy, light massage, and rest, this spasm may disappear in 24 to 48 hours.

If the pain, spasm and restricted and painful elbow motion persist, additional treatment with a synchronized sound-stimulator unit can be used to relieve pain and spasm and restore motion. If pain is significantly disturbing to the adult athlete, analgesics and muscle relaxants may be used beneficially provided that sound clinical judgment determines their need.

The use of anesthetic injections locally with or without the combined use of a corticosteroid is an important therapeutic tool in the management and treatment of such clinical conditions. Injections should be reserved for chronic, protracted, and recurrent cases that do not respond to rest and physical therapy. When I decide to inject a painful, tender tendinomyositis, I employ a long-acting corticosteroid. I inject 1 to 1.5 ml accurately into the tender site under aseptic conditions, but not into the joint, using a disposable syringe with a 22 gauge, 1½-inch needle. A maximum of three injections are given, spaced about 7 to 10 days apart. Each injection is followed by cryotherapy for 24 hours. If relief is forthcoming, it usually occurs by the third injection. If not, do not inject again.

Rest is also important in the treatment of these injuries. The amount of rest depends on the extent of the injury and its progress with treatment. Slings, padded-molded-posterior plaster splints and padded long-arm casts are used. In all of these, the elbow is held at a right angle. At first I use a sling to provide rest, but if the elbow does not improve within a week, I switched over to a padded long-arm cast with the elbow and wrist immobilized and the fingers free. I believe in resting an elbow in a cast before I entertain the use of injections. There is no one best way to treat these conditions; only the doctor's experience, skill, and success determine how he manages and treats these difficult and at times chronic injuries.

CHAPTER-11

TREATMENT AND CARE OF HAND, WRIST, AND FINGER INJURIES

There are more than 20 joints in the wrist, hand, and fingers, which are formed by 28 bones bound together by a complicated system of ligaments, strengthened at points by insertions of tendons. These small and closely fitted joints are moved by 33 muscles, most of which originate at the elbow and forearm and insert as long slender tendons near the joints they move. These muscles offer no protective padding to direct injury of these parts. These moving parts have snugly fitted surfaces with little tolerance for any derangement and anything altering the shape of the joint surfaces or the consistency of the soft parts limits motion.

Because these parts are complex, exposed, and vulnerable to injury, and considering their importance to an athlete in athletic and his social and economic well being practical prophylactic measures must be taken to prevent injuries and reduce the severity of those that do occur. The incidence of injuries is materially reduced if a protective wrapping is used, similar to the bandages used by boxers for their hands and wrists. Such a wrapping adds extra padding to the thinly muscled metacarpals and strength to the ligaments. As a result, the likelihood of contusions, fractures, sprains and dislocations is reduced. In the event of fractures or dislocations, serious displacement of bone ends usually does not occur. Consequently, with the anxiety of injuring the hands reduced, the athlete uses them more efficiently for both offence and defence. This is especially true for football linemen as well as boxers. This use of commercial forearm and hand pads prevents a multitude of minor contusions, abrasions, and bruising of the forearm, wrists, and hands.

FIRST-AID MEASURES

Step 1.

As with other injuries, the trainer takes a complete history, placing special emphasis on the mechanism of the injury. Was the hand stepped on? Was it contused or sqeezed? Was the part pulled, bent or twisted? What was the position of the part at the time of injury? The trainer also makes a careful examination of the injured part or parts, looking for swelling and deformities. He gently palpates these areas for tenderness and swelling. He gently tests for range of motion, immediately stopping if the pain is great with any attempted motion.

Step 2.

If the trainer feels reasonably certain that there are no fractures or dislocations, he renders first-aid care similar to that for other injured joints, the emphasis being directed to checking the hemorrhage and extravasation of traumatic exudates into tissues by ice water or ice packs and compression bandaging where feasible. This is extremely important in preventing stiffness and fibrosis of joints, which occur rapidly if the movable parts remain bathed in serofibrinous exudate. If the pain, tenderness, swelling, and joint restriction are greater than dull or annoying, he refers the athlete to the team physician with instruction to see him before going to bed. If the trainer suspects a fracture or dislocation, he immediately puts in a call to the attending physician for further instruction. The physician will decide whether an x-ray picture is indicated. The trainer notes all his observations in a permanent training room record.

DEFINITIVE TREATMENT

Contusions

Contusions are common everyday occurrences in most sports, many of which are trivial and ignored. Fewer would result if wraps and flexible pads were used more commonly. Such protection is especially necessary for those athletes who must use the hands aggresively in both offensive and defensive play in body contact sports. If the injury is serious enough to produce pain, swelling, tenderness, and marked restriction of wrist, hand, or finger motion, the athlete should consult the trainer or doctor.

The trainer immerses the injured part in ice water or applies ice packs for 30 minutes. After thorough drying, the injured part is splinted and wrapped with an elastic bandage and put in a sling, with the injured part positioned higher than the elbow. If the wrist, hand or several of the fingers have been moderately contused, splinting of these parts for 24 to 48 hours with an appropriately sized padded plaster splint secured with an elastic bandage is recommended. The hand and forearm are placed in a sling with the hand positioned higher than the elbow, which helps to relieve painful motion and limit swelling. During sleep the hand and forearm should be placed on a sloping bed of pillows.

The use of whirlpool or moist hot packs, massage and exercises for these injured joints 48 hours following injury is suggested. Pain tenderness, and swelling have lessened by this time, and these modalities aid in the absorption of traumatic exudates. Early physical therapy and especially joint mobilization reduce the likelihood of fibrosis, adhesions and stiffness in the wrist, hands and fingers. Squeezing a rubber sponge in lukewarm water is an efficient and inexpensive method to aid maximal restoration of wrist, hand and finger function.

SPRAINS

Sprains of the fingers and thumbs commonly occur in athletics when fingers are bent or twisted beyond their normal range of motion or are jammed by an external force. They are usually accompanied by pain, swelling, and restricted, painful motion commensurate with the injury, which may require x-ray films to rule out fractures. An important component in finger sprains is partial or complete rupture of the collateral ligament or capsule of these small joints leading to instability and/or capsulitis, which may persist for months and lead to permanent limitation of motion. These must be protected and treated by a physician familiar with these injuries. Stress testing of the collateral ligament will confirm the diagnosis.

Therapy is started to limit the swelling by immersing the hand in ice water. After thorough drying either adhesive tape or a metal finger splint, such as aluminium with foam rubber padding, is applies, depending on the extent of the injury. If adhesive tape is used, the finger is immobilized in 20° to 30° flexion by taping it to the neighbouring finger. The mobile, uninjured finger allows use of the injured finger, but at the same time protects it. If a thumb has been jammed or sprained at the metacarpal-phalangeal joint, it is splinted to the hand and wrist by a figure-eight adhesive tape or bandage application/ It is best not to splint fingers in extension if more than one joint is involved. Splinting is discontinued after local tenderness and painful motion have subsided, and is followed by whirlpool, massage and active exercises. Protective strapping of the finger or thumb should be continued when the athlete returns to competition to prevent re-injury.

PROTECTIVE SPLINTING FOR FINGER SPRAINS

For mild to moderate sprains of finger joints, the injured finger can be splinted to its neighbouring finger with three pieces of ½-inch adhesive tape, which is kept on for several days. Athletes may continue to compete with the dressing with some guarding of the finger. The splint is kept on until all local tenderness and painful motion have disappeared.

For severe sprains, more rigid fixation is necessary, and metal splints such as aluminium with foam rubber padding are popular provided no fractures were present. The metal splint is bent slightly to allow positioning of the finger in 20° to 30° flexion. The finger is secured to the splint with several strips of ½ inch adhesive tape and kept on for 7 to 10 days. No participation is allowed during this phase of treatment.

SPRAINED THUMB

Most physicians fail to diagnose the area of the thumb that is painful. Is It is a dorsal or volar sprain? Does it hurt in abduction or adduction? Fractures, dislocations, and especially collateral-ligament injuries of the thumb are frequent and should not be overlooked. Stress x-ray films are useful for diagnosing ligament injuries.

PROTECTIVE STRAPPING FOR A SPRAINED THUMB

An underwrap or skin protectant is first applied to the thumb and wrist. The idea is to tape the thumb to prevent painful motion. A 1 inch adhesive tape strapping is applied as a figure eight spica of the thumb and wrist these parts are held in a position of function. This dressing prevents extremes of abduction and extension of the thumb. Such protection is continued until tenderness has been eliminated and normal, pain-free motion has returned. Fractures and dislocations of these parts are frequent and should not be overlooked.

TENDON INJURY

Although "baseball fingers" are most commonly seen in baseball players, especially catchers, this injury occurs not infrequently in other sports. The most common mechanism of injury is when the tip any finger is struck a direct blow, causing a forced flexion of the distal phalanx of the finger while the tendon is actively contracted. This produces an avulsion or disinsertion of the extensor tendon with or without an attached fragment of bone from it insertion in the base of the terminal phalanx.

A deformity of the distal phalanx at the distal interphalangeal joint result, described as a "drop finger." The same injury may also result when the extensor tendon has been contused sufficiently. The athlete complains of local pain, tenderness, and inability to actively extend the terminal phalanx.

Fresh ruptures can be treated adequately by the application of a volar or dorsal metal splint with the distal interphalangeal joint in slight hyperextension. X-ray films are taken before and after the application of the immobilization, which is maintained for 6 to 8 weeks. For successful reattachment of the tendon, treatment must be started within 7 to 10 days. Surgical procedures do not produce sufficient relief from the deformity and disability to warrant their frequent use. In reliable athlete, the position of slight hyperextension is maintained with an intramedullary pin across the joint.

Cut or Lacerated Finger or Torn Fingernail. For emergency care, medicated cream is put on the cut. A finger cap made commercially or made with 1½-to 2-inch adhesive tape 5 to 6 inches in length is placed on the cut. In order to make a finger cap, the tape is twisted around the distal phalanx of the finger with ½ inch on and off finger. The open end is molded and trimmed in the shape of the finger.

WRIST SPRAINS

The wrist is frequently sprained when it is accidentally put through a range of motion greater than that which is normal. This may occur from a multitude of events, resulting in stretched or sprained radial or ulnar collateral, volar, dorsocarpal, and distal radio-ulnar ligaments. The intensity of the pain, tenderness, swelling, and joint restriction varies with the severity of trauma. Those cases that are mild quickly with early application of cold compresses or ice water for about ½ hour, followed by splinting with elastic bandages or adhesive tape. A padded, molded, removable metal or plastic splint may also be used. The wrist is placed in a functional position of extension of 15°. The splint is secured to the wrist with an elastic bandage with fingers left free to move. Heat, massage, and exercises to the wrist begin the day following the injury.

A protective strapping of three overlapping strips of 1½ inch tape is place about the wrist daily following treatment, and also to prevent re-injury when the athlete returns to competition. The attending physician examines the wrist daily the determine its progress and when the athlete may resume play.

If the wrist does not respond to such treatment or if there is point tenderness, x-ray films should be taken to determine the presence of any bony or periosteal pathology. The application of a padded plaster cast with the wrist extended 15° for 10 to 14 days or longer gives a moderately or severely sprained wrist the complete immobilization so necessary to achieve maximal restoration. The fingers are left free to move. A word of caution: the wrist that remains "sprained" should make the doctor suspect a fracture of the carpal navicular, and requires follow-up x-ray examinations of the wrist from multiple views. Early diagnosis can be aided by bone scan in difficult cases.

After removal of the cast, whirlpool, massage, and exercises are necessary to aid in the absorption of traumatic exudates. Early joint mobility reduces the likelihood of fibrosis, adhesions and stiffness in the wrist. Exercises facilitate restoration of normal muscle strength. Athletic participation may be resumed when the wrist is neither tender nor painful upon effort and has a normal range of motion and muscle strength. Protective strapping and appropriate of the wrist and forearm are indicated to prevent reinjury.

CHAPTER-12

TREATMENT AND CARE OF MUSCLE INJURIES

The second largest category of athletic injuries involves the muscles and tendons and infrequently the fascial covering of some muscles. Muscle injuries predominate in this category and result from strains and contusions. Frequently, muscles may become disabled by going into painful spasm or cramp for a variety of reasons.

A muscle strain can occur at any point from its origin to insertion: tendon, musculotendinous junction, or muscle belly. Sometimes they are referred to as a pulled muscle or tendon depending on the site. Fascial tears with muscle herniation are almost clinically indistinguishable from muscle tears. The severity of the injury ranges from a tear of a few or many fibres as a result of overstretching to a complete rupture of the muscle or tendon.

For the purposes of our discussion, it is sufficient to know that these injuries result when the tensile strength of the muscle or tendon fibres is exceeded by the forces to which these tissues are subjected.

Strains can result after a vigorous contraction against resistance, as is frequently seen in back injuries of weight lifters following a lifting incident. In tendons, excessive force can cause overstretching and even rupture of a tendon at or near a point of maximal length, as is seen in a skier who falls forward without release of his bindings and can severely stretch or even rupture his Achilles tendon. This is also seen in football and basketball players. Conditions predisposing to both muscle and tendon injuries are insufficient conditioning, myostatic contractures, limited joint function, incoordination between opposing muscle groups, fatigue, improper warm-up, lack of skill, and pre-existing degenerative changes in the muscle and tendon.

These injuries are usually sudden, painful, and immediately disabling. However, pain and disability may develop later. The nature and extent of disability depends on the location and the number of muscle and tendon fibres, and blood vessels ruptured at the site of the injury. Tenderness, swelling and ecchymosis are the most frequent signs of these injuries. The athlete may hear a sharp snap or tear emanating from the injured tissue at the time of the injury. Testing the strength of a single muscle group against resistance aids in localizing the injury.

Muscle strains occur at many anatomic sites. Some strains are characteristic of specific sports; others may occur in several types of athletic activity. No athlete is immune from strains, regardless of his sport. The preponderance of injuries are minor muscle strains that heal in 1 to 7 days, depending on the extent of the injury. Only the more frequent muscle strains and pulled tendons are discussed here.

MUSCLE STRAINS AND PULLED TENDONS

In muscle strains, the torn muscle fibres and their blood vessels hemorrhage, resulting in swelling, ecchymosis, and restricted function. In order to prevent the formation of excessive restrictive fibrous scarring when these torn muscles heal, hemorrhage and swelling must be immediately checked with cold applications for no less than 30 minutes and preferably longer, compression bandaging, and elevation where possible. These techniques should be continued at home. Slings, splints, crutches and other supportive measures should be used to rest or limit activity of the other supportive measures should be used to rest or limit activity of the injured part when indicated. Analgesic and anti-inflammatory medication should also be used.

Following these first-aid measures, healing of the injured muscle by the formation of a strong mobile scar is hastened with heat, massage, and gentle exercises if swelling has stopped. Activity is graded until the scar in the muscle is more mature. After the injured muscle has developed maximal flexibility and strength, the athlete is then fit to return to his sport. A protective strapping may be used to prevent reinjury. Premature return to sports can result in reinjury and a chronic problem.

TRAPEZIUS MUSCLE

This is a superficial, large, trapezoidal muscle located on the back of the neck, shoulders, and upper back; it is easily palpated. It has widespread origins from the occiput, ligamentum nuchae, and spinous processes of C7 to D12 and insertions into the clavicle, acromion, and spine of the scapula. Because of its location, the trapezius is intimately associated with movements of the head, neck, shoulder girdle, and arm. Strains of the trapezium occur most frequently in football, wrestling, and gymnastics.

In football, the trapezius muscle may become strained as a result of being suddenly stretched while in a contracted state in a variety of situations. In wrestling, it may result from attempting to break a securely held head-hold. The trapezius may also be strained as a result of a gymnast not flexing his head and neck properly in a forward roll. Tears of this muscle most frequently occur at the angle of the neck and at the clavicular attachments. In boxing, the trapezius may severely strained when a powerful punchs is thrown and misses its target. In this case, the whole muscle may be torn off the spine of the scapula, with severe bleeding.

Pain, tenderness, and swelling at the site of the injury usually depend on the trauma. Frequently, this muscle goes into spasm following injury, causing a kink in the neck, a stiff neck, and even an inability to move the injured shoulder and the upper extremity on the same side. Testing neck movements as well as the different portions of the trapezius muscle against resistance aids in localizing the injury.

Severe strain with marked bleeding requires the immediate application of cold compresses, compression dressings and rest in a sling to stop the hemorrhage. This treatment may be combined with an adhesive strapping and a sling applied between treatment if the shoulder sags on the injured side. Analgesic and anti-inflammatory medication may be given. If swelling is anticipated, cold compresses are continued. If not, cold compresses are replaced by heat application and followed by massage and exercise. The exercise program is graded progressively until normal strength and flexibility are obtained. The sling and adhesive strappings are discarded when the shoulder can be supported normally without discomfort.

ROTATOR CUFF MUSCLES

The subscapularis, teres minor, infraspinatus and supraspinatus muscles are collectively called the "rotator cuff" and envelop the humeral head at their insertions into the humerus. In addition to activating rotation and abduction movements of the shoulder, these muscles also impart strength and stability to the relatively unstable shoulder joint. This effect is accomplished by making the joint snug when these muscles are contracted. These muscles are most frequently strained near their bony insertions into the humerus as a result of a violent contraction of any or all the muscular components during weightlifting or when an athlete falls on an arm or outstretched hand. Football players and baseball pitchers may incur this injury as a result of throwing a football or baseball. Although any of the rotator cuff muscles may tear, the supraspinatus muscle is most frequently injured.

SUPRASPINATUS MUSCLE

In addition to the acute pain and tenderness usually localized to the cuff that is injured, active motion of the shoulder is restricted. Testing abduction of the shoulder against resistance causes increased pain and the arm falls limp to the side.

The immediate first aid is to apply cold compresses to the injured muscle. Rest and support of the injured muscle can be accomplished by an adhesive strapping and a sling. The following day cold packs, massage and gentle exercises are started and then the adhesive strapping and sling are replaced. The supportive strapping and sling can be reapplied daily when rest and restricted activity of the injured muscle and upper extremity are necessary. This regimen is continued until acute symptoms subside. Then heat, massage, and a graded exercise program are started. We use the pendulum exercise holding a 1-pound weight because it is easy to understand and do, and it provides an objective measure of improvement.

Following a pendulum exercise routine, active assistive exercises using a towel and broomstick are recommended. Isometrics and strengthening exercises are later instituted for total rehabilitation of the shoulder. Disability varies from a few days to a few weeks, depending on the sport. An x-ray study of the shoulder is indicated if any bony or periosteal pathology is suspected. Surgical repair is necessary if a complete disruption of the rotator cuff is present.

DELTOID MUSCLE

This large, triangular, and superficially placed muscle fits over the shoulder joint like the cap of a sleeve. It has a widespread origin from the clavicle, acromion, and scapular spine and inserts into the deltoid tuberosity of the humerus. Because this muscle consists of anterior, middle, and posterior parts, it can raise the arm at the shoulder in forward, sideward, and backward directions respectively. The anterior part is most frequently strained, especially in football, when an arm tackle fails to bring the runner down but the force of the speeding runner succeeds in stretching the deltoid muscle without levering the head of the humerus out of the shoulder joint. The middle and posterior deltoid may be strained in any sport following movements of the arm against resistance in the lateral and posterior directions respectively.

Pain, tenderness, swelling, and localization of the pain by the athlete as well as testing active motion of the arm against resistance help to make the diagnosis. The first aid is the same regardless of which part of the deltoid is injured. Cold applications and adhesive strapping support similar to that used for supraspinatus strains may be used with a sling if immobilization is necessary for 24 hours or longer. The exercise program is similar to that described for supraspinatus strain.

INTERCOSTAL MUSCLES

Each side of the rib cage is enclosed by a thin, two-layered sheath of 11 adjacent internal external intercostal muscles that occupy the entire length of the intercostal spaces. Their primary function is to aid in respiration. These muscles lift the ribs during inspiration and may contract during voluntary expiratory efforts. Violent and repeated coughing can cause strain in these muscles.

This muscle injury may be so excruciatingly painful that the athlete restricts his breathing and takes shallow breaths to ease the pain brought on by regular respiratory excursion. At times, an actual tearing can be felt and the athlete may be rendered immobile, afraid to move his trunk or arm because of the pain. Point tenderness is usually present and perhaps even some swelling.

The best treatment is immediate application of an adhesive strapping of the injured part, extending from just beyond the midline in front or from just beyond midline in the back to support the chest and limit the chest excursion. This gives the injured muscle a chance to heal. Cold compresses may be applied to the injured site of the chest muscle for 30 minutes or more; these may be continued at home. The tape should not be removed for 3 to 7 days. The strapping should be reinforced if it starts to pull away at the edges, and may be removed when acute symptoms have subsided. Following removal, moist hot packs, massage, and breathing exercises can be started. The use of rib cage protector may prove beneficial following removal of the tape. Pulmonary problems such as pneumonia may complicate these injuries.

If a rib fracture is suspected, an x-ray picture should be taken of the rib cage. If the x-ray picture do not show a fracture, a follow-up x-ray study should be done in 10 days if the pain in the chest continues. It is not unusual for follow-up x-ray picture to reveal a rib fracture that was not present on the original study.

TENNIS ELBOW

This condition is most frequently seen in tennis players, but is not confined to them. There is no unanimity among authors as to its pathology; it has been variously described as a radio-humeral bursitis, radiohumeral synovitis, epicondylitis and epicondylalgia. This ambiguous pathologic condition may account for a group of clinical conditions that occur about the lateral aspect of the elbow, having a similar onset, symptoms, and signs. In more experienced players, the pain can be felt on the medial side as well. Such conditions have been noted in golfers, fishermen, handball, racquet-ball paddle-ball, badminton, and squash players, pitchers, and others. There is, however, agreement that these ailments stem from the repeated demands of these sports on the elbow, by which it is subjected to sudden, changing, forcible and, at times, unnatural motions. The experts agree that beginner's backhand frequently causes lateral epicondylitis, whereas the advanced player's extremely hard severe can cause medial epicondylitis. Players who use the two-handed backhand develop fewer elbow problems from tennis.

We treat the "tennis elbow" as a localized condition of tendinomyositis of the supinator-extensor group of muscles that arise from the lateral epicondyle of the humerus. We believe this condition occurs in tennis players not only from repeated forceful pronation and supination of the forearm with an extended elbow but also represents the sum of microtraumatic injuries resulting from the complicated biomechanics of gripping a tennis racket, carrying out the stroke, and striking the tennis ball. Not only is it important to put the ball over the net, but it must also be hit to a particular portion of the court, frequently with enough speed and spin to make it difficult and at best, impossible to return. The racket must properly fit the player's hand in order to strike the ball properly.

The proper grip size of a tennis racket will help prevent twisting or knocking the racket out of the hand by the impact of the ball. The best grip is accomplished by a synergistic contraction of the forearm muscles, with the wrist held locked in slight extension and ulnar deviation; this places an additional load on the extensor group of forearm muscles and increases the exposure to trauma. The limb velocity of the stroke, the rotary movements of the forearm during a stroke motion, and the speed of the approaching ball determine the sprains and shocks to which the forearm muscles are subjected, both in their bodies and at their condylar origins. The wrist and elbow joints also share in this trauma, but fortunately are only rarely injured.

Development of the "tennis elbow" is one of the hazards of playing tennis regularly. Faulty stroke mechanics hasten the development of tennis elbow. A spin severe accomplished by wrist flexion and ulnar or radial deviations causes additional tension and strains of the extensor muscle group. The forehand and especially backhand strokes, when converted into forearm pronation and supination respectively during the follow-through to produce spin on the ball, are also conducive to this tennis condition. In the forehand stroke, the elbow ends slightly bent, and in the backhand, the elbow ends extended. Chop or slice strokes, especially backhand slices, place even greater stress on the forearm muscles. In a well-executed stoke, there is only a minimum of movement at the elbow and wrist. The wrist should be flexed in slight extension and in slight ulnar deviation at impact.

Clinically, the athlete complains most commonly of pain or about the lateral epicondyle and in the body of the extensor muscle. The pain may be dull or sharp. Tenderness is usually present about the conjoined tendon of the muscle, and tender areas may also be noted in other muscles about the elbow. The pain in increased by activity and lessened by rest and restricted activity. Pain and weakness radiating down the forearm are commonly experienced when lifting objects with the forearm in pronation and the elbow fully or partially extended. Pain is usually absent when lifting in supination. Testing a dorsiflexed wrist against resistance usually causes pain at the condylar origin of the muscle or in the body itself. Gripping with the forearm pronated causes pain, as when turning a door knob by pronating the hand and opening the door against resistance.

The conservative treatment that was recommended for the tendinomyositis of the muscle arising from the medial epicondyle for baseball pitchers is also indicated for tennis elbow. A counterforce forearm brace is frequently helpful.

Fortunately, prophylactic measures can be taken to prevent these injuries and avoid recurrences. The player must pay proper attention to the selection of a proper racquet and handle size, racquet flexibility and weight, and string tension. The arm and forearm muscles must be exercised to obtain maximal flexibility and strength. In the arm, the brachialis, brachioradialis, and triceps muscles participate more significantly than the biceps. In the forearm, the supinator-extensor muscles and especially the extensor carpi radialis work harder than the pronator-flexor muscles. All of these exercises to develop flexibility and strength are equally useful in handball, paddleball, racquet-ball, and squash. Proper stroke mechanics are essential. Play should cease when fatigue, improper warm-up, illness, or tension states increase the risk of injury. Warm-up with stretching and flexibility exercises prior to practice or competition reduces the incidence and extent of sprains and strains of the musculoskeletal system.

LOW BACK

The lumbar paraspinal muscles are located in the lumbar area of the back. They comprise the large muscle mass located between the spinous and transverse processes of the vertebrae, which even extend beyond the transverse process to cover partly the posterior portion of the thorax. These paraspinal muscles are concerned with extension, lateral bending and rotation of the trunk. They are frequently strained in weight lifting as well as other sports, usually from a lifting incident in which a powerful contraction of these muscles is made against resistance. Movement of the back may or may not accompany this muscular effort. Pain and disability may be felt immediately upon straining, sometimes accompanied by snapping, popping or tearing sounds emanating from the back. However, in many instance the symptoms and abnormal physical findings present themselves the following day or even later. Usually, the pain is localized to one side of the back, and tenderness is felt at the site of the injury. Swelling is not uncommon is most low back strains. The appearance of painful muscle spasm splints the back, adding to the athlete's discomfort and requiring the use of muscle relaxants. Frequently, low back strains are complicated by intervertebral joint sprains.

When a low back has been strained sufficiently to produce pain and disability, some physicians usually apply adhesive tape strapping to the low back if they see the athlete soon after the injury. Bed rest for 48 to 72 hours or longer is mandatory, depending on the severity of the injury. Bed rest is best accomplished in a hospital with a board under a firm mattress. However, this may be impractical, so conscientious bed rest on a firm mattress at home and bathroom privileges only are acceptable. Analgesics and muscle relaxants must be prescribed. After the acute symptomatology has lessened, the tape is removed and heat, massage and gentle back exercises may be started. Electrical stimulation of muscles combined with ultrasound may be used if pain or muscle spasm does not lessen with hand massage. This apparatus works well with trigger points and painful muscle spasm in the low back. When the athlete has regained a full range of back mobility and muscle strength, he is ready to return to the game.

GROIN

The adductor group of muscles located on the medial aspect of the thigh and the iliopsoas muscles amount for the bulk of groin strains that occur in athletics. The following muscles comprise the adductor group: adductor magnus, adductor longus, gracilis, adductor brevis, and pectineus. Because of their origin from either the pubic or ischial rami and their insertion into the femoral shaft, their principal action is to adduct the thigh and hip; however, these muscles perform additional movements, depending on the degree of hip flexion. For example, the adductor magnus muscle is able to inwardly rotate the hip. This is used in such actions as "stemming" in skiing and gripping the sides of a horse while riding.

The iliopsoas muscle is comprised of the psoas major and the iliacus muscles. These muscles have separate origins but a common insertion. The psoas muscle arises from the anterior surfaces of the transverse processes, the sides of the vertebral bodies and the corresponding intervertebral biscs from T12 to L5. This muscle runs distally in the posterior wall of the abdomen to the iliac fossa, where it joins the iliacus muscle that arises here. Together they insert into the lesser trochanter of the femur, acting as flexors and internal rotators of the hip joint. Acting alone, the psoas major can flex and laterally bend the lumbar spine.

Although pulled groin muscles occur most frequently in running sports, they do occur in other sports. There muscles are strained either as a result of stretching a contracted muscle or an over-contraction mechanism. In horse riders who become unbalanced, these muscles become strained in the process of overcontracting to maintain equilibrium. Gymnasts who land heavily on parallel bars in a straddle position often strain the adductors.

The weather plays a decided influence in the incidence of these injuries. In rainy weather, hyperabduction and hyperextension movements of the hip because of slipper footing result in ground pulls. When an athlete is insufficiently warmed-up in cold weather, quick change in direction, such as a lineman pulling out, results in similar hip movements and groin injuries. *Characteristically,* this injury is seen early in football practice and in early basketball season. Fatigue, poor posture, uneven muscle strength, poor flexibility, and overstretching are the primary causes leading to such strains.

Most athletes find this injury disturbing because of its location and interference with mobility. The presenting complaint may be pain or tightness in the groin. Usually the injury can be localized by palpating the point of maximal tenderness. With the athlete in a supine position, testing the hip against resistance primarily in flexion and adduction helps localize the injured muscle because of increased pain and weakness. The hip is also tested in abduction and extension to determine the status of the muscles concerned with those movements. A complete tear of the origin of one of the adductor muscles can produce a painful lump in the groin which should not be confused with an inguinal hernia.

Treatment is started to check hematoma by use of ice therapy and the application of a single hip spica compression bandage with the hip in 10 to 15° flexion. Bed rest and limitation of activity until all bleeding has ceased is mandatory. The use of moist hot packs or whirlpool may be started on the second or third day provided this does not start the bleeding again. When the symptoms subside, the athlete may be allowed to resume activities gradually.

The activity of the athlete is determined by his response to treatment. His progress should be evaluated daily. The supportive groin bandaging enables the athlete to move about and even run without pain. It prevents further tearing of the injured groin muscles, and should be continued until the athlete has achieved the maximal benefits from treatment.

If an avulsion fracture of the lesser trochanteric or any other sites of muscle attachments to bone in the groin are suspected, x-ray studies should be made.

QUADRICEPS

This muscle has already been adequately described. Because of its function and location it is easily strained in sprinters and hurdles. However, this injury is not confined to track and field athletes, but may experienced in all sports when a violent contraction or injuries stretch of this muscle occurs during an athletic activity.

Although pain usually depends on the severity of the injury, in general, quadriceps pulls are not as painful as hamstring pulls. The initial step is to control the bleeding with ice therapy and a compression wrap.

For functional testing of the injured quadriceps, and treatment, including the supportive strapping.

HAMSTRING

This is a powerful group of three posterior femoral muscles located on the lateral, posterior, and medial aspects of the thigh. They arise from the ischial tuberosity and insert on the lateral and medial aspects of the lower leg. One of these muscles is the biceps femoris, also known as the lateral hamstring. This is made up of two parts: a long head that arises from the ischial tuberosity, which is joined by a short head that stems from the back of the femur. Together the two heads combine and insert into the head of the fibula and lateral condyle of the tibia. The medial hamstring consists of the semitendinosus muscle, which also arises from the ischial tuberosity and inserts on the medial aspects of the tibia near the knee joint. The semi-membranosus is the other muscle of the medial hamstring group, which also arises from the ischial tuberosity and inserts into the medial condyle, of the tibia. These muscles act as powerful flexors and rotators of the knee; they can also act as hip extensors.

Hamstring pulls are most commonly seen in any of the running sports, especially in track and field competition. Sprinters who uncoil off their starting blocks with maximal effort may pull up lame as a result of a pulled hamstring. This injury may also occur when a runner makes a determined effort to overtake a competitor. Thus, these muscle pulls are appropriately called "sprinter's strain." Swimmers also suffer from hamstring pulls, but not of the intensity experienced by trackmen. Swimmers develop their injuries as a result of a maximal push-off from their starting blocks. Unlike trackmen, football players, and others, swimmers can continue to swim because their main leg effort is powered by the quadriceps and calf muscles. In track, however, the athlete may drop to the ground because of the severity of the pain or may limp to a halt.

The injury occurs anywhere in the muscle, but most frequently it is located at or near the ischial tuberosity. In addition to the pain, swelling and ecchymosis may also appear, depending on the location and extent of the injury. Careful palpation will localize the point of greatest tenderness. The injured muscle usually goes into spasm. Contraction of the hamstring while testing for knee flexion against resistance produces pain and helps localize the site of the injury. A straight leg raising test, with the athlete in a supine position with the knee extended, also aids in determining the site and severity of the injury.

If the injury is a minor one, the use of cold compresses, compression dressing and restricted activity for 24 hours may be sufficient. This is followed by moist hot packs, hand massage, and a supportive adhesive strapping for a few days.

If the injury is moderate or severe, immediate treatment consists of continuous ice therapy, compression bandaging, bed rest, elevation, analgesics, and anti-inflammatory medications. A painful lump may develop. Bed rest is continued until bleeding has stopped. Ambulation is done with crutches and no weight-bearing is permitted until active knee motion can be done without pain. Physical therapy consisting of moist hot packs or whirlpool treatment and active range-or-motion exercise for the knee is started after all bleeding has stopped.

A supportive strapping to the back of the thigh may be used as part of the therapeutic program as well as prevention of re-injury. Because recurrence is not infrequent, resumption of activity depends on the extent of the injury and the response to treatment. Return to competition may be achieved by graded activity to normal flexibility and strength.

SHIN SPLINTS

This is a unique ailment of the lower leg peculiar to athletics. Although there is no unanimity as to the pathologic disorder, clinically the diagnosis presents no difficulty. Trackmen in both outdoor and indoor seasons, basketball, football and baseball players, and divers have their share of shin splints. This injury is usually associated with running and jumping on hard surface or running on uneven terrain, as in cross-country. Clinically, pain and tenderness are experienced in the muscles that hug the tibia on all its surfaces. If the foreleg pain is not too intense, the athlete may become aware of aches and pains in various sites of the foot. There is pain in the lower leg accompanied with ankle restriction when the foot is dorsiflexed.

We consider this condition a painful and disabling overuse syndrome of the lower leg usually localized along the inner distal 2/3 of the tibia. It is caused by a strain of the anterior and/or posterior tibial muscles where they hug the tibial shaft and attach to the interosseous membrane. These muscles react in this manner because of a variety of biomechanical factors such as poor conditioning, running on hard surfaces, banked tracks, or shoulder of the road, malalignment problems, hyperpronation of the feet, and others. These cause repetitive abnormal pulls of the tendons and periosteal attachments of these muscles on the bone and interosseous membrane. Initially, a tendonitis develops that, if unsuccessfully treated, may become a chronic periostitis. This is usually seen at the beginning of a training cycle.

Most athletes describe a dull ache in the shin of the lower leg that can be steady or intermittent and increasing to a sharp pain upon activity that is severe enough to completely disable an athlete. Symptoms vary with the athletes. Some complain of a tenderness when the sore or painful area is palpated. Some complain of swelling that if present is only minimal by examination. Walking, especially on stairs, may increase pain. Ankle motion may or may not affect pain. Resistance to inversion and plantar flexion of foot and ankle usually causes increased pain. The symptoms of shin splints are numerous and as varied as the athletes who complain of them.

Treatment initially includes rest, cryotherapy, and application of elastic bandaging of he entire lower leg including foot held in a neutral position. Physicians use ultrasound therapy, which reduces the pain within the muscles. An orthotic device such as an arch support when indicated has been helpful. When symptoms subside, the athlete should return to running on soft, level surfaces, wearing proper shoes and an orthotic device when indicated.

If pain and disability continue, diagnostic steps must be taken to rule in or out subacute compartment syndromes and stress fracture of the tibia. At that point, proper therapeutic steps are instituted.

TENNIS LEG

The calf of the lower leg is composed of the gastrocnemius, soleus, and plantaris muscles. The last arises just above the lateral condyle of the femur. It has a small belly and a long ribbon-like tendon that runs between the fleshy triceps surae muscles and inserts with the tendo Achilles into the posterior part of the so calcis. There is agreement that this injury results from a violent dorsiflexion of the foot with the knee extended or a single violent contraction of the calf muscle as the player rises on his toes to serve or start running, injuring the medial gastrocnemius.

Another mechanism that can use this injury results from minimal traumatic forces. This occurs when leg muscles tensed to move an athlete in one direction are reflexly and suddenly changed because new visual stimuli require an automatic move into a different direction. The requires activation of antagonistic muscles, resulting in an uncoordinated movement.

Physicians believe that any of the aforementioned mechanisms may cause a rupture of the medial gastrocnemius, which accounts for the sharp pain deep in the calf that is frequently associated with an audible pop or snap. The athlete often relates that the calf felt as if it were hit with a baseball bat. Increased pain is felt because of vascular impairment. A heel elevation may be helpful.

The pain is acute, localized, and intense. Immediate limping occurs. The athlete avoids walking running or rising up on his toes because increased pain results. The calf swells. Careful palpation will localize the point of acute tenderness-this is the site of injury. Ecchymosis is not infrequently present. Testing for plantar flexion of the ankle reveals restricted activity and pain. Tear of the medial gastrocnemius should be carefully distinguished from acute phlebitis and ruptured. Achilles tendon, which is an acute surgical emergency.

Treatment consists of cold compresses, physical therapy, compression bandaging, elevation, and crutches. Physical therapy consists of whirlpool, massage, and gentle active exercises. Combined electrical stimulation and ultrasound may also be used. In most cases, early ambulation with taping is most effective. The tape is changed every 3 or 4 days. Plaster cast immobilization is applied only in severe cases, since the resulting disuse atrophy and muscle weakness present additional problems in rehabilitation and duration of disability.

Tennis shoes with proper medial and counter supports must be selected and flexibility and strengthening exercises of the lower extremities must be done prophylactically to minimize the risk of lower leg ankle, and foot injuries.

PULLED ACHILLES TENDON

The gastrocnemius and soleus muscles join about the middle of the back of the foreleg to form the Achilles tendon, which runs distally to insert in the posterior portion of the so calcis. Not only do these muscles chiefly provide the propelling force of locomotion, but this force is enhanced by the excellent leverage provided by the posterior projection of the so calcis. Because this tendon is the thickest and strongest in the body, it is pulled much more frequently than ruptured. The musculotendinous junction is strained more frequently than at the bony insertion. However, both strains are quite painful and disabling.

Cryotherapy, compression bandaging, elevation, and rest are started immediately to check swelling and to minimize the formation of a painful scar. In mild injuries, an adhesive tape strapping helps considerably. The use of whirlpool, massage, and gentle active exercise is started, usually on the second day, to achieve healing without the formation of a painful scar. Rest and limited activity of this part aid considerably in lessening the formation of scar. Stretching of the tendon after pain has subsided prevents contractures of the muscle and recurrence. Crutches should be used if ambulation is too painful.

A substantial extrinsic overload force is usually required to cause a rupture of this tendon. However, rupture may occur with minimal trauma if local degenerative processes of attrition following years of competitive demand are already present in the tendon. A ruptured tendon is usually obvious clinically by a deformity in the contours of the tendon. A defect or gap between the ruptured ends may be palpated, associated with a Thompson test, which is positive when manual compression of an injured calf does not result in ankle plantar flexion. Pain, tenderness and swelling frequently accompany this injury. Rupture is best treated in the hospital with either surgical repair or plaster cast immobilization in plantar flexion.

FOOT STRAIN

This condition, as expected, is seen more frequently in running sports. It gives rise to essentially the same signs and symptoms of painful flatfoot. However, flatfoot and other static conditions are frequently absent. The size, shape, contours and static deformities in the feet, if present, usually have no bearing on a young athlete's performance unless the feet have been injured forcibly or gradually.

There is no unanimity concerning the pathology of this condition among physicians conversant with athletic medicine. However, most agree that this is a painful and disabling condition that requires treatment. We believe that this condition results from an overstretching of the plantar structure of the foot due to an overuse syndrome.

Although the plantar and spring ligaments may be injured, the plantar fascia bears the real brunt of this injury. These bands are overstretched either by a severe direct force or by a cumulative effect of repeated strains. Weakening of this plantar structure predisposes to the traumatic injury of these tissues. The plantar fascia is made up of spindle-shaped fibres that break like bamboo when subjected to sufficient stress. An inflammatory reaction results with hemorrhage and swelling. The ends of the torn fascial fibres curl up and become painful and tender nodules on the plantar surface of the foot which are palpable when the foot is dorsiflexed. The plantar fascia may go into spasm and stand out cord-like on the sole of the foot. There are two types of predisposing factors: (1) intrinsic, such as that caused by latent development, overweight or a malfunctional problem; (2) extrinsic and traumatic, such as that caused by improperly fitted shoes or by landing on the tarsus instead of the ball of the foot. Excessive demands made on these feet before they are conditioned to the task invariably bring on the strain syndrome.

Clinically, both feet are usually affected, but the amount of pain and discomfort may vary between feet. There are multiple areas of pain and tenderness located on the plantar surface of the foot. Ecchymosis may occasionally be present. Weight-bearing is painful and causes a limp. Stiffness of the foot may also cause a limp. The calf muscles may shorten secondarily and not infrequently develop cramps, which also occur in the foot. The painful and tender elongated fascial nodules and the spastic plantar fascia have already been described.

First-aid treatment with cold compresses locally for 30 minutes or more is started to check the swelling. If the pain is great and weight-bearing is too painful, crutches should be provided the athlete, who is given instructions not to bear weight on the injured foot. If the pain is severe, bed rest is prescribed until acute pain has subsided. Adhesive tape rest straps for the foot are recommended. The tape starts at the metatarsal phalangeal joints and is taped to the plantar surface of the foot, with the ends crossing each other over dorsum of the foot. The tape extends to the insertion of the plantar fascia into the os clacis. This can be removed daily and reapplied after whirlpool and massage. Manipulation of the foot also contributes to relief. The adhesive strapping is continued until the acute condition subsides. Some physicians and trainers use felt pads secured to the long arch; this is unnecessary once the pain has subsided and the athlete has exercised his weak and strained muscle back to normal strength and flexibility. X-ray films of the foot are taken to rule in or rule out stress fractures or other bony or periosteal disorders.

COMMON MUSCLE CONTUSIONS

These are minor injuries that are common to all sports; in training room jargon they are known as bruises. Contusions occur in all the muscles described in the section on muscle strains as well as other muscles of the body vulnerable to blow. They heal in 1 to 7 days, depending on the number of muscle fibres and blood vessels injured and the hemorrhage that ensures. Optimal healing can be achieved by minimizing hemorrhage with cold compresses and compression dressings for 24 to 48 hours. Rest and restricted activity of the injured part and elevation where feasible are also indicated. The following day, physical therapy consisting of heat, whirlpool where feasible, hand massage and gentle active exercise are started to facilitate the absorption of the traumatic exudate. Electrical muscle stimulation and ultrasound may be used with contusions of deep muscles. Muscle relaxants may be prescribed if painful muscle spasm is present. Slings, splints, crutches, appropriate protective pads, adhesive tape strapping, or elastic bandage wrapping should be used to immobilize and rest the injured part. Supportive strapping may be used to prevent re-injury.

SHOULDER POINTER

This injury results from a direct blow to the top of the shoulder in the area of the acromioclavicular joint and the adjacent deltoid and trapezius muscles. It is seen mainly in football when the shoulder pad does not fit or is worn improperly. This condition may be confused with a minor acromioclavicular joint injury, but it can be distinguished from joint injury in that the pain, tenderness and swelling are noted in the lateral fibres of the deltoid and the middle fibres of the trapezius muscles, and no demonstrable laxity occurs at the acromioclavicular joints.

These injuries respond satisfactorily with ice compresses, shoulder cap adhesive strapping, and the use of sling for a few days. Complete restoration is aided by moist hot packs, massage, and active exercises of the injured area. Re-injury can be prevented by the use of a properly fitted shoulder pad overlying a foam rubber pad taped to the injured area. The athlete should be ready to return to competition in less than a week.

HIP POINTER

This injury results from a contusion to the iliac crest and the insertions of the anterior and lateral abdominal muscles. It is seen most frequently in football following a blow to this superficial exposed area because of an improperly fitted hip pad. A hip pointer is a more painful and disabling condition to treat than a shoulder pointer because the insertions of the anterior and lateral trunk muscles are further strained with forward, lateral, and rotary trunk movements. Increased intra-abdominal pressure brought on by coughing, sneezing, or laughing also aggravates these injured muscles.

Treatment is directed to comforting the athlete and checking the swelling. The application of an adhesive tape strapping not only restricts the activity of the area, but also aids in compression. Cryotherapy is applied directly to the injured area followed by strapping. Bed rest for one to several days is certainly helpful in restricting and limiting activity. The use of analgesic and anti-inflammatory medication and injections of local anesthesia and corticosteroids are indicated depending on the severity of the injury. Heat and active exercise may be used after the acute symptoms have diminished. Whirlpool baths can also be used. However, following return to competition, the iliac crest must be protected by a sponge rubber pad and regulation hip pads that fit properly.

LOW BACK

Because of its incapacitating nature, contusion of the low back may cause immediate cessation of play. It is not unusual for an athlete to sink to the ground or stay on his feet with his trunk half-flexed. In both instance, the athlete usually puts his hand on his back to protect it against further injury. This type of injury usually follows a kick or hard blow to the back. In addition to the soft tissue injury, it is necessary to check out any suspected bony injury by x-ray study. Kidney involvement can be evaluated clinically and by urinalysis. Pain, tenderness, and painfully restricted trunk motion are usually present. Hematoma and ecchymosis are present if the blow is hard enough.

Because of the disabling nature of the injury, we believe in immediated bed rest that aids in reducing pain. The pressure of the back on the mattress also aids in preventing swelling. Analgesics and muscle relaxants are prescribed for painful muscle spasm, which is usually present. When pain and spasm have lessened, active exercises may be started in bed and gradually increased until maximal restoration of muscle strength and flexibility have been obtained. As soon as hemorrhage has been controlled, heat and light massage are given to the low back. The use of the whirlpool baths, electrical muscle stimulation, and ultrasound for low-back muscle injuries has been especially useful in achieving optimal results. Conscientious bed rest at home on a firm mattress and bathroom privileges are acceptable, but the athlete must be warned against abusing the privilege of not being under the direct surveillance of the medial and coaching staff while at home. However, his progress will indicate how honest he has been in following orders.

If moderate to severe back pain persists, x-ray may be necessary to rule out fractures, especially of the transverse processes.

CHARLEY HORSE

This is a common disabling condition in athletics seen predominantly in contact sports such as football, soccer, basketball, and field hockey; it usually follows a direct blow to the anterior thigh. Depending on the magnitude of the blow, this force either contuses or crushes the entire soft tissue contents of the anterior compartment of the thigh against the femur. This happens frequently in football when the front of an athlete's thigh is struck a blow by another player's head, shoulder, knee, or foot. A loose or improperly fitted thigh pad increases the likelihood of such an injury. Although the brunt of the trauma is borne by the quadriceps muscles, resulting in the rupture of a varying number of muscle fibres and their blood vessels, the subcutaneous tissue with its frailly supported fat cells and blood vessels are concomitantly traumatized as well. This adds to the hemorrhage and ecchymotic discoloration at the site of injury.

Some authors state that a "charley horse" may occur in muscles other than the quadriceps and may also follow a tear or rupture of muscle fibres as result of violent muscular contraction. Although there is no unanimity about the mechanism of injury, there is agreement on the treatment.

The quadriceps muscle, consisting of the rectus femoris, vastus inter-medius, vastus lateralis, and vastus medialis, is a large fleshy muscle that covers the front of the thigh and spans the hip; it activates two joints. Because it is a hip flexor as well as a knee extensor, it is an important antigravity muscle vital to maintaining the erect position. This has been discussed earlier in this chapter. When the muscle is contused, the severity of the condition is directly proportionate to the number of muscular fibres and blood vessels ruptured and the amount of hemorrhage and traumatic exudate that escapes. The thigh becomes swollen, painful, and diffusely tender. Limping is an expected sign, and running is not attempted.

The hemorrhagic exudate in the thigh may become organized during the process of repair and takeon a stone-like consistency when palpated. Active contraction of the quadriceps is quite painful, causing the athlete to avoid actively extending or lifting the leg or having the quadriceps stretched passively when the knee is bent. The quadriceps may even go into spasm reflexly following the blow to it.

The trainer takes a complete history, placing emphasis on the mechanism of the injury. If the thigh muscle became painful while running in the absence of direct trauma, the athlete probably "pulled" the muscle rather than suffering a "charley horse." The trainer makes a careful examination, looking for swelling, deformities, and ecchymosis. He compares the injured limb with the normal one. He gently palpates for tenderness, muscle spasm, and contour changes in the muscle, and gently tests the range of hip and knee motion in a supine and prone position. These movements stretch the quadriceps muscle, and if it was injured, pain is elicited and knee motion is restricted. If the knee has almost a normal range of motion, the injury may be treated in the same manner described for usual contusions and strains. If the knee bends 90° or less in either a supine or prone position, the athlete has suffered a moderately or severe contusion of the thigh.

The first-aid treatments that the trainer renders are the same as for other injuries of the musculoskeletal system-rest, compression, and ice. In this case, the application of cryotherapy for 30 minutes intervals to the injured thigh is followed by elastic compression bandaging. The elastic bandage is applied in a spiral manner from groin to knee. With minor and mild contusions, the athlete may wait until the following day to consult with the team doctor.

However, he should continue to apply ice packs at home during the night. With moderate or severe contusions to the thigh, some trainers use large pieces of sponge rubber pads to aid in the compression. The athlete should be given a pair of crutches with instructions to avoid weight-bearing on the injured leg. He is instructed to see the doctor the same day.

For moderate or severe contusions, we believe in complete bed rest at home or preferably in the hospital for 7 to 10 days or longer, depending on the extent of the injury. Continuous ice packs, elastic compression dressings and leg elevation for 48 hours are ordered. Analgesics and anti-inflammatory medications are prescribed. Muscle relaxants are prescribed when indicated. Bathroom privileges with crutches and no weight-bearing on the injured leg are permitted. As soon as pain, swelling and tenderness have been significantly reduced, physical therapy to the injured leg can be started in 72 hours. This consists of moist hot packs or whirlpool to the injured leg for 30 minutes followed by light massage. Ultrasonic therapy may be substituted for massage, either following moist hot packs or while the leg is immersed in the whirlpool bath.

Active exercises of he quadriceps to pain tolerance are encouraged hourly for 5 minutes throughout the waking day. Movement of the adjacent joints may be started when this does not cause pain and should be done along with the exercise routine. Progressive-resistance exercises for the quadriceps muscle may also be used in the manner previously described for insufficiency of this muscle. The use of a stationary bicycle with controls for wheel resistance is beneficial in helping to obtain a full range of knee motion and muscular strength. This treatment is continued until all the soreness and hardness has disappeared from the quadriceps and a full range of knee motion and normal muscular strength has been obtained. Swimming is helpful in the rehabilitation of these injuries, commencing by walking through waist-high water and progressing to swimming.

The attending physician examines the injured leg daily to determine its progress. He also guards against resumption of bleeding during this active and vigorous treatment, and is on the lookout for myositis ossificans, which frequently complicates these injuries. He decides when the athlete is fit to return to competition. The athlete is not allowed to bear weight until he can extend his knee against a resistance of 10 to 15 pounds. He must not compete until he has obtained normal range of knee motion and quadriceps strength.

Since a number of these condition result from blows to thighs that are inadequately protected by thigh pads that are too small or have shifted in position, re-injury can be prevented by taping the pad directly to the thigh. If a larger pad is necessary, it can be fashioned from rigid material that is contoured to the injured thigh and secured with adhesive tape.

MYOSITIS OSSIFICANS

This complication is seen not infrequently following a severe blow to the anterior thigh muscles, thigh adductors and brachialis and others. When an injured quadriceps fails to respond in 3 to 4 weeks, myositis ossificans should be suspected. This is accompanied by pain, tenderness, swelling, and induration of the anterior thigh muscles. Restricted knee bending and especially straightening usually provide ample evidence that some calcium has been deposited in this injured muscle. Early x-ray pictures will show linear calcific streaks, which later coalesce and mature into a mass with bony density. This accounts for the persistent signs and symptoms. When this condition is diagnosed, all physical therapy is stopped. An elastic bandage is applied about the injured thigh.

The athlete is placed on crutches with no weight-bearing permitted on the injured leg. Isometric exercises to the point of pain are encouraged. Knee motion is started to pain tolerance. Treatment is directed toward reduction of pain, cessation of bleeding and maintenance of muscle tone. Maturation of the bony mass may take as long as 12 months.

MUSCLE SPASMS AND MUSCLE CRAMPS

The outstanding physiologic characteristics of muscle function are its ability to contract to stimuli and overcome resistance, its ability to yields to passive stretch, and its ability to relax and give up its tension. These basic properties of muscle function are integrated and coordinated to permit reciprocal contraction-relaxation of opposing muscles and activation of adjacent joints.

When a muscle responds to a stimulus, it reacts by contracting a sufficient number of muscle fibres to move or stabilize a musculotendinous unit to overcome or resist the presenting resistance. Such a reaction is initiated by the muscle's sensory organ or muscle spindle. A discussion of muscle spindle structure and function is beyond the scope of this book. If a greater amount of work is to be done, an increased number of muscle fibres are brought into play. This gradation of muscle contraction is made possible by the recruitment of a number of activate motor neurons. Motor neurons are nerve cells located in the anterior horn of the spinal cord that innervate the skeletal muscle fibre by a motor nerve. Normal motor performance depends on the right degree of motor neuron activation; the latter depends on the correct balance between excitatory and inhibitory influences impinging upon the motor nerve pool.

Trauma, dietary deficiencies, drugs, fatigue, fasciculating illness, myotonic disorders, nerve-root irritation, and psychic stress may interfere with or eliminate this balance and cause muscle spasms or cramps that are quite disabling.

In athletics, painful muscle spasm most frequently results from an acutre injury, which need not be severe, or fatigue. The pain resulting from trauma irritates the lower motor neurons, and this leads to reflex protective muscle spasm that splints and limits painful motion of an adjacent joint. The muscle spasm also may become painful, to set up a vicious pain-spasm pain cycle. Injuries to the neck, shoulder, low back and legs frequently cause painful muscle spasm of the area musculature. Treatment is directed toward correcting the disturbances of the sensory-motor reflex arc. This is done with surface anesthesia, injections, muscle relaxants, moist hot packs, cold packs and electrotherapy. Gentle active motion to pain tolerance accompanies this treatment.

Painful hypertonic muscle contractions that lead to cramps are listed as follows:

1. Fasciculating illness.
2. Myotonic disorders.
3. Metabolic disorders.
4. Psychogenic cramps.

The classification takes into account the diversity of cramps and the varying mechanisms responsible for their appearance. However, this grouping, except for No. 3, does not encompass or explain the appearance of this common athletic occurrence in the healthy athlete.

No athlete is immune to this usually short-lived and disabling condition. The occurrence of cramps in athletics usually results from the following causes:

1. Loss of salt as a result of excessive sweating.
2. Hyperventilation, causing a carbon dioxide gas loss and respiratory alkalosis.
3. Fatigued state leading to an inability to relax.
4. Circulatory impairment resulting from a tight supportive strap, improperly fitted equipment or shoes.
5. Without any apparent reason.

The following additional circumstances may be associated with the development of cramps:

1. Overstretched and tight muscles anywhere in the musculoskeletal system.

2. Overwork in early season when there is a lack of physical conditioning.

3. A sudden, sharp blow causing intense pain and temporary cramp.

4. Assuming unnatural positions, such as standing at attention for a prolonged period of time.

5. Loss of potassium as a result of urination.

6. Loss or dietary deficiency of other trace elements such as MG, ZN, and CHR.

In the prevention and treatment of cramps, elimination of the cause is the primary consideration. For instance, it is well known that abdominal cramps may occur if a swimmer eats shortly before competing the implications should be obvious. In cases of excessive sweating with loss of salt, replacement of salt is indicated. Cramps may result from respiratory alkalosis as a result of overexertion in long distance and cross-country running; this can be corrected only by conditioning.

Although cramps are experienced more frequently in the legs, breast strokes can relate many occurrences of cramped cupped hands following trying competition. It is not unusual to see an athlete who is running stop short because of a cramped calf; however, swimmer who maintain their feet in marked plantar flexion while doing a flutter kick instead of using a loose ankle also suffer calf cramps quite similar to those of athletes running on the ground.

CHAPTER-13

TREATMENT AND CARE OF FRACTURES AND DISLOCATIONS

The third largest group of athletic injuries includes fractures and dislocations. Fortunately, the incidence of these injuries is relatively low, although the athlete who suffers such an injury could not care less about this low incidence. He is concerned only with getting well quickly and back into the game.

Diagnosis and treatment offer no great problem in most fractures. Since so many excellent texts cover the diagnosis, treatment and rehabilitation of fractures and dislocations, these topics are discussed only in general terms. However, the reaction of athletes to these types of injuries requires some discussion because they differ considerably from patients usually seen in a medical practice.

An athlete seems not to be aware that treatment and healing varies with the bone that is fractured or the joint that is dislocated. Because of his youthful exuberance, impatience, and excellent potential for restoration, he expects a quick and miraculous recovery, whether he is unable to ambulate because of a fractured ankle or unable to use his shoulder because it is dislocated. In addition to the overt demands and expectations made by the injured athlete on the doctor and the trainer, other pressures, some subtle and some not so subtle, are exerted by the athletic director, the coach and even the parents to accelerate the treatment and heal the athlete in less time than the specialized structures normally need to heal. These lay sources may even offer medical recommendations, usually citing the use of a well-known product or technique. To assist our readers in warding off the questions, suggestions and pressures that are sure to follow fractures and dislocations, some general principles are covered.

A WORD OF CAUTION

Attending physician must have a high index of suspicion of fractures at unusual sites and in particular should look for avulsion fractures. In some cases, the patient oftenly reported an avulsion fracture of the lesser trochanter caused by the contraction of the iliopsoas muscle in the jacknifing motion of serving in tennis that was missed for 14 months despite examinations by four orthopedists and four radiologists. Dependence on x-ray pictures and not on clinical tests, such as a Ludluff's sign, inability to flex the hip while in a sitting position, or the presence of swelling or ecchymosis or both at the base of Scarpa's triangle, leaves reason to believe that the attending physicians did not suspect such a fracture. Unfortunately, by not resting sufficiently, the patient was left with a chronic condition.

In athletics, the major dislocations involves the shoulder, elbow, and ankles. These should be immobilized for no less than 4 weeks to allow satisfactory healing of the torn ligamentous and capsular tissues. The high incidence of recurrences in shoulder dislocations has already been noted.

When an extremity is encased in a plaster cast or dressing, atrophy of the muscles of the immobilized limb is certain to follow even when an athlete makes a vigorous effort to exercise the restricted muscles. The middle fibres of the deltoid and the quadriceps muscle of the thigh atrophy rapidly when the upper and lower extremities, respectively, are immobilized. When the shoulder, arm, or forearm are casted or immobilized with a Velpeau dressing or a sling and swathe, vigorous isometric exercises of the muscles of these parts must be started as soon as the pain subsides. After the period of immobilization, Codman exercises for the injured shoulder provide both isotonic and stretching exercises aided by the force of gravity. This increases the range of motion of the shoulder as well as strengthening of the muscles about the shoulder.

When the lower extremity is immobilized in plaster, the antigravity muscles atrophy more rapidly in size and strength than the other muscles of the leg. This is the price they pay for escaping so late from their evolutionary bonds. Active isometric exercises of all the muscles of the immobilized limb are started as soon as the pain subsided. However, greater emphasis is directed to the quadriceps than the other muscles. If only the lower leg is encased, the quadriceps is still vigorously exercised as well as the calf and anterior leg muscles. The joints that are not immobilized are also put through a range-of-motion exercise. These maintain the strength, shape, and size of the restricted muscles and minimize the limp after the cast is removed.

BURSITIS

This is an inflammation of the bursal sac that causes pain and swelling. The most common sites of bursitis in athletics are the shoulder, knee area, and hell. X-ray study of these sites before starting therapy rules out or confirms the presence of any bony, periosteal, or soft tissue disorder.

SUBDELTOID OR SUBACROMIAL BURSITIS

This bursa is composed of an upper subacromial portion, located beneath the upper end of the deltoid muscle and acromion, and a larger subdeltoid part, which is located over the greater tuberosity and rotator cuff and is also covered by the deltoid. This bursa is interposed between the deltoid muscle and the acromion and the humeral head and the rotator cuff; it is frequently inflamed in baseball and basketball players as a result of excessive repetitive throwing motions. Other athletes may relate a history of injury to the shoulder area by a direct blow or a fall on an outstretched hand or point of the shoulder.

In acute cases, the player complains of severe shoulder pain that becomes worse with any shoulder movement, either active or passive. Shoulder motion is moderately restricted, especially abduction and internal rotation. If the bursa is markedly distended, it may cause swelling of the shoulder.

These are progressively increased until range-of-motion exercises, such as Codman, ladder climb, and shoulder wheel exercises, can be done to pain tolerance. For those athletes who cannot tolerate cold therapy, Hydrocollator packs, ultrasound and electrical muscle stimulation, and a sling may be used instead, along with the therapeutic exercises. Some physicians inject the site of maximal tenderness with a local anesthetic combined with a corticosteroid. However, I reserve this type of treatment for acute exacerbations of chronic cases that usually show some x-ray therapy may give considerable relief and must be remembered as an effective mode of therapy.

PREPATELLAR BURSITIS

This bursa lies between the skin and the patella. Bursitis at this site results frequently in football and soccer players from direct blows or falls on the knees. To a lesser extent, it is also seen in hurdlers. Prepatellar bursal swelling characterizes the injury, along with redness, warmth, and tenderness. Pain and discomfort may develop along with bursal distention. The swelling is usually localized directly over the front of the patella, but may extend beyond these limits. The knee joint is practically never involved. This condition must be examined, diagnosed and a course of treatment prescribed by a physician.

The immediate treatment in acute injuries is the application of an ice compress followed by a compression bandage, continued until swelling has been checked. Although swelling may continue is spite of such measures, it is considerably lessened. Pain and discomfort are also diminished.

A sizable effusion extending beyond the confines of the patella usually warrants hospitalization, where repeated aspirations can be performed with strict asepsis.

RETROCALCANEAL BURSITIS

This bursa is situated between the postero-superior surface of the clacaneus and the tendo Achilles. It frequently becomes inflamed from friction and pressure caused by ill-fitting shoes. Retrocalcaneal bursitis also stems from kicks to this site and tight heel cords. The athlete complains of pain and discomfort in the back of the heel, which increases with motion and is usually eliminated with no weight-bearing.

This condition must be examined and diagnosed by the physician. In acute cases, complete rest, whirlpool and ultrasound therapy are effective. Raising the bursa above the level of the shoe by the use of sponge rubber heel inside the shoe eliminates the pressure and friction of the shoe counter on the bursa. A full-length molded insert arch placed inside a regular shoe to distribute the weight over the entire foot sometimes helps. If the condition does not respond to treatment, the bursa may be injected with a combination of local anethetic and corticosteroid once weekly for 3 weeks. This and other foot disorders are on the rise with the present boom in running and jogging.

PART 8

PHYSICAL EDUCATION— A HANDBOOK FOR TEACHERS

1

INTRODUCTION TO PHYSICAL EDUCATION

PHYSICAL EDUCATION IN THE BEGINNING

Physical education in the nineteenth century presents a dismal picture of drill masters, ustads and superannuated army gymnasts who knew very little of modified Swedish gymnastics and nothing more than what the army had taught them for the conditioning of uncultured adult recruits. No serious effort was made either by the Government or the educational authorities to the question of health, efficiency and harmonious development of the whole man.

ADVENT OF PHYSICAL EDUCATION ON OUR SOIL

With the dawn of the twentieth century, the first rays of light shone upon this continent to enlighten people of the importance of physical fitness and a scientific physical education. It was the YMCAs in India which played a major role in spreading the new concept.

It goes to the credit of America which produced great physical educational missionaries and the United Kingdom which sent great educationists to India. Many leaders trained at the International College of Physical Education of YMCA at Springfield (Mass) USA, have done pioneering work in the field of physical education in India and other countries in the East.

AN INSTITUTION FOR PHYSICAL EDUCATION

With the arrival in 1908 of Dr. Henry Gray as the first Physical Director of the National YMCA at Calcutta a new emphasis was given to physical education. Through lectures, demonstrations and through a programme of physical training, games and sports in the various YMCAs in India, Dr. Grey and his associated created a new interest in Physical Education of modern lines. Later, Dr. A.G. Noehren as the National Physical Director of YMCAs of India, continued the work of Dr. Gray.

A young American, H.C. Buck, then doing physical education work at Wichita, Kansas, came to India in September 1918 to take service as Physical Director at the Central YMCA, Madras. He studies the existing situation in the country, felt the great need for training leadership in the field, and established a School of Physical Education in the year 1920 at Madras, which has today blossomed into the YMCA College of Physical Education.

PHYSICAL EDUCATION FROM H.C. BUCK'S POINT OF VIEW

H.C. Buck found in physical education a field where all the races and creeds of the world can come together and meet in the worship of those qualities of love and forgiveness, beauty and splendour, truth and justice, equanimity and kindness which are essential for a good life.

In 1919, he started as a humble worker as Physical Director and co-worker with Dr. Noehren at the Central YMCA Madras, and was soon able to indicate in his statements orderliness, discipline, respect for rules and a host of other qualities essential for sportsmen and a good citizen. Buch's vision, his faith and optimism, his tenacity of purpose, his interring zeal, his geniality and inherent goodness, his limitless industry and immense capacity for leadership, were the materials which contributed to the stately steel frame of that edifice which he raised and endowed with strength and richness to the traditions it created and treasured for the betterment of the youth of India. Till about the twenties physical education was unknown to this country and its educational system. Educationists did indeed believe in the old adage "Men Sana in Corpore Sano", but all that was done in schools to put that saying into practice was to give the pupils as occasional hour of drill in the week and, where convenience permitted and facilities could be had without trouble, a team of star players in football or badminton was trained.

The instructors were ignorant and ill-paid. There was no attempt to provide for, and much less to teach games to pupils. Drill was done only outside the school hours and even that was more or less unrelated to the school curriculum. The drill master was accordingly the Cinderella of the school staff and could often be bought off or placated without difficulty by influential pupils. The drill master often used language and adopted methods which we should associate with the back streets of olden days. Even the check that drill masters wore spike of their outlook and attitude, for when they did not choose to wear their old army uniforms, they generally donned the familiar but grotesque dress peculiar to circus ringmasters of games. These drill masters knew little or nothing, nor were they interested. Further, where an attempt was made to provide facilities for play they were left to the care of someone among the teachers of the three R's and the drill masters could hardly poach upon the preserves of honorary superintendents of games. Despite the lack of any general provision for games for all pupils, headmasters and principals, book-inspired and anxious to emulate British examples, talked glibly of the many virtues of team games and the benefits accruing from pupil participation in sports.

In fact, even in this country it was a common belief that the Battle of Waterloo was won on the playfields of Eton and Harrow. No serious effort was, however, made to give thought to the questions of the health and efficiency of the school child. This cannot be considered strange in a country where not only education but even administration has tended till quite recently to function according to the convenience of the rulers, whose main aim naturally centred directly or indirectly on their own interests, rather than on the health and progress of the people.

BASIC GOALS OF PHYSICAL EDUCATION

Physical education should aim to provide skilled leadership, adequate facilities and ample time for affording full opportunity for individuals and groups to participate in situation that are physically wholesome, mentally stimulating and satisfying and socially sound. This implies a thorough understanding of the nature and needs of the participants and the implementation of a programme utilising activities and facilities catering to these interests and needs.

THE FUNDAMENTAL OBJECTIVES OF PHYSICAL EDUCATION

1. Protection and improvement of health and the development of organic fitness.
2. Increase in strength and neuro-muscular control.
3. Development of desirable social attitudes and standards or conduct.
4. Acquisition of skills, habits and attitudes in a variety of physical activities which will contribute to wholesome and enjoyable leisure pursuits.

INTERPRETATION IN PHYSICAL EDUCATION

Physical education is that part of the general education programme which is concerned with the growth, development and education of children through the medium of muscular activities. It is education of the whole child by means of physical activities. They are so selected and conducted as to influence every aspect of the child's life physically, mentally, emotionally and morally.

Some of the reasons why physical education and scientifically trained physical educators are necessary in India are the following:

1. General disinclination to exercises which develop hardihood.
2. Need of training in high ideals of sportsmanship.
3. Ignorance of sex matters.
4. Child marriage.
5. Lack of attention to sanitation.
6. Improper diet.
7. Widespread use of drugs and other forms of addiction. N.K. Mia says in his articles: "Buck and the Y.M.C.A. College of Physical Education":

But in the last analysis, if India is to be saved, she must save herself. No body cannot for ever bear all her burdens. India and Indians are best understood by her own people. This being so it seems only proper that this programme of physical regeneration should be carried on by the sons of India—Our attempt at depending upon foreign Physical Directors to do the job has been futile and the solution lies in training indigenous leadership.

We need help from developed countries like America which has the money, the manpower and the experience. All these are needed in helping India to help herself, and our prayer is that individuals in America may be made to see this opportunity to serve, each according to his talents. In spite of an abundance of acceptable interpretations and advice from authoritative writers and speakers, there is still a tendency to cling to outmoded methods and systems of physical education. Therefore, whether physical education has any place in the present social order and whether it can contribute anything of value to modern life, will depend entirely upon our intention to continue to cling tenaciously to the traditionally formalised and standardised schemes of physical education based on some artificial system of exercises.

We may assume at the outset that in any educational procedure the sensible thing to do is to be guided by the facts obtained from a study of human nature and to build up our programme in the light of the facts so discovered. It is education of the whole man, through the medium of physical activities. As such, the activities should be carefully selected and conducted.

Physical education in the past has suffered from the same defects as general education. There has been too great a tendency to follow the line of least resistance and to fit individuals and groups to preconceived schemes of work instead of fitting the programme to the interests and needs of those being educated. Such misguided procedures are not likely to bring the desired results. Both education and physical education must provide experiences that are life like and which will produce personalities capable of adjusting to the present-day social order. A study of the history of physical education reveals that much valuable time has been wasted in squabbles over the merits and demerits of various systems.

RESEARCH, EDUCATION AND PHYSICAL EDUCATION

A variety of research fronts established in the industrial sphere were the causative factor for the industrial that has taken place. In the field of humanities or the human sciences, research has contributed new frontiers of knowledge.

This is particularly true in the area of medicine, engineering, sociology and psychology. In India, physical education is a growing field and if is to be made scientific and comparable with other advanced fields such as medicine, engineering, science, agriculture, etc., it is essential that more and more research should be undertaken in this field under the available conditions.

There is no doubt that numerous research studies can be carried out on the playfield itself. Yet adequate and appropriate space is needed where sophisticated instruments can be installed and research studies conducted under controlled conditions. Education is usually regarded as acquisition of knowledge. It is defined as "the art of making available to each generation the organised knowledge of the past". It also involves "the aggregate of all the processes by means of which a person develops abilities, attitudes and other forms of positive faculties in the society in which he lives".

More than acquiring knowledge, it cultivates a cluster of attitudes and skills. The ability to think independently and clearly is of major importance. Education thus becomes a means to and end, not and end by itself. It is with a view to developing the overall personality of youth that physical education has been made a part of general education. "Education is control of the development of knowledge and formation of the whole structure of man." "Physical education is now being recognised as a part of total education, as a phase of general education and as a way of real education." Of all animals, man has been the most successful in the constant struggle against the environment. Even though he cannot run as fast as some quadrupeds, swim like dolphins, climb like apes, fly as birds do, he has been the only creature capable of defying the forces of gravity and reaching the realms of outer space.

The one factor that has enabled him to accomplish this feat is his ingenuity and intelligence in understanding the mysteries of nature. Man has consistently striven to run faster, jump higher, throw farther and have greater speed, power and strength. Physical education and sports alter the very essence of life. They shape social and human needs, bring greater goodwill and closer contact in the comity of nations. Physical education is extremely essential for helping to remove the differences between mental and physical work. The study of man and motion is a complex task. We cannot comprehend man as a whole. We know him as the macrocosm of distinct parts and the cream of creation. Today, research enjoys a prestigious place in physical education and coaching programmes.

The scholar should be fully aware of the purposes to be served by the research which he undertakes, whether it is applied or pure research. He should be able to conduct the research in an objective way. He should be able to communicate his experience, observations and findings in a cogent and clear-cut manner. Then only case the scholar justify his placement. The research worker's mission should be to conduct a research programme which will benefit the discipline of area selected by him.

The ability to analyse critically is a necessary attribute of a successful researcher.

The problems the scholars face are:

(i) Problems related to time : in the majority of cases, the completion of research takes at least four years;

(ii) Problems related to the sources of information; reference books are the only commonly available aid to research; equipment and other facilities have not been strengthened to a satisfactory extent;

(iii) The majority of scholars feel that their research has no practical application, but just serves as a stop-gap arrangement;

(iv) There is more confusion in selecting the topic than in selecting the director.

PLAY AND CHILD

In the modern world, the objective of education is the development of intellectual skills like thinking, planning and imagination, achieving social skills like competition, cooperative feeling, endurance and emotional maturity besides psychomotor skills and abilities like grip, coordination, strength, etc. In this respect, the educational objectives and processes have a great impact on physical education.

The scholarly learning which the students acquire in the classroom can have tremendous relevance and impact in the playground. The quantum and quality of learning differ from age to age. As the child grows physically and mentally, he exhibits variations of learning level. In the initial stage, educational perspective is a conglomeration of certain measures like action and rest, success and failure, nervousness and fear of facing competition.

The child may not be fully aware of the competition and may not be equipped to participate in serious competitions in all aspects. A fully grown (individual) student is mature enough to make himself ready and fit for participation in physical activities and to analyse his own performance for further rectification and improvement. A seasoned sportsman is far advanced in playing techniques, anticipating the type and nature of performance of the opponents and entering into the playfield in a well-prepared manner to face tactfully the opposing sportsman. There is every possibility for a shrewd and strategic sportsman to transform and apply the classroom knowledge and fruitful experience in the playfield and also throughout his lifetime, in whichever walk of life he may choose.

Ultimately it is quite obvious that the educational perspective of physical education programmes does help a student to lead a meaningful and disciplined life with the right convictions and attitude. It is quite clear that every child, when entering the playfield considers himself, consciously or unconsciously, as a separate and individualised entity during every moment of play. The child is demonstrating his actions with the force of his physiological and academic background. The personality traits and the knowledge learnt in the classroom are reflected in his play. Every sportsman needs a basic or minimum level of literacy and communicative skills because physical activity is controlled by written and verbal commands. Nowadays, a sportsman has to operate or use sophisticated sports equipment or gadgets for advanced training and better performance.

So, it becomes all the more important for personnel involved in games and sports, chiefly for the sportsman, to have the unique personality, basic educational status and novel scientific ideas to explore and exploit new method and openings in the vista of physical education and sports. A child is exposed to several kinds of experiences, many situations and opportunities which mould his thinking, imagination and deeds.

In the educational institutions, the educational perspective helps him to interpret and understand the experiences and outcomes of the playfields. The practical experiences from physical activities apply to a great extent in the effective performance in the classroom also. The attitude, and action of a student should be analysed in totality, taking into consideration both classroom performance and playground achievements. The psychological disorders such as dejection and frustration which affect students may be due to the direct or indirect effect of the interaction of the pleasant or unpleasant experiences that the students may have undergone. The physical educator should take the utmost care to diagnose these correctly and extend guidance and counselling. The partial and incomplete approach by the physical educator may impair the physical and psychological constitution of the child.

The crux of the problem is that the classroom teachers do not have any active hand in the practical affairs of the field and, likewise, the physical educators do not take part in the classroom teaching and other curricular programmes. So there is a yawning gap between these two. They must plan an effective solution to bridge the gap so that the students acquire harmonious, healthy and rich knowledge from the teachers of both general education and physical education. Physical education is an unparalleled domain, because it helps students to reap maximum benefits.

There have to be certain preconditions like positive biological endowment, creating positive educational goals and appropriate opportunities for the child to interact with the school in a positive manner and to be conscious of the educational outcome of such interaction. The learning of the child is dependent upon nature, environment, facilities of the educational institution, etc. There are noticeable differences between a child from a school with all the facilities and the one from a school which is not equipped with the necessary amenities and facilities. A child who emerges out of a rural school will lag behind the other children in almost every aspect. Moreover, the invaluable and formative ideas and experiences that a child learns from the inter-school and intra-school competitions also differ from situation to situation. Traits such as presence of mind, intelligence, performance in the field surely will have an impact and carry-over value and will definitely have a 'say' in their later life. The playfield can be described as a miniature classroom where many of the educational processes are going on to help them to achieve skills, performance and character traits through play interaction. Sports and games provide numerous opportunities for the players to strike up interaction between various personalities.

A player has to move with the manager, coach, referee, captains, playmates, etc. This interaction may help or hinder the purpose of physical development and educational growth. The physical educators and coaches must bear in mind factors such as individual difference and the interaction between the player and the physical activity. Then only can they render service effectively. The individual difference may be of many kinds-physiological, social, psychological, physical and educational, capacities, resources and limitations that an individual exhibits from time to time. The playfield is an open laboratory which does not have physical boundaries. Here the sky is the limit.

The playground activities inspire many young ones to fight in a healthy manner in order to achieve victory. This correlates the educational goal with that of physical education. The open-field classroom help young children to adapt themselves to failures, and frustration, victory and defeat, individual honour and group triumph and emotional ups and downs. The playfield can reject players, push them to its boundaries and make them wish to lose. It also, at times depresses, exhilarates and stimulates. It sorts out the individual players according to their capacity, performance and status. The educational aim of play at a given moment may be to teach the rules of the games, to teach the physical activities, etc. The educative atmosphere in the institutions may create a spirit of competition and cooperation, domination, democracy, stimulation and depression.

The participants may not have the same mental calibre or interest in physical events. The intensity of seriousness, and the degree of genuine interest on the part of the participant sportsman may vary according to the personality and ature of the sportsman. It is high time that we plan meticulously the various ways to learn the physical activities in a scientific manner, like our predecessors, so that we can hand over a standardised knowledge to our younger generation.

Hence, physical activities become sufficiently educational, if they develop this capacity to inherit from our predecessors and extend to our progeny. The continuous emphasis of the moral approach and attempt of the physical education policy will bring about solid progress. Physical education helps to provide this continuity in action and thought. The learning that is taking place inside the classroom should be continued and carried on outside also. No doubt, the playground is the agency and medium that offers continuity to education.

There are other agencies such as the family, neighbourhood, professional playgroups, government, mass media, to give continuity and perpetuate the career of people by inducting them into the educational sphere. The physical educator and coach should select appropriate physical activities, and ancillary equipment that will improve the spirit of commitment of the professional. The general pattern of sports and games and all the inherent programmes have been structured from the sphere of general education. The policies, and programmes of physical education should always be in accordance with general education policies. The school and the playground play a predominant role in the formation of a strong personality in children as they spend the major part of the day time in schools.

GENERAL POINT OF VIEW

In ancient times, physical activity was part and parcel of man behaviour in his every endeavour. The modern man, even after realising and relishing the higher values and fruits of physical education, unfortunately neglects physical activity. Trained leaders of physical education have failed in advocating or defining the concept of physical education. They have defined it in terms of sports and games.

Thus, the tremendous effects and sacred values of physical education have been reduced to the very minimum. In the recent times, the concept of physical education has been accorded due importance, attention and recognition.

Experts from various quarters have started patronising the one-time neglected field on realising its merits. The old-timers are of the opinion that physical education was meant for those who were gifted with physical strength and prowess. Such misconceptions are no more valid. Now the trend is that physical education is a must for every human being at all age levels for a complete life. It has wonderful potentialities and tremendous a virtues to give to every man under the sun.

As time passes, there occurred very constructive literary works on themes like specialised and specific games, its history and contribution to health and recreation, growth and development of physical education and allied fields. But, to our surprise, it has still not been considered as an academic subject in the true sense and remains simply either an extracurricular or extra-educational activity despite the considerable amount of literature on the subject. It is a healthy indication if a discipline grows in its structure, dimension and application.

The expansion of physical education is quite possible if it draws concepts and laws from other allied branches of knowledge. Physical education has enriched its content and scope by deriving sports from medicine and yoga, from philosophy. A part from such induction of allied knowledge, there have been developments of the principal concepts, improvements of the pattern of games, in the design of equipments, playing conditions, techniques of coaching methods, methodical organisation and administration, the use of tests and measurements in physical education, etc.

This remarkable improvement has helped those who are directly or indirectly involved in the field of physical education. Researches in physical education conducted all over the world in the past years, have provided highly beneficial ideas and novel advantages. In the hoary past, all over the world exercises were mostly associated with the rigorous training of the military services. Man and his actions should be in accordance with mother nature for a healthy and happy existence. Physical education is largely advocated in western countries to promote the well-being of the population at large, right from the young stage for effective functioning of the human internal systems as well as effective functioning of the body and for efficient performance on the sports arena.

The basic principles of natural movement are consistent with that of general education and were formulated as a direct response to the recognition that out older practices and ideas in physical education were consistent with the modern philosophy of education. Philosophy and physical education are as interrelated and inseparable as two sides of the same coin and they play a dynamic role in shaping the life of an individual or an individual of in a group. The spectacular professional career of a physical educator enlivens and enlightens the mentality and mode of action of the young students in the high school and colleges, particularly in the matters relating to sports career.

The impact of concrete and compact concepts of physical education eventually makes a break through in their outlook and day to day life.

As the first phase, the physical educators are expected to develop mental attitudes and skills and undergo hardship, stress and strain besides sacrifices. The physical educators should take the initiative to render the service of uplifting the profession and the young student community at large, bearing in mind the following key points; code of behaviour, professional attitude, philosophy of the profession, professional commitment and job satisfaction which are to be given due stress in the course of his accomplishments.

The physical educator has to march a long way for transforming his personal and technical personality for the cause of the cherished field of physical education, as well as the positive transformation of the domain of physical education. The physical educator has been entrusted with a great mission of teaching for the betterment of his students and his profession. However, he has not been provided with the ideal type of professional training. He does not enjoy the privilege of having well-defined clients to render service to. His clients are in a way vague, willy nilly and general in nature. The clients do not come forward with specific and clearcut defects, deficiencies and problems. In spite of these drawbacks most of the physical educators do spot out the innate and latent talents of the students and inspire and encourage them to specialise in specific areas. They enrich the trainees or students by feeding appropriate theoretical knowledge as well.

EDUCATIONAL POINT OF VIEW

Educational principles are patterned in such a way that the students in schools and colleges are moulded into complete personalities by means of guided participation. The child has to be looked after and nourished systematically and scientifically by the teachers at various levels. The medium for this sacred task is the well-designed and balanced physical education programmes.

According to scientific educational techniques, the teachers should pick out the positive as well as negative aspects of the students under them, and do their best to analyse and synthesise the psychological and emotional demands of the students. Guidance and counselling can be rendered to the students for their betterment by the physical education teachers. The students should be trained to transfer the skills or talents acquired to the other domains in which they may involve themselves in later phases of life. It is quite appropriate to have strict and stipulated norms of physical efficiency for admitting the students into educational institutions, though it may sound rigid, unconventional and impractical in day-to-day life.

This pattern of admission will hold good in due course and help to realise the true aims and objectives of physical education and make use reap the real fruits there of. We can then produce totally developed personalities more easily. Educational commentators, academic experts and other critics question the contributory role of physical education and its related subjects in vogue in producing a substantial positive effect in the mind and behaviour of the people. If it does not prove to be good, competitive sports and games can be brought to a halt, which are just a national waste.

It is more purposeful if we plan meticulously for mass participation, group involvement, and mass level fitness and health programmes along with great emphasis on recreational activities which are highly conductive in making a strong, solid, cultured and healthy society. Education has been defined as a change, modification of an adjustment on the part of the student as a result of fruitful experiments and experiences.

Physical education is called an integral part of the total educational process which combines the physical, social and psychological aspects of man's life, through well-directed physical activities. There are other sciences like physics and medicine which have enriched the core and content of physical education.

The educational principles chiefly aim at producing well bread and well-balanced children who will adjust with and adapt to the real problems in their future lifestyle. The planned programme should be congenial to the philosophy and goal of the individuals, groups or communities for whom it is designed. Meaningless theory and unsuitable activities should be eliminated because they fail to satisfy and fulfil the requirement of the pupils for personality growth.

The original thrust of the educational policy is aimed at the improvement of academic standards thereby enriching the intellectual spheres of the students. This concept, when put into practice in the past, did not come up to expectations for reasons like imbalanced character development and other serious handicaps which could have been avoided, to a great extent, if combined efforts had been undertaken to influence the young children as well as college-going students in the right academic perspectives. The total development of the individual is of prime importance.

The experts in the field of education must find out ideal means, methods and agencies through which the total development can be achieved in practical life. The various physical activities are the media, which are considered as educational objectives and means to achieve the total objective of integrated development. The physical education policies and programmes, along with education-oriented approaches, will successfully create the required personality traits among the students.

It is high time that we totally discard the traditional concepts of physical education which develop mutual indifference, confrontation and isolation between education and physical education. Education with its dynamic nature and thrust towards improvement should concentrate on imparting valuable knowledge in health education, movement education, recreation, physical education, vocational education, fine arts, etc., to the children at early period of their lives.

If we look back to the concepts of education of the ancient Spartan government, we come to know that the aim of education was to produce men of action and individual physical excellence so that the individual could be put to the service of the country especially in times of emergency and war. In those days, human power was chiefly utilised for military purposes as countries were waging wars for survival constantly, and to establish their supremacy over the others. Apparently the idea was to keep the citizens physically sound so as to live life to the flues and they sought wholesome activities that aimed at harmonious development of the body. In short, the whole educational pattern was to channelise the youth towards military objectives.

However, the aim today is to develop the total personality of man for a better life. These above said educational objectives can be achieved provided the programmes of physical education fit into the educational perspective of the total system. The dynamic operations of the educational system should be well understood by men who are entrusted with the work of gearing up the administrative machinery of physical education. The physical educators should take utmost care that they must not over emphasize the importance of the physical aspects of the game situation and the educational values should be developed among the students for fuller growth. Students may become completely balanced and grown up in every aspect only if both the values are developed hand in hand.

As a matter of fact, physical education has not been given educational orientation because the recreational aspects enjoy more importance than the educational aspects. The formulation of the various physical activities must be done taking the educational principles into account. The general education pattern must yield to certain positive changes and transformation in its structure and policy for this purpose. The key points such as the developmental characteristics of students, the principle of correlation between academic subjects and physical activities, the principle of student-teacher ratio, etc., should be give due place in the physical education curriculum. The sole purpose of physical activities should be the fulfilment of the higher values of general education.

PHYSICAL EDUCATION

Physical movements are a biological necessity. Physical education has devised organised games and sports in a systematic way within the educational institutions. A student learns a lot when he takes part in any event. He gradually learns to perform in a perfect manner, after repetition. He understands the nature and inherent techniques of a phenomenon by the trial and error methods, thereby mastering the do's and don'ts of a particular area. Thus, an individual is facilitated in having a wide scope of learning by himself through the medium of physical activities in an educational atmosphere. This may be called the self-analysis function of scientific physical activity.

The educational values of physical education can be acquired in the open classroom, i.e., the playground where the instructor conducts various types of activities which provide ample opportunities for character development, play-interaction, shouldering responsibility and practising the art acquired before. The participation in the field activities direct and educates the students. The classroom and the playground are the twin places where the students can experiment with their innate talents in order to evaluate themselves and put into practice their worth.

There is the possibility also to compensate by performing well in the field in case anybody is weak in classroom achievements, or a student may even retain the same high position in both the places. Physical education is a superb field wherein ample opportunities are created for the development of complete personality through coordinated physical activities.

The unique feature of physical education programmes is that participants willingly engage themselves without any kind of hesitation, inhibitions and reservation. No doubt, other academic and social media of the school like the curriculum, classroom, administrative machinery and examination system also play a significant role in the formation of wholesome personality, but physical education contributes a vital part of the total general education pattern. Physical Education had to pass through a number of ordeals, and tribulations to its achieve present prestigious status.

Physical education programmes were considered to be the extracurricular and evening-hour recreational activities in those days, whereas it enjoys an enviable position now because researches and innovations were made in curricula and in implementation of the designed activities.

Moreover, it has been proved that there is a direct relationship between scholastic standing and the physical performance in the field. So, also, the physical educators in schools and colleges now enjoy honour and professional status and they are on the faculty councils and university committees.

This clearly indicates that physical education has been recognised and universally accepted as being on part with other departments of knowledge. Physical education has many wings such as athletics associations, amateur associations, professional units, coaching centres, etc., in which specialised personnel are working hard for the improvement of the specific purposes.

It is a healthy sign if there is meaningful and coordinated integration for the overall prosperity of the entire field. The question arises: Is there integration and coordination between general education and physical education? Undoubtedly, a congenial atmosphere has been established between physical education and general education.

Moreover, the wide gap has been almost bridged. In schools and colleges, physical education programmes have been made compulsory for all the students and thus a mutual interdependence between them has been well established. It is not wrong to say that physical education and general education are inspirable. The physical educators of today have been entrusted with greater responsibilities in keeping with the changed curriculum. In the past, physical education was thought of as improving the physique, strength and motor skills, whereas it now aims at improving the overall personality of a man. It is a healthy sign that physical education has been accorded the right place which has enlarged its aims and objective. It is the moral duty of the whole physical education machinery to tone itself so as to make a breakthrough in this field.

The main and very important aim of physical education is to create ideal opportunities for young students at various levels to acquire the true and all-round perfection and development in every aspect. The main objectives of the multifarious programmes of physical education is to produce responsible and rational citizen who act wisely throughout their lives. We have not yet succeeded in this particular aspect and angle. There is no shadow of doubt that we have to go a long way in order to realise the goals of physical education.

GENERAL EDUCATION AND PHYSICAL EDUCATION

The progress of life and physical education are inseparable. Physical education is an integral part of general education as well as that of our life. In view of the vital role that it plays in our very life, we should have recognised it and adopted it effectively in general education. It is high time that we give it the right status. There cannot be good results in the limited time allotted to the physical education classes. The time must be sufficiently increased for the efficient and effective learning of the higher values of physical education.

It should get the academic status of a full-fledged branch of knowledge which will pave the way for a renaissance in all spheres of general education. The leaders of physical education blesses with foresight are striving hard to achieve this ideal. The ideal changes and reformative amendments in the principles of physical education should be carried out after deep thought and analytical scrutiny, taking into consideration three vital aspects, namely, the scope of physical education as a full-fledged academic discipline, professional ethics and the relationship with other domains.

Physical education has a relationship and correlation with different academic fields. It has to draw various physical, biochemical and mechanical laws from other disciplines for its enrichment. Thus the content of this field is abundantly rich. Professional ethic should take a new dimensional approach and physical education can no more be an island away from the mainstream of education. The chief aim is the all round development and fuller growth of children.

Physical education cannot survive unless it receives unstinted co-operation and generous help from other disciplines. The affinity and relationship between general education and physical education have fallen into oblivion in the practical sense. Thus both exist physically together but are functionally apart. Both must go hand in hand in order to produce the desired result in the personality development of children at all levels. The physical educators should be conscious of the importance to be given to the educational perspective in physical activity. Opportunities should be open to all the pupils in educational institutions for fuller growth and prosperity.

It is important that carefully chosen and meticulously planned physical activities should be included in the curriculum to enhance the active participation of the children for this development of their personality traits. It is important to evaluate the contribution of general education to the development of the culture, attitude and behaviour of the people of this country. Have we succeeded in this great task? We have made considerable improvement in the physical education programmes which have really played an important role in discriminating knowledge, liberating the mind and improving skills, promoting free thinking and encouraging creative talents and developing positive attitudes towards change and order. Society is expecting a long from general education. A player should be analysed and judged from several angles. The physical educator should scout the all round performance of a player not only in the sportsfield but also in the classroom and elsewhere. The player's behaviour patterns must be scrutinised for further psychological stabilisation.

There should be an ideal relationship between the classroom teachers and physical educators so that both can arrive at an analytical conclusion about the abilities, interest, limitations and scope of each individual student and his participation in the school activities. This system of studying the students helps the physical educator to assess the motor skills of the individual before the individual is permitted to practise in the specialised area. The physical educator establishes a close relationship with the teachers of other disciplines regarding nutrition, health, diseases, safety measures, first aid, etc.

The physical educator has to cover the topics like physiology, physics, sports, medicine, first aid and he is also involved in mathematical concepts like duration of time, counting measurements, sequences, evaluation, etc. Further, he has to evolve social concepts that may be developed during healthy athletic competitions and games. He should ask the students to give their views and comments after the game is over.

In this way, physical education is a part of general education. Physical education is passing through a difficult period because the State and policy makers do not come forward enthusiastically to make it an essential part of general education. The time allotted for students at lower levels as well as higher levels is not sufficient at all. Naturally, the students cannot benefit much from physical education in most schools and colleges. If at all students spend their evenings on the games field, it may be the "chosen group" participating in the school games, inter-class matches and inter-school tournaments which are purely carried on a voluntary basis.

The pity is that the fruits of physical education do not reach all the students. Moreover, there is no uniform pattern in the schools regarding the effective thrust on physical education with the result that it is not given the due place and importance and has thus become and matter of convenience.

Generally, the teachers of general education as well as of physical education feel that general education and physical education are distinct and separate entities and do not have common educational elements. This is the cause for several serious misconceptions among the educated masses as well as the public. They fail to recognise the interrelationship and interdependence without which the very purpose of general education is defeated. It is very interesting to note that both the subject teacher and the physical educator deal with the same material, namely the student. The unity of organism, and the interaction between the parts are confirmed in research findings.

The integration of youth personalities in educational institutions is safeguarded and promoted to the optimum level only if the forces, of these twin, related fields act on the student community. It is a fact that the examination system and the present pattern of education contribute in making the student panic-stricken, perturbed and crippled as regards the spontaneous development of personality traits.

General education cannot afford to forego the unique services of the physical educator. He is an asset not only to the educational institutions but also to the students because his chief work is to promote their physical health as well as their intellects, emotions, sociable character, cognitive and recreational abilities.

The days are not far off when physical education will identify itself with general education. At present, this ideal identification is mostly at a verbal level. Though it is popularly said that physical education is an integral part of general education, yet it is so only theoretically. It is however very gratifying to know that a favourable climate is now gradually being created to establish a close rapport. It is necessary that physical education should have devised a clear-cut basic concept which is conductive for such renovative outcome and mutual enrichment. This healthy relationship between general subjects and physical education should blossom in the day-to-day routine of schools and colleges which will contribute to the balanced growth, psychological stability and positive outlook of the young students.

The terms "physical education" make us understand the educational perspective as well as physical values. But in practice, unfortunately, we are prone to missing the educational value that are derived from physical education. In this way we miss the right perspective. The foundations of physical education and the preconditions of a proper educational perspective have not been efficiently planned and effectively executed.

This deficient condition has led to academic chaos and confusion in its implementation, as result of which a corrective formula is to be sought to put physical education on the right track. It is obvious that physical education has a great role to play in order to achieve the goals of education. But the physical educators are not aware of the potentialities it possesses.

The correct approach, practical manipulations and organisational devices are not to be carried out in every educational institution by the individual physical educator alone. Both physical education and general education are inseparable and the existence and execution of one is not only unhealthy but also creates undesirable tendencies among the children.

Physical education should always produce an educational value which is superb and ideal in every respect. The necessary prerequisites should made available for the successful implementation of physical education. Here educational perspective is a precondition. There is no guarantee that we may succeed to a great extent just because of the existence of the educational perspective. Moreover, there are other factor which determine the possibility of the correct educational perspective.

They are:-

(i) certain physiological and biological endowments,

(ii) The educational institution and its multifarious on-going activities,

(iii) The ample scope for interaction between groups and individuals.

These three factors can make a correlation between physical education and education for the purpose of transfer of learning from one to another which may not always be simple in practical situations. The educational values that the children learn from physical activities are different depending upon the teachers coaches, facilities, playmates and available equipments.

The type of educational experience acquired differs from one game to the other according to the nature, movement pattern, equipment and ground as different technical and biomechanical principle are involved in them. The scoring procedures, strategy and technical personnel vary according to the game.

Thus the students engaged in different physical activities receive several kinds of educational values. A gifted and brilliant student may excel both in academic performance as well as in the spheres of games and sports. It is a golden opportunity for the students to have the playing field as the educating unit where they are exposed to educative phenomena such as trial and error learning, goals and achievements levels, appreciation and punishment, psychological stability and sportsmanship qualities. If physical activities are efficiently organised, they may positively improve the physical standards of students. Physical education program, like competitions between the various groups in and out of the educational institutions really help to enrich their psychological aspects.

In schools and colleges, a meritorious sports performance is given due importance in matters of admission and promotions. Physical education promotes educational perspectives as it produces direct impact on the teaching learning process, organisational and administrative aspects. This inductive function of physical education is possible only if the activities are properly planned and strictly implemented. It is not possible to give a clear-cut definition of the term "education". It may mean more than an ocean.

It is incorrect to say that education takes place inside physical buildings or only in a limited area. It may occur in any place. The educational institutions provide opportunities for the students to spend a major portion of their time and learn the programmed and framed knowledge. In everybody's case, the institutionalised education has great impact on the formation of personality. The motto, systems and customs followed in a particular institution are reflected in the attitude and behaviour of a student' life. Though physical education is an integral part of general education, it also, to a great extents supports and supplements the aims and objectives of general education.

It is a heavenly blessing that the coordinated work of general education and physical education do not contradict each other at any juncture; thus there is a greater possibility of realising the aims of education is general through the various designed programmes of physical education.

Thus, it goes without saying that every physical educator should be well-versed with the precepts of general education. Physical education should not be restricted to training in sports and games. It should play a wider role in overall education of society. It is high time that the essential values and idealistic principles of various domains of learning should be brought into the mainstream of physical education to frame an integrated programme of schooling to achieve complete and comprehensive values in the educational set-up. Both general education and physical education have a common task, i.e., to promote the all-round development of the child, in their respective ways. The product to be shaped and moulded is the child.

The physical educator should possess necessary prerequisites for interpreting the psychological, social and physical aspects of the total structure of schooling so that physical activities can be selected on the basis of the need, interest and abilities of the individual students and the educational objectives of the school.

The educational basis of physical education should define the scope of physical education as well as form the proper guidelines to match the student with the activities relevant to schooling. Physical education, which is indeed a dynamic field, cannot afford to function in isolation in schools and colleges without associating itself with other connected disciplines. The field of physical education involves not only students at various levels but also several personnel like the participants, parent, audience, administrators, and physical educators. So physical education is unique in this aspect because it establishes the interaction and also the interpersonal relationship between many personalities through physical activities, thus playing a predominant role in the total educational process. The physical educator must possess positive insight into his profession and have thorough knowledge about physical education as an educational process. It makes him view the player from an educational point of view.

The player who faces victory or defeat well, who walks out of the field in protest, the physically disadvantaged, the student who withdraws from the field, the school champion, his playmates and his opponents, his captain, his coach, his officials and audience are all part of the play. So it is better that the physical educator masters the educational forces and the influences of the educational atmosphere on the player's performance and on his own coaching or training.

The competitions conducted on the field should inculcate the spirit of sportsmanship and healthy competition. The constructive competitions are designed to produce among the players educative values. The higher values emerge through the interaction of individual participants in the sports and games.

Thus, strong character is and exemplary personalities are evolved on the playfield. The behavioural methods and social science have long been of importance and interest to those concerned with sports and physical education. Great emphasis has been laid on the intensification of academic study in physical education with respect to educational objectives and their interpretation which has resulted exciting experience novel ideas, meaning, concepts and workable suggestions are evolved for physical educator in the classroom and the coach in the playground.

The physical educator should be prepared to accept and adapt to these innovative ideas. The playfield is an open-air classroom where the children go with their unique ways of life, abilities and limitation and acquire emotional stability, trial and error learning and character formation. The physical educator creates through various physical activities, an educative climate from which the children learn a lot for life along, with health habits and recreative values. A physical educator should therefore have knowledge of both physical and general education.

INTERDISCIPLINE RELATIONSHIP

No nascent discipline is rich in its structure and content. It has to grow with time. The experiments and research conducted explore the possibilities for further growth and enrichment. In this process, it has to make collaborative work with other disciplines from which concepts and professional formulae can be borrowed for its enlargement and application. The interdisciplinary sharing of ideas and joint efforts are applicable to any profession.

Physical education is not an exception because if it acts in isolation its scope and growth are adversely affected. Some sort of mutual analysis and collaborative research work will therefore help to enrich the profession substantially. The field of physical education is ever, growing in all aspects. It is in the process of enriching its major principles and premises deriving the related concepts and laws from other domains so that it can become an independent academic discipline.

The physical education teacher must be quite conversant with the new scientific formulae that are adopted from time to time to impart up-to-date qualitative education. Valuable information in the form of various physical and scientific laws becomes a part and parcel of physical education. The physical educator should earnestly strive to learn the fresh knowledge and techniques so that he can teach the students and can himself be recognised as an asset of the institution, not only by the student community but also by the staff who belong to other departments and by the community at large. He should not be content with the knowledge that he has acquired from the professional institutions as well as from books and training courses. The physical educator should also strive hard to evolve his own methods to realise the aims and objectives of our field.

In reality society expects more from the physical educators than what is being rendered by them. This calls for greater interest, dedicated service and genuine commitments on the part on the physical educators. The educational set up in the schools and colleges will yield the desired result only if general education and physical education make a wholehearted coordinated effort in implementing the programmes successfully.

General education cannot alone accomplish the onerous task of effectively educating the younger ones. There is no doubt that physical education is part and parcel of the mainstream of general education. Physical educators stress more on active participation and not on winning or losing. The matter in which the participants take part in competitions is more commended and appreciated. This applied to any profession. But qualitative work is admired and recognized in any walk of life rather than more quantity and volume of work personal gain is not the criterion but service to the common man and profession is all the more important. Idealistic principles will make the physical educators more dedicated towards developing the character of student.

The pleasure and satisfaction that we derive from hard work, dedicated service and professional commitments are definitely unique and unparalleled. A committed individual considers his profession a field where he has to put in wholehearted effort and genuinely attempt to explore new avenues of advancement. It is a thrilling experience for a dedicated physical educator to engage himself in the development of the profession. No doubt, the job satisfaction is personal and subjective. The professional curriculum must be planned in such a way that the trainees are given ample opportunities to educate themselves.

PROFESSIONALISM AND PROFESSIONAL ETHICS

Physical education aims at the all-round development of human being, i.e., young children and adults. In the field of physical education higher virtues and sacred and sublime qualities are instilled in the minds of the students. Physical educators play a predominant role in this aspect. They rank next to the parents in imparting decency and decorum to young ones. So, the physical educator should understand that his profession needs a specific type of professional behaviour. An individual can afford to lose both wealth and health, but certainly not his character. So also an individual profession cannot afford to lose its character, namely "professional image" which emerges from the plans and behaviour of the profession as well as the professional.

The community at large must certify the worth and condition of any profession and not the personnel within the profession itself. The combined and coordinated efforts of all the persons at all levels can build up a positive professional image. A single man, can by no means, succeed in this great task. Honesty and integrity of the physical educators will do a lot in this regard. The professional image is nothing but the general view that people have about a profession. Inherently, it is a psychological impression after constant and careful scrutiny of the profession. If a particular individual does not observe the code of professional ethics faithfully, he not only harms his own personal image but also ruins the already established image of the profession. Professionalisation opens up a good number of opportunities and advantageous vistas for the physical education teacher to recognise and face new problems connected with his subject in an appropriate manner.

The physical educators are trained in such a way that they are well equipped professionally to adjust and adapt to the new changes and professional regulations that are introduced from time to time. It is evident that the regulations can participate in a healthy manner in the interdisciplinary approaches and intellectual discussions with the teachers of other academic disciplines.

At present, this intellectual interaction is not very much in practice, because of the language problem or the limited acquaintance with other disciplines. Hence to further our own interest of getting accepted by other professionals from other disciplines, we should be professionalised in our discipline and be recognised with due honour as fellow teachers in the totality of the entire educational system.

It is clearly understood now that professional ethics include

(i) a code of conduct,

(ii) the philosophy of the profession,

(iii) a dignity of work,

(iv) a professional attitude,

(v) a commitment and

(vi) job satisfaction

Professional ethics can be called a psychological state of mind derived out of a voluntary exposure to a profession. Hasty action, likes and dislikes, personal attachments, sentimental influences and biased opinions have no place in a profession and an individual must take up his profession as a noble one and give it his due regard and respect.

A true and ideal professional always seeks to do something in his cherished field as his contribution and this professional thirst does not end till he creates a suitable environment for the betterment of the existing conditions of the profession. A committed physical educator is an asset to his discipline and he can be entrusted with confidential responsibilities and professional commitments because he will be prepared to make all-out attempts for utilising his potentialities and talents for the betterment of his profession.

The achievement in any academic discipline is due to such committed individuals. It is quite obvious that a trained professional in any branch of knowledge, especially in physical education, is bound to develop and possess his or her own attitude about the profession he has embraced for either livelihood or service. The physical educator should avoid forming subjective attitudes. The individual must analyse the overall situation and the impact of it before forming final attitudes, judgement and decisions.

This can be achieved only when an individual is able to estimate the real situations, and infer or interpret them with an open mind and welcome these situations irrespective of his personal likes and dislikes. Professional ethic includes the practical attitudes of the person towards his profession and the estimation and value that he attaches to it. The healthy attitudes about the profession to which an individual is wedded must duly generate the right type of spirit, drive which ultimately leads to the desired target.

Physical education involves group competition, the social gathering and togetherness of a host of individuals who try hard for individual as well as common goals wherein we find mixed causes and effects such as competition and cooperation, winning and losing, risk and safety. The element of risk involved in the field of physical education right from the training phase till the actual competition is to be borne in mind by the different personnel involved in physical education and sports namely of coaches, managers and sportsmen.

The ethical aspects of a profession should be flexible, functional and operational so as to be conductive to attaining higher and holistic virtues and values. A rigid set of professional ethics may not produce the desired result. Moreover the tremendous toil and dedicated service rendered by many become futile and fruitless. The physical educators must, as far as possible, try to follow these ethics. It is necessary to provide better working conditions and privileges to the physical educators so as to motivate them. The distribution of duties and responsibilities amongst various segments of the community makes the administrative machinery strong and smooth. The real strength of any profession lies not only in its productivity but perhaps, more so, in its ethical behaviour. Productivity is discernible whereas the effect of ethical behaviour assumes long-term significance.

Physical education can in no way boast of having the professional ethics that every other profession has been fortunate enough to possess. To cite an example, professions like medicine and law have well laid out codes of professional ethic which enhance their morale and promote their image.

As these two professions have unique roles to play in the modern world, numerous other professions too have got a predominant part to play. Physical education ethics do inspire the physical educators to participate in the professional programmes and variety of commitments in wholesome ways in order to achieve the aims and objectives of physical education.

When the physical educators fail to follow the professional ethics, they are bound to create problems of great magnitude. They may not understand the disadvantage and serious ill-effects that arise on account of the breach of the professional ethics in the beginning but in the long run it leads to the disorganisation of their own personality because of the continuous development of themselves complex and finally their behaviour cannot be justified either by themselves or by observes. It is no exaggeration to say that the absence of professional ethics causes inconsistent attitude and behaviour patterns among the physical educators. This sorry state of affairs in the field of physical education breeds conflicts, chaos, unwanted comments from others and an unpleasant atmosphere at the end.

It is crystal clear that physical educators should strictly follow the ethical values and virtues. Professional ethics denotes professional standards and norms of conduct for people who have dedicated themselves to serve the community at large through these coordinated programmes. The rules and regulations that are farmed in any profession serve like a guiding star to the people who are directly or indirectly involved.

The ethical formulate maintain the moral standard of the general social attitude and way of life. The professionals have personal ambition to achieve. In this process of dedicated service, the physical educators have to sacrifice their personal benefits. Such sacrifices and dedicated involvement by the physical educators contribute a lot to the growth of the profession.

The individual should be prepared to accept the great task for the sake of bringing honour and glory to the profession. The codes of a field are a strong base on which the future of the profession, as well as of the personnel, involved is dependent to a great extent. Professional ethics should be given top priority especially in the organisation and administration of professional concepts in an educational institution.

It vividly points out the do's and don'ts thereby helping the physical educators to get rid of the areas of conflicts and controversy. The physical educators are quite aware of, and conversant with the ideal ways and means of putting into practice the systematic approaches and ideal method of the profession. The guiding principles of professional ethics are a "must" for specific action and accomplishment in the everchanging routine and roles of physical educators. The physical educators should welcome and appreciate the professional codes for the betterment of their profession. It is important to note that rules and concepts are for the profession.

The professional ethics emerge within the framework of the profession itself which may be the result of the experiences acquired and the amalgamated opinions and constructive views of the co-physical educators of various correlated backgrounds. The physical educators are morally bound to observe professional ethics as there are no hard and fast rules to punish the defaulters in case they fail to follow. But the social pressures from the professional associations, etc., are the usual social penalties for violating professional ethics. Every physical educator is expected to be more responsible to adhere to the ethics framed. Though the code of professional ethics is applicable to teachers in general, the physical educators are particularly expected to practice it sincerely so as to set a good example for others.

There are lot of opportunities in physical education programmes such as fair play, good sportsmanship, cooperation, unselfishness, regard for rules of games and fellowship, etc. The physical educators should lead a clean academic as well as social life, failing which they earn a bad name for the physical education community and the profession too.

PHILOSOPHY

The most important professional hurdle that we find in the world of today is that interested and dedicated individuals do not join the field of physical education. The physical educators are therefore largely misfits who may not be competent enough to deliver the goods.

Physical education is the last resort for incompetent individuals who have no aptitude for the profession. Some individuals knowingly take temporary shelter under its fold. This sorry state of affairs generates wavering minds and indifference on the part of these. These professionals can always contribute something positively to the profession and not the wayward individuals. This type of superficial expansion is temporary and detrimental to the health and improvement of the profession.

The precondition for any professional growth is thus the number of committed professionals who can discharge their professional responsibilities diligently and willingly. An individual can switch over to another profession but an intentional stay in a profession as a "pastime" may considerably ruin the growth of the profession and its very existence. In these days, physical educators work mainly for monetary benefits. If not all, most of them do not have or develop the requisite enthusiasm, sincerity and dedication. If we trace the development of any profession, we find that it is because many dedicated souls have worked relentlessly.

It is, no doubt, a challenging and tough task for those who wish to make physical education an independent academic discipline in this vast nation. Such sagacious leaders may have to face troubles and initial impediments, but they can gradually achieve their goal provided they have strong will to face the hurdles in their path.

PHILOSOPHY AND PHYSICAL EDUCATION

Invariably all the branches of knowledge emerge from philosophy which vividly indicates the vital role that philosophy plays at every phase in all walks of life. We cannot separate or segregate philosophy from any discipline.

Physical education has or has to have the essential elements and tenets of philosophy, as it has a predominant part in the development of the total personality of a child. General education does have the relevant maximum relationship with philosophy. Philosophical analysis and values have contributed considerably to the formation of educational practice.

Motivation plays a vital part in encouraging the students, trainees and the physical educators themselves to gain inspiration and intellectual information and must work towards providing an independent status to the subject but not at the cost of discarding the role of philosophy in physical education.

In today's changing society, there must be a sound philosophy of physical education for the profession to survive and flourish. Philosophy is a process through which physical educators search for truths, reality and values. It is only through philosophy that physical educators are able to stuck the meaning, nature, importance and source of values in physical education. Philosophy guides the physical educator in determining the aims, objectives, principles and content of physical education and provides a logical means of determining whether or not it is providing worth while services in the education of human beings. A professional philosophy has the superb inherent ability to inspire the professional to act with vigour and vitality, conviction and contemplation to the fullest possible extent.

The essential elements of philosophy are eventually reflected in his mind, words and deed. The mind, local system and psychomotor system generate positive thinking, positive speaking and positive doing. The congenial blend of these three vital aspects, goes astray if the individual does not strictly follow the professional ethics and philosophical values in actual practice. It is of the utmost importance that the training systems include both the professional ethics as well as the philosophy along with other departments of knowledge in the professional institutions. Otherwise, the training is an incomplete one which produces imbalances and inconsistencies among the physical educators.

Ever since the recorded history, philosophy has solid and strong foundation for almost all domains of knowledge. Physical education is no exception. Educational thought is influenced by the five major philosophies, viz., idealism, realism, pragmatism, naturalism and existentialism. A physical educator must have the basic knowledge of the concept of philosophy that can be practised in everyday life.

Any physical educator who has mastered or has been blessed inherently with this gift can successfully do a better job in the institutions and can better match the students and sports appropriately, instead of falling into the trap of mechanical and routine working. The physical educator should strive to inculcate in the young minds of the students a well-balanced philosophical outlook vis-a-vis the overall sports programmes. The field and concept of physical education do not enjoy any remarkable reputation and important status as most people are not convinced of the importance of physical education in day-to-day life.

There have been many great men in every field who were not physically strong. So, there is a school of thought that the physical weakness may not be a hindrance or hurdle to achieving greatness or name. It is not correct to say that physically weak people develop other compensatory capacities either to be on par with the normal ones or to excel them in every aspect. Most people are not conscious of the necessity of living a wholesome and healthy life. In ordinary life, men like to reach the pinnacle of greatness by hook or by crook.

The vital point of healthy living is ignored or totally discarded. But the very same people whole heartedly practise the physical fitness assignments. It is of interest to trace the historical development of physical education. Many scientists, philosophers and psychologists have propounded theories of physical education in depth and breadth in the light of scientific principles. Aristotle made an extensive study of the systems of the human body and its practical functions in relation to physical activities.

Physical education vividly depicts the ever-growing social changes and the changes caused in the structure and implementation of objectives of education. Its nature and content open new avenues for experimentation and exploration in the field which will pave the way for its total development. It cannot be accorded the status of an academic discipline as it does not satisfy the prerequisites at present.

But physical educators are striving ceaselessly to establish its worth. Though we may succeed in making physical education a full-fledged academic discipline, it will not function as an independent discipline unless there is a drastic move on the part of the government to promote it. Physical educators have arrived at the conclusion, after serious discussions and analysis, that physical activities have definite correlation and interrelationship with other branches of knowledge.

This had led to the promotion of the nature, purpose status and scope of physical education. The leaders of physical education have done their best to explore the influences of various social, physical, cultural and psychological phenomena upon physical activities. This is not sufficient. A strong nation wide educational policy is required to amalgamate the various factors to bring about sequential coherence among the various faculties which can stir up human activity and the acquisition of skills.

We cannot but admit the fact that vital concepts such as motivational methods, aspiration levels and self-evaluation have not attained significance and due place in practice. The concept of physical education and its programmes at various levels have to be restructured and modified according to the present conditions and needs so as to enable the modern child to enjoy the fullest possible benefits of physical education. Then only can it become a meaningful part of general education.

The present move is to establish physical education as a compact and complete academic subject which can magnificently kindle the spark and bring out the hidden talents and aspirations in a consecutive constructive manner. At present, physical educators have resolved to change the age-old concept of physical education as it was considered to be the one-hour-evening programme.

In other words, it is nothing but one-period physical exercises or events. In reality, it is not so. It has hot a tremendous role to play at school, college and university levels. The potentialities and idealistic virtues of men should be spotted out and exploited to the maximum or else the aims and objectives of education and physical education are totally defeated.

Moreover, the physical educators should not be content with their professional services in the educational institutions, if they fail to contribute to the actual development of personalities at their disposal. It is a period of transition for both education and physical education. They have to cope with the new changes and satisfy the pressing demands. They should unhesitatingly adopt newly discovered ways and means in their approaches to shape the personality of a growing child. Then they can deliver the goods in a fitting manner.

Today the world is highly competitive in nature. Physical education is no exception. It goes without saying that the programmes of physical education should be restyled and tailored to suit the present conditions in the educational institutions. Unless every facet of academic discipline is given the right place, education cannot but be a dismal failure.

Physical education promotes the whole being of man namely the body, mind and spirit to suitable and necessary highest level. So, it is to make physical education an academic discipline. Invariably all the physical educators are giving a clarion call for standardising the academic status of physical education. They try all out means to make it a full-fledged academic discipline.

Unfortunately various efforts like well intended seminars, etc., have not helped in getting physical education a respectable status in educational institution. It has been deprived of its legitimate, right and was made to have a secluded existence for name's sake, which did not create high esteem among physical educators themselves.

Conversely, they were more likely to develop an inferiority complex. The physical educators were openly branded and treated as second rate persons compared to the classroom teachers. The prime work to be undertaken is to make them feel strongly that physical education is on par with other branches and faculties of knowledge. They should have the necessary conviction on this point.

Unless physical education marches majestically along with other disciplines, the realisation of the goals of education in the true sense is impossible. A dynamic masterplan should be evolved to rearrange the course of action for making physical education an effective medium to achieve the desired ends of general education. The following suggestion may bring about good results.

SUGGESTED MASTER PLAN FOR PHYSICAL EDUCATION

a. The aims and objectives of physical education should be defined in clear-cut terms.

b. The close-knit relationship of physical education with other disciplines should be understood and established in an appropriate way so as to obtain the maximum benefits.

c. The concept and utility of movement patterns which form the basis of all types of labour and managerial affairs should be rightly appreciated.

d. Different bodies and individuals should be amalgamated to make united effort to achieve the full-fledged academic status for physical education.

e. It is of prime importance that experts and stalwarts from other fields are requested to put their heads and hearts together to make a better design for physical education by making them participate in lectures, seminars and workshops.

f. Short refresher courses may be held for physical educators to raise the standard of physical education as well as maximise their contribution to the field.

g. The various quarters should be convinced of the importance and need of physical education so that they will whole heartedly patronise the steps that the physical educators undertake. The governments at the centre and states should give priority to the physical educators in the matters of employment.

Physical education is a unique field where there are ample opportunities for demonstration of action and strict observance of rules. It is not to be found in other disciplines. The importance of "self" is stressed emphatically though the ultimate goal is to inculcate the feelings of group-spirit, group-interaction and group-welfare and service before self.

This is, no doubt, a special feature of physical education. The potentialities and scope of physical education are tremendous and they should be realised, and the conceptual framework and foundation should also be rationalized to pave the way for a renaissance in physical education. It is possible only through reformulating the theoretical perspective.

Physical education grows naturally, provided it has a strong academic status which helps in fear and fuller growth. Apart from this, status help to bring about an intellectual harmony, understanding and cooperation between the various personalities, agencies and associations involved in this field.

This naturally facilitates the evolution of a sound and practicable theory for the purpose of learning these activities effectively. Educational objectives are carefully planned in such a way as to inculcate social, moral and holistic virtues in the minds of young children, thereby making them fit personalities in this complicated and competitive world. Education as well as physical education plays a vital role to achieve this unique ambition.

No doubt, in modern life, parents cannot always afford to spare sufficient attention towards educating the young ones. The teachers are also not in a position to do justice as there is limited time at their disposal. Even if the teachers are prepared to render dedicate their selfless service to educate the students in a special and better manner, the students are not only unreceptive but they look down upon both the physical education teachers and the entire programme as it does not enjoy a reputation like other subjects.

The students also do not consider physical education as part of general education. These programmes are distinctly and decidedly alienated from the mainstream of education as they have been eternally branded, in practice, as the optional and extra evening hour programmes which have no value and significance in the academic, social and professional spheres.

Physical education has unfortunately lost its significance as it is not a subject for examination and graduation in the strictest sense. Invariably, the students, the society and even the teaching community give it stepmotherly treatment and less importance in curriculums at all levels. Everybody is privileged and entitled to choose his or her own branch of knowledge and pursue for personal and social betterment.

Educational institutions which have the moral and legal duty to cater to the genuine needs of the growing students according to their capacity and capability and resources and aspirations neither provide adequate facilities, amenities, and congenial atmosphere for young ones to take up a sporting career, nor regularise the time meant for physical education programmes. In this aspect, we have utterly disappointed the students of our days and they have been deprived of the privilege of enjoying the benefits of physical education.

The result is that they do not flock with enthusiasm to the fields nor do they stick to physical education activities for a long time. We cannot blame the students for their lack of ability or interest. The underlying reason for this is the present status of physical education. There is a great need therefore, to put physical education or par with other subjects.

2

FUNCTIONS OF PHYSICAL EDUCATION

PHYSICAL EDUCATION AND THE TASKS OF THE BODY

Even before the human embryo is as large as a finger-nail, a tube has formed within it, enlarged at a certain point, and begun to pulsate. Thus the human heart has its beginning. It develops into a four-chambered organ which circulates the life blood for 80 years, without a stop in the pulsations which commenced in that tiny tube.

This is one of the tasks of the body–to develop and maintain an organ which is necessary to life. The body does this all unconsciously, and in the right timing and placing with respect to the other body organs.

In addition to the internal and unconscious tasks, the body also accomplishes a series of visible tasks of which a person is more conscious and which affect his feelings about himself as well as the attitudes of others toward him. These visible tasks of the body constitute the process, in part, of growing up and growing through the life cycle.

Consider, for example, the tasks of learning to walk. Sometimes between the ages of nine and fifteen months the bones, muscles and nerves of the legs and trunk have developed to the point where they are equal to the task of walking. Then the infant learns to walk with varying amounts of help and stimulation from other people. This task is followed by those of running, jumping and skipping.

The child learns to walk almost unconsciously. But even at this early level the gives evidence of being pleased with himself at this accomplishment, and he certainly experience the approval of others as he masters this task. From this time on, the tasks of the body are accomplished with a growing awareness and interest in them by the individual.

Although the body continues in its silent and organic way to accomplish the tasks of growth, such as readying the eyes for the task of reading, and preparing the gonads for the task of reproduction, the result is visible to the individual and to the people around him and they pay a great deal of attention to it.

The child soon learns that he will be judged by what his body accomplishes, and so he tries to make it do well, and he makes the best of whatever it does. This is one of the lessons of life - that we are judged by our bodies and can improve them.

This is true all through life. It is true of the events which constitute puberty, and of the events which take place in men and women around the age of fifty. It is true of the bodily reading apparatus at the age of 6, as well as at the age of 45. It is true of sweet sixteen and of bitter sixty-six.

The human boys is never left alone to achieve its visible uncriticized, as presumably is the case among oysters, ants, and butterflies. Among these organisms it seems unlikely that there is any social expectation about how one's body should develop, and therefore the individual oyster, ant, or butterfly is not likely to feel either social stigma or social approval for the way he looks. But with humans there is always a social judgment.

A person is always judged by the way he looks, and he knows and feels this judgment. The extent to which a society judges people by their appearance varies from one society to another. The ancient Greeks were more conscious of their bodies perhaps than many others; but probably no society exceeds the present-day American in the emphasis it places on looks.

Therefore there are two aspects of physical development, both of which are important for the happiness of people. One, which we have been considering, is the development of the body as it is perceived and valued by other people. Society judges people, and gives them approval or disapproval, partly by the way they look.

The other aspect is that of health and performance. For obvious reasons it is desirable to have good health and for the body to perform acceptably the physical tasks expects of it.

One might easily say that good physical health and bodily performance are more important than having a physical appearance which pleases people, and in a sense this true; but a person who is out of fashion because he has a big nose, or a receding chin, or is very tall or very short or very fat may feel this as keenly as someone else who has chronic ill health. Both aspects are important to the happiness of people, and physical education may well be concerned with both aspects.

Education can do three things for a person in relation to the tasks of the body:

(1) Help a person to achieve these tasks through physical training, proper diet, cosmetics, and grooming.

(2) Help a person to understand and accept inevitable bodily disadvantages, and to correct them as far as possible through instruments to aid the body, and to correct as braces for teeth, and glasses for eyes.

(3) Help a person to prepare for bodily changes in the course of physical growth.

We shall illustrate these three functions of education in relation to the physical changes of adolescence, which is the period when the body is of greatest concern to people.

BODY TASKS OF ADOLESCENCE

The human body grows from childhood to adulthood with such dramatic changes that everyone is aware of them, both the adolescents experiencing the changes and the remainder of the society witnessing them. Those who observe the changes expect adolescents to behave in accordance with their physical appearance, even though this may belie their chronological age. An early maturing 14-year old girl will be treated by older girls and boys as their equal, and they will often say and do things to her which are beyond her understanding and experience. A 15-year old, slow-maturing boy will be treated as a child by his own age-mates and those slightly older.

Most people remember their own adolescence with pleasure or discomfort depending on how well their own bodies met the expectations of the social group. Counsellors and medical practitioners report the concerns of boys and girls with their physical maturation and their physical appearance.

The fear that boys have of physical inadequacy is attested by many studies of adolescent personality difficulties. For instance, Schonfeld reported on the developmental and psychiatric evaluation of 258 boys aged 9 to 16 who presented personality difficulties and emotional conflicts associated with fears of physical inadequacy. He says that during the early part of the second decade of life personality conflicts and psychosomatic complaints may result from an apparent or actual delay in the age of onset of sexual maturation, or inadequacy of masculine development.

A recent questionnaire study of high schools students in confirms the prevalence of adolescent concerns with physique, both with the timing of maturation and with specific physical blemishes. Boys were concerned over being short, girls over being tall. Girls were concerned over having to wear glasses, with freckles and size of their noses, while both sexes were concerned over acne.

Physical appearance was a source of embarrassment to two girls, for different reasons.

During the junior high and high school days, the student was extremely sensitive about his physical appearance. He was short and stocky and awkward. He wore glasses, and acne, and wore braces on my teeth. He was particularly self-conscious about my rather prominent nose. Two of the boys in junior high school indulged in teasing me about my nose and as a result he was very miserable during that period. He withdrew from his companions and had only a few friends. He spent a great deal of time in the library reading books which were usually of an adult level. He compensated, also, by studying hard and standing at the top of my class scholastically. His feelings of inferiority in so far as my physical appearance was concerned never quite left me, although he developed into a person who was average physically, and he realize that he no longer stand out as different from most people.

The physical changes accompanying adolescence were a source of constantly painful embarrassment to him. He was much fatter than anyone else in my group. He was mortified by the development of my breasts, which were very large. Menarche, while accompanied by no physical discomfort, seemed so disgusting to him that he tried desperately to conceal the fact of menstruation from everyone, even his mother. He was as ashamed of it as if it had been syphilis. His coming of age was a period of intense unhappiness.

As one becomes aware of the difficulties that some boys and girls have in adolescence of accepting their bodies and making the most of them, one sees how physical education might help them, through preparing them for the bodily changes of puberty, through helping them to understand and accept certain inevitable disadvantages, and through helping them to achieve the physical skills that are valued in adolescence and to make the most of their physical appearance through grooming and cosmetics. Specifically, there are three things which every high school department of physical education might do.

In biology or hygiene, teach about the physical changes of adolescence, stressing the normality of variability. This has not yet been done to any appreciable extent. Yet this kind of knowledge would set at rest the worries about their normality of all boys and girls except the few who have serious emotional disturbances.

Make it easy for a student to ask for information and assurance with respect to his own physical development. Every school and college should have someone who is easily approached and who is prepared by personality and by training to discuss with students their concerns about their physical development. This person will usually be a doctor, a nurse, a teacher of biology or physical education.

THIS STATE OF THE BODY IS ONLY ONE OF THE IMPORTANT FACTORS

The foregoing discussion might be interpreted by the unwary reader to support the proposition that the body takes priority; that the way it accomplishes its growth tasks determines the social and emotional functioning of the adolescent. There is no question that a tendency in this direction does exist —a tendency expressed by a correlation coefficient that is reliably positive, but not very high. But there are many individual exceptions to such as general proposition, as was pointed out by More in his study of the relations of the physical to other aspects of development in adolescence. He found a number of early-maturing boys and girls who were not particularly early in their social development, even though the general rule was for early maturity to be associated with early social and emotional maturity. This tendency he found more pronounced in girls than in boys. The reason for the low order of relationship between physical, social and emotional aspects of maturity in adolescence is probably partly that the social and emotional qualities of a person are established by middle childhood and tend to carry over through adolescence, so that a child with an easy social personality and a stable emotionality moves through adolescence with these qualities regardless of how his body matures unless it is drastically deviant.

Partly, also, the reason for the relatively low relationship of the physical to the social and emotional aspects of living in adolescence is that teachers and counsellors and parents have been relatively successful in helping boys and girls to accept their bodies and thus to adjust to physical deviations within the fairly wide range that can be called normal.

This discussion raises the question of maturation versus learning, or heredity versus environment. Physical education theory must be continually responding to our knowledge and our biases on the topic of the relative significance of heredity or environment in shaping a person's life. Heredity held sway until the early of the 20th century, and then gave way to environmentalism which must have required a major reorientation of physical education theory.

·Now there appears to be something of a swing of the pendulum away from environmentalism though it does not approach the hereditarism of 50 years ago. Physical educators are in a good situation to draw usefully and impartially from the growing knowledge and genetic and constitutional factors in human development as well as from the growing knowledge of the effects of the family and the peer group and the educational environment on the person.

BODY TASKS AT OTHER AGE LEVELS

The tasks of the body have their special forms at the several age periods, and consequently the functions of health and physical education should be carried out differently in the different age periods. There is something important to be done through education, however, in relation to the body tasks at all ages from 6 to the last years of life.

Middle Childhood, 6-12

During middle childhood our society sets two major for children which involves their bodies.

One is the task of learning the physical skills that are necessary for the games and physical activities of childhood-such skills as throwing and catching, kicking, tumbling, swimming and handling simple tools. The body prepares to accomplish these tasks through growth of bone and muscle, but they have to be learned, and they are learned partly from the peer group and partly through school. Boys are expected to do a better job of learning these skills than girls.

The other task in to learn wholesome attitudes and habits concerning the care of the body, which give a sense of physical normality and adequacy, the ability to enjoy using the body, and a wholesome attitude toward sex.

Early Adulthood, 20-40

In early adulthood the sexes differ most widely in their bodily tasks, because at this time the female task of child-bearing takes priority over the other feminine. tasks for most women. To perform this task well, both mentally and physically, a woman needs a variety of kinds of preparation, some of which can only come through health and physical education. It is not claimed here that preparation for the physical act of motherhood should be a part of high school or college education, though some interesting educational experiments have been made in this direction. Rather, this preparation is most likely to come in early adulthood through the informal means of coaching by one's mother and doctor and by reading, or through the more formal means of classes for expectant mothers maintained by adult education agencies. The preparation takes the form of exercises before and after childbirth, of diet, and of learning the pros and cons of nursing a child.

For both sexes there is the everyday but all-important task of learning to use the body wisely and effectively-to conserve one's energy and maintain one's health during the physical prime of life. This is the time when women and men can look their best, and when their success and satisfaction in life is dependent in a major way on their making the best of their bodies.

Middle Age, 40-60

In middle age there is a fundamental task of accepting and adjusting to the physiological changes that characterize this period. Aging of the body tissues has been going on, mostly unnoticed, since early adulthood. Muscular strength has been diminishing, neuromuscular skills have been fading, and the body has been slowing down. Some of the physical symptoms of aging are:

Growth of stiff hair in the nose, ears, and eyelashes of men.

Growth of hair on the upper lip of women.

Drying and wrinkling of the skin.

Deposition of fat around the middle.

Presbyopia-loss of accommodative power of the lens of the eye. The elasticity of the lens decreases steadily from childhood to old age, and by the age of seventy-five the lens is ordinarily completely inelastic, making it impossible for the eye to adjust itself unaided to the task of focusing on objects at varying distances.

The menopause, or climacterium, occurs in women over a period of several years, usually between forty-five and fifty-five. Menstruation gradually ceases and the ovaries become mere masses of connective tissue. With the cessation of ovarian activity, the delicate balance of the endocrine system is disturbed. Physical symptoms may take the form of hot and cold flashes, dizziness, sweating, insomnia, and excitability.

Thus the body accomplishes its natural task of growing older, but this tends to create real problems of adjustment as great or greater than those of adolescence. The exercise habits of men sometimes have to be changes. There are profound effects on the sexual activities and interests of men and women. A minority of people suffer from more or less severe psychological depression associated with physiological changes.

Women and men can make this period of life much more comfortable for themselves by understanding what is taking place in their bodies, by using various devices to keep their physical abilities up to earlier levels and to defend themselves against the attacks of physical middle-aging. For instance, it is a definite fact that a great many people at about age 50 cease to read more than a few minutes a day because "their eyes hurt", when a suitable adjustment of reading glasses or bifocals would clear up the trouble.

A most valuable kind of adult education is given through books, lectures, and classes on the conservation of personal physical resources in middle age.

Later Maturity, 60+

The slow downward trend of physical vigour and physical beauty which starts in middle age continues in the years of later maturity, sometimes just as slowly, and sometimes more swiftly. Most people maintain very good health and vigour well past the age of 70. Still, the body is aging, but the rate of aging varies enormously among individuals, and it seems likely that medical science will soon find ways to control and decrease the rate of aging in those people who now age most rapidly. The characteristic illnesses of later maturity-cancer, heart disease, and arthritis- are coming gradually under some degree of medical control

No doubt people can aid their bodies to perform more effectively in later maturity by paying attention to their diet, to exercise, to grooming, and to the doctor's advice. An important part of any program of counselling or group study in preparation for retirement should be some lessons on the maintenance of heath.

Conclusion

This we see that throughout the life cycle the body has its tasks to perform, appropriate tasks to each stage of life. The body has its own wisdom, but it can be aided by the kind of wisdom which we get from medical science.

The person has a great stake in how well his body performs its tasks, and he can help his body do better, given the kind of information and training which modern health and physical education provide. However, all people will have to accept the fact that their bodies are not performing as well as they would like, or that their physical appearance is not as good as they would like to be. To some this comes early in life-to all it comes eventually. They can be helped by physical education to accept these unfavourable facts, and to do their best in the face of these facts.

The tasks of the body are especially important to personal wellbeing in the present-day American society, because out society sets such great store on the physical appearance of people. Possibly there will be less emphasis on sheer looks as time goes on, and as the proportion of older people in the society increases. But there is not likely to be any decrease in the social emphasis on health, and people will be expected more and more to make the most of their bodies. Perhaps there will develop a public opinion which blames people for their own ill health, as Samuel Butler suggested in Erewhon. In his Utopia Butler said that people might be severely censured if they became ill, because they were expected to know how to keep healthy, and illness could only come through gross negligence.

In any case it appears that the tasks of the body will be better performed at all ages if people accept the help of health and physical education, and if this profession does what appears to be its manifest duty.

3

PRINCIPLES OR FOUNDATIONS OF PHYSICAL EDUCATION

RAISON D'ETRE

Beginning with some sort of physical activities in the past-unsympathetic and unorganized physical education today has developed into an academic discipline with a sound 'body of knowledge.' It has also grown into a profession which draws its technical tenets from a variety of professional and scientific fields on the one hand, and code of ethics from social sciences on the other.

The academician and the professional in the physical educator have to understand the foundations of the policies, practices and programmes of physical education. Precisely, foundations of a discipline are made of fundamental beliefs and convocations which have been verified. Facts and only facts are the building blocks of beliefs and convictions. Research is the main instrument through which facts are known and theories formulated.

Theories, in turn, are subjected to more rigorous research so that they could be verified in order to take the shape of laws or principles. Theories are modified in the light of new facts or observations which can explain a phenomenon more rationally and logically. The search for truth—the ultimate reality - is an arduous job. It requires the use of scientific method which deftly blends two great epistemological approaches, empiricism and rationalism.

In simple words, we can learn about the universe of ideas, objects or phenomena by using our powers of observation. We can try to understand what these observations mean by using our power of reason, and test our reasoning power against a new set of observations.

The application of scientific method to the study of 'man and movement' in the modern era has resulted in tremendous amount of knowledge. The sciences of 'life, matter and mind' and humanities have contributed 'facts' hitherto unknown to the physical educators. The scientists and scholars working under these fields are not directly concerned with physical education and sport. Their approach, therefore, is fragmentary. The emergence of specialities and sub-specialities of various branches of knowledge such as sport-medicine, sport physiology, sport psychology, sport sociology, bio-mechanics etc. as an interface between physical education and pure sciences has brought physical education to the brink of a unique discipline the roots of which lie in the science laboratories and boughs and branches on the play fields.

The facts received from various sort bio-sciences and art disciplines are to be synthesized and made applicable to the process of building of an enduring edifice of principles which should serve as a guiding light for practices to physical educators alone. It is their prerogative to justify their policies on the basis of scientific principles on the one hand and social value-system on the other.

PRINCIPLES: DEFINITION AND SOURCES

The word principle is defined as "a fundamental truth, a law, a promotive force, a general law or rule as a guide to action." A tentatively organized body of facts is generally called a theory. When verified, either through personal experience or experimentation, a theory takes the shape of a principle. So principles are basic beliefs or fundamental truths which guide and direct actions. A philosophical belief may be relative or absolute in terms of its validity with reference to time and place but a scientific principle is characterized by its universality and a sort of permanence. One of the important things about principles is that they have a universal appeal and mass following.

Physical education is a unique field. In comparison to other fields, it stands apart for its multi-faced form. In one way physical education is an art, in another it is a science, yet in another way it is an organized activity programme so essential for human growth and development. The origin of physical education is traced to the information coming from a wide variety of art and science disciplines. Barrow believes that principles of physical education are chiefly derived from (i) basic sciences (ii) humanities and (iii) social heritage of man. Their virtue lies in the fact that they are founded on human nature, and insight, experience and understanding. The three sources of principles are interrelated. The categorization is simply a matter or convenience rather than rule because whatever man believes or knows to be true is the result of interplay of internal and external forces. In other to have a better understanding of the principles, let us classify them into (i) philosophical beliefs, and (ii) scientific principles.

Philosophy is principally reflective and contemplative in nature. Therefore, philosophical beliefs are the result of 'human observation, experience, understanding and insight'—both personal and collective. The individual and society cannot exist without each other. The personal philosophy and social philosophy influence each other. The personal philosophy and social society cannot exist without each other. The personal philosophy and social philosophy influence each other and direct human thought and action. Powerful beliefs of the "big brains" of a culture often become part of the social philosophy.

Ordinary thoughts and beliefs are good enough for individual consumption i.e. to regulate the day to day behaviour. Philosophic beliefs held by intellectual giants life Aristotle, Plato, Socrates, Chanakya, Manu, Patanjali,

Gemini and a host of others have guided human society through the centuries. However, a large number of these philosophic beliefs have become invalid and lost their sanctity in the light of more reliable observations and innovations. Philosophic beliefs are considered tentative in the sense that change with the time flux. What was considered true and right centuries ago, may not fit into the overall scheme of things today. Paradoxically, they are dynamic and progressive on the one hand,'they are rigid and dogmatic on the other because they draw their strength and sanctity from customs, traditions, social and religious taboos. Customs and traditions are hard to change because they have mass-following.

A philosopher may be very rational in his outlook, a commoner invariably is more sentimental in his approach to life. That, perhaps, is the reason why the common man holds fast to the philosophic beliefs handed over to him as a part of social fast to the philosophic beliefs handed over to him as a part of social legacy and cultural heritage.

In some ways, the truth is fundamental even though its interpretation may change from time to time and situation to situation, in other ways, the truth is relative i.e. what is true for one may not be true for another. So is man's faith in the philosophic beliefs. The changing face of the world on account of scientific discoveries and inventions, socio-economic upheavals, urbanization and industrialization, is bringing about catastrophic changes in the well-established values of life and well-entrenched philosophic beliefs. Contemporary political, social, economic, religious philosophies have attained a new meaning. So much is the impact of change on our life that we find every new generation coming out with new ideas and beliefs about life and social, economic and religious systems. Education as well as physical education cannot remain unaffected in this fast-changing environs and ideas.

Scientific principles are those generalizations the validity and reliability of which have been proved through empirical and/or experimental techniques. Although scientists, in general, don't consider scientific beliefs to be unchangeable, their faith in well-established principles is absolute. Law of Gravitation, Newton's laws of Motion, Archimede's principles etc. are irrefutable principles because they are the result of unchallengeable scientific evidence. They will change only when more substantial and enduring facts are known about the phenomena which these principles govern. Except for a few "missing links, " a large number of sciences of life and matter have developed to such an extent that the possibility of replacing the hitherto gathered knowledge with new facts is simply remote.

The sciences of behaviour and mind are still caught in the web of theories. There is more than adequate scope for many hypotheses to be tested and verified in subjects like psychology, motor behaviour etc. More precise methodologies and refined techniques are required to fill gaps in knowledge in the field of science. The emergence of sport-specific sciences like exercise and sport physiology, sport psychology, bio-mechanics, kinesiology etc. is a step in the right direction. The sport scientists are trying hard to close the gaps between scientific facts about human movement and the methodologies which govern the process of training. The scientific principles bring physical educators much closer to the realities.

The worth of physical education lies in its reliance on the principles—both philosophic and scientific. Williams argues that "one difference between a profession and a trade is that the former is guided by principles based upon scientific facts and/or philosophical concepts while a trade is guided only by rules, methods and directions. The main characteristic of a profession is its reliance upon facts of nature and/or philosophy as the basis for determination of procedure." While philosophic beliefs help the physical educators to formulate aim, objectives and goals of physical education on the basis of values which the individual and society cherish, the scientific principles give him an insight into the realities which govern processes, procedures, methods and methodologies of professional practices.

NEED OF PRINCIPLES IN PHYSICAL EDUCATION

Principles serve numerous purposes in physical education:

1. They form the foundations of physical education as an academic discipline. The entire edifice of activity programme is constructed on the bedrock of principles. Principles provide strength to physical education to stand on its own legs and justify its academic policies and practices.

2. They assist the physical educators to set realistic objectives and goals as well as justify the means to achieve the ends. Professional practices based on solid scientific principles and firm convictions are difficult to challenge.

3. Principles make physical education a socially relevant endeavour, and the physical educators earn a respectable status in the academe as well as in the society. The greater the reliance on principles, the higher the status for the physical educator.

4. Principles provide authority to the physical educators to challenge those administrative directives which go against professional ethics, interests of the participants in physical activity programmes, and well-established universal practices.

5. They serve as guidelines for planning and construction of curricula and course-content for various physical education course,, and set criteria for their evaluation from time to time.

4

BIOLOGICAL FOUNDATIONS OF PHYSICAL EDUCATION

INTRODUCTION

Biological sciences deal with life and life-processes. Microbiology, zoology, botany, anthropology, anatomy and physiology are a few disciplines and sub-disciplines of biological sciences. Through sustained observation, rational thinking and empirical evidence biologists have been able to explode myths about origin and propagation of life on the Earth. The 'story of life' makes an interesting reading but it has been an uphill task for the biologists to construct this story from the 'mute' and fragmentary evidence recorded in fossils, rocks, cases etc.

Moreover, the evidence is so much scattered in terms of time and space that it leaves many vital questions about life unanswered. This gap in knowledge is generally filled with theoretical explanations. That, perhaps, is the reason why the history of life is still perforated.

Since in physical education, our direct concern is man and his movement, the focus of discussion, in this chapter, would be those biological facts which have relevance to the understanding of the biological nature of man and its bearing on physical activity programmes.

To begin with, it has more or less, been accepted that man was not dropped from Heaven but is a product of biological evolution which spanned our billions of years. In the beginning, there existed the cosmic matter on the earth. After a long period, the inorganic material dramatically became organic and laid the foundation for "a new order".

About two thousand million years ago life evolved out of the organic matter and manifested itself in the form of protozoa. Catastrophic environmental changes went on the earth for hundreds of millions of years as a consequence of which more complex organisms evolved. Invertebrates that are said to have appeared on the science some five hundred million years ago, were simply unicellular organisms. From unicellular to multi-cellular, organism to prosimilar, to humanoids, to home spines etc., life evolved in stages.

The apeman, the cave man and the civilized man are links in the biological evolution as well as cultural revolution. Approximately, five hundred thousand years ago evolved the 'intelligent man' and there from began the story of civilization and culture. For a considerably long period of time did man remain slave to natural forces and adapted himself to the changing understand the forces of nature and make the environment conducive for his living.

Interaction between man and his environment was instrumental in the development of man's mental faculties. The nett result of this phenomenal change was that in the 'struggle for existence' man began to rely more on his brain than the 'brawn' which gave him an edge over other animals.

Biologists are of the considered opinion that the major factors which assisted the transition from ape to man were (1) natural selection (2) mitosis—the reproduction of cells through cell-division, (3) meiosis of the sex cell or sexual selection, (4) use and disuse of organs, (5) environmental changes, and (6) other correlative factors/changes. Biologists are also unanimous in accepting the hypothesis of 'Survival to the Fittest'. It lays down that animals and animal-species which could not brave the onslaughts of the changing environment or catastrophic occurrences such as scarcity of food, endemics, climatic upheavals etc. could not survive and became extinct. Those that were "fit" and adapted themselves to the sudden of gradual changes could continue to live. Genetic variations and transmission of traits are also explained on the basis of this widely accepted principle.

Connecting the loose ends of the biological story of man's development, Darwin emphasized: " In the course of evolution, man's ancestors lost certain characteristics either fully or in part; a keen sense of smell, the hairy covering on the body, the majority of the dermal muscles, the tail, prehensile feet, pointed aerobes etc." In discussing the causes that led man to adopt erect mode of locomotion, he assumed that "change of feeding" was of great importance. That occurred when hominoids began spending more and more time in "search of food." Genetic variation and environmental changes are cited as the chief agents causing the development of 'modern man'.

Even though no perceptible change seems to have occurred to man in the last thirty-thousand years the evolutionary process has been going on uninterruptedly like an under—current. Biologically all human beings have similar physical characteristics, racial variations are due to geographical and ecological factors.

Upright body posture and adoption of erect mode of locomotion are considered significant stepping stones in the ascent of man to the apex of biological hierarchy. Revolutionary as these changes proved, they led to the freedom of of re-limbs and development of cerebrum in man. When the arms became free they developed greater mobility and enabled man to perform variety of bodily movements such as hanging, throwing, hitting, carrying things from one place to another etc. As a quadruped man used mouth, like other animals, to carry objects and also fight the opponent (s). The freedom of mouth is said to become responsible for development of language in the human race.

Consequently, man had a number of advantages over other animals. He could protect himself better from animal attacks and natural calamities and procure food more conveniently. He had enough time to 'think' and attend to other things. With the greater mobility of limbs and versatility of 'mind' man laid the foundation for a sort of civilization- the civilization of the primitive man. The accidental or international discovery of fire, wheel, axe, hammer and the like brought about highly significant changes in man's life style and initiated cultural revolution.

The biological evolution and sociocultural revolution have mixed up so well that it has become difficult to discuss on aspect of life on the Earth without reference to other(s). Evolution and revolution have proved a blessing and a bane at the same time. They created the new and destroyed the old. They will create something newer to destroy what is today new.

After having developed a keen intellect and intelligence man began to change the environment with urbanization and industrialization. He left his natural habitat which required to make use of body and its powers. The changed environment - his own creation - forced him to rely too much on his mental powers and machines, and neglect the body that had helped him weather a thousand storms since origin of life. Undoubtedly, man is the master of his destiny because he has numerous techniques and methodologies at his command to combat and tame the forces of nature and lives life the way he likes. On the other hand, it is undeniable fact that both biologic evolution and cultural revolution have brought about certain weaknesses in the human body and its working system as a result of which man looks inferior to animals in many respects although he is far superior to them in intelligence:

Some of these biological weaknesses are listed below:-

1. The physical fitness level in man is now considerably lower than what it was in the past.

2. With the invention of tools, man's manual skills i.e., combative dexterity, sensing danger etc. have been pushed back.

3. The rate of incidence of hypo-kinetic diseases has gone up beyond measure. Heart diseases, despite best medical care, are on the ascendance.

4. Pursuit of materialistic philosophy has added to the woes of man. Constantly increasing stresses and strains on human mind have become an instrument of psycho-somatic disorders.

5. Posture and body mechanics have been adversely affected due to the changes human anatomy underwent during evolution.

6. Man has fallen victim to malnutrition. The rich and the poor suffer from it alike. There is artificiality in producing and consuming food.

With this 'weak' biologic legacy and accelerating mechanization of life, it would be difficult for the mankind to live a qualitative life and survive for long. Great damage has already been done to the human body and the Earth's ecology. The tide of deterioration—whether in health and fitness or in environment—has to be stemmed. The only silver lining in the cloud is the 'right education' which, at this crucial juncture, must consist of understanding and following, in letter and spirit, the principles of physical activity, fitness and health. This is the greatest need of the hour for 'the brave new world'.

PHYSICAL ACTIVITY : BASIS OF LIFE

All living beings are naturally active :they move and they live: they live because they move. Life is characterized by movement. Even the plants which seem obviously inert, also move. All functions of the organism depend upon movement. Movement is the cosmic principle of matter and mind. The inherent energy in the matter generates movement and movement, in turn, generates and sustains life. Each atom of the universe and each cell of the organism are blessed with vital energy which causes them 'move'.

From the moment of conception i.e., fertilization of the female egg by the sperm, to death life is nothing but an endless series of movement. The process of reproduction-fertilization, cell division, cell-multiplication, cell-differentiation, birth of a new organism - is based on movement. Movement is an inborn quality of the organism. When movement ceases, life ceases to exist.

The biologists assert that activity—whether survival or developmental—is a part and parcel of man's biological inheritance. In the primitive past, activity helped man to survive, in the modern day world it assists him to live vigorously and enjoy the blessings of Nature and fruit of his endeavours. Play, games, sports etc. are legacy of the past and justify physical activity as the basis for a qualitative life.

EXERCISE : A DAILY NECESSITY

Not only is physical activity a basic organic necessity, it is a daily requirement. Like food, it must be taken every day. Preponderance of scientific evidence indicates that walking, jogging, playing vigorous games and sports and manual work stimulate growth, processes, and keep the individual physically fit. Williams points out that "all life functions depend upon physical fitness, and greater the physical fitness, the greater the potential life efficiency."

A golden principle of health and fitness is regular physical activity. In general, physical activity improves body posture and strengthens musculature. It causes better digestion, efficient elimination of toxins and other waste products, greater vascularization, stabilized respiration, and greater output of energy. It needs to be emphasized that the real benefits from physical activity are derived only when regularity is strictly observed and the activity to be engaged in calls for a supreme effort. Bortz observed, "There is no drug in current or perspective use that holds as much for sustained health as a life time program of physical exercise."

The human body consists of billions of tiny cells of different types such as muscular cells, skeletal cells, cardiac cells, smooth-muscle cells, nerve cells etc. The cells are not only building blocks of the body , they are also "store-house of energy." These cells perform all vital life functions like digestion, elimination of waste products etc. Regular physical activity stimulates them to perform their respective "duties" at the optimal level thereby enhancing the individual's capacity to work more efficiently and for a longer time. The regular exercisers are significantly healthier and fitter than non-exercisers. The researchers feels that "....if we maintain adequate levels of muscular strength, endurance, flexibility, heart-lung efficiency, balance, bone integrity, and nervous system function, we can retain good performance levels to meet the physical and mental demands required for independent living, well into the chronological 80s and 90s."

From infancy to old age, all human beings perform daily chores, and attend to routines. All the involves physical activity, its quantity and quality being dependent on age, sex, vocation, profession etc. This routine physical activity is hopelessly inadequate to maintain a high degree of health and fitness because the systems of the body are not goaded and geared to work at a higher level of load. Besides this, the modern lifestyle is a paradox in itself. On the one hand, it is sedentary, on the other it is plagued by hurrying-surrying. The routine physical activity is not "exercise" in the real sense of the term. It is simply coping with the necessities of life.

The qualitative exercise is one which is done for its own sake and performed in a tension-free atmosphere. A balanced exercise and activity programme must necessarily include five components viz., (i) Relaxation movements for they help reduce stress and tension, (ii) Endurance exercises which stimulate cardio-respiratory processes, (iii) Muscle-strengthening exercises that provide force for movement, (iv) Stretching exercise which enhance joint mobility, and (v) Balance exercises which reduce the risk of falling and injury.

BENEFITS OF PHYSICAL EXERCISE

Anatomic, physiological and psychological benefits of the large-muscle activity are numerous. *First,* physical activity performed in accordance with the laws of bio-mechanics, helps in developing a correct posture and maintaining it. Sitting, standing, sleeping, walking and running postures are extremely important in life for they allow us to economise on energy and add to the aesthetic value. People with pastoral deviations become a laughing stock and feel inferior in the presence of others, thus aggravating their miseries.

Second, repeated powerful contraction of the skeletal muscles causes increase in their girth, size and efficiency. When a muscle fibre is stimulated, it produces the maximal tension or none at all; the higher the frequency, the greater the tension and also greater the rate at which tension can be developed.

Endurance of the neuro-muscular system is closely related to the ability of a muscle to maintain tension when its is repeatedly stimulated. Through exercise, muscles develop greater contracting ability, strength, capacity for energy storage, endurance and beautiful shape.

Third, the powerful exercise causes chemical change in the muscle i.e., increase in phosphorescent content, glycogen, non-nitrogenous substances and haemoglobin. The nerve impulse travels more rapidly across the motor-end plate in the muscle fibre due to which reaction time improves.

Fourth, through muscular exercise, the cardiac muscle becomes stronger so as the contract more powerfully to push out more blood to the arteries. The heart which is about the size of man's closed fist is the finest pump ever known. In an average adult, it beats 40 million times a year, and more than 2.8 billion times in a life time. It pumps 4,300 gallons of blood daily through 60,000 miles of blood vessels.

Precisely, a normal heart pumps out 10.2 litres of blood a minute in normal conditions while a trained "athletic heart" pumps out 22 litres. The athletic heart is so muscular that it can pump the same amount of blood with 50 beats per minute the average heart pumps with 75 beat per minute. Thus, the athletic heart will beat 13 million fewer times per year. It works less, rests more, and consequently takes a much times per year. It works less, rests more, and consequently takes a much longer time to wear out.

Fifth, physical exercise enlarges all the coronary arteries which feed the heart. It increases collateral circulation so that more than one blood vessel will supply a given area of the heart. Physiologists observes: "Exercise could open up the blood vessels supplying the heart making them less liable to obstruction, and where a partial blockade has developed, vigorous effort could encourage the development of new alternative pathways for the blood." This will prevent the possibility of a heart attack. It lowers the concentration of cholesterol in the blood vessels and fat in the blood.

Sixth, sustained physical activity not only lowers the blood pressure but also it teaches the heart how to extract oxygen from the blood more efficiently. The congestive heart appears large because the muscle is stretched with fluid. The athlete's heart is large because it is muscular. Pavo Nurmi who won nine gold medals in long distance running, had a muscular heart three times the normal size.

Seventh, physical activity causes numerical increase in the RBCs and WBCs thereby ensuring more efficient transportation of food and oxygen to various parts of the body and potentiating individual's ability to combat disease respectively. The greater capitalization, due to exercise, accelerates cell-metabolism and smoothens the road for sturdy growth of the cells.

Eighth, exercise helps regulate breathing. Accepting that the effect of strenuous exercise on respiratory functions is not very clear, researchers hypothesize that "the trained subject demonstrates (a) a decrease in the minute volume of breathing required for the performance of a given load, indicating an improvement required for the performance of a given load, indicating an improvement in the efficiency of ventilation, (b) an increase in maximal respiratory minute volume that can be achieved during very strenuous exertion.

It is probable that the respiratory superiority of the athlete lies not so much in a large vital capacity as in a greater ability to utilize his maximal lung capacity... when exertion is severe, both the minute volume and the frequency of breathing may continue to increase throughout the period of work although there may be a slight decrease in the tidal volume......."

Finally, strenuous activity improves digestion and hastens evacuation process. Increased mobility in the intestinal tract may be due to the fact that exercise causes the body to release increased amount of magnesium into the intestinal tract. The transit time for most people is usually twelve to twenty four hours whereas the marathon runners find that a meal can pass through their systems in as little as four to six hours.

Individual psychological benefits of physical activity. Include: positive changes in self-perceptions and well-being, improvement in self-confidence and awareness, positive changes in mood, relief of tension, relief of feelings such as depression and anxiety, influence on premenstrual tension, increased mental well-being, increased alertness and clear thinking, increased energy and ability to cope with daily activity, increased enjoyment of exercise and social contacts, and the development of positive coping strategies.

GROWTH & DEVELOPMENT AND PHYSICAL ACTIVITY

Activity is the basis of growth and development. The faster the child moves, the faster it grows is an oft-quoted biological dictum. The entire process of reproduction—fertilization, cell-division, cell-multiplication, cell-differentiation—is based on innate biological activity. Functional changes accompany structural transformation and help the organism to adjust and adopt to the environment. Movement and growth processes are directly and closely related. It is impossible to think of one without the other.

Most animals are organically complete at birth. They acquire no appendages in life. However, they grow in stature and size. It is interesting that chronological advancement does not cause significant behavioural changes in animals. They continue to depend upon their instinctive urges and follow the dictates of nature for their survival. In the case of man, things are different. As the human child grows in years, he acquires knowledge and skills chiefly due to quantitative and qualitative changes in his physical structure. His behavioural patterns become more complex. He develops mentally too. Rather, his physical and mental growth curves move up concurrently.

The words growth and development are often used interchangeably. Putting aside the semantic debate, suffice to say that growth is only one aspect of development which is a life-long process. Precisely, growth is a concrete biological process in which the organism gains in size, volume, girth, height and weight. It underscores enlargement of cells, fibres, muscles, bones and organs day by day and year by year. Anatomically, growth is a quantitative change in structure and form observed and objectively measured over a time span. Development, on the other hand, is a much wider term indicating "advancement, more unfoldment, a progressive change—a sort of growing towards greater maturity" . It is a qualitative change in the structural, functional and behavioural aspects of the organism.

Growth is controlled and determined by genetic factors, development is dependent upon external factors such as nutrition, health care, physical activity etc. Benedick considers development to be a "process in which the internal physiological changes and the psychological processes stimulated by them are integrated in a way which enable the individual to master further and a new environmental stimulations". Growth reaches its peak by the time a boy or a girl crosses "teens" but development processes continue further. Growth mostly is physical while development covers also mental, intellectual, emotional and social aspects. Growth is objectively and directly measured; measurement of development is possible only through measured; measurement of development is possible only through indirect means. Growth is an orderly phenomenon characteristic of species: it involves structural changes. Though there are individual differences in growth pattern, various predefined periods of growth the common to all individuals of the same species. Development is characterized by inter-linked and interdependent processes of differentiation, integration and learning. Differentiation refers to cellular specialization and integration denotes co-ordination of various cellular systems.

Learning—a psycho-physiological phenomenon—underlines 'acquisition of new responses or modification of old responses as a result of experience or practice'. Chronological growth may be important in numerous ways e.g., deciding one's admission in school, categorization in minor or major under constitutional provision etc. From the viewpoint of curriculum planning in physical education and training for competitive sport, chronological growth is not a valid yardstick for knowing one's abilities, qualities and capabilities.

GENERAL PRINCIPLES GOVERNING GROWTH

The human growth is governed by several general principles, the knowledge of which helps teachers to plan academic as well as activity curriculum accordingly.

- The growth is a result of interaction between the germ-plasm and environment. The seed which is a gift of nature, contains all the essential characteristics which a child shall have by it is incapable of transforming itself into an adult in the absence of conducive environmental factors such as nutrition, air, water, protection, activity etc. It is all a matter of seed-soil relationship.
- The growth follows an orderly sequence. The development of structure and function is progressive. A simple-to-complex order is uniformly maintained through out. The growth is cephalo-caudal as well as proximo-distal, As astute progression is discernible in the acquisition of motor and mental skills. Every child, says Gessell, "sits before he stands; he babbles before he talks, he fabricates before he tells the truth: he draws a circle before he draws a square; he is selfish before he is altruistic ; he is dependent on others before he achieves dependence on self."
- The growth is a continuous but gradual process. From the stage of zygotic formation to adulthood, a child passes through well-demarcated periods of accelerated growth and consolidation alternately. However, various stages of growth fuse into one

another, thereby making the whole affair a single and smooth continuum. 'Sudden spurts' of growth emerge from the quieter and less dramatic periods. The developmental gains of one stage are carried on to the next stage without hurdle. It takes roughly eighteen long year for the human nonage to become an adult.

- The growth is a creative process. From conception to the completion of adolescence dramatic changes occur in the human organism anatomically, physiologically and behaviourally. The acquisition of new motor skills, habits, concepts, attitudes and the like is part of this creative process.
- The growth in some direction is inevitable. The zygote transforms itself into an embryo and foetus from an impulsion. Lack of ideal nutrition, oxygen and protection from disease may retard developmental processes but it hardly impedes growth.
- Different aspects of growth proceed at different rate to speed. The physical, mental, emotional, intellectual and social aspects of growth, though closely related, have different pace of movement. If children of the same age were compared on various parameters of growth, marked variations would be found. Some are early mutterer in one aspect but late mutterer in the other. It may be true in reverse order. Complete synchronization among all aspects of growth is a rare phenomenon.
- Each individual grows in his own unique way. Though the broad sequence of growth in the same in all individuals the rate of growth varies from individual to individual, depending upon genetic and environmental factors. To quote Gessell again "Some children are tall and some short, some slender others stocky; some are physically strong, others are weak;

some are intellectually keen others are dull. There are the energetic and the phlegmatic, the agile and the awkward, the courageous and the fearful, the outgoing and the in-going personality."

- Growth is affected by internal and external factors. What an individual receives from his parents, grandparents and fore-fathers is nurtured by the environment in which he is brought up. Heredity sets limits for development in terms of potential. No ideal environment can help the child transgress these limits.
- Anatomically, various organs of the body grow at different rate of speed. Each organ reaches its maximal dimension at a certain period of time. Even though this seems to be a chaos, geneticists have found some order in it. The feet, for instance, speed up first reaching their peak growth rate only after about three months after the adolescence spurt has begun. In another six months, it is the turn of the calf muscles and the thighs. Four months later the hips and chest begin to broaden at an accelerated speed, followed by shoulders, In both sexes, the length of the trunk and the depth of the chest reach peak growth last of al. In infancy and childhood, many children look disproportionate but with the passage of time, body dimensions settle down.
- Growth is characterized by fluctuation. The road to development is not smooth but undulated, Genetic and environment factors such as dietary habits, physical and mental stresses and strains, lack of parental and health care might cause fluctuation in growth. The fluctuation is neither a drawback nor disqualification but an inevitability, the impact of which can be attenuated by exerting controls over factors causing it.

- Although rate and pattern of growth are fairly predefined in each case, they can be modified to some extent by improving living conditions.
- With the knowledge of broad generalizations about growth and its influencing factors geneticists can predict future growth and development of a child. Prediction equations have rather been worked out for almost all aspects of growth.

FORCES INFLUENCING GROWTH

Two major forces which influence an individual's growth and development are heredity and environment. While heredity is fixed and unchangeable factor, environment is flexible and modifiable. Every individual can be differentiated and identified on the basis of his genetic material which he inherits from his biological parents. This genetic material called DNA of which the genes are made is transmitted from generation to generation strictly according to natural laws, determines the basic traits of every individual both physiologenic and ontogenic.

Therefore, the hereditary characteristics are unmodifiable and unchangeable. There is substantial empirical evidence to prove that children born and brought up under most appropriate environmental conditions, reach the usual physical stature prevalent in the family. Height-weight patterns, complexion, susceptibility to certain physical ailments and psych-somatic disorders, motor and physiological capacity and many more characteristics are contained in the genetic material which the individual inherits.

No external influence can change or modify them. The individual variations in growth are largely due to these factors. It is said that if one wanted to be an Olympic athlete, one must choose one's parents carefully. Certain races are predisposed to grow taller and heavier than others.

Environmental factors include family atmosphere, parental care, medical facilities, neighbourhood, school, culture, society, climate, surroundings, shelter etc. The children from colder environments appear to grow healthier and stronger. It has been observed that the children belonging to poor, disturbed, and under-nourished families are significantly poorer in growth and health standards than children belonging to well-nourished and less disturbed families.

Similarly parental roles, peers, opportunity for education, society, culture influence growth. Environment factors and conditions affecting growth can be manipulated and modified but they cannot transgress heredity limits in terms of potential which is pre-determined. They simply add or substract to what one is endowed with. Researchers emphasises that innate capacity for growth "is a gift of nature. It can be guided, but is cannot be transcended by an educational agency."

MOTOR DEVELOPMENT

In order to have a better estimation of the role of physical activity in the development of a child, it is necessary to know a few vital facts about motor development through various periods of growth.

Infancy, as explained before, is a period of tremendous growth. In the beginning the general movements of the infant are uncoordinated. When a sensory stimulus is applied to one part of the body, the entire body is activated and the energy is diffused through out. The infant cannot make differentiated responses.

However, the general responses of the babe are visual-fixation on light, spontaneous eye movements, shuddering, shedding tears, sucking, swallowing, cheek and lip movements, sucking of the fingers, yawning, hiccuping, rhythmic mouthing movements, frowning and wrinkling of the brow, tuning and lifting the head, turning the trunk, body jerk, hand and arms movements, prancing and kicking legs etc. As the nervous system gains strength, during the first year of his life, the baby performs such motor activities as lifting his head while lying on his stomach, rolling from stomach to back, sitting, crawling, standing, assisted walking and finally unassisted walking. Essentially guided by cephalocaudal, proximo—distal and mass-to-specific principles, the motor development in infancy initiates adaptive and adoptive processes which bring the child face to face with realities of the world.

In childhood, rate of growth decelerates. As a consequence, the child starts learning new movements and has an urge for independent action. A child can jump off the floor at 37.3 months, stand on one foot alone at 29.3 months, hop at 49.3 months and throw into the basket at 61.5 months. He learns literally no new activity after fifth year but through repetition and practice, he over-learns various motor skills, with the result that there is gradual but sure improvement in the quality of performance.

By the time, the child enters puberty, he can perform variety of motor activities with equal dexterity, if he had been exposed to activity-environment early. Acquisition of high-coordination motor skills greatly depends on the interest, aptitude and opportunity in which children at this stage of life differ from one another significantly.

Adolescence is again a period of accelerated growth more in terms of bull and size rather than motor abilities. Due to increase in muscular strength, children can perform more vigorous activities and for longer duration. Motor development reaches its peak during adolescence. A close relationship is discernible between body-build and motor activities. The mesomorphic child who develops bulky muscles and thick bones likes to engage in games and sports requiring strength and speed. The ectomorph with thin and slender body frame goes in for endurance—type activities. The children with endomorphic heavy build get interested in activities. The children with endomorphic heavy build get interested in activities which require enormous strength like weightlifting, throwing, wrestling etc. Those who were deprived of opportunity for organized physical activity in early years show clumsy motor movements and are least inclined to sports. Such children have the tendency to become bookworms. Physical and motor strengths and weaknesses are clearly visible in the adolescents.

EXERCISE AND GROWTH RELATIONSHIP

Of all the factors which influence child's growth, physical activity is the most dynamic as well as important factor. The effects of physical activity on the organism are observable and measurable objectively. It is interesting to note that genetic factors generally resist digression from the normal growth pattern and strive to hold the original developmental scheme. Consequently, the effects of exercise tend to gradually disappear after the cessation of exercise.

Therefore, the continuity in growth and continuity in exercise are simply hand in glove. Recent research indicates that improvement in muscular development and efficiency is not due to growth of new muscle fibres but on account of activation of the inactive fibres and thickening of existing ones, chiefly due to vigorous physical exercise. It is obvious that muscle potential is greatly dependent on intensity rather than duration of exercise.

Although the morphological structure is predetermined yet it appears that endurance-type exercises stimulate more muscular vascularization because of the greater demands of circulation imposed by aerobic work on the cardiovascular system. On the other hand, more intense exercise seems to improve the muscle contents like proteins, myoglobin, muscle glycogen etc. and also the size of the muscle. However, it is not clear at present whether the muscular improvement, is due to mechanical involvement of tension and pressure or due to chemical phenomenon. Certain studies, especially of the German physiologists, show that exercise stimulates growth in the muscle only when oxygen debt occurs. Another view is that exercise causes changes in the muscle and when the muscle starts recovering, it overcompensates i.e., its recovery is more than what it has lost, resulting in improvement. Another important feature of the growth influences of exercise is that exercise causes reduction in the fat content of the body which is more in males than in females.

Exercise-physiologist also assert that the physical force affecting the orientation of muscle matrix of cell may alter the structural design of the muscles. Because of this reason the muscles developed in aerobic exercise are usually slender, thinner and longer and the muscles developed in anaeorobic exercises are stronger, shorter, and more spherical carrying more of explosive power.

The shape of muscles can be changed by switching over to either type of exercises. The most convincing explanation for this phenomenon is that exercise brings about certain definite positive changes in the central nervous system which plays a dominant role in growth and development.

It has also come to light that the weight of the internal organs, bone-strength and length are improved by exercise. It appears that the pressure-effects of exercise on the epiphytes of bones stimulates growth. But, if the exercise pressure is in excess, the growth of the bone retards Inactivity results in the slender, lighter and longer bones. The decline in structural growth is mainly due to loss of calcium and nitrogen as a result of inactivity or sedentary life-style.

As the shape of a muscle is modified by the quality of exercise; the shape of the bones also appears to be modified by variation in the quality of exercise. Heavy and resistance exercises develop stronger and thicker bones while light and long-duration exercises develop longer and thinner bones. As the angle of pressure application on the bones varies from exercise to exercise, the bony discs are rearranged according to the pressure application affecting the structure and shape of the bones.

Exercise and growth, therefore, are very closely related. All things being equal, the exercisers have more qualitative growth than non-exercisers.

PRIMACY OF MUSCULAR SYSTEM

Although all the systems of the body are interrelated and interdependent, the muscular system is considered as the prime instrument of movement. In the evolution of life, muscular system seems to have played an extremely important role.

In the living organisms, muscular system was the first to appear. The other systems developed only in relation to the activity of the muscular system. Differentiation in cells came about much later. This process was responsible for the creation of new animal species and made the higher animals like man extremely complex in structure and function. Protozoa and amoeba from which shot off other animal species in the beginnings are still a muscle. The visceral organs in higher animals developed in relation to the activity of the large muscles of the trunk.

The movement of a newborn child are largely big-muscle movements initially controlled by reflexes. The control over trunk muscles is more accurate and comes much earlier than control over extremities and fine muscles. The reason for this phenomenon is to be sought in the order and sequence of the foetal growth as well as evolutionary process. The trunk muscles, therefore, are the oldest. They play a pivotal role in the growth and development of the muscles of the extremities. 80% or the bulk of human body is all muscle. That is, perhaps the reason why muscular system should take precedence over other systems of the body.

More importantly, the cardiac, respiratory, mesentric and peristaltic muscles are not within the voluntary control of the individual. They are controlled primarily by reflexes. The skeletal muscles exert indirect control over these highly specialized muscles. The functional efficiency of the visceral muscles and organs is traced to efficient movement of the skeletal muscles.

The muscular system serves as an axis of man's life activity. On the basis of their structure and function, the muscles of the human body are categorized under the following heads:-

(i) Smooth muscles;

(ii) Cardiac muscles;

(iii) Striated muscles.

The smooth cells make smooth muscles which comprise the intestinal track. The cardiac cell make myocardium of which the heart is made. The digestive and cardiac musculature performs highly specialized functions of supplying food stuff and oxygen to all parts of the body for performing their respective functions.

The smooth muscles and cardiac muscles are not under the voluntary control of the individual but they are intimately related to the skeletal muscles. The visceral organs are not capable of improving their own efficiency, they depend on muscular system. The large muscles, when exercised vigorously, stimulate the visceral muscles to work at optimal efficiency.

From the skeletal musculature rather than the visceral muscles. By virtue of their structure, striated muscles are capable of producing powerful contractions. Each muscle fibre is composed of functional units referred to as sacromeres, which give the muscle fibre its striated appearance. Striations are caused by a repetitive and specific organization of the myofibriller proteins, actin and myocin and regulatory proteins within each sacromere. Skeletal muscles are attached to the bones: they have their origins and insertions. They exert their effect by moving parts to which they are attached or by compressing the parts they surround. When attached to the bones, the contracting muscle draws its two ends towards the centre and one or both attachments move. When the muscle is in the wall of the organ the contraction causes compression or movement, depending upon the position of the muscle cells.

MUSCLE TONE

The quality of the muscles to "remain in a state of semicontraction even when no activity is being performed", is called muscle tone or tunas. No powerful movement can occur unless the muscles are in a state of readiness. In simple words, the muscle tone is tension—a sort of tightness which keeps the muscle "set" for action. The muscle tone depends upon electrical stimulation from the nervous system and is a reflex phenomenon.

It is established beyond doubt that if the nerve that innervates a muscle is severed, the muscle becomes exceedingly flaccid. Endurance of the neuro-muscular system is closely related to the ability of a muscle to maintain tension when it is repetitively stimulated. All the living organisms even when completely relaxed, remain in a state of semi-preparedness, more popularly known as the semi-contraction phase.

During powerful contraction phases, there is rush of blood to the affected muscle and through chemical processes, heat is produced. The tonus is actually the cause of muscle development but if the tension so developed crosses the required level, it causes fatigue, makes the muscle stale, negatively affects movement-precision and impedes performance.

The only way to keep the muscles toned is to exercise them correctly and adequately. It is a fact that the muscles lose tone in old age. They also lose tone in bound age when one does not extract work out of them. Inactivity is the greatest enemy of the muscle tone. Frequent strains, sprains and pulls occur in the muscles because they are not properly toned through exercise.

Recent research had has revealed that the muscles get better toned through isogonic and isokinetic exercise rather than by long endurance-type activities. The well-toned muscles are of great advantage to man.

First, they help to maintain good posture in all situations. Not only do they give a beautiful look to the human body, they add to the work efficiency of the individual. The exercisers and non-exercisers have been found to differ significantly in this respect.

Second, a good muscle tone improves reaction tune, thereby enabling the sport-persons to perform better especially in short-duration speed events.

Third, improvement in neuro-muscular coordination is possible only when muscles are kept well-toned through exercise. This postpones early fatiguing and aging so that one can maintain good health and fitness even in old age.

RECIPROCAL INNERVATION

The muscles are arranged in pairs i.e. agonists and antagonists, in order to work in a cooperative and synchronized way. Biceps-triceps and quadriceps-hamstring are excellent examples of paired muscles. The agonists are called *prime movers* and antagonists controllers. When a group of agonists is stimulated and is initiating a movement, its opposite group acts as a counter force to regulate and control movement by relaxing.

This role of the paired muscles is reversed when the movement is performed in the exactly opposite direction.

While the movement of one group of muscles is guided by excitatory processes, the movement of its opponents is controlled by inhibitory processes. This natural phenomenon of checks and balances is called Reciprocal Innervation and is programmed through neural impulses.

Muscles are known to be servants of the brain and the volitional movements are initiated by impulses that are discharged from certain areas of the cerebral cortex. An important feature of this reflex activity is that stimulation of a particular muscle is associated with inhibition of the antagonistic muscle. The more intense the impulse, the more powerful the contraction in muscles and more violent the movement. A reticular formation in the brain is said to be the switchboard for excitatory and inhibitory processes in the muscles. Some muscles are called as fixators or stabilizers.

During a complex movement, when numerous group of muscles operate the anatomical levers, fixators hold these levers in their proper position. A wholesome activity programme must strengthen reciprocal innervation. The largely reflex-controlled movement of infants and children look clumsy in the beginning because their antagonists are not strong enough to control the movement and relax properly when agonists are contracting.

The principle of reciprocal innervation also underlines the fact that children should not be motivated beyond permissible limits and exercises involving too much of suppleness should not be given to very bound children because such exercises exert undue pressure on the spinal muscles and ligaments thereby severely affecting the inhibitory processes.

USE, DISUSE AND OVER USE

Free and unrestricted movement of muscles is a biological hunger. Life appears to go much better with vigorous motion than with inactivity. Biologists have conclusively proved that organs of the body which are in constant use, develop and remain efficient and those which are not used atrophy and become defunct.

The eternal law of use and disuse is said to be responsible for appearance of numerous characteristics in man and animals, and disappearance of others during the biological evolution. An astounding difference between an organism and a machine is that the former develops with use, the latter wears out. This does not rule out degeneration of the human body. The body does degenerate with age but the rate of wear and tear of cells can be minimized considerably and the repair work speeded up through well planned physical activity.

The exerciser does not turn old fast and continues to remain fighting fit even in declining years. 'Use' means proper and adequate movement of the body and its parts. 'Disuse' means cessation of activity or inadequate movement. So long a person is alive, there is no cessation of activity by simply attending to daily chores cannot be considered adequate if one is to enjoy the blessings of life.

The changed earthly—environment and the emergence of 'push-button culture' have considerably reduced the demands on the human body resulting in lower levels of health and organic fitness. The 'civilized' man is not required to jump a stream, climb a tree throw a stone in order to escape from danger or hunt for food. The challenges of modern civilization are entirely different from those encountered by man during evolutionary and revolutionary periods of life.

Yet challenges are challenges and they have to be met with verve and vigour if the human race has to survive as a virile master of creation rather its lazy-servant. The greatest danger to mankind is from physical inactivity and self-complacency about fitness and health. In a sense, modern life many be active but it certainly is not vigorous.

'Overuse' means working the muscles beyond their latent capacity. This generally happens when a commoner continues to work overtime to make both ends meet and an athlete trains hard and continuously without giving opportunity to the muscles to relax and recover from fatigue.

Stress fracture, muscle-soreness and staleness are some effects of overuse of muscles. Over using is overdoing, a consequence of over-motivation and over-enthusiasm. Physical exercise becomes a killer if the work-out is not properly planned. Training schedules planned without reference to nutrition, rest, load, intensity, capacity etc. not only retard performance, they pose a great threat to health and well-being of the athletes.

Physical education must teach people how to make judicious use of the muscles in order to receive benefits in terms of fitness for life and sport, health and wellness. Both disuse and overuse of muscles are dangerous in as much as one results in atrophy the other in hypertrophy. The middle path, therefore, is use—proper and adequate.

LOAD, CREST LOAD AND OVER LOAD

It has been scientifically established that real benefits from physical activity accrue only when its intensity and load are progressively increased. The principle of load has, therefore, great significance for physical educators. It is directly related to the cardio-respiratory system of the body. A load is considered as normal if the intake of oxygen is just adequate to meet the demands of the body.

During vigorous physical effort, when the entire cardio-respiratory machinery is working at a high rate, and the intake of oxygen is sufficient to continue work without problem, it is normal load. A load is considered to the be the crest load if the intake of oxygen is adequate to meet the demands of the body but the cardio-respiratory machinery is working at its optimum capacity without further prospectus of increase at that moment.

A load is considered over-load when the intake of oxygen is insufficient to meet its demand in the body even though the cardio-respiratory machinery works at its maximal capacity. This situation, when continued for sometime creates an imbalance in the demand and supply of oxygen and the oxygen debt results.

A few common signs and symptoms of over-loading physical activity are persistent soreness and stiffness in the muscles, tendons and joints, heaviness in legs, headache, nausea, loss of appetite, fatigue, sluggishness, loss of weight, swelling of the lemonades in the neck, groin and armpits, nervousness, depression, gasping for air, and unexplained drop in performance. During hard days of training , muscle fuel called glycogen is used up. It takes the body ten hours to ten days to replenish it. Potassium, a mineral released from the muscle cell to control heat is also depleted. It requires upto forty-eight hours to restore the supply.

Notwithstanding the serious athletic training where tow much overloading has to be the rule, the normal daily physical exercise is not adequate for optimum growth and development of a normal person. Although in the process of maturation various organs of the body develop yet more than normal work-load should be given on the body if greater efficiency and capacity are to be built up.

In the process of maturation, muscles and organs grow up in a normal way. For higher than the normal level of fitness and efficiency, sport scientists believe, muscles should be exercised at a higher than the normal work load. The optimal development of all parts of the body cannot be assured without application of this principle in letter and spirit. With repetition and practice i.e. through a psycho-physiological adaptation over a period of time, what is overload today, may become crestload tomorrow, and the crest load normal load day after. Progression is the keynote to the load-principle.

In training for competitive sports, overload is a rule rather than exception. Almost all serious sports require the athletes to be superfit. Unbelievable performance-records have been established in the Olympic games simply because the winning athletes had trained at a much higher load simply because the winning athletes had trained at a much higher load than required, thereby pushing up their physiological efficiency to the levels hitherto unknown, and extending frontiers of human body beyond the known horizons. For example, Paavo Nurmi—the hero of 1920 Olympics trained himself by running 50 fast miles a week while Emil Zetopack of 1956 Olympics, ran 70 fast miles per week so as be able to show unprecedented excellence in endurance running.

An important implication of the overload principle for the physical educators is that the physical activity load for various age groups and two sexes should be worked out in such a manner that physical activity assists growth and does not stunt it. Overloading of children when they are passing through accelerated periods of growth, is dangerous because it results in burning up.

A lot many promising athletes reach the deadened of their sporting career because over-enthusiastic teachers overload them with hard training and make them win junior competitions. Educationally this is not at all sound.

AGE : CRITERION OF PUPIL-CLASSIFICATION

From cradle to coffin, the human beings pass through various periods of growth and development. Each period of growth is unique in terms of its span and the characteristics of behaviour associated with it. From the viewpoint of universal norms of growth infants, children and adolescents differ from one another significantly in almost all characteristics. So classifying pupils into various groups on the basis of their chronological age poses no problem. The greatest difficulty comes from the individual differences amongst children of the same age group. Normally, chronological age is used as a yardstick for measuring growth of children and assigning to them social status. From the viewpoint of curriculum planning in physical education this socially recognized age-old practice has not been found very sound chiefly due to acute individual differences in growth and development. The geneticists, therefore, suggest that alongwith chronological age, developmental characteristics should also be taken into consideration when classifying pupils and assigning them to various groups.

A reference to anatomical, physiological and mental ages, which reflect various developmental characteristics, is a necessity. In common parlance, age virtually refers to chronological age which is reckoned in years, months and days.

Beginning with the day of birth and terminating with the death of an individual, the chronological age is guided by the moving hands of the clock. Traditionally, chronological age is a legally valid criterion for categorizing an individual into a minor or major person, seeking admission in a school, being eligible for a job, getting assigned to an athletic group—sub-junior, junior or senior—for sport competitions. Some physiologist reports that age is an important consideration upto almost seventeen years by which time a child is said to have grown upto 95%. After this, it should be discounted for classifying pupils solely on the basis of chronological age. Before a child reaches the top of maturity, chronological age as a criterion of classification might be misleading because various aspects of development do not necessarily move in a synchronized way. Some clever parents deliberately hide the actual age of their children with some ulterior motive. The sport associations do the same thing on purpose.

Anatomical age is concerned with ossification of bones—a process by which the elastic bones of the child become harder and stronger over a period of time with marked changes in their chemical composition. X-rays are generally used to determine the extent to which a child has matured structurally. Dentition—the number of teeth a child has at a particular point of time—is also considered as an index of anatomical age. This process of skeletal examination does not only lend credibility to the chronological age especially when the vested interests attempt to hoodwink the selectors for selecting subjunior and junior athletic teams but also help the physical educators to assess the suitability of children for strenuous physical activity and hard heavy weight training.

Determining anatomical age of a child is a highly technical task and should be left to the competent medical personnel. The physical educators should not resort to this technique without medical support. Physiological age is inferred from the signs and symptoms connected with puberty. It takes cognizance of the functional condition of the organs of the body more specifically the reproductive and the glandular systems.

The quality and quantity of hair on the pubis and in arm pits, onset of menarche in girls and night ejaculation in boys are sure indices of age-related developmental changes and physiological maturity of children. Even though a valid yardstick of pupil classification, physiological age is rarely calculated unless clinical situations so warrant. Besides, determining physiological age of a child is a cumbersome task. The teachers/parents have to venture into the private life of the children to assure themselves of maturity level. Despite all this, physiological readiness/maturity is an important consideration in working our activity load for each child especially when he/she is inducted into the arena of competitive sport at a relatively young age.

Mental age indicates maturity of the human mind especially cognitive, perceptual and affective abilities. Developmental psychologists consider mental age as an important classification—criterion. In skill-acquisition, mental maturity is of great value. Mentally backward children find it difficult to acquire sports skills speedily. Even though mental age is rarely used as a yard stick for pupil classification in sport activity circles, numerous performance and paper-and-pencil tests are available which can help the physical educators to differentiate deviant mental growth curve from the normal one. Physical educators should be well advised not to lean too heavily on chronological age even though it serves as a handy tool for pupil classification.

Other variables such as high as height, weight strength, aerobic/anaerobic capacity, mental maturity etc. require serious consideration while classifying pupils and assigning them to various groups.

HEALTH AND EXERCISE

Generally, health means 'freedom from disease'. When discussed in relation to human movement, health seems to be a much broader concept and this definition is found lopsided. Health, is "that quality of life which enables one to live are two different things. There are many who have rarely fallen prey to any serious disease in life but this does not at all mean that they really 'live most and serve best.' Health, therefore, has mental, social and spiritual implications.

The crux of the matter is that 'freedom from disease' is only one aspect of health. One needs to have a fairly high level of physical fitness to perform one's duties to the best of one's ability, to be free from mental tensions, to have a healthy attitude towards life, and to have an excellent rapport with one's environment. Only then one would certainly enjoy the blessings of nature and live optimally. A healthy person should not live for himself, he must significantly contribute to create a healthy environment—both physical and social—in order to make the world a better place to live in. This exactly is the underlying spirit of the phrase 'live most and serve best'. It is wisely said that a healthy person is an asset to the society, a sick person a liability. The one commands and the other simply demands.

SEX AND AGE DIFFERENCES

Biologically, the sex of a child is determined at the very moment of conception and a neonate enters this world wither as a male or female. Nature has ordained the sexes to play their respective roles according to biological requirements especially in the matter of procreation. Structural and functional differences between the genders are innate. They have a great bearing on the social roles the sexes play in their life.

From the view-point of growth and development, except for distinction in reproductive system, the differences in physical structure and function of female and male child are hardly manifest until puberty. With the onset of puberty which is about two years earlier for the female child, the secondary sex characteristics begin to appear and become quite pronounced during "teens" in the two sexes. From here onward does the parting-of-ways commence for the male and the female.

The differences characterizing sexes are not merely superficial but significant because even a layman considers them so profound that it is regarded as an insult to refer to a person to the other sex than that to which he or she rightly belongs. "It is here", say Lindhard "that the object of their education must differ in the same degree because the boys must be brought up to be men and girls to be women."

The structural, physiological and emotional differences that surface during adolescence are essentially due to the functioning of sex glands and the effects that follow transform delicate girls into beauteous women and boys into virile young men, both capable of reproductive activity. The gonads not only produce the germ-plasm—the material cause of a new life—but also secrete hormones which give respective secondary characteristics to the sexes.

Characteristically, girls have a faster growth rate in the early stages of adolescence. They are ahead of boys atleast by two years. The growth-spurt begins by 10-11 years in girls and 11-13 in boys. Even by 14-16 years, boys are behind girls in maturity. After that the boys not only grow faster but also they overtake girls. By 16-17 years, girls reach the peak of their growth when the boys are still midway. The greatest impact of growth-spurt, both in boys and girls, is found in the anatomical and physiological regions.

When the growth-curves of the two sexes are compared, it would not be difficult to find that (1) the girls mature earlier than boys, and (2) they temporarily surpass the boys in physical dimensions around mid-adolescence. The faster growth-rate and shorter growth-span make the girls look maturer than boys. By 16-17 years the female growth-rate slackens down considerably, while the male growth-curve continues to show an upward trend well upto 19-20 years.

On this account, women are said to be "aging" faster and their life-span, on average, is found to be shorter in comparison to that of man.

ANATOMICAL DIFFERENCES

- The skeletal height, which is genetically determined, is the most important index of growth. By nature, man is taller and heavier than woman. Even at birth, an average male infant is longer by an inch or so than the female child.
- The female bones are comparatively shorter and weaker. As a result, the entire female skeleton is shorter, less angular and more delicate. Since much of the female muscle is all-fat, the skeleton shows

marked muscle traces. This makes women susceptible to negative effects of hard manual labour.

- The proportion between torso and extremities in both the sexes is different. While women have a comparatively longer torso and shorter limbs, men have shorter torso and longer limbs. This structural arrangement may not be an oddity but this creates many a mechanical complication for women in activities which necessitate 'body reach' and frequent change of centre of gravity. Shorter limbs and longer body makes the female centre of gravity. Shorter limbs and longer body makes the female centre of gravity fall lower. That is why, women have a greater stability in body balance better than men.
- The lumber region of the female spine is comparatively longer and the thoracic region shorter. The narrow thoracic cavity makes no room for bigger visceral organs as in man. Woman's heart, lungs, stomach etc. are smaller than those of man.
- The greater difference is in the pelvic region. The female pelvis is much roomy and broader. It is so because women have to rear children inside their body. The uterus on this account is distensible so that even the pelvic bone itself is broader. Thus, the abdominal wall which is the main support of viscera, is a wailer part in women especially those who have given birth to children. The greater and stronger use of lower extremities requires a fairly strong and solid pelvic girdle which is not there in women. In this respect, women are not stronger or even equal to men.
- Woman's shoulder is much weaker than that of man. Not only the bones of the shoulder joint but also the muscles and cartilages controlling the movement of the shoulder joint, are weaker. The clavicles are comparatively long and slender. Consequently

women are far inferior to man in shoulder strength. That is, perhaps, the reason why hanging exercises in gymnastics and pole vault are not prescribed for women. In swinging bat or racquet and throwing a ball women are far behind man.

- Because of the pelvic bone being broader and longer, the comparatively greater convergence of the thigh bones result in knees being slightly inward, and that on crux, when the position of the femur is more vertical as in running, points obliquely downward-outward. Due to this skeletal arrangement, the female lower extremities lose both force and precision. Broader hips, unlike those of men, are a hindrance in running and also in movements requiring more of agility. The sway of hips in walking impinges upon the energy cost.
- Slender bones and rounded fatty muscles make women inferior to men in almost all the regions of strength, i.e., grip strength, explosive strength, dynamic strength etc. Their punch, thrust, kick, hit pull, push etc. much lighter than those of men.

PHYSIOLOGICAL DIFFERENCES

- On the whole, muscular strength in women is far less than in men. Due to slightly different composition of muscles and abundance of adipose tissue, no amount of weight training can help women improving muscular strength and power. Man is much stronger to woman in pulling, pushing punching, slapping, kicking, striking, and squeezing.
- Not only are women misfit for hard manual labour but even at light physical duties, they do not have the same staying power as men. Their aerobic capacity is very low and during vigorous activity their muscle glycogen gets depleted at a much faster rate as compared to men. Asmussan, a Danish

physiologist, has set the strength of the average female at 60% of the male figure, with only about a half of this deficiency being attributed to her shorter stature.

- Comparatively smaller cardio—respiratory apparatus of women is greatly responsible for their low vital capacity and stroke volume. Their heart rate is faster. Variations in their blood composition favour certain biological functions which women perform. All this affects their endurance capacity.

- Menstrual-period, which bogs down a woman atleast for five days in a month, has been a debatable point with exercise physiologists as well as female athletes for a long time. Not withstanding sociological merits and demerits of the case, the medicos are in agreement that except in extreme pathological cases, the 'periods' do not affect women's physical strength. The menstrual period has greater psychological implications than physiological complications. Headache, nausea, sluggishness, inaptitude for vigorous activity etc. are observed in menstruating women.

- Interestingly, in normal circumstances, atleast one woman in seven is liable to be menstruating on any day. Sport physiologists have, therefore, been able to alter the menstrual periods of female competitors so that this inevitable biological activity does not create hurdles during international fixtures. Surprisingly, some women athletes are said to have successfully spell. Still the medical world does not react favourably to women's tendency of subjecting themselves to hard physical training and competition during the menstrual period on hygienic and health grounds.

- Pregnancy and child-bearing are very sensitive situations in the life of a woman during which she cannot be subjected to hard physical activity. These biological functions make women different to men and restrict their freedom of movement. During pregnancy and especially after childbirth light exercise is essentially necessary for women but not without consultation of a doctor. No wonder, some mothers compete in international sports competitions. These are exceptions. The average woman cannot dream of it. General health condition—both internal and external is the major consideration in this matter.

- Even though average man's brain weights 3 pounds, the average woman's two pounds, the relation of the brain to body is about the same in both sexes and, in any case, it does not make woman inferior to man in intelligence. However, women are found to be inferior to man in reaction time and less predisposed to aggressiveness. Women are slower in motor reactions such as in applying brakes to speeding automobiles.

- Women have also been found emotionally weak. The effect of injury, accident, victory or defeat is far greater on women than on men. Women may not be lacking in self-control but once they breakdown under stress, they take more time to recover from shocks and traumas. Manifestation and effects of nervous breakdown are far stronger in women than in men. That is perhaps, why experts do not advise women exposing themselves to activities which disturb emotional equipoise such as boxing where a hard punch from the opponent may set the athlete bleeding.

- Sex and age differences are not at all a quash for anxiety because spheres of sports competition and physical activity for men and women are clearly demarcated. Age groups and sexes do not clash with one another on the sports field but compete in their own categories. The knowledge of sex and age differences serves as an excellent guidelines for planning exercise and sport curricula for various slices of population and organizing competition for them.

5

THE IMPORTANCE OF PHYSICAL TRAINING IN PHYSICAL EDUCATION

Physical training means planned physical exercises performed systematically in schools and youth organization for educational purposes. Its aims are manifold. The emphasis is generally laid on its preventive medical aspect: physical training should promote health and develop-physical strength and endurance. It also has subsidiary aims the importance of which varies from one country to another, such as pre-military training, social training, character and will formation and training in posture and efficiency.

Physical training as an educational subject did not become worldwide until the last two centuries with the advent of compulsory education. Very few schools or youth organization do not nowadays include it in their syllabus. In different countries it takes a variety of form corresponding to its subsidiary aims.

It is highly complex, but the one factor common to all it forms is movement. Physical movements effort and performance are always its foundations and its essential characteristics. The idea that physical movement is an important factor in education has now spread to all parts of the world.

The diversity of physical training and its lack of uniformity throughout the world are due to its historical development. Modern physical training is a river fed from many sources. Its oldest source and its most beautiful manifestation in the European countries are the gymnastics of ancient Greece.

Besides those it comprises many popular forms of games, contests and dance coming from all over the world: gymnastics from the monasteries of China; Indian breathing and concentration exercises; ball games from the Indians and from the Middle ages in Europe; the tournaments of chivalry; the swimming sports of the South Sea Islanders; skiing from the Lapps and Scandinavians; canoeing from the Eskimos.

Those early forms of local culture have converged from all sides to stimulate physical training and to be adopted by it and transformed.

In this nineteenth century it received powerful impetus from the German gymnastic movement, from Swedish gymnastics and from the sports and games of English life. The English development in particular spread its influence throughout the world. The sports and games of the British nobility passed in unbroken succession to the middle classes and during the nineteenth century to the workers, preserving the ethical, social and spiritual values of chivalry but adapting them to the needs of the times. Sociologists agree that modern sport as it developed in Great Britain between 1880 and 1900 was a by-product of the industrial revolution.

Every country that has developed industries and become an industrial nation can show a parallel development of sport. The latest evidence for this observation comes from the Soviet Union and Bharat. We can see today that the form of English sport, with its contests and games and its spirit of "fairness", has spread to nearly every country in the world probably as one manifestation of a uniform and universal culture. This modern sport has also decisively influenced physical training, in many lands very much, in others for the time being not at all.

Throughout the world, however, discussion takes place on the influence of sport on physical training, and a modern physical training without sport is today inconceivable.

In the twentieth century, moreover, physical training has received a new access of strength from modern gymnastics and modern dancing, which first appeared in Central Europe and were then developed on a large scale in the schools of Great Britain.

When, as a consequence of compulsory education physical training appeared in all countries in the nineteenth century, its national components were preponderant. In Prussian Germany for instance German "school gymnastics" with their strictly formal and intellectual structure made headway against the great political difficulties of the anti-democratic restoration; in Sweden there grew up a system of health and pustular gymnastics that was adopted in many other countries; the public schools of England developed a training based on games which helped to shape the English national character. There appeared for the first time in the twentieth century a tendency for national systems of physical training to influence one another, which now seems to have reached some kind of settlement.

The German youth movement generated fresh impulses which brought physical training and gymnastics out of their dusty buildings back into nature. In Austria there grew up the "natural gymnastics" which overcame the rigid forms of gymnastics instruction and gave new life to physical training.

In France He'bert introduced his "method naturelle", which had a similar effect, Sweden likewise started to reform its unduly rigid methods. All these new movements spread their influence beyond the national frontiers. The Austrian innovations strongly influenced physical training in Holland and also in Germany. The reforms in Sweden and Germany were reflected in countries which had originally learnt physical training from them.

Two world wars brought upheaval and devastation but also strengthened the bonds between peoples. Physical training now manifests a general tendency to become uniform in all countries, and similar results of change can be observed in many places. The problems of physical training which confront us today are much the same over most of the world.

This statement sounds surprising, but at the first UNESCO seminar on physical training and sports held in Gauting Munich, in September 1957 it was generally agreed to be true.

What points are covered by agreement?

1. It is apparent in all countries that their large cities and industrial areas have so little room in which children can play and move that special measures have to be taken to promote children's active physical life. The most important measure of this kind is compulsory physical training in the schools.
2. It is also apparent everywhere that, to prevent our children from becoming intellectualized, these school which go in for nothing but book-learning must yield to the cultivation of physical, artistic and manual skills.
3. It is admitted in all industrial States that in free communities sports and games make an important contribution to social and moral training, which is now inadequate in communities using only traditional methods.
4. All State and municipal educational authorities therefore now agree in demanding a stronger, deeper and more vital physical training in schools and youth organizations.

That is the scope of agreement concerning the postulates of physical training. It is, however, interesting to note that the problems which physical training authorities have to tackle nowadays are much the same in all countries. They relate to methods, the training of instructors, and the finding of money for playgrounds and premises. The differences life merely in the matter which shall be taught, where historical and national factors are as important as ever.

I. Methods

It is a surprising thing that in the last ten years the old conflict over the best method of physical training has come to an end. Discussion always brings to the fore the "natural method"; it has various names and concepts according to language and national characteristics, but emphasis is always laid on freedom, the differences between individuals, pleasure, and indirect effects. It is widely known in Europe as the "movement lesson" though it has by no means been introduced into all schools. It allows the child independence, freedom of will, freedom of choice and freedom of fantasy development, but demands of him discipline and inward order. It is a democratic form of physical training and is therefore banned in the dictator States.

To develop it further is a universal task in which all nations participate in peaceful emulation and which is certain to bear precious fruit.

II. THE TRAINING OF INSTRUCTORS

The proper training of instructor for physical education is also a matter discussed in all countries. A final solution has not yet been reached any where, should physical-training instructors be trained in universities and teacher-training colleges, or in special high schools? Should the instructor be a specialist, or should he teach other subjects as well and be trained in these also? Should primary schools have physical-training instructors, or should the form masters give all the instruction, including that of physical training? What happens to physical training if, as in many countries, most of the teaching is done by women? These are the worldwide problems in this field. In Europe it is becoming increasingly probable that they will be solved along the following lines.

(i) In the higher schools the system of specialization in teaching prevails; the physical training instructor teacher other subjects as well, especially when he grows older.

(ii) The primary-school teacher must be thoroughly instructed in physical training so that he can teach it later in his own class.

(iii) Women who have been suitably trained are perfectly capable of conducting physical training in schools for boys only.

The standing of physical training in relation to other school subjects depends less on the teacher's practical ability than on his skill as a teacher and his moral attitude and character. Modern schools of all sorts need physical training instructors who know their subject inside out and are keen on it, and who at the same time are, as teachers and instructors, intellectually and scientifically equal and superior to their pupils.

III. PREMISES

The most difficult problem of physical training in all countries is that of premises and equipment. War damage has made it just as accrue in many European countries as it is in countries such as Turkey and Egypt where physical-training organization is new. The construction of playgrounds, halls, swimming baths and playing field needs a big capital outlay and their maintenance means a continuing expense. For instance in Germany, with its unfavourable climate, an ideal programme for the building of gymnasia would cost DM3,000 million, or 7.5 percent of the national budget. How can parliaments and parties be convinced that such expenses are vital for the future of our people?

In Great Britain the Education Act, 1944, has shown that they can be so convinced. The most powerful help in this fight for money for physical training comes from the doctors, who throughout the world are ardent champions of physical training as a weapon against the menacing disease of civilization. It is also important to develop a sound, convincing scientific theory of physical training, without which such a vital movement can nowadays make no headway.

It is absolutely necessary to press forward with the development of the practical side of teaching but theory in research and instruction must no be neglected. An international physical-training research institution, perhaps within the scope of UNESCO, would be for many countries an inestimable aid and support in the campaign for sound physical training.

IV. THE SCOPE OF INSTRUCTION

The difference between countries in the choice of the subjects to be taught in physical training is relatively wide. Historical development, with its national and popular origins and forms, is here especially conspicuous. That however, is certainly no disadvantage.

On the contrary, modern methods of physical training do not depend on any hard-and-fast code of exercises and performance but can be applied to all forms of movement. The more varied the material offered, the better is the chance of making all children enthusiasts for movement. Physical training throughout the world has hitherto been shaped too preponderantly by Europe; we are now expecting it to receive a strong access of new life from the hitherto little-known ancient and popular forms of movement practised in , for instance, India, Japan and western Asia.

If we allow free competition, physical training will be enriched precisely by the interaction of national physical exercises with modern sports, and its results. We Europeans look with amusement and reverence on the methods and result of Yoga, and on the old Indian dances which have been so beautifully revived. The inner movement of meditation, and the artistic shaping of movements, are forms which ought to be brought within the reach of physical training.

It would be lamentable-and this is the last thing I have to say- if modern sport with its Anglo-Saxon stamp, though indispensable for physical training were to become the only prevailing form, the sole principle of physical training for the whole world. The Olympic games, based on the principles of sport, definitely guide the physical training of every country in this direction. There is most oftenly three principles operating in physical training: there is the principle of sport, the essence of which is the competitive comparison of measurable performance, and alongside it is the principle of true play, so well as the principle of gymnastic dancing, in essence the artistic moulding of movement. Until all three principles can stand side by side, equal in rights and rank and interpenetrate one another, we shall no have a physical training that is really effective and educationally, psychologically and biologically sound.

In addition, the physical training of every land should cultivate the traditional forms of the nation and people : in Germany gymnastics and walking, in Austria mountain climbing and skiing in England rowing and sailing, in Japan archery and club-fighting, in India perhaps Mallkhamb.

The great games of basketball, volleyball and football, track athletics and swimming have already made such headway in the world that there is now no danger that in any country, at least of the free world, physical training will recede into national restriction and one-sidedness.

The best way to encourage physical training in all countries is, however, for all those who have authority and knowledge in this domain to work together and pool their experience and knowledge in mutual help and support and in sporting comradeship and brotherhood.

6

THE IMPORTANCE OF GUIDANCE AND EDUCATION IN PHYSICAL EDUCATION

Perhaps the most marked features of a developed and industrialised culture are its fluidity and its complexity. Many of the highly developed cultures of the past were complex but, because of caste of class systems, they were relatively static; and the place in them of the individual participant was determined by the accident of birth. From then on, his education, his vocation, his marriage even, and much, if not all, of his moral and emotional life were determined for him by a series of rules and by a continuous social conditioning that allowed little possibility of emerging from "the station to which God had called him". Upward social mobility was restricted frequently to the most able or confined to periods of social disintegration under the impact usually of war, famine or pestilence, or it was permitted in one or two directions only-for example the artist craftsman of the Renaissance in Italy. It was always possible to fall from high estate, but such falls rarely meant a change of class. It is indeed possible to argue that the decline of many ancient cultures was marked by an incipient fluidity and upward mobility which undermined the social structure without allowing it to transform itself sufficiently. The Renaissance in Europe, on the contrary, by generalizing in Western culture the concepts of individualism of the uniqueness of the individual and by digesting in social terms the judo-Christian concept of the value of a human being in and for himself, may have provided the only possible psych-social situation in which social mobility, cultural complexity, and humanism are compatible with maintenance of steady evolution in society and the enrichment of personal life.

By values consciously and unconsciously determined and accepted, every culture makes a series of choices which, by facilitation of exclusion, guide individuals in their growth; and education is one of the major means of inculcating the "rightness" of these choices and of ensuring that the individual accepts them. We tend, however, naturally in our education of children-whether as parents or as teachers-to transmit the values of our culture and its choices in terms of our own childhood and adolescent experience.

On the other hand one of the features of contemporary life, whether in Western communities or in the so-called developing countries, is the rapidity of social change, the telescoping into a generation or even half a generation, of the growth and enlargement of material and personal possibilities which have been spread over centuries. It is important here to emphasize a fact that is frequently forgotten, namely that this is not merely a raising of the material standard of life, not merely a matter of better nutrition, protection from disease the accumulation of objects and instruments of use and beauty; it is an enlargement of the possibilities of riches in the emotional, intellectual and spiritual life. The bewilderment of choice, the hunger for possession, the apparent materialism are the superficial aspects of a process which should permit a flowering of the human spirit hitherto confined to a privileged few in exactly the same way as the motor car provides a chance of enlargement of experience which was frequently denied even to princes in their horse-drawn carriages

It is often stated that "you can't change human nature." In fact of course human nature does change and contemporary man is considerably different psychologically as well as socially from his medieval counterpart, or even from the nineteenth century man. The twentieth century may well prove ultimately to be more remarkable for the development of the human sciences, especially that of psychology, than for advances in the application of the physical sciences. One thing is certainly becoming clear from our growing knowledge of the way in which personality develop : that, while perhaps there may be biologically determined limitations upon personal growth and tendencies towards particular mental structures and rigidities, human nature is infinitely more modifiable than has hitherto been recognized or than at present we know how to exploit. Indeed it may well be hat the nature versus nurture controversies will seem academic not many years from hence as will some if not all of our conceptions of conditioning , learning and the like.

If the line of thought outlined above is correct, then the contemporary problem is that of exploiting the richness of possibilities offered by a fluid, complex culture of great mobility and in process of rapid change, by exploiting and developing the personal resources of contemporary man. In other words, whereas in the past we could accept relatively few variations in personality structure and a relatively short period of growth, conditioning, and adaptation, we can now envisage the possibility, even the desirability, of a widening range of differences in personal development and a longer period of growth leading to a more flexible, richer and more fully exploited use of the potential resources of each individual. Just as contemporary man is heavier and taller than his medieval counterpart, we may look to see an increase in creativity, imagination, subtlety and delicacy of intellectual and emotional response if the resources inherent in human psychology can be effectively exploited.

It is into this line of thought that our concepts of guidance should be fitted; and the idea is not a new one that education should aim to achieve the fullest possible realization of the possibilities inherent in the individual. The difficulty lies partly in our ignorance of human potentialities; partly in the resistances which develop in growing adult; and partly in our incapacity to exploit the techniques of education as a means of guiding and fostering the growth of the individual and through him of his society. The tendency of guidance in the past fifty years has been to concentrate upon the rehabilitation of the abnormal-the delinquent, maladjusted, or pathological individual-or it has sought an adaptation to circumstances, usually of work, which it does not seek to charge or even to modify. Thus one finds much discussion of vocational guidance as essentially a means of helping the individual to fit into the world of work and of selection or allocation to various forms of secondary studies considered mainly as a more or less efficient process of enabling the schools to receive the kind of pupils which they can educate in a predetermined way. "Child Guidance" too has become almost synonymous with the treatment of problem children. As is perhaps natural in such circumstances, the various kinds of services of guidance and those who staff them have tended more and more to become specialized and to be separated from the schools and from responsibility for the growth of society itself. Instead of becoming increasingly aware of the needs and directions of their social group and attempting to harmonize the potentialities of the young with the circumstances of a changing life, they are specialists concerned with a narrow sector in time.

However, in rare cases very clearly indeed, the educator sees that such guidance is not enough. The pioneers of active methods were certainly concerned with the immediate ease with which children could be brought to learn what adults thought it fit they should learn; but they were also concerned with fostering the kind of creativity peculiar to each child, and which, if exploited, night lead him to make an individual contribution to the growth of his community.

In this sense, guidance cannot be separated from the total educational process, even though some of its more complex functions may be discharged by specialists. Nor can it be a snapshot process. It must take account of what has made each child what he is and of what society wishes him to become—that is, at once of the social and environmental pressures that shape us, of the ways and means of modifying them, and finally of the ends, values, exigencies and choices of society. It derives from an implicit value system; it should be concerned with the analysis of this system and if necessary, participate in changing it progressively.

This is a point the implication of which may perhaps be illustrated by a negative example. We can now within fairly narrow limits select from among all children at the threshold of puberty, those most likely to profit from an academic type of secondary education. What in fact we do is to accept criteria of success as determined by the school or by examining bodies and proceed to develop tests or other procedures which give the best possible prediction. As this "guidance", become more efficient, the schools receive more and more children who are suitable to their methods and curricula. The danger is twofold : implicitly the values represented by the criteria come to be accepted as sacrosanct; and there are fewer and fewer of those partial misfits who constitute the challenge to educational method and the motive for improvement and rethinking. This is not to say that efficient selection or guidance is undesirable: far from it. It is to suggest that any should scheme of guidance-whether in the educational field or in the vocational field-must consider in value-term as well as in psychological ones, not only the child, his abilities and aptitudes but the situation of education or work, to which we wish him to adapt. It is not a simple affair of static matching, so many abilities or qualities in the subject, so many demands made by the situation. Both in the subject and in the situation there is or should be a process of modification, education in one sense, which finally fits them together leaving neither as it was before. We must also ask whether the criteria of successful adaptation ensure the real values which our society is seeking; or whether in efficiently adapting children to a situation which is intrinsically imperfect or even outmoded, we are not contributing rather to the stagnation or deterioration of society than it its dynamic improvement. Put in another way, we may say that long with the guidance of the individual should go a constant attempt to bring about evolution in the situation towards which we orient him.

But the development or stagnation of a society does not depend solely on what happens in its schools: nor can we be content at some stage in life merely to task children as the chances of their growth and experience have made them. At the time of beginning school, at eleven or twelve, when the child is on the threshold of adolescence with all its possibilities, at the end of compulsory schooling, and at many an other stage in his growth, we become aware that he is an individual with a history, and that many of the foundations of his personality and many of his attitudes and capacities depend upon events in his early childhood and upon what has gone on in his family, and in the streets, in his life outside the classroom.

We are not yet fully aware of how different kinds of experience may favourably or unfavourably modify growth; nor of what implications certain kinds of environmental pressure or facilitation may have for subsequent education and adjustment. We do, however, know many things : we know, for example, that if a child be deprived of certain experiences under the age of live, it is difficult if not impossible for him to grow satisfactorily later. If he lives in an environment where he gets little verbal stimulus we know that he will have difficulty in the early stages of learning to read. We know too that if he is prevented by circumstances from play in as he should with all kinds of objects and substances, he will suffer severely later on and may well lose not only the capacity to play but any creative or constructive tendency whatever. In the past for most children, more or less by accident, the circumstances, of life in the country or in a small community provided them with what was necessary for relatively satisfactory psychological growth. In the huge urban concentrations of the present day, children do not get such things as space and materials for play, chances to explore their environment and the like, accidentally. They are lacking or severely curtailed, and they have to be provided. Just as manufactured food may be deficient in vitamins and just as these have to be supplied artificially ; so childhood's experiences may be deprived of the vitamins of effective and intellectual growth and we should recognize this and take steps to replace them.

Thus our concept of guidance as an intrinsic aspect of education must also include an analyst's of the environment in terms of the needs of children, the attempt to determine how these needs may be supplied by the family, by the school or by some other means, and the necessary help to parents and teachers which will enable them to discharge their functions. Again, however, the fundamental principle is illustrated that we cannot confine ourselves to bringing about an adaptation to the status quo on the one hand or to the treatment of exceptional case on the other. The circumstances in which many children grow up, the pressures, economic, social and psychological, upon them through their families and through the surrounding community are not ideal, may well be unacceptable.

There is thus the inescapable social responsibility of asking ourselves how the family may be adapted to contemporary life and how its surrounding circumstances may be ameliorated so that the values upon which we are agreed may be preserved and developed and at the same time the experiences of childhood may pave the way for the full flowering of creative human beings later on. This is not likely to be achieved by a kind of laissez-faire paternalism nor by focusing our effort on the so-called problem families, urgent as such first aid may be. It can only be done if our knowledge of sociology, of social psychology and of child development is put at the disposal of parents themselves, not in the form of easy instructions on child-rearing, but as an active instrument which enables them to achieve ends which they have consciously chosen for themselves and their children.

The need for this kind of guidance is perhaps most clearly seen in the technical assistance field. Here communities-or at least their leaders-have chosen certain objectives of economic and social development. As means to these ends they have attempted to develop certain kinds of educational system. In many cases, however, these systems do not achieve the ends sought because the implications of technology in psychological terms, or the content of curricula and of educational method do not square with the kinds of personality structure which the culture hitherto has favoured. Technological development, the spirit, of free scientific enquiry as it is understood by the West, an economy, based upon activity, competitiveness and aggression, may all require certain attitudes in the individual, themselves based upon the intangible pressures of childhood, which are absent in a particular culture. This does not mean that the ends of social or economic development should not be sought; it does mean that the way to achieve them may not be that of simply importing superficial aspects of systems which have apparently been successful elsewhere. One must search for and recognize the essentials; and these essentials are almost always psychological, tissues of disposition and attitudes in individuals and groups, reaching back deep into the culture and stemming from the unstructured experiences on early childhood, play with comrades, the pressures and predilections frequently unconscious, of the community within which each adult has grown. It may well be that the essential means of introducing any particular social or economic change is that of influencing the basic psychological climate in which the young grow up and which the adult takes for granted.

Just as a child cannot learn arithmetic unless he has first gone through the casual preschool experiences of counting, enumerating, weighing and measuring, upon which depend his basic concepts of number, size, weight, area and the like, so it may be that a community cannot have the aeroplane, the motor car, the refrigerator, sanitation, and a relatively healthy environment unless a considerable proportion of those who compose it have gone through some at least of the psychological experiences which led mankind to invent them. The problem is to determine the nature of these basic experiences, whether for the individual or for the culture, and then to ensure that they are provided.

The upshot of this rather discursive and undetailed discussion is to underline the idea that guidance is implicit in education-whether we are considering the guidance of parents, of school children, or of adolescents at the threshold of their career. But it should also be explicit. That is to say that it should increasingly become a continuous process of analysis and re-synthesis, a means whereby the insights of psychology, whether of the individual, his group, or of his society, are consciously used as a means to the enrichment of human life. Just as better nutrition and the removal of physical inhibiting factors have contributed to greater life span, to heavier, taller, and healthier human beings, so we should be able to attempt the subtler and more difficult task of releasing the human spirit from the psychological inhibitions which dampen or destroy the capacity for creativity and joy.

Much of this is a workaday task, requiring good journeyman common sense; and much of it is being done already. In Europe and North America, for example, the need for easing the transition from home to school has been recognized. Tests of school readiness of reading readiness, reception classes, nursery schools and classes all exist and are becoming more and more widely used. Many schools, in America, Austria, Canada, Britain, France and elsewhere, make use of cumulative record cards which serve as a means of recording the observations of different teachers upon the growth of their pupils and which may be the basis of curricular or methodological modifications. In some countries, guidance, on the basis mainly of objective tests, is given at the threshold of secondary education in order to aid children in the code of alternatives according to their aptitudes; and in most, there are service of vocational guidance, some highly developed like those of Belgium and Holland. Almost every country in Europe, North America, and a good many others in the rest of the world, alarmed at the increasing numbers of children who show marked signs of maladjustment or who become delinquent, has set up services of diagnosis and treatment, child guidance clinics and the like.

From such activities much good has resulted; and the study of the process of adjustment is bound to draw attention to many factor in human psychology which imply a criticism either of educational value or of the pressure exerted by society itself. Yet, as has been suggested earlier, we have yet to take two essential steps. The first is the integration of all services of guidance-whether for the preschool child and his parents, for the school child, or for the adolescent on the threshold of work-into a comprehensive and coordinated process conceived as the essential ancillary to the effort of the teacher. This step would recognize at once the integrity of the individual and the wide range of differences between individuals-a range which, since it is the source of riches in the life of a community-the service may be said to exist to foster.

The second step is perhaps more essential; it is certainly more difficult. Communities change, for good or for ill; they offer more or fewer possibilities to individual participants. We in Europe and probably in the world generally, are committed to rapid change and to the humanistic concept that all human being are of equal value though of different capacities. This implies that guidance services must also be concerned with the situations towards which the individual is guided. They must therefore, not become merely efficient means of selection; but instruments whereby the situation in which the child or adolescent finds himself-the family, the school, the working environment—is analysed in terms of how far it favours the full development of which he is capable and fosters a dynamic social contribution rather than deadens-as at present-his power to live fully.

7

THE ROLE OF GUIDANCE AND COUNSELLING IN PHYSICAL EDUCATION

There have been countless voices, down through the ages, which have posed this problem-have presented this perennial dilemma. Ever since human beings have lived together in groups there have been conflict of interests and confusion of authorities. Only by the help the receives from other can the decisions of life be made : such help is *Guidance.* Those who are wiser and who have travelled the road before show the way to others.

Often, however, the word 'guidance' is used in a more restricted sense, to indicate a set of professional techniques. These includes methods such as the maintenance of records; the construction and application of tests; the use of various types of interviews-depth, non-directive, psychoanalytical; the use of questionnaires; role-playing, psycho-drama, even hypnosis, the use of rating system; the full bag of tricks of the classroom teacher, Socratic questioning, audio-visual aids, the use of the library and museum resources, laboratory practice, work experience. Some of these techniques are designed merely to transmit knowledge: to make available to the person seeking guidance the factual information necessary to his decision.

Others are designed to teach him the procedures of making choice, the methods of logical reasoning the canons of aesthetic discrimination the ethics of moral decision. Still others may be techniques to induce tranquillity of spirit, and produce social adjustment, mental health, or personal development. These techniques in turn may be either preventive or therapeutic.

There is also the field of vocational guidance, one of the most important of the traditional specialization. It has now been divided and subdivided so that there are vocational guidance experts who specialize on individual industries, and others who are experts on one stratum only of personnel, for example, 'middle management development'—there are even some who specialize on advising on the specific management courses which are most suitable for industrial executives within such a stratum. Specialization, however, has not limited itself to areas of interest, such as vocational, educational, or remedial. It has identified itself also, with institutions and age levels. Thus, there is the elementary school guidance officer, the home room guidance teacher, the specialist in reading clinics, the residence-halls expert, the juvenile court guidance officer, the clinician connected with an institution for the abnormal, and a dozen other categories. Within these areas there is beginning to grow up a sort of super specialization in the form of functional experts-the technician skilled in psychological tests, interview techniques, religious counselling, family life and marriage counselling, or inter-group relations.

It is perhaps inevitable hat with the growth of specialization and all the technical trapping of tests and techniques, there should develop a vigorous and at times militant professional movement. Priests have been advising adherents and parents have been guiding their children since prehistoric times, and on the record they have not done too badly. Teachers who themselves tend to be belligerently professional on occasion, have used many, if not most, of the recognised guidance techniques for centuries. There is one powerful school of though in the profession which feels the most guidance responsibilities should be centred in the classroom teacher, since only he can adequately known the individual from daily contact. But there is an equally powerful school which maintains that guidance is far too intricate to be permitted to any but the trained and presumably licensed specialist. The potential danger of bad advice has been widely recognized for some time, and the complexity of some of the esoteric techniques currently used by clinical guidance technicians is not to be denied. But the degree of mystery in which the whole process has been wrapped by enthusiastic participants is hardly warranted by the facts. One of America's leading educators, in commenting upon the speed with wh ich the field of guidance has been developing, wrote, "Like the Red Queen, you have to run as fast as you can to stay in the same place". Perhaps guidance, like religious conversion, or tribal initiation, or some forms of psycho-analysis, has to be experienced in order to be understood, and perhaps it is developing so rapidly that intelligent laymen cannot understand current advance. But the evidence does not appear to support either contention.

It is almost certainly due to this growth of professional vested interest that there has been created in the educational world something which might be termed guidance with a big 'G'. In the western countries especially in USA, there has grown up an attitude of possessiveness which at times is a little disconcerting. Thus, it is sometimes held that guidance is really only that which is traditionally considered to be guidance in the educational system. This comes perilously close to a definition of guidance as "those functions which the trained guidance official performs". More than once an American-trained guidance specialist has categorically dismissed the efforts of a foreign educational system with the sweeping generalization-"No guidance process exists." Nothing could be farther from the truth. Guidance exists, almost by definition, in every educational system, and in the vast majority of human relations. But it may both exist in forms which are familiar to a specialist preoccupied with tests and records and interview techniques and professional attitudes. To an unfortunately large number of American guidance technicians the counselling efforts of a typical British public school head master appear appealingly old-fashioned, slipshod and non-objective. But the educator knows that the very essence of the head master's task is guidance. The confusion, however, is more than merely a difficulty in semantics. It stems from the mistake of identifying the guidance process with currently fashionable techniques of collecting and systematizing the information which is considered useful in the process.

The inescapable truth is that the most distinguished guidance has always been that imparted by the world's greatest teachers—by the Christ walking with his disciples near the Sea of Galilee, by a Confucius writing his Analects, by a Machiavelli instructing his Prince, or by a parent rearing his child. Every person who succeeds in guiding another utilizes elements which appear indispensable. He must know the individual whether by scientific testing or by the apperception which comes from intimate daily contact. He must know the cultural setting, and in particular those areas specifically interesting to the individual, whether he amasses vast files of sociological data, or whether he gets it by the intuitive understanding of a sensitive participant in life's activities. He must have a world view, a Wellanschauung, a comprehensive philosophy, which enables to correlate particular aspects of the individual's problem with the wider significance of social trends and ideal. He must have a certain humility as, through the instrument of his suggestion, he sets loose forces whose results he may not foresee. He must be a man of honour, who lives by the ethics acceptable to himself, to the individual seeking help, and to society. Some would add that these ethics must above all satisfy the profession, and perhaps they must where professional guidance is used. But for the rest, the criterion of a sympathetic heart, of a deep humanity, must suffice.

Finally, these guidance people whether they be professionals trained in universities, or devoted amateurs learned in the ways of men, must have the power of communicating with those they would help. With some it will be a coldly analytical transmittal of data or logical persuasion. With others only the receptive ear, sympathetically noting the pent-up urges of the individual, gently guiding him into safer, more desirable channels. But all must give to the individual the sense of their willingness and ability to help.

SEARCH FOR A DEFINITION OF GUIDANCE

Thus, there is much overlap between the connotation of the terms 'education' and 'guidance'. In all human societies guidance has been provided, but the agencies through which it has operated have changed and are changing. So are the problem-areas with which guidance is concerned.

At about this stage in our editorial thinking, we attempted to frame a definition of 'guidance' so as to focus the efforts of our contributors. We said : The word 'guidance' is used to denote efforts deliberately organized by groups to direct their members towards desired patterns of behaviour-desired because they are considered good either for the group as a whole, or for both. Guidance may be general and informal through agencies like the family, the Church, the school, the political party. It is carried on by procedures such as example, admonition, imitation, participation. In advanced and complex societies, it becomes increasingly specific in nature and is then the responsibility of experts. We wish to distinguish between 'guidance' and 'influence' and 'teaching', though both of the latter may be used as guidance procedure."

This attempt quite failed to secure the approval of those we consulted. As a result of many discussions we therefore proposed a fresh 'working definition'. Guidance, we said, is "a process of helping individuals through their own efforts to discover and develop their potentialities both for personal happiness and social usefulness."

Our later definition was, without doubt, an improvement on our first attempt. It suffered, however, from a great drawback. It might be taken to denote a corpus of knowledge, a set of techniques, a social control, a fad, a professional movement or, in fact, the whole of education. So we had to limit the scope of our treatment by applying severe criteria of exclusion.

First, there was a criterion of degree. We have attempted to present in this *Year Book* a panorama of services, techniques, and theories which are of general interest to guidance personnel connected with organized education as well as to all teachers. Efforts have been made to avoid massive detail which would enable the professional psychologist or guidance officer to do his job better.

Next, there was a criterion of extension. There are four broad areas of behaviour-influencing factors. These are : (a) entirely unformalized and non-institutionalized factors which influenced behaviour and attitudes, (b) commercially and politically instigated propaganda or advertising designed to guide persons in choice of products or in political allegiance, (c) the whole area of negative guidance, and (d) the consideration of guidance by restraint or compulsion.

Finally, there was a criterion of reference. It is repeatedly indicated that guidance is a process which reflects a social philosophy and the culture in which it is located. We have attempted to record in this volume the important characteristics of a particular type of guidance which we believe to be applicable to free and thinking men in a free and fundamentally democratic world. Where we have dealt with systems of guidance in areas which do not fully attain these standards, we have done so in the hope and belief that even in the most totalitarian society the individual does retain some measure of choice. We have seen the processes of guidance through eyes conditioned by our own freedom. Our working definition of guidance itself reveals a philosophical commitment to freedom and self-direction. We hold that the individual has the fundamental right to make choice which are neither efficient nor in his own best interests. And we deny that society has the right to impose upon the individual certain choice, merely for the sake of an efficiency which he or family reject. In adopting this position we as educators, reveal that we work within the frame of reference of a philosophy which protects the rights of minorities and elevates the individual to a position of importance which in some thing comes above that of the State.

CONCLUSIONS

1. The Spreading of Professionalized Guidance Services

From the monographs collected in this *Year Book* four general conclusion emerge quite clearly. The first is that professionalized guidance services are everywhere being established and are spreading chiefly because important and necessary functions are no longer effectively discharged by traditional agencies. The profound changes that are going on in the occupational structure, in the structure of the family, in habits and mores, in religion and ideology and in political situation-all these make it abundantly clear that the older, informal modes of providing guidance are failing to meet current needs or, even, breaking down altogether; so that there are good reasons for intensive study, for the activities of professionally trained specialists, and for structuring the whole business more coherently.

Let take an instance: adolescents in western societies feel a need for the guidance given by older and wiser persons. This was at one stage provided in english boarding schools by the head master or the house master, who knew the boy and his parents and was acquainted with their background and financial position, with the occupational opportunities available, the social codes in vogue, and so on. Nowadays, secondly grammar schools in England, as in U.S.A., have become mass institutions so that teachers hardly know more than the names of their pupils-who in any case are drawn from all ranks and classes. In these circumstances, is it strange that a specialist should be put in charge of guidance or that special techniques for gathering information about the young person being guided should be devoted? There is here no question about 'imitating other western countries', but rather of reacting to a situation which inhabitants encountered earlier than others.

2. Changing Role of the Secondary School in the Guidance Process

Traditionally, one of the aims of the secondary schools in days gone by was to provide guidance in the affairs of life by developing the power of reason and then showing how it could be applied to human affairs. But, however magnificent it may be, this ideal is not one which the secondary school of modern industrial societies can easily accept as attainable. One may say, indeed, that to pursue it in this twentieth century is to chase a will-o'the-wisp. For the new mass secondary schools are, rather characteristically, institutions which assist the total mobilization of the population for social and industrial ends. By their very structure, the school systems allocate the young into occupational groups and guide or even direct them towards accepted objectives.

In its modern form, the guidance given by school system seems to accept the notion that there are basic innate differences between individuals. It seems to be assumed that according to their capacities they can be fitted into their correct niche. Justice, happiness, social harmony, and efficiency depends on finding the right place for the right person. The basis of 'guidance' is then thought of in terms of (a) discovering the aptitudes and capacities of each individual and then, (b) placing him in society in such a position that he will be socially useful and happy. The vast number of specialisms today makes such a task extremely difficult. In some educational systems, like that of England, three broad groups are still being thought of and initial selection is in terms of these groups. England differs in this from many countries only in the early age (11+) at which the broad selection takes place. There is increasingly a process of further differentiation as pupils go through the educational system. At each stage the range of information imparted becomes smaller but-so it seems-its depth in increased. Having completed a course of formal education the student may find himself qualified only for a very limited range of occupation. On the other hand, if his education has been rather broader, he may find himself competing-to his disadvantage-with others who have had a more specialized training.

We have here an illustration of the way in which guidance may be provided by structuring a situation. The school system of a country is such that children are guided into different streams and there presented with specific life possibilities. If they do not fit into the ordinary categories, because they are too bright or too dull, special forms of guidance are provided, such as schools 'for handicapped until they learn to adapt themselves. Social control is applied, while an illusion of personal choice may persist.

3. GUIDANCE IS CONDITIONED BY SOCIAL ASSUMPTIONS

The most basic conclusion to be drawn from the material gathered in this Year Book, and one on the importance of which we cannot insist too much, is that 'guidance' is always deeply conditioned by the assumptions made by those in charge of the process. This conclusion may be unpalatable, since many technicians are convinced that they keep themselves entirely out of the business, leaving perfect freedom to their clients. Our statement, therefore, needs elucidation.

Let begin by asking about an individual whose mental health and tranquillity of spirit seem to demand a course a action which is normal, antisocial, or politically treasonable. The brilliant scientist who disclosed his nation's atomic secrets to an unfriendly power is a spectacular case in point. Such an individual, undeniably same in the legal sense, is driven to a course of action which is unacceptable to the society in which he lives. Yet this course seems essential to his peace of conscience in the murky half-light of his view of world peace. If such an individual should seek guidance from a counsellor prior to his treasonable act, what would be the advice given? Would it be truly non-directive, neutral in its morality, uncommitted in its political allegiance? Obviously not-for complete neutrality in guidance would be a denial in terms. Yet, if the guidance process is to be politically biased, if it is to take sides and attempt to lead the client to a specific decision, then it has ceased to be solely a technique, a method, and has become an end, a goal. What this goal will be is inevitably conditioned by the total culture, and hence guidance becomes in the end still another thing-a social control. It is not of importance that the example just given happens to be lurid and extreme. It would apply equally if the guidance were to help rehabilitate a juvenile deliquent or to prevent adolescent gang activity, or to channel youthful energies into 'proper' activities, or to build democratic loyalties, or combat the excesses of competitiveness or social consciousness. For in each, there has come into play some cultural standard or norm, a moral choice has been made.

What is 'guidance' then, as a social control ? It is surely an instrument for the achievement of some ideological goal or other. Thus, in the example just cited, the 'guidance' may incite the troubled scientist to betray his country on the grounds that he will then make a contribution to the dream of a world social revolution, or it may restrain his treason on the grounds of nationalism and patriotism, or perhaps it may invoke religious sanctions against his broken oaths. But whatever the specific direction of the counselling, such guidance acts as a social control since it specifically guides the subject into a socially accepted pattern, into a path of action and a set of attitudes which are determined by social organization and mores. And all this remains perfectly true even when the 'guide' or counsellor eschews all temptation to use authority or to issue directives.

Even when he merely helps his client, to discover the semi-conscious pre-judices or habits latent in his mind, leaving the ultimate decision absolutely to him, doing no more than helping the person in trouble to understand himself, even then the mores and the society come into action. There is, in truth, no absolutely 'non-directive' guidance, however one may try to create it. Guidance in a Communist society could not conceivably be the same as guidance in a Fascist society, and none of these could be called guidance in a democracy or in monarchic society.

4. General Trends in Guidance

In identifying trends which appear to represent the best current thought and practice within the profession, Professor Ruth Strang mentions four.

The first is a trend towards more participation by teachers in the guidance programmes, a reversal of the former policy of restricting the guidance activities to trained professionals. In this there seems to be a recognition of the importance of continued and daily contacts with the person seeking guidance and a lessening of the emphasis on difficult testing techniques and clinical methods.

The second is a trend towards development guidance. This is in part an effort to apply the guidance process to the whole personality of the individual rather than to fragmented elements such as his vocation, health, education, etc. In part too it is an effort to continue the process through the years so that the individual receives help when he needs it and in manner which is consistent with his physical and social maturation.

The third is a trend towards client-centered counselling. This was recognised as basic from the first planning of the volume, and is included in the working definition adopted. But in the sense that Professor Strang uses it, client-centred counselling includes not only a social context of freedom and self-direction, but also newly developed techniques which are presumed to be helpful in achieving this goal. The guidance officer attempts to set the stage so that the client sees for himself the basic issues and makes his choice for himself-always from among socially acceptable perceived alternative. And prominent among the new techniques are non-directive counselling, permissive guidance activities, and various elements drawn from the field of group dynamics, such as shared leadership.

The fourth is a trend towards what Professor Strang calls the "team approach". In the complexity of modern life, few if any individuals are equipped to give adequate guidance in many fields or to collect information through many specialized techniques. This makes almost inevitable the use of various facilities, sometimes grouped in a clinic, sometimes drawn from various agencies of the community If the client is to achieve the desideratum of continuity in his relationship and coordination between the many behaviour conditioning agencies. It will be necessary to establish some unifying binding force. Fundamental of course, is a common and recognized social philosophy-so that, in different agencies and different times, the guidance process is not applied to conflicting and antagonistic ends.

Almost equally essential will be some systematic continuity in the service, the maintenance of record, the wise use of guidance information tempered by charity and controlled by professional ethics.

To this analysis, we would add one reflection. We have been impressed by the degree to which the experimental approach has been effective in discovering new and fruitful techniques, such as the various group and community methods of diagnosis and treatment. We are impressed too, by the way in which new insights gained by psychiatrists in remedial work throw light on the problems and difficulties of ordinary people. Here, as in surgery and in psychology, it seems that the study of the diseased and abnormal helps one to understand better the usual and normal.

In closing this brief examination of the guidance process in its relation to education today, one may well be puzzled at the apparent simplicity of the area which has been advanced as a new and important educational discipline. Here is no profound and esoteric corpus of knowledge to master. With one or two notable exceptions, the tests and techniques are relatively simple in theory, even though at time of questionable validity in practice. In the past the major emphasis has been placed on collecting and verifying the knowledge, and it is only relatively recently that the more important and more difficult technique of acting upon the knowledge has become the principal focus of attention. In the limited area of communication much has been done, and guidance officer is today better equipped to transmit to the student his analysis of the pertinent data, and even his evaluation of the intangible and emotional factors. Group techniques and counselling methods may be invoked and personal decisions taken by the client. These are influenced by the guidance leader, who is not and cannot be truly neural. Yet in theory, and largely in practice these techniques are not difficult to understand. But in spite of its apparent simplicity the new orientation is highly promising and may transform education.

Successful guidance depends upon a skill infinitely more difficult to acquire than formal techniques. It depends upto warmth of personality, a depth of humanity, and a breadth of personal experience which only the gifted few possess. These men, whether they be the 'Mr. Chips' of the English public school or the professionally trained technicians of the guidance clinic, will find their reward in the enriched lives of those they "help through their own efforts to discover and develop their potentialities, both for personal happiness and social usefulness.

8

THE NEED FOR GUIDANCE AND COUNSELLING IN PHYSICAL EDUCATION

Guidance, or counselling, as an idea, has a long history and in the educational tradition of all countries there are to be found notable attempts to define it and practice it. Plato said, there may well be an art whose aim would be to effect this very thing, the conversion of the soul in the readiest way; not to put the power of slight into the soul's eye, which already has it, but to ensure that, instead of looking in the wrong direction, it is turned they way it ought to be":-

(1) Nowadays we tend to think of guidance as "a process of helping individuals through their own efforts to discover and develop their potentialities for personal happiness and social usefulness". (2) Looked at in this way it may not be obvious in what way guidance differs from education itself, nor why the concept of guidance has become such an important one at the present time. Although guidance has to be distinguished from education, for it is only one aspect of educational activity, yet it comes close to being the central or cardinal aspect of it. It is one of the main themes of this article that education, as the means of growth of the individual person within a community of persons, succeeds in its aim only in so for it is informed throughout by the spirit of guidance.

It is in the emphasis on the individual in our definition of guidance that we find the clue to what distinguishes it as an educational activity in its own right, and a clue to why it is of vital importance today. Speaking of the hindrances which exist to the full development of the individual, some eminent researchers admits that: "the individual needs some specialized assistance in understanding the nature of these hindrances, as well as in discovering his own potentialities to meet them. The heart of guidance lies in providing the individual with this specialized help". (3) Thūs guidance is a specialized activity directed to helping individuals overcome their difficulties in personal development, and we may hazard the opinion that its contemporary significance derives essentially from the plight of the individual person in face the impersonal character of modern mass society and its every-increasing and changing demands upon him.

EVIDENCE OF THE NEED FOR GUIDANCE

This plight of the individual person in the modern world in plain to see, if we are prepared to look at modern life unflinchingly and with eyes undazzled by the great achievements of our scientific age. To accept this, it is unnecessary either to assert that the individual's plight is worse than in past ages, or to deny the immense benefits which applied science has brought and is bringing, for example, through material prosperity and the conquest of disease.

We are dealing with an absolute fact-the fact of stress, unhappiness and misery, manifested through social disruption, and maladjustments in personal and working life, and evidenced by the statistics for refugees and homeless persons, occupational unsettlement, divorce, children in need of care and protection, psychosomatic illness, neurotic and psychotic disorders, crime, and destructive and violent behaviour generally.

This under two of misery and maladjustment, found in all modern societies and not least in those in course of rapid transition to a modern condition, has its counterpart also in the aimlessness and inner emptiness of the lives of millions of ordinary people who are never ill in the ordinary sense, never offend against society and who in outward appearances are fully occupied—perhaps too fully and too feverishly occupied. Where leisure exists and is increasing, there is a great misuse of it or failure to use it constructively.

There is everywhere a great and increasingly conscious pressure towards conformity of life patterns, and towards the uncritical acceptance of ready made values and the political myths created by ruling groups. There is in brief a widespread failure by modern man to accept the challenge of his birthright to think and feel for himself, and to embrace constructively, but critically, his responsibilities and privileges as a citizen of the world. This is the familiar cry of every social critic and reformer of our age, but it is worth repetition if we go on to realize that this "failure" of modern man is a failure brought about by our social failure to understand the overwhelming nature of the task which the individual now faces, and to provide him with an education which will fit to carry it out.

Modern social life demands a level of personal maturity which the majority of mankind have not attained, and cannot attain without an education which sees as its central concern the nurture of the individual and understands what this nurture entails in terms of personal guidance.

Evidence for this educational failure is to be found in plenty by a study of educational systems themselves, and ironically, but inevitably, it is manifested most clearly precisely at those points where we can claim the greatest educational advances, namely in the ever-increasing provision of educational facilities for all the children of all the people, everywhere. Our vast and growing educational enterprises are vast in their administrative and external aspects, but from time to time we become vividly aware that there is a certain hollowness within, where as yet out efforts to enable our pupils to develop to maturity through the education they receive can claim only very modest success.

There is overwhelming testimony to be found in all countries, of the extent to which what we offer, in the way we offer it, is unsuited to a very large proportion of our children. This appears most readily when we examine the gap between our alleged standard and the genuine achievements of children, and when we discover for example the proportion of the children admitted to our academic secondary schools who are unsuccessful in their studies when judged by the examination standards set up by these schools themselves to symbolize their aims. In England itself nearly forty percent of grammar school entrants leave without securing a worthwhile general certificate of education (4). The most damaging revelation, however, comes when we contrast examination success with the extent to which those who succeed in these examinations have progressed in acquiring the basic arts of living, as distinct from a mere knowledge of "subject". Knowledge is increasing at an alarming rate and we can show how our pupils are becoming increasingly stuffed with it at all levels up to and including the universities, but evidence to show that it is being effectively transmuted into what Whitehead called "active wisdom" is much harder to come by.

CAUSES OF EDUCATIONAL FAILURE

It is possible to point outside the school to many causes of difficulty and failure in the personal development of modern man. The vastness and speed of social change, and its disruptive effects on the traditional means of personal growth and nourishment is the most general cause, with the breakdown of the traditional family unit and the growth in complexity of occupational opportunity as its most general effects. In this situation the adolescent particularly is exposed to conflicts and perplexities with which we have not equipped him to deal. With the increasing emancipation of women and the spread of coeducation, a set of specially perplexing factors is added. But it is idle to blame our changing society, for such change has come to stay as a permanent feature of modern life and it is the task of the school to answer the challenge which it presents.

When we look within the school itself we can at once see some of the ways in which we are failing to meet the challenge and to some extent, as has been noted, these appear to be the direct result of our greatest efforts to expand educational provision and raise educational standards. There is the atmosphere of intense competition to be found both in the primary school, and in the academic secondary schools, particularly in Wester countries. Only the fittest survive this pressure and practically none survive it emotionally undamaged. There is the tremendous emphasis on standardized attainment, which tends to neglect the varying needs, temperaments and abilities of individual children. Above all there is the growing impersonality of the school itself, particularly as it become a bigger and more comprehensive unit-an impersonality also exaggerated, particularly at the primary stages, by the large size of classes. At the secondary stage one important factor making for impersonality and lack of concern for the child as an individual, and particularly as whole individual, is the organization of secondary work around subjects. Some organization of this kind is inevitable, but its effect is that teachers are more and more forced to be teachers of subjects rather than of children. And it is very rarely that a Head is in a position to know well even a majority of the pupils.

It could perhaps be said that the essence of this modern problem lies in the fact of the loosening and weakening of the personal environment of home and community outside the school, taken in conjunction with the relative failure to provide an educational environment within the school which is capable of supplying the missing personal nourishment. The nourishment needed is essentially to be thought about in terms of personal relationships, and of the guidance which springs out of such relationships, and it is here therefore within the school that we find the imperative need to develop our guidance and counselling services.

GUIDANCE WITHIN THE SCHOOL

The tendencies toward intense competition, standardized achievement and impersonality which are now prominent features of all our educational system, can be counteracted in the first instance only by the creation of an effective special guidance and counselling service within the schools themselves. Such services, of course, already exist in many places, but they are still mainly in the embryo stage. The U.S.A. may perhaps be cited as an exception, but while what has happened there is a potent, it is not necessarily an example to be followed elsewhere. Each country must develop means suited to its own educational situation and aims. While the creation of a special guidance service within schools is a necessary step, it is by itself by no means a sufficient one.

On the one hand it has to be related to the still more specialized services both clinical and vocational outside the school, which are becoming more and more recognized as essential ancillary agents of the educational system. On the other hand, a guidance service within the school must be supported by the whole of the school, and its existence, if it does its work well, must necessarily in time come to modify the school's whole approach to its educational function.

What are the special duties of a guidance officer or counsellor, for example within a large secondary school? Ideally he should have a major say in working out the course to be followed by each child, whether the organization permits only of guidance by "classification" into streams or sets or whether it permits guidance of a much more fundamental and individual kind. He should have the surveillance of the teaching of the more backward and difficult children and should do some of this teaching himself. By his role he is also ideally fitted to carry out that aspect of vocational guidance which is the proper function of the school, and in doing this he must establish sound relationships with all those community agencies which interest themselves in job placement and the welfare of young people after leaving school. He must also be closely linked with the area's clinical services and be ready to call on specialized psychological aid when this is necessary. Not least, he must, wherever necessary and possible, establish relations with parents. But above all, he must be a person in the school who by virtue of his unique role and special skills is naturally and at need consulted by staff and also by pupils. His door must be always open to everyone. It is specially important that he acts always as a guide and consultant, and that he himself does not take executive action. Executive power must remain with the Head of the school, and with the teaching staff under his direction. This is quite fundamental. It is fundamental that the Head and staff should retain their authority.

The counsellor must never usurp their functions. Not only would such action be intolerable for them, it would also destroy the counsellor's own role which ultimately depends on his not being a wielder of authority, a judge of right and wrong. Just how fundamental this point is will appear in a moment.

It will, however, be obvious that the work of the counsellor will depend absolutely on the degree of co-operation he can obtain from Head and staff. On the teaching staff he must rely for much of his information and in turn they must be prepared to give sympathetic consideration to his views, if his work is to count for anything. In order to do this they must begin to understand something of his work and approach. In fact it is to be hoped and indeed expected (if he is successful) that through his influence, his attitude and the needs of his job, there will in time come about a subtle change in the attitude of teaching staff to their roles as educators. In the case of any given child, the counsellor's interventions are bound to be episodic, but one of the essentials of effective guidance is its continuity. Such continuity can only be attained if the guidance attitude comes to permeate the work of the school as a whole, and thus comes to re-fashion the relations between teachers and pupils. It is for this reason that the creation of a specialized guidance service within a school cannot be a complete answer to the need for guidance.

Ultimately all educators must come to see their supreme function as that of guides to the growing person, not only in relation to learning in the school sense but to the wider learnings which mark his growth to maturity. Within the school itself the essential change that is needed is the development of a view of education which sees the acquisition of knowledge and skills as only means towards the growth of persons to maturity. Emotional and social development them become primary aims of education. Clearly, if special guidance and counselling services are to become effective educational instruments in spreading the spirit of guidance, the training of the teachers of the future must seek above all things to secure the development of those attitudes towards education which lie at the heart of the guidance function.

THE ESSENCE OF GUIDANCE

It is only too easy to suppose that the essential skills of the counsellor or of the teacher who approaches education in the spirit of guidance are mainly those manipulative skills derived from technical developments in the field of psychological measurement and assessment. Children are tested and assessed and their educational environment is fashioned or re-fashioned to suit their needs. Such work is a necessary part of guidance, but it is only the outer husk. It is that part of guidance which may be called "contrivance" (5) through which the external stresses and strains to which the individual is subjected may be modified. The kernel of guidance however lies in the relationship which the counsellor establishes with his clients and through which they are enabled to develop further their own powers of dealing with both inner and outer problems. It is not so much what he does, but what he is to them, and enables them to do, which is important. It is their inner freedom, their own understanding, their powers of decision and of embracing purposes of their own, which have to be strengthened.

The essential skills of guidance therefore lie within the counsellor's or teacher's own personality, in the extent of his insight into the problems and conflicts which beset the growing person, and which for him were first exemplified in his own growth to maturity. His first and most fundamental need is to understand himself and the relation in which he stands to children. If the relationship is to nourish their growth, it is essential that he becomes to some extent the ally of the child's own ego, the central part of his personality, rather than of the child's moral function or superego, to use Freud's term. It is difficult for the teacher to establish this relationship in any strength-but it can be done-all "good" teachers achieve it. Generally the teacher functions most readily as an external or ancillary super-ego for the child, in the same way as his parents did in his early years. It is fundamentally in this sense that the teacher is a parent substitute-a source of authority. The teacher can not but embody many aspects of authority for the child, no matter how "permissive" and non-authoritarian he may be, but he can also establish himself as a guide or friend, who seeks to understand rather than to judge, just as, and even more easily than the good parent can. The counsellor, by virtue of his special ról e, is in a position to maximise the extent to which he appears to the child as someone who will always befriend him, and to minimise the extent to which he appears as only an additional figure in authority over him. It is for this reason that the counsellor should not assume executive functions. The counsellor's role is therefore a difficult one and calls for special personal qualities-qualities which all good teachers must possess, but which the counsellor must and can exemplify to a especially high degree.

While our perception of the need for guidance in education may at first arise from a consideration of the external complexities of modern society, an understanding of the real nature of this need cannot be reached unless we perceive that the essential problem is the nourishment of those powers of the individual by virtue of which he becomes more able to withstand the pressures, external (the opinions and exhortations of others) and internal (his own feelings) which beset him, and more able to take his destiny into his own hands. It is only as individuals can progressively come to master their own passions and fears, and to command their powers of rational thought and decision, that they can enter into fruitful and cooperative relations with one another. Otherwise these relations become distorted through outward duress and/or inner compulsion. We have therefore to look to a form of guidance in education which seeks to help the individual to achieve his own maturity, as one of the essential means by which men may eventually grow out of this age of anxiety and confusion and lay claim to their birthright of rational freedom.

9

THE ROLE OF PSYCHOLOGICAL GUIDANCE IN NATIONAL PLANNING

Though, India has received the political independence but yet we are often reminded that we have a long way to go yet. Achievement of political freedom was the first step. Economic and social freedom has still to be acquired. To attain this end national planning has been adopted as the means. We seem to believe in five-year periods of attempts. We have made one such effort and are in the midst of the second. The emphasis in the first plan was on food. In the second, it is on industry, particularly on the heavy variety.

One of the essential requirements of industrial development is technically trained manpower. We are short of technicians and engineers. To overcome this difficulty new Institutes of Technology are being opened. The number of Engineering Colleges is being increased and the training capacity of the existing institutions is being enlarged.

But how are we to find the lads who are to go into these institutions? By selection from those available? "Yes" seems to be the answer to this question. But selection presupposes abundant supply of suitable people. If the supply is less than the demand the question of selection does not arise. One has to take what one gets and be content with it. To produce an abundant supply for technical training institutes Psychological Guidance in schools will be found of service. To find out the potentialities of young people and to guide them into suitable vocations is the essence of Psychological

Guidance. An extensive School Psychological Service will contribute substantially to the successful completion of the National Plans.

In the present economic context of our country it will be wise to broaden the concept of guidance. Normally guidance is understood to mean the finding out of the youth's potentialities by Psychometric and projective Tests, Questionnaires and Interview and telling him what particular vocation he is best suited for. It will be helpful to include counselling also under the term guidance. I feel it is necessary in the present economic and social setup of the country.

It is needed to remove the prejudices and widen the vision of the youth. There is still a prejudice amongst us against working with hands. We still want white-collar jobs. We are averse to putting on dirty overalls, soiling our hands and sweating while we work. The prejudice is unconsciously passed on to the youth. Majority of the young lads, found suitable for technical training, are desirous of becoming engineers. They are shy of being workmen even though their potentialities do not promise them anything better.

Prejudice against working with hands holds them back. Most of them ultimately drift into offices to become inefficient and discontented clerks. Counselling, if properly done, will help to remove the prejudice and will, perhaps, be successful in diverting a large number from the army of clerks to the army of technically trained workmen who are so urgently needed for the success of our plans.

It is not enough to tell the young boy what particular job he is best suited for. Our diagnosis tells him where he will be successful. But we have to be careful and prepare him for failure also. By telling the boy that he will make a good engineer we are perhaps raising his hopes. Under the present, conditions it is quite possible that the he may not be able to secure admission in an Engineering College. That means frustration- a frustration greatly intensified by the consciousness that he has the potentiality of becoming a good engineer. Unfortunately, the number of such young people is quite large under the present state of unemployment in the country. A large body of frustrated youth is more likely to hinder than to help the successful completion of the plan. It is true that the plan itself is trying to remove unemployment, but it is going to take a long time before this objective is achieved.

Unemployment will exist in the country for some time to come, and the youth will continue to be frustrated. Frustration in youth, followed by a negative attitude and antisocial activities, could be fought by Psychological Guidance. This can best be done by counselling. Through counselling the young people should be taught to face defeat and not to lose their mental balance in the struggle for employment. They could be encouraged to start at a lower rung of the ladder and work their way up. If they have potentialities of being successful at the top, those very potentialities will help them to rise quicker. What they require is patience, and patience is better than frustration. Counselling, therefore, seems to be urgently needed to be included in the technique of guidance.

If our plans have to be successfully completed we will have to have enthusiastic young men. No matter how good the plan, if we have diffident and frustrated young men to work it the result is obvious. We have to produce self-confidence and enthusiasm in the youth. Psychological Guidance can help to achieve this aim. But the concept of Guidance must be widened. It has a heavy mathematical bias at present. If it is to help national planning it must include a little more Psychology.

10

THE ROLE OF GUIDANCE AND COUNSELLING IN MANPOWER PLANNING

Before the industrial revolution, which really began with the invention of the steam engine, the social and economic life of all countries was much simpler than it is today. The population of the world was smaller, the tempo of life much slower and space had not been conquered by modern methods of travel. To a large extent, the life of the average person was dominated by the conditions in his immediate environment and such population and occupational adjustments as had to be made could usually be achieved within each locality. Of course, what has been said is a generalization to which there was inevitable exception, but it is certainly true that in those earlier and more leisurely days, the need for manpower planning was practically nil.

This last century, however, has brought a complete revolution in the life of mankind. Space and time have been shortened enormously. The tempo of life has increased. Populations now uninhibited in their growth as a result of modern system of medicine, better nutrition and a more varied and interesting life, have grown enormously. At the same time thousands of new occupations have been created, with the result that manpower planning has become an essential part of a well-organized society.

Manpower planning like any other form of planning is an adjustment of supply and demand. In this case it is a process whereby the essential characteristics and abilities of the population are studied in detail and related to or adapted to the day-to-day manpower requirements of modern society. In a vague way the need for this has been appreciated for some years, but only more recently, as the complexity of modern economic life has grown, and as the number of occupations into which individuals can enter has increased, has the need for detailed manpower planning become imperative. Great strides are being made in this direction in all countries and India is by no means lagging behind.

In fact, quite a number of foreign observers who have come in contact with those engaged in manpower planning in this country have commented very favourably and with some surprise on the techniques and methods which are being adopted to develop manpower planning programmes. It is against this background that we must consider the role of guidance and counselling in manpower planning.

It will be readily realized that manpower planning, however good it may be, will prove quite infructious unless there are agencies capable of turning the manpower plan into a reality in terms of human aspirations and abilities.

A manpower plan will fail unless it not only appeals to the imagination of the people, but is also able, demonstrably, to give happiness and satisfaction to the average citizen. It is not an over-simplification to say that the average human being is not very hard to please and to make happy. The needs of most of us can be stated in fairly simple terms. Our first need is perhaps a sense of security; freedom from want, freedom from fear in our social and political relationships, and freedom from sickness. Another strongly felt need of the average man is the need to feel what we are doing is worthwhile. Another elementary desire of most of us is the desire to continually better ourselves, economically, socially and intellectually. In other words, whatever may be the manpower or economic plan of a country, it should set out to meet these elemental requirements of the average individual. Human beings are not and should not be pawns in political, social and economic games, and it is at this point that there is need to develop sound systems of vocational guidance and counselling.

It is axiomatic that no two human beings are alike, each one of us differs in physical, intellectual and social attributes. We are all motivated by different impulses, physical, psychological and intellectual and the aim of those responsible for guiding us should be to ensure that at a young age, our feet are set on a road which will lead to the maximum use of all our abilities and characteristics.

Square pegs must go in square holes, round pegs in round holes and all the other intermediate shapes suitably adapted. This is the ideal and, as the reader will readily realize, it is an ideal which it will probably take a long time to achieve. The encouraging thing is that the need for such achievement is being increasingly recognized. Evidence of this is to be found in the development of vocational and educational guidance and counselling and the interest being taken in the welfare of workers.

Despite the difficulty of the task before us, there are several obvious lines of development which can be fairly readily taken up. For instance, India's rapidly developing industrial life will require more and more engineers, craftsmen and technicians during the years to come. Among our many millions of population, there will be tens of thousands of young people whose aptitudes, inclination and physical characteristics make them more suitable for such work than their contemporaries. The task of the vocational guidance worker and counsellor is to acquire detailed knowledge of the task to be performed and to locate those of our young people who have the necessary aspirations, aptitudes and abilities to take up such work. Similarly, our need to bring education to all our people will require, during the coming years, an estimation of the number of educationists required for the purpose. It is for those concerned with manpower planning to estimate the numbers required and suggest the phasing of the programme. When that has been done it is for those who are engaged in educational and other forms of guidance to locate those of our young people most suited for this work. The nature of the task to be done and the characteristics which are essential for a teacher or a professor are vastly different from those required of an engineer, a craftsman or a technician. The difference in characteristics, abilities and aptitudes are capable of analysis and it is to this task that those engaged in guidance and counselling should direct their activities. What has been said of engineers, craftsmen, technicians, and educationists, is not less true of all other occupations which go to make up the complex society in which we live.

From what has been said it will be seen that a good deal of basic study has yet to be done if our objectives are to be achieved. At present for instance, very little is yet known about our occupational life. Before we can utilize any utilize any conclusions with regard to the abilities or aptitudes of individuals, we must have a far clearer picture of the jobs which have to be filled. It is for this reason that the Government of India, in the Ministry of Labour and Employment, is busily at work preparing not only an occupational classification, but also an analysis and description of each job which is commonly performed in the country. Having got this information it is then essential to make the material readily available to those who are responsible for giving guidance and counselling both to young people and to adults together with estimates of the numbers required.

This is being done by producing and distributing career pamphlets and information about careers and trainings facilities in the country. It is only when our young people are in a position to readily read about a variety of occupations that they will be able to make an intelligent choice of a career. Even then they will need wise counsel from their teachers, their parents, their Employment Officers and their friend so that they can match, realistically, their ambitions and aspirations with their abilities.

It is perhaps, desirable at this point to sound a word of warning. Although Vocational and Educational Guidance and Counselling are given a precise connotation by various experts, it needs, perhaps, to be recognized that, however good might be a system of Vocational Guidance and Counselling through the medium of experts, their activity cannot be a substitute for the collective wisdom of society as represented by, shall we say, parents, friends, relatives, teachers, the writers of books and magazines and the press. All these agencies are continually giving guidance good, bad or indifferent, to young people. It is important, therefore, that all these agencies must, of necessity, become increasingly enlightened, if each succeeding generation of young people is to quickly reach vocational maturity and make sound choices of careers.

It is also no less desirable to emphasize that because each one of us in an individual and will never cease to be so, it is essential that in the last analysis it is for each boy or girl, to make his or her own choice of career, whatever may be the wishes of those engaged in manpower planning, education of vocational guidance or counselling. Guidance should lead to self-choice.

Despite what I have said above, however, it can hardly be disputed, in view of very widespread ignorance, conservatism, prejudice and lack of knowledge of the basic facts of our social and economic life, that there is need for the development of specialized services through which expert guidance can be given to our young people. Such services will, it is hoped, set an example to the community as a whole. It is to be hoped, therefore, that there will be a rapid increase in the number of teachers in schools, who are specially trained to give guidance to school children. Similarly, it is desirable that at Employment Exchanges specially trained staff should be increasingly engaged in the task of helping employment seekers to make suitable occupational choices when they are looking for work. It is, for this reason that recent developments under the Central and State Governments to provide such expert guidance are being increasingly developed. Such agencies are essential collaborators with those engaged in manpower planning, and it is their role to endeavour that the guidance that they give is related, on the one side, to the essential manpower requirements of the country and on the other to the wholesome development and he achievement of contentment of each individual that comes to them.

11

THE IMPORTANCE OF OCCUPATIONAL INFORMATION PROGRAMME IN PHYSICAL EDUCATION

It has been estimated that every year some two million new people enter into the already over crowded employment market in India. In the beginning of the Second Five-Year Plan there were over five million people seeking employment. With the annual influx of two million additional men and women to the market the problem becomes so huge that it cannot be satisfactorily handled without the development of large-scale industries and without some kind of social and economic revolution.

Fortunately for us the social and economic revolution is taking place peacefully through the well-phased five-year plans. It is true that the unemployment problem has, in spite of all possible measures having been taken to halt it, continued to deteriorate, but it cannot be denied that the rate of deterioration has been checked.

According to a survey conducted in 1955-56, 154.84 million people were engaged in India in gainful employment. They included 110.61m. in agriculture, animal husbandry, etc.; 3.15 m. in factories; 94 m. in forestry, fisheries, etc.; 1.56 m. in railways and communications, 0.79 m. in mining, 10.18 m. in commerce including bank, insurance and transport, 7.56 m. in professions, in liberal arts, 3.50 m. in domestic services, 4.70 m. in Government services (administration) and 11.85 m. in small and cottage industries.

Besides this huge number of people engaged in work it is proposed that 6 million new employments would be created during the Second Plan period. A number of large-scale and small-scale industries are being established in different parts of the country. In the fields of social welfare, health, education, agriculture and horticulture, mining, new employment opportunities are being created. In the community development projects thousands of people will be required for rural upliftment work.

In spite of the development schemes that we have the available employment opportunities in the country when compared with the available manpower are hopelessly inadequate. That in itself is a serious problem. But besides this there is another important problem—the problem regarding dearth of facilities for occupational information necessary for employment seekers. It is true that due to slow progress in industrial development the number of occupation in our country is still much less than the number of occupations developed in other industrially developed countries.

In the United States 40,000 distinguishable occupations have been put on record. In the United Kingdom also where the people do not like to make hair-split distinctions in many cases between one occupation and another, it is estimated that 10,000 occupations exist. It our country industrial revolution has just started. Still there no less than 4,000 occupations from which a young man or woman may make a selection.

As the industry is growing and the scientific technology is developing old methods of work are being abandoned, old tools, implements and machines are being replaced with new ones and old techniques are giving way to modern ones. In this process new jobs are being created for new types of people who can learn new techniques of production and who can adjust themselves in new environments. These days when young men and women come out to make their choice of career they are confronted with numerous complicated problems. They do not know what occupations are suitable for them, where the suitable occupations are available, how to prepare themselves for those occupations and so on. Moreover, they like to know something about a number of occupations so that they may compare the prospect in all these occupations to avoid the risk of entering a blind alley job.

The selection of right occupation on the part of a new entrant in the world of work is important not only for him, but also for the management and the nation at large. It is a well-known fact that unless a worker gets maximum job satisfaction his output cannot be optimum. A worker can enjoy his work if he selects a career where he suffers neither from excessive strain on him nor from overplay of idle imagination.

With a view to help individuals to make judicious choice of careers, to assist parents and teachers to guide their children in going to the right field of work, to help employers to select persons who are conscious of the hazards and risks in their employment, several agencies both public and private are trying to disseminate objective occupational information to those who seek for it. Amongst the public agencies, it may be said that the Directorate General of Resettlement and Employment under the Ministry of Labour and Employment is the pioneer in this field. The D.G.R. and E. are collecting employment market information of the whole country through the network of Employment Exchanges and are publishing a series of Career Pamphlets on a very wide range of occupations.

In these pamphlets information is given on educational and physical requirements for the job, on place of work, training facilities, average income, future prospects, and employment outlook. Besides these, Youth Employment

Offices and Adult Counselling Centres have been opened in a number of big cities in the country to give occupational information to employment seekers. D.G.R. and E. publish Occupational Field Reviews and National Classification of Occupations which are of great value to any occupational information centre. The Handbooks on Training facilities in the State and the two volume of the Hand-books on Training Facilities in India are also considered to be unique publications in the country.

Education authorities are also, in a few cases, giving out some occupational information to school-leavers through talks on careers and through organized visits to industries and other places of work. The Ministry of Defence and the Ministry of Commerce and Industry also publish brochures and charts which contain valuable information on occupation in Defence Forces and in small-scale and cottage industries.

There are some private agencies which have made considerable contribution to the dissemination of occupational information to young people. Amongst them Y. M. C. A. Publishing House, Calcutta, Rotary Club, Bombay, Vocational Guidance Bureau, Bombay, and other Vocational Guidance Bureaux in the States are worth mentioning.

That the objective occupational information is of great value to a young person, when he is confronted with the problem of choosing a career, cannot be denied by anybody. The process of colleting, collating, and giving out the information, however, is very complex in a vast country like ours where development is uneven and occupations have not been standardized as yet. Some people think that useful occupational information on a national basis cannot be given at this stages as all the necessary data cannot be collected.

There may be some truth in this argument. Nevertheless, when partial information is collected from different parts of the country after watching some workers on the job, interrogating workers, supervisors, and instructors in industries and after going through relevant literature, it is bound to be useful to employment seekers. The agency that undertakes the collection of occupational information, however, takes all possible precautions to see that the field staff permit only minimum personal factor to play in their study of occupations. With these objects in view, training courses for field staff are organized and they are trained to sift out the useful and objective information on occupation.

There is no doubt that as the country progresses, more and more industries will be developed and more and more people will look for wage employment. The Occupational Information Programme will then have much more importance than what it has today. Their future is not very much distant. Occupational Information Programme, started recently in this country is still in the preparatory stage.

Those, who are trying to make the young people of the country careers conscious by disseminating objective occupational information in a scientific manner, are doing a great service to the nation. Those, who subscribe to the view that the Five-Year Plan can be saved by the Vocational Guidance Programme of which occupational information programme is the most important part, do not possibly exaggerate it.

12

THE SIGNIFICANCE OF PLANNING, PRINCIPLES, POLICIES, AND STANDARD PRACTICES IN PHYSICAL EDUCATION

THE ROLE OF PLANNING

The role of planning is to take action in the present that will influence the future. Administrators outline steps that must be taken to achieve the objectives that will advance the organization toward its goals. Planning precedes organizing and plays an important part in decision making. Policy planning, organizational planning, procedural planning, curricular planning and activity planning all have their own particular role descriptions and specific meanings.

Planning has been found to be important in the following ways:

- Sound and thorough planning tends to lessen the number of arbitrary actions. The path is clearly laid out.
- Systematic planning can help avoid role ambiguity and therefore role conflict.
- Effective planning with regard to salaries and fringe benefits can reduce dissatisfaction among the staff

and tends to diminish the number of arbitrary promotions and dismissals.

- The process of planning leads to more frequent reviews of current situations and subsequent maintenance, repair, or reconstruction.
- Careful planning will include meticulous care of records that contain objectives and goals. Perennial review of objectives and goals will do much to improve the entire operation.

Planning is essentially a special case of decision making with constant consideration of the future. Its basic steps are the same as those listed for problem solving. Planning has futuristic overtones. The final selection of any plan must be based on conditions and facts that are valid both today and tomorrow.

In every phase of the planning process, there are certain steps that must be included. These are the development of goals, objective, policies, procedures, and programs.

Obviously the size of the entire operation must be assessed. The basic fact on which everything else depends must be the enrolment, current and projected. The size of each class must be determined, the facilities to handle the projected enrolment considered, the financial resources carefully analysed, and the local and state rules and regulations thoroughly understood.

POLICIES AND STANDARD PRACTICES

Policies are essential to the efficient administration of any department, school, business, or other organization. Without them, there is little to guide the activities and conduct of the establishment in the pursuit of its goals. With well-reasoned policies, the organization can function efficiently and effectively, and its members will better understand what is expected of them.

Individuals are generally quite sensitive to treatment that they conserve discriminatory. They believe justice requires that the punishment be appropriate to the offence, that all persons be treated impartially, and that people should be informed about the behaviour expected of them. Goods laws are a part of the answer.

In any enterprise, it is important that the operation be efficient, and effective. Undue waste of time, money, and resources is deplored. Standard operating practices increase efficiency.

In educational institutions, as in other large organizations, some standardization is desirable. While individual differences should receive appropriate attention, correct and incorrect solutions and methods must be identified. Specific instruction and procedural requirements that are clearly spelled out result in a more productive organization.

System and organization, when not emphasized to the extreme, are to be preferred to anarchy and chaos. Authority, rightfully delegated or assumed, must be exercised if all efforts are to be coordinated and effective. Well-founded policies are helpful.

Many problems, tasks, and circumstances are repetitious. It is wasteful to spend time, energy, and resources to study them over and over again when a similar decision in each case is best. Suitable written guidelines help in economizing on time and energy.

To deal martially with people, to avoid waste of energy and resources, to bring about desirable standardization of procedures, to use what is learned in one instance to improve future decision, and to eliminate chaos, institutions establish and utilize guidelines of several kinds.

Depending upon the nature of the guidelines and the hierarchical level at which they are formulated and utilized, they are variously termed policies, standard procedures, standard practices, standard methods, guiding principles, rules, or just general guidelines. Well will use the terms policies, standard practices, and guidelines

THE NATURE OF POLICIES

A policy is a guiding principle that serves as a basis for a course of action. A policy does not spell out in detail exactly what is to be done, but it does point the direction. It should assist those who must make executive decisions, but it should not be so inflexible as to leave little latitude for individual judgment.

Policy making is often a major function of school committees, boards of trustees, athletic committees, and other legislative bodies. Policy may also be formulated and established at lower administrative levels. As one narrows the group to which they are addressed, finally coming right down to the individual, policies become more specific. As one ascends the hierarchical ladder or increases the scope of one's public, policies become more general.

It can readily be seen, then, that a policy might be formulated by a school committee, spelled out in a set of more specific statements by the superintendent of schools, and developed in even greater details by the athletic department. For example, a college board of trustees might establish a policy to the effect that "purchasing should be a centralized function". The president would then formulate a policy stating that all purchases should clear through the office of the controller.

The controller, in turn, would delegate the authority to select physical education equipment to the director of that department while establishing a policy stating that all requisitions must be countersigned in the controller's office. The director of physical policies and procedures relating to the selection and purchase of equipment.

STANDARD PRACTICES

A policies are promulgated and authority is delegated, one eventually arrives at the operating level. By this time, directions and guidelines have become so specific that they can no longer rightly be termed policies but rather standard practices or procedures.

Standard practices are rather specific instructions about how to proceed with a given task. Within the framework of established policies, a coach might be taking a track team on a trip. In a well-organized department, there would be specific guidelines about how many players could be carried, the maximum allowance for food, the method of accounting for expenditures, procedures for dealing with series injuries, and the conduct of athletes on trips, These and more would be spelled out in written standard practices or similar guidelines.

In many instances, it is difficult to determine just when instructions are policies and at what point they become standard practices. It is impossible to draw a hard and fast line. For this reason, some institutions prefer to use the term guidelines for their sets of instructions.

POLICIES AND PLANNING

It is impossible to separate policy formulation from planning, since it is, in fact, a very important part of planning. When goals have been established and directions determined, policies that guide that enterprise toward them should be formulated. Whenever a legislative or controlling body formulates a general statement of philosophy and direction, it is formulating policy.

At lower her archical levels, policy statements emerge when decisions are made about priorities in the use of facilities, criteria for salary increments, disciplinary measures for students, limits on faculty loads, requirements for graduation, guidelines for grades, or eligibility rules for athletes. Most of these are established in advance, and all of them are intended to guide future action. They are, then, an integral part of planning.

POLICIES AND DECISION-MAKING

Not all decisions can be based on established policies. Most situations have unique elements that require individual study and decisions appropriate to the particular circumstances. Nevertheless decisions should be made in light of policies that exist. If a pending decision is not compatible with an established policy, it should be studies carefully to determine whether or not the specific circumstances merit special consideration.

In many instances, the director of physical education and athletics is put in an intermediary position between his or her immediate superior or an established policy on the one hand and the athletes and/or coaches on the other. In such cases, decisions and actions will be strengthened by a firm policy and superiors who will back the director. Policies are often unpopular, but they are usually less objectionable than an arbitrary decision by one individual.

Executives responsible for athletic programs have a large number of difficult decisions to make. The eligibility of athletes, the recruitment practices of coaches, the interference by alumni, the emphasis on winning records, and the temptations to exploit athletes are potential trouble spots. Thoughtfully prepared policies and conscientious adherence to them will help the athletic director avoid many pitfalls.

In all institutions, some control over decision making is necessary. Defining the purpose of an organization, ensuring that decisions are guided by reason, prescribing lines of authority, and establishing guidelines are ways of accomplishing this.

POLICIES AND ORGANIZING

Organizing consists of grouping tasks and individuals related by common responsibilities. Without some guidelines, it is difficult to avoid duplication of effort, and without general principles, misunderstanding regarding duties and responsibilities are much more apt to arise.

As an example, policies, concerning the use of the gymnasium are essential. Such policies should indicate what the priorities are, who is the final authority in case of conflicts, where the master schedule is kept, and which activities should be scheduled during each hour of the day.

If coaches teach and teachers coach, there must be guiding policies for the division of labour, the manner of computing teacher local, and compensation for extra duty. There must also be a clear understanding about who reports to whom; otherwise two superiors may claim the same time for a given employee.

Policies should also cover use of funds. If the budget is to cover all activities, it is important that the sports with small spectator appeal be protected. Clearly defined relationships and carefully planned budgets will help. Departmental and program organization must also take into account the educational values for all the students. They should not be influenced unduly by dramatic appeals and popular demand.

Good communications system help executives in the process of coordination. They also assist managers who are striving to unite the work of different people in their efforts to achieve the objectives that have been developed for the organization. The success of any enterprise depends to a large extent on how well administrators organize individual tasks so that they are joined into a combined, purposeful action.

POLICIES AND DIRECTING OR COORDINATING

Policies, rightly used, are an effective way of communicating. Relevant and carefully formulated policies can serve as an effective means of directing. Inasmuch as the policies are generally disseminated to all units of an organization, they serve as coordinating devices as well as directives. They also speed up communications for they not only pass along the "channel of command" but they provide multiple channels by which message flow in all direction and to all units of the organization.

Few modern business, however, can tolerate having communication flow only through the channel of command. Each manager would be a potential bottleneck for the flow of essential information. The sheer mass of detail in most departments makes direct communication between operators necessary. Once an activity passes beyond the ability of a man to attend to every detail, routine and standard information must flow from one operator to another without managerial attention. An executive would be forced to neglect other duties if he tried to make himself the exclusive transmitter of information.

STANDARD PRACTICES, POLICIES, AND CONTROLLING

Controlling is the process of assessing performance and outcomes on the basis of established criteria. These criteria consist of hopes and plans articulated in the form of goals, policies, and standard practices. If the plans have been carefully laid, the policies thoughtfully formulated, and the standard practices meticulously followed, the results should approach or even exceed expectations. Policies and standard practices, in situations where the persons involved in implementation have also had an important role in their formulation, serve as guidelines and instructions for almost every phase of the operation. Individuals who feel that these were arrived at democratically and are soundly conceived will generally work energetically and enthusiastically to see that they are followed.

Basic policies in physical education and athletics should emphasize the key role of the student in education. The governing factor in many important decisions should be "the most good for the most students." This idea can be formulated as a statement of policy and can be used as a yardstick in the evaluation of the program. If inordinate attention is given the talented student, the great musician, or the star athlete, it may be noted as a weakness.

Disproportionate importance attached to special education for the handicapped, with too little energy and resources for other aspects of the program, will also be considered in the process of controlling. If he two extremes, the talented and the handicapped, are given so much consideration that there is little left for the middle eighty percent, this too will be seen as a flaw. If careful thought is given to the basic policy, all segments of the student body will receive consideration.

Personnel policies may include a statement to the effect that there will be no discrimination in employment or compensation on the basis of sex, race, or religion. Standard practices will spell out procedures for implementing that policy and evaluative steps for determining compliance.

A departmental policy may state that in the conduct of athletics the health and safety of the athletes are of primary concern. Standard practices may consist of instructions in case of injury and safety procedures to prevent accidents.

It becomes obvious that policies and standard practices are indispensable to the processes of evaluating and controlling and are necessary for a sound administration.

FORMULATING POLICIES

Preparing policies is an important task that is usually carried out at the administrative level. The dean of students is generally responsible for decisions regarding student life. The athletic director and the comptroller are both involved with regulations concerning the expenditure of money for team travel. Staff members responsible for other activities must likewise be included in the groups assigned to formulate policies for the conduct of those activities. Each committee engaged in writing policies and other regulations should include at least one member who has the ability to express ideas in a clear and concise manner.

All members of a policy-writing committee should be instructed to research all pertinent facts thoroughly before making their report to the organizational unit involved.

Well-written policies provide security to members of an organization. One of the chief causes of confusion in large organizations is the lack of clear-cut rules, regulations, and policies.

THE ADMINISTRATIVE HANDBOOK

Institutions and their subdivisions have found administrative handbooks (also referred to as policy books or administrative guides) both useful and effective. Smaller institutions may place all guidelines in one book. As institutions become larger and the organizations more complex, it becomes necessary to have a major handbook containing general policies for the entire institution, leaving departmental or program handbooks for the subdivision. Such books may contain only policies or a combination of policies and standard practices. If they contain a combination, they may be organized so that after each policy there will be found the standard practices that will implement it or so that the policies may be found in the first part of the book, with the standard practices following in the last part.

Those who have used loose-leaf notebooks have found that they permit changes to be made with the test confusion. Alphabetized index tabs with the subject indicated will assist in the organization of the handbook.

SAMPLE POLICIES AND STANDARD PRACTICES

As illustrations of how policies and standard practices might be written for an administrative handbook, four hypothetical examples are presented.

Policy I-Public Relations

All staff members have a responsibility for good public relations. Educational programs to be successful need the support of the many public. A sound program is the basis upto which good public relations rest.

Standard Practices

- Students who feel they are receiving something worthwhile and who are treated with the dignity that should be accorded all individuals are the most effective public relations agents. Teachers and coaches should avail themselves of opportunities to assist in this effort.
- Teachers and coaches should watch for opportunities to interpret programs to the public. All should participate in affairs where parents and other members of the general public are present. Within appropriate limits, opportunities to speak at civic functions should be accepted.
- Good human relations result in good public relations, Sincerity, integrity, and friendliness will pay dividends in acceptance by the public.

Policy II-Purchasing Equipment

The director of the division of physical education and athletics is ultimately responsible for the purchasing of physical education and athletic equipment. However, each staff member has a role. Every teacher and coach must assist in the assessment of needs and recommendations for the best and most appropriate equipment. All staff members must follow the specific procedures outlined in the standard practices when initiating purchases.

Standard Practices

- Each staff member responsible for initiating a purchase must investigate the costs, possible sources, and quantities needed. A check on the inventory should be made when necessary.
- All purchase must be initiated on the standard requisition form, which should be completed in every detail. The signature of the initiator should be affixed in the appropriate place.
- Requisitions must be approved and signed by the director of the division and will then be forwarded to the central purchasing office, where the purchase order will be completed.
- The initiator is responsible for examing the equipment when received and also for indicating approval for payment on the appropriate form. This should be sent to the director's office, which will then forward it to the controller for payment.

Policy III-Employment of Personnel

The basic principle for guiding the employment of personnel will be "the best person for the job." This implies a careful analysis of the education, experience, and personal qualifications of the candidates.

- Unless it is obviously impossible or inappropriate, a committee of staff members intimately concerned will be appointed as a "search committee" to seek candidates from many sources and to review the problems carefully.

- The search committee will present in writing to the director two or three names ranked in order of preference. These individuals will normally be brought in for personal interviews.
- The director will confer with the academic dean or principal regarding the committee's recommendations. The final selection will then be made.
- Qualification considered especially important are integrity, teaching competence, diligence, sincerity, commitment to the students' welfare, interest in people, intelligence, tact, and friendliness. These should be assessed to the extent possible.

Policy IV—Affirmative Action

The basic purpose of the affirmative action plan is to ensure that all personnel are treated fairly. There will be no discrimination on the basis of creed, race, ethnic background, or gender. All individuals will be given equal opportunities to succeed and advance to the degree that their performance, qualifications, and worth to the institution merit.

Standard Practices

- When employing personnel, the announcements of vacancies will be distributed so they will reach all individuals who may be qualified and interested.
- There will be no discrimination against minority groups when administering the programs of promotions, salary increments, and advancement.
- When employing new personnel, there should be an effort to strike a reasonable balance between persons of the various races, creeds, ethnic groups, and sexes.

- There will be compensatory and tutorial programs established to help disadvantaged students meet admission requirements.

These are partial examples of how policies and standard practices might be developed and placed in an administrative handbook. Each topic should begin on a new page so a single policy can be replace without disturbing others.

SUGGESTED SUBJECTS FOR POLICIES AND STANDARD PRACTICES

Policies and standard practices that might be included in departments of physical education and athletics are listed under the following headlines:

PERSONNEL POLICIES

- Tenure and dismissal
- Contracts
- Sick leave
- Leave of absence
- Classification and promotion
- Salary schedules and policies
- Retirement
- Credit unions
- Vacations
- Work load
- Teacher evaluation
- Affirmative action
- Collective bargaining

STAFF WORK

- Importance of complete fact-finding
- Written reports
- Appropriate coordination

CLASS ORGANIZATION AND CONDUCT

- Attire
- Attendance and make-up
- Record books
- Use of student leaders
- Grading and evaluating
- Changing class sections

HEALTH SERVICE

- Reporting of accidents, injuries, and sickness
- School nurse
- School physician
- Injury care
- Student health

FACILITIES

- For classes
- For curricular activities
- Outside group usage
- For free play (not class or curricular)
- Priorities, assignment, etc.

TEACHERS' OR COACHES' ABSENCES

- Reporting
- Sickness
- Trips
- Substitute teachers
- Other arrangements

ATHLETICS

- Scheduling
- Athletic trips
- Eligibility
- Insurance
- Personal car
- Training rules
- Playing on outside teams
- Parking during contests
- Recruiting
- Fund raising
- Safety of athletes

EQUIPMENT

- Purchase
- Care
- Custody
- Checking out and in
- Responsibility and accountability

KEYS

- Responsibility
- Accountability

IN-SERVICE EDUCATION

- Travel to conferences, etc.
- Advanced study
- Professional leaves
- Remuneration

DEPARTMENTAL MEETINGS

- Attendance
- Agenda
- Participation

REPORTS

- Special (injuries, unusual events)
- Trips and convention
- Annual
- Seasonal

COMMITTEE WORK

- Assignments
- Reporting
- Service limit

FINANCIAL ADMINISTRATION

- Budgeting
- Financial aid

- Accounting

PROFESSIONAL ETHICS COMMUNICATION

- Interdepartmental
- Extradepartmental
- Channels

OUTSIDE RELATIONSHIPS

- Municipal government
- Civic organizations
- Grants
- General public

SUPERVISION

- Philosophy
- Responsibility
- Student-teacher relationships

FORMULATING AND ESTABLISHING POLICIES AND STANDARD PRACTICES

- The philosophy, policies, and edicts of the institution should be carefully studies. All departmental guidelines should be compatible with those of the institution.
- State and local laws, municipal regulations, and any other pertinent rules and practices should be reviewed for their relevance to new policies.
- Departmental staff members should be involved on the basis of their special responsibilities their ability to write or edit, their role in implementation, and their interest in the project.

- An overall editorial committee should be formed and changed with the responsibility for uniformity of format, clarity of statements, and good writing.
- Subcommittees should be appointed for each area or topic for which guidelines are being written.
- Individuals with some executive responsibilities should be involved in the formulation of policies; persons at the operating level should have most to say about standard practices.
- When policies have been formulated by individual committees, they shall be presented to the department for discussion and approval. Revisions can be made at that time.
- The department director should present new policies to superiors for their approval. When approved by the institution, they become effective.
- Policies should be flexible enough to allow some leeway for those who implement them. They shall be reviewed periodically for needed changes.

SUMMARY

The role of planning is to take action in the present that will serve as a guide for the future. Administrators outline the steps that advance the organization toward its goals.

Thorough planning tends to lessen the number of random action, to avoid role conflict, to reduce dissatisfaction, and to diminish the number of arbitrary promotions and dismissals. It also leads to more consistent review of current actions and to meticulous care of important records.

The planning process includes the development of objectives, policies, standard practices, and programs. In a school system, the entire operation is dependent on the enrolment and the resources. These must be assessed before the program can be set in motion.

Policies are guiding principles that have been approved by a supervisory or legislative body for the operation of a department or other unit of a school or college. Executive functions include responsibility for the implementation of policies. This usually results in the promulgation of more specific policies or standard practices at the operational level.

Policies will be implemented more willingly if those who are responsible for implementing them have a voice in the formulation of the policies. Administrators at each level of the hierarchical organization should provide for the necessary representation.

Clearly articulated policies and carefully spelled-out standard will prevent misunderstandings and lead to more efficient and effective operation. They are also very important as criteria upon which evaluation and controlling can be based.

13

NEW DIRECTIONS IN SPORTS AS A FIELD OF STUDY

Until the 1960s the dominant steam of research in sporting areas was in physical education or in practical matters related to sporting practices. During the 1960s a new direction appeared in physical education: a growing scholarly interest in the study of sport. The result has been a startling change in research directions and concentration during the last decade and a half. This chapter will look at the rise of the disciplines in the field of physical education, along with the idea of sport as a legitimate field of scholarly study, and then briefly discuss some of the new fields of study in sport.

THE EMERGENCE OF A DISCIPLINE IN PHYSICAL EDUCATION

We have already discussed the emergence of the discipline side of physical education in the first chapter, but a short review will help in understanding developments in sports study in the 1970s. We defined a discipline as "an area of knowledge and theory that can exist purely for itself" that is, with no need to show that it has a practical application. The interest in this side of physical education began to develop in the mid-1960s.

The interest in a discipline centred around Henry's 1964 article and its implications. While various scholars, such as Kenyon, worked to define a discipline and its area of study, AAPER worked to organize and present a document which would demonstrate physical education's body of knowledge." At the same time, scholars in the Big Ten Conference schools organized a series of annual conference to discuss the different newly emerging disciplines or subdisciplines in what some scholars were beginning to call "sport studies." By the early 1970s publication had appeared from AAHPER which attempted to organize the theoretical base underlying physical education. Meanwhile, the American Academy of Physical Education debated whether a new name was needed for physical education, one which would better demonstrate the true focus of its study.

In this year since Henry's article first appeared and spurred interest in a discipline many changes in direction have affected-and are continuing to affect-physical education. The first notable change has been the split in physical education between the professional interests and the disciplinary interest. Many conflicts have arisen which seem to pit physical education against sport studies and "teachers" against "researchers." The more practical appearance of the profession side of studies has created problems with those interested in the discipline or research side, as each sometimes question the other's validity or importance.

In truth, both groups contribute to physical education in important ways. Their conflicts often seem to be little more than arguments of different points of view, though sometimes the real argument has bee over which group wields the power in a department. However, the scholarly side of physical education is far more prominently displayed today than it has been in the past.

A second notable change has been the appearance of new professional societies representing the disciplinary subgroups and their particular scholarly focus of interests. These new societies, which represent areas such as sport philosophy, sport sociological, sport history and sport psychology, have promoted scholarship in their areas by initiating national conferences and by publishing journals that provide more scholarly and wide-raging outlets of research than provided by the older organizations of physical education. By the mid-1970s AAHPERD and recognized the growth of the scholarly interests and had stared "Academies" within its professional structure.

A third notable change in the direction of physical education has been evident in the last decade or so. These years have seen a great burst of scholarly research and writing. Books of readings in scholarly areas have reflected this growth by their need of extensive revising as the quality and quantity of research continues to radically increase. This growth of scholarship has perhaps done the most in terms of reviving physical education and in presenting it to the outside world as an academically respectable field of study and work.

SPORT—A LEGITIMATE FIELD OF ACADEMIC STUDY

Sport holds a prominent place in modern life. Millions of people participate in sporting activities, watch and read about them, and spend billions of dollars annually on sports-related activities and equipment. Though this massive interest in sport was noticed many decades ago, little attention was paid to actually studying except by sport journalists and by the occasional scholar, whose professional co-workers often considered the pursuit of such interests as scholarly "slumming." Indeed, scholarly suspicion of the idea of a "scholarly" interest in sport still exists. But the impact of sport on modern society has made it clear that sport is a very legitimate field of academic study. As Max Scheler noted over half a century ago, "Scarcely an international phenomenon of the day deserves social and psychological study to the degree that sport does. Sport has gown immeasurably in scope and in social importance, but the meaning of sport has received little in the way of serious attention."

We now see sport used at the international level for many blatantly political purposes; prestige, a show of friendship, a show of international acceptance, and so forth. China invited the United States to send a table-tennis team on a tour as a sign of improving relations between the countries. Cuba used the 1976 Olympic victories of Alberto Junatorena as an argument for the superiority of their political system in improving life in their nation. Just as Hitler used the 1936 Olympics to show the "superiority" of his Nazi system, so did the Soviet union use the 1980 Olympics to serve the same flagrant propaganda purposes for their communist system. The Soviets published many articles stating that the awarding of the games to Moscow showed that the world had accepted the legitimacy of their communist government and, indeed, had approved of Moscow's approach to world peace, which included sending an army into an adjoining nation prior to the games. The obvious political nature of sport was made more clear when the games.

The obvious political nature of sport was made clear when the United States and many other nations withdrew from those games, using their absence as a protest of the Soviet Union's political actions more than as a political perversion of the purpose of the Olympics. Indeed, just as in 1936, the International Olympic Committee showed no sign of protest at the use of the game for political means by the host nation.

Sometimes we fail to realize the extent of our interest in sport in modern times. As Guttmann notes:

One reason that sports are not understood is that familiarity has made their significance seem obvious when its is not. Another reason is that the philosophers, historians, sociologists, and psychologist who have concerned themselves with sports have only rarely written for the ordinary reader. They have communicated mainly with each other.

Over the last decade and a half we have seen the rise of "sport science," the discipline arm of physical education. Though arguments for human movement as the focus of the discipline were advanced, more popularity seems to have settled on sport as the focus. Human movement has been called too broad, as it can include things such as learning to hold a pencil or to walk, while sport is more specific to the types of activities which are actually used in the field.

THE DISCIPLINES IN PHYSICAL EDUCATION

The fields of study or subdisciplines of sport are shown in the figure. Similar groupings have been suggested by other scholars, though Siedentop is one of the few who has called for the inclusion of pedagogy in the disciplines. The figure attempts to show the show the generally accepted subdisciplines within sport science and, at the same time, to show something of their relationships to each other. Sport pedagogy is concerned with teaching, particularly the skills used in sporting situations. It includes teaching methods and many elements tied to the concern of the profession of physical education. As the profession and professional preparation are discussed later, they will not be discussed further at this point. Discussions of the other six components follow.

Sport Biomechanics. Sport biomechanics is concerned with the effects of natural law and forces on the body in sport. It has developed from the field of kinesiology, which is also a study of movement. Kinesiology has two basic areas: anatomical kinesiology, which is concerned with the construction and working mechanisms of the body, and mechanical kinesiology, which is biomechanics or the mechanics of the human body. In sum, sport biomechanics is the study of the human body how the laws of physics apply to it.

Research in biomechanics breaks down into two large categories: fundamental study of the process of simple movements, and analysis of motor skills, which are far more complex and pertinent to sport skills. J. Ann Carr discusses seven types of research found in biomechanics. They are cinematography, stroboscope, force platform studies, electrogonimetry, electromyography, telemetry, and computer-based studies.

Cinematography uses motion picture photography to study movement. High-speed individual pictures are taken of many parts of a single continuing motion. Stroboscopy employs a similar photographic technique, except that an entire skill is captured in a single picture. A stroboscopic light flashes at preselected intervals of time during the performance. Only the positions at preselected intervals of time during the performance. Only the positions of the body photographed during the light flashes will show up on the picture, thus providing a representative view of the entire pattern of motion.

A force platform measures the force pushing against it, such as the amount of push a jumper uses in leaving the ground. It is used in studying the size and direction of forces, as well as their duration, and helps give a clearer idea of the variables in performances of skills such as the sprint start.

Electrogoniometry records changes in joint angles with electrical instruments, giving a clearer idea of the sequence and ranges of motion followed in performing a skill. Electromyography uses electrical instruments to record the work of muscles during the performance of skills. It can tell what muscles are used in performing a complex skill. Telemetry uses electrical instruments to record electrical "events" in the body, which means any physical activity that can be converted into an electrical signal such as a heartbeat. Small radio transmitters are then used to send the signal to recording instrument so that the performer can be studied while actually taking part in a normal performance, such as recording the activity of the heart of someone competing in a one-mile race.

Computers are being increasingly used to help analyse complied skill performance. In fact, they can now be used to simulate skill activities. The mechanical characteristics of a performer, such as a discus thrower, can be fed into a computer and displayed on a screen, along with information on the thrower's performance. The computer then can simulate or predict how far the discus would have been thrown if certain improvements in the thrower's technique had been made. This gives the performer a clearer idea of how a skill be improved and the potential gain which might come from this improvement.

The motion analyses of biomechanics look at two aspects of motion study: kinematics and kinetics. Kinematics seeks information on the motion of the body, regardless of what causes the motion. Kinetics studies what causes the body to move the way it does. There are many other subdivisions of areas within biomechanics, such as mechanics and dynamics, and even lower subdivisions, such as fluid mechanics, but these are better discussed in a biomechanics course. Kinetics and kinematics themselves are subdivision of dynamics, which is simply the study of motion.

Many groups are concerned with sport biomechanics, and numerous meetings are held at the national and international level to discuss research in the field. In addition, many biomechanical studies are published each year in the Research Quarterly for Exercise and Sport, a publication of AAHPERD. Within AAHPERD there is a discipline-oriented academy in kinesiology, which is devoted to encouraging scholarship in this area.

The future of biomechanics should include more joint research projects with either motor-learning specialists interested in determining how skills are learned and what are the most efficient teaching procedures, or with coaches interested in improving the technical performances of athletes through utilization of the scientific expertise and research capabilities of modern programs. The sport-and-athletics-oriented use of biomechanics is already a conspicuous part of Eastern European athletics, with East Germany and the Soviet Union leading the way in the application of research capabilities to athletic performance.

SPORT PHYSIOLOGY

Sport physiology is concerned with how the body functions during exercise. The effects of training are a critical facet of sport physiology research, which makes it perhaps the most important of the sport studies, for it is concerned with all aspects of how the body adapts to exercise: This includes such concerns as the function and contraction of the muscles, the workings of the nervous system during physical activity, the functions of the respiratory system, and the working of the cardiovascular system.

At the same time, this area of study if often considered to include sport medicine, an equally important and growing area of study. Sport medicine is concerned with both treating and preventing athletic injuries. In turn, this broad interest in the health or the physically active body also can include adapted physical education, or developmental activities for the physically of mentally handicapped or disabled. The sports medicine specialist is concerned with preventive training, treatment, and equipment that assist the performer in staying healthy; nutrition; drugs and erogogenic aids; the treatment and rehabilitation of injuries; and ethical matters related to the training, exercise, and treatment of athletes.

The sport physiologist conducts research studies in a physiology laboratory, using such equipment as treadmills, exercise bicycles, oxygen measuring equipment, and equipment that measures chemical characteristics of the body. Where the sport biomechanics specialist works in areas of physics, the sport physiologist works basically in areas related to chemistry. More or the work of the sport physiologist takes place in the laboratory than of the sport biomechanics specialist. Yet, the importance of the research of the physiologist is great, for the work cuts to the heart of the training system; unless an athlete is trained to a fine edge and to the highest level, good mechanics will not result in high-level performances.

Groups interested in the study of sport physiology include the Exercise physiology. Academy of AAHPERD, which encourages scholarly study among the professional membership; the American College of Sports Medicine, which encourages and publishes research in that area; and the National Athletic Trainer's Association, which encourages study in that area. The American Medical Association has a Committee on the Medical Aspects of Sports that actively works with physicians and keeps them informed of matters relating to sports problems, injury, and treatment. The work of this committee ha become especially important due to the great in crease in participation in competitive sports and to the related rise in sports injuries, many of which are treated by doctors who normally do not work with sports injuries.

Publications in the field include the Research Quarterly for Exercise and Sport, published by AAHPERD; the periodical Medicine and Science in Sports, published by the ACSM; and the book the Encyclopedia of Sport Sciences and Medicine, also published by the ACSM. Many national and international conferences on the subject are help each year by different groups interested in sports physiology.

The future of sport physiology will probably include more coordinated studies with coaches that are designed to learn how to determine and properly monitor optimal training levels in exercise programs. These studies will utilize testing of the cardio-respiratory system and of blood chemistry. Much work in this area has already been done in East Germany and the Soviet union.

Currently, much research is being conducted by sport physiologists in the prevention of athletic injuries and in the development of better programs to prepare people for exercise programs and to help people recover swiftly from injuries. At the same time, work is also being done to prepare more athletic trainers and to educate more doctors in sports medicine so that prevention and treatment will be raised to a higher level in the United States.

In addition, work is being done by sport physiologists in areas related to the needs of the physically handicapped. This work includes the development of rehabilitation methods and programs and the development of more "normal" programs of physical education and sport for the handicapped. The impetus provided by federal regulations, such as PL 94-142, which require the "main streaming" of handicapped individuals into non-handicapped programs, has resulted in far more attention and money for this area than at any time in the past.

OTHER DISCIPLINES

Sport philosophy has been discussed at some length, so it will not be discussed within this chapter. The areas of sport psychology, sport sociology and sport history will be discussed within the context of the social sciences.

STUDYING SPORT IN THE SOCIAL SCIENCES

Physical education and sporty studies have been traditionally associated with scientific studies, but in recent years increasing attention has been paid to the potential of sport research in the social sciences. We can simplify the distinction between the sciences and the social sciences by looking at the sciences as concerned basically with physical phenomena, while the social sciences are concerned with social phenomena. The most commonly understood social sciences in sport studies are psychology, sociology, and history. We will briefly discuss each of these social sciences in order to give a fuller idea of the focus and method of each in sport studies.

SPORT PSYCHOLOGY

Sport psychology is concerned with studying human behaviour in the sport setting. In the realm of sport studies, psychology is often studied in two aspects: motor sill learning and performance, which is common to both physical education and sport and to sport is concerned with the psychological factors affecting the learning and performance of physical skills—with how individuals are affected by both internal and external factors.

Among the earliest works in sport psychology were two books by Coleman R. Griffith, Psychology of Coaching and Psychology and Athletics. Clearance Ragsdle published an dearly work, The psychology of Motor Learning, and John Lawther published The Psychology of Coaching in 1951. Even so , sport psychology was a relatively new territory when large-scale interest began to develop in the 1960s.

The International Society of sports Psychology was organized at the First International Congress of Psychology of Sport in Rome in 1965, while the North American Society for the Psychology of Sport and Physical activity was founded in 1966. When the idea of discipline-centred academies to promote scholarship appeared in the early 1970s, the Sport Psychology Academy was begun in 1975, with the somewhat related Motor Development Academy following in 1979. Both within the professional arm of physical education, AAHPERD.

While articles relating to sport psychology may be found frequently in the Research Quarterly for Exercise and Sport and occasionally in Quest, the primary scholarly publications are the *International Journal of Psychology of Sport*, the *Journal of Sport Psychology the Journal of Motor Behaviour,* and *Perceptual and Motor Skills.*

Sports psychology studies such issues as the nature of motor skill, performance and learning ,and the psychological characteristics of the performer. The factors that are studied include those affecting physical performance such as motivation, the distribution of practice, and the specificity. The difference in these factors in the teaching situation and the coaching situation is primarily one of the level of skill and intensity of the performer, as the basic factors and principles are the same.

Some sport psychologists are debating the direction to be taken in sport psychology research, particularly in methodology. Rainer Martens has called for more emphasis on "field" research—that is, research which studies performance where it takes place, on the track or playing field, rather than traditional laboratory research. In the past most research has been with individuals or groups in a laboratory setting which is a carefully monitored environment. Martens notes the existence of the question of why sport psychologists spend so little time actually studying sport, or applied research. In response, he suggests that more theory-building work is necessary and that doing it will require more time studying sport where and as it takes place.

Martens does note that research can be just as erroneous as any other type of research, but says that laboratory research often is not useful in the field situation. The essential problem is the complexity of human behaviour. So many factors can affect a single situation that it may be impossible to determine how to change the factors if we want to increase or decrease some element of performance.

Siedentop agrees with Marten's suggestions that the field would be the best place for research in psychology and with the idea that new theories would be more likely to develop from field research which is concerned with applied problems. However, Siedentop does not agree with all of Marten's ideas. He notes that "sport psychology will become more accepted in the 'field' if it adopt a more client-centred approach. Sport psychologists are beginning to react to this call for more applied research into the actual sporting practice instead of lab experiments that often bear little fruit in the in the field.

Sport psychology is a field that is receiving growing interest. To date, psychologists in the Western world have only moderately active in working with athletes and teams, but in the Eastern socialist countries sport psychology has been increasingly present in the preparation of high-level athletes. This is the direction of the future. Coaches, teachers, and parents are becoming more concerned not only about preparing athletes for highly skilled performance, but also about protecting the emotional-psychological health of athletes.

Much work remains to be done by sport psychologists in terms of field and laboratory research; actual work coaches, athletes, and teams; the monitoring of programs, such as youth sports.

SPORT SOCIOLOGY

Sport sociology is concerned with the social behaviour of people in the sport setting, both individual and group behaviour. This broad area is sometimes described as studying the sociocultural processes and institutions as they relate to and are affected by sport and sport in behaviour. Sport is a significant part of our social order; it is often described as a "microcosm of society," that is, a small-scale model of what the whole society is like. The sport sociologist, studies how people interact with each other in a sport setting in order to determine how the process of sport affects their development and socialization, or how they fit into society.

Two aspects of society are studied by sport sociologists: social institutions, such as schools or other organizations, and social processes, such as the development of social status or prestige within a group or community. Social aspects of life are difficult to research, for they provide little truly objective data. Group and individual behaviour are studied by using sources such as interviews, official statistics, questionnaires, documents, observation, and experimentation. Such sources are rarely objective, however, since they require the opinion of an individual or group to group to determine a status or change.

As a result, sociological research results often are considered controversial. At the same time, the important part played by sport in the schools and in the community as children grow up requires that we learn as much as we can about how sport affects the social aspects of the growing process. Only with such knowledge in hand can sport be used in the most beneficial way in helping children grow into healthy, socially useful adults.

Areas of research in sport sociology include sport and social institutions social stratification, and socialization. Among the many sub-topics that are studied in relation to individuals and groups in sport are sexual differences and roles, racism, religion, values and ethics, economics, politics, leisure and work habits, ethnic groups, and social change.

Sport sociology is still a newer area of sport research, though a few of its scholarly works go back to the early years of this century such as Steinitzer's Sport and Culture, Rise's Sociology of Sport, Huizinga's Homo Ludens, and Caillois's Man, play, and games. Early suggestions for sport sociology as a subdiscipline in the United States were made by Gerald Kenyon and John Loy in 1965, and more specific explanations of the subject by Loy followed in 1968. Indeed, sport sociology was one of the first of the sporting disciplines or subdisciplines to develop its own scholarly organizations and publications apart from the usual small groups of physical educations that operate strictly within larger general conventions.

The Committee for the Sociology of Sport was an early branch of the International Council of Sport and Physical Education, and it was followed by the International Committee of Sport Sociology, which was founded in 1964. The ICSS has regular international sport sociology seminars and sponsors the International Review of Sport Sociology. The ICSS was followed by the North American Society for the Sport and by the Sport Sociology Academy, which was formed in the NASPE area of AAHPERD. Other sport sociology publications include the Sport Sociology Bulletin and the Journal of sport and Social Issues. Some sport history meetings and periodicals publish studies that can be termed sport sociology since areas of sociology may be studied in their historical context, such as whether sports participation was widely used in blending early immigrant groups into the existing communities in the United States.

SPORT HISTORY

Sport history is the study of sport in the past. It can serve to teach us how things have come to be as they are today, and it can direct us to problems that need to be solved. There are two today, and it can direct us to problems that need to be solved. There are types of historical research descriptive and interpretive. Descriptive historical research is the early groundwork for study, for it simply determines the facts of the matter—the "what" of history—and reports them. Early historical works are usually descriptive.

The more advanced level of historical research is interpretive: the attempt to tell or determine why something happened or what is important about an event or trend. Evidence must be not only analysed but also interpreted; this injects the issue of values and value systems into the research.

Sources for historical research are generally called primary of secondary sources. A primary source is any person or thing that was a direct witness to the event being studied. It may be the account of a person who was there, or it may be official record kept during the event. In short, the primary source is first-hand information. The secondary source is any source not directly involved in the event when it happened, such as the report of a person who interviewed someone who was a participant.

Historical research involves three basic concepts; change, development, and progress. Change is a simple concept—a difference from an earlier state or condition. Change can be documented easily because no values are involved. Either a rule did or did not change; the evidence is usually clear. Development is a series of changes in a direction; it, too is not difficult to establish with evidence. The speed of change in a direction can range from slow to fast and if it is consistent in a single direction, it can be documented to show a trend. Again, no values are involved. Simple facts can establish direction.

The third concept of historical research is progress, which does require value judgments and is thus less grounded in facts. Change and development are descriptive ideas, but progress is always interpretive because it assumes improvement. One of the difficulties of historical research is that many ideas are based on the concept of progress, which Robert Nisbet says has been an accepted concept for three thousand years of western history. Yet, the validity of progress as a concept is beginning to be questioned because it is so value-laden. As Nisbet summarizes it, "The idea of progress holds that man kind has advanced in the past—from some aboriginal condition of primitiveness, barbarism, or even nullity—is now advancing, and will continue to advance through the foreseeable future."

This idea, clearly is a value judgment, for one must believe in the idea of progress to begin with. The concept is critical to sport, since modern sport is very concerned with records and their breaking; only the belief in the idea of progress makes those records worth keeping, for they are goals to be surpassed, which is possible only if there is a belief in progress.

One of the early history books was Joseph Strutt's sports and Pastimes of the People of England. John A. Krout's annals of American Sport was the first scholarly book on sport history in the United States, though earlier writings on the subjects are available. Many of the sources on sport history are cited in a booklet produced in 1980 by the History of Sport and Physical Education Academy of the AAHPERD, Getting Started in the History of Sport and Physical Education. Excellent works on research methods also are available, such as the one by Jacques Barzun and Henry F. Graaf, while other works serve as an introduction to the problems of sport history research itself, such as the one by Allen Guttmann.

Sport history, with its concern about the when, where and how of sport, serves to complete the circle of studies covered in sport science. Obviously, not all of the components are sciences; for those areas of study not strictly considered science, the term "sport arts and sciences" for those areas of study not strictly considered science, the term " sport arts and sciences" has been suggested as has the term "sport social sciences." Sport history serves to show us where we have been, how we got where we are today, and, with a little luck, perhaps where we may be going and what we should look for.

A SUMMATION

We now have looked briefly at each of the disciplines or subdisciplines generally accepted as part of the field of sport science or sport studies. Scholars accept either six or seven areas as separate: sport biomechanics, sport physiology, sport philosophy, sport psychology, sport sociology, sport history, and sport pedagogy.

14

CONTRIBUTION AND RELATIONSHIPS OF HEALTH, PHYSICAL EDUCATION AND RECREATION TO FITNESS

The name, American Association for Health, Physical Education and Recreation, involves a number of varied, intricate and sometimes vague relationships. To the title physical education in our association's name, the world health was added, but no one stopped to ask what it included. An individual possesses health; associations are concerned with health education. More recently, the word recreation was added; and here again definitions became varied, ranging from concepts of sports and games to a wide gamut of creative activities, or to some it means recreation education.

We are involved in the meaning of terms and confusion reigns. A word means one thing to one and another to his neighbour, another to his professional associate, and still another to an administrator or to the public. This paper is an attempt to clarify this situation. As we move through the discussion, words and phrases will be defined and relationships established, from the viewpoint of the speaker.

PHASES OF DEVELOPMENT

Man may be thought of in terms of four phases of development: organic; neuromuscular; interpretive; and emotional. It is evident that all developments are bound into an integrated whole but the word fitness should be reserved for a quality of organic power. Yet, when fitness is discussed someone inevitably raises the question, "What about mental fitness? Does it involve native intelligence, the I.Q., educational advancement, emotional balance, or just what is it? Then someone raises the question of moral and spiritual fitness. Unfortunately, there is no clear cut meaning for these words, though apparently many people have. Is there a standard definition for these terms which has eluded me or are they qualities differing for each man?

The word fitness should be reserved for organic development optimum health. "Fit as a fiddle" is understood. When an athlete is "in the pink", we know what this means.

Total fitness is too vague a term. Such broad terms as "total" or "well-rounded" can be applied to all education, to life itself; but as the whole is the sum of its parts, can we not discuss the relationship of parts? If so, we must isolate physical fitness as the primary objective of physical education.

The physical education, health and recreation aspects of our education have been criticized for attempting to be all things to all men. Physical education and its associated areas cannot be all things to all men, but there are some things which they must be to all men.

Total fitness is the responsibility of all society-home, church, school and community. It seems to me that physical education should concern itself largely with the physical organism-optimum health. There will occur voices to defend fringe contributions of physical education and it should be agreed, but in the breakdown of responsibilities, our major task is the development of an organism capable of performing sustained effort.

Various phases of education are assigned specific points of emphasis. One stresses history and literature; another, the sciences; another languages; another citizenship and still another the arts of vocational training. All are, or should be, interested in the health and physical fitness of an individual and, likewise, physical education should be interested in and contribute to all educational objectives. The physical educator's primary responsibility, however, should remain focuses. One group of educators can select only a small portion of the total problem.

It would be better to talk about a man skilled in a specific activity rather than skill-fitness; the thinking, problem solving man rather than mental-fitness; the man who lives on an emotionally high level rather than moral-fitness. Health is only one phase of total man, and our responsibilities must be confined to this one phase though we, like every other discipline, contribute to the whole.

Men, throughout the ages, have been high on one or two of the four phases of development but seldom high on all four. Let us consider some examples. Gandhi was low on the organic level to the point of frailty. He wanted to weave but said, "My finger are all thumbs." Intellectually, he was fairly high though he failed as a lawyer. Emotionally, however, he was a mountain peak. He helped to free 150 million untouchables in India; he preached tolerance for which his enemies took his life.

In a like manner, mountain climbers and athletes while high on the organic and neuromuscular level may be at the same time either very low or very high on the intellectual and emotional levels. Examples of uneven development multiply with the names of Robert Louis Stevenson, Roosevelt and Elizabeth Barrett Browning all of who were frail but maintained peaks of achievement on other levels. There are, on the other hand, classic examples of people high on all levels, such as Robert Frost, Carl Sandburg, Winston Churchill, Jean Sibelius and Justice William O. Douglas. One could also cite many who are low on all the four levels of development. It is obvious that one can be skilful and intellectual yet not be high in other phases of development.

It is obvious too that one can be high or low in all. The point is that superiority in one phase of development does not guarantee the same pre-eminence in another.

ORGANIC DEVELOPMENT

This is the ability of the human organism to resist fatigue and to sustain effort. We need people, for war and peace, high on this level. With the high standard set by the armed forces, rejections will never be much lower than in World War-I1 because of hereditary backgrounds, accidents, or specific handicaps such as in eyes and ears and nerves.

We might think of health or physical fitness on a thermometer with the mercury moving up and down. Health is a condition of the organism. There are numerous factors which help to raise the mercury in this thermometer. Some are: protection from infections; good medical and dental advice and care; high hereditary background; good habits of nutrition, rest and sheep; adapted exercise; etc.

When the individual functions in an atmosphere of joy, happiness and challenge, he is training for fitness or optimum health-the mercury reading is high, but when he operates without these requisites, he causes the mercury on his health scale to lower. A high reading on this thermometer is to be desired.

Health or fitness, then, should be considered as a condition of the organism and not in terms of total life outcomes or objectives.

In a similar manner we might think of skills, the ability to think, and emotional status as thermometers with many elements tending to raise the mercury while others lower it. Illness and handicaps, hereditary or acquired, may readily lower or raise the skill-level or the thinking-level and may produce either bitterness or great faith. Elizabeth Barrett Browning when urged by her friends to stop working because of her ill health said, "If work means headaches, perforce it prefer headaches."

NEURO-MUSCULAR DEVELOPMENT

One may be highly or poorly skilled in any one of many areas-athletics, crafts, mechanics, science, painting, sculpturing, written or spoken language, picking pockets, or dozens more. The doers may be skilful and may be healthy but may not necessarily be ideal citizens. Skill ranges all the way from the beginning of gross movement to the performance of the artist. Skilful performance in strenuous activities helps the body to conserve energy and, hence, is closely related to organic development.

INTERPRETIVE DEVELOPMENT

This is the ability to think in one or more areas, to see relationships, to solve problems, to associate and remember, and to make sound judgements. A high rating on an intelligence test is not the sole criterion for this development. There are many kinds of intelligences, not just one. We think in terms of past experiences so we are largely a product of where we have been and what we have done. Skills give meaning to words and relationships. The hands are the "eye of the brain". Thinking in one area, however, seldom assures competency in another.

EMOTIONAL DEVELOPMENT

This involves the problem of attitudes and feelings. One the highest level, it may assume a religious concepts involving the mountain peaks of brotherhood and respect for all men. On the lower level it may be expressed in prejudice, hearted and intolerance.

These four developments are all related and the ideal is to be high on each of them but this attainment for all would be a utopia beyond the dream of the science fictionist.

DEFINITIONS

The next step is to discuss the meaning of several words which too often are taken for granted.

Physical education must be defined in terms of certain objectives. It can be illustrated, and desirable outcomes may be cited. It involves the total body: nerves, organs, muscles, the master brain and the emotions. Activities, other than physical education, are also dependent on these same physical sources. The farmer, the dock worker, and the bank president utilize similar body-brain-nerve and emotional connections, but physical education involves, activities whose primary outcome is in terms of organic and skill development. It is the training a man undergoes for the purpose of developing hid body, with all its related processes to function so that he may live to his fullest capacity.

Emotionally development is and should be a by-product of physical education. Exercise involved in games and sports, swimming and gymnastics, coming and outdoor education have specific objectives in terms of body power, endurance and behaviour. The objective here is exercise for health and organic development, while with the farmer, the carpenter and the dock worker the exercise involved in the pursuit of each and its outcomes is not the primary objective. The results in the finished product becomes the desired outcome.

Re-physical education has been used as a substitute for the term rehabilitation. Here again the object of the exercise is re-educating the body, not papering a board.

Recreation education, one of the primary responsibilities of teacher training, refers to the process of exposing young and old to satisfying recreational pursuits, of helping them skilfully in leisure and of providing good facilities for them.

Health is the ability to sustain effort and recover from fatigue quickly. It should be thought of, ideally, in terms of optimum organic functioning.

Health education on the other hand, involves a total educational process and is the result of the efforts of many people who try to raise the health status of man on the mercury scale.

RELATIONSHIPS

There are three relationships which must be considered: the relationship of health to physical education; the relationship of physical education to recreational; and the relationship of recreation to health.

HEALTH AND PHYSICAL EDUCATION

This is primarily a relationship of exercise to optimum health within the individual's capacity. If you prefer, call it fitness. Many facets which promote optimum health and longevity are outside the physical education domain. Optimum health is promoted by the doctor, dentist, nurse, sanitation and public health officials, nutritionists and others who provide a wholesome atmosphere in which a person lives.

Exercise contributes in at least five areas. When many variables affects the health of man it is always difficult to prove this-did-that or if-he-had-done-this, the-result-would-have-been-that. It is very difficult to draw always or never conclusions. Man must take the advice of experts for they, by training and experience, are in the best position to know the truth. The expert source from which the following was drawn is exercise and health, published by the American Medical Association.

A general conclusion of the relationships of the physical education type of exercise and health is provided in a joint statement made by the American Medical Association and the American Association for health, physical education, and Recreation:

1. Exercise is one of the most important factors contributing to total fitness.

2. The contributions of exercise to fitness include the development and maintenance of strength, speed, agility, endurance, and skill in persons who are physiologically sound. Active games, sports, swimming, rhythmic activities, prescribed exercises, and vigorous hobbies, such as gardening and other work around the home, all can make distinctive as well as worthwhile general contributions to fitness.

3. Individuals differ in their capacity to enjoy and benefit from participation in exercise because of constitutional variations in body size, strength, and structure as well as differences in previous experience and present condition.

4. Exercise should be graded according to age, individual reaction to activity, and the state of the person's fitness. After age 40, more frequent medical evaluation of the individual's capacity for exercise is imperative.

5. Activities for girls and women should be selected with regard for their psychological as well as physiological characteristics. Those which involves a minimum of body contact and do not stress heavy lifting should be favoured. Regularity of exercise should be stressed, with activity continued. If it is well tolerated, during the menstrual period.

6. The training involved in preparation for athletic competition contributes as much to fitness as participation in the contests themselves. Systematic training for any activity contributes effectively to fitness.

7. Time and care taken to condition the body for sports and athletics through appropriate activities will improve enjoyment, upgrade performance, and increase the ability to continue participation over a period of years.

8. Certain types of exercises are appropriate to certain conditions of weather and climate. Common sense suggests that a person should not set excessive performance goals under unfavourable conditions.

9. The proper use of protective equipment is essential to safe and effective participation in certain sports. Careful maintenance and proper control of facilities for athletics and other types of participation will help to prevent accidents and reduce injuries.

10. The rules of the game or specifications for play in an activity are made to protect participants and to enhance enjoyment. They should be properly interpreted, scrupulously observed, and vigorously enforced.

11. The vigour with which an individual participates in an activity will have more to do with outcomes for fitness than the activities or events in which he elects to participate.

PHYSICAL EDUCATION AND RECREATION

There is a vital relationship between physical education and certain phases of recreation but always keep in mind that recreation in a much broader term than is implied in sports and games. For activity to have any value there must be sustained effort. In order to sustain effort there must be drive, interest and fun. Recreation, therefore, which takes one camping and in the out-of-doors, which gives a person enjoyment in a game of tennis, badminton or swimming, form a real point of articulation with physical education.

Even at retirement, slowing up a little should not mean coming to a complete stop. Life has a quick way of disposing of non-workers and inactive persons. Retirement should never be the lazy man's dream of doing nothing. Explosive types of exercises or exercise too long sustained or engaged in at high altitudes should be avoided but other exercises should be carried on not just to the age of forty but to seventy-five and eighty-five. Recreation-fun is the catalyst which sets off desirable fitness outcomes.

RECREATION AND HEALTH

There is a physiological rule called the "law of attention"-namely, when the organism gives its attention to an activity (to grasp a fishing rod, or a golf club, or a lathe or a violin), worries and tensions disappear. The 20th century killers are fears, insecurities and tensions. We are living in a coronary-stomach ulcer-decade and excessive tensions are the cause relaxing recreation, hobbies in the best sense, is needed.

We need some tensions, of course, as in the uncertainty of the game, the thrill of a new struggle, the hope of success. Boredom has many of the characteristics of fatigue. The answer to many a health problem is to get into action, do something in which you are interested, find a hobby, get going! The other end of the scale from boredom is undue tension.

Man has a quality of oneness. Happiness, just old-fashioned joy, which means the absence of stress, supports buoyant health in a positive way and helps to keep the body resistance high. Happiness is associated with challenge, accomplishment and mastery. Happiness involves hope and faith.. Hope, faith and joy are medicinal. They are therapeutic. They represent the difference between living and existing and often, between life and death. Happiness, however, is more than entertainment and amusement, money or "eat, drink and be merry." The basic need is to have a goal in work and recreation, a feeling of being wanted, of belonging, of sacrificing for a worthwhile cause.

CHALLENGE

We now have ample support from scientists that health has a relationship to the religious, spiritual, work and recreational phases of life. One must see meaning in life. One must have a goal and travel hopefully to live and be healthy.

It is recognized that there are many other relationships between physical education and various life outcomes, following philosophical and physiological principles of living, but still the main objective of physical education remains organic development-health.

It must be apparent that desirable outcomes of education and of life and the outcomes of physical education cannot be adequately tested by any quantitative measurements. We can test speed, strength, agility, and to some extent, endurance, but we cannot test the will to live, the will to do and the will to conquer.

We have heard a great deal about the necessity of health and fitness, particularly since 1918; but so far as the schools are concerned, it has been mostly talk. As Russia increased the pressure of studies in the school-room, it correspondingly increased the time devoted to physical education. Rear Admiral H. G. Rickover commented wisely, "While you are developing the minds of children develop also their bodies through physical education. These, too, are paramount."

We still need today, however, some things to help people. In the modern school program we must have a longer day. This extended time should lay the basis for a health-fitness-exercise program; it should also give children some leisure time opportunities in the performing arts. We could have a longer school week. Most European schools carry on for six days. In this time our children could master one or two foreign languages, improve their English and arouse curiosity through science.

There could even be a longer school year. Summers could be utilized for work experience in factory, shop and farm, or in well organized private and school camps. Boys and girls could get experience in conservation, in preserving and replanting national and state forests and in working on public lands. These areas of educational could be as valuable as those in the class rooms.

For total development, education must recognize the many talents of young and old- the many phases of development: organic, neuromuscular, interpretive and emotional. There would be no drop-outs if the school curriculum were broad enough to meet the interests and abilities of all children. We need redirection of outcomes. Thus optimum health-fitness-citizenship and joy in living would be encouraged.

The boys and girls of this country deserve administrative backing from our state and local boards of education and from all school administrative officials. Our young people have the will and all life is reborn with every child. We must not falter now.

15

SIGNIFICANT EXPERIENCES—A CHALLENGE TO PHYSICAL EDUCATION

The word "significant" comes from two root words "signum," which means sign or mark, and "facere," to make, therefore an experience that makes a mark is a significant experience. Everybody wants to make a mark in the world. The kind of mark seems to vary with age. A boy wants to be a circus clown. Then he wants to be like his dad-that doesn't last very long! Then he wants to be a fireman, then he wants to make All State, then he wants to get rich; later on he wants to make both ends meet, and finally he hopes to get his old age pension. So really these marks vary.

Another way to think about this is to inquire what experiences are remembered. There is a school of psychology that places great emphasis on what you remember from your early childhood. A person stuck his neck out once to tell another person that he remembered a fight at age 5 with his brother in which each of them got hold of the same rocking chair and ended by pulling it apart. Of course, the fellow analysed it to show aggressiveness because the incident remembered was a fight. But since the recollection is that we came apart each with his share, like breaking up a wishbone, may be we were interested in sharing.

Every significant experience is in some way connected with strong feeling tone and this feeling tone makes it significant. Let us say the "heat" of the feeling burns the mark into our memory.

NEUROLOGY OF A SIGNIFICANT EXPERIENCE

In a model brain one sees the parts of the brain that react in what is called a significant experience. It would have taken more than this brain to answer this question in old testament days when, you remember, God searched the reins and the heart of man. The reins-that is the kidneys-were the seat of the mind and the heart the location of the sound. In New Testament times, we would have needed to bring along also the "bowels of tender mercy." Saint Paul speaks of the emotions being in the abdomen. But today we have it all localized up here in the head. Gall and Spurzheim in 1829 stood before the Society of Biology in Paris to enunciate the principles of phrenology. These gentlemen had left bumps on peoples' heads and were quite sure that by feeling around up there they could tell what was wrong or what was right with a person. Thus, they located the liberty axis up on top and to one side of it religion and the other side love. What could be nicer to encircle liberty. In high school my physiology teacher told us that bumps behind the ears meant that you were destructive. So all of us Lane Tech Indians felt behind our ears and found we were destructive.

The significant fact of phrenology is its attempt to connect parts of the brain with character traits-loyalty, honesty, purity, observing power, etc. This is the older viewpoint which now is found only where somebody sells rattlesnake oil with a picture of the brain as a backdrop.

Today we know the motor cortex, where stimulation causes movement in muscles of the other side. We know the sensory cortex where stimulation gives rise to sensations of touch in various parts of the body. Back of this is an area which is necessary for sight and just in front of it is one for the interpretation of sight. On the anterior missal surface there is something for smell and taste, and here on the temporal lobe is something for hearing. Other areas are less well understood.

This is fairly good evidence that memories are stored in the cortex, and that these memories can be brought out by electrical stimulation. They are also brought out by the stimulation accompanying epileptic attacks and account for the aura that precedes the attack. To know where to operate, the surgeon now stimulates until he finds a spot that produces an experience similar to the aura that regularly precedes an attack. Removal of this area often brings relief from epileptic seizures.

But that is only part of the story. Simultaneously with these advances regarding the cortex some astonishing discoveries were made in the basal part of the brain. It goes back to the 30's when professor Hess of Zurich found some 4,000 spots in the cat's brain stem which when stimulated gave rise to different actions in the cat, such as blinking, purring, falling asleep, and combinations of some activities. Here was uncovered a rudimentary brain that must have existed millions of years ago before this top cortex business arrived to make us human. This rudimentary brain still works in us.

Near the front end of the brain stem are centres for anger, rage, and pain, in the diencephalon. Just above these are pleasure centres. An electrode placed into this part of the brain can be wired so that when a cat touches a certain button it apparently feels a sensation of pleasure. Now this cat might, in the course of an hour, accidentally touch the button 15 to 20 times but when a circuit is connected so that it stimulates itself, it will do it 5000 times an hour to get this sensation of pleasure. So we know "pleasure" is located in the brain stem. We know pain is in there, too. We know other reactions of the body connected with the viscera are located here. This is the great new discovery-the reticular formation as it is called. We know that this part is connected with the cortex for two way communication. So every idea, if we could think of it that way, is connected with feelings down in this part and the feeling centres in turn communicate with the cortex. There is thus continuous interrelationship between ideas and the centres for feeling tone, and we begin to see what happen if we want feelings connected with experiences, so that when either is activated the other, also, reacts.

Then, also, there is a rather peculiar bump up front called the prefrontal lobe which is one of the most recent developments of the brain not found in the China man, at least not as far as we can reconstruct from his skull. Thus prefrontal lobe has a few interesting stories connected with it.

In 1848 Phineas Gage, a very sedate, Puritan-like man living in New England, while tamping gun powder into a blasting hole had the powder explode and drive the tamping rod into his prefrontal lobe. This has become the famous crowbar case of Harvard Medical School. This caused Phineas to change his nature completely. Previously a very honest, home-loving, well-disciplined, conscientious man, now with the piece of metal in his prefrontal lobe he was an entirely different person-no more a good Puritan as you would picture such a person. He lost interest in his family and became in a sense a loose liver.

Sometime later a woman became much depressed. So she put a gun to the side of her head and shot. She didn't die. When the haemorrhage cleared out or her eyes she recovered to appear rather normal. Instead of being completely depressed, she was now outgoing. She had shot off her worry bump.

It is not evident whether she was depuritanized as was good old Phineas, but there have been many operations like that since. It is called *psycho-surgery*. The prefrontal lobe of the brain is in a very special way connected with the diencephalon where nerve centres controlling emotional tone are lodged. Too much connection with these centres results in overloading our experiences with affective states, sometimes resulting in withdrawal. Consequently, an operation to sever this connection may bring relief. This was first done on may be Portuguese neurologist, Moniz, in 1936.

Through the prefrontal lobes there are nerve paths that connect the cortex where ideas are stored with the centres of feeling. Incidentally, removal of the prefrontal lobes doesn't change your IQ by the ordinary tests; but you are not as wise as you were before. Knowing facts and being able to answer an examination is knowledge. Wisdom is knowing how to use these facts and this is in some way connected with feeling. When you begin to connect feelings with ideas then you may sense that one is better than other. When you connect pain with one kind of action and pleasure with another, you have the beginning of conscience. Dr. Dandy, one of the early surgeons on this part of the brain, had removed the prefrontal lobe from a patient whom he retained at the hospital as a handyman. One day Dr. Dandy assigned this handyman without a prefrontal lobe to show some noted visiting neuro-surgeons around the hospital grounds before bringing them to his office. These surgeons noted nothing unusual in the handyman.

People who lack prefrontal lobes often do a lot of bragging and punning, but who doesn't sometimes! May be they just lack structurally what some of us lack functionally. Thus far we have seen that in man's brain they are opportunities for all connections necessary to make a significant experience, i.e., to tie ideas up with feeling tone and to inject feeling tone back into the ideas. This is the neurological basis of significant experiences.

SIGNIFICANT EXPERIENCE AND AGE LEVELS

Let us go beyond neurology to think in terms of significant experiences at various ages in life, particularly those experiences about which physical education can do something and which therefore are a challenge to physical education. Let us think of the child that is just beginning to crawl in its crib. It raises its head and moves around, it pulls up one arm and finally it stands up very proudly. Of course it doesn't say, "I'm proud"; but look at it and you can tell that it feels proud of what it can do.

Then pretty soon it starts to climb. A little later it climbs up and jumps down. Then it climbs a little higher and a little higher before jumping. Imagine what is happening in the brain of this child. We know that the cortex is very poorly developed. The child cannot write a letter to its Senator, it cannot debate with its parents. All it can do, at least all that can be mentioned in public, is jump, struggle, spit, and cry. These are all muscular activities. Now imagine that this child has climbed up on a rock. Now look at it. The child is excited, leaning forward. You can see expressions of pleasure, of excitement, and a little fear all in that same face. Here it faces a challenge. It calls, "Mama, look." No! No! No! Let me help you down!" That's one kind of mother. Another mother controls herself and says, "Okay, jump."

At this age it is very important what kind of physical education a child gets; and the mother is the physical educator. The girls who are now in your college classes are the physical educators of tomorrow's preschool child. What does this jump mean to the child? Obviously, the only way it can express itself is by doing something within its ability. Modern psychology has taught us that very early in life we develop our feelings of self-worth, our feelings of acceptance or non-acceptance of self.

It is important to that child to jump, to feel it is somebody. Long before it can say, "I am somebody," it feels that way. If it is constantly told, "No, no, no, let me help you down; you can't do that; you will hurt yourself," what kind of a child are we raising? Here is the great remaining "gold mine" for physical education to exploit in its effort to influence the character, the personality, the traits or courage, or whatever you want to call them-of the adult to come. As the twig is bent, so grows the tree. It is also true that one who has never learned to accept himself, cannot accept others, because he will project on others the feelings he has about himself.

We must help to bring such experiences into the lives of more children long before they come to school. Watch kids in the first and second grade when their classmates urge them to attempt a daring feat. Some come running and then turn black; others go to it with abandon. They may trip but what's the difference, they go on. Similarly some adults are constantly holding back while others are trying. We must touch the lives of these young children, through our present high school and college girls, the mothers of tomorrow. This is physical education for the pre-school child.

Then there is the first time a child played in a game with official rules where one might have gotten away with something when the official wasn't looking or when the teacher was not very observant. That was a significant experience. Was there then a coach who said, "This does not go; you've got to play the right way or you don't play." Was there someone back there who gave that boy the first real feeling of respect for rules, perhaps connecting it with diencephalic pain connected through the prefrontal lobes to the ideas in the cortical part of the brain when he said, "This thing doesn't go! If you don't play right, you're out! You're a disgrace!" For this reason there is no such thing as "Just a kid's basketball game that doesn't count." The first game is perhaps the most important one.

These significant experiences in the lives of youngsters that may start them in one direction or another, are a challenge to us in physical education. They make it important that even in elementary school there be somebody in charge who knows the rules and sportsmanship, and who is both capable and alert to make sure that the right thing happens.

Moving up a bit, let us look in on a high school. Visualize a boy sitting in a literature class where Shakespeare must be read. What is he doing? His lips are moving a bit. Especially when the teacher is looking, he goes through motions of being interested; but somewhere in his subconscious he is thinking of something else. He has a bit of athlete's itch on one foot; so one foot is scratching the other. The bell rings and Henry-VIII goes out the mental window. This is no pretty picture of integrated activity. But watch this same boy in the closing minutes of a basketball game with the score tied and you will see the whole boy playing, completely integrated with but one purpose.

We've said a lot about the whole child going to school; but what do we do with the whole child? In the lower grades we can perhaps occupy him. Here they read a story and then act it out. But in that high school literature class, the boy's eyes and lips may be there, but the rest of him is most likely some other place. There is little that demands he give himself, totally. This leads me to say that an integrated activity is a significant experience.

Unfortunately, we have less and less of that as we go up the academic ladder in our schools. The only place where the average fellow still gets a totally integrating experience, one in which the whole individual acts, thinks, and feels together—eyes, ears, muscles, brain, glands—everything, is in the gymnasium or on the athletic field. Maybe this is why play is so important to people; this is why youngsters like it so much.

Too much of modern day life depends on the use of the eyes and ears only. But we know that ideas in our minds, concepts, if you wish to call them that, are composed of everything that comes into the cortex from the sense organs-from eyes and ears, yes, but these are not enough. What comes in from the muscles may often be just the feeling of sitting on one's seat. This does not ensure formation of a true-to-life concept because a related, true-to-reality proprioceptive component is lacking. The child that cannot distinguish between the moon, a cookie, and a ball that are held before it may grab for each but soon learns to distinguish between the moon, a cookie, and a ball that are held before it may grab for each but soon learns to distinguish between the moon on the one hand, and the cookie and the ball on the other when he can or cannot reach them or get his hands on or around them. Until he gets his hands around a ball he does not really know what a ball is and even though he can't get them around the moon, his appreciation of the roundness of the moon depends on the fact that he has had a ball in his hands. The third dimension experience, the depth dimension of our concepts comes to us from muscle and joint senses, i.e., the proprioceptive system. Too much of modern life is limited by two dimensions. Too much is just seeing picture and reading the printed page. It is short on muscle and joint experiences.

Elementary education is better in this important respect than is secondary and higher education except for laboratory work. Active out stories bring much more meaning to Macbeth or to Robin Hood than just reading the words. Could you imagine a nation going wild over a world's series game reported by radio if its people had never actually played some kind of ball game? Denied such experiences some people develop a deep-seated hunger for them, others have so often ignored the feeling that they have lost the craving.

Many people cannot express their feelings as did the artist. People find these concept-fulfilling experiences, not only in physical education activities, but also in gardening, in handicrafts, and in many other physical activities. This is terrifically important, lest we come to live in a completely unrealistic, flat world; and has far reaching significance.

Too often, instead of doing the thing with our hands, we just write a check and somebody else gets the real experience. Thus deprived of bodily experiences with reality our concept forming mind suffers a kind of malnutrition due to a deficiency in the proprioceptive component of the diet of sensory experiences—the muscle and joint component. The resulting sickly formed concepts may account for some cockeyed thinking and failure to cope decisively with problems even in high places. In times of national and international crisis, a farmer, a foot soldier, a miner, or even a paper hanger may rise to replace the talkers. Probably combinations such as rail splitter-lawyer or carpenter-teacher dedicated to high values would be even better. In a time when such experiences are disappearing from urbanized American life our concepts may well become correspondingly "anaemic" and unrealistic. But this is no propaganda for a "back-to-the farm movement." The farm is also becoming push-button. It does argue for supplementing the unbalanced sensory diet of civilized life with consciously selected dosages of muscular experience.

There are other ways in which modern life destroys integration. If you get mad at somebody, you don't dare show it, lest you get into trouble, especially if he's your boss. But let's go to the zoo and stand in front of the monkey cage. Do something to make the monkey mad. There'll be no question about it, he'll display his anger so everybody knows it. We call this honesty. Let us call it integrity or "oneness." When John was a youngster a Jewish friend told him, "There's something about him he like. He is what we call one." It took him years to grasp the real meaning of what he said. He meant that he said what he felt and felt what he said. In this sense the monkey is also one.

Obviously, this does not happen regularly in modern life. You have had people call you wonderful and yet you were afraid to leave the room for fear of what they would say when you were gone. It's good that people don't always tell him what they think about him. He couldn't take it. This kind of behaviour is found only on one tiny twig of the animal tree. It's the schizic branch where man sits at the top where behaviour is split—where we say one thing when we feel another. It is civilization. One can have only a few friends to whom one can talk as he feels. How awkward it would be otherwise.

A young woman who in the summer of 1937 sat in class at the University of California gave the instructor a good idea. It was in the days when some of us swore at modern dance and others swore by it. She was all for it. "Tell me," the instructor said, "why are you so crazy about this modern dance?" She gave this very significant answer. Well, since I'm a woman, I'm supposed to act like a lady; I must take short steps and I have to be dainty whether I want to or not. But in modern dance I feel big, I can make a big movement and if I want to stamp, I can stamp. It's okay." Dance gave her the opportunity to do and feel as one. Dance gave her the wonderful feel of integration. Could we say that modern dance brings to man the healing balm of monkey wholeness?

But you don't have to do modern dance to get the feel of such as experience. You can get it with a minimum of activity. Will all of you please say, "flat." Now say "point" and move your lips back. Say "flat" and point your lips. It's true also in other languages. Always if you speak simple words like "up," "down," "flat," and "point," the face moves with it. I've discovered another interesting and related fact. If you ask a person to repeat the word "spitz" for instance, and he imitates the sound without knowing what he is saying he will very likely do it poorly. But if you tell him "spitz means point" he'll do a much better job. This reminds me of what I've been taught by my modern dance friends. They say, "If you imitate, it isn't modern dance. But if you feel it first and then do it, it's modern dance." This is the way the instructor learned the meaning of modern dance and how to understand the ladies who do it so well.

We men may get the same feeling in other ways. Recalling one case in which some young boys were playing football in a snow storm, over forty years ago. As offensive tackle it was the individual's job to block the opposing line men. Hitting the line again and again with almost bone crushing force with body, mind, and emotion all together hellbent with others on going in one direction, provided such an experience that one never forgets.

Similarly when a piece of wood connects squarely with horse hide and the ball goes places, the whole individual operating with split second perfection gets this feeling of togetherness. All of us have such experiences once in a while. Many of us don't have them often enough. One explanation for satisfaction gained from swatting a ball involves imagining it's your mother-in-law to get all the aggressions out of you. To anyone that is an unnecessarily complicated explanation. One can get something very direct from hitting the ball just right without anthropomorphizing the little sphere. It may help some people but not him. Perhaps this is a tribute to one's mother-in-law.

We don't yet fully understand the implications to mental health of thus constantly splitting ourselves rather than acting as one. It has not been proven, but it is felt fear that such continual splitting must weaken the force of one's personality. Continuous ambivalence or something approaching that must put a strain on the structure of mind. Efforts have been put to coin a companion term of "monovalence" or "univalence" but the nearest one can get to it is "integration" or "wholeness" as the contrasting condition that builds inner strength. When we centre attention on feelings we sometimes speak of mixed feeling. That is the feeling one is supposed to has when his mother-in-law drives his brand new Cadillac over a cliff. If we insist on taking mother-in-law for a ride in our analogies, then think of mother-in-law driving him old, decrepit Chevrolet on which he has plenty of insurance over the cliff. That would be all feelings going in the same direction.

If a given object or experience makes us feel two ways, for example, if an individual has to feel nice toward somebody and at the same time he do feel another way, this disintegrating. The boy who wants to win so badly that he's willing to do anything to win, even though his own code of ethics says it's wrong is having a disintegrating experience. It's like a woman falling in love with a married man. That's an awfully disintegrating experience because the object, the man, calls out two feeling in her—one which says "go" and the other which says "no". This tears things apart. But this need not be in sports. In good sports, properly coached, we learn to play hard and fair, to win-but not at any cost; if winning has not been pitched too high.

Obviously it is most important that the right kind of leadership is given to the youngsters at the time when feelings are tied up with what is right and wrong in sports. Then all goes together in the right direction.

Why are boys so crazy about playing ball or playing on a team? It isn't because they like to run around. It isn't only because they enjoy the game. There is something else about it. It is this feeling of being needed, this feeling of being a part of something that is greater than One's self and feeling important to it. These are significant experiences. These are the experiences that often keep a boy in high school when he otherwise would drop out. No doubt there are comparable experiences in the lives of girls, experiences that provide a genuine feeling of worth not for personal aggrandisement with arrogance, but in service to a group or to the school. We can provide many opportunities for such significant experiences to our young people. We must learn to make each such experience provide 100% significance in the finest sense possible. This happens best when somebody in position of leadership understands what should happen and helps it to go that way.

Athletes as a whole do their best work at about age 25. That's roughly when most of the athletic records are made. Skilled labourers reach their peak at age 35. Brain workers at age 45. Inventions come most commonly between the ages of 31 and 35. Poets and dramatists ripen between 44 and 50. Of course there are always exceptions, but these are the averages. And after 50 there is nothing left for us but to become philosophers. That explains why you asked me to speak, which, by the way, has also shown me another time when one can have a significant experience. That is when some big idea takes hold of one.

The older we get the more pieces should come to fit together to ensure for us a satisfying philosophy for our profession, for our life. The philosophy is the picture, the facts are the parts. The mind sits in front of the pieces, unhappy, until they begin to fit together. The mind wants to see the picture, it is confused by the disjointed parts. The bringing together of more and more facts into an ever enlarging consistent and satisfying philosophy of our task, of our profession, of our place in the larger scheme of things, is the most difficult and never ending task for the human mind. Progress in its accomplishment brings feelings of satisfaction commensurate with the significance of the experience.

RESEARCH IMPLICATION—THEN AND NOW

A discussion of the topic, Research-then and now, should begin with a clarification of terms. For "Then," two periods, in which research had a definite characteristic, have been selected. It is logical on this the seventy-fifth anniversary of our national association to begin the first "Then" in 1885 and, as will be seen later, to mark its close in the first decade of the twentieth century. There followed a period of transition from the one type of research to another which began in the 20's and extended to the 40's. This again was followed by a period of readjustment in research and it is interesting to note that during both transitional stages this country was engaged in war. "Now" will be considered as beginning in the 50's.

Was there research in each of these three periods and if so, what was its chief characteristic? What were the influences which shaped the investigation? It has been said, "Science owes many of its spectacular advances to improvement in methodology and the introduction of new techniques." As each period is summarized, these two factors, methodology and techniques, will be seen as important in research our field.

It will be well, as the three areas are surveyed, have in mind the meaning and the nature of research. Briefly, research is a search for truth. Note that the word is a combination of search and the prefix re-Current truth is scrutinized and re-examined to determine whether it is still true or whether a new statement should replace or expand the old. Steinhaus, in describing research to physical educators, said, "The methods of research, though endlessly different in their specific application, are fundamentally simple. Essentially they comprise four steps: (1) observation; (2) recording and treating the observed data; (3) generalization to the formulation of a theory; (4) testing the new formulation with further observations."

Looking now at the first then, were physical educators searching for truth in the late 1800's? Certainly they were making observations, were recording these, and to some degree treating the data. No well-trained physical educator in that day would begin classes until students had been measured and tested. In many an institution physical education classes did not begin until two or three weeks after the opening of school. This did not mean that the physical educator was idle; on the contrary, she was perhaps the busiest person on campus. From the time of the opening bell until the dinner hour, she was measuring heights, weights, sitting heights, girth of forearm, upper arm, necks, thighs, calves, length of arms and legs, strength of backs, legs, chests, and volumes of lung capacity. And if there was a right and left, both measures were taken.

The interest of the profession in this type of measure is show in the appointment of committees on Statistics and Measurement, the first in 1885, the last in 1903. The final report of this committee was made at the national convention in 1905, thus providing a closing date for this Anthropocentric Age. These successive committees, during their quarter century of existence, suggested and approved items which were to be tested or measured; at one time the list included 50 items. Thus, making observations, the first step in research as listed by Steinhaus, was a large scale, almost universal, operation.

Did the physical educator carry out the second step, recording and treating the observed data? With the limited statistical techniques which were available, scores were recorded and treated. Based on hundreds and even thousands of measures, chart showing averages and percentile ranges were published for men by Hitchocock, Sargent and Seaver, and, for women, at wellesley, Oberlin and the University of Nebraska. Each student was given a chart of these group measures and on it were plotted his own scores, thus showing individual standing in comparison to his peers. Using these charts, the instructor planned a program of gymnastic exercises for each student. This profile of individual status and needs is today considered sound and desirable. Our profession can take pride in these pioneer procedures and would do well to continue them. The items measured will differ; the general procedures are sound.

Reports on gains made as a result of participation in physical education would be as commendable and as desirable in 1960 as it was in the beginning of the century. Each of us would like to present such figures, but we can be assured that whatever the gain, questions would be asked. Are the gains significant and can they be attributed to physical education classes? Did the Wisconsin student of 1912 gain in leg strength because she exercised in the gymnasium or because each day she climbed the hill on the Madison campus?

From the treatment of the data, it can be assumed

that the physical educator implied that gymnastic exercises increased strength and lung capacity. This was an accepted theory before the observations were made; the theory was not tested. Research of this first then was limited to the first two of the four steps in research.

In research, facilities are important. There must be personnel capable of conducting investigations; there must be time for observation, for organizing data, time for thinking and theorizing; there must be space and there must be equipment for making the desired observation. This list does not name funds specifically, but it is obvious that if time, space and equipment are not adequate, often these lacks can be attributed to insufficient funds. Even adequate personnel may depends on the budget.

Equipment was not costly. The most expensive were the dynamometers, but these were long-lived. Many purchased before 1900 are usable today. Neither space nor time were problems. The entire department staff and the entire department space were available for the measurement period. Perhaps some staff member sat up all night to calculate averages without the aid of a calculator; yet college enrolments were small, as were those in secondary school and wholesale measurements in elementary schools were not common.

The last report of a national committee on Anthropomorphic marks a significant date in the Measurement of Man. It was in 1905 that a French psychologist, Alfred Binet, published his first series of tests to measure human intelligence. Binet made provisions of his tests up to the time of his death in 1911. Educators in this country were interested in the new device and during the first World War, with the availability of the service men, the first large scale measurement of intelligence was conducted with the administration of the Army Alpha Test. Binet's tests were revised for use in American schools, courses in measurement were added to psychology and education departments, and became a necessary part of teacher training.

By the 20's some colleges and universities offered an undergraduate major in physical education leading to a Bachelor's degree. In 1925, a national committee recommended that all directors and supervisors of physical education should have a bachelor's degree, and that all college teachers, with the exception of specialists, such as coaches and teachers of dance and swimming, should have equal preparation. With professional training in the colleges and universities, the student in physical education came in contact with the rapidly developing tests for mental ability. One of the early statisticians, McCall of Teacher College, Columbia University, enthusiastically proclaimed that anything which exists can be measured. Physical educators are not likely to ignore a challenge. If mental capacity and ability could be measured, why not motor ability, native and acquired? And so began the Motor Measurement Millennium.

Physical educators following the pattern set by psychologists and educators undertook the task of devising tests to measure human ability. Preliminary observations had already been made. It was and is common knowledge that individuals have motor abilities and that the degree of ability differs. Even a child in choosing players for his team makes his selection on a judgment of skill.

However, such judgments are not scored numerically and experts may disagree on ratings. Investigators undertook to find test situations in which numerical scores could be obtained and in which differences of judgment would be minimized.

Their methods of procedures in devising tests followed a general pattern; analysis of the elements of the skill, selecting and devising situations in which performance could be objectively scored and then subjecting the scores to statistical analysis. Young and Moser's presentation of the process of obtaining a battery of tests to measure basketball ability illustrate these steps. The elements contributing to successful performance are according to their analysis, (1) ability to handle the ball, throwing and catching; (2) ability to handle the body in relation to the ball, to move quickly, to change direction, to jump; (3) ability to make baskets. As a result of the ingenuity of the investigators and search through basketball literature, 36 situations were listed as possible measurement devices. These were administered to classes and on the basis of subjective evaluation and statistical treatment, seventeen tests were studies more intensively. Finally, on the basis of statistical evidence of reliability and validity, five tests were recommended as a battery which would measure the ability to play basketball.

Investigators of motor ability have generalized from their observations and treatment of data, step three in methods of research. Many such batteries to measure ability in various sports were presented in this period, as were measures of more general abilities. The fourth step in research, testing the new formulation with further testing, was not common. Most of the batters were the outcomes of Master's these and Doctoral dissertations.

During the 20's and 30's, there had been a rapid increase in the number of colleges offering graduate majors in physical education. In the first decade of the century, three schools offered courses leading to an advanced degree-Columbia, Oberlin and Sringfield College. During the 20's, eleven more schools offered such courses and by 1942 the number had increased to fifty-six. Had it not been for the need of presenting a thesis for the these degrees, perhaps such batteries as Brace's Motor Ability Test, Humiston's and Scott's Tests of Motor Ability, Dyer's Test for Tennis, and the French and Cooper's Volleyball tests and many others would not have been developed. Once a battery had been proposed and the thesis completed, there was no demand for the fourth step of further testing and evaluation of the hypothesis.

Not only was there no demand for this step, there was often active opposition. Survivors of the Anthropometric Age were still members of the teaching staff; for many of them such terms as reliability and validity, standard deviation and correlation had little meaning. Development of test batteries took precious time from teaching. The measures of this period never were used as universally as were the anthropometric and strength measures. For the staff members reluctant to us the new devices, these years were anything but a millennium.

With disagreement within the profession, there was no longer time allotted to research projects. Time was available only for the graduate student because it was a part of the study load. There was little demand for special research equipment. The batteries were devised for use in classes, and equipment for testing was limited to that which was needed for the game itself.

Some insight into the facilities which would stimulate research was obtained in 1937 from a questionnaire which Dr. Frances Hellebrandt sent to all member institutions of the National Association of the Directors of Physical Education for College Women. Replies were received from 91 schools and of this number 10 indicated that faculty members had a definite time on their schedules for research. In two cases the amount was not defined; in one college, it ranged from 1 to 4 per cent; in seven colleges, from 10 to 30 per cent. Only two schools indicated that space was set aside for research; in 6, there was special research equipment; 7 had research funds in the budget-these were $10, $25, and $75; others were $300 and $650. Only two schools reported research assistants. There was one each on half-time in these schools and the salaries were $500 and $600 for 10 months.

The investigators who developed the test batteries were exploring a new field. They were usually experienced teachers, but not experienced in research. They learned techniques as they developed their problem. These advisors had little more experience than did the students; few had a doctoral degree. Perhaps the most valuable outcome of the period was not the research, but the training which it gave to students and faculty. These individuals were to become the investigators of the present period, the now of this discussion. They are among the chief influence which make now a period of promise.

The present is promising because research facilities are better than they have been at any time in our history. Facilities, as stated earlier, include personnel, time space, and equipment. This one situation will illustrate the status of departments offering advanced degree. Some will be better equipped than is the example, some not as well.

First, the personnel. In 1930, there were on the staff one doctor of medicine, four women with Master's degrees, and the remainder of the staff had bachelor's degrees. Today, there is one doctor of medicine, four staff members have Doctor of Philosophy degrees, and, in general, only those women who have Master's degrees are taken on as full-time staff members. The qualifications for scientific investigation of the staff are now vastly superior to those of the 1930's, not only because there have been longer periods of preparation, but because the training in research procedures through which the staff members achieved their degrees is superior to that which the 1930 staff had experienced.

Second, the time for research. In the 30's whatever research was done by staff members was done in addition to a full teaching load. Many a midnight hour and many Sunday was spent in the laboratory and office attempting to follow some line of investigation intriguing at the time. Today, the department is attempting to develop a schedule which will include time for research as a part of the teaching load. Each staff member of professorial rank, and there are ten of these—three full professors and three associate and four assistant—will have such time for a given period. If at the end of the period she has demonstrated no drive for investigation, research time will not be allowed.

Frequently, research grant makes possible additional time. At present, such arrangement has made a 40 per cent reduction in one staff member's teaching load.

Research assistants can also be considered as adding to the staff member's research time, for these assistants do the routine work and take over many details of projects, thus enabling the staff member to accomplish more in the investigations. In the 30's there was one half-time assistant in the department; today there are eight. Three of these are supported by university funds, not considered a part of the department's budget, and five are supported by grants from off-campus organizations. Thus, it might be said that the research time is equivalent to the total load of at least six people.

Third, the space. In 1930, there was no space which the investigator could consider his own. Today, there are two large laboratories assigned to research projects. In addition, when the study demands, the entire staff is cooperative in making available space which is ordinarily used for other purposes. In a recent study which involved volume measures of the human body, tank was set up in one of the gang showers because a ready supply of water and a drain to carry off the water was needed. Another study required the use of the gymnasium for a two day period. Not only did the instructors of classes give up the space allocated to them, but they acted as assistants in that two day project, as members of their classes were measured in the overarm and underarm throws and in the standing broad jump.

The projects of one of the staff is concerned with strength studies. The dynamometers purchased in the early part of the century are still available, but the investigator prefers the tensiometer. That was purchased some ten years ago, and for the past six years that investigator has moved the testing table and the tensiometer to a neighbouring elementary school where 8 muscle groups have been measured on the same group of children during that period. At other time the equipment is used for studies with college students.

There are also ergographs for measuring the among of work which can be accomplished if a muscle group is exercised until fatigued. The distance a load is lifted and the time for lifting are recorded on another piece of equipment. These provide means of studying and comparing methods of improving strength.

For measurement of energy expenditure in exercise, there are Douglas bags to collect expired air. There are recorders to measure the intake of oxygen. These have long been used by physiologists.

In one of the laboratories, a small space has been insulated to permit electromyographic studies. It has long been recognized that a logical analysis of muscle action is not a valid picture of functioning muscles. Except for studies of walking, there have been no sound reports of muscle action in the skills which comprise physical education curricula. A recent electromyo-graphical study reports an observation which is of interest to those attempting to develop motor skill. It was found that when the free foot was planter flexed, the initial activity appeared in the peroneus lounges if the performer thought of pushing the forefoot downward.

On the other hand, if the performer thought of bringing the heel upward, the resulting planter flexion was initiated by contraction of the soleus. This suggests that the idea which is in the mind of the performer may be important in bringing into action the desired muscles and could be important in bringing into action the desired muscles and could be important to all teachers of motor skill.

And last in this list is the photographic equipment. Picture of motion taken at high speeds are essential for the physical educator as is the microscope for the biologist. Most descriptions of sports skills and locomotor skills are based on what the eye can see or on what the performer thinks he does. Both have been shown to be erroneous. Our equipment includes a 16mm, camera, which can expose 4,000 frames per minute and which is equipped with a wide one inch lens and a three inch lens. For studying film, there is a time-motion study projector, by which one frame can be projected for unlimited time without danger of burning the film and which can be turned by hand.

It can also be run at various speeds, forward or backward. More satisfactory for tracing film is the Recorder. Six of these are in our laboratory, three of which expose three frames at a time; the others, one frame. The projection is at table height convenient for tracing, and the film can be turned forward or backward by a handle within easy reach.

The ball velocity was measured from the film also and was 98.5 feet per second. The slight difference of 3.5 feet per second could be due to error in measurement or to failure to include some contributing factor.

Analysis of the joint action in the standing broad jump has shown that the action cannot be understood if the explanation is vigorous extension of hip, knee and ankle. Film study shows that the knee extensors and gravitational force are the main contributors to projection of the body. Ankle and hip extension maintain the direction of projection. To see that the downward force of gravity can pull the foot upward is to gain in appreciation of the Wisdom of the Body in motor performance, as Cannon saw that wisdom in physiological functioning in the early part of this century.

Film study shows that the performer uses joint action of which he is not aware. If these actions are not voluntarily controlled, how is the movement brought about? A possible explanation is that the human nervous system is equipped with inherent motor patterns, that the voluntary part of the skill is only the decision to perform and that the details of the act are taken over by that part of the nervous system which is below the level of consciousness. Inherent patterns have been recently studies in forms of life other than Man. Lorenz has indicated that patterns are inherited as surely as are physical features and Sperry has suggested that an affinity between specific muscles and specific neurones determine possible coordinations. Broer has shown pictorially the similarity of pattern in underarm throw, the volleyball and the badminton serve; in the overarm throw, the badminton clear, and the tennis serve; in the sidearm throw, the tennis drive and batting. If such patterns are inherent in Man, how early do they appear?

In observation of boys of pre-school age, we have found in a three year old the sidearm, overarm, and the underarm pattern in well established coordination. Teaching may well begin with the basic pattern, rather than with a description of detail.

These many avenues of study make possible a pooling of the findings of each in an attempt to look at motor development and skill from many angles. It is attack on the Unknown from many aspects rather than effort along one line only as was characteristic of the Anthropometric Age and the Motor Measurement Millennium. For example, when our photographic studies indicated that the principle projecting force in the standing broad jump was that due to contraction of the knee extensors, the staff member who was studying strength in the same subject reported that the correlation between the distance of the jump and the strength of knee extensors was greater than it was with either ankle or hip muscles.

Each line of investigation now requires special apparatus, which in many cases is designed for the project. Each investigator will develop technical methods which will result from long experience. Those who study by means of photography will have skills and information which differ from those of the student of strength. The department which was used as an illustration is only one of many. In each, there will be other special lines of investigation. Each investigator, confident in his ability to conduct research, will follow the leads suggested by his findings. Results from all parts of the country will attack the Unknown from many more aspects than will any one department. Research in physical education has reached maturity and the years ahead are indeed a Period of Promise.

